BUS 5601: Essentials of Business Development I

D1616525

Warren | Reeve | Duchac | Gwartney | Stroup | Macpherson
Scott | Pride | Ferrell | McGuigan | Moyer | Harris

CENGAGE
Learning·

Australia • Brazil • Japan • Korea • Mexico • Singapore • Spain • United Kingdom • United States

BUS 5601: Essentials of Business Development I

Senior Manager, Custom Production:
Donna Brown
Linda deStefano

Manager, Custom Production:
Terri Daley
Louis Schwartz

Marketing Manager:
Rachael Kloos

Manager, Premedia:
Kim Fry

Manager, Intellectual Property Project
Management:
Brian Methe

Manager, Manufacturing & Inventory:
Spring Stephens

Financial & Managerial Accounting, 12 edition
Warren | Reeve | Duchac

© 2014 Cengage Learning. All rights reserved.

Macroeconomics: Private and Public Choice, 15 Edition
Gwartney | Stroup | Macpherson | Sobel

© 2015 Cengage Learning. All rights reserved.

Managerial Economics: Applications, Strategies and Tactics, 13 Edition
McGuigan | Moyer | Harris

© 2015 Cengage Learning. All rights reserved.

College Accounting: A Career Approach, 12 Edition
Scott

© 2015 Cengage Learning. All rights reserved.

Foundations of Marketing, 6 Edition
Pride | Ferrell

© 2015 Cengage Learning. All rights reserved.

For product information and technology assistance, contact us at
Cengage Learning Customer & Sales Support, 1-800-354-9706

For permission to use material from this text or product,
submit all requests online at **cengage.com/permissions**
Further permissions questions can be emailed to
permissionrequest@cengage.com

This book contains select works from existing Cengage Learning resources and was produced by Cengage Learning Custom Solutions for collegiate use. As such, those adopting and/or contributing to this work are responsible for editorial content accuracy, continuity and completeness.

Compilation © 2015 Cengage Learning

ISBN: 978-1-3052-8974-1

WCN: 01-100-101

Cengage Learning
20 Channel Center Street
Boston, MA 02210
USA

Cengage Learning is a leading provider of customized learning solutions with office locations around the globe, including Singapore, the United Kingdom, Australia, Mexico, Brazil, and Japan. Locate your local office at:
www.international.cengage.com/region.

Cengage Learning products are represented in Canada by Nelson Education, Ltd.

For your lifelong learning solutions, visit **www.cengage.com/custom.**

Visit our corporate website at **www.cengage.com.**

Table of Contents

FOUNDATIONS OF MARKETING

chapter 1

Customer-Driven Strategic Marketing

© marcnorman/iStockphoto.com

OBJECTIVES

1. Define *marketing*.
2. Be aware of the marketing concept.
3. Understand the importance of building customer relationships.
4. Understand the role of marketing in our global economy.

MARKETING INSIGHTS

Chipotle Grill—Where Relationships Matter

Chipotle Mexican Grill seems to do things a bit differently from other fast-food chains. Chipotle spends very little on advertising compared to the competition. Chipotle spends only $6 million on ad campaigns in a year. Comparatively, Arby's—considered the smallest of the fast-food chains—spends nearly $100 million. Instead of paid advertising, Chipotle strives to form relationships with customers to encourage positive word of mouth and gather marketing research. For instance, Chipotle offers an invitation-only loyalty program to customers willing to take the time to answer questions about the company's philosophy.

Furthermore, Chipotle's "food with integrity" products use fresh food with ingredients grown naturally and sustainably from local farmers whenever possible, increasing positive relationships with local suppliers. Chipotle attempts to create high customer satisfaction by ensuring that products are of the best quality. The company also spends a great deal of time investigating ways to improve the taste and quality of its products. For instance, the company's owner had a team of engineers create a new machine that heats tortillas evenly after he couldn't convince his distributor to make one according to acceptable standards.

Advancing technology offers new opportunities for Chipotle Grill to connect with customers—but the restaurant chain is being cautious. While the company is investigating other marketing platforms like iPhone apps and social media tools, it wants to retain human interaction in the Chipotle experience. This is demonstrated in its practices—selecting only the cheeriest of applicants. Chipotle continues to be successful because of its innovative and unique approach to marketing and stakeholder relationships.[1]

Like all organizations, Chipotle Grill attempts to provide products that customers want, communicate useful information about them to excite interest, price them appropriately, and make them available when and where customers want to buy them. Even if an organization does all these things well, however, competition from marketers of similar products, economic conditions, and other factors can impact the company's success. Such factors influence the decisions that all organizations must make in strategic marketing.

This chapter introduces the strategic marketing concepts and decisions covered throughout the text. First, we develop a definition of *marketing* and explore each element of the definition in detail. Next, we explore the importance of value-driven marketing. We also introduce the marketing concept and consider several issues associated with its implementation. Additionally, we take a look at the management of customer relationships and relationship marketing. Finally, we examine the importance of marketing in global society.

DEFINING *MARKETING*

LO1. Define *marketing*.

If you ask several people what *marketing* is, you are likely to hear a variety of descriptions. Although many people think marketing is advertising or selling, marketing is much more complex than most people realize. In this book we define **marketing** as the process of creating, distributing, promoting, and pricing goods, services, and ideas to facilitate satisfying exchange relationships with customers and to develop and maintain favorable relationships with stakeholders in a dynamic environment. Our definition is consistent with that of the American Marketing Association (AMA), which defines *marketing* as "the activity, set of institutions, and processes for creating, communicating, delivering, and exchanging offerings that have value for customers, clients, partners, and society at large."[2]

Marketing Focuses on Customers

As the purchasers of the products that organizations develop, price, distribute, and promote, **customers** are the focal point of all marketing activities (see Figure 1.1). Organizations have to define their products not as what the companies make or produce but as what they do to satisfy customers. The Walt Disney Company is not in the business of establishing theme parks; it is in the business of making people happy. At Disney World, customers are guests, the crowd is

marketing The process of creating, distributing, promoting, and pricing goods, services, and ideas to facilitate satisfying exchange relationships with customers and to develop and maintain favorable relationships with stakeholders in a dynamic environment

customers The purchasers of organizations' products; the focal point of all marketing activities

Appealing to Target Markets
Marvel provides online entertainment to satisfy its customers.

Figure 1.1 Components of Strategic Marketing

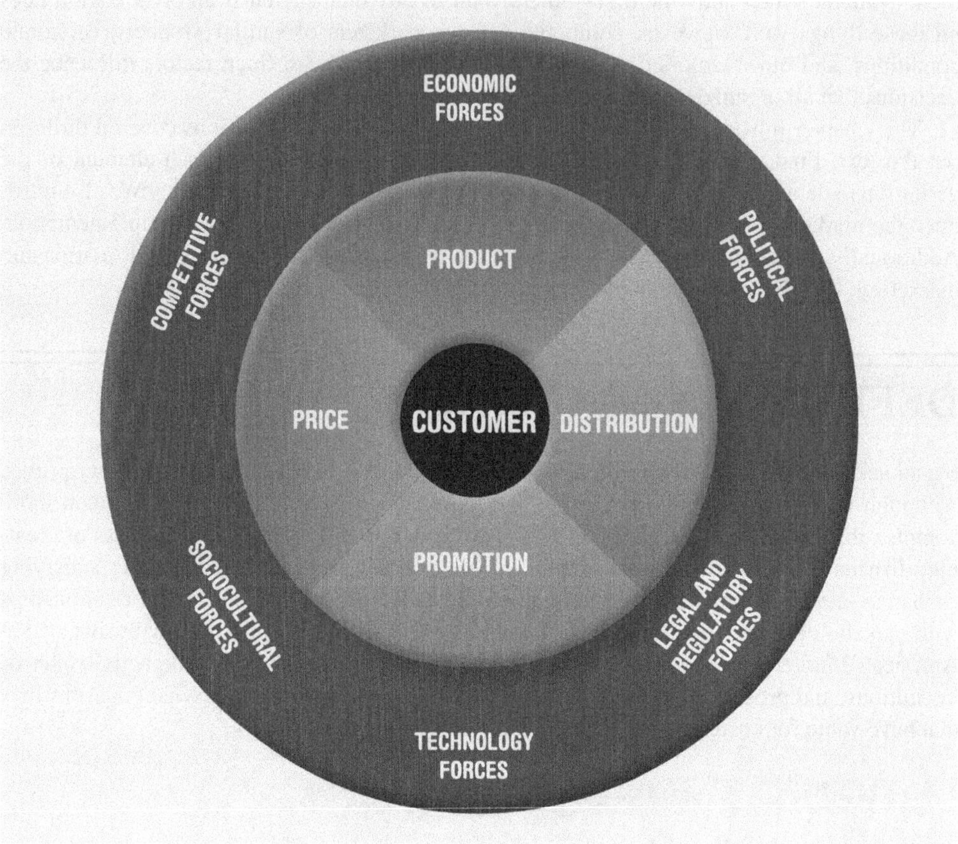

© Cengage Learning

an audience, and employees are cast members. Customer satisfaction and enjoyment can come from anything received when buying and using a product.

The essence of marketing is to develop satisfying exchanges from which both customers and marketers benefit. The customer expects to gain a reward or benefit greater than the costs incurred in a marketing transaction. The marketer expects to gain something of value in return, generally the price charged for the product. Through buyer–seller interaction, a customer develops expectations about the seller's future behavior. To fulfill these expectations, the marketer must deliver on promises made. Over time, this interaction results in relationships between the two parties. Fast-food restaurants such as Taco Bell and Subway depend on repeat purchases from satisfied customers—many often live or work a few miles from these restaurants—whereas customer expectations revolve around tasty food, value, and dependable service.

Organizations generally focus their marketing efforts on a specific group of customers, called a **target market**. Marketing managers may define a target market as a vast number of people or a relatively small group. Often companies target multiple markets with different products, promotions, prices, and distribution systems for each one. Vans shoes targets a fairly narrow market segment, especially compared to more diverse athletic shoe companies such as Nike and Reebok. Vans targets skateboarders and snowboarders between the ages of 10 and 24, whereas Nike and Reebok target most sports, age ranges, genders, and price points.[3]

target market A specific group of customers on whom an organization focuses its marketing efforts

Marketing Deals with Products, Distribution, Promotion, and Price

Marketing is more than simply advertising or selling a product; it involves developing and managing a product that will satisfy customer needs. It focuses on making the product available in the right place and at a price acceptable to buyers. It also requires communicating information that helps customers determine if the product will satisfy their needs. These activities are planned, organized, implemented, and controlled to meet the needs of customers within the target market. Marketers refer to these activities—product, pricing, distribution, and promotion—as the **marketing mix** because they decide what type of each element to use and in what amounts. Marketing creates value through the marketing mix. A primary goal of a marketing manager is to create and maintain the right mix of these elements to satisfy customers' needs for a general product type. Note in Figure 1.1 that the marketing mix is built around the customer.

Marketing managers strive to develop a marketing mix that matches the needs of customers in the target market. For example, Zumiez targets teenage girls and boys with snowboarding and skateboarding clothes targeted toward this age group.[4] Marketing managers must constantly monitor the competition and adapt their product, pricing, promotion, and distribution decisions to create long-term success.

Before marketers can develop a marketing mix, they must collect in-depth, up-to-date information about customer needs. Such information might include data about the age, income, ethnicity, gender, and educational level of people in the target market, their preferences for product features, their attitudes toward competitors' products, and the frequency with which they use the product. Zumiez has to closely monitor trends to adjust its marketing mix to provide constant fashion changes. Armed with market information, marketing managers are better able to develop a marketing mix that satisfies a specific target market.

Let's look more closely at the decisions and activities related to each marketing mix variable.

The Product Variable

Successful marketing efforts result in products that become part of everyday life. Consider the satisfaction customers have had over the years from Coca-Cola, Levi's jeans, Visa credit cards, Tylenol pain relievers, and 3M Post-it Notes. The product variable of the marketing mix deals with researching customers' needs and wants and designing a product that

marketing mix Four marketing activities—product, pricing, distribution, and promotion— that a firm can control to meet the needs of customers within its target market

Marketing Debate

The Truth about Organic Products

ISSUE: Do consumers understand organic food?

Many consumers equate the title organic with healthy. However, most research has proven that purchasing organic products generally has no significant effect upon an individual's health, although in some cases organic food has been shown to contribute less toward food poisoning. Some organic foods, such as organic potato chips, are just as fattening as non-organic.

So is the term organic misleading? It depends upon how consumers interpret the term. Synthetic chemicals and pesticides are not used on organic produce, although organic pesticides can be used. Organic farming is also more beneficial to the environment. Whatever might be true about organic food, demand for organically grown products has continually risen and shows no signs of slowing down.[a]

Types of Products   Vizio produces 3D technology, a tangible good, to allow consumers a differentiated product experience, while Verizon provides an intangible product through its cellular services.

product A good, a service, or an idea

satisfies them. A **product** can be a good, a service, or an idea. A good is a physical entity you can touch. Oakley sunglasses, Seven for All Mankind jeans, and Axe body spray are all examples of products. A service is the application of human and mechanical efforts to people or objects to provide intangible benefits to customers. Air travel, education, haircutting, banking, medical care, and day care are examples of services. Ideas include concepts, philosophies, images, and issues. For instance, a marriage counselor, for a fee, gives spouses ideas to help improve their relationship. Other marketers of ideas include political parties, churches, and schools.

The product variable also involves creating or modifying brand names and packaging and may include decisions regarding warranty and repair services. For example, the lawn care company TruGreen was originally branded as "Chemlawn." The company adapted its branding and products to provide a healthier and "greener" product offering.

Product variable decisions and related activities are important because they are directly involved with creating products that address customers' needs and wants. To maintain an assortment of products that helps an organization achieve its goals, marketers must develop new products, modify existing ones, and eliminate those that no longer satisfy enough buyers or that yield unacceptable profits.

The Distribution Variable

To satisfy customers, products must be available at the right time and in convenient locations. Subway, for example, locates not only in strip malls but also inside Walmarts, Home Depots, Laundromats, churches, and hospitals, as well as inside Goodwill stores, car dealerships, and appliance stores. There are more than 37,000 Subways worldwide, surpassing McDonald's as the world's largest chain.[5]

In dealing with the distribution variable, a marketing manager makes products available in the quantities desired to as many target-market customers as possible,

Distribution
Starbucks increases its distribution channels by offering its coffee products through retail organizations, such as Barnes & Noble.

Emerging Trends

The Demand for Single-Serve Coffee Is Brewing

Starbucks is at it again, taking over the coffee world one mug at a time. In an attempt to diversify itself, Starbucks has begun to pursue efforts to tackle the emerging trend of Verismo single-serve coffee machines. It has set its sights on introducing brewers that enable consumers to make single shots of espresso along with espresso-based drinks and lattes.

One of the ways in which Starbucks promoted the product was by having Starbucks baristas demonstrate how it worked at Williams-Sonoma stores countrywide. The coffee machines are being distributed to specialty home stores as this is a specialty product for Starbucks. The company

named the machine Verismo after a style of Italian opera to spark interest among consumers. Direct competition for Verismo includes Kraft Foods Tassimo, Nestle's Nespresso, and Green Mountain's Keurig machines.

The product itself is quite innovative since it is the first single cup machine that can make brewed coffee, espresso, and lattes with fresh milk. The machine is technically not the first venture Starbucks has made into the single-serve coffee market. The company entered with a single-serve instant coffee packet, which was a highly successful product. If the past is an indicator of how Verisimo will perform, Starbucks may be adding another profitable venture to its portfolio.[b]

keeping total inventory, transportation, and storage costs as low as possible. A marketing manager also may select and motivate intermediaries (wholesalers and retailers), establish and maintain inventory control procedures, and develop and manage transportation and storage systems. The advent of the Internet and electronic commerce also has dramatically influenced the distribution variable. Companies now can make their products available throughout the world without maintaining facilities in each country. Apple has benefitted from the ability to download songs and apps over the Internet. The company has supported growth and global success beyond the presence of physical Apple stores by selling phones, computers, iPads, and accessories online. We examine distribution issues in Chapters 13 and 14.

The Promotion Variable

The promotion variable relates to activities used to inform individuals or groups about the organization and its products. Promotion can aim to increase public awareness of the organization and of new or existing products. Century 21 Real Estate, for example, wanted to increase brand preference among young adults between the ages of 25 and 34. The company released a mobile game called We City that gave players the opportunity to build their own virtual cities. Players could choose to place Century 21-branded buildings in their cities as well as watch a 30-second advertisement for Century 21. More than 90 percent choose to insert Century 21-branded buildings into their virtual cities.[6]

Promotional activities also can educate customers about product features or urge people to take a particular stance on a political or social issue, such as smoking or drug abuse. For example, the National Highway Safety Traffic Administration released an ad campaign to deter drunk driving during the holiday season. The campaign carried the message that cops "would see you before you see them." In the advertisement, a transparent cop watches a drunk couple as they leave a party, only to have them arrested as they are driving home.[7]

Promotion can help to sustain interest in established products that have been available for decades, such as Arm & Hammer baking soda or Ivory soap. Many companies are using the Internet to communicate information about themselves and their products. Campbell's Kitchen provides a diverse array of recipes, coupons, and discussion boards online to support the sales of their soups.[8]

The Price Variable

The price variable relates to decisions and actions associated with establishing pricing objectives and policies and determining product prices. Price is a critical component of the marketing mix because customers are concerned about the value obtained in an exchange. Price is often used as a competitive tool, and intense price competition sometimes leads to price wars. Higher prices can be used competitively to establish a product's premium image. Waterman and Mont Blanc pens, for example, have an image of high quality and high price that has given them significant status. Other companies are skilled at providing products at prices lower than competitors (consider Walmart's tagline "Save Money, Live Better"). Amazon uses its vast network of partnerships and cost efficiencies to provide products at low prices. Brick-and-mortar retailers have not been able to offer comparable products with prices that low, providing Amazon with a considerable competitive advantage.

The marketing-mix variables are often viewed as controllable because they can be modified. However, there are limits to how much marketing managers can alter them. Economic conditions, competitive structure, and government regulations may prevent a manager from adjusting prices frequently or significantly. Making changes in the size, shape, and design of most tangible goods is expensive; therefore, such product features cannot be altered very often. In addition, promotional campaigns and methods used to distribute products ordinarily cannot be rewritten or revamped overnight.

Marketing Creates Value

Value is an important element of managing long-term customer relationships and implementing the marketing concept. We view **value** as a customer's subjective assessment of benefits relative to costs in determining the worth of a product (customer value = customer benefits–customer costs). Consumers develop a concept of value through the integration of their perceptions of product quality and financial sacrifice.[9] From a company's perspective, there is a trade-off between increasing the value offered to a customer and maximizing the profits from a transaction.[10]

Customer benefits include anything a buyer receives in an exchange. Hotels and motels, for example, basically provide a room with a bed and bathroom, but each firm provides a different level of service, amenities, and atmosphere to satisfy its guests. Hampton Inn offers the minimum services necessary to maintain a quality, efficient, low-price overnight accommodation. In contrast, the Ritz-Carlton provides every imaginable service a guest might desire.

value A customer's subjective assessment of benefits relative to costs in determining the worth of a product

Value-Driven Marketing
Cadbury provides a high-quality chocolate bar that satisfies customer desires at a premium price point.

The hotel even allows its staff members to spend up to $2,000 to settle customer complaints.[11] Customers judge which type of accommodation offers the best value according to the benefits they desire and their willingness and ability to pay for the costs associated with the benefits.

Customer costs include anything a buyer must give up to obtain the benefits the product provides. The most obvious cost is the monetary price of the product, but nonmonetary costs can be equally important in a customer's determination of value. Two nonmonetary costs are the time and effort customers expend to find and purchase desired products. To reduce time and effort, a company can increase product availability, thereby making it more convenient for buyers to purchase the firm's products. Another nonmonetary cost is risk, which can be reduced by offering good basic warranties or extended warranties for an additional charge.[12] Another risk-reduction strategy is the offer of a 100 percent satisfaction guarantee. This strategy is increasingly popular in today's catalog/telephone/Internet shopping environment. L.L.Bean, for example, uses such a guarantee to reduce the risk involved in ordering merchandise from its catalogs.

The process people use to determine the value of a product is not highly scientific. All of us tend to get a feel for the worth of products based on our own expectations and previous experience. We can, for example, compare the value of tires, batteries, and computers directly with the value of competing products. We evaluate movies, sporting events, and performances by entertainers on the more subjective basis of personal preferences and emotions. For most purchases, we do not consciously try to calculate the associated benefits and costs. It becomes an instinctive feeling that Kellogg's Corn Flakes is a good value or that McDonald's is a good place to take children for a quick lunch. The purchase of an automobile or a mountain bike may have emotional components, but more conscious decision making also may figure in the process of determining value.

In developing marketing activities, it is important to recognize that customers receive benefits based on their experiences. For example, many computer buyers consider services such as fast delivery, ease of installation, technical advice, and training assistance to be important elements of the product. Customers also derive benefits from the act of shopping and selecting products. These benefits can be affected by the atmosphere or environment of a store, such as Red Lobster's nautical/seafood theme. Even the ease of navigating a website can have a tremendous impact on perceived value. For this reason, General Motors has developed a user-friendly way to navigate its website for researching and pricing vehicles. Using the Internet to compare a Chevrolet to a Mercedes could result in different users viewing each automobile as an excellent value. Owners have rated Chevrolet as providing reliable transportation and having dealers who provide acceptable service. A Mercedes may cost twice as much but has been rated as a better-engineered automobile that also has a higher social status than the Chevrolet. Different customers may view each car as being an exceptional value for their own personal satisfaction.

The marketing mix can be used to enhance perceptions of value. A product that demonstrates value usually has a feature or an enhancement that provides benefits. Promotional activities can also help to create image and prestige characteristics that customers consider in their assessment of a product's value. In some cases value may be perceived simply as the lowest price. Many customers may not care about the quality of the paper towels they buy; they simply want the cheapest ones for use in cleaning up spills because they plan to throw them in the trash anyway. On the other hand, more people are looking for the fastest, most convenient way to achieve a goal and therefore become insensitive to pricing. For example, many busy customers are buying more prepared meals in supermarkets to take home and serve quickly, even though these meals cost considerably more than meals prepared from scratch. In such cases the products with the greatest convenience may be perceived as having the greatest value. The availability or distribution of products also can enhance their value. Taco Bell wants to have its Mexican fast-food products available at any time and any place people are thinking about consuming food. It therefore has introduced Taco Bell products into supermarkets, vending machines, college campuses, and other convenient locations. Thus, the development of an effective marketing strategy requires understanding the needs and desires of customers and designing a marketing mix to satisfy them and provide the value they want.

Marketing Builds Relationships with Customers and Other Stakeholders

Marketing also creates value through the building of stakeholder relationships. Individuals and organizations engage in marketing to facilitate **exchanges**, the provision or transfer of goods, services, or ideas in return for something of value. Any product (good, service, or even idea) may be involved in a marketing exchange. We assume only that individuals and organizations expect to gain a reward in excess of the costs incurred.

For an exchange to take place, four conditions must exist. First, two or more individuals, groups, or organizations must participate, and each must possess something of value that the other party desires. Second, the exchange should provide a benefit or satisfaction to both parties involved in the transaction. Third, each party must have confidence in the promise of the "something of value" held by the other. If you go to a Coldplay concert, for example, you go with the expectation of a great performance. Finally, to build trust, the parties to the exchange must meet expectations.

Figure 1.2 depicts the exchange process. The arrows indicate that the parties communicate that each has something of value available to exchange. An exchange will not necessarily take place just because these conditions exist; marketing activities can occur even without an actual transaction or sale. You may see an ad for a Sub-Zero refrigerator, for instance, but you might never buy the luxury appliance. When an exchange occurs, products are traded for other products or for financial resources.

Marketing activities should attempt to create and maintain satisfying exchange relationships. To maintain an exchange relationship, buyers must be satisfied with the good, service, or idea obtained, and sellers must be satisfied with the financial reward or something else of value received. A dissatisfied customer who lacks trust in the relationship often searches for alternative organizations or products. The customer relationship often endures over an extended time period, and repeat purchases are critical for the firm.

Marketers are concerned with building and maintaining relationships not only with customers but also with relevant stakeholders. **Stakeholders** include those constituents who have a "stake," or claim, in some aspect of a company's products, operations, markets, industry, and outcomes; these include customers, employees, investors and shareholders, suppliers,

exchanges The provision or transfer of goods, services, or ideas in return for something of value

stakeholders Constituents who have a "stake," or claim, in some aspect of a company's products, operations, markets, industry, and outcomes

Satisfying Stakeholder Needs
Apple continues to excel at creating products that satisfy customers, generate jobs, create shareholder wealth, and contribute to greater life enjoyment.

Figure 1.2 Exchange between Buyer and Seller

Something of value

Money, credit, labor, goods

Buyer

Seller

Something of value

Goods, services, ideas

© Cengage Learning

governments, communities, and many others. Developing and maintaining favorable relations with stakeholders is crucial to the long-term growth of an organization and its products.

Marketing Occurs in a Dynamic Environment

Marketing activities do not take place in a vacuum. The **marketing environment**, which includes competitive, economic, political, legal and regulatory, technological, and sociocultural forces, surrounds the customer and affects the marketing mix (see Figure 1.1). The effects of these forces on buyers and sellers can be dramatic and difficult to predict. Their impact on value can be extensive as market changes can easily impact how stakeholders perceive certain products. They can create threats to marketers but also can generate opportunities for new products and new methods of reaching customers.

The forces of the marketing environment affect a marketer's ability to facilitate value-driven marketing exchanges in three general ways. First, they influence customers by affecting their lifestyles, standards of living, and preferences and needs for products. Because a marketing manager tries to develop and adjust the marketing mix to satisfy customers, effects of environmental forces on customers also have an indirect impact on marketing-mix components. Second, marketing environment forces help to determine whether and how a marketing manager can perform certain marketing activities. Third, environmental forces may affect a marketing manager's decisions and actions by influencing buyers' reactions to the firm's marketing mix.

Marketing environment forces can fluctuate quickly and dramatically, which is one reason why marketing is so interesting and challenging. Because these forces are closely interrelated, changes in one may cause changes in others. For example, evidence linking children's consumption of soft drinks and fast foods to health issues has exposed marketers of such products to negative publicity and generated calls for legislation regulating the sale of soft drinks in public schools. Some companies have responded to these concerns by voluntarily reformulating products to make them healthier or even introducing new products. McDonald's began featuring calorie counts on its menus, while Coca-Cola reduced the calories in some of its soft drinks by 30 percent.[13]

Changes in the marketing environment produce uncertainty for marketers and at times hurt marketing efforts, but they also create opportunities. For example, when oil prices increase, consumers shift to potential alternative sources of transportation including bikes, buses, light rail, trains, carpooling, more energy-efficient vehicle purchases, or telecommuting when possible. Marketers who are alert to changes in environmental forces not only can adjust to and influence these changes but can also capitalize on the opportunities such changes provide. Marketing-mix variables—product, price, distribution, and promotion—are factors over

marketing environment The competitive, economic, political, legal and regulatory, technological, and sociocultural forces that surround the customer and affect the marketing mix

which an organization has control; the forces of the environment, however, are subject to far less control. Even though marketers know that they cannot predict changes in the marketing environment with certainty, however, they must nevertheless plan for them. Because these environmental forces have such a profound effect on marketing activities, we explore each of them in considerable depth in Chapter 3.

UNDERSTANDING THE MARKETING CONCEPT

LO2. Be aware of the marketing concept.

Some firms have sought success by buying land, building a factory, equipping it with people and machines, and then making a product they believe buyers need. However, these firms frequently fail to attract customers with what they have to offer because they define their business as "making a product" rather than as "helping potential customers satisfy their needs and wants." On the other hand, Daisy-brand cottage cheese recognizes that consumers want healthy foods that are convenient to enjoy. Daisy's low-fat, 2-percent cottage cheese has no additives, preservatives, or growth hormones and markets itself as an excellent source of protein and calcium. To emphasize the healthful image of the product, the organization's advertising provides visuals of healthy foods that can be enjoyed with its cottage cheese.

marketing concept
A managerial philosophy that an organization should try to satisfy customers' needs through a coordinated set of activities that also allows the organization to achieve its goals

According to the **marketing concept**, an organization should try to provide products that satisfy customers' needs through a coordinated set of activities that also allows the organization to achieve its goals. Customer satisfaction is the major focus of the marketing concept. To implement the marketing concept, an organization strives to determine what buyers want and uses this information to develop satisfying products. It focuses on customer analysis, competitor analysis, and integration of the firm's resources to provide customer value and satisfaction, as well as to generate long-term profits.[14] The firm also must continue to alter, adapt, and develop products to keep pace with customers' changing desires and preferences. Howard Schultz, founder and CEO of Starbucks, demonstrates the company's grasp on the marketing concept by explaining that Starbucks is not a coffee business that serves people, but rather a "people business serving coffee." Starbucks' leadership sees the company as being "in the business of humanity," emphasizing the fact that Starbucks is not only concerned about customers but society as well.[15] Thus, the marketing concept emphasizes that marketing begins and ends with customers. Research has found a positive association between customer satisfaction and shareholder value,[16] and high levels of customer satisfaction also tend to attract and retain high-quality employees and managers.[17]

The marketing concept is not a second definition of marketing. It is a management philosophy guiding an organization's overall activities. This philosophy affects all organizational activities, not just marketing. Production, finance, accounting, human resources, and marketing departments must work together.

The marketing concept is also not a philanthropic philosophy aimed at helping customers at the expense of the organization. A firm that adopts the marketing concept must satisfy not only its customers' objectives but also its

Courtesy of Daisy Brand LLC

Implementing the Marketing Concept
Daisy-brand low-fat, 2-percent cottage cheese satisfies consumers' needs for a low-calorie snack that can be combined with a variety of other foods.

Entrepreneurship in Marketing

Build-a-Bear Entrepreneur Creates Innovative Way to Enable Children's Creativity

Maxine Clark, CEO of Build-a-Bear Workshops, has always been an entrepreneur at heart. After conquering the retail industry as president of Payless ShoeSource, Clark naturally wondered what was next. One day while shopping, she conceived a business idea that would enable children to take a hands-on approach at using their creativity. The idea would allow children to choose a stuffed bear, stuff it, and even give it a heart. After formulating a business plan and acquiring capital through investors, Clark began to work on opening the first store in the St. Louis Galleria.

The store was a success that enabled room for growth throughout the country and the world. Currently, the company operates in 19 countries and is continually looking for further expansion. The operation grew from bears and clothes to shoes, accessories, and additional options for other animals. The company is consistently focused on their customers and their experiences, which has built a loyal following globally with more than $390 million in revenue.[c]

© iStockphoto.com/CRTd

own, or it will not stay in business long. The overall objectives of a business might relate to increasing profits, market share, sales, or a combination of all three. The marketing concept stresses that an organization can best achieve these objectives by being customer oriented. Thus, implementing the marketing concept should benefit the organization as well as its customers.

It is important for marketers to consider not only their current buyers' needs but also the long-term needs of society. Striving to satisfy customers' desires by sacrificing society's long-term welfare is unacceptable. For instance, there is significant demand for large SUVs and trucks. However, environmentalists and federal regulators are challenging automakers to produce more fuel-efficient vehicles with increased mpg standards. The question that remains is whether or not Americans are willing to give up their spacious SUVs for the good of the environment.

Evolution of the Marketing Concept

The marketing concept may seem like an obvious approach to running a business. However, businesspeople have not always believed that the best way to make sales and profits is to satisfy customers.

The Production Orientation

During the second half of the 19th century, the Industrial Revolution was in full swing in the United States. Electricity, rail transportation, division of labor, assembly lines, and mass production made it possible to produce goods more efficiently. With new technology and new ways of using labor, products poured into the marketplace, where demand for manufactured goods was strong.

The Sales Orientation

While sales have always been needed to make a profit, during the first half of the 20th century competition increased and businesses realized that they would have to focus more on selling products to buyers. Businesses viewed sales as the major means of increasing profits, and this period came to have a sales orientation. Businesspeople believed that the most important marketing activities were personal selling, advertising, and distribution. Today, some people incorrectly equate marketing with a sales orientation.

The Market Orientation

By the early 1950s, some businesspeople began to recognize that efficient production and extensive promotion did not guarantee that customers would buy products. These businesses, and many others since, found that they must first determine what customers want and then produce those products rather than making the products first and then trying to persuade customers that they need them. As more organizations realized the importance of satisfying customers' needs, U.S. businesses entered the marketing era, one of market orientation.

A **market orientation** requires the "organizationwide generation of market intelligence pertaining to current and future customer needs, dissemination of the intelligence across departments, and organizationwide responsiveness to it."[18] Market orientation is linked to new-product innovation by developing a strategic focus to explore and develop new products to serve target markets.[19] For example, with an increasing "green attitude" in this country, consumers like environmentally responsible products offered at fair prices. To meet this demand, Method laundry detergent is eight times more concentrated and can clean 50 loads of laundry from a container the size of a small soft-drink bottle. Top management, marketing managers, nonmarketing managers (those in production, finance, human resources, and so on), and customers are all important in developing and carrying out a market orientation. Trust, openness, honoring promises, respect, collaboration, and recognizing the market as the raison d'etre are six values required by organizations striving to become more market oriented.[20] Unless marketing managers provide continuous customer-focused leadership with minimal interdepartmental conflict, achieving a market orientation will be difficult. Nonmarketing managers must communicate with marketing managers to share information important to understanding the customer. Finally, a market orientation involves being responsive to ever-changing customer needs and wants. To accomplish this, eBay, the online auction and shopping site, acquired the online platform Hunch to help the ecommerce site create better product recommendations for its users. Hunch uses online data to make predictions based on users' likes and interests. It follows buyers' online purchases and recommends related topics.[21] Trying to assess what customers want, which is difficult to begin with, is further complicated by the speed with which fashions and tastes can change. Today, businesses want to satisfy customers and build meaningful long-term buyer–seller relationships. Doing so helps a firm boost its own financial value.[22]

Implementing the Marketing Concept

A philosophy may sound reasonable and look good on paper, but this does not mean that it can be put into practice easily. To implement the marketing concept, a market-oriented organization must accept some general conditions and recognize and deal with several problems. Consequently, the marketing concept has yet to be fully accepted by all businesses.

Management must first establish an information system to discover customers' real needs and then use the information to create satisfying products. For example, Rubbermaid is using a social commerce platform (customer/business interaction mechanism) that impacts product development and education as to how to use the product. In reviewing customer interaction, Rubbermaid noted that many consumers did not understand how to use its "Produce Saver" food storage container properly. When the company added use and care instructions to its website, the average star rating (a notation of satisfaction) increased significantly. Listening and responding to consumers' frustrations and appreciation is the key in implementing the marketing concept.[23] An information system is usually expensive; management must commit money and time for its development and maintenance. Without an adequate information system, however, an organization cannot be market oriented.

To satisfy customers' objectives as well as its own, a company also must coordinate all of its activities. This may require restructuring its internal operations, including production, marketing, and other business functions. This requires the firm to adapt to a changing external environment, including changing customer expectations. Companies who monitor the

market orientation An organizationwide commitment to researching and responding to customer needs

external environment can often predict major changes and adapt successfully. For instance, while the majority of Internet companies failed after the dot-com bubble burst in 2000, Amazon.com continued to thrive because it understood its customers and had created a website customized to their wants.[24] The company continues to expand its products and add new features to its website to serve its customers better. On the other hand, when Hewlett-Packard announced it intended to sell its personal computer business, company share prices plummeted. Investors felt HP's livelihood depended upon its PC sales. Additionally, because personal computers are such an integral part of HP, such a decision would require major changes in company operations and strategic direction. The plan was eventually scrapped.[25] If marketing is not included in the organization's top-level management, a company could fail to address actual customer needs and desires. Implementing the marketing concept demands the support not only of top management but also of managers and staff at all levels of the organization.

CUSTOMER RELATIONSHIP MANAGEMENT

LO3. Understand the importance of building customer relationships.

Customer relationship management (CRM) focuses on using information about customers to create marketing strategies that develop and sustain desirable customer relationships. Achieving the full profit potential of each customer relationship should be the fundamental goal of every marketing strategy. Marketing relationships with customers are the lifeblood of all businesses. At the most basic level, profits can be obtained through relationships in the following ways: (1) by acquiring new customers, (2) by enhancing the profitability of existing customers, and (3) by extending the duration of customer relationships. In addition to retaining customers, companies also should focus on regaining and managing relationships with customers who have abandoned the firm.[26] Implementing the marketing concept means optimizing the exchange relationship, otherwise known as the relationship between a company's financial investment in customer relationships and the return generated by customers' loyalty and retention.

Maintaining positive relationships with customers is an important goal for marketers. The term **relationship marketing** refers to "long-term, mutually beneficial arrangements in which both the buyer and seller focus on value enhancement through the creation of more satisfying exchanges."[27] Relationship marketing continually deepens the buyer's trust in the company, and as the customer's confidence grows, this, in turn, increases the firm's understanding of the customer's needs. Buyers and marketers can thus enter into a close relationship in which both participate in the creation of value.[28] Successful marketers respond to customer needs and strive to increase value to buyers over time. Eventually, this interaction becomes a solid relationship that allows for cooperation and mutual dependency. Whole Foods has implemented relationship marketing with the view that customers are its most important stakeholder. One of the company's core values involves "satisfying the customer first."[29]

Relationship marketing strives to build satisfying exchange relationships between buyers and sellers by gathering useful data at all customer contact points and analyzing that data to better understand customers' needs, desires, and habits. It focuses on building and using databases and leveraging technologies to identify strategies and methods that will maximize the lifetime value of each desirable customer to the company. It is imperative that marketers educate themselves about their customers' expectations if they are to satisfy their needs; customer dissatisfaction will only lead to defection.[30]

To build these long-term customer relationships, marketers are increasingly turning to marketing research and information technology. By increasing customer value over time, organizations try to retain and increase long-term profitability through customer loyalty, which results from increasing customer value. The airline industry is a key player in CRM efforts

customer relationship management (CRM) Using information about customers to create marketing strategies that develop and sustain desirable customer relationships

relationship marketing Establishing long-term, mutually satisfying buyer–seller relationships

with its frequent-flyer programs. Frequent-flyer programs enable airlines to track individual information about customers, using databases that can help airlines understand what different customers want and treat customers differently depending on their flying habits. Relationship-building efforts like frequent-flyer programs have been shown to increase customer value.[31]

Through the use of Internet-based marketing strategies (e-marketing), companies can personalize customer relationships on a nearly one-on-one basis. A wide range of products, such as computers, jeans, golf clubs, cosmetics, and greeting cards, can be tailored for specific customers. Customer relationship management provides a strategic bridge between information technology and marketing strategies aimed at long-term relationships. This involves finding and retaining customers by using information to improve customer value and satisfaction.

LO4. Understand the role of marketing in our global economy.

THE IMPORTANCE OF MARKETING IN OUR GLOBAL ECONOMY

Our definition of marketing and discussion of marketing activities reveal some of the obvious reasons the study of marketing is relevant in today's world. In this section we look at how marketing affects us as individuals and at its role in our increasingly global society.

Marketing Costs Consume a Sizable Portion of Buyers' Dollars

Studying marketing will make you aware that many marketing activities are necessary to provide satisfying goods and services. Obviously, these activities cost money. About one-half of a buyer's dollar goes toward marketing costs. If you spend $16 on a new CD, 50 to 60 percent goes toward marketing expenses, including promotion and distribution, as well as profit margins. The production (pressing) of the CD represents about $1, or 6 percent of its price. A family with a monthly income of $3,000 that allocates $600 to taxes and savings spends about $2,400 for goods and services. Of this amount, $1,200 goes toward marketing activities. If marketing expenses consume that much of your dollar, you should know how this money is being used.

Marketing Is Used in Nonprofit Organizations

Although the term *marketing* may bring to mind advertising for Burger King, Volkswagen, and Apple, marketing is also important in organizations working to achieve goals other than ordinary business objectives (such as profit). Government agencies at the federal, state, and local levels engage in marketing activities to fulfill their mission and goals. For instance, the National Highway Traffic Safety Administration releases ads to warn consumers about the dangers associated with drinking and driving. The advertisement featuring champagne glasses and a broken Christmas bulb reinforces the message that a festive occasion like the holidays can easily turn into a tragedy as more people are inclined to consume alcohol. In addition, universities and colleges engage in marketing activities to recruit new students, as well as to obtain donations from alumni and businesses.

In the private sector, nonprofit organizations also employ marketing activities to create, price, distribute, and promote programs that benefit particular segments of society. The Red Cross provides disaster relief throughout the world and offers promotional messages to encourage donations to support their efforts. For example, when Hurricane Sandy hit the East Coast of the United States, the Red Cross released many promotional messages encouraging people to donate money for those impacted by the disasters.

DURING THE HOLIDAYS

2–3 TIMES
MORE PEOPLE DIE
IN ALCOHOL-RELATED
CRASHES
&
40% OF TRAFFIC FATALITIES
INVOLVE A DRIVER
WHO IS IMPAIRED BY
ALCOHOL

Source: National Highway Traffic Safety Administration, Traffic Safety Facts, December 2007.

AP Photo/PR NEWSWIRE

Nonprofit Organization
The National Highway Traffic Safety Administration creates awareness of the risks associated with drinking and driving during the holiday season.

Marketing Is Important to Businesses and the Economy

Businesses must engage in marketing to survive and grow, and marketing activities are needed to reach customers and provide products. Financial resources generated from sales are necessary for the operations of a firm and to provide financial returns to investors. Innovation in operations and products drive business success and customer loyalty. Even nonprofit businesses need to understand and use marketing to serve their audience.

Marketing activities help to produce the profits that are essential to the survival of individual businesses. Without profits, businesses would find it difficult, if not impossible, to buy more raw materials, hire more employees, attract more capital, and create additional products that, in turn, make more profits. Without profits, marketers cannot continue to provide jobs and contribute to social causes. Therefore, marketing helps create a successful economy and contributes to the well-being of society.

Marketing Fuels Our Global Economy

Marketing is necessary to advance a global economy. Advances in technology, along with falling political and economic barriers and the universal desire for a higher standard of living, have made marketing across national borders commonplace while stimulating global economic growth. As a result of worldwide communications and increased international travel, many U.S. brands have achieved widespread acceptance around the world. At the same time, customers in the United States have greater choices among the products they buy because foreign brands such as Toyota (Japan), Bayer (Germany), and Nestlé (Switzerland) sell alongside U.S. brands such as General Motors, Tylenol, and Chevron. People around the world watch CNN and MTV on Samsung and Sony televisions they purchased at Walmart. Electronic commerce via the Internet now enables businesses of all sizes to reach buyers worldwide. We explore the international markets and opportunities for global marketing in Chapter 8.

Marketing Knowledge Enhances Consumer Awareness

Besides contributing to the well-being of our economy, marketing activities help to improve the quality of our lives. Studying marketing allows us to understand the importance of marketing to customers, organizations, and our economy. Thus, we can analyze marketing efforts that need improvement and how to attain that goal. Today the consumer has more power from information available through websites, social media, and required disclosure. As you become more knowledgeable, it is possible to improve purchasing decisions. In general, you have more accurate information about a product before you purchase it than at any other time in history. Understanding marketing enables us to evaluate corrective measures (such as laws, regulations, and industry guidelines) that could stop unfair, damaging, or unethical marketing practices. Thus, understanding how marketing activities work can help you to be a better consumer and increase your ability to maximize value from purchases.

Marketing Connects People through Technology

Technology, especially computers and telecommunications, helps marketers to understand and satisfy more customers than ever before. Over the phone and online, customers can provide feedback about their experiences with a company's products. Even products such as Dasani bottled water provide a customer service number and a website for questions or comments. This feedback helps marketers refine and improve their products to satisfy customer needs better. Today marketers must recognize the impact not only of websites but of instant messaging, blogs, online forums, online games, mailing lists, and wikis, as well as text messaging via cell phones and interacting through Facebook. Increasingly, these tools are facilitating marketing

Marketing Connects People through Technology
Social media sites, such as Facebook, allow consumers to share information on marketers' successes and failures through technology.

AP Images/Paul Sakuma

Table 1.1   **Selected Smartphone Activities of U.S. Citizens**

Activity	All Cell Owners
Check weather reports and forecasts	77%
Use a social networking site	68
Get turn-by-turn navigation or direction while driving	65
Get news online	64
Play a game	64
Upload photos online so that others can see them	58
Listen to an online radio or music service, such as Pandora or Spotify	53
Check your bank balance or any online banking	44
Visit a local, state, or federal government website	31
Get coupons on deals to use at local businesses	24

Source: Pew Research Center's Internet & American Life Project, March 15–April 3, 2012 Tracking Survey. N = 2,254 adults ages 18 and older, including 903 interviews conducted on respondent's cell phone. Margin of error is +/−2.6 percentage points based on cell phone owners (n = 1,954).

exchanges. For example, new apps are being released that allow consumers to pay for their purchases using their smartphones. These apps contain "virtual replicas" of the consumer's credit or debit cards that can be used in lieu of plastic. Recognizing the convenience of this new method, more and more companies are adapting their operations to accept mobile payments.[32]

The Internet allows companies to provide tremendous amounts of information about their products to consumers and to interact with them through e-mail and websites. A consumer shopping for a new car, for example, can access automakers' webpages, configure an ideal vehicle, and get instant feedback on its cost. Consumers can visit Autobytel, Edmund's, and other websites to find professional reviews and obtain comparative pricing information on both new and used cars to help them find the best value. They can also visit a consumer opinion site, such as Yelp, to read other consumers' reviews of the products. They can then purchase a vehicle online or at a dealership. A number of companies employ social media to connect with their customers, using blogs and social networking sites such as Facebook and Twitter. We consider social networking and other digital media in Chapter 9. Table 1.1 shows some of the most common smartphone activities. We will discuss mobile marketing in more detail in Chapter 9.

Socially Responsible Marketing: Promoting the Welfare of Customers and Stakeholders

The success of our economic system depends on marketers whose values promote trust and cooperative relationships in which customers and other stakeholders are treated with respect. The public is increasingly insisting that social responsibility and ethical concerns be considered in planning and implementing marketing activities. Although some marketers' irresponsible or unethical activities end up on the front pages of *USA Today* or *The Wall Street Journal*, more firms are working to develop a responsible approach to developing long-term relationships with customers and other stakeholders.

In the area of the natural environment, companies are increasingly embracing the notion of **green marketing**, which is a strategic process involving stakeholder assessment to create

green marketing A strategic process involving stakeholder assessment to create meaningful long-term relationships with customers while maintaining, supporting, and enhancing the natural environment

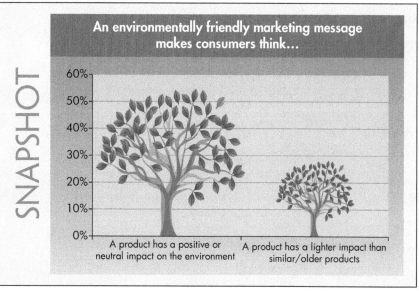

Source: 2012 Cone Green Gap Tracker Survey of 1,019 consumers.

meaningful long-term relationships with customers while maintaining, supporting, and enhancing the natural environment. Safeway and Whole Foods, for example, have been recognized by Greenpeace as the supermarket chains with the most sustainable seafood buying practices. Understanding that overfishing is a major concern, these supermarkets discontinued sales of several threatened fish populations.[33] Such initiatives not only reduce the negative impact that businesses have on the environment but also serve to enhance their reputations as sustainability concerns continue to grow. By addressing concerns about the impact of marketing on society, a firm can contribute to society through socially responsible activities as well as increase its financial performance.

Marketing Offers Many Exciting Career Prospects

From 25 to 33 percent of all civilian workers in the United States perform marketing activities. The marketing field offers a variety of interesting and challenging career opportunities throughout the world, such as personal selling, advertising, packaging, transportation, storage, marketing research, product development, wholesaling, and retailing. In the most recent recessionary period when unemployment was high, sales positions remained among the most attractive job opportunities. Marketing positions are among the most secure positions because of the need to manage customer relationships. In addition, many individuals working for nonbusiness organizations engage in marketing activities to promote political, educational, cultural, church, civic, and charitable activities. Whether a person earns a living through marketing activities or performs them voluntarily for a nonprofit group, marketing knowledge and skills are valuable personal and professional assets.

Going Green

Garbage Takes On an Entirely New Meaning

Levi Strauss is taking on a new initiative and it involves recycling. Levi's, the largest producer of jeans in the world, has developed an eco-friendly product line that incorporates at minimum 20 percent of recycled plastic into its jeans. The Waste<Less denim collection is reducing the company's carbon footprint by starting at the beginning. Its sustainability efforts began when Levi's wanted to improve methods of cotton growing. The company joined the Better Cotton Initiative that educates farmers on how to grow cotton with less water. It also began to focus on reducing its energy use.

For Levi's spring collection 3.5 million recycled plastic bottles were used to create the line. Not only are the products more eco-friendly but they are also stylish. The fiber used from the different plastic bottles enables the denim to attain a different sheen then most jeans. Levi's found that the more an individual wears the denim, the more the color of the denim will resemble the color of the bottle used to produce it. This gives consumers an idea of the process and what was used to make their clothing. Levi's has realized that many consumers enjoy participating in eco-friendly initiatives that add hope for a better tomorrow.[d]

Chapter Review

1. Define *marketing.*

Marketing is the process of creating, pricing, distributing, and promoting goods, services, and ideas to facilitate satisfying exchange relationships with customers and to develop and maintain favorable relationships with stakeholders in a dynamic environment. The essence of marketing is to develop satisfying exchanges from which both customers and marketers benefit. Organizations generally focus their marketing efforts on a specific group of customers called a target market.

To understand how marketing focuses on consumers, it is necessary to know several key marketing terms. A target market is the group of customers toward which a company directs a set of marketing efforts. Marketing involves developing and managing a product that will satisfy customer needs, making the product available at the right place and at a price acceptable to customers, and communicating information that helps customers determine if the product will satisfy their needs. These activities—product, price, distribution, and promotion—are known as the marketing mix because marketing managers decide what type of each element to use and in what amounts. Marketing managers strive to develop a marketing mix that matches the needs of customers in the target market. Before marketers can develop a marketing mix, they must collect in-depth, up-to-date information about customer needs. The product variable of the marketing mix deals with researching customers' needs and wants and designing a product that satisfies them. A product can be a good, a service, or an idea. In dealing with the distribution variable, a marketing manager tries to make products available in the quantities desired to as many customers as possible. The promotion variable relates to activities used to inform individuals or groups about the organization and its products. The price variable involves decisions and actions associated with establishing pricing policies and determining product prices. These marketing mix variables are often viewed as controllable because they can be changed, but there are limits to how much they can be altered.

Individuals and organizations engage in marketing to facilitate exchanges—the provision or transfer of goods, services, and ideas in return for something of value. Four conditions must exist for an exchange to occur. First, two or more individuals, groups, or organizations must participate, and each must possess something of value that the other party desires. Second, the exchange should provide a benefit or satisfaction to both parties involved in the transaction. Third, each party must have confidence in the promise of the "something of value" held by the other. Finally, to build trust, the parties to the exchange must meet expectations. Marketing activities should attempt to create and maintain satisfying exchange relationships.

The marketing environment, which includes competitive, economic, political, legal and regulatory, technological, and sociocultural forces, surrounds the customer and the marketing mix. These forces can create threats to marketers, but they also generate opportunities for new products and new methods of reaching customers. These forces can fluctuate quickly and dramatically.

2. Be aware of the marketing concept.

According to the marketing concept, an organization should try to provide products that satisfy customers' needs through a coordinated set of activities that also allows the organization to achieve its goals. Customer satisfaction is the marketing concept's major objective. The philosophy of the marketing concept emerged in the United States during the 1950s after the production and sales eras. Organizations that develop activities consistent with the marketing concept become market-oriented organizations. To implement the marketing concept, a market-oriented organization must establish an information system to discover customers' needs and use the information to create satisfying products. It must also coordinate all its activities and develop marketing mixes that create value for customers in order to satisfy their needs.

3. Understand the importance of building customer relationships.

Relationship marketing involves establishing long-term, mutually satisfying buyer–seller relationships. Customer relationship management (CRM) focuses on using information about customers to create marketing strategies that develop and sustain desirable customer relationships. Managing customer relationships requires identifying patterns of buying behavior and using that information to focus on the most promising and profitable customers. A customer's value over a lifetime represents an intangible asset to a marketer that can be augmented by addressing the customer's varying needs and preferences at different stages in his or her relationship with the firm. Customer lifetime value is a key measurement that forecasts a customer's lifetime economic contribution based on continued-relationship marketing efforts. Knowing a customer's potential lifetime value can help marketers determine how to best allocate resources to marketing strategies to sustain that customer over a lifetime.

4. Understand the role of marketing in our global economy.

Marketing is important to our economy in many ways. Marketing costs absorb about half of each buyer's dollar. Marketing activities are performed in both business and nonprofit organizations. Marketing activities help business organizations to generate profits, and they help fuel the increasingly global economy. Knowledge of marketing enhances consumer awareness. New technology improves marketers' ability to connect with customers. Socially responsible marketing can promote the welfare of customers and society.

Green marketing is a strategic process involving stakeholder assessment to create meaningful long-term relationships with customers while maintaining, supporting, and enhancing the natural environment. Finally, marketing offers many exciting career opportunities.

> **Go to www.cengagebrain.com for resources to help you master the content in this chapter as well as for materials that will expand your marketing knowledge!**

Key Concepts

marketing 3
customers 3
target market 4
marketing mix 5

product 6
value 8
exchanges 10
stakeholders 10

marketing
  environment 11
marketing concept 12
market orientation 14

customer relationship
  management (CRM) 15
relationship marketing 15
green marketing 19

Issues for Discussion and Review

1. What is *marketing*? How did you define the term before you read this chapter?
2. What is the focus of all marketing activities? Why?
3. What are the four variables of the marketing mix? Why are these elements known as variables?
4. What is value? How can marketers use the marketing mix to enhance the perception of value?
5. What conditions must exist before a marketing exchange can occur? Describe a recent exchange in which you participated.
6. What are the forces in the marketing environment? How much control does a marketing manager have over these forces?
7. Discuss the basic elements of the marketing concept. Which businesses in your area use this philosophy? Explain why.
8. How can an organization implement the marketing concept?
9. What is customer relationship management? Why is it so important to "manage" this relationship?
10. Why is marketing important in our society? Why should you study marketing?

Marketing Applications

1. Identify several businesses in your area that have *not* adopted the marketing concept. What characteristics of these organizations indicate nonacceptance of the marketing concept?
2. Identify possible target markets for the following products:
   a. Kellogg's Corn Flakes
   b. Wilson tennis rackets
   c. Disney World
   d. Diet Pepsi
3. Discuss the variables of the marketing mix (product, price, promotion, and distribution) as they might relate to each of the following:
   a. A trucking company
   b. A men's clothing store
   c. A skating rink
   d. A campus bookstore
4. There are seemingly hundreds of different cell phones available on the market today. How do consumers choose? The answer is simple: consumer value.

Compare the value of an Apple iPhone and a Samsung Galaxy smartphone. Begin by identifying the benefits and costs that you consider when evaluating cell phones—factors like ease of texting, overall look and feel, or purchasing price. Assign a weighting coefficient to each factor that reflects its importance to you. You could use 0–5, for example, with 0 meaning *no importance*

whatsoever and 5 meaning *absolutely important*. Using the equation value = benefits − costs, calculate the value for the iPhone and the Samsung Galaxy. Do these results match actual cell phone sales for the two products?

5. Develop your analytical and communication skills using the Role-Play Exercises online at **www.cengagebrain.com**.

Internet Exercise

The American Marketing Association

The American Marketing Association (AMA) is the marketing discipline's primary professional organization. In addition to sponsoring academic research, publishing marketing literature, and organizing meetings of local businesspeople with student members, it helps individual members to find employment in member firms. Visit the AMA website at **www.marketingpower.com**.

1. What type of information is available on the AMA website to assist students in planning their careers and finding jobs?
2. If you joined a student chapter of the AMA, what benefits would you receive?
3. What marketing-mix variable does the AMA's Internet marketing effort exemplify?

developing your marketing plan

Successful companies develop strategies for marketing their products. The strategic plan guides the marketer in making many of the detailed decisions about the attributes of the product, its distribution, promotional activities, and pricing. A clear understanding of the foundations of marketing is essential in formulating a strategy and in the development of a specific marketing plan. To guide you in relating the information in this chapter to the development of your marketing plan, consider the following:

1. Discuss how the marketing concept contributes to a company's long-term success.

2. Describe the level of market orientation that currently exists in your company. How will a market orientation contribute to the success of your new product?
3. What benefits will your product provide to the customer? How will these benefits play a role in determining the customer value of your product?

The information obtained from these questions should assist you in developing various aspects of your marketing plan. Develop your marketing plan online using the Interactive Marketing Plan at **www.cengagebrain.com**.

video case 1.1
Cruising to Success: The Tale of New Belgium Brewing

In 1991, electrical engineer Jeff Lebesch and Kim Jordan began making Belgian-style ales in their basement. The impetus for the brewery occurred after Lebesch had spent time in Belgium riding throughout the country on his

mountain bike. He believed he could manufacture high-quality Belgian beers in America. After spending time in the Colorado Rockies deciding the values and directions of their new company, the two launched New Belgium Brewing

(NBB), with Kim Jordan as marketing director. The company's first beer was named Fat Tire in honor of Lebesch's Belgian mountain biking trek. Fat Tire remains one of NBB's most popular ales.

NBB has come far from its humble basement origins. Today, the Fort Collins–based brewery is the third-largest craft brewer in the country with products available in 30 states. Kim Jordan helms the company as one of the few female CEOs of a large beer firm. "This entrepreneurial thing sneaks up on you," Jordan states. "And even after 20 years, I still have those pinch me moments where I think, wow, this is what we've created here together." While total beer sales are dropping in the United States, sales in the craft beer industry have increased to $8.7 billion. NBB has a sales growth rate of 15 percent.

Creating such success required a corporate culture that stressed creativity and an authentic approach to treating all stakeholders with respect. While the New Belgium product is a quality craft beer, just as important to the company is how it treats employees, the community, and the environment. Each element of the marketing mix was carefully considered. The company spends a significant amount of time researching and creating its beers, even collaborating with Seattle-based Elysian Brewing to co-create new products. This collaBEERation has led to products such as Ranger IPA and Kick. NBB's culture is focused on making a quality product and satisfying customers. It has even ventured into organic beer with its creation of Mothership Wit Organic Wheat Beer. The company has several product line varieties, including its more popular beers Fat Tire, 1554, and Sunshine Wheat; seasonal beers such as Dig and Snow Day; and its Lips of Faith line, a series of experimental beers including La Folie and Prickly Passion produced in smaller batches.

The distribution element of the product mix was complex at the outset. In her initial role as marketing director, Jordan needed to convince distributors to carry their products. Often, new companies must work hard to convince distributors to carry their brands as distributors are fearful of alienating more established rivals. However, Jordan tirelessly got NBB beer onto store shelves, even delivering beer in her Toyota station wagon. As a craft brewer, NBB uses a premium pricing strategy. Its products are priced higher than domestic brands such as Coors or Budweiser and have higher profit margins. The popularity of NBB beers has prompted rivals to develop competitive products such as MillerCoors' Blue Moon Belgian White.

Perhaps the most notable dimension of NBB's marketing mix is promotion. From the beginning the company based its brand on its core values, including practicing environmental stewardship and forming a participative environment in which all employees can exert their creativity. "For me brand is absolutely everything we are. It's the people here. It's how we interact with one another. And then there's the other piece of that creativity, obviously, which is designing beers," Kim Jordan said. NBB promotion has attempted to portray the company's creativity and its harmony with the natural environment. For instance, one NBB video features a tinkerer repairing a bicycle and riding down the road, while another features NBB "rangers" singing a hip-hop number to promote the company's Ranger IPA ale. The company has also heavily promoted its brand through Facebook and Twitter. This "indie" charm has served to position NBB as a company committed to having fun and being a socially responsible company.

NBB also markets itself as a company committed to sustainability. Sustainability has been a core value at NBB from day one. The company was the first fully wind-powered brewery in the United States. NBB recycles cardboard boxes, keg caps, office materials, and amber glass. The brewery stores spent barley and hop grains in an on-premise silo and invites local farmers to pick up the grains, free of charge, to feed their pigs. The company also provides employees with a cruiser bicycle after one year of employment so they can bike to work instead of drive.

NBB's popularity is allowing it to expand on the East Coast with plans to continue expanding throughout the United States. The combination of a unique brand image, strong marketing mix, and an orientation that considers all stakeholders has turned NBB into a multi-million-dollar success.[34]

Questions for Discussion

1. How has New Belgium implemented the marketing concept?
2. What has Kim Jordan done to create success at New Belgium?
3. How does New Belgium's focus on sustainability as a core value contribute to its corporate culture and success?

NOTES

[1] Jim Edwards, "How Chipotle's Business Model Depends On NEVER Running TV Ads," *Business Insider*, March 16, 2012, http://articles.businessinsider.com/2012-03-16/news/31199897_1_chipotle-advertising-marketing (accessed September 13, 2012); "Chipotle Selects MicroStrategy as its Enterprise Business Intelligence Solution," *Market Watch*, August 21, 2012, www.marketwatch.com/story/chipotle-selects-microstrategy-as-its-enterprise-business-intelligence-solution-2012-08-21 (accessed September 13, 2012); Jefferson Graham, "Chipotle Resists Tech Automation at Restaurants," *USA Today*, August 16, 2012, www.usatoday.com/tech/columnist/talkingtech/story/2012-08-15/talking-tech-chipotle-app/57079794/1 (accessed September 13, 2012); Joel Stein, "The Fast Food Ethicist," *Time*, July 23, 2012, pp. 39–44.

[2] Definition of Marketing," American Marketing Association, www.marketingpower.com/AboutAMA/Pages/DefinitionofMarketing.aspx (accessed July 7, 2010).

[3] "Vans, Inc.,"www.jiffynotes.com/a_study_guides/book_notes/cps_03/cps_03_00479.html (accessed December 27, 2010).

[4] "Recreational Equipment Incorporated (REI): A Responsible Retail Cooperative," in O. C. Ferrell, John Fraedrich, and Linda Ferrell, *Business Ethics: Ethical Decision Making and Cases*, 9th ed. (Mason, OH: South-Western Cengage Learning, 2013), 466–475.

[5] "The History of Subway," www.subway.com/subwayroot/About_Us/History.aspx?icid=About%20Us:%20Promo:%20Unit%201:%20History:%20W6:%202012 (accessed December 7, 2012).

[6] Molly Soat, "Virtual Development," *Marketing News*, May 31, 2012, p. 10.

[7] "Impaired Driving," NHTSA, www.nhtsa.gov/Impaired (accessed December 7, 2012).

[8] Campbell's Kitchen, www.campbellskitchen.com/RecipeCategoryHome.aspx?fbid=DKtnA8n1vQ0 (accessed December 7, 2012).

[9] Rajneesh Suri, Chiranjeev Kohli, and Kent B. Monroe, "The Effects of Perceived Scarcity on Consumers' Processing of Price Information," *Journal of the Academy of Marketing Science* 35 (2007): 89–100.

[10] Natalie Mizik and Robert Jacobson, "Trading Off Between Value Creation and Value Appropriation: The Financial Implications and Shifts in Strategic Emphasis," *Journal of Marketing* (January 2003): 63–76.

[11] Kasey Wehrum, "How May We Help You?" *Inc.*, March 2011, 63–68.

[12] O. C. Ferrell and Michael Hartline, *Marketing Strategy*. (Mason, OH: South-Western, 2005), 108.

[13] Mike Esterl, "With Soda on Defensive, Machines Will List Calories," *The Wall Street Journal*, October 9, 2012, p. B3.

[14] Ajay K. Kohli and Bernard J. Jaworski, "Market Orientation: The Construct, Research Propositions, and Managerial Implications," *Journal of Marketing* (April 1990): 1–18; O. C. Ferrell, "Business Ethics and Customer Stakeholders," *Academy of Management Executive* 18 (May 2004): 126–129.

[15] "Starbucks CEO Howard Schultz Is All Abuzz," *CBS News*, March 27, 2011, www.cbsnews.com/stories/2011/03/27/business/main20047618.shtml (accessed March 30, 2011).

[16] Eugene W. Anderson, Claes Fornell, and Sanal K. Mazvancheryl, "Customer Satisfaction and Shareholder Value," *Journal of Marketing* (October 2004): 172–185.

[17] Xeuming Luo and Christian Homburg, "Neglected Outcomes of Customer Satisfaction," *Journal of Marketing* 70, April 2007.

[18] Kohli and Jaworski, "Market Orientation: The Construct, Research Propositions, and Managerial Implications."

[19] Kwaku Atuahene-Gima, "Resolving the Capability-Rigidity Paradox in New Product Innovation," *Journal of Marketing* 69 (October 2005): 61–83.

[20] Gary F. Gebhardt, Gregory S. Carpenter, and John F. Sherry Jr., "Creating a Market Orientation," *Journal of Marketing* 70 (October 2006), www.marketingpower.com.

[21] "eBay Acquires Recommendation Engine Hunch.com," Business Wire, November 21, 2011, www.businesswire.com/news/home/20111121005831/en/eBay-Acquires-Recommendation-Engine-Hunch.com (accessed January 11, 2012).

[22] Sunil Gupta, Donald R. Lehmann, and Jennifer Ames Stuart, "Valuing Customers," *Journal of Marketing Research* (February 2004): 7–18.

[23] "Bazaarvoice Enables Rubbermaid to Listen, Learn, and Improve Products Based on Customer Conversations," Business Wire, January 21, 2010, www.businesswire.com/portal/site/home/permalink/?ndmViewId=news_view&newsId=20100121005613&newsLang=en (accessed January 12, 2012); "User-Generated R&D: Clay Shirky Explains How to Feed Innovation with Customer Insights," Bazaarvoice, May 3, 2011, www.bazaarvoice.com/blog/2011/05/03/user-generated-rd-clay-shirky-explains-how-to-feed-innovation-with-customer-insights/ (accessed January 12, 2012).

[24] Pradeep Korgaonkar and Bay O'Leary, "Management, Market, and Financial Factors Separating Winners and Losers in e-Business," *Journal of Computer-Mediated Communication* 11, no. 4 (2006): article 12.

[25] "Hewlett-Packard Replaces Leo Apotheker with Meg Whitman," BBC News, September 23, 2011, www.bbc.co.uk/news/business-15028509 (accessed February 3, 2012); James B. Stewart, "For Seamless Transitions, Don't Look to Hewlett," *The New York Times*, August 26, 2011, www.nytimes.com/2011/08/27/business/for-seamless-transitions-at-the-top-dont-consult-hewlett-packard.html?pagewanted=all (accessed February 3, 2012).

[26] Jacquelyn S. Thomas, Robert C. Blattberg, and Edward J. Fox, "Recapturing Lost Customers," *Journal of Marketing Research* (February 2004): 31–45.

[27] Jagdish N. Sheth and Rajendras Sisodia, "More Than Ever Before, Marketing Is under Fire to Account for What It Spends," *Marketing Management* (Fall 1995): 13–14.

[28] Stephen L. Vargo and Robert F. Lusch, "Service-Dominant Logic: Continuing the Evolution," *Journal of the Academy of Marketing Science* 36(2008): 1–10.

[29] "Whole Foods Market's Core Values," Whole Foods, www.wholefoodsmarket.com/values/corevalues.php (accessed January 10, 2012).

[30] Chezy Ofir and Itamar Simonson, "The Effect of Stating Expectations on Customer Satisfaction and Shopping Experience," *Journal of Marketing Research* XLIV (February 2007), 164–174.

[31] Robert W. Palmatier, Lisa K. Scheer, and Jan-Benedict E. M. Steenkamp, "Customer Loyalty to Whom? Managing the Benefits and Risks of Salesperson-Owned Loyalty," *Journal of Marketing Research* XLIV (May 2007), 185–199.

[32] Edward C. Baig, "Mobile Payments Gain Traction," *USA Today*, August 11, 2011, 1A–2A; Jefferson Graham, "Starbucks Expands Mobile Payments to 6,800 Sites," *USA Today*, January 19, 2011, 1B.

[33] "Carting Away the Oceans Infographic," *Greenpeace*, 2012, www.greenpeace.org/usa/en/campaigns/oceans/seafood/Carting-Away-the-Oceans-Infographic/ (accessed December 7, 2012).

[34] New Belgium website, newbelgium.com (accessed March 27, 2012); "New Belgium Brewing: Ethical and Environmental Responsibility," in O. C. Ferrell, John Fraedrich, and Linda Ferrell, *Business Ethics: Ethical Decision Making and Cases*, 9th ed. (Mason, OH: South-Western Cengage Learning, 2013), 355–363; "New Belgium Brewery," Amalgamated, http://amalgamatednyc.com/project/tinkerer/ (accessed March 27, 2012);Norman Miller, "Craft Beer Industry Continues to Grow," *PJ Star*, March 26, 2012, www.pjstar.com/community/blogs/beer-nut/x140148153/Craft-Beer-industry-continues-to-grow (accessed March 27, 2012); "COLLABEERATIONS," Elysian Brewing

Company, www.elysianbrewing.com/elysian-beers/collabeerations (accessed March 27, 2012); Devin Leonard, "New Belgium and the Battle of the Microbrews," *Bloomberg Businessweek*, December 1, 2011, www.businessweek.com/magazine/new-belgium-and-the-battle-of-the-microbrews-12012011.html (accessed March 27, 2012); "Our Joy Ride," www.newbelgium.com/Community/videos.aspx?id=1e15e412-9153-433d-9249-85134c24befa (accessed March 27, 2012).

Feature Notes

[a] Lauran Neergaard, "Organic Food Is Not Healthier Than Conventional Produce: Study," *Huffington Post*, September 4, 2012, www.huffingtonpost.com/2012/09/04/organic-food-health-produce-food_n_1853995.html (accessed November 10, 2012); Mayo Clinic Staff, "Nutrition and Healthy Eating," *Mayo Clinic*, www.mayoclinic.com/health/organic-food/NU00255 (accessed November 10, 2012); Marissa Lippert, "Organic or Not? Is Organic Produce Healthier Than Conventional?"

Eating Well, 2009, www.eatingwell.com/food_news_origins/green_sustainable/organic_or_not_is_organic_produce_healthier_than_conventional (accessed December 7, 2012).

[b] Kim Bhasin, "We Tasted the Lattes from Starbucks' New Verismo Machine—Here's the Verdict," *Business Insider*, September 20, 2012, www.businessinsider.com/starbucks-verismo-taste-test-2012-9#ixzz28GbWVIlQ (accessed October 3, 2012); Chris Barth, "Starbucks' New Verismo Machine Sinks Green Mountain. Will You Buy It," *Forbes Inc*, September 20, 2012, www.forbes.com/sites/chrisbarth/2012/09/20/starbucks-new-verismo-machine-sinks-green-mountain-will-you-buy-it/ (accessed October 3, 2012); Julie Jargon, "Starbucks Gives Single-Serve a Shot," *The Wall Street Journal*, September 20, 2012, B9.

[c] Dinah Eng, "How Maxine Clark Built Build-a-Bear," *Fortune*, March 19, 2012, pp. 49–52; Ann C. Logue, "Warm, Fuzzy, and Business Savvy," *NYSE*, 2005, www.nyse.com/pdfs/NYSE_OCT_NOV_05_B_A_B.pdf (accessed October 24, 2012); "Build-A-Bear's Founder Shares Her Story," *Businessweek*, September 17, 2007, www.businessweek.com/stories/2007-09-17/build-a-bears-founder-shares-her-storybusinessweek-business-news-stock-market-and-financial-advice (accessed October 24, 2012).

[d] James E. Ellis, "Levi's Has a New Color For Blue Jeans: Green," *Bloomberg Businessweek*, October 22–28, 2012, pp. 26–28; Robyn Griggs Lawrence, "Corporations are Going Green-Slowly But Surely," *Mother Earth News*, February 4, 2011, www.motherearthnews.com/natural-home-living/corporations-are-going-green-slowly-but-surely.aspx (accessed November 2, 2012); Jessica Misener, "Levi Strauss Aims to Use Less Water in Jeans-Making Process," *The Huffington Post*, November 2, 2011, www.huffingtonpost.com/2011/11/02/levi-strauss-jeans-water-environment-levis_n_1071454.html (accessed November 2, 2012).

chapter 2

Planning, Implementing, and Evaluating Marketing Strategies

OBJECTIVES

1. Understand the strategic planning process.
2. Examine what is necessary to effectively manage the implementation of marketing strategies.
3. Describe the major elements of strategic performance evaluation.
4. Understand the development of a marketing plan.

© iStockphoto.com/jfmdesign

MARKETING INSIGHTS

Procter & Gamble Plans for More Billion-Dollar Brands

Cincinnati-based Procter & Gamble introduced its first product, Ivory Soap, more than 175 years ago. Today, the company rings up $84 billion in worldwide annual sales of personal care and household products. From Pampers disposable diapers to Pantene shampoo, Duracell batteries to Downy fabric softener, its many billion-dollar brands can be found in every supermarket, coast to coast.

Over the years, Procter & Gamble has developed a reputation for marketing excellence because of its intense focus on satisfying customer needs. For example, as part of its plan to boost sales of Pampers, company researchers moved in with families to see how parents of infants and toddlers actually use disposable diapers. The insights they gained prompted Procter & Gamble to make Pampers more absorbent so babies would sleep comfortably through the night—and parents could get much-needed sleep. By promoting the product's innovative features and the benefits for babies and parents, Procter & Gamble was able to increase yearly sales of Pampers beyond $10 billion.

Procter & Gamble's brand managers are responsible for setting specific objectives for their products, formulating plans to achieve these objectives, and establishing performance measures. They can call on a team of "innovation facilitators" for guidance in exploring new marketing possibilities. And if a plan doesn't achieve the expected results, they're ready to get back on track by making changes to the marketing mix. Watch for more billion-dollar brands as Procter & Gamble applies its marketing know-how to boost its market share and sales year by year, especially in developing countries where the company projects significant future growth.[1]

Whether it's Procter & Gamble or Subway, an organization must be able to create customer value and achieve its goals. This occurs through successful strategic marketing management. **Strategic marketing management** is the process of planning, implementing, and evaluating the performance of marketing activities and strategies, both effectively and efficiently. Effectiveness and efficiency are key concepts to understanding strategic marketing management. *Effectiveness* is the degree to which long-term customer relationships help achieve an organization's objectives. *Efficiency* refers to minimizing the resources an organization uses to achieve a specific level of desired customer relationships. Thus, the overall goal of strategic marketing management is to facilitate highly desirable customer relationships and to minimize the costs of doing so.

We begin this chapter with an overview of the strategic planning process and a discussion of the nature of marketing strategy. These elements provide a framework for an analysis of the development, implementation, and evaluation of marketing strategies. We conclude with a discussion of how to create a marketing plan.

LO1. Understand the strategic planning process.

THE STRATEGIC PLANNING PROCESS

Through the process of **strategic planning**, a company establishes an organizational mission and formulates goals, a corporate strategy, marketing objectives, and a marketing strategy.[2] A market orientation should guide the process of strategic planning to ensure that a concern for customer satisfaction is an integral part of the entire company, leading to the development of successful marketing strategies and planning processes.[3]

Figure 2.1 shows the various components of the strategic planning process, which begins with the establishment or revision of an organization's mission and goals. The corporation

Figure 2.1 Components of the Strategic Planning Process

strategic marketing management The process of planning, implementing, and evaluating the performance of marketing activities and strategies, both effectively and efficiently

strategic planning The process of establishing an organizational mission and formulating goals, corporate strategy, marketing objectives, marketing strategy, and a marketing plan

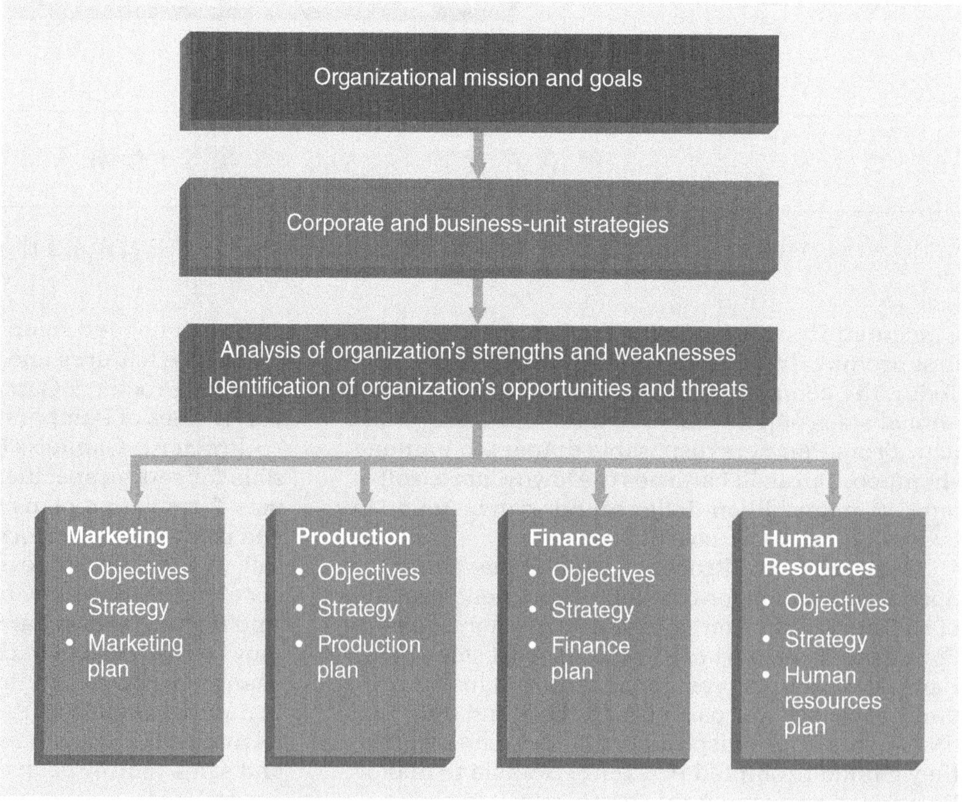

From Pride/Ferrell, *Marketing* 2014, 17E. © 2014 Cengage Learning.

and individual business units then develop strategies to achieve these goals. The company performs a detailed analysis of its strengths and weaknesses and identifies opportunities and threats within the external marketing environment. Next, each functional area of the organization (marketing, production, finance, human resources, etc.) establishes its own objectives and develops strategies to achieve them, which must support the organization's overall goals and mission and should be focused on market orientation. Because this is a marketing book, we are most interested in marketing objectives and strategies. We will examine the strategic planning process by taking a closer look at each component, beginning with organizational mission statements and goals.

Establishing Organizational Mission Statements and Goals

Once an organization has assessed its resources and opportunities, it can begin to establish goals and strategies to leverage them. The goals of any organization should derive from its **mission statement**, a long-term view, or vision, of what the organization wants to become. For example, Starbucks' mission, "to inspire and nurture the human spirit—one cup and one neighborhood at a time," speaks to a desire to be a gathering place in every neighborhood.[4]

Developing Corporate and Business-Unit Strategies

In most organizations, strategic planning begins at the corporate level and proceeds downward to the business-unit and marketing levels. However, organizations are increasingly developing and conducting strategic planning that moves in both directions. When conducting strategic planning, a firm is likely to seek out experts from many levels of the organization to take advantage of in-house expertise and a variety of opinions.

Figure 2.2 shows the relationships between the three planning levels: corporate, business unit, and marketing. Corporate strategy is the broadest of the levels and should be developed

mission statement A long-term view, or vision, of what the organization wants to become

Bloomberg/Getty Images

Strategic Marketing
Android engages in strategic marketing by identifying and analyzing its target market and then developing a marketing mix to meet customers' needs.

Figure 2.2 **Levels of Strategic Planning**

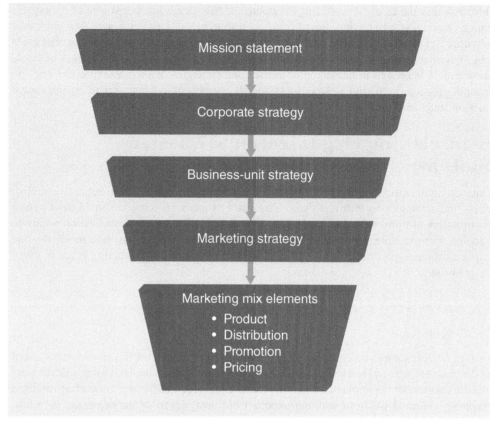

From Pride/Ferrell, *Marketing* 2014, 17E. © 2014 Cengage Learning.

with the organization's overall mission in mind. Business-unit strategy should be consistent with the corporate strategy while also serving the unit's needs. Marketing strategy utilizes the marketing mix to develop a message that is consistent with the business-unit and corporate strategies.

Corporate Strategies

Corporate strategy determines the means for utilizing resources in the functional areas of marketing, production, finance, research and development, and human resources to achieve the organization's goals. A corporate strategy outlines the scope of the business and such considerations as resource deployment, competitive advantages, and overall coordination of functional areas. Top management's level of marketing expertise and ability to deploy resources to address the company's markets can affect sales growth and profitability. Corporate strategy addresses the two questions posed in the organization's mission statement: *Who are our customers?* and *What is our core competency?* The term *corporate* does not apply solely to corporations. In this context, it refers to the top-level (i.e., highest) strategy and is used by all organizations of all sizes.

corporate strategy A strategy that determines the means for utilizing resources in the various functional areas to reach the organization's goals

Corporate strategy planners are concerned with broad issues such as corporate culture, competition, differentiation, diversification, interrelationships among business units, and environmental and social issues. They attempt to match the resources of the organization with the opportunities and threats in the environment. KiOR, for example, is a biofuels company whose corporate strategy planners identified a demand for ecofriendly fuels and a need for a biofuel not developed from corn or sugar-cane. These two fuel sources can cause food shortages and deforestation, respectively. KiOR developed a biofuel using waste, not food—addressing a waste disposal problem while producing fuel the nation needs.[5] Corporate strategy planners are also concerned with defining the scope and role of the company's business units so the units are coordinated to reach the ends desired. The proactive nature of a company's corporate strategy can affect its capacity to innovate.

Business-Unit Strategies

After analyzing corporate operations and performance, the next step in strategic planning is to determine the direction of the business and develop strategies for individual business units. A **strategic business unit (SBU)** is a division, product line, or other profit center within the parent company. Nestlé, for example, has SBUs for Confectionaries and Beverages. Each SBU sells a distinct set of products to an identifiable group of customers and each competes with a well-defined set of competitors. The revenues, costs, investments, and strategic plans of an SBU can be separated from those of the parent company and evaluated. SBUs face different market growth rates, opportunities, competition, and profit-making potential. Business strategy should seek to create value for the company's target markets and attain greater performance, which marketing research suggests requires implementing appropriate strategic actions and targeting appropriate market segments.[6]

Corporate Strategy
Samsung's corporate strategy includes frequent introductions of newly designed, technologically advanced products.

Strategic planners should recognize the performance capabilities of each SBU and carefully allocate resources among them. Several tools allow a company's portfolio of SBUs, or even individual products, to be classified and visually displayed according to the attractiveness of markets and the business's relative market share. A **market** is a group of individuals and/or organizations that have needs for products in a product class and have the ability, willingness, and authority to purchase those products. The percentage of a market that actually buys a specific product from a particular company is referred to as that product's (or business unit's) **market share**. Google, for example, controls 67 percent of the U.S. search engine market share.[7] Product quality, order of entry into the market, and market share have all been associated with SBU success.[8]

One of the most helpful tools for a marketer is the **market growth/market share matrix**, developed by the Boston Consulting Group (BCG). This approach is based on the philosophy that a product's market growth rate and its market share are important considerations in determining marketing strategy. To develop such a tool, all of the company's SBUs and products are integrated into a single matrix and compared and evaluated to determine appropriate strategies for individual products and overall portfolio strategies. Managers use this model to determine and classify each product's expected future cash contributions and future cash requirements. However, the BCG analytical approach is more of a diagnostic tool than a guide for making strategy prescriptions.

Figure 2.3, which is based on work by the BCG, enables a strategic planner to classify a company's products into four basic types: stars, cash cows, dogs, and question marks. *Stars* are products with a dominant share of the market and good prospects for growth. However, they use more cash than they generate in order to finance growth, add capacity, and increase

strategic business unit (SBU) A division, product line, or other profit center within the parent company

market A group of individuals and/or organizations that have needs for products in a product class and have the ability, willingness, and authority to purchase those products

market share The percentage of a market that actually buys a specific product from a particular company

market growth/market share matrix A helpful business tool, based on the philosophy that a product's market growth rate and its market share are important considerations in determining its marketing strategy

Marketing Debate

Question Marks versus Stars: How to Decide?

ISSUE: What happens to customer choice when companies put their marketing dollars primarily into stars rather than funding question marks?

Stars have high market share and bright prospects for future sales and profits, although they require cash infusions to continue their growth trajectory. Especially when economic conditions are challenging, companies may prefer to direct money toward stars rather than investing in question marks that need a big budget to advance from a small market share position. Competition is also a factor: Some corporate giants such as Unilever have been concentrating their marketing investments in high-potential products, with an eye toward surpassing rivals and setting the stage for long-term returns.

Even though question marks have low market share, they do satisfy the needs of some customers, and they also round out customer choice. Should companies invest to further develop and promote these products, even if their current outlook isn't as promising as for higher-growth products? Both General Motors and Nissan face such decisions with their electric vehicles. Several years after introducing the Chevrolet Volt electric car, General Motors has not achieved the hoped-for market share, and Nissan has had a similar experience with its electric car, the Leaf. Are electric vehicles question marks or stars? What should companies do when they must choose where to invest their marketing dollars?[a]

market share. An example of a star might be Amazon's Kindle. *Cash cows* have a dominant share of the market, but low prospects for growth. They typically generate more cash than is required to maintain market share. Bounty paper towels represent a cash cow for Procter & Gamble because it is a product that consistently sells well. *Dogs* have a subordinate share of the market and low prospects for growth. Dogs are often found in established markets. The cathode ray tube television would probably be considered a dog by a company like Panasonic, as most customers prefer flat screens. *Question marks,* sometimes called

Figure 2.3 **Growth Share Matrix Developed by the Boston Consulting Group**

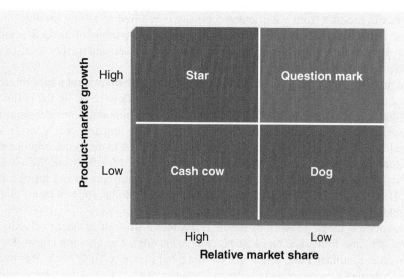

"problem children," have a small share of a growing market and require a large amount of cash to build market share. Mercedes bicycles, for example, are a question mark relative to Mercedes' automobile products.

The long-term health of an organization depends on having a range of products, some that generate cash (and generate acceptable profits) and others that use cash to support growth. The major indicators of a firm's overall health are: the size and vulnerability of the cash cows, the prospects for the stars, and the number of question marks and dogs. Particular attention should be paid to products that require large cash flows, as most firms cannot afford to sponsor many such products. If resources are spread too thin, the company will be unable to finance promising new product entries or acquisitions.

Assessing Organizational Resources and Opportunities

The strategic planning process begins with an analysis of the marketing environment, including the industry in which the company operates or intends to sell its products. As we will see in Chapter 3, the external marketing environment, which includes economic, competitive, political, legal and regulatory, sociocultural, and technological forces, can threaten an organization and influence its overall goals. These forces affect the amount and type of resources the company can acquire, but can also create favorable opportunities that can help an organization achieve its goals and marketing objectives.

Any strategic planning effort must take into account the organization's available financial and human resources and capabilities and how these resources are likely to change over time, as changes may affect the organization's ability to achieve its mission and goals. Adequate resources can help a firm generate customer satisfaction and loyalty, goodwill, and a positive reputation, all of which impact marketing through creating well-known brands and strong financial performance. Coca-Cola, Apple, and Google all benefit from high brand recognition and goodwill. Such strengths also include **core competencies**, things a company does extremely well—sometimes so well that they give the company an advantage over competition.

Analysis of the marketing environment also includes identifying opportunities in the marketplace, which requires a solid understanding of the company's industry. When the right combination of circumstances and timing permits an organization to take action to reach a particular target market, a **market opportunity** exists. For example, Amazon recently identified a market opportunity to enter into small business banking. As more small businesses are engaging in online retailing, Amazon has begun to offer banking opportunities to businesses that sell their goods through the Amazon website. Amazon believes that it can lend financing to small companies more quickly and easily than a bank or commercial lender.[9] Such opportunities are often called **strategic windows**, temporary periods of optimal fit between the key requirements of a market and the particular capabilities of a company competing in that market.[10] When a company matches a core competency to opportunities it has discovered in the marketplace, it is said to have a **competitive advantage**. Some companies possess manufacturing, technical, or marketing skills that they can tie to market opportunities to create a competitive advantage. Note in the Dyson vacuum advertisement that the company focuses on promoting the product's advantages over competing brands. The advertisement indicates that the vacuum does not lose suction from any angle, something other vacuum brands cannot

core competencies Things a company does extremely well, which sometimes give it an advantage over its competition

market opportunity A combination of circumstances and timing that permits an organization to take action to reach a particular target market

strategic windows Temporary periods of optimal fit between the key requirements of a market and the particular capabilities of a company competing in that market

competitive advantage The result of a company matching a core competency to opportunities it has discovered in the marketplace

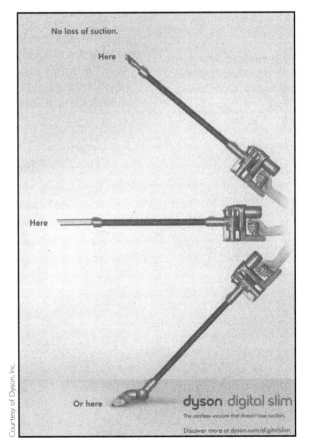

Courtesy of Dyson, Inc.

Competitive Advantage
Dyson has gained a competitive advantage through a combination of product features relative to those of competing brands.

claim. This model is also very compact and lightweight, making for easy maneuvering and storage, an important selling point for some consumers. These factors combine to give Dyson a competitive advantage.

A SWOT analysis can be helpful for gauging a firm's capabilities and resources relative to the industry. It can provide a firm with insights into such factors as timing market entry into a new geographic region or product category.

SWOT Analysis

The **SWOT analysis** is used to assess an organization's strengths, weaknesses, opportunities, and threats. It is depicted as a four-cell matrix, as in Figure 2.4, and shows how marketers must seek to convert weaknesses into strengths, threats into opportunities, and match internal strengths with external opportunities to develop competitive advantages. Strengths and weaknesses are internal factors that can influence an organization's ability to satisfy target markets. *Strengths* refer to competitive advantages, or core competencies, that give the company an advantage over other firms in meeting the needs of its target markets. *Weaknesses* are limitations a company faces in developing or implementing a marketing strategy. For example, Best Buy's sales and cash flow began to dwindle after relying too heavily for too long on sales of computers and entertainment. Marketing research revealed that the company was focusing marketing activities on the wrong products and the wrong target market, as its sales had shifted to tablets and e-readers. This necessitated a revamped marketing strategy and a reassessment of the company's best target market.[11] Marketers must keep in mind that strengths and weaknesses are only meaningful when they help or hinder the company in meeting customer needs and desires.

Opportunities and threats affect all organizations within an industry, market, or geographic region because they exist outside of and independently of the company. *Opportunities* refer to favorable conditions in the environment that could produce rewards for the organization if acted upon. Opportunities are situations that exist but must be exploited for the company to benefit from them. *Threats,* on the other hand, refer to barriers that could prevent the company from reaching its objectives. Opportunities and threats can stem from many sources within

SWOT analysis Assessment of an organization's strengths, weaknesses, opportunities, and threats

Figure 2.4 The Four-Cell SWOT Matrix

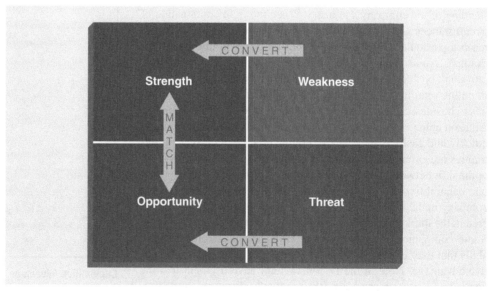

From Pride/Ferrell, *Marketing 2014*, 17E. © 2014 Cengage Learning.

Going Green

GE's Ecomagination Saves and Earns Billions

General Electric launched Ecomagination as part of its corporate strategy to "imagine and build innovative solutions to today's environmental challenges while driving economic growth." Since embracing this green strategy, GE has saved billions of dollars through energy and water conservation, generated billions in new revenue, and polished its image as a socially responsible firm.

Ecomagination combines GE's strengths in customer knowledge, design, and manufacturing to create and market dozens of green products for consumers and business customers. "This design signal we're getting from the marketplace is affordability, efficiency, and environmental sensitivity," says Mark Vachon, who heads Ecomagination.

Given GE's global business presence, any green products it develops in one region can be distributed or adapted for distribution in other regions. For example, an energy-efficient portable ultrasound scanner designed for China was later introduced worldwide. Another product, the WattStation, is a user-friendly electric car charging station designed for use in suburban parking lots or on city streets.

Although Ecomagination products already account for 12 percent of GE's $150 billion annual revenue, the company is inviting new ideas from consumers and businesses. Watch for more green to flow to GE's bottom line as it continues its successful green strategy in the coming years.[b]

© iStockphoto.com/CRTd

the marketing environment. When a competitor's introduction of a new product threatens a company, a firm may require a defensive strategy. If the company can develop and launch a new product that meets or exceeds the competition's offering, it can transform the threat into an opportunity.

First-Mover and Late-Mover Advantage

An important factor that marketers must consider when identifying organizational resources and opportunities is whether the firm has the resources to cultivate a first-mover advantage, or is in a position to choose between developing a first-mover or late-mover advantage. A **first-mover advantage** is the ability of an innovative company to achieve long-term competitive advantages by being the first to offer a certain product in the marketplace. Being the first to enter a market helps a company build a reputation as a pioneer and market leader. For a first mover, the market is, for at least a short period, free of competition as potential competitors work to develop a rival product. Because consumers have no choice initially, being a first mover also helps establish customer brand loyalty in cases when switching to another brand later, when there are more options, may be costly or difficult for the consumer. The first to develop a new product can also protect secrets and technology through patents.

There are risks, however, of being the first to enter a market. There are usually high outlays associated with creating a new product, including market research, product development, production, and marketing—or buyer education—costs. Also, early sales growth may not match predictions if the firm overestimates demand or fails to target marketing efforts properly. The company runs the risk that the product will fail due to market uncertainty, or that the product might not completely meet consumers' expectations or needs.

A **late-mover advantage** is the ability of later market entrants to achieve long-term competitive advantages by not being the first to offer a certain product in a marketplace. Competitors that enter the market later can benefit from the first mover's mistakes and have a chance to improve on the product design and marketing strategy. A late mover is also likely to have lower initial investment costs than the first mover because the first mover has already

first-mover advantage The ability of an innovative company to achieve long-term competitive advantages by being the first to offer a certain product in the marketplace

late-mover advantage The ability of later market entrants to achieve long-term competitive advantages by not being the first to offer a certain product in a marketplace

First-Mover Advantage
The Kindle was the first e-reader to be introduced. What advantages did Amazon, the maker of the Kindle, experience by being first to market?

Kristoffer Tripplaar/Alamy

developed a distribution infrastructure and educated buyers about the product. By the time a late mover enters the market, there is also more data, and therefore more certainty, about product success.

There are disadvantages of being a late mover too, though. The company that entered the market first may have patents and other protections on its technology and trade secrets that prevent the late mover from producing a similar product. If customers who have already purchased the first mover's product believe that switching to the late mover's product will be expensive or time-consuming, it may be difficult for the late mover to gain market share.

It is important to note that the timing of entry into the market is crucial. Companies that are relatively quick to enter the market after the first mover generally have a greater chance of building market share and brand loyalty. Companies that enter the market later on, after many other companies have done so, face strong competition and have more disadvantages.

Developing Marketing Objectives and Marketing Strategies

The next phase in strategic planning is the development of marketing objectives and marketing strategies, which are used to achieve marketing objectives. A **marketing objective** states what is to be accomplished through marketing activities. These objectives can be given in terms of product introduction, product improvement or innovation, sales volume, profitability, market share, pricing, distribution, advertising, or employee training activities. A marketing objective of Ritz-Carlton hotels, for example, is to have more than 90 percent of its customers express that they had a memorable experience at the hotel. Marketing objectives should be based on a careful study of the SWOT analysis, matching strengths to opportunities, eliminating weaknesses, and minimizing threats.

Marketing objectives should possess certain characteristics. First, a marketing objective should be expressed in clear, simple terms so that all marketing and nonmarketing personnel in the company understand exactly what they are trying to achieve. Second, an objective

marketing objective
A statement of what is to be accomplished through marketing activities

should be measurable, which allows the organization to track progress and compare outcomes against beginning benchmarks. For instance, if an objective is to increase market share by 10 percent in the United States, the company should be able to measure market share changes accurately to ensure that it is making gains toward that objective. Third, a marketing objective should specify a time frame for its accomplishment, such as six months or one year. Finally, a marketing objective should be consistent with both business-unit and corporate strategies. This ensures that the company's mission is carried out consistently at all levels of the organization by all personnel. Marketing objectives should be achievable and use company resources effectively, and successful accomplishment should contribute to the overall corporate strategy. A marketing strategy ensures that the firm has a plan in place to achieve its marketing objectives.

A **marketing strategy** is the selection of a target market and the creation of a marketing mix that will satisfy the needs of target market members. A marketing strategy articulates the best use of the company's resources to accomplish its marketing objectives.

Selecting the Target Market

Selecting an appropriate target market may be the most important decision a company makes in the strategic planning process and is a key to strategic success. The target market must be chosen before the organization can adapt its marketing mix to meet the customers' needs and preferences. Take a look at the advertisement for the Dominican Republic Tourism Board. You see a charter fishing boat and the question "What's on your mind?" in a text message-style bubble. Based on the image and the words in this ad, you can assume that the marketers are trying to reach a target market that is seeking to unplug from the office and from the demands of everyday life. If a company selects the wrong target market, all other marketing decisions are likely to be in vain. Toyota, for example, did not properly identify its target market when introducing the Yaris sedan in China. A success with middle-class consumers ages 18 to 34 elsewhere around the world, the Yaris was a spectacular flop in China. Toyota failed to realize until it was too late that young, middle-class Chinese consumers are very price sensitive and the Yaris was priced beyond their reach. Those Chinese consumers who could afford the car tended not to like the styling.[12]

Careful and accurate target market selection is crucial to productive marketing efforts. Products, and even whole companies, sometimes fail because marketers misidentify the best target market for their products. Organizations that try to be all things to all people rarely satisfy the needs of any customer group very well. Identification and analysis of a target market provide a foundation on which the company can develop its marketing mix.

When exploring possible target markets, marketing managers try to evaluate how entry could affect the company's sales, costs, and profits. Marketing information should be organized to facilitate a focus on the chosen target customers. Accounting and information systems, for example, can be used to track revenues and costs by customer (or customer group). The firm should offer rewards to managers and employees who focus efforts on profitable customers. Firms should develop teamwork skills that promote a flexible customer orientation that allows the firm to adapt to changes in the marketing environment.

AP Photo/PR NEWSWIRE

Having the camera ready for "the big one".
DOMINICAN REPUBLIC. CLOSER THAN YOU THINK.

Dominican Republic
Has it all
GoDominicanRepublic.com

Marketing Objectives
What is the Dominican Republic Tourism Board hoping to achieve with this ad?

marketing strategy A plan of action for identifying and analyzing a target market and developing a marketing mix to meet the needs of that market

Target Market Selection   Are Holiday Inn Express and the Four Seasons Hotel aiming at the same target market?

Marketers should determine whether a selected target market aligns with the company's overall mission and objectives. If it does, they should assess whether the company has the appropriate resources to develop a marketing mix (product, price, promotion, and distribution) that meets the needs of that target market. The size and number of competitors already marketing products in potential target markets are concerns as well. For example, the market for mobile apps, which consumers can download to their mobile devices, has exploded in recent years. The market has become so competitive that any new entrants must carefully evaluate whether their product represents a new product that would be in demand by the target market or a genuine improvement over what already exists.[13]

Creating Marketing Mixes

Using all relevant information available to conduct in-depth research allows a firm to select the most appropriate target market, which is the basis for creating a marketing mix that satisfies the needs of that market. Thus, the organization should analyze demographic information, customer needs, preferences, and behaviors with respect to product design, pricing, distribution, and promotion. For example, Tide learned through conducting marketing research that men increasingly help with household chores, but that women continue to distrust their ability to complete chores satisfactorily. In order to take advantage of this situation, Tide developed a series of products, such as pre-portioned laundry detergent capsules, and marketing promotions aimed at helping men contribute to chores in a way that satisfies the women in their lives.[14]

Marketing mix decisions should have two additional characteristics: consistency and flexibility. All marketing mix decisions should be consistent with the business-unit and corporate strategies. Such consistency allows the organization to achieve its objectives on all three levels of planning. Flexibility, on the other hand, permits the organization to alter the marketing mix in response to changes in market conditions,

SNAPSHOT

Increase in the Percent of Fortune Global 100 Companies that Use Social Media as a Part of Their Marketing Strategies

Twitter: 65, 82
Facebook: 54, 74
YouTube: 50, 79

■ 2 Years Ago (in percentage)
■ This Year (in percentage)

Source: Burson-Marsteller, 2012.

competition, and customer needs. Marketing strategy flexibility has a positive influence on organizational performance.

Utilizing the marketing mix as a tool set, a company can detail how it will achieve a sustainable competitive advantage. A **sustainable competitive advantage** is one that the competition cannot copy in the foreseeable future. Walmart, for example, maintains a sustainable competitive advantage in groceries over supermarkets because of its highly efficient and low-cost distribution system. This advantage allows Walmart to offer lower prices and has helped it to maintain the largest share of the supermarket business. Maintaining a sustainable competitive advantage requires flexibility in the marketing mix when facing uncertain environments.

MANAGING MARKETING IMPLEMENTATION

LO2. Examine what is necessary to effectively manage the implementation of marketing strategies.

Marketing implementation is the process of putting marketing strategies into action. Through planning, marketing managers provide purpose and direction for an organization's marketing efforts and are positioned to implement specific marketing strategies. The effective implementation of any and all marketing activities depends on a well-organized marketing department that is capable of motivating personnel, effective communication, good coordination efforts, and setting reasonable and attainable timetables for activity completion.

Organizing the Marketing Unit

The structure and relationships of a marketing unit, including establishing lines of authority and communication that connect and coordinate individuals, strongly affect marketing activities. Companies that truly adopt the marketing concept develop an organizational culture that

sustainable competitive advantage An advantage that the competition cannot copy

marketing implementation The process of putting marketing strategies into action

Emerging Trends

Watch That Weather Forecast!

To avoid being crippled by weather-related complications, such as a hurricane, blizzard, or tornado, some major marketers consult staff meteorologists as they work on marketing plans and implementation. For example, Walmart's meteorologists constantly monitor weather developments and update marketing planners and store personnel who must be ready to respond to bad weather systems. "It's great to have somebody in-house who can evaluate that information so that we can give real-time information to our associates, not only here at headquarters but out in the field," explains Walmart's head of emergency management. Planners analyze historical sales from each store in the affected area and then send out trucks filled with the specific goods each store will need during that type of storm (such as snow blowers for a blizzard or sump pumps for a hurricane).

Similarly, Home Depot's weather watchers keep the home improvement retailer ready for any type of storm, knowing that customers will need certain supplies before the bad weather and other supplies in its aftermath. When hurricane season opens, Home Depot has tractor-trailers preloaded with plywood, generators, and other products to restock stores in a storm's path. As a result, Home Depot is ready and able to remain open during a weather emergency.

Both FedEx and UPS have meteorologists on staff to help the delivery firms decide when their trucks should wait out a storm and how to reroute their cargo jets around severe weather systems. To maintain good customer relations, both firms alert customers as soon as they know pickups and deliveries will be delayed by bad weather.[c]

is based on a shared set of beliefs that places the customer's needs at the center of decisions about strategy and operations. Technology can help companies adopt the marketing concept. For example, firms increasingly use online Web tracking to improve information flows and their understanding of customers' needs and wants. While some feel that this technology is a violation of privacy, tracking companies have helped marketers create very detailed profiles for their target markets, which helps all members of the marketing unit more effectively address the needs of the target market.[15]

Firms must decide whether operations should be centralized or decentralized, a choice that directly affects marketing decision making and strategy. In a **centralized organization**, top-level managers delegate little authority to lower levels. In a **decentralized organization**, decision-making authority is delegated as far down the chain of command as possible. In centralized organizations, marketing decisions are made at the top levels. However, centralized decision making may prove ineffective in firms that must respond quickly to fluctuations in customer demand. In these organizations, decentralized authority allows the company to adapt more rapidly to customer needs.

How effectively a company's marketing management can implement marketing strategies also depends on how the marketing unit is organized. Organizing marketing activities to align with the overall strategic marketing approach enhances organizational efficiency and performance. A marketing department should clearly outline the hierarchical relationships between personnel and who is responsible for performing certain activities and making decisions.

Motivating Marketing Personnel

People work to satisfy physical, psychological, and social needs. To motivate marketing personnel, managers must address their employees' needs to maintain a high level of workplace satisfaction. It is crucial that the plan to motivate employees be fair, ethical, and well understood by members of the organization. Employee rewards should also be tied to organizational goals. A firm can motivate its workers through a variety of methods, including by linking pay with performance, informing workers how their performance affects department and corporate results and how it affects their own compensation, providing appropriate and competitive compensation, implementing a flexible benefits program, and adopting a participative management approach.

centralized organization
A structure in which top-level managers delegate little authority to lower levels

decentralized organization
A structure in which decision-making authority is delegated as far down the chain of command as possible

Recognition
Recognizing outstanding performance is one approach to motivating marketing personnel.

Jon Feingersh/Jupiter Images

Diversity in the workplace can complicate employee motivational strategies, as different generations and cultures may be motivated by different things. For example, an employee might value autonomy or recognition more than a pay increase. Managers can reward employees, not just with money and fringe benefits, but also with nonfinancial rewards, such as prestige or recognition, job autonomy, skill variety, task significance, increased feedback, or even a more relaxed dress code. It is crucial for management to show that it takes pride in its workforce and to motivate employees to take pride in their company.

Communicating within the Marketing Unit

Marketing managers must be in clear communication with the firm's upper-level management to ensure that they are aware of the firm's goals and achievements and that marketing activities are consistent with the company's overall goals. The marketing unit should also take steps to ensure that its activities are in synch with those of other departments, such as finance or human resources. For example, marketing personnel should work with the production staff to design products that have the features that marketing research indicates are what customers desire.

It is important that communication flow up, from the front lines of the organization to upper management. Customer-contact employees are in a unique position to understand customers' wants and needs, and pathways should be open for them to communicate this knowledge to marketing managers. In this way, marketing managers can gain access to a rich source of information about what customers require, how products are selling, the effectiveness of marketing activities, and any issues with marketing implementation. Upward communication also allows marketing managers to understand the problems and requirements of lower-level employees, a critical group to keep satisfied, as they are the ones who interface with customers.

Training is a key part of communicating with marketing employees. An effective training program provides employees with a forum to learn and ask questions, and results in employees who are empowered and can be held accountable for their performance. Many firms utilize a formalized, high-tech information system that tracks data and facilitates communication between marketing managers, sales managers, and sales personnel. Information systems expedite communications within and between departments and support other activities, such as allocating scarce organizational resources, planning, budgeting, sales analyses, performance evaluations, and report preparation.

Coordinating Marketing Activities

Marketing managers must coordinate diverse employee actions to achieve marketing objectives and must work closely with management in many areas, including research and development, production, finance, accounting, and human resources to ensure that marketing activities align with other functions of the firm. They must also coordinate the activities of internal marketing staff with the marketing efforts of external organizations, including advertising agencies, resellers (wholesalers and retailers), researchers, and shippers. Marketing managers can improve coordination by making each employee aware of how his or her job relates to others and how his or her actions contribute to the achievement of marketing objectives.

Establishing a Timetable for Implementation

Successful marketing implementation requires that employees know the specific activities for which they are responsible and the timetable for completing them. Establishing an implementation timetable involves several steps: (1) identifying the activities to be performed, (2) determining the time required to complete each activity, (3) separating the activities to be performed in sequence from those to be performed simultaneously, (4) organizing the activities in the proper order, and (5) assigning responsibility for completing each activity to one or more employees, teams, or managers. Completing all implementation activities on schedule requires tight coordination within the marketing unit and among other departments that contribute to marketing activities, such as production. Pinpointing which activities can be performed simultaneously will reduce the total amount of time needed to put a given marketing strategy into practice. Since scheduling is a complicated task, most organizations use sophisticated computer programs to plan the timing of marketing activities. HP, for example, uses its own software to monitor sales, Web traffic, schedule orders and production, and schedule marketing activities.[16]

LO3. Describe the major elements of strategic performance evaluation.

EVALUATING MARKETING STRATEGIES

To achieve marketing objectives, marketing managers must evaluate marketing strategies effectively. **Strategic performance evaluation** consists of establishing performance standards, measuring actual performance, comparing actual performance with established standards, and modifying the marketing strategy, if needed.

Establishing Performance Standards

A **performance standard** is an expected level of performance against which actual performance can be compared. A performance standard might be a 20 percent reduction in customer complaints, a monthly sales quota of $150,000, or a 10 percent increase per month in new-customer accounts. Performance standards are derived from marketing objectives that are set while developing the marketing strategy. By establishing marketing objectives, a firm indicates what a marketing strategy is supposed to accomplish. Marketing objectives directly or indirectly set forth performance standards, usually in terms of sales, costs, or communication dimensions, such as brand awareness or product feature recall. Actual performance should be measured in similar terms to facilitate comparisons.

Analyzing Actual Performance

The principle means by which a marketer can gauge whether a marketing strategy has been effective in achieving objectives is by analyzing the actual performance of the marketing strategy. Take, for example, the advertisement for Renova, a company that sells high-end household paper products. While measuring the cost of this advertisement is not difficult, evaluating the overall effectiveness of the marketing strategy can be complicated. In this advertisement, you can see that the marketer has built in several mechanisms for attracting consumer interest and tracking it. To start, the image in the advertisement is difficult to interpret. The bright color and extreme close-up incites curiosity in the viewer because you do not at first realize what it is (toilet paper), so you examine the image. Once the advertisement has the viewer's interest, it offers a couple of means of gaining more information, namely the matrix barcode, which can be scanned with a smartphone, and the URL, where consumers without smartphones can go to shop for products. Once consumers have visited the website, the company can track the volume of visitors and purchases. While still crude measures, these techniques are an improvement over previous technology and allow marketers to get an approximate idea of the success of an advertisement. Generally speaking, technological advancements have made it easier for firms to analyze actual performance.

Another means of analyzing actual performance is by conducting customer research and surveys. In this section, we focus on two bases—sales and cost—for evaluating the actual performance of marketing strategies.

Sales Analysis

strategic performance evaluation Establishing performance standards, measuring actual performance, comparing actual performance with established standards, and modifying the marketing strategy, if needed

performance standard An expected level of performance against which actual performance can be compared

sales analysis Analysis of sales figures to evaluate a firm's performance

Sales analysis uses sales figures to evaluate a firm's current performance. It is a common method of evaluation because sales data are readily available, at least in aggregate form, and can reflect the target market's reactions to a marketing mix. If sales spike after a particular marketing mix is implemented, marketers can be reasonably certain that the marketing mix was effective at reaching the target audience. Information from sales data alone is not sufficient, however. To provide useful information, marketers must compare current sales data with forecasted sales, industry sales, specific competitors' sales, and the costs incurred from marketing efforts to achieve the sales volume. For example, if Renova, the paper company in the ad above, had forecasted $550,000 in sales for next quarter but nets $600,000, marketers can assume that the advertisement had a positive impact on sales. This is especially true if more sales than expected were from the company's website, since the advertisement directs customers there. Furthermore, if the advertisement came in under budget because there were no props or actors required, marketers may deem this a very effective advertisement indeed.

Although sales may be measured in several ways, the basic unit of measurement is the sales transaction. A sales transaction results in an order for a specified quantity of the organization's product sold under specified terms by a particular salesperson or sales team on a certain date. Organizations should record all information related to a transaction so that they can analyze sales in terms of dollar volume or market share. Firms frequently use dollar volume in their sales analyses because the dollar is a common denominator of sales, costs, and profits. A marketing manager who uses dollar-volume analysis should factor out the effects of price changes, which can skew the numbers by making it seem that more or fewer sales have been made than is the case.

A firm's market share is the sales of a product stated as a percentage of total industry sales of competing products. Market share analysis lets a company compare its marketing strategy with competitors' strategies. The primary reason for using market share analysis is to estimate whether sales changes have resulted from the firm's marketing strategy or from uncontrollable environmental forces. When a company's sales volume declines, but its share of the market stays the same, the marketer can assume industry sales declined because of outside factors. However, if a company experiences a decline in both sales and market share, it should consider making changes to its marketing strategy to make it more effective.

Even though market share analysis can be helpful in evaluating the performance of a marketing strategy, the user must exercise caution when interpreting results. When attributing a sales decline to uncontrollable factors, a marketer must keep in mind that factors in the external marketing environment do not impact all firms equally because firms have varying strategies and objectives. Changes in the strategies of one company can affect the market shares of one or all companies in that industry. Within an industry, the entrance of new firms, the launch of new products by competing firms, or the demise of established products also affect a firm's market share. Market share analysts should attempt to account for these effects. Apple, for example, caused its competitors to reevaluate their marketing strategies when it introduced the iPad, spurring competitor innovation and revised marketing strategies.

Courtesy of Renova

Performance Evaluation
Measuring the cost of an advertising campaign is not difficult. Evaluating the effectiveness of an advertising campaign is challenging.

Marketing Cost Analysis

Although sales analysis is critical for evaluating the performance of a marketing strategy, it provides only a partial picture. A marketing strategy that successfully generates sales may not be deemed effective if it is extremely costly. A firm must take into account the marketing costs associated with a strategy to gain a complete understanding of its effectiveness at achieving a desired sales level. **Marketing cost analysis** breaks down and classifies costs to determine which are associated with specific marketing efforts. Comparing costs of previous marketing activities with results allows a marketer to better allocate the firm's resources in the future. Marketing cost analysis lets a company evaluate the performance of a marketing strategy by comparing sales achieved and costs sustained. By pinpointing exactly where a company incurs costs, this form of analysis can help isolate profitable or unprofitable customers, products, and geographic areas.

A company that understands and manages costs appropriately has a competitive advantage. A low-cost provider is in a position to engage in aggressive price competition, for example. The Internet offers low-cost marketing options, such as e-mail, social media, and viral videos. It is also the medium where it is easiest for consumers to compare prices, making it a suitable medium to engage in price competition. Bazaarvoice is a company that helps firms create more effective marketing strategies by utilizing social media, targeting key markets, and allowing customers to create and share information about products and brands. Firms like Bazaarvoice help companies efficiently utilize new technological tools in marketing in order to maximize impact and keep costs low, while also creating methods for marketers to track customer responses to marketing activities.[17]

One way to analyze costs is by comparing a company's costs with industry averages. Many companies check the amount of money they spend on marketing efforts and other operations against average levels for the industry to identify areas in need of improvement. When looking at industry averages, however, a company should take into account its own unique situation. The company's costs can differ from the industry average for several reasons, including its own marketing objectives, cost structure, geographic location, types of customers, and scale of operations.

Costs can be categorized in different ways when performing marketing cost analysis. One way is to identify which costs are affected by sales or production volume. Some costs are fixed, meaning they do not change between different units of time, regardless of a company's production or sales volume. Fixed costs are variables such as rent and employees' salaries, which will not be affected by fluctuations in production or sales. Fixed costs are generally not very illuminating when determining how to utilize marketing funds more effectively. It does little good, for example, to know that a firm spends $80,000 on rent annually. The marketing analyst must conduct additional research to determine that, of the $80,000 spent on rent, $32,000 is spent on facilities associated with marketing efforts.

Some costs are directly attributable to production and sales volume. These are known as variable costs and they are stated in terms of a per quantity (or unit) cost. Variable costs include the cost to produce or sell each unit of a specific product, such as the materials and labor, or the amount of commissions that are paid to salespeople when they sell products.

Another way to categorize costs is based on whether or not they can be linked to a specific business function. Costs that can be linked are allocated, using one or several criteria, to the functions that they support. For example, if the firm spends $80,000 to rent space for production, storage, and sales facilities, the total rental cost can be allocated to each of the three functions using a measurement, such as square footage. Some costs cannot be assigned according to any logical criteria. These are such costs as interest paid on loans, taxes paid to the government, and the salaries of top management.

Comparing Actual Performance with Performance Standards and Making Changes, If Needed

marketing cost analysis
Analysis of costs to determine which are associated with specific marketing efforts

When comparing actual performance with established performance standards, a firm may find that it exceeded or failed to meet performance standard benchmarks. When actual performance exceeds performance standards, marketers will likely be satisfied and a marketing

Entrepreneurship in Marketing

Samuel Adams: Helping Others Brew the American Dream

Jim Koch is helping small businesses brew their American dreams. His Boston Beer Company, maker of Samuel Adams Beer, is an entrepreneurial success story, with annual revenue of nearly $600 million. In the early days, Koch faced many daunting marketing challenges, such as how to connect with suitable distributors. Even today, he and his managers maintain a small-business mindset because they recognize that Boston Beer's share of the U.S. beer market is tiny compared with the much larger shares held by deep-pocketed multinational rivals.

To help other small businesses plan for the future, Koch has partnered with the microlender Accion to create Brewing the American Dream. The program offers marketing advice, management mentoring, and small loans to entrepreneurs in the food and beverage industries.

Just as valuable as the funding is the opportunity to turn to Koch and his team for guidance when facing tough decisions. The owner of Delectable Desires, for example, borrowed $4,000 (which she repaid) and benefited from hours of consultation with a Boston Beer finance expert, who helped her assess pricing options for her cheesecakes.

Brewing the American Dream also works with local sponsors to host speed coaching sessions around the country. For 20 minutes at a time, entrepreneurs can sit down with a marketing expert or some other functional specialist to discuss their firms' weaknesses, opportunities, and competitive situation. After changing tables to consult with coaches in multiple functions, they walk away with new ideas for solving today's problems and building toward the profits of tomorrow.[d]

strategy will be deemed effective. It is important that a firm seek to gain an understanding of why the strategy was effective because this information may allow marketers to adjust the strategy tactically to be even more effective.

When actual performance fails to meet performance standards, marketers should seek to understand why the marketing strategy was less effective than expected. For example, perhaps a marketing mix variable such as price was not ideally suited to the target market, which could result in lower performance. Environmental changes or aggressive competitive behavior can both cause a marketing strategy to underperform.

When a marketer finds that a strategy is underperforming expectations, a question sometimes arises as to whether the marketing objective, against which performance is measured, is realistic. After studying the problem, the firm may find that the marketing objective is indeed unrealistic. In this case, marketers must alter the marketing objective to bring it in line with more sensible expectations. It is also possible that the marketing strategy is underfunded, which can result in lower performance.

CREATING THE MARKETING PLAN

LO4. Understand the development of a marketing plan.

The strategic planning process ultimately yields a marketing strategy that is the framework for a **marketing plan**, a written document that specifies the marketing activities to be performed to implement and evaluate the organization's marketing strategies. Developing a clear, well-written marketing plan, though time consuming, is important. It provides a uniform marketing vision for the firm and is the basis for internal communications. It delineates marketing responsibilities and tasks and outlines schedules for implementation. The plan presents objectives and specifies how resources are to be allocated to achieve them. Finally, the marketing plan helps managers monitor and evaluate the performance of a marketing strategy.

marketing plan A written document that specifies the activities to be performed to implement and control the organization's marketing activities

A single marketing plan can be developed and applied to the business as a whole, but it is more likely that a company will choose to develop multiple marketing plans, with each relating to a specific brand or product. Multiple marketing plans are part of a larger strategic business plan and are used to implement specific parts of the overall strategy.

Organizations use many different formats when producing a marketing plan. They may be written for strategic business units, product lines, individual products or brands, or specific markets. The key is to make sure that the marketing plan aligns with corporate and business-unit strategies and is accessible to and shared with all key employees. A marketing plan represents a critical element of a company's overall strategy development, and it should reflect the company's culture and be representative of all functional specialists in the firm.

Marketing planning and implementation are closely linked in successful companies. The marketing plan provides a framework to stimulate thinking and provide strategic direction. Implementation is an adaptive response to day-to-day issues, opportunities, and unanticipated situations—for example, an economic slowdown that dampens sales—that cannot be incorporated into marketing plans.

Table 2.1 describes the major elements of a typical marketing plan. Each component builds on the last. The first component is the executive summary, which provides an overview of the entire plan so that readers can quickly identify the key issues and their roles in the planning and implementation processes. The executive summary includes an introduction, an explanation of the major aspects of the plan, and a statement about costs. The next component of the marketing plan is the environmental analysis, which supplies information about the company's current situation with respect to the marketing environment, the target market, and the firm's current objectives and performance. The environmental analysis includes an

Table 2.1   Components of the Marketing Plan

Plan Component	Component Summary	Highlights
Executive Summary	One- to two-page synopsis of the entire marketing plan	1. Stress key points 2. Include one to three key points that make the company unique
Environmental Analysis	Information about the company's current situation with respect to the marketing environment	1. Assess marketing environment factors 2. Assess target market(s) 3. Assess current marketing objectives and performance
SWOT Analysis	Assessment of the organization's strengths, weaknesses, opportunities, and threats	1. Company strengths 2. Company weaknesses 3. Opportunities in the environment and industry 4. Threats in the environment and industry
Marketing Objectives	Specification of the company's marketing objectives	1. Qualitative measures of what is to be accomplished 2. Quantitative measures of what is to be accomplished
Marketing Strategies	Outline of how the company will achieve its objectives	1. Target market(s) 2. Marketing mix
Marketing Implementation	Outline of how the company will implement its marketing strategies	1. Marketing organization 2. Activities and responsibilities 3. Implementation timetable
Performance Evaluation	Explanation of how the company will evaluate the performance of the implemented plan	1. Performance standards 2. Financial controls 3. Monitoring procedures (audits)

assessment of all the environmental factors—competitive, economic, political, legal, regulatory, technological, and sociocultural—that can affect marketing activities. The analysis then examines the current needs of the organization's target markets. In the final section of the environmental analysis, the company evaluates its marketing objectives and performance to ensure that objectives are consistent with the changing marketing environment. The next component of the marketing plan is the SWOT analysis (strengths, weaknesses, opportunities, and threats), which utilizes the information gathered in the environmental analysis. The marketing objectives section of the marketing plan states what the company wants to accomplish through marketing activities, using the SWOT analysis as a guide of where the firm stands in the market. The marketing strategies component outlines how the firm plans to achieve its marketing objectives and discusses the company's target market selection(s) and marketing mix. The marketing implementation component of the plan outlines how marketing strategies will be executed. The success of a marketing strategy depends on the feasibility of marketing implementation. Finally, the performance evaluation establishes the standards for how results will be measured and evaluated, and what actions the company should take to reduce the differences between planned and actual performance.

It is important to note that most organizations utilize their own formats and terminology to describe the marketing plan. Every marketing plan is, and should be, unique to the organization for which it was created.

Creating and implementing a marketing plan allows the organization to achieve its marketing objectives and its business-unit and corporate goals. However, a marketing plan is only as good as the information it contains and the effort and creativity that went into its development. Therefore the importance of having a good marketing information system that generates robust and reliable data cannot be overstated. Equally important is the role of managerial judgment throughout the strategic planning process. While the creation of a marketing plan is an important milestone in strategic planning, it is by no means the final step. To succeed, a company must have a plan that is closely followed, yet flexible enough to adapt to the changing marketing environment.

Chapter Review

1. Understand the strategic planning process.

Through the process of strategic planning, a company identifies or establishes an organizational mission and goals, corporate strategy, marketing goals and objectives, marketing strategy, and a marketing plan. To achieve its marketing objectives, an organization must develop a marketing strategy, which includes identifying a target market and creating a plan of action for developing, distributing, promoting, and pricing products that meet the needs of customers in that target market. The strategic planning process ultimately yields the framework for a marketing plan, a written document that specifies the activities to be performed for implementing and controlling an organization's marketing activities.

An organization's goals should align with its mission statement—a long-term view, or vision, of what the organization wants to become. A well-formulated mission statement gives an organization a clear purpose and direction, distinguishes it from competitors, provides direction for strategic planning, and fosters a focus on customers. An organization's goals, which focus on desired results, guide the remainder of its planning efforts.

Corporate strategy determines the means for utilizing resources in the areas of production, finance, research and development, human resources, and marketing to reach the organization's goals. Business-unit strategy focuses on strategic business units (SBUs)—divisions, product lines, or other profit centers within the parent company used to define areas for consideration in a specific strategic marketing plan. The Boston Consulting Group's market growth/market share matrix integrates a company's products or SBUs into a single, overall matrix for evaluation to determine appropriate strategies for individual products and business units.

The marketing environment, including economic, competitive, political, legal and regulatory, sociocultural, and technological forces, can affect the resources available to a company to create favorable opportunities. Resources may help a firm develop core competencies, which are things that a company does extremely well—sometimes so well that it gives the company an advantage over its competition. When the right combination of circumstances and timing permits an organization to take action toward reaching a particular target market, a market opportunity exists. Strategic windows are temporary periods of optimal fit between the key requirements of a market and the particular capabilities of a company competing in that market. When a company matches a core competency to opportunities in the marketplace, it is said to have a competitive advantage. A marketer can use SWOT analysis to assess a firm's ability to achieve a competitive advantage.

If marketers want to understand how the timing of entry into a marketplace can create competitive advantage, they can examine the comparative benefits of first-mover versus late-mover advantages. The next phase of strategic planning involves the development of marketing objectives and strategies. Marketing objectives state what is to be accomplished through marketing activities, and should be consistent with both business-unit and corporate strategies. Marketing strategies, the most detailed and specific of the three levels, are composed of two elements: the selection of a target market and the creation of a marketing mix that will satisfy the needs of the target market. Marketing mix decisions should also be consistent with business-unit and corporate strategies and be flexible enough to respond to changes in market conditions, competition, and customer needs. Marketers can alter elements of the marketing mix to accommodate different marketing strategies.

2. Examine what is necessary to effectively manage the implementation of marketing strategies.

Marketing implementation is the process of executing marketing strategies. Through planning, marketing managers provide purpose and direction for an organization's marketing efforts. Marketing managers must understand the problems and elements of marketing implementation before they can implement specific marketing activities effectively. Proper implementation requires creating efficient organizational structures, motivating marketing personnel, properly communicating within the marketing unit, coordinating the marketing activities, and establishing a timetable for implementation.

The marketing unit must have a coherent internal structure in order to organize direct marketing efforts. In a centralized organization, top-level managers delegate very little authority to lower levels, whereas in decentralized organizations, decision-making authority is delegated as far down the chain of command as possible. Motivating marketing employees is crucial to effectively implementing marketing strategies. Marketing managers learn marketing employees' needs and develop methods to motivate them to help the organization meet its goals. Proper communication within the marketing unit is a key element in successful marketing implementation. Communication should move down (from top management to the lower-level employees) and up (from lower-level employees to top management). Marketing managers must also be able to effectively coordinate marketing activities. This entails both coordinating the activities of the marketing staff within the firms and integrating those activities with the marketing actions of external organizations that

are also involved in implementing the marketing strategies. Finally, successful marketing implementation requires that a timetable be established. Establishment of an implementation timetable involves several steps and ensures that employees know the specific activities for which they are responsible and the timeline for completing each activity. Completing all activities on schedule requires tight coordination among departments. Many organizations use sophisticated computer programs to plan the timing of marketing activities.

3. Describe the major elements of strategic performance evaluation.

Strategic performance evaluation consists of establishing performance standards, analyzing actual performance, comparing actual performance with established standards, and modifying the marketing strategy when needed. When actual performance is compared with performance standards, marketers must determine whether a discrepancy exists and, if so, whether it requires corrective action, such as changing the standard or improving actual performance. Two possible ways to evaluate the actual performance of marketing strategies are sales analysis and marketing cost analysis.

Sales analysis uses sales figures to evaluate a firm's current performance. It is the most common method of evaluation because sales data are a good indication of the target market's reaction to a marketing mix. Marketers analyze sales by comparing current sales to forecasted sales, industry sales, specific competitors' sales, or the costs incurred to achieve the sales volume. Companies can analyze sales in terms of the dollar volume or market share.

Marketing cost analysis breaks down and classifies costs to determine which are associated with specific marketing efforts. Marketing cost analysis helps marketers decide how to best allocate the firm's marketing resources. Companies can use marketing cost analysis to identify profitable or unprofitable customers, products, and geographic areas. Marketers can compare current costs to previous years, forecasted costs, industry averages, competitors' costs, or to the results generated by costs. Companies should identify which of its costs are variable and therefore affected by sales or production volumes, and which are fixed and therefore not related to sales volume. Companies should also categorize costs based on whether or not they can be linked to a specific business function, specifically marketing.

4. Understand the development of a marketing plan.

A key component of marketing planning is the development of a marketing plan, which outlines all the activities necessary to implement marketing strategies. The plan fosters communication among employees, assigns responsibilities and schedules, specifies how resources are to be allocated to achieve objectives, and helps marketing managers monitor and evaluate the performance of a marketing strategy.

Go to www.cengagebrain.com for resources to help you master the content in this chapter as well as for materials that will expand your marketing knowledge!

Key Concepts

strategic marketing
    management 28
strategic planning 28
mission statement 29
corporate strategy 30
strategic business unit
    (SBU) 31
market 31
market share 31

market growth/market share
    matrix 31
core competencies 33
market opportunity 33
strategic windows 33
competitive
    advantage 33
SWOT analysis 34
first-mover advantage 35

late-mover advantage 35
marketing objective 36
marketing strategy 37
sustainable competitive
    advantage 39
marketing
    implementation 39
centralized
    organization 40

decentralized
    organization 40
strategic performance
    evaluation 42
performance standard 42
sales analysis 42
marketing cost
    analysis 44
marketing plan 45

Issues for Discussion and Review

1. Identify the major components of strategic planning, and explain how they are interrelated.
2. Explain how an organization can create a competitive advantage at the corporate strategy level and at the business-unit strategy level.
3. What are some issues to consider in analyzing a company's resources and opportunities? How do these issues affect marketing objectives and marketing strategy?
4. What is SWOT analysis and why is it important?
5. How can an organization make its competitive advantages sustainable over time? How difficult is it to create sustainable competitive advantages?
6. How should organizations set marketing objectives?

7. What are the two major parts of a marketing strategy?
8. When considering the strategic planning process, what factors influence the development of a marketing strategy?
9. Identify and explain the major managerial actions that are a part of managing the implementation of marketing strategies.
10. Which element of the strategic planning process plays a major role in the establishment of performance standards? Explain.
11. When assessing actual performance of a marketing strategy, should a marketer perform marketing cost analysis? Why or why not?
12. Identify and explain the major components of a marketing plan.

Marketing Applications

1. You probably are quite familiar with Apple and its highly popular products. You may even own an iPad, iPhone, or iPod. Create a SWOT analysis for Apple. If you need additional information, feel free to visit the company's investor relations webpage at: **http://investor.apple.com/**. Here you will find annual reports, financial performance information, and other data that might help you with your SWOT analysis. When you are finished, find a partner and share your work. Do your SWOT analyses look similar, or are they very different? What did you not think about that your partner did?

2. Contact three local companies that appear to be successful (maybe they are expanding to new locations or post financial data online that looks promising). Visit the company's website or contact a company manager to find the company's mission statement and/or organizational goals. Obtain as much information as possible about the mission statement and organizational goals. Discuss how the statement matches the criteria outlined in the text.
3. Assume you own a new, family-style restaurant that will open for business in the coming year. Formulate a long-term goal for the restaurant, and then develop short-term goals to help you achieve the long-term goal.

4. Amazon.com identified an opportunity to capitalize on the convenience of online shopping. Many consumers would rather shop from home and avoid stores. Entering the market during a strategic window gave Amazon.com a competitive advantage in a new market. Consider the opportunities that may be present in your city or your region. Identify a strategic window, and discuss how a company could take advantage of this opportunity. What types of core competencies are necessary?

5. Marketing units may be organized according to functions, products, regions, or types of customers. Describe how you would organize the marketing units for the following:

   a. A toothpaste with whitener, a toothpaste with sensitivity protection, a toothpaste with cinnamon flavor

   b. A national line offering winter and summer sports clothing for men and women

   c. A life insurance company that provides life, health, and disability insurance

6. Develop your analytical and communication skills using the Role-Play Exercises online at **www.cengagebrain.com**.

Internet Exercise

Apple

You conducted a SWOT analysis for Apple in Exercise 1, so you should feel quite familiar with the company's strengths, weaknesses, opportunities, and threats. One of Apple's strengths is its website, which is considered to be very well organized and informative. See why by accessing **www.apple.com**.

1. Based on the information provided on the website, describe Apple's SBUs. Does Apple have SBUs that are divisions, product lines, or some other profit-center structure within the parent company?

2. Based on your existing knowledge of Apple as an innovative leader in the consumer electronics industry, describe the company's primary competitive advantage (i.e., what makes Apple strategically unique?). How does Apple's website support this competitive advantage?

3. Assess the quality and effectiveness of Apple's website. Specifically, perform a preliminary SWOT analysis comparing Apple's website with other high-quality websites you have visited.

developing your marketing plan

One of the foundations of a successful marketing strategy is a thorough analysis of your company. To make the best decisions about what products to offer, which markets to target, and how to reach those target market members, you must recognize your company's strengths and weaknesses. The information collected in this analysis should be referenced when making many of the decisions in your marketing plan. While writing the beginning of your plan, the information in this chapter can help you with the following issues:

1. Can you identify the core competencies of your company? Do they currently contribute to a competitive advantage? If not, what changes could your company make to establish a competitive advantage?

2. Conduct a SWOT analysis of your company to identify its strengths and weaknesses. Continue your analysis to include the business environment, discovering any opportunities that exist or threats that may impact your company.

3. Using the information from your SWOT analysis, have you identified any opportunities that are a good match with your company's core competencies? Likewise, have you discovered any weaknesses that could be converted to strengths through careful marketing planning?

The information obtained from these questions should assist you in developing various aspects of your marketing plan. Develop your marketing plan online using the Interactive Marketing Plan at **www.cengagebrain.com**.

video case 2.1

How White Rock Adds Marketing Sparkle

Larry Bodkin had a tough road ahead of him when he became president of White Rock Beverages. Founded in the late 1800s, White Rock's sparkling water reached its heyday in the early 20th century as the water of the upper class. However, by the end of the century, White Rock was struggling to survive in the face of intense competition from global brands with gigantic marketing budgets.

Now more than 140 years old, White Rock has used a combination of different marketing strategies to revitalize itself. For years it utilized a hybrid distribution system to sell to distributors in some markets and to retailers in other markets. In the process, White Rock uses customer service as a differentiator between its beverages and its competitors. Because customers find the company responsive to their needs, many stay loyal to the White Rock brand.

Another way in which White Rock differentiates itself from companies like Coca-Cola and Pepsi is by its branding strategy. The company recognizes that one of its key strengths is as a premium brand for a niche market segment. White Rock targets the health-food segment by marketing itself as a unique, healthy brand. It also capitalizes on its history as one of the oldest sparkling beverage companies in America. This brand appeal has become so important that White Rock challenged Coca-Cola after Coke claimed that it created today's modern image of Santa Claus. Bodkin demanded an apology from Coca-Cola when it was revealed that White Rock had been using the modern Santa Claus ad two decades prior to Coca-Cola's Santa ads. By developing a strong, authentic image for each of its brands, White Rock is building on recent trends toward "artisanal" foods that emphasize quality and distinctive traditions.

White Rock's marketing efforts have been successful in stimulating revenue growth. However, since the brand has matured (meaning that growth will likely be minimal), the company is adapting its strategy by introducing White Rock in new containers and sizes. For instance, it developed the White Rock Punch 'n' Fruity juice boxes, which are meant to appeal to on-the-go consumers and parents. Additionally, White Rock is breaking into the organic industry with its line of White Rock organics, made with cane sugar and natural fruit extracts.

White Rock is also pursuing an acquisition strategy of other brands. In addition to the White Rock brand, the company owns the Sioux City and Olde Brooklyn brands, brand names that seem connected to a bygone era. White Rock credits its nationally distributed Sioux City brand as one of the first brands of soft drinks to carry a Western theme. Olde Brooklyn's flavors are named after Brooklyn neighborhoods, a nostalgic appeal that connects with customers seeking brands with authenticity and history. Olde Brooklyn also lacks preservatives, which helps it appeal to the health-food market. By using brands such as Olde Brooklyn to gain entry into health-food stores and other retail segments, White Rock has expanded its distribution to 40 states and is already planning for future growth.[18]

Questions for Discussion

1. How would you describe White Rock's strengths, weaknesses, opportunities, and threats?
2. What do you think White Rock should do to gain competitive advantage?
3. What elements of the marketing mix could White Rock change to improve its marketing strategy?

NOTES

[1] Based on information in "P&G Expands Experience to Make More Innovation Experts," *Fast Company*, January 15, 2013, www.fastcompany. com; "P&G Vows Stepped-Up Marketing, Cost Cutting," *Advertising Age*, October 25, 2012, www .adage.com; Patricia Odell, "P&G's CMO on Three Key Strategies, Mistakes, and Anthropologists," *Chief Marketer*, October 12, 2012, http:// chiefmarketer.com; Jack Neff, "Talking the (Internal) Talk at P&G," *Advertising Age*, October 29, 2012, www.adage.com; www.pg.com

[2] O. C. Ferrell andMichael Hartline, *Marketing Strategy*, 5th ed. (Mason, OH: Cengage Learning, 2011), 10.

[3] Christian Homburg, Karley Krohmer, and John P. Workman Jr., "A Strategy Implementation Perspective of Market Orientation," *Journal of Business Research* 57 (2004): 1331–1340.

[4] "Our Starbucks Mission Statement," Starbucks, www.starbucks.com/about-us/company-information/ mission-statement (accessed January 10, 2013).

[5] Matthew L. Wald, "Fuel From Waste, Poised at a Milestone," *New York Times*, November 14, 2012, www.nytimes.com/2012/11/14/business/energy-environment/alternative-fuels-long-delayed-promise-might-be-near-fruition.html; KiOR, www.kior.com (accessed January 10, 2013).

[6] Stanley F. Slater, G. Tomas M. Hult, and Eric M. Olson, "On the Importance of Matching Strategic Behavior and Target Market Selection to Business Strategy in High-Tech Markets," *Journal of the Academy of Marketing Science* 35 (2007): 5–17.

[7] Tess Stynes, "Google, Microsoft Increase U.S. Search Market Shares in November," NASDAQ, December 12, 2012, www.nasdaq.com/article/comscore-google-microsoft-increase-us-search-market-shares-in-november-20121212-01189#.UO-Ni3djGoM.

[8] Robert D. Buzzell, "The PIMS Program of Strategy Research: A Retrospective Appraisal," *Journal of Business Research* 57 (2004): 478–483.

[9] Sarah E. Needleman and Craig Bensinger, "Small Businesses are Finding an Unlikely Banker: Amazon," *Wall Street Journal*, October 4, 2012, http://online.wsj.com/article/SB10000872396390443493304578034103049644978.html (accessed January 11, 2013).

[10] Derek F. Abell, "Strategic Windows," *Journal of Marketing* (July 1978): 21.

[11] Joan E. Solsman, "Best Buy Shares Rally on Holiday Sales," *Wall Street Journal*, January 11, 2013, http://online.wsj.com/article/SB10001424127887323442804578235402334803068.html.

[12] Norihiko Shirouzu, "Toyota's Misfire in China Offers Lesson in Local Market Savvy," *Wall Street Journal*, October 29, 2012, www.nytimes.com/2012/10/30/business/global/toyotas-misfire-in-china-offers-lesson-in-local-market-savvy.html (accessed January 11, 2013).

[13] Claire Cain Miller, "Mobile Apps Drive Rapid Changes in Searches," *New York Times*, January 7, 2013, www.nytimes.com/2013/01/08/business/mobile-apps-drive-rapid-changes-in-search-technology.html.

[14] Ellen Byron, "A Truce in the Chore Wars," *Wall Street Journal*, December 4, 2012, http://online.wsj.com/article/SB100014241278873234021904578157500316162398.html

[15] Jennifer Valentino-Devries and Jeremy Singer-Vine, "They Know What You're Shopping For," *Wall Street Journal*, December 7, 2012, http://online.wsj.com/article/SB10001424127887324784404578143144132736214.html (accessed January 14, 2013).

[16] Clint Boulton, "H-P Using Its Analytics Software to Grow Sales," *Wall Street Journal*, January 11, 2013, http://blogs.wsj.com/cio/2013/01/11/h-p-using-its-analytics-software-to-grow-sales/ (accessed January 15, 2013).

[17] Bazaarvoice, www.bazaarvoice.com (accessed January 13, 2013).

[18] Joel Rose, "White Rock Beverages Still Thirsty After 140 Years," NPR, December 5, 2011, www.npr.org; "After 140 Years, White Rock Still Solid," BevNet, July 6, 2011, BevNET.com; White Rock, www.whiterockbeverages.com; "Creative Beverage Merchandising," Creative Beverage, April/May 2005, www.creativemag.com; PR Newswire, "Coca-Cola's Santa Claus: Not the Real Thing!" PR News Online, December 15, 2006, www.prnewsonline.com; Patricia Olsen, "At the Helm: Larry Bodkin," *Family Business Magazine*, May-June 2012, www.familybusinessmagazine.com (accessed January 16, 2013).

Feature Notes

[a] Based on information in Bill Vlasic, "2 Makers Press the Case for Electric Cars," *New York Times*, January 15, 2013, www.nytimes.com; Matthew Boyle, "Unilever Wants to Be America's Ice Cream King," *Bloomberg Businessweek*, August 23, 2012, www.businessweek.com; "Struggling Sales of Cars Like the Chevrolet Volt, Nissan Leaf Show Weakness in Electric Vehicle Market," *New York Daily News*, October 9, 2012, www.nydailynews.com.

[b] Based on information in Todd Woody, "GE's New Ecomagination Chief: Green Tech Innovation Goes Global," *Forbes*, May 3, 2011, www.forbes.com; Kate Maddox, "'B to B' Names GE's Boff Digital Marketer of the Year," BtoB, October 3, 2011, 3; "GE's Ecomagination Challenge Phase Two to Focus on Eco-Home Technology," TechCrunch, January 7, 2011, www.techcrunch.com; Kerry A. Dolan, "Yves Behar's Latest Design: GE's WattStation," *Forbes*, July 13, 2010, www.forbes.com; www.ecomagination.com.

[c] Based on information in Dhanya Skariachan and Phil Wahba, "Home Depot, Walmart, Grocers Get Boost from Irene," Reuters, August 26, 2011, www.reuters.com; John Hamilton, "Big-Box Stores' Hurricane Prep Starts Early," NPR, August 26, 2011, www.npr.org; J. Cashman, "Generators, Batteries Big Sellers Ahead of Irene," *New England Post*, August 27, 2011, www.newenglandpost.com; "Snow Disrupts Package Pickup, Delivery in Oklahoma," *Oklahoman*, February 2, 2011, http://newsok.com; Arielle Kass, "Georgia Companies Prepared for Hurricane Well in Advance," *Atlanta Journal Constitution*, August 26, 2011, www.ajc.com/business.

[d] Robb Mandelbaum, "What Big Companies Get from Helping Small Companies," *New York Times*, November 26, 2012, www.nytimes.com; Robb Mandelbaum, "Making Small Business a Cause," *New York Times*, November 14, 2012, www.nytimes.com; Jay Goltz, "Speed Counseling for Struggling Business Owners," *New York Times*, August 2, 2012, www.nytimes.com (accessed January 17, 2013).

chapter 3

The Marketing Environment, Social Responsibility, and Ethics

© iStockphoto.com/EdStock

MARKETING INSIGHTS

Companies Win with Cause-Related Marketing

For many companies, linking their product to a social cause is becoming not only a way to build rapport with customers through support of a social cause, but also a way to build upon the company's core competencies and values. Effective cause-related marketing initiatives can create a positive image of a company among consumers, particularly as consumers are increasingly expecting companies to support social or environmental causes. One study revealed that 85 percent of consumers view companies that engage in cause-related marketing in a more positive light.

While some firms make one-time donations or decide to temporarily adopt a community project, others have successfully incorporated cause-related marketing into their programs. For instance, IBM established a community service program, Corporate Service Corps, which allows more than 200 teams of twelve people to volunteer domestically and globally. AT&T has invested more than $100

million in the education system, while its employees have volunteered 270,000 hours of mentoring for students. These programs have bolstered employee satisfaction and job performance and have also demonstrated how corporations can produce positive results within their communities.

Additionally, cause-related marketing has enabled organizations to achieve strong linkages between their support for causes and the products they offer. For instance, American Express created a special edition United Way Gift Card in which the company donates the purchase fee for the card to support United Way's work. American Express benefits from both the sale of the gift card as well as the positive perception it generates by aligning its product with a good cause. Aligning marketing activities with a social cause utilizing core competencies of the firm has proven to be an effective way of creating strong associations between company and cause.[1]

To succeed in today's highly competitive marketplace, companies must respond to changes in the marketing environment, particularly changes in customer and public desires and competitors' actions. Increasingly, success also requires that marketers act responsibly and ethically. Because recognizing and responding to such changes in the marketing environment are crucial to marketing success, this chapter explores in some detail the forces that contribute to these changes.

The first half of this chapter explores the competitive, economic, political, legal and regulatory, technological, and sociocultural forces that make up the marketing environment. This discussion addresses the importance of scanning and analyzing the marketing environment, as well as how each of these forces influences marketing strategy decisions. The second half of the chapter considers the role of social responsibility and ethics. These increasingly important forces raise several issues that pose threats and opportunities to marketers, such as the natural environment and consumerism.

THE MARKETING ENVIRONMENT

The marketing environment consists of external forces that directly or indirectly influence an organization's acquisition of inputs (human, financial, natural resources and raw materials, and information) and creation of outputs (goods, services, or ideas). As indicated in Chapter 1, the marketing environment includes six such forces: competitive, economic, political, legal and regulatory, technological, and sociocultural.

Whether fluctuating rapidly or slowly, environmental forces are always dynamic. Changes in the marketing environment create uncertainty, threats, and opportunities for marketers. For instance, firms providing digital products such as software, music, and movies face many environmental threats as well as opportunities. Advancing technology enables digital delivery of these products, which is an efficient and effective way to reach global markets. On the other hand, sites such as Pirate Bay allow peer-to-peer transfers and are referred to as file-sharing sites or cyberlockers. The movie and music industries want more effective legislation in place to crack down on the theft of their products. Most of these developments involve trying to influence controls to stop this threat, including arresting individuals involved in the development of these piracy sites such as Pirate Bay co-founder Gottfrid Svartholm Warg.[2] Monitoring the environment is therefore crucial to an organization's survival and to the long-term achievement of its goals.

To monitor changes in the marketing environment effectively, marketers engage in environmental scanning and analysis. **Environmental scanning** is the process of collecting information about forces in the marketing environment. Scanning involves observation; secondary sources such as business, trade, government, and Internet sources; and marketing research. The Internet has become a popular scanning tool because it makes data more accessible and allows companies to gather needed information quickly.

Environmental analysis is the process of assessing and interpreting the information gathered through environmental scanning. A manager evaluates the information for accuracy; tries to resolve inconsistencies in the data; and, if warranted, assigns significance to the findings. By evaluating this information, the manager should be able to identify potential threats and opportunities linked to environmental changes. A threat could be rising interest rates or commodity prices. An opportunity could be increases in consumer income, decreases in the unemployment rate, or adoption of new technology related to the Internet.

Understanding the current state of the marketing environment and recognizing threats and opportunities arising from changes within it help companies with strategic planning. In particular, they can help marketing managers assess the performance of current marketing efforts and develop future marketing strategies.

environmental scanning
The process of collecting information about forces in the marketing environment

environmental analysis
The process of assessing and interpreting the information gathered through environmental scanning

Responding to the Marketing Environment

Marketing managers take two general approaches to environmental forces: accepting them as uncontrollable or attempting to influence and shape them.[3] An organization that views

Responding to the Marketing Environment
The sponsors of this ad are trying to educate drivers about the dangers associated with texting and driving.

environmental forces as uncontrollable remains *passive* and *reactive* toward the environment. Instead of trying to influence forces in the environment, its marketing managers adjust current marketing strategies to environmental changes. They approach with caution market opportunities discovered through environmental scanning and analysis. On the other hand, marketing managers who believe that environmental forces can be shaped adopt a more *proactive* approach. For example, if a market is blocked by traditional environmental constraints, proactive marketing managers may apply economic, psychological, political, and promotional skills to gain access to and operate within it. Once they identify what is blocking a market opportunity, they assess the power of the various parties involved and develop strategies to overcome the obstructing environmental forces. Microsoft, Intel, and Google, for example, have responded to political, legal, and regulatory concerns about their power in the computer industry by communicating the value of their competitive approaches to various publics. The computer giants contend that their competitive success results in superior products for their customers with benefits to society.

A proactive approach can be constructive and bring desired results. To exert influence on environmental forces, marketing managers seek to identify market opportunities or to extract greater benefits relative to costs from existing market opportunities. The advertisement launched by the National Highway Traffic Safety Commission attempts to bring about desired results by showing the dangers of texting and driving. The advertisement purposefully covers the face of the man texting to demonstrate how texting can distract or "blind" people when they are on the road. Political action is another way to affect environmental forces. The pharmaceutical industry, for example, has lobbied very effectively for fewer restrictions on prescription drug marketing. However, managers must recognize that there are limits on how much environmental forces can be shaped. Although an organization may be able to influence legislation through lobbying—as the movie and music industries are doing to try and stop the piracy of their products—it is unlikely that a single organization can significantly change major economic factors such as recessions, interest rates, or commodity prices.

Competitive Forces

Few firms, if any, operate free of competition. In fact, for most products, customers have many alternatives from which to choose. For example, while the five best-selling soft drinks in the United States are Coke Classic, Diet Coke, Pepsi-Cola, Mountain Dew, and Diet Pepsi, soft-drink sales in general have flattened as consumers have turned to alternatives such as bottled water, flavored water, fruit juice, and iced tea products.[4] Thus, when marketing managers define the target market(s) their firm will serve, they simultaneously establish a set of competitors.[5] The number of firms that supply a product may affect the strength of competitors.

Brand Competition
Coke and Pepsi compete head-to-head in the soft-drink market.

competition Other firms that market products that are similar to or can be substituted for a firm's products in the same geographic area

brand competitors Firms that market products with similar features and benefits to the same customers at similar prices

product competitors Firms that compete in the same product class but market products with different features, benefits, and prices

total budget competitors Firms that compete for the limited financial resources of the same customers

When just one or a few firms control supply, competitive factors exert a different sort of influence on marketing activities than when many competitors exist.

Broadly speaking, all firms compete with one another for customers' dollars. More practically, however, a marketer generally defines **competition** as other firms that market products that are similar to or can be substituted for its products in the same geographic area. These competitors can be classified into one of four types. **Brand competitors** market products with similar features and benefits to the same customers at similar prices. For example, a thirsty, calorie-conscious customer may choose a diet soda such as Diet Coke or Diet Pepsi from the soda machine. However, these sodas face competition from other types of beverages. **Product competitors** compete in the same product class but market products with different features, benefits, and prices. The thirsty dieter, for instance, might purchase iced tea, juice, a sports beverage, or bottled water instead of a soda. Generic competitors provide very different products that solve the same problem or satisfy the same basic customer need. Our dieter, for example, might simply have a glass of water from the kitchen tap to satisfy his or her thirst. Total budget competitors compete for the limited financial resources of the same customers.[6] **Total budget competitors** for Diet Coke, for example, might include gum, a newspaper, and bananas. Although all four types of competition can affect a firm's marketing performance, brand competitors are the most significant because buyers typically see the different products of these firms as direct substitutes for one another. Consequently, marketers tend to concentrate environmental analyses on brand competitors.

50 Essential Experiences
The Travel Bucket List

A Collection of Travel Stories to Inspire Your Next Journey

Competitive Structures
The cruise ship industry is an example of an oligopoly.

Table 3.1   Selected Characteristics of Competitive Structures

Type of Structure	Number of Competitors	Ease of Entry into Market	Product	Example
Monopoly	One	Many barriers	Almost no substitutes	Water utilities
Oligopoly	Few	Some barriers	Homogeneous or differentiated (with real or perceived differences)	UPS, FedEx, Postal Service (package delivery)
Monopolistic competition	Many	Few barriers	Product differentiation, with many substitutes	Wrangler, Levi Strauss (jeans)
Pure competition	Unlimited	No barriers	Homogeneous products	Vegetable farm (sweet corn)

© Cengage Learning

When just one or a few firms control supply, competitive factors exert a different form of influence on marketing activities than when many competitors exist. Table 3.1 presents four general types of competitive structures: monopoly, oligopoly, monopolistic competition, and pure competition. A **monopoly** exists when an organization offers a product that has no close substitutes, making that organization the sole source of supply. Because the organization has no competitors, it controls supply of the product completely and, as a single seller, can erect barriers to potential competitors. In reality, most monopolies surviving today are local utilities, which are heavily regulated by local, state, or federal agencies. An **oligopoly** exists when a few sellers control the supply of a large proportion of a product. In this case, each seller considers the reactions of other sellers to changes in marketing activities. Products facing oligopolistic competition may be homogeneous, such as aluminum, or differentiated, such as package delivery services. The cruise ship industry is an example of an oligopoly. However, even an industry dominated by a few companies must still compete and release promotional materials. The Princess Cruises advertisement promotes the exciting travel experiences posted on its blog by its employees. By sharing 50 travel stories from the past year, the company hopes to demonstrate to viewers that they too can have an amazing travel experience with Princess Cruises. **Monopolistic competition** exists when a firm with many potential competitors attempts to develop a marketing strategy to differentiate its product. For example, Wrangler and Seven 4 All Mankind have established an advantage for their blue jeans through well-known trademarks, design, advertising, and a reputation for quality. Wrangler is associated with a cowboy image, while Seven 4 All Mankind tries to maintain a premium designer image. Although many competing brands of blue jeans are available, these firms have carved out market niches by emphasizing differences in their products, especially style and image. **Pure competition**, if it existed at all, would entail a large number of sellers, none of which could significantly influence price or supply. The closest thing to an example of pure competition is an unregulated farmers' market, where local growers gather to sell their produce. Pure competition is an ideal at one end of the continuum; monopoly is at the other end. Most marketers function in a competitive environment somewhere between these two extremes.

Marketers need to monitor the actions of major competitors to determine what specific strategies competitors are using and how those strategies affect their own. Price is one of the marketing strategy variables that most competitors monitor. When Delta or Southwest Airlines lowers the fare on a route, most major airlines attempt to match the price. Monitoring guides marketers in developing competitive advantages and aids

monopoly A competitive structure in which an organization offers a product that has no close substitutes, making that organization the sole source of supply

oligopoly A competitive structure in which a few sellers control the supply of a large proportion of a product

monopolistic competition A competitive structure in which a firm has many potential competitors and tries to develop a marketing strategy to differentiate its product

pure competition A market structure characterized by an extremely large number of sellers, none strong enough to significantly influence price or supply

them in adjusting current marketing strategies and planning new ones. When an airline such as Southwest acquires a competitor such as AirTran, then there is the potential for less competition.

In monitoring competition, it is not enough to analyze available information; the firm must develop a system for gathering ongoing information about competitors. Understanding the market and what customers want, as well as what the competition is providing, will assist in maintaining a market orientation.[7] Information about competitors allows marketing managers to assess the performance of their own marketing efforts and to recognize the strengths and weaknesses in their own marketing strategies. Data about market shares, product movement, sales volume, and expenditure levels can be useful. However, accurate information on these matters is often difficult to obtain. We explore how marketers collect and organize such data in Chapter 4.

Economic Forces

Economic forces in the marketing environment influence both marketers' and customers' decisions and activities. In this section, we examine the effects of buying power and willingness to spend, as well as general economic conditions.

Buying Power and Willingness to Spend

buying power Resources, such as money, goods, and services, that can be traded in an exchange

disposable income After-tax income

discretionary income Disposable income available for spending and saving after an individual has purchased the basic necessities of food, clothing, and shelter

The strength of a person's **buying power** depends on economic conditions and the size of the resources—money, goods, and services that can be traded in an exchange—that enable the individual to make purchases. The major financial sources of buying power are income, credit, and wealth.

For an individual, *income* is the amount of money received through wages, rents, investments, pensions, and subsidy payments for a given period, such as a month or a year. Normally, this money is allocated among taxes, spending for goods and services, and savings. Marketers are most interested in the amount of money left after payment of taxes because this **disposable income** is used for spending or saving. Because disposable income is a ready source of buying power, the total amount available in a nation is important to marketers. Several factors determine the size of total disposable income, including the total amount of income—which is affected by wage levels, the rate of unemployment, interest rates, and dividend rates—and the number and amount of taxes. Disposable income that is available for spending and saving after an individual has purchased the basic necessities of food, clothing, and shelter is called discretionary income. People use **discretionary income** to purchase entertainment, vacations, automobiles, education, pets, furniture, appliances, and so on. Breitling sells products that would be purchased with discretionary income. It uses celebrity soccer player David Beckham in its advertisements to lend an air of prestige to its watches, which helps it to justify its $11,200 price tag for its Breitling Transocean Chronograph Unitime traveler's watch. Changes in total discretionary income affect sales of these products, especially automobiles, furniture, large appliances, and other costly durable goods.

Credit is also important because it enables people to spend future income now or in the near future. However, credit increases

Discretionary Income
Consumers may use their discretionary income to purchase the Breitling Transocean Chronograph Unitime, touted as the ultimate watch for travelers.

current buying power at the expense of future buying power. Several factors determine whether people acquire, use, or forgo credit. After the last recession, obtaining credit loans for homes has been more difficult for consumers due to the number of consumers who defaulted on their loans. Banks have tightened the requirements for loans. Interest rates affect buyers' decisions to use credit, especially for expensive purchases such as homes, appliances, and automobiles. When interest rates are low, the total cost of automobiles and houses becomes more affordable. In contrast, when interest rates are high, consumers are more likely to delay buying such expensive items. Use of credit is also affected by credit terms, such as size of the down payment and amount and number of monthly payments.

Wealth is the accumulation of past income, natural resources, and financial resources. It exists in many forms, including cash, securities, savings accounts, gold, jewelry, and real estate. The significance of wealth to marketers is that as people become wealthier, they gain buying power in three ways: they can use their wealth to make current purchases, to generate income, and to acquire large amounts of credit.

People's **willingness to spend**—their inclination to buy because of expected satisfaction from a product—is related, to some degree, to their ability to buy. That is, people are sometimes more willing to buy if they have the buying power. However, several other elements also influence willingness to spend. Some elements affect specific products; others influence spending in general. A product's price and value influence almost all of us. Cross pens, for example, appeal to customers who are willing to spend more for fine writing instruments even when lower-priced pens are readily available. The amount of satisfaction received from a product already owned also may influence customers' desires to buy other products. Satisfaction depends not only on the quality of the currently owned product but also on numerous psychological and social forces. The American Customer Satisfaction Index, computed by the National Quality Research Center at the University of Michigan (see Figure 3.1), offers an indicator of customer satisfaction with a wide variety of businesses. The American Customer Satisfaction Index helps marketers understand how consumers perceive their industries and businesses. By understanding how satisfied (or dissatisfied) customers are with their business or industry, marketers can take this information and adapt their marketing strategies accordingly.

Economic Conditions

The overall state of the economy fluctuates in all countries. Changes in general economic conditions affect (and are affected by) supply and demand, buying power, willingness to spend, consumer expenditure levels, and the intensity of competitive behavior. Therefore, current economic conditions and changes in the economy have a broad impact on the success of organizations' marketing strategies.

Fluctuations in the economy follow a general pattern, often referred to as the **business cycle**. In the traditional view, the business cycle consists of four stages: prosperity, recession, depression, and recovery. During *prosperity,* unemployment is low, and total income is relatively high. Assuming a low inflation rate, this combination ensures high buying power. During a *recession,* however, unemployment rises, while total buying power declines. Pessimism accompanying a recession often stifles both consumer and business spending. A prolonged recession may become a *depression,* a period in which unemployment is extremely high, wages are very low, total disposable income is at a minimum, and consumers lack confidence in the economy. During *recovery,* the economy moves from depression or recession to prosperity. During this period, high unemployment begins to decline, total disposable income increases, and the economic gloom that reduced consumers' willingness to buy subsides. Both the ability and willingness to buy increase.

The business cycle can enhance the success of marketing strategies. In the prosperity stage, for example, marketers may expand their product offerings to take advantage of increased buying power. They may be able to capture a larger market share by intensifying distribution

willingness to spend
An inclination to buy because of expected satisfaction from a product, influenced by the ability to buy and numerous psychological and social forces

business cycle A pattern of economic fluctuations that has four stages: prosperity, recession, depression, and recovery

Figure 3.1 **National Customer Satisfaction Benchmark**

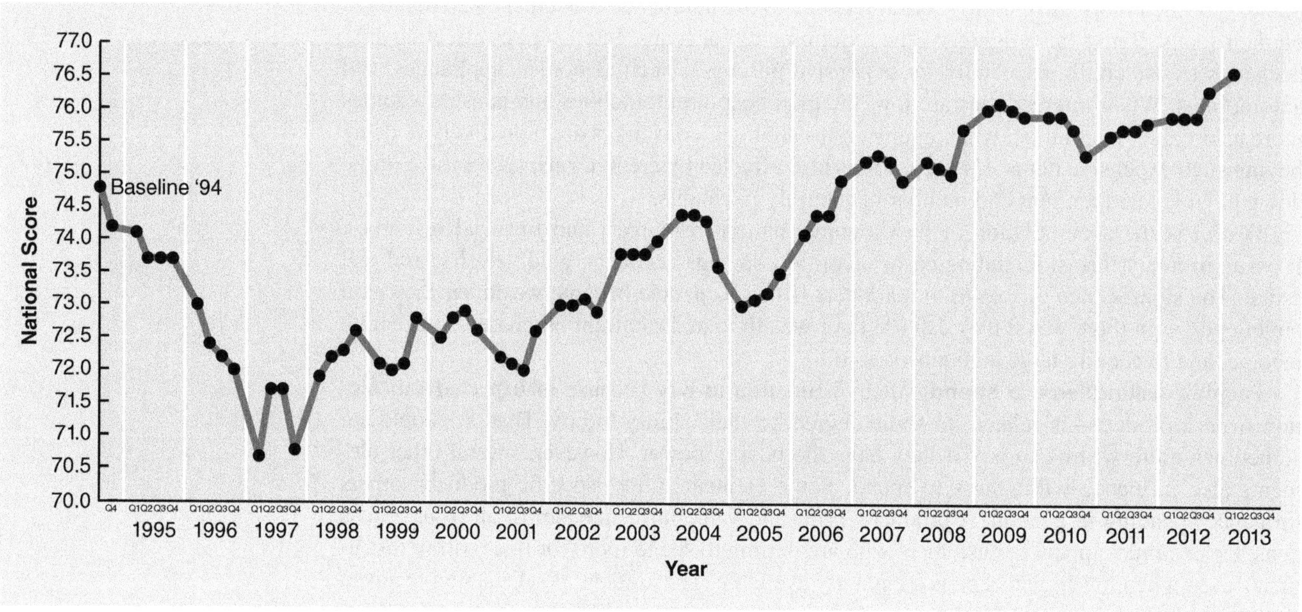

Source: Data from American Customer Satisfaction Index, "National Quarterly Benchmarks," www.theacsi.org/national-economic-indicator/national-quarterly-benchmarks (accessed May 2013).

and promotion efforts. In times of recession or depression, when buying power decreases, many customers may become more price conscious and seek more basic, functional products. For example, when buying power decreased during the most recent recession, department store sales dropped. Consumers began shopping at off-price retailers such as T.J.Maxx and Ross. These stores attracted middle-income consumers because they sell brand-name goods at a discount. Even during the recovery cycle, many consumers opted to continue shopping at off-price retailers to take advantage of the lower prices.[8]

During economic downturns, a company should focus its efforts on determining precisely what functions buyers want and ensure that these functions are available in its product offerings. Promotional efforts should emphasize value and utility. Some firms make the mistake of drastically reducing their marketing efforts during a recession, harming their ability to compete. The United States and most of the world experienced a period of prosperity in 2004–2007. During this time, household net worth increased by almost 6 percent a year, with rapidly increasing home values, low unemployment, low interest rates, and expanding credit availability. The decision by the government and financial institutions to grant subprime loans (higher-interest loans to people with poor credit ratings) triggered the default of these loans. In 2008, the United States experienced an economic downturn due to higher energy prices, falling home values, increasing unemployment, the financial crisis in the banking industry, and fluctuating currency values. That recession was the longest since the Great Depression of the 1930s.

Political Forces

Political, legal, and regulatory forces of the marketing environment are closely interrelated. Legislation is enacted; legal decisions are interpreted by courts; and regulatory agencies are created and operated, for the most part, by elected or appointed officials. Legislation and regulations (or their lack) reflect the current political outlook. For instance, after the financial crisis caused a worldwide recession, the government passed the Dodd-Frank Wall Street Reform and Consumer Protection Act of 2010. This act was created to increase accountability and transparency in the financial industry.[9] The legislation established a new Consumer Financial

Protection Bureau to protect consumers from deceptive financial practices.[10] Consequently, the political forces of the marketing environment have the potential to influence marketing decisions and strategies.

Reactive marketers view political forces as beyond their control and simply adjust to conditions arising from those forces. Some firms are more proactive, however, and seek to influence the political process. In some cases, organizations publicly protest the actions of legislative bodies. More often, organizations help elect to political offices individuals who regard them positively. Much of this help is in the form of campaign contributions. AT&T is an example of a company that has attempted to influence legislation and regulation over a long period of time. Since 1990, AT&T has made more than $50 million in corporate donations for use in supporting the campaign funds of political candidates.[11] For years, legislators and other groups have sought to limit the amount of corporate campaign contributions. In the 2010 ruling *Citizens United v. Federal Election Commission*, the Supreme Court ruled that the government is not authorized to ban corporate spending in candidate elections.[12] This means that future elections can be affected by large corporate donations to candidates. Marketers also can influence the political process through political action committees (PACs) that solicit donations from individuals and then contribute those funds to candidates running for political office.

Companies also can participate in the political process through lobbying to persuade public and/or government officials to favor a particular position in decision making. Many companies concerned about the threat of legislation or regulation that may negatively affect their operations employ lobbyists to communicate their concerns to elected officials. For instance, as the United States government debates whether to pass stricter laws regulating marketing activities over the Internet, social media firms such as Google are sending lobbyists to give their respective viewpoints regarding the proposed legislation.

Legal and Regulatory Forces

A number of federal laws influence marketing decisions and activities. Table 3.2 lists some of the most significant pieces of legislation. Regulatory agencies and self-regulatory forces also affect marketing efforts.

Protesting against Business and Government
Protestors carry a banner to protest the sale of genetically modified food during a demonstration at a biotechnology industry conference.

Table 3.2   **Major Federal Laws Affecting Marketing Decisions**

Act (Date Enacted)	Purpose
Procompetitive legislation	
Sherman Antitrust Act (1890)	Prohibits contracts, combinations, or conspiracies to restrain trade; calls monopolizing or attempting to monopolize a misdemeanor offense.
Clayton Act (1914)	Prohibits specific practices such as price discrimination, exclusive dealer arrangements, and stock acquisitions in which the effect may notably lessen competition or tend to create a monopoly.
Federal Trade Commission Act (1914)	Created the Federal Trade Commission; also gives the FTC investigatory powers to be used in preventing unfair methods of competition.
Robinson-Patman Act (1936)	Prohibits price discrimination that lessens competition among wholesalers or retailers; prohibits producers from giving disproportionate services of facilities to large buyers.
Wheeler-Lea Act (1938)	Prohibits unfair and deceptive acts and practices, regardless of whether competition is injured; places advertising of foods and drugs under the jurisdiction of the FTC.
Celler-Kefauver Act (1950)	Prohibits any corporation engaged in commerce from acquiring the whole or any part of the stock or other share of the capital assets of another corporation when the effect substantially lessens competition or tends to create a monopoly.
Consumer Goods Pricing Act (1975)	Prohibits the use of price-maintenance agreements among manufacturers and resellers in interstate commerce.
Antitrust Improvements Act (1976)	Requires large corporations to inform federal regulators of prospective mergers or acquisitions so that they can be studied for any possible violations of the law.
Consumer protection legislation	
Pure Food and Drug Act (1906)	Prohibits the adulteration and mislabeling of food and drug products; established the Food and Drug Administration.
Fair Packaging and Labeling Act (1966)	Makes illegal the unfair or deceptive packaging or labeling of consumer products.
Consumer Product Safety Act (1972)	Established the Consumer Product Safety Commission; protects the public against unreasonable risk of injury and death associated with products.
Magnuson-Moss Warranty (FTC) Act (1975)	Provides for minimum disclosure standards for written consumer product warranties; defines minimum consent standards for written warranties; allows the FTC to prescribe interpretive rules in policy statements regarding unfair or deceptive practices.
Nutrition Labeling and Education Act (1990)	Prohibits exaggerated health claims and requires all processed foods to contain labels showing nutritional information.
Telephone Consumer Protection Act (1991)	Establishes procedures to avoid unwanted telephone solicitations; prohibits marketers from using an automated telephone dialing system or an artificial or prerecorded voice to certain telephone lines.
Children's Online Privacy Protection Act (2000)	Regulates the online collection of personally identifiable information (name, mailing address, e-mail address, hobbies, interests, or information collected through cookies) from children under age 13.

(continued)

Table 3.2   Major Federal Laws Affecting Marketing Decisions   (*continued*)

Act (Date Enacted)	Purpose
Consumer protection legislation	
Do Not Call Implementation Act (2003)	Directs the Federal Communications Commission (FCC) and the FTC to coordinate so that their rules are consistent regarding telemarketing call practices, including the Do Not Call Registry and other lists, as well as call abandonment.
Credit Card Act (2009)	Implements strict rules on credit card companies regarding topics such as issuing credit to youths, terms disclosure, interest rates, and fees.
Dodd-Frank Wall Street Reform and Consumer Protection Act (2010)	Promotes financial reform to increase accountability and transparency in the financial industry, protects consumers from deceptive financial practices, and established the Bureau of Consumer Financial Protection.
Trademark and copyright protection legislation	
Lanham Act (1946)	Provides protections and regulation of brand names, brand marks, trade names, and trademarks.
Trademark Law Revision Act (1988)	Amends the Lanham Act to allow brands not yet introduced to be protected through registration with the Patent and Trademark Office.
Federal Trademark Dilution Act (1995)	Gives trademark owners the right to protect trademarks and requires relinquishment of names that match or parallel existing trademarks.
Digital Millennium Copyright Act (1998)	Refines copyright laws to protect digital versions of copyrighted materials, including music and movies.

© Cengage Learning

Regulatory Agencies

Federal regulatory agencies influence many marketing activities, including product development, pricing, packaging, advertising, personal selling, and distribution. Usually, these bodies have the power to enforce specific laws, as well as some discretion in establishing operating rules and regulations to guide certain types of industry practices.

Of all the federal regulatory units, the **Federal Trade Commission (FTC)** influences marketing activities most. Although the FTC regulates a variety of business practices, it allocates considerable resources to curbing false advertising, misleading pricing, and deceptive packaging and labeling. When it receives a complaint or otherwise has reason to believe that a firm is violating a law, the commission issues a complaint stating that the business is in violation. If a company continues the questionable practice, the FTC can issue a cease-and-desist order demanding that the business stop doing whatever caused the complaint. The firm can appeal to the federal courts to have the order rescinded. However, the FTC can seek civil penalties in court, up to a maximum penalty of $10,000 a day for each infraction if a cease-and-desist order is violated. The FTC also assists businesses in complying with laws and files lawsuits against those engaging in deceptive marketing practices. For instance, the FTC investigated whether Google had engaged in anticompetitive practices by unfairly favoring its own products while making it more difficult for competing products to be displayed prominently in its search results.[13]

Unlike the FTC, other regulatory units are limited to dealing with specific products or business activities. For example, the Food and Drug Administration (FDA) enforces regulations prohibiting the sale and distribution of adulterated, misbranded, or hazardous food and drug products. The Consumer Product Safety Commission (CPSC) ensures compliance with the Consumer Product Safety Act and protects the public from unreasonable risk of injury from any consumer product not covered by other regulatory agencies.

Federal Trade Commission (FTC) An agency that regulates a variety of business practices and curbs false advertising, misleading pricing, and deceptive packaging and labeling

Consumer Credit Card Security
Credit card theft has created the need for consumer vigilance and regulatory agencies' assistance in preventing fraud.

In addition, laws have also been created to prevent businesses from gaining an unfair advantage through bribery. The U.S. Foreign Corrupt Practices Act (FCPA) prohibits American companies from making illicit payments to foreign officials in order to obtain or keep business. Siemens AG paid $1.6 billion to the United States and Germany to settle allegations that it had bribed government officials in different countries to win contracts.[14] The FCPA does allow for small facilitation ("grease") payments to expedite routine government transactions. However, the passage of the U.K. Bribery Act did not initially allow for facilitation payments, although the U.K. government has decided to review this prohibition, because it is often necessary in developing countries to pay low-level government officials small gratuities for them to carry out their duties.[15] The U.K. Bribery Act is more encompassing than the FCPA and has significant implications for global business. Under this law companies can be found guilty of bribery even if the bribery did not take place within the U.K., and company officials without explicit knowledge about the misconduct can still be held accountable. The law applies to any business with operations in the U.K.[16] It also can hold companies liable if its joint-venture partners or subsidiaries are found guilty of bribery. However, the U.K. Bribery Law does allow for leniency if the company has an effective compliance program and undergoes periodic ethical assessments.[17] In response to the law, companies have begun to strengthen their compliance programs related to bribery. For instance, Kimberly-Clark now requires some of its business partners to consent to audits and keep thorough documentation of their payments.[18]

State consumer protection laws offer an opportunity for state attorneys general to deal with marketing issues related to fraud and deception. Most states have consumer protection laws that are very general in nature and provide enforcement when new schemes evolve that injure consumers. For example, the New York Consumer Protection Board is very proactive in monitoring consumer protection and providing consumer education. More recently, the New York Consumer Protection Board has taken measures to protect consumers from scams or data breaches. It provided information to warn consumers against falling for Hurricane Sandy scams after the disaster struck.[19]

Self-Regulation

In an attempt to be good corporate citizens and prevent government intervention, some businesses try to regulate themselves. Several trade associations have also developed self-regulatory

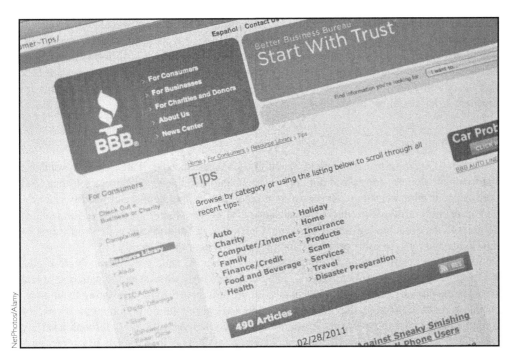

Self-Regulation
The Better Business Bureau is one of the best-known self-regulatory programs.

programs. Although these programs are not a direct outgrowth of laws, many were established to stop or stall the development of laws and governmental regulatory groups that would regulate the associations' marketing practices. Sometimes trade associations establish ethics codes by which their members must abide or risk censure or exclusion from the association. For instance, the Pharmaceutical Research and Manufacturers of America released its "Guiding Principles" to function as a set of voluntary industry rules for drug companies to follow when advertising directly to consumers.[20]

Perhaps the best-known nongovernmental regulatory group is the **Better Business Bureau**, a local regulatory agency supported by local businesses. About 113 bureaus help to settle problems between consumers and specific business firms in the United States and Canada. Each bureau also acts to preserve good business practices in a locality, although it usually lacks strong enforcement tools for dealing with firms that employ questionable practices. When a firm continues to violate what the Better Business Bureau believes to be good business practices, the bureau warns consumers through local newspapers or broadcast media. If the offending organization is a Better Business Bureau member, it may be expelled from the local bureau. For example, the St. Louis Better Business Bureau expelled three firms for failing to respond to complaints or requests.[21]

The National Advertising Division (NAD) of the Council of Better Business Bureaus operates a self-regulatory program that investigates claims regarding alleged deceptive advertising. For example, NAD recommended that Comcast stop marketing its XFINITY Internet service as "the fastest in the nation" because it felt Comcast did not have evidence to back up its claim.[22] Another self-regulatory entity, the **National Advertising Review Board (NARB)**, considers cases in which an advertiser challenges issues raised by the National Advertising Division (NAD) about an advertisement. Cases are reviewed by panels drawn from NARB members representing advertisers, agencies, and the public. For example, the NARB determined that companies using the Fair Trade USA seal on its labeling must specify the percentage of fair trade ingredients on the label.[23] The NARB, sponsored by the Council of Better Business Bureaus and three advertising trade organizations, has no official enforcement powers. However, if a firm refuses to comply with its decision, the NARB may publicize the questionable practice and file a complaint with the FTC.

Self-regulatory programs have several advantages over governmental laws and regulatory agencies. Establishment and implementation are usually less expensive, and guidelines

Better Business Bureau
A local, nongovernmental regulatory agency, supported by local businesses, that helps settle problems between customers and specific business firms

National Advertising Review Board (NARB) A self-regulatory unit that considers challenges to issues raised by the National Advertising Division (an arm of the Council of Better Business Bureaus) about an advertisement

are generally more realistic and operational. In addition, effective self-regulatory programs reduce the need to expand government bureaucracy. However, these programs have several limitations. When a trade association creates a set of industry guidelines for its members, non-member firms do not have to abide by them. Furthermore, many self-regulatory programs lack the tools or authority to enforce guidelines. Finally, guidelines in self-regulatory programs are often less strict than those established by government agencies.

Technological Forces

The word *technology* brings to mind scientific advances such as iPads, electric vehicles, smartphones, cloning, lifestyle drugs, the Internet, radio-frequency identification tags, and more. Such developments make it possible for marketers to operate more efficiently and provide an exciting array of products for consumers. However, even though these innovations are outgrowths of technology, none of them *is* technology. **Technology** is the application of knowledge and tools to solve problems and perform tasks more efficiently.

Technology determines how we, as members of society, satisfy our physiologic needs. In various ways and to varying degrees, eating and drinking habits, sleeping patterns, sexual activities, health care, and work performance are all influenced by both existing technology and advances in technology. Because of the technological revolution in communications, for example, marketers can now reach vast numbers of people more efficiently through a variety of media. Social networks, smartphones, and tablet computers help marketers to interact with customers, make appointments, and handle last-minute orders or cancellations. Currently, about one-third of Americans have exchanged their landlines for cell phones.[24] An estimated 46 percent of American adults own the more advanced smartphones.[25]

The proliferation of cell phones, most with text-message capabilities, has led marketers to employ text and multimedia messaging on cell phones to reach their target markets. Restaurants, for example, can send their lunch specials to subscribers' cell phones.

Computers have become a staple in American homes, but the type of computer has been changing drastically in this past decade. Traditional desktop computers appear to be on the decline. Laptops became immensely popular due to their mobility, but analysts estimate that laptops might be entering the maturity stage of the product life cycle. Conversely, tablet computers such as the iPad and the Samsung Galaxy Tab are experiencing immense growth and may soon supersede laptops in sales.[26] In response many companies are creating apps specifically made for the iPad and similar devices. The rapidly evolving state of technology requires marketers to familiarize themselves with the latest technological changes.

technology The application of knowledge and tools to solve problems and perform tasks more efficiently

Marketing Debate

Copycats or Innovators?

ISSUE: Is Rocket Internet a hub for innovation or just another copycat?

Copying has been around for years, but has one company taken it too far? Rocket Internet is a German-based company that clones successful U.S Internet-based business models and launches them on an international scale. Rocket Internet has launched numerous duplicated businesses, most famously Citydeal, copied from Groupon. Citydeal was eventually acquired by Groupon.

Critics have discredited Rocket Internet by saying the company is uninspired and lacking in originality. However, company models cannot be patented, and trademarks only apply within the country issued. In a sense, Rocket Internet's approach seems unethical. On the other hand, it could be seen as an innovative way to take a successful business plan and capitalize on it in an untapped market. Technically, Rocket Internet is operating legally.[a]

The effects of technology relate to such characteristics as dynamics, reach, and the self-sustaining nature of technological progress. The *dynamics* of technology involve the constant change that often challenges the structures of social institutions, including social relationships, the legal system, religion, education, business, and leisure. *Reach* refers to the broad nature of technology as it moves through society. Consider the impact of cellular and wireless telephones. The ability to call from almost any location has many benefits but also has negative side effects, including increases in traffic accidents, increased noise pollution, and fears about potential health risks.[27] The *self-sustaining* nature of technology relates to the fact that technology acts as a catalyst to spur even faster development. As new innovations are introduced, they stimulate the need for more advancements to facilitate further development. Apple, for instance, advances the capabilities of each new model of its iPhone and iPad. Research in Motion, on the other hand, failed to update technology for its BlackBerry as fast as Apple did for its products, losing market share as a result. Technology initiates a change process that creates new opportunities for new technologies in every industry segment or personal life experience that it touches. At some point there is even a multiplier effect that causes still greater demand for more change to improve performance.[28] It is important for firms to determine when a technology is changing an industry and define the strategic influence of the new technology. For example, wireless devices in use today include radios, cell phones, laptop computers, TVs, pagers, and car keys. To remain competitive, companies must keep up with and adapt to these technological advances. Through a procedure known as *technology assessment,* managers try to foresee the effects of new products and processes on their firms' operations, on other business organizations, and on society in general. With information obtained through a technology assessment, management tries to estimate whether benefits of adopting a specific technology outweigh costs to the firm and to society at large. The degree to which a business is technologically based also influences its managers' response to technology.

Sociocultural Forces

Sociocultural forces are the influences in a society and its culture(s) that bring about changes in attitudes, beliefs, norms, customs, and lifestyles. Profoundly affecting how people live, these forces help to determine what, where, how, and when people buy products. Like the other environmental forces, sociocultural forces present marketers with both challenges and opportunities.

sociocultural forces The influences in a society and its culture(s) that change people's attitudes, beliefs, norms, customs, and lifestyles

Changes in a population's demographic characteristics—age, gender, race, ethnicity, marital and parental status, income, and education—have a significant bearing on relationships and individual behavior. These shifts lead to changes in how people live and ultimately in their consumption of products such as food, clothing, housing, transportation, communication, recreation, education, and health services. We look at a few of the changes in demographics and diversity that are affecting marketing activities.

One demographic change affecting the marketplace is the increasing proportion of older consumers. According to the U.S. Bureau of the Census, the number of people age 65 and older is expected to more than double by the year 2050, reaching 88.5 million.[29]

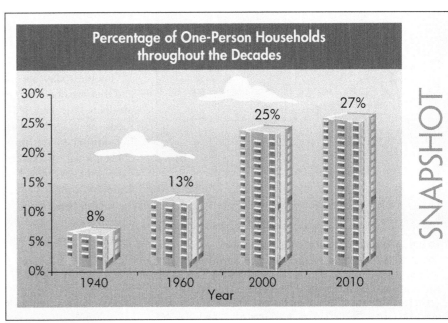

Source: U.S. Census Bureau

Consequently, marketers can expect significant increases in the demand for health-care services, recreation, tourism, retirement housing, and selected skin-care products.

The number of singles is also on the rise. Singles currently comprise 49 percent of American households.[30] Single people have quite different spending patterns than couples and families with children. They are less likely to own homes and thus buy less furniture and fewer appliances. They spend more heavily on convenience foods, restaurants, travel, entertainment, and recreation. In addition, they tend to prefer smaller packages, whereas families often buy bulk goods and products packaged in multiple servings.

The United States is entering another baby boom, with 27.3 percent of the total population age 18 or younger; the original baby boomers, born between 1946 and 1964, account for about 26 percent.[31] The children of the original baby boomers differ from one another radically in terms of race, living arrangements, and socioeconomic class. Thus, the newest baby boom is much more diverse than previous generations.

Despite this trend, the birthrate has begun to decline. The U.S. population experienced the slowest rate of growth in the last decade since the Great Depression. The population grew 9.7 percent to almost 310 million. While the birthrate is declining, new immigrants help with population gains.[32] This represents another noteworthy population trend: the increasingly multicultural nature of U.S. society. The number of immigrants into the United States has risen steadily during the past 40 years. By the turn of the 20th century, the U.S. population had shifted from one dominated by whites to one consisting largely of three racial and ethnic groups: whites, blacks, and Hispanics. The U.S. government projects that by the year 2050, more than 133 million Hispanics, 66 million blacks, and 41 million Asians will call the United States home.[33]

Marketers recognize that these profound changes in the U.S. population bring unique problems and opportunities. For example, it is projected that Hispanic purchasing power will be $1.5 trillion by 2015.[34] But a diverse population means a more diverse customer base, and marketing practices must be modified—and diversified—to meet its changing needs. In an effort to target this expanding demographic, MillerCoors is sponsoring a Mexican soccer league and placing more Spanish language on its cartons and labels. The company hopes to create a rapport with Hispanic consumers in order to gain their loyalty.[35]

Changes in social and cultural values have dramatically influenced people's needs and desires for products. Although these values do not shift overnight, they do change at varying speeds. Marketers try to monitor these changes because knowing this information can equip them to predict changes in consumers' needs for products, at least in the near future.

People today are more concerned about the foods they eat and thus are choosing more low-fat, organic, natural, and healthy products. Marketers have responded with a proliferation of foods, beverages, and exercise products that fit this new lifestyle. In addition to the proliferation of new organic brands, many conventional marketers have introduced organic versions of their products, including Orville Redenbacher, Heinz, and even Walmart. Yoplait yogurt has capitalized on this trend by touting the health benefits of its yogurt. The company has launched an advertisement featuring half of a yogurt and half of a donut to emphasize that although Yoplait's yogurt is low-fat, it is also a sweet, tasty treat.

The major source of values is the family. Values about the permanence of marriage are changing, but children remain important. Marketers have responded with safer, upscale baby gear and supplies, children's electronics, and family entertainment products.

Courtesy of Yoplait

Changing Trends in Social and Cultural Values
The growing concern for obesity has caused a renewed interest in healthy and low-fat foods. This ad compares Yoplait yogurt with a frosted cake doughnut with sprinkles. While both of these foods are sweet, Yoplait promotes the 90 calories of its yogurt compared to the 350 calories of the doughnut.

Emerging Trends

How Restaurants Are Responding to the Health Trend

Less sodium and more calorie information are becoming an emerging trend that is sweeping throughout fast-food chains across the nation. As obesity rates continue to rise, patrons are trying to take control of their health and become conscious of what they put into their bodies. With this consciousness has come an adaptation from marketers who are trying to grow with their consumers by providing information to make healthy choices easier. With the publishing of calories, restaurants seem to be reformulating menu items to enable healthier alternatives when dining out.

For instance, Boston Market is lowering the sodium within three of its signature items by 20 percent. The company is also removing salt shakers from in-store dining tables. These efforts attempt to address issues consumers have raised about the amount of salt within their products.

McDonald's has taken similar steps to bring awareness to consumers regarding calorie information about items on their menu. McDonald's is the largest restaurant chain and the first fast-food company to menu label on a national level. The emerging trend of menu-labeling is soon to become a requirement for restaurants with 20 or more outlets throughout the nation. As environmental trends continue to change, marketers at fast-food restaurants must be prepared to meet them head on.[b]

© iStockphoto.com/CRTd

Marketers are also aiming more marketing efforts directly at children because children often play pivotal roles in purchasing decisions. Children and family values are also a factor in the trend toward more eat-out and takeout meals. Busy families generally want to spend less time in the kitchen and more time together enjoying themselves. Beneficiaries of this trend primarily have been fast-food and casual restaurants like McDonald's, Taco Bell, Boston Market, and Applebee's, but most supermarkets have added more ready-to-cook or ready-to-serve meal components to meet the needs of busy customers. Some, like Whole Foods, also offer eat-in cafés.

SOCIAL RESPONSIBILITY AND ETHICS IN MARKETING

LO2. Understand the concept and dimensions of social responsibility in marketing.

In marketing, **social responsibility** refers to an organization's obligation to maximize its positive impact and minimize its negative impact on society. Social responsibility thus deals with the total effect of all marketing decisions on society. In marketing, social responsibility includes the managerial processes needed to monitor, satisfy, and even exceed stakeholder expectations and needs.[36] Remember from Chapter 1 that stakeholders are groups that have a "stake," or claim, in some aspect of a company's products, operations, markets, industry, and outcomes. CEOs such as Indra Nooyi, chairman and CEO of PepsiCo, are increasingly recognizing that businesses must take their social responsibilities more seriously.[37]

Ample evidence demonstrates that ignoring stakeholders' demands for responsible marketing can destroy customers' trust and even prompt government regulations. Irresponsible actions that anger customers, employees, or competitors may not only jeopardize a marketer's financial standing, but have legal repercussions as well. For instance, GlaxoSmithKline paid $90 million to settle claims that it had marketed the diabetes drug Avandia illegally.[38] In contrast, socially responsible activities can generate positive publicity and boost sales. IBM's corporate volunteer program has helped Kenya reform its postal system and has aided Tanzania in developing eco-tourism opportunities. It has also generated millions of dollars in new business.[39]

social responsibility
An organization's obligation to maximize its positive impact and minimize its negative impact on society

Socially Responsible Products
Many car companies are embracing the electric car as a long-term, socially responsible benefit to their product offerings.

Socially responsible efforts such as IBM's have a positive impact on local communities; at the same time, they indirectly help the sponsoring organization by attracting goodwill, publicity, and potential customers and employees. Thus, while social responsibility is certainly a positive concept in itself, most organizations embrace it in the expectation of indirect long-term benefits.

Socially responsible organizations strive for **marketing citizenship** by adopting a strategic focus for fulfilling the economic, legal, ethical, and philanthropic social responsibilities that their stakeholders expect of them. Companies that consider the diverse perspectives of stakeholders in their daily operations and strategic planning are said to have a *stakeholder orientation,* an important element of corporate citizenship.[40] A stakeholder orientation in marketing goes beyond customers, competitors, and regulators to include understanding and addressing the needs of all stakeholders, including communities and special-interest groups. As a result, organizations are now under pressure to undertake initiatives that demonstrate a balanced perspective on stakeholder interests.[41] Pfizer, for example, has secured stakeholder input on a number of issues, including rising health-care costs and health-care reform.[42] As Figure 3.2 shows, the economic, legal, ethical, and philanthropic dimensions of social responsibility can be viewed as a pyramid.[43] The economic and legal aspects have long been acknowledged, but ethical and philanthropic issues have gained recognition more recently.

Economic Dimension

At the most basic level, all companies have an economic responsibility to be profitable so that they can provide a return on investment to their owners and investors, create jobs for the community, and contribute goods and services to the economy. How organizations relate to stockholders, employees, competitors, customers, the community, and the natural environment affects the economy.

Marketers also have an economic responsibility to compete fairly. Size frequently gives companies an advantage over others. Large firms often can generate economies of scale that

marketing citizenship
The adoption of a strategic focus for fulfilling the economic, legal, ethical, and philanthropic social responsibilities expected by stakeholders

Figure 3.2 **The Pyramid of Corporate Social Responsibility**

RESPONSIBILITIES

Philanthropic
*Be a good
corporate citizen*
• Contribute resources to the
community; improve quality of life

Ethical
Be ethical
• Obligation to do what is right, just, and fair
• Avoid harm

Legal
Obey the law
• Law is society's codification of right and wrong
• Play by the rules of the game

Economic
Be profitable
• The foundation upon which all others rest

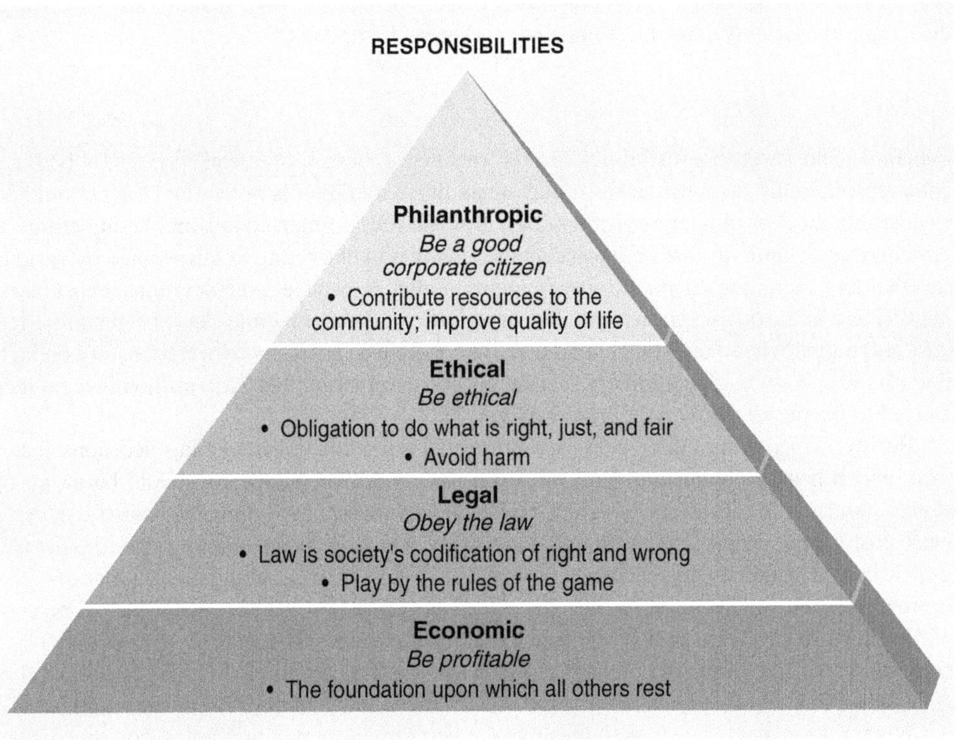

Source: From Archie B. Carroll, "The Pyramid of Corporate Social Responsibility: Toward the Moral Management of Organizational Stakeholders," adaptation of Figure 3, p. 42. Reprinted from *Business Horizons,* July/August 1991, by the Foundation for the School of Business at Indiana University. Reprinted with permission.

allow them to put smaller firms out of business. Consequently, small companies and even whole communities may resist the efforts of firms such as Walmart, Home Depot, and Best Buy to open stores in their vicinity. These firms can operate at such low costs that small, local firms often cannot compete. Such issues create concerns about social responsibility for organizations, communities, and consumers.

Legal Dimension

Marketers are also expected to obey laws and regulations. The efforts of elected representatives and special-interest groups to promote responsible corporate behavior have resulted in laws and regulations designed to keep U.S. companies' actions within the range of acceptable conduct. Although most of the cases in the news deal with serious misconduct, not all legal cases are a violation of law. Sometimes, they are an attempt to interpret the law. Laws can be ambiguous, and new situations arise that create a need for courts to interpret whether the situation should be allowed or regulated. For instance, Internet tracking and privacy issues have caused lawmakers to consider whether to develop legislation limiting the types of information marketers can gather over the Internet.

When marketers engage in deceptive practices to advance their own interests over those of others, charges of fraud may result. In general, fraud is any purposeful communication that deceives, manipulates, or conceals facts in order to create a false impression. It is considered a crime, and convictions may result in fines, imprisonment, or both. In one global business study, nearly one-third of organizations who were victims of fraud experienced losses of more than $500,000, with one-fourth facing losses of more than $1 million. While asset misappropriation was the most common type of fraud cited, financial statement fraud resulted in the highest losses.[44]

When customers, interest groups, or businesses become outraged over what they perceive as irresponsibility on the part of a marketing organization, they may urge their legislators to draft new legislation to regulate the behavior, or they may engage in litigation to force the organization to "play by the rules." Deceptive advertising in particular causes consumers to become defensive toward all promotional messages and become distrustful of all advertising; thus, it harms not only consumers but also marketers themselves.[45]

Ethical Dimension

Economic and legal responsibilities are the most basic levels of social responsibility for a good reason: failure to consider them may mean that a marketer is not around long enough to engage in ethical or philanthropic activities. Beyond these dimensions is marketing ethics—principles and standards that define acceptable conduct in marketing as determined by various stakeholders, including the public, government regulators, private-interest groups, consumers, industries, and the organization itself. The most basic of these principles have been codified as laws and regulations to encourage marketers to conform to society's expectations of conduct. For instance, an Avon global bribery scandal cost the firm more than $250 million in legal fees and led to the ouster of Avon CEO Andrea Jung.[46]

However, marketing ethics goes beyond legal issues. Ethical marketing decisions foster trust, which helps to build long-term marketing relationships. Marketers should be aware of ethical standards for acceptable conduct from several viewpoints—company, industry, government, customers, special-interest groups, and society at large. When marketing activities deviate from accepted standards, the exchange process can break down, resulting in customer dissatisfaction, lack of trust, and lawsuits. The 2013 Edelman Trust Barometer revealed that 62 percent of American respondents trust businesses to do what is right. Figure 3.3 compares American consumers' trust of business compared to citizens of other countries. The figure reveals that Americans' trust in business is lower than China, Brazil, the United Arab Emirates, and India.[47]

When managers engage in activities that deviate from accepted principles, continued marketing exchanges become difficult, if not impossible. The best time to deal with such problems is during the strategic planning process, not after major problems materialize. For example,

---

Figure 3.3 Trust in Business for Selected Countries

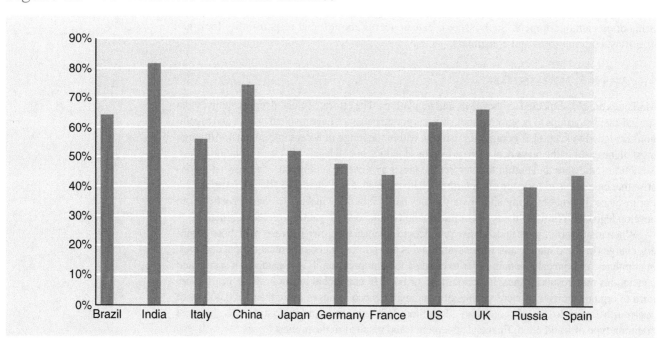

Source: Edelman Insights, *Global Deck: 2013 Trust Barometer*, http://www.slideshare.net/fullscreen/EdelmanInsights/global-deck-2013-edelman-trust-barometer-16086761/5 (accessed July 24, 2013).

Entrepreneurship in Marketing

True Office Provides an Innovative Way to Approach Ethical Training

Adam Sodowick, entrepreneur and CEO of True Office, has developed a new method of interactive video game storytelling to engage employees during ethics training programs. After conducting a series of trials, True Office found that employees retain more knowledge of the topic when it is presented through visually interactive methods. This "gamification" has the potential to impact ethical training in a positive way. With higher retention rates, employees are more likely to engage and motivate people to solve problems according to what they learned about the company's ethics and compliance standards presented in the video game.

On average companies annually spend $60 billion on corporate training, and the payoff can sometimes seem small if employees are not engaged in the program. Yet True Office claims that through its program, companies can monitor employee passing rates and areas that require additional training. This feature could help marketing managers that are responsible for teaching employees about ethical issues such as bribery, conflicts of interest, and misuse of company resources.[c]

team members at Whole Foods are expected to contribute insight and make recommendations on how to address problems before they become major issues as well as how to improve compliance at stores.[48]

An **ethical issue** is an identifiable problem, situation, or opportunity requiring an individual or organization to choose from among several actions that must be evaluated as right or wrong, ethical or unethical. Any time an activity causes marketing managers or customers in their target market to feel manipulated or cheated, a marketing ethical issue exists, regardless of the legality of that activity. For example, the Girl Scouts have been criticized because their three most popular cookies—Samoas, Tagalongs, and Thin Mints—contain partially hydrogenated oils (trans fat). Yet the company has carried a "0 percent trans fat" label on their cookie boxes since 2007. By law, companies are allowed to label their food products as containing 0 percent trans fat as long as the product contains less than 0.5 grams of trans fat per serving. Even though the cookies' labels are legal, the ethics involved are debatable.[49]

Regardless of the reasons behind specific ethical issues, marketers must be able to identify these issues and decide how to resolve them. To do so requires familiarity with the many kinds of ethical issues that may arise in marketing. Research suggests that the greater the consequences associated with an issue, the more likely it will be recognized as an ethics issue, and the more important it will be to making an ethical decision.[50] Some examples of ethical issues related to product, promotion, price, and distribution (the marketing mix) appear in Table 3.3.

Philanthropic Dimension

At the top of the pyramid are philanthropic responsibilities. These responsibilities, which go beyond marketing ethics, are not required of a company, but they promote human welfare or goodwill, as do the economic, legal, and ethical dimensions of social responsibility. After natural disasters such as Hurricane Sandy, for example, many corporations—including Comcast, Goldman Sachs, Target, General Motors, and Kellogg—provided support to victims, waived certain fees, and/or aided in cleanup efforts.[51] Philanthropy is not limited to large companies, however. For example, Charlotte Street Computers in Asheville, North Carolina, has developed a refurbishing center that refurbishes computers and then donates them to those in need. The small business also sponsors several community events and fundraising for charities.[52]

More companies than ever are adopting a strategic approach to corporate philanthropy. Many firms link their products to a particular social cause on an ongoing or short-term basis,

ethical issue An identifiable problem, situation, or opportunity requiring a choice among several actions that must be evaluated as right or wrong, ethical or unethical

Table 3.3   **Ethical Issues in Marketing**

Issue Category	Examples
Product	• Failing to disclose risks associated with a product • Failing to disclose information about a product's function, value, or use • Failing to disclose information about changes in the nature, quality, or size of a product
Distribution	• Failing to live up to the rights and responsibilities associated with channel member roles • Manipulating product availability • Using coercion to force other intermediaries to behave in a certain way
Promotion	• False or misleading advertising • Using manipulative or deceptive sales promotions, tactics, and publicity • Offering or accepting bribes in personal selling situations
Pricing	• Price fixing • Predatory pricing • Failing to disclose the full price of a purchase

© Cengage Learning

a practice known as **cause-related marketing**. Target, for example, contributes significant resources to education through its Take Charge of Education program. Customers using a Target REDcard can designate a specific school to which Target donates 1 percent of their total purchase.[53] A Cone study revealed that 85 percent of respondents have a more positive image of companies that support causes they care about.[54] Some companies are beginning to extend the concept of corporate philanthropy beyond financial contributions by adopting a **strategic philanthropy approach**, the synergistic use of organizational core competencies and resources to address key stakeholders' interests and achieve both organizational and social benefits. Strategic philanthropy involves employees; organizational resources and expertise; and the ability to link these assets to the concerns of key stakeholders, including employees, customers, suppliers, and society in general. Strategic philanthropy involves both financial and nonfinancial contributions to stakeholders (employee time, goods and services, and company technology and equipment, as well as facilities), but it also benefits the company. Salesforce.com, for example, believes in the benefits of strategic philanthropy so strongly that it incorporates community service into its corporate culture. Salesforce.com allows employees to take up to 1 percent of their time to volunteer in their communities, it sets aside 1 percent of the company's capital for the Salesforce.com Foundation, and it donates or discounts licenses of its CRM (Customer Relationship Management) software to thousands of nonprofits worldwide.[55] The synergistic use of organizational core competencies and resources to address key stakeholders' interests achieve both organizational and social benefits.

Although social responsibility may seem to be an abstract ideal, managers make decisions related to social responsibility every day. To be successful, a business must determine what customers, government regulators, and competitors, as well as society in general, want or expect in terms of social responsibility. Two major categories of social responsibility issues are sustainability and consumerism.

Sustainability

One of the more common ways marketers demonstrate social responsibility is through programs designed to protect and preserve the natural environment. Most Fortune 500 companies now engage in recycling activities and make significant efforts to reduce waste and conserve

cause-related marketing
The practice of linking products to a particular social cause on an ongoing or short-term basis

strategic philanthropy approach The synergistic use of organizational core competencies and resources to address key stakeholders' interests and achieve both organizational and social benefits

Green Product Offerings
Whole Foods focuses on sustainable, locally-sourced food products when possible. Local sourcing reduces greenhouse gases by reducing transportation.

energy. Many companies are making contributions to environmental protection organizations, sponsoring and participating in cleanup events, promoting recycling, retooling manufacturing processes to minimize waste and pollution, employing more environmentally friendly energy sources, and generally reevaluating the effects of their products on the natural environment. This approach to the environment is to reduce, reuse, and recycle.

As mentioned in Chapter 1, green marketing is a strategic process involving stakeholder assessment to create meaningful long-term relationships with customers while maintaining, supporting, and enhancing the natural environment. Many products have been certified as

Going Green

Google's New Venture: Going Green

Can a multi-billion-dollar corporation really become a zero-carbon operation? According to Google's CEO Larry Page, it is certainly going to try. In 2007, Google established the green initiative RE<C, which stands for renewable energy is cheaper than coal, to reduce the company's carbon footprint. The company is taking proactive steps to reduce carbon emissions from its day-to-day operations. It plans to achieve this goal by investing in solar and wind producers, purchasing carbon offsets, and constructing its data centers more efficiently.

The company has marketed its green efforts as something new, innovative, and ambitious that other companies can potentially emulate. For Google, going green has been an initiative that has proven its commitment toward social responsibility. The company realizes that it can give back not only technologically but also proactively by essentially eliminating greenhouse gas emissions. Google began these efforts by marketing the benefits of going green to its employees. It provides its employees with energy-efficient modes of transportation and has installed the largest network of electric vehicle charging stations in the United States. Google's green initiatives also enhance its reputation with its target market, as many companies and consumers prefer doing business with sustainable firms. If its carbon-efficient blueprint becomes a successful endeavor, Google may have found an inadvertent way to market social responsibility by just doing the right thing.[d]

"green" by environmental organizations such as Green Seal and carry a special logo identifying their organization as green marketers. Lumber products at Home Depot, for example, may carry a seal from the Forest Stewardship Council to indicate that they were harvested from sustainable forests using environmentally friendly methods.[56]

Consumerism

Consumerism consists of organized efforts by individuals, groups, and organizations seeking to protect consumers' rights. The movement's major forces are individual consumer advocates, consumer organizations and other interest groups, consumer education, and consumer laws.

To achieve their objectives, consumers and their advocates write letters or send e-mails to companies, lobby government agencies, broadcast public-service announcements, and boycott companies whose activities they deem irresponsible. Some consumers choose to boycott firms and products out of a desire to support a cause and make a difference.[57] For example, several organizations evaluate children's products for safety, often announcing dangerous products before Christmas so that parents can avoid them. Other actions by the consumer movement have resulted in seat belts and air bags in automobiles, dolphin-safe tuna, the banning of unsafe three-wheel motorized vehicles, and numerous laws regulating product safety and information.

Also of great importance to the consumer movement are four basic rights spelled out in a "consumer bill of rights" drafted by President John F. Kennedy. These rights include the right to safety, the right to be informed, the right to choose, and the right to be heard. Ensuring consumers' *right to safety* means that marketers have an obligation not to market a product that they know could harm consumers. This right can be extended to imply that all products must be safe for their intended use, include thorough and explicit instructions for proper and safe use, and have been tested to ensure reliability and quality. Consumers' *right to be informed* means that consumers should have access to and the opportunity to review all relevant information about a product before buying it. Many laws require specific labeling on product packaging to satisfy this right. In addition, labels on alcoholic and tobacco products inform consumers that these products may cause illness and other problems. The Federal Trade Commission provides a wealth of consumer information at its website (www.ftc.gov/bcp/consumer.shtm) on a variety of topics ranging from automobiles and the Internet to diet, health, and fitness. The *right to choose* means that consumers should have access to a variety of products at competitive prices. They also should be assured of satisfactory quality and service at a fair price. Activities that reduce competition among businesses in an industry might jeopardize this right. The *right to be heard* ensures that consumers' interests will receive full and sympathetic consideration in the formulation of government policy. The right to be heard also promises consumers fair treatment when they complain to marketers about products. This right benefits marketers too because when consumers complain about a product, the manufacturer can use this information to modify the product and make it more satisfying.

Incorporating Social Responsibility and Ethics into Strategic Planning

Although the concepts of marketing ethics and social responsibility are often used interchangeably, it is important to distinguish between them. *Ethics* relates to individual and group decisions—judgments about what is right or wrong in a particular decision-making situation—whereas *social responsibility* deals with the total effect of marketing decisions on society. The two concepts are interrelated because a company that supports socially responsible decisions and adheres to a code of conduct is likely to have a positive effect on society. Because ethics and social responsibility programs can be profitable as well, an increasing number of companies are incorporating them into their overall strategic market planning.

consumerism Organized efforts by individuals, groups, and organizations to protect consumers' rights

AP Images/Associated Press

Social Responsibility and Strategic Planning
Walmart deals with consumer environmental concerns through reducing waste in the supply chain and using alternative fuel in some fleet trucks.

Without compliance programs and uniform standards and policies for conduct, it is hard for a company's employees to determine what conduct is acceptable within the company. In the absence of such programs and standards, employees generally will make decisions based on their observations of how their peers and superiors behave. To improve ethics, many organizations have developed **codes of conduct** (also called *codes of ethics*) consisting of formalized rules and standards that describe what the company expects of its employees. The New York Stock Exchange now requires every member corporation to have a formal code of conduct. Codes of conduct promote ethical behavior by reducing opportunities for unethical behavior; employees know both what is expected of them and what kind of punishment they face if they violate the rules. Such codes are important in preventing misconduct within the organization. Effective content, the frequency of communication regarding the code, the quality of communication, and the incorporation of the code into the organization by senior and local management can result in less instances of observed unethical behavior.[58] Codes help marketers deal with ethical issues or dilemmas that develop in daily operations by prescribing or limiting specific activities. Codes of conduct often include general ethical values such as honesty and integrity, general legal compliance, harmful acts, and obligations related to social values, as well as more marketing-specific issues such as confidentiality, responsibilities to employers and clients, obligations to the profession, and marketing-specific legal and technical compliance issues.[59]

It is important that companies consistently enforce standards and impose penalties or punishment on those who violate codes of conduct. Barrett-Jackson, an auction company specializing in classic and collector cars, recognizes the importance of ethical conduct to its customers. Ethical standards are such a significant part of the company's culture that it hired a top auditing firm to conduct an independent examination of its practices. To create an effective compliance program and to stave off the types of misconduct found in similar organizations, Barrett-Jackson constantly reviews and updates it policies.[60] Table 3.4 lists some commonly observed types of misconduct as reported in the National Business Ethics Survey (NBES). To succeed, a compliance program must be viewed as part of the overall marketing strategy implementation. If ethics officers and other executives are not committed to the principles and initiatives of marketing ethics and social responsibility, the program's effectiveness will be in question.

codes of conduct Formalized rules and standards that describe what the company expects of its employees

Table 3.4 **Observed Misconduct**

Behaviors	Employees Observing It (%)
Misuse of company time	33%
Abusive behavior	21
Lying to employees	20
Company resource abuse	20
Violating company Internet use policies	16
Discrimination	15
Conflicts of interest	15
Inappropriate social networking	14
Health or safety violations	13
Lying to outside stakeholders	12
Stealing	12
Falsifying time reports or hours worked	12

Source: Ethics Resource Center, *2011 National Business Ethics Survey: Workplace Ethics in Transition* (Washington, DC: Ethics Resource Center, 2012), p. 39. © Ethics Resource Center, Washington, DC.

Increasing evidence indicates that being ethical and socially responsible pays off. Social responsibility has a synergistic effect on market orientation that leads to improved business performance.[61] More firms are moving beyond market orientation that focuses on customers and competitors and are adopting a stakeholder orientation that focuses on all constituents. Such a relationship implies that being ethically and socially concerned is consistent with meeting the demands of customers and other stakeholders. By encouraging their employees to understand their markets, companies can help them respond to stakeholders' demands.[62]

There is a direct association between corporate social responsibility and customer satisfaction, profits, and market value.[63] In a survey of consumers, 80 percent indicated that when quality and price are similar among competitors, they would be more likely to buy from the company associated with a particular cause. In addition, young adults ages 18 to 25 are especially likely to take a company's citizenship efforts into account when making not only purchasing but also employment and investment decisions.[64]

Thus, recognition is growing that the long-term value of conducting business in a socially responsible manner far outweighs short-term costs.[65] Companies that fail to develop strategies and programs to incorporate ethics and social responsibility into their organizational culture may pay the price with poor marketing performance and the potential costs of legal violations, civil litigation, and damaging publicity when questionable activities are made public.

Chapter Review

1. Recognize the importance of the marketing environment.

The marketing environment consists of external forces that directly or indirectly influence an organization's acquisition of inputs and creation of outputs. To monitor changes in the marketing environment effectively, marketers engage in environmental scanning and analysis. Environmental scanning is the process of collecting information about the forces in the marketing environment; environmental analysis is the process of assessing and interpreting the information gathered through environmental scanning. This information helps marketing managers to minimize uncertainty and threats and capitalize on opportunities presented by environmental factors.

Marketers need to monitor the actions of competitors to determine what strategies competitors are using and how those strategies affect their own. Economic conditions influence consumers' buying power and willingness to spend. Legislation is enacted, legal decisions are interpreted by courts, and regulatory agencies are created and operated by elected or appointed officials. Marketers also can choose to regulate themselves. Technology determines how members of society satisfy needs and wants and helps improve the quality of life. Sociocultural forces are the influences in a society that bring about changes in attitudes, beliefs, norms, customs, and lifestyles. Changes in any of these forces can create opportunities and threats for marketers.

2. Understand the concept and dimensions of social responsibility in marketing.

Social responsibility refers to an organization's obligation to maximize its positive impact and minimize its negative impact on society. Whereas social responsibility is achieved by balancing the interests of all stakeholders in an organization, ethics relates to acceptable standards of conduct in making individual and group decisions. At the most basic level, companies have an economic responsibility to be profitable so that they can provide a return on investment to their stockholders, create jobs for the community, and contribute goods and services to the economy. Marketers are also expected to obey laws and regulations. Marketing ethics refers to principles and standards that define acceptable conduct in marketing as determined by various stakeholders. Philanthropic responsibilities go beyond marketing ethics; they are not required of a company but promote human welfare and goodwill.

> Go to www.cengagebrain.com for resources to help you master the content in this chapter as well as for materials that will expand your marketing knowledge!

Key Concepts

environmental scanning 54
environmental analysis 54
competition 56
brand competitors 56
product competitors 56
total budget competitors 56
monopoly 57
oligopoly 57

monopolistic
   competition 57
pure competition 57
buying power 58
disposable income 58
discretionary income 58
willingness to spend 59
business cycle 59

Federal Trade Commission
   (FTC) 63
Better Business Bureau 65
National Advertising Review
   Board (NARB) 65
technology 66
sociocultural forces 67
social responsibility 69

marketing citizenship 70
ethical issue 73
cause-related
   marketing 74
strategic philanthropy
   approach 74
consumerism 76
codes of conduct 77

Issues for Discussion and Review

1. Why are environmental scanning and analysis important to marketers?
2. What are four types of competition? Which is most important to marketers?
3. Define *income, disposable income,* and *discretionary income.* How does each type of income affect consumer buying power?
4. What factors influence a buyer's willingness to spend?

5. What are the goals of the Federal Trade Commission? List the ways in which the FTC affects marketing activities. Do you think that a single regulatory agency should have such broad jurisdiction over so many marketing practices? Why or why not?
6. Name several nongovernmental regulatory forces. Do you believe that self-regulation is more or less effective than governmental regulatory agencies? Why?
7. Discuss the impact of technology on marketing activities.
8. In what ways are cultural values changing? How are marketers responding to these changes?
9. What is social responsibility, and why is it important?
10. What are four dimensions of social responsibility? What impact do they have on marketing decisions?
11. What are some major social responsibility issues? Give an example of each.
12. Describe consumerism. Analyze some active consumer forces in your area.
13. What is the difference between ethics and social responsibility?

Marketing Applications

1. Assume that you are opening *one* of the following retail businesses. Identify publications at the library or online that provide information about the environmental forces likely to affect the business. Briefly summarize the information each provides.
   1. Convenience store
   2. Women's clothing store
   3. Grocery store
   4. Fast-food restaurant
   5. Furniture store
2. Identify at least one technological advancement and one sociocultural change that have affected you as a consumer. Explain the impact of each on your needs as a customer.
3. Identify an organization in your community that has a reputation for being ethical and socially responsible. What activities account for this image? Is the company successful? Why or why not?
4. Competitive forces are very important to companies, particularly those that operate in many different countries. However, the importance of each competitive force might vary depending upon the industry. For instance, legal and regulatory forces limit many of the activities of cigarette firms. While rising prices might impact the purchase of luxury goods, necessities such as diapers and antibiotics will not experience as much of an impact, as people require them whether the prices are high or not. With this in mind, examine the impacts that economic forces, political forces, legal and regulatory forces, technological forces, and sociocultural forces have upon Exxon Mobil, General Motors, and Procter & Gamble. Rate each of these factors on a scale of 1–5, with 5 being most important and 1 as least important. Based on these three companies, which environmental variable do you think would be the highest priority for each company and why? And which environmental variable do you feel would be most important for marketers?
5. Develop your analytical and communication skills using the Role-Play Exercises online at **www.cengagebrain.com**.

Internet Exercise

Business for Social Responsibility

Business for Social Responsibility (BSR) is a non-profit organization for companies desiring to operate responsibly and demonstrate respect for ethical values, people, communities, and the natural environment. Founded in 1992, BSR offers members practical information, research, educational programs, and technical assistance, as well as the opportunity to network with peers on current social responsibility issues. Visit **http://www.bsr.org**.

1. What types of businesses join BSR, and why?
2. Describe the services available to member companies. How can these services help companies improve their performances?
3. Peruse the "BSR Conference—Overview" tab, located at the top of the home page. What are some advantages to attending the BSR conference and listening to industry leaders and experts in corporate social responsibility?

developing your marketing plan

A marketing strategy is dynamic. Companies must continually monitor the marketing environment not only to create their marketing strategy, but also to revise it if necessary. Information about various forces in the marketplace is collected, analyzed, and used as a foundation for several marketing plan decisions. The following questions will help you to understand how the information in this chapter contributes to the development of your marketing plan:

1. Describe the current competitive market for your product. Can you identify the number of brands or market share that they hold? Expand your analysis to include other products that are similar or could be substituted for yours.
2. Using the business cycle pattern, in which of the four stages is the current state of the economy? Can you identify any changes in consumer buying power that would affect the sale and use of your product?
3. Referring to Tables 3.2 and 3.3, do you recognize any laws or regulatory agencies that would have jurisdiction over your type of product?
4. Conduct a brief technology assessment, determining the impact that technology has on your product, its sale, or use.
5. Discuss how your product could be affected by changes in social attitudes, demographic characteristics, or lifestyles.

The information obtained from these questions should assist you in developing various aspects of your marketing plan. Develop your marketing plan online using the Interactive Marketing Plan at **www.cengagebrain.com**.

video case 3.1
TOMS Shoes Expands One for One® Model to Eyewear

While many organizations try to incorporate cause-related marketing into their business operations, TOMS Shoes takes the concept of philanthropy one step further. TOMS blends a for-profit business with a philanthropic component in what it terms the one for one model®. For every pair of shoes sold, another pair is provided to a child in need. Recently, TOMS has also expanded into eyewear. For every pair of eyewear sold, a person with vision problems in developing countries receives surgery, prescription glasses, or medical treatment to help restore his or her sight. Unlike many nonprofits, TOMS' for-profit business enables the company to support its philanthropic component, which keeps the company from having to solicit donations.

The idea for TOMS Shoes occurred after founder Blake Mycoskie witnessed the immense poverty in Argentinean villages, poverty so bad that many families could not afford to purchase shoes for their children. Recognizing the importance of shoes to health and education, Mycoskie decided to create a new business that would consist of two parts: TOMS Shoes, a for-profit business that would sell the shoes, and Friends of TOMS, the company's nonprofit subsidiary that would distribute shoes to those in need.

For his original product, Mycoskie decided to adopt the *alpargata* shoe worn in Argentina. The *alpargata* is a slip-on shoe made from canvas or fabric with rubber soles. After a *Los Angeles Times* article featured Mycoskie's new business, demand for the shoes exploded. Unfortunately for Mycoskie, he did not have enough shoes to fill the orders. Mycoskie was able to work out the product shortage, and today TOMS is a thriving business.

After distributing its one-millionth pair of shoes in 2010, TOMS began to consider other products that could be used in the one for one model. "When I thought about launching another product with the TOMS model, vision seemed the most obvious choice," Blake Myscoskie explained. Because 80 percent of vision impairment in developing countries is preventable or curable, TOMS decided that for every pair of eyewear it sold, the company would provide treatment or prescription glasses for those in need. TOMS chose Nepal as the first country for which to apply its one for one model.

TOMS takes its obligations for social responsibility seriously. The company builds the cost of the extra pair of shoes and eye care into the price of the products it sells. TOMS also works closely with local humanitarian organizations. "With TOMS we always work with local nonprofits or NGOs to understand what the need is in a community before we just go in and start giving," said Liza De La Torre, VP of Sales and Marketing at TOMS.

Customers who do business with TOMS feel committed to the company because they know that their purchases are going toward a good cause, even if they might pay a bit more in the process. TOMS goes to great lengths to educate the public about the importance of its mission. Although it does not have a marketing budget, the company provides internship opportunities and engages brand ambassadors at universities to spread the TOMS message. Every year the company promotes the One Day Without Shoes campaign, in which participants spend one day without shoes to understand what children in developing countries must undergo daily. These events have been supported by celebrities such as Charlize Theron, Kris Ryan, and the Dallas Cowboys Cheerleaders.

Despite TOMS' clear philanthropic component, risks for misconduct still exist. The company uses factories in China, Argentina, and Ethiopia for manufacturing, which creates complex supply chain relationships that must be carefully managed. TOMS created a set of manufacturing standards based upon International Labor Organization compliance standards for its manufacturers. The company regularly performs audits to check that the factories are complying with company standards. TOMS also seeks to create a strong organizational relationship with its employees and volunteers. The company often allows employees to participate in Shoe Drops (distributing the shoes to children) so they can see firsthand how their efforts are helping others.

Despite its success, TOMS' mission is far from complete. As its expansion into eyewear demonstrates, the company is looking for new opportunities to apply its one for one model. TOMS demonstrates how an innovative concept and the ability to incorporate philanthropy into business operations can create a successful company that can make a difference.[66]

Questions for Discussion

1. Do you think TOMS is successful because of its unique products, or is it the firm's approach to social responsibility?
2. How does TOMS manage its supply chain in order to ensure ethical and socially responsible conduct?
3. How does TOMS' business model relate to the understanding of stakeholders and strategic philanthropy?

NOTES

1 Diane Brady, "Volunteerism as a Core Competency," *Bloomberg Businessweek*, November 12-18, 2012, pp. 53–54; David Gould, "Cause Marketing—Where CSR Meets CRM," Special Advertising Section, *Businessweek*, 2012, S8; Arianna Huffington, "Companies and Causes: Social Media Jumpstart a Marketing Revolution," *Huffington Post*, April 6, 2011, www.huffingtonpost.com/arianna-huffington/companies-and-causes-soci_b_845657.html (accessed November 16, 2012); K. Adiwijaya and R. Fauzan, "Cause-Related Marketing: The Influence of Cause-Brand Fit, Firm Motives and Attribute Altruistic to Consumer Inferences and Loyalty and Moderation Effect of Consumer Values," *2012 International Conference on Economics Marketing and Management*, Vol. 28, Singapore; IACSIT Press.

2 "Dotcom Bust," *Economist*, January 28, 2012, p. 66; Sven Grundberg, The Pirate Bay Co-Founder Faces New Allegations, *The Wall Street Journal*, September 11, 2012, http://online.wsj.com/article/SB10000872396390443884104577645153822983344.html (accessed December 7, 2012).

3 P. Varadarajan, Terry Clark, and William M. Pride, "Controlling the Uncontrollable: Managing Your Market Environment," *Sloan Management Review* (Winter 1992): 39–47.

4 Jon Sicher, "Top 10 CSD Results for 2008," *Beverage Digest*, March 30, 2009; Natalie Zmuda, "Major Changes at PepsiCo as Marketing Department Reorganizes," *Ad Age*, June 16, 2011, http://adage.com/article/cmo-strategy/pepsico-reorganizes-marketing-department-beverages/228259/ (accessed January 12, 2012).

5 O. C. Ferrell and Michael D. Hartline, *Marketing Strategy* (Mason, OH: South-Western, 2008), p. 58.

6 Ibid.

7 Ibid.

8 John Jannarone, "Discounters Are Still in Fashion" *The Wall Street Journal*, February 25, 2011, C8.

9 Joshua Gallu, "Dodd–Frank May Cost $6.5 Billion and 5,000 Workers," *Bloomberg*, February 14, 2011, www.bloomberg.com/news/2011-02-14/ dodd-frank-s-implementation-calls-for-6-5-billion-5-000-staff-in-budget.html (accessed February 22, 2011); Binyamin Appelbaum and Brady Dennis, "Dodd's Overhaul Goes Well Beyond Other Plans," *The Washington Post*, November 11, 2009, www.washingtonpost.com/wp-dyn/content/article/2009/11/09/AR2009110901935.html?hpid=topnews&sid=ST2009111003729 (accessed February 22, 2011).

10 "Wall Street Reform: Bureau of Consumer Financial Protection (CFPB)," U.S. Treasury, www.treasury.gov/initiatives/Pages/cfpb.aspx (accessed February 22, 2011).

11 "Top All-Time Donors, 1989-2012," OpenSecrets.org, www.opensecrets.org/orgs/list.php (accessed December 11, 2012).

12 "Campaign Finance," *The New York Times*, October 8, 2010, http://topics.nytimes.com/top/reference/timestopics/subjects/c/campaign_finance/index.html (accessed January 24, 2011).

13 Steve Lohr, "Drafting Antitrust Case, F.T.C. Raises Pressure on Google," *The New York Times*,

www.nytimes.com/2012/10/13/technology/ftc-staff-prepares-antitrust-case-against-google-over-search.html?pagewanted=all&_r=0 (accessed December 11, 2012).

[14] Chad Bray, "U.S. Charges Ex-Siemens Executives in Alleged Bribery Scheme," *The Wall Street Journal*, December 14, 2011, http://online.wsj.com/article/SB10001424052970203430404577096283680373586.html?KEYWORDS=Siemens+bribery (accessed February 7, 2012).

[15] Dionne Searcey, "U.K. Law on Bribes Has Firms in a Sweat," *The Wall Street Journal*, December 28, 2010, B1; Julius Melnitzer, "U.K. Enacts 'Far-Reaching' Anti-Bribery Act," *Law Times*, February 13, 2011, www.lawtimesnews.com/201102148245/Headline-News/UK-enacts-far-reaching-anti-bribery-act (accessed March 28, 2011); Samuel Rubenfeld, "The Morning Risk Report: Bribery Act Review Considers Facilitation Payment Exception," *The Wall Street Journal*, May 31, 2013, http://blogs.wsj.com/riskandcompliance/2013/05/31/the-morning-risk-report-bribery-act-review-considers-facilitation-payment-exception/ (accessed June 14, 2013) .

[16] Julius Melnitzer, "U.K. Enacts 'Far-Reaching' Anti-Bribery Act," *Law Times*, February 13, 2011, www.lawtimesnews.com/201102148245/Headline-News/UK-enacts-far-reaching-anti-bribery-act (accessed March 28, 2011).

[17] Ibid.

[18] Sarah Johnson, "Don't Trust, Verify," *CFO*, February 1, 2012, www.cfo.com/article.cfm/14615752?f=singlepage (accessed February 7, 2012).

[19] "Welcome to the Division of Consumer Protection," Department of State, Division of Consumer Protection, www.dos.ny.gov/consumerprotection/ (accessed December 11, 2012).

[20] "PhRMA Guiding Principles: Direct to Consumer Advertisements," Pharmaceutical Research and Manufacturers of America, December 2008, www.phrma.org.

[21] "Council of Better Business Bureaus," Better Business Bureau, http://www.bbb.org/us/cbbb/ (accessed June 24, 2013); "BBB Expels Three Firms for Accreditation Violations," *Better Business Bureau*, November 30, 2012, http://stlouis.bbb.org/article/bbb-expels-three-firms-for-accreditation-violations-38561 (accessed December 11, 2012).

[22] "NAD Recommends Comcast Discontinue Unqualified 'Fastest in the Nation' Claims, Following Verizon Challenge," *ASRC*, June 12, 2012, www.asrcreviews.org/2012/06/nad-recommends-comcast-discontinue-unqualified-fastest-in-the-nation-claims-following-verizon-challenge/ (accessed December 11, 2012).

[23] Ryan Zinn, "National Advertising Review Board Determines that Fair Trade USA's 'Fair Trade Certified' Labels Should Reveal Percentage of Fair Trade Content in Body Care Products," Organic Consumers Association, September 18, 2012, www.organicconsumers.org/articles/article_26281.cfm (accessed December 11, 2012).

[24] David Goldman, "Are Landlines Doomed?," *CNN*, April 10, 2012, http://money.cnn.com/2012/04/10/technology/att-verizon-landlines/index.htm (accessed December 11, 2012).

[25] Aaron Smith, "Nearly Half of American Adults Are Smartphone Owners," Pew Internet, May 1, 2012, http://pewinternet.org/Reports/2012/Smartphone-Update-2012/Findings.aspx (accessed January 13, 2012).

[26] David Sarno, "The Rise of Tablet Computers," *Los Angeles Times*, May 6, 2011, http://articles.latimes.com/2011/may/06/business/la-fi-tablet-era-20110506 (accessed January 13, 2012).

[27] Debbie Thorne, O. C. Ferrell, and Linda Ferrell, *Business and Society*, 3rd ed. (New York: Houghton Mifflin, 2008), p. 36.

[28] Debbie McAlister, Linda Ferrell, and O.C. Ferrell, *Business and Society* (Mason, OH: South-Western Cengage Learning, 2011), 352-353.

[29] "Grayson K. Vincent and Victoria A. Velkoff, "The Next Four Decades: The Older Population in the United States: 2010 to 2050," May 2010, www.census.gov/prod/2010pubs/p25-1138.pdf (accessed January 13, 2012).

[30] Eric Klinenberg, "Solo Nation: American Consumers Stay Single," *CNNTimes*, January 25, 2012, http://finance.fortune.cnn.com/2012/01/25/eric-klinenberg-going-solo/ (accessed December 11, 2012).

[31] "State & County Quick Facts," United States Census Bureau, http://quickfacts.census.gov/qfd/states/00000.html (accessed December 11, 2012); "10,000 Baby Boomers Retire," Pew Research Center: The Data Bank, December 11, 2012, http://pewresearch.org/databank/dailynumber/?NumberID=1150 (accessed December 11, 2012).

[32] U.S. Bureau of the Census, *Statistical Abstract of the United States, 2010*, 58.

[33] U.S. Bureau of the Census, "Projections of the Population by Sex, Race, and Hispanic Origin for the United States: 2010 to 2050," August 14, 2008, www.census.gov/population/www/projections/summarytables.html.

[34] Sam Fahmy, "Despite Recession, Hispanic and Asian Buying Power Expected to Surge in U.S., According to Annual UGA Selig Center Multicultural Economy Study," Terry College of Business, November 4, 2010, www.terry.uga.edu/news/releases/2010/minority-buying-power-report.html (accessed January 13, 2012).

[35] David Kesmodel, "Brewers Go Courting Hispanics," *The Wall Street Journal*, July 12, 2011, B8.

[36] Isabelle Maignan and O. C. Ferrell, "Corporate Social Responsibility and Marketing: An Integrative Framework," *Journal of the Academy of Marketing Science* (January 2004): 3–19.

[37] Indra Nooyi, "The Responsible Company," *The Economist*, March 31, 2008, 132.

[38] Jeanne Whalen and Kristin Jones, "Glaxo to Pay States $90 Million in Avandia Settlement," *The Wall Street Journal*, November 5, 2012, http://online.wsj.com/article/SB10001424127887324556304578121314190446632.html (accessed December 11, 2012).

[39] Anne Tergesen, "Doing Good to Do Well," *The Wall Street Journal*, January 9, 2012, B7.

[40] Debbie Thorne, O. C. Ferrell, and Linda Ferrell, *Business and Society*, 3rd ed. (New York: Houghton Mifflin, 2008), pp. 48–50.

[41] O. C. Ferrell, "Business Ethics and Customer Stakeholders," *Academy of Management Executive* (May 2004): 126–129.

[42] "2005 Corporate Citizenship Report," Pfizer, www.pfizer.com/pfizer/subsites/corporate_citizenship/report/stakeholders_table.jsp (accessed January 19, 2007).

[43] Archie Carroll, "The Pyramid of Corporate Social Responsibility: Toward the Moral Management of Organizational Stakeholders," *Business Horizons* (July/August 1991): 42.

[44] Association of Certified Fraud Examiners, *Report to the Nations on Occupational Fraud and Abuse*, 2010, www.acfe.com/rttn/rttn-2010.pdf (accessed January 25, 2011).

[45] Sundar Bharadwaj, "Do Firms Pay a Price for Deceptive Advertising?" *Knowledge@Emory*, October 15, 2009, http://knowledge.emory.edu/article.cfm?articleid=1275(accessed November 3, 2009)

[46] Joe Palazzolo, Emily Glazer, and Joann S. Lublin. "Prosecutors Ask to Meet Jung in Avon Bribery Probe." *The Wall Street Journal*. July 29, 2012. http://online.wsj.com/article/SB10000872396390444840104577553683406542666.html (accessed December 3, 2012).

[47] Edelman Insights, *Global Deck: 2013 Trust Barometer*, www.slideshare.net/fullscreen/EdelmanInsights/global-deck-2013-edelman-trust-barometer-16086761/5 (accessed January 23, 2013).

[48] "2010 World's Most Ethical Companies—Company Profile: Whole Foods Market," *Ethisphere*, Q1, p. 32.

[49] Monica Eng, "Girl Scout Cookies and Other Sweets Offer Confusing Labeling on Trans Fats," *Los Angeles Times*, January 25, 2011, www.latimes.com/health/ct-met-girl-scout-cookies-trans-fat-20110125,0,1426933.story (accessed January 26, 2011).

[50] Tim Barnett and Sean Valentine, "Issue Contingencies and Marketers' Recognition of Ethical Issues, Ethical Judgments and Behavioral Intentions," *Journal of Business Research* 57 (2004): 338–346.

[51] Laura Stampler, "What These Companies Did in the Wake of Hurricane Sandy Will Restore Your Faith in Big Business," Yahoo Finance! November 2, 2012, http://finance.yahoo.com/news/what-these-companies-did-in-the-wake-of-hurricane-sandy-will-restore-your-faith-in-big-business.html (accessed December 11, 2012).

[52] Lindsay Blakely, "Erasing the Line between Marketing and Philanthropy," *CBS News*, April 21, 2011, www.cbsnews.com/8301-505143_162-40244368/erasing-the-line-between-marketing-and-philanthropy/ (accessed January 17, 2012); "The Best of 2011," Charlotte Street Computers, http://charlottestreetcomputers.com/the-best-of-2011/ (accessed January 17, 2012).

[53] "Take Charge of Education," Target, https://sites.target.com/site/en/corporate/page.jsp?contentId=PRD03-005174&ref=sr_shorturl_tcoe (accessed January 26, 2011).

[54] "Cone LLC Releases the 2010 Cone Cause Evolution Study," Cone, www.coneinc.com/cause-grows-consumers-want-more (accessed January 26, 2011).

[55] "2010 World's Most Ethical Companies—Company Profile: Salesforce.com," *Ethisphere*, Q1, p. 32.

[56] "Welcome to Eco Options: Sustainable Forestry," Home Depot, www.homedepot.com/ecooptions/index.html? (accessed February 5, 2010).

[57] Jill Gabrielle Klein, N. Craig Smith, and Andrew John, "Why We Boycott: Consumer Motivations for Boycott Participation," *Journal of Marketing* (July 2004): 92–109.

[58] Muel Kaptein, "Toward Effective Codes: Testing the Relationship with Unethical Behavior," *Journal of Business Ethics*, 99 (2011): 233–251.

[59] Bruce R. Gaumnitz and John C. Lere, "Contents of Codes of Ethics of Professional Business Organizations in the United States," *Journal of Business Ethics* 35 (2002): 35–49.

[60] "2010 World's Most Ethical Companies—Company Profile: Barrett-Jackson," *Ethisphere*, Q1, p. 32.

[61] Anis Ben Brik, Belaid Rettab, and Kamel Mellahi, "Market Orientation, Corporate Social Responsibility, and Business Performance," *Journal of Business Ethics* 99 (2011): 307–324.

[62] O. C. Ferrell and Michael Hartline, *Marketing Strategy*, 4th ed. (Mason, OH: Cengage Learning, 2008), pp. 76–79.

[63] Marjorie Kelly, "Holy Grail Found: Absolute, Definitive Proof That Responsible Companies Perform Better Financially," *Business Ethics*, Winter 2005, www.business-ethics.com/current_issue/winter_2005_holy_grail_article.html; Xueming Luo and C. B. Bhattacharya, "Corporate Social Responsibility, Customer Satisfaction, and Market Value," *Journal of Marketing* 70 (October 2006), www.marketingpower.com; Isabelle Maignan, O. C. Ferrell, and Linda Ferrell, "A Stakeholder Model for Implementing Social Responsibility in Marketing," *European Journal of Marketing* 39 (September/October 2005): 956–977.

[64] "Cone LLC Releases the 2010 Cone Cause Evolution Study."

[65] Maignan, Ferrell, and Ferrell, "A Stakeholder Model for Implementing Social Responsibility in Marketing."

[66] Athima Chansanchai, "Happy Feet: Buy a Pair of TOMS Shoes and a Pair Will Be Donated to a Poor Child Abroad," *Seattle Pi*, June 11, 2007, www.seattlepi.com/default/article/Happy-feet-Buy-a-pair-of-TOMS-shoes-and-a-pair-1240201.php (accessed June 3, 2011); Patrick Cole, "Toms Free Shoe Plan, Boosted by Clinton, Reaches Million Mark," *Bloomberg*, September 15, 2010, www.bloomberg.com/news/2010-09-16/toms-shoe-giveaway-for-kids-boosted-by-bill-clinton-reaches-million-mark.html (accessed June 2, 2011); "Don't Be an Intern at TOMS," TOMS, www.toms.com/our-movement/intern (accessed June 9, 2011); "How We Give," TOMS, www.toms.com/how-we-give (accessed June 3, 2011); "How We Wear Them," TOMS, www.toms.com/how-we-wear-them/ (accessed June 3, 2011); Booth Moore, "Toms Shoes' Model Is Sell a Pair, Give a Pair Away," *Los Angeles Times*, April 19, 2009, www.latimes.com/features/image/la-ig-greentoms19-2009apr19,0,3694310.story (accessed June 9, 2011); "One Day Without Shoes," TOMS, www.onedaywithoutshoes.com/ (accessed June 3, 2011); "One for One," TOMS, www.toms.com/our-movement/movement-one-for-one (accessed June 3, 2011); "Our Movement," TOMS, www.toms.com/our-movement/ (accessed March 5, 2012); Stacy Perman, "Making a Do-Gooder's Business Model Work," *Bloomberg Businessweek*, January 23, 2009, www.businessweek.com/smallbiz/content/jan2009/sb20090123_264702.htm (accessed June 3, 2011); Michelle Prasad, "TOMS Shoes Always Feels Good," *KENTON Magazine*, March 19, 2011, http://kentonmagazine.com/toms-shoes-always-feel-good/ (accessed June 3, 2011); Craig Sharkton, "Toms Shoes—Philanthropy As a Business Model," sufac.com, August 23, 2008, http://sufac.com/2008/08/toms-shoes-philanthropy-as-a-business-model/ (accessed June 3, 2011); *TOMS Campus Club Program*, http://images.toms.com/media/content/images/campus-clubs-assets/TOMSCampushandbook_082510_International_final.pdf (accessed June 2, 2011); "TOMS Company Overview," TOMS, www.toms.com/corporate-info/ (accessed June 3, 2011); "TOMS Manufacturing Practices," TOMS, www.toms.com/manufacturing-practices (accessed June 3, 2011); *TOMS One for One Giving Report*, http://images.toms.com/media/content/images/giving-report/TOMS-Giving-Report-2010.pdf (accessed June 3, 2011); TOMS Shoes, www.toms.com/ (accessed June 3, 2011); Mike Zimmerman, "The Business of Giving: TOMS Shoes," *Success Magazine*, September 30, 2009, www.success-magazine.com/the-business-of-giving/PARAMS/article/852 (accessed June 3, 2011); "TOMS Eyewear," www.toms.com/eyewear/ (accessed March 5, 2012); "TOMS Founder Shares Sole-ful Tale," *North Texas Daily*, April 14, 2011, www.ntdaily.com/?p=53882 (accessed March 5, 2012).

Feature Notes

[a] Max Chafkin, "The Sincerest Form of Flattery," *Inc. magazine*, May 29, 2012, www.inc.com/magazine/201206/max-chafkin/oliver-samwer-european-king-of-the-company-cloners.html (accessed August 29, 2012); Caroline Winter, "How Three Germans Are Cloning the Web," *Businessweek*, February 29, 2012, www.businessweek.com/articles/2012-02-29/the-germany-website-copy-machine (accessed August 29, 2012).

[b] Julie Jargon and Bill Tomson, "Highest-Calorie Menu Item at McDonald's? Not a Burger," *Wall Street Journal*, September 13, 2012, http://online.wsj.com/article/SB10000872396390443884104577647400959492314.html (accessed October 8, 2012); Bruce Horovitz, "Boston Market Shakes Salt Habit," *USA Today*, August 21, 2102, A1; Saabira Chaudhuri, "McDonald's to List Calories on Menus; Tests Healthier Menus," *Wall Street Journal*, September 12, 2012, http://online.wsj.com/article/BT-CO-20120912-709004.html (accessed October 5, 2012).

[c] Melaine Rodier, "A Game Called Compliance," *Wall Street Tech*, July 25, 2012, www.wallstreetandtech.com/regulatory-compliance/a-game-called-compliance/240004357 (accessed October 28, 2012); Alex Konrad, "Pong For Corporate Training," *Fortune*, May, 15, 2012, http://tech.fortune.cnn.com/2012/05/15/gamification-true-office/ (accessed October 28, 2012); John Adams, "Corporate Compliance Is a Game for Cristobal Conde," *American Banker*, August 24, 2012, www.americanbanker.com/issues/177_165/corporate-compliance-is-a-game-for-cristobal-conde-1052126-1.html?pg=1 (accessed October 28, 2012).

[d] Brian Dumaine, "Google's Zero-Carbon Quest," Fortune Tech, http://tech.fortune.cnn.com/2012/07/12/google-zero-carbon/ (accessed August 17, 2012); Bill Weihl, "Reducing Our Carbon Footprint" Google, May 6, 2009, http://googleblog.blogspot.com/2009/05/reducing-our-carbon-footprint.html#!/2009/05/reducing-our-carbon-footprint.html/ (accessed August 17, 2012).

chapter 4

Marketing Research and Information Systems

OBJECTIVES

1. Gain perspective on the importance of marketing research.
2. Differentiate between the two major types of marketing research—exploratory and conclusive research.
3. Describe the basic steps in conducting marketing research.
4. Understand how technology is used to facilitate information gathering and analysis.
5. Identify key ethical and international considerations in marketing research.

© iStockphoto.com/sandramo

MARKETING INSIGHTS

LEGO Discovers an Overlooked Target Market—Girls!

LEGO, the world's third-largest toy company, is well known for its plastic building block sets. Especially since its introduction of block kits and video games featuring characters and situations from hit movie franchises like *Star Wars* and *Harry Potter*, LEGO has enjoyed strong sales and profits. The Danish firm's toys were mostly geared toward boys until CEO Jorgen Vig Knudstorp decided to expand LEGO's appeal by creating products specifically for girls of kindergarten age and up.

LEGO's researchers began by observing girls at play and interviewing their families about likes and dislikes. One finding was that girls tend to enjoy role-playing and telling stories that evolve minute by minute. The researchers also learned how much attention girls pay to color and other aesthetic details. Finally, they discovered that girls like to project themselves into role-play situations and identify with the minifigures in LEGO kits.

Based on research with 3,500 girls over four years, the company's international team of designers developed LEGO Friends, building sets featuring five female minifigures living in fictional Heartlake City, which includes a café, veterinary clinic, beauty salon, and horse stables. The designers also developed six bright new block colors, including lavender and turquoise, specifically for Friends sets.

Despite some controversy over whether this new product line was reinforcing gender stereotypes, LEGO Friends have become extremely popular. During the first year alone, LEGO sold twice as many Friends sets as it expected, giving a big boost to company revenues and setting the stage for future product introductions.[1]

Marketing research enables firms such as LEGO to implement the marketing concept by helping them acquire information about whether and how their goods and services satisfy the desires of target-market customers. When used effectively, such information facilitates relationship marketing by helping marketers focus their efforts on trying to anticipate and meet the needs of their customers. Marketing research and information systems that provide practical and objective information to help firms develop and implement marketing strategies are therefore essential to effective marketing.

In this chapter, we focus on how marketers gather the information needed to make marketing decisions. First, we define marketing research and examine the individual steps of the marketing research process, including the various methods of collecting data. Next, we look at how technology aids in collecting, organizing, and interpreting marketing research data. Finally, we consider ethical and international issues in marketing research.

marketing research
The systematic design, collection, interpretation, and reporting of information to help marketers solve specific marketing problems or take advantage of marketing opportunities

THE IMPORTANCE OF MARKETING RESEARCH

LO1. Gain perspective on the importance of marketing research.

Marketing research is the systematic design, collection, interpretation, and reporting of information to help marketers solve specific marketing problems or take advantage of marketing opportunities. As the word *research* implies, it is a process for gathering the information needed that is not already available to decision makers. The purpose of marketing research is to inform an organization about customers' needs and desires, marketing opportunities for particular goods and services, and changing attitudes and purchase patterns of customers. Market information increases the firm's ability to make informed decisions and respond to customer needs, which can lead to improved organizational performance. Detecting shifts in buyers' behaviors and attitudes helps companies react to the ever-changing marketplace. Strategic planning requires marketing research to facilitate the process of assessing such opportunities or threats.

Marketing research can help a firm better understand market opportunities, ascertain new products' potential for success, and determine the feasibility of a marketing strategy. It can also reveal trends. For example, mobile retailing, meaning shopping on smartphones and other devices, is booming. The marketing for mobile retailing is expected to double in fewer than five years.[2] This means that marketers must take smartphone compatibility into account when designing advertisements and in-store displays. For instance, marketers may want to include a matrix barcode that pushes customers to the company website when they scan it with their mobile device. Failing to keep up with trends can ruin companies because they will not maintain a competitive advantage.

The real value of marketing research is measured by improvements in a marketer's ability to make informed decisions. Many types of organizations use marketing research to help them develop marketing mixes that address the needs of customers. It is important in today's rapidly changing marketing environment that firms have the necessary organizational speed and agility to adapt to changes quickly. To improve research-gathering capacity

Courtesy of Accenture

Importance of Marketing Research
Firms such as Accenture can help companies improve their data-gathering and assessing capabilities, helping them to make better decisions about marketing strategies and to improve performance.

and decision-making ability, some firms may choose to hire a consultant that can assist with gathering and assessing the data involved in marketing research. Take a look at the advertisement, for instance. Accenture is a high-tech consulting firm that helps companies to improve performance through improved data-gathering and assessing methods. As the advertisement indicates, understanding opportunities and successes and capitalizing on them is critical to a firm's ability to succeed. Having a full understanding of issues can help a company increase performance and develop an advantage over competitors. Accenture has been hired by many firms, such as fashion retailers, to improve their website design, interactivity, and response time to customer complaints—resulting in increased customer satisfaction and revenues.[3] Marketers should treat information as one of its resources, just as finances and human capital are resources, and they must weigh the costs and benefits of obtaining information. Information should be considered worthwhile if it results in marketing activities that better satisfy the firm's target customers, lead to increased sales and profits, or help the firm achieve some other goal.

L02. Differentiate between the two major types of marketing research—exploratory and conclusive research.

TYPES OF RESEARCH

The nature and type of research a firm conducts will vary depending on the research design and the hypotheses under investigation. Marketing research can involve two forms of data. *Qualitative data* yields descriptive, nonnumerical information. *Quantitative data* yields information that can be communicated through numbers. Marketers may choose to collect either or both, depending upon the information desired. To collect data, marketers conduct either exploratory research or conclusive research. Although each has a distinct purpose, they vary in levels of formalization and flexibility. Table 4.1 summarizes the differences.

Table 4.1 **Differences between Exploratory and Conclusive Research**

Research Project Components	Exploratory Research	Conclusive Research
Research purpose	General: to generate insights about a situation	Specific: to verify insights and aid in selecting a course of action
Data needs	Vague	Clear
Data sources	Ill-defined	Well-defined
Data collection form	Open-ended, rough	Usually structured
Sample	Relatively small, subjectively selected to maximize generalization of insights	Relatively large, objectively selected to permit generalization of findings
Data collection	Flexible, no set procedure	Rigid, well-laid-out procedure
Data analysis	Informal, typically not quantitative	Formal, typically quantitative
Inferences/ recommendations	More tentative than final	More final than tentative

Source: A. Parasuraman, *Marketing Research*, Second Edition. © 2007 South-Western, a part of Cengage Learning, Inc. Reproduced by permission, www.cengage.com/permissions.

Exploratory Research

When marketers need more information about a problem or want to make a tentative hypothesis more specific, they conduct **exploratory research**. The main purpose of exploratory research is to better understand a problem or situation and/or to help identify additional data needs or decision alternatives.[4] For example, China is the world's largest auto producer and has made great strides in developing high-efficiency vehicles, yet exports practically none of them. Chinese automakers have begun to see opportunities abroad as countries increase fuel-efficiency standards and demand for efficient cars grows. Geely Group, which acquired Volvo Cars of Sweden, for instance, has begun conducting exploratory research in major Western markets, such as Britain, to determine which of its low-cost and high-fuel-efficiency models would be most popular there.[5] Exploratory research can help marketers better understand how consumers view a topic or a product, which can assist a firm as it develops better products and more targeted marketing mixes.

Some organizations utilize **customer advisory boards**, which are small groups of actual customers who serve as sounding boards for new product ideas and offer researchers insights into their feelings and attitudes toward a firm's marketing strategy, including products, promotion, pricing, and distribution. While these advisory boards can help companies maintain strong relationships with valuable customers, they can also generate a greater understanding of marketing research questions. For example, Modulo, a major IT and risk and compliance contractor, formed a customer advisory board to help the firm confront the fast-changing environment of IT security. The board meets quarterly and helps the firm identify opportunities and threats facing international security and banking, and to identify changes in governance for the markets in which it has clients.[6]

One common method for conducting exploratory research is through a focus group. A **focus group** brings together multiple people to discuss a specific topic in a group setting facilitated by a moderator. Focus groups are often conducted informally, without a structured questionnaire. They allow customer attitudes, behaviors, lifestyles, needs, and desires to be explored in a flexible and creative manner. Questions are open-ended and stimulate respondents to answer in their own words. A traditional focus group session consists of 8 to 12 individuals and is led by a moderator, who is an independent individual hired by the research firm or the company. The moderator encourages all of the participants to engage in the conversation and directs the discussion by asking questions when needed.

Focus groups can provide companies with ideas for new products or can be a forum to test marketing strategies for existing products. This format can yield detailed information, including on topics about which researchers might not have thought to ask participants because they can engage with one another.

In-person focus groups have some disadvantages, however. For instance, sometimes the focus group's discussion can be hindered by overly talkative, confrontational, or shy individuals. Some participants might be less than honest in an effort to be sociable or to receive money

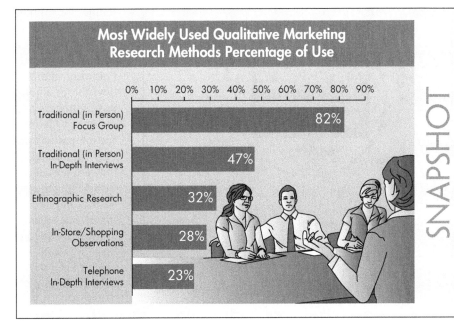

SNAPSHOT

Most Widely Used Qualitative Marketing Research Methods Percentage of Use

Traditional (in Person) Focus Group — 82%
Traditional (in Person) In-Depth Interviews — 47%
Ethnographic Research — 32%
In-Store/Shopping Observations — 28%
Telephone In-Depth Interviews — 23%

Source: GreenBook Research Industry Trends Report Spring 2012, www.greenbookblog.org/GRIT-Spring-2012/

exploratory research Research conducted to gather more information about a problem or to make a tentative hypothesis more specific

customer advisory boards Small groups of actual customers who serve as sounding boards for new-product ideas and offer insights into their feelings and attitudes toward a firm's products and other elements of its marketing strategy

focus group An interview that is often conducted informally, without a structured questionnaire, in small groups of 8 to 12 people, to observe interaction when members are exposed to an idea or a concept

Conduct Live Focus Groups Online with a Webcam

Sometimes you need to go outside a research facility to broaden the respondent pool. InterVu Online Focus Groups enable you to reach participants anywhere in the world at any time.

With InterVu, you can get the same face-to-face exchange you get from traditional focus groups. Moderators and respondents log in to the InterVu web portal through their computer and transmit their image with a personal web cam.

This *live* focus group exchange allows all participants to see, hear and react to each other in the same way as a traditional group interview only online. InterVu Focus Groups are transmitted in real-time to any number of viewers, world wide.

FocusVision
WORLDWIDE

Schedule a Demo or Book a Project today.

For more information, call 888-536-2878
or email request@focusvision.com

STAMFORD   LONDON   SINGAPORE
www.focusvision.com

FocusVision Worldwide, Inc.

Focus Groups
Companies like FocusVision help administer video-enabled online focus groups with the use of platforms such as InterVu.

and/or food in exchange for their participation.[7] Furthermore, focus groups do not provide quantitative data, and are thus best used to uncover issues that can be explored using quantifiable marketing research techniques.

Because of their ease of use, online focus groups are a growing research trend. Participants either sign in to a website and insert their responses in the fields provided, or log into a video chat. Online focus groups can be a cost-effective way to gather data from large and geographically diverse groups. Technology exists to make conducting online focus groups easy and cost-effective. Take a look, for example, at the advertisement for FocusVision. It is a company that offers video transmission that enables companies to conduct online video focus groups using its platform, InterVu. The advertisement visually emphasizes how the product brings disparate individuals together by positioning them around a central focal point containing a computer. Online focus groups are much more convenient for the participants than traditional focus groups because they can participate in their own homes, no matter where they are located. However, this method is not well-adapted to asking participants about a product's smell or taste, so it is not suitable for all goods. When using a website login, researchers also cannot observe the participants' nonverbal cues and body language, which can often reveal "gut" reactions to questions or topics discussed. Marketers should keep these characteristics in mind when designing a research project for a particular product.

Conclusive Research

Conclusive research is designed to verify insights through an objective procedure to help marketers make decisions. It is used in the final stages of decision making, when the marketer has narrowed his or her decision down to a few alternatives. Conclusive research is helpful when a marketer requires a well-defined and structured research project to help decide which of a set of approaches is best for a specific product and target consumers. Conclusive research studies are typically quantitative, formal, specific, and have verifiable methods. Two such types of conclusive research are descriptive research and experimental research.

If marketers need to understand the characteristics of certain phenomena to solve a particular problem, **descriptive research** can aid them. Descriptive research may range from general surveys of customers' educations, occupations, or ages to seeking out specific information on how often teenagers consume sports drinks or how often customers buy new shoes. For example, if Nike and Reebok wanted to target more young women, they might ask 15- to 35-year-old females how often they work out, how frequently they wear athletic shoes, and how many pairs of athletic shoes they buy in a year. Such descriptive research could be used to develop specific marketing strategies for the athletic shoe market. Descriptive studies generally demand significant prior knowledge and assume that the problem or issue is clearly defined. Some descriptive studies require statistical analysis and predictive tools. The marketer's primary task is to choose adequate methods for collecting and measuring data.

Descriptive research does not provide sufficient information to allow researchers to make causal inferences (i.e., that variable X causes a variable Y). **Experimental research** allows

conclusive research Research designed to verify insights through objective procedures and to help marketers in making decisions

descriptive research Research conducted to clarify the characteristics of certain phenomena to solve a particular problem

experimental research Research that allows marketers to make causal inferences about relationships

marketers to make these causal deductions about relationships between variables. Such experimentation requires that an independent variable (Variable X, one that is not influenced by or acted on by other variables) be manipulated and the resulting changes to a dependent variable (Variable Y, one that is influenced by the dependent variable) be measured. Manipulation of the dependent variable while controlling for other variables is what makes experimental research different from descriptive research. In this way, researchers can determine causality, which is highly important when developing marketing strategy.

THE MARKETING RESEARCH PROCESS

LO3. Describe the basic steps in conducting marketing research.

To maintain the control needed to obtain accurate information, a firm should approach marketing research as a process with logical steps: (1) locating and defining problems or issues, (2) designing the research project, (3) collecting data, (4) interpreting research findings, and (5) reporting research findings (see Figure 4.1). These steps should be viewed as adaptable and as part of an overall approach to conducting research, rather than as a rigid set of rules. Marketers must consider each step and determine how they can be adapted to resolve the issues at hand.

Locating and Defining Problems or Research Issues

The first step in launching a research study is defining the problem or issue. This will encourage researchers to focus on the true nature and boundaries of a situation as it relates to marketing strategy or implementation. The first sign of a problem is typically a departure from normal functioning, such as the failure to meet an objective that was previously attainable. If a corporation's objective is a 12 percent sales increase and there was only a 6 percent increase under the current marketing strategy, marketers should analyze this discrepancy to adapt the marketing strategy to be more effective. Declining sales, increasing expenses, and decreasing profits all signal problems for a firm. Conversely, a dramatic increase in sales or another positive event should prompt marketers to research the reasons for the change in order to leverage opportunities.

Marketing research often focuses on identifying and defining market opportunities or changes in the environment. When a firm discovers a market opportunity, it should conduct research to understand the situation and craft an appropriate marketing strategy. Customer relationship management (CRM) is essential to attracting and retaining loyal customers, and also requires research to be effective. CRM involves taking advantage of opportunities in the marketing environment. It is frequently based on an analysis of existing customers and their needs and wants because understanding existing loyal customers helps a firm design a marketing strategy to maintain them while reaching out to new customers.

In order to identify and define an issue correctly, marketers must be careful not to be distracted by superficial symptoms. Addressing symptoms of the problem will not help

Figure 4.1 The Five Steps of the Marketing Research Process

alleviate it, leading to unnecessary expenses and a continuation of the underlying issue. For example, companies that market eco-friendly products such as hybrid cars and CFL light bulbs have found that shifting marketing strategy to highlight convenience first and sustainability second has improved sales. The real problem causing slow sales was not a defect in the products, but that consumers still want to know about how the product is an improvement over previous products, after which they will be happy to pay a price premium for eco-friendliness.[8]

Researchers and decision makers should remain in the problem or issue definition stage as long as needed, until they are certain they have designed a research plan that addresses the issue. Taking the necessary steps to allow researchers to refine a broad, indefinite problem or issue into a precise and testable research statement is a prerequisite for the next step in the research process. Some companies hire firms such as Booshaka to assist them. As you can see in the advertisement, Booshaka helps companies to understand the problem, define the issue, learn how to leverage customer feedback, and manage data gathered from word-of-mouth marketing online. Word-of-mouth is an increasingly important element of many firm's marketing strategies, yet many marketers do not understand how to manage the tool and require outside experts.

Designing the Research Project

Once the problem or issue has been defined, the next step is to create a **research design**, an overall plan for obtaining the information needed to address the issue. This step requires formulating a hypothesis and determining what type of research is most appropriate for testing the hypothesis to ensure the results are reliable and valid.

research design An overall plan for obtaining the information needed to address a research problem or issue

hypothesis An informed guess or assumption about a certain problem or set of circumstances

Developing a Hypothesis

The objective statement of a marketing research project should include a hypothesis based on both previous research and expected research findings. A **hypothesis** is an informed guess or assumption about a certain problem or set of circumstances. It is what a researcher seeks to prove or disprove and is based on all the insight and knowledge available about the problem

Locating and Defining Research Issues and Problems
Companies like Booshaka can identify market opportunities or changes in the competitive environment, which can assist marketing researchers in defining a problem.

Build your team of superfans with booshaka!

Booshaka simplifies word of mouth marketing — your superfans are your best marketers. Marketing on Facebook is **not** about the **rap** but the **rapport** that you have with your fans.

Already registered? Login

f Install — Top Fans is Free
b Buy — 7-day Trial for Top Fans Pro

Understand · Activate · Reward · Amplify
Community to Fans to Relationships to Advocates to Community

1 2 3 **TOP FANS** Free Leaderboard for Facebook.

TOP FANS PRO Social Rewards & Analytics Dashboard.

FIRST CLASS Advanced Insights & Custom Solutions.

Courtesy of Booshaka.com

or circumstances from previous research studies and other sources. As information is gathered, the researcher tests the hypothesis. For example, a food marketer such as H.J. Heinz might propose the hypothesis that children today have considerable influence on their families' buying decisions regarding Heinz products. A marketing researcher would then gather data, perhaps through surveys of children and their parents and observing families shop, analyze the data, and draw conclusions as to whether the hypothesis is correct. Sometimes, several hypotheses are developed over the course of a research project. The hypotheses that are accepted or rejected become the study's conclusions.

Research Reliability and Validity

In designing research, marketing researchers must ensure that research techniques are both reliable and valid. A research technique has **reliability** if it produces almost identical results in repeated trials. To have **validity**, the research method must measure what it is supposed to measure, not something else. This means than not all reliable research findings are valid. For example, although a group of customers may express the same level of satisfaction based on a rating scale, as individuals they may not exhibit the same repurchase behavior because of different personal characteristics. If the purpose of rating satisfaction was to estimate potential repurchase behavior, this result may cause the researcher to question the validity of the satisfaction scale.[9] A study to measure the effect of advertising on sales is valid if advertising can be isolated from other factors and from variables that affect sales. Research projects should be replicable as well, otherwise it is impossible to establish reliability.

Collecting Data

The next step in the marketing research process is collecting data to help prove (or disprove) the research hypothesis. The research design must specify what types of data to collect and how they will be collected.

Types of Data

Marketing researchers have two types of data at their disposal. **Primary data** are observed and recorded or collected directly from respondents. Primary data must be gathered by observing phenomena or surveying people of interest. **Secondary data** are compiled both inside and outside the organization for some purpose other than the current investigation. Secondary data include general reports compiled by other organizations and internal and online databases. Reports might address a variety of topics, including market share, retail inventory levels, and customers' buying behavior. They are useful for research if the information contained is pertinent to the hypothesis marketers are testing. Most marketing research comes from secondary sources, as they often provide the needed information at relatively low cost and effort. The Internet has increased the amount of secondary data available exponentially, making research both easier and more complicated. Now researchers are faced with the task of sorting through large volumes of secondary data, some of it of questionable quality, in order to find the information they need. There remain, however, large and reputable publications and databases that are useful.

Sources of Secondary Data

Marketers often begin the data-collection phase of the marketing research process by gathering secondary data. They may use available reports and other information from both internal and external sources to study a marketing problem.

Internal sources of secondary data, such as databases, sales records, and research reports, can be helpful because they provide information on the firm's own marketing activities. This

reliability A condition that exists when a research technique produces almost identical results in repeated trials

validity A condition that exists when a research method measures what it is supposed to measure

primary data Data observed and recorded or collected directly from respondents

secondary data Data compiled both inside and outside the organization for some purpose other than the current investigation

information can be used to test hypotheses and pinpoint problems. From sales reports, for example, a firm can gather information such as the most popular times of the year for products, and which colors and sizes sell best. Marketers should look at any available tools for marketing, management, or financial purposes in their data search. Accounting records are often overlooked but can be a rich source of quantitative data. While they generally do not flow automatically to other departments, these records offer detailed information about costs, sales, customer accounts, and profits. Another source of internal secondary data is competitive information gathered by the sales force.

External sources of secondary data (see Table 4.2) include trade associations, periodicals, government publications, unpublished sources, and online databases. Trade associations, such as the American Marketing Association, offer guides and directories that are full of information. Periodicals such as *Bloomberg Businessweek, The Wall Street Journal, Sales and Marketing*

Table 4.2   **Sources of Secondary Information**

Government Sources	
Economic census	www.census.gov
Export.gov—country and industry market research	www.export.gov/mrktresearch/index.asp
National Technical Information Services	www.ntis.gov
Strategis—Canadian trade	www.strategis.ic.gc.ca
Trade Associations and Shows	
American Society of Association Executives	www.asaecenter.org
Directory of Associations	www.marketingsource.com/associations
Trade Show News Network	www.tsnn.com
Magazines, Newspapers, Video, and Audio News Programming	
Google Video Search	www.google.com/videohp?hl=en
Media Jumpstation	www.directcontactpr.com/jumpstation
Google News Directory	www.google.com/Top/News
Yahoo! Video Search	www.video.search.yahoo.com
Corporate Information	
The Public Register Online	www.annualreportservice.com
Bitpipe	www.bitpipe.com
Business Wire—press releases	www.businesswire.com
Hoover's Online	www.hoovers.com
Open Directory Project	www.dmoz.org
PR Newswire—press releases	www.prnewswire.com

Source: Adapted from "Data Collection: Low-Cost Secondary Research," *KnowThis.com*, www.knowthis.com/principles-of-marketing-tutorials/data-collection-low-cost-secondary-research/ (accessed January 24, 2013).

Going Green

Green Marketing

Electric cars—both all-electric plug-ins and electric-gasoline hybrids—are being marketed as good for the environment and, in the long run, good for the buyer's wallet. Unfortunately, as Nissan, General Motors, Ford, and other automakers have found out, these benefits haven't yet translated into widespread acceptance of electric cars. Sales of Nissan's Leaf are running well below the company's projections, and sluggish demand has prompted General Motors to temporarily halt Volt production on occasion.

Why aren't sales of electric cars stronger, given the benefits? One reason, according to research, is "sticker shock." A survey by the Indiana University School of Public and Environmental Affairs found that buyers tend to underestimate how much more an electric car will cost compared to a traditional gas-powered car. Confronted by a higher-than-expected price tag, buyers may not realize how much money they'll save on fuel expenditures over the life of the car. Nissan is addressing this issue by introducing a new Leaf priced 18 percent below the original model. At the other end of the price spectrum, General Motors is introducing an electric Cadillac for upscale drivers willing to pay for a green luxury car.

Another reason consumers hesitate to buy plug-ins is "range anxiety," concern over the limited range an electric car can travel between charge-ups. Early electric cars had a range of less than 100 miles and required nearly eight hours to recharge. Thanks to technical advances, newer electric vehicles have a longer range and recharge in only a few hours—sometimes via wireless charging. By promoting these improvements, automakers hope to attract more eco-minded buyers in the coming years.[a]

Management, Advertising Age, Marketing Research, and *Industrial Marketing* publish general information that can help marketers define problems and develop hypotheses. Many marketers also consult federal government publications such as the *Statistical Abstract of the United States* and publications by the U.S. Census Bureau on Business, Agriculture, and the Population. Marketers can use searchable online databases, available through the Census website, to gather data on many different topics. Although the government only conducts its primary census every 10 years, it also conducts the American Community Survey (ACF), which is sent to population samples annually. The ACF is not as comprehensive as the decennial Census, but it can provide marketers with an up-to-date picture of the nation's population. A company might use census data to determine, for example, whether the demographics, education, and income levels of a population in a specific area would make it a good place to construct a shopping mall.

The Internet is a very useful research tool. Search engines help marketers to locate quickly many types of secondary data or news and scholarly information research topics of interest. Of course, companies can also mine their own websites for useful information by using CRM tools. Many online retailers, for example, track customer purchases in order to gain a more complete understanding of their needs, desires, lifestyles, and income level. With this information, companies are able to cater recommendations to individuals based on the customer's previous purchases. Such a marketing system helps companies track the changing desires and buying habits of the most valuable customers. Furthermore, marketing researchers are increasingly monitoring blogs to discover what consumers are saying about their products—both positive and negative. Many retailers will send out products to popular bloggers with the hope that they will use them and feature the products and a review on their websites.

Methods of Collecting Primary Data

Collecting primary data is a lengthier, more expensive, and more complex process than collecting secondary data. To gather primary data, researchers use sampling procedures, survey methods, and observation. These efforts can be handled in-house by the firm's own research department or contracted to a private research firm such as ACNielsen or SymphonyIRI Group.

population All the elements, units, or individuals of interest to researchers for a specific study

sample A limited number of units chosen to represent the characteristics of a total population

sampling The process of selecting representative units from a total population

probability sampling A type of sampling in which every element in the population being studied has a known chance of being selected for study

random sampling A form of probability sampling in which all units in a population have an equal chance of appearing in the sample, and the various events that can occur have an equal or known chance of taking place

Sampling Because the time and resources available for research are limited, it is almost impossible to investigate all the members of a target market or other population. A **population**, or "universe," includes all the elements, units, or individuals of interest to researchers for a specific study. Consider a Gallup poll designed to predict the results of a presidential election. All registered voters in the United States constitute the population. By selecting a limited number of units—a **sample**—to represent the characteristics of a total population, researchers can predict the behaviors of the total population. **Sampling** in marketing research, therefore, is the process of selecting representative units from a population. Sampling techniques allow marketers to predict buying behavior fairly accurately without having to collect responses from a total population. Because it would be impossible in most situations to collect reactions from the entire market or market segment, most types of marketing research employ sampling techniques.

There are two basic types of sampling: probability sampling and nonprobability sampling. With **probability sampling**, every element in the population being studied has a known chance of being selected for study. Random sampling is a form of probability sampling. When marketers employ **random sampling**, all the units in a population have an equal chance of appearing in the sample. Likewise, the various events that can occur have an equal or known chance of taking place. For example, a specific card in a regulation playing deck has a 1 in 52 probability of being drawn. Sample units are ordinarily chosen by selecting from a table of random numbers statistically generated so that each digit, 0 through 9, will have an equal probability of occurring in each position in the sequence. The sequentially numbered elements of a population are sampled randomly by selecting the units whose numbers appear in the table of random numbers. There are random number generators available for free online, such as Random.org, that will generate lists of random numbers for this purpose.

Another type of probability sampling is **stratified sampling**, in which the population of interest is divided into groups according to a common attribute, and a random sample is then chosen within each subgroup. A stratified sample may reduce some of the error that is a risk of a completely random sample, ensuring that a group is not accidentally overrepresented. By segmenting a population into groups, the researcher makes sure that each segment receives its proportionate share of sample units and helps investigators avoid including too many or too few sample units from each subgroup. Samples are usually stratified when researchers believe there may be variations among different types of respondents. For instance, many political opinion surveys are stratified by gender, race, age, and/or geographic location.

The second type of sampling, **nonprobability sampling**, is more subjective than probability sampling because there is no way to calculate the probability that a specific element of the population being studied will be chosen. Quota sampling, for example, is highly judgmental because the final choice of participants is left to the researchers. In **quota sampling**, researchers divide the population into groups and then arbitrarily choose participants from each segment. In quota sampling, researchers impose some controls—usually limited to two or three variables, such as age, gender, or race—over the selection of participants to ensure that representative categories of respondents are included. A study of people who wear eyeglasses, for example, may be conducted by interviewing equal numbers of men and women. However, because quota samples are not probability samples, not everyone has an equal chance of being selected and sampling error therefore cannot be measured statistically. Quota samples are used most often in exploratory studies, when researchers have not yet generated hypotheses to test. In this

Courtesy of Tobii Technology, Inc.

Collecting Data
Tobii Technology assists clients in providing technology to study eye movements on screen to collect primary data and gain insight into customers' responses to marketing communications.

case, the findings may provide valuable insights into a problem but cannot be extrapolated to the total population.

Survey Methods Marketing researchers often employ sampling to collect primary data through mail, telephone, personal interview, online, or social networking surveys. Table 4.3 summarizes and compares the advantages of the various survey methods. The results of such surveys are used to describe and analyze buying behavior. The survey method chosen depends on a variety of factors, including: the nature of the problem or issue, the data needed to test the hypothesis, and the resources available to the researcher (e.g., funding and personnel). Marketers may employ more than one survey method depending on the goals of the research project. Surveys can be quite expensive, although online survey services have made the method much more affordable even for small firms. There are many companies that offer free or low-cost survey services, such as SurveyMonkey, Constant Contact, and KwikSurveys.[10]

Gathering information through surveys can be difficult because many people believe responding to surveys requires too much scarce personal time and may have concerns about invasions of privacy and how personal information will be used. The unethical use of selling techniques disguised as marketing surveys has also led to decreased cooperation. Hence, firms that choose to conduct surveys should anticipate a fairly high nonresponse rate. A danger in relying on survey responses when the nonresponse rate is high is that the results will not be representative of the sample as a whole.[11]

In a **mail survey**, questionnaires are sent to respondents who are encouraged to complete and return them. Mail surveys are used most often when the individuals in the sample are

stratified sampling A type of probability sampling in which the population is divided into groups with a common attribute and a random sample is chosen within each group

nonprobability sampling A sampling technique in which there is no way to calculate the likelihood that a specific element of the population being studied will be chosen

quota sampling A nonprobability sampling technique in which researchers divide the population into groups and then arbitrarily choose participants from each group

mail survey A research method in which respondents answer a questionnaire sent through the mail

Table 4.3   Comparison of the Four Basic Survey Methods

	Mail Surveys	**Telephone Surveys**	**Online Surveys**	**Personal Interview Surveys**
Economy	Potentially lower in cost per interview than telephone or personal surveys if there is an adequate response rate.	Avoids interviewers' travel expenses. Is less expensive than in-home interviews.	The least expensive method if there is an adequate response rate.	The most expensive survey method. Shopping mall and focus-group interviews have lower costs than in-home interviews.
Flexibility	Inflexible. The questionnaire must be short and easy for respondents to complete.	Flexible because interviewers can ask probing questions, but observations are impossible.	Less flexible. The survey must be easy for online users to receive and return; short, dichotomous, or multiple-choice questions work best.	The most flexible method. Respondents can react to visual materials. Demographic data are more accurate. In-depth probes are possible.
Interviewer bias	Interviewer bias is eliminated. Questionnaires can be returned anonymously.	Some anonymity, but it may be hard to develop trust in respondents.	Interviewer bias is often eliminated with e-mail, but an e-mail address on the return eliminates anonymity.	Interviewers' personal characteristics or inability to maintain objectivity may result in bias.
Sampling and respondents' cooperation	Obtaining a complete mailing list is difficult. Nonresponse is a major disadvantage.	Sample limited to respondents with telephones. Devices that screen calls, busy signals, and refusals are a problem.	The available e-mail address list may not be a representative sample for some purposes. Social media surveys might be skewed as fans may be more likely to take the survey.	Not-at-homes are a problem, which may be overcome by focus-group and shopping mall interviewing.

spread over a wide area and funds for the survey are limited. A mail survey is less expensive than a telephone or personal interview survey, as long as the response rate is high enough to produce reliable results.

Premiums, or incentives, that encourage respondents to return questionnaires can be effective in encouraging mail survey response rates and developing panels of respondents who are interviewed regularly. Such mail panels, selected to represent a target market or market segment, are especially useful in evaluating new products and providing general information about customers, as well as records of their purchases (in the form of purchase diaries). Mail panels and purchase diaries are much more widely used than custom mail surveys, but both panels and purchase diaries have shortcomings. People who take the time to fill out a diary may differ from the general population based on income, education, or behavior, such as the time available for shopping activities. Internet and social networking surveys have also greatly gained in popularity, although they are similarly limited—given that not all demographics utilize these media equally.

In a **telephone survey**, an interviewer records respondents' answers to a questionnaire over the phone. A telephone survey has some advantages over a mail survey. The rate of response is higher because it takes less effort to answer the telephone and talk than to fill out and return a questionnaire. If enough interviewers are available, a telephone survey can be completed very quickly. Political candidates or organizations that want an immediate reaction to an event may choose this method. In addition, a telephone survey permits interviewers to gain rapport with respondents and ask probing questions. Automated telephone surveys, also known as interactive voice response or "robosurveys," rely on a recorded voice to ask the questions while a computer program records respondents' answers. The primary benefit of automated surveys is the elimination of any bias that might be introduced by a live researcher. However, because of abuse of robosurveys during events such as political campaigns, many people have negative associations with them.

Another option is the **telephone depth interview**, which combines the traditional focus group's ability to probe with the confidentiality provided by a telephone survey. This type of interview is most appropriate for qualitative research projects among a small targeted group. This method can be appealing to busy respondents because they can choose the time and day for the interview. Although this method is difficult to implement, it can yield revealing information from respondents who otherwise would be unwilling to participate in marketing research.

A major shortcoming is that only a small proportion of the population likes to participate in telephone surveys or interviews. Many households are excluded from telephone directories by choice (unlisted numbers) or because the residents moved after the directory was published. Potential respondents often use telephone answering machines, voice mail, or caller ID to screen or block calls, Millions have also signed up for "Do Not Call Lists." Additionally, a shrinking proportion of the population has landlines, making conducting phone surveys more difficult. In fact, more than one in four homes in the U.S. has no landline at all.[12] These factors can significantly limit participation and distort representation. Moreover, surveys and interviews conducted over the telephone are limited to oral communication and cannot include visual aids or observation.

In a **personal interview survey**, participants respond to questions face-to-face. Various audiovisual aids—pictures, products, diagrams, or prerecorded advertising copy—can be incorporated into a personal interview. Rapport gained through direct interaction usually permits more in-depth interviewing, including probes, follow-up questions, or psychological tests. In addition, because personal interviews can be longer than other survey types, they may yield more information. Respondents can be selected more carefully, and reasons for nonresponse can be explored. One such research technique is the **in-home (door-to-door) interview**. The in-home interview offers a clear advantage when thoroughness of self-disclosure and elimination of group influence are important. In an in-depth interview of 45 to 90 minutes, respondents can be probed to reveal their true motivations, feelings, behaviors, and aspirations.

telephone survey A research method in which respondents' answers to a questionnaire are recorded by an interviewer on the phone

telephone depth interview An interview that combines the traditional focus group's ability to probe with the confidentiality provided by telephone surveys

personal interview survey A research method in which participants respond to survey questions face-to-face

in-home (door-to-door) interview A personal interview that takes place in the respondent's home

Over time, the nature of personal interviews has changed. In the past, most personal interviews, which were based on random sampling or prearranged appointments, were conducted in the respondent's home. Today, many personal interviews are conducted in shopping malls or other public areas. **Shopping mall intercept interviews** involve interviewing a percentage of individuals who pass by an "intercept" point in a mall. Like any face-to-face interviewing method, mall intercepts have advantages. The interviewer is in a position to recognize and react to respondents' nonverbal indications of confusion. Respondents can view product prototypes, videotapes of commercials, and other materials, and provide their opinions. Also, the mall environment lets the researcher control for complex situational variables that may be present in individuals' homes.

An **on-site computer interview** is a variation of the shopping mall intercept interview in which respondents complete a self-administered questionnaire displayed on a computer monitor. A computer software package can be used to conduct such interviews. After a brief lesson on how to operate the software, respondents proceed through the survey at their own pace. Questionnaires can be adapted so that respondents see only those items (usually a subset of an entire scale) that may provide useful information about their attitudes.

Online and Social Media Surveys As more and more consumers have Internet access and connect regularly, the Internet has become an increasingly important research and marketing resource. Internet surveys are quickly becoming the predominant tool for general population sampling, in part because of their relatively low cost and ability to target specific samples. In an **online survey**, questionnaires can be transmitted to respondents either through e-mail or via a website. Marketing researchers often send these surveys to online panel samples purchased from professional brokers or compiled by the company. E-mail is semi-interactive, meaning recipients can ask for question clarification or pose questions of their own. The potential advantages of online surveys are quick response time and lower cost than traditional mail, telephone, and personal interview surveys, if the response rate is adequate. Increasingly, firms use their websites to conduct surveys. They may include a premium, such as a chance to win a prize, to encourage participation.

Social networking sites are also used to conduct surveys. Marketers can also utilize digital media forums such as chat rooms, blogs, newsgroups, and research communities to identify trends in consumer interests and consumption patterns. However, using these forums for conducting surveys has limitations. Consumers must choose to visit a particular social media site or blog, which eliminates sample randomness, and it may be difficult to obtain a representative sample size if site traffic or participation rates are low. On the other hand, they can provide marketers with a general idea of consumer trends and preferences. Movies, consumer electronics, food, and computers are popular topics in many online communities. Indeed, by merely monitoring ongoing online conversations, marketers may be able to identify new-product opportunities and consumer needs. Free and low-cost services, such as Google Analytics, can help a firm to monitor online traffic to a website and to track whether users have linked from a social networking site, such as Pinterest. Tracking consumer conversations and movements on the Internet can help a firm better understand consumer needs and behaviors, as well as how to target them better. A major advantage of online data is that it can be gathered at little incremental cost compared to alternative data sources.

Crowdsourcing combines the words *crowd* and *outsourcing* and calls for taking tasks usually performed by a marketer or researcher and outsourcing them to a crowd, or potential market, through an open call. In the case of digital marketing, crowdsourcing is often used to obtain the opinions or needs of the crowd (or potential markets). There are entire sites dedicated to crowdsourcing. DesignCrowd.com, for instance, is a website that allows firms to crowdsource product, website, and other design projects.[13] Crowdsourcing is a way for marketers to gather input straight from willing consumers and to actively listen to people's ideas and evaluations on products.

Marketing research will likely rely heavily on online surveys in the future, particularly as negative attitudes toward other survey methods, such as telephone surveys, render them less representative and more expensive. Internet surveys have especially strong potential within

shopping mall intercept interviews A research method that involves interviewing a percentage of individuals passing by "intercept" points in a mall

on-site computer interview A variation of the shopping mall intercept interview in which respondents complete a self-administered questionnaire displayed on a computer monitor

online survey A research method in which respondents answer a questionnaire via e-mail or on a website

crowdsourcing Combines the words *crowd* and *outsourcing* and calls for taking tasks usually performed by a marketer or researcher and outsourcing them to a crowd, or potential market, through an open call

Entrepreneurship in Marketing

Baldwin& Ad Agency Does Good with Güd

When David Baldwin started Baldwin& in 2009, he set a goal of doubling the ad agency's size every year for the first five years. Three years later, his North Carolina–based agency received *Advertising Age*'s "Small Agency of the Year" award, bringing nationwide attention to its creativity and jump-starting its already rapid rate of growth.

Baldwin& uses insights gained from consumer and retailer research to develop attention-getting campaigns for clients like Burt's Bees and the BMW PGA Golf. When Burt's Bees prepared to introduce the güd (pronounced "good") brand of shampoos and skin lotions for women in the 18-to-30 age group, it worked with Target, Kroger, and Walgreens to obtain shoppers' input about fragrance preferences. These key retailers also reviewed güd's proposed packaging and provided their reactions, an

important step because of the need to make personal care products stand out on store shelves.

For the launch, Baldwin& created a digital-heavy campaign based on its knowledge of the target market's usage of social media and cell phones. In addition to quick response (QR) codes on packaging for obtaining more product information using smartphones, the agency arranged for coupons and free samples to be distributed to Facebook users who clicked to "like" the brand. To highlight the brand's personality, the agency prepared YouTube videos focusing on the unique fragrances and posted clever tweets about the new products. The engaging campaign not only attracted customers for güd, it attracted inquiries from potential clients for Baldwin&.[b]

organizations whose employees are networked and for associations that publish members' e-mail addresses. However, there are some ethical issues to consider when using e-mail for marketing research, such as unsolicited e-mail, which could be viewed as "spam," and privacy, as some survey respondents fear their personal information will be given or sold to third parties without their knowledge or permission. Some firms are Internet experts and can help firms conduct online primary research in ways that receive less backlash. C+R Research is one of these firms, as you can see in the advertisement. C+R has experience helping companies gather online qualitative data from a variety of sources, including large consumer panels, in-depth discussions, diaries, online chats, and video journals. Firms like this can help marketing researchers better leverage all of the data available online when conducting research.

A serious challenge for firms conducting online surveys is obtaining a sample that is representative of the population. While Internet surveys allow respondents to retain their anonymity and flexibility, it can also enable survey takers to abuse the system. For instance, some survey takers respond multiple times or pose as other people, particularly when the survey pays or offers a reward to respondents. To get around this problem, companies are developing screening mechanisms and instituting limits on how many surveys one person can take.[14] Survey programs, such as Qualtrics, automatically delete surveys that appear suspicious.

Questionnaire Construction A carefully constructed questionnaire is essential to the success of any survey. Questions must be clear, easy to understand, and directed toward a specific objective, meaning they must be designed to elicit information that meets the study's data requirements. Defining the objective of a questionnaire before construction will provide a guide to the substance of the questions and ensure that they yield useful information that contributes to the research project. The most important rule in composing questions is to maintain impartiality.

The questions are usually of three kinds: open-ended, dichotomous, and multiple-choice. Open-ended questions should be used carefully, as it is very difficult to code the responses in such a way as to easily analyze the data later. Problems may develop in the analysis of dichotomous or multiple-choice questions when responses for one outcome outnumber others. For example, a dichotomous question that asks respondents to choose between "buy" or "not buy" might require additional sampling from the disproportionately smaller group if there were not enough responses to analyze.[15] Researchers must also be very careful about questions that a respondent might consider too personal or that might require an admission of activities that other people are likely to condemn. Researchers must word questions carefully so as not to offend respondents.

Observation Methods When observing subjects of a research sample, researchers record individuals' overt behavior, taking note of physical conditions and events. They avoid direct contact with subjects and instead monitor their actions systematically. For instance, researchers might use observation methods to answer the question, "How long does the average McDonald's restaurant customer have to wait in line before being served?" Observation may include the use of ethnographic techniques, such as watching customers interact with a product in a real-world environment. Observation may also be combined with interviews. For instance, during a personal interview, the condition of a respondent's home or other possessions may be observed and recorded. The interviewer can also directly observe and confirm such demographic information as race, approximate age, and gender.

Data gathered through observation can sometimes be biased if the subject is aware of the observation process and adapts his or her behavior accordingly. However, a researcher can place an observer in a natural market environment, such as a grocery store, without influencing shoppers' actions. If the presence of a human observer is likely to bias the outcome or if human sensory abilities are inadequate, mechanical means may be used to record behavior. Mechanical observation devices include cameras, recorders, counting machines, scanners, and equipment that records physiological changes. A special camera can be used to record the eye movements of people as they look at an advertisement. The camera detects the sequence of reading and the parts of the advertisement that receive the greatest attention. The electronic scanners used in supermarkets are another mechanical means of gathering observational data. They provide accurate data on sales and customers' purchase patterns. In many cases, marketing researchers are able to buy the data from stores. Retailers such as Target have turned observation into a science, keeping vast databases of all individual shoppers' purchases and demographic information in order to assemble an aggregate overview of their shoppers, as well as a complete picture of each individual customer's lifestyle, habits, and product needs and how they change over time.[16]

Observation is straightforward and avoids a central problem of survey methods: motivating respondents to state their true feelings or opinions. However, observation tends to be descriptive and may not provide insights into causal relationships. Another drawback is that analyses based on observation are subject to the observer's biases or the limitations of the device being used.

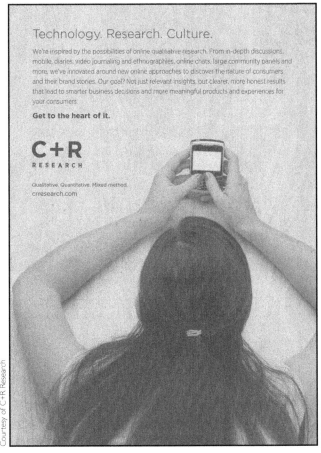

Courtesy of C+R Research

Online and Social Media Surveys
Firms like C+R Research can help marketing researchers learn about and leverage all the tools available on the Internet that assist with gathering the kind of qualitative research on consumers that leads to better marketing strategies.

Interpreting Research Findings

After collecting data to test their hypotheses, marketers need to interpret the research findings. Interpretation of the data is easier if marketers carefully plan their data analysis methods early in the research process. They should allow for continual evaluation of the data during the entire collection period. In this way, marketers gain valuable insights into areas that should be probed during the formal analysis.

ANALYTICS

Know what's hot.

The topic of analytics is on fire right now. With SAS, you can discover innovative ways to increase profits, reduce risk, predict trends and turn data assets into competitive advantage. Decide with confidence.

Scan the QR code* with your mobile device to view a video or visit sas.com/know for a free Harvard Business Review report.

§.sas

THE POWER TO KNOW.

*Requires reader app to be installed on your mobile device

Courtesy of SAS Institute

Statistical Interpretation
SAS is a major producer of analytics software, which can assist a firm with data analysis and interpretation—an essential element of drawing the correct conclusions on which to build a firm's marketing strategy.

In most cases, the first step researchers will take is to assemble the data into a table format. Cross-tabulation may be useful, especially in tabulating joint occurrences, for data that will be used across categories of things or people studied. For example, using the two variables of gender and purchase rates of automobile tires, a cross-tabulation will show how men and women differ in purchasing automobile tires.

After the data are tabulated, they must be analyzed. **Statistical interpretation** focuses on what is typical and what deviates from the average. It indicates how widely responses vary and how they are distributed in relation to the variable being measured. When marketers interpret statistics, they must take into account estimates of expected error or deviation from the true values of the population. The analysis of data may lead researchers to accept or reject their hypothesis. Data require careful interpretation and a firm may choose to enlist an expert consultant or computer software to ensure accuracy. In a marketing environment increasingly filled with data, errors are possible and it is ever more important to interpret data correctly. Look at the advertisement for SAS, a leading producer of business analytics software. This advertisement underscores the importance of correct data analysis in this ad with an image of chili peppers and the phrase "Analytics. Know what's hot." If a researcher improperly analyzes data, he or she could reach the wrong conclusion, leading to a cascade of effects that might render a marketing strategy useless. Because so many firms engage in high-tech analysis, a firm must take steps to ensure that it has competitive tools at its disposal.

If the results of a study are valid, the decision maker should take action. If a question has been incorrectly or poorly worded, however, the results may produce poor decisions. Consider the research conducted for a food marketer that asked respondents to rate a product on criteria such as "hearty flavor," as well as how important each criterion was to the respondent. Although such results may have had utility for advertising purposes, they are less helpful in product development because it is not possible to objectively determine a meaning for the subjective phrase "hearty flavor." Managers must understand the research results and relate them to a context that permits effective decision making.

Reporting Research Findings

The final step in the marketing research process is to report the research findings. Before preparing the report, the marketer must objectively analyze the findings to determine whether the research is as complete as it can be and how well the data answer the research question and support or negate the hypothesis. Most research will not have answered the research question completely. Thus, the researcher must point out deficiencies and their causes in the report. While writing, researchers must keep the report's audience in mind and ensure that findings are relevant to the firm. They should also determine before writing how much detail and supporting data to include. Research is not useful unless it supports the organization's overall strategy and objectives.

If an outside research agency was contracted, it is important that it fully understand the client's business. Those responsible for preparing the report must facilitate adjusting the findings to the environment, as it can change over time. The report must be helpful to marketers and managers on an ongoing basis.[17]

statistical interpretation
Analysis of what is typical and what deviates from the average

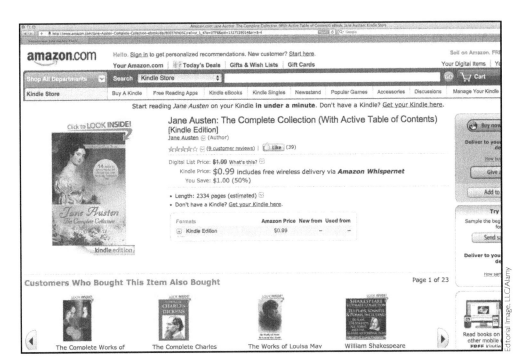

Editorial Image, LLC/Alamy

Using Technology
Amazon and other online retailers have developed technology that makes recommendations to a customer for books or movies that he or she might like based on prior purchases.

The report is usually a formal, written document. Researchers must allocate sufficient time when they plan and schedule the project for compiling and writing it, since this task can be time-consuming. Report writers should keep in mind that corporate executives prefer reports that are short, clear, and simply expressed. To address this desire, researchers often give their recommendations first, in an executive summary, followed by details on how the results were obtained. This way, executives can easily see the results of the report without spending time on the details. A technical report allows its users to analyze data and interpret recommendations because it describes the research methods and procedures and the most important data gathered. Thus, researchers must recognize the needs and expectations of the report user and adapt to them.

USING TECHNOLOGY TO IMPROVE MARKETING INFORMATION GATHERING AND ANALYSIS

LO4. Understand how technology is used to facilitate information gathering and analysis.

Technology and the Internet have made the information required for marketing decisions more accessible than ever. Marketers can easily track customer buying behavior, obtain detailed demographic profiles, and anticipate what buyers want—making it possible to fine-tune marketing mixes to satisfy customers. Information technology permits for easy internal research and quick information gathering to help marketers better understand and satisfy customers. CRM has been enhanced by the ability to integrate and access data from all customer contacts.

Consumer feedback is an important aspect of marketing research, and new technology has enhanced this process. Most consumers read online product reviews on a myriad of sites, from Amazon to Yelp!, when making purchase decisions. While this represents a tremendous opportunity for firms to generate new customers, they must also be aware of fake product reviews and the potentially negative effect they can have on consumer perception. Increasingly, too, while consumers utilize product reviews, they are also wary of them; companies recently have been found guilty of paying people to write positive reviews of products and services, claiming to be unbiased customers.[18] Thus, as with any other resource, firms must manage digital resources with caution to maintain a high level of consumer trust and satisfaction.

Finally, companies of all sizes have unprecedented access to industry forecasts, business trends, and customer buying behavior—which improves communication, understanding of the marketing environment, and marketing research capabilities. Many firms use marketing information systems, CRM technologies, and cloud computing to network technologies and organize the marketing data available to them. In this section, we look at marketing information systems and specific technologies that are helping marketing researchers obtain and manage marketing research data.

Marketing Information Systems

A **marketing information system (MIS)** is a framework for the day-to-day management and structuring of information gathered regularly from sources both inside and outside the organization. As such, an MIS provides a continuous flow of information about prices, advertising expenditures, sales, competition, and distribution expenses and can be an important asset for developing effective marketing strategies. The main focuses of an MIS are on data storage and retrieval, as well as on computer capabilities and management's information requirements. MIS can help with producing regular sales reports by product or market categories, data on inventory levels, and records of salespeople's activities, which can all help in marketing decision making.

An effective MIS starts by determining the objective of the information—that is, by identifying decision needs that require certain information. The firm then specifies an information system for continuous monitoring to provide regular, pertinent information on both the external and internal environment. Shipping companies such as FedEx have interactive marketing information systems that provide instantaneous communication between the company and customers. Customers can track their packages via the Internet and receive immediate feedback concerning delivery. The company's website provides researchers with information about customer usage and allows customers to convey opinions on company services. The evolving telecommunications and computer technologies allow marketers to use information systems to cultivate one-to-one relationships with customers.

marketing information system (MIS) A framework for managing and structuring information gathered regularly from sources inside and outside the organization

---

Emerging Trends

The Billboard of the Future

Traditionally, when a person looks at a billboard, information goes one way: from billboard to consumer. However, new marketing research technology now allows information to go two ways. The consumer collects information from the billboard's message, and the billboard in turn collects information about the consumer.

In Japan, digital billboards have been invented that estimate a consumer's age and gender. Based on the estimated age and gender, the display then creates advertising tailored to the appropriate demographic. An East Japan Railway subsidiary introduced vending machines with this technology that use information gleaned from consumers to suggest drinks.

Similar billboards are appearing across the world. In the United States, marketers are creating displays that

recognize gestures and facial expressions of consumers. This data can determine whether the consumer is actually looking at the display. For marketers, the technology can help them understand who is attracted to their messages and perhaps create customized messages for each consumer based upon this data collection. However, privacy advocates are wary of this technology. They fear that it can be misused to identify people, a violation of individual privacy. So far there is little regulation to limit how marketers will use information collected from billboards. As this technology becomes more popular, clearer laws will be needed to allow marketers to gather information without abusing consumer privacy.[c]

Databases

Most marketing information systems include internal databases. A **database** is a collection of information arranged for easy access and retrieval. Databases allow marketers to tap into an abundance of information useful in making marketing decisions—internal sales reports, newspaper articles, company news releases, government economic reports, and bibliographies—often accessed through a computer system.

Improvements in information technology have made it possible for firms to develop databases that are vastly enhanced in their speed and storage capacity, to guide strategic planning and improve customer service. For instance, think about the advertisement for the SAP HANA database. It uses 21st-century technology to consolidate all the data contained in a database in order to speed processing and to allow a firm to retrieve answers more quickly. The HANA database model reduces redundancies and makes it easier for marketers to retrieve the information that they need to make sound marketing decisions and improve customer relationship marketing.

Customer relationship management (CRM) employs database marketing techniques to identify different types of customers and develop specific strategies for interacting with each customer. CRM incorporates these three elements:

1. Identifying and building a database of current and potential consumers, including a wide range of demographic, lifestyle, and purchase information.
2. Delivering differential messages according to each consumer's preferences and characteristics through established and new media channels.
3. Tracking customer relationships to monitor the costs of retaining individual customers and the lifetime value of their purchases.[19]

Nearly all firms collect customer information in databases. For instance, many commercial websites require consumers to register and provide personal information before accessing

Courtesy of SAP America, Inc.

Databases
SAP produces a revolutionary database, called HANA, which reduces information redundancies, improves speed, and makes marketing decision making more efficient and accurate.

database A collection of information arranged for easy access and retrieval

the site or making a purchase. Frequent-flyer programs ask loyal customers to participate in surveys about their needs and desires and to track their best customers' flight patterns by time of day, week, month, and year. Supermarkets frequently offer store discount cards, which allow them to gain consumer data on purchases through checkout scanners.

Marketing researchers can also use databases, such as LexisNexis or online commercial databases, for a fee, to obtain useful information for marketing decisions. To find research within a database, a user typically searches by keyword, topic, or company, and the database service generates abstracts, articles, or reports. Information provided by a single firm on household demographics, purchases, television viewing behavior, and responses to promotions such as coupons and free samples is called **single-source data**. For example, BehaviorScan, offered by SymphonyIRI Group, screens the television and purchasing habits of markets with populations between 75,000 and 215,000.[20] It is important that marketers gather longitudinal (long-term) information on customers to maximize the usefulness of single-source data.

Marketing Decision Support Systems

A **marketing decision support system (MDSS)** is customized computer software that aids marketing managers in decision making by helping them anticipate the effects of certain decisions. An MDSS has a broader range and offers greater computational and modeling capabilities than spreadsheets and lets managers explore a broad range of alternatives. For instance, an MDSS can determine how sales and profits might be affected by higher or lower interest rates or how sales forecasts, advertising expenditures, or production levels might affect overall profits. For this reason, MDSS software is often a major component of a company's MIS. Some decision support systems incorporate artificial intelligence and other advanced computer technologies.

LO5. Identify key ethical and international considerations in marketing research.

ISSUES IN MARKETING RESEARCH

Marketers should identify and be aware of concerns that can influence the integrity of research, such as ethical issues and the international environment. Ethical issues are a constant risk in gathering and maintaining consistently high-quality information. International issues relate to environmental differences, such as culture, legal requirements, level of technology, and economic development.

The Importance of Ethical Marketing Research

Marketing managers and other professionals increasingly rely on marketing research, marketing information systems, and new technologies to make better decisions. Therefore, it is essential that professional standards be established by which to judge the reliability of marketing research. Such standards are necessary because of the ethical and legal issues that can develop in gathering marketing research data. For example, many consumers are wary of how their personal information collected by marketers will be used, especially whether it will be sold to third parties.

It is important that marketers remain ethical at all times, to retain consumer and stakeholder trust and a positive reputation. To provide standards and guidelines, organizations such as the Marketing Research Association have developed codes of conduct and guidelines that promote ethical marketing research. To be effective, such guidelines must instruct marketing researchers on how to avoid misconduct. Table 4.4 provides sample steps researchers should follow when introducing a questionnaire to a customer in order to ensure respondent cooperation and satisfaction.

As increasing amounts of personal information can be found online, consumer privacy remains a significant issue. Firms have the ability to purchase tremendous amounts of detailed data on customer demographics, interests, and more personal matters such as bankruptcy

single-source data Information provided by a single marketing research firm

marketing decision support system (MDSS) Customized computer software that aids marketing managers in decision making

Table 4.4   Guidelines for Questionnaire Introduction

- Allow interviewers to introduce themselves by name.

- State the name of the research company.

- Indicate that this questionnaire is a marketing research project.

- Explain that no sales will be involved.

- Note the general topic of discussion (if this is a problem in a "blind" study, a statement such as "consumer opinion" is acceptable).

- State the likely duration of the interview.

- Assure the anonymity of the respondent and the confidentiality of all answers.

- State the honorarium, if applicable (for many business-to-business and medical studies, this is done up-front for both qualitative and quantitative studies).

- Reassure the respondent with a statement such as, "There are no right or wrong answers, so please give thoughtful and honest answers to each question" (recommended by many clients).

Source: Reprinted with the permission of The Marketing Research Association.

filings and past marriages. This information has allowed companies to predict customer behavior and life changes more accurately, but many feel it infringes upon consumer privacy.[21] For instance, when consumers visit retail sites online, companies collect data on their purchases and what they view. Many companies use this to their advantage. For instance, Amazon, Netflix, and eBay all use data to provide customized recommendations based on customers' interests, ratings, or past purchases. Companies such as Capital One Financial use data collected by firms that specialize in tracking consumers' online behavior. While such data enable companies to offer more personalized services, policy makers fear that it could also allow them to discriminate against consumers who do not appear to be "valuable" customers.[22] Many consumers also believe that their online behavior could be used to identify them personally. Google, for instance, collects and stores data from individual users' searches. These search queries are kept indefinitely, although Google claims that the data is "anonymized" after 18 months.[23]

International Issues in Marketing Research

As we shall see in Chapter 8, sociocultural, economic, political, legal, and technological forces vary in different regions of the world. These variations create challenges for the organizations that are attempting to understand foreign customers through marketing research. While the marketing research process is generally the same around the world, some regional differences exist. To make certain that firms are sufficiently aware of global and regional differences, many companies retain a research firm, or at least a researcher, with experience in the country of interest. Most of the largest marketing research firms derive a significant share of their revenues from research conducted outside the United States. For example, the Nielsen Company, the largest marketing research firm in the world, is a U.S. company but has a market presence in over 100 different countries.[24]

Experts recommend a two-pronged approach to conducting international marketing research. The first phase involves a detailed search for and analysis of secondary data to gain a greater understanding of a particular marketing environment and to pinpoint key regional issues that could affect primary research data. Secondary data can be particularly helpful in building

International Issues
Firms such as Intage can help researchers gain an insider perspective on new international markets through local consultants and international experience.

a general understanding of the market, including economic, legal, cultural, and demographic issues, as well as in assessing the opportunities and risks of doing business in that market, and in forecasting demand. Marketing researchers often begin by gaining a general overview through country trade reports from the U.S. Department of Commerce, trade and general business publications such as *The Wall Street Journal,* and country-specific publications and websites. These sources can offer insights into a country's marketing environment and might indicate untapped market opportunities.

The second phase involves field research using many of the methods described earlier, including focus groups and telephone surveys, to refine a firm's understanding of specific customer needs and preferences. Differences between countries can have a profound influence on data-gathering techniques. For instance, in-home (door-to-door) interviews are illegal in some places. In developing countries, many people only have cell phones, making telephone surveys less practical and less representative of the total population. Primary data gathering generally will have a greater chance of success if the firm employs local researchers who understand how to approach potential respondents and can do so in their own languages.[25]

Some firms specialize in international marketing research, such as Intage, which is featured in the advertisement. Intage guarantees insider knowledge of Asia, particularly the region's countries, customs, and people. Intage promises to provide firms with local experts on any country a company seeks to enter. This type of insider knowledge can be of critical importance to a firm conducting marketing research in a region such as Asia, particularly for a Western firm that is based in a very different cultural environment. Without it, a firm will have little direction on how to develop a marketing strategy that will be effective. Regardless of the specific methods used to gather primary data, whether in the United States or abroad, the goal is to recognize the needs of specific target markets to craft the best possible marketing strategy to satisfy the needs of customers in each market, as we will see in the next chapter.

Chapter Review

1. Gain perspective on the importance of marketing research.

Marketing research is a critical step in developing a marketing strategy. It is the systematic design, collection, interpretation, and reporting of information to help marketers solve specific marketing problems or take advantage of marketing opportunities. It is a process for gathering information not currently available to decision makers. Marketing research can help a firm better understand market opportunities,

ascertain the potential for success of new products, and determine the feasibility of a particular marketing strategy. The value of marketing research is measured by improvements in a marketer's ability to make decisions.

To maintain the control needed to obtain accurate information, marketers approach marketing research as a process with some basic logical steps: (1) locating and defining problems or issues, (2) designing the research project, (3) collecting data, (4) interpreting research findings, and (5) reporting research findings.

2. Differentiate between the two major types of marketing research—exploratory and conclusive research.

Marketers conduct exploratory research when they need more information about a problem or want to make a tentative hypothesis more specific. It can help marketers better understand how consumers view a topic or a product, which can help a firm develop better products and more targeted marketing mixes. The main purpose of exploratory research is to better understand a problem or situation and/or to help identify additional data needs or decision alternatives.

Conclusive research, on the other hand, is used to verify insights through an objective procedure. It is used in the final stages of decision making, when the marketer has narrowed his or her decision down to a few alternatives.

3. Describe the basic steps in conducting marketing research.

The first step in launching a research study, problem or issue definition, focuses on uncovering the nature and boundaries of a situation or question related to marketing strategy or implementation. When a firm discovers a market opportunity, it may need to conduct research to understand the situation more precisely so it can craft an appropriate marketing strategy.

In the second step, marketing researchers design a research project to obtain the information needed to address it. This step requires formulating a hypothesis and determining what type of research to employ to test the hypothesis so the results are reliable and valid. A hypothesis is an informed guess or assumption about a problem or set of circumstances. Research is considered reliable if it produces almost identical results in repeated trials. It is valid if it measures what it is supposed to measure.

For the third step of the research process, collecting data, two types of data are available. Primary data are observed and recorded or collected directly from respondents. Secondary data are compiled inside or outside the organization for some purpose other than the current investigation. Sources of secondary data include an organization's own database and other internal sources, periodicals, government publications, unpublished sources, and online databases. Methods of collecting primary data include sampling, surveys, observation, and experimentation. Sampling involves selecting representative units from a total population. In probability sampling, every element in the population being studied has a known chance of being selected

for study. Nonprobability sampling is more subjective than probability sampling because there is no way to calculate the likelihood that a specific element of the population being studied will be chosen. Marketing researchers employ sampling to collect primary data through mail, telephone, online, or personal interview surveys. A carefully-constructed questionnaire is essential to the success of any survey. In using observation methods, researchers record respondents' overt behavior and take note of physical conditions and events. In an experiment, marketing researchers attempt to maintain certain variables while measuring the effects of experimental variables.

To apply research data to decision making, marketers must interpret and report their findings—the final two steps in the marketing research process. Statistical interpretation focuses on what is typical or what deviates from the average. After interpreting the research findings, the researchers must prepare a report on the findings that the decision makers can understand and use. Researchers must also take care to avoid bias and distortion.

4. Understand how technology is used to facilitate information gathering and analysis.

Technology is essential to effective information gathering and analysis. Firms that do not utilize up-to-date technological tools are at a disadvantage. Many firms use technology to create a marketing information system (MIS), a framework for managing and structuring information gathered regularly from sources both inside and outside the organization. A database is a collection of information arranged for easy access and retrieval. A marketing decision support system (MDSS) is customized computer software that aids marketing managers in decision making by helping them anticipate the effects of certain decisions. Online information services and the Internet also enable marketers to communicate with customers and obtain information.

5. Identify key ethical and international considerations in marketing research.

Eliminating unethical marketing research practices and establishing generally acceptable procedures for conducting research are important goals of marketing research. Both domestic and international marketing use the same marketing research process, but international marketing may require modifying data-gathering methods to address regional differences.

Go to www.cengagebrain.com for resources to help you master the content in this chapter as well as materials that will expand your marketing knowledge!

Key Concepts

marketing research 87
exploratory research 89
customer advisory
  boards 89
focus group 89
conclusive research 90
descriptive research 90
experimental research 90
research design 92
hypothesis 92
reliability 93

validity 93
primary data 93
secondary data 93
population 96
sample 96
sampling 96
probability sampling 96
random sampling 96
stratified sampling 97
nonprobability
  sampling 97

quota sampling 97
mail survey 97
telephone survey 98
telephone depth
  interview 98
personal interview
  survey 98
in-home (door-to-door)
  interview 98
shopping mall intercept
  interview 99

on-site computer
  interview 99
online survey 99
crowdsourcing 99
statistical interpretation 102
marketing information
  system (MIS) 104
database 105
single-source data 106
marketing decision support
  system (MDSS) 106

Issues for Discussion and Review

1. What is marketing research? Why is it important?
2. Describe the five steps in the marketing research process.
3. What is the difference between defining a research problem and developing a hypothesis?
4. Describe the different types of approaches to marketing research, and indicate when each should be used.
5. Where are data for marketing research obtained? Give examples of internal and external data.
6. What is the difference between probability sampling and nonprobability sampling? In what situation would random sampling be best? Stratified sampling? Quota sampling?
7. Suggest some ways to encourage respondents to cooperate in mail surveys.

8. If a survey of all homes with listed telephone numbers is to be conducted, what sampling design should be used?
9. Describe some marketing problems that could be solved through information gained from observation.
10. What is a marketing information system, and what should it provide?
11. Define a database. What is its purpose, and what does it include?
12. How can marketers use online services and the Internet to obtain information for decision making?
13. What role do ethics play in marketing research? Why is it important that marketing researchers be ethical?
14. How does marketing research in other countries differ from marketing research in the United States?

Marketing Applications

1. Suppose you are opening a health insurance brokerage firm and want to market your services to small businesses with fewer than 50 employees. Determine the information you must pull from your database and analyze in order to pursue your marketing efforts. What variables did you select and why?
2. After observing customers' traffic patterns, Bashas' Markets repositioned the greeting card section in its stores, and card sales increased substantially. To increase sales for the following types of companies, what

information might marketing researchers want to gather from customers?
a. Furniture stores
b. Gasoline outlet service stations
c. Investment companies
d. Medical clinics

3. When a company wants to conduct research, it must first identify a problem or possible opportunity to market its goods or services. Choose a company in your city

that you think might benefit from a research project. Develop a research question and outline a method to approach this question. Explain why you think the research question is relevant to the organization and why the particular methodology is suited to the question and the company.

4. Input for marketing information systems can come from internal or external sources. Nielsen Corporation is the largest provider of single-source marketing research in the world. Identify two firms in your city that might benefit from internal sources and two that might benefit from external sources. Explain why these sources would be useful to these companies. Suggest the type of information each company should gather.

5. You work as a marketing researcher for a manufacturer of energy drinks. Your company is designing a new product that will be targeted at college and university students. In order to learn more about energy drink consumption habits, the company plans to conduct a survey of the target market. After conducting some research, you determine that the best survey method that fits your firm's budget is a mail survey. You know from past experience that the response rate for mail surveys is approximately 10 percent. Your manager tells you that he wants at least 550 completed surveys in order to make an informed decision. You also know that approximately 14 percent of respondents who mail surveys back to you fail to answer certain questions. Given the low response rate and the rate of unfinished surveys, how large will the sample size need to be to comply with your manager's request? With this estimated response rate and the number of surveys that the company plans to distribute, do you feel that this sample will be representative of the entire population of college and university students?

6. Develop your analytical and communication skills using the Role-Play Exercises online at **www.cengagebrain.com**.

Internet Exercise

ESOMAR

ESOMAR, the European Society for Opinion and Marketing Research, was founded in 1948. It is a non-profit association for marketing research professionals. ESOMAR promotes the use of opinion and marketing research to improve marketing decisions in companies worldwide and works to protect personal privacy in the research process. Visit the association's website at **www.esomar.org**.

1. How can ESOMAR help marketing professionals conduct research to guide marketing strategy?

2. How can ESOMAR help marketers to protect the privacy of research subjects when conducting marketing research in other countries?

3. ESOMAR introduced the first professional code of conduct for marketing research professionals in 1948. The association continues to update the document to address new technology and other changes in the marketing environment. According to ESOMAR's code, what are the specific professional responsibilities of marketing researchers?

developing your marketing plan

Decisions about which market opportunities to pursue, what customer needs to satisfy, and how to reach potential customers are not made in a vacuum. The information provided by marketing research activities is essential in developing both the strategic plan and the specific marketing mix. Focus on the following issues as you relate the concepts in this chapter to the development of your marketing plan.

1. Define the nature and scope of the questions you must answer with regard to your market. Identify the types of information you will need about the market to answer those questions. For example, do you need to know about the buying habits, household income levels, or attitudes of potential customers?

2. Determine whether or not this information can be obtained from secondary sources. Visit the websites

provided in Table 4.3 as possible resources for the secondary data.

3. Using Table 4.4, choose the appropriate survey method(s) you would use to collect primary data for one of your information needs. What sampling method would you use?

The information obtained from these questions should assist you in developing various aspects of your marketing plan. Develop your marketing plan online using the Interactive Marketing Plan at **www.cengagebrain.com**.

video case 4.1

Marketing Research Reveals Marketing Opportunities in the Baby Boomer Generation

For many years, marketers have focused upon consumers between the ages of 18 and 34 to promote products. Marketers feel that wooing consumers early in life will ensure that they become lifetime loyal customers. While this seems logical, research is revealing that Baby Boomers might be a more profitable demographic. Statistics show that while spending for Millennials is actually shrinking, Baby Boomer spending has been increasing. Baby Boomers are estimated to have $3.4 trillion in annual buying power.

The Baby Boomer generation is vastly different from the generations preceding it. Baby Boomers desire to have a variety of products available to them. Many of the products traditionally thought to belong to the younger generation are actually bought the most by older generations, such as cars and technological products. With approximately 20 percent of the U.S. population estimated to be 65 years or older by 2030, marketers are beginning to research better ways for marketing to Baby Boomers.

In one study researchers attempted to understand how older consumers shop and interact in stores. Because store marketers often target younger generations of consumers, little thought has been given to how accessible these stores are for older generations. The research design involved equipping a person with gloves, neck braces, helmets, blurry goggles, and other equipment to simulate how a person in his or her 70s with arthritis is feeling. Researchers would then observe how the person takes items off of shelves, gets into his or her car, and gets up from chairs.

This research has been shared with many businesses, who have interpreted the findings to create a retail environment better suited to this demographic. CVS, for instance, has lowered its shelves, made its store lighting softer, and installed magnifying glasses for hard-to-read labels. Other businesses are using this information to redesign their products. Diamond Foods Inc., for example, has designed the packaging of its Emerald snack nuts to be easier to open, a great help for older consumers whose hands become less mobile as they age. The company also studied consumers with arthritis and decreased the time it takes to rotate the caps to open its products.

Additionally, Baby Boomers have created an opportunity for businesses to market entirely new products. Baby Boomers tend to embrace fitness and exercise regimens as a way to stay fit and prolong their lives. Technology firms are seeing an opportunity to develop products to be installed in the homes of older consumers. These products monitor the movements of the inhabitants and alert family or experts if there are any changes in the inhabitants' movements. A decrease in mobility could signal a change in the person's physical and mental state, which may require medical attention. Although these devices might otherwise seem intrusive, Baby Boomers' desires to stay healthy and prolong life are increasing their demand. Many Baby Boomers are also concerned with preserving their more youthful appearance. Lingerie maker Maidenform has created shapewear, or clothes that help to "tone" the body, targeted toward those ages 35 to 54.

There is one description that marketers must avoid when marketing to Baby Boomers: any words or phrases that make them feel old. Marketing research has revealed that Baby Boomers do not like to be reminded that they are aging. Therefore, many marketing initiatives aimed at older consumers must be subtle. For this reason, Diamond Foods does not market the fact that its packages are easier to open because it does not want to make Baby Boomers feel aged. Even marketers of products that are for older people have overhauled their promotional campaigns to focus less on the concept of aging. Kimberly-Clark's Depend brand for incontinence was widely regarded as "adult diapers." This negative connotation led many to avoid them. To try to counteract this view, Kimberly-Clark released commercials that discussed the benefits of the product but also tried to "de-myth" the brand by discussing its similarity in look and feel to

underwear. Many other businesses that sell similar products are following suit.

Although marketers have long focused on Millennials, the demand for products by Baby Boomers is changing the ways that businesses market to consumers. Marketing research is key to understanding the Baby Boomer demographic and creating the goods and services that best meet their needs.[26]

Questions for Discussion

1. Why are Baby Boomers such a lucrative market?
2. How has the marketing research process been used to understand how Baby Boomers shop and interact in stores?
3. How have stores used marketing research findings to tailor their stores and products to appeal to Baby Boomers?

NOTES

[1] Based on information in "Legos for Girls Sell at Twice the Expected Volume," *New Haven Register*, January 5, 2013, http://nhregister.com; Dan Milmo, "Lego's 'Sexist' Friends Range for Girls Spurs 35% Profit Rise," *Guardian (U.K.)*, August 31, 2012, www.guardian.co.uk; Brad Wieners, "Lego Is for Girls," *Bloomberg Businessweek*, December 14, 2011, www.businessweek.com; "Lego Bucks Toy Slump," *Wall Street Journal*, December 19, 2012, www.wsj.com; www.lego.com.

[2] Lilly Vitorovich, Retailers to Ring Up Sales Via Mobile, January 23, 2013, http://blogs.wsj.com/tech-europe/2013/01/23/retailers-to-ring-up-sales-via-mobile-marketing.

[3] "Fashion Retailer: Helping Increase Sales and Website Traffic Project Snapshot," Accenture, www.accenture.com/us-en/Pages/success-fashion-retailer-helping-increase-sales-website-traffic.aspx (accessed January 27. 2013).

[4] Dhruv Grewal Parasuraman and R. Krishnan, *Marketing Research* (Boston: Houghton Mifflin, 2007).

[5] Keith Bradsher, "Next Made-in-China Boom: College Graduates," *New York Times*, January 17, 2013, www.nytimes.com/2013/01/17/business/chinas-ambitious-goal-for-boom-in-college-graduates.html.

[6] Press release, "Top Corporate and Government Leaders in Risk Management and Cybersecurity Highlight Key Themes for 2013 at Modulo's

First International Executive Customer Conference," MarketWatch, January 11, 2013, www.marketwatch.com/story/top-corporate-and-government-leaders-in-risk-management-and-cybersecurity-highlight-key-themes-for-2013-at-modulos-first-international-executive-customer-conference-2013-01-11.

[7] Daniel Gross, "Lies, Damn Lies, and Focus Groups," *Slate*, October 10, 2003, www.slate.com/articles/business/moneybox/2003/10/lies_damn_lies_and_focus_groups.html (accessed February 3, 2013).

[8] Bryn Nelson, "Marketing Plan: Solve a Problem, Then Spread the Word," *New York Times*, April 11, 2012, http://green.blogs.nytimes.com/2012/04/11/marketing-plan-solve-a-problem-then-spread-the-word/ (accessed January 27, 2013).

[9] Vikas Mittal and Wagner A. Kamakura, "Satisfaction, Repurchase Intent, and Repurchase Behavior: Investigating the Moderating Effects of Customer Characteristics," *Journal of Marketing Research* (February 2001): 131–142.

[10] Melinda F. Emerson, "Using Social Media to Test Your Idea Before You Try to Sell It," *New York Times*, August 3, 2012, http://boss.blogs.nytimes.com/2012/08/03/using-social-media-to-test-your-idea-before-you-try-to-sell-it/ (accessed January 27, 2013).

[11] Robert M. Graves, "Nonresponse Rate and Nonresponse Bias in Household Surveys," *Public

Opinion Quarterly*, 2006, 70(5), 646–675, http://poq.oxfordjournals.org/content/70/5/646.ful (accessed February 3, 2013).

[12] Mike Snider, "More People Ditching Home Phone for Mobile," *USA Today*, April 20, 2011, http://usatoday30.usatoday.com/tech/news/2011-04-20-cellphone-study.htm (accessed January 26, 2013).

[13] DesignCrowd, www.designcrowd.com, accessed January 27, 2013.

[14] Sue Shellenbarger, "A Few Bucks for Your Thoughts?" *Wall Street Journal*, May 18, 2011, http://online.wsj.com/article/SB10001424052748703509104576329110724411724.html (accessed January 27, 2013).

[15] Bas Donkers, Philip Hans Franses, and Peter C. Verhoef, "Selective Sampling for Binary Choice Models," *Journal of Marketing Research* (November 2003): 492–497.

[16] Charles Duhigg, "How Companies Learn Your Secrets," *The New York Times*, February 19, 2012, www.nytimes.com/2012/02/19/magazine/shopping-habits.html (accessed January 26, 2013).

[17] Piet Levy, "10 Minutes with…Gregory A. Reid," *Marketing News*, February 28, 2010, 34.

[18] Mike Deri Smith, "Fake Reviews Plague Consumer Websites," *The Guardian*, January 26, 2013, www.guardian.co.uk/money/2013/jan/26/fake-reviews-plague-consumer-websites.

[19] David Aaker, V. Kumar, George Day, and Robert Lane, *Marketing Research*, 10th ed. (New York: Wiley & Sons, 2010).

[20] *BehaviorScan® Testing*, 2013, www.symphonyiri .com/LinkClick.aspx? fileticket=da0Vpb7a728%3D&tabid=348 (accessed January 26, 2013).

[21] Chares Duhigg, "How Companies Learn Your Secrets," *The New York Times*, February 15, 2012, www.nytimes.com/2012/02/19/magazine/ shopping-habits.html (accessed January 27, 2013).

[22] Emily Steel and Julia Angwin, "The Web's Cutting Edge, Anonymity in Name Only," *The Wall Street Journal*, August 4, 2010, http://online.wsj. com/article/SB10001424052748703294904575385 532109190198.html (accessed January 27, 2013).

[23] Morgan Downs (Producer), *Inside the Mind of Google* [DVD], United States: CNBC Originals, 2010.

[24] Corporate Profile, Nielson, http://ir.nielsen.com/ GenPage.aspx?IID=4260029&GKP=1073745941 (accessed January 26, 2013).

[25] Reprinted with permission of The Marketing Research Association, P.O. Box 230, Rocky Hill, CT 06067-0230, 860-257-4008.

[26] Ellen Byron, "'From Diapers to 'Depends': Marketers Discreetly Retool for Aging Boomers," *The Wall Street Journal*, February 5, 2011, http:// online.wsj.com/article/SB1000142405274870 4013604576104394209062996.html (accessed March 30, 2012); Bruce Horovitz, "Big-Spending Baby Boomers Bend the Rules of Marketing," *USA Today*, November 16, 2010, www.usatoday.com/ money/advertising/2010-11-16-1Aboomerbuyers 16_CV_N.htm (accessed February 3, 2013).

Feature Notes

[a] Based on information in David Shepardson and Karl Henkel, "'Electric Car Is Not Dead,' GM Says," *Detroit News*, January 17, 2013, www .detroitnews.com; Mike Ramsey, "Nissan to Build Lower-Cost Leaf Electric Car in U.S.," *Wall Street Journal*, January 9, 2013, www.wsj .com; Bill Vlasic, "2 Makers Press the Case for Electric Cars," *New York Times*, January 15, 2013, www.nytimes.com; "Wireless Charging May Be Key to Electric Vehicle Success, BMW and Nissan Already Developing Technology," *New York Daily News*, December 28, 2012, www.nydaily.com.

[b] Based on information in Amy Corr, "Passersby Help Burt's Bees Billboard Show Before-and-After Effect," *Media Post*, January 7, 2013, www .mediapost.com; Edgar Allen Beem, "Beyond the Bottom Line: Baldwin&, an Award-Winning, Three-Year-Old Indie Agency," *Photo District News*, January 2013, p. 68; "Personal Care Line Aimed at Gen Y Flaunts Attitude, Aroma, Digital Deftness," *Packaging Strategies*, February 29, 2012, p. 6; Allison Schiff, "Gud's Integrated 'Aromavision' Campaign Engages the Senses," *DM News*, June 2012, p. 37; www.baldwinand.com.

[c] Daisuke Wakabayashi and Juro Osawa, "Billboard That Can See You," *The Wall Street Journal*, September 3, 2010, B5; Emily Steel, "The Billboard That Knows," *The Wall Street Journal*, February 29, 2011, B5.

[d] Emily Steel, "Using Credit Cards to Target Web Ads," *The Wall Street Journal*, October 25, 2011, A1, A16; "U.S. Senator Wants Details on How MasterCard, Visa Use Customer Data," *The Wall Street Journal*, October 27, 2011, http://blogs.wsj.com/digits/2011/10/27/u-s-senator-wants-details-on-how-mastercard-visa-use-customer-data/ (accessed February 3, 2013).

chapter 5

OBJECTIVES

1. Understand what markets are and how they are generally classified.
2. Grasp an overview of the five steps of the target market selection process.
3. Understand the differences among general targeting strategies.
4. Become familiar with the major segmentation variables.
5. Know what segment profiles are and how they are used.
6. Understand how to evaluate market segments.
7. Identify the factors that influence the selection of specific market segments for use as target markets.
8. Become familiar with sales forecasting methods.

Target Markets: Segmentation and Evaluation

Craig Yates/Alamy

MARKETING INSIGHTS

Magnum Is Irresistible to Any Demographic

The supermarket freezer aisle has become a red-hot battleground for companies seeking a bigger bite of the $85 billion global ice-cream market. The worldwide leader is Unilever, which owns popular brands like Ben & Jerry's, Breyers, and Klondike. In the United States, however, Nestlé dominates the ice-cream aisle—a situation that Unilever is planning to change with the marketing of its Magnum premium ice-cream brand.

Magnum is for adults who want to indulge themselves with a rich, creamy ice-cream pop, topped with a coating of fine Belgian chocolate. Even if they're not jet-setters, consumers who admire or aspire to a luxurious lifestyle can get a small taste of it at home by treating themselves to a Magnum pop. Unilever is aiming its marketing toward adults who can afford to pamper themselves with an ice-cream

dessert to cap off a special meal or as an everyday indulgence right out of the freezer.

Introduced in Europe in 1989, Magnum is now available in 50 countries and has grown into one of Unilever's billion-dollar brands. When Unilever launched Magnum in the U.S. market a few years ago, the product became so popular so quickly that the company had to import more from Europe to keep up with demand. Today, Magnum's U.S. sales exceed $100 million annually. Unilever has also created Magnum Minis, smaller pops with fewer calories, to tempt U.S. consumers who might otherwise choose competing ice-cream novelties. With 5 million Facebook likes and more than 53,000 Twitter followers, Magnum is building on its social media presence to promote the luxury lifestyle, one ice-cream pop at a time.[1]

Like Magnum, most organizations trying to compete effectively must identify specific customer groups toward which they will direct marketing efforts. This includes developing and maintaining marketing mixes that satisfy the needs of those customers. In this chapter, we define and explore the concepts of markets and market segmentation. First we discuss the major requirements of a market. Then we examine the steps in the target market selection process, including identifying the appropriate targeting strategy, determining which variables to use for segmenting consumer and business markets, developing market segment profiles, evaluating relevant market segments, and selecting target markets. We conclude with a discussion of the various methods for developing sales forecasts.

WHAT ARE MARKETS?

LO1. Understand what markets are and how they are generally classified.

In Chapter 2, we defined a *market* as a group of individuals and/or organizations that have a desire or needs for products in a product class and have the ability, willingness, and authority to purchase those products. You, as a student, for example, are part of the market for textbooks. You are part of other markets as well, such as for computers, clothes, food, and music. To truly be a market, they must possess all four characteristics. For example, teenagers are not part of the market for alcohol. They may have the desire, willingness, and ability to buy liquor, but they do not have the authority to do so because teenagers are prohibited by law from buying alcoholic beverages.

Markets fall into one of two categories: consumer markets and business markets. These categories are based on the characteristics of the individuals and groups that make up a specific market and the purposes for which they buy products. A **consumer market** consists of purchasers and household members who intend to consume or benefit from the purchased products and do not buy products to make a profit. Consumer markets are sometimes also referred to as *business-to-consumer (B2C) markets.* Each of us belongs to numerous consumer markets for all the purchases we make in categories such as housing, food, clothing, vehicles, personal services, appliances, furniture, recreational equipment, and so on, as we shall see in Chapter 6.

consumer market Purchasers and household members who intend to consume or benefit from the purchased products and do not buy products to make profits

Types of Markets   Dockers advertises to consumer markets, whereas Xerox advertises to business markets.

A **business market** consists of individuals or groups that purchase a specific kind of product for one of three purposes: resale, direct use in producing other products, or use in general daily operations. For instance, a producer that buys electrical wire to use in the production of lamps is part of a business market for electrical wire. Some products can be part of the business or consumer market, depending on their end use. For instance, if you purchase a chair for your home, that chair is part of the consumer market. However, if an office manager purchases the same chair for use in a business's office, it is part of the business market. Business markets may be called *business-to-business (B2B), industrial,* or *organizational markets* and can be subclassified into producer, reseller, government, and institutional markets, as we shall see in Chapter 7.

Compare the two advertisements for Dockers and Xerox. Although you may like to wear khakis to work, Dockers targets the consumer market as it would be unlikely that a business would require khaki pants for use in producing other products or in business operations. Xerox, however, targets businesses in this advertisement. While consumers can purchase Xerox-brand products for home use, business customers tend to make much larger and more frequent purchases, making them a profitable target market. In this ad, Xerox is pointing out that it performs other services in addition to producing copy machines, such as automating global invoices for Marriot Hotels.

TARGET MARKET SELECTION PROCESS

LO2. Grasp an overview of the five steps of the target market selection process.

As indicated earlier, the first of two major components of developing a marketing strategy is selecting a target market. Although marketers may employ several methods for target market selection, they generally follow a five-step process. This process is shown in Figure 5.1, and we discuss it in the following sections.

STEP 1: IDENTIFY THE APPROPRIATE TARGETING STRATEGY

LO3. Understand the differences among general targeting strategies.

A target market is a group of people or organizations for which a business creates and maintains a marketing mix specifically designed to satisfy the needs of group members. The strategy used to select a target market is affected by target market characteristics, product attributes, and the organization's objectives and resources. Figure 5.2 illustrates the three basic targeting strategies: undifferentiated, concentrated, and differentiated.

Undifferentiated Targeting Strategy

An organization sometimes defines an entire market for a product as its target market. When a company designs a single marketing mix and directs it at the entire market for a particular product, it is using an **undifferentiated targeting strategy**. As Figure 5.2 shows,

business market Individuals or groups that purchase a specific kind of product for resale, direct use in producing other products, or use in general daily operations

undifferentiated targeting strategy A strategy in which an organization designs a single marketing mix and directs it at the entire market for a particular product

Figure 5.1 **Target Market Selection Process**

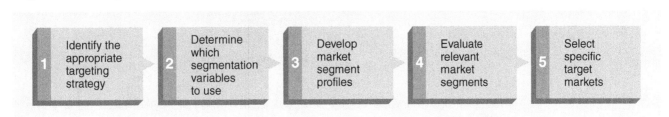

| 1 Identify the appropriate targeting strategy | 2 Determine which segmentation variables to use | 3 Develop market segment profiles | 4 Evaluate relevant market segments | 5 Select specific target markets |

Figure 5.2 **Targeting Strategies**

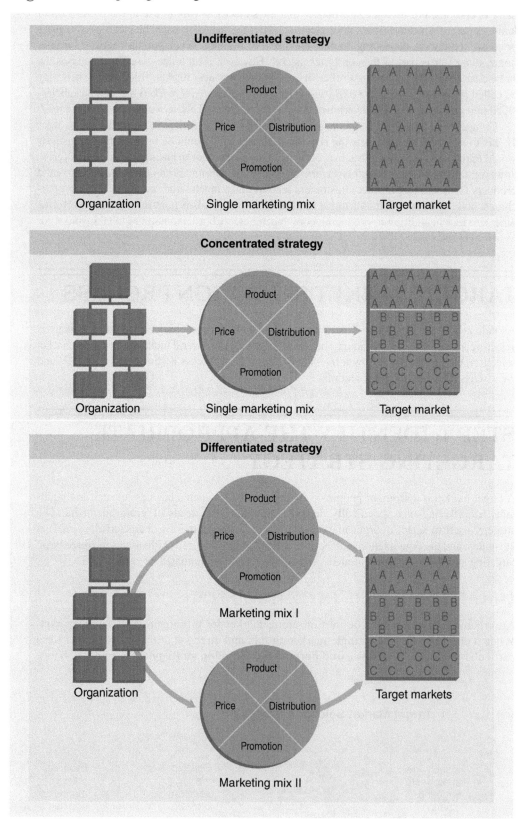

The letters in each target market represent potential customers. Customers with the same letters have similar characteristics and similar product needs.

© Cengage Learning

the strategy assumes that all customers in the target market have similar needs, and thus the organization can satisfy most customers with a single marketing mix with little or no variation. Products marketed successfully through the undifferentiated strategy include commodities and staple food items, such as sugar and salt and conventionally raised produce.

The undifferentiated targeting strategy is effective under two conditions. First, a large proportion of customers in a total market must have similar needs for the product, a situation termed a **homogeneous market**. A marketer using a single marketing mix for a total market of customers with a variety of needs would find that the marketing mix satisfies very few people. For example, marketers would have little success using an undifferentiated strategy to sell a "universal car" because different customers have varying needs. Second, the organization must have the resources to develop a single marketing mix that satisfies customers' needs in a large portion of a total market and the managerial skills to maintain it.

The reality is that, although customers may have similar needs for a few products, for most products their needs are different enough to warrant separate marketing mixes. In such instances, a company should use a concentrated or a differentiated strategy.

Concentrated Targeting Strategy through Market Segmentation

While most people will be satisfied with the same white sugar, not everyone needs the same car, furniture, or clothes. A market comprised of individuals or organizations with diverse product needs is called a **heterogeneous market**. For example, some individuals want a Ford truck because they have to haul heavy loads for their work, while others live in the city and enjoy the ease of parking and good gas mileage of a Smart car. The automobile market thus is heterogeneous.

homogeneous market
A market in which a large proportion of customers have similar needs for a product

heterogeneous market
A market made up of individuals or organizations with diverse needs for products in a specific product class

Concentrated Targeting Strategy   Both Mont Blanc and Bic pens use a concentrated targeting strategy to aim at a different, single market segment. They are not competing for the same customers.

For heterogeneous markets, market segmentation is the best approach. **Market segmentation** is the process of dividing a total market into groups, or segments, that consist of people or organizations with relatively similar product needs. The purpose is to enable a marketer to design a marketing mix that more precisely matches the needs of customers in the selected market segment. A **market segment** consists of individuals, groups, or organizations that share one or more similar characteristics that cause them to have relatively similar product needs. The total market for blue jeans is divided into multiple segments. Price-sensitive customers can buy bargain jeans at Walmart or Ross. Others may need functional jeans, like Carhartt brand, for work. Still other customers wear jeans as a fashion statement and are willing to spend hundreds of dollars on an exclusive brand such as 7 for All Mankind.

The rationale for segmenting heterogeneous markets is that a company will be most successful in developing a satisfying marketing mix for a portion of a total market, since customers' needs tend to vary. The majority of organizations use market segmentation to best satisfy the needs of their customers.

For market segmentation to succeed, five conditions must exist. First, customers' needs for the product must be heterogeneous, otherwise there is no reason to waste resources segmenting the market. Second, segments must be identifiable and divisible. The company must be able to find a characteristic, or variable, for effectively separating a total market into groups comprised of individuals with relatively uniform product needs. Third, the marketer must be able to compare the different market segments with respect to estimated sales potential, costs, and profits. Fourth, at least one segment must have enough profit potential to justify developing and maintaining a special marketing mix for it. Finally, the company must be able to reach the chosen segment with a particular marketing mix. Some market segments may be difficult or impossible to reach because of legal, social, or distribution constraints. For instance, producers of Cuban rum and cigars cannot market to U.S. consumers because of a trade embargo.

When an organization directs its marketing efforts toward a single market segment using one marketing mix, it is employing a **concentrated targeting strategy**. Notice in Figure 5.2 that the organization using the concentrated strategy is aiming its marketing mix only at "B" customers. Take a look at the two advertisements for Mont Blanc and Bic pens. Both of these brands are using a concentrated marketing strategy to reach a specific target market, but are aiming their advertisements at very different market segments. Mont Blanc is a very high-end pen company with products that sell for thousands of dollars. The simplicity and elegance of the advertisement speak to the luxury of the product. Bic, on the other hand, is a brand of cheap, disposable pens. They come in multipacks, are purchased by people who want a reliable and functional pen but do not care about the experience of writing, and are meant to be used and thrown away, not treasured for generations.

As you can see with the two pen brands, the chief advantage of the concentrated strategy is that it allows a firm to specialize. The firm analyzes the characteristics and needs of a distinct customer group and then focuses all its energies on satisfying that group's needs. If the group is big enough, a firm may generate a large sales volume by reaching a single segment. Concentrating on a single segment can also permit a firm with limited resources to compete with larger organizations that have overlooked smaller market segments.

Specialization, however, means that a company allocates all its resources for one target segment, which can be hazardous. If a company's sales depend on a single segment and the segment's demand for the product declines, the company's financial health also deteriorates. The strategy can also prevent a firm from targeting segments that might be successful, because when a firm penetrates one segment, its popularity may keep it from extending its marketing efforts into other segments.

Differentiated Targeting Strategy through Market Segmentation

With a **differentiated targeting strategy**, an organization directs its marketing efforts at two or more segments by developing a marketing mix for each segment (see Figure 5.2).

market segmentation The process of dividing a total market into groups with relatively similar product needs to design a marketing mix that matches those needs

market segment Individuals, groups, or organizations sharing one or more similar characteristics that cause them to have similar product needs

concentrated targeting strategy A market segmentation strategy in which an organization targets a single market segment using one marketing mix

differentiated targeting strategy A strategy in which an organization targets two or more segments by developing a marketing mix for each segment

Marketing Debate

Is Anything Gained by Gender Targeting?

ISSUE: Does targeting children by gender reinforce stereotypes or limit play possibilities?

After 50 years of targeting only girls for its Easy-Bake Oven, Hasbro has announced a gender-neutral version and is airing commercials showing boys playing with the toy oven. This change made headlines because of a teenage girl who wanted to give her little brother the oven as a gift but couldn't find it in boy-friendly colors. She presented Hasbro with a petition signed by 44,000 supporters and told its marketers that boys shouldn't be discouraged from cooking.

This illustrates one side of the debate over whether toymakers should target children by gender. Some parents seek to encourage creative play unconfined by typical gender roles. Advocacy groups like Pinkstinks worry that gender targeting will cause children to avoid toys and play activities traditionally associated with the opposite gender and possibly influence career choices through stereotyping. Hasbro isn't the only company that has faced such objections. After the Swedish government forced Top Toy to change its stereotyped gender targeting, the company's promotions began featuring girls with military toys and boys with household appliance toys.

For their part, toymakers target by gender so they can understand the specific needs and preferences of boys and girls and respond with appropriate marketing-mix elements. In fact, Hasbro knows that pink and purple aren't the only colors girls like—which is why it has offered its Easy-Bake Ovens in green, teal, orange, and yellow over the years. So is it acceptable to target by gender if the marketer doesn't exclude nontargeted children and doesn't promote a negative view of the other gender?[a]

© iStockphoto.com/CRTd

After a firm uses a concentrated targeting strategy successfully in one market segment, it may expand its efforts to include additional segments. For instance, the yoga brand lululemon first became popular as a clothing company for women. However, lululemon's marketers identified growth opportunities among male consumers and now pursue a differentiated targeting strategy, investing substantial marketing resources into the men's yoga segment.[2]

A benefit of a differentiated approach is that a firm may increase sales in the aggregate market because its marketing mixes are aimed at more customers. For this reason, a company with excess production capacity may find a differentiated strategy advantageous because the sale of products to additional segments may absorb excess capacity. On the other hand, a differentiated strategy often demands more production processes, materials, and people because the different ingredients in each marketing mix will vary. Thus, production costs may be higher than with a concentrated strategy.

STEP 2: DETERMINE WHICH SEGMENTATION VARIABLES TO USE

LO4. Become familiar with the major segmentation variables.

Segmentation variables are the characteristics of individuals, groups, or organizations used to divide a market into segments. Location, age, gender, and rate of product usage can all be bases for segmenting markets. Marketers may use several variables in combination when segmenting a market. For example, Silk, maker of nondairy soy and almond milks, segments the market for Unsweetened Vanilla Almondmilk two ways: by those who are allergic to or do not like the taste of dairy milk and by those looking to reduce the amount of calories in their diet while still getting the calcium and vitamins found in regular milk.[3]

segmentation variables Characteristics of individuals, groups, or organizations used to divide a market into segments

To select a segmentation variable, marketers consider several factors. The segmentation variable should relate to customers' needs for, uses of, or behavior toward the product. It is likely a television marketer will segment television viewers for primetime television by income and age but not by religion, for example, because people's television viewing does not vary much because of religion. Marketers must select measurable segmentation variables, such as age, location, or gender, if individuals or organizations in a total market are to be classified accurately.

There is no best way to segment markets, and the approach will vary depending on a number of factors. A company's resources and capabilities affect the number and size of segment variables used. The type of product and degree of variation in customers' needs also dictate the number and size of segments targeted. No matter what approach is used, choosing one or more segmentation variables is a critical step in effectively targeting a market. Selecting an inappropriate variable limits the chances of developing a successful marketing strategy. To help you better understand potential segmentation variables, we next examine the differences between the major variables used to segment consumer and business markets.

Variables for Segmenting Consumer Markets

A marketer that is using segmentation to reach a consumer market can choose one or several variables. As Figure 5.3 shows, segmentation variables can be grouped into four major categories: demographic, geographic, psychographic, and behavioristic.

Demographic Variables

Demographers study aggregate population characteristics such as the distribution of age and gender, fertility rates, migration patterns, and mortality rates. Demographic characteristics that marketers commonly use include age, gender, race, ethnicity, income, education, occupation, family size, family life cycle, religion, and social class. Marketers segment markets by demographic characteristics because they are often closely linked to customers' needs and purchasing behaviors and can be readily measured.

Figure 5.3 **Segmentation Variables for Consumer Markets**

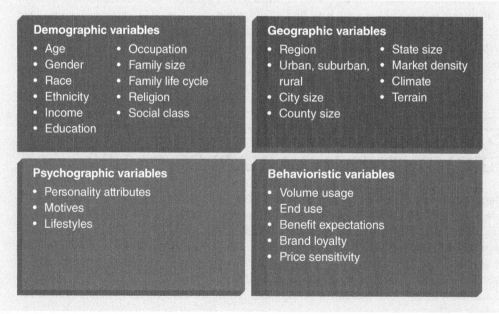

Demographic variables
- Age
- Gender
- Race
- Ethnicity
- Income
- Education
- Occupation
- Family size
- Family life cycle
- Religion
- Social class

Geographic variables
- Region
- Urban, suburban, rural
- City size
- County size
- State size
- Market density
- Climate
- Terrain

Psychographic variables
- Personality attributes
- Motives
- Lifestyles

Behavioristic variables
- Volume usage
- End use
- Benefit expectations
- Brand loyalty
- Price sensitivity

Age is a common variable for segmentation purposes. A trip to the shopping mall high-lights the fact that many retailers, including Zara, Aeropostale, and American Eagle Outfitters, target teens and young adults. If considering segmenting by age, marketers need to be aware of age distribution, how that distribution is changing, and how it will affect the demand for different types of products. The proportion of consumers under the age of 55 is expected to continue to decrease over time as Baby Boomers (born between 1946 and 1964) age. In 1970, the average age of a U.S. citizen was 27.9. It is currently 37.3.[4] Because of the increasing average age of Americans, many marketers are searching for ways to market their products toward older adults. As Figure 5.4 shows, Americans in different age groups have different product needs because of their different lifestyles and health situations. Citizens 65 and older, for instance, spend the most on health care, while those between 35 and 64 spend the most on housing and food.

Gender is another demographic variable that is commonly used to segment markets for many products, including clothing, soft drinks, nonprescription medications, magazines, some food items, and personal care products. For example, after years of being pressured to create marketing strategies that are not targeted by gender, U.S. toymakers are again moving toward segmenting toys by gender. Marketers made this decision based on sales data and customer responses to marketing mixes, but also looked to cognitive science research that indicates how boys and girls do indeed have different preferences.[5]

Figure 5.4 **Spending Levels by Age Groups for Selected Product Categories**

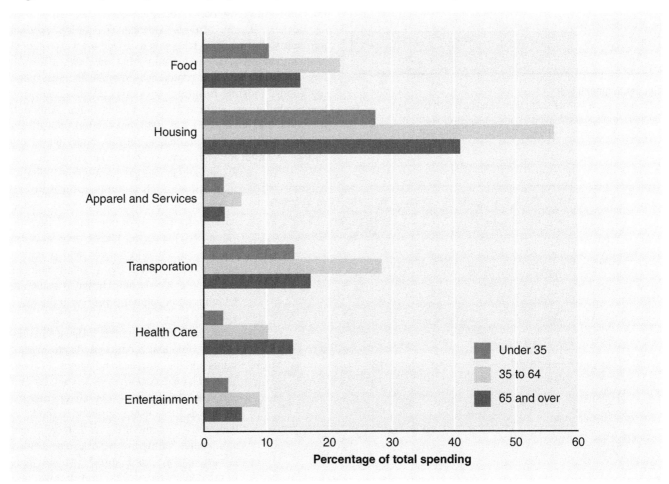

Source: Consumer Expenditure Survey, U.S. Department of Labor, Bureau of Labor Statistics, www.bls.gov/cex/#tables (accessed January 19, 2013).

Gender Segmentation
New Balance segments some of its running shoes based on gender, emphasizing feminine colors and design elements.

The U.S. Census Bureau reports that females account for 50.8 percent and males for 49.2 percent of the total U.S. population.[6] Although they represent only slightly more than half of the population, women disproportionately influence buying decisions. It is estimated that women account for 85 percent of all consumer purchases, causing many marketers to consider female customers when making marketing decisions.[7] Take a look at the advertisement for the New Balance sneaker. The marketers at New Balance are clearly segmenting this product by gender, given the bright pink color. Furthermore, the ad shows a man sketching, as if for a fashion line. This is an image more common in a fashion magazine than an athletic one and underscores that New Balance paid attention to feminine details in designing this product. The New Balance 870v2 is clearly a running shoe that is targeted solely at females.

Marketers also use race and ethnicity as variables for segmenting markets for many products. Cosmetics, for example, is an industry where it is important to match the shade of the products with the skin color of customers. Iman Cosmetics is a line created by the Ethiopian supermodel Iman, with deeper colors designed to flatter the skin tones of women of color, be they Black, Hispanic, or Asian. These products are not made for, nor marketed to, light-skinned women.[8]

Because income strongly influences people's product purchases, it often provides a way to divide markets. Income affects customers' lifestyles and what they can afford to buy. Product markets segmented by income include sporting goods, housing, furniture, cosmetics, clothing, jewelry, home appliances, automobiles, and electronics. Although it may seem obvious to target higher-income consumers because of their larger purchasing power, many marketers choose to target lower-income segments because they represent a much larger population globally. Increasingly, online retailers measure the worth of consumers using a metric called an e-score that ranks consumers' lifetime values to the firm, taking into account credit score, buying power, and purchase history. Calculated by a small number of firms, e-scores help firms to calculate which market segments represent the most valuable targets.[9]

Among the factors that influence household income and product needs are marital status and the presence and age of children. These characteristics, often combined and called the *family life cycle,* affect consumers' needs for housing, appliances, food and beverages, automobiles, and recreational equipment. Family life cycles can be divided in various ways, as Figure 5.5 shows. This figure depicts the process broken down into nine categories.

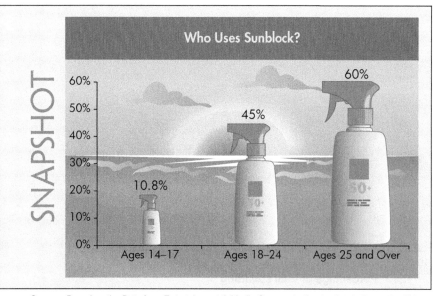

SNAPSHOT

Who Uses Sunblock?

- Ages 14–17: 10.8%
- Ages 18–24: 45%
- Ages 25 and Over: 60%

Source: Based on the Data from Entertainment & Media Communication Institute's Center for Skin Cancer Prevention.

Figure 5.5 Family Life Cycle Stages as a Percentage of All Households

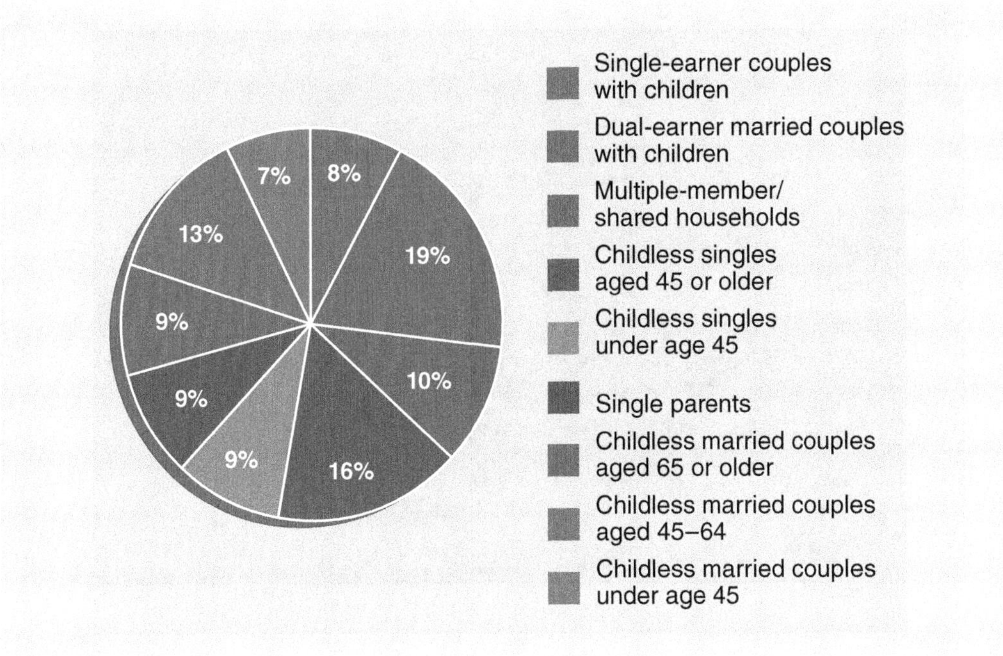

Single-earner couples with children

Dual-earner married couples with children

Multiple-member/shared households

Childless singles aged 45 or older

Childless singles under age 45

Single parents

Childless married couples aged 65 or older

Childless married couples aged 45–64

Childless married couples under age 45

© Cengage Learning

   The composition of the U.S. household in relation to the family life cycle has changed considerably over the last several decades. Single-parent families are on the rise, meaning that the "typical" family no longer necessarily consists of a married couple with children. In fact, husband-and-wife households only account for 48.4 percent of all households in the United States, whereas they used to account for a majority of living arrangements. An estimated 26.7 percent of Americans live alone. Recently, previously small groups have risen in prominence, prompting an interest from marketers. For example, unmarried households represent 6.6 percent of the total, an increase of 41 percent since 2000. Same-sex partners represent 0.6 percent of households, which is a small proportion of the total, but an increase of more than 81 percent since 2000.[10] People live in many different situations, all of which have different requirements for goods and services. Tracking demographic shifts such as these helps marketers be informed and prepared to satisfy the needs of target markets through new marketing mixes that address their changing lifestyles.

Geographic Variables

Geographic variables—climate, terrain, city size, population density, and urban/rural areas—also influence consumer product needs. Markets may be divided using geographic variables, because differences in location, climate, and terrain will influence consumers' needs. Consumers in the South, for instance, rarely have a need for snow tires. A company that sells products to a national market might divide the United States into Pacific, Southwest, Central, Midwest, Southeast, Middle Atlantic, and New England regions. A firm that is operating in one or several states might regionalize its market by counties, cities, zip code areas, or other units.

   City size can be an important segmentation variable. Many firms choose to limit marketing efforts to cities above a certain size because small populations have been calculated to generate inadequate profits. Other firms actively seek opportunities in smaller towns. A classic example is Walmart, which initially was located only in small towns and even today can

Geographic Segmentation
Climate affects numerous markets. Customers' needs for automotive accessories, such as tires, vary based on climate.

be found in towns where other large retailers stay away. If a marketer chooses to divide by a geographic variable, such as by city size, the U.S. Census Bureau provides reporting on population and demographics that can be of considerable assistance to marketers.

Market density refers to the number of potential customers within a unit of land area, such as a square mile. Although market density relates generally to population density, the correlation is not exact. For example, in two different geographic markets of approximately equal size and population, market density for office supplies would be much higher in an area containing a large number of business customers, such as a city downtown, than in another area that is largely residential, such as a suburb. Market density may be a useful segmentation variable for firms because low-density markets often require different sales, advertising, and distribution activities than do high-density markets.

Marketers may also use geodemographic segmentation. **Geodemographic segmentation** clusters people by zip codes or neighborhood units based on lifestyle and demographic information. Targeting this way can be effective because people often choose to live in an area that shares their basic lifestyle and political beliefs. Information companies such as Donnelley Marketing Information Services and Claritas provide geodemographic data services called Prospect Zone and PRIZM, respectively. PRIZM, for example, classifies zip code areas into 66 different cluster types, based on demographic information of residents.[11]

Geodemographic segmentation allows marketers to engage in micromarketing. **Micromarketing** involves focusing precise marketing efforts on very small geographic markets, such as communities and even individual neighborhoods. Providers of financial and health-care services, retailers, and consumer product companies use micromarketing. Many retailers use micromarketing to determine the merchandise mix for individual stores. Increasingly, firms can engage in micromarketing in online retailing, given the Internet's ability to target precise interest groups. Unlike traditional micromarketing, online micromarketing is not limited by geography. The wealth of consumer information available online allows marketers to appeal efficiently and effectively to very specific consumer niches.

Climate is commonly used as a geographic segmentation variable because of its broad impact on people's behavior and product needs. Product markets affected by climate include air-conditioning and heating equipment, fireplace accessories, clothing, gardening equipment, recreational products, and building materials.

market density The number of potential customers within a unit of land area

geodemographic segmentation A method of market segmentation that clusters people in zip code areas and smaller neighborhood units based on lifestyle and demographic information

micromarketing An approach to market segmentation in which organizations focus precise marketing efforts on very small geographic markets

Psychographic Variables

Marketers sometimes use psychographic variables, such as personality characteristics, motives, and lifestyles, to segment markets. A psychographic variable can be used by itself or in combination with other types of segmentation variables.

Personality characteristics can be a useful means of segmentation when a product resembles many competing products and consumers' needs are not significantly related to other segmentation variables. However, segmenting a market according to personality traits can be risky. Although marketing practitioners have long believed consumer choice and product use vary with personality, marketing research has generally indicated only a weak relationship. It is difficult to measure personality traits accurately, especially because most personality tests were developed for clinical use, not for market segmentation purposes.

When appealing to a personality characteristic, a marketer almost always selects one that many people view positively. Individuals with this characteristic, as well as those who aspire to have it, may be influenced to buy the marketer's brand. Marketers taking this approach do not worry about measuring how many people have the positively valued characteristic. They assume a sizable proportion of people in the target market either have it or aspire to have it.

When motives are used to segment a market, the market is divided according to consumers' reasons for making a purchase. Personal appearance, affiliation, status, safety, and health are examples of motives affecting the types of products purchased and the choice of stores in which they are bought. Marketing efforts based on particular motives can be a point of competitive advantage for a firm. Take, for example, the advertisement for luxury Italian menswear brand Ermenegildo Zegna. This is a brand known for its classic styling and high quality, underscored in the slogan "passion for details." The luxurious quality of this brand is emphasized in the close-up of a man wearing a classically tailored suit and loafers, holding plaid and leather briefcases. This advertisement is clearly appealing to customers who are motivated by personal appearance and status and who care about fashion. These customers wish to associate with a luxury lifestyle and want others to notice that they dress in Italian couture brands.

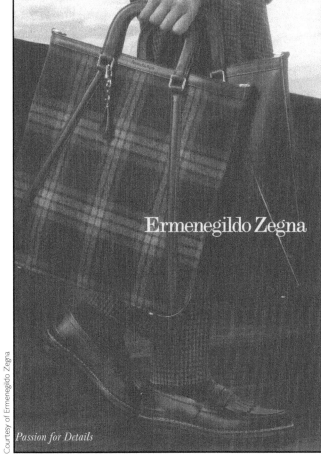

Courtesy of Ermenegildo Zegna

Segmentation Based on Motives
This Ermenegildo Zegna advertisement for men's luxury clothing and accessories is clearly appealing to customers who are motivated by personal appearance and status and who care about fashion.

Lifestyle segmentation groups individuals according to how they spend their time, the importance of things in their surroundings (homes or jobs, for example), beliefs about themselves and broad issues, and some demographic characteristics, such as income and education.[12] Lifestyle analysis provides a broad view of buyers because it encompasses numerous characteristics related to people's activities (e.g., work, hobbies, entertainment, sports), interests (e.g., family, home, fashion, food, technology), and opinions (e.g., politics, social issues, education, the future).

One of the most popular psychographic systems is VALS™ from Strategic Business Insights (SBI), a spin-off of SRI International. VALS classifies consumers based on psychological motivations validated to correlate with purchase behavior and four key demographics. The VALS classification questionnaire, which is used to determine consumers' VALS types, can be integrated into larger research projects to discover more about the underlying drivers of consumer choice. Figure 5.6 is an example of VALS data that shows the proportion of each VALS group that own a tablet/e-reader, a dog, or buy food labeled natural or organic. VALS research can be used to create new products as well as to segment existing markets. Additional VALS frameworks have been developed for different geographic markets, including the United States, Japan, the United Kingdom, Venezuela, the Dominican Republic, Nigeria, and China.[13]

Figure 5.6 VALS Types and Selected Consumer Preferences

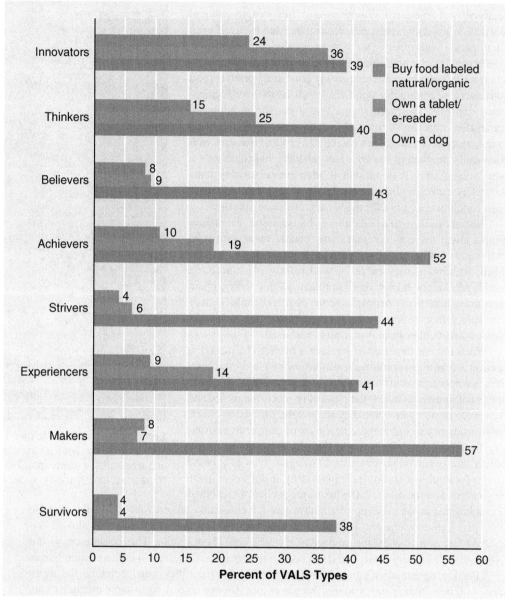

Source: VALS™/GfK MRI, Spring 2012.
To Receive an Accurate VALS Type: By design, the questions are for use by people whose first language is American English. If you are not a citizen of the United States or Canada, residency should be for enough time to know the culture and its idioms. If you do not meet these conditions, your VALS type will not be valid.

Behavioristic Variables

Firms can divide a market according to consumer behavior toward a product, which commonly involves an aspect of consumers' product use. For example, a market may be separated into users—classified as heavy, moderate, or light—and nonusers. To satisfy a specific group, such as heavy users, marketers may create a distinctive product and price, or initiate special promotion and distribution activities. Per capita consumption data can help determine different levels of usage by product category. To satisfy customers who use a product in a certain way, some feature—packaging, size, texture, or color—may be designed precisely to make the product easier to use, safer, or more convenient.

Benefit segmentation is the division of a market according to benefits that consumers want from the product. Although most types of market segmentation assume a relationship between the variable and customers' needs, benefit segmentation differs in that the benefits customers seek *are* their product needs. Consider that a customer who purchases over-the-counter cold relief medication may be interested in two benefits: stopping a runny nose and relieving chest congestion. By determining desired benefits, marketers can divide people into groups by the benefits they seek. The effectiveness of such segmentation depends on three conditions: (1) the benefits sought must be identifiable, (2) using these benefits, marketers must be able to divide people into recognizable segments, and (3) one or more of the resulting segments must be accessible to the firm's marketing efforts.

Marketers can segment consumer markets using many characteristics. They do not, however, use the same variables to segment business characteristics. We will learn about business market segmentation in the next section.

Variables for Segmenting Business Markets

Like consumer markets, business markets are frequently segmented for marketing purposes. Marketers segment business markets according to geographic location, type of organization, customer size, and product use.

Geographic Location

Earlier we noted that the demand for consumer products can vary considerably among geographic areas due to differences in climate, terrain, or regional customer preferences. Demand for business products also varies according to geographic location. For instance, producers of lumber may divide their markets geographically because customers' needs vary by region. Geographic segmentation may be especially appropriate for producers seeking to reach industries concentrated in certain locations, such as furniture and textile producers concentrated in the Southeast.

benefit segmentation The division of a market according to benefits that consumers want from the product

IKEA Adds to the Green Lifestyle

IKEA, the global retailer known for its stylish, affordable, assemble-it-yourself furniture, has added interest in sustainability as a key element in its segmentation strategy. Spotlighting environmental efforts gives IKEA an edge with the growing segment of eco-minded customers and helps the company's bottom line as well. "What is good for our customers is also good for us in the long run," says CEO Mikael Ohlsson.

Consumers who want to live a greener lifestyle appreciate the way IKEA puts its environmental values into practice, making its stores, its products, and even its shipping materials more eco-friendly every year. More than three-quarters of IKEA's U.S. stores and distribution centers are equipped with solar panels to generate clean energy. Instead of the wooden pallets traditionally used for shipping merchandise, IKEA now uses single-use pallets made from recyclable cardboard. The new pallets are more compact and much lighter than wooden pallets, which means less fuel is consumed when they're transported—and IKEA pays less for transportation.

IKEA recently began rating its products using an 11-point sustainability scorecard, tracking attributes such as the product's percentage of recycled content and the amount of clean energy used in production. Such detailed information appeals to customers seeking a greener lifestyle, who are interested in each product's environmental impact.[b]

For over 15 years, the gold standard still remains.

When quality matters, reach for the gold standard of coated paper — Sappi McCoy. And with affordable pricing, it's never been easier for your brand to look its best. McCoy boasts a remarkably rich, tactile feel that captures fine details, cool crisp blue tones, and provides unparalleled readability and clarity. All of which you can see in the pages of our latest edition of The Standard.

 At Sappi, we're always looking to help you raise the design bar. That's why you should get your own copy of *The Standard 5: Special Effects* through your local Sappi Sales Representative. You can also read more about The Standard series at sappi.com/na or request previous editions at sappisamples.com.

sappi   For more information please contact your Sappi sales representative, or call 800.882.4332.

Courtesy of Sappi

Segmenting Business Markets
Sappi produces high-quality paper products. It segments based on product use, focusing marketing efforts on companies that produce design work that requires a high grade of paper.

Type of Organization

A company sometimes segments a market by types of organization within that market because they often require different product features, distribution systems, price structures, and selling strategies. Given these variations, a firm may either concentrate on a single segment with one marketing mix (a concentration targeting strategy) or focus on several groups with multiple mixes (a differentiated targeting strategy). A carpet producer, for example, could segment potential customers into several groups, such as automobile makers, commercial carpet contractors (firms that carpet large commercial buildings), apartment complex developers, carpet wholesalers, and large retail carpet outlets.

Customer Size

An organization's size may affect its purchasing procedures and the types and quantities of products it needs. Size can thus be an effective variable for segmenting a business market. To reach a segment of a specific size, marketers may have to adjust one or more marketing mix ingredients. For example, marketers may want to offer customers who buy in large quantities a discount as a purchase incentive. Personal selling is common and expected in business markets, where a higher level of customer service may be required—larger customers may require a higher level of customer service because of the size and complexity of their orders. Because the needs of large and small buyers tend to be distinct, marketers frequently use different marketing practices to reach target customer groups.

Product Use

Certain products, particularly basic raw materials such as steel, petroleum, plastics, and lumber, can be used numerous ways in the production of goods. These variations will affect the types and amounts of products purchased, as well as the purchasing method. Consider the advertisement for Sappi, for example. Paper is a product that can be used for a variety of purposes and targeted at many different markets. Sappi, a producer of high-quality paper, is targeting its McCoy line of coated papers at businesses that do design work and that care about crisp colors and paper feel. As part of its marketing strategy, you can see in this ad that Sappi produces its own educational publication, *The Standard*, featuring articles on printing and design. The magazine gives the firm added credibility among its target audience, while physically showcasing the product, paper.

LO5. Know what segment profiles are and how they are used.

STEP 3: DEVELOP MARKET SEGMENT PROFILES

A market segment profile describes the similarities among potential customers within a segment and explains the differences among people and organizations in different segments. A profile may cover such aspects as demographic characteristics, geographic factors, product benefits sought, lifestyles, brand preferences, and usage rates. Individuals and organizations within a market segment should be relatively similar with respect to several of their characteristics and product needs and differ considerably from those within other market segments. Marketers use market segment profiles to assess the degree to which their products fit potential customers' product needs. Market segment profiles help marketers understand how a business can use its capabilities to serve potential customer groups.

Market segment profiles help a marketer determine which segment or segments are most attractive relative to the firm's strengths, weaknesses, objectives, and resources. Although marketers may initially believe certain segments are attractive, a market segment profile may yield contrary information. Market segment profiles can be useful in helping a firm make marketing decisions relating to a specific market segment or segments.

STEP 4: EVALUATE RELEVANT MARKET SEGMENTS

LO6. Understand how to evaluate market segments.

After analyzing the market segment profiles, a marketer should be able to narrow his or her focus to several promising segments that warrant further analysis. Marketers should examine sales estimates, competition, and estimated costs associated with each of these segments.

Sales Estimates

Potential sales for a market segment can be measured along several dimensions, including product level, geographic area, time, and level of competition.[14] With respect to product level, potential sales can be estimated for a specific product item (e.g., Diet Coke) or an entire product line (e.g., Coca-Cola Classic, Diet Coke, and Coke Zero comprise goods in a product line). A manager must also determine the geographic area to include in the estimate. In relation to time, sales estimates can be short range (one year or less), medium range (one to five years), or long range (longer than five years). The competitive level specifies whether sales are being estimated for a single firm or for an entire industry.

Market potential is the total amount of a product that customers will purchase within a specified period at a specific level of industry-wide marketing activity. Market potential can be stated in terms of dollars or units. A segment's market potential is affected by economic, sociocultural, and other environmental forces. The specific level of marketing effort will vary from one firm to another, but each firm's marketing activities together add up to the industry-wide marketing effort total. A marketing manager must also estimate whether and to what extent industry marketing efforts will change over time.

Company sales potential is the maximum percentage share of a market that an individual firm within an industry can expect to capture for a specific product. Several factors influence company sales potential for a market segment. First, the market potential places an absolute limit on the size of the company's sales potential—a firm cannot exceed the market potential. Second, the magnitude of industry-wide marketing activities has an indirect but definite impact on the company's sales potential. For instance, when Domino's Pizza advertises home-delivered pizza, it indirectly promotes pizza in general. Maybe you see the ad and it sparks a craving for pizza, but you call the Pizza Hut down the street because it is more familiar to you. Third, the intensity and effectiveness of a company's marketing activities relative to competitors' activities affect the size of the company's sales potential. If a company spends twice as much as any of its competitors on marketing efforts, and if each dollar spent is more effective in generating sales, the firm's sales potential will be high relative to competitors'.

Two general approaches that measure company sales potential are breakdown and buildup. In the **breakdown approach**, the marketing manager first develops a general economic forecast for a specific time period. Next, the manager estimates market potential based on this

market potential The total amount of a product that customers will purchase within a specified period at a specific level of industry-wide marketing activity

company sales potential The maximum percentage of market potential that an individual firm within an industry can expect to obtain for a specific product

breakdown approach Measuring company sales potential based on a general economic forecast for a specific period and the market potential derived from it

Emerging Trends

New Moves in Marketing Movie Rentals

Redbox, Netflix, and Amazon, among other movie rental marketers, are dividing the ever-evolving market for movie rentals according to customer behavior and lifestyle. The result: Customers have new choices for renting movies where and when they want. Although movie rental stores are few and far between these days, customers who prefer DVDs can find a movie at one of Redbox's 42,000 DVD kiosks nationwide. Redbox sees ongoing demand for DVDs and continues to install thousands of new kiosks in supermarkets and other high-traffic locations. It has also teamed with Verizon to offer Redbox Instant movie streaming, priced by monthly subscription or individual rental.

Netflix, a DVD-rentals-by-mail pioneer, sees the market moving away from DVDs. It has therefore been promoting subscription rentals of movies streamed through Internet-connected televisions and game consoles, although it still rents DVDs by mail. Netflix sets itself apart from competitors through its vast library of titles and through original programming such as the *House of Cards* series offered first to streaming subscribers.

The online retail giant Amazon sells DVDs and also offers online access to streamed movies and programs, rented one by one or by subscription. Customers who join Amazon Prime get unlimited streaming for one flat annual fee (as well as receiving free two-day delivery on Amazon purchases). Finally, for customers with on-the-go lifestyles, Amazon—like its major competitors—has apps for renting and viewing movies on iPhones and other mobile devices.[c]

forecast. The manager derives the company's sales potential from the forecast and an estimate of market potential. In the **buildup approach**, the marketing manager begins by estimating how much of a product a potential buyer in a specific geographic area, such as a sales territory, will purchase in a given period. The manager then multiplies that amount by the total number of potential buyers in that area. The manager performs the same calculation for each geographic area in which the firm sells products and then adds the totals to calculate market potential. To determine company sales potential, the manager must estimate, based on planned levels of company marketing activities, the proportion of the total market potential the company can reasonably attain.

Competitive Assessment

Besides obtaining sales estimates, it is crucial to assess competitors that are already operating in the segments being considered. A market segment that initially seems attractive based on sales estimates may turn out to be much less so after a competitive assessment. Such an assessment should ask several questions about competitors: How many exist? What are their strengths and weaknesses? Do several competitors already have major market shares and together dominate the segment? Can our company create a marketing mix to compete effectively against competitors' marketing mixes? Is it likely that new competitors will enter this segment? If so, how will they affect our firm's ability to compete successfully? Answers to such questions are important for proper assessment of the competition in potential market segments.

Cost Estimates

To fulfill the needs of a target segment, an organization must develop and maintain a marketing mix that precisely meets the wants and needs of that segment, which can be expensive. Distinctive product features, attractive package design, generous product warranties, extensive

buildup approach Measuring company sales potential by estimating how much of a product a potential buyer in a specific geographic area will purchase in a given period, multiplying the estimate by the number of potential buyers, and adding the totals of all the geographic areas considered

advertising, attractive promotional offers, competitive prices, and high-quality personal service use considerable organizational resources. In some cases marketers may conclude that the costs to reach some segments are so high that they are basically inaccessible. Marketers also must consider whether the organization can reach a segment at costs equal to or below competitors' costs. If the firm's costs are likely to be higher, it will be unable to compete in that segment in the long run.

STEP 5: SELECT SPECIFIC TARGET MARKETS

LO7. Identify the factors that influence the selection of specific market segments for use as target markets.

Assuming one or more segments offer significant opportunities to achieve organizational objectives, marketers must decide which offer the most potential at reasonable costs. Ordinarily, information gathered in the previous step—concerning sales estimates, competitors, and cost estimates—requires careful review in this final step to determining long-term marketing opportunities. At this time, the firm's management must investigate whether the organization has sufficient financial resources, managerial skills, employee expertise, and facilities to compete effectively in the selected segments. The firm must also consider the possibility that the requirements of some market segments are at odds with the firm's overall objectives, and that possible legal problems, conflicts with interest groups, and technological advancements will render certain segments unattractive. Finally, marketers must consider long-term versus short-term growth. If long-term prospects look poor, a marketer may ultimately choose not to target a segment because it would be difficult to recoup expenses.

Selecting appropriate target markets is important to an organization's effective adoption and use of the marketing concept philosophy. Identifying the right target market is the key to implementing a successful marketing strategy. Failure to do so can lead to low sales, high costs, and severe financial losses. A careful target market analysis places an organization in a strong position to serve customers' needs and achieve its objectives.

DEVELOPING SALES FORECASTS

LO8. Become familiar with sales forecasting methods.

After a company selects a target market or markets, it must develop a **sales forecast**—the amount of a product the company expects to sell during a specific period at a specified level of marketing activity. The sales forecast differs from the company sales potential in that it concentrates on what actual sales will be at a certain level of company marketing effort. The company sales potential assesses what sales are possible at various levels of marketing activities, assuming certain environmental conditions exist. Businesses use the sales forecast for planning, organizing, implementing, and controlling activities. The success of numerous activities depends on the forecast's accuracy. Common problems in failing companies are improper planning and lack of realistic sales forecasts. For example, overly ambitious sales forecasts can lead to overbuying, overinvestment, and higher costs that can weaken a firm's strength and position.

To forecast sales, a marketer can choose from a number of forecasting methods, some arbitrary and quick and others more scientific, complex, and time consuming. A firm's choice of method, or methods, depends on the costs involved, type of product, market characteristics, time span and purpose of the forecast, stability of the historical sales data, availability of required information, managerial preferences, and forecasters' areas of expertise and experience.[15] Common forecasting techniques fall into five categories: executive judgment, surveys, time series analysis, regression analysis, and market tests.

sales forecast The amount of a product a company expects to sell during a specific period at a specified level of marketing activities

Entrepreneurship in Marketing

How Skullcandy Segments Its Market

Rick Alden, an avid snowboarder, founded Skullcandy in 2003 with the idea of making trendy, functional headphones for music lovers who enjoy active sports and want to look stylish. The iPod era was in full swing, and consumers could now take their digital music collections anywhere and everywhere—even on snow-capped mountains. "I wanted to integrate headphones into backpacks, beanies, helmets—to make an easier music delivery device," he remembers.

Although age was a consideration—many of the consumers in his target market were in their teens or twenties—lifestyle and attitude turned out to be more important variables for segmenting the overall market.

Skullcandy's headphones and earbuds are specially made for snowboarders and others who listen to music while engaging in snow or sun sports. Instead of the usual black or white earbuds, Skullcandy's earbuds are brightly colored to appeal to sports-minded consumers with fashion flair.

With more than $200 million in annual revenue and distribution in 70 countries, Skullcandy now competes against global giants such as Sony. To continue growing, the company has adjusted its segmentation to reach consumers involved in a wider variety of active-sports lifestyles, including skateboarders, surfers, inline skaters, and motocrossers.[d]

Executive Judgment

Executive judgment is the intuition of one or more executives. This is an unscientific but expedient and inexpensive approach to sales forecasting. It is not a very accurate method, but executive judgment may work reasonably well when product demand is relatively stable and the forecaster has years of market-related experience. However, because intuition is heavily influenced by recent experience, the forecast may weight recent sales booms or slumps excessively. Another drawback to intuition is that the forecaster has only past experience as a guide for deciding where to go in the future.

Surveys

executive judgment A sales forecasting method based on the intuition of one or more executives

customer forecasting survey A survey of customers regarding the types and quantities of products they intend to buy during a specific period

sales force forecasting survey A survey of a firm's sales force regarding anticipated sales in their territories for a specified period

expert forecasting survey Sales forecasts prepared by experts outside the firm, such as economists, management consultants, advertising executives, or college professors

Another way to forecast sales is to question customers, sales personnel, or experts regarding their expectations about future purchases. In a **customer forecasting survey**, marketers ask customers what types and quantities of products they intend to buy during a specific period. This approach may be useful to a business with relatively few customers. Consider Lockheed Martin, the U.S. government's largest contractor. Because most of its contracts come from the same customer, the government, Lockheed Martin could conduct customer forecasting surveys effectively. PepsiCo, by contrast, has millions of customers and could not feasibly use a customer survey to forecast future sales.

In a **sales force forecasting survey**, the firm's salespeople estimate anticipated sales in their territories for a specified period. The forecaster combines these territorial estimates to arrive at a tentative forecast. A marketer may survey sales staff for several reasons, the most important being that the sales staff is the company personnel closest to customers on a daily basis. They therefore have first-hand knowledge about customers' product needs. Moreover, when sales representatives assist in developing the forecast, they are invested in the process and are more likely to work toward its achievement.

When a company wants an **expert forecasting survey**, it hires professionals to help prepare the sales forecast. These experts are usually economists, management consultants, advertising executives, college professors, or other individuals outside the firm with experience in a specific market. Drawing on this experience and their analyses of available information about the company and the market, experts prepare and present forecasts or answer questions. Using experts is a quick way to get information and is relatively inexpensive. However, because they work outside the firm, these forecasters may be less motivated than company personnel to do an effective job.

A more complex form of the expert forecasting survey incorporates the Delphi technique. In the **Delphi technique**, experts create initial forecasts, submit them to the company for averaging, and have the results returned to them so they can make individual refined forecasts. When making calculations using the Delphi technique, experts use the averaged results to eradicate outliers and to refine predictions. The procedure may be repeated several times until the experts, each working separately, reach a consensus. Because this technique gets rid of extreme data, the ultimate goal in using the Delphi technique is to develop a highly reliable sales forecast.

Time Series Analysis

With **time series analysis**, the forecaster uses the firm's historical sales data to discover a pattern, or patterns, in sales over time. If a pattern is found, it can be used to forecast sales. This forecasting method assumes that past sales patterns will continue into the future. The accuracy, and thus usefulness, of time series analysis hinges on the validity of this assumption.

In a time series analysis, a forecaster usually performs four types of analyses: trend, cycle, seasonal, and random factor. **Trend analysis** focuses on aggregate sales data, such as the company's annual sales figures, covering a period of many years to determine whether annual sales are generally rising, falling, or staying about the same. Through **cycle analysis**, a forecaster analyzes sales figures (often monthly sales data) for a three- to five-year period to ascertain whether sales fluctuate in a consistent, periodic manner. When performing a **seasonal analysis**, the analyst studies daily, weekly, or monthly sales figures to evaluate the degree to which seasonal factors, such as climate and holiday activities, influence sales. In a **random factor analysis**, the forecaster attempts to attribute erratic sales variations to random, nonrecurring events, such as a regional power failure, a natural disaster, or political unrest in a foreign market. After performing each of these analyses, the forecaster combines the results to develop the sales forecast. Time series analysis is an effective forecasting method for products with reasonably stable demand, but not for products with erratic demand.

Regression Analysis

Like time series analysis, regression analysis requires the use of historical sales data. In **regression analysis**, the forecaster seeks to find a relationship between past sales (the dependent variable) and one or more independent variables, such as population, per capita income, or gross domestic product. Simple regression analysis uses one independent variable, whereas multiple regression analysis includes two or more independent variables. The objective of regression analysis is to develop a mathematical formula that accurately describes a relationship between the firm's sales and one or more variables. However, the formula indicates only an association, not a causal relationship. Once an accurate formula is established, the analyst plugs the necessary information into the formula to derive the sales forecast.

Regression analysis is useful when a precise association can be established. However, a forecaster seldom finds a perfect correlation. Furthermore, this method can be used only when available historical sales data are extensive. Thus, regression analysis is not useful for forecasting sales of new products.

Market Tests

A **market test** involves making a product available to buyers in one or more test areas and measuring purchases and consumer responses to the product, distribution, promotion, and price. Test areas are often mid-sized cities with populations of 200,000 to 500,000, but they

Delphi technique A procedure in which experts create initial forecasts, submit them to the company for averaging, and then refine the forecasts

time series analysis A forecasting method that uses historical sales data to discover patterns in the firm's sales over time and generally involves trend, cycle, seasonal, and random factor analyses

trend analysis An analysis that focuses on aggregate sales data over a period of many years to determine general trends in annual sales

cycle analysis An analysis of sales figures for a three- to five-year period to ascertain whether sales fluctuate in a consistent, periodic manner

seasonal analysis An analysis of daily, weekly, or monthly sales figures to evaluate the degree to which seasonal factors influence sales

random factor analysis An analysis attempting to attribute erratic sales variations to random, nonrecurrent events

regression analysis A method of predicting sales based on finding a relationship between past sales and one or more independent variables, such as population or income

market test Making a product available to buyers in one or more test areas and measuring purchases and consumer responses to marketing efforts

can be towns or small cities with populations of 50,000 to 200,000. Test areas are chosen for their representativeness of a firm's target markets.

A market test provides information about consumers' actual, rather than intended, purchases. In addition, purchase volume can be evaluated in relation to the intensity of other marketing activities such as advertising, in-store promotions, pricing, packaging, and distribution. Forecasters base their sales estimates for larger geographic units on customer response in test areas. For example, McDonald's launched a new menu addition, chicken wings, in response to its popularity. The company chose Atlanta as the test market for the product, expanding the test to a very different market, Chicago, after receiving positive feedback in the South.[16]

Because it does not require historical sales data, a market test is effective for forecasting sales of new products or of existing products in new geographic areas. A market test also gives a marketer an opportunity to test the success of various elements of the marketing mix. However, these tests are often time consuming and expensive. In addition, a marketer cannot be certain that consumer response during a market test represents the total market response, or that the same response will continue in the future.

Using Multiple Forecasting Methods

Although some businesses depend on a single sales forecasting method, most firms use several techniques. Sometimes a company is forced to use multiple methods when marketing diverse product lines, but even a single product line may require several forecasts, especially when the product is sold to different market segments. Thus, a producer of automobile tires may rely on one technique to forecast tire sales for new cars and on another to forecast sales of replacement tires. Variation in the length of forecasts may call for several forecasting methods as well. A firm that employs one method for a short-range forecast may find it inappropriate for long-range forecasting. Sometimes a marketer verifies results of one method by using one or more other methods and comparing outcomes.

Chapter Review

1. Understand what markets are and how they are generally classified.

A market is a group of people who, as individuals or as organizations, have needs for products in a product class and have the ability, willingness, and authority to purchase such products. Markets can be categorized as consumer markets or business markets, based on the characteristics of the individuals and groups that make up a specific market and the purposes for which they buy products. A consumer market, also known as a *business-to-consumer (B2C) market,* consists of purchasers and household members who intend to consume or benefit from the purchased products and do not buy products for the main purpose of making a profit. A business market, also known as *business-to-business (B2B), industrial,* or *organizational market,* consists of individuals or groups that purchase a specific kind of product for one of three purposes: resale, direct use in producing other products, or use in general daily operations.

2. Grasp an overview of the five steps of the target market selection process.

In general, marketers employ a five-step process when selecting a target market. Step one is to identify the appropriate targeting strategy. Step two is determining which segmentation variables to use. Step three is to develop a market segment profile. Step four is evaluating relevant market segments. Finally, step five is selecting specific target markets. Not all marketers will follow all of these five steps in this order, but this process provides a good general guide.

3. Understand the differences among general targeting strategies.

Step one of the target market selection process is to identify the appropriate targeting strategy. When a company designs a single marketing mix and directs it at the entire market for a particular product, it is using an undifferentiated targeting strategy. The undifferentiated strategy is effective in a homogeneous market, whereas a heterogeneous market needs to be segmented through a concentrated targeting strategy or a differentiated targeting strategy. Both of these strategies divide markets into segments consisting of individuals, groups, or organizations that have one or more similar characteristics and thus can be linked to similar product needs. When using a concentrated strategy, an organization directs marketing efforts toward a single market segment through one marketing mix. With a differentiated targeting strategy, an organization directs customized marketing efforts at two or more segments.

Certain conditions must exist for market segmentation to be effective. First, customers' needs for the product should be heterogeneous. Second, the segments of the market should be identifiable and divisible. Third, the total market should be divided so segments can be compared with respect to estimated sales, costs, and profits. Fourth, at least one segment must have enough profit potential to justify developing and maintaining a special marketing mix for that segment. Fifth, the firm must be able to reach the chosen segment with a particular marketing mix.

4. Become familiar with the major segmentation variables.

The second step is determining which segmentation variables to use, which are the characteristics of individuals, groups, or organizations used to divide a total market into segments. The segmentation variable should relate to customers' needs for, uses of, or behavior toward the product. Segmentation variables for consumer markets can be grouped into four categories: demographic (e.g., age, gender, income, ethnicity, family life cycle), geographic (e.g., population, market density, climate), psychographic (e.g., personality traits, motives, lifestyles), and behavioristic (e.g., volume usage, end use, expected benefits, brand loyalty, price sensitivity). Variables for segmenting business markets include geographic location, type of organization, customer size, and product use.

5. Know what segment profiles are and how they are used.

Step three in the target market selection process is to develop market segment profiles. Such profiles describe the similarities among potential customers within a segment and explain the differences among people and organizations in different market segments. They are used to assess the degree to which the firm's products can match potential customers' product needs. Segments, which may seem attractive at first, may be shown to be quite the opposite after a market segment profile is completed.

6. Understand how to evaluate market segments.

Step four is evaluating relevant market segments. Marketers analyze several important factors, such as sales estimates, competition, and estimated costs associated with each segment. Potential sales for a market segment can be measured along several dimensions, including product level, geographic area, time, and level of competition. Besides obtaining sales estimates, it is crucial to assess competitors that are already operating in the segments being considered. Without competitive information, sales estimates may be misleading. The cost of developing a marketing mix that meets the wants and needs of individuals in that segment must also be considered. If the firm's costs to compete in that market are very high, it may be unable to compete in that segment in the long run.

7. Identify the factors that influence the selection of specific market segments for use as target markets.

The final step involves the actual selection of specific target markets. In this step, the company considers whether customers' needs differ enough to warrant segmentation and which segments to target. If customers' needs are heterogeneous, the decision of which segment to target must be made, or whether to enter the market at all. Considerations such as the firm's available resources, managerial skills, employee expertise, facilities, the firm's overall objectives, possible legal problems, conflicts with interest groups, and technological advancements must be considered when deciding which segments to target.

8. Become familiar with sales forecasting methods.

A sales forecast is the amount of a product the company actually expects to sell during a specific period at a specified level of marketing activities. To forecast sales, marketers can choose from a number of methods. The choice depends on various factors, including the costs involved, type of product, market characteristics, and time span and purposes of the forecast. There are five categories of forecasting techniques: executive judgment, surveys, time series analysis, regression analysis, and market tests. Executive judgment is based on the intuition of one or more executives. Surveys include customer, sales force, and expert forecasting. Time series analysis uses the firm's historical sales data to discover patterns in the firm's sales over time and employs four major types of analysis: trend, cycle, seasonal, and random factor. With regression analysis, forecasters attempt to find a relationship between past sales and one or more independent variables. Market testing involves making a product available to buyers in one or more test areas and measuring purchases and consumer responses to distribution, promotion, and price. Many companies employ multiple forecasting methods.

Go to www.cengagebrain.com for resources to help you master the content in this chapter as well as materials that will expand your marketing knowledge!

Key Concepts

consumer market 116
business market 117
undifferentiated targeting
   strategy 117
homogeneous market 119
heterogeneous market 119
market segmentation 120
market segment 120
concentrated targeting
   strategy 120

differentiated targeting
   strategy 120
segmentation
   variables 121
market density 126
geodemographic
   segmentation 126
micromarketing 126
benefit segmentation 129
market potential 131

company sales
   potential 131
breakdown approach 131
buildup approach 132
sales forecast 133
executive judgment 134
customer forecasting
   survey 134
sales force forecasting
   survey 134

expert forecasting
   survey 134
Delphi technique 135
time series analysis 135
trend analysis 135
cycle analysis 135
seasonal analysis 135
random factor analysis 135
regression analysis 135
market test 135

Issues for Discussion and Review

1. What is a market? What are the requirements for a market?
2. In your local area, identify a group of people with unsatisfied product needs who represent a market. Could this market be reached by a business organization? Why or why not?
3. Outline the five major steps in the target market selection process.
4. What is an undifferentiated strategy? Under what conditions is it most useful? Describe a present market situation in which a company is using an undifferentiated strategy. Is the business successful? Why or why not?
5. What is market segmentation? Describe the basic conditions required for effective segmentation. Identify several firms that use market segmentation.
6. List the differences between concentrated and differentiated strategies, and describe the advantages and disadvantages of each.
7. Identify and describe four major categories of variables that can be used to segment consumer markets. Give examples of product markets that are segmented by variables in each category.

8. What dimensions are used to segment business markets?
9. Define *geodemographic segmentation*. Identify several types of firms that might employ this type of market segmentation, and explain why.
10. What is a market segment profile? Why is it an important step in the target market selection process?
11. Describe the important factors that marketers should analyze to evaluate market segments.
12. Why is a marketer concerned about sales potential when trying to select a target market?
13. Why is selecting appropriate target markets important for an organization that wants to adopt the marketing concept philosophy?
14. What is a sales forecast? Why is it important?
15. What are the two primary types of surveys a company might use to forecast sales? Why would a company use an outside expert forecasting survey?
16. Under what conditions are market tests useful for sales forecasting? What are the advantages and disadvantages of market tests?
17. Under what conditions might a firm use multiple forecasting methods?

Marketing Applications

1. Despite customers using cell phones to tell the time, the U.S. watch market is still worth about $10 billion. A new watch company that manufactures classic American watches in the style of the Elgin and Hamilton brands has identified five main segments in the U.S. watch market, using a combination of demographic, psychographic, and behavioristic variables.

Carrie is a 25- to 40-year-old woman. She might be single or married, with or without children, but she values her independence. She is a professional, living an urban lifestyle. She is brand conscious and makes well-informed purchasing decisions. She is often a fashion leader. Her annual household income exceeds $100,000. She enjoys jazz, opera, ballet, and more "intellectual" popular music. She dines out often, usually at the most fashionable restaurants. She watches television, especially PBS, Discovery Channel, and HGTV. She has three watches, each of which is priced around $500: a stylish daytime watch for the office, a glamorous watch for evening events, and a sporty watch for weekends and recreational pursuits.

Brittney is a 12- to 18-year-old female. She is all about fashion. She has about $50 to spend per week, either from a part-time job or as an allowance from her parents. She enjoys spending time with her friends and can often be seen at malls or cafés, chatting or texting. She is very aware of different brands and tries to imitate the latest fashions from her favorite celebrities. Her musical taste is mainstream, and she is addicted to reality programs and MTV. She has six watches, each of which costs less than $100. Watches to her are an accessory, and she replaces them frequently when fashion changes.

Skater Boy is a 12- to 23-year-old male. He is a self-described "individual." He thinks of himself as being different, and his style and activities are beyond the mainstream. He often buys clothing at "underground" shops, and his favorite clothing items are often not branded at all or are from anti-establishment brands. He has a part-time job or receives an allowance but spends the majority of this money on music, games, and other lifestyle pursuits. He watches some television, mostly extreme sports, cartoons, and comedy programs. He has one watch, which he wears as a statement of his personality. It is rugged and clunky and costs less than $200.

Executives are men and women, age 45 and above. They are married with children and consider themselves elite, with annual household incomes of more than $400,000. They belong to exclusive clubs and sit on boards of not-for-profit organizations. They have a high regard for quality and often buy products that are somewhat exotic. They watch little television, preferring evenings out at the opera, ballet, or symphony, for which they have season tickets. Like **Carrie**, they have three watches (daytime, evening, and weekend), but each is worth more than $1,000.

Joe Lunchbox is a 25- to 65-year-old man. He is married with two children and earns about $40,000 per year. He is very family-oriented and spends his spare time camping, attending sporting events, and working on do-it-yourself projects. He often buys American and prefers the basic casual style of jeans, T-shirts, and running shoes. His music tastes range from country to classic rock. He loves television, especially sports. He has one watch, which was received as a gift. It serves only one function—telling time.

Develop a rating scale of 1–5, with 1 as the most desirable market segment and 5 as the least desirable. If you decided to market a watch that was under $100 and would

compete against lower-priced Swatch or Timex watches, rate the attractiveness of each market based on these criteria. What will be the unique features that will give your watch a competitive advantage?

What if you wanted to develop a higher-priced watch that targets those individuals with an active lifestyle? Which market segment would you choose, and why?

2. Cable channels, such as Lifetime and Spike TV, each target a specific market segment. Identify another product marketed to a distinct target market. Describe the target market, and explain how the marketing mix appeals specifically to that group.

3. Generally, marketers use one of three basic targeting strategies to focus on a target market: undifferentiated, concentrated, or differentiated. Locate an article that discusses the target market for a specific product. Describe the target market, and explain the targeting strategy used to reach that target market.

4. The car market may be segmented according to income and age. Discuss two ways the market for each of the following products might be segmented.
   a. Candy bars
   b. Travel services
   c. Bicycles
   d. Cell phones

5. If you were using a time series analysis to forecast sales for your company for the next year, how would you use the following sets of sales figures?

a.

Year	Sales	Year	Sales
2003	$145,000	2008	$149,000
2004	$144,000	2009	$148,000
2005	$147,000	2010	$180,000
2006	$145,000	2011	$191,000
2007	$148,000	2012	$227,000

b.

	2010	2011	2012
Jan.	$12,000	$14,000	$16,000
Feb.	$13,000	$14,000	$15,500
Mar.	$12,000	$14,000	$17,000
Apr.	$13,000	$15,000	$17,000
May	$15,000	$17,000	$20,000
June	$18,000	$18,000	$21,000
July	$18,500	$18,000	$21,500
Aug.	$18,500	$19,000	$22,000
Sep.	$17,000	$18,000	$21,000
Oct.	$16,000	$15,000	$19,000
Nov.	$13,000	$14,000	$19,000
Dec.	$14,000	$15,000	$18,000

c. In 2010, sales increased 21.2 percent. In 2011, sales increased 18.8 percent. New stores were opened in 2010 and 2011.

6. Develop your analytical and communication skills using the Role-Play Exercises online at **www.cengagebrain.com**.

Internet Exercise

iExplore

iExplore is an Internet company that offers a variety of travel and adventure products. Learn more about its goods, services, and travel advice through its website at **www.iexplore.com**.

1. Based on the information provided at the website, what are some of iExplore's basic products?
2. What market segments does iExplore appear to be targeting with its website? What segmentation variables is the company using to segment these markets?
3. How does iExplore appeal to comparison shoppers?

developing your marketing plan

Identifying and analyzing a target market is a major component of formulating a marketing strategy. A clear understanding and explanation of a product's target market is crucial to developing a useful marketing plan. References to various dimensions of a target market are likely to appear in several locations in a marketing plan. To assist you in understanding how information in this chapter relates to the creation of your marketing plan, focus on the following considerations:

1. What type of targeting strategy is being used for your product? Should a different targeting strategy be employed?
2. Select and justify the segmentation variables that are most appropriate for segmenting the market for your product. If your product is a consumer product, use Figure 5.3 for ideas regarding the most appropriate segmentation variables. If your marketing plan focuses on a business product, review the information in the section entitled "Variables for Segmenting Business Markets."
3. Discuss how your product should be positioned in the minds of customers in the target market relative to the product positions of competitors.

The information obtained from these questions should assist you in developing various aspects of your marketing plan. Develop your marketing plan online using the Interactive Marketing Plan at **www.cengagebrain.com**.

video case 5.1
Raleigh Wheels into a New Era for Bicycle Marketing

From its 19th-century roots as a British bicycle company, Raleigh has developed a worldwide reputation for marketing sturdy, comfortable, steel-frame bicycles. The firm, named for the street in Nottingham, England, where it was originally located, was a trendsetter in designing and manufacturing bicycles. When Raleigh introduced steel-frame bicycles equipped with three-speed gear hubs in 1903, it revolutionized the industry and set off a never-ending race to improve the product's technology. In the pre-auto era, its bicycles became a two-wheeled status symbol for British consumers, and the brand maintained its cachet for decades. Although Raleigh's chopper-style bicycles were hugely popular in the 1970s, international competition and changing consumer tastes have taken a toll during the past few decades.

Now owned by Netherlands-based Accell Group, Raleigh markets a wide variety of bicycles to consumers in Europe, Canada, and the United States. Its U.S. division, based in Kent, Washington, has been researching new bicycles for contemporary consumers and developing models that are lighter, faster, and better. Inspired by the European lifestyle and tradition of getting around on bicycles, and its long history in the business, Raleigh is looking to reinvigorate sales and capture a larger share of the $6 billion U.S. bicycle market.

Raleigh's U.S. marketers have been observing the "messenger market," customers who ride bicycles through downtown streets to deliver documents and small packages to businesses and individuals. They have also noted that many everyday bicycle riders dress casually, in T-shirts and jeans, rather than in special racing outfits designed for speed. Targeting consumers who enjoy riding bicycles as a lifestyle, Raleigh's marketers are focusing on this segment's specific needs and preferences as they develop, price, promote, and distribute new models.

In recent years, Raleigh's marketers have stepped up the practice of bringing demonstration fleets to public places where potential buyers can hop on one of the company's bicycles and pedal for a few minutes. The idea is to allow consumers who enjoy bicycling to actually experience the fun feeling of riding a Raleigh. The marketers are also fanning out to visit bicycle races and meet bicyclists in cities and towns across America, encouraging discussions about Raleigh and about bicycling in general and seeking feedback about particular Raleigh products.

Listening to consumers, Raleigh's marketers recognized that many had misperceptions about the weight of steel-frame bicycles. Although steel can be quite heavy, Raleigh's bicycles are solid yet light, nimble, and easy to steer. Those who have been on bicycles with steel frames praise the quality of the ride, saying that steel "has a soul," according to market research.

To stay in touch with its target market, Raleigh is increasingly active in social media. Ten thousand fans visit its Facebook page to see the latest product concepts and post their own photos and comments about Raleigh bicycles. It also uses Twitter to keep customers informed and answer questions about its bicycles and upcoming demonstration events. The company's main blog communicates the latest news about everything from frame design and new bike colors under consideration to product awards and racing activities. It has a separate blog about both the fun and the challenges of commuting on bicycle, a topic in which its customers are intensely interested because so many do exactly that. By listening to customers and showing that it understands the daily life of its target market, Raleigh is wheeling toward higher sales in a highly competitive marketplace.[17]

Questions for Discussion

1. Of the four categories of variables, which is most important to Raleigh's segmentation strategy, and why?
2. How would you describe Raleigh's positioning for its steel-frame bicycles?
3. Raleigh sells exclusively through retail dealers, not directly to consumers. How does this affect its ability to segment the bicycle market using geographic variables?

NOTES

[1] Based on information in Matthew Boyle, "In Emerging Markets, Unilever Finds a Passport to Profit," *Bloomberg Businessweek*, January 3, 2013, www.businessweek.com; Matthew Boyle, "Unilever Wants to Be America's Ice Cream King," *Bloomberg Businessweek*, August 23, 2012, www.businessweek.com; "Unilever Maintains Pole Position," *Grocer*, September 22, 2012, S57; "Keep Your Cool," *Convenience Store*, October 12, 2012, 52; "Media Headliner: Di Como Seeks to Discover Unilever's Sweet Spot," *Campaign*, November 30, 2012, 21.

[2] Katie Smith, "Lululemon Targets Men's Wear for Future Growth," just-style, January 18, 2013, www.just-style.com/analysis/lululemon-targets-mens-wear-for-future-growth_id116702.aspx.

[3] Unsweetened Vanilla Almondmilk, Silk, http://silk.com/products/unsweetened-vanilla-almond-milk, accessed January 28, 2013.

[4] American Community Survey, U.S. Census Bureau, 2011, www.census.gov/compendia/statab/cats/population.html (accessed January 19, 2013).

[5] Elizabeth Sweet, "Guys and Dolls No More?" *New York Times*, December 21, 2012, www.nytimes.com/2012/12/23/opinion/sunday/gender-based-toy-marketing-returns.html.

[6] American Community Survey, U.S. Census Bureau, 2011, www.census.gov/compendia/statab/cats/population.html (accessed January 19, 2013).

[7] "Marketing to Women—Quick Facts," She-Conomy, http://she-conomy.com/report/marketing-to-women-quick-facts/ (accessed January 19, 2013).

[8] "FAQ," Iman Cosmetics, www.imancosmetics.com/faq (accessed January 19, 2013).

[9] Natasha Singer, "Secret E-Scores Chart Consumers' Buying Power," *New York Times*, August 19, 2012, www.nytimes.com/2012/08/19/business/electronic-scores-rank-consumers-by-potential-value.html (accessed January 19, 2013).

[10] "*Households and Families: 2010*," U.S. Census Briefs, www.census.gov/prod/cen2010/briefs/c2010br-14.pdf (accessed January 19, 2013).

[11] "My Best Segments," Claritas, www.claritas.com/MyBestSegments/Default.jsp?ID=0&menuOption=home&pageName=Home (accessed January 20, 2013).

[12] Joseph T. Plummer, "The Concept and Application of Life Style Segmentation," *Journal of Marketing* (January 1974): 33.

[13] SRI Consulting Business Intelligence, "About VALS™," www.strategicbusinessinsights.com/vals/international.shtml (accessed February 3, 2013).

[14] Philip Kotler and Kevin Keller, *Marketing Management*, 14th ed. (Englewood Cliffs, NJ: Prentice Hall, 2012).

[15] Charles W. Chase Jr., "Selecting the Appropriate Forecasting Method," *Journal of Business Forecasting* (Fall 1997): 2, 23, 28–29.

[16] Alix Bryan, "McDonald's 'Mighty Chicken' Wings Take Flight to a New Test Market," WTVR, January 7, 2013, http://wtvr.com/2013/01/07/mcdonalds-chicken-wings-take-flight-to-a-new-test-market/.

[17] Mark Sutton, "Raleigh Trade Show: Teaching an Old Bike New Tricks," Bike Biz, March 16, 2012, www.bikebiz.com; "BRAINy Awards Honor Individuals," Bicycle Retailer and Industry News, April 15, 2010, www.bicycleretailer.com; Francis Lawell, "Raleigh: Cycling to Success?" Business Review (UK), February 2009, 16ff; "Industry Overview 2008," National Bicycle Dealers Association, http://nbda.com; www.raleighusa.com; "Accell Group Stops Raleigh Production in Canada," *Bike Europe*, January 15, 2013, www.bike-eu.com.

Feature Notes

[a] Based on information in Tanja Tricarico, "Toymakers Challenges on Gender Stereotypes," *Financial Times*, January 3, 2013, www.ft.com; Heidi Glenn, "Girls, Boys, and Toys: Rethinking Stereotypes in What Kids Play With," *National Public Radio*, December 17, 2012, www.npr.org; Victoria Cavaliere, "Hasbro Easy-Bake Oven to Be Marketed to Girls and Boys in 2013 Following Petition for Change by 13-Year-Old Girl," *New York Daily News*, December 18, 2012, www.nydailynews.com.

[b] Based on information in "Ikea Adding Solar Power in Canton, Other Midwest Stores," CBS Detroit, January 12, 2012, http://Detroit.cbslocal.com; "Ikea: Stock Market Pressures Hinder Sustainability," Environmental Leader, September 20, 2011, www.environmentalleader.com; Ola Kinnander, "Ikea's Challenge to the Wooden Shipping Pallet," *Bloomberg Businessweek*, November 23, 2011, www.businessweek.com; "Ikea Installs Electric Car Charging Stations in Costa Mesa," Los Angeles Business, December 7, 2011, www.bizjournals.com; Jonathan Bardelline, "IKEA Boosting Stock of Sustainable Goods with Eco Scoreboard," Green Biz, March 30, 2011, www.greenbiz.com.

[c] Based on information in Brian Stelter, "A Drama's Streaming Premiere," *New York Times*, January 18, 2013, www.nytimes.com; Lauren Goode, "Netflix, Redbox, and More: What You Need to Know," *All Things D*, January 21, 2013, http://allthingsd.com; Brad Stone, "This Theater Is Getting Awfully Crowded," *Bloomberg Businessweek*, January 21, 2013, 36–37; Richard McGill Murphy, "Cashing in on Kiosks," *Fortune*, December 3, 2012, 44.

[d] Based on information in Richard Nieva, "Skullcandy's Delicious Ride," *Fortune*, November 22, 2011, www.fortune.com; Margaret Heffernan, "Skullcandy: How a Small Company Reaches a Big Market," *CBS Marketwatch*, January 11, 2011, www.cbsnews.com; Steven Oberbeck, "Utah's Skullcandy Continues Turnaround in Q2," *Salt Lake City Tribune*, August 16, 2011, www.sltrib.com; "The Service Dude," *Fortune*, December 26, 2011, 21.

chapter 6

Consumer Buying Behavior

Vicki Beaver/Alamy

MARKETING INSIGHTS

Pretty Ugly's Pretty Popular

Are Uglydolls really ugly? Discovering that custom- ers of all ages are charmed by the colorful felt dolls with personality, consider them part of the family, and view them as an expression of individuality has helped David Horvath and Sun-Min Kim build their company, appropriately named Pretty Ugly, into a multi-million-dollar business.

It all started with Horvath's doodle of a playful- looking monster nicknamed Wage, which he included in a love letter to Kim in 2001. The two met while classmates at Parsons School of Design, and they wrote to each other when Kim returned home to South Korea. After Kim surprised Horvath by making a felt doll based on his doodle, Horvath showed Wage to a retailer friend in Los Angeles and walked away with an order for 20 more. Kim sewed

the dolls, and kept sewing as order after order sold out, snapped up on impulse by consumers with an affinity for felt critters with big eyes and tiny fangs. The entrepreneurs knew they were on the right track when they received photos showing Uglydolls keeping customers company at the dinner table and riding in the car on family outings.

Soon Kim and Horvath, now married, hired a factory to handle production so they could concen- trate on dreaming up adorably ugly dolls along with whimsical descriptions of what makes each charac- ter tick. They licensed their brand for party goods, backpacks, watches, calendars, and other merchan- dise. Digital and entertainment products are also on the way as Pretty Ugly breaks into new categories for long-term growth.[1]

Pretty Ugly and many other traditional and online marketers go to great lengths to understand their customers' needs and gain a better grasp of **buying behavior**, which is the decision processes and actions of people involved in buying and using products. **Consumer buying behavior** refers to the buying behavior of ultimate consumers—those who purchase products for personal or household use and not for business purposes. Marketers attempt to understand buying behavior for several reasons. First, customers' overall opinions and attitudes toward a firm's products have a great impact on the firm's success. Second, as we saw in Chapter 1, the marketing concept stresses that a firm should create a marketing mix that meets customers' needs. To find out what satisfies consumers, marketers must examine the main influences on what, where, when, and how they buy. Third, by gaining a deeper understanding of the factors that affect buying behavior, marketers are better positioned to predict how consumers will respond to marketing strategies.

In this chapter, we first examine the major stages of the consumer buying decision process, beginning with problem recognition, information search, and evaluation of alternatives, and proceeding through purchase and postpurchase evaluation. We follow this with an examination of how the customer's level of involvement affects the type of decision making they use and discuss the types of consumer decision-making processes. Next, we examine situational influences—surroundings, time, purchase reason, and buyer's mood and condition—that affect purchasing decisions. We go on to consider psychological influences on purchasing decisions: perception, motives, learning, attitudes, personality and self-concept, and lifestyles. Next, we discuss social influences that affect buying behavior, including roles, family, reference groups and opinion leaders, social classes, and culture and subcultures. We conclude with a discussion of consumer misbehavior.

buying behavior The decision processes and actions of people involved in buying and using products

consumer buying behavior The decision processes and purchasing activities of people who purchase products for personal or household use and not for business purposes

consumer buying decision process A five-stage purchase decision process that includes problem recognition, information search, evaluation of alternatives, purchase, and postpurchase evaluation

CONSUMER BUYING DECISION PROCESS

LO1. Recognize the stages of the consumer buying decision process.

The **consumer buying decision process**, shown in Figure 6.1, includes five stages: problem recognition, information search, evaluation of alternatives, purchase, and postpurchase evaluation. Before we examine each stage, consider these important points. First, as shown

Figure 6.1 Consumer Buying Decision Process and Possible Influences on the Process

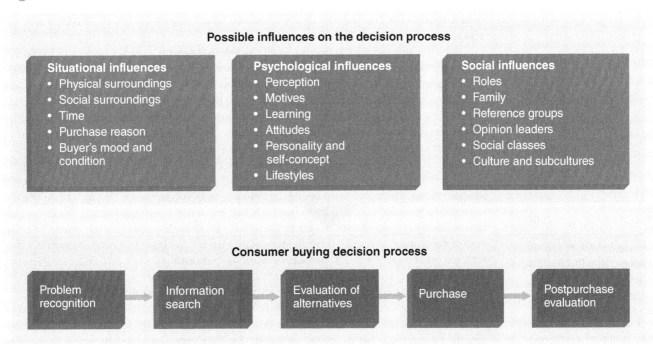

Possible influences on the decision process

Situational influences	Psychological influences	Social influences
• Physical surroundings • Social surroundings • Time • Purchase reason • Buyer's mood and condition	• Perception • Motives • Learning • Attitudes • Personality and self-concept • Lifestyles	• Roles • Family • Reference groups • Opinion leaders • Social classes • Culture and subcultures

Consumer buying decision process

Problem recognition → Information search → Evaluation of alternatives → Purchase → Postpurchase evaluation

© Cengage Learning

Problem Recognition
This advertisement is attempting to stimulate problem recognition regarding the protection of one's computer.

in Figure 6.1, this process can be affected by numerous influences, which are categorized as situational, psychological, and social. Second, the actual act of purchasing is usually not the first stage of the process. Third, not all decision processes lead to a purchase. Individuals may end the process at any stage. Finally, not all consumer decisions include all five stages.

Problem Recognition

Problem recognition occurs when a buyer becomes aware of a difference between a desired state and an actual condition. The speed of consumer problem recognition can be rapid or slow. It is possible that a person has a problem or need but is unaware of it until marketers point it out. Marketers use sales personnel, advertising, and packaging to help trigger recognition of such needs or problems. Take a look at the advertisement for Carbonite, a company that provides computer backup services, for an example of a common consumer problem. The advertisement is making the viewer aware of a possible future scenario in which a liquid spills on a laptop, ruining it. This is a fairly common experience among users of electronics, but something that most people do not consider until it is too late. This advertisement is admonishing consumers to be proactive and to back up data in preparation for the day that something bad happens to their computer.

Information Search

After recognizing the problem or need, the buyer will decide whether or not to pursue satisfying that need. If the consumer chooses to move forward, he or she will next search for product information to help resolve the problem or satisfy the need. For example, if a consumer realizes that he does, indeed, need to back up the files on his computer, he will conduct a search on different products and services that could fulfill this need.

An information search has two aspects. In an **internal search**, buyers search their memories for information about products that might solve their problem. If they cannot retrieve enough information from memory to make a decision, they seek additional information from outside sources in an **external search**. The external search may focus on communication with friends or relatives, comparison of available brands and prices, marketer-dominated sources, and/or public sources. An individual's personal contacts—friends, relatives, and coworkers—often are influential sources of information because the person trusts and respects them. However, consumers should be wary not to overestimate the product knowledge of family and friends. Consumers may also use marketer-dominated sources of information, such as salespeople, advertising, websites, package labeling, and in-store demonstrations and displays because they typically require little effort. The Internet has become a major resource during the consumer buying decision process, with its many sources for product descriptions and reviews and the ease of comparing prices. Buyers can also obtain information from independent sources—for instance, government reports, news presentations, publications such as *Consumer Reports,* and reports from product-testing organizations. Consumers frequently view information from these sources as credible because of their factual and unbiased nature.

Repetition, a technique well-known to advertisers, increases consumers' information retention and recall. When they see or hear an advertising message for the first time, recipients may not grasp all of its important details, but they recall more details as the message is

internal search An information search in which buyers search their memories for information about products that might solve their problem

external search An information search in which buyers seek information from sources other than their memories

repeated. However, marketers should be wary not to repeat a message too many times, as consumers can grow tired of it and begin to respond unfavorably. Information can be presented verbally, numerically, or visually. Marketers pay great attention to the visual components of their advertising materials.

Evaluation of Alternatives

A successful information search within a product category yields a group of brands that a buyer views as possible alternatives. This group of brands is sometimes called a **consideration set** (or an *evoked set*). Consumers assign a greater value to a brand they have heard of than to one they have not—even when they do not know anything else about the brand other than the name. For example, a consideration set of computers might include laptop, notebook, and tablet computers from Dell, Toshiba, and Apple. A consumer will probably initially lean toward the one with which he or she is most familiar, or which his or her friends prefer, before conducting any additional searches.

To assess the products in a consideration set, the buyer uses **evaluative criteria**: objective characteristics (such as the size) and subjective characteristics (such as style) that are important to him or her. Consider that one buyer may want a large display, whereas another may want a computer with a lot of memory. The buyer assigns a certain level of importance to each criterion. However, some features and characteristics carry more weight than others, depending on consumer preferences. The buyer rates and eventually ranks brands in the consideration set using the selected evaluative criteria. It is possible that the evaluation stage may yield no brand the buyer is willing to purchase. In that case, a further information search may be necessary.

Marketers can influence consumers' evaluations by *framing* the alternatives—that is, describing the alternatives and their attributes in a certain manner. Framing can make a characteristic seem more important to a consumer and facilitate its recall from memory. For example, by stressing a car's superior comfort and safety features over those of a competitor's, a carmaker can direct consumers' attention toward these points. You have experienced the framing effect if you have ever walked into a gourmet grocery or high-end clothing store where the displays make the products seem so appealing you just have to buy them, only to return home and be less satisfied than you were in the store. Framing has a stronger influence on the decision processes of inexperienced buyers. If the evaluation of alternatives yields one or more brands that the consumer is willing to buy, he or she is ready to move on to the next stage of the decision process: the purchase.

consideration set A group of brands within a product category that a buyer views as alternatives for possible purchase

evaluative criteria Objective and subjective product characteristics that are important to a buyer

Purchase

In the purchase stage, the consumer chooses to buy the product or brand yielded by the evaluation of alternatives. However, product availability may influence which brand is ultimately purchased. If the brand that ranked highest in evaluation is unavailable and the buyer is unwilling to wait until it is available again, the buyer may choose to purchase the brand that ranked second. For example, if a consumer is at the mall shopping for jeans and the preferred Levis in her size are out of stock, but the Lucky brand jeans are not, the consumer may opt to purchase the Lucky brand to save another trip to the mall later.

Buying on the Weekend: How Much Does It Cost?

SNAPSHOT

Source: Jae Yang and Paul Trap.

Going Green

How Green Is That Product? Check the App!

In a world filled with alternatives, how do you evaluate products or brands that offer similar benefits? The answer, for many consumers, is to check a product's environmental record before making a buying decision. There's an app for that—actually, any number of mobile apps are available to help consumers determine which goods or services are the greenest alternatives.

Consumers who download the GoodGuide app, for example, first select the criteria they want to apply to a product, such as how energy efficient it is and whether it contains natural ingredients. Next, they scan the product's bar code with a cell phone. The app instantly checks

GoodGuide's database of 140,000 products and displays a numerical score, from 0 to 10. The higher the score, the greener the product.

The Green Fuel app helps consumers find the nearest gas station offering alternative fuels such as compressed natural gas. The Light Bulb Finder app suggests energy-efficient alternatives to traditional incandescent light bulbs, personalized for each user's zip code and power situation. The Find Green app directs users toward local businesses that offer green goods and services. And the eLabel app reveals a product's carbon and water footprint.[a]

During this stage, buyers also pick the seller from which they will buy the product—it could be a specific retail shop, chain, or online retailer. The choice of seller may affect final product selection and therefore the terms of sale, which, if negotiable, are determined at this stage. Consumers also settle other issues, such as price, delivery, warranties, maintenance agreements, installation, and credit arrangements, at this time. Finally, the actual purchase takes place (although the consumer can still decide to terminate the buying decision process even at this late stage).

Postpurchase Evaluation

After the purchase, the buyer evaluates the product to ascertain if its actual performance meets expected levels. Many criteria used in evaluating alternatives are applied again during postpurchase evaluation in order to make a comparison. The outcome of this stage is either satisfaction or dissatisfaction, which influences whether the consumer will repurchase the brand or product, complain to the seller, or communicate positively or negatively with other possible buyers.

This stage is especially important for high-priced items. Shortly after the purchase of an expensive product, evaluation may result in **cognitive dissonance**; doubts in the buyer's mind about whether purchasing the product was the right decision. Cognitive dissonance is most likely to arise when a person recently bought an expensive, high-involvement product that is found lacking compared to desirable features of competing brands. A buyer who is experiencing cognitive dissonance may attempt to return the product or may seek out positive information, such as reviews, to justify choosing it. Marketers sometimes attempt to reduce cognitive dissonance by having salespeople call or e-mail recent customers to make sure they are satisfied with their new purchases. Salespeople may send recent buyers results of studies demonstrating that other consumers are very satisfied with the brand.

As Figure 6.1 shows, three major categories of influences are believed to affect the consumer buying decision process: situational, psychological, and social. In the remainder of this chapter, we focus on these influences. Although we discuss each major influence separately, their effects on the consumer decision process are interrelated.

cognitive dissonance
A buyer's doubts shortly after a purchase about whether the decision was the right one

TYPES OF CONSUMER DECISION MAKING AND LEVEL OF INVOLVEMENT

LO2. Understand the types of consumer decision making and the level of involvement.

To acquire products that satisfy their current and future needs, consumers engage in different types of decision-making processes that vary depending on the nature of the product. The amount of effort, both mental and physical, that buyers expend in solving problems also varies considerably with the cost and type of product. A major determinant of the type of decision-making process employed depends on the customer's **level of involvement**; the degree of interest in a product and the importance the individual places on that product. High-involvement products tend to be those that are visible to others (such as real estate, high-end electronics, or automobiles) and are more expensive. High-importance issues, such as health care, are also associated with high levels of involvement. Low-involvement products are much less expensive and have less associated social risk, such as grocery or drugstore items. A person's interest in a product or product category that is ongoing and long-term is referred to as *enduring involvement*. Most consumers have an enduring involvement with only a very few activities or items—these are the product categories in which they have the most interest. Many consumers, for instance, have an enduring involvement with Apple products, a brand that inspires loyalty and trust. Consumers will expend a great deal of effort to purchase and learn about Apple products, waiting in line for the latest iPhone release and reading articles about the various features of the newest iPad. In contrast, *situational involvement* is temporary and dynamic and results from a particular set of circumstances, such as the sudden need to buy a new bathroom faucet after the current one starts leaking and will not stop. For a short time period, the consumer will research different faucet models, retailers, and prices, but will settle on a choice relatively quickly because the consumer needs a functional bathroom again soon. Once the purchase is made, the consumer's interest and involvement taper off quickly. Consumer involvement may be attached to product categories (such as sports), loyalty to a specific brand, interest in a specific advertisement (e.g., a funny commercial) or a medium (such as a television show), or to certain decisions and behaviors (e.g., a love of shopping). Interest, such as finding an advertisement entertaining, does not necessarily mean the consumer will become involved with the brand. It may not satisfy a need the customer currently has, or he or she may be loyal to another brand. There are three types of consumer decision making, which vary in involvement level and other factors: routinized response behavior, limited decision making, or extended decision making (see Table 6.1).

A consumer uses **routinized response behavior** when buying frequently purchased, low-cost items that require very little search-and-decision effort. A consumer may have a

level of involvement An individual's degree of interest in a product and the importance of the product for that person

routinized response behavior A consumer problem-solving process used when buying frequently purchased, low-cost items that require very little search-and-decision effort

Table 6.1   Consumer Decision Making

	Routinized Response	Limited	Extended
Product cost	Low	Low to moderate	High
Search effort	Little	Little to moderate	Extensive
Time spent	Short	Short to medium	Lengthy
Brand preference	More than one is acceptable, although one may be preferred	Several	Varies, usually many

© Cengage Learning

Low-Involvement Products
Soft drinks are low-involvement products because they are inexpensive and purchased frequently. When buying soft drinks, consumers usually employ routinized response behavior.

brand preference, but will be satisfied with several brands in the product class. Typically, low-involvement products are bought through routinized response behavior—that is, almost automatically. For example, most buyers spend very little time or effort selecting soft drinks or chips.

Buyers engage in **limited decision making** when they purchase products occasionally or from unfamiliar brands in a familiar product category. This type of decision making requires slightly more time for information gathering and deliberation. For instance, if Procter & Gamble introduces an improved Pantene shampoo, interested buyers will seek additional information about the product, perhaps by asking a friend who has used it, watching a commercial about it, or visiting the company's website, before making a trial purchase.

The most complex type of decision making, **extended decision making**, occurs with high-involvement, unfamiliar, expensive, or infrequently purchased items—for instance, a car, home, or college education. The buyer uses many criteria to evaluate alternative brands or choices and spends much time seeking information and deciding before making the purchase.

Purchase of a specific product does not elicit the same type of decision-making process every time. We may engage in extended decision making the first time we buy a product, but find that limited decision making suffices when we buy it again. If a routinely purchased brand is discontinued or no longer satisfies us, we may use limited or extended decision making to switch to a new brand. Thus, if we notice that the brand of pain reliever we normally buy is no longer working well, we may seek out a different brand through limited decision making. Most consumers occasionally make purchases solely on impulse and not on the basis of any of these three decision-making processes. **Impulse buying** involves no conscious planning and stems from a powerful urge to buy something immediately.

limited decision making
A consumer problem-solving process used when purchasing products occasionally or needing information about an unfamiliar brand in a familiar product category

extended decision making
A consumer problem-solving process employed when purchasing unfamiliar, expensive, or infrequently bought products

impulse buying An unplanned buying behavior resulting from a powerful urge to buy something immediately

SITUATIONAL INFLUENCES ON THE BUYING DECISION PROCESS

Situational influences result from circumstances, time, and location that affect the consumer buying decision process. Imagine buying an automobile tire after noticing, while washing your car, that the current tire is badly worn. This is a different experience from buying a tire right after a blowout on the highway spoils your road trip. Situational factors can influence the buyer during any stage of the consumer buying decision process and may cause the individual to shorten, lengthen, or terminate the process. Situational factors can be classified into five categories: physical surroundings, social surroundings, time perspective, reason for purchase, and the buyer's momentary mood and condition.[2]

Physical surroundings include location, store atmosphere, scents, sounds, lighting, weather, and other factors in the physical environment in which the decision-making process occurs. Retail chains try to design their store environment and layout in a way that makes shopping as enjoyable and easy as possible, so consumers are more inclined to linger and make purchases. Take Louis Vuitton, featured in the advertisement. The brand is known for high-end bags, luggage, and accessories and conveys an air of luxury in the advertisement and in its physical stores. In this advertisement you see a woman in a balloon landing in what appears to be

situational influences
Influences that result from circumstances, time, and location that affect the consumer buying decision process

a European square, indicated by the large stone building behind her. This is an appropriate image to capture for a brand known for its luxury bags, including suitcases. This image of glamorous travel is captured in Louis Vuitton's physical stores as well, which are frequently located in glamorous cities such as Rome, Shanghai, and Paris, and create an environment where people dream of romantic vacations and are put in a mood to shop. Marketers at banks, department stores, and specialty stores go to considerable effort and expense to create physical settings that are conducive to making purchase decisions. Restaurant chains, such as Olive Garden and Chili's, invest heavily in facilities, often building from the ground up, to provide surroundings that are distinctive to the chain and that enhance customers' experiences.

However, in some settings, dimensions such as weather, traffic sounds, and odors are clearly beyond the marketers' control. General climatic conditions, for example, may influence a customer's decision to buy a specific type of vehicle (such as an SUV) with certain features (such as a four-wheel drive). Current weather conditions, or other external factors, may be either encouraging or discouraging to consumers when they seek out specific products.

Social surroundings include characteristics and interactions of others who are present during a purchase decision, such as friends, relatives, salespeople, and other customers. Buyers may feel pressured to behave in a certain way because they are in a public place such as a restaurant, store, or sports arena. Thoughts about who will be around when the product is used or consumed are another dimension of the social setting. Negative elements of physical surroundings, such as an overcrowded store or an argument between a customer and a salesperson, may cause consumers to leave the store before purchasing anything.

Courtesy of Louis Vuitton

Situational Influences
Because physical surroundings are a situational influence, retailers such as Louis Vuitton expend considerable resources on making their storefronts and interiors inviting and consistent with the brand's image.

The time dimension influences the buying decision process in several ways. It takes varying amounts of time to progress through the steps of the buying decision process, including learning about, searching for, purchasing, and using a product. Time also plays a role when consumers consider the frequency of product use, the length of time required to use it, and the overall product life. Other time dimensions that can influence purchases include time of day, day of the week or month, seasons, and holidays. For example, a customer under time constraints is likely to either make a quick purchase decision or delay a decision.

The reason for purchase involves what the product purchase should accomplish and for whom. Generally, consumers purchase an item for their own use, for household use, or as a gift. Purchase choices are likely to vary depending on the reason. For example, you will likely choose a nicer product brand for a gift than you would for yourself. If you own a Mont Blanc pen, which is a very expensive brand, it is likely that you received it as a gift from someone very close to you.

The buyer's moods (e.g., anger, anxiety, or contentment) or conditions (e.g., fatigue, illness, or having cash on hand) may also affect the consumer buying decision process. Such moods or conditions are momentary and occur immediately before the situation where a buying decision will be made. They can affect a person's ability and desire to search for or receive information, or seek and evaluate alternatives. Moods can also significantly influence a consumer's postpurchase evaluation. If you are happy immediately after purchase, you may be more likely to attribute the mood to the product and will judge it favorably.

LO4. Understand the psychological influences that may affect the consumer buying decision process.

PSYCHOLOGICAL INFLUENCES ON THE BUYING DECISION PROCESS

Psychological influences partly determine people's general behavior and thus influence their behavior as consumers. Primary psychological influences on consumer behavior are perception, motives, learning, attitudes, personality and self-concept, and lifestyles. Even though these psychological factors operate internally, they are strongly affected by external social forces.

Perception

People perceive the same event or thing at the same time in different ways. When you first look at the illustration do you see fish or birds? Similarly, the same individual may perceive an item in different ways at different times. **Perception** is the process of selecting, organizing, and interpreting information inputs to produce meaning. **Information inputs** are sensations received through sight, taste, hearing, smell, and touch. When we hear an advertisement on the radio, see a friend, smell food cooking at a restaurant, or touch a product, we receive information inputs. Perception is complicated and can be influenced and compounded by different factors. For instance, research has shown that advertisements for food items that appeal to multiple senses at once are more effective than ones that focus on taste alone.[3]

Perception can be interpreted different ways because, although we constantly receive pieces of information, only a few reach our awareness. We would be completely overwhelmed if we paid equal attention to all sensory inputs, so we select some and ignore others. This process is called **selective exposure** because an individual selects (mostly unconsciously) which inputs will reach awareness. If you are concentrating on this paragraph, you probably are not aware that cars outside are making noise, that the room light is on, that a song is playing on your MP3 player, or even that you are touching the page. Even though you receive these inputs, they do not reach your awareness until they are brought to your attention. An individual's current set of needs affects selective exposure. Information inputs that relate to one's strongest needs are more likely to reach conscious awareness. It is not by chance that many fast-food commercials are aired near mealtimes. Customers are more likely to pay attention to these advertisements at these times.

The selective nature of perception may also result in two other conditions: selective distortion and selective retention. **Selective distortion** is changing or twisting received information.

psychological influences Factors that in part determine people's general behavior, thus influencing their behavior as consumers

perception The process of selecting, organizing, and interpreting information inputs to produce meaning

information inputs Sensations received through sight, taste, hearing, smell, and touch

selective exposure The process by which some inputs are selected to reach awareness and others are not

selective distortion An individual's changing or twisting of information that is inconsistent with personal feelings or beliefs

It occurs when a person receives information inconsistent with personal feelings or beliefs and he or she interprets the information, changing its meaning to align more closely with expectations. Selective distortion explains why people will reject logical information, even when presented with supporting evidence. Selective distortion can both help and hurt marketers. For example, a consumer may become loyal to a brand and remain loyal, even when confronted with evidence that another brand is superior. However, selective distortion can also lessen the impact of the message on the individual substantially. In **selective retention**, a person remembers information inputs that support personal feelings and beliefs and forgets inputs that do not. After hearing a sales presentation and leaving a store, for example, a customer may quickly forget many selling points if they contradict personal beliefs or preconceived notions about a product.

The second step in the process of perception is perceptual organization. Information inputs that reach awareness are not received in an organized form. To produce meaning, an individual must organize and integrate new information with what is already stored in memory. People use several methods to achieve this. One method, called *closure*, occurs when a person fills in missing information in a way that conforms to a pattern or statement. In an attempt to draw attention to its brand, an advertiser may capitalize on closure by using incomplete images, sounds, or statements in its advertisements.

Interpretation, the third step in the perceptual process, involves assigning meaning to what has been organized. A person interprets information according to what he or she expects or what is familiar. For this reason, a manufacturer who

Fish or Fowl?
Do you see fish or birds?

selective retention
Remembering information inputs that support personal feelings and beliefs and forgetting inputs that do not

---

Marketing Debate

Digital Stalking: Your Choice?

ISSUE: Should consumers have to take the initiative to opt out of online tracking, or should they be excluded unless they opt in?

Since the dawn of the Internet age, marketers have studied online behavior to better understand what consumers do and why. The goal is to deliver relevant online marketing messages when and where a consumer is likely to be interested.

Privacy advocates worry that consumers don't know how much data marketers actually collect online. Few people dig deeply into privacy policies or learn about the tracking techniques being used to follow their activities online. That's why critics say consumers should be tracked only if they consent by opting in.

Legal or regulatory action may result in a "Do Not Track" list similar to the "Do Not Call" list that currently prevents consumers from receiving unwanted telemarketing calls.

Marketers point out that tracking adds convenience, allowing them to personalize pages and offers according to consumers' preferences. Still, the online advertising industry has set up a program to more prominently disclose tracking and make it easier to opt out. In addition, most Internet browsers can be configured to detect tracking and let consumers opt out. Finally, by offering special privileges or other incentives, marketers have found many consumers very willing to provide personal data and allow tracking.[b]

changes a product or its package may face consumer backlash from customers looking for the old, familiar product or package and who do not recognize, or do not like, the new one. Unless a product or package change is accompanied by a promotional program that makes people aware of the change, an organization may suffer a sales decline.

Although marketers cannot control buyers' perceptions, they often try to influence them. Several problems may arise from such attempts, however. First, a consumer's perceptual process may operate such that a seller's information never reaches the target. For example, a buyer may entirely block out and not notice an advertisement in a magazine. Second, a buyer may receive information but perceive it differently than was intended, as occurs in selective distortion. For instance, when a toothpaste producer advertises that "35 percent of the people who use this toothpaste have fewer cavities," a customer could infer that 65 percent of users have more cavities. Third, a buyer who perceives information inputs to be inconsistent with prior beliefs is likely to forget the information quickly, as is the case with selective retention.

Motives

motive An internal energizing force that directs a person's behavior toward satisfying needs or achieving goals

Maslow's hierarchy of needs The five levels of needs that humans seek to satisfy, from most to least important

A **motive** is an internal energizing force that directs a person's activities toward satisfying needs or achieving goals. Buyers are affected by a set of motives rather than by just one. At any point in time, certain motives will have a stronger influence on a person than others. For example, the sensation of being cold is a strong motivator on the decision to purchase a new coat, making the feeling more urgent in the winter than it is in the summer.

Motives can be physical feelings, states of mind, or emotions. Some motives may help an individual achieve his or her goals, whereas others create barriers to achievement. Motives also affect the direction and intensity of behavior.

Abraham Maslow, an American psychologist, conceived a theory of motivation based on a hierarchy of needs. According to Maslow, humans seek to satisfy five levels of needs, from most to least basic to survival, as shown in Figure 6.2. This pyramid is known as **Maslow's hierarchy of needs**. Maslow proposed that people are constantly striving to move up the hierarchy, fulfilling one level of needs, then aspiring to fulfill the next.

At the most basic level are *physiological needs,* requirements for survival such as food, water, sex, clothing, and shelter, which people try to satisfy first. Food and beverage marketers often appeal to physiological needs, such as sex appeal or hunger. Carl's Jr. is famous for its commercials of lingerie models eating burgers, appealing to two physiological needs at once—hunger and sex appeal. Look at this advertisement for Breathe Right nasal strips. The ad consists of the word "sleep," with the word congestion wedged between each letter. It tells customers that congestion can inhibit sound sleep, and Breathe Right strips can help people sleep better when they are congested. Since sleep is one of the most basic functions, this advertisement appeals to our physiological needs.

At the next level are *safety needs,* which include security and freedom from physical and emotional pain and suffering. Life insurance, automobile air bags, carbon monoxide detectors, vitamins, and decay-fighting toothpastes are products that consumers purchase to ensure their safety needs are met.

Don't let nasal congestion get in between you and your sleep.

Opens your nose to relieve nighttime congestion the instant you put it on. For as long as you have it on.

It's your right to Breathe Right. **GET 2 FREE STRIPS AT BREATHERIGHT.COM**

Physiological Needs
Breathe Right nasal strips help an individual sleep better by facilitating improved breathing. This product contributes to achieving physiological needs, since sleep is a basic function of survival.

Figure 6.2 Maslow's Hierarchy of Needs

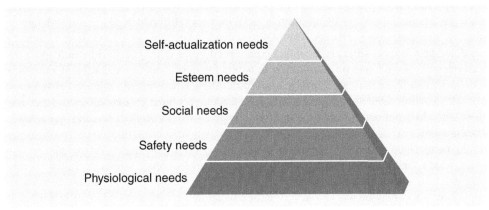

© Cengage Learning

Next are *social needs:* the human requirements for love and affection and a sense of belonging. Advertisements for cosmetics and other beauty products, jewelry, and even cars often suggest that purchasing these products will bring love and social acceptance, and are therefore appealing to social needs. Certain types of clothing, such as items emblazoned with logos or slogans, appeal to the customer's need to belong by displaying their affinity for popular brands.

At the level of *esteem needs,* people require respect and recognition from others as well as self-esteem, a sense of one's own worth. Owning a Lexus automobile, purchasing an expensive handbag, or flying first class can satisfy esteem needs. Purchasing products from firms that have reputations for being socially responsible can be motivated by a customer's desire to be perceived as a caring individual, thus contributing to satisfying esteem needs.

At the top of the hierarchy are *self-actualization needs.* These refer to people's needs to grow and develop and to become all they are capable of becoming. Many people never reach this level of the hierarchy, but it can be motivating to try. Some products that may send messages that they satisfy these needs include fitness center memberships, educational institutions, and self-improvement workshops. In its recruiting advertisements, the U.S. Army told its audience to "be all that you can be," a message that implies that people can reach their full potential by enlisting in the U.S. Army.

Motives that influence which establishments a customer frequents are called **patronage motives**. A buyer may shop at a specific store because of such patronage motives as price, service, location, product variety, or friendliness of salespeople. To capitalize on patronage motives, marketers try to determine why regular customers shop at a particular store and to emphasize these characteristics in the marketing mix.

Learning

Learning refers to changes in a person's thought processes and behavior caused by information and experience. Consequences of behavior strongly influence the learning process. Behaviors that result in positive consequences tend to be repeated. For example, a consumer who buys a Snickers candy bar, enjoys the taste, and feels satisfied after eating it is more likely to buy Snickers bars again. The individual will probably continue to purchase that product until it no longer provides satisfaction. When outcomes of the behavior are no longer satisfying or no longer contribute to achieving a desired goal, such as weight loss, the person may switch to a less fattening brand or stop eating candy bars altogether.

patronage motives Motives that influence where a person purchases products on a regular basis

learning Changes in an individual's thought processes and behavior caused by information and experience

Purchasing decisions require that customers process information, an ability that varies by individual. The type of information inexperienced buyers use may differ from the type used by experienced shoppers who are familiar with the product and purchase situation. Thus, two potential buyers of an antique desk may use different types of information in making their purchase decisions. The inexperienced buyer may judge the desk's value by price and appearance, whereas the more experienced buyer may seek information about the manufacturer, period, and place of origin to assess the desk's quality and value. Consumers who lack experience may seek information from others when making a purchase and even take along an informed "purchase pal." Experienced buyers have greater self-confidence and more knowledge about the product and can recognize which product features are reliable cues to quality.

Marketers help customers learn about their products by helping them gain experience with them, which makes customers feel more comfortable. Free samples, sometimes coupled with coupons, can successfully encourage trial and reduce purchase risk. For instance, because some consumers may be wary of new or exotic menu items, restaurants may offer free samples. In-store demonstrations foster knowledge of product uses. A software producer may use point-of-sale product demonstrations to introduce a new product. Test drives give potential new-car purchasers some experience with the automobile's features.

Consumers also learn by experiencing products indirectly through information from salespeople, advertisements, websites, friends, and relatives. Through sales personnel and advertisements, marketers offer information before (and sometimes after) purchases that can create favorable consumer attitudes toward the product. However, marketers may encounter problems in attracting and holding consumers' attention, providing them with information for making purchase decisions, and convincing them to try the product.

Attitudes

An **attitude** is an individual's enduring evaluation of feelings about and behavioral tendencies toward an object or idea. The things toward which we have attitudes may be tangible or intangible, living or nonliving. For example, we have attitudes about sex, religion, politics, and music, just as we do toward cars, football, and breakfast cereals. Although attitudes can change over time, they generally remain stable and do not vary, particularly in the short term. A person's attitudes toward different things do not have equal impact at any one time and some are stronger than others. Individuals acquire attitudes through experience and interaction with other people.

An attitude consists of three major components: cognitive, affective, and behavioral. The cognitive component is the person's knowledge and information about the object or idea. The affective component comprises the individual's feelings and emotions toward the object or idea. Emotions involve both psychological and biological elements. They relate to feelings and can create visceral responses that result in behaviors. Love, hate, and anger are emotions that can influence behavior. For some people, certain brands, such as Google, Starbucks, or REI, elicit an emotional response. Firms that successfully create an emotional experience or connection with customers establish a positive brand image that can result in customer loyalty. This means it is important for marketers to generate authentic, genuine messages that consumers can relate to on an emotional level. The behavioral component manifests itself in the person's actions regarding the object or idea. Changes in cognitive, affective, or behavioral components may possibly affect other components.

Consumer attitudes toward a company and its products greatly influence success or failure of the firm's marketing strategy. When consumers have strongly negative attitudes toward one or more aspects of a firm's marketing practices, they may not only stop using its products, but also urge relatives and friends to do likewise. Because attitudes play an important part in determining consumer behavior, marketers should regularly measure consumer attitudes toward prices, package designs, brand names, advertisements, salespeople, repair services, store locations, features of existing or proposed products, and social responsibility efforts.

attitude An individual's enduring evaluation of feelings about and behavioral tendencies toward an object or idea

Emerging Trends

Keeping Customers Connected Everywhere

Free Wi-Fi isn't limited to coffee shops and fast-food restaurants anymore. In this wireless world, many consumers with mobile devices expect to be a click away from social media and news updates at all times. As a result, a growing number of department stores, supermarkets, and even sports stadiums are providing free Wi-Fi to keep customers happily connected to the Internet.

Saks Fifth Avenue offers free Wi-Fi in its 44 stores, along with an in-store shopping app that makes it easy for customers to browse and buy. Although some stores are concerned about shoppers comparing prices online and buying from Internet retailers, Saks recognizes that customers also use the Web to make better buying decisions by researching product details and reading consumer reviews. Nordstrom, Macy's, and Target are among the many retailers that now have free Wi-Fi. Woodman's Food Markets in Wisconsin has also joined the wireless world with a free shopping-list app for iPhones to streamline shopping and free Wi-Fi in its stores.

Most National Football League stadiums are now set up for free Wi-Fi so fans can check other sports results and post social media comments or photos directly from their seats. Making it easy to live the connected lifestyle at the stadium encourages fans to go to the game rather than staying home to watch.[c]

Seeking to understand attitudes has resulted in two major academic models: the attitude toward the object model (the Fishbein model) and the behavioral intentions model (also known as the Theory of Reasoned Action). These models provide an understanding of the role of attitudes in decision making. The attitude toward the object model can be used to understand, and possibly predict, a consumer's attitude. It consists of three elements: beliefs about product attributes, the strength of beliefs, and the evaluation of beliefs. These elements combine to form what is called the overall attitude toward the object.[4]

The behavioral intentions model, rather than focusing on attributes, focuses on intentions to act or purchase. This model considers consumer perceptions of what other people, particularly peers, believe is the best choice among a set of alternatives. As its name indicates, this model focuses on attitudes toward the buying behavior, not toward the object. The subjective norm component is important in recognizing that individuals live in an inherently social environment and are influenced by what others think and believe. Consider attitudes toward personal appearance (such as what clothes people wear, hairstyles, or piercings or tattoos). Consumers will take into account what others will think of their decisions. Many people are motivated to comply with what others hold to be an acceptable norm and stay in close communication through traditional word-of-mouth communications, media, and online social networking.

Several methods help marketers gauge consumer attitudes. One of the simplest ways is to question people directly. The Internet and social networking sites are useful tools for marketers seeking to garner information on attitudes directly from consumers. Using sites such as Facebook, companies can ask consumers for feedback and product reviews.

Marketers also evaluate attitudes through attitude scales. An **attitude scale** usually consists of a series of adjectives, phrases, or sentences about an object. Respondents indicate the intensity of their feelings toward the object by reacting to the adjectives, phrases, or sentences. For example, a marketer who is measuring people's attitudes toward shopping might ask respondents to indicate the extent to which they agree or disagree with a number of statements, such as "shopping is more fun than watching television."

When marketers determine that a significant number of consumers have negative attitudes toward an aspect of a marketing mix, they may try to improve those attitudes. This task is generally lengthy, expensive, and difficult and can require extensive promotional efforts. To alter responses so that more consumers purchase a certain brand, a firm might launch

attitude scale A means of measuring consumer attitudes by gauging the intensity of individuals' reactions to adjectives, phrases, or sentences about an object

LET'S LIGHT UP OUR CITIES WITH A CLEANER SOURCE OF ELECTRICITY.

We all need electricity to power our lives. Shell is helping to deliver natural gas to more countries than any other energy company. When used to generate electricity, it emits around half the CO₂ of coal. It's one of the most abundant sources of energy available today and, with our continued innovation, it could provide us with cleaner energy for around the next 250 years. Let's power our future with gas. Search: Shell let's go

LET'S GO.

Communication to Influence Attitudes
Shell is seeking to change consumer attitudes about energy companies by promoting its eco-friendlier energy sources in this advertisement, which shows people enjoying an all-American game of baseball.

an information-focused campaign to change the cognitive component of a consumer's attitude, or a persuasive (emotional) campaign to influence the affective component. Distributing free samples can help change the behavioral component by offering customers a no-cost means of trying out a product.

Both business and nonbusiness organizations try to change people's attitudes about many things using marketing messages, from health and safety to prices and product features. For example, look at the Shell advertisement. To counter attitudes that energy companies are corrupt or polluting, marketers at Shell created an advertising campaign featuring eco-friendly and socially responsible themes. It is particularly important to energy companies to maintain their reputations in the wake of the 2010 BP Deepwater Horizon oil leak in the Gulf of Mexico, which eroded consumer trust in BP and harmed the economies of Gulf states. This Shell advertisement does not promote a specific product or region, but rather seeks to change consumer attitudes about the company. The ad touts that Shell uses natural gas as a cleaner form of electricity (influencing the cognitive component of an attitude) to generate, in this case, the power to run the lights at an all-American baseball game on a summer night (evoking positive thoughts and influencing the emotional component of an attitude).

Personality and Self-Concept

Personality is a set of internal traits and distinct behavioral tendencies that result in consistent patterns of behavior in certain situations. An individual's personality is a unique combination of hereditary characteristics and personal experiences. Personalities typically are described as having one or more characteristics, such as compulsiveness, ambition, gregariousness, dogmatism, authoritarianism, introversion, extroversion, and competitiveness. Marketing researchers look for relationships between such characteristics and buying behavior. Even though a few links between several personality traits and buyer behavior have been determined, studies have not proven a definitive link. However, the weak association between personality and buying behavior may be the result of unreliable measures, rather than a true lack of a relationship.

Many marketers are convinced that personalities do influence types and brands of products purchased. Because of this believed relation, marketers aim advertising at specific personality types. For example, truck commercials often highlight rugged, all-American individualism. Marketers generally focus on positive personality characteristics, such as security consciousness, sociability, independence, or competitiveness, rather than on negatively valued ones, such as insensitivity or timidity.

A person's self-concept is closely linked to personality. **Self-concept** (sometimes called *self-image*) is one's perception or view of oneself. Individuals develop and alter their self-concepts based on an interaction between psychological and social dimensions. Research shows that buyers purchase products that reflect and enhance their self-concepts and that purchase decisions are important to the development and maintenance of a stable self-concept.[5] For example, consumers who feel insecure about their self-concept may purchase products that they believe will help bolster the qualities they would like to project. Consumers' self-concepts can influence whether they buy a product in a specific product category and may affect brand selection as well as the retailers they frequent.

personality A set of internal traits and distinct behavioral tendencies that result in consistent patterns of behavior in certain situations

self-concept A perception or view of oneself

Entrepreneurship in Marketing

Birchbox Helps Eliminate Guesswork from Beauty Products

Katia Beauchamp and Hayley Barna know how difficult it is to sort through the blizzard of beauty items on store shelves and find just the right cosmetics without investing a lot of time and money. As classmates at Harvard Business School, they founded Birchbox to deliver a box of sample-size beauty products by mail to customers every month for one low monthly fee. Once subscribers tried the samples and saw the results, they could buy full-size products from the Birchbox website whenever they ran out.

When a customer starts a subscription, she completes a profile questionnaire to guide Birchbox in selecting cosmetics, shampoos, moisturizers, and other products that fit her preferences. Each monthly shipment contains a variety of samples chosen for individual subscribers, with additional product tips available from Birchbox's online magazine, Facebook page, and YouTube channel. Not knowing exactly what will arrive adds to customers' anticipation, and the low cost reduces the risk of trying something new. Just as important, customers have the opportunity to experience each product's benefits firsthand and then decide whether to purchase it in the future, a process that Birchbox's founders call "try, learn, and buy."

Barely two years after launching Birchbox, Beauchamp and Barna had attracted 100,000 subscribers. More recently, they've expanded into Europe and are testing sample boxes for men. Customers like the convenience of receiving samples by mail, and many brands that have distributed samples via Birchbox are happy with the sales results, too.[d]

Lifestyles

As we saw in Chapter 4, many marketers attempt to segment markets by lifestyle. A **lifestyle** is an individual's pattern of living expressed through activities, interests, and opinions. Lifestyle patterns include the ways people spend time, the extent of their interaction with others, and their general outlook on life. People partially determine their own lifestyles, but lifestyle is also affected by personality and by demographic factors such as age, education, income, and social class. Lifestyles have a strong impact on many aspects of the consumer buying decision process, from problem recognition to postpurchase evaluation. Lifestyles influence consumers' product needs and brand preferences, types of media they use, and how and where they shop. A number of companies, such as CopperBridge Media, offer lifestyle analysis to business organizations.[6]

SOCIAL INFLUENCES ON THE BUYING DECISION PROCESS

L05. Examine the social influences that may affect the consumer buying decision process.

Forces that other people exert on buying behavior are called **social influences**. As Figure 6.1 (located at the beginning of this chapter) shows, they are divided into five major groups: roles, family, reference groups and opinion leaders, social classes, and culture and subcultures.

Roles

All of us occupy positions within groups, organizations, and institutions. In these positions we play one or more **roles**, which are sets of actions and activities a person in a particular position is supposed to perform based on the expectations of both the individual and surrounding persons. Because every person occupies numerous positions, they have many roles.

lifestyle An individual's pattern of living expressed through activities, interests, and opinions

social influences The forces other people exert on one's buying behavior

roles Actions and activities that a person in a particular position is supposed to perform based on expectations of the individual and surrounding persons

For example, a man may perform the roles of son, husband, father, employee or employer, church member, civic organization member, and student in an evening college class. Thus, multiple sets of expectations are placed on each person's behavior.

An individual's roles influence both general behavior and buying behavior. The demands of a person's many roles may be diverse and even at times inconsistent or at odds. Consider the various types of clothes that you buy and wear depending on whether you are going to class, to work, to a party, or to the gym. You and others in these settings have expectations about what is acceptable attire for these events. Thus, the expectations of those around us affect our purchases of many different types of clothing and other products.

Family Influences

consumer socialization The process through which a person acquires the knowledge and skills to function as a consumer

Family influences have a direct impact on the consumer buying decision process. Parents teach their children how to cope with a variety of problems, including those that help them deal with purchase decisions. **Consumer socialization** is the process through which a person acquires the knowledge and skills to function as a consumer. Often, children gain this knowledge and set of skills by observing parents and older siblings in purchase situations.

Children observe brand preferences and buying practices in their families and, as adults, will retain some of these brand preferences and buying practices as they establish and raise their own families. Buying decisions made by a family are a combination of group and individual decision making.

The extent to which family members take part in family decision making varies among families and product categories. Traditionally, family decision-making processes have been grouped into four categories: autonomic, husband dominant, wife dominant, and syncratic, as shown in Table 6.2. Although female roles have changed over time, women still make the majority of purchase decisions in households. Indeed, research indicates that women are the primary decision makers for 85 percent of all consumer buying decisions.[7]

The family life-cycle stage affects individual and joint needs of family members. For example, consider how the car needs of recently married twenty-somethings differ from those of the same couple when they are forty-somethings with a 13-year-old daughter and a 17-year-old son. Family life-cycle changes can affect which family members are involved in purchase decisions and the types of products purchased. Children also have a strong influence on household purchase decisions.

When two or more family members participate in a purchase, their roles may dictate that each is responsible for performing certain purchase-related tasks, such as initiating the idea, gathering information, determining if the product is affordable, deciding whether to buy the product, or selecting the specific brand. The specific purchase tasks performed depend on the types of products being considered, the kind of family purchase decision process typically employed, and the presence and amount of influence children have in the decision process. Thus, different family members play different roles in the family buying process.

Fuse/Jupiter Images

Family Influences
The decision process related to purchasing a home is influenced by parents and children. In addition, children learn about buying housing, which they will apply when making similar decisions when they are adults.

Table 6.2   Types of Family Decision Making

Decision-Making Type	Decision Maker	Types of Products
Husband dominant	Male head of household	Lawn mowers, hardware and tools, stereos, automobile parts
Wife dominant	Female head of household	Children's clothing, women's clothing, groceries, household furnishings
Autonomic	Equally likely to be made by the husband or wife, but not by both	Men's clothing, luggage, toys and games, sporting equipment, cameras
Syncratic	Made jointly by husband and wife	Vacations, TVs, living room furniture, carpets, financial planning services, family cars

© Cengage Learning

Within a household, an individual may perform one or more roles related to making buying decisions. The gatekeeper is the household member who collects and controls information, including price and quality comparisons, locations of sellers, and assessment of which brand best suits the household's needs. For example, if a family is planning a summer vacation, the gatekeeper will compare prices for hotels and airfare to determine the best deal. The influencer is a family member who tries to impact buying decisions by expressing his or her opinions. In the vacation example, an influencer might be a child who wants to go to Disney World or a teenager who wants to go snowboarding. The decider is a member who makes the buying choice. This role switches depending on the type and expense of the product being purchased. In the case of a vacation, the decider will more likely be the adults, who possess information, influence, and their own preferences. The buyer is the family member who actually makes the purchase. The user is a household member who consumes or uses the product. In the Disney World example, all members of the family are users.

Reference Groups

A **reference group** is a group, either large or small, with which a person identifies so strongly that he or she adopts the values, attitudes, and behavior of group members. Most people have several reference groups, such as families, work-related groups, fraternities or sororities, civic clubs, professional organizations, or church-related groups.

In general, there are three major types of reference groups: membership, aspirational, and disassociative. A membership reference group is one to which an individual actually belongs, with which the individual identifies intensely enough to take on the values, attitudes, and behaviors of people in that group. An aspirational reference group is one to which a person aspires to belong. The aspiring member desires to be like group members. A group that a person does not wish to be associated with is a disassociative or negative reference group. The individual does not want to take on the values, attitudes, and behavior of group members.

A reference group may serve as an individual's point of comparison and source of information. A customer's behavior may change over time to be more in line with the actions and beliefs of group members. For instance, a person may switch to a different brand of shirt based on reference group members' advice and preferences. An individual may also seek information from the reference group about other factors regarding a prospective purchase, such as where to buy a certain product.

reference group A group that a person identifies with so strongly that he or she adopts the values, attitudes, and behavior of group members

Reference groups can affect whether a person does or does not buy a product at all, buys a type of product within a product category, or buys a specific brand. The extent to which a reference group affects a purchase decision depends on the product's conspicuousness and on the individual's susceptibility to reference group influence. Generally, the more conspicuous a product, the more likely that reference groups will influence a consumer's purchase decision. A product's conspicuousness is determined by whether others can see it and whether it attracts attention. A marketer sometimes tries to use reference group influence in advertisements by suggesting that people in a specific group buy a product and are satisfied with it. Whether this kind of advertising succeeds depends on three factors: how effectively the advertisement communicates the message, the type of product, and the individual's susceptibility to reference group influence. In this type of appeal, the advertiser hopes that many people will accept the suggested group as a reference group and buy (or react more favorably to) the product.

Opinion Leaders

An **opinion leader** is a member of an informal group who provides information about a specific topic, such as smartphones, to other group members seeking information. The opinion leader is in a position or has knowledge or expertise that makes him or her a credible source of information on a few topics. Opinion leaders are easily accessible and they are viewed by other group members as being well-informed about one or multiple topics. Opinion leaders are not the foremost authority on all topics, but because such individuals know they are opinion leaders, they feel a responsibility to remain informed about specific topics, and thus seek out advertisements, manufacturers' brochures, salespeople, and other sources of information. Opinion leaders have a strong influence on the behavior of others in their group, particularly relating to product adoption and purchases.

An opinion leader is likely to be most influential when consumers have high product involvement but low product knowledge, when they share the opinion leader's values and attitudes, and when the product details are numerous or complicated. Possible opinion leaders and topics are shown in Table 6.3.

Social Classes

In all societies, people rank others into higher or lower positions of respect. This ranking process, called social stratification, results in social classes. A **social class** is an open aggregate of people with similar social rank. A class is referred to as *open* because people can move into and out of it. Criteria for grouping people into classes vary from one society to

opinion leader A member of an informal group who provides information about a specific topic to other group members

social class An open group of individuals with similar social rank

---

Table 6.3   Examples of Opinion Leaders and Topics

Opinion Leader	Possible Topics
Local religious leader	Charities to support, political ideas, lifestyle choices
Sorority president	Clothing and shoe purchases, hair styles, nail and hair salons
"Movie buff" friend	Movies to see in theaters, rent, or buy, television programs to watch
Family doctor	Prescription drugs, vitamins, health products
"Techie" acquaintance	Computer and other electronics purchases, software purchases, Internet service choices, video game purchases

© Cengage Learning

another. In the United States, we take into account many factors, including occupation, education, income, wealth, race, ethnic group, and possessions. A person who is ranking someone into a class does not necessarily apply all of a society's criteria. Sometimes, too, the role of income tends to be overemphasized in social class determination. Although income does help determine social class, the other factors also play a role. Within social classes, both incomes and spending habits can differ significantly among members.

Analyses of social class in the United States commonly divide people into either three to seven categories. Social scientist Richard P. Coleman suggests that, for purposes of consumer analysis, the population is divided into the three major status groups shown in Table 6.4, which are upper, middle, and lower classes. However, he cautions marketers that considerable diversity exists in people's life situations within each status group.

To some degree, individuals within social classes develop and assume common behavioral patterns. They may have similar attitudes, values, language patterns, and possessions. Social class influences many aspects of people's lives. Because people most frequently interact with others within their own social class, people are more likely to be influenced by others within their own class than by those in other classes. Social class can influence choice of religion, financial planning decisions, access to education, occupation, and leisure time activities.

Social class also influences people's spending, saving, and credit practices. It can determine the type, quality, and quantity of products a person buys and uses. For instance, it affects purchases of clothing, foods, financial and health-care services, travel, recreation, entertainment, and home furnishings. Behaviors within a social class can influence others as well. Most common is the "trickle-down" effect, in which members of lower classes attempt to emulate members of higher social classes, such as purchasing desirable automobiles, large homes, and even selecting certain names for their children. Couture fashions designed for the upper class influence the styles of the clothing sold in department stores frequented by the middle class, which eventually is sold to the working class who shop at discount clothing stores. Less often, status float will occur, when a product that is traditionally associated with a lower class gains status and popularity among upper classes. Social class also affects an individual's shopping patterns and types of stores patronized. In some instances, marketers attempt to focus on certain social classes through store location and interior design, product design and features, pricing strategies, personal sales efforts, and advertising. Many companies focus on the middle and working classes because they account for such a large portion of the population. Outside the United States, the middle class is growing rapidly in places such as India, China, and Brazil, making these consumers increasingly desirable targets for marketing messages.

Some firms target different classes with a range of products at different price points. Even designers who previously only made clothing for the wealthy have learned about the benefits of offering items at different price points. Numerous fashion houses, such as Lanvin and Jason Wu, have produced collaborations with retailers such as Target and H&M, coming out with affordable lines for the middle class.[8]

Culture and Subcultures

Culture is the accumulation of values, knowledge, beliefs, customs, objects, and concepts that a society uses to cope with its environment and passes on to future generations. Culture permeates most things you do and objects you interact with, from the style of buildings in your town, to the education you receive, to the laws governing your country. Culture also includes society-specific core values and the degree of acceptability of a wide range of behaviors. For example, in U.S. culture, customers and businesses are expected to behave ethically.

Culture influences buying behavior because it saturates our daily lives. Our culture determines what we wear and eat and where we reside and travel. Society's interest in the healthfulness of food affects food companies' approaches to developing and promoting their products. Culture also influences how we buy and use products and the satisfaction we derive from them.

culture The accumulation of values, knowledge, beliefs, customs, objects, and concepts that a society uses to cope with its environment and passes on to future generations

Table 6.4   **Social Class Behavioral Traits and Purchasing Characteristics**

Class (Percent of Population)	Behavioral Traits	Buying Characteristics
Upper Americans		
Upper-upper (0.5)	Social elite Of aristocratic, prominent families Inherited their position in society	Children attend private preparatory schools and best colleges Do not consume ostentatiously Spend money on private clubs, various causes, and the arts
Lower-upper (3.8)	Newer social elite Successful professionals earning very high incomes Earned their position in society	Purchase material symbols of their status, such as large, suburban houses and expensive automobiles Provide a substantial market for luxury product offerings Visit museums and attend live theater Spend money on skiing, golf, swimming, and tennis
Upper-middle (13.8)	Career-oriented, professional degree holders Demand educational attainment of their children	Provide a substantial market for quality product offerings Family lifestyle characterized as gracious yet careful Spend money on movies, gardening, and photography
Middle Americans		
Middle class (32.8)	"Typical" Americans Work conscientiously and adhere to culturally defined standards Average-pay, white-collar workers Attend church and obey the law Often very involved in children's school and sports activities	Greatly value living in a respected neighborhood and keep their homes well furnished Generally price sensitive Adopt conventional consumption tastes and consult category experts Spend on family-oriented, physical activities, such as fishing, camping, boating, and hunting
Working class (32.3)	Average-pay, blue-collar workers Live a routine life with unchanging day-to-day activities Hold jobs that entail manual labor and moderate skills Some are union members Socially not involved in civic or church activities, limit social interaction to close neighbors and relatives	Reside in small houses or apartments in depressed areas Impulsive as consumers yet display high loyalty to national brands Seek best bargains Enjoy leisure activities such as local travel and recreational parks
Lower Americans		
Upper-lower (9.5)	Low-income individuals who generally fail to rise above this class Reject middle-class morality	Living standard is just above poverty Seek pleasure whenever possible, especially through impulse purchases Frequently purchase on credit
Lower-lower (7.3)	Some are on welfare and may be homeless Poverty stricken Some have strong religious beliefs Some are unemployed In spite of their problems, often good-hearted toward others May be forced to live in less desirable neighborhoods	Spend on products needed for survival Able to convert discarded goods into usable items

Sources: Roger D. Blackwell, Paul W. Miniard, and James F. Engel, *Consumer Behavior*, 10th ed. (Mason, OH: Cengage Learning, 2005); "The Continuing Significance of Social Class Marketing," *Journal of Consumer Research* 10 (Dec. 1983): 265–280; Eugene Sivadas, George Mathew, and David J. Curry, "A Preliminary Examination of the Continued Significance of Social Class in Marketing," *Journal of Consumer Marketing* 14, no. 6 (1997): 463–469.

When U.S. marketers sell products in other countries, they must be aware of the tremendous impact specific cultures have on product purchases and use. Global marketers will find that people in other regions of the world have different attitudes, values, and needs, which call for different methods of doing business and different marketing mixes. Some international marketers fail because they do not or cannot adjust to cultural differences.

A culture consists of various subcultures. A **subculture** is a group of individuals whose characteristics, values, and behavioral patterns are similar within the group and different from those of people in the surrounding culture. Subcultural boundaries are often based on geographic designations and demographic characteristics, such as age, religion, race, and ethnicity. U.S. culture is marked by many different subcultures. Among them are punk, gamer, biker, endurance sports enthusiast, and cowboy. Within subcultures, greater similarities exist in people's attitudes, values, and actions than within the broader culture. Relative to other subcultures, individuals in one subculture may have stronger preferences for specific types of clothing, furniture, food, or consumer electronics. Take, for example, this advertisement for Brooks-brand PureDrift running shoes. Marketers are appealing to a subculture of athletes who like to train with minimal gear. These people tend to like to run barefoot, engage in endurance athletic feats, and follow a special diet such as "paleo," wherein adherents only eat foods that existed in prehistoric times. Some athletes believe emulating an ancient lifestyle helps them to be healthier, perform better, and increase their stamina. The PureDrift is a minimalist shoe, for runners within this subculture who would like some foot protection without the normal cushioning of running shoes.

subculture A group of individuals whose characteristics, values, and behavioral patterns are similar within the group and different from those of people in the surrounding culture

Subcultures can play a significant role in how people respond to advertisements, particularly when pressured to make a snap judgment. It is important for marketers to understand that a person can be a member of more than one subculture and that the behavioral patterns and values attributed to specific subcultures do not necessarily apply to all group members.

The percentage of the U.S. population consisting of ethnic and racial subcultures has grown and is expected to continue to grow. By 2050, about one-half of the U.S. population will be members of racial and ethnic minorities. The U.S. Census Bureau reports that the three largest and fastest-growing ethnic U.S. subcultures are African Americans, Hispanics, and Asians.[9] Nearly 50 percent of children under the age of 5 are minorities.[10] The population growth of these ethnic and racial subcultures represents a potential opportunity for marketers because of cultural-specific tastes and desires. Businesses recognize that, to succeed, their marketing strategies have to take into account the values, needs, interests, shopping patterns, and buying habits of these various subcultures.

African American Subculture

In the United States, the African American subculture represents 13.7 percent of the population.[11] Like all subcultures, African American consumers possess distinct buying patterns. For example, African American consumers spend much of their money on depreciable products such as phone services, children's clothing, and shoes. The combined buying power of African American consumers is projected to reach $1.1 trillion by 2015.[12]

Many companies are increasing their focus on the African American community. For example, State Farm

Courtesy of Brooks

Subcultures
Athletic shoe companies, such as Brooks, have released minimalist shoes, such as the PureDrift, to appeal to a subculture of athletes who wish to train with minimal gear.

auto insurance has featured African American basketball superstars such as LeBron James and Chris Paul in their advertisements as the insurance provider seeks to appeal to a younger and more ethnically diverse audience and to draw in new customers.[13]

Hispanic Subculture

Hispanics represent 16.7 percent of the U.S. population.[14] Hispanic buying power is expected to reach $1.5 trillion by 2015.[15] Hispanics represent a large and powerful subculture, and are an attractive consumer group for marketers.

When considering the buying behavior of Hispanics, marketers must keep in mind that this subculture is really composed of many diverse cultures coming from a huge geographic region that encompasses nearly two dozen nationalities, including Cuban, Mexican, Puerto Rican, Caribbean, Spanish, and Dominican. Each has its own history and unique culture that affect consumer preferences and buying behavior. Marketers should also recognize that the terms *Hispanic* and *Latino* refer to an ethnic category rather than a racial distinction. In spite of its complexity, because of the group's growth and purchasing power, understanding the Hispanic subculture is critical to marketers. Like African American consumers, Hispanics spend more of their income on groceries, phone services, clothing, and shoes, while they spend less than average on health care, entertainment, and education.[16]

Recognizing that half of children under age 5 are minorities, and that about 25 percent of children are Hispanic, marketers for Huggies Pull-Ups training pants developed two parallel advertising campaigns. One features a white family and one features a Hispanic family. Through research, marketers learned that the Hispanic subculture had slightly different issues and needs with toilet training. While white parents are reluctant to start the process, Hispanic parents are impatient to get through it. To this end, the English campaign features the line "Celebrate the first flush," while the Spanish campaign uses "Celebrate every flush."[17] It is through capitalizing on subtle but important differences such as this that marketers can attract a target market and retain them as loyal customers.

Asian American Subculture

The term *Asian American* includes Filipinos, Chinese, Japanese, Asian Indians, Koreans, and Vietnamese, encompassing people from more than 15 ethnic groups. This group represents 5.7 percent of the U.S. population.[18] The individual language, religion, and value system of each group influences its members' purchasing decisions. Some traits of this subculture, however, carry across ethnic divisions, including an emphasis on hard work, strong family ties, and a high value on education. The combined buying power of Asian American consumers is projected to reach $1 trillion by 2017.[19] Asian Americans are the fastest growing demographic, increasing by 50 percent in a decade, and a valuable target market because, as a group, Asian Americans are more educated and have household incomes that are 28 percent higher than the median income.

LO6. Examine consumer misbehavior.

CONSUMER MISBEHAVIOR

Approaching the topic of inappropriate consumer behavior requires some caution because of varying attitudes and cultural definitions of what comprises misbehavior. However, it is generally agreed that some conduct, such as shoplifting or purchasing illegal drugs, falls under the category of activities that are unacceptable by established norms. Therefore, we will define **consumer misbehavior** as behavior that violates generally accepted norms of a particular society. Shoplifting is one of the most obvious misconduct areas, with organized retail crime (where people are paid to shoplift goods from retail stores) on the rise. For example, theft of Tide detergent has become a national problem, with some grocery stores losing up to $15,000 a month. Tide is a premium detergent and thieves use it as a form of currency to buy drugs, with the dealers then turning around and selling single-use servings of Tide at Laundromats for high

consumer misbehavior
Behavior that violates generally accepted norms of a particular society

Table 6.5   Motivations for Unethical or Illegal Misbehavior

• Justification/rationalization	• The thrill of getting away with it
• Economic reasons	• There is little risk of getting caught
• It is accepted by peers	• People think they are smarter than others

Source: Kevin J. Shanahan and Michael J. Hyman, "Motivators and Enablers of SCOURing: A Study of Online Piracy in the US and UK," *Journal of Business Research* 63 (September–October 2010): 1095–1102.

profits. Participants in these crime rings have been spotted filling their carts and walking right out of stores. It has become such a problem that many stores now lock up their Tide detergent.[20] Experts estimate that organized retail crime alone costs businesses between $15 billion and $37 billion annually.[21] Aside from selling goods on the black market, consumer motivation for shoplifting includes the low risk of being caught, a desire to be accepted by a group of peers (particularly among young people), and the excitement associated with the activity.

Consumer fraud includes purposeful actions to take advantage of and/or damage others. Fraudulently obtaining credit cards, checks, bank accounts, or false insurance claims fall into this category. Even large companies with sophisticated security systems can be vulnerable to consumer fraud. Major banks, newspapers, governments, and even Twitter have been hacked and mined by criminals for the data their computer systems hold.[22] Some consumers engage in identity theft, which is a serious and growing legal problem—particularly as more shopping is conducted online, where regulations and security are more difficult to enforce. A type of consumer fraud that some consumers might not even consider a crime would be purchasing a dress for a special event, wearing it once, and then returning it.

Piracy is copying computer software, video games, movies, or music. It is a growing legal problem that some estimate costs the electronics and entertainment industries $59 billion annually, although the number is difficult to calculate precisely.[23] The recording industry broadcasts messages explaining why sharing music is not acceptable, but it remains a serious problem. Understanding motivations for piracy can be helpful in developing a plan to combat the issue (see Table 6.5).

Yet another area of concern with consumer misbehavior is abusive consumers. Rude customers engage in verbal or physical abuse, can be uncooperative, and may even break policies. Airlines remove abusive customers if they represent a threat to employees and other passengers. Belligerently drunk customers, especially in environments such as bars and restaurants, have to be removed in order to protect others. Understanding the psychological and social reasons for consumer misconduct can be helpful in preventing or responding to the problem.

Chapter Review

1. Recognize the stages of the consumer buying decision process.

The consumer buying decision process includes five stages: problem recognition, information search, evaluation of alternatives, purchase, and postpurchase evaluation. Not all decision processes culminate in a purchase, nor do all consumer decisions include all five stages. Problem recognition occurs when buyers become aware of a difference between a desired state and an actual condition. After recognizing the problem or need, buyers search for information about products to help resolve the problem or satisfy the need. In the internal search, buyers search their memories for information about products that might solve the problem. If they cannot retrieve from memory sufficient information to make a decision, they seek additional information through an external search. A successful search yields a group of brands, called a consideration set, which a buyer views as possible alternatives. To evaluate the products in the consideration set, the buyer establishes certain criteria by which to compare, rate, and rank different products. Marketers can influence consumers' evaluations by framing alternatives. In the purchase stage, consumers select products or brands on the basis of results from the evaluation stage and on other dimensions. Buyers also choose the seller from whom they will purchase the product. After the purchase, buyers evaluate the product to determine if actual performance meets expected levels.

2. Understand the types of consumer decision making and the level of involvement.

Buying behavior consists of the decision processes and acts of people involved in buying and using products. Consumer buying behavior is the buying behavior of ultimate consumers. An individual's level of involvement—the importance and intensity of interest in a product in a particular situation—affects the type of decision-making process used. Enduring involvement is an ongoing interest in a product class because of personal relevance, whereas situational involvement is a temporary interest that stems from the particular circumstance or environment in which buyers find themselves. There are three kinds of consumer decision making: routinized response behavior, limited decision making, and extended decision making. Consumers rely on routinized response behavior when buying frequently purchased, low-cost items requiring little search-and-decision effort. Limited decision making is used for products purchased occasionally or when buyers need to acquire information about an unfamiliar brand in a familiar product category. Consumers engage in extended decision making when purchasing an unfamiliar, expensive, or infrequently bought product. Purchase of a certain product does not always elicit the same type of decision making. Impulse buying is not a consciously planned buying behavior but involves a powerful urge to buy something immediately.

3. Explore how situational influences may affect the consumer buying decision process.

Three major categories of influences affect the consumer buying decision process: situational, psychological, and social. Situational influences are external circumstances or conditions existing when a consumer makes a purchase decision. Situational influences include surroundings, time, reason for purchase, and the buyer's mood and condition.

4. Understand the psychological influences that may affect the consumer buying decision process.

Psychological influences partly determine people's general behavior, thus influencing their behavior as consumers. The primary psychological influences on consumer behavior are perception, motives, learning, attitudes, personality and self-concept, and lifestyles. Perception is the process of selecting, organizing, and interpreting information inputs (sensations received through sight, taste, hearing, smell, and touch) to produce meaning. The three steps in the perceptual process are selection, organization, and interpretation. Individuals have numerous perceptions of packages, products, brands, and organizations that affect their buying decision processes.

A motive is an internal energizing force that orients a person's activities toward satisfying needs or achieving goals. Learning refers to changes in a person's thought processes and behavior caused by information and experience. Marketers try to shape what consumers learn in order to influence what they buy. An attitude is an individual's enduring evaluation, feelings, and behavioral tendencies toward an object or idea and consists of three major components: cognitive, affective, and behavioral. Personality is the set of traits and behaviors that make a person unique. Self-concept, closely linked to personality, is one's perception or view of oneself. Researchers have found that buyers purchase products that reflect and enhance their self-concepts. Lifestyle is an individual's pattern of living expressed through activities, interests, and opinions. Lifestyles influence consumers' needs, brand preferences, and how and where they shop.

5. Examine the social influences that may affect the consumer buying decision process.

Social influences are forces that other people exert on buying behavior. They include roles, family, reference groups and opinion leaders, electronic networks, social class, and culture and subcultures. Everyone occupies positions within groups, organizations, and institutions, and each position involves playing a role—a set of actions and activities that a person in a particular position is supposed to perform based on expectations of both the individual and surrounding persons. In a family, children learn from parents and older siblings how to make decisions, such as purchase decisions. Consumer socialization is the process through which a person acquires the knowledge and skills to function as a consumer. The consumer socialization process is partially accomplished through family influences.

A reference group is a group that a person identifies with so strongly that he or she adopts the values, attitudes, and behavior of group members. The three major types of reference groups are membership, aspirational, and disassociative. An opinion leader is a member of an informal group who provides information about a specific topic to other group members. A social class is an open group of individuals with similar social rank.

Social class influences people's spending, saving, and credit practices. Culture is the accumulation of values, knowledge, beliefs, customs, objects, and concepts that a society uses to cope with its environment and passes on to future generations. A culture is made up of subcultures, groups of individuals whose characteristic values and behavior patterns are similar to one another but different from those of the surrounding culture. U.S. marketers focus on three major ethnic subcultures: African American, Hispanic, and Asian American.

6. Examine consumer misbehavior.

Consumer misbehavior is defined as behavior that violates generally accepted norms of a particular society. One form of consumer misbehavior involves shoplifting, or stealing goods from retail stores. Organized retail crime is on the rise and involves people paying others to shoplift certain goods from retail stores, which are then usually sold on the black market. Another form of consumer misbehavior is consumer fraud, which involves purposeful actions to take advantage of and/or damage others. Common examples of consumer fraud are false insurance claims, identity theft, returning an item of clothing after wearing it, and fraudulently obtaining credit cards, checks, and bank accounts. Another form of consumer misbehavior is piracy, the copying or sharing of music, movies, video games, and computer software. One final area of concern with regards to consumer misbehavior is abusive consumers, which include customers who are rude, verbally or physically abusive, and/or uncooperative, which may violate some companies' policies. In order to respond to or even prevent these growing problems, organizations need to understand the psychological and social reasons for consumer misbehavior.

> Go to www.cengagebrain.com for resources to help you master the content in this chapter as well as materials that will expand your marketing knowledge!

Key Concepts

buying behavior 145
consumer buying behavior 145
consumer buying decision process 145
internal search 146
external search 146
consideration set 147
evaluative criteria 147
cognitive dissonance 148
level of involvement 149

routinized response behavior 149
limited decision making 150
extended decision making 150
impulse buying 150
situational influences 151
psychological influences 152
perception 152
information inputs 152

selective exposure 152
selective distortion 152
selective retention 153
motive 154
Maslow's hierarchy of needs 154
patronage motives 155
learning 155
attitude 156
attitude scale 157
personality 158

self-concept 158
lifestyle 159
social influences 159
roles 159
consumer socialization 160
reference group 161
opinion leader 162
social class 162
culture 163
subculture 165
consumer misbehavior 166

Issues for Discussion and Review

1. What are the major stages in the consumer buying decision process? Are all these stages used in all consumer purchase decisions? Why or why not?
2. How does a consumer's level of involvement affect his or her choice of decision-making process?
3. Name the types of consumer decision-making processes. List some products you have bought using each type. Have you ever bought a product on impulse? If so, describe the circumstances.
4. What are the categories of situational factors that influence consumer buying behavior? Explain how each of these factors influences buyers' decisions.
5. What is selective exposure? Why do people engage in it?
6. How do marketers attempt to shape consumers' learning?
7. Why are marketers concerned about consumer attitudes?
8. In what ways do lifestyles affect the consumer buying decision process?

9. How do roles affect a person's buying behavior? Provide examples.
10. What are family influences, and how do they affect buying behavior?
11. What are reference groups? How do they influence buying behavior? Name some of your own reference groups.
12. How does an opinion leader influence the buying decision process of reference group members?
13. How might consumer behavior be influenced by digital networks?
14. In what ways does social class affect a person's purchase decisions?
15. What is culture? How does it affect a person's buying behavior?
16. Describe the subcultures to which you belong. Identify buying behavior that is unique to one of your subcultures.
17. What is consumer misbehavior? Describe the various forms of consumer misbehavior.

Marketing Applications

1. Assume that Reebok has developed two new types of athletic shoes. One is designed for distance runners, and the other has been developed for skateboarders. As a marketer, you need to evaluate the potential psychological influences for each of these distinct target markets.

   Rank each of the following on a scale of 1 to 5 in order of importance for distance runners versus skateboarders. Consider 1 as the most important and 5 as the least important.

   - Roles
   - Family influences
   - Reference groups
   - Opinion leaders
   - Social classes
   - Culture and subcultures

   Are your top two ranks for the distance runner and skateboarder markets the same or different? If they're dissimilar, explain why various social influences affect contrasting target markets.

2. Consumers use one of three decision-making processes when purchasing goods or services: routinized response behavior, limited decision making, or extended decision making. Describe three buying experiences you have had (one for each type of decision making), and identify which decision-making type you used. Discuss why that particular process was appropriate.

3. The consumer buying process consists of five stages: problem recognition, information search, evaluation of alternatives, purchase, and postpurchase evaluation. Not every buying decision goes through all five stages, and the process does not necessarily conclude in a purchase. Interview a classmate about the last purchase he or she made. Report the stages used and those skipped, if any.

4. Attitudes toward products or companies often affect consumer behavior. The three components of an attitude are cognitive, affective, and behavioral. Briefly describe how a beer company might alter the cognitive and affective components of consumer attitudes toward beer products and toward the company.

5. An individual's roles influence that person's buying behavior. Identify two of your roles, and give an example of how they have influenced your buying decisions.

6. Select five brands of toothpaste and explain how the appeals used in advertising these brands relate to Maslow's hierarchy of needs.

7. Develop your analytical and communication skills using the Role-Play Exercises online at **www.cengagebrain.com**.

Internet Exercise

Amazon

Some mass-market e-commerce sites, such as Amazon, have extended the concept of customization to their customer base. The company has created an affinity group by drawing on certain users' likes and dislikes to make product recommendations to other users. Check out this pioneering online retailer at **www.amazon.com**.

1. What might motivate some consumers to read a "Top Selling" list?
2. Is the consumer's level of involvement with an online book purchase likely to be high or low?
3. Discuss the consumer buying decision process as it relates to a decision to purchase from Amazon.

developing your marketing plan

Understanding the process that an individual consumer goes through when purchasing a product is essential for developing marketing strategy. Knowledge about the potential customer's buying behavior will become the basis for many of the decisions in the specific marketing plan. Using the information from this chapter, you should be able to determine the following:

1. See Table 6.1. What type of decision making are your customers likely to use when purchasing your product?

2. Determine the evaluative criteria that your target market(s) would use when choosing between alternative brands.
3. Using Table 6.2, what types of family decision making, if any, would your target market(s) use?

4. Identify the reference groups or subcultures that may influence your target market's product selection.

The information obtained from these questions should assist you in developing various aspects of your marketing plan. Develop your marketing plan online using the Interactive Marketing Plan at **www.cengagebrain.com**.

video case 6.1

Starbucks Refines the Customer Experience

Starbucks—the Seattle-based company that popularized the "coffee culture"—is brewing up higher sales through new beverages and new cafés in global markets. A stop at Starbucks has become part of many consumers' daily routines. Some are attracted by the high-quality, brewed-to-order coffees, while others look forward to relaxing and socializing in the "third place" between home and work.

Starbucks has researched and refined every aspect of the customer experience, from the size of its coffees ("tall" is actually "small") to the number of minutes that customers spend waiting in line. To speed up purchases, it offers a pay-by-cell phone option called "mobile pay." Consumers with iPhone or Android cell phones simply download the app and let cashiers scan the Starbucks code on the screen during checkout. The app links to the customer's Starbucks Card, which combines the rewards of a loyalty program with the convenience of a prepaid card for making purchases. Mobile pay is a big hit: in its first 15 months, customers used their cell phones to make more than 42 million payments to Starbucks.

Well established in the intensely competitive U.S. market, Starbucks is growing much more quickly in Asian markets. The company will soon have 1,500 cafés and 30,000 employees in China, where consumers drink, on average, just three cups of coffee every year. By opening in more locations and encouraging consumers to bring their friends for coffee and conversation, Starbucks aims to increase demand and boost sales throughout China. In Japan, where Starbucks now has more than 1,000 cafés, consumers have long enjoyed the tradition of meeting in neighborhood coffee shops.

Through market research, Starbucks stays in touch with what its customers like and what their lifestyles are like. Coffee lovers are still buying their espressos or lattes, but they're also "looking for a healthier lifestyle," says a Starbucks executive. In response to this trend, the company bought Evolution Fresh, which makes premium juices, and opened

its first Evolution Fresh store in Bellevue, Washington. On the menu are all-natural, freshly blended drinks from nutritious fruits and vegetables, plus salads and wraps. Over time, Starbucks is adding Evolution Fresh drinks to the menu in all of its cafés and opening additional Evolution Fresh stores on the East and West Coasts. Although expanding into fresh juices means competing with Jamba Juice and other rivals, Starbucks is relying on its brand-building expertise to juice up this part of its business.

Taking note of consumer interest in energy drinks, which has blossomed into an $8 billion market, Starbucks has also launched Starbucks Refreshers, a line of carbonated drinks with more than half the caffeine content of an espresso shot. Available in supermarkets and in Starbucks cafés, these all-natural drinks combine green, unroasted coffee with fruit juices for a fruity, non-coffee flavor. To gain significant market share, Starbucks must battle Red Bull, Rockstar, and other well-known marketers of energy drinks.

Starbucks also believes in social responsibility. It offers health-insurance benefits to both part-time and full-time employees and donates generously to community projects. It also protects the environment by recycling in every café and constructing buildings designed to save energy and water. Finally, the company follows ethical purchasing practices to ensure that coffee growers get a fair price for their premium beans.[24]

Questions for Discussion

1. In terms of situational influences and level of involvement, what are the benefits of mobile pay?
2. With Evolution Fresh, which psychological influences on consumer buying decisions does Starbucks seem to be addressing?
3. Why would Starbucks want customers to know that it believes in social responsibility?

NOTES

[1] Based on information in Marc Graser, "Universal Licensing Unit Turns Ugly," *Variety*, January 7, 2013, www.variety.com; Gendy Alimurung, "David Horvath and Sun-Min Kim: The Doll Makers," *Los Angeles Weekly*, May 22, 2012, www.laweekly.com; Nicole Carter, "How to Build an Empire," *Inc.*, May 23, 2011, www.inc.com; Sarah E. Needleman, "A Love Letter Begets Dolls," *Wall Street Journal*, December 19, 2012, www.wsj.com; www.uglydolls.com.

[2] Russell W. Belk, "Situational Variables and Consumer Behavior," *Journal of Consumer Research* (December 1975): 157–164.

[3] Ryan S. Elder and Ariadna Krishna, "The Effects of Advertising Copy on Sensory Thoughts and Perceived Taste," *Journal of Consumer Research* 36, no. 5 (February 2010): 748–756.

[4] Barry J. Babin and Eric G. Harris, *CB3* (Mason, OH: Cengage Learning, 2012), 130.

[5] Aric Rindfleisch, James E. Burroughs, and Nancy Wong, "The Safety of Objects: Materialism, Existential Insecurity, and Brand Connection," *Journal of Consumer Research* 36, no. 1 (June 2009): 1–16.

[6] www.copperbridgemedia.com/industries/spirituality-wellness/lifestyle-analysis/.

[7] "Fast Facts," Marketing to Women Conference, www.m2w.biz/fast_facts.php (accessed February 2, 2013).

[8] About H&M, http://about.hm.com/content/hm/AboutSection/en/About/Facts-About-HM/People-and-History/Our-History.html (accessed February 2, 2013); "Target Designer Collaborations," *Huffington Post*, www.huffingtonpost.com/news/target-designer-collaboration (accessed February 2, 2013).

[9] "2010 Census Shows Asians Are Fastest-Growing Race Group," U.S. Census, March 21, 2012, www.census.gov/newsroom/releases/archives/2010_census/cb12-cn22.html (accessed February 2, 2013).

[10] "Most Children Younger Than Age 1 are Minorities," U.S. Census Newsroom, May 17, 2012, www.census.gov/newsroom/releases/archives/population/cb12-90.html (accessed February 2, 2013).

[11] African-American Consumers: Still Vital, Still Growing," Neilson, 2012, www.nielsen.com/africanamerican (accessed February 2, 2013).

[12] African-American Consumers: Still Vital, Still Growing," Neilson, 2012, www.nielsen.com/africanamerican (accessed February 2, 2013).

[13] Andrew Adam Newman, "A Basketball Star and His 'Twin' Sell Insurance," *New York Times*, December 18, 2012, www.nytimes.com/2012/12/19/business/media/chris-paul-to-star-in-state-farm-insurance-ads.html (accessed February 2, 2013).

[14] American Community Survey, U.S. Census Bureau, 2011.

[15] Hispanic Fast Facts, AHAA, http://ahaa.org/default.asp?contentID=161 (accessed February 2, 2013).

[16] Jeffrey M. Humphreys, "The Multicultural Economy 2010," Selig Center for Economic Growth, www.terry.uga.edu/selig/buying_power.html (accessed February 11, 2013).

[17] Tanzina Vega, "Celebrating the 'First Flush' with Parades and Pull-Ups," *New York Times*, January 3, 2013, www.nytimes.com/2013/01/04/business/huggies-pull-ups-ad-campaign-aims-to-celebrate-toilet-training.html (accessed February 2, 2013).

[18] American Community Survey, U.S. Census Bureau, 2011.

[19] Rosa Ramirez, "Asian American Purchasing Power to Rise to $1 Trillion," *National Journal*, November 21, 2012, www.nationaljournal.com/thenextamerica/economy/asian-american-purchasing-power-to-rise-to-1-trillion-20121121 (accessed February 2, 2013).

[20] Ben Paynter, "Suds for Drugs," *New York Magazine*, January 6, 2013, http://nymag.com/news/features/tide-detergent-drugs-2013-1/.

[21] "New Smartphone App Developed to Fight Retail Crime," PR Web, January 29, 2013, www.prweb.com/releases/2013/1/prweb10355345.htm.

[22] Michael Chertoff, "How Safe Is Your Data?" *Wall Street Journal*, January 18, 2013, http://online.wsj.com/article/SB100014241278873239683045782460426853037734.html.

[23] Eduardo Porter, "The Perpetual War: Pirates and Creators," *New York Times*, February 4, 2013, www.nytimes.com/2012/02/05/opinion/sunday/perpetual-war-digital-pirates-and-creators.html.

[24] Rose Yu, "Starbucks to Brew a Bigger China Pot," *The Wall Street Journal*, April 1, 2012, www.wsj.com; Bruce Horovitz, "Starbucks to Jolt Consumers with Refreshers Energy Drink," *USA Today*, March 22, 2012, www.usatoday.com; Bruce Horovitz, "Starbucks to Open First Evolution Fresh Juice Store," *USA Today*, March 18, 2012, www.usatoday.com; Jennifer Van Grove, "Starbucks Apps Account for 42M Payments," *VentureBeat*, April 9, 2012, www.venturebeat.com.

Feature Notes

[a] Based on information in "Values for Money," *Economist*, November 19, 2011, 66; "New Devices for an 'Appy' Environment," *Environmental Technology Online*, December 23, 2011, www.envirotech-online.com; Jefferson Graham, "Mobile Apps Make It Easier to Go Green," *USA Today*, May 12, 2011, www.usatoday.com; Jefferson Graham, "GoodGuide App Helps Navigate Green Products," *USA Today*, May 13, 2011, www.usatoday.com.

[b] Based on information in Byron Acohido, "Consumers Turn to Do-Not-Track Software to Maintain Privacy," *USA Today*, December 29, 2011, www.usatoday.com; Byron Acohido, "Internet Advertisers Begin Offering New Do Not Track Icon," *USA Today*, August 29, 2011, www.usatoday.com; Ryan LaSalle and Rafae Bhatti, "A Privacy-Centered Economy," *TechWorld*, January 13, 2012, www.techworld.com.

[c] Based on information in Michael Garry, "Woodman's Launches Mobile Scanning App," *Supermarket News*, January 14, 2013, http://supermarketnews.com; Verne Kopytoff, "Why Stores Are Finally Turning on to WiFi," *Fortune*, December 14, 2012, http://tech.fortune.cnn.com; Bill Siwicki, "Saks Fifth Avenue Rolls Out Wi-Fi Nationwide," *Internet Retailer*, September 19, 2012, www.internetretailer.com; Drake Bennett, "The Next Best Thing to Not Being There," *Bloomberg Businessweek*, September 24, 2012, 40–42.

[d] Based on information in Rip Empson and Ingrid Lunden, "Birchbox Rebrands in the UK, Hopes to Take a Little Shine off Glossybox and Other Beauty Box Rivals," *Techcrunch*, January 10, 2013, http://techcrunch.com; Olga Kharif, "A Surprise in Every Birchbox," *Bloomberg Businessweek*, February 16, 2012, www.businessweek.com; Allen Adamson, "Birchbox, Like Apple and Amazon and Google, Is a Hit Because Its Founders Hit on the Right Question," *Forbes*, September 12, 2012, www.forbes.com.

MICROECONOMICS

CHAPTER 1
The Economic Approach

FOCUS

- What is scarcity, and why is it important even in relatively wealthy economies?

- How does scarcity differ from poverty? Why does scarcity necessitate rationing and cause competition?

- What is the economic way of thinking? What is different about the way economists look at choices and human decision-making?

- What is the difference between positive and normative economics?

Economist, n.–A scoundrel whose faulty vision sees things as they really are, not as they ought to be.
—Daniel K. Benjamin, after Ambrose Bierce

Welcome to the world of economics. In recent years, economics has often been front-page news, and it affects all of our lives. The housing market's boom and bust, the recession and financial troubles of 2008–2009, the weak recovery and continuation of high unemployment rates, the soaring costs of a college education, and poor job opportunities even for college graduates—all of these have been in the news and have turned the lives of many Americans upside down. Economics will enhance your understanding of all of these topics and many more. You will soon see that economics is about much more than just financial markets and economic policy. In fact, a field trip to the fruits and vegetables section at your local grocery store could well be filled with more economics lessons than a trip to the New York Stock Exchange.

In a nutshell, economics is the study of human behavior, with a particular focus on human decision-making. It will introduce you to a new and powerful way of thinking that will both help you make better decisions and enhance your understanding of how the world works.

You may have heard some of the following statements: The federal government's debt has soared to historic highs, and trouble lies ahead if we do not get it under control. More government spending is necessary in order to speed up economic recovery. Americans would be better off if we did not buy so many things from foreigners. A higher minimum wage will help the poor. Government action is needed to ensure that health care is affordable and available to all. Are these statements true? This course will provide you with knowledge that will enhance your understanding of issues like these and numerous others. It may even alter the way you think about them.

The origins of economics date back to Adam Smith, a Scottish moral philosopher, who expressed the first economic ideas in his breakthrough book, *An Inquiry into the Nature and Causes of the Wealth of Nations*, published in 1776. As the title of his book suggests, Smith sought to explain why people in some nations were wealthier than those in others. This very question is still a central issue in economics. It is so important that throughout this book we will use a special "Keys to Economic Prosperity" symbol in the margin to highlight sections that focus on this topic. A listing of the major keys to prosperity is presented inside the front cover of the book. These keys and accompanying discussions will help you understand what factors enable economies, and their citizens, to grow wealthier and prosper.

OUTSTANDING ECONOMIST

THE IMPORTANCE OF ADAM SMITH, THE FATHER OF ECONOMIC SCIENCE

Economics is a relatively young science. The foundation of economics was laid in 1776, when Adam Smith (1723–1790) published *An Inquiry into the Nature and Causes of the Wealth of Nations.*

Smith was a lecturer at the University of Glasgow, in his native Scotland. Before economics, morals and ethics were actually his concern. His first book was *The Theory of Moral Sentiments*. For Smith, self-interest and sympathy for others were complementary. However, he did not believe that charity alone would provide the essentials for a good life.

Smith stressed that free exchange and competitive markets would harness self-interest as a creative force. He believed that individuals *pursuing their own interests* would be directed by the "invisible hand" of market prices toward the production of those goods that were most advantageous to society. He argued that the wealth of a nation does not lie in gold and silver, but rather in the goods and services produced and consumed by people. According to Smith, competitive markets would lead to coordination, order, and efficiency without the direction of a central authority.

These were revolutionary ideas at the time, but they had consequences. Smith's ideas greatly influenced not only Europeans but also those who developed the political economy structure of the United States. Further, Smith's notion of the "invisible hand" of the market continues to enhance our understanding of why some nations prosper while others stagnate.[1]

[1]For an excellent biographical sketch of Adam Smith, see David Henderson, ed., *The Fortune Encyclopedia of Economics* (New York: Warner Books, 1993), 836–38. The entire text of this useful encyclopedia is now available online, free of charge, at http://www.econlib.org.

1-1 WHAT IS ECONOMICS ABOUT?

Economics is about scarcity and the choices we have to make because our desire for goods and services is far greater than their availability from nature. Would you like some new clothes, a nicer car, and a larger apartment? How about better grades and more time to watch television, go skiing, and travel? Do you dream of driving your brand-new Porsche into the driveway of your oceanfront house? As individuals, we have a desire for goods that is virtually unlimited. We may want all of these things. Unfortunately, both as individuals and as a society we face a constraint called scarcity that prevents us from being able to completely fulfill our desires.

Scarcity is present whenever there is less of a good or resource freely available from nature than people would like. There are some things that are not scarce—seawater comes to mind; nature has provided as much of it as people want. But almost everything else you can think of—even your time—is scarce. In economics, the word *scarce* has a very specific meaning that differs slightly from the way it is commonly used. Even if large amounts of a good have been produced, it is still scarce as long as there is not as much of it *freely available from nature* as we would all like. For example, even though goods like apples and automobiles are relatively abundant in the United States, they are still scarce because we would like to have more of them than nature has freely provided. In economics, we generally wish to determine only if a good is scarce or not, and refrain from using the term to refer to the relative availability or abundance of a good or resource.

Because of scarcity, we have to make choices. Should I spend the next hour studying or watching TV? Should I spend my last $20 on iTunes downloads or on a shirt? Should this factory be used to produce clothing or furniture? Choice, the act of selecting among alternatives, is the logical consequence of scarcity. When we make choices, we constantly face trade-offs between meeting one desire or another. To meet one need, we must let another go unmet. The basic ideas of *scarcity* and *choice*, along with the *trade-offs* we face, provide the foundation for economic analysis.

Resources are the ingredients, or inputs, that people use to produce goods and services. Our ability to produce goods and services is limited precisely because of the limited nature of our resources.

Exhibit 1 lists a number of scarce goods and the limited resources that might be used to produce them. There are three general categories of resources. First, there are *human resources*—the productive knowledge, skill, and strength of human beings. Second, there are *physical resources*—things like tools, machines, and buildings that enhance our ability to produce goods. Economists often use the term capital when referring to these human-made resources. Third, there are *natural resources*—things like land, mineral deposits,

Scarcity
Fundamental concept of economics that indicates that there is less of a good freely available from nature than people would like.

Choice
The act of selecting among alternatives.

Resource
An input used to produce economic goods. Land, labor, skills, natural resources, and human-made tools and equipment provide examples. Throughout history, people have struggled to transform available, but limited, resources into things they would like to have—economic goods.

Capital
Human-made resources (such as tools, equipment, and structures) used to produce other goods and services. They enhance our ability to produce in the future.

EXHIBIT 1

A General Listing of Scarce Goods and Limited Resources

History is a record of our struggle to transform available, but limited, resources into goods that we would like to have.

SCARCE GOODS	LIMITED RESOURCES
Food (bread, milk, meat, eggs, vegetables, coffee, etc.)	Land (various degrees of fertility)
Clothing (shirts, pants, blouses, shoes, socks, coats, sweaters, etc.)	Natural resources (rivers, trees, minerals, oceans, etc.)
Household goods (tables, chairs, rugs, beds, dressers, television sets, etc.)	Machines and other human-made physical resources
Education	Nonhuman animal resources
National defense	Technology (physical and scientific "recipes" of history)
Leisure time	Human resources (the knowledge, skill, and talent of individual human beings)
Entertainment	
Clean air	
Pleasant environment (trees, lakes, rivers, open spaces, etc.)	
Pleasant working conditions	

oceans, and rivers. The ingenuity of humans is often required to make these natural resources useful in production. For example, until recently, the yew tree was considered a "trash tree," having no economic value. Then, scientists discovered that the tree produces taxol, a substance that could be used to fight cancer. Human knowledge and ingenuity made yew trees a valuable resource. As you can see, natural resources are important, but knowing how to use them productively is just as important.

As economist Thomas Sowell points out, cavemen had the same natural resources at their disposal that we do today. The huge difference between their standard of living and ours reflects the difference in the knowledge they could bring to bear on those resources versus what we can.[1] Over time, human ingenuity, discovery, improved knowledge, and better technology have enabled us to produce more goods and services from the available resources. Nonetheless, our desire for goods and services is still far greater than our ability to produce them. Thus, scarcity is a fact of life today, and in the foreseeable future. As a result, we confront trade-offs and have to make choices. This is what economics is about.

1-1a SCARCITY AND POVERTY ARE NOT THE SAME

Think for a moment about what life was like in 1750. People all over the world struggled 50, 60, and 70 hours a week to obtain the basic necessities of life—food, clothing, and shelter. Manual labor was the major source of income. Animals provided the means of transportation. Tools and machines were primitive by today's standards. As the English philosopher Thomas Hobbes stated in the seventeenth century, life was "solitary, poor, nasty, brutish, and short." [2]

Throughout much of South America, Africa, and Asia, economic conditions today continue to make life difficult. In North America, Western Europe, Oceania, and some parts of Asia, however, economic progress has substantially reduced physical hardship and human drudgery. In these regions, the typical family is more likely to worry about financing its summer vacation than about obtaining food and shelter. As anyone who has watched the TV reality show *Survivor* knows, we take for granted many of the items that modern technological advances have allowed us to produce at unbelievably low prices. Contestants on *Survivor* struggle with even basic things like starting a fire, finding shelter, and catching fish. They are thrilled when they win ordinary items like shampoo, rice, and toilet paper.

The degree to which modern technology and knowledge allow us to fulfill our desires and ease the grip of scarcity is often taken for granted—as the castaways on the CBS reality series Survivor quickly find out when they have to struggle to meet even basic needs, such as food, shelter, and cleaning their bodies and clothes.

Monty Brinton/CBS Photo Archive/Getty Images

---

[1] Thomas Sowell, *Knowledge and Decisions* (New York: Basic Books, 1980), 47.

[2] Thomas Hobbes, *Leviathan* (1651), Part I, Chapter 13.

During one episode, a contestant eagerly paid over $125 for a small chocolate bar and spoonful of peanut butter at an auction—and she considered it a great bargain!

It is important to note that scarcity and poverty are not the same thing. Scarcity is an **objective** concept that describes a factual situation in which the limited nature of our resources keeps us from being able to completely fulfill our desires for goods and services. In contrast, poverty is a **subjective** concept that refers to a personal opinion of whether someone meets an arbitrarily defined level of income. This distinction is made even clearer when you realize that different people have vastly different ideas of what it means to be poor. The average family in the United States that meets the federal government's definition of being "in poverty" would be considered wealthy in most any country in Africa. A family in the United States in the 1950s would have been considered fairly wealthy if it had air conditioning, an automatic dishwasher or clothes dryer, or a television set. Today, the majority of U.S. families officially classified as poor have many items that would have been viewed as symbols of great wealth just 65 years ago.

People always want more and better goods for themselves and others about whom they care. Scarcity is the constraint that prevents us from having as much of *all* goods as we would like, but it is not the same as poverty. Even if every individual were rich, scarcity would still be present.

1-1b SCARCITY NECESSITATES RATIONING

Scarcity makes **rationing** a necessity. When a good or resource is scarce, some criterion must be used to determine who will receive it and who will go without. The choice of which method is used will, however, have an influence on human behavior. When rationing is done through the government sector, a person's political status and ability to manipulate the political process are the key factors. Powerful interest groups and those in good favor with influential politicians will be the ones who obtain goods and resources. When this method of rationing is used, people will devote time and resources to lobbying and favor seeking with those who have political power, rather than to productive activities.

When the criterion is first-come, first-served, goods are allocated to those who are fastest at getting in line or willing to spend the longest time waiting in line. Many colleges use this method to ration tickets to sporting events, and the result is students waiting in long lines. Sometimes, as at Duke University during basketball season, they even camp out for multiple nights to get good tickets! Imagine how the behavior of students would change if tickets were instead given out to the students with the highest grade point average.

In a market economy, price is generally used to ration goods and resources only to those who are willing and able to pay the prevailing market price. Because only those goods that are scarce require rationing, in a market economy, one easy way to determine whether a good or resource is scarce is to ask if it sells for a price. If you have to pay for something, it is scarce.

1-1c THE METHOD OF RATIONING INFLUENCES THE NATURE OF COMPETITION

Competition is a natural outgrowth of scarcity and the desire of human beings to improve their conditions. Competition exists in every economy and every society. But the criteria used to ration scarce goods and resources will influence the competitive techniques employed. When the rationing criterion is price, individuals will engage in income-generating activities that enhance their ability to pay the price needed to buy the goods and services they want. Thus, one benefit of using price as a rationing mechanism is that it encourages individuals to engage in the production of goods and services to generate income. In contrast, rationing on the basis of first-come, first-served encourages individuals to waste a substantial amount of time waiting in line, while rationing through the political process encourages individuals to waste time and other resources in competing with others to influence the political process.

Objective
A fact based on observable phenomena that is not influenced by differences in personal opinion.

Subjective
An opinion based on personal preferences and value judgments.

Rationing
Allocating a limited supply of a good or resource among people who would like to have more of it. When price performs the rationing function, the good or resource is allocated to those willing to give up the most "other things" in order to get it.

Within a market setting, the competition that results from scarcity is an important ingredient in economic progress. Competition among business firms for customers results in newer, better, and less expensive goods and services. Competition between employers for workers results in higher wages, benefits, and better working conditions. Further, competition encourages discovery and innovation, two important sources of growth and higher living standards.

1-2 THE ECONOMIC WAY OF THINKING

One does not have to spend much time around economists to recognize that there is an "economic way of thinking." Admittedly, economists, like others, differ widely in their ideological views. A news commentator once remarked that "any half-dozen economists will normally come up with about six different policy prescriptions." Yet, in spite of their philosophical differences, the approaches of economists reflect common ground.

That common ground is economic theory, developed from basic principles of human behavior. Economic researchers are constantly involved in testing and seeking to verify their theories. When the evidence from the testing is consistent with a theory, eventually that theory will become widely accepted among economists. Economic theory, like a road map or a guidebook, establishes reference points indicating what to look for and how economic issues are interrelated. To a large degree, the basic economic principles are merely common sense. When applied consistently, however, these commonsense concepts can provide powerful and sometimes surprising insights.

It [economics] is a method rather than a doctrine, an apparatus of the mind, a technique of thinking which helps its possessor to draw correct conclusions.

—*John Maynard Keynes[3]*

Economic theory
A set of definitions, postulates, and principles assembled in a manner that makes clear the "cause-and-effect" relationships.

1-2a EIGHT GUIDEPOSTS TO ECONOMIC THINKING

The economic way of thinking requires incorporating certain guidelines—some would say the building blocks of basic economic theory—into your own thought process. Once you incorporate these guidelines, economics can be a relatively easy subject to master. Students who have difficulty with economics have almost always failed to assimilate one or more of these principles. The following are eight principles that characterize the economic way of thinking. We will discuss each of these principles in more depth throughout the book so that you will be sure to understand how and when to apply them.

1. The use of scarce resources is costly, so decision-makers must make trade-offs. Economists sometimes refer to this as the "there is no such thing as a free lunch" principle. Because resources are scarce, the use of resources to produce one good diverts those resources from the production of other goods. A parcel of undeveloped land could be used for a new hospital or a parking lot, or it could simply be left undeveloped. No option is free of cost—there is always a trade-off. A decision to pursue any one of these options means that the decision-maker must sacrifice the others. The highest valued alternative that is sacrificed is the opportunity cost of the option chosen. For example, if you use one hour of your scarce time to study economics, you will have one hour less time to watch television, spend social networking, sleep, work at a job, or study other subjects. Whichever one of these options you would have chosen had you *not* spent the hour studying economics is your highest valued option forgone. If you would have slept, then the opportunity cost of this hour spent studying economics is a forgone hour of sleep. In economics, the opportunity cost of an action is the highest valued option given up when a choice is made.

It is important to recognize that the use of scarce resources to produce a good is always costly, regardless of who pays for the good or service produced. In many countries, various kinds of schooling are provided free of charge *to students*. However, provision of the

Opportunity cost
The highest valued alternative that must be sacrificed as a result of choosing an option.

---

[3]John Maynard Keynes (1883–1946) was an English economist whose writings during the 1920s and 1930s exerted an enormous impact on both economic theory and policy. Keynes established the terminology and the economic framework that are still widely used when economists study problems of unemployment and inflation.

When a scarce resource is used to meet one need, other competing needs must be sacrificed. The forgone shoe store is an example of the opportunity cost of building the new drugstore.

schooling is not free *to the community as a whole*. The scarce resources used to produce the schooling—to construct the building, hire teachers, buy equipment, and so on—could have been used instead to produce more recreation, entertainment, housing, medical care, or other goods. The opportunity cost of the schooling is the highest valued option that must now be given up because the required resources were used to produce the schooling.

By now, the central point should be obvious. As we make choices, we always face trade-offs. Using resources to do one thing leaves fewer resources to do another.

Consider one final example. Mandatory air bags in automobiles save an estimated 400 lives each year. Economic thinking, however, forces us to ask ourselves if the $50 billion spent on air bags could have been used in a better way—perhaps say, for cancer research that could have saved *more* than 400 lives per year. Most people don't like to think of air bags and cancer research as an "either/or" proposition. It's more convenient to ignore these trade-offs. But if we want to get the most out of our resources, we have to consider all of our alternatives. In this case, the appropriate analysis is not simply the lives saved with air bags versus dollars spent on them, but also the number of lives that could have been saved (or other things that could have been accomplished) if the $50 billion had been used differently. A candid consideration of hard trade-offs like this is essential to using our resources wisely.

2. Individuals choose purposefully—they try to get the most from their limited resources. People try not to squander their valuable resources deliberately. Instead, they try to choose the options that best advance their personal desires and goals at the least possible cost. This is called **economizing behavior**. Economizing behavior is the result of purposeful, or rational, decision-making. When choosing among things of equal benefit, an economizer will select the cheapest option. For example, if a pizza, a lobster dinner, and a sirloin steak are expected to yield identical benefits for Mary (including the enjoyment of eating them), economizing behavior implies that Mary will select the cheapest of the three alternatives, probably the pizza. Similarly, when choosing among alternatives of equal cost, economizing decision-makers will select the option that yields the greatest benefit. If the prices of several dinner specials are equal, for example, economizers will choose the one they like the best. Because of economizing behavior, the desires or preferences of individuals are revealed by the choices they make.

Economizing behavior
Choosing the option that offers the greatest benefit at the least possible cost.

Purposeful choosing implies that decision-makers have some basis for their evaluation of alternatives. Economists refer to this evaluation as **utility**—the benefit or satisfaction that an individual expects from the choice of a specific alternative. Utility is highly subjective, often differing widely from person to person. The steak dinner that delights one person may be repulsive to another (a vegetarian, for example).

Utility
The subjective benefit or satisfaction a person expects from a choice or course of action.

The idea that people behave rationally to get the greatest benefit at the least possible cost is a powerful tool. It can help us understand their choices. However, we need to realize that a rational choice is not the same thing as a "right" choice. If we want to understand people's choices, we need to understand their own subjective evaluations of their options *as they see them*. As we have said, different people have different preferences. If Joan prefers $50 worth of chocolate to $50 worth of vegetables, buying the chocolate would be the rational choice for her, even though some outside observer might say that Joan is making a "bad" decision. Similarly, some motorcycle riders choose to ride without a helmet because they believe the enjoyment they get from riding without one is greater than the cost (the risk of injury). When people weigh the benefits they receive from an activity against its cost, they are making a rational choice—even though it might not be the choice you or I would make in the same situation.

3. Incentives matter—changes in incentives influence human choices in a predictable way. Both monetary and nonmonetary incentives matter. If the personal cost of an option increases, people will be less likely to choose it. Correspondingly, when an option becomes more attractive, people will be more likely to choose it. This vitally important guidepost, sometimes called the basic postulate of economics, is a powerful tool because it applies to almost everything that we do.

Think about the implications of this proposition. When late for an appointment, a person will be less likely to take time to stop and visit with a friend. Fewer people will go picnicking on a cold and rainy day. Higher prices will reduce the number of units sold. Attendance in college classes will be below normal the day before spring break. In each case, the explanation is the same: As the option becomes more costly, less is chosen.

Similarly, when the payoff derived from a choice increases, people will be more likely to choose it. A person will be more likely to bend over and pick up a quarter than a penny. Students will attend and pay more attention in class when the material is covered extensively on exams. Customers will buy more from stores that offer low prices, high-quality service, and a convenient location. Senior voters will be more likely to support candidates who favor higher Social Security benefits. All of these outcomes are highly predictable, and they merely reflect the "incentives matter" postulate of economics.

Noneconomists sometimes argue that people respond to incentives only because they are selfish and greedy. This view is false. People are motivated by a variety of goals, some humanitarian and some selfish, and incentives matter equally in both. Even an unselfish individual would be more likely to attempt to rescue a drowning child from a three-foot swimming pool than the rapid currents approaching Niagara Falls. Similarly, people are more likely to give a needy person their hand-me-downs rather than their favorite new clothes.

Just how far can we push the idea that incentives matter? If asked what would happen to the number of funerals performed in your town if the price of funerals rose, how would you respond? The "incentives matter" postulate predicts that the higher cost would reduce the number of funerals. While the same number of people will still die each year, the number of funerals performed will still fall as more people choose to be cremated or buried in cemeteries in other towns. Substitutes are everywhere—even for funerals. Individuals also respond to incentives when committing crimes—precisely the reason why people put signs in their yard saying "This house protected by XYZ security."

4. Individuals make decisions at the margin. When making a choice between two alternatives, individuals generally focus on the *difference* in the costs and benefits between alternatives. Economists describe this process as marginal decision-making, or "thinking at the margin." The last time you went to eat fast food, you probably faced a decision that highlights this type of thinking. Will you get the $1.50 cheeseburger and the $1.00 medium drink, or instead get the $3.00 value meal that has the cheeseburger and drink and also comes with a medium order of fries? Naturally, individual decision-making focuses on the difference between the alternatives. The value meal costs 50 cents more (its marginal cost) but will give you one extra food item—the fries (its marginal benefit). Your marginal decision is whether it is worth the extra 50 cents to have the fries. If you pay attention, you'll notice yourself frequently thinking at the margin. Next time you find yourself asking a salesclerk, "How much *more* is this one?" when you are choosing between two items, you are doing a marginal analysis.

Marginal choices always involve the effects of net additions to or subtractions from current conditions. In fact, the word *additional* is often used as a substitute for *marginal*. For example, a business decision-maker might ask, "What is the additional (or marginal)

Because consumers respond to incentives, store owners know they can sell off excess inventory by reducing prices.

Marginal
Term used to describe the effects of a change in the current situation. For example, a producer's marginal cost is the cost of producing an additional unit of a product, given the producer's current facility and production rate.

cost of producing one more unit?" Marginal decisions may involve large or small changes. The "one more unit" could be a new factory or a new stapler. It is marginal because it involves additional costs and additional benefits. Given the current situation, what marginal benefits (additional sales revenues, for example) can be expected from the new factory, and what will be the marginal cost of constructing it? What is the marginal benefit versus marginal cost of purchasing a new stapler? The answers to these questions will determine whether building the new factory or buying the new stapler is a good decision.

It is important to distinguish between *average* and *marginal*. A manufacturer's average cost of producing automobiles (which would be the total cost of production divided by the total number of cars the manufacturer produces) may be $25,000, but the marginal cost of producing an additional automobile (or an additional 1,000 automobiles) might be much lower, say, $10,000 per car. Costs associated with research, testing, design, molds, heavy equipment, and similar factors of production must be incurred whether the manufacturer is going to produce 1,000 units, 10,000 units, or 100,000 units. Such costs will clearly contribute to the average cost of an automobile, but they will change very little as additional units are produced. Thus, the marginal cost of additional units may be substantially less than the average cost. Should production be expanded or reduced? That choice should be based on marginal costs, which indicate the *change* in total cost due to the decision.

People commonly ignore the implications of marginal thinking in their comments, but seldom in their actions. Thus, the concept is far better at explaining how people act than what they say. Students are often overheard telling other students that they shouldn't skip class because they have paid to enroll in it. Of course, the tuition is not a factor relevant at the margin—it will be the same whether or not the student attends class on that particular day. The only real marginal considerations are what the student will miss that day (a quiz, information for the exam, etc.) versus what he or she could do with the extra time by skipping class. This explains why even students who tell others they paid too much for the class to skip it will ignore the tuition costs when they themselves decide to skip class.

Decisions are made at the margin. That means that they almost always involve additions to, or subtractions from, current conditions. If we are going to get the most out of our resources, activities that generate more benefits than costs should be undertaken, while those that are more costly than they are worth should not be undertaken. This principle of sound decision-making applies to individuals, businesses, governments, and for society as a whole.

5. Although information can help us make better choices, its acquisition is costly.
Information that helps us make better choices is valuable. However, the time needed to gather it is scarce, making information costly to acquire. As a result, people economize on their search for information just like they do anything else. For example, when you purchase a pair of jeans, you might evaluate the quality and prices of jeans at several different stores. At some point, though, you will decide that additional comparison-shopping is simply not worth the trouble. You will make a choice based on the limited information you already have.

The process is similar when individuals search for a restaurant, a new car, or a roommate. They will seek to acquire some information, but at some point, they will decide that the expected benefit derived from gathering still more information is simply not worth the cost. When differences among the alternatives are important to decision-makers, they will spend more time and effort gathering information. People are much more likely to read a consumer ratings magazine before purchasing a new automobile than they are before purchasing a new can opener. Because information is costly for people to acquire, limited knowledge and uncertainty about the outcome generally characterize the decision-making process.

6. Beware of the secondary effects: economic actions often generate indirect as well as direct effects.
In addition to direct effects that are quickly visible, people's decisions often generate indirect, or "secondary," effects that may be

observable only with time. Failure to consider secondary effects is one of the most common economic errors because these effects are often quite different from initial, or direct, effects. Frédéric Bastiat, a nineteenth-century French economist, stated that the difference between a good and a bad economist is that the bad economist considers only the immediate, visible effects, whereas the good economist is also aware of the **secondary effects**. The true cause of these secondary effects might not be seen, even later, except by those using the logic of good economics.

Perhaps a few simple examples that involve both immediate (direct) and secondary (indirect) effects will help illustrate the point. The immediate effect of an aspirin is a bitter taste in one's mouth. The secondary effect, which is not immediately observable, is relief from a headache. The short-term direct effect of drinking twelve cans of beer might be a warm, jolly feeling. In contrast, the secondary effect is likely to be a sluggish feeling the next morning, and perhaps a pounding headache.

Sometimes, as in the case of the aspirin, the secondary effect—headache relief—is actually an intended consequence of the action. In other cases, however, the secondary effects are unintended. Changes in government policy often alter incentives, indirectly affecting how much people work, earn, invest, consume, and conserve for the future. When a change alters incentives, *unintended consequences* that are quite different from the intended consequences may occur.

Let's consider a couple of examples that illustrate the potential importance of unintended consequences. In an effort to reduce gasoline consumption, the federal government mandates that automobiles be more fuel efficient. Is this regulation a sound policy? It may be, but when evaluating the policy's overall impact, one should not overlook its secondary effects. To achieve the higher fuel efficiency, auto manufacturers reduced the size and weight of vehicles. As a result, there are more highway deaths—about 2,500 more per year—than would otherwise occur because these lighter cars do not offer as much protection for occupants. Furthermore, because the higher mileage standards for cars and light trucks make driving cheaper, people tend to drive more than they otherwise would. This increases congestion and results in a smaller reduction in gasoline consumption than was intended by the regulation. Once you consider the secondary effects, the fuel efficiency regulations are much less beneficial than they might first appear.

Trade restrictions between nations have important secondary effects as well. The proponents of tariffs and quotas on foreign goods almost always ignore the secondary effects of their policies. Import quotas restricting the sale of foreign-produced sugar in the U.S. market, for example, have resulted in domestic sugar prices that have often been two or three times the price in the rest of the world. The proponents of this policy—primarily sugar producers—argue that the quotas "save jobs" and increase employment. No doubt, the employment of sugar growers in the United States is higher than it otherwise would be. But what about the secondary effects? The higher sugar prices mean it's more expensive for U.S. firms to produce candy and other products that use a lot of sugar. As a result, many candy producers, including the makers of Life Savers, Jaw Breakers, Red Hots, and Fannie May and Fanny Farmer chocolates, have moved to countries like Canada and Mexico, where sugar can be purchased at its true market price. Thus, employment among sugar-using firms in the United States is reduced. Further, because foreigners sell less sugar in the United States, they have less purchasing power with which to buy products we export to them. This, too, reduces U.S. employment.

Once the secondary effects of trade restrictions like the sugar quota program are taken into consideration, we have no reason to expect that U.S. employment will increase as a result. There may be more jobs in favored industries, but there will be less employment in others. Trade restrictions reshuffle employment rather than increase it. But those who unwittingly fail to consider the secondary effects will miss this point. Clearly, consideration of the secondary effects is an important ingredient of the economic way of thinking.

THE FAMILY CIRCUS®   **By Bil Keane**

"Everybody wants to be sick.
I'm using M&M's for pills."

Bil Keane, Inc. King Features Syndicate

Sometimes actions change the incentives people face and they respond accordingly, creating secondary effects that were not intended.

Secondary effects
The indirect impact of an event or policy that may not be easily and immediately observable. In the area of policy, these effects are often both unintended and overlooked.

7. The value of a good or service is subjective. Preferences differ, sometimes dramatically, between individuals. How much is a ticket to see a performance of the Bolshoi Ballet worth? Some people would be willing to pay a very high price, while others might prefer to stay home, even if tickets were free! Circumstances can change from day to day, even for a given individual. Alice, a ballet fan who usually would value the ticket at more than its price of $100, is invited to a party and suddenly becomes uninterested in attending the ballet. Now what is the ticket worth? If she knows a friend who would give her $40 for the ticket, it is worth at least that much. If she advertises the ticket on eBay and gets $60 for it, a higher value is created. But if someone who doesn't know of the ticket would have been willing to pay even more, then a potential trade creating even more value is missed. If that particular performance is sold out, perhaps someone in town would be willing to pay $120. One thing is certain: The value of the ticket depends on several things, including who uses it and under what circumstances.

Economics recognizes that people can and do value goods differently. Mike may prefer to have a grass field rather than a parking lot next to his workplace and be willing to bear the cost of walking farther from his car each day. Kim, on the other hand, may prefer the parking lot and the shorter walk. As a science, economics does not place any inherent moral judgment or value on one person's preferences over another's—in economics, all individuals' preferences are counted equally. Because the subjective preferences of individuals differ, it is difficult for one person to know how much another will value an item.

Think about how hard it is to know what would make a good gift for even a close friend or family member. Thus, arranging trades, or otherwise moving items to higher valued users and uses, is not a simple task. The entrepreneurial individual, who knows how to locate the right buyers and arranges for goods to flow to their highest valued use, can sometimes create huge increases in value from existing resources. In fact, moving goods toward those who value them most and combining resources into goods that individuals value more highly are primary sources of economic progress.

Scientific thinking
Developing a theory from basic principles and testing it against events in the real world. Good theories are consistent with and help explain real-world events. Theories that are inconsistent with the real world are invalid and must be rejected.

8. The test of a theory is its ability to predict. Economic thinking is scientific thinking. The proof of the pudding is in the eating. How useful an economic theory is depends on how well it predicts the future consequences of economic action. Economists develop economic theories using scientific thinking based on basic principles. The idea is to predict how incentives will affect decision makers and compare the predictions against real-world events. If the events in the real world are consistent with a theory, we say that the theory has *predictive value* and is therefore valid.

If it is impossible to test the theoretical relationships of a discipline, the discipline does not qualify as a science. Because economics deals with human beings who can think and respond in a variety of ways, can economic theories really be tested? The answer to this question is yes, if, on average, human beings respond in predictable and consistent ways to changes in economic conditions. The economist believes that this is the case, even though not all individuals will respond in the specified manner. Economists usually do not try to predict the behavior of a specific individual; instead, they focus on the general behavior of a large number of individuals.

In the 1950s, economists began to do laboratory experiments to test economic theories. Individuals were brought into laboratories to see how they would act in buying and selling situations, under differing rules. For example, cash rewards were given to individuals who, when an auction was conducted, were able to sell at high prices and buy at low prices, thus approximating real-world market incentives. These experiments have verified many of the important propositions of economic theory.

Laboratory experiments, however, cannot duplicate all real economic interactions. How can we test economic theory when controlled experiments are not feasible? This is a problem, but economics is no different from astronomy in this respect. Astronomers can use theories tested in physics laboratories, but they must also deal with the world as it is. They cannot change the course of the stars or planets to see what impact the change would have on the gravitational pull of Earth. Similarly, economists cannot arbitrarily change the prices of cars or unskilled-labor services in real markets just to observe the effects on quantities purchased or levels of employment. However, economic conditions (for example, prices, production costs, technology, and transportation costs), like the location of the planets, do change from time to time. As actual conditions change, an economic theory can be tested by comparing its predictions with real-world outcomes. Just as the universe is the main laboratory of the astronomer, the real-world economy is the primary laboratory of the economist.

1-3 POSITIVE AND NORMATIVE ECONOMICS

As a social science, economics is concerned with predicting or determining the impact of changes in economic variables on the actions of human beings. Scientific economics, commonly referred to as positive economics, attempts to determine "what is." Positive economic statements involve potentially verifiable or refutable propositions. For example, "If the price of gasoline rises, people will buy less gasoline." We can statistically investigate (and estimate) the relationship between gasoline prices and gallons sold. We can analyze the facts to determine the correctness of a positive economic statement. Remember, a positive economic statement need not be correct; it simply must be testable.

In contrast, normative economics is about "what ought to be," given the preferences and philosophical views of the advocate. Value judgments often result in disagreement about normative economic matters. Two people may differ on a policy matter because one is from one political party and the other is from another, or because one wants cheaper food while the other favors organic farming (which is more expensive), and so on. They may even agree about the expected outcome of altering an economic variable (that is, the positive economics of an issue), but disagree as to whether that outcome is desirable.

Unlike positive economic statements, normative economic statements can neither be confirmed nor proven false by scientific testing. "Business firms should not be concerned with profits." "We should have fewer parking lots and more green space on campus." "The price of gasoline is too high." These normative statements cannot be scientifically tested because their validity rests on value judgments.

Normative economic views can sometimes influence our attitude toward positive economic analysis, however. When we agree with the objectives of a policy, it's easy to overlook the warnings of positive economics. Although positive economics does not tell us which policy is best, it can provide evidence about the likely effects of a policy. Sometimes proponents unknowingly support policies that are actually in conflict with their own goals and objectives. Positive economics, based on sound economic logic, can help overcome this potential problem.

Economics can expand our knowledge of how the real world operates, in both the private and the public (government) sectors. However, it is not always easy to isolate the impact of economic changes. Let's now consider some pitfalls to avoid in economic thinking.

Positive economics
The scientific study of "what is" among economic relationships.

Normative economics
Judgments about "what ought to be" in economic matters. Normative economic views cannot be proved false because they are based on value judgments.

1-4 PITFALLS TO AVOID IN ECONOMIC THINKING

1-4a VIOLATION OF THE *CERTERIS PARIBUS* CONDITION CAN LEAD ONE TO DRAW THE WRONG CONCLUSION

Economists often qualify their statements with the words *ceteris paribus*. *Ceteris paribus* is a Latin term meaning "other things constant." An example of a *ceteris paribus* statement would be the following: "*Ceteris paribus*, an increase in the price of housing will cause buyers to reduce their purchases of housing." Unfortunately, we live in a dynamic world, so things seldom remain constant. For example, as the price of housing rises, the income of consumers might also increase for unrelated reasons. Each of these factors—higher housing prices and increasing consumer income—will have an impact on housing purchases. In

Ceteris paribus
A Latin term meaning "other things constant" that is used when the effect of one change is being described, recognizing that if other things changed, they also could affect the result. Economists often describe the effects of one change, knowing that in the real world, other things might change and also exert an effect.

fact, we would generally expect them to have opposite effects: Higher prices are likely to reduce housing purchases, whereas higher consumer incomes are likely to increase them. We point out this pitfall because sometimes statistical data (or casual observations) appear inconsistent with economic theories. In most of these cases, the apparent contradictions reflect the effects of changes in other factors (violations of the *ceteris paribus* conditions). The observed effects are the result of the combination of the changes.

The task of sorting out the effects of two or more variables that change at the same time is difficult. However, with a strong grip on economic theory, some ingenuity, and enough data, it can usually be done. This is, in fact, precisely the day-to-day work of many professional economists.

1-4b GOOD INTENTIONS DO NOT GUARANTEE DESIRABLE OUTCOMES

There is a tendency to believe that if the proponents of a policy have good intentions, their proposals must be sound. This is not necessarily the case. Proponents may be unaware of some of the adverse secondary effects of their proposals, particularly when they are indirect and observable only over time. Even if their policies would be largely ineffective, politicians may still find it advantageous to call attention to the severity of a problem and propose a program to deal with it. In other cases, proponents of a policy may actually be seeking a goal other than the one they espouse. They may tie their arguments to objectives that are widely supported by the general populace. Thus, the fact that an advocate says a program will help the economy, expand employment, help the poor, increase wages, improve health care, or achieve some other highly desirable objective does not necessarily make it so.

Let's begin with a couple of straightforward examples. Federal legislation has been introduced that would require all children, including those under age two, to be fastened in a child safety seat when traveling by air. Proponents argue the legislation will increase the survival rate of children in the case of an airline crash and thereby save lives. Certainly, saving lives is a highly desirable objective, but will this really be the case? *Some* lives will probably be saved. But what about the secondary effects? The legislation would mean that a parent traveling with a small child would have to purchase an additional ticket, which will make it more expensive to fly. As a result, many families will choose to travel by auto rather than by air. Because the likelihood of a serious accident per mile traveled in an automobile is several times higher than for air travel, more automobile travel will result in more injuries and fatalities. In fact, studies indicate that the increase in injuries and fatalities from additional auto travel will exceed the number of lives saved by airline safety seats.[4] Thus, even though the intentions of the proponents may well be lofty, there is reason to believe that the net impact of their proposal will be more fatalities and injuries than would be the case in the absence of the legislation.

The stated objective of the Endangered Species Act is to protect various species that are on the verge of extinction. Certainly, this is an admirable objective, but there is nonetheless reason to question the effectiveness of the act itself. The Endangered Species Act allows the government to regulate the use of individual private property if an endangered species is found present on *or* near an individual's land. To avoid losing control of their property, many landowners have taken steps to make their land less attractive as a natural habitat for these endangered species. For example, the endangered red-cockaded woodpecker nests primarily in old trees within southern pine ecosystems. Landowners have responded by cutting down trees the woodpeckers like to nest in to avoid having one nest on their land, which would result in the owner losing control of this part of their property. The end result is that the habitat for these birds has actually been disappearing more rapidly.

---

[4]For a detailed analysis of this subject, see Thomas B. Newman, Brian D. Johnston, and David C. Grossman, "Effects and Costs of Requiring Child-Restraint Systems for Young Children Traveling on Commercial Airplanes," *Archives of Pediatrics and Adolescent Medicine* 157 (October 2003): 969–74.

As you can see, good intentions are not enough. An unsound proposal will lead to undesirable outcomes, even if it is supported by proponents with good intentions. In fact, many economists believe that the recent financial crisis was a secondary effect of well-intended government regulations and policies that lowered mortgage lending standards in order to expand homeownership. Sound economic reasoning can help us better anticipate the secondary effects of policy changes and avoid the pitfall of thinking that good intentions are enough.

1-4c ASSOCIATION IS NOT CAUSATION

In economics, identifying cause-and-effect relationships is very important. But statistical association alone cannot establish this causation. Perhaps an extreme example will illustrate the point. Suppose that each November, a witch doctor performs a voodoo dance designed to summon the gods of winter, and that soon after the dance is performed, the weather in fact begins to turn cold. The witch doctor's dance is associated with the arrival of winter, meaning that the two events appear to have happened in conjunction with one another. But is this really evidence that the witch doctor's dance actually caused the arrival of winter? Most of us would answer no, even though the two events seemed to happen in conjunction with one another.

Those who argue that a causal relationship exists simply because of the presence of statistical association are committing a logical fallacy known as the *post hoc propter ergo hoc* fallacy. Sound economics warns against this potential source of error.

1-4d THE FALLACY OF COMPOSITION: WHAT'S TRUE FOR ONE MIGHT NOT BE TRUE FOR ALL

What is true for the individual (or subcomponent) may not be true for the group (or the whole). If you stand up for an exciting play during a football game, you will be better able to see. But what happens if everyone stands up at the same time? Will everyone be better able to see? The answer is, of course, no. Thus, what is true for a single individual does not necessarily apply to the group as a whole. When everyone stands up, the view for individual spectators fails to improve; in fact, it may even become worse.

People who mistakenly argue that what is true for the part is also true for the whole are said to be committing the fallacy of composition. What is true for the individual can be misleading and is often fallacious when applied to the entire economy. The fallacy of composition highlights the importance of considering both a micro view and a macro view in the study of economics. Microeconomics focuses on the decision-making of consumers, producers, and resource suppliers operating in a narrowly defined market, such as that for a specific good or resource. Because individual decision-makers are the moving force behind all economic action, the foundations of economics are clearly rooted in a micro view.

As we have seen, however, what is true for a small unit may not be true in the aggregate. Macroeconomics focuses on how the aggregation of individual micro-units affects our analysis. Like microeconomics, it is concerned with incentives, prices, and output. Macroeconomics, however, aggregates markets, lumping together all 117 million households in this country. Macroeconomics involves topics like total consumption spending, saving, and employment, in the economy as a whole. Similarly, the nation's 28 million business firms are lumped together in "the business sector." What factors determine the level of aggregate output, the rate of inflation, the amount of unemployment, and interest rates? These are macroeconomic questions. In short, macroeconomics examines the forest rather than the individual trees. As we move from the microcomponents to a macro view of the whole, it is important that we beware of the fallacy of composition.

Fallacy of composition
Erroneous view that what is true for the individual (or the part) will also be true for the group (or the whole).

Microeconomics
The branch of economics that focuses on how human behavior affects the conduct of affairs within narrowly defined units, such as individual households or business firms.

Macroeconomics
The branch of economics that focuses on how human behavior affects outcomes in highly aggregated markets, such as the markets for labor or consumer products.

LOOKING AHEAD

The primary purpose of this book is to encourage you to develop the economic way of thinking so that you can separate sound reasoning from economic nonsense. Once you have developed the economic way of thinking, economics will be relatively easy. Using the economic way of thinking can also be fun. Moreover, it will help you become a better citizen. It will give you a different and fascinating perspective on what motivates people, why they act the way they do, and why their actions sometimes go against the best interest of the community or nation. It will also give you valuable insight into how people's actions can be rechanneled for the benefit of the community at large.

KEY POINTS

- Scarcity and choice are the two essential ingredients of economic analysis. A good is scarce when the human desire for it exceeds the amount freely available from nature. Scarcity requires us to choose among available alternatives. Every choice entails a trade-off.

- Every society will have to devise some method of rationing scarce resources among competing uses. Markets generally use price as the rationing device. Competition is a natural outgrowth of the need to ration scarce goods.

- Scarcity and poverty are not the same thing. Absence of poverty implies that some basic level of need has been met. An absence of scarcity implies that our desires for goods are fully satisfied. We may someday eliminate poverty, but scarcity will always be with us.

- Economics is a way of thinking that emphasizes eight points:
  1. The use of scarce resources to produce a good always has an opportunity cost.
  2. Individuals make decisions purposefully, always seeking to choose the option they expect to be most consistent with their personal goals.
  3. Incentives matter. The likelihood of people choosing an option increases as personal benefits rise and personal costs decline.

  4. Economic reasoning focuses on the impact of marginal changes because it is the marginal benefits and marginal costs that influence choices.
  5. Because information is scarce, uncertainty is a fact of life.
  6. In addition to their direct impact, economic changes often generate secondary effects.
  7. The value of a good or service is subjective and varies with individual preferences and circumstances.
  8. The test of an economic theory is its ability to predict and explain events in the real world.

- Economic science is positive; it attempts to explain the actual consequences of economic actions or "what is." Normative economics goes further, applying value judgments to make suggestions about what "ought to be."

- Microeconomics focuses on narrowly defined units, while macroeconomics is concerned with highly aggregated units. When shifting focus from micro to macro, one must beware of the fallacy of composition: What's good for the individual may not be good for the group as a whole.

- The origin of economics as a science dates to the publication of *An Inquiry into the Nature and Causes of the Wealth of Nations* by Adam Smith in 1776. Smith believed a market economy would generally bring individual self-interest and the public interest into harmony.

CRITICAL ANALYSIS QUESTIONS

1. Indicate how each of the following changes would influence the incentive of a decision-maker to undertake the action described.

   a. A reduction in the temperature from 80° to 50° on one's decision to go swimming
   b. A change in the meeting time of the introductory economics course from 11:00 A.M. to 7:30 A.M. on one's decision to attend the lectures
   c. A reduction in the number of exam questions that relate directly to the text on the student's decision to read the text

   d. An increase in the price of beef on one's decision to buy steak
   e. An increase in the rental rates of apartments on one's decision to build additional rental housing units

2. "The government should provide such goods as health care, education, and highways because it can provide them for free." Is this statement true or false? Explain your answer.

3. a. What method is used to ration goods in a market economy? How does this rationing method influence the incentive of individuals to supply goods, services, and resources to others?

b. How are grades rationed in your economics class? How does this rationing method influence student behavior? Suppose the highest grades were rationed to those whom the teacher liked best. How would this method of rationing influence student behavior?

4. *In recent years, the child tax credit has been increased in the United States. According to the basic principles of economics, how will the birthrate be affected by policies that reduce the taxes imposed on those with children?

5. *"The economic way of thinking stresses that good intentions lead to sound policy." Is this statement true or false? Explain your answer.

6. Self-interest is a powerful motivator. Does this necessarily imply that people are selfish and greedy? Do self-interest and selfishness mean the same thing?

7. A restaurant offers an "all you can eat" lunch buffet for $10. Shawn has already eaten three servings, and is trying to decide whether to go back for a fourth. Describe how Shawn can use marginal analysis to make his decision.

8. *"Individuals who economize are missing the point of life. Money is not so important that it should rule the way we live." Evaluate this statement.

9. *"Positive economics cannot tell us which agricultural policy is better, so it is useless to policy makers." Evaluate this statement.

10. *"I examined the statistics for our basketball team's wins last year and found that, when the third team played more, the win-ning margin increased. If the coach played the third team more, we would win by a bigger margin." Evaluate this statement.

11. Which of the following are positive economic statements and which are normative?

a. The speed limit should be lowered to 55 miles per hour on interstate highways.

b. Higher gasoline prices cause the quantity of gasoline that consumers buy to decrease.

c. A comparison of costs and benefits should not be used to assess environmental regulations.

d. Higher taxes on alcohol result in less drinking and driving.

12. Why can't we consume as much of each good or service as we would like? If we become richer in the future, do you think we will eventually be able to consume as much of everything as we would like? Why or why not?

13. Suppose that in an effort to help low-skill workers the government raises the permissible minimum wage to $15 per hour. Can you think of any unintended secondary effects that will result from this action? Will all low-skill workers be helped by the minimum wage law?

14. Should the United States attempt to reduce air and water pollution to zero? Why or why not?

*Asterisk denotes questions for which answers are given in Appendix B.

CHAPTER 3
Demand, Supply, and the Market Process

FOCUS

- What are the laws of demand and supply?
- How do consumers decide whether to purchase a good? How do producers decide whether to supply it?
- How do buyers and sellers respond to changes in the price of a good?
- What role do profits and losses play in an economy? What must a firm do to make a profit?
- How is the market price of a good determined?
- How do markets adjust to changes in demand? How do they adjust to changes in supply?
- What is the "invisible hand" principle?

I am convinced that if [the market system] were the result of deliberate human design, and if the people guided by the price changes understood that their decisions have significance far beyond their immediate aim, this mechanism would have been acclaimed as one of the greatest triumphs of the human mind.
—Friedrich Hayek, Nobel Laureate[1]

From the point of view of physics, it is a miracle that [7 million New Yorkers are fed each day] without any control mechanism other than sheer capitalism.
—John H. Holland, scientist, Santa Fe Institute[2]

[1]Friedrich Hayek, "The Use of Knowledge in Society," *American Economic Review* 35 (September 1945): 519–30.
[2]As quoted by Russell Ruthen in "Adapting to Complexity," *Scientific American* 268 (January 1993): 132.

To those who study art, the *Mona Lisa* is much more than a famous painting of a woman. Looking beyond the overall picture, they see and appreciate the brush strokes, colors, and techniques embodied in the painting. Similarly, studying economics can help you to gain an appreciation for the details behind many things in your everyday life. During your last visit to the grocery store, you probably noticed the fruit and vegetable section. Next time, take a moment to ponder how potatoes from Idaho, oranges from Florida, apples from Washington, bananas from Honduras, kiwi fruit from New Zealand, and other items from around the world got there. Literally thousands of different individuals, *working independently*, were involved in the process. Their actions were so well coordinated, in fact, that the amount of each good was just about right to fill exactly the desires of your local community. Furthermore, even the goods shipped from halfway around the world were fresh and reasonably priced.

How does all this happen? The short answer is that it is the result of market prices and the incentives and coordination that flow from them. To the economist, the operation of markets—including your local grocery market—is like the brush strokes underlying a beautiful painting. Reflecting on this point, Friedrich Hayek speculates that if the market system had been deliberately designed, it would be "acclaimed as one of the greatest triumphs of the human mind." Similarly, computer scientist John H. Holland argues that, from the viewpoint of physics, the feeding of millions of New Yorkers day after day with very few shortages or surpluses is a miraculous feat (see the chapter-opening quotations).

Amazingly, markets coordinate the actions of millions of individuals *without* central planning. There is no individual, political authority, or central planning committee in charge. Considering that there are more than 300 million Americans with widely varying skills and desires, and roughly 28 million businesses producing a vast array of products ranging from diamond rings to toilet paper, the coordination derived from markets is indeed an awesome achievement.

The produce section of your local grocery store is a great place to see economics in action. Literally millions of individuals from around the world have been involved in the process of getting these goods to the shelves in just the right quantities. Market prices underlie this feat.

This chapter focuses on demand, supply, and the determination of market prices. For now, we will analyze the operation of competitive markets—that is, markets in which buyers and sellers are free to enter and exit. We will also assume that the property rights are well defined. Later, we will consider what happens when these conditions are absent.

On eBay, sellers enter their reserve prices—the minimum prices they will accept for goods; buyers enter their maximum bids—the maximum prices they are willing to pay for goods. The process works the same way when a person runs a newspaper ad to sell a car. The seller has in mind a minimum price he or she will accept for the car. A potential buyer, on the other hand, has in mind a maximum price he or she will pay for the car. If the buyer's maximum price is greater than the seller's minimum price, the exchange will occur at a price somewhere in between. As these examples show, the buyers' and sellers' desires and incentives determine prices and make markets work. We will begin with the demand (buyer's) side, and then turn to the supply (seller's) side of the market.

3-1 CONSUMER CHOICE AND THE LAW OF DEMAND

Clearly, prices influence our decisions. As the price of a good increases, we have to give up more of *other* goods if we want to buy it. Thus, as the price of a good rises, its opportunity cost increases (in terms of other goods that must be forgone to purchase it).

Law of demand
A principle that states there is an inverse relationship between the price of a good and the quantity of it buyers are willing to purchase. As the price of a good increases, consumers will wish to purchase less of it. As the price decreases, consumers will wish to purchase more of it.

Substitutes
Products that serve similar purposes. An increase in the price of one will cause an increase in demand for the other (examples are hamburgers and tacos, butter and margarine, Chevrolets and Fords).

This basic principle underlies the law of demand. *The law of demand states that there is an inverse (or negative) relationship between the price of a good or service and the quantity of it that consumers are willing to purchase.* This inverse relationship means that price and the quantity consumers wish to purchase move in opposite directions. As the price increases, buyers purchase less—and as the price decreases, buyers purchase more.

The availability of substitutes—goods that perform similar functions—helps explain this inverse relationship. No single good is absolutely essential; everything can be replaced with something else. A chicken sandwich can be substituted for a cheeseburger. Wood, aluminum, bricks, and glass can take the place of steel. Going to the movies, playing tennis, watching television, and going to a football game are substitute forms of entertainment. When the price of a good increases, people cut back on their purchases of it and turn to substitute products.

3-1a THE MARKET DEMAND SCHEDULE

The lower portion of Exhibit 1 shows a hypothetical *demand schedule* for pizza delivery in a city. A demand schedule is simply a table listing the various quantities of something consumers are willing to purchase at different prices. When the price of a large pizza delivery is $35, only 4,000 people per month order pizza delivery. As the price falls to $25, the quantity of pizza deliveries demanded rises to 8,000 per month; when the price falls to $10, the quantity demanded increases to 14,000 per month.

EXHIBIT 1

Law of Demand

As the demand schedule shown in the table indicates, the number of people ordering pizza delivery (just like the consumption of other products) is inversely related to price. The data from the table are plotted as a demand curve in the graph. The inverse relationship between price and amount demanded reflects the fact that consumers will substitute away from a good as it becomes more expensive.

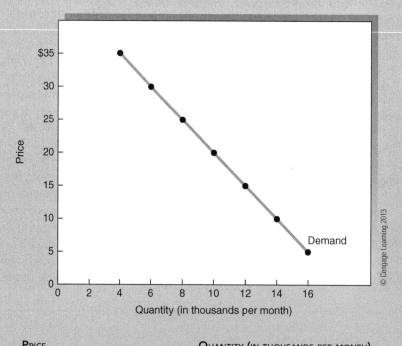

© Cengage Learning 2013

PRICE	QUANTITY (IN THOUSANDS PER MONTH)
$35	4
30	6
25	8
20	10
15	12
10	14
5	16

The upper portion of Exhibit 1 shows what the demand schedule would look like if the various prices and corresponding quantities were plotted on a graph and connected by a line. This is called the *demand curve*. When representing the demand schedule graphically, economists measure price on the vertical or *y*-axis and the amount demanded on the horizontal or *x*-axis. Because of the inverse relationship between price and amount purchased, the demand curve will have a negative slope—that is, it will slope downward to the right. More of a good will be purchased as its price decreases. This is the law of demand.

Read horizontally, the demand curve shows how much of a particular good consumers are willing to buy at a given price. Read vertically, the demand curve shows how much consumers value the good. The height of the demand curve at any quantity shows the maximum price consumers are willing to pay for an additional unit. If consumers value highly an additional unit of a product, they will be willing to pay a large amount for it. Conversely, if they place a low value on the additional unit, they will be willing to pay only a small amount for it.

Because the amount a consumer is willing to pay for a good is directly related to the good's value to them, the height of the demand curve indicates the marginal benefit (or value) consumers receive from additional units. (Recall that we briefly discussed marginal benefit in Chapter 1.) When viewed in this manner, the demand curve reveals that as consumers have more and more of a good or service, they value additional units less and less.

3-1b CONSUMER SURPLUS

Previously, we indicated that voluntary exchanges make both buyers and sellers better off. The demand curve can be used to illustrate the gains to consumers. Suppose you value a particular good at $50, but you are able to purchase it for only $30. Your net gain from buying the good is the $20 difference. Economists call this net gain of buyers **consumer surplus**. Consumer surplus is simply the difference between the maximum amount consumers would be willing to pay and the amount they actually pay for a good.

Exhibit 2 shows the consumer surplus for an entire market. The height of the demand curve measures how much buyers in the market value each unit of the good. The price indicates the amount they actually pay. The difference between these two—the triangular area below the demand curve but above the price paid—is a measure of the total consumer surplus generated by all exchanges of the good. The size of the consumer surplus, or

Consumer surplus
The difference between the maximum price consumers are willing to pay and the price they actually pay. It is the net gain derived by the buyers of the good.

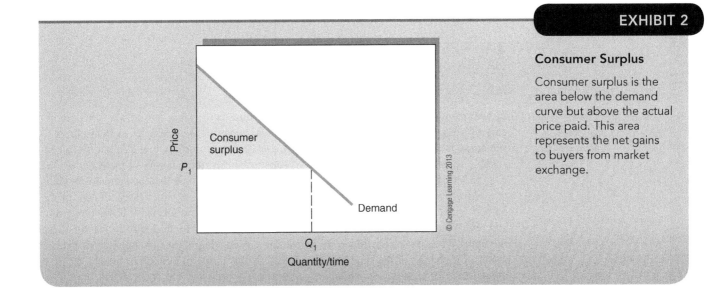

EXHIBIT 2

Consumer Surplus

Consumer surplus is the area below the demand curve but above the actual price paid. This area represents the net gains to buyers from market exchange.

triangular area, is affected by the market price. If the market price for the good falls, more of it will be purchased, resulting in a larger surplus for consumers. Conversely, if the market price rises, less of it will be purchased, resulting in a smaller surplus (net gain) for consumers.

Because the value a consumer places on a particular unit of a good is shown by the corresponding height of the demand curve, we can use the demand curve to clarify the difference between the *marginal value* and *total value* of a good—a distinction we introduced briefly in Chapter 1. Returning to Exhibit 2, if consumers are currently purchasing Q_1 units, the marginal value of the good is indicated by the height of the demand curve at Q_1—the last unit consumed (or purchased). So at each quantity, the height of the demand curve shows the marginal value of that unit, which as you can see declines along a demand curve. The *total value* of the good, however, is equal to the combined value of all units purchased. This is the sum of the value of each unit (the heights along the demand curve) on the *x*-axis, out to and including unit Q_1. This total value is indicated graphically as the entire area under the demand curve out to Q_1 (the triangular area representing consumer surplus *plus* the unshaded rectangular area directly below it).

You can see that the total value to consumers of a good can be far greater than the marginal value of the last unit consumed. When additional units are available at a low price, the marginal value of a good may be quite low, even though its total value to consumers is exceedingly high. This is usually the case with water. The value of the first few units of water consumed per day will be exceedingly high. The consumer surplus derived from these units will also be large when water is plentiful at a low price. As more and more units are consumed, however, the *marginal value* of even something as important as water will fall to a low level. When water is cheap, then, people will use it not only for drinking, cleaning, and cooking but also for washing cars, watering lawns, flushing toilets, and maintaining fish aquariums. Thus, although the total value of water is rather large, its marginal value is quite low.

Consumers will tend to expand their consumption of a good until its price and *marginal value* are equal (which occurs at Q_1 in Exhibit 2 at a price of P_1). Thus, the price of a good (which equals marginal value) reveals little about the *total value* derived from the consumption of it. This is the reason that the market price of diamonds (which reflects their high marginal value) is greater than the market price of water (which has a low marginal value), even though the total value of diamonds is far less than the total value of water. Think of it this way: Beginning from your current levels of consumption, if you were offered a choice between one diamond or one gallon of water right now, which would you take? You would probably take the diamond, because at the margin it has more value to you than additional water. However, if given a choice between giving up *all* of the water you use or *all* of the diamonds you have, you would probably keep the water over diamonds, because water has more total value to you.

3-1c RESPONSIVENESS OF QUANTITY DEMANDED TO PRICE CHANGES: ELASTIC AND INELASTIC DEMAND CURVES

As we previously noted, the availability of substitutes is the main reason why the demand curve for a good slopes downward. Some goods, however, are much easier than others to substitute away from. As the price of tacos rises, most consumers find hamburgers a reasonable substitute. Because of the ease of substitutability, the quantity of tacos demanded is quite sensitive to a change in their price. Economists would say that the demand for tacos is relatively *elastic* because a small price change will cause a rather large change in the amount purchased. Alternatively, goods like gasoline and electricity have fewer close substitutes. When their prices rise, it is harder for consumers to find substitutes for these products. When close substitutes are unavailable, even a large price change may not cause much of a change in the quantity demanded. In this case, an economist would say that the demand for such goods is relatively *inelastic*.

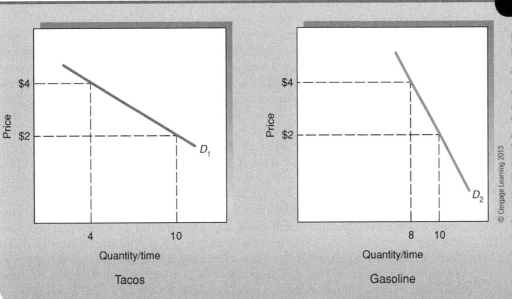

EXHIBIT 3

Elastic and Inelastic Demand Curves

The responsiveness of consumer purchases to a change in price is reflected in the steepness of the demand curve. The flatter demand curve (D_1) for tacos shows a higher degree of responsiveness and is called relatively elastic, while the steeper demand curve (D_2) for gasoline shows a lower degree of responsiveness and is called relatively inelastic

Graphically, this different degree of responsiveness is reflected in the steepness of the demand curve, as shown in Exhibit 3. The flatter demand curve (D_1, left frame) is for a product like tacos, for which the quantity purchased is highly responsive to a change in price. As the price increases from $2.00 to $4.00, the quantity demanded falls sharply from ten to four units. The steeper demand curve (D_2, right frame) is for a product like gasoline, for which the quantity purchased is much less responsive to a change in price. For gasoline, an increase in price from $2.00 to $4.00 results in only a small reduction in the quantity purchased (from ten to eight units). An economist would say that the flatter demand curve D_1 is "relatively elastic," whereas the steeper demand curve D_2 is "relatively inelastic." The availability of substitutes is the main determinant of a product's elasticity or inelasticity and thus how flat or steep its demand curve is.

What would a demand curve that was perfectly vertical represent? Economists refer to this as a "perfectly" inelastic demand curve, meaning that the quantity demanded of the product never changes—regardless of its price. Although it is tempting to think that the demand curves are vertical for goods essential to human life (or goods that are addictive), this is inaccurate for two reasons. First, in varying degrees, there are substitutes for everything. As the price of a good rises, the incentive increases for suppliers to invent even more substitutes. Thus, even for goods that currently have few substitutes, if the price were to rise high enough, alternatives would be invented and marketed, reducing the quantity demanded of the original good. Second, our limited incomes restrict our ability to afford goods when they become very expensive. As the price of a good rises to higher and higher levels, if we do not cut back on the quantity purchased, we will have less and less income to spend on other things. Eventually, this will cause us to cut back on our purchases of it. Because of these two reasons, the demand curve for every good will slope downward to the right.

3-2 CHANGES IN DEMAND VERSUS CHANGES IN QUANTITY DEMANDED

The purpose of the demand curve is to show what effect a price change will have on the quantity demanded (or purchased) of a good. Economists refer to a change in the quantity of a good purchased in response solely to a price change as a "change in *quantity demanded*." A change in quantity demanded is simply a movement along a demand curve from one point to another.

Changes in factors other than a good's price—such as consumers' income and the prices of closely related goods—will also influence the decisions of consumers to purchase a good. If one of these other factors changes, the entire demand curve will *shift* inward or outward. Economists refer to a shift in the demand curve as a "change in *demand*."

Failure to distinguish between a change in demand and a change in quantity demanded is one of the most common mistakes made by beginning economics students.[3] *A change in demand is a shift in the entire demand curve. A change in quantity demanded is a movement along the same demand curve.* The easiest way to distinguish between these two concepts is the following: If the change in consumer purchases is caused by a change in the price of the good, it is a change in quantity demanded—a movement along the demand curve; if the change in consumer purchases is due to a change in anything other than the price of the good (a change in consumer income, for example), it is a change in demand—a shift in the demand curve.

Let us now take a closer look at some of the factors that cause a "change in demand"—an inward or outward shift in the entire demand curve.

1. Changes in consumer income. An increase in consumer income makes it possible for consumers to purchase more goods. If you were to win the lottery, or if your boss were to give you a raise, you would respond by increasing your spending on many products. Alternatively, when the economy goes into a recession, falling incomes and rising unemployment cause consumers to reduce their purchases of many items. A change in consumer income will result in consumers buying more or less of a product at all possible prices. When consumer income increases, in the case of most goods, individuals will purchase more of the good even if the price is unchanged. This is shown by a shift to the right—an outward shift—in the demand curve. Such a shift is called an *increase in demand*. A reduction in consumer income generally causes a shift to the left—an inward shift—in the demand curve, which is called a *decrease in demand*. Note that the appropriate terminology here is an increase or a decrease in demand, not an increase or a decrease in quantity demanded.

Exhibit 4 highlights the difference between a change in demand and a change in quantity demanded. The demand curve D_1 indicates the initial demand curve for tablet

EXHIBIT 4

Change in Demand versus Change in Quantity Demanded

Panel (a) shows a change in quantity demanded, a movement along the demand curve D_1, in response to a change in the price of tablet computers. Panel (b) shows a change in demand, a shift of the entire curve, in this case due to an increase in consumer income.

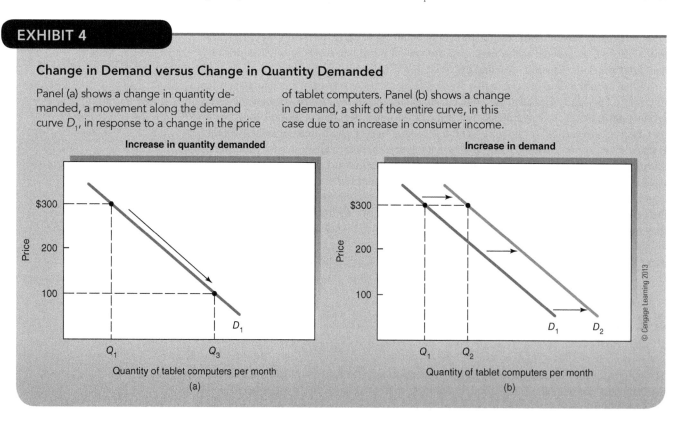

(a)

(b)

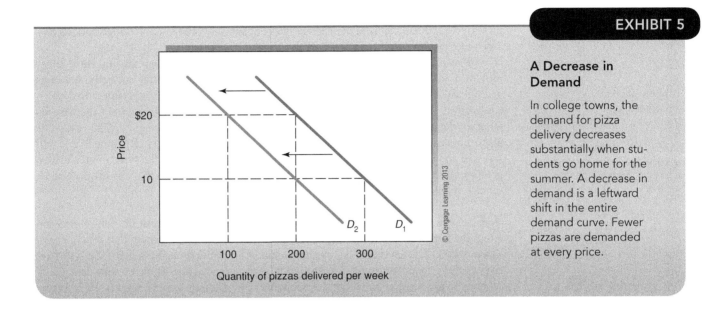

EXHIBIT 5

A Decrease in Demand

In college towns, the demand for pizza delivery decreases substantially when students go home for the summer. A decrease in demand is a leftward shift in the entire demand curve. Fewer pizzas are demanded at every price.

computers. At a price of $300, consumers will purchase Q_1 units. If the price were to decline to $100, the *quantity demanded* would increase from Q_1 to Q_3. The arrow in panel (a) indicates the change in *quantity demanded*—a movement along the original demand curve D_1 in response to the change in price. Now, alternatively suppose there were an increase in income that caused the *demand* for tablet computers to shift from D_1 to D_2. As indicated by the arrows in panel (b), the entire demand curve would shift outward. At the higher income level, consumers would be willing to purchase more tablet computers than before. This is true at a price of $300, $200, $100, and every other price. The increase in income leads to an increase in *demand*—a shift in the entire curve.

2. Changes in the number of consumers in the market. Businesses that sell products in college towns are greatly saddened when summer arrives. As you might expect in these towns, the demand for many items—from pizza delivery to beer—falls during the summer. Exhibit 5 shows how the falling number of consumers in the market caused by students going home for the summer affects the demand for pizza delivery. With fewer customers, the demand curve shifts inward from D_1 to D_2. There is a decrease in demand; pizza stores sell fewer pizzas than before regardless of what price they originally charged. Had their original price been $20, then demand would fall from 200 pizzas per week to only 100. Alternatively, had their original price been $10, then demand would fall from 300 pizzas to 200. When autumn arrives and the students come back to town, there will be an increase in demand that will restore the curve to about its original position. As cities grow and shrink, and as international markets open up to domestic firms, changes in the number of consumers affect the demand for many products.

3. Changes in the price of a related good. Changes in prices of closely related products also influence the choices of consumers. Related goods may be either substitutes or complements. When two products perform similar functions or fulfill similar needs, they are substitutes. Economists define goods as substitutes when there is a direct relationship between the price of one and the demand for the other—meaning an increase in the price of one leads to an increase in demand for the other (they move in the same direction). For example, margarine is a substitute for butter. If the price of butter rises, it will increase the demand for margarine as consumers substitute margarine for the more expensive butter. Conversely, lower butter prices will reduce the demand for margarine, shifting the entire demand curve for margarine to the left.

Gasoline and hybrid cars provide another example of a substitute relationship. As gasoline prices have risen in recent years, the demand for gas–electric hybrid cars has increased. Beef and chicken, pencils and pens, apples and oranges, and coffee and tea provide other examples of goods with substitute relationships.

Other products are consumed jointly, so the demands for them are linked together as well. Examples of goods that "go together" include peanut butter and jelly, hot dogs and hot dog buns, and tents and other camping equipment. These goods are called **complements**. For complements, a decrease in the price of one will not only increase its quantity demanded; it will also increase the demand for the other good. The reverse is also true. As a complement becomes more expensive, the quantity demanded of it will fall, and so will the demand for its complements. For example, if the price of steak rises, grocery stores can expect to sell fewer bottles of steak sauce, even if the price of steak sauce remains unchanged.

Complements
Products that are usually consumed jointly (for example, bread and butter, hot dogs and hot dog buns). A decrease in the price of one will cause an increase in demand for the other.

4. Changes in expectations.
Consumers' expectations about the future also can affect the current demand for a product. If consumers begin to expect that a major hurricane will strike their area, the current demand for batteries and canned food will rise. Expectations about the future direction of the economy can also affect current demand. If consumers are pessimistic about the economy, they start spending less, causing the current demand for goods to fall. Perhaps most important is how a change in the expected future price of a good affects current demand. When consumers expect the price of a product to rise in the near future, their current demand for it will increase. Gasoline is a good example. If you expect the price to increase soon, you'll want to fill up your tank now before the price goes up. In contrast, consumers will delay a purchase if they expect the item to decrease in price. No doubt you have heard someone say, "I'll wait until it goes on sale." When consumers expect the price of a product to fall, current demand for it will decline.

5. Demographic changes.
The demand for many products is strongly influenced by the demographic composition of the market. An increase in the elderly population in the United States in recent years has increased the demand for medical care, retirement housing, and vacation travel. The demand curves for these goods have shifted to the right. During the 1980s, the number of people aged 15 to 24 fell by more than 5 million. Because young people are a major part of the U.S. market for jeans, the demand for jeans fell by more than 100 million pairs over the course of the decade.[4] More recently, the increased use of cell phones and iPods among teenagers has led to a dramatic reduction in the demand for wristwatches.

6. Changes in consumer tastes and preferences.
Why do preferences change? Preferences change because people change and because people acquire new information. Consider how consumers respond to changing trends in popular diet programs. The demand for high-carbohydrate foods like white bread has fallen substantially, whereas the demand for low-carbohydrate foods like beef has risen. This is a major change from the past, when the demand for beef fell because of the "heart-healthy" eating habits consumers preferred then. Trends in the markets for clothing, toys, collectibles, and entertainment are constantly causing changes in the demand for these products as well. Firms may even try to change consumer preferences for their own products through advertising and information brochures.

The accompanying **Thumbnail Sketch** summarizes the major factors that cause a change in *demand*—a shift of the entire demand curve—and points out that quantity *demanded* (but not demand) will change in response to a change in the price of a good.

---

[4]These figures are from Suzanne Tregarthen, "Market for Jeans Shrinks," *The Margin* 6, no. 3 (January–February 1991): 28.

Thumbnail Sketch
Factors That Cause Changes in Demand and Quantity Demanded

This factor changes the quantity demanded of a good:

1. The price of the good: A higher price decreases the quantity demanded; a lower price increases the quantity demanded.

These factors change the demand for a good:

1. Consumer income: Lower consumer income will generally decrease demand; higher consumer income will generally increase demand.
2. Number of consumers in the market: Fewer consumers decreases demand; more consumers increases demand.
3a. Price of a substitute good: A decrease in the price of a substitute decreases the demand for the original good; an increase in the price of a substitute increases the demand for the original good.

3b. Price of a complementary good: An increase in the price of a complement decreases the demand for the original good; a decrease in the price of a complement increases the demand for the original good.
4. Expected future price of the good: If the price of a good is expected to fall in the future, the current demand for it will decrease; if the price of a good is expected to rise in the future, the current demand for it will increase.
5. Demographic changes: Population trends in age, gender, race, and other factors can increase or decrease demand for specific goods.
6. Consumer preferences: Changes in consumer tastes and preferences can increase or decrease demand for specific goods.

3-3 PRODUCER CHOICE AND THE LAW OF SUPPLY

Now let's shift our focus to producers and the supply side of the market. How does the market process determine the amount of each good that will be produced? To figure this out, we first have to understand what influences the choices of producers. Producers convert resources into goods and services by doing the following:

1. organizing productive inputs and resources, like land, labor, capital, natural resources, and intermediate goods;
2. transforming and combining these inputs into goods and services; and
3. selling the final products to consumers.

Producers have to purchase the resources at prices determined by market forces. Predictably, the owners of these resources will supply the resources only at prices at least equal to what they could earn elsewhere. Put another way, each resource the producers buy to make their product has to be bid away from all other potential uses. Its owner has to be paid its opportunity cost. The sum of the producer's cost of each resource used to produce a good will equal the **opportunity cost of production**.

There is an important difference between the opportunity cost of production and standard accounting measures of cost. Accountants generally do not count the cost of assets owned by the firm when they calculate the firm's cost. But economists do. Economists consider the fact that the assets owned by the firm could be used some other way—in other words, that they have an opportunity cost. Unless these opportunity costs are covered, the resources will eventually be used in other ways.

The opportunity cost of the assets owned by the firm is the earnings these assets could have generated if they were used in another way. Consider a manufacturer that invests $100 million in buildings and equipment to produce shirts. Instead of buying buildings and equipment,

Opportunity cost of production
The total economic cost of producing a good or service. The cost component includes the opportunity cost of all resources, including those owned by the firm. The opportunity cost is equal to the value of the production of other goods sacrificed as the result of producing the good.

the manufacturer could simply put the $100 million in the bank and let it draw interest. If the $100 million were earning, say, 5 percent interest, the firm would make $5 million on that money in a year's time. This $5 million in forgone interest is part of the firm's opportunity cost of producing shirts. Unlike an accountant, an economist will take that $5 million opportunity cost into account. If the firm plans to invest the money in shirt-making equipment, it had better earn more from making the shirts than the $5 million it could earn by simply putting the money in the bank. If the firm can't generate enough to cover all of its costs, including the opportunity cost of assets owned by the firm, it will not continue in business. If the firm were earning only $3 million producing shirts, it might be earning profit on its accounting statement, but it would be suffering a $2 million economic loss relative to simply putting the money in the bank.

3-3a THE ROLE OF PROFITS AND LOSSES

KEYS TO ECONOMIC PROSPERITY

Profits and Losses

Profits direct producers toward activities that increase the value of resources; losses impose a penalty on those who reduce the value of resources.

Profit
An excess of sales revenue relative to the opportunity cost of production. The cost component includes the opportunity cost of all resources, including those owned by the firm. Therefore, profit accrues only when the value of the good produced is greater than the value of the resources used for its production.

Firms earn a **profit** when the revenues from the goods and services that they supply exceed the opportunity cost of the resources used to make them. Consumers will not buy goods and services unless they value them at least as much as their purchase price. For example, Susan would not be willing to pay $40 for a pair of jeans unless she valued them by at least that amount. At the same time, the seller's opportunity cost of supplying a good will reflect the value consumers place on *other* goods that could have been produced with those same resources. This is true precisely because the seller has to bid those resources away from other producers wanting to use them.

Think about what it means when, for example, a firm is able to produce jeans at a cost of $30 per pair and sell them for $40, thereby reaping a profit of $10 per pair. The $30 opportunity cost of the jeans indicates that the resources used to produce the jeans could have been used to produce other items worth $30 to consumers (perhaps a denim backpack). In turn, the profit indicates that consumers value the jeans more than other goods that might have been produced with the resources used to supply the jeans.

The willingness of consumers to pay a price greater than a good's opportunity cost indicates that they value the good more than other things that could have been produced with the same resources. Viewed from this perspective, profit is a reward earned by entrepreneurs who use resources to produce goods consumers value more highly than the other goods those resources could have produced. In essence, this profit is a signal that an entrepreneur has increased the value of the resources under his or her control.

Business decision makers will seek to undertake production of goods and services that will generate profit. However, things do not always turn out as expected. Sometimes business firms are unable to sell their products at prices that will cover their costs. **Losses** occur when the revenue derived from sales is insufficient to cover the opportunity cost of the resources used to produce a good or service. Losses indicate that the firm has reduced the value of the resources it has used. In other words, consumers would have been better off if those resources had been used to produce something else. In a market economy, losses will eventually cause firms to go out of business, and the resources they previously utilized will be directed toward other things valued more highly, or to other firms who can produce those same goods at a lower cost.

Profits and losses play a very important role in a market economy. They determine which products (and firms) will expand and survive and which will contract and be driven from the market. Clearly, there is a positive side to business failures. As our preceding discussion highlights, losses and business failures free up resources being used unwisely so they can be put to use by other firms providing consumers with more value.

Loss
A deficit of sales revenue relative to the opportunity cost of production. Losses are a penalty imposed on those who produce goods even though they are valued less than the resources required for their production.

3-3b SUPPLY AND THE ENTREPRENEUR

Entrepreneurs organize the production of new products. In doing so, they take on significant risk in deciding what to produce and how to produce it. Their success or failure depends on how much consumers eventually value the products they develop relative to other products that could have been produced with the resources. Entrepreneurs figure out which projects are likely to be profitable and then try to persuade a corporation, a banker, or individual investors to invest the resources needed to give their new idea a chance. Studies indicate, however, that only about 55 to 65 percent of the new products introduced are still on the market five years later. Being an entrepreneur means you have to risk failing.

Entrepreneurs who buy raw land, put in streets and sewer lines, and divide up the land into lots for sale will earn a profit if the revenues derived from the lot sales exceed the opportunity cost of the project. Profit is a reward for increasing the value of the resources.

To prosper, entrepreneurs must convert and rearrange resources in a manner that will increase their value. A person who purchases 100 acres of raw land, puts in streets and a sewage-disposal system, divides the plot into 1-acre lots, and sells them for 50 percent more than the opportunity cost of all resources used is clearly an entrepreneur. This entrepreneur profits because the value of the resources has increased. Sometimes entrepreneurial activity is less complex, though. For example, a 15-year-old who purchases a power mower and sells lawn services to his neighbors is also an entrepreneur seeking to profit by increasing the value of his resources—time and equipment.

3-3c MARKET SUPPLY SCHEDULE

How will producer–entrepreneurs respond to a change in product price? Other things constant, a higher price will increase the producer's incentive to supply the good. Established producers will expand the scale of their operations, and over time new entrepreneurs, seeking personal gain, will enter the market and begin supplying the product, too. *The law of supply states that there is a direct (or positive) relationship between the price of a good or service and the amount of it that suppliers are willing to produce. This direct relationship means that the price and the quantity producers wish to supply move in the same direction. As the price increases, producers will supply more—and as the price decreases, they will supply less.*

Like the law of demand, the law of supply reflects the basic economic principle that incentives matter. Higher prices increase the reward entrepreneurs get from selling their products. The more profitable it is to produce a product, the more of it entrepreneurs will be willing to supply. Conversely, as the price of a product falls, so does its profitability and the incentive to supply it. Just think about how many hours of tutoring services you would be willing to supply for different prices. Would you be willing to spend more time tutoring students if instead of $8 per hour, tutoring paid $50 per hour? The law of supply suggests you would, and producers of other goods and services are no different.

Exhibit 6 illustrates the law of supply. The curve shown in the exhibit is called a *supply curve*. Because there is a direct relationship between a good's price and the amount offered for sale by suppliers, the supply curve has a positive slope. It slopes upward to the right. Read horizontally, the supply curve shows how much of a particular good producers are willing to produce and sell at a given price. Read vertically, the supply curve reveals important information about the cost of production. The height of the supply curve indicates both (1) the minimum price necessary to induce producers to supply that additional unit and (2) the opportunity cost of producing that additional unit. These are both measured by the height of the supply curve because the minimum price required to induce a supplier to sell a unit is precisely the marginal cost of producing it.

Law of supply
A principle that states there is a direct relationship between the price of a good and the quantity of it producers are willing to supply. As the price of a good increases, producers will wish to supply more of it. As the price decreases, producers will wish to supply less.

EXHIBIT 6

Supply Curve

As the price of a product increases, other things constant, producers will increase the amount of the product supplied to the market.

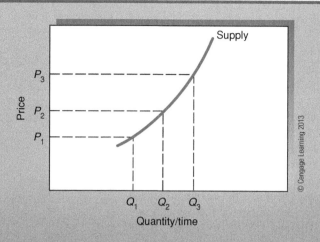

3-3d PRODUCER SURPLUS

We previously used the demand curve to illustrate consumer surplus, the net gains of buyers from market exchanges. The supply curve can be used in a similar manner to illustrate the net gains of producers and resource suppliers. Suppose that you are an aspiring musician and are willing to perform a two-hour concert for $500. If a promoter offers to pay you $750 to perform the concert, you will accept, and receive $250 more than your minimum price. This $250 net gain represents your **producer surplus**. In effect, producer surplus is the difference between the amount a supplier actually receives (based on the market price) and the minimum price required to induce the supplier to produce the given units (their marginal cost). The shaded area of Exhibit 7 illustrates the measurement of producer surplus for an entire market.

　　It's important to note that producer surplus represents the gains received by all parties contributing resources to the production of a good. In this respect, producer surplus is fundamentally different from profit. Profit accrues to the owners of the business firm producing the good, whereas producer surplus encompasses the net gains derived by all people who help produce the good, including those employed by or selling resources to the firm.

Producer surplus
The difference between the price that suppliers actually receive and the minimum price they would be willing to accept. It measures the net gains to producers and resource suppliers from market exchange. It is not the same as profit.

EXHIBIT 7

Producer Surplus

Producer surplus is the area above the supply curve but below the actual sales price. This area represents the net gains to producers and resource suppliers from production and exchange.

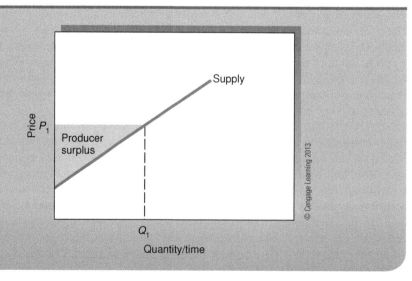

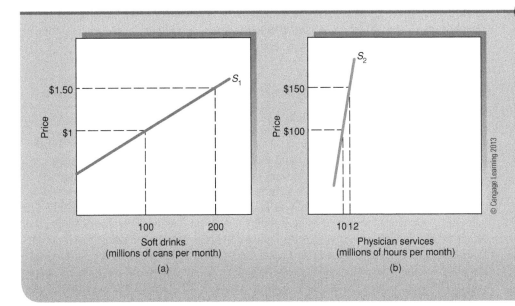

© Cengage Learning 2013

EXHIBIT 8

Elastic and Inelastic Supply Curves

Frame (a) illustrates a supply curve that is relatively elastic and therefore the quantity supplied is highly responsive to a change in price. Soft drinks provide an example. Frame (b) illustrates a relatively inelastic supply curve, one in which the quantity supplied increases by only a small amount in response to a change in price. This is the case for physician services.

3-3e RESPONSIVENESS OF QUANTITY SUPPLIED TO PRICE CHANGES: ELASTIC AND INELASTIC SUPPLY CURVES

Like the quantity demanded, the responsiveness of the quantity supplied to a change in price is different for different goods. The supply curve is said to be elastic when a modest change in price leads to a large change in quantity supplied. This is generally true when the additional resources needed to expand output can be obtained with only a small increase in their price. Consider the supply of soft drinks. The contents of soft drinks—primarily carbonated water, sugar, and flavoring—are abundantly available. A sharp increase in the use of these ingredients by soft drink producers is unlikely to push up their price much. Therefore, as Exhibit 8 illustrates, if the price of soft drinks were to rise from $1 to $1.50, producers would be willing to expand output sharply from 100 million to 200 million cans per month. A 50 percent increase in price leads to a 100 percent expansion in quantity supplied. The larger the increase in quantity in response to a higher price, the more elastic the supply curve. The flatness of the supply curve for soft drinks reflects the fact that it is highly elastic.

In contrast, when the quantity supplied is not very responsive to a change in price, supply is said to be inelastic. Physicians' services are an example. If the earnings of doctors increase from $100 to $150 per hour, there will be some increase in the quantity of the services they provide. Some physicians will work longer hours; others may delay retirement. Yet, these adjustments are likely to result in only a small increase in the quantity supplied because it takes a long time to train a physician and the number of qualified doctors who are working in other occupations or who are outside of the labor force is small. Therefore, as Exhibit 8 (right frame) shows, a 50 percent increase in the price of physician services leads

OUTSTANDING ECONOMIST

ALFRED MARSHALL (1842–1924)

British economist Alfred Marshall was one of the most influential economists of his era. Many concepts and tools that form the core of modern microeconomics originated with Marshall in his famous *Principles of Economics*, first published in 1890. Marshall introduced the concepts of supply and demand, equilibrium, elasticity, consumers' and producers' surplus, and the idea of distinguishing between short-run and long-run changes.

to only a 20 percent expansion in the quantity supplied. Unlike soft drinks, higher prices for physician services do not generate much increase in quantity supplied. Economists would say that the supply of physician services is relatively inelastic.

3-4 CHANGES IN SUPPLY VERSUS CHANGES IN QUANTITY SUPPLIED

Like demand, it is important to distinguish between a change in the *quantity supplied* and a change in *supply*. When producers change the number of units they are willing to supply in response to a change in price, this movement along the supply curve is called a "change in *quantity supplied*." A change in any factor *other than the price* shifts the supply curve and is called a "change in *supply*."

As we previously discussed, profit-seeking entrepreneurs will produce a good only if its sales price is expected to exceed its opportunity cost of production. Therefore, changes that affect the opportunity cost of supplying a good will also influence the amount of it producers are willing to supply. These other factors, such as the prices of resources used to make the good and the level of technology available, are held constant when we draw the supply curve. The supply curve itself reflects quantity changes only in response to price changes. Changes in these other factors shift the supply curve. Factors that increase the opportunity cost of providing a good will discourage production and decrease supply, shifting the entire curve inward to the left. Conversely, changes that lower the opportunity cost of producers will encourage production and increase supply, shifting the entire curve outward to the right.

Let us now take a closer look at the primary factors that will cause a change in supply and shift the entire curve right or left.

1. Changes in resource prices. How will an increase in the price of a resource, such as wages of workers or the materials used to produce a product, affect the supply of a good? Higher resource prices will increase the cost of production, reducing the profitability of firms supplying the good. The higher cost will induce firms to reduce their output. With time, some may even be driven out of business. As Exhibit 9 illustrates, higher resource prices will reduce the supply of the good, causing a shift to the left in the supply curve from S_1 to S_2. Alternatively, a reduction in the price of a resource used to produce a good will cause an increase in supply—a rightward shift in the supply curve—as firms expand output in response to the lower costs and increased profitability of supplying the good.

2. Changes in technology. Like lower resource prices, technological improvements—the discovery of new, lower-cost production techniques—reduce production costs, and thereby increase supply. Technological advances have affected the cost of almost everything.

EXHIBIT 9

A Decrease in Supply

Crude oil is a resource used to produce gasoline. When the price of crude oil rises, it increases the cost of producing gasoline and results in a decrease in the supply of gasoline.

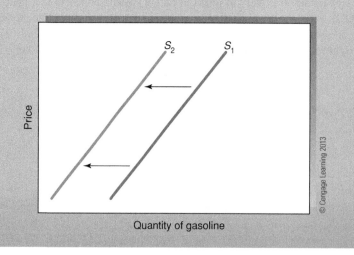

Thumbnail Sketch

Factors That Cause Changes in Supply and Quantity Supplied

This factor changes the quantity supplied of a good:

1. The price of the good: A lower price decreases the quantity supplied; a higher price increases the quantity supplied.

These factors change the supply of a good:

1. Resource prices (the prices of things used to make the good): Lower resource prices increase supply; higher resource prices decrease supply.

2. Technological change: A technological improvement increases supply; a technological setback decreases supply.

3. Weather or political conditions: Favorable weather or good political conditions increase supply; adverse weather conditions or poor political conditions decrease supply.

4. Taxes imposed on the producers of a good: Lower taxes increase supply; higher taxes decrease supply.

©iStockphoto.com/baianliang

Before the invention of the printing press, books had to be handwritten. Just imagine the massive reduction in cost and increase in the supply of books caused by this single invention. Similarly, improved farm machinery has vastly expanded the supply of agricultural products through the years. The field of robotics has reduced the cost of producing airplanes, automobiles, and other types of machinery. Better computer chips have drastically reduced the cost of producing electronics. Forty years ago, a simple calculator cost more than $100 and a microwave oven almost $500. When introduced in the mid-1980s, a cellular telephone cost more than $4,000. You have probably noticed that the prices of flat-screen computer monitors and plasma-screen televisions have fallen substantially in recent years. Again, technological advances explain these changes.

3. Elements of nature and political disruptions. Natural disasters and changing political conditions can also alter supply, sometimes dramatically. In some years, good weather leads to "bumper crops," increasing the supply of agricultural products. At other times, freezes or droughts lead to poor harvests, reducing supply. War and political unrest in the Middle East region have had a major impact on the supply of oil several times during the past few decades. Factors such as these will alter supply.

4. Changes in taxes. If the government increases the taxes on the sellers of a product, the result will be the same as any other increase in the cost of doing business. The added tax that sellers have to pay will reduce their willingness to sell the product at any given price. Each unit must now be sold for a price that covers not only the opportunity cost of production, but also the tax. For example, a special tax is levied on commercial airline tickets, partially to cover the cost of airport security. This tax increases the cost of air travel and thereby reduces the supply (a shift to the left in the supply curve.)

The accompanying **Thumbnail Sketch** summarizes the major factors that change *supply* (a shift of the entire supply curve) and quantity supplied (a movement along the supply curve).

3-5 HOW MARKET PRICES ARE DETERMINED: DEMAND AND SUPPLY INTERACT

Consumer–buyers and producer–sellers make decisions independent of each other, but market prices coordinate their choices and influence their actions. To the economist, a **market** is not a physical location but an abstract concept that encompasses the forces generated

Market
An abstract concept encompassing the forces of demand and supply and the interaction of buyers and sellers with the potential for exchange to occur.

by the decisions of buyers and sellers. A market may be quite narrow (for example, the market for grade A jumbo eggs), or it may be quite broad like when we lump diverse goods into a single market, such as the market for all "consumer goods." There is also a wide range of sophistication among markets. The New York Stock Exchange is a highly formal, computerized market. Each weekday, buyers and sellers, who seldom meet, electronically exchange corporate shares they own worth billions of dollars. In contrast, a neighborhood market for babysitting services or tutoring in economics may be highly informal, bringing together buyers and sellers primarily by word of mouth.

Equilibrium *is a state in which the conflicting forces of demand and supply are in balance. When a market is in equilibrium, the decisions of consumers and producers are brought into harmony with one another, and the quantity demanded will equal the quantity supplied.* In equilibrium, it is possible for both buyers and sellers to realize their choices simultaneously. What could bring these diverse interests into harmony? We will see that the answer is market prices.

Equilibrium
A state in which the conflicting forces of demand and supply are in balance. When a market is in equilibrium, the decisions of consumers and producers are brought into harmony with one another, and the quantity demanded will equal the quantity supplied.

3-5a MARKET EQUILIBRIUM

As we have learned, a higher price will reduce the quantity of a good demanded by consumers. Conversely, a higher price will increase the quantity of a good supplied by producers. The market price of a good will tend to change in a direction that will bring the quantity of a good consumers want to buy into balance with the quantity producers want to sell. If the price is too high, the quantity supplied by producers will exceed the quantity demanded. Producers will be unable to sell as much as they would like unless they reduce their price. Alternatively, if the price is too low, the quantity demanded by consumers will exceed the quantity supplied. Some consumers will be unable to get as much as they would like, unless they are willing to pay a higher price to bid some of the good away from other potential customers. Thus, there will be a tendency for the price in a market to move toward the price that brings the two into balance.

People have a tendency to think of consumers wanting lower prices and producers wanting higher prices. Although this is true, price changes frequently trend toward the middle of the two extremes. When a local store has an excess supply of a particular item, how does it get rid of it? By having a sale or otherwise lowering its price. Firms often lower their prices in order to get rid of excess supply.

In contrast, excess demand is solved by consumers bidding up prices. Children's toys around Christmas provide a perfect example. When first introduced, items such as the Nintendo Wii, Webkinz, and the video game Rock Band were immediate successes. The firms producing these products had not anticipated the overwhelming demand; every child wanted one for Christmas. Some stores raised their prices, but the demand was so strong that lines of parents were forming outside stores before they even opened. Often, only the first few in line were able to get the toys (a sure sign that the store had set the price below equilibrium). Out in the parking lots, in the classified ads, and on eBay, parents were offering to pay even higher prices for these items. If stores were not going to set the prices right, parents in these informal markets would! These examples show that rising prices are often the result of consumers bidding up prices when excess demand is present. A similar phenomenon can be seen in the market for tickets to a World Series game or a popular music group's upcoming concert, as the immediate value of a ticket on the resale market can be much higher than the original retail price if, at that price, the original quantity supplied is not adequate to meet the quantity demanded.

As these examples illustrate, whenever quantity supplied and quantity demanded are not in balance, there is a tendency for price to change in a manner that will correct the imbalance. It is possible to show this process graphically with the supply and demand curves we have developed in this chapter. Exhibit 10 shows the supply and demand curves in the market for a basic calculator. At a high price—$12, for example—producers will plan to supply 600 calculators per day, whereas consumers will choose to purchase only 450. An excess supply of 150 calculators (shown by distance *ab* in the graph) will result. Unsold calculators will push the inventories of producers upward. To get rid of some of their calculators in inventory, some producers will cut their price to increase their sales. Other firms will have to lower their price,

EXHIBIT 10

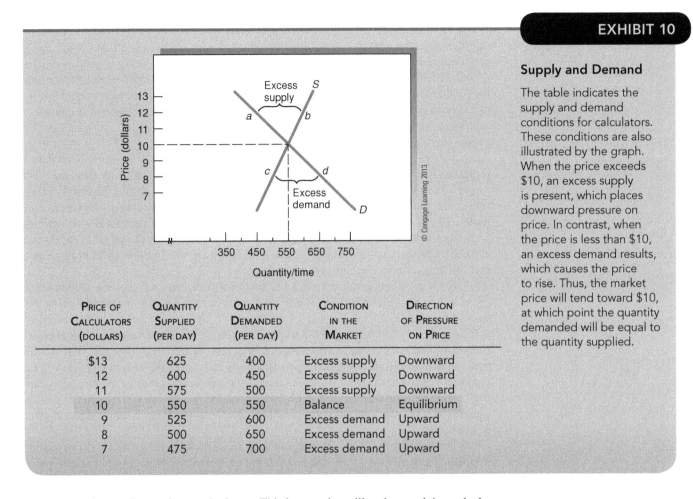

Supply and Demand

The table indicates the supply and demand conditions for calculators. These conditions are also illustrated by the graph. When the price exceeds $10, an excess supply is present, which places downward pressure on price. In contrast, when the price is less than $10, an excess demand results, which causes the price to rise. Thus, the market price will tend toward $10, at which point the quantity demanded will be equal to the quantity supplied.

PRICE OF CALCULATORS (DOLLARS)	QUANTITY SUPPLIED (PER DAY)	QUANTITY DEMANDED (PER DAY)	CONDITION IN THE MARKET	DIRECTION OF PRESSURE ON PRICE
$13	625	400	Excess supply	Downward
12	600	450	Excess supply	Downward
11	575	500	Excess supply	Downward
10	550	550	Balance	Equilibrium
9	525	600	Excess demand	Upward
8	500	650	Excess demand	Upward
7	475	700	Excess demand	Upward

too, as a result, or sell even fewer calculators. This lower price will make supplying calculators less attractive to producers. Some of them will go out of business. Others will reduce their output or perhaps produce other products. How low will the price of calculators go? As the figure shows, when the price has declined to $10, the quantity supplied by producers and the quantity demanded by consumers will be in balance at 550 calculators per day. At this price ($10), the quantity demanded by consumers just equals the quantity supplied by producers, and the choices of the two groups are brought into harmony.

What will happen if the price per calculator is lower—$8, for example? In this case, the amount demanded by consumers (650 units) will exceed the amount supplied by producers (500 units). An excess demand of 150 units (shown by the distance *cd* in the graph) will be the result. Some consumers who are unable to purchase the calculators at $8 per unit because of the inadequate supply would be willing to pay a higher price. Recognizing this fact, producers will raise their price. As the price increases to $10, producers will expand their output and consumers will cut down on their consumption. At the $10 price, equilibrium will be restored.

3-5b EFFICIENCY AND MARKET EQUILIBRIUM

When a market reaches equilibrium, all the gains from trade have been fully realized and **economic efficiency** is present. Economists often use economic efficiency as a standard to measure outcomes under alternative circumstances. The central idea of efficiency is a cost-versus-benefit comparison. On the one hand, undertaking an economic action will be efficient only if it generates more benefit than cost. On the other hand, undertaking an action that generates more cost than benefit is inefficient. For a market to be efficient, all trades that generate more benefit than cost need to be undertaken. In addition, economic efficiency requires that no trades creating more cost than benefit be undertaken.

Economic efficiency
A situation in which all of the potential gains from trade have been realized. An action is efficient only if it creates more benefit than cost. With well-defined property rights and competition, market equilibrium is efficient.

A closer look at the way that markets work can help us understand the concept of efficiency. The supply curve reflects producers' opportunity cost. Each point along the supply curve indicates the minimum price for which the units of a good could be produced without a loss to the seller. Assuming no other third parties are affected by the production of this good, then the height of the supply curve represents the opportunity cost to society of producing and selling the good. On the other side of the market, each point along the demand curve indicates how consumers value an extra unit of the good—that is, the maximum amount the consumer is willing to pay for the extra unit. Again assuming that no other third parties are affected, the height of the demand curve represents the benefit to society of producing and selling the good. Any time the consumer's valuation of a unit (the benefit) exceeds the producer's minimum supply price (the cost), producing and selling the unit is consistent with economic efficiency. The trade will result in mutual gain to both parties. When property rights are well defined and only the buyers and sellers are affected by production and exchange, competitive market forces will automatically guide a market toward an equilibrium level of output that satisfies economic efficiency.

Exhibit 11 illustrates why this is true. Suppliers of bicycles will produce additional bicycles as long as the market price exceeds their opportunity cost of production (shown by the height of the supply curve). Similarly, consumers will continue to purchase additional bikes as long as their benefit (shown by the height of the demand curve) exceeds the market price. Eventually, market forces will result in an equilibrium output level of *Q* and a price of *P*. At this point, all the bicycles providing benefits to consumers that exceed the costs to suppliers will be produced. Economic efficiency is met because all of the potential consumer and producer gains from exchange (shown by the shaded area) have occurred. As you can see, the point of market equilibrium is also the point where the combined area showing consumer and producer surplus is the greatest.

When fewer than *Q* bicycles are produced, some bicycles valued more by consumers than the opportunity cost of producing them are not being produced. This is not consistent with economic efficiency. On the other hand, if output is expanded beyond *Q*, inefficiency will also result because some of the bicycles cost more to produce than consumers are willing to pay for them. Prices in competitive markets eventually guide producers and consumers to the level of output consistent with economic efficiency.

EXHIBIT 11

Economic Efficiency

When markets are competitive and property rights are well defined, the equilibrium reached by a market satisfies economic efficiency. All units that create more benefit (the buyer's valuation shown by the height of the demand curve) than cost (opportunity cost of production shown by the height of the supply curve) are produced. This maximizes the total gains from trade, the combined area represented by consumer and producer surplus.

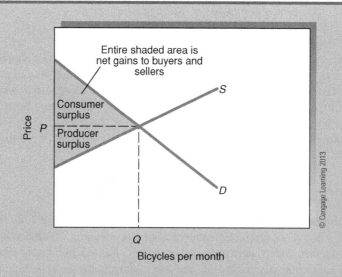

© Cengage Learning 2013

3-6 HOW MARKETS RESPOND TO CHANGES IN DEMAND AND SUPPLY

How will a market adjust to a change in demand? Exhibit 12 shows the market adjustment to an increase in the demand for eggs around Easter. Demand D_1 and supply S are typical throughout much of the year. During the two weeks before Easter, however, consumer demand for eggs rises because people purchase them to decorate, too. This shifts egg demand from D_1 to D_2 during that time of year. As you can see, the increase in demand pushes the price upward from P_1 to P_2 (typically by about 20 cents per dozen) and results in a larger equilibrium quantity traded (Q_2 rather than Q_1—an increase of typically around 600 million eggs). There is a new equilibrium at point b around Easter (versus point a during the rest of the year).

The tradition of coloring and hunting for eggs causes an increase in demand for eggs around Easter. As Exhibit 12 illustrates, this leads to higher egg prices and costly actions by producers to supply a larger quantity during this period.

Although consumers may not be happy about paying a higher price for eggs around Easter, the higher price serves two essential purposes. First, it encourages consumers to conserve on their usage of eggs. Some consumers may purchase only two dozen eggs to color, rather than three; other consumers may skip having an omelet for breakfast and have yogurt instead. These steps on the consumer side of the market help make the eggs that are available around Easter go further. Second, the higher price is precisely what results in the additional 600 million eggs being supplied to the market to satisfy this increased consumer demand. Without the price increase, excess demand would be present, and many consumers would simply be unable to find eggs to purchase around Easter. If the price remained at P_1 (the equilibrium price throughout most of the year), consumers at Easter-time would want to purchase more eggs than producers would be willing to supply. At the higher P_2 price, however, the quantity suppliers are willing to sell is again in balance with the quantity consumers wish to purchase.

Why were suppliers unwilling to supply the additional 600 million eggs at the original price of P_1? Because at the original equilibrium price of P_1, suppliers were already

---

EXHIBIT 12

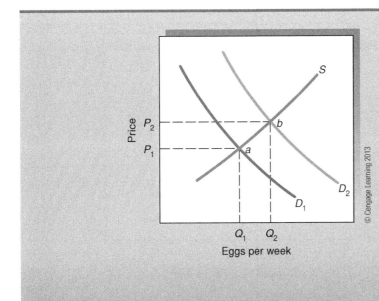

Market Adjustment to Increase in Demand

Here, we illustrate how the market for eggs adjusts to an increase in demand such as generally occurs around Easter. Initially (before the Easter season), the market for eggs reflects demand D_1 and supply S. The increase in demand (shift from D_1 to D_2) pushes price up and leads to a new equilibrium at a higher price (P_2 rather than P_1) and larger quantity traded (Q_2)

producing and selling all the eggs that cost less to produce than that price. The additional eggs desired by consumers around Easter all cost more to produce than the old market price of P_1. The higher price of P_2 is what allows suppliers to cover their higher production costs associated with these extra eggs. Around Easter, farmers take costly steps to avoid having the hens molt because hens lay fewer eggs when they are molting. They do this by changing the quantity and types of feed and by increasing the lighting in the birds' sheds—both of which mean higher production costs. Farmers also try to build up larger than normal inventories of eggs before Easter. Eggs are typically about two days old when consumers buy them at the store, but can be up to seven days old around Easter time. Building up and maintaining this additional inventory are costly, too.

In a market economy, when the demand for a good increases, its price will rise, which will (1) motivate consumers to search for substitutes and cut back on additional purchases of the good and (2) motivate producers to supply more of the good. These two forces will eventually bring the quantity demanded and quantity supplied back into balance.

It's important to note that this response on the supply side of the egg market is not a shift in the supply curve. The supply curve remains unchanged. Rather, there is a movement along the original supply curve—a change in *quantity* supplied. The only reason suppliers are willing to alter their behavior (produce more eggs) is because the increased demand has pushed up the price of eggs. Notice that it is the change in demand (a shift of the demand curve) that leads to the change in quantity supplied (a movement along the supply curve). Producers are simply responding to the price movement caused by the change in demand. A movement along one curve (a change in quantity supplied *or* a change in quantity demanded) happens in response to a shift in the other curve (a change in demand or a change in supply).

When the demand for a product declines, the adjustment process sends buyers and sellers just the opposite signals. Take a piece of paper and see if you can diagram a decrease in demand and how it will affect price and quantity in a market. If you've done it correctly, a decline in demand (a shift to the left in the demand curve) will lead to a lower price and a lower quantity traded. What's going on in the diagram is that the lower price (caused by lower consumer demand) is reducing the incentive of producers to supply the good. When consumers no longer want as much of a good, falling market prices signal producers to cut back production. The reduced output allows these resources to be freed up to go into the production of other goods consumers want more.

How will markets respond to changes in supply? Exhibit 13 shows the market's adjustment to a decrease in the supply of lemons, such as happened during January 2007 when freezing temperatures in California destroyed a large portion of the lemon crop. A reduction

EXHIBIT 13

Market Adjustment to a Decrease in Supply

Here, using lemons as an example, we illustrate how a market adjusts to a decrease in supply. Assume adverse weather conditions substantially reduce the supply (shift from S_1 to S_2) of lemons. The reduction in supply leads to an increase in the equilibrium price (from P_1 to P_2) and a reduction in the equilibrium quantity traded (from Q_1 to Q_2).

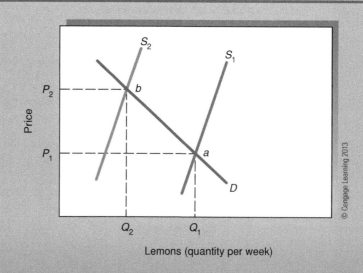

© Cengage Learning 2013

Thumbnail Sketch
How Changes in Demand and Supply Affect Market Price and Quantity

Changes in Demand

1. An increase in demand—shown by a rightward shift of the demand curve—will cause an increase in both the equilibrium price and the equilibrium quantity.

2. A decrease in demand—shown by a leftward shift of the demand curve—will cause a decrease in both the equilibrium price and the equilibrium quantity.

Changes in Supply

1. An increase in supply—shown by a rightward shift of the supply curve—will cause a decrease in the equilibrium price and an increase in the equilibrium quantity.

2. A decrease in supply—shown by a leftward shift of the supply curve—will cause an increase in the equilibrium price and a decrease in the equilibrium quantity.

©iStockphoto.com/baianliang

in supply (shift from S_1 to S_2) will cause the price of lemons to increase sharply (P_1 to P_2). Because of the higher price, consumers will cut back on their consumption of lemons (the movement along the demand curve from a to b). Some will switch to substitutes—in this case, probably other varieties of citrus. The higher price also encourages the remaining lemon suppliers to take additional steps—like more careful harvesting techniques or using more fertilizer—that allow them to produce more lemons than otherwise would be the case. The higher prices will rebalance the quantity demanded and quantity supplied.

As the lemon example illustrates, a decrease in supply will lead to higher prices and a lower equilibrium quantity. How do you think the market price and quantity would adjust to an increase in supply, as might be caused by a breakthrough in the technology used to harvest the lemons? Again, try to draw the appropriate supply and demand curves to illustrate this case. If you do it correctly, the graph you draw will show an increase in supply (a shift to the right in the supply curve) leading to a lower market price and a larger equilibrium quantity.

The accompanying **Thumbnail Sketch** summarizes the effect of changes—both increases and decreases—in demand and supply on the equilibrium price and quantity. The cases listed in the sketch, however, are for when only a single curve shifts. But sometimes market conditions simultaneously shift both demand and supply. For example, consumer income might increase at the same time that a technological advance in production occurs. These two changes will cause both demand and supply to increase at the same time—both curves will shift to the right. The new equilibrium will definitely be at a larger quantity, but the direction of the change in price is indeterminate. The price may either increase or decrease, depending on whether the increase in demand or increase in supply is larger—which curve shifted the most, in other words.

What will happen if supply increases but demand falls at the same time? Price will definitely fall, but the new equilibrium quantity may either increase or decrease. Draw the supply and demand curves for this case and make sure that you understand why.

3-6a INVISIBLE HAND PRINCIPLE

KEYS TO ECONOMIC PROSPERITY

Invisible Hand Principle

Market prices coordinate the actions of self-interested individuals and direct them toward activities that promote the general welfare.

©iStockphoto.com/malerapaso

More than 235 years ago, Adam Smith, the father of economics, stressed that personal self-interest *when directed by market prices* is a powerful force promoting economic progress. In a famous passage in his book *An Inquiry into the Nature and Causes of the Wealth of Nations*, Smith put it this way:

> Every individual is continually exerting himself to find out the most advantageous employment for whatever [income] he can command. It is his own advantage, indeed, and not that of the society which he has in view. But the study of his own advantage naturally, or rather necessarily, leads him to prefer that employment which is most advantageous to society. . . . He intends only his own gain, and he is in this, as in many other cases, led by an invisible hand to promote an end which was not part of his intention. By pursuing his own interest he frequently promotes that of the society more effectually than when he really intends to promote it.[5]

The "invisible hand" to which Smith referred was the pricing system—prices determined by the forces of supply and demand. Smith's fundamental insight was that market prices tend to bring the self-interest of individuals into harmony with the betterment of society. Moreover, when it is directed by market prices, personal self-interest is a powerful force promoting growth and prosperity.

The tendency of market prices to channel the actions of self-interested individuals into activities that promote the prosperity of the society is now known as the **invisible hand principle**. Let's take a closer look at this important principle.

Invisible hand principle
The tendency of market prices to direct individuals pursuing their own interests to engage in activities promoting the economic well-being of society.

3-6b PRICES AND MARKET ORDER

The invisible hand principle can be difficult to grasp because there is a natural tendency to associate order with central direction and control. Surely some central authority must be in charge. But this is not the case. The pricing system, reflecting the choices of literally millions of consumers, producers, and resource owners, provides the direction. Moreover, the market process works so automatically that most of us give little thought to it. We simply take it for granted.

Perhaps an example from your everyday life will help you better understand the invisible hand principle. Visualize a busy retail store with 10 checkout lanes. No one is assigning shoppers to checkout lanes. Shoppers are left to choose for themselves. Nonetheless, they do not all try to get in the same lane. Why? Individuals are always alert for adjustment opportunities that offer personal gain. When the line at one lane gets long or is held up by a price check, some shoppers will shift to other lanes and thereby smooth out the flow among the lanes. Even though central planning is absent, this process of mutual adjustment by self-interested individuals results in order and social cooperation. A similar phenomenon occurs on busy interstate highways as drivers switch between lanes for personal gain, with the end result being the quickest flow of traffic for everyone and for the group as a whole.

The incentive structure generated by markets is a lot like that accompanying the checkout at a busy retail store or driving on the freeway. Like the number of people in a lane, profits and losses provide market participants with information about the advantages and disadvantages of different economic activities. Losses indicate that an economic activity is congested, and, as a result, producers are unable to cover their costs. In such a case, successful market participants will shift their resources away from such activities toward other, more valuable uses. Conversely, profits are indicative of an open lane, the opportunity to experience gain if one shifts into an activity in which the price is high relative to the per-unit cost. As producers and resource suppliers shift away from activities characterized by congestion and into those characterized by the opportunity for profit, they enlarge the flow of economic activity.

Consider the following three vitally important functions performed by market prices.

---

[5]Adam Smith, *An Inquiry into the Nature and Causes of the Wealth of Nations* (New York: Modern Library, 1937), 423.

1. Market prices communicate information to both buyers and sellers that will promote efficient use of resources and proper response to changing conditions. Prices provide producers with up-to-date information about which goods consumers most intensely desire and with important information about the abundance of the resources used in the production process. The cost of production, driven by the opportunity cost of resources, tells the business decision-maker the relative importance others place on the alternative uses of those resources. A boom in the housing market might cause lumber prices to rise. In turn, furniture-makers seeing these higher lumber prices will utilize substitute raw materials such as metal and plastic in their production processes. Because of market prices, furniture-makers will conserve on their use of lumber, just as if they had known that lumber was now more urgently needed for constructing new housing.

Consider another example. Suppose a drought in Brazil severely reduces the supply of coffee. Coffee prices will rise. Even if consumers do not know about the drought, the higher prices will provide them with all the information they need to know—it's time to cut back on coffee consumption. *Market prices register information derived from the choices of millions of consumers, producers, and resource suppliers, and provide them with everything they need to know to make wise decisions.*

2. Market prices coordinate the actions of market participants. Market prices also coordinate the choices of buyers and sellers, bringing their decisions into line with each other. Excess supply will lead to falling prices, which discourage production and encourage consumption until the excess supply is eliminated. Alternatively, excess demand will lead to price increases, which encourage consumers to economize on their uses of the good and suppliers to produce more of it, eliminating the excess demand. Changing market prices induce responses on both sides of the market that will correct imbalances.

3. Market prices motivate economic players. Market prices establish a reward–penalty (profit–loss) structure that encourages people to work, cooperate with others, use efficient production methods, supply goods that are intensely desired by others, and invest for the future. Self-interested entrepreneurs will seek to produce only the goods consumers value enough to pay a price sufficient to cover production cost. Self-interest will also encourage producers to use efficient production methods and adopt cost-saving technologies because lower costs will mean greater profits. Firms that fail to do so will be unable to compete successfully in the marketplace.

At the beginning of this chapter, we asked you to reflect on why the grocery stores in your local community generally have on hand about the right amount of milk, bread, vegetables, and other goods. Likewise, how is it that refrigerators, automobiles, and CD players, produced at different places around the world, make their way to stores near you in approximately the same numbers that they are demanded by consumers? The invisible hand principle provides the answer, and it leads to an amazing degree of social cooperation.

Is the concept of the invisible hand really valid? Next time you sit down to have a nice dinner, think about all the people who help make it possible. It is unlikely that any of them, from the farmer to the truck driver to the grocer, was motivated by a concern that you have an enjoyable meal. Market prices, however, bring their interest into harmony with yours. Farmers who raise the best beef or turkeys receive higher prices, truck drivers and grocers earn more money if their products are delivered fresh and in good condition, and so on. An amazing degree of cooperation and order is created by market exchanges—all without the central direction of any government official.

3-6c COMPETITION AND PROPERTY RIGHTS

As we noted earlier in this chapter, our focus so far has been on markets in which rival firms can freely enter and exit, and private-property rights are clearly defined and enforced. *The efficiency of market organization is, in fact, dependent upon these two things: (1) competitive markets and (2) well-defined and enforced private-property rights.*

Competition, the great regulator, can protect both buyer and seller. It protects consumers from sellers who would charge a price substantially above the cost of production or withhold a vital resource for an exorbitant amount of money. Similarly, it protects employees (sellers of their labor) from the power of any single employer (the buyers of labor). When markets are competitive, both buyers and sellers have alternatives and these alternatives provide them with protection against ill treatment by others.

When property rights are well defined, secure, and tradable, suppliers of goods and services have to pay resource owners for their use. They will not be permitted to seize and use scarce resources without compensating the owners. Neither will they be permitted to use violence (for example, to attack or invade the property of another) to get what they want. The efficiency of markets hinges on the presence of property rights—after all, people can't easily exchange or compete for things they don't have or can't get property rights to. Without well-defined property rights, markets simply cannot function effectively.

LOOKING AHEAD

Although we incorporated numerous examples designed to enhance your understanding of the supply-and-demand model throughout this chapter, we have only touched the surface. In various modified forms, this model is the central tool of economics. The next chapter will explore several specific applications and extensions of this important model.

KEY POINTS

- The law of demand states that there is an inverse (or negative) relationship between the price of a good or service and the quantity of it that consumers are willing to purchase. The height of the demand curve at any quantity shows the maximum price that consumers are willing to pay for that unit.

- The degree of responsiveness of consumer purchases to a change in price is shown by the steepness of the demand curve. The more responsive buyers are to a change in price, the flatter, or more elastic, the demand curve will be. Conversely, the less responsive buyers are to a change in price, the steeper, or more inelastic, the demand curve will be.

- A movement along a demand curve is called a change in quantity demanded. A shift of the entire curve is called a change in demand. A change in *quantity demanded* is caused by a change in the price of the good (generally in response to a shift of the supply curve). A change in *demand* can be caused by several things, including a change in consumer income or a change in the price of a closely related good.

- The opportunity cost of producing a good is equal to the cost incurred by bidding the required resources away from alternative uses. Profit indicates that the producer has increased the value of the resources used, whereas a loss indicates that the producer has reduced the value of the resources used.

- The law of supply states that there is a direct (or positive) relationship between the price of a good or service and the quantity of it that producers are willing to supply. The height of the supply curve at any quantity shows the minimum price necessary to induce suppliers to produce that unit—that is, the opportunity cost of producing it.

- A movement along a supply curve is called a change in quantity supplied. A change in *quantity supplied* is caused by a change in the price of the good (generally in response to a shift of the demand curve). A shift of the entire supply curve is called a change in supply. A change in *supply* can be caused by several factors, such as a change in resource prices or an improvement in technology.

- The responsiveness of supply to a change in price is shown by the steepness of the supply curve. The more willing producers are to alter the quantity supplied in response to a change in price, the flatter, or more elastic, the supply curve. Conversely, the less willing producers are to alter the quantity supplied in response to a change in price, the steeper, or less elastic, the supply curve.

- Prices bring the conflicting forces of supply and demand into balance. There is an automatic tendency for market prices to move toward the equilibrium price, at which the quantity demanded equals the quantity supplied.

- Consumer surplus represents the net gain to buyers from market trades. Producer surplus represents the net gain to producers and resource suppliers from market trades. In equilibrium, competitive markets maximize these gains, a condition known as economic efficiency.

- Changes in the prices of goods are caused by changes in supply and demand. An increase in demand will cause the price and quantity supplied to rise. Conversely, a decrease in demand will cause the price and quantity supplied to fall. An increase in supply, however, will cause the price to fall and quantity demanded to rise. Conversely, a decrease in supply will cause the price to rise and quantity demanded to fall.

- Market prices communicate information, coordinate the actions of buyers and sellers, and motivate decision makers to act. As the invisible hand principle indicates, market prices are generally able to bring the self-interest of individuals into harmony with the general welfare of society. The efficiency of the system is dependent upon two things, however: (1) competitive market conditions and (2) well-defined and secure property rights.

CRITICAL ANALYSIS QUESTIONS

1. *Which of the following do you think would lead to an increase in the current demand for beef?
   a. higher pork prices
   b. higher consumer income
   c. higher prices of feed grains used to feed cattle
   d. widespread outbreak of mad cow or hoof-and-mouth disease
   e. an increase in the price of beef

2. What is being held constant when a demand curve for a specific product (shoes or apples, for example) is constructed? Explain why the demand curve for a product slopes downward to the right.

3. What is the law of supply? How many of the following "goods" do you think conform to the general law of supply? Explain your answer in each case.
   a. gasoline
   b. cheating on exams
   c. political favors from legislators
   d. the services of heart specialists
   e. children
   f. legal divorces

4. *Are prices an accurate measure of a good's total value? Are prices an accurate measure of a good's marginal value? What's the difference? Can you think of a good that has high total value but low marginal value? Use this concept to explain why professional wrestlers earn more than nurses, despite the fact that it is virtually certain that nurses create more total value for society than do wrestlers.

5. What is being held constant when the supply curve is constructed for a specific good like pizza or automobiles? Explain why the supply curve for a good slopes upward to the right.

6. Define consumer surplus and producer surplus. What is meant by economic efficiency, and how does it relate to the gains of consumers and producers?

7. How is the market price of a good determined? When the market for a product is in equilibrium, how will consumers value an additional unit compared to the opportunity cost of producing that unit? Why is this important?

8. *"The future of our industrial strength cannot be left to chance. Somebody has to develop notions about which industries are winners and which are losers." Is this statement by a newspaper columnist true? Who is the "somebody"?

9. What factors determine the cost of producing a good or service? Will producers continue to supply a good or service if consumers are unwilling to pay a price sufficient to cover the cost?

10. *"Production should be for people and not for profit." Answer the following questions concerning this statement:
    a. If production is profitable, are people helped or harmed? Explain.
    b. Are people helped more if production results in a loss than if it leads to profit? Is there a conflict between production for people and production for profit?

11. What must an entrepreneur do to earn a profit? How do the actions of firms earning profits influence the value of resources? What happens to the value of resources when losses are present? If a firm making losses goes out of business, is this bad? Why or why not?

12. *What's wrong with this way of thinking? "Economists claim that when the price of something goes up, producers increase the quantity supplied to the market. But last year, the price of oranges was really high and the supply of them was really low. Economists are wrong!"

13. What is the invisible hand principle? Does it indicate that self-interested behavior within markets will result in actions that are beneficial to others? What conditions are necessary for the invisible hand to work well? Why are these conditions important?

14. What's wrong with this way of thinking? "Economists argue that lower prices will result in fewer units being supplied. However, there are exceptions to this rule. For example, in 1972, a very simple 10-digit electronic calculator sold for $120. By 2000, the price of the same type of calculator had declined to less than $5. Yet business firms produced and sold many more calculators in 2000 than they did in 1972. Lower prices did not result in less production or in a decline in the number of calculators supplied."

15. What is the difference between substitutes and complements? Indicate two goods that are substitutes for each other. Indicate two goods that are complements.

16. Do business firms operating in competitive markets have a strong incentive to serve the interest of consumers? Are they motivated by a strong desire to help consumers? Are "good intentions" necessary if individuals are going to engage in actions that are helpful to others? Discuss.

*Asterisk denotes questions for which answers are given in Appendix B.

CHAPTER 7
Consumer Choice and Elasticity

FOCUS

- What are the fundamental postulates underlying consumer choice?
- How does the law of diminishing marginal utility help explain the law of demand?
- How do the demand curves of individuals translate into a market demand curve?
- What is demand elasticity? What does it measure? Why is it important?

The most famous law in economics, and the one economists are most sure of, is the law of demand. On this law is built almost the whole edifice of economics. —**David R. Henderson**[1]

A thing is worth whatever a buyer will pay for it.
—**Publilius Syrus, first century B.C.**[2]

[1]David R. Henderson, "Demand," in *The Concise Encyclopedia of Economics*, ed. David R. Henderson (http://www.econlib.org/library/CEE.html).

[2]Quoted in Michael Jackman, ed., *Macmillan Book of Business and Economic Quotations* (New York: Macmillan, 1984), 150.

The statement of David Henderson highlights the central position of the law of demand in economics. As Publilius Syrus noted more than 2,000 years ago, demand reflects the willingness of individuals to pay for what is offered in the marketplace. In this section, we begin our

examination of microeconomic markets for specific products with an analysis of the demand side of markets. In essence, we will be going "behind" the market demand curve to see how it is made up of individual consumer demands and what factors determine the choices of individual consumers.[3]

7-1 FUNDAMENTALS OF CONSUMER CHOICE

Each of us must decide how to allocate our limited income among the many possible things we would like to buy. The prices of goods, *relative to each other,* are important determining factors. If your favorite cereal doubled in price, would you switch to a different brand? Would your decision be different if all cereals, not just yours, doubled in price? Your choice *between* brands of cereal will be affected only by the change in relative prices. If the prices of all cereals rose by a proportional amount, you might quit purchasing cereal, but this would not give you a strong reason to switch to a different brand. Relative prices measure opportunity cost. If cereal is $5 per box when movie tickets are $10, you must give up two boxes of cereal to purchase one movie ticket.

Several fundamental principles underlie the choices of consumers. Let's take a closer look at the key factors influencing consumer behavior.

1. Limited income necessitates choice. Because of scarcity, we all have limited incomes. The limited nature of our income requires us to make choices about which goods we will and will not buy. When more of one good or service is bought, we must buy less of some other goods if we are to stay within our budget.

2. Consumers make decisions purposefully. The goals that underpin consumer choice can usually be met in alternative ways. If two products cost the same, a consumer will choose to buy the one expected to have the higher benefit. Conversely, if two products yield equal benefits, the consumer will choose to buy the less expensive one. Fundamentally, economics assumes that consumers are rational—that they are able to weigh the costs and benefits of alternative choices.

3. One good can be substituted for another. Consumers can achieve *utility*—that is, satisfaction—from many different alternatives. Either a hamburger or a taco might satisfy your hunger, whereas going either to a movie or to a football game might satisfy your desire for entertainment. With $600, you might either buy a new TV set or take a short vacation. No single good is so precious that some of it will not be given up in exchange for a large enough quantity of other goods. Even seemingly unrelated goods are sometimes substituted one for another. For example, high water prices in Southern California have led residents there to substitute cactus gardens and reduced flow showerheads for water.

4. Consumers must make decisions without perfect information, but knowledge and past experience will help. In Chapter 1, we noted that information is costly to acquire. Asking family and friends, searching through magazines such as *Consumer Reports,* and contacting your local Better Business Bureau are all ways of gathering information about products and potential sellers. The time and effort consumers spend acquiring information will be directly related to the value derived from it. Predictably, consumers will spend more time and money to inform themselves when they are

---

[3]You may want to review the section on demand in Chapter 3 before proceeding with this chapter.

© Tatiana Volgutova/Shutterstock.com

Consumers will seek to spend their income in a manner that will provide them with the maximum value (total utility).

buying "big ticket" items such as automobiles or air-conditioning systems than when they are buying pencils or paper towels.

While no one has perfect foresight, your own experiences—and those of others—will help you make better-informed choices. You have a pretty good idea of what to expect when you buy a cup of coffee and a bagel at your favorite restaurant. Your expectations might not always be fulfilled precisely the same way every time (for example, the coffee may be weak or the bagel too crispy), but even then, you will gain valuable information that will help you project the outcome of future choices more accurately.

5. The law of diminishing marginal utility applies: As the rate of consumption increases, the marginal utility gained from consuming additional units of a good will decline. Utility is a term economists use to describe the subjective personal benefits that result from taking an action. The **law of diminishing marginal utility** states that the **marginal (or additional) utility** derived from consuming successive units of a product will eventually decline as the rate of consumption increases. For example, the law says that even though you might like ice cream, your marginal satisfaction from additional ice cream will eventually decline as you eat more and more of it. Ice cream at lunchtime might be great. An additional helping for dinner might also be good. However, after you have had it for lunch and dinner, another serving as a midnight snack will be less attractive. When the law of diminishing marginal utility sets in, the additional utility derived from still more units of ice cream declines.

The law of diminishing marginal utility explains why, even if you really like a certain product, you will not spend your entire budget on it. As you increase your consumption of any good, the utility you derive from each additional unit will become smaller and smaller, eventually becoming less than the price. At that point, you will not want to purchase any more units of the good.

Law of diminishing marginal utility
The basic economic principle that as the consumption of a product increases, the marginal utility derived from consuming more of it (per unit of time) will eventually decline.

Marginal utility
The additional utility, or satisfaction, derived from consuming an additional unit of a good.

7-2 MARGINAL UTILITY, CONSUMER CHOICE, AND THE DEMAND CURVE OF AN INDIVIDUAL

The law of diminishing marginal utility helps us understand the law of demand and the shape of the demand curve. The height of an individual's demand curve at any specific unit is equal to the maximum price the consumer would be willing to pay for that unit—its **marginal benefit** to the consumer—given the number of units he or she has already purchased. Although marginal benefit is measured in dollars, the dollar amount reflects the opportunity cost of the unit in terms of other goods forgone. If a consumer is willing to pay, at most, $5 for an additional unit of the product, this indicates a willingness to give up, at most, $5 worth of other goods. *Because a consumer's willingness to pay for a unit of a good is directly related to the utility derived from consuming the unit, the law of diminishing marginal utility implies that a consumer's marginal benefit, and thus the height of the demand curve, falls as the quantity consumed increases.*

Exhibit 1 shows this relationship for a hypothetical consumer Jones, relative to her weekly consumption of pizza. Because of the law of diminishing marginal utility, each additional pizza consumed per week will generate less marginal utility for Jones than did the previous pizza. For this reason, Jones's maximum willingness to pay—her marginal benefit—will fall as the quantity consumed increases. In addition, the steepness of Jones's demand curve, or its responsiveness to a change in price—its elasticity—is a reflection of how rapidly Jones's marginal utility diminishes with additional consumption. An individual's demand curve for a good whose marginal value declines more rapidly, will be steeper.

Given what we now know about a consumer's maximum willingness to pay for additional units of a good, we are in a position to discuss how many units the consumer will choose to purchase at various prices. *At any given price, consumers will purchase all units of a good for which their maximum willingness to pay—their marginal benefit—is greater than the price.* They will stop at the point at which the marginal benefit of the next unit would be less than the price. Although there are some problems related to dividing up certain kinds of goods (for example, it is hard to purchase half a car), we can generally say that a consumer will purchase all units of a good up to the point at which the marginal benefit from it equals the price of the good ($MB = P$).

Marginal benefit
The maximum price a consumer will be willing to pay for an additional unit of a product. It is the dollar value of the consumer's marginal utility from the additional unit, and therefore it falls as consumption increases.

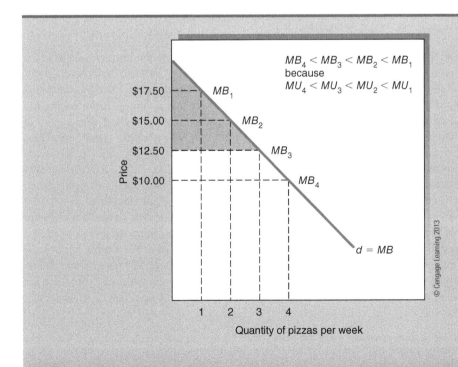

EXHIBIT 1

Diminishing Marginal Utility and the Individual's Demand Curve

An individual's demand curve, Jones's demand for personal pizzas in this case, reflects the law of diminishing marginal utility. Because marginal utility (*MU*) falls with increased consumption, so does the consumer's maximum willingness to pay— marginal benefit (*MB*). A consumer will purchase until *MB* = Price, so at a price of $12.50 per pizza, Jones would purchase three pizzas and receive a consumer surplus shown by the shaded triangle.

Returning to Exhibit 1, if the price of pizza were $12.50, Jones would purchase three pizzas per week.[4] Remember from Chapter 3 that consumer surplus is defined as the difference between the maximum price the consumer is willing to pay and the price actually paid, summed over all units consumed. Because the height of the demand curve reflects Jones's maximum willingness to pay for pizza, the shaded triangle that lies above the price shows the total consumer surplus derived from her consumption of the three pizzas. When a consumer has purchased all units to the point at which $MB = P$, total consumer surplus is maximized.

Within this framework, how would a consumer respond to a decrease in the price of a good? The consumer will increase purchases to the point at which marginal benefit diminishes to the level of the new lower price. If marginal utility declines rapidly with consumption, the consumer will expand his or her purchases only slightly. If marginal utility declines less rapidly, it will take a larger expansion in purchases to reach this point. The law of diminishing marginal utility underlies a person's demand curve for a product. The shape and steepness of the curve, for example, depend on his or her marginal utility.

7-2a CONSUMER EQUILIBRIUM WITH MANY GOODS

The last time you were at the mall, you probably saw something that you liked, perhaps a nice shirt. After all, there are many things we would like—many different alternatives that would give us utility. Next, you looked at the price tag: "Fifty dollars, wow! That's too much." What you were really saying was, "I like the shirt, but not as much as the $50 worth of other goods that I would have to give up for it." Consumer choice is a constant comparison of value relative to price. Consider another example: Perhaps you prefer expensive steak to a hamburger. Even if you do, your happiness may often be better served if you buy the hamburger and then spend the savings on something else.

The idea that consumers choose among products by comparing their relative marginal utility (MU) to price (P) can be expressed more precisely. A consumer with a limited amount of income to spend on a group of products is not likely to do the following math, but will act as though he or she had, and will end up consuming a bundle of goods and services such that

$$\frac{MU_A}{P_A} = \frac{MU_B}{P_B} = \cdots = \frac{MU_n}{P_n}$$

In this formula, MU represents the marginal utility derived from the last unit of a product, and P represents the price of the good. The subscripts $_{A, B, \ldots, n}$ indicate the different products available to the consumer. *This formula implies that the consumer will maximize his or her satisfaction (or total utility) by ensuring that the last dollar spent on each good purchased yields an equal degree of marginal utility.* Alternatively stated, the last unit of each item purchased should provide the same marginal utility *per dollar spent on it.* Thus, if the price of a gallon of ice cream is twice as high as the price of a smoothie, the ice cream should provide twice the marginal benefits to justify its purchase. Thus, a consumer will purchase these items to the point at which the marginal utility of the last gallon of ice cream is exactly twice as high as the marginal utility derived from the last smoothie.

Perhaps the best way to grasp this point is to think about what happens when your ratios of marginal utility to price are not equal for two goods. Suppose that you are at a local restaurant eating buffalo chicken wings and drinking Coke. For simplicity, assume that a large Coke and an order of wings each costs $2. With your $10 budget, you decide to purchase four orders of wings and one large Coke. When you finish your Coke, there are still lots of wings left. You have already eaten so many wings, though, that those remaining

---

[4]Jones would certainly purchase the first and second pizzas because $MB > P$. For the third pizza, $MB = P$, so Jones would be indifferent to buying the unit or not purchasing it. For a good that is easily divisible, say, pounds of roast beef, the consumer could continue purchasing up to 2.9999 pounds at a deli counter. Thus, economists are comfortable with simply concluding that the consumer will purchase this final unit, implying that Jones will purchase three pizzas.

do not look as attractive. You could get more utility with fewer wings and another Coke, but it is too late. You have not spent your $10 in a way that gets you the most for your money. Instead of satisfying the preceding condition, you find that the marginal utility of wings is lower than the marginal utility of a Coke, and because they both have the same price ($2), this implies that

$$\frac{MU_{\text{WINGS}}}{P_{\text{WINGS}}} < \frac{MU_{\text{COKE}}}{P_{\text{COKE}}}$$

If you had purchased fewer wings and more Coke, your total utility would have been higher. Consuming the added Coke would have lowered its marginal utility, decreasing the value of the right side of the equation. Simultaneously, spending less on wings would have raised the marginal utility of wings, increasing the value of the left side of the equation. You will maximize your utility—and get the most "bang for the buck" from your budget—when you make these values (the ratios) equal.

The equation can also be used to illustrate the law of demand. Beginning with a situation in which the two sides were equal, suppose that the price of wings increased. It would lower the value of *MU/P* for wings below the *MU/P* for Coke. In response, you would reallocate your budget, purchasing fewer of the more costly wings and more Coke. Thus, we have the law of demand—as the price of wings rises, you will purchase less of them. When people try to spend their money in a way that gives them the greatest amount of satisfaction, the consumer decision-making theory outlined here is difficult to question. In the next section, we will take the theory a little further.

7-2b PRICE CHANGES AND CONSUMER CHOICE

The demand curve or schedule shows the amount of a product that consumers are willing to buy at alternative prices during a specific time period. The law of demand states that the amount of a product bought is inversely related to its price. We have seen how the law of demand can be derived from fundamental principles of consumer behavior. Now, we go further and distinguish two different phenomena underlying a consumer's response to a price change. First, as the price of a product declines, the lower opportunity cost will induce consumers to buy more of it—even if they have to give up some other products, whose price had not fallen. This tendency to substitute a product that has become cheaper for goods that are now relatively more expensive is called the substitution effect of a price change.

Second, if a consumer's money income is unchanged, a reduction in the price of a product they consume will increase his or her real income—the amount of goods and services he or she is able to purchase with that fixed amount of money income. If your rent were to decline by $100 per month, for example, that would allow you to buy more of many other goods. This increase in your real income has the same effect as if the rent had remained the same but your income had risen by $100 per month. As a result, this second way in which a price change affects consumption is called the income effect. Typically, consumers will respond to the income effect by buying more of the cheaper product and other products as well because they can better afford to do so. Substitution and income effects generally work in the same direction: They both cause consumers to purchase more of a good as its price falls and less of a good as its price rises.[5]

7-2c TIME COSTS AND CONSUMER CHOICE

You may have heard the saying that "time is money." It is certainly true that time has value and that this value can sometimes be measured in dollars. As we have learned, the monetary price of a good is not always a complete measure of its cost to the consumer. Consuming

Substitution effect
That part of an increase (decrease) in amount consumed that is the result of a good being cheaper (more expensive) in relation to other goods because of a reduction (increase) in price.

Income effect
That part of an increase (decrease) in amount consumed that is the result of the consumer's real income being expanded (contracted) by a reduction (rise) in the price of a good.

---

[5]The substitution effect will always work in this direction. The income effect, however, may work in the reverse direction for some types of goods known as inferior goods. These will be addressed later in this chapter.

most goods requires not only money but also time; and time, like money, is scarce to the consumer. So a lower time cost, like a lower money price, will make a product more attractive. For example, one study showed that patients in a dentist's office are willing to pay more than $5 per minute saved to shorten their time spent in waiting rooms.[6] Similarly, fast food and air travel are demanded mainly for the time savings they offer.

Time costs, unlike money prices for goods, differ among individuals. They are higher for people with higher wage rates, for example. Other things being equal, high-wage consumers choose more time-saving commodities than do people with lower time costs and wages. For example, high-wage consumers are overrepresented among airplane and taxicab passengers but underrepresented among television watchers, chess players, and long-distance bus travelers.

Failure to account for time costs can lead to bad decisions. For example, which is cheaper for consumers: (1) waiting in line three hours to purchase a $25 concert ticket or (2) buying the same ticket for $40 without standing in line? A consumer whose time is worth more than $5 per hour will find that $40 without the wait in line is less costly. As you can see, time costs matter. For example, when government-imposed price ceilings (discussed in Chapter 4) create shortages, rationing by waiting occurs. For many consumers, the benefit of the lower price due to the ceiling will be largely, if not entirely, offset by their increased time cost of having to wait in line.

7-2d MARKET DEMAND REFLECTS THE DEMAND OF INDIVIDUAL CONSUMERS

The market demand schedule is the relationship between the market price of a good and the amount demanded by all the individuals in the market area. Because individual consumers purchase less at higher prices, the amount demanded in a market area as a total is also inversely related to price.

Exhibit 2 shows the relationship between individual demand and market demand for a hypothetical two-person market. The individual demand curves for both Jones and Smith are shown. Jones and Smith each consume three pizzas per week at a price of $12.50. The

EXHIBIT 2

Individual and Market Demand Curves

The market demand curve is merely the horizontal sum of the individual demand curves. It will slope downward to the right just as individual demand curves do.

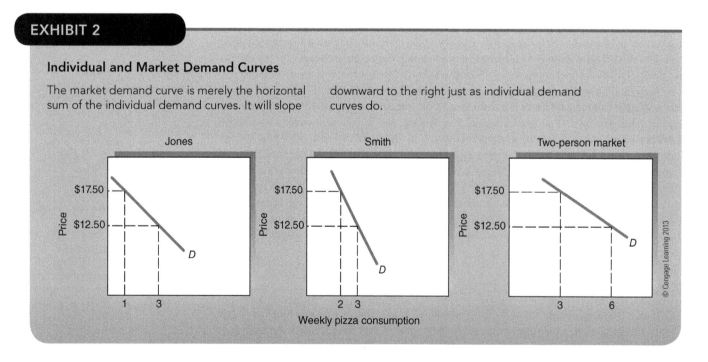

© Cengage Learning 2013

---

[6]Rexford E. Santerre and Stephen P. Neun, *Health Economics: Theories, Insights and Industry Studies* (Orlando, FL: Harcourt, 2000), 113.

amount demanded in the two-person market is six pizzas. If the price rises to $17.50 per pizza, the amount demanded in the market will fall to three pizzas, one demanded by Jones and two by Smith. ***The market demand is simply the horizontal sum of the individual demand curves of consumers—in this case, Smith and Jones.***

In the real world, there can be millions of consumers in a market. But the relationship between the demand curves of individuals and the market demand curve will still be just like the one shown in Exhibit 2. At any given price, the amount purchased in the market will be the sum of the amounts purchased by each consumer in the market. Furthermore, the total amount demanded in the market will decline as price increases because individual consumers will purchase fewer units at the higher prices. The market demand curve reflects the collective choices of the individual consumers.

7-3 ELASTICITY OF DEMAND

Although it is important to recognize that consumers will buy less of a product as its price increases, it is also often important to know whether the increase will lead to a large or small reduction in the amount purchased. Economists have designed a tool called the price elasticity of demand to measure this sensitivity of amount purchased in response to a change in price. The equation for the price elasticity of demand is as follows:

$$\text{Price elasticity of demand} = \frac{\text{Percentage change in quantity demanded}}{\text{Percentage change in price}} = \frac{\%\Delta Q}{\%\Delta P}$$

Price elasticity of demand
The percentage change in the quantity of a product demanded divided by the percentage change in the price that caused the change in quantity. The price elasticity of demand indicates how responsive consumers are to a change in a product's price.

This ratio is often called the *elasticity coefficient*. To express it more briefly, we use the notation %ΔQ to represent percentage change in quantity and %ΔP to represent percentage change in price. (The Greek letter delta [Δ] means "change in.") The law of demand states that an increase in a product's price lowers the quantity of it purchased, whereas a decrease in price raises it. ***Because a change in price causes the quantity demanded to change in the opposite direction, the price elasticity coefficient is always negative, although economists often ignore the sign and use the absolute value of the coefficient.***

To see how the concept of elasticity works, suppose that the price of the Ford Explorer rises 10 percent, while other prices remain the same. Ford could expect Explorer sales to fall substantially—perhaps 30 percent—as sport-utility vehicle (SUV) buyers respond by switching to other SUVs whose prices have not changed. This strong response by buyers means that the demand for the Explorer is elastic.

Now consider a different situation. Suppose that, because of a new tax, the price of not only the Explorer *but of all new SUVs* rises 10 percent. In this case, consumers' options are much more limited. They can't simply switch to a cheaper close substitute as they could when the price of the Explorer alone rose. They might either simply pay the extra money for a new SUV or settle for a used SUV instead. Because of this, the 10 percent rise in the price of all new SUVs will lead to a smaller consumer response, perhaps a 5 percent decline in sales of new SUVs.

To calculate the elasticity coefficient for the Explorer in the initial example, we begin with the 30 percent decline in quantity demanded and divide it by the 10 percent increase in the price. Thus, the elasticity of demand for the Explorer would be

$$\frac{\%\Delta Q}{\%\Delta P} = \frac{-30\%}{+10\%} = -3$$

(or 3.0 if we ignore the minus sign). This means that the percentage change in quantity demanded is three times the percentage change in price.

To calculate the demand elasticity for *all* SUVs (our second example), we see that the percentage change in quantity, 5 percent, divided by the percentage change in price, 10 percent, gives us –1/2, or –0.5. When it comes to the price elasticity of demand for all SUVs, the percentage change in quantity demanded (using our hypothetical numbers) is only half the percentage change in price, not three times the percentage change in price as it was with the Explorer.

Often, we will have to derive the percentage change in quantity and price. If you know the quantities that will be purchased at two different prices, you can then derive the percentage change in both the price and the quantity. For example, suppose that a price change from P_0 to P_1 causes a change in quantity demanded from Q_0 to Q_1. The change in quantity demanded would therefore be $Q_0 - Q_1$. To calculate the percentage change in quantity, we divide the actual change by the midpoint (or average) of the two quantities.[7] Although it is often easy to find the midpoint without a formula (halfway between $4 and $6 is $5), it can also be found as $(Q_0 + Q_1)/2$. Finally, because 0.05 is simply 5 percent, we multiply by 100. Thus, we can express the percentage change in quantity demanded as

$$\frac{(Q_0 - Q_1)}{[(Q_0 + Q_1)/2]} \times 100$$

Similarly, when the change in price is $P_0 - P_1$, the *percentage* change in price is

$$\frac{(P_0 - P_1)}{[(P_0 + P_1)/2]} \times 100$$

Dividing the resulting percentage change in quantity by the percentage change in price gives us the elasticity.

Using substitution, it is possible to derive a version of the elasticity formula that incorporates these two percentage calculations. Because each term is multiplied by 100 and the denominator of each term contains a 2, these factors cancel out of the final expression. After simplification this version is

$$\frac{[(Q_0 - Q_1)/(Q_0 + Q_1)]}{[(P_0 - P_1)/(P_0 + P_1)]}$$

A numerical example will help you understand this. Suppose that Trina's Cakes can sell fifty specialty cakes per week at $7 each, or it can sell seventy specialty cakes per week at $6 each. The percentage difference in quantity is the difference in the quantity demanded ($50 - 70 = -20$) divided by the midpoint (60) times 100. The result is a -33.33 percent change in quantity ($-20 \div 60 \times 100 = -33.33$).

Now that we've calculated the percentage change in quantity demanded of cakes, let's calculate the percentage change in the price. The percentage change in price is the difference in the two prices ($7 - $6 = $1) divided by the midpoint price ($6.50) times 100, or a 15.38 percent change in price ($1 \div 6.5 \times 100 = 15.38$). Dividing the percentage change in quantity by the percentage change in price ($-33.33 \div 15.38$) gives an elasticity coefficient of -2.17. Alternatively, we could have expressed this directly as

$$\frac{[(50 - 70)/(50 + 70)]}{[(7 - 6)/(7 + 6)]} = \frac{(-20/120)}{(1/13)} = \frac{(-1/6)}{(1/13)} = \frac{-13}{6} = -2.17$$

The same result is obtained either way. The elasticity of 2.17 (ignoring the sign) indicates that the percentage change in quantity is just over twice the percentage change in price.

The elasticity coefficient lets us make a precise distinction between elasticity and inelasticity. When the elasticity coefficient is greater than 1 (ignoring the sign), as it was for the demand for Trina's Cakes, demand is elastic. When it is less than 1, demand is inelastic. Demand is said to be of *unitary elasticity* if the price elasticity is exactly 1.

---

[7]This formula uses the average of the starting point and the ending point of the change so that it will give the same result whether we start from the lower or the higher price. This arc elasticity formula is not the only way to calculate elasticity, but it is the most frequently used.

7-3a GRAPHIC REPRESENTATION OF PRICE ELASTICITY OF DEMAND

Exhibit 3 presents demand curves of varying elasticity. A demand curve that is completely vertical is said to be *perfectly inelastic*, shown in part (a) of Exhibit 3. In the real world, such demand does not exist because the substitutes for a good become more attractive as the price of that good rises. Moreover, because of the income effect, we should expect that a higher price will always reduce the quantity demanded, other things remaining the same.

EXHIBIT 3

Price Elasticity of Demand

(a) Perfectly inelastic: Despite an increase in a product's price, consumers still purchase the same amount of it. Substitution and income effects prevent this from happening in the real world, though.

(b) Relatively inelastic: A percentage increase in a product's price results in a smaller percentage reduction in its sales. The demand for cigarettes has been estimated to be highly inelastic.

(c) Unit elastic: The percentage change in quantity demanded of a product is equal to the percentage change in its price. A curve with a decreasing slope results. Sales revenue (price times quantity sold) is constant.

(d) Relatively elastic: A percentage increase in a product's price leads to a larger percentage reduction in purchases of it. When good substitutes are available for a product (as in the case of apples), the amount of it purchased will be highly sensitive to price changes.

(e) Perfectly elastic: Consumers will buy all of Farmer Jones's wheat at the market price, but none will be sold above the market price.

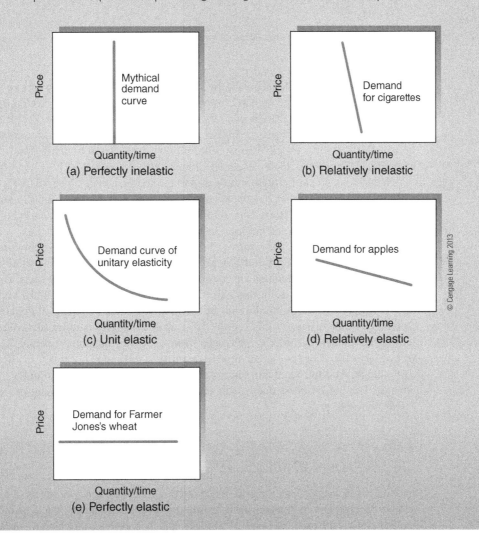

Slope of the Demand Curve versus Price Elasticity

With this straight-line (constant slope) demand curve, demand is more elastic in the high price range. The formula for elasticity shows that, when price rises from $1 to $2 and quantity falls from 110 to 100, demand is inelastic. A price rise of the same magnitude (but of a smaller percentage), from $10 to $11, leads to a decline in quantity of the same size (but of a larger percentage), so that elasticity is much greater. (Price elasticities are negative, but economists often ignore the sign and look only at the absolute value.)

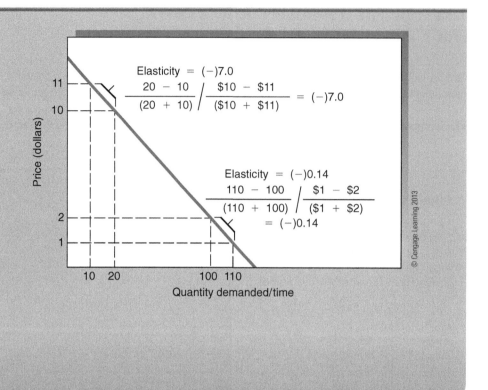

The more inelastic the demand, the steeper the demand curve *over any specific price range*. As you can see, the demand for cigarettes (shown in part b of Exhibit 3) is highly inelastic; a big change in price doesn't change quantity demanded much. People who crave nicotine will be willing to pay the higher price. Conversely, the demand for apples (shown in part d) is relatively elastic. People will find it easy to switch to oranges or bananas, for example, if the price of apples increases dramatically.

When demand elasticity is unitary, as part (c) shows, a demand curve that is convex to the origin will result. When a demand curve is completely horizontal, an economist would say that it is *perfectly elastic*. Demand for the wheat marketed by a single wheat farmer, for example, would approximate perfect elasticity (part e).

Because elasticity is a relative concept, the elasticity of a straight-line demand curve will differ at each point along the demand curve. As Exhibit 4 shows, the elasticity of a straight-line demand curve (one with a constant slope) will range from highly elastic to highly inelastic. In this exhibit, when the price rises from $10 to $11, sales decline from 20 to 10. According to the formula, the price elasticity of demand is –7.0. Demand is very elastic in this region. In contrast, demand is quite inelastic in the $1 to $2 price range. As the price increases from $1 to $2, the amount demanded declines from 110 to 100. The ten-unit change in quantity is the same, but it is a smaller *percentage* change. And the $1 change in price is the same, but it is now a larger *percentage* change. The elasticity of demand in this range is only –0.14; demand in this case is highly inelastic.

7-3b HOW LARGE ARE THE DEMAND ELASTICITIES OF VARIOUS PRODUCTS?

Economists have estimated the price elasticity of demand for many products. As Exhibit 5 shows, the elasticity of demand varies substantially among products. The demand is highly inelastic for several products—salt, toothpicks, matches, coffee, and gasoline (short-run)—in

EXHIBIT 5

Estimated Price Elasticity of Demand for Selected Products

INELASTIC		APPROXIMATELY UNITARY ELASTICITY	
Salt	– 0.1	Movies	– 0.9
Matches	– 0.1	Housing, owner occupied, long run	– 1.2
Toothpicks	– 0.1	Shellfish, consumed at home	– 0.9
Airline travel, short run	– 0.1		
Gasoline, short run	– 0.2	Oysters, consumed at home	– 1.1
Gasoline, long run	– 0.7		
Residential natural gas, short run	– 0.1	Private education	– 1.1
		Tires, short run	– 0.9
Residential natural gas, long run	– 0.5	Tires, long run	– 1.2
Coffee	– 0.25	Radio and television receivers	– 1.2
Fish (cod), consumed at home	– 0.5	**ELASTIC**	
Tobacco products, short run	– 0.45	Restaurant meals	– 2.3
		Foreign travel, long run	– 4.0
Legal services, short run	– 0.4	Airline travel, long run	– 2.4
Physician services	– 0.6	Fresh green peas	– 2.8
Dental services	– 0.7	Automobiles, short run	– 1.2–1.5
Taxi, short run	– 0.6	Chevrolet automobiles	– 4.0
Automobiles, long run	– 0.2	Fresh tomatoes	– 4.6
Cigarette consumption, long run, Canada	– 0.3	Hospital care in California	– 4.8

Sources: Hendrick S. Houthakker and Lester D. Taylor, *Consumer Demand in the United States, 1929–1970* (Cambridge, MA: Harvard University Press, 1966, 1970); Douglas R. Bohi, *Analyzing Demand Behavior* (Baltimore: Johns Hopkins University Press, 1981); Hsaing-tai Cheng and Oral Capps Jr., "Demand for Fish," *American Journal of Agricultural Economics* 70, no. 3 (1988): 533–42; Rexford E. Santerre and Stephen P. Neun, *Health Economics: Theories, Insights and Industry Studies* (Orlando, FL: Harcourt, 2000); Martin Gaynor and William Vogt, "Competition among Hospitals," *The RAND Journal of Economics* (Winter 2003): 764–85; and Nikolay Gospodinov and Ian Irvine, "A 'Long March' Perspective on Tobacco use in Canada," *Canadian Journal of Economics* 38, no. 2 (2005): 366–93.

their normal price range. In contrast, the demand curves for fresh tomatoes, Chevrolet automobiles, and fresh green peas are highly elastic. The demand for movies, housing, private education, radios, and television sets is near 1.0 (unitary).

7-3c WHY DO THE PRICE ELASTICITIES OF DEMAND VARY?

The primary determinants of a product's price elasticity of demand are the availability of good substitutes and to the share of the typical consumer's total budget expended on a product. Let's consider each of these factors.

Availability of Substitutes *The most important determinant of the price elasticity of demand is the availability of substitutes. When good substitutes for a product are available, a price increase induces many consumers to switch to other products. Demand is elastic.* For example, if the price of apples increases consumers might substitute oranges or bananas.

When good substitutes for a product are unavailable, the demand for it will tend to be inelastic. Medical services are an example. When we are sick, most of us find witch doctors, faith healers, palm readers, and aspirin to be highly imperfect substitutes for the services of a physician. Not surprisingly, the demand for physician services is inelastic.

The availability of substitutes increases as the product class becomes more specific, thus increasing price elasticity. For example, as Exhibit 5 shows, the price elasticity of Chevrolets, a narrow product class, exceeds that of the broad class of automobiles in general. If the price of Chevrolets alone rises, many substitute cars are available. But if the prices of all automobiles rise together, consumers have fewer good substitutes.

Product's Share of the Consumer's Total Budget If the expenditures on a product are quite small relative to the consumer's budget, the income effect will be small even if there is a substantial increase in the price of the product. This will make demand less elastic. Compared to one's total budget, expenditures on some commodities are minor. Matches, toothpicks, and salt are good examples. Most consumers spend less than a couple of dollars per year on each of these items. A doubling of their price would exert little influence on a family's budget. Therefore, even if the price of such a product were to rise sharply, consumers would still not find it worthwhile to spend much time and effort looking for substitutes.

Exhibit 6 provides a graphic illustration of both elastic and inelastic demand curves. In part (a), the demand curve for fast-food hamburgers is elastic because there are good substitutes—for example, tacos, burritos, salads, chicken, and other sandwiches. Therefore, when the price of the hamburgers increases from $4.00 to $6.00, the quantity purchased declines sharply from 100 million to only 25 million. The calculated price elasticity equals –3.0. The fact that the absolute value of the coefficient is greater than 1 confirms that the demand for hamburgers is elastic over the price range shown.

Part (b) of Exhibit 6 shows the demand curve for cigarettes. Because most smokers do not find other products to be a good substitute, the demand for cigarettes is highly inelastic. As the price of cigarettes increases from $4.00 to $6.00, the number of packs purchased falls by only a small amount (from 100 million to 90 million). The price elasticity coefficient is –0.26, substantially less in absolute value than 1, confirming that the demand for cigarettes is inelastic. (*Exercise:* Use the price elasticity formula to verify the values of these elasticity coefficients.)

EXHIBIT 6

Inelastic and Elastic Demand

As the price of fast-food hamburgers (a) rose from $4 to $6, the quantity purchased fell sharply from 100 million to 25 million. The percentage reduction in quantity is larger than the percentage increase in price. Thus, the demand for the hamburgers is elastic. In contrast, an increase in the price of cigarettes from $4 to $6 leads to only a small reduction in the number of packs purchased (b). Because the percentage reduction in quantity is smaller than the percentage increase in price, demand is inelastic.

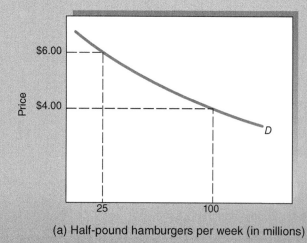

(a) Half-pound hamburgers per week (in millions)

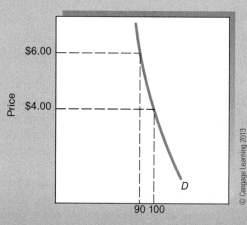

(b) Cigarette packs per week (in millions)

7-3d TIME AND DEMAND ELASTICITY

As changing market conditions raise or lower the price of a product, both consumers and producers will respond. However, the response will not be instantaneous, and it is likely to become larger over time. *In general, when the price of a product increases, consumers will reduce their consumption by a larger amount in the long run than in the short run. Thus, the demand for most products will be more elastic in the long run than in the short run. This relationship between elasticity and the length of the adjustment period is sometimes referred to as the second law of demand.*

The first law of demand says that buyers will respond predictably to a price change, purchasing more when the price is lower than when the price is higher, if other things remain the same. The second law of demand says that the response of buyers will be greater after they have had time to adjust more fully to a price change.

7-4 HOW DEMAND ELASTICITY AND PRICE CHANGES AFFECT TOTAL EXPENDITURES (OR REVENUES) ON A PRODUCT

By looking at demand elasticity, we can determine changes in total consumer spending on a product when its price changes. We can do this in three different ways: by looking at (1) changes in an individual's total spending, using the demand elasticity from his or her demand curve for the product; (2) changes in the total combined spending of all consumers, using the elasticity from the total market demand curve; or (3) changes in total consumer spending on the product, using the demand curve facing the firm that produces it. This third method allows us to look at elasticity based not on what consumers spend, but on what the producer receives from selling the product.

Total expenditures (or revenues) simply amount to the price of the product times the number of units of it purchased (or sold). Because total expenditures are equal to the price times the quantity, and because the price and the quantity move in opposite directions, the net effect of a price change on the total spending on a product depends on whether the (percentage) price change or the (percentage) quantity change is greater.

CHANGE IN TOTAL EXPENDITURES	=	PRICE	×	QUANTITY
?	=	↑	×	↓
?	=	↓	×	↑

When demand is inelastic, the price elasticity coefficient is less than 1. This means that the percentage change in price is greater than the percentage change in quantity. *Therefore, when demand is inelastic, the change in the price will dominate and, as a result, the price and total expenditures will change in the same direction.* In other words, when the price of an inelastic product (say, cigarettes) increases, spending on it will increase, too—and vice versa. Conversely, when demand is elastic, the change in quantity will be greater than the change in the price. *As a result, the impact of the change in quantity will dominate, and therefore the price and expenditures will move in opposite directions.* In other words, when the price of a product with an elastic demand (say, fast-food hamburgers) increases, spending on it will decrease.

When demand elasticity is unitary, the change in quantity demanded will be equal in magnitude to the change in price. With regard to their impact on total expenditures, these two effects will exactly offset each other. *Thus, when price elasticity of demand is equal to 1, total expenditures will remain unchanged as price changes.*

EXHIBIT 7

Demand Elasticity and How Changes in Price Affect Total Consumer Expenditures or a Firm's Total Revenue

PRICE ELASTICITY OF DEMAND	NUMERICAL ELASTICITY COEFFICIENT (IN ABSOLUTE VALUE)	IMPACT OF RAISING PRICE ON TOTAL CONSUMER EXPENDITURES OR A FIRM'S TOTAL REVENUE	IMPACT OF LOWERING PRICE ON TOTAL CONSUMER EXPENDITURES OR A FIRM'S TOTAL REVENUE
Elastic	1 to ∞	decrease	increase
Unit Elastic	1	unchanged	unchanged
Inelastic	0 to 1	increase	decrease

Exhibit 7 summarizes the relationship between changes in the price of a product and changes in total spending on it when demand is elastic, inelastic, and unit elastic. The demand curves shown in Exhibit 6 can also be used to show the link between elasticity and changes in total spending. When the price of cigarettes (part b), increases from $4.00 to $6.00, the price elasticity of demand is 0.26, indicating that demand is inelastic. This increase in cigarette prices leads to an increase in spending on the product from $400 million ($4.00 × 100 million units) to $540 million ($6.00 × 90 million units). If the change had occurred in the opposite direction, with the price falling from $6.00 to $4.00, total expenditures would have declined.

The price elasticity of demand for fast-food hamburgers when the price increases from $4.00 to $6.00 (part a of Exhibit 6) is 3.0, indicating that demand is elastic. In this case, price and expenditures will move in opposite direction. The increase in the price of hamburgers lowers total consumer spending on the product from $400 million ($4.00 × 100 million hamburgers) to $150 million ($6.00 × 25 million hamburgers). If the price change had been in the opposite direction, with the price falling from $6.00 to $4.00, total expenditures would have risen.

When a firm increases the price of its product, its revenues may rise, fall, or remain the same. If the demand for the firm's product is inelastic, the higher price will expand the firm's total revenue. However, if the demand for the firm's product is elastic, a price increase will lead to substantially lower sales and a decline in total revenue. In the case of unitary elasticity, the price increase will leave total revenue unchanged.

Beyond the price elasticity of demand, two other elasticity relationships are important. We therefore end this chapter with a brief discussion of income elasticity of demand and price elasticity of supply.

Income elasticity
The percentage change in the quantity of a product demanded divided by the percentage change in consumer income that caused the change in quantity demanded. It measures the responsiveness of the demand for a good to a consumer's change in income.

Normal good
A good that has a positive income elasticity, so that as consumer income rises, demand for the good rises, too.

7-5 INCOME ELASTICITY

Increases in consumer income will increase the demand (the quantity demanded at each price) for most goods. Income elasticity tells us how responsive the demand for a product is to income changes. Income elasticity is defined as

$$\text{Income elasticity} = \frac{\text{Percentage change in quantity demanded}}{\text{Percentage change in income}}$$

As Exhibit 8 shows, although the income elasticity coefficients for products vary from one good to another, they are normally positive. In fact, the term normal good refers to any good with a positive income elasticity of demand. Some normal goods have lower income elasticities than others, however. In general, goods that people

EXHIBIT 8

Estimated Income Elasticity of Demand for Selected Products

LOW-INCOME ELASTICITY		HIGH-INCOME ELASTICITY	
Margarine	−0.20	Private education	2.46
Fuel	0.38	New cars	2.45
Electricity	0.20	Recreation and amusements	1.57
Fish (haddock)	0.46	Alcohol	1.54
Food	0.51		
Tobacco	0.64		
Hospital care	0.69		

Sources: Hendrick S. Houthakker and Lester D. Taylor, *Consumer Demand in the United States, 1929–1970* (Cambridge, MA: Harvard University Press, 1966); L. Taylor, "The Demand for Electricity: A Survey," *Bell Journal of Economics* 6, no. 1 (1975): 74–110; F. W. Bell, "The Pope and the Price of Fish," *American Economic Review* 58, no. 5 (1968): 1346–50; and Rexford E. Santerre and Stephen P. Neun, *Health Economics: Theories, Insights and Industry Studies* (Orlando, FL: Harcourt, 2000).

regard as "necessities" will have low income elasticities (between 0 and 1). Significant quantities are purchased even at low incomes, and, as income increases, spending on these items will increase by less than a proportional amount. It is understandable that items such as fuel, electricity, bread, tobacco, economy clothing, and potatoes have a low income elasticity.

Goods that consumers regard as "luxuries" generally have a high (greater than 1) income elasticity. For example, private education, new automobiles, swimming pools, and vacation travel are all highly income-elastic. As the consumer's income increases, the demand for these goods expands even more rapidly, and therefore spending on these items increases as a proportion of income.

A few commodities, such as margarine, low-quality meat cuts, and bus travel, actually have a negative income elasticity. Economists refer to goods with a negative income elasticity as inferior goods. As income expands, the demand for inferior goods will decline. Conversely, as income declines, the demand for inferior goods will increase.

Inferior good
A good that has a negative income elasticity, so that as consumer income rises, the demand for the good falls.

7-6 PRICE ELASTICITY OF SUPPLY

The price elasticity of supply is the percentage change in quantity supplied, divided by the percentage change in the price causing the supply response. Because this measures the responsiveness of sellers to a change in price, it is analogous to the price elasticity of demand. However, the price elasticity of supply will be positive because the quantity producers are willing to supply is directly related to price. As in demand elasticity, time plays a role. In the next two chapters, we will discuss more fully the factors that determine supply elasticity. For now, it is important simply to recognize the concept of supply elasticity and the fact that suppliers (like buyers) will be more responsive to a price change when they have had more time to adjust to it.

Price elasticity of supply
The percentage change in quantity supplied, divided by the percentage change in the price that caused the change in quantity supplied.

LOOKING AHEAD Market demand indicates how strongly consumers desire a good or service. In the following chapter, we will turn to a firm's costs of production—costs that arise because resources are demanded for alternative uses. These two topics—consumer demand and the cost of production—are central to understanding how markets work and the conditions necessary for the efficient allocation of resources.

KEY POINTS

- Consumers will try to allocate their limited incomes among a multitude of goods in a way that maximizes their utility. The role of relative prices, information, and preferences, as well as the law of diminishing marginal utility, help explain the choices consumers make and the downward slope of a person's demand curve for products.

- The market demand curve for a product is the horizontal sum of the demand curve of the individuals for the product.

- The price elasticity of demand measures the responsiveness of the quantity of a product purchased to a change in its price.

- The availability of substitutes is the primary determinant of the price elasticity of demand for a product. When there are good substitutes available, and the item is a sizable component of the consumer's budget, its demand will tend to be elastic. When only poor substitutes are available, demand will tend to be inelastic.

- Typically, the price elasticity of a product will increase as consumers have had more time to adjust to a change in its price. This direct relationship between the size of the elasticity coefficient and the length of the adjustment period is often referred to as the *second law of demand*.

- The concept of elasticity helps us determine how a change in price will affect total consumer expenditures on a product or a firm's total revenues derived from it. When the demand for a product is elastic, a price change will cause total spending on it to change in the opposite direction. When demand for a product is inelastic, a change in price will cause total spending on it to change in the same direction.

- The concept of elasticity can also be applied to consumer income (which is called the income elasticity of demand) and supply (which is called the price elasticity of supply).

CRITICAL ANALYSIS QUESTIONS

1. Suppose that, in an attempt to raise more revenue, Nowhere State University (NSU) increases its tuition. Will this necessarily result in more revenue? Under what conditions will revenue (a) rise, (b) fall, or (c) remain the same? Explain this, focusing on the relationship between the increased revenue from students who enroll at NSU despite the higher tuition and the lost revenue from lower enrollment. If the true price elasticity were –1.2, what would you suggest the university do to expand revenue?

2. *A bus ticket between two cities costs $150 and the trip will take 25 hours, whereas an airplane ticket costs $450 and takes five hours. Kathy values her time at $12 per hour, and Rachel values her time at $18 per hour. Will Kathy take the bus or the plane? Which will Rachel take? Explain.

3. *Recent research confirms that the demand for cigarettes is not only inelastic, but it also indicates that smokers with incomes in the lower half of all incomes respond to a given price increase by reducing their purchases by amounts that are more than four times as large as the purchase reductions made by smokers in the upper half of all incomes. How can the income and substitution effects of a price change help explain this finding?

4. A consumer is currently purchasing three pairs of jeans and five T-shirts per year. The price of jeans is $30, and T-shirts cost $10. At the current rate of consumption, the marginal utility of jeans is 60, and the marginal utility of T-shirts is 30. Is this consumer maximizing his or her utility? Would you suggest that he buy more jeans and fewer T-shirts, or more T-shirts and fewer jeans?

5. When residential electricity in the state of Washington cost about half as much as in nearby Montana, the average household in Washington used about 1,200 kilowatt-hours per month, whereas Montanans used about half that much per household. Do these data provide us with two points on the average household's demand curve for residential electricity in this region? Why or why not?

6. *People who are wealthy are widely believed to have more leisure time than people who are poor. However, even though we are a good deal wealthier today than our great-grandparents were 100 years ago, we appear to live more hectic lives and have less free time. Can you explain why?

7. What are the major determinants of a product's price elasticity of demand? Studies indicate that the demand for Florida oranges, Bayer aspirin, watermelons, and airfares to Europe are elastic. Why?

8. Most systems of medical insurance substantially lower the out-of-pocket costs consumers have to pay for additional units of physician services and hospitalization. Some reduce these costs to zero. How does this method of payment affect the consumption levels of medical services? Might this method of organization result in "too much" consumption of medical services? Discuss.

9. Are the following statements true or false? Explain your answers.

   a. A 10 percent reduction in price that leads to a 5 percent increase in the amount purchased indicates a price elasticity of more than 1.

b. A 10 percent reduction in price that leads to a 2 percent increase in total expenditures (or total revenue) indicates a price elasticity of more than 1.

c. If the percentage change in price is less than the resultant percentage change in quantity demanded, demand is inelastic.

10. *Respond to the following questions: If you really like pizza, should you try to consume as much pizza as possible? If you want to succeed, should you try to make the highest possible grade in your economics class?

11. *Sue loves ice cream but cannot stand frozen-yogurt desserts. In contrast, Carole likes both foods and can hardly tell the difference between the two. Who will have the more elastic demand for yogurt?

12. *Jill's Sausage Dog Stand projects the following demand for Jill's sausage dogs:

PRICE ($)	QUANTITY PURCHASED (per day)
2	50
4	40
6	20

a. Calculate the price elasticity of demand between $2 and $4. Is demand in this range elastic or inelastic?

b. Calculate the price elasticity of demand between $4 and $6. Is demand in this range elastic or inelastic?

13. Suppose John, the owner-manager of a local hotel projects the following demand for his rooms:

PRICE ($)	QUANTITY PURCHASED (per Night)
90	100
110	90
130	70

a. Calculate the price elasticity of demand between $90 and $110.

b. Is the price elasticity of demand between $90 and $110 elastic, unit elastic, or inelastic?

c. Will John's total revenue rise if he increases the price from $90 to $110?

d. Calculate the price elasticity of demand between $110 and $130.

e. Is the price elasticity of demand between $110 and $130 elastic, unit elastic, or inelastic?

f. Will John's total revenue rise if he increases the price from $110 to $130?

*Asterisk denotes questions for which answers are given in Appendix B.

CHAPTER 8
Costs and the Supply of Goods

FOCUS

- Why are business firms used to organize production? How do market incentives influence the operation of businesses?

- What are explicit and implicit costs, and how do they guide the behavior of the firm?

- How does economic profit differ from accounting profit? Why is this difference important?

- How will increases in output influence the firm's costs in the short run? How will costs vary with output in the long run?

- What are the major factors that would cause the firm's costs to change?

From the standpoint of society as a whole, the "cost" of anything is the value that it has in alternative uses.
—**Thomas Sowell**[1]

[1]Thomas Sowell, *Basic Economics* (New York: Basic Books, 2000), 10.

Demand and supply interact to determine the market price of a product. In the preceding chapter, we showed that the demand for a product reflects the strength of consumer desire for that product. In this chapter, we will focus on the cost of production. The resources needed to produce one good could be used to produce other goods instead. As Thomas Sowell says in the quotation that begins this chapter, the cost to society of anything is the value that it has in alternative uses. The market price for resources makes that cost clear to producers as they must bid resources away from alternative uses. The maker of soccer balls, for example, must compete against producers of other goods when purchasing the machines, raw materials, and labor needed to produce the balls.

Costs carry an important message: They tell producers the value of the resources if left in their alternative uses. If the per-unit cost of producing a good exceeds its price, producers will suffer losses, reduce output, and some may go out of business. Only when a producer can generate enough value for consumers to allow the price to exceed production costs, will the firm be profitable and survive. This chapter lays the foundation for a detailed investigation of the links between costs, business output, and market supply.

8-1 THE ORGANIZATION OF THE BUSINESS FIRM

The business firm is an entity designed to organize raw materials, labor, and machines with the goal of producing goods and/or services. Firms (1) purchase productive resources from households and other firms, (2) transform them into a different commodity, and (3) sell the transformed product or service to consumers. In market economies, business firms choose their own price, output level, and methods of production. They not only reap the benefits of sales revenues, but they also must pay the costs of the resources they use.

8-1a INCENTIVES, COOPERATION, AND THE NATURE OF THE FIRM

In privately owned firms, owners risk their wealth on the success of the business. If the firm is successful and earns profits, these financial gains go to the owners. Conversely, if the firm suffers losses, the owners must bear the consequences.

The property right of owners to the residual income of the firm plays a very important role: It provides owners with a strong incentive to organize and operate their business in a manner that will maximize the value of their output to consumers while keeping the cost of producing output low. The wealth of these residual claimants is directly influenced by the success or failure of the firm. Thus, they have both the authority and a strong incentive to see that resources under their direction are used efficiently and directed toward production of goods that are valued more highly than their costs.

There are two ways of organizing productive activity: contracting and team production. In principle, all production could be accomplished solely through contracting. For example, a builder might have a house built by contracting with one person to pour the concrete, another to construct the wooden part of the house, a third to install the roofing, a fourth to do the electrical wiring, and so on. No employees would have to be involved in such a project. More commonly, though, goods and services are produced with some combination of contracting and the use of team production.

Team production involves the employment of workers operating under the supervision of the owner, or the owner's representative—a manager. While team production can often reduce transaction costs, it leads to another set of problems. Team members—the employees working for the firm—must be monitored and given incentives to avoid shirking, or working at less than the expected rate of productivity. Taking long work breaks, paying more attention to their own convenience than to work results, and wasting time when diligence is called for are examples of shirking. Hired managers, even including those at the top, must be monitored and given incentives to avoid shirking.

Residual claimants
Individuals who personally receive the excess, if any, of revenues over costs. Residual claimants gain if the firm's costs are reduced or revenues increase.

Team production
A production process in which employees work together under the supervision of the owner or the owner's representative.

Shirking
Working at less than the expected rate of productivity, which reduces output. Shirking is more likely when workers are not monitored, so that the cost of lower output falls on others.

Principal–agent problem
The incentive problem that occurs when the purchaser of services (the principal) lacks full information about the circumstances faced by the seller (the agent) and cannot know how well the agent performs the purchased services. The agent may to some extent work toward objectives other than those sought by the principal paying for the service.

Imperfect monitoring and imperfect incentives are always a problem with team production. It is part of a larger class of what economists call principal–agent problems. If you have ever taken a car to an auto mechanic, you have confronted this problem. The mechanic wants to get the job done quickly and make as much money as possible. The car owner not only wants to get the job done quickly also, but wants the problem fixed in a lasting way, at the lowest possible cost. Because the mechanic typically knows far more about the job than the customer, it is hard for the customer to monitor the mechanic's work. Therefore, the mechanic (the agent) may not act in the best interest of the customer (the principal).

The owner of a firm is in a similar situation. It is often difficult to monitor the performance of individual employees and motivate them to work together productively. If it is going to keep costs low and the value of output high, a firm must discover and adopt an incentive structure that motivates executives, managers, and workers to cooperate productively and discourages shirking. An effective incentive structure will align the costs and benefits faced by employees making decisions with those of the firm as a whole. Ultimately, it is the job of the owners, as residual claimants, to develop an effective incentive structure that will minimize the principal–agent problem.

8-1b THREE TYPES OF BUSINESS FIRMS

Business firms can be organized in one of three primary ways: as a proprietorship, a partnership, or a corporation. The structure chosen determines how the owners share the risks and liabilities of the firm and how they participate in making decisions.

Proprietorship
A business firm owned by an individual who possesses the ownership right to the firm's profits and is personally liable for the firm's debts.

Partnership
A business firm owned by two or more individuals who possess ownership rights to the firm's profits and are personally liable for the debts of the firm.

A proprietorship is a business firm owned by a single individual who is fully liable for the debts of the firm. In addition to assuming the responsibilities of ownership, the proprietor often works directly for the firm, providing managerial and other labor services. Many small businesses, including restaurants, barbershops, and farms, are business proprietorships. As Exhibit 1 shows, proprietorships account for 72 percent of the business firms in the United States. Because most proprietorships are small, however, they account for only 4 percent of all business revenues.

A partnership consists of two or more people who are co-owners of a business firm. The partners share risks and responsibilities in an agreed-upon manner. There is no difference between a proprietorship and a partnership in terms of owner liability. In both cases, the owners are fully liable for all business debts incurred by the firm. Many law, medical,

---

EXHIBIT 1

How Business Firms Are Organized

Nearly three out of every four firms are proprietorships, but only 4 percent of all business revenue is generated by proprietorships. Corporations account for about one out of every five firms but generate 82 percent of all revenues.

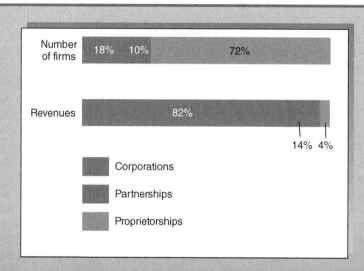

Source: *Statistics of Income Tax Stats Integrated Business Data*, Internal Revenue Service, Table 1. (Data are for 2008.)

and accounting firms are organized along partnership lines. However, this form of business structure accounts for only 10 percent of the total number of firms and 14 percent of all business revenues.

The business firms that are **corporations** account for 82 percent of total business revenue, even though they constitute only 18 percent of all firms. What accounts for the attractiveness of this business structure? From its start, by an act of the British Parliament in 1862, the corporation, or "joint stock company," as it is also called, grew in importance for two main reasons. First, although the stockholders of the corporation are the legal owners, their liability is limited to the value of their shares of the corporation. If a corporation owes you money, you cannot directly sue the stockholders. Of course, you can sue the corporation. However, if a corporation goes bankrupt, you and others to whom the firm owes money may simply be out of luck. This limited liability makes it possible for corporations to attract investment funds from a large number of "owners" who do not participate in the day-to-day management of the firm.

Second, ownership can easily be transferred under the corporate structure. The shares, or ownership rights, of an owner who dies can be sold by the heirs to another owner without disrupting the business firm. Because of this, the corporation is an ongoing concern. Similarly, stockholders who become unhappy with the way a corporation is run can bail out simply by selling their stock.

While there are advantages to the corporate form of business organization, large corporations with many stockholders—millions in some cases—are also more likely to suffer from principal–agent problems. The stockholders elect a board of directors, which in turn appoints the company's high-level managers. Internal corporate policies and competition for control of the firm by outsiders can be used to reduce these principal–agent problems.

Another disadvantage of the corporate form of business organization is higher taxation. While the incomes of sole proprietors and partnerships are taxed as ordinary personal income, the income of corporations is taxed twice—once as corporate income and again as personal income when it accrues to the owners in the form of dividends or capital gains. Since 1977, an increasing number of states allow a hybrid form of business organization called the *limited liability company* (LLC), which combines the advantages of limited liability of a corporation but the tax advantages of a sole proprietorship or partnership.

> **Corporation**
> A business firm owned by shareholders who possess ownership rights to the firm's profits, but whose liability is limited to the amount of their investment in the firm.

8-2 HOW WELL DOES THE CORPORATE STRUCTURE WORK?

Do corporations serve the interests of consumers? Are corporate managers in a position to serve themselves at the expense of their customers and stockholders? When thinking about these questions, keep three points in mind.

First, in a market economy, firms must compete for investment funds and for customers. Investors are free to buy and sell the shares of corporations. Similarly, consumers are free to choose among firms, including both corporate and noncorporate businesses. This competitive process greatly limits the ability of managers to benefit personally at the expense of either customers or stockholders. If a business firm is not managed in a manner that serves the interests of both its shareholders and customers, they will choose other options. Moreover, investor-driven changes in a company's stock price and consumer-driven changes in sales revenue provide channels through which managerial performance can be judged, and managers can be held accountable, by shareholders and the board of directors.

Second, the compensation of managers can be structured in a manner that will bring their interests into harmony with those of the shareholder-owners. This is generally the case. The salary increases and bonuses of most high-level managers are directly related to the firm's profitability and the price of its shares. In recent years, salaries have constituted only about 10 percent of the compensation of chief executive officers (CEOs). The other 90 percent has been in the form of bonuses, often stock awards and stock options (the right to buy shares at a certain price) related to company performance.

Corporate managers have a strong incentive to serve the interests of customers and stockholders because of the following: competition for investment funds and consumer sales, the linkage of their compensation to company performance, and the threat of takeover if the company is run poorly.

Third, the threat of corporate takeover helps keep current managers from straying too far from a profit-maximization strategy. Managers who do not serve the interests of their shareholders leave the firm vulnerable to a takeover, a move by an outside person or group to gain control of the firm. Poor management will cause market value of the firm's stock to decline, making it an attractive prospect for takeover specialists shopping for a poorly run business, the value of which could be substantially increased by a new and better management team.

The prevalence of the corporate form of business organization provides strong evidence that it is an effective form of business organization in many sectors of the economy. Rival forms of business organization, including proprietorships, partnerships, consumer cooperatives, employee ownership, and mutually owned companies, can and do compete in the marketplace for investment funds and customers. Nonetheless, the corporate structure is the dominant form of business organization (see Exhibit 1). If the corporation was not generally a cost-efficient and consumer-sensitive form of organization, this would not be the case.

8-3 THE ECONOMIC ROLE OF COSTS

Consumers would like to have more economic goods, but resources to produce them are scarce. How much of each desired good should be produced? In a market economy, consumer demand and production costs are central to performing this balancing function. *The demand for a product represents the voice of consumers instructing firms to produce the good. Conversely, a firm's costs represent the desire of consumers not to sacrifice goods that could be produced if the same resources were employed elsewhere.* A profit-seeking firm will try to produce only those units of output for which buyers are willing to pay full cost. Proper measurement and interpretation of costs by the firm are critical to both the firm's profitability and its efficient use of resources.

8-3a CALCULATING ECONOMIC COSTS AND PROFITS

Profit directs the actions of business firms. Profit is simply the firm's total revenue minus its total costs. But to calculate profit correctly, costs must be measured properly. Most people think of costs as amounts paid for raw materials, labor, machines, and similar inputs. However, this concept of cost, which stems from accounting procedures, excludes some important components.

The key to understanding the economist's concept of profit is to remember the idea of *opportunity cost*—the highest valued alternative forgone by the resource owner when the resource is used. These costs may be either explicit or implicit. Explicit costs result when the firm makes a monetary payment to resource owners. Money wages, interest, and rental payments are a measure of what the firm gives up to employ the services of labor and capital resources. These are relatively easy to track. But firms also incur implicit costs—those associated with the use of resources owned by the firm. For example, the owners of small proprietorships often work for their own businesses, for little or no pay. These businesses incur an implicit cost—an opportunity cost—associated with the use of this resource (the owners' labor services). The highest valued alternative forgone in this case is the maximum amount of money the owners could have earned doing something else. The total cost of production is the sum of these explicit and implicit costs incurred by the employment of all resources involved in the production process.

Accounting statements also generally omit the implicit cost of equity capital—the cost of funds supplied by the firm's owners. If a firm borrows financial capital from a bank or other private source, it will have to pay interest. Accountants properly record this interest expense as a cost. In contrast, when the firm acquires financial capital by issuing shares of stock, accountants don't record this as an expense. Essentially, this is because the stockholders *are* the firm's owners. Either way, acquiring capital has an opportunity cost. Banks will demand interest payments, and shareholders will expect a return from their investment in the form of dividend payments or rising share value.

Economists use the normal return on financial capital as a basis for determining the implicit opportunity cost of equity capital. If the normal rate of return on financial capital is 10 percent, for example, investors will not continue to supply equity capital unless they can earn this normal return. Thus, it is an opportunity cost of equity capital.

8-3b HOW DO ECONOMIC AND ACCOUNTING PROFIT DIFFER?

Economic profit is total revenues minus total costs, including both the explicit and implicit cost components. Economic profit will be positive only if the earnings of the business exceed the opportunity cost of all the resources used by the firm, *including the opportunity cost of assets owned by the firm and any unpaid labor services supplied by the owner*. In contrast, economic losses result when the earnings of the firm are insufficient to cover explicit and implicit costs. That is why the normal profit rate is zero economic profit, yielding just the competitive rate of return on the capital (and labor) of owners. A higher rate would draw more competitors and their investors into the market; a lower rate would cause competitors and their investors to exit the market.

Remember, zero economic profits do not imply that the firm is about to go out of business. On the contrary, they indicate that the owners are receiving exactly the normal profit rate, or the competitive market rate of return on their investment.

Whenever accounting procedures omit implicit costs, like those associated with owner-provided labor services or equity capital, the firm's opportunity costs of production will be understated. This understatement of cost leads to an overstatement of profits. Therefore, the accounting profits of a firm are generally greater than the firm's economic profits (see the Applications in Economics feature on accounting costs). For most large corporations, though, omitting the implicit costs of services provided by an owner isn't an issue. In this case, the accounting profits approximate the returns to the firm's equity capital. High accounting profits (measured as a rate of return on a firm's assets), relative to those of other firms, suggest that a firm is earning an economic profit. Correspondingly, a low rate of accounting profit implies economic losses. Either positive or negative economic profits, of course, call for a change in output. Such a change, however, will take time.

Explicit costs
Payments by a firm to purchase the services of productive resources.

Implicit costs
The opportunity costs associated with a firm's use of resources that it owns. These costs do not involve a direct money payment. Examples include wage income and interest forgone by the owner of a firm who also provides labor services and equity capital to the firm.

Total cost
The costs, both explicit and implicit, of all the resources used by the firm. Total cost includes a normal rate of return for the firm's equity capital.

Opportunity cost of equity capital
The rate of return that must be earned by investors to induce them to supply financial capital to the firm.

Economic profit
The difference between the firm's total revenues and its total costs, including both the explicit and implicit cost components.

Normal profit rate
Zero economic profit, providing just the competitive rate of return on the capital (and labor) of owners. An above-normal profit will draw more entry into the market, whereas a below-normal profit will lead to an exit of investors and capital.

Accounting profits
The sales revenues minus the expenses of a firm over a designated time period, usually one year. Accounting profits typically make allowances for changes in the firm's inventories and depreciation of its assets. No allowance is made, however, for the opportunity cost of the equity capital of the firm's owners, or other implicit costs.

APPLICATIONS IN ECONOMICS

Economic and Accounting Costs: A Hypothetical Example

The revenue–cost statement for a corner grocery store owned and operated by Emily Blake is presented here.

TOTAL REVENUE	
Sales (groceries)	$170,000
Costs (explicit)	
Groceries, wholesale	$76,000
Utilities	4,000
Taxes	6,000
Advertising	2,000
Labor services (employees)	12,000
Total (explicit) costs	$100,000
Net (accounting) profit	$70,000
Additional (implicit) costs	
Interest (personal investment)	$7,000
Rent (Emily's building)	18,000
Salary (Emily's labor)	50,000
Total (implicit) costs	$75,000
TOTAL EXPLICIT AND IMPLICIT COSTS	$175,000
ECONOMIC PROFIT (TOTAL REVENUE MINUS EXPLICIT AND IMPLICIT COSTS)	−$5,000

Emily works full-time as the manager, chief cashier, and janitor. She has $140,000 worth of refrigeration and other equipment invested in the store. Last year, her total sales were $170,000, and suppliers and employees were paid $100,000. Emily's revenues therefore exceeded explicit costs by $70,000. This is what was recorded on the accounting statements as profit.

But did Emily really make a profit last year? Let's look at her opportunity costs and see: If Emily didn't have $140,000 of her own money invested in equipment, she could be earning 5 percent interest on the money in the bank, which would add up to $7,000 each year. Similarly, if the building she owns weren't being used as a grocery store, it could be rented to someone else for $1,500 per month. Rental income forgone is therefore $18,000 per year. In addition, because Emily is tied up working in the grocery store, a $50,000 managerial position she could hold at another local grocery store is forgone. Considering the interest, rental, and salary income that Emily had to forgo to operate the grocery store last year, her implicit costs were $75,000. This makes her total costs—both explicit and implicit—$175,000. (Recall that explicit costs were $100,000.) That's $5,000 *less* than her actual revenues of $170,000. As a result, Emily incurred an economic loss of $5,000, despite the accounting profit of $70,000 recorded on the store's books.

8-4 SHORT-RUN AND LONG-RUN TIME PERIODS

Short run (in production)
A time period so short that a firm is unable to vary some of its factors of production. The firm's plant size typically cannot be altered in the short run.

Time plays an important role in the production process. All of a firm's resources can be expanded (or contracted) over time, but for specialized equipment, expanding (and contracting) availability quickly is likely to be very expensive or even impossible. Economists often speak of the short run as a time period so short that the firm is unable to alter its present plant size. In the short run, the firm is typically stuck with its existing plant and heavy equipment. These assets are "fixed" for a given time period, in other words. The firm can alter output, however, by applying larger or smaller amounts of "variable" resources, like labor and raw materials. In this way, the existing plant capacity can be used more or less intensively in the short run.

How long is the short run? *The short run is that period of time during which at least one factor of production, usually the size of the firm's plant, cannot be changed.* The length varies across industries and firms. A trucking firm might be able to hire more drivers and buy or rent more trucks and double its hauling capacity in a few months. In other industries, particularly those that use assembly lines and mass-production techniques, increasing production capacity may take several years.

Long run (in production)
A time period long enough to allow the firm to vary all of its factors of production.

The long run is a time period long enough for existing firms to alter the size of their plants and for new firms to enter (or exit) the market. *All of the firm's resources are variable in the long run.* In the long run, firms can expand their output by increasing the sizes of their plants—perhaps by adding on to them or by constructing entirely new facilities.

An example may help you understand the distinction between the short- and long-run time periods: If a tablet computer manufacturer hired 200 additional workers and ordered more raw materials in order to squeeze more production out of its existing plant, it would be making a short-run adjustment. In contrast, if the manufacturer built an additional plant (or expanded the size of its current facility) and installed additional heavy equipment, it would be making a long-run adjustment.

8-5 CATEGORIES OF COSTS

In the short run, we can break a firm's costs into two categories—fixed and variable. Each category of costs behaves differently. Seeing that behavior graphically will help us understand how the profit-maximizing level of the firm's output is determined. It will also be important to distinguish between a firm's total costs and its per-unit costs, which we call "average" costs.

Each of the firm's fixed costs, and their sum, called total fixed cost (*TFC*), will remain unchanged when output rises or falls in the short run. For example, a firm's insurance premiums; its property taxes; and, most significantly, the opportunity cost of using its fixed assets will be present whether the firm produces a large or small amount of output. These costs will not vary with output. They can be avoided only if the firm goes out of business.

What will happen to average fixed cost (*AFC*), which is fixed cost *per unit*, as output expands? Remember that the firm's fixed cost will be the same whether output is 1, or 100, or 1,000. The *AFC* is simply fixed cost divided by output. As output increases, *AFC* declines because the fixed cost will be spread over more and more units (see part a of Exhibit 2).

Some costs vary with output. For example, additional output can usually be produced by hiring more workers and buying more raw materials. The sum of those and other costs that rise as output increases is the firm's total variable cost (*TVC*). At any given level of output, the firm's average variable cost (*AVC*), which is variable cost *per unit*, is the total variable cost divided by output.

A firm's total cost (*TC*) is the sum of the fixed and variable costs. At zero output a firm has no variable costs, thus total cost will be equal to total fixed cost. As output expands from zero, variable costs begin to increase, causing total cost to rise with output even though fixed costs are remaining unchanged. Average total cost (*ATC*), sometimes referred to as unit cost, can be found by dividing total cost by the total number of units produced. *ATC* is also equal to the sum of the average fixed and average variable costs. One way to look at ATC is that it is the amount of revenue needed per unit of output to cover total cost.

The economic way of thinking focuses on what happens "at the margin." How much does it cost to produce an additional unit? Marginal cost (*MC*) is the change in

Total fixed cost
The sum of the costs that do not vary with output. They will be incurred as long as a firm continues in business and the assets have alternative uses.

Average fixed cost
Total fixed cost divided by the number of units produced. It always declines as output increases.

Total variable cost
The sum of those costs that rise as output increases. Examples of variable costs are wages paid to workers and payments for raw materials.

Average variable cost
The total variable cost divided by the number of units produced.

Average total cost
Total cost divided by the number of units produced. It is sometimes called per-unit cost.

Marginal cost
The change in total cost required to produce an additional unit of output.

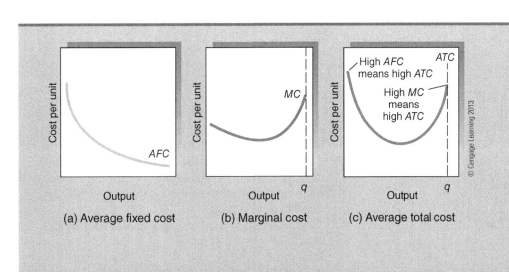

EXHIBIT 2

The General Characteristics of Short-Run Cost Curves

Average fixed costs (a) will be high for small rates of output, but they will always decline as output expands. Marginal cost (b) will rise sharply as the plant approaches its production capacity, q. As graph (c) shows, ATC will be a U-shaped curve because AFC will be high for small rates of output, and MC will be high as the plant's production capacity is approached.

total cost that results from the production of one additional unit. The profit-conscious decision-maker recognizes *MC* as the addition to cost that must be covered by additional revenue if producing the marginal unit is to be profitable. In the short run, as illustrated by part (b) of Exhibit 2, *MC* will generally decline at first if output is increased, reach a minimum, and then increase. The rising *MC* simply reflects the fact that it becomes increasingly difficult to squeeze additional output from a plant as the facility's maximum capacity (the dotted line of part b of Exhibit 2) is approached. The accompanying **Thumbnail Sketch** summarizes how the firm's various costs are related to one another.

8-6 OUTPUT AND COSTS IN THE SHORT RUN

As a firm changes its rate of output in the short run, how will its unit cost be affected? In the short run, the firm can vary its output by using its fixed plant size more (or less) intensively. Exhibit 2 shows two ways that this can result in high unit costs. First, when the output rate of a plant is small relative to its capacity, the facility is being underutilized, causing *AFC* to be high and *ATC* to be high, too. It will be costly to operate a large plant, with its high fixed costs, substantially below its production capacity. Alternatively, overutilization can also cause high unit costs. An overutilized plant will mean congestion—time spent by workers waiting for machines and similar costly delays. Requiring output beyond the least-cost, or designed, output level of a plant will lead to high *MC* and therefore to high *ATC*.

Thus, the ATC curve will be U-shaped, as pictured in part (c) of Exhibit 2. ATC will be high for both an underutilized plant and an overutilized plant. It will be high for an underutilized plant because average fixed cost will be high. It will be high for an overutilized plant because marginal cost will be high.

Thumbnail Sketch
Compact Glossary on Cost

Term	Symbol	Equation	Definition
Fixed cost			Cost that is independent of the output level
Variable cost			Cost that varies with the output level
Total fixed cost	TFC		Cost of the fixed inputs (equals sum of quantity times unit price for each fixed input)
Total variable cost	TVC		Cost of the variable inputs (equals sum of quantity times unit price for each variable input)
Total cost	TC	$TC = TFC + TVC$	Cost of all inputs (equals fixed costs plus variable costs)
Marginal cost	MC	$MC = \Delta TC \div \Delta q$	Change in total cost resulting from a one-unit rise in output (q) [equals the change in total cost divided by the change in output]
Average fixed cost	AFC	$AFC = TFC \div q$	Total fixed cost per unit of output (equals total fixed cost divided by total output)
Average variable cost	AVC	$AVC = TVC \div q$	Total variable cost per unit of output (equals total variable cost divided by total output)
Average total cost	ATC	$ATC = AFC + AVC$	Total cost per unit of output (equals average fixed cost plus average variable cost)

8-6a DIMINISHING RETURNS AND PRODUCTION IN THE SHORT RUN

Our analysis of the changes in unit cost as the output rate rises reflects a long-established economic law. This **law of diminishing returns** states that, as more and more units of a variable factor are applied to a fixed amount of other resources, output will eventually increase by smaller and smaller amounts. Therefore, the impact on output of additional units of the variable factor will diminish. The cost per unit of adding the variable factor may be the same, but the added output per dollar spent falls. The impact on cost per unit of output is clear: When the returns to the variable factor are rising, marginal costs (the additions to total variable cost needed to add a unit of output) are falling. Similarly, when the returns to the variable factor are falling, marginal cost is rising.

The law of diminishing returns is as famous in economics as the law of gravity is in physics. It is based on common sense and real-life observation. Have you ever noticed that as you apply a single resource more intensively, the resource eventually tends to accomplish less and less? Consider a wheat farmer who applies fertilizer (a variable resource) more and more intensively to an acre of land (a fixed factor). At some point, the application of additional 100-pound units of fertilizer will expand the wheat yield by successively smaller amounts.

Essentially, the law of diminishing returns is a constraint imposed by nature. If it were not valid, it would be possible to raise all the world's food in a flowerpot. We would be able to increase output simply by applying another unit of labor and fertilizer to the world's most fertile flowerpot! In the real world, of course, this is not the case; the law of diminishing returns is valid, reflecting a constraint we all must face.

Exhibit 3 illustrates the law of diminishing returns numerically. Column 1 indicates the quantity of the variable resource, labor in this example, which is combined with a specified amount of the fixed resource. Column 2 shows the **total product** that will result as the utilization rate of labor increases. Column 3 provides data on the **marginal product**, the change in total output associated with each additional unit of labor. Without the application of labor, output will be zero. As additional units of labor are applied, total product (output) rises. As the first three units of labor are applied, total product increases by successively larger amounts (8, then 12, then 14). Beginning with the fourth unit, however, diminishing returns

Law of diminishing returns
The postulate that as more and more units of a variable resource are combined with a fixed amount of other resources, using additional units of the variable resource will eventually increase output only at a decreasing rate. Once diminishing returns are reached, it will take successively larger amounts of the variable factor to expand output by one unit.

Total product
The total output of a good that is associated with each alternative utilization rate of a variable input.

Marginal product
The increase in the total product resulting from a unit increase in the employment of a variable input. Mathematically, it is the ratio of the change in total product to the change in the quantity of the variable input.

EXHIBIT 3

The Law of Diminishing Returns (Hypothetical Data)

(1) UNITS OF THE VARIABLE RESOURCE, LABOR (PER DAY)	(2) TOTAL PRODUCT (OUTPUT)	(3) MARGINAL PRODUCT	(4) AVERAGE PRODUCT
0	0		—
		8	
1	8		8.0
		12	
2	20		10.0
		14	
3	34		11.3
		12	
4	46		11.5
		10	
5	56		11.2
		8	
6	64		10.7
		6	
7	70		10.0
		4	
8	74		9.3
		1	
9	75		8.3
		−2	
10	73		7.3

© Cengage Learning 2013

are confronted. When the fourth unit of labor is added, marginal product—the change in the total product—declines to 12 (down from 14, when the third unit was applied). As additional units of labor are applied, marginal product continues to decline. It is increasingly difficult to squeeze a larger total product from the fixed resources (for example, plant size and equipment). Eventually, marginal product becomes negative (beginning with the tenth unit).

Column 4 of Exhibit 3 provides data for the **average product** of labor, which is simply the total product divided by the units of labor applied. Note that the average product increases as long as the marginal product is greater than the average product. Whenever the marginal unit's contribution is greater than the average, it must cause the average to rise. (A good analogy would be your grade point average. If the grade you get in this course is higher than your overall grade point average, your grade in this class will increase your overall average.) Here, marginal product rises through the first four units. The marginal product of the fifth unit of labor, though, is 10, less than the average product for the first four units of labor (11.5). Therefore, beginning with the fifth unit, the average product declines as additional labor is applied. When marginal productivity is below the average, it brings down the average product.

Using the data from Exhibit 3, Exhibit 4 illustrates the law of diminishing returns graphically. Initially, the total product curve (part a) increases quite rapidly. As diminishing marginal returns are confronted (beginning with the fourth unit of labor), total product increases more slowly. Eventually, a maximum output (75) is reached with the application of the ninth unit of labor. The marginal product curve (part b) reflects the total product curve. Geometrically, marginal product is the slope—the rate of increase—of the total product

Average product
The total product (output) divided by the number of units of the variable input required to produce that output level.

EXHIBIT 4

The Law of Diminishing Returns

As units of variable input (labor) are added to a fixed input, total product will increase, first at an increasing rate and then at a declining rate (a). This will cause both marginal and average product curves (b) to rise at first and then decline. Note that the marginal product curve intersects the average product curve at its maximum (when four units of labor are used). The smooth curves indicate that labor can be increased by amounts of less than a single unit.

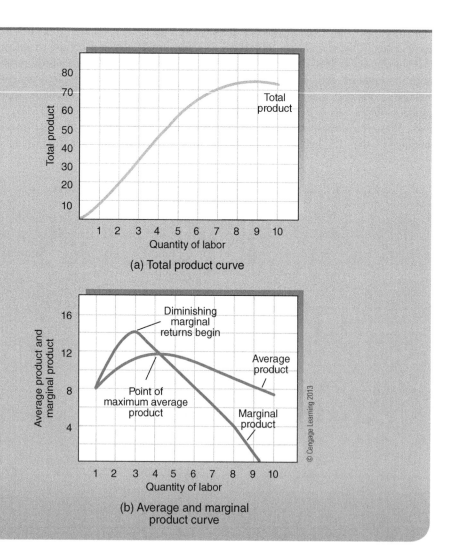

(a) Total product curve

(b) Average and marginal product curve

© Cengage Learning 2013

curve. That slope, the marginal product, reaches its maximum here with the application of three units of labor. Beyond three units, diminishing returns are present. Eventually, at ten units of labor, the marginal product becomes negative. When marginal product becomes negative, total product is necessarily declining. The average product curve rises as long as the marginal product curve is above it, because each added unit of labor is raising the average. The average product reaches its maximum at four units of labor. Beyond that, each additional unit of labor brings down the average product, and the curve slopes downward.

8-6b DIMINISHING RETURNS AND THE SHAPE OF THE COST CURVES

What impact will diminishing returns have on a firm's costs? Once a firm confronts diminishing returns, larger and larger additions of the variable factor are required to expand output by one unit. This will cause marginal cost (MC) to rise. As MC continues to increase, eventually it will exceed average total cost. Until that point, MC is below ATC, bringing ATC down. When MC is greater than ATC, the additional units cost more than the average, and ATC must increase. Think about what happens when you get a grade on an exam above your current class average. Your class average goes up. What happens if a unit of above-average cost is added to output? Average total cost rises. The firm's *MC* curve therefore crosses the *ATC* curve at the *ATC*'s lowest point. For output rates beyond the minimum *ATC,* the rising *MC* causes *ATC* to increase.

Exhibit 5 numerically illustrates the effect of the law of diminishing returns on a firm's short-run cost curve. Here, we assume that Royal Roller Blades, Inc., combines units of a variable input with a fixed factor to produce units of output (pairs of inline skates). Columns 2, 3, and 4 indicate how the total cost schedules vary as output is expanded. Total fixed costs (*TFC*), representing the opportunity cost of the fixed factors of production, are $50 per day at all levels of output. For the first four units of output, total variable costs (*TVC*) increase at a decreasing rate—by $15 with the production of the first unit, $10 with the production of the second unit, $9 with the third, and so on. Why? In this range, there are increasing returns to the variable input. Beginning with the fifth unit of output, however, diminishing marginal returns are present. From this point on, *TVC* and *TC* increase by successively larger amounts as output is expanded.

EXHIBIT 5

The Numerical Short-Run Cost Schedules of Royal Roller Blades, Inc.

	TOTAL COST DATA (PER DAY)			AVERAGE/MARGINAL COST DATA (PER DAY)			
(1) OUTPUT PER DAY	(2) TFC	(3) TVC	(4) TC (2) + (3)	(5) AFC (2) ÷ (1)	(6) AVC (3) ÷ (1)	(7) ATC (4) ÷ (1)	(8) MC $\Delta(4) \div \Delta(1)$
0	$50	$0	$50	—	—	—	—
1	50	15	65	$50.00	$15.00	$65.00	$15
2	50	25	75	25.00	12.50	37.50	10
3	50	34	84	16.67	11.33	28.00	9
4	50	42	92	12.50	10.50	23.00	8
5	50	52	102	10.00	10.40	20.40	10
6	50	64	114	8.33	10.67	19.00	12
7	50	79	129	7.14	11.29	18.43	15
8	50	98	148	6.25	12.25	18.50	19
9	50	122	172	5.56	13.56	19.11	24
10	50	152	202	5.00	15.20	20.20	30
11	50	202	252	4.55	18.36	22.91	50

EXHIBIT 6

Costs in the Short Run

Using data from Exhibit 5, this exhibit shows the general shape of the firm's short-run total cost curves (a), and average and marginal cost curves (b). Note that when output is small (for example, two units), *ATC* will be high because the *AFC* is so high. Similarly, when output is large (for example, eleven units), per-unit cost (*ATC*) will be high because additional units will be extremely costly to produce at this point. Thus, the short-run *ATC* curve will be U-shaped.

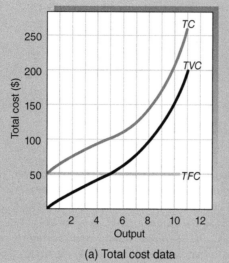

(a) Total cost data

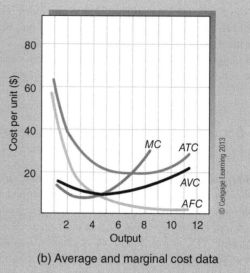

(b) Average and marginal cost data

Columns 5 through 8 of Exhibit 5 are the average and marginal cost schedules. For small output rates, the *ATC* of producing roller blades is high, primarily because of the high *AFC*. Initially, *MC* is less than *ATC*, so *ATC* is falling. When diminishing returns set in for output rates beginning with five units, however, *MC* rises. Beginning with the sixth unit of output, *MC* exceeds *AVC*, causing *AVC* to rise. Beginning with the eighth unit of output, *MC* exceeds *ATC*, causing it also to rise. *ATC* thus reaches its minimum at seven units of output. Look carefully at the data of Exhibit 5 to be sure that you fully understand the relationships among the various cost curves. Do you understand how columns 4 to 8 are derived from columns 1 to 3?

Using the numeric data of Exhibit 5, Exhibit 6 graphically illustrates the total, the average, and the marginal cost curves. Note that the *MC* curve intersects both the *AVC* and *ATC* curves at their minimum points (part b). As *MC*, driven up by diminishing returns, continues to rise above *ATC*, unit costs rise higher and higher as output increases beyond seven units.

In sum, the firm's short-run cost curves reflect the law of diminishing marginal returns. Assuming that the price of the variable resource is constant, *MC* declines so long as the marginal product of the variable input is rising. This results because, in this range, smaller and smaller additions of the variable input are required to produce each extra unit of output. The situation is reversed, however, when diminishing returns are confronted. Once diminishing returns set in, more and more units of the variable factor are required to generate each additional unit of output. *MC* will rise because the marginal product of the variable resource is declining. Eventually, *MC* exceeds *AVC* and *ATC*, causing these costs also to rise. A U-shaped, short-run average total cost curve results.

8-7 OUTPUT AND COSTS IN THE LONG RUN

The short-run analysis relates costs to output *for a specific size of plant*. Firms, though, are not committed forever to their existing plants. In the long run, all resources used by the firm are variable, thus there are no long-run fixed costs.

EXHIBIT 7

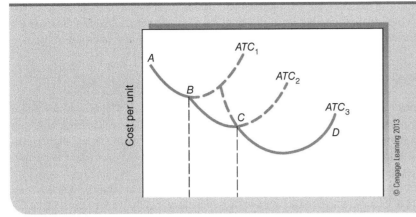

Long-Run Average Total Cost

The short-run average total cost curves are shown for three alternative plant sizes. If these three were the only possible plant sizes, the long-run average total cost curve would be *ABCD*.

How will the firm's choice of plant size affect per-unit production costs? Exhibit 7 illustrates the short-run *ATC* curves for three different plant sizes, ranging from small to large. If these three plant sizes were the only possible choices, which one should the firm choose as it plans for the future? The answer depends on the rate of output the firm expects to produce from the plant. The smallest plant would have the lowest cost if an output rate of less than q_1 were produced. The medium-size plant would provide the least cost method of producing output rates between q_1 and q_2. For any output level greater than q_2, the largest plant would be the most cost efficient.

The long-run* ATC *curve shows the minimum average cost of producing each output level when the firm is free to choose among all possible plant sizes. It can best be thought of as a planning curve because it reflects the expected per-unit cost of producing alternative rates of output while plants are still in the blueprint stage.

Exhibit 7 illustrates the long-run *ATC* curve when only three plant sizes are possible, and the planning curve *ABCD* is thus mapped out. Of course, given sufficient time, firms can usually choose among many plants of various sizes. Exhibit 8 presents the long-run planning curve under these circumstances. It is a smooth curve, with each short-run *ATC* curve tangent to it.

It is important to keep in mind that no single plant size could produce the alternative output rates at the costs indicated by the planning curve *LRATC* in Exhibit 8. Any of the planning curve options are, of course, available to the firm before a plant size is chosen and the plant is built.

EXHIBIT 8

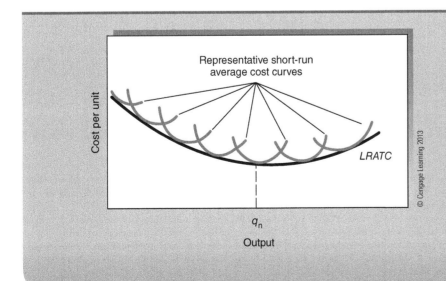

The Planning Curve (LRATC)

When many different plant sizes are possible, the long-run average total cost curve (*LRATC*) can be mapped out. When firms are able to plan large volumes of output, using mass-production methods will generally lead to lower per-unit costs. This helps explain why the *LRATC* has a downward-sloping portion.

But it can *operate* in the short run only *after* a plant size has been chosen and put in place. The *LRATC* curve outlines the *possibilities* available in the planning stage. It shows the expected output and average total costs of production for the firm depending on the plant size it chooses.

8-7a ECONOMIES AND DISECONOMIES OF SCALE

Do larger firms have lower minimum unit costs than smaller ones?[2] There are three major reasons why planning a larger volume of output generally reduces, at least initially, unit costs: (1) economies accompanying the use of mass-production methods, (2) higher productivity as a result of specialization and "learning by doing," and (3) economies in promotion and purchasing.[3] Let's consider each of these factors.

Mass-production techniques usually are economical only when large volumes of output are planned, because they tend to involve large development and setup costs. Once the production methods are established, though, marginal costs are low. For example, the use of molds, dies, and assembly line production methods reduce the per-unit cost of automobiles only when the planned volume of output is in the millions. High-volume methods, although cheaper to use for high rates of output and high volumes, will typically require high fixed costs and therefore cause unit costs to be far higher for low volumes of production.

Large-scale operation also allows the specialized use of labor and machines. In a giant auto plant, hundreds of different jobs must be done, and many of them require a training period for each worker. In a small plant, a single worker might do ten or twenty of these jobs, so each worker would have a much longer, more costly training period. Even then, the worker doing so many tasks might never fully develop the same level of

Mass-production methods can often reduce average costs for firms planning higher output volumes.

REUTERS/SUKREE SUKPLANG/LANDOV

---

[2]Throughout this section, we assume that firms with larger plants necessarily plan a larger volume of output than do their smaller counterparts. Reality approximates these conditions. Firms choose large plants because they are planning to produce a large volume.

[3]Note the distinction between rate and volume of output. Rate of output is the number of units produced during a specific period (for example, the next six months). Volume is the total number of units produced during all time periods. For example, Boeing might produce two 787 airplanes per month (rate of output) while planning to produce a volume of two hundred 787s during the expected life of the model. Increasing the rate (reducing the time period during which a given output is produced) tends to raise costs, whereas increasing the volume (total amount produced) tends to lower costs per unit.

proficiency of the more specialized worker. Baseball players improve by playing baseball, and pianists by playing the piano. Similarly, the employees of a firm improve their skills as they experience "learning by doing" in their jobs. Even better, concentration on a narrower range of tasks can help workers discover or develop cost-reducing techniques. The result of greater size and specialization is often more output per unit of labor.

Large firms are also able to achieve lower costs by spreading fixed costs (like the costs of advertising, developing specialized equipment, and searching out and negotiating better input prices, for example) over many more units. For example, both McDonald's and General Motors are able to spread these costs over a large number of stores and volume of sales. The cost advantages of scale come in many forms.

Economic theory explains why, at least initially, larger firms have lower unit costs than comparable smaller firms. Declining unit costs mean that **economies of scale** are present over the initial range of outputs. The long-run *ATC* curve is falling.

What about *dis*economies of scale? As output continues to expand, is there reason to believe that larger firms will eventually have higher average total costs than smaller ones? The underlying causes of diseconomies of scale are less obvious, but they do occur. As a firm gets bigger and bigger, beyond some point bureaucratic inefficiencies *may* result. Inflexible procedures tend to replace managerial genius. Innovation requires clearance from more levels of management and becomes more difficult and costly. Motivating the workforce, carrying out managerial directives, and monitoring results of plans are also more complex when the firm is larger, and principal–agent problems grow as the number of employees increases and more levels of communication and monitoring are needed.

Circumstances vary, so diseconomies of scale set in at smaller firm sizes for some kinds of firms than for others. For example, firms in the fast-food industry can be very large and remain efficient; economies of scale apparently outweigh the diseconomies, even for giants like McDonald's. But in the fine-dining segment of the restaurant industry, the best restaurants seem to be small. Customers demand individual attention, and a constantly changing, innovative menu that takes advantage of the continually changing array of locally available fresh ingredients—with consistently high quality as the only constant—is important. There are few truly gourmet restaurant chains because diseconomies seem to set in at a much smaller size at these firms. The bottom line for diseconomies of scale is this: For some firms, bureaucratic inefficiencies, principal–agent problems, difficulties with innovation, and similar problems that increase with firm size cause long-run average total costs to rise beyond some output level. However, there is considerable variation among industries and even among firms in the same industry concerning the precise output level at which diseconomies of scale begin to occur.

It is important to note that scale economies and diseconomies stem from sources different from those of increasing and diminishing returns. Economies and diseconomies of scale are long-run concepts. They relate to conditions of production when all factors are variable. In contrast, increasing and diminishing returns are short-run concepts, applicable only when the firm has at least one fixed factor of production.

Economies of scale
Reductions in the firm's per–unit costs associated with the use of large plants to produce a large volume of output.

The consistently high quality of gourmet restaurants like 18 Seaboard in Raleigh, North Carolina, can seldom be duplicated by chain restaurants, in part because a gourmet chef must make decisions daily about which locally available fresh ingredients will be used and how they will be used to produce a constantly innovative menu, delivered by an attentive and dedicated staff. Thus, diseconomies of scale limit the size of firms like 18 Seaboard.

Rick Stroup/18 Seaboard

8-7b ALTERNATIVE SHAPES OF THE *LRATC*

Exhibit 9 outlines three different long-run average total cost (*LRATC*) curves, each describing real-world conditions in differing industries. For a firm described by the cost curve in part (a), both economies and diseconomies of scale are present. Higher per-unit costs will result if the firm chooses a plant size other than the one that minimizes the cost of producing output *q*. If each firm in an industry faces the same cost conditions, we can generalize and say that all plants larger or smaller than this ideal size will experience higher unit costs. A very narrow range

Three Different Types of Long-Run Average Total Cost Curves

For one type of *LRATC* curve, economies of scale are present for output levels less than *q*, but immediately beyond *q*, diseconomies of scale occur (a). In another instance, economies of scale are important until some minimum output level (q_1) is attained. Once the minimum level has been attained, there is a wide range of output levels (q_1 to q_2) consistent with the minimum *LRATC* for the industry (b). In the third situation, economies of scale exist for all relevant output levels (c). As we will see later, this type of *LRATC* curve has important implications for how industries are structured.

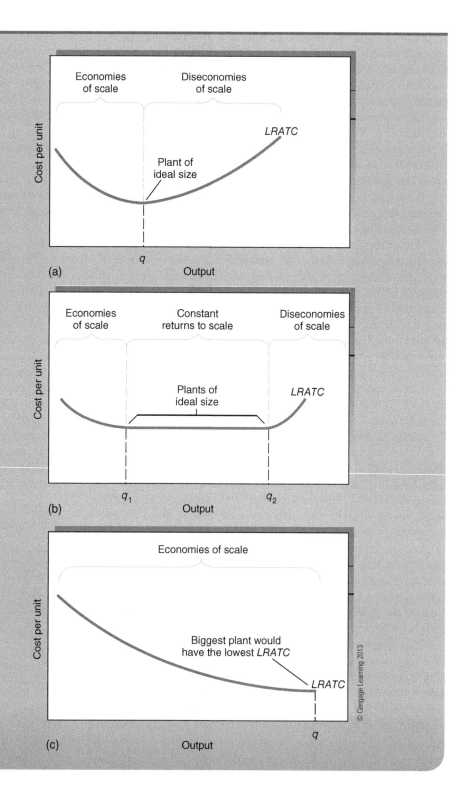

(a)

(b)

(c)

of plant sizes would be expected in industries with the *LRATC* depicted by part (a). Some agricultural products and retail lines approximate these conditions.

Part (b) demonstrates the general shape of the *LRATC* that economists believe is present in most industries. Initially, economies of scale exist, but once a minimum efficient scale is reached, wide variation in firm size is possible. Firms smaller than the minimum efficient size would have higher per-unit costs, but firms larger than that would not gain a cost advantage. **Constant returns to scale** are present for a broad range of output rates

Constant returns to scale Unit costs that are constant as the scale of the firm is altered. Neither economics nor diseconomies of scale are present.

(between q_1 and q_2), in other words. This situation is consistent with real-world conditions in many industries. For example, small firms can be as efficient as larger ones in the apparel, lumber, and publishing industries, as well as in several retail industries.

In part (c) of Exhibit 9, economies of scale exist for all relevant output levels. The larger the firm size, the lower the per-unit cost. The *LRATC* for local telephone service can approximate the curve shown here.

8-8 WHAT FACTORS CAUSE COST CURVES TO SHIFT?

When we drew the general shapes of a firm's cost curves in both the long run and short run, we assumed that certain other factors—resource prices, taxes, regulations, and technology—remained constant as the firm altered its rate of output. Let's now consider how changes in these factors affect the firm's costs.

8-8a PRICES OF RESOURCES

If the price of resources used should rise, the firm's cost curves will shift upward, as Exhibit 10 shows. Higher resource prices will increase the cost of producing each alternative output level. For example, what happens to the cost of producing automobiles when the price of steel rises? The cost of producing automobiles also rises. Conversely, lower resource prices will reduce costs and shift the cost curves downward at each level of output.

8-8b TAXES

Taxes are a component of a firm's cost. Suppose that an excise tax of 20 cents were levied on the seller for each gallon of gasoline sold. What would happen to the seller's costs? They would increase, just as they did in Exhibit 10. The firm's average total and marginal cost curves would shift upward by the amount of the tax. If the tax were an annual business license fee instead, it would raise the average cost, but not the variable cost. Can you explain why?

8-8c REGULATIONS

The government often imposes health, safety, environmental, and production regulations on business firms. Federal regulations under the Americans with Disabilities Act compel

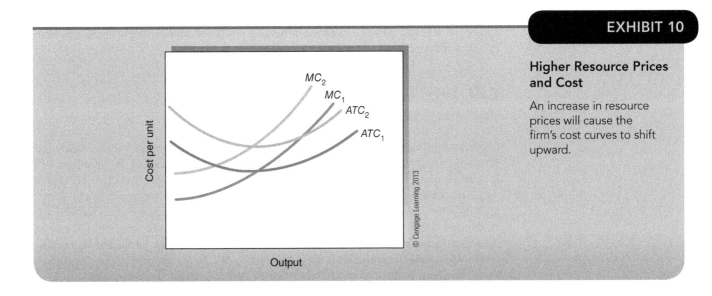

EXHIBIT 10

Higher Resource Prices and Cost

An increase in resource prices will cause the firm's cost curves to shift upward.

© Cengage Learning 2013

EXHIBIT 11

Egg Production Costs and Technological Change

Suppose an egg producer discovers (or develops) a "super" mineral water that makes it possible to get more eggs from the same number of chickens. Because of this technological improvement, various output levels of eggs can now be produced with less feed, space, water, and labor. Costs will be reduced. The egg producer's *ATC* and *MC* curves will shift downward.

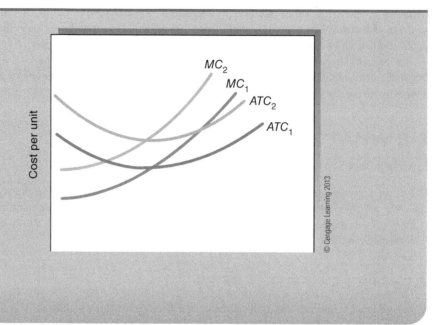

many firms to make their facilities accessible to people in wheelchairs, and the Patient Protection and Affordable Care Act (PPACA) requires certain firms to provide health benefits to full-time workers. Other regulations force firms to build certain features into their products. Strong bumpers and air bags in automobiles are examples. Although regulations provide benefits, they are also costly. Just processing the paperwork that must be submitted to regulators is costly, and so are the compulsory changes themselves. Like tax increases, increases in regulatory compliance costs will shift cost curves upward. In some cases, only fixed costs will be affected; in other instances, variable costs will be altered as well. In both cases, the firm's *ATC* will be higher.

8-8d TECHNOLOGY

Improvements in technology often make it possible to produce a specific amount of output with fewer resources. Computers and robotics have lowered costs in many industries. The Internet has made it easy to find and outsource many business-to-business services, ranging from building maintenance and bookkeeping to software development to the purchase of manufacturing components. As Exhibit 11 shows, a technological improvement will shift the firm's cost curves downward, reflecting the lower amount of resources needed to produce different levels of output.

8-9 THE ECONOMIC WAY OF THINKING ABOUT COSTS

Think for a moment about what the cost curves developed in this chapter really mean. The firm's short-run *MC* curve represents the opportunity cost of expanding output, *given the firm's current plant size*. The firm's long-run *ATC* curve represents the opportunity cost per unit of output associated with varying plant sizes and rates of output, *given that the alternative plants are still on the drawing board*. Costs are associated with choices, and they are forward-looking. At the time decisions must be made, neither the short-run *MC* nor the long-run *ATC* can be determined from accounting records, because accounting costs look backward. Accounting figures yield valuable information about historical costs, but, as the following section illustrates, they must be interpreted carefully when they are used to forecast future costs.

8-9a WHAT ARE SUNK COSTS?

Sunk costs are the historical costs of past decisions that cannot be reversed. Sunk costs give managers hindsight when it comes to making current decisions, but the specific costs themselves are no longer relevant. When past choices cannot be reversed—no refund is available, for example—money that has been spent is gone for good. Today's choices must be based on the costs and benefits expected under *current and future* market conditions, if mistakes are to be avoided (see the accompanying Myths of Economics feature).

To minimize costs, business decision-makers need to realize that sunk costs are, indeed, *sunk*. A simple example will emphasize this point. Suppose that the firm in Exhibit 5 pays $100,000 to purchase and install a roller blade–producing machine. The machine is expected to last ten years. The company's books record the cost of the machine as $10,000 each year under the heading of depreciation. The machine can be used only to make roller blades, though. Because dismantling and reinstallation costs are high, it cannot be leased or sold to another firm. Also, it has no scrap value. In other words, there are no alternative uses for the machine. The machine's annual production of roller blades will generate $50,000 of revenues for the firm when it is employed with raw materials and other factors of production that cost $46,000. Thus, the net revenue generated by the machine is $4,000.

Should the firm continue to use the machine? Its depreciation figures suggest that the machine is costing the firm $10,000 annually, compared to the $4,000 net revenue it generates. Put another way, accounting costs indicate that the machine is reducing the firm's profit by $6,000 annually. The machine's depreciation cost, however, is a sunk cost. It was incurred when the machine was purchased and installed, which is over and done with now. The *current* opportunity cost of the machine is therefore precisely zero. Because using the machine generates $4,000 of additional net revenue, the firm can gain by continuing with its operation. Of course, if market conditions are not expected to improve, the firm will not

Sunk costs
Costs that have already been incurred as a result of past decisions. They are sometimes referred to as historical costs.

MYTHS OF ECONOMICS

"A Good Business Decision-Maker Will Never Sell a Product for Less Than Its Production Costs."

This statement contains a grain of truth. A profit-seeking entrepreneur will not undertake a project knowing the costs can't be covered. However, the statement fails to emphasize (1) the time dimension of the production process and (2) the uncertainty associated with business decisions. The production process takes time. Raw materials must be purchased, employees hired, and plants equipped. Retailers must contract with suppliers. As these decisions are made, costs result. Many of the firm's costs of production are incurred long before its product is ready for marketing.

Even a good business decision-maker is not always able to predict the future because market conditions can change quickly and unexpectedly. At the time the product is ready for sale, buyers might be unwilling to pay a price that will cover the seller's past costs of production. These past costs, however, are now sunk costs and no longer relevant. Decisions must now be made on the basis of the firm's current costs of delivering value to buyers, and the revenues to be gained by doing so.

Should a grocer refuse to sell oranges that are about to spoil because their wholesale cost cannot be covered? The grocer's current opportunity cost of selling the oranges at this point is nearly zero. The alternative would be to throw them in the garbage next week. Almost any price, even one far below past costs, will be better than letting the oranges spoil.

Consider another example. Suppose a couple that owns a house plans to relocate temporarily. Should they refuse to rent the house they're moving out of for $500 (if this is the best offer available) because their monthly house payment is $800? Of course not. The house payment will go on, regardless of whether they rent the house. If the homeowners can cover their opportunity costs (perhaps the expected wear and tear plus a $60 monthly fee for a property management service), they will gain by renting rather than leaving the house vacant.

Past mistakes provide useful lessons for the future, but they cannot be reversed. Bygones are bygones, even if they resulted in business loss. There is no need to fret over spilt milk, burnt toast, or yesterday's business losses.

franckreporter/E+/Getty Images

purchase a similar machine or replace the machine when it wears out, but this should not influence its decision whether to continue operating the one it already has.

8-9b HOW WILL COST INFLUENCE SUPPLY?

Costs underpin the firm's supply decisions. A strictly profit-maximizing firm will compare the expected revenues derived from a decision or a course of action with the expected costs. If the anticipated revenues exceed costs, then the course of action will be chosen because it is expected to expand profits (or reduce losses).

For short-run supply decisions, the marginal cost of producing additional units is the relevant cost to consider. To maximize profits, the decision-maker should compare the expected marginal costs with the expected additional revenue from larger sales. If the latter exceeds the former, output (the quantity supplied) should be expanded.

While marginal costs are central in the short run, average total costs are the relevant cost consideration in the long run. Before entering an industry (or purchasing capital assets for expansion or replacement), a profit-maximizing decision-maker will compare the expected market price with the expected long-run average total cost. Profit-seeking potential entrants will supply the product if, and only if, they expect the market price to exceed their long-run average total cost. Similarly, existing firms will continue to supply a product in the long run only if they expect that the market price will enable them at least to cover their long-run average total cost.

LOOKING AHEAD

This chapter focused on the relationship between output and cost in both the short and long runs. The next three chapters will use these general principles to analyze the price and output decisions of firms under alternative market conditions.

KEY POINTS

- The business firm is used to organize productive resources and transform them into goods and services. There are three major types of business structure—proprietorships, partnerships, and corporations.

- The principal–agent problem tends to reduce efficiency within the firm. Monitoring and the structure of incentives can be used to minimize inefficiencies arising from this source.

- The demand for a product indicates the intensity of consumers' desires for the item. The (opportunity) cost of producing the item indicates the intensity of consumers' desires for other goods that could have been produced instead, with the same resources.

- In economics, total cost includes not only explicit payments for resources employed by the firm, but also the implicit costs associated with the use of productive resources owned by the firm (like the opportunity cost of the firm's equity capital or owner-provided services) that could be used elsewhere.

- Because accounting methods omit the cost of equity capital (and sometimes other implicit costs), they tend to understate the opportunity cost of producing a good and overstate the firm's economic profit.

- Economic profit (or loss) results when a firm's sales revenues exceed (or are less than) its total costs, both explicit and implicit.

- Firms that are earning the market (or "normal") rate of return on their assets will therefore make zero economic profit.

- The firm's short-run average total cost (*ATC*) curve will tend to be U-shaped.

- The law of diminishing returns explains why a firm's short-run marginal and average total costs will eventually rise. When diminishing marginal returns are present, successively larger amounts of the variable input will be required to increase output by one more unit. As this happens, marginal cost will rise.

- The long-run *ATC* (*LRATC*) reflects the costs of production for plants of various sizes. When economies of scale are present, *LRATC* will decline. When constant returns to scale are experienced, *LRATC* will be constant. When diseconomies of scale are present, *LRATC* will rise.

- Changes in (1) resource prices, (2) taxes, (3) regulations, and (4) technology will cause the cost curves of firms to shift.

- Sunk costs are costs that have already been incurred and cannot be recovered. Sunk costs give managers hindsight when it comes to making current decisions, but the specific costs themselves are no longer directly relevant for current and future decisions.

CRITICAL ANALYSIS QUESTIONS

1. The owners of a firm are residual income claimants. How does their property right to the residual income affect their incentive to (a) produce efficiently and keep cost low and (b) supply goods that consumers value highly relative to cost? Why is this important?

2. Which of the following statements do you think reflect sound economic thinking? Explain your answer.
   a. "I paid $400 for this economics course. Therefore, I'm going to attend the lectures even if they are useless and boring."
   b. "Because we own rather than rent, and the house is paid for, housing doesn't cost us anything."
   c. "I own 100 shares of stock that I can't afford to sell until the price goes up enough for me to get back at least my original investment."
   d. "Private education is costly to produce, whereas public schooling is free."

3. Suppose a firm produces bicycles. Will the firm's accounting statement reflect the opportunity cost of the bicycles? Why or why not? What costs would an accounting statement reveal? Should current decisions be based on accounting costs? Explain.

4. What is the principal–agent problem? When will the principal–agent problem be most severe? Why might there be a principal–agent problem between the stockholder owners and the managers of a large corporation?

5. *"If a firm maximizes profit, it must minimize the cost of producing the profit-maximizing output." Is this statement true or false? Explain your answer.

6. What are some of the advantages of the corporate business structure of ownership for large business firms? What are some of the disadvantages? Is the corporate form of business ownership cost efficient? In a market economy, how would you tell whether the corporate structural form was efficient?

7. Explain the factors that cause a firm's short-run average total costs initially to decline but eventually to increase as the rate of output rises.

8. Which of the following are relevant to a firm's decision to increase output: (a) short-run average total cost, (b) short-run marginal cost, (c) long-run average total cost? Justify your answer.

9. Economics students often confuse (a) diminishing returns related to the variable factors of production and (b) diseconomies of scale. Explain the difference between the two, and give one example of each.

10. "Firms that make a profit have increased the value of the resources they used; their actions created wealth. In contrast, the actions of firms that make losses reduce wealth. The discovery and undertaking of profit-making opportunities are key ingredients of economic progress." Evaluate the statement.

11. *Is profit maximization consistent with the self-interest of corporate owners? Is it consistent with the self-interest of corporate managers? Is there a conflict between the self-interests of owners and those of managers?

12. *What is the opportunity cost of (a) borrowed funds and (b) equity capital? Under current tax law, firms can record as an expense the opportunity cost of borrowed funds, but not equity capital. How does this tax law affect the amount of debt the firm wants to incur, compared with the amount of money it raises by selling equity?

13. Why do economists consider normal returns to capital to be a cost? How does economic profit differ from normal profit?

14. *Draw a U-shaped, short-run *ATC* curve for a firm. Construct the accompanying *MC* and *AVC* curves.

15. What is shirking? If the managers of a firm are attempting to maximize its profits, will they have an incentive to limit shirking? How might they go about doing so?

16. What are implicit costs? Do implicit costs contribute to the opportunity cost of production? Should an implicit cost be counted as cost? Give three examples of implicit costs. Does the firm's accounting statement take implicit costs into account? Why or why not?

17. *Consider a machine purchased one year ago for $12,000. The machine is being depreciated $4,000 per year over a three-year period. Its current market value is $5,000, and the expected market value of the machine one year from now is $3,000. If the interest rate is 10 percent, what is the expected cost of holding the machine during the next year?

18. *Investors seeking to take over a firm often bid a positive price for the business even though it is currently experiencing losses. Why would anyone ever bid a positive price for a firm operating at a loss?

19. Fill in the blanks in the accompanying table shown at the bottom of page and answer the following questions:
   a. What happens to total product when marginal product is negative?
   b. What happens to average product when marginal product is greater than average product?
   c. What happens to average product when marginal product is less than average product?
   d. At what point does marginal product begin to decrease?
   e. At what point does marginal cost begin to increase?
   f. Summarize the relationship between marginal product and marginal cost.
   g. What happens to marginal costs when total product begins to fall?
   h. What is happening to average variable costs when they equal marginal costs?
   i. Marginal costs equal average variable costs between what output levels?
   j. What is happening to average total costs when they equal marginal costs?
   k. Marginal costs equal average total costs between what output levels?

*Asterisk denotes questions for which answers are given in Appendix B.

Units of Variable Input	Total Product	Marginal Product	Average Product	Price of Input	Total Variable Cost	Average Variable Cost	Total Fixed Cost	Total Cost	Average Total Cost	Marginal Cost
0	0	____	____	$1	____	____	$2	____	____	____
1	6	____	____	$1	____	____	$2	____	____	____
2	15	____	____	$1	____	____	$2	____	____	____
3	27	____	____	$1	____	____	$2	____	____	____
4	37	____	____	$1	____	____	$2	____	____	____
5	45	____	____	$1	____	____	$2	____	____	____
6	50	____	____	$1	____	____	$2	____	____	____
7	52	____	____	$1	____	____	$2	____	____	____
8	50	____	____	$1	____	____	$2	____	____	____

APPENDIX A

General Business and Economics Indicators for the United States

Section 1

Year	Personal Consum Expend	Gross Private Domestic Invest	Govt Consumpand Gross Invest	Net Exports	Gross Domestic Product	Real GDP 2005 Prices	Annual Real Rate	Real GDP Per Capita
1960	$331.8	$78.9	$111.5	$4.2	$526.4	$2,830.9	2.5	$15,661
1961	342.2	78.2	119.5	4.9	544.8	2,896.9	2.3	15,766
1962	363.3	88.1	130.1	4.1	585.7	3,072.4	6.1	16,466
1963	382.7	93.8	136.4	4.9	617.8	3,206.7	4.4	16,940
1964	411.5	102.1	143.2	6.9	663.6	3,392.3	5.8	17,675
1965	443.8	118.2	151.4	5.6	719.1	3,610.1	6.4	18,576
1966	480.9	131.3	171.6	3.9	787.7	3,845.3	6.5	19,559
1967	507.8	128.6	192.5	3.6	832.4	3,942.5	2.5	19,836
1968	558.0	141.2	209.3	1.4	909.8	4,133.4	4.8	20,590
1969	604.5	173.6	240.4	1.4	1,019.9	4,707.9	13.9	23,222
1970	647.7	170.1	254.2	4.0	1,075.9	4,717.7	0.2	23,003
1971	701.0	196.8	269.3	0.6	1,167.8	4,873.0	3.3	23,463
1972	769.4	228.1	288.2	–3.4	1,282.4	5,128.8	5.2	24,432
1973	851.1	266.9	306.4	4.1	1,428.5	5,418.2	5.6	25,565
1974	932.0	274.5	343.1	–0.8	1,548.8	5,390.2	–0.5	25,200
1975	1,032.8	257.3	382.9	16.0	1,688.9	5,379.5	–0.2	24,907
1976	1,150.2	323.2	405.8	–1.6	1,877.6	5,669.3	5.4	25,996
1977	1,276.7	396.6	435.8	–23.1	2,086.0	5,930.6	4.6	26,922
1978	1,426.2	478.4	477.4	–25.4	2,356.6	6,260.4	5.6	28,120
1979	1,589.5	539.7	525.5	–22.5	2,632.1	6,459.2	3.2	28,694
1980	1,754.6	530.1	590.8	–13.1	2,862.5	6,443.4	–0.2	28,295
1981	1,937.5	631.2	654.7	–12.5	3,210.9	6,610.6	2.6	28,741
1982	2,073.9	581.0	710.0	–20.0	3,345.0	6,484.3	–1.9	27,923
1983	2,286.5	637.5	765.7	–51.7	3,638.1	6,784.7	4.6	28,953
1984	2,498.2	820.1	825.2	–102.7	4,040.7	7,277.2	7.3	30,784
1985	2,722.7	829.6	908.4	–114.0	4,346.7	7,585.7	4.2	31,805
1986	2,898.4	849.1	974.5	–131.9	4,590.1	7,852.1	3.5	32,624
1987	3,092.1	892.2	1,030.8	–144.8	4,870.2	8,123.9	3.5	33,453
1988	3,346.9	937.0	1,078.2	–109.4	5,252.6	8,465.4	4.2	34,544
1989	3,592.8	999.7	1,151.9	–86.8	5,657.7	8,777.0	3.7	35,479
1990	3,825.6	993.5	1,238.4	–77.9	5,979.6	8,945.4	1.9	35,756
1991	3,960.2	944.3	1,298.2	–28.6	6,174.0	8,938.9	–0.1	35,258
1992	4,215.7	1,013.0	1,345.4	–34.8	6,539.3	9,256.7	3.6	36,029
1993	4,471.0	1,106.8	1,366.1	–65.2	6,878.7	9,510.8	2.7	36,540
1994	4,741.0	1,256.5	1,403.7	–92.5	7,308.7	9,894.7	4.0	37,557
1995	4,984.2	1,317.5	1,452.2	–89.8	7,664.0	10,163.7	2.7	38,125
1996	5,268.1	1,432.1	1,496.4	–96.4	8,100.2	10,549.5	3.8	39,114
1997	5,560.7	1,595.6	1,554.2	–102.0	8,608.5	11,022.9	4.5	40,383
1998	5,903.0	1,735.3	1,613.5	–162.7	9,089.1	11,513.4	4.4	41,692
1999	6,316.9	1,884.2	1,726.0	–261.4	9,665.7	12,071.4	4.8	43,216
2000	6,801.6	2,033.8	1,834.4	–380.1	10,289.7	12,565.2	4.1	44,495
2001	7,106.9	1,928.6	1,958.8	–369.0	10,625.3	12,684.4	0.9	44,472
2002	7,385.3	1,925.0	2,094.9	–425.0	10,980.2	12,909.7	1.8	44,832
2003	7,764.4	2,027.9	2,220.8	–500.9	11,512.2	13,270.0	2.8	45,660
2004	8,257.8	2,276.7	2,357.4	–614.8	12,277.0	13,774.0	3.8	46,968
2005	8,790.3	2,527.1	2,493.7	–715.7	13,095.4	14,235.6	3.4	48,094
2006	9,297.5	2,680.6	2,642.2	–762.4	13,857.9	14,615.2	2.7	48,910
2007	9,744.4	2,643.7	2,801.9	–709.8	14,480.3	14,876.8	1.8	49,311
2008	10,005.5	2,424.8	3,003.2	–713.2	14,720.3	14,833.6	–0.3	48,708
2009	9,842.9	1,878.1	3,089.1	–392.2	14,417.9	14,417.9	–2.8	46,927
2010	10,201.9	2,100.8	3,174.0	–518.5	14,958.3	14,779.4	2.5	47,710
2011	10,711.8	2,232.1	3,158.7	–568.7	15,533.8	15,052.4	1.8	48,239
2012	11,149.6	2,475.2	3,167.0	–547.2	16,244.6	15,470.7	2.8	49,226

Source: http://www.bea.gov

Section 2

	GDP Deflator		Consumer Price Index	
Year	Index (2005 = 100)	Annual Percentage Change	Index	Percentage Change
1960	20.2	1.4	29.6	1.0
1961	20.5	1.1	29.9	1.1
1962	20.7	1.4	30.3	1.2
1963	21.0	1.1	30.6	1.2
1964	21.3	1.6	31.0	1.3
1965	21.7	1.8	31.5	1.6
1966	22.3	2.8	32.5	3.0
1967	23.0	3.1	33.4	2.8
1968	23.9	4.3	34.8	4.3
1969	23.6	−1.5	36.7	5.5
1970	24.8	5.3	38.8	5.8
1971	26.1	5.1	40.5	4.3
1972	27.2	4.3	41.8	3.3
1973	28.7	5.4	44.4	6.2
1974	31.3	9.0	49.3	11.1
1975	34.2	9.3	53.8	9.1
1976	36.0	5.5	56.9	5.7
1977	38.3	6.2	60.6	6.5
1978	41.0	7.0	65.2	7.6
1979	44.3	8.3	72.6	11.3
1980	48.4	9.0	82.4	13.5
1981	52.9	9.4	90.9	10.3
1982	56.1	6.1	96.5	6.1
1983	58.3	3.9	99.6	3.2
1984	60.4	3.6	103.9	4.3
1985	62.3	3.2	107.6	3.5
1986	63.6	2.0	109.6	1.9
1987	65.2	2.4	113.6	3.7
1988	67.4	3.5	118.3	4.1
1989	70.1	3.9	124.0	4.8
1990	72.7	3.7	130.7	5.4
1991	75.1	3.3	136.2	4.2
1992	76.8	2.3	140.3	3.0
1993	78.6	2.4	144.5	3.0
1994	80.3	2.1	148.2	2.6
1995	82.0	2.1	152.4	2.8
1996	83.5	1.8	156.9	2.9
1997	84.9	1.7	160.5	2.3
1998	85.8	1.1	163.0	1.6
1999	87.0	1.4	166.6	2.2
2000	89.0	2.3	172.2	3.4
2001	91.1	2.3	177.1	2.8
2002	92.5	1.5	179.9	1.6
2003	94.3	2.0	184.0	2.3
2004	96.9	2.7	188.9	2.7
2005	100.0	3.2	195.3	3.4
2006	103.1	3.1	201.6	3.2
2007	105.8	2.7	207.3	2.8
2008	107.8	1.9	215.3	3.8
2009	108.7	0.8	214.5	−0.4
2010	110.0	1.2	218.1	1.6
2011	112.2	2.0	224.9	3.1
2012	114.2	1.7	229.6	2.1

Source: http://www.bea.gov and http://www.bls.gov

Section 3

Year	Civilian Pop	Civilian Labor Force	Civilian Labor Force Participation	Civilian Employment/ Population	Unemployment Rates		
					All	Age 16 to 19	Men Age 20+	Women Age 20+
1960	117.2	69.6	59.4	56.1	5.5	14.7	4.7	5.1
1961	118.8	70.5	59.3	55.4	6.7	16.8	5.7	6.3
1962	120.2	70.6	58.8	55.5	5.5	14.7	4.6	5.4
1963	122.4	71.8	58.7	55.4	5.7	17.2	4.5	5.4
1964	124.5	73.1	58.7	55.7	5.2	16.2	3.9	5.2
1965	126.5	74.5	58.9	56.2	4.5	14.8	3.2	4.5
1966	128.1	75.8	59.2	56.9	3.8	12.8	2.5	3.8
1967	129.9	77.3	59.6	57.3	3.8	12.9	2.3	4.2
1968	132.0	78.7	59.6	57.5	3.6	12.7	2.2	3.8
1969	134.3	80.7	60.1	58.0	3.5	12.2	2.1	3.7
1970	137.1	82.8	60.4	57.4	4.9	15.3	3.5	4.8
1971	140.2	84.4	60.2	56.6	5.9	16.9	4.4	5.7
1972	144.1	87.0	60.4	57.0	5.6	16.2	4.0	5.4
1973	147.1	89.4	60.8	57.8	4.9	14.5	3.3	4.9
1974	150.1	91.9	61.3	57.8	5.6	16.0	3.8	5.5
1975	153.2	93.8	61.2	56.1	8.5	19.9	6.8	8.0
1976	156.2	96.2	61.6	56.8	7.7	19.0	5.9	7.4
1977	159.0	99.0	62.3	57.9	7.1	17.8	5.2	7.0
1978	161.9	102.3	63.2	59.3	6.1	16.4	4.3	6.0
1979	164.9	105.0	63.7	59.9	5.8	16.1	4.2	5.7
1980	167.7	106.9	63.8	59.2	7.1	17.8	5.9	6.4
1981	170.1	108.7	63.9	59.0	7.6	19.6	6.3	6.8
1982	172.3	110.2	64.0	57.8	9.7	23.2	8.8	8.3
1983	174.2	111.6	64.0	57.9	9.6	22.4	8.9	8.1
1984	176.4	113.5	64.4	59.5	7.5	18.9	6.6	6.8
1985	178.2	115.5	64.8	60.1	7.2	18.6	6.2	6.6
1986	180.6	117.8	65.3	60.7	7.0	18.3	6.1	6.2
1987	182.8	119.9	65.6	61.5	6.2	16.9	5.4	5.4
1988	184.6	121.7	65.9	62.3	5.5	15.3	4.8	4.9
1989	186.4	123.9	66.5	63.0	5.3	15.0	4.5	4.7
1990	189.2	125.8	66.5	62.8	5.6	15.5	5.0	4.9
1991	190.9	126.3	66.2	61.7	6.8	18.7	6.4	5.7
1992	192.8	128.1	66.4	61.5	7.5	20.1	7.1	6.3
1993	194.8	129.2	66.3	61.7	6.9	19.0	6.4	5.9
1994	196.8	131.1	66.6	62.5	6.1	17.6	5.4	5.4
1995	198.6	132.3	66.6	62.9	5.6	17.3	4.8	4.9
1996	200.6	133.9	66.8	63.2	5.4	16.7	4.6	4.8
1997	203.1	136.3	67.1	63.8	4.9	16.0	4.2	4.4
1998	205.2	137.7	67.1	64.1	4.5	14.6	3.7	4.1
1999	207.8	139.4	67.1	64.3	4.2	13.9	3.5	3.8
2000	212.6	142.6	67.1	64.4	4.0	13.1	3.4	3.6
2001	215.1	143.7	66.8	63.7	4.7	14.7	4.2	4.1
2002	217.6	144.9	66.6	62.7	5.8	16.5	5.2	5.1
2003	221.2	146.5	66.2	62.3	6.0	17.5	5.4	5.1
2004	223.4	147.4	66.0	62.3	5.5	17.0	4.9	4.9
2005	226.1	149.3	66.0	62.7	5.1	16.6	4.5	4.6
2006	228.8	151.4	66.2	63.1	4.6	15.4	4.1	4.1
2007	231.9	153.1	66.0	63.0	4.6	15.7	4.1	4.0
2008	233.8	154.3	66.0	62.2	5.8	18.7	5.4	4.9
2009	235.8	154.1	65.4	59.3	9.3	24.8	9.6	7.5
2010	237.8	153.9	64.7	58.5	9.6	25.9	9.8	8.0
2011	239.6	153.6	64.1	58.4	8.9	24.4	8.7	7.9
2012	243.3	155.0	63.7	58.6	8.1	24.0	7.5	7.3

Source: www.bls.gov

Section 4

						FEDERAL BUDGET			NATIONAL DEBT[1]	
						FISCAL	FISCAL		BILLIONS	PERCENT
		ANNUAL		ANNUAL	AAA	YEAR	YEAR	SURPLUS/	OF	OF
YEAR	M1	CHANGE	M2	CHANGE	BONDS	OUTLAYS	RECEIPTS	DEFICIT	DOLLARS	GDP
1960	$140.3	−0.1	$304.3	3.8	4.4	$92.2	$92.5	$0.3	$210.3	40.5%
1961	143.1	2.0	324.8	6.7	4.4	97.7	94.4	(3.3)	211.1	39.8%
1962	146.5	2.4	350.1	7.8	4.3	106.8	99.7	(7.1)	218.3	38.5%
1963	150.9	3.0	379.6	8.4	4.3	111.3	106.6	(4.8)	222.0	37.0%
1964	156.8	3.9	409.4	7.8	4.4	118.5	112.6	(5.9)	222.1	34.6%
1965	163.5	4.2	442.5	8.1	4.5	118.2	116.8	(1.4)	221.7	32.2%
1966	171.0	4.6	471.4	6.5	5.1	134.5	130.8	(3.7)	221.5	29.3%
1967	177.7	3.9	503.6	6.8	5.5	157.5	148.8	(8.6)	219.9	27.1%
1968	190.1	7.0	545.3	8.3	6.2	178.1	153.0	(25.2)	237.3	27.3%
1969	201.4	5.9	578.7	6.1	7.0	183.6	186.9	3.2	224.0	23.6%
1970	209.1	3.8	601.4	3.9	8.0	195.6	192.8	(2.8)	225.5	22.3%
1971	223.2	6.7	674.4	12.1	7.4	210.2	187.1	(23.0)	237.5	22.0%
1972	239.0	7.1	758.1	12.4	7.2	230.7	207.3	(23.4)	251.0	21.3%
1973	256.4	7.2	831.8	9.7	7.4	245.7	230.8	(14.9)	265.7	20.3%
1974	269.2	5.0	880.7	5.9	8.6	269.4	263.2	(6.1)	263.1	18.3%
1975	281.4	4.5	963.7	9.4	8.8	332.3	279.1	(53.2)	309.7	19.8%
1976	297.2	5.6	1,086.6	12.8	8.4	371.8	298.1	(73.7)	382.7	22.0%
1977	320.0	7.7	1,221.4	12.4	8.0	409.2	355.6	(53.7)	444.1	22.5%
1978	346.3	8.2	1,322.4	8.3	8.7	458.7	399.6	(59.2)	491.6	22.2%
1979	372.7	7.6	1,425.8	7.8	9.6	504.0	463.3	(40.7)	524.7	21.0%
1980	395.7	6.2	1,540.4	8.0	11.9	590.9	517.1	(73.8)	591.1	21.7%
1981	424.9	7.4	1,679.6	9.0	14.2	678.2	599.3	(79.0)	664.9	21.8%
1982	453.0	6.6	1,831.4	9.0	13.8	745.7	617.8	(128.0)	790.1	24.5%
1983	503.2	11.1	2,054.8	12.2	12.0	808.4	600.6	(207.8)	981.7	28.5%
1984	538.6	7.0	2,219.3	8.0	12.7	851.8	666.4	(185.4)	1,151.9	30.0%
1985	587.0	9.0	2,416.7	8.9	11.4	946.3	734.0	(212.3)	1,337.5	32.3%
1986	666.4	13.5	2,613.5	8.1	9.0	990.4	769.2	(221.2)	1,549.8	35.2%
1987	743.5	11.6	2,783.8	6.5	9.4	1,004.0	854.3	(149.7)	1,677.7	36.1%
1988	774.8	4.2	2,933.4	5.4	9.7	1,064.4	909.2	(155.2)	1,822.4	36.4%
1989	782.2	1.0	3,056.1	4.2	9.3	1,143.7	991.1	(152.6)	1,970.6	36.5%
1990	810.6	3.6	3,223.6	5.5	9.3	1,253.0	1,032.0	(221.0)	2,177.1	38.0%
1991	859.0	6.0	3,342.2	3.7	8.8	1,324.2	1,055.0	(269.2)	2,430.4	41.0%
1992	965.9	12.5	3,403.6	1.8	8.1	1,381.5	1,091.2	(290.3)	2,703.3	43.3%
1993	1,078.5	11.7	3,438.0	1.0	7.2	1,409.4	1,154.3	(255.1)	2,922.7	44.4%
1994	1,145.2	6.2	3,482.1	1.3	8.0	1,461.8	1,258.6	(203.2)	3,077.9	44.1%
1995	1,143.1	−0.2	3,552.7	2.0	7.6	1,515.7	1,351.8	(164.0)	3,230.3	44.0%
1996	1,106.5	−3.2	3,722.8	4.8	7.4	1,560.5	1,453.1	(107.4)	3,343.1	43.3%
1997	1,070.1	−3.3	3,909.8	5.0	7.3	1,601.1	1,579.2	(21.9)	3,347.8	40.8%
1998	1,080.6	1.0	4,188.9	7.1	6.5	1,652.5	1,721.7	69.3	3,262.9	37.7%
1999	1,102.3	2.0	4,496.9	7.4	7.0	1,701.8	1,827.5	125.6	3,135.7	34.1%
2000	1,103.6	0.1	4,769.3	6.1	7.6	1,789.0	2,025.2	236.2	2,898.4	29.5%
2001	1,140.3	3.3	5,179.4	8.6	7.1	1,862.8	1,991.1	128.2	2,785.5	27.2%
2002	1,196.7	4.9	5,562.4	7.4	6.5	2,010.9	1,853.1	(157.8)	2,936.2	27.8%
2003	1,273.8	6.4	5,950.1	7.0	5.7	2,159.9	1,782.3	(377.6)	3,257.3	29.7%
2004	1,344.3	5.5	6,236.0	4.8	5.6	2,292.8	1,880.1	(412.7)	3595.2	30.8%
2005	1,371.6	2.0	6,504.3	4.3	5.2	2,472.0	2,153.6	(318.3)	3855.9	31.0%
2006	1,374.7	0.2	6,845.3	5.2	5.6	2,655.1	2,406.9	(248.2)	4060.0	30.7%
2007	1,372.6	−0.1	7,267.1	6.2	5.6	2,728.7	2,568.0	(160.7)	4255.5	30.7%
2008	1,434.9	4.5	7,763.7	6.8	5.6	2,982.5	2,524.0	(458.6)	5311.9	37.1%
2009	1,637.7	14.1	8,385.3	8.0	5.3	3,517.7	2,105.0	(1,412.7)	6775.5	48.5%
2010	1,742.3	6.4	8,593.4	2.5	5.0	3,457.1	2,162.7	(1,294.4)	8207.2	57.2%
2011	2,010.0	15.4	9,221.3	7.3	4.6	3,603.1	2,303.5	(1,299.6)	8463.5	56.7%
2012	2,310.9	15.0	10,006.9	8.5	3.7	3,537.1	2,450.2	(1,087.0)	9635.8	62.0%

Source: www.economagic.com and www.whitehouse.gov/omb/

[1]National debt is debt held by private investors.

Section 5

| YEAR | SIZE OF GOVERNMENT AS A PERCENT OF GDP[1] | | | | |
	EXPENDITURES	REVENUES	PURCHASES	NONDEFENSE	TRANSFER
1960	31.8	25.9	23.0	14.9	5.3
1961	33.2	25.9	23.8	15.7	5.9
1962	33.2	26.1	24.1	15.8	5.6
1963	33.1	26.6	23.9	15.8	5.6
1964	32.4	25.5	23.4	15.7	5.3
1965	31.8	25.5	22.9	15.4	5.3
1966	32.7	26.2	23.7	15.6	5.3
1967	34.8	26.5	25.0	16.1	6.0
1968	35.2	28.1	24.9	16.0	6.4
1969	33.6	28.1	23.6	15.5	6.3
1970	35.1	27.0	23.6	16.0	7.2
1971	35.2	26.4	23.1	16.0	7.9
1972	34.8	27.5	22.5	15.9	8.0
1973	33.8	27.7	21.4	15.5	8.1
1974	35.2	28.2	22.2	16.4	8.8
1975	37.2	26.5	22.7	17.1	10.1
1976	35.8	27.3	21.6	16.4	9.8
1977	34.7	27.6	20.9	15.9	9.4
1978	33.8	27.7	20.3	15.5	8.9
1979	33.6	28.0	20.0	15.3	9.0
1980	35.5	28.2	20.6	15.7	9.8
1981	35.7	28.9	20.4	15.3	9.9
1982	37.9	28.4	21.2	15.7	10.6
1983	37.8	27.7	21.0	15.6	10.5
1984	36.6	27.8	20.4	15.1	9.8
1985	37.1	28.2	20.9	15.6	9.7
1986	37.5	28.4	21.2	15.9	9.7
1987	37.2	29.1	21.2	15.8	9.5
1988	36.3	28.9	20.5	15.3	9.4
1989	36.2	29.0	20.4	15.3	9.5
1990	36.9	28.9	20.7	15.8	9.9
1991	37.7	28.8	21.0	16.0	10.2
1992	38.4	28.5	20.6	15.9	11.6
1993	37.7	28.6	19.9	15.5	11.7
1994	36.5	28.9	19.2	15.2	11.5
1995	36.5	29.2	18.9	15.2	11.5
1996	35.7	29.7	18.5	14.9	11.5
1997	34.6	30.0	18.1	14.7	11.1
1998	33.6	30.4	17.8	14.6	10.8
1999	33.1	30.4	17.9	14.7	10.5
2000	32.6	30.8	17.8	14.8	10.4
2001	33.7	29.7	18.4	15.4	11.0
2002	34.6	27.3	19.1	15.8	11.6
2003	35.0	26.7	19.3	15.7	11.8
2004	34.7	26.8	19.2	15.6	11.7
2005	34.7	28.2	19.0	15.4	11.7
2006	34.8	29.1	19.1	15.5	11.8
2007	35.5	29.2	19.3	15.7	12.1
2008	37.2	27.7	20.4	16.4	13.0
2009	40.6	25.8	21.4	17.2	15.1
2010	40.8	26.1	21.2	16.9	15.4
2011	39.7	26.3	20.3	16.1	15.0
2012	38.4	26.4	19.5	15.5	14.7

Source: http://www.bea.gov

[1]There are some differences across reporting agencies with regard to accounting procedures and the treatment of government enterprises. This results in some differences in statistical measures of the size of government.

Section 6

Year	Top 1	Top 5	Top 10	Next 40	Bottom 50
1980	19.1	36.8	49.3	43.7	7.0
1981	17.6	35.1	48.0	44.6	7.5
1982	19.0	36.1	48.6	44.1	7.3
1983	20.3	37.3	49.7	43.1	7.2
1984	21.1	38.0	50.6	42.1	7.4
1985	21.8	38.8	51.5	41.4	7.2
1986	25.7	42.6	54.7	38.9	6.5
1987	24.8	43.3	55.6	38.3	6.1
1988	27.6	45.6	57.3	37.0	5.7
1989	25.2	43.9	55.8	38.4	5.8
1990	25.1	43.6	55.4	38.8	5.8
1991	24.8	43.4	55.8	38.7	5.5
1992	27.5	45.9	58.0	36.9	5.1
1993	29.0	47.4	59.2	36.0	4.8
1994	28.9	47.5	59.4	35.8	4.8
1995	30.3	48.9	60.7	34.6	4.6
1996	32.3	51.0	62.5	33.2	4.3
1997	33.2	51.9	63.2	32.5	4.3
1998	34.8	53.8	65.0	30.8	4.2
1999	36.2	55.5	66.5	29.5	4.0
2000	37.4	56.5	67.3	28.8	3.9
2001	33.9	53.3	64.9	31.1	4.0
2002	33.7	53.8	65.7	30.8	3.5
2003	34.3	54.4	65.8	30.7	3.5
2004	36.9	57.1	68.2	28.5	3.3
2005	39.4	59.7	70.3	26.6	3.1
2006	39.9	60.1	70.8	26.2	3.0
2007	40.4	60.6	71.2	25.9	2.9
2008	38.0	58.7	70.0	27.3	2.7
2009	36.7	58.7	70.5	27.3	2.3

APPENDIX B

Answers to Selected Critical Analysis Questions

CHAPTER 1: THE ECONOMIC APPROACH

4. For most taxpayers, the change will reduce the after-tax cost of raising children. Other things being constant, one would predict an increase in the birthrate.

5. False. Intentions do not change the effect of the policy. If the policy runs counter to sound economics, it will lead to a counterproductive outcome even if that was not the intention of the policy. Bad policies are often advocated by people with good intentions.

8. Money has nothing to do with whether an individual is economizing. Any time a person chooses, in an attempt to achieve a goal, he or she is economizing.

9. Positive economics can help one better understand the likely effects of alternative policies. This will help one choose alternatives that are less likely to lead to disappointing results.

10. Association is not causation. It is likely that a large lead, near the end of the game, caused the third team to play more, rather than the third team causing the lead.

14. This is a question that highlights the importance of marginal analysis. In responding to the question, think about the following. After pollution has already been reduced substantially, how much will it cost to reduce it still more? If the quality of air and water were already high, how much gain would result from still less pollution?

CHAPTER 2: SOME TOOLS OF THE ECONOMIST

2. This is an opportunity cost question. Even though the productivity of brush painters has changed only slightly, rising productivity in other areas has led to higher wages in other occupations, thereby increasing the opportunity cost of being a house painter. Because people would not supply house-painting services unless they were able to meet their opportunity costs, higher wages are necessary to attract house painters from competitive (alternative) lines of work.

8. Yes. This question highlights the incentive of individuals to conserve for the future when they have private ownership rights. The market value of the land will increase in anticipation of the future harvest as the trees grow and the expected day of harvest grows closer. Thus, with transferable private property, the tree farmer will be able to capture the value added by his planting and holding the trees for a few years, even if the actual harvest does not take place until well after his death.

9. In general, it sanctions all forms of competition except for the use of violence (or the threat of violence), theft, or fraud.

12. Those who get tickets at the lower price gain, whereas those who are prevented from offering a higher price to ticket holders may not get a ticket even though both the prospective buyer and some ticket holders would have gained from the exchange at the higher price. Ticket holders may simply break the law or may sell at the regulated price only to buyers willing to provide them with other favors. Price controls, if they are effective, always reduce the gains from trade.

17. The opportunity cost of those individuals will rise, and they will likely consume less leisure.

CHAPTER 3: SUPPLY, DEMAND, AND THE MARKET PROCESS

1. Choices (a) and (b) would increase the demand for beef; (c) and (d) would affect primarily the supply of beef, rather than the demand; (e) leads to a change in quantity demanded, not a change in demand.

4. Prices reflect marginal value, not total value. The marginal value of a good is the maximum amount a consumer would be willing to pay for a specific unit. The height of the

demand curve reflects the value that consumers place on each unit. The total value is the total benefit consumers derive from all units consumed. The area under the demand curve for the number of units consumed reflects the total value. Water provides an example of a good with high total value but low marginal value. With regard to the last question, are there more nurses or professional wrestlers?

8. Neither markets nor the political process leaves the determination of winners and losers to chance. Under market organization, business winners and losers are determined by the decentralized choices of millions of consumers who use their dollar votes to reward firms that provide preferred goods at a low cost and penalize others who fail to do so. Under political decision-making, the winners and losers are determined by political officials who use taxes, subsidies, regulations, and mandates to favor some businesses and penalize others.

10. **a.** Profitable production increases the value of resources owned by people and leads to mutual gain for resource suppliers, consumers, and entrepreneurs. **b.** Losses reduce the value of resources, which reduces the well-being of at least some people. There is no conflict.

12. The supply curve is constructed under the assumption that other things are held constant. A reduction in the supply of oranges such as would occur under adverse weather conditions would lead to both a higher price and smaller total quantity supplied. This is perfectly consistent with economic theory.

CHAPTER 4: SUPPLY AND DEMAND: APPLICATIONS AND EXTENSIONS

1. An increase in demand for housing will also increase the demand for the resources required for its production, including the services of carpenters, plumbers, and electricians. This will lead to higher wages and an increase in employment for people in these groups.

4. Agreement of both buyer and seller is required for an exchange. Price ceilings push prices below equilibrium and thereby reduce the quantity sellers are willing to offer. Price floors push prices above equilibrium and thereby reduce the quantity consumers wish to buy. Both decrease the actual quantity traded in the market.

6. **a.** Decreases; **b.** Increases; **c.** Decreases; **d.** Increases

11. The deadweight loss is the loss of the potential gains of buyers and sellers emanating from trades that are squeezed out by the tax. It is an excess burden because even though the exchanges that are squeezed out by the tax impose a cost on buyers and sellers, they do not generate tax revenue (because the trades do not take place).

12. The employment level of low-skilled workers with large families would decline. Some would attempt to conceal the presence of their large family in order to get a job.

14. No. As the tax rate approaches the revenue maximum point, the higher rates substantially reduce the number of trades that take place. This is why the higher rates do not raise much additional revenue. As rates increase toward the revenue maximum point, the lost gains from trade are large and the additions to revenue are small. Thus, rates in this range are highly inefficient.

CHAPTER 5: DIFFICULT CASES FOR THE MARKET, AND THE ROLE OF GOVERNMENT

1. When payment is not demanded for services, potential customers have a strong incentive to attempt a "free ride." However, when the number of nonpaying customers becomes such that the sales revenues of sellers are diminished (and in some cases eliminated), the sellers' incentive to supply the good is thereby reduced (or eliminated).

9. By reducing output below the efficient level, sellers of toasters would no longer produce or exchange some units of the good, despite the fact that the consumers value the marginal units more than it costs to produce them.

11. A public good reflects the characteristics of the good, not the sector in which it is provided. Elementary education is not a public good because it is relatively easy to exclude nonpaying customers and to establish a one-to-one link between payment for and receipt of the good.

CHAPTER 6: THE ECONOMICS OF POLITICAL ACTION

2. Corporate officers, although they surely care about the next few months and the profits during that time, also care about the value of the firm and its stock price. If the stock price rises sufficiently in the next few months—as it will if investors believe that current investments in future-oriented projects (planting new trees, for example) are sound—then the officers will find their jobs secure even if current profits do not look good. Rights to the profits from those (future) trees are salable now in the form of the corporation's stock. There is no such mechanism to make the distant fruits of today's investments available to the political entrepreneurs who might otherwise fight for the future-oriented project. Only if the project appeals to today's voters, and only if they are willing to pay today for tomorrow's benefits, will the program be a political success. In any case, the wealth of the political official is not directly enhanced by his or her successful fight for the project.

4. The problem is not so much that the "wrong guys" won the last election as it is the incentive structure confronted by political decision-makers. Even if the "right people" were elected, they would be unlikely to improve the efficiency of government, at least not very much, given the strong incentive to support special-interest and shortsighted policies and the weak incentives for operational efficiency when decisions are made by the political process.

8. It is difficult for the voter to know what a candidate will do once elected, and the rationally ignorant voter is usually unwilling to spend the time and effort required to understand issues because the probability that any single vote will decide the issue is exceedingly small. Special-interest voters, in contrast, will know which candidate has promised them the most on their issue. Also, the candidate who is both competent and prepared to ignore special interests will have a hard time getting these facts to voters without financial support from special-interest groups. Each voter has an incentive to be a "free rider" on the "good government" issue. Interestingly, controlling government on behalf of society as a whole is a public good. As in the case of other public goods, there is a tendency for too little of it to be supplied.

10. No. The government is merely an alternative form of organization. Government organization does not permit us to escape either scarcity or competition. It merely affects the nature of the competition. Political competition (for example, voting, lobbying, political contributions, and politically determined budgets) replaces market competition. Neither is there any reason to believe that government organization modifies the importance of personal self-interest.

12. When the welfare of a special-interest group conflicts with that of a widely dispersed, unorganized majority, the legislative political process can reasonably be expected to work to the benefit of the special interest.

CHAPTER 7: CONSUMER CHOICE AND ELASTICITY

2. If your opportunity cost of time is more than $15, it will make sense to take the plane. Thus, Kathy will take the bus and Rachel the plane.

3. It is likely that the income effect of cigarette price changes is much larger for low-income smokers than for high-income smokers, perhaps because expenditures on

cigarettes are a larger proportion of the household budget for those with lower incomes. Thus, the income effect will be larger for this group.

6. Both income and time constrain our ability to consume. Because, in a wealthier society, time becomes more binding and income less binding, time-saving actions will be more common in a wealthier society. As we engage in time-saving actions (fast food, automatic appliances, air travel, and so on) in order to shift the time restraint outward, our lives become more hectic.

10. The answer to the first question is "No." Even for things we like, we will experience diminishing returns. Eventually, the cost of additional units of pizza will exceed their benefits. And, in answer to the second question, perfection in any activity is generally not worth the cost. For example, reading every page of this text three, four, or five times may improve your grade, but it may not be worth it. One function of a text is to structure the material (highlighted points, layout of graphs, and so on) so that the reader will be able to learn quickly (at a lower cost).

11. Carole

12. **a.** −0.33; inelastic **b.** −1.67 elastic

CHAPTER 8: COSTS AND THE SUPPLY OF GOODS

2. **a.** The amount paid for the course is a sunk cost. It is not directly relevant to whether one should attend the lectures. **b.** There is an opportunity cost of one's house even if it is paid for. **c.** The decline in the price of the stock is a sunk cost and therefore it is not directly relevant to whether or not to sell at this time. **d.** There is an opportunity cost of public education even if it is provided free to the consumer.

5. True. If it could produce the output at a lower cost, its profit would be greater.

7. At low output, the firm's plant (a fixed cost) is underutilized, implying a high average cost. As output rises toward the designed output level, average cost falls, but then rises as the designed or optimal output for that size plant is surpassed and diminishing returns set in.

11. Because owners receive profits, clearly profit maximization is in their interest. Managers, if they are not owners, have no property right to profit and therefore no direct interest in profit maximization. Because a solid record of profitability tends to increase the market value (salary) of corporate managers, they do have an indirect incentive to pursue profits. However, corporate managers may also be interested in gaining power, having nice offices, hiring friends, expanding sales, and other activities, which may conflict with profitability. Thus, owners need to provide incentives for managers to seek profits and to monitor the results.

12. **a.** The interest payments; **b.** The interest income forgone. The tax structure encourages debt rather than equity financing because the firm's tax liability is inversely related to its debt–equity ratio.

14. Check list. Did your marginal cost curve cross the *ATC* and *AVC* curves at their low points? Does the vertical distance between the *ATC* and *AVC* curves get smaller and smaller as output increases? If not, redraw the three curves correctly. See Exhibit 6b.

17. $2,500: the $2,000 decline in market value during the year plus $500 of potential interest on funds that could be obtained if the machine were sold new. Costs associated with the decline in the value of the machine last year are sunk costs.

18. Because they believe they will be able to restructure the firm and provide better management so that the firm will have positive net earnings in the future. If the firm is purchased at a low enough price, this will allow the new owners to cover the opportunity cost of their investment and still earn an economic profit. Alternatively, they may expect to sell off the firm's assets, receiving more net revenue than the cost of purchasing the firm.

CHAPTER 9: PRICE TAKERS AND THE COMPETITIVE PROCESS

1. In a highly competitive industry such as agriculture, lower resource prices might improve the rate of profit in the short run, but in the long run, competition will drive prices down until economic profit is eliminated. Thus, lower resource prices will do little to improve the long-run profitability in such industries.

2. The market price will decline because the profits will attract new firms (and capital investment) into the market and supply will increase, driving down the price until the profits are eliminated.

5. **a.** Increase; **b.** Increase; **c.** Increase: firms will earn economic profit; **d.** Rise (compared with its initial level) if coffee is an increasing-cost industry, but return to initial price if it is a constant-cost industry; **e.** Increase even more than it did in the short run; **f.** Economic profit will return to zero.

6. **a.** Decline; **b.** Increase; **c.** Decline; **d.** Decline

9. Competition virtually forces firms to operate efficiently and produce goods and services that consumers value highly relative to cost. Firms that fail to do so will find it difficult to compete and eventually losses will drive them from the market.

11. **a.** The reduction in supply led to higher prices. **b.** Because demand is inelastic, the total revenue from sales increased. **c.** Overall, the profitability of farming increased, although some of the producers that were hardest hit by the drought experienced losses because of their sharp reduction in output.

15. **b.** Six or seven tons—$250 profit; **c.** seven or eight tons—$600 profit; **d.** five or six tons—$50 loss. Because the firm can cover its variable cost, it should stay in business if it believes that the low ($450) price is temporary.

CHAPTER 10: PRICE-SEARCHER MARKETS WITH LOW ENTRY BARRIERS

3. The amount of variety is determined by the willingness of consumers to pay for variety relative to the cost of providing it. If consumers value variety highly and the added costs of producing different styles, designs, and sizes is low, there will be a lot of variety. Alternatively, if consumers desire similar products, or if variation can be produced only at a high cost, little variety will be present. Apparently, consumers place a substantial value (relative to cost) on variety in napkins but not in toothpicks.

7. No. A firm that maximizes *total* revenue would expand output as long as marginal revenue is positive. When marginal costs are positive, the revenue-maximizing price would be lower (and the output greater) than the price that would maximize the firm's profits.

8. In any of these cases, the answer is competition. To survive, a given type and size of firm must be able to produce at a low cost. Those firms with high per-unit cost will be driven from the market.

10. Building the new resort is more risky (and less attractive) because if the market analysis is incorrect, and demand is insufficient, it probably will be difficult to find other uses for the newly built resort. If the airline proves unprofitable, however, the capital (airplanes) should be extremely mobile. However, the resort would have one offsetting advantage: If demand were stronger than expected, and profits larger, it would take competitors longer to enter the market (build a new resort), and they would be more reluctant to make the more permanent investment.

12. In a competitive setting, only the big firms will survive if economies of scale are important. When economies of scale are unimportant, small firms will be able to compete effectively.

14. Competition provides the answer. If McDonald's fails to provide an attractively priced, tasty sandwich with a smile, people will turn to Burger King, Wendy's, Dairy Queen, and other rivals. If Walmart does not provide convenience and value, people will turn to Kmart, Target, and other retailers. Similarly, as recent experience has shown, even a firm as large as General Motors will lose customers to Ford, Honda, Toyota, Chrysler, Volkswagen, and other automobile manufacturers if it fails to please the customer as much as rival suppliers do.

17. **a.** Total revenue: $0; $8,000; $14,000; $18,000; $20,000; $20,000; Total cost: $0; $5,000; $10,000; $15,000; $20,000; $25,000; Economic profit: $0; $3,000; $4,000; $3,000; $0; $5,000 (loss). **b.** Marginal revenue: $8,000; $6,000; $4,000; $2,000; $0; Marginal cost: $5,000; $5,000; $5,000; $5,000; $5,000. **c.** Profit-maximizing price: $7,000. **d.** Rod will sell two boats at the profit-maximizing price of $7,000. **e.** Rod's economic profits will be $4,000 per week. Sales volume will be 2. **f.** Yes, boats 1 and 2 are the only boats for which marginal revenue is higher than marginal cost. **g.** Because of the existence of economic profit, more boat dealers will open up in the area. This will result in more competition and lower prices. The entry will continue until boat dealers' economic profits fall to zero. **h.** When demand is elastic, lowering price increases total revenue; thus, Rod's demand is elastic between the prices of $9,000 and $5,000. When demand is unitary elastic, lowering price leaves revenue unchanged; thus, Rod's demand is unitary elastic between the prices of $5,000 and $4,000. One could also assume that Rod's demand would eventually become inelastic below a price of $4,000 because the elasticity of demand keeps falling as one moves down along a demand curve. When this happens, Rod's total revenue will begin to fall as he continues to lower price. For example, at a price of $3,000, Rod may sell six boats per week, resulting in only $18,000 in revenue, which is less than the revenue Rod receives at a price of $4,000.

CHAPTER 11: PRICE-SEARCHER MARKETS WITH HIGH ENTRY BARRIERS

1. The statement is true. Profits cannot exist in the long run without barriers to entry because without barriers new entrants seeking the profits would increase supply, drive down price, and eliminate the profits. But barriers to entry are no guarantee of profits. Sufficient demand is also a necessary condition.

3. No; No; No.

8. Because use of product variation and quality improvements to obtain a larger share of the market will be more difficult to monitor and control than a simple price reduction.

11. Reductions in the cost of transportation generally increase competition because they force firms to compete with distant rivals and permit consumers to choose among a wider range of suppliers. As a result, the U.S. economy today is generally more competitive, in the rivalry sense, than it was hundred years ago.

12. The stock price, when the uncle bought the stock, no doubt reflected the well-known profits. The previous owners of the stock surely would not have sold it at a price that failed to reflect its high expected rate of future profit. Thus, there is no reason to believe that the stock purchase will earn a high rate of return for the uncle.

13. **a.** $15, profit = $140,000; **b.** $10.

CHAPTER 12: THE SUPPLY OF AND DEMAND FOR PRODUCTIVE RESOURCES

3. **a.** Five; **b.** $350; **c.** Four. The firm will operate in the short run, but it will go out of business in the long run unless the market prices rise.

4. Yes. General increases in the productivity of the labor force will cause a general increase in wages. The higher general wage rates will increase the opportunity cost of barbering and cause the supply of barbers to decline. The reduction in the supply of barbers will place upward pressure on the wages of barbers, even if technological change and worker productivity have changed little in barbering.

6. The job opportunities outside of teaching are more attractive for people with math and science training than for those with English and history degrees. Therefore, the same salary that attracts a substantial number of English and history teachers will be insufficient to attract the required number of math and science teachers.

8. No. The dressmaker needs to employ more capital and less labor because the marginal dollar expenditures on the former are currently increasing output by a larger amount than the latter.

12. **a.** MP 14; 12; 11; 9; 7; 5; 4. TR 70; 130; 185; 230; 265; 290; 310. MRP 70; 60; 55; 45; 35; 25; 20. **b.** 4; **c.** Employment would decline to 3.

CHAPTER 13: EARNINGS, PRODUCTIVITY, AND THE JOB MARKET

2. U.S. workers are more productive. By investing in human capital, the laborers are somewhat responsible, but the superior tools and physical capital that are available to U.S. workers also contribute to their higher wages.

6. Although this statement, often made by politicians, sounds true, in fact, it is false. Output of goods and services valued by consumers, not jobs, is the key to economic progress and a high standard of living. Real income cannot be high unless real output is high. If job creation were the key to economic progress, it would be easy to create millions of jobs. For example, we could prohibit the use of farm machinery. Such a prohibition would create millions of jobs in agriculture. However, it would also reduce output and our standard of living.

9. False. Several additional factors, including differences in preferences (which would influence time worked, the trade-off between money wage and working conditions, and evaluation of alternative jobs), differences in jobs, and imperfect labor mobility, would result in variations in earnings.

11. Hourly wages will be highest in B because the higher wages will be necessary to compensate workers in B for the uncertainty and loss of income during layoffs. Annual earnings will be higher in A in order to compensate workers in A for the additional hours they will work during the year.

CHAPTER 14: INVESTMENT, THE CAPITAL MARKET, AND THE WEALTH OF NATIONS

1. All the changes would increase interest rates in the United States.

4. No. The average outstanding balance during the year is only about half of $1,000. Therefore, the $200 interest charge translates to almost a 40 percent annual rate of interest.

6. *Hints:* Which has been considered to be more risky—purchasing a bond or a stock? How does risk influence the expected rate of return?

8. 6 percent.

10. **a.** Mike; **b.** Yes, people who save a lot are able to get a higher interest rate on their savings as the result of people with a high rate of time preference; **c.** Yes, people who want to borrow money will be able to do so at a lower rate when there are more people (like Alicia) who want to save a lot.

11. They are helped. This question is a lot like prior questions involving Alicia and Mike. Potential gains from trade are present. If obstacles do not restrain trade, the

low-income countries will be able to attract savings (from countries with a high saving rate) at a lower interest rate than would exist in the absence of trade. Similarly, people in the high-income countries will be able to earn a higher return than would otherwise be possible. Each can gain because of the existence of the other.

12. **a.** Approximately $1.277 million; **b.** Yes; **c.** The lottery earnings are less liquid. Because there is not a well-organized market transforming lottery earnings into present income, the transaction costs of finding a "buyer" (at a price equal to the present value of the earnings) for the lottery earnings "rights" may be higher than for the bond, if one wants to sell in the future.

14. No. The present value of the $500 annual additions to earnings during the next ten years is less than the cost of the schooling.

16. Consider the following when answering this question: Whose money is being invested by each of the two entities? If a private investment project goes bad, who is hurt? If a private project is successful, who reaps the gain? Answer the same two questions for political officials.

CHAPTER 15: INCOME INEQUALITY AND POVERTY

2. Differences in family size, age of potential workers, nonmoney "income," taxes, and cost-of-living among areas reduce the effectiveness of annual money income as a measure of economic status. In general, high-income families are larger, are more likely to be headed by a prime-age worker, have less nonmoney income (including leisure), pay more taxes, and reside in higher-cost-of-living areas (particularly large cities). Thus, money income comparison between high- and low-income groups often overstates the economic status of the former relative to the latter.

4. If there were no intergenerational mobility, the diagonal numbers would all be 100 percent. If there were complete equality of opportunity and outcomes, the numbers in each column and row would be 20 percent.

6. No. The increase in marginal tax rates will reduce the incentive of the poor to earn income. Therefore, their income will rise by $1,000 minus the reduction in their personal earnings due to the disincentive effects of the higher marginal tax rates.

7. 67 percent

CHAPTER 16: GAINING FROM INTERNATIONAL TRADE

2. Availability of goods and services, not jobs, is the source of economic prosperity. When a good can be purchased cheaper abroad than it can be produced at home, a nation can expand the quantity of goods and services available for consumption by specializing in the production of those goods for which it is a low-cost producer and trading them for the cheap (relative to domestic costs) foreign goods. Trade restrictions limiting the ability of Americans to purchase low-cost goods from foreigners stifle this process and thereby reduce the living standard of Americans.

4. Statements (a) and (b) are not in conflict. Because trade restrictions are typically a special-interest issue, political entrepreneurs can often gain by supporting them even when they promote economic inefficiency.

6. True. The primary effect of trade restrictions is an increase in domestic scarcity. This has distributional consequences, but it is clear that, as a whole, a nation will be harmed by the increased domestic scarcity that accompanies the trade restraints.

10. In thinking about this issue, consider the following points. Suppose that the Japanese were willing to give products such as automobiles, electronic goods, and clothing to us free of charge. Would we be worse off if we accepted the gifts? Should we try to keep the free goods out? What is the source of real income—jobs or goods and services? If the gifts make us better off, doesn't it follow that partial gifts would also make us better off?

12. Although trade reduces employment in import-competing industries, it expands employment in export industries. On balance, there is no reason to believe that trade

either promotes or destroys jobs. The major effect of trade is to permit individuals, states, regions, and nations to generate a larger output by specializing in the things they do well and trading for those things that they would produce only at a high cost. A higher real income is the result.

16. True. If country A imposes a tariff, other countries will sell less to A and therefore acquire less purchasing power in terms of A's currency. Thus, they will have to reduce their purchases of A's export goods.

SPECIAL TOPIC 1: GOVERNMENT SPENDING AND TAXATION

1. Taxes reduce economic efficiency because they eliminate some exchanges and thereby reduce the gains from these transactions. Because of (a) the deadweight losses accompanying the elimination of exchanges and (b) the cost of collecting taxes, the costs of additional tax revenue will be greater than the revenue transferred to the government. Studies indicate that it costs between $1.20 and $1.30 for each dollar of tax revenue raised by the government.

5. As we discussed in Chapter 6, the political process works better when there is a close relationship between who pays for and who benefits from government programs. An increase in the number of people who pay no income taxes is likely to weaken this relationship. Whereas those with low incomes pay payroll taxes, the revenues from this tax are earmarked for the finance of the Social Security and Medicare programs. Thus, expansions in government are financed primarily by the personal income tax. In the future, exemption of large numbers of people from this tax is likely to make it more difficult to control the growth of government. If you do not have to help pay for more government spending, why would you oppose it?

SPECIAL TOPIC 2: THE ECONOMICS OF SOCIAL SECURITY

2. The pay-as-you-go Social Security system is facing a crisis because the inflow of tax revenue is insufficient to cover the promised benefits. Although the Social Security Trust Fund has bonds, they are merely an IOU from the Treasury to the Social Security Administration. To redeem these bonds and provide additional funds to finance Social Security benefits, the federal government will have to raise taxes (or pay the interest on additional Treasury bonds it sells), or cut other expenditures, or both. Thus, the presence of the SSTF bonds does not do much to alleviate the crisis.

SPECIAL TOPIC 3: THE STOCK MARKET: ITS FUNCTION, PERFORMANCE, AND POTENTIAL AS AN INVESTMENT OPPORTUNITY

1. History shows that in the U.S. stock market, fairly high returns can be gained at a relatively low risk by people who hold a diverse portfolio of stocks in unrelated industries for a period of twenty years or more. An indexed equity mutual fund is an option that would allow a person to purchase a diverse portfolio while keeping commission costs low.

3. The expectation of high profits in the future drove up the price of the stock, despite the lack of a dividend payment in the first years of the firm. Investors are equally happy with high dividends or the equivalent in rising stock value due to the firm's retaining its profits for further investment.

5. Investors are buying such a stock for its rising value (price), which reflects expected future earnings and dividends.

SPECIAL TOPIC 4: GREAT DEBATES IN ECONOMICS: KEYNES VERSUS HAYEK

1. Keynes is arguing that it does not matter much how the government spends stimulus funds. According to the Keynesian view, the key consideration is to spend the funds so they will generate income for those undertaking the project, and as those funds are spent, a multiple expansion in income and aggregate demand will result.

SPECIAL TOPIC 5: THE CRISIS OF 2008: CAUSES AND LESSONS FOR THE FUTURE

3. The less equity the owner has in his or her house, the more likely he or she will default. This is particularly true in the United States because most home mortgages here are nonrecourse loans: The owner is not responsible for the debt beyond turning the property over to the lender in case of default. The lender has no legal claim on assets of the borrower beyond the asset that was mortgaged. Thus, when the value of a house falls below the outstanding loan, the borrower will often gain by simply abandoning the property. This is precisely what many have done in recent years.

5. The incentive to evaluate the borrower's creditworthiness carefully is reduced. If the mortgage originator had to keep the loan until it was repaid, there would be greater incentive for the lender to evaluate the creditworthiness of the borrower more diligently.

SPECIAL TOPIC 6: LESSONS FROM THE GREAT DEPRESSION

5. The statement reflects a failure to recognize the secondary effects of limiting imports. If we buy less from foreigners, they will have fewer dollars that are required for the purchase of our exports. Therefore, a reduction in imports will also reduce exports and there is no reason to expect any net increase in employment. Instead, trade restraints lead to less output and lower incomes.

SPECIAL TOPIC 7: THE ECONOMICS OF HEALTH CARE

2. Health insurance benefits are a component of the employee's compensation package. Unless the employer values the services of the employee by an amount greater than or equal to the total cost of the employee's compensation, the worker will not be hired. Thus, like other components of the compensation package, health insurance benefits are earned by employees.

4. Medicare and Medicaid increased both total health care spending and the share of that spending paid by a third party. Both of these factors increased the demand for and prices of medical services, thereby making them more expensive for people who do not qualify for these programs.

6. Personal choices exert a major impact on health care expenditures. Individuals who smoke, consume alcohol, and eat excessively; fail to exercise and control their weight; use recreational drugs; and engage in other risky behavior will have higher health care costs. Under systems in which all are charged the same premium, the incentive

to adopt a healthy lifestyle is reduced. Persons who make choices that promote good health are forced to subsidize those who do not. This perverse incentive structure also pushes health care costs upward.

8. The incentive to purchase insurance when you are healthy will be reduced.

SPECIAL TOPIC 8: EARNINGS DIFFERENCES BETWEEN MEN AND WOMEN

2. **a.** The average years of work experience of women relative to men would decline because many of the women entering the labor force would have little prior work experience. **b.** The average hours of work of women would also decline because many of the married women would be looking for part-time employment and hours that were complementary with their historic household responsibilities. **c.** The increased labor force participation of married women would cause the female–male earnings ratio to fall.

4. Not necessarily. Compared with married men, single men tend to be younger, have fewer dependents, be more likely to drop out of the labor force, and be less likely to receive earnings-enhancing assistance from another person. All these factors will reduce their earnings relative to married men.

SPECIAL TOPIC 9: DO LABOR UNIONS INCREASE THE WAGES OF WORKERS?

1. If the union is able to raise the wages of the farm workers: (a) The cost of Florida oranges will rise, causing supply to decline and price to rise in the long run; (b) profits of the Florida orange growers will decline in the short run, but in the long run they will return to the normal rate; (c) mechanization will be encouraged; and (d) the employment of fruit pickers will decline—particularly in the long run.

3. If only part of an industry is unionized, if the union pushes up the wages of the unionized firms, this will increase their cost and make it difficult for them to compete effectively with their nonunion rivals. Thus, the union will be unable to increase wages much without experiencing a substantial reduction in the employment of its members.

5. False. Competition constrains both employers and employees. Employers must compete with other employers for labor services. To gain the labor services of an employee, an employer must offer a compensation package superior to one that the employee can get elsewhere. If the employer does not offer a superior package, the employee will work for a rival employer or choose self-employment. Similarly, employees must compete with other employees. Therefore, their ability to demand whatever wage they would like is also restrained. Thus, competition prevents both the payment of low (below-market) wages by employers and the imposition of high (above-market) wages by employees.

6. Not necessarily. Adjustment must be made for differences in (a) the productivity characteristics of the union and nonunion workers and (b) the types of jobs they occupy (for example, work environment, job security, likelihood of layoff, and so on). Adjustment for these factors may either increase or reduce the $1.50 differential.

7. Remember, union members compete with other workers, including less-skilled workers. An increase in the minimum wage makes unskilled, low-wage workers more expensive. A higher minimum wage increases the demand for high-skilled employees who are good substitutes for the low-skilled workers. Union members are overrepresented among the high-skilled group helped by an increase in the minimum wage. Therefore, although union leaders will generally pitch their support for a higher minimum wage in terms of a desire that all workers be paid a "decent wage," the effect

of the legislation on union members suggests that self-interest rather than altruism underlies their support for the legislation.

SPECIAL TOPIC 10: THE QUESTION OF RESOURCE EXHAUSTION

2. When demand expands in resource markets, prices send signals and provide the incentives that will reduce future demand relative to supply. These forces will avoid lasting shortages.

5. If any resource, including water, is bought and sold, then market signals will automatically be provided to signal the desires of users to have, and the abilities of suppliers to supply, more. A market provides productive incentive to all concerned. Users conserve more when a market price rises, suppliers provide more, and there is greater incentive to develop and use substitutes for the higher priced resource. If markets are not used to allocate a resource, these benefits will be lost.

SPECIAL TOPIC 11: DIFFICULT ENVIRONMENTAL CASES AND THE ROLE OF GOVERNMENT

1. The ITQ would allow fishers to fish at their own speed without fear of losing their quota to others.

3. The cost of stopping the buildup would be very large. Avoiding the buildup would be very costly. That large opportunity cost could accomplish instead much else that would help future generations. The forecasted risks are only speculatively the result of the buildup and would occur mostly far in the future. And a warmer world has advantages as well as disadvantages.

4. In a market with strong property rights in place, a polluter would have to be concerned about harming others and being sued by them for damages. Without strong property rights in place, regulation might help. Or it might not. In any case, regulators need information available only in a market to judge how tightly to regulate if the regulator is seeking efficiency.

MACROECONOMICS

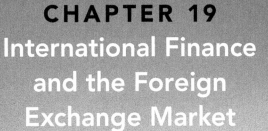

CHAPTER 19
International Finance and the Foreign Exchange Market

FOCUS

- What determines the exchange rate value of the dollar relative to other currencies? Why do exchange rates change?

- What are the alternative types of exchange rate systems? Which types work well and which will lead to financial problems?

- What information is included in the balance-of-payments accounts of a nation? Will the balance-of-payments accounts of a country always be in balance?

- Is a balance-of-trade deficit bad?

Currencies, like tomatoes and football tickets, have a price at which they are bought and sold. An exchange rate is the price of one currency in terms of another.
—Gary Smith[1]

[1]Gary Smith, *Macro Economics* (New York: W. H. Freeman, 1985), 514.

Trade across national boundaries is complicated by the fact that nations generally use different currencies to buy and sell goods in their respective domestic markets. The British use pounds; the Japanese, yen; the Mexicans, pesos; 18 European countries, the euro; and so on. Therefore, when a good or service is purchased from a seller in another country, it is generally necessary for someone to convert one currency to another.

As we previously discussed, the forces of supply and demand will determine the exchange rate value of currencies in the absence of government intervention. This chapter focuses more directly on the foreign exchange market. We will consider how exchange rates both exert an impact on and are influenced by the flow of trade and the flow of capital across national boundaries. We will also analyze alternative exchange rate regimes and consider some of the recent changes in the structure of currency markets around the world.

©iStockphoto.com/nicoolay

19-1 FOREIGN EXCHANGE MARKET

Foreign exchange market
The market in which the currencies of different countries are bought and sold.

When trading parties live in different countries, an exchange will often involve a currency transaction. Currency transactions take place in the foreign exchange market, the market where currencies of different countries are bought and sold. Suppose that you own a sporting goods shop in the United States and are preparing to place an order for athletic shoes. You can purchase them from either a domestic or foreign manufacturer. If you decide to purchase the shoes from a British firm, either you will have to change dollars into pounds at a bank and send them to the British producer or the British manufacturer will have to go to a bank and change your dollar check into pounds. In either case, purchasing the British shoes will involve an exchange of dollars for pounds.

Exchange rate
The domestic price of one unit of foreign currency. For example, if it takes $1.80 to purchase one English pound, the dollar–pound exchange rate is 1.80.

Suppose the British producer has offered to supply the shoes for 30 pounds per pair. How can you determine whether this price is high or low? To compare the price of the British-supplied shoes with the price of those produced domestically, you must know the exchange rate between the dollar and the pound. *The exchange rate is one of the most important prices because it enables consumers in one country to translate the prices of foreign goods into units of their own currency. Specifically, the dollar price of a foreign good is determined by multiplying the foreign product price by the exchange rate (the dollar price per unit of the foreign currency).* For example, if it takes $1.80 to obtain 1 pound, then the British shoes priced at 30 pounds would cost $54 (30 times the $1.80 price of the pound).

Suppose the exchange rate is $1.80 = 1 pound and that you decide to buy 200 pairs of athletic shoes from the British manufacturer at 30 pounds ($54) per pair. You will need 6,000 pounds in order to pay the British manufacturer. If you contact an American bank that handles foreign exchange transactions and write the bank a check for $10,800 (the $1.80 exchange rate multiplied by 6,000), it will supply the 6,000 pounds. The bank will typically charge a small fee for handling the transaction.

Where does the American bank get the pounds? The bank obtains the pounds from British importers who want dollars to buy things from Americans. Note that the U.S. demand for foreign currencies (such as the pound) is generated by the demand of Americans for things purchased from foreigners. In contrast, the supply of foreign currencies in exchange for dollars reflects the demand of foreigners for things bought from Americans.

Exhibit 1 presents data on the exchange rate—the cents required to purchase a European euro, Japanese yen, British pound, and Canadian dollar—from 1990 to 2013. Under the flexible rate system present in most industrial countries, the exchange rate between currencies changes from day to day and even from hour to hour. The exchange rate figures for years prior to 2013 are the average for the year. The 2013 figures are for exchange rates as of May 31, 2013.

Appreciation
An increase in the value of the domestic currency relative to foreign currencies. An appreciation makes foreign goods cheaper for domestic residents.

An appreciation in the value of a nation's currency means that fewer units of the currency are now required to purchase one unit of a foreign currency. For example, as Exhibit 1 shows, it took 151.85 cents to purchase a British pound in 2013, down from

EXHIBIT 1

Foreign Exchange Rates, 1990–2013

Year	Euro	Japanese Yen	British Pound	Canadian Dollar	Index of Exchange Rate Value of the Dollar[a] (26 Currencies)
1990	—	0.690	178.41	85.7	71.4
1992	—	0.789	176.63	82.7	76.9
1994	—	0.979	153.19	73.2	90.9
1996	—	0.919	156.07	73.3	97.5
1998	—	0.763	165.73	67.4	115.9
2000	92.3	0.928	151.56	67.3	119.6
2001	89.5	0.823	143.96	64.6	126.1
2002	94.5	0.799	150.25	63.7	126.8
2003	113.2	0.863	163.47	71.4	119.3
2004	124.4	0.925	183.30	76.8	113.8
2005	124.5	0.908	182.04	82.5	110.8
2006	125.6	0.860	184.34	88.2	108.7
2007	137.1	0.849	200.20	93.2	103.6
2008	147.3	0.967	185.45	93.8	99.9
2009	139.4	1.067	156.61	87.6	105.7
2010	132.6	1.139	154.52	97.1	101.8
2011	139.3	1.255	160.43	101.1	97.2
2012	128.6	1.253	158.53	100.1	99.8
2013	129.9	0.992	151.85	96.7	101.9

[a]2013 figures are as of May 31, 2013.
Source: http://research.stlouisfed.org/fred2/

185.45 cents in 2008. Thus, the dollar appreciated against the pound during this period. As the result of this appreciation, goods purchased from British suppliers became less expensive to Americans.[2] At the same time, the prices of American goods to British consumers moved in the opposite direction. An appreciation of the U.S. dollar relative to the British pound is the same thing as a depreciation in the British pound relative to the dollar.

When a depreciation occurs, it will take more units of the domestic currency to purchase a unit of foreign currency. During the 2002–2008 period, the dollar depreciated against all of the major currencies (see Exhibit 1). In 2008, it took 185.45 cents to purchase a British pound, up from 143.96 in 2001. Similarly, it took 147.3 cents to purchase a euro in 2008, up from only 89.5 in 2001. The number of cents required to purchase a Canadian dollar and a Japanese yen also increased during this time frame. As the number of cents required to purchase a unit of foreign currency increases, the dollar depreciates, and foreign goods become more expensive for Americans.

Exhibit 1 also provides an index of the foreign exchange value of the dollar against 26 major currencies. This broad index provides evidence on what is happening to the dollar's general exchange rate value.[3] An increase in the index implies an appreciation in the dollar, whereas a decline is indicative of a depreciation. Between 1996 and 2002, the dollar appreciated by approximately 30 percent against these twenty-six currencies. Between 2002 and 2013, however, the index indicates that the dollar depreciated by approximately

Depreciation
A reduction in the value of the domestic currency relative to foreign currencies. A depreciation makes foreign goods more expensive for domestic residents.

[2]Because an appreciation means a lower price of foreign currencies, some may think it looks like a depreciation. Just remember that a lower price of the foreign currency means that one's domestic currency will buy more units of the foreign currency and thus more goods and services from foreigners.
[3]In the construction of this index, the exchange rate of each currency relative to the dollar is weighted according to the proportion of U.S. trade with the country. For example, the index weights the U.S. dollar–Japanese yen exchange rate more heavily than the U.S. dollar–Swiss franc exchange rate because the volume of U.S. trade with Japan exceeds the volume of trade with Switzerland.

20 percent (down to 101.9 from 126.8) relative to this broad bundle of currencies. Frequently, people will use the terms *"strong"* and *"weak"* when referring to the exchange rate value of a currency. A currency is said to be strong when it has been appreciating in value, whereas a weak currency is one that has been depreciating on the foreign exchange market.

A pure flexible exchange rate system is one in which market forces alone determine the foreign exchange value of the currency. The exchange rate system in effect since 1973 might best be described as a managed flexible rate regime. It is flexible because all the major industrial countries allow the exchange rate value of their currencies to float. But the system is also "managed" because the major industrial nations have from time to time attempted to alter supply and demand in the foreign exchange market by buying and selling various currencies. Compared with the total size of this market, however, these transactions have generally been small. Thus, the exchange rate value of major currencies like the U.S. dollar, British pound, Japanese yen, and the European euro is determined primarily by market forces. Several countries link their currency to major currencies like the U.S. dollar or European euro. As we proceed, we will investigate alternative methods of linking currencies and analyze the operation of different regimes.

Flexible exchange rates
Exchange rates that are determined by the market forces of supply and demand. They are sometimes called floating exchange rates.

19-2 DETERMINANTS OF THE EXCHANGE RATE

To simplify our explanation of how the exchange rate is determined, let's assume that the United States and Great Britain are the only two countries in the world. When Americans buy and sell with each other, they use dollars. Therefore, American sellers will want to be paid in dollars. Similarly, when the British buy and sell with each other, they use pounds. As a result, British sellers will want to be paid in pounds.

In our two-country world, the demand for pounds in the exchange rate market originates from the purchases by Americans of British goods, services, and assets (both real and financial). For example, when U.S. residents purchase men's suits from a British manufacturer; travel in the United Kingdom; or purchase the stocks, bonds, or physical assets of British business firms, they demand pounds from (and supply dollars to) the foreign exchange market to pay for these items.

Correspondingly, the supply of foreign exchange (pounds in our two-country case) originates from sales by Americans to foreigners. When Americans sell goods, services, or assets to the British, for example, the British buyers will supply pounds (and demand dollars) in the exchange rate market in order to acquire the dollars to pay for the items purchased from Americans.[4]

Exhibit 2 illustrates the supply and demand curves of Americans for foreign exchange—British pounds in our two-country case. The demand for pounds is downward sloping because a lower dollar price of the pound—meaning a dollar will buy more pounds—makes British goods cheaper for American importers. The goods produced by one country are generally good substitutes for the goods of another country. This means that when foreign (British) goods become cheaper, Americans will increase their expenditures on imports (and therefore the quantity of pounds demanded will increase). Thus, as the dollar price of the pound declines, Americans will both buy more of the lower-priced (in dollars) British goods and demand more pounds, which are required for the purchases.

Similarly, the supply curve for pounds is dependent upon the sales by Americans to the British (i.e., the purchase of American goods by the British). An increase in the dollar price of the pound means that a pound will purchase more dollars and more goods priced in dollars. Thus, the price (in pounds) of American goods, services, and assets to British

---

[4]We analyze the foreign exchange market in terms of the demand for and supply of foreign currencies. Alternatively, this analysis could be done in terms of the supply of and demand for dollars. Because one currency is traded for another, the same actions that generate a demand for foreign exchange simultaneously generate a supply of dollars. Correspondingly, the same exchanges that create a supply of foreign currencies simultaneously generate a demand for dollars in the foreign exchange market.

EXHIBIT 2

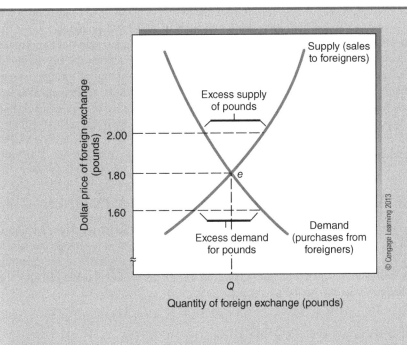

Equilibrium in the Foreign Exchange Market

The dollar price of the pound is measured on the vertical axis. The horizontal axis indicates the flow of pounds to the foreign exchange market. The equilibrium exchange rate is $1.80 = 1 pound. At the equilibrium price, the quantity of pounds demanded just equals the quantity supplied. On the one hand, a higher dollar price per pound ($2.00 = 1 pound) will lead to an excess supply of pounds, causing the dollar price of the pound to fall. On the other hand, a lower dollar price per pound ($1.60 = 1 pound) will result in an excess demand for pounds, causing the pound to appreciate.

purchasers declines as the dollar price of the pound increases. As this happens, the British will purchase more from Americans and therefore supply more pounds to the foreign exchange market. Thus, the supply curve for pounds will slope upward to the right.

As Exhibit 2 shows, equilibrium is present at the dollar price of the pound that brings the quantity demanded and quantity supplied of pounds into balance, $1.80 in this case. *The market-clearing price of $1.80 per pound not only equalizes demand and supply in the foreign exchange market but also equalizes (1) the value of U.S. purchases of items supplied by the British with (2) the value of items sold by U.S. residents to the British.* Demand and supply in the currency market are simply the mirror images of these two factors.

What would happen if the price of the pound were above equilibrium—$2.00 = 1 pound, for example? At the higher dollar price of the pound, British goods would be more expensive for Americans. Americans would cut back on their purchases of shoes, glassware, textile products, financial assets, and other items supplied by the British, and the quantity of pounds demanded by Americans would therefore decline. Simultaneously, the higher dollar price of the pound would make U.S. exports cheaper for the British. For example, an $18,000 American automobile would cost British consumers 10,000 pounds when 1 pound trades for $1.80, but it would cost only 9,000 pounds when 1 pound exchanges for $2.00. If the dollar price of the pound were $2.00, the British would supply more pounds to the foreign exchange market than Americans would demand. As you can see in Exhibit 2, this excess supply of pounds would cause the dollar price of the pound to decline until equilibrium is restored at the $1.80 = 1 pound price.

At a below-equilibrium price, such as $1.60 = 1 pound, an opposite set of forces would be present. The lower dollar price of the pound would make British goods cheaper for Americans and American goods more expensive for the British. At the $1.60 price for a pound, the purchases of Americans from the British would exceed their sales to them, leading to an excess demand for pounds. In turn, the excess demand would cause the dollar price of the pound to rise until equilibrium was restored at $1.80 = 1 pound.

The implications of the analysis are general. In our multicountry and multicurrency world, the demand for foreign currencies in exchange for dollars reflects the purchases by Americans of goods, services, and assets from foreigners. The supply of foreign currencies in exchange for dollars reflects the sales by Americans of goods, services, and assets to foreigners. The equilibrium exchange rate will bring the quantity of foreign exchange demanded by Americans into balance with the quantity supplied by foreigners. It will also bring the purchases by Americans from foreigners into balance with the sales by Americans to foreigners.

19-3 WHY DO EXCHANGE RATES CHANGE?

When exchange rates are free to fluctuate, the market value of a nation's currency will appreciate and depreciate in response to changing market conditions. Any change that alters the quantity of goods, services, or assets bought from foreigners relative to the quantity sold to them will alter the exchange rate. Let's consider the major factors that will alter the foreign exchange value of a nation's currency.

19-3a CHANGES IN INCOME

An increase in domestic income will encourage the nation's residents to spend a portion of their additional income on imports. When the income of a nation grows rapidly, the nation's imports tend to rise rapidly as well. As Exhibit 3 illustrates, an increase in imports also increases the demand for foreign exchange (the pound in our two-country case). As the demand for pounds increases, the dollar price of the pound rises (from $1.80 to $2.00). This depreciation of the dollar reduces the incentive of Americans to import British goods and services, while increasing the incentive of the British to purchase U.S. exports. These two forces will restore equilibrium in the foreign exchange market at a new, higher dollar price of the pound.

Just the opposite takes place when the income of a trading partner (Great Britain in our example) increases. Rapid growth of income abroad will lead to an increase in U.S.

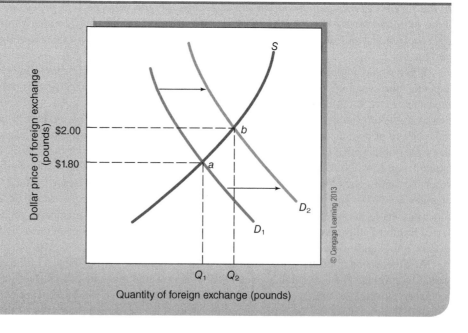

EXHIBIT 3

The Growth of U.S. Income and Imports

Other things constant, if incomes grow in the United States, U.S. imports will grow. The increase in the imports will increase the demand for pounds, causing the dollar price of the pound to rise (from $1.80 to $2.00).

© Cengage Learning 2013

exports, causing the supply of foreign exchange (and demand for dollars) to increase. This will cause the dollar to appreciate—the dollar price of the pound will fall, in other words.

What will happen if both countries are growing? Other things constant, it is the relative growth rate that matters. A country that grows more rapidly than its trading partners will increase its imports relative to its exports, which will cause the exchange rate value of its currency to fall. Conversely, sluggish growth of a country's income relative to its trading partners will lead to a decline in imports relative to exports, which will cause the exchange rate value of its currency to rise. Granted, it seems paradoxical that sluggish growth relative to one's trading partners will cause a country's currency to appreciate, but that's in fact what happens.

19-3b DIFFERENCES IN RATES OF INFLATION

Other things constant, domestic inflation will cause the value of a nation's currency to depreciate, whereas deflation will cause its currency to appreciate. Suppose prices in the United States rise by 50 percent while our trading partners are experiencing stable prices. The domestic inflation will cause U.S. consumers to increase their demand for imported goods (and foreign currency). In turn, the inflated domestic prices will cause foreigners to reduce their purchases of U.S. goods, thereby reducing the supply of foreign currency to the exchange market. As Exhibit 4 illustrates, the exchange rate will adjust to this set of circumstances. In our two-country example, the dollar will depreciate relative to the pound.

Exchange rate adjustments permit nations with even high rates of inflation to engage in trade with countries experiencing relatively stable prices.[5] A depreciation in a nation's currency in the foreign exchange market compensates for the nation's inflation rate. For example, if inflation increases the price level in the United States by 50 percent and the value of the dollar in exchange for the pound depreciates (such that the value of the foreign currency increases 50 percent), then the prices of American goods measured in pounds are unchanged to British consumers. Thus, when the exchange rate value of the dollar changes

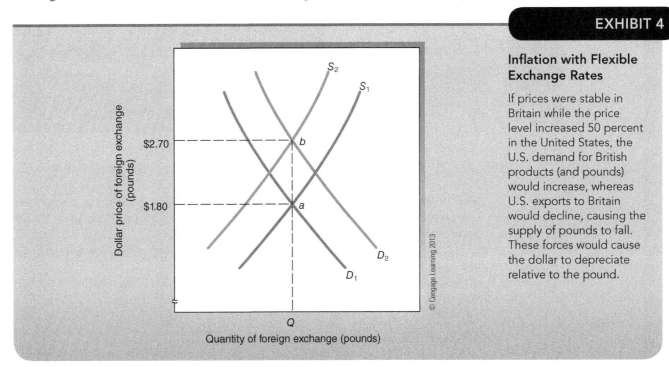

EXHIBIT 4

Inflation with Flexible Exchange Rates

If prices were stable in Britain while the price level increased 50 percent in the United States, the U.S. demand for British products (and pounds) would increase, whereas U.S. exports to Britain would decline, causing the supply of pounds to fall. These forces would cause the dollar to depreciate relative to the pound.

© Cengage Learning 2013

---

[5]However, high rates of inflation are likely to cause greater variability in the foreign exchange value of a currency across time periods. In turn, this increased variability of the exchange rate will generate uncertainty and reduce the volume of international trade—particularly transactions involving a time dimension. Thus, exchange rate instability is generally harmful to the health of an economy.

American consumer purchases an auto from a Japanese manufacturer.

American vacationer buys a ticket on British Airways.

Foreign student pays tuition to Harvard.

Foreign investor purchases a bond from a U.S. corporation.

How will each of these transactions influence the demand for and supply of foreign currencies in exchange for the dollar?

from $1.80 = 1$ pound to $2.70 = 1$ pound, the depreciation in the dollar restores the original prices of U.S. goods to British consumers even though the price level in the United States has increased by 50 percent.

On the one hand, when domestic prices are increasing more rapidly than those of one's trading partners, the value of the domestic currency will tend to depreciate in the foreign exchange market. On the other hand, if a nation's inflation rate is lower than that of its trading partners, then its currency will tend to appreciate.

19-3c CHANGES IN INTEREST RATES

Financial investments will be quite sensitive to changes in real interest rates—that is, interest rates adjusted for the expected rate of inflation. International loanable funds will tend to move toward areas where the expected real rate of return (after compensation for differences in risk) is highest. ***Thus, increases in real interest rates relative to a nation's trading partners will tend to cause that nation's currency to appreciate.*** For example, if real interest rates rise in the United States relative to Britain, British citizens will demand dollars (and supply their currency, pounds) in the foreign exchange market to purchase the high-yield American assets. The increase in demand for the dollar and supply of pounds will then cause the dollar to appreciate relative to the British pound.

In contrast, when real interest rates in other countries increase relative to rates in the United States, short-term financial investors will move to take advantage of the higher yields abroad. As investment funds move from the United States to other countries, there will be an increase in the demand for foreign currencies and an increase in the supply of dollars in the foreign exchange market. A depreciation in the dollar relative to the currencies of the countries with the higher real interest rates will be the result.

19-3d CHANGES IN THE BUSINESS AND INVESTMENT CLIMATE

The inflow and outflow of capital will also be influenced by the quality of the business and investment environment. The monetary, legal, regulatory, and tax climates are particularly important here. Countries that follow a monetary policy consistent with price stability, protect property rights, keep taxes low, and treat people impartially will tend to attract capital. In turn, the inflow of capital will strengthen the demand for the domestic currency and thereby cause it to appreciate. In contrast, when investors are concerned about the stability of the monetary climate, fairness of the legal system, high taxes, and excessive regulation, many will choose to do business elsewhere. As they do so, an outflow of capital and depreciation in the foreign exchange value of the domestic currency will result. Thus, other things constant, the foreign exchange value of a nation's currency will tend to appreciate when its policy environment is improving, while it will tend to depreciate if investors believe that the policy climate is deteriorating.

The accompanying **Thumbnail Sketch** summarizes the major forces that cause a nation's currency to appreciate or depreciate when exchange rates are determined by market forces.

19-4 INTERNATIONAL FINANCE AND ALTERNATIVE EXCHANGE RATE REGIMES

There are three major types of exchange rate regimes: (1) flexible rates; (2) fixed rate, unified currency; and (3) pegged exchange rates. So far, we have focused on the operation of a flexible rate regime. We now consider the other two.

Thumbnail Sketch
What Factors Cause a Nation's Currency to Appreciate or Depreciate?

These Factors Will Cause a Nation's Currency to Appreciate:

1. Slow growth of income (relative to one's trading partners) that causes imports to lag behind exports
2. A rate of inflation that is lower than that of one's trading partners
3. Domestic real interest rates that are higher than real interest rates abroad
4. A shift toward sound policies that attract an inflow of capital

These Factors Will Cause a Nation's Currency to Depreciate:

1. Rapid growth of income (relative to one's trading partners) that stimulates imports relative to exports
2. A rate of inflation that is higher than that of one's trading partners
3. Domestic real interest rates that are lower than real interest rates abroad
4. Movement toward unsound policies that cause an outflow of capital

19-4a FIXED RATE, UNIFIED CURRENCY SYSTEM

Currency board
An entity that (1) issues a currency with a fixed designated value relative to a widely accepted currency (for example, the U.S. dollar), (2) promises to continue to redeem the issued currency at the fixed rate, and (3) maintains bonds and other liquid assets denominated in the other currency that provide 100 percent backing for all currency issued.

Obviously, the 50 states of the United States have a unified currency, the dollar. In addition, the U.S. dollar has been the official currency of Panama for more than a century. Ecuador adopted the U.S. dollar as its official currency in 2000, and El Salvador did so in 2001. The currency of Hong Kong is also closely linked to the U.S. dollar. Hong Kong has a **currency board** that has the power to create currency only in exchange for a specific quantity of U.S. dollars (7.7 HK dollars = 1 U.S. dollar).[6] Countries that adopt the currency board approach do not conduct monetary policy. Instead, they merely accept the monetary policy of the nation to which their currency is tied—the U.S. policy in the case of Hong Kong. Thus, the United States, Panama, Ecuador, El Salvador, and Hong Kong have a unified currency regime.

Eighteen countries of the European Union—Austria, Belgium, Cyprus, Estonia, Finland, France, Germany, Greece, Ireland, Italy, Latvia, Luxembourg, Malta, Netherlands, Portugal, Slovakia, Slovenia, and Spain—have also established a unified currency regime. The official currency in each of these countries is the euro. Several other European countries, including Bulgaria, Lithuania, Bosnia, and Herzegovina use a currency board to link their domestic currency to the euro. Thus, the euro is a unified currency in all of these countries. In turn, the foreign exchange value of the euro relative to other currencies, such as the dollar, the British pound, and the Japanese yen, is determined by market forces (flexible exchange rates).

The distinguishing characteristic of a fixed rate, unified currency regime is the presence of only one central bank with the power to expand and contract the supply of money. For the dollar, that central bank is the Federal Reserve System; for the euro, it is the European Central Bank. Those linking their currency at a fixed rate to the dollar or the euro do not conduct monetary policy; they merely accept the monetary policy of the central bank for their currency. For example, the former central banks of the countries now using the euro no longer have the power to create money. In essence, they are now branches of the European Central Bank, much like the regional and district Federal Reserve banks are branches of the Fed. Similarly, currency boards do not create additional currency. They merely agree to exchange their domestic currency for the currency to which it is linked at a fixed rate.

A pure gold standard system, in which each country agrees to exchange units of its domestic currency for gold at a designated price and fully backs its domestic money supply with gold, is also a fixed rate, unified system. In this case, the world supply of gold (rather than a central bank) determines the total supply of money. If a country's purchases from foreigners exceeded its sales to them, its supply of gold would fall, which would reduce the domestic supply of money. This would put downward pressure on the domestic price level and bring the payments to and receipts from foreigners back into balance. Things would change in the opposite direction if a country were selling more to foreigners than it was purchasing from them. In this case, the excess of sales relative to purchases would lead to an inflow of gold, expansion in the domestic money supply, and higher domestic prices. International financial arrangements approximated those of a gold standard during the period between the U.S. Civil War and the establishment of the Federal Reserve System in 1913.

Fixed exchange rate
An exchange rate that is set at a determined amount by government policy.

Between 1944 and 1971, most of the world operated under a system of **fixed exchange rates**, where each nation fixed the price of its currency relative to others. In essence, this was a quasi-unified system. It was unified in the sense that the value of one currency was fixed relative to others over lengthy time periods. But it was not a fully unified system because each country continued to exercise control over its monetary policy. Nations maintained

---

[6]A currency board like that of Hong Kong does two things. First, it issues domestic currency at a fixed rate in exchange for a designated foreign currency. Second, the foreign currency is then invested in bonds denominated in that currency. This means that the money issued by the currency board is backed 100 percent by the foreign currency. Therefore, the holders of the money issued by the currency board know that it will always have sufficient funds to exchange the domestic currency for the foreign one at the fixed rate. In essence, the country with a currency board accepts the monetary policy of the nation to which its currency is tied.

reserves with the International Monetary Fund (IMF), which could be drawn on when payments to foreigners exceeded receipts from them. This provided each with some leeway in the conduct of monetary policy. However, countries running persistent payment deficits would eventually deplete their reserves. This constrained the country's monetary independence and provided its policy-makers with an incentive to keep its monetary policy approximately in line with that of its trading partners. Under this fixed exchange rate regime, nations often imposed tariffs, quotas, and other trade barriers in an effort to keep their payments and receipts in balance at the fixed rate. Various restrictions on the convertibility of currencies were also common. These problems eventually led to the demise of the system.

19-4b PEGGED EXCHANGE RATE REGIME

A pegged exchange rate system is one in which a country commits itself to the maintenance of a specific exchange rate (or exchange-rate range) relative to another currency (like the U.S. dollar) or a bundle of currencies. In contrast with the currency board approach, however, countries adopting the pegged exchange rate continue to conduct monetary policy. Thus, an excess of purchases from foreigners relative to sales to them does not automatically force the country to reduce its domestic money supply.

However, maintaining the pegged rate will restrict the independence of monetary policy. A country can either (1) follow an independent monetary policy and allow its exchange rate to fluctuate or (2) tie its monetary policy to maintain the fixed exchange rate. It cannot, however, maintain the convertibility of its currency at the fixed exchange rate while following a monetary policy more expansionary than the country to which its currency is tied. Attempts to do so will lead to a financial crisis—a situation in which falling foreign currency reserves eventually force the country to forgo the pegged exchange rate.

This is precisely what happened in Mexico during 1989–1994. Mexico promised to exchange the peso for the dollar at a pegged rate, but it also expanded its domestic money supply much more rapidly than the United States. In the early 1990s, this led to a higher rate of inflation in Mexico than in the United States. Responding to the different inflation rates, more and more people shifted away from the Mexican peso and toward the dollar. By December 1994, Mexico's foreign exchange reserves were virtually depleted. As a result, it could no longer maintain the fixed exchange rate with the dollar. Mexico devalued its currency, triggering a crisis that affected several other countries following similar policies.

In 1997–1998, much the same thing happened in Brazil, Thailand, and Indonesia. Like Mexico, these countries sought to maintain fixed exchange rates (or rates within a narrow band), while following monetary and fiscal policies that were inconsistent with the fixed rate. As their reserves declined, they were forced to abandon their exchange rate pegs. This was extremely disruptive to these economies. Imports suddenly became much more expensive and therefore less affordable. Businesses (including banks) that had borrowed money in dollars (or some other foreign currency) were unable to repay their loans as the result of the sharp decline in the exchange rate value of the domestic currency. In turn, these disruptions led to severe economic declines.

Both economic theory and real-world experience indicate that either a purely flexible exchange rate regime or a fixed rate, unified regime with a single central bank will work reasonably well. In contrast, a pegged exchange rate regime is something like a time bomb. Pushed by political considerations, monetary policy makers in most countries are unable to follow a course consistent with the maintenance of pegged rates. Failure to do so, however, eventually leads to abandonment of the peg and a financial crisis.

19-5 BALANCE OF PAYMENTS

Just as countries calculate their gross domestic product (GDP) so that they have a general idea of their domestic level of production, most countries also calculate their balance of international payments in order to keep track of transactions across national boundaries. The

International Monetary Fund (IMF)
An international banking organization, currently with more than 185 member nations, designed to oversee the operation of the international monetary system. Although it does not control the world supply of money, it does hold currency reserves for member nations and makes currency loans to national central banks.

Pegged exchange rate system
A commitment to use monetary and fiscal policy to maintain the exchange rate value of the domestic currency at a fixed rate or within a narrow band relative to another currency (or bundle of currencies).

Balance of payments
A summary of all economic transactions between a country and all other countries for a specific time period, usually a year. The balance-of-payments account reflects all payments and liabilities to foreigners (debits) and all payments and obligations received from foreigners (credits).

balance of payments summarizes the transactions of the country's citizens, businesses, and governments with foreigners. Balance-of-payments accounts are kept according to the principles of basic bookkeeping. Any transaction that creates a demand for foreign currency (and a supply of the domestic currency) in the foreign exchange market is recorded as a debit, or minus, item. Imports are an example of a debit item. Transactions that create a supply of foreign currency (and demand for the domestic currency) on the foreign exchange market are recorded as a credit, or plus, item. Exports are an example of a credit item. *Because the foreign exchange market will bring quantity demanded and quantity supplied into balance, it will also bring the total debits and total credits into balance.*

Exhibit 5 summarizes the balance-of-payments accounts of the United States for 2012. As the exhibit shows, the transactions can be grouped into one of three separate categories: the current account, capital account, or the official reserve account. Let's take a look at each of these major categories.

EXHIBIT 5

U.S. Balance of Payments, 2012 (in billions of dollars)

		DEBITS	CREDITS	BALANCE
CURRENT ACCOUNT				
1	U.S. merchandise exports		1,564.1	
2	U.S. merchandise imports	−2,299.4		
3	Balance of merchandise trade (1 + 2)			−735.3
4	U.S. service exports		630.4	
5	U.S. service imports	−434.6		
6	Balance on service trade (4 + 5)			195.8
7	Balance on goods and services (3 + 6)			−539.5
8	Income receipts of Americans from abroad		742.0	
9	Income receipts of Foreigners in the United States	−543.4		
10	Net income receipts			198.6
11	Net unilateral transfers			−134.1
12	Balance on current account (7 + 10 + 11)			−475.0
CAPITAL ACCOUNT				
13	Foreign investment in the United States (capital inflow)		11.3	
14	U.S. investment abroad (capital outflow)	−62.7		
15	Net Other Currency Transactions[a]		157.2	
16	Balance on capital account (13 + 14 + 15)			105.8
OFFICIAL RESERVE TRANSACTIONS				
17	U.S. official reserve assets	−4.5		
18	Foreign official assets in the U.S.		373.7	
19	Balance, Official Reserve Account (17 + 18)			369.2
20	Total (12 + 16 + 19)			0.0

Source: http://www.bea.gov.

[a]Statistical discrepancy is included in this figure.

19-5a CURRENT-ACCOUNT TRANSACTIONS

Current-account transactions involve only current exchanges of goods and services and current income flows (and gifts). They do not involve changes in the ownership of either real or financial assets. Current-account transactions are dominated by the trade in goods and services. The export and import of merchandise goods are the largest components in the current account. When U.S. producers export their products, foreigners will supply their currency in exchange for dollars in order to pay for the U.S.-produced goods. Because U.S. exports generate a supply of foreign exchange and demand for dollars in the foreign exchange market, they are a credit (plus) item. In contrast, when Americans import goods, they will demand foreign currencies and supply dollars in the foreign exchange market. Thus, imports are a debit (minus) item.

In 2012, the United States exported $1,564.1 billion of merchandise goods compared with imports of $2,299.4 billion. The difference between the value of a country's merchandise exports and the value of its merchandise imports is known as the **balance of merchandise trade** (or *balance of trade*). If the value of a country's merchandise exports falls short of the value of its merchandise imports, it is said to have a balance-of-trade deficit. In contrast, the situation in which a nation exports more than it imports is referred to as a trade surplus. In 2012, the United States ran a merchandise-trade deficit of $735.3 billion (line 3 of Exhibit 5).

The export and import of services are also sizable. Service trade involves the exchange of items like insurance, transportation, banking services, and items supplied to foreign tourists. Like the export of merchandise goods, service exports generate a supply of foreign exchange and demand for dollars. For example, a Mexican business that is insured by an American company will supply pesos and demand dollars to pay its premiums for the service. Thus, service exports are recorded as credits in the balance-of-payments accounts of exporting nations. Conversely, the import of services from foreigners generates a demand for foreign currency and a supply of dollars in the exchange market. Therefore, service imports are a debit item.

As Exhibit 5 illustrates, in 2012, U.S. service exports were $630.4 billion, compared with service imports of $434.6 billion. Thus, the United States ran a $195.8 billion surplus on its service trade transactions (line 6 of Exhibit 5). When we add the balance of service exports and imports to the balance of merchandise trade, we obtain the **balance on goods and services**. In 2012, the United States ran a $539.5 billion deficit (the sum of the $735.3 billion merchandise-trade deficit and the $195.8 billion service surplus) in the goods and services account.

Two other relatively small items are also included in current-account transactions: (1) net income from investments and (2) unilateral transfers. Americans have made substantial investments in stocks, bonds, and real assets in other countries. As these investments abroad generate income, dollars will flow from foreigners to Americans. This flow of income to Americans will supply foreign currency (and create a demand for dollars) in the foreign exchange market. Thus, the net income to Americans is entered as a credit in the U.S. current account. Correspondingly, foreigners earn income from their investments in the United States. This net income to foreigners is recorded as a debit in the U.S. current account because the supply of dollars to the foreign exchange market creates a demand for foreign exchange.

As Exhibit 5 shows, in 2012, Americans earned $742.0 billion from investments abroad, whereas foreigners earned $543.4 billion from their investments in the United States. On balance, Americans earned $198.6 billion more on their investments abroad than foreigners earned on their investments in the United States. This $198.6 billion net inflow of investment income reduced the size of the deficit on current-account transactions.

Gifts to foreigners, like U.S. aid to a foreign government or private gifts from U.S. residents to their relatives abroad, generate a demand for foreign currencies and supply of dollars in the foreign exchange market. Thus, they are a debit item. Correspondingly, gifts to Americans from foreigners are a credit item. Because the U.S.

Current account
The record of all transactions with foreign nations that involve the exchange of merchandise goods and services, current income derived from investments, and unilateral gifts.

Balance of merchandise trade
The difference between the value of merchandise exports and the value of merchandise imports for a nation. It is also called simply the *balance of trade* or *net exports*. The balance of merchandise trade is only one component of a nation's total balance of payments and its current account.

Balance on goods and services
The exports of goods (merchandise) and services of a nation minus its imports of goods and services.

government and private U.S. citizens gave $134.1 billion more to foreigners than we received from them, this net unilateral transfer was entered as a debit item on the current account in 2012.

19-5b BALANCE ON CURRENT ACCOUNT

Balance on current account
The import–export balance of goods and services, plus net investment income earned abroad, plus net private and government transfers. If the value of the nation's export-type items exceeds (is less than) the value of the nation's import-type items plus net unilateral transfers to foreigners, a current-account surplus (deficit) is present.

The difference between (1) the value of a country's current exports (both goods and services) and earnings from its investments abroad and (2) the value of its current imports (again, both goods and services) and the earnings of foreigners on their domestic assets (plus net unilateral transfers to foreigners) is known as the balance on current account. The current-account balance provides a summary of all current-account transactions. As with the balance of trade, when the value of the current-account debit items (import-type transactions) exceeds the value of the credit items (export-type transactions), we say that the country is running a current-account deficit. Alternatively, if the credit items are greater than the debit items, the country is running a current-account surplus. In 2012, the United States ran a current-account deficit of $475.0 billion.

Because trade in goods and services dominates current-account transactions, the trade- and current-account balances are closely related. Countries with large trade deficits (surpluses) almost always run substantial current-account deficits (surpluses).

19-5c CAPITAL-ACCOUNT TRANSACTIONS

Capital account
The record of transactions with foreigners that involve either (1) the exchange of ownership rights to real or financial assets or (2) the extension of loans.

In contrast with current-account transactions, capital-account transactions focus on changes in the ownership of real and financial assets. These transactions are composed of (1) direct investments by Americans in real assets abroad (or by foreigners in the United States) and (2) loans to and from foreigners. When foreigners make investments in the United States—for example, by purchasing stocks, bonds, or real assets from Americans—their actions will supply foreign currency and generate a demand for dollars in the foreign exchange market. Thus, these capital inflow transactions are a credit.

Conversely, capital outflow transactions are recorded as debits. For example, if a U.S. investor purchases a shoe factory in Mexico, the Mexican seller will want to be paid in pesos. The U.S. investor will supply dollars (and demand pesos) on the foreign exchange market. Because U.S. citizens will demand foreign currency (and supply dollars) when they invest in stocks, bonds, and real assets abroad, these transactions enter into the balance-of-payments accounts as a debit. In 2012, foreign investments in the United States (capital inflow) summed to 11.3 billion, while U.S. investments abroad (capital outflow) totaled $62.7 billion. In 2012, there was also a net capital inflow of $157.2 billion from other currency transactions including financial derivatives and changes in U.S. currency abroad. Because the capital inflow exceeded the outflow, the United States ran a $105.8 billion capital-account surplus in 2012.

19-5d OFFICIAL RESERVE ACCOUNT

Official reserve account
The record of transactions among central banks.

As we noted earlier, the current exchange rate regime is not a pure flexible rate system. Countries with pegged exchange rates will often engage in official reserve transactions in an effort to maintain their pegged rate. These transactions are debited and credited in a country's official reserve account. Even countries with flexible exchange rates may engage in official reserve transactions in order to influence their exchange rate. When a nation's currency is appreciating rapidly, a country may try to slow the appreciation by purchasing foreign financial assets. Conversely, when a currency is depreciating, the country may attempt to halt the depreciation by using some of its foreign currency reserves to purchase the domestic currency in the foreign exchange market. Because of the credibility and widespread use of the U.S. dollar, these official reserve transactions often involve assets denominated in dollars, particularly bonds issued by the U.S. Treasury.

The official reserve transactions are usually small relative to the size of the foreign exchange market, but they were sizable in 2012. As the financial market turmoil continued after the 2008–2009 recession, foreign central banks purchased $373.7 billion of dollar assets, mostly Treasury bonds. The U.S. purchases of foreign reserves were small, only $4.5 billion. Thus, the United States ran a surplus of $369.2 billion on official reserve transactions in 2012. (*Note:* the transactions in the capital and official reserve accounts are sometimes labeled Financial Account transactions.)

What impact do these purchases of U.S. Treasury bonds by foreign central banks have on the U.S. economy? Their impact is much like that of other capital inflows. These foreign purchases, like other capital inflows, will increase the demand for the dollar in the foreign exchange market, causing the foreign exchange value of the dollar to be higher than would otherwise be the case. They will also lead to lower domestic interest rates. Domestic interest rates will fall because the capital inflow will raise the supply of loanable funds. There is a positive side to these official reserve purchases of the dollar. If foreign central banks did not have confidence in both the economy and the monetary policy of the United States, they would not want to purchase and hold U.S. financial assets.

19-5e THE BALANCE OF PAYMENTS MUST BALANCE

The sum of the debit and credit items of the balance-of-payments accounts must balance. Thus, the following identity must hold:

Current-Account Balance + Capital-Account Balance + Official Reserve-Account Balance = 0

However, the specific components of the accounts need not balance. For example, the debit and credit items of the current account need not be equal. Specific components may run either a surplus or a deficit. Nevertheless, because the balance of payments as a whole must balance, a deficit in one area implies an offsetting surplus in other areas. Similarly, even though market forces will bring about an overall balance, there is no reason to expect that the trade flows between any two countries will be in balance. See the accompanying Myths of Economics box feature on this topic.

If a nation is experiencing a current-account deficit, it must experience an offsetting surplus on the sum of its capital-account and official reserve-account balances. This has been the case for the United States in recent years.

In 2012, the United States ran a $475.0 billion current-account deficit and a $105.8 billion capital-account surplus. The difference between these two figures—a $369.2 billion deficit—was exactly offset by a $369.2 billion surplus in the official reserve account. Thus, the deficits and surpluses of the current-, capital-, and official reserve accounts summed to zero as is shown in Exhibit 5 (line 20).

Under a pure flexible rate system, official reserve transactions would be zero. Under these conditions, a capital-account surplus (inflow of capital) would mean that the current account must have a deficit. Similarly, a capital-account deficit (outflow of capital) would mean that the current account must have a surplus.

With flexible exchange rates, changes in the net inflow of capital will influence the current-account balance. If a nation is experiencing an increase in net foreign investment, perhaps as the result of attractive investment opportunities, this increase in the capital-account surplus (inflow of capital) will enlarge the current-account deficit. In contrast, capital flight (outflow of capital) will move the current account toward a surplus.

19-6 EXCHANGE RATES, CURRENT ACCOUNT BALANCE, AND CAPITAL INFLOW

Exhibit 6 presents data on the foreign exchange value of the dollar, current-account balance, and inflow of capital for the United States since 1978. (*Note:* While the data in the

The Exchange Rate, Current-Account Balance, and Net Foreign Investment

Here, we show the relationship between the exchange rate, the current-account deficit, and net foreign investment (capital inflow). The shaded areas represent recessions.

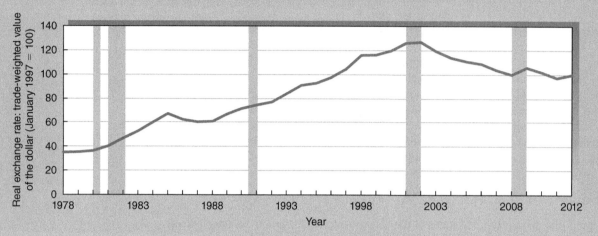

(a) Exchange-rate value of the dollar (compared with 26 currencies)

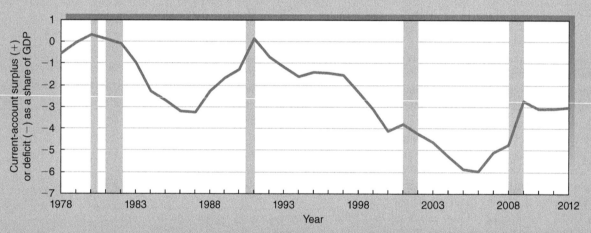

(b) Current-account balance as a share of GDP

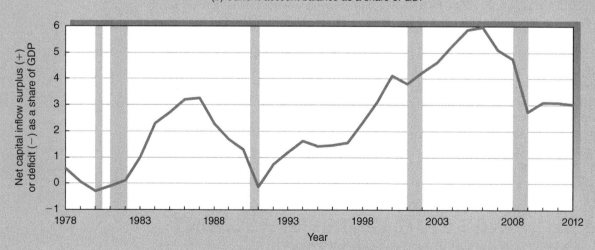

(c) Net capital inflow as a share of GDP

Note: Data are given in billions of dollars.

Source: http://research.stlouisfed.org/fred2/

MYTHS IN ECONOMICS

"If Other Countries Are Treating Us Fairly, Our Exports to Them Should Be Approximately Equal to Our Imports from Them."

Politicians like to bash countries like Japan and China that export much more to us than they import from us. Some have even called for trade restraints to limit imports from these countries until our exports to and imports from them are brought into balance. This view is based on a misconception about bilateral trade balances. Flexible exchange rates will bring total purchases from foreigners into balance with total sales to them. However, there is no reason to expect that imports and exports with any specific country will be in balance.

Consider the trade "deficits" and "surpluses" of a doctor who likes to golf. The doctor can be expected to run a trade deficit with sporting goods stores, golf caddies, and course operators. Why? These suppliers sell items that the golfer–doctor purchases in sizable quantities. The doctor, on the other hand, probably sells few items the sporting goods store purchases. Similarly, the doctor can be expected to run trade surpluses with medical insurers, elderly patients, and those with chronic illnesses. These trading partners are major purchasers of the services provided by the doctor, although the doctor might purchase very little from them.

The same principles are at work across nations. A nation will tend to run trade deficits with countries that are low-cost suppliers of items it imports and trade surpluses with countries that buy a lot of the things it exports. Japan is a major importer of resources like oil and a major exporter of high-tech manufacturing goods. Americans import a lot of the latter, but they export very little of the former. Similarly, China is a low-cost producer of labor-intensive items like toys and textile products, items that are costly for a high-wage country like the United States to produce domestically. On the other hand, the United States is a low-cost producer of high-tech products and grains like wheat and corn that are purchased only in small quantities by poor countries like China. The bottom line is this: Japan and China are low-cost producers of many items that we import, and the United States is not a major exporter of items imported intensively by Japan and China. Thus, our bilateral trade deficits with them are perfectly understandable.

In recent years, the United States has run trade surpluses with Netherlands, Australia, Belgium, Luxembourg, Brazil, and the United Kingdom. Do these bilateral trade surpluses indicate that the United States treats these countries unfairly? Of course not. The surpluses merely reflect that these countries import substantial amounts of items supplied economically by U.S. producers and export only small amounts of items imported intensively by Americans. It may be good politics to bash those with whom we run bilateral trade deficits, but the argument is nonetheless based on a fallacious view of trade balances between countries.

franckreporter/E+/Getty Images

middle frame are for the current-account balance, the trade balance figures would be virtually identical because trade in goods and services is the dominant component of the current account.) The link between the inflow of capital and the current-account deficit is clearly visible. As the middle and lower panels illustrate, the two are mirror images. When the inflow of capital increases, the current-account (trade) balance shifts toward a deficit. Correspondingly, when net capital inflow shrinks, so, too, does the current-account deficit. This is the expected outcome under a flexible rate system. With flexible rates, the overall payments to and receipts from foreigners must balance. Thus, a deficit in one area is not an isolated event. If a nation runs a current-account (trade) deficit, it must also run a capital-account (plus official reserve account) surplus of equal magnitude.

Prior to 1981, net capital inflow in the United States was relatively small, and so too was the current-account deficit. However, as the U.S. economy grew briskly following the 1982 recession, net capital inflow (bottom panel) in the United States increased sharply. Simultaneously, the U.S. dollar appreciated and the current-account deficit widened. As the U.S. economy slowed during the late 1980s and the recession of the early 1990s, net capital inflow fell to a trickle, and the current account actually registered a small surplus in 1991. But as the U.S. economy recovered from the 1990 recession and grew rapidly during the 1990s, once again net capital inflow increased substantially, the U.S. dollar appreciated, and the current account moved toward a large deficit.

As during the expansions of the 1980s and 1990s, there was also an inflow of capital and a substantial increase in the U.S. current-account deficit during the expansion that began in 2002. However, there was also an important difference. While the dollar appreciated during the two earlier recoveries, it depreciated during the most recent expansion. Furthermore, more than half of the inflow of capital reflects dollar purchases by foreign central banks. In many cases, these purchases were motivated by foreigners' desire to slow the depreciation of the dollar (and the appreciation of their domestic currency). As we noted in Exhibit 1, during 2002–2013, the dollar depreciated by 20 percent against an index of 26 currencies, and the depreciations relative to the euro and Canadian dollar were even greater. Had it not been for the sizable purchases of U.S. Treasury bonds by foreign central banks in recent years, the depreciation of the dollar would surely have been larger.

As Exhibit 6 shows, trade (and current account) deficits are closely linked to the inflow of capital. When foreigners are making more "investments" in a country than the residents of the country are making abroad, a capital account surplus will occur. In turn, the capital account surplus generally leads to a trade (and current account) deficit. In essence, trade (and current-account) deficits are the flip side of capital inflows.

Whether an inflow of capital is good or bad depends on the source of the inflow and how the funds are used. When the inflow of capital occurs because the investment environment of the country is attractive and foreigners are providing the funds for productive investments, this is a positive development. The investments will increase the machines, tools, and other capital assets available to domestic workers, which will increase both their future productivity and earnings. Clearly, trade and current account deficits arising from this source will exert a positive impact on both the country's current and future income.

However, if the inflow of capital is used to increase current consumption or for the finance of unproductive projects, it will reduce future income. In recent years, a substantial portion of the capital inflow to the United States has been used to finance federal budget deficits. This borrowing has made it possible for Americans to consume more today, but the interest expenses will mean less consumption in the future. Moreover, political decision-makers have channeled a large share of these borrowed funds into counterproductive projects and subsidies for favored businesses and interest groups. Use of capital inflow in this manner will reduce the future income of Americans. In addition, as the recent financial troubles of Greece illustrate, when this process is taken to a high level, it can lead to indebtedness to foreigners that will even endanger the creditworthiness of a government.

When considering the significance of the U.S. trade deficit, one should keep two points in mind. First, no legal entity is responsible for the trade deficit. It reflects an aggregation of the voluntary choices of businesses and individuals.[7] Thus, it is not like a business loss or even the budget deficit of a government. Second, to a large degree, the inflow of capital reflects the confidence of investors in both the U.S. economy and the policies of the United States. If either should become less attractive in the future, the situation would change. For example, if the United States continued to run large deficits that push the federal debt to high levels, the confidence of both domestic and foreign investors would diminish. This would lead to a decline in the capital inflow and a reduction in the trade deficit. As the experience of Greece indicates, this is not an attractive way to shift the trade balance toward a surplus.

---

[7]As the late Herbert Stein, a former chair of the President's Council of Economic Advisers, once put it: "The trade deficit does not belong to any individual or institution. It is a pure-statistical aggregate, like the number of eggs laid in the U.S. or the number of bald-headed men living here." See Herbert Stein, "Leave the Trade Deficit Alone," *The Wall Street Journal* (March 11, 1987).

KEY POINTS

- Because countries generally use different currencies, international trade usually involves the conversion of one currency to another. The currencies of different countries are bought and sold in the foreign exchange market. The exchange rate is the price of one national currency in terms of another.

- The dollar demand for foreign exchange arises from the purchase (import) of goods, services, and assets by Americans from foreigners. The supply of foreign currency in exchange for dollars arises from the sale (export) of goods, services, and assets by Americans to foreigners. The equilibrium exchange rate will bring these two forces into balance.

- With flexible exchange rates, the following will cause a nation's currency to appreciate: (1) rapid growth of income abroad (and/or slow domestic growth), (2) low inflation (relative to one's trading partners), (3) rising domestic real interest rates (and/or falling rates abroad), and (4) improvement in the business and investment environment. The reverse of these conditions will cause a nation's currency to depreciate.

- There are three major types of exchange rate regimes: (1) flexible rates; (2) fixed rate, unified currency; and (3) pegged exchange rates. Both flexible rate and fixed rate, unified currency systems work quite well. Pegged rate systems, however, often lead to problems because they require that the nation follow a monetary policy consistent with maintaining the pegged rate. Political pressure often makes this difficult to do.

- The balance-of-payments accounts provide a summary of transactions with foreigners. There are three major balance-of-payments components: (1) the current account, (2) capital account, and (3) the official reserve account. The balances of these three components must sum to zero, but the individual components of the accounts need not be in balance.

- Under a pure flexible rate system, there will be no official reserve-account transactions. Under these circumstances, the current and capital accounts must sum to zero. This implies that an inflow of capital will shift the current account toward a deficit, while an outflow of capital will move the current account toward a surplus.

- Trade deficits are not necessarily bad. Countries that grow rapidly and follow policies that investors find attractive will tend to experience an inflow of capital and a trade deficit. However, if the inflow of capital is used to finance a higher level of current consumption or channeled into unproductive projects, future income will be adversely affected

- There is no reason to expect that bilateral trade between countries will balance. A country will tend to run a bilateral trade deficit with countries that are low-cost producers of items that it imports in large quantities.

CRITICAL ANALYSIS QUESTIONS

1. If the dollar depreciates relative to the Japanese yen, how will this affect the dollar price of a Japanese camera produced by Nikon, for example? How will this change influence the quantity of Nikon cameras purchased by Americans?

2. How will the purchases of items from foreigners compare with the sales of items to foreigners when the foreign exchange market is in equilibrium? Explain.

3. Will a flexible exchange rate bring the imports of goods and services into balance with the exports of goods and services? Why or why not?

4. *The accompanying chart indicates an actual newspaper quotation of the exchange rate of various currencies. On February 2, did the dollar appreciate or depreciate against the British pound? How did it fare against the Canadian dollar?

U.S. DOLLAR EQUIVALENT

	FEBRUARY 1	FEBRUARY 2
British pound	1.755	1.746
Canadian dollar	0.6765	0.6775

5. *Suppose the exchange rate between the United States and Mexico freely fluctuates in the open market. Indicate whether each of the following would cause the dollar to appreciate or depreciate relative to the peso.

   a. an increase in the quantity of drilling equipment purchased in the United States by Pemex, the Mexican oil company, as a result of a Mexican oil discovery

   b. an increase in the U.S. purchase of crude oil from Mexico as a result of the development of Mexican oil fields

   c. higher real interest rates in Mexico, inducing U.S. citizens to move some of their financial investments from U.S. to Mexican banks

   d. lower real interest rates in the United States, inducing Mexican investors to borrow dollars and then exchange them for pesos

   e. inflation in the United States and stable prices in Mexico

   f. an increase in the inflation rate from 2 percent to 10 percent in both the United States and Mexico

   g. an economic boom in Mexico, inducing Mexicans to buy more U.S.-made automobiles, trucks, electric appliances, and manufacturing equipment

   h. attractive investment opportunities in Mexico, inducing U.S. investors to buy stock in Mexican firms

6. Explain why the current-account balance and capital-account balance must sum to zero under a pure flexible rate system.

7. Rapidly growing strong economies often experience trade deficits, whereas economies with sluggish growth often have trade surpluses. Can you explain this puzzle?

8. *In recent years, a substantial share of the domestic capital formation in the United States has been financed by foreign investors. Is this dependence on foreign capital dangerous? What would happen if the inflow of foreign capital came to a halt?

9. *Suppose that the United States were running a current-account deficit. How would each of the following changes influence the size of the current-account deficit?

   a. a recession in the United States

   b. a decline in the attractiveness of investment opportunities in the United States

   c. an improvement in investment opportunities abroad

10. If taxes imposed on personal and corporate income increased substantially in the United States and the monetary policy of the United States was less stable and more inflationary than other countries, how would these policies affect the trade deficit? Why?

11. If foreigners have confidence in the U.S. economy and therefore move to expand their investments in the United States, how will the U.S. current-account balance be affected? How will the exchange-rate value of the dollar be affected?

12. Is a trade surplus indicative of a strong, healthy economy? Why or why not?

13. *"Changes in exchange rates will automatically direct a country to a current-account balance under a flexible exchange rate system." Is this statement true or false?

14. *Several members of Congress have been highly critical of Japan and China because U.S. imports from these countries have persistently been substantially greater than our exports to them.

   a. Under a flexible exchange rate system, is there any reason to expect that the imports from a given country will tend to equal the exports to that country?

   b. Can you think of any reason why the United States might persistently run a trade deficit with these countries?

15. *In recent years, the central banks of both Japan and China have purchased large amounts of U.S. Treasury bonds. These purchases increase the exchange rate value of the dollar relative to the Japanese yen and Chinese yuan. Are these purchases harmful to the U.S. economy? Why or why not?

*Asterisk denotes questions for which answers are given in Appendix B.

APPENDIX A

General Business and Economics Indicators for the United States

Section 1

Year	Personal Consum Expend	Gross Private Domestic Invest	Govt Consumpand Gross Invest	Net Exports	Gross Domestic Product	Real GDP 2005 Prices	Annual Real Rate	Real GDP Per Capita
1960	$331.8	$78.9	$111.5	$4.2	$526.4	$2,830.9	2.5	$15,661
1961	342.2	78.2	119.5	4.9	544.8	2,896.9	2.3	15,766
1962	363.3	88.1	130.1	4.1	585.7	3,072.4	6.1	16,466
1963	382.7	93.8	136.4	4.9	617.8	3,206.7	4.4	16,940
1964	411.5	102.1	143.2	6.9	663.6	3,392.3	5.8	17,675
1965	443.8	118.2	151.4	5.6	719.1	3,610.1	6.4	18,576
1966	480.9	131.3	171.6	3.9	787.7	3,845.3	6.5	19,559
1967	507.8	128.6	192.5	3.6	832.4	3,942.5	2.5	19,836
1968	558.0	141.2	209.3	1.4	909.8	4,133.4	4.8	20,590
1969	604.5	173.6	240.4	1.4	1,019.9	4,707.9	13.9	23,222
1970	647.7	170.1	254.2	4.0	1,075.9	4,717.7	0.2	23,003
1971	701.0	196.8	269.3	0.6	1,167.8	4,873.0	3.3	23,463
1972	769.4	228.1	288.2	−3.4	1,282.4	5,128.8	5.2	24,432
1973	851.1	266.9	306.4	4.1	1,428.5	5,418.2	5.6	25,565
1974	932.0	274.5	343.1	−0.8	1,548.8	5,390.2	−0.5	25,200
1975	1,032.8	257.3	382.9	16.0	1,688.9	5,379.5	−0.2	24,907
1976	1,150.2	323.2	405.8	−1.6	1,877.6	5,669.3	5.4	25,996
1977	1,276.7	396.6	435.8	−23.1	2,086.0	5,930.6	4.6	26,922
1978	1,426.2	478.4	477.4	−25.4	2,356.6	6,260.4	5.6	28,120
1979	1,589.5	539.7	525.5	−22.5	2,632.1	6,459.2	3.2	28,694
1980	1,754.6	530.1	590.8	−13.1	2,862.5	6,443.4	−0.2	28,295
1981	1,937.5	631.2	654.7	−12.5	3,210.9	6,610.6	2.6	28,741
1982	2,073.9	581.0	710.0	−20.0	3,345.0	6,484.3	−1.9	27,923
1983	2,286.5	637.5	765.7	−51.7	3,638.1	6,784.7	4.6	28,953
1984	2,498.2	820.1	825.2	−102.7	4,040.7	7,277.2	7.3	30,784
1985	2,722.7	829.6	908.4	−114.0	4,346.7	7,585.7	4.2	31,805
1986	2,898.4	849.1	974.5	−131.9	4,590.1	7,852.1	3.5	32,624
1987	3,092.1	892.2	1,030.8	−144.8	4,870.2	8,123.9	3.5	33,453
1988	3,346.9	937.0	1,078.2	−109.4	5,252.6	8,465.4	4.2	34,544
1989	3,592.8	999.7	1,151.9	−86.8	5,657.7	8,777.0	3.7	35,479
1990	3,825.6	993.5	1,238.4	−77.9	5,979.6	8,945.4	1.9	35,756
1991	3,960.2	944.3	1,298.2	−28.6	6,174.0	8,938.9	−0.1	35,258
1992	4,215.7	1,013.0	1,345.4	−34.8	6,539.3	9,256.7	3.6	36,029
1993	4,471.0	1,106.8	1,366.1	−65.2	6,878.7	9,510.8	2.7	36,540
1994	4,741.0	1,256.5	1,403.7	−92.5	7,308.7	9,894.7	4.0	37,557
1995	4,984.2	1,317.5	1,452.2	−89.8	7,664.0	10,163.7	2.7	38,125
1996	5,268.1	1,432.1	1,496.4	−96.4	8,100.2	10,549.5	3.8	39,114
1997	5,560.7	1,595.6	1,554.2	−102.0	8,608.5	11,022.9	4.5	40,383
1998	5,903.0	1,735.3	1,613.5	−162.7	9,089.1	11,513.4	4.4	41,692
1999	6,316.9	1,884.2	1,726.0	−261.4	9,665.7	12,071.4	4.8	43,216
2000	6,801.6	2,033.8	1,834.4	−380.1	10,289.7	12,565.2	4.1	44,495
2001	7,106.9	1,928.6	1,958.8	−369.0	10,625.3	12,684.4	0.9	44,472
2002	7,385.3	1,925.0	2,094.9	−425.0	10,980.2	12,909.7	1.8	44,832
2003	7,764.4	2,027.9	2,220.8	−500.9	11,512.2	13,270.0	2.8	45,660
2004	8,257.8	2,276.7	2,357.4	−614.8	12,277.0	13,774.0	3.8	46,968
2005	8,790.3	2,527.1	2,493.7	−715.7	13,095.4	14,235.6	3.4	48,094
2006	9,297.5	2,680.6	2,642.2	−762.4	13,857.9	14,615.2	2.7	48,910
2007	9,744.4	2,643.7	2,801.9	−709.8	14,480.3	14,876.8	1.8	49,311
2008	10,005.5	2,424.8	3,003.2	−713.2	14,720.3	14,833.6	−0.3	48,708
2009	9,842.9	1,878.1	3,089.1	−392.2	14,417.9	14,417.9	−2.8	46,927
2010	10,201.9	2,100.8	3,174.0	−518.5	14,958.3	14,779.4	2.5	47,710
2011	10,711.8	2,232.1	3,158.7	−568.7	15,533.8	15,052.4	1.8	48,239
2012	11,149.6	2,475.2	3,167.0	−547.2	16,244.6	15,470.7	2.8	49,226

Source: http://www.bea.gov

Section 2

	GDP Deflator		Consumer Price Index	
Year	Index (2005 = 100)	Annual Percentage Change	Index	Percentage Change
1960	20.2	1.4	29.6	1.0
1961	20.5	1.1	29.9	1.1
1962	20.7	1.4	30.3	1.2
1963	21.0	1.1	30.6	1.2
1964	21.3	1.6	31.0	1.3
1965	21.7	1.8	31.5	1.6
1966	22.3	2.8	32.5	3.0
1967	23.0	3.1	33.4	2.8
1968	23.9	4.3	34.8	4.3
1969	23.6	−1.5	36.7	5.5
1970	24.8	5.3	38.8	5.8
1971	26.1	5.1	40.5	4.3
1972	27.2	4.3	41.8	3.3
1973	28.7	5.4	44.4	6.2
1974	31.3	9.0	49.3	11.1
1975	34.2	9.3	53.8	9.1
1976	36.0	5.5	56.9	5.7
1977	38.3	6.2	60.6	6.5
1978	41.0	7.0	65.2	7.6
1979	44.3	8.3	72.6	11.3
1980	48.4	9.0	82.4	13.5
1981	52.9	9.4	90.9	10.3
1982	56.1	6.1	96.5	6.1
1983	58.3	3.9	99.6	3.2
1984	60.4	3.6	103.9	4.3
1985	62.3	3.2	107.6	3.5
1986	63.6	2.0	109.6	1.9
1987	65.2	2.4	113.6	3.7
1988	67.4	3.5	118.3	4.1
1989	70.1	3.9	124.0	4.8
1990	72.7	3.7	130.7	5.4
1991	75.1	3.3	136.2	4.2
1992	76.8	2.3	140.3	3.0
1993	78.6	2.4	144.5	3.0
1994	80.3	2.1	148.2	2.6
1995	82.0	2.1	152.4	2.8
1996	83.5	1.8	156.9	2.9
1997	84.9	1.7	160.5	2.3
1998	85.8	1.1	163.0	1.6
1999	87.0	1.4	166.6	2.2
2000	89.0	2.3	172.2	3.4
2001	91.1	2.3	177.1	2.8
2002	92.5	1.5	179.9	1.6
2003	94.3	2.0	184.0	2.3
2004	96.9	2.7	188.9	2.7
2005	100.0	3.2	195.3	3.4
2006	103.1	3.1	201.6	3.2
2007	105.8	2.7	207.3	2.8
2008	107.8	1.9	215.3	3.8
2009	108.7	0.8	214.5	−0.4
2010	110.0	1.2	218.1	1.6
2011	112.2	2.0	224.9	3.1
2012	114.2	1.7	229.6	2.1

Source: http://www.bea.gov and http://www.bls.gov

Section 3

Year	Civilian Pop	Civilian Labor Force	Civilian Labor Force Participation	Civilian Employment/ Population	Unemployment Rates			
					All	Age 16 to 19	Men Age 20+	Women Age 20+
1960	117.2	69.6	59.4	56.1	5.5	14.7	4.7	5.1
1961	118.8	70.5	59.3	55.4	6.7	16.8	5.7	6.3
1962	120.2	70.6	58.8	55.5	5.5	14.7	4.6	5.4
1963	122.4	71.8	58.7	55.4	5.7	17.2	4.5	5.4
1964	124.5	73.1	58.7	55.7	5.2	16.2	3.9	5.2
1965	126.5	74.5	58.9	56.2	4.5	14.8	3.2	4.5
1966	128.1	75.8	59.2	56.9	3.8	12.8	2.5	3.8
1967	129.9	77.3	59.6	57.3	3.8	12.9	2.3	4.2
1968	132.0	78.7	59.6	57.5	3.6	12.7	2.2	3.8
1969	134.3	80.7	60.1	58.0	3.5	12.2	2.1	3.7
1970	137.1	82.8	60.4	57.4	4.9	15.3	3.5	4.8
1971	140.2	84.4	60.2	56.6	5.9	16.9	4.4	5.7
1972	144.1	87.0	60.4	57.0	5.6	16.2	4.0	5.4
1973	147.1	89.4	60.8	57.8	4.9	14.5	3.3	4.9
1974	150.1	91.9	61.3	57.8	5.6	16.0	3.8	5.5
1975	153.2	93.8	61.2	56.1	8.5	19.9	6.8	8.0
1976	156.2	96.2	61.6	56.8	7.7	19.0	5.9	7.4
1977	159.0	99.0	62.3	57.9	7.1	17.8	5.2	7.0
1978	161.9	102.3	63.2	59.3	6.1	16.4	4.3	6.0
1979	164.9	105.0	63.7	59.9	5.8	16.1	4.2	5.7
1980	167.7	106.9	63.8	59.2	7.1	17.8	5.9	6.4
1981	170.1	108.7	63.9	59.0	7.6	19.6	6.3	6.8
1982	172.3	110.2	64.0	57.8	9.7	23.2	8.8	8.3
1983	174.2	111.6	64.0	57.9	9.6	22.4	8.9	8.1
1984	176.4	113.5	64.4	59.5	7.5	18.9	6.6	6.8
1985	178.2	115.5	64.8	60.1	7.2	18.6	6.2	6.6
1986	180.6	117.8	65.3	60.7	7.0	18.3	6.1	6.2
1987	182.8	119.9	65.6	61.5	6.2	16.9	5.4	5.4
1988	184.6	121.7	65.9	62.3	5.5	15.3	4.8	4.9
1989	186.4	123.9	66.5	63.0	5.3	15.0	4.5	4.7
1990	189.2	125.8	66.5	62.8	5.6	15.5	5.0	4.9
1991	190.9	126.3	66.2	61.7	6.8	18.7	6.4	5.7
1992	192.8	128.1	66.4	61.5	7.5	20.1	7.1	6.3
1993	194.8	129.2	66.3	61.7	6.9	19.0	6.4	5.9
1994	196.8	131.1	66.6	62.5	6.1	17.6	5.4	5.4
1995	198.6	132.3	66.6	62.9	5.6	17.3	4.8	4.9
1996	200.6	133.9	66.8	63.2	5.4	16.7	4.6	4.8
1997	203.1	136.3	67.1	63.8	4.9	16.0	4.2	4.4
1998	205.2	137.7	67.1	64.1	4.5	14.6	3.7	4.1
1999	207.8	139.4	67.1	64.3	4.2	13.9	3.5	3.8
2000	212.6	142.6	67.1	64.4	4.0	13.1	3.4	3.6
2001	215.1	143.7	66.8	63.7	4.7	14.7	4.2	4.1
2002	217.6	144.9	66.6	62.7	5.8	16.5	5.2	5.1
2003	221.2	146.5	66.2	62.3	6.0	17.5	5.4	5.1
2004	223.4	147.4	66.0	62.3	5.5	17.0	4.9	4.9
2005	226.1	149.3	66.0	62.7	5.1	16.6	4.5	4.6
2006	228.8	151.4	66.2	63.1	4.6	15.4	4.1	4.1
2007	231.9	153.1	66.0	63.0	4.6	15.7	4.1	4.0
2008	233.8	154.3	66.0	62.2	5.8	18.7	5.4	4.9
2009	235.8	154.1	65.4	59.3	9.3	24.8	9.6	7.5
2010	237.8	153.9	64.7	58.5	9.6	25.9	9.8	8.0
2011	239.6	153.6	64.1	58.4	8.9	24.4	8.7	7.9
2012	243.3	155.0	63.7	58.6	8.1	24.0	7.5	7.3

Source: www.bls.gov

Section 4

Year	M1	Annual Change	M2	Annual Change	Aaa Bonds	Federal Budget Fiscal Year Outlays	Federal Budget Fiscal Year Receipts	Surplus/ Deficit	National Debt[1] Billions of Dollars	National Debt[1] Percent of GDP
1960	$140.3	−0.1	$304.3	3.8	4.4	$92.2	$92.5	$0.3	$210.3	40.5%
1961	143.1	2.0	324.8	6.7	4.4	97.7	94.4	(3.3)	211.1	39.8%
1962	146.5	2.4	350.1	7.8	4.3	106.8	99.7	(7.1)	218.3	38.5%
1963	150.9	3.0	379.6	8.4	4.3	111.3	106.6	(4.8)	222.0	37.0%
1964	156.8	3.9	409.4	7.8	4.4	118.5	112.6	(5.9)	222.1	34.6%
1965	163.5	4.2	442.5	8.1	4.5	118.2	116.8	(1.4)	221.7	32.2%
1966	171.0	4.6	471.4	6.5	5.1	134.5	130.8	(3.7)	221.5	29.3%
1967	177.7	3.9	503.6	6.8	5.5	157.5	148.8	(8.6)	219.9	27.1%
1968	190.1	7.0	545.3	8.3	6.2	178.1	153.0	(25.2)	237.3	27.3%
1969	201.4	5.9	578.7	6.1	7.0	183.6	186.9	3.2	224.0	23.6%
1970	209.1	3.8	601.4	3.9	8.0	195.6	192.8	(2.8)	225.5	22.3%
1971	223.2	6.7	674.4	12.1	7.4	210.2	187.1	(23.0)	237.5	22.0%
1972	239.0	7.1	758.1	12.4	7.2	230.7	207.3	(23.4)	251.0	21.3%
1973	256.4	7.2	831.8	9.7	7.4	245.7	230.8	(14.9)	265.7	20.3%
1974	269.2	5.0	880.7	5.9	8.6	269.4	263.2	(6.1)	263.1	18.3%
1975	281.4	4.5	963.7	9.4	8.8	332.3	279.1	(53.2)	309.7	19.8%
1976	297.2	5.6	1,086.6	12.8	8.4	371.8	298.1	(73.7)	382.7	22.0%
1977	320.0	7.7	1,221.4	12.4	8.0	409.2	355.6	(53.7)	444.1	22.5%
1978	346.3	8.2	1,322.4	8.3	8.7	458.7	399.6	(59.2)	491.6	22.2%
1979	372.7	7.6	1,425.8	7.8	9.6	504.0	463.3	(40.7)	524.7	21.0%
1980	395.7	6.2	1,540.4	8.0	11.9	590.9	517.1	(73.8)	591.1	21.7%
1981	424.9	7.4	1,679.6	9.0	14.2	678.2	599.3	(79.0)	664.9	21.8%
1982	453.0	6.6	1,831.4	9.0	13.8	745.7	617.8	(128.0)	790.1	24.5%
1983	503.2	11.1	2,054.8	12.2	12.0	808.4	600.6	(207.8)	981.7	28.5%
1984	538.6	7.0	2,219.3	8.0	12.7	851.8	666.4	(185.4)	1,151.9	30.0%
1985	587.0	9.0	2,416.7	8.9	11.4	946.3	734.0	(212.3)	1,337.5	32.3%
1986	666.4	13.5	2,613.5	8.1	9.0	990.4	769.2	(221.2)	1,549.8	35.2%
1987	743.5	11.6	2,783.8	6.5	9.4	1,004.0	854.3	(149.7)	1,677.7	36.1%
1988	774.8	4.2	2,933.4	5.4	9.7	1,064.4	909.2	(155.2)	1,822.4	36.4%
1989	782.2	1.0	3,056.1	4.2	9.3	1,143.7	991.1	(152.6)	1,970.6	36.5%
1990	810.6	3.6	3,223.6	5.5	9.3	1,253.0	1,032.0	(221.0)	2,177.1	38.0%
1991	859.0	6.0	3,342.2	3.7	8.8	1,324.2	1,055.0	(269.2)	2,430.4	41.0%
1992	965.9	12.5	3,403.6	1.8	8.1	1,381.5	1,091.2	(290.3)	2,703.3	43.3%
1993	1,078.5	11.7	3,438.0	1.0	7.2	1,409.4	1,154.3	(255.1)	2,922.7	44.4%
1994	1,145.2	6.2	3,482.1	1.3	8.0	1,461.8	1,258.6	(203.2)	3,077.9	44.1%
1995	1,143.1	−0.2	3,552.7	2.0	7.6	1,515.7	1,351.8	(164.0)	3,230.3	44.0%
1996	1,106.5	−3.2	3,722.8	4.8	7.4	1,560.5	1,453.1	(107.4)	3,343.1	43.3%
1997	1,070.1	−3.3	3,909.8	5.0	7.3	1,601.1	1,579.2	(21.9)	3,347.8	40.8%
1998	1,080.6	1.0	4,188.9	7.1	6.5	1,652.5	1,721.7	69.3	3,262.9	37.7%
1999	1,102.3	2.0	4,496.9	7.4	7.0	1,701.8	1,827.5	125.6	3,135.7	34.1%
2000	1,103.6	0.1	4,769.3	6.1	7.6	1,789.0	2,025.2	236.2	2,898.4	29.5%
2001	1,140.3	3.3	5,179.4	8.6	7.1	1,862.8	1,991.1	128.2	2,785.5	27.2%
2002	1,196.7	4.9	5,562.4	7.4	6.5	2,010.9	1,853.1	(157.8)	2,936.2	27.8%
2003	1,273.8	6.4	5,950.1	7.0	5.7	2,159.9	1,782.3	(377.6)	3,257.3	29.7%
2004	1,344.3	5.5	6,236.0	4.8	5.6	2,292.8	1,880.1	(412.7)	3595.2	30.8%
2005	1,371.6	2.0	6,504.3	4.3	5.2	2,472.0	2,153.6	(318.3)	3855.9	31.0%
2006	1,374.7	0.2	6,845.3	5.2	5.6	2,655.1	2,406.9	(248.2)	4060.0	30.7%
2007	1,372.6	−0.1	7,267.1	6.2	5.6	2,728.7	2,568.0	(160.7)	4255.5	30.7%
2008	1,434.9	4.5	7,763.7	6.8	5.6	2,982.5	2,524.0	(458.6)	5311.9	37.1%
2009	1,637.7	14.1	8,385.3	8.0	5.3	3,517.7	2,105.0	(1,412.7)	6775.5	48.5%
2010	1,742.3	6.4	8,593.4	2.5	5.0	3,457.1	2,162.7	(1,294.4)	8207.2	57.2%
2011	2,010.0	15.4	9,221.3	7.3	4.6	3,603.1	2,303.5	(1,299.6)	8463.5	56.7%
2012	2,310.9	15.0	10,006.9	8.5	3.7	3,537.1	2,450.2	(1,087.0)	9635.8	62.0%

Source: www.economagic.com and www.whitehouse.gov/omb/

[1]National debt is debt held by private investors.

Section 5

	SIZE OF GOVERNMENT AS A PERCENT OF GDP[1]				
YEAR	EXPENDITURES	REVENUES	PURCHASES	NONDEFENSE	TRANSFER
1960	31.8	25.9	23.0	14.9	5.3
1961	33.2	25.9	23.8	15.7	5.9
1962	33.2	26.1	24.1	15.8	5.6
1963	33.1	26.6	23.9	15.8	5.6
1964	32.4	25.5	23.4	15.7	5.3
1965	31.8	25.5	22.9	15.4	5.3
1966	32.7	26.2	23.7	15.6	5.3
1967	34.8	26.5	25.0	16.1	6.0
1968	35.2	28.1	24.9	16.0	6.4
1969	33.6	28.1	23.6	15.5	6.3
1970	35.1	27.0	23.6	16.0	7.2
1971	35.2	26.4	23.1	16.0	7.9
1972	34.8	27.5	22.5	15.9	8.0
1973	33.8	27.7	21.4	15.5	8.1
1974	35.2	28.2	22.2	16.4	8.8
1975	37.2	26.5	22.7	17.1	10.1
1976	35.8	27.3	21.6	16.4	9.8
1977	34.7	27.6	20.9	15.9	9.4
1978	33.8	27.7	20.3	15.5	8.9
1979	33.6	28.0	20.0	15.3	9.0
1980	35.5	28.2	20.6	15.7	9.8
1981	35.7	28.9	20.4	15.3	9.9
1982	37.9	28.4	21.2	15.7	10.6
1983	37.8	27.7	21.0	15.6	10.5
1984	36.6	27.8	20.4	15.1	9.8
1985	37.1	28.2	20.9	15.6	9.7
1986	37.5	28.4	21.2	15.9	9.7
1987	37.2	29.1	21.2	15.8	9.5
1988	36.3	28.9	20.5	15.3	9.4
1989	36.2	29.0	20.4	15.3	9.5
1990	36.9	28.9	20.7	15.8	9.9
1991	37.7	28.8	21.0	16.0	10.2
1992	38.4	28.5	20.6	15.9	11.6
1993	37.7	28.6	19.9	15.5	11.7
1994	36.5	28.9	19.2	15.2	11.5
1995	36.5	29.2	18.9	15.2	11.5
1996	35.7	29.7	18.5	14.9	11.5
1997	34.6	30.0	18.1	14.7	11.1
1998	33.6	30.4	17.8	14.6	10.8
1999	33.1	30.4	17.9	14.7	10.5
2000	32.6	30.8	17.8	14.8	10.4
2001	33.7	29.7	18.4	15.4	11.0
2002	34.6	27.3	19.1	15.8	11.6
2003	35.0	26.7	19.3	15.7	11.8
2004	34.7	26.8	19.2	15.6	11.7
2005	34.7	28.2	19.0	15.4	11.7
2006	34.8	29.1	19.1	15.5	11.8
2007	35.5	29.2	19.3	15.7	12.1
2008	37.2	27.7	20.4	16.4	13.0
2009	40.6	25.8	21.4	17.2	15.1
2010	40.8	26.1	21.2	16.9	15.4
2011	39.7	26.3	20.3	16.1	15.0
2012	38.4	26.4	19.5	15.5	14.7

Source: http://www.bea.gov

[1]There are some differences across reporting agencies with regard to accounting procedures and the treatment of government enterprises. This results in some differences in statistical measures of the size of government.

Section 6

Year	Top 1	Top 5	Top 10	Next 40	Bottom 50
1980	19.1	36.8	49.3	43.7	7.0
1981	17.6	35.1	48.0	44.6	7.5
1982	19.0	36.1	48.6	44.1	7.3
1983	20.3	37.3	49.7	43.1	7.2
1984	21.1	38.0	50.6	42.1	7.4
1985	21.8	38.8	51.5	41.4	7.2
1986	25.7	42.6	54.7	38.9	6.5
1987	24.8	43.3	55.6	38.3	6.1
1988	27.6	45.6	57.3	37.0	5.7
1989	25.2	43.9	55.8	38.4	5.8
1990	25.1	43.6	55.4	38.8	5.8
1991	24.8	43.4	55.8	38.7	5.5
1992	27.5	45.9	58.0	36.9	5.1
1993	29.0	47.4	59.2	36.0	4.8
1994	28.9	47.5	59.4	35.8	4.8
1995	30.3	48.9	60.7	34.6	4.6
1996	32.3	51.0	62.5	33.2	4.3
1997	33.2	51.9	63.2	32.5	4.3
1998	34.8	53.8	65.0	30.8	4.2
1999	36.2	55.5	66.5	29.5	4.0
2000	37.4	56.5	67.3	28.8	3.9
2001	33.9	53.3	64.9	31.1	4.0
2002	33.7	53.8	65.7	30.8	3.5
2003	34.3	54.4	65.8	30.7	3.5
2004	36.9	57.1	68.2	28.5	3.3
2005	39.4	59.7	70.3	26.6	3.1
2006	39.9	60.1	70.8	26.2	3.0
2007	40.4	60.6	71.2	25.9	2.9
2008	38.0	58.7	70.0	27.3	2.7
2009	36.7	58.7	70.5	27.3	2.3

APPENDIX B
Answers to Selected Critical Analysis Questions

CHAPTER 1: THE ECONOMIC APPROACH

4. For most taxpayers, the change will reduce the after-tax cost of raising children. Other things being constant, one would predict an increase in the birthrate.

5. False. Intentions do not change the effect of the policy. If the policy runs counter to sound economics, it will lead to a counterproductive outcome even if that was not the intention of the policy. Bad policies are often advocated by people with good intentions.

8. Money has nothing to do with whether an individual is economizing. Any time a person chooses, in an attempt to achieve a goal, he or she is economizing.

9. Positive economics can help one better understand the likely effects of alternative policies. This will help one choose alternatives that are less likely to lead to disappointing results.

10. Association is not causation. It is likely that a large lead, near the end of the game, caused the third team to play more, rather than the third team causing the lead.

14. This is a question that highlights the importance of marginal analysis. In responding to the question, think about the following. After pollution has already been reduced substantially, how much will it cost to reduce it still more? If the quality of air and water were already high, how much gain would result from still less pollution?

CHAPTER 2: SOME TOOLS OF THE ECONOMIST

2. This is an opportunity cost question. Even though the productivity of brush painters has changed only slightly, rising productivity in other areas has led to higher wages in other occupations, thereby increasing the opportunity cost of being a house painter. Because people would not supply house-painting services unless they were able to meet their opportunity costs, higher wages are necessary to attract house painters from competitive (alternative) lines of work.

8. Yes. This question highlights the incentive of individuals to conserve for the future when they have private ownership rights. The market value of the land will increase in anticipation of the future harvest as the trees grow and the expected day of harvest grows closer. Thus, with transferable private property, the tree farmer will be able to capture the value added by his planting and holding the trees for a few years, even if the actual harvest does not take place until well after his death.

9. In general, it sanctions all forms of competition except for the use of violence (or the threat of violence), theft, or fraud.

12. Those who get tickets at the lower price gain, whereas those who are prevented from offering a higher price to ticket holders may not get a ticket even though both the prospective buyer and some ticket holders would have gained from the exchange at the higher price. Ticket holders may simply break the law or may sell at the regulated price only to buyers willing to provide them with other favors. Price controls, if they are effective, always reduce the gains from trade.

17. The opportunity cost of those individuals will rise, and they will likely consume less leisure.

CHAPTER 3: SUPPLY, DEMAND, AND THE MARKET PROCESS

1. Choices (a) and (b) would increase the demand for beef; (c) and (d) would affect primarily the supply of beef, rather than the demand; (e) leads to a change in quantity demanded, not a change in demand.

4. Prices reflect marginal value, not total value. The marginal value of a good is the maximum amount a consumer would be willing to pay for a specific unit. The height of the

demand curve reflects the value that consumers place on each unit. The total value is the total benefit consumers derive from all units consumed. The area under the demand curve for the number of units consumed reflects the total value. Water provides an example of a good with high total value but low marginal value. With regard to the last question, are there more nurses or professional wrestlers?

8. Neither markets nor the political process leaves the determination of winners and losers to chance. Under market organization, business winners and losers are determined by the decentralized choices of millions of consumers who use their dollar votes to reward firms that provide preferred goods at a low cost and penalize others who fail to do so. Under political decision-making, the winners and losers are determined by political officials who use taxes, subsidies, regulations, and mandates to favor some businesses and penalize others.

10. **a.** Profitable production increases the value of resources owned by people and leads to mutual gain for resource suppliers, consumers, and entrepreneurs. **b.** Losses reduce the value of resources, which reduces the well-being of at least some people. There is no conflict.

12. The supply curve is constructed under the assumption that other things are held constant. A reduction in the supply of oranges such as would occur under adverse weather conditions would lead to both a higher price and smaller total quantity supplied. This is perfectly consistent with economic theory.

CHAPTER 4: SUPPLY AND DEMAND: APPLICATIONS AND EXTENSIONS

1. An increase in demand for housing will also increase the demand for the resources required for its production, including the services of carpenters, plumbers, and electricians. This will lead to higher wages and an increase in employment for people in these groups.

4. Agreement of both buyer and seller is required for an exchange. Price ceilings push prices below equilibrium and thereby reduce the quantity sellers are willing to offer. Price floors push prices above equilibrium and thereby reduce the quantity consumers wish to buy. Both decrease the actual quantity traded in the market.

6. **a.** Decreases; **b.** Increases; **c.** Decreases; **d.** Increases

11. The deadweight loss is the loss of the potential gains of buyers and sellers emanating from trades that are squeezed out by the tax. It is an excess burden because even though the exchanges that are squeezed out by the tax impose a cost on buyers and sellers, they do not generate tax revenue (because the trades do not take place).

12. The employment level of low-skilled workers with large families would decline. Some would attempt to conceal the presence of their large family in order to get a job.

14. No. As the tax rate approaches the revenue maximum point, the higher rates substantially reduce the number of trades that take place. This is why the higher rates do not raise much additional revenue. As rates increase toward the revenue maximum point, the lost gains from trade are large and the additions to revenue are small. Thus, rates in this range are highly inefficient.

CHAPTER 5: DIFFICULT CASES FOR THE MARKET, AND THE ROLE OF GOVERNMENT

1. When payment is not demanded for services, potential customers have a strong incentive to attempt a "free ride." However, when the number of nonpaying customers becomes such that the sales revenues of sellers are diminished (and in some cases eliminated), the sellers' incentive to supply the good is thereby reduced (or eliminated).

9. By reducing output below the efficient level, sellers of toasters would no longer produce or exchange some units of the good, despite the fact that the consumers value the marginal units more than it costs to produce them.

11. A public good reflects the characteristics of the good, not the sector in which it is provided. Elementary education is not a public good because it is relatively easy to exclude nonpaying customers and to establish a one-to-one link between payment for and receipt of the good.

CHAPTER 6: THE ECONOMICS OF COLLECTIVE DECISION-MAKING

2. Corporate officers, although they surely care about the next few months and the profits during that time, also care about the value of the firm and its stock price. If the stock price rises sufficiently in the next few months—as it will if investors believe that current investments in future-oriented projects (planting new trees, for example) are sound—then the officers will find their jobs secure even if current profits do not look good. Rights to the profits from those (future) trees are salable now in the form of the corporation's stock. There is no such mechanism to make the distant fruits of today's investments available to the political entrepreneurs who might otherwise fight for the future-oriented project. Only if the project appeals to today's voters, and only if they are willing to pay today for tomorrow's benefits, will the program be a political success. In any case, the wealth of the political official is not directly enhanced by his or her successful fight for the project.

4. The problem is not so much that the "wrong guys" won the last election as it is the incentive structure confronted by political decision-makers. Even if the "right people" were elected, they would be unlikely to improve the efficiency of government, at least not very much, given the strong incentive to support special-interest and shortsighted policies and the weak incentives for operational efficiency when decisions are made by the political process.

8. It is difficult for the voter to know what a candidate will do once elected, and the rationally ignorant voter is usually unwilling to spend the time and effort required to understand issues because the probability that any single vote will decide the issue is exceedingly small. Special-interest voters, in contrast, will know which candidate has promised them the most on their issue. Also, the candidate who is both competent and prepared to ignore special interests will have a hard time getting these facts to voters without financial support from special-interest groups. Each voter has an incentive to be a "free rider" on the "good government" issue. Interestingly, controlling government on behalf of society as a whole is a public good. As in the case of other public goods, there is a tendency for too little of it to be supplied.

10. No. The government is merely an alternative form of organization. Government organization does not permit us to escape either scarcity or competition. It merely affects the nature of the competition. Political competition (for example, voting, lobbying, political contributions, and politically determined budgets) replaces market competition. Neither is there any reason to believe that government organization modifies the importance of personal self-interest.

12. When the welfare of a special-interest group conflicts with that of a widely dispersed, unorganized majority, the legislative political process can reasonably be expected to work to the benefit of the special interest.

CHAPTER 7: TAKING THE NATION'S ECONOMIC PULSE

1. Choices (a), (c), (f), (g), and (h) will exert no effect on GDP; (b) and (d) will increase GDP by the amount of the expenditure; and (e) will increase GDP by $250 (the commission on the transaction).

3. Because the furniture was produced last year, the sale does not affect GDP this year. It reduces inventory investment by $100,000 and increases consumption by $100,000, leaving GDP unchanged.

7. $8.31
9. **a.** $1,000; **b.** $600; **c.** $200; **d.** 0; **e.** $20,000
11. **a.** False. Inventory investment indicates whether the holdings of unsold goods are rising or falling. A negative inventory investment merely indicates that there was a reduction in the size of inventories during the period. **b.** False. If gross investment is less than the depreciation of capital goods during the period, net investment would be negative. Net investment in the United States was negative for several years during the Great Depression of the 1930s. **c.** Not necessarily. Rather, it may be the result of an increase in prices, population, or hours worked.
12. Neither the receipts nor the expenditures on payouts would count toward GDP because they are merely transfers—they do not involve production. However, expenditures on operations, administration, and government-provided goods and services from lottery proceeds would add to GDP.
16. **a.** $2,30.1 billion; **b.** $4,272.8 billion; **c.** 47.8; **d.** $5,800.5 billion; **e.** 88.6; **f.** $12,638.4 billion; **g.** $13,591.7 billion

CHAPTER 8: ECONOMIC FLUCTUATIONS, UNEMPLOYMENT, AND INFLATION

2. Job seekers do not know which employers will offer them the more attractive jobs. They find out by searching. Job search is "profitable" and consistent with economic efficiency as long as the marginal gain from search exceeds the marginal cost of searching. The job search process will lead to a better match between the skills of employees and the requirements of the available jobs.
3. Individuals (e) and (f) would be classified as employed; (a), (b), and (c) would be classified as unemployed; (d) is not in the labor force.
6. When the actual unemployment rate is equal to the natural rate of unemployment, cyclical unemployment is absent and potential GDP is at its sustainable rate.
7. **a.** 60 percent; **b.** 8.3 percent; **c.** 55 percent
8. No. It means that there were no jobs available at wage rates acceptable to the potential workers who were unemployed. Thus, they continued to search for more attractive opportunities.
13. The wages people earn are also prices (prices for labor services) and, like other prices, they usually rise as the general level of prices increases. The statement ignores this factor. It implicitly assumes that money wages are unaffected by inflation—that they would have increased by the same amount (6 percent) even if prices would have been stable. Generally, this will not be the case.

CHAPTER 9: AN INTRODUCTION TO BASIC MACROECONOMIC MARKETS

4. When the price level is higher than anticipated, real wages will decline and employment expands. Profit rates will be higher than normal, and the actual rate of unemployment will fall below the natural rate. The abnormally high rate of output will not be sustainable, because the real wage rates will rise when the long-term contracts expire and are renegotiated.
6. An increase in the real interest rate will make it more attractive for foreigners to purchase bonds and make other investments in the United States. As a result, there will be an increase in the inflow of capital from abroad.
10. They are all equal.
12. $10,000; $20,000
15. **a.** 5,700; **b.** No, because the actual price level will be 110, higher than what was

anticipated. **c.** Actual unemployment will be less than the natural rate because the unexpected high level of prices will improve profit margins, reduce real wage rates, and cause the firms to expand output in the short run.

CHAPTER 10: DYNAMIC CHANGE, ECONOMIC FLUCTUATIONS, AND THE *AD–AS* MODEL

1. Choice (a) would decrease *AD*; (b), (c), and (d) would increase it; and (e) would leave it unchanged. For the "why" part of the question, see the Factors That Shift Aggregate Demand section at the beginning of the chapter.
2. Choices (a), (b), (c), and (d) will reduce *SRAS*; (e) will increase it.
8. Tightness in resource markets will result in rising resource prices relative to product prices, causing the *SRAS* to shift to the left. Profit margins will decline, output rates will fall, and long-run equilibrium will be restored at a higher price level. The above-normal output cannot be maintained because it reflects input prices that people would not have agreed to and output decisions they would not have chosen if they had anticipated the current price level (and rate of inflation). Once they have a chance to correct these mistakes, they do so; output returns to the economy's long-run potential.

CHAPTER 11: FISCAL POLICY: THE KEYNESIAN VIEW AND HISTORICAL PERSPECTIVE

3. The multiplier principle is the concept that a change in one of the components of aggregate demand—investment, for example—will lead to a far greater change in the equilibrium level of income. Because the multiplier equals $1/(1 - MPC)$, its size is determined by the marginal propensity to consume. The multiplier makes stabilizing the economy more difficult, because relatively small changes in aggregate demand have a much greater effect on equilibrium income.
6. Either an increase in government expenditures or a reduction in taxes should be employed to shift the budget toward a larger deficit (or smaller surplus).

CHAPTER 12: FISCAL POLICY, INCENTIVES, AND SECONDARY EFFECTS

2. The crowding-out effect is the theory that budget deficits will lead to higher real interest rates, which retard private spending. The crowding-out effect indicates that fiscal policy will not be nearly as potent as the simple Keynesian model implies. The new classical theory indicates that anticipation of higher future taxes (rather than higher interest rates) will reduce private spending when government expenditures are financed by debt.
10. In the Keynesian model, investment is determined by factors other than the interest rate. Thus, budget deficits would not exert much effect on capital formation. In the crowding-out model, capital formation would be reduced because the budget deficits would lead to higher interest rates, which would crowd out private investment. In the new classical model, households will save more, and, as a result, budget deficits could be financed without either an increase in the interest rate or a reduction in capital formation.
13. Yes. Only the lower rates would increase the incentive to earn marginal income and thereby stimulate aggregate supply.
15. No. If it takes more workers to generate a specific amount of energy with wind power, this implies that wind power is a more costly method of generating energy than either coal or natural gas. Thus, the implications of the statement are exactly the opposite of what the wind energy proponents imply.

CHAPTER 13: MONEY AND THE BANKING SYSTEM

1. A liquid asset is one that can easily and quickly be transformed into money without experiencing a loss of its market value. Assets such as high-grade bonds and stocks are highly liquid. In contrast, illiquid assets cannot be easily and quickly converted to cash without some loss of their value. Real estate, a family-owned business, business equipment, and artistic works are examples of illiquid assets.

3. Money is valuable because of its scarcity relative to the availability of goods and services. The use of money facilitates (reduces the cost of) exchange transactions. Money also serves as a store of value and a unit of account. Doubling the supply of money while holding output constant would simply cause its purchasing power to fall without enhancing the services that it performs. In fact, fluctuations in the money supply generally create uncertainty about the future value of money and thereby reduce its ability to serve as a reliable store of value, accurate unit of account, and medium of exchange for time-dimension contracting.

6. **a.** There is no change; currency held by the public increases, but checking deposits decrease by an equal amount. **b.** Bank reserves decrease by $100. **c.** Excess reserves decrease by $100, minus $100 multiplied by the required reserve ratio.

8. Answers (b), (e), and (f) will reduce the money supply; (a) and (c) will increase it. If the Treasury's deposits (or the deposits of people who receive portions of the Treasury's spending) are considered part of the money supply, then (d) will leave the money supply unchanged.

10. Whereas the transformation of deposits into currency does not directly affect the money supply, it does reduce the excess reserves of banks. The reduction in excess reserves will cause banks to reduce their outstanding loans and thereby shrink the money supply. Therefore, an increase in the holding of currency relative to deposits will tend to reduce the supply of money.

12. There are two major reasons. First, the money supply can be altered quietly via open market operations, whereas a reserve requirement change focuses attention on Fed policy. Second, open market operations are a fine-tuning method, whereas a reserve requirement change is a blunt instrument. Generally, the Fed prefers quiet, marginal changes to headline-grabbing, blunt changes that are more likely to disrupt markets.

16. **a.** Money supply increases by $100,000; **b.** $80,000; **c.** $500,000; **d.** no; there will be some leakage in the form of additional currency holdings by the public and additional excess reserve holdings by banks.

18. **a.** Money supply will increase by $2 billion; **b.** $1.8 billion; **c.** $20 billion.

CHAPTER 14: MODERN MACROECONOMICS AND MONETARY POLICY

2. Choices (a) and (c) would increase your incentive to hold money deposits; (b) and (d) would reduce your incentive to hold money.

3. **a.** The cost of obtaining the house is $100,000. **b.** The cost of holding it is the interest forgone on the $100,000 sales value of the house. **c.** The cost of obtaining $1,000 is the amount of goods one must give up in order to acquire the $1,000. For example, if a pound of sugar sells for 50 cents, the cost of obtaining $1,000 in terms of sugar is 2,000 pounds. **d.** As in the case of the house, the cost of holding $1,000 is the interest forgone.

7. **a.** Bank reserves will decline; **b.** Real interest rates will rise; **c.** Spending on consumer durables will fall; **d.** The dollar will appreciate because the higher interest rates will attract bond purchases by foreigners; **e.** Exports will decline because the appreciation of the dollar will make U.S. goods more expensive for foreigners; **f.** The higher real interest rates will tend to reduce real asset prices; **g.** Real GDP will fall.

10. If the time lag is long and variable (rather than short and highly predictable), it is less likely that policy makers will be able to time changes in monetary policy so that they

will exert a countercyclical effect on the economy. The policy makers will be more likely to make mistakes and thereby exert a destabilizing influence.

11. Association does not reveal causation. Decision-makers, including borrowers and lenders, will eventually anticipate a high rate of inflation and adjust their choices accordingly. As the expected rate of inflation increases, the demand for loanable funds will increase and the supply will decrease. This will lead to higher nominal interest rates. Thus, economic theory indicates that the causation tends to run the opposite direction from that indicated by the statement.

CHAPTER 15: STABILIZATION POLICY, OUTPUT, AND EMPLOYMENT

2. Compared with earlier periods, the United States has experienced less economic instability since 1960. This has been particularly true during the past twenty-five years. An increase in the stability of monetary policy deserves much of the credit for the more stable economic conditions of recent decades.

5. For (a) and (b), the actual and natural rates of unemployment will be equal. For (c), the actual rate will be less than the natural rate. For (d), the actual rate will exceed the natural rate.

11. **a.** Keep the inflation rate at a low and highly predictable level; **b.** No; **c.** Both nominal interest rates and the general level of prices will rise.

CHAPTER 16: CREATING AN ENVIRONMENT FOR GROWTH AND PROSPERITY

3. If poor countries follow sound policies and provide an attractive economic environment, foreigners will be willing to supply investment funds. Propelled by foreign investment, some poor countries have achieved exceedingly high rates of both investment and growth during recent decades.

8. When considering the answer to this question, think about the following: Is there an opportunity cost of the capital used by government firms? Do government firms have a strong incentive to keep costs low? Are government firms innovative?

12. The increase in diversity provides consumers with more options and thereby improves their welfare. For the most part, the GDP figures fail to capture the impact of this factor.

13. Regulations such as price ceilings, price floors, and mandated product characteristics will generally reduce the volume of gains from trade. Simultaneously, they will encourage rent-seeking activities, which will increase the contributions available to political officials.

CHAPTER 17: INSTITUTIONS, POLICIES, AND CROSS-COUNTRY DIFFERENCES IN INCOME AND GROWTH

6. Gains from trade, technological improvements, discovery of high value products (relative to cost) and lower-cost production methods, and capital formation are the major sources of economic growth. Institutions that protect property rights, enforce contracts in an even-handed manner, and promote open markets are crucial to the realization of the gains from the key sources of growth. Countries that adopt sound institutions and policies grow, while those that fail to do so stagnate.

8. It is hard to see how the less-developed economies could have grown so rapidly without borrowing technologies and ideas from the high-income countries. The high-income countries also provided both investment capital and markets for the sale of products for the LDCs. Historical growth records buttress this view. The per capita incomes of several economies including Hong Kong, Singapore, South Korea, and China have

grown at annual rates of 5 percent or more over periods of twenty-five years or more. Prior to 1960, no country was able to achieve long-term growth anywhere near such a rate. By way of comparison, per capita income in the United Kingdom and the United States grew at an annual rate of approximately 1 percent during the nineteenth century when countries with significantly higher incomes were absent.

10. A country does not have to be democratic in order to be economically free. Hong Kong illustrates this point. Neither does democracy guarantee economic freedom. India was democratic, but it was one of the world's least free economies prior to 1990.

12. Quality of the legal system: Does it protect property rights and enforce contracts fairly; tax rates; freedom to trade with others; onerous regulations, to list a few of the factors.

13. Poor economic institutions and policies provide the primary reason.

14. Because citizens can move elsewhere at a low cost. When significant numbers vote with their feet by leaving an area, the tax base will erode, and this confronts politicians with an incentive to change their ways.

CHAPTER 18: GAINING FROM INTERNATIONAL TRADE

2. Availability of goods and services, not jobs, is the source of economic prosperity. When a good can be purchased cheaper abroad than it can be produced at home, a nation can expand the quantity of goods and services available for consumption by specializing in the production of those goods for which it is a low-cost producer and trading them for the cheap (relative to domestic costs) foreign goods. Trade restrictions limiting the ability of Americans to purchase low-cost goods from foreigners stifle this process and thereby reduce the living standard of Americans.

4. Statements (a) and (b) are not in conflict. Because trade restrictions are typically a special-interest issue, political entrepreneurs can often gain by supporting them even when they promote economic inefficiency.

6. True. The primary effect of trade restrictions is an increase in domestic scarcity. This has distributional consequences, but it is clear that, as a whole, a nation will be harmed by the increased domestic scarcity that accompanies the trade restraints.

10. In thinking about this issue, consider the following points. Suppose that the Japanese were willing to give products such as automobiles, electronic goods, and clothing to us free of charge. Would we be worse off if we accepted the gifts? Should we try to keep the free goods out? What is the source of real income—jobs or goods and services? If the gifts make us better off, doesn't it follow that partial gifts would also make us better off?

12. Although trade reduces employment in import-competing industries, it expands employment in export industries. On balance, there is no reason to believe that trade either promotes or destroys jobs. The major effect of trade is to permit individuals, states, regions, and nations to generate a larger output by specializing in the things they do well and trading for those things that they would produce only at a high cost. A higher real income is the result.

16. True. If country A imposes a tariff, other countries will sell less to A and therefore acquire less purchasing power in terms of A's currency. Thus, they will have to reduce their purchases of A's export goods.

CHAPTER 19: INTERNATIONAL FINANCE AND THE FOREIGN EXCHANGE MARKET

4. On February 2, the dollar appreciated against the British pound and depreciated against the Canadian dollar.

5. Scenarios (a) and (g) would cause the dollar to appreciate; (b), (c), (d), (e), and (h) would cause the dollar to depreciate; (f) would leave the exchange rate unchanged.

8. Some people fear that foreign investment makes the United States vulnerable because foreigners might decide to sell their assets and leave suddenly. When you consider this argument, it is important to recognize that foreign and domestic investors are influenced by pretty much the same considerations. Anything that would cause foreigners to withdraw funds would also cause domestic investors to do likewise. In fact, the vulnerability runs the other way. If foreign investors were to leave, the assets financed by their funds would remain. Thus, they would be in a weak position to impose harm on the U.S. economy.

9. Each of the changes would reduce the size of the current-account deficit.

13. False. Flexible exchange rates bring the sum of the current and capital accounts into balance, but they do not necessarily lead to balance for either component.

14. **a.** No. The exchange rate will bring the overall purchases and sales into balance, but there is no reason to expect the imports and exports to any given country to be in balance. **b.** The United States imports large quantities of goods Japan and China produce at a low cost (for example, electronic products, and labor intensive goods like toys and textiles), but it is not a major exporter of goods purchased intensively by these countries (natural resources, building materials, and inexpensive consumer items).

15. These purchases increase the foreign exchange value of the dollar, which makes imports cheaper relative to exports and thereby enlarges the trade deficit. Politicians often charge that this reduces output and employment. However, the bond purchases are an inflow of capital that will also result in lower U.S. interest rates, which will tend to stimulate output and employment. Thus, there is little reason to believe that the net effect will be either substantial or harmful.

SPECIAL TOPIC 1: GOVERNMENT SPENDING AND TAXATION

1. Taxes reduce economic efficiency because they eliminate some exchanges and thereby reduce the gains from these transactions. Because of (a) the deadweight losses accompanying the elimination of exchanges and (b) the cost of collecting taxes, the costs of additional tax revenue will be greater than the revenue transferred to the government. Studies indicate that it costs between $1.20 and $1.30 for each dollar of tax revenue raised by the government.

5. As we discussed in Chapter 6, the political process works better when there is a close relationship between who pays for and who benefits from government programs. An increase in the number of people who pay no income taxes is likely to weaken this relationship. Whereas those with low incomes pay payroll taxes, the revenues from this tax are earmarked for the finance of the Social Security and Medicare programs. Thus, expansions in government are financed primarily by the personal income tax. In the future, exemption of large numbers of people from this tax is likely to make it more difficult to control the growth of government. If you do not have to help pay for more government spending, why would you oppose it?

SPECIAL TOPIC 2: THE ECONOMICS OF SOCIAL SECURITY

2. The pay-as-you-go Social Security system is facing a crisis because the inflow of tax revenue is insufficient to cover the promised benefits. Although the Social Security Trust Fund has bonds, they are merely an IOU from the Treasury to the Social Security Administration. To redeem these bonds and provide additional funds to finance Social Security benefits, the federal government will have to raise taxes (or pay the interest on

additional Treasury bonds it sells), or cut other expenditures, or both. Thus, the presence of the SSTF bonds does not do much to alleviate the crisis.

SPECIAL TOPIC 3: THE STOCK MARKET: ITS FUNCTION, PERFORMANCE, AND POTENTIAL AS AN INVESTMENT OPPORTUNITY

1. History shows that in the U.S. stock market, fairly high returns can be gained at a relatively low risk by people who hold a diverse portfolio of stocks in unrelated industries for a period of twenty years or more. An indexed equity mutual fund is an option that would allow a person to purchase a diverse portfolio while keeping commission costs low.
3. The expectation of high profits in the future drove up the price of the stock, despite the lack of a dividend payment in the first years of the firm. Investors are equally happy with high dividends or the equivalent in rising stock value due to the firm's retaining its profits for further investment.
5. Investors are buying such a stock for its rising value (price), which reflects expected future earnings and dividends.

SPECIAL TOPIC 4: GREAT DEBATES IN ECONOMICS: KEYNES VERSUS HAYEK

1. Keynes is arguing that it does not matter much how the government spends stimulus funds. According to the Keynesian view, the key consideration is to spend the funds so they will generate income for those undertaking the project, and as those funds are spent, a multiple expansion in income and aggregate demand will result.

SPECIAL TOPIC 5: THE CRISIS OF 2008: CAUSES AND LESSONS FOR THE FUTURE

3. The less equity the owner has in his or her house, the more likely he or she will default. This is particularly true in the United States because most home mortgages here are nonrecourse loans: The owner is not responsible for the debt beyond turning the property over to the lender in case of default. The lender has no legal claim on assets of the borrower beyond the asset that was mortgaged. Thus, when the value of a house falls below the outstanding loan, the borrower will often gain by simply abandoning the property. This is precisely what many have done in recent years.
5. The incentive to evaluate the borrower's creditworthiness carefully is reduced. If the mortgage originator had to keep the loan until it was repaid, there would be greater incentive for the lender to evaluate the creditworthiness of the borrower more diligently.

SPECIAL TOPIC 6: LESSONS FROM THE GREAT DEPRESSION

5. The statement reflects a failure to recognize the secondary effects of limiting imports. If we buy less from foreigners, they will have fewer dollars that are required for the purchase of our exports. Therefore, a reduction in imports will also reduce exports and there is no reason to expect any net increase in employment. Instead, trade restraints lead to less output and lower incomes.

SPECIAL TOPIC 7: THE FEDERAL BUDGET AND THE NATIONAL DEBT

1. No. Both private corporations and governments can, and often do, have continual debt outstanding. Borrowers can continue to finance and refinance debt as long as lenders have confidence in their ability to pay. This will generally be the case as long as the interest liability is small relative to income (or the potential tax base).

3. No. Remember, trade is a positive-sum game. Bonds are sold to foreigners because they are offering a better deal (acceptance of a lower interest rate) than is available elsewhere. Prohibiting the sale of bonds to foreigners would result in higher real interest rates and less investment, both of which would adversely affect Americans.

5. Lower; voters do not enjoy paying taxes and, therefore, voter dissatisfaction places a restraint on higher taxes, which would also restrain expenditures if the budget had to be balanced. More efficiently, the restraint of tax increases would tighten the budget constraint and make the reality of opportunity cost more visible to both voters and politicians.

MANAGERIAL
ECONOMICS

Fundamental Economic Concepts

CHAPTER PREVIEW

A few fundamental microeconomic concepts provide cornerstones for all of the analysis in managerial economics. Four of the most important are demand and supply, marginal analysis, net present value, and the meaning and measurement of risk. We will first review how the determinants of demand and supply establish a market equilibrium price for gasoline, crude oil, and hybrid electric cars. Marginal analysis tools are central when a decision maker is seeking to optimize some objective, such as maximizing cost savings from changing a lightbulb (e.g., from normal incandescent to compact fluorescent lights [CFL] or light-emitting diodes [LED]). The net present value concept makes alternative cash flows occurring at different points in time directly comparable. In so doing, it provides the linkage between the timing and risk of a firm's projected profits and the shareholder wealth-maximization objective. Risk-return analysis is important to an understanding of the many trade-offs that managers must consider as they introduce new products, expand capacity, or outsource overseas in order to increase expected profits at the risk of greater variation in profits.

Two appendices elaborate these topics for those who want to know more analytical details and seek exposure to additional application tools. Appendix C develops the relationship between marginal analysis and differential calculus. Web Appendix F shows how managers incorporate explicit probability information about the risk of various outcomes into individual choice models, decision trees, risk-adjusted discount rates, simulation analysis, and scenario planning.

MANAGERIAL CHALLENGE
Why Charge $25 per Bag on Airline Flights?

In May 2008, American Airlines (AA) announced that it would immediately begin charging $25 per bag on all AA flights, not for extra luggage but for the first bag! Crude oil had nearly doubled from $70 to $130 per barrel in the previous 12 months, and jet fuel prices had accelerated even faster. AA's new baggage policy applied to all ticketed passengers except first class and business class. On top of incremental airline charges for sandwiches and snacks introduced the previous year, this

new announcement stunned the travel public. Previously, only a few deep discount U.S. carriers with very limited route structures such as People Express had charged separately for both food and baggage service. Since American Airlines and many other major carriers had belittled that policy as part of their overall marketing campaign against deep discounters, AA executives faced a dilemma.

Jet fuel surcharges had recovered the year-over-year average variable cost increase for jet fuel expenses, but

Cont.

MANAGERIAL CHALLENGE *Continued*

incremental variable costs (the marginal cost) remained uncovered. A quick back-of-the-envelope calculation outlines the problem. If total variable costs for a 500-mile flight on a 180-seat 737-800 rise from $22,000 in 2007 Q2 to $36,000 in 2008 Q2 because of $14,000 of additional fuel costs, then competitively priced carriers would seek to recover $14,000/180 = $78 per seat in jet fuel surcharges. The average variable cost rise of $78 would be added to the price for each fare class. For example, the $188 Super Saver airfare, restricted to 14-day advance purchase and Saturday night stayovers, would go up to $266. Class M airfares, requiring 7-day advance purchase but no Saturday stayovers, would rise from $289 to $367. Full coach economy airfares without purchase restrictions would rise from $419 to $497, and so on.

The problem was that by 2008 Q2, the marginal cost for jet fuel had risen to approximately $1 for each pound transported 500 miles. Carrying an additional 170-pound passenger in 2007 had resulted in $45 of additional fuel costs. By May 2008, the marginal fuel cost was $170 – $45 = $125 higher! So although the $78 fuel surcharge was offsetting the accounting expense increase when one averaged in cheaper earlier fuel purchases, additional current purchases were much more expensive. Managers realized they should focus on this much higher $170 marginal cost when deciding on incremental seat sales and deeply discounted prices.

And similarly, this marginal $1 per pound for 500 miles became the focus of attention in analyzing baggage cost. A first suitcase was traveling free under the prior baggage policy, as long as it weighed less than 42 pounds. But that maximum allowed suitcase imposed $42 of marginal cost in May 2008. Therefore, in mid-2008, American Airlines (and now other major

carriers) announced a $25 baggage fee for the first bag in order to cover the marginal cost of the representative suitcase on AA, which weighs 25.4 pounds.

Discussion Questions

■ How should the airline respond when presented with an overweight bag (more than 42 pounds)?

■ Explain whether or not each of the following should be considered a variable cost that increases with each additional airline seat sale: baggage costs, crew costs, commissions on ticket sales, airport parking costs, food costs, and additional fuel costs from passenger weight.

■ If jet fuel prices reverse their upward trend and begin to decline, fuel surcharges based on average variable cost will catch up with and surpass marginal costs. How should the airlines respond then?

DEMAND AND SUPPLY: A REVIEW

Demand and supply simultaneously determine equilibrium market price (P_{eq}). P_{eq} equates the desired rate of purchase Q_d/t with the planned rate of sale Q_s/t. Both concepts address intentions—that is, purchase intentions and supply intentions. Demand is therefore a potential concept often distinguished from the transactional event of "units sold." In that sense, demand is more like the potential sales concept of customer traffic than it is the accounting receivables concept of revenue from completing an actual sale. Analogously, supply is more like scenario planning for operations than it is like actual production, distribution, and delivery. In addition, supply and demand are explicitly rates per unit time period (e.g., autos per week at a Chevy dealership and the aggregate purchase intentions of the households in the surrounding target market). Hence, P_{eq} is a market-clearing equilibrium concept, a price that equates the flow rates of intended purchase and planned sale.

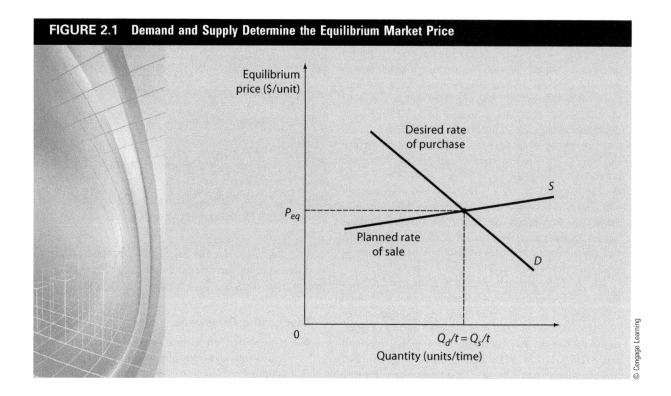

FIGURE 2.1   Demand and Supply Determine the Equilibrium Market Price

When the order flow to buy at a given price (Q_d/t) in Figure 2.1 just balances against the order flow to sell at that price (Q_s/t), P_{eq} has emerged, but what ultimately determines this metric of "value" in a marketplace? Among the earliest answers can be found in the Aristotelian concept of intrinsic use value. Because diamonds secure marriage covenants and peace pacts between nations, they provide enormous use value and should therefore exhibit high market value. The problem with this theory of value taken alone arises when one considers cubic zirconium diamonds. No one other than a jewel merchant can distinguish the artificial cubic zirconium from the real thing, and therefore the intrinsic uses of both types are identical. Yet, cubic zirconium diamonds sell for many times less than natural stones of like grade and color. Why? One clue arose at the end of the Middle Ages, when Catholic monasteries produced beautiful hand-copied Bibles and sold them for huge sums (i.e., $22,400 in 2012 dollars) to other monasteries and the nobility. In 1455, Johannes Gutenberg offered a "mass produced" printed facsimile that could be put to exactly the same intrinsic use, and yet the market value fell almost one-hundredfold to $250 in 2010 dollars. Why?

Equilibrium market price results from the interaction of demanders and suppliers involved in an exchange. In addition to the use value demanders anticipate from a product, a supplier's variable cost will also influence the market price observed. Ultimately, therefore, what minimum asking price suppliers require to cover their variable costs is just as pivotal in determining value in exchange as what maximum offer price buyers are willing to pay. Gutenberg Bibles and cubic zirconium diamonds exchange in a marketplace at lower "value" not because they are intrinsically less useful than prior copies of the Bible or natural diamonds, but simply because the bargain struck between buyers and sellers of these products will likely be negotiated down to a level that just covers their lower variable cost plus a small profit. Otherwise, preexisting competitors are likely to win the business by asking less.

Even when the cost of production is nearly identical and intrinsic use value is nearly identical, equilibrium market prices can still differ markedly. One additional determinant of value helps to explain why. Market value depends upon the relative scarcity of resources. Hardwoods are scarce in Japan, but plentiful in Sweden. Even though the cost of timber cutting and sawmill planing is the same in both locations, hardwood trees have scarcity value as raw material in Japan that they do not have in Sweden where they are plentiful. To take another example, whale oil for use in lamps throughout the nineteenth and early twentieth centuries stayed at a nearly constant price until whale species began to be harvested at rates beyond their sustainable yield. As whale resources became scarcer, the whalers who expended no additional cost on better equipment or longer voyages came home with less oil from reduced catches. With less raw material on the market, the input price of whale oil rose quickly. Consequently, despite unchanged other costs of production, the scarcer input led to a higher final product price. Similar results occur in the commodity market for coffee beans or orange juice when climate changes or insect infestations in the tropics cause crop projections to decline and scarcity value to rise.

Example

Discovery of Jojoba Bean Causes a Collapse of Whale Oil Lubricant Prices[1]

Until the last decade of the twentieth century, the best-known lubricant for high friction machinery with repeated temperature extremes like fan blades in aircraft jet engines, contact surfaces in metal cutting tools, and gearboxes in auto transmissions was a naturally occurring substance—sperm whale oil. In the early 1970s, the United States placed sperm whales on the endangered species list and banned their harvest. With the increasing scarcity of whales, the world market price of whale oil lubricant approached $200 per quart. Research and development for synthetic oil substitutes tried again and again but failed to find a replacement. Finally, a California scientist suggested the extract of the jojoba bean as a natural, environmentally friendly lubricant. The jojoba bean grows like a weed throughout the desert of the southwestern United States on wild trees that can be domesticated and cultivated to yield beans for up to 150 years.

After production ramped up from 150 tons in 1986 to 700 tons in 1995, solvent-extracted jojoba sold for $10 per quart. When tested in the laboratory, jojoba bean extract exhibits some lubrication properties that exceed those of whale oil (e.g., thermal stability over 400°F). Although 85 to 90 percent of jojoba bean output is used in the production of cosmetics, the confirmation of this plentiful substitute for high-friction lubricants caused a collapse in whale lubricant prices. Sperm whale lubricant has the same cost of production and the same use value as before the discovery of jojoba beans, but the scarcity value of the raw material input has declined tenfold. Consequently, a quart of sperm whale lubricant now sells for under $20 per quart.

---

[1]Based on "Jojoba Producers Form a Marketing Coop," *Chemical Marketing Reporter* (January 8, 1995), p. 10.

The Diamond-Water Paradox and the Marginal Revolution

So equilibrium price in a marketplace is related to (1) intrinsic use value, (2) production cost, and (3) input scarcity. In addition, however, most products and services have more than one use and more than one method of production. And often these differences relate to how much or how often the product has already been consumed or produced. For example, the initial access to e-mail servers or the Internet for several hours per day is often essential to maintaining good communication with colleagues and business associates. Additional access makes it possible to employ search engines such as Google for information related to a work assignment. Still more access affords an opportunity to meet friends in a chat room. Finally, some households might purchase even more hours of access on the chance that a desire to surf the Web would arise unexpectedly. Each of these uses has its own distinct value along a continuum starting with necessities and ending with frivolous nonessentials. Accordingly, what a customer will pay for another hour of Internet access depends on the incremental hour in question. For any given item or service, the greater the utilization already, the lower the use value remaining.

marginal use value The additional value of the consumption of one more unit; the greater the utilization already, the lower the use value remaining.

This concept of a **marginal use value** that declines as the rate of consumption increases leads to a powerful insight about consumer behavior. The question was posed: "Why should something as essential to human life as water sell for low market prices while something as frivolous as cosmetic diamonds sell for high market prices?" The initial answer was that water is inexpensive to produce in most parts of the world while diamonds require difficult search and discovery, expensive mining, and extensive transportation and security expenses. In other words, diamonds cost more than water, so minimum asking prices of suppliers dictate the higher market value observed for diamonds. However, recall that supply is only one of what Alfred Marshall famously called "two blades of the scissors" representing demand and supply. You can stab with one blade but you can't cut paper, and using supply alone, you can't fully explain equilibrium market price.

marginal utility The use value obtained from the last unit consumed.

The diamond-water paradox was therefore restated more narrowly: "Why should consumers bid low offer prices for something as essential as water while bidding high offer prices for something as frivolous as diamonds?" The resolution of this narrower paradox hinges on distinguishing marginal use value (**marginal utility**) from total use value (total utility). Clearly, in some circumstances and locales, the use value of water is enormous. At an oasis in the desert, water does prevent you from thirsting to death. And even in the typical city, the first couple of ounces of some liquid serve this same function, but that's the first couple of ounces. The next couple of dozen gallons per day remain at high use value for drinking, flushing indoor plumbing, cooking, body washing, and so forth. Thereafter, water is used for clothes washing, landscape watering, car washing, and sundry lesser purposes. Indeed, if one asks the typical American household (which consumes 80–100 gallons per person per day) to identify its least valuable use of water each day, the answer may come back truly frivolous—perhaps something like the water that runs down the sink drain while brushing teeth. In other words, the *marginal use value* of water in most developed countries is the water that saves the consumer the inconvenience of turning the water taps (on and off) twice rather than just once. And it is this marginal use value at the relevant margin, not the total utility across all uses, that determines a typical water consumer's meager willingness to pay.

Marginal Utility and Incremental Cost Simultaneously Determine Equilibrium Market Price

Alfred Marshall had it right: demand and supply do simultaneously determine market equilibrium price. On the one hand, marginal utility determines the maximum offer price consumers are willing to pay for each additional unit of consumption on the demand side of the market. On the other hand, variable cost at the margin (an incremental cost concept sometimes referred to as "marginal cost") determines the minimum asking price producers are willing to accept for each additional unit supplied. Water is

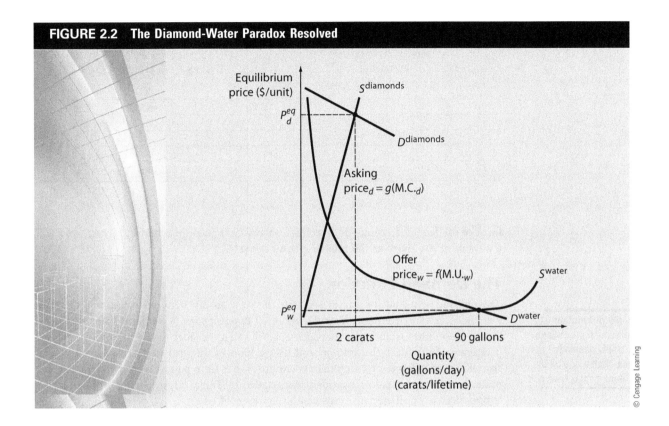

FIGURE 2.2   The Diamond-Water Paradox Resolved

both cheaper to produce and more frivolous than diamonds *at the relevant margin*, and hence water's market equilibrium price is lower than that of diamonds. Figure 2.2 illustrates this concept of marginal use value for water varying from the absolutely essential first few ounces to the frivolous water left running while brushing one's teeth.

At the same time, the marginal cost of producing water remains low throughout the 90-gallon range of a typical household's daily consumption. In contrast, diamonds exhibit steeply rising marginal cost even at relatively small volume, and customers continue to employ cosmetic diamonds for highly valuable uses even out to the relevant margin (one to three carats) where typical households find their purchases occurring. Therefore, diamonds *should* trade for equilibrium market prices that exceed the equilibrium market price of water.

Individual and Market Demand Curves

We have seen that the market-clearing equilibrium price (P_{eq}) that sets the desired rate of purchase (Q_d/t) equal to the planned rate of sale (Q_s/t) is simultaneously both the maximum offer price demanders are willing to pay (the "offer") and the minimum asking price sellers are willing to accept (the "ask"). But what determines the desired rate of purchase Q_d/t and planned rate of sales Q_s/t? The demand schedule (sometimes called the "demand curve") is the simplest form of the demand relationship. It is merely a list of prices and corresponding quantities of a commodity that would be demanded by some individual or group of individuals at uniform prices. Table 2.1 shows the demand schedule for regular-size pizzas at a Pizza Hut restaurant. This demand schedule indicates that if the price were $9.00, customers would purchase 60 per night. Note that the lower the price, the greater the quantity that will be demanded. This is the strongest

TABLE 2.1 SIMPLIFIED DEMAND SCHEDULE: PIZZA HUT RESTAURANT	
PRICE OF PIZZA ($/UNIT)	QUANTITY OF PIZZAS SOLD (UNITS PER TIME PERIOD)
10	50
9	60
8	70
7	80
6	90
5	100

© Cengage Learning

form of the law of demand—if a product or service is income superior, a household will always purchase more as the relative price declines.

The Demand Function

demand function A relationship between quantity demanded per unit of time and all the determinants of demand.

The demand schedule (or curve) specifies the relationship between prices and quantity demanded, *holding constant the influence of all other factors.* A **demand function** specifies all these other factors that management will often consider, including the design and packaging of products, the amount and distribution of the firm's advertising budget, the size of the sales force, promotional expenditures, the time period of adjustment for any price changes, and taxes or subsidies. As detailed in Table 2.2, the demand function for hybrid-electric or all-electric autos can be represented as

$$Q_D = f(P, P_S, P_C, Y, A, A_C, N, C_P, P_E, T_A, T/S \ldots) \qquad [2.1]$$

where Q_D = quantity demanded of (e.g., Toyota Prius or Chevy Volt)
  P = price of the good or service (the auto)
  P_S = price of **substitute goods** or services (e.g., the popular gasoline-powered Honda Accord or Chevy Cruze)
  P_C = price of **complementary goods** or services (replacement batteries)
  Y = income of consumers
  A = advertising and promotion expenditures by Toyota or General Motors (GM)
  A_C = competitors' advertising and promotion expenditures (e.g., Honda)
  N = size of the potential target market (demographic factors)
  C_P = consumer tastes and preferences for a "greener" form of transportation
  P_E = expected future price appreciation or depreciation of hybrid autos
  T_A = purchase adjustment time period
  T/S = taxes or subsidies on hybrid autos

substitute goods Alternative products whose demand increases when the price of the focal product rises.

complementary goods Complements in consumption whose demand decreases when the price of the focal product rises.

The demand schedule or demand curve merely deals with the price-quantity relationship itself. Changes in the price (P) of the good or service will result only in movement along the demand curve, whereas changes in any of the other demand determinants in the demand function (P_S, P_C, Y, A, A_C, N, C_P, P_E, and so on) shift the demand curve. This is illustrated graphically in Figure 2.3. The initial demand relationship is line DD'. If the original price were P_1, quantity Q_1 would be demanded. If the price declined to P_2, the quantity demanded would increase to Q_2. If, however, changes occurred in the other determinants of demand, we would expect to have a shift in the entire demand curve. If, for example, a subsidy to hybrids were enacted, the new demand curve might become

TABLE 2.2 PARTIAL LIST OF FACTORS AFFECTING DEMAND

DEMAND FACTOR	EXPECTED EFFECT
Increase (decrease) in price of substitute goods[a] (P_S)	Increase (decrease) in demand (Q_D)
Increase (decrease) in price of complementary goods[b] (P_C)	Decrease (increase) in Q_D
Increase (decrease) in consumer income levels[c] (Y)	Increase (decrease) in Q_D
Increase (decrease) in the amount of advertising and marketing expenditures (A)	Increase (decrease) in Q_D
Increase (decrease) in level of advertising and marketing by competitors (A_C)	Decrease (increase) in Q_D
Increase (decrease) in population (N)	Increase (decrease) in Q_D
Increase (decrease) in consumer preferences for the good or service (C_P)	Increase (decrease) in Q_D
Expected future price increases (decreases) for the good (P_E)	Increase (decrease) in Q_D
Time period of adjustment increases (decreases) (T_A)	Increase (decrease) in Q_D
Taxes (subsidies) on the good increase (decrease) (T/S)	Decrease (increase) in Q_D

© Cengage Learning

[a]Two goods are substitutes if an increase (decrease) in the price of Good 1 results in an increase (decrease) in the quantity demanded of Good 2, holding other factors constant, such as the price of Good 2, other prices, income, and so on, or vice versa. For example, margarine may be viewed as a rather good substitute for butter. As the price of butter increases, more people will decrease their consumption of butter and increase their consumption of margarine.

[b]Goods that are used in conjunction with each other, either in production or consumption, are called *complementary goods*. For example, DVDs are used in conjunction with DVD players. An increase in the price of DVD players would have the effect of decreasing the demand for DVDs, *ceteris paribus*. In other words, two goods are complementary if a decrease in the price of Good 1 results in an increase in the quantity demanded of Good 2, *ceteris paribus*. Similarly, two goods are complements if an increase in the price of Good 1 results in a decrease in the quantity demanded of Good 2.

[c]The case of inferior goods—that is, those goods that are purchased in smaller total quantities as income levels rise—will be discussed in Chapter 3.

FIGURE 2.3 Shifts in Demand

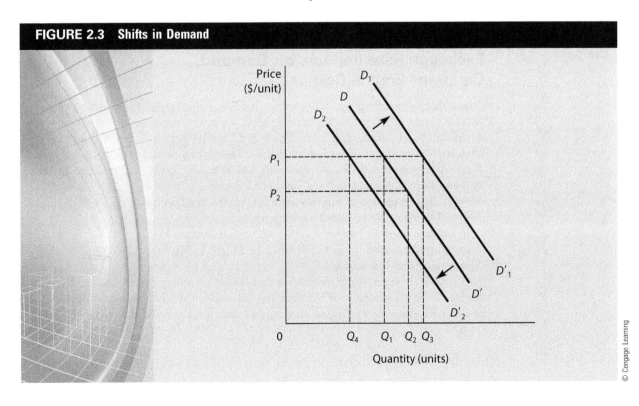

© Cengage Learning

$D_1D'_1$. At any price, P_1, along $D_1D'_1$, a greater quantity, Q_3, will be demanded than at the same price before the subsidy on the original curve DD'. Similarly, if the prices of substitute products such as the Honda Civic or Chevy Cruze were to decline sharply, the demand curve would shift downward and to the left. At any price, P_1, along the new curve D'_2D_2, a smaller quantity, Q_4, would be demanded than at the same price on either DD' or $D_1D'_1$.

In summary, movement along a demand curve is often referred to as *a change in the quantity demanded*, while holding constant the effects of factors other than price that determine demand. In contrast, a shift of the entire demand curve is often referred to as a *change in demand* and is always caused by some demand determinant other than price.

Import-Export Traded Goods

In addition to the previous determinants of demand, the demand for goods traded in foreign markets is also influenced by external factors such as exchange rate fluctuations. When Microsoft sells computer software overseas, it prefers to be paid in U.S. dollars. This is because a company like Microsoft incurs few offshore expenses beyond advertising and therefore cannot simply match payables and receivables in a foreign currency. To accept euros, Japanese yen, or Australian dollars in payment for software purchase orders would introduce an exchange rate risk exposure for which Microsoft would want to be compensated in the form of higher prices on its software. Consequently, the foreign exports of Microsoft are typically transacted in U.S. dollars and are therefore tied inextricably to the price of the dollar against other currencies. As the value of the dollar rises, offshore buyers must pay a larger amount of their own currency to obtain the U.S. dollars required to complete a purchase order for Microsoft's software, and this decreases the export demand. Even in a large domestic market like the United States, companies often find that these export demand considerations are key determinants of their overall demand.

Example

Exchange Rate Impacts on Demand: Cummins Engine Company

Cummins Engine Company of Columbus, Indiana, is the largest independent manufacturer of new and replacement diesel engines for heavy trucks and for construction, mining, and agricultural machinery. Volvo and Daimler-Benz are their major competitors, and 53 percent of sales occur offshore. The Cummins and Daimler-Benz large diesel truck engines sell for approximately $40,000 and €35,000, respectively. In the 2002 recession, Cummins *suffered* substantial declines in cash flow. One reason was obvious: diesel replacement engines are not needed when fewer goods are being delivered, and therefore fewer diesels are wearing out.

In addition, however, between 1999 and 2002, the value of the U.S. dollar (€ per $) increased by 30 percent from €.85/$ to €1.12/$. This meant that a $40,000 Cummins diesel engine that had sold for €34,000 in Munich in 1999 became €44,800, whereas the €35,000 Mercedes diesel alternative that had been selling for $41,176 in Detroit declined to $31,250 because of the stronger U.S. dollar. Cummins faced two unattractive options, either of which would reduce its cash flow. It could either cut its profit

(continued)

margins and maintain unit sales, or maintain margins but have both offshore and domestic sales collapse. The company chose to cut margins and maintain sales. By 2005, the dollar's value had eroded, returning to €.85/$, and Cummins' sales performance markedly improved. In the interim, demand for Cummins engines was adversely affected by the temporary appreciation of the U.S. dollar.

In 2009, with the U.S. dollar at a still lower value of €.64/$, the Cummins Engine Co. could barely keep up with export demand since diesels to Europe were priced at €25,600 versus Mercedes' €32,000. Similarly, in Cleveland, St. Louis, and Atlanta, Cummins $40,000 diesels were up against $54,688 Mercedes substitutes. What a great time to be an American company competing against European manufacturers.

Individual and Market Supply Curves

What determines the planned rate of sale Q_s/t? Like the demand schedule, the supply schedule is a list of prices and corresponding quantities that an individual or group of sellers desires to sell at uniform prices, *holding constant the influence of all other factors.* A number of these other determinants of supply that management will often need to consider are detailed in Table 2.3. The **supply function** can be represented as

supply function
A relationship between quantity supplied and all the determinants of supply.

$$Q_S = f(P, P_I, P_{UI}, T, EE, F, RC, P_E, T_A, T/S \ldots) \qquad [2.2]$$

where Q_s = quantity supplied (e.g., of domestic autos)
  P = price of the autos
  P_I = price of inputs (e.g., sheet metal)
  P_{UI} = price of unused substitute inputs (e.g., fiberglass)
  T = technological improvements (e.g., robotic welding)
  EE = entry or exit of other auto sellers
  F = accidental supply interruptions from fires, floods, etc.
  RC = costs of regulatory compliance
  P_E = expected (future) changes in price
  T_A = adjustment time period
  T/S = taxes or subsidies

TABLE 2.3 PARTIAL LIST OF FACTORS AFFECTING SUPPLY

SUPPLY FACTOR	EXPECTED EFFECT AT EVERY PRICE
Increase (decrease) in the price of inputs (P_I)	Decrease (increase) in supply
Increase (decrease) in the price of unused substitute inputs (P_{UI})	Decrease (increase) in supply
Technological improvements (T)	Increase in supply
Entry (Exit) of other sellers (EE)	Increase (decrease) in supply
Supply disruptions (F)	Decrease in supply
Increase (decrease) in regulatory costs (RC)	Decrease (increase) in supply
Expected future price increases (decreases) (P_E)	Decrease (increase) in supply
Time period of adjustment lengthens (shortens) (T_A)	Increase (decrease) in supply
Taxes (subsidies) (T/S)	Decrease (increase) in supply

© Cengage Learning

NAFTA and the Reduced Labor Costs of Ford Assembly Plants in Detroit

The North American Free Trade Agreement (NAFTA) made it possible to buy sub-assemblies like axles and engine blocks from Mexican suppliers like Cifunsa, S.A., without paying any import tariff when the parts arrived in the United States. United Auto Worker (UAW) labor in a Detroit auto assembly plants making axle subassemblies can be thought about as an unused substitute input from the point of view of Ford Motor Company. NAFTA in effect lowered the input cost of substitute inputs for Ford. This means fewer employers would pursue labor contracts with the UAW and instead shift some of their production south across the Mexican border. Less demand implies lower equilibrium wages. Hence, the indirect effect of NAFTA was a reduction in the input costs for UAW labor that the Ford Motor Co. did utilize. As usual, lower input cost implies a shift of the supply curve down and to the right, an increase in supply.

---

supply curve

A relationship between price and quantity supplied per unit time, holding other determinants of supply constant.

Again, changes in the price (P) of the good or service will result only in movement along the given **supply curve**, whereas changes in any of the other independent variables (P_I, P_{UI}, T, EE, F, RC, P_E, T_A, and so on) in the function shift the supply curve. As with demand, a movement *along* a supply curve is referred to as *a change in the quantity supplied*, while holding constant other determinants of supply. A shift of the entire supply curve is often referred to as a change *in supply* and is always caused by some supply determinant other than price.

Equilibrium Market Price of Gasoline

In April–July 2008, Americans woke up to a new reality about gasoline that markedly affected their driving habits as well as U.S. energy policy. The price of a gallon of regular octane gasoline skyrocketed from $3.00 per gallon to $4.10 (see Figure 2.4). The previous summer, when gas prices had hovered around $3 per gallon, Americans had cut back

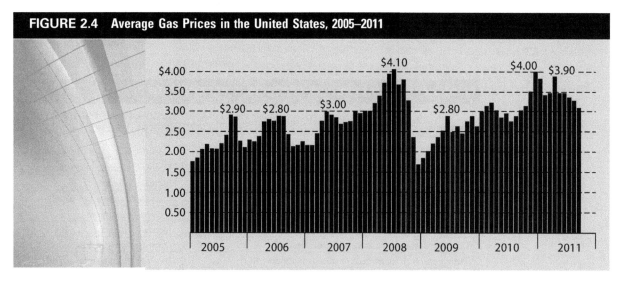

FIGURE 2.4   Average Gas Prices in the United States, 2005–2011

Source: AAA Carolinas.

only slightly on nonessential driving. In the summer of 2008, however, not only summer vacations but urban commuting itself changed in extraordinary ways. Overall, customer demand by the typical two-person urban household shrank from 16 gallons per week to 11.5 gallons as the price rose. As a result, for the first time in U.S. history, gasoline expenditure by U.S. households declined despite a rising price at the pump—that is, 16 gallons/week at $3 in 2007 (Q3) = $48 > 11.5 gallons per week at $4.10 in 2008 (Q3) = $47.15.

Several determinants of demand and supply were identified as possible explanations for the spike in gasoline's equilibrium market price. First, much was written about the fact that no new refinery had been built in the United States in more than 30 years, suggesting that refinery capacity shortages or pipeline bottlenecks might be responsible. Declining capacity does shift the supply curve in Figure 2.2 to the left, which would imply a higher equilibrium price. But no refinery closings or pipeline disruptions could be identified that summer. And the U.S. Department of Energy found refineries command only $0.36 per gallon of the final product price of gasoline in order to achieve cost recovery plus earn a profit. Therefore, refineries could not be responsible for the $1.10 increase in the equilibrium price between July 2007 and July 2008.

Second, retail gas station owners were accused of gouging the driving public. Higher markups at retail also would shift the supply curve for gasoline back to the left, raising the equilibrium market price. But again, retail markup and indeed all gasoline marketing were found to add only $0.28 per gallon to the $4.10 price, much less than could be responsible for the $1.10 run-up that summer in gasoline's equilibrium market price. Third, excise taxes on gasoline (earmarked for bridge building and road maintenance) are levied by both the federal and state governments. Gasoline taxes constitute $0.41 per gallon on average across the United States. Any new excise taxes would have shifted the supply curve leftward, resulting in a higher equilibrium market price for gasoline. President George W. Bush's Council of Economic Advisors in 2007 did explore levying an additional $1 per gallon tax on gasoline to reduce the dependence of the United States on foreign oil, but no tax increase was ever initiated. So what was responsible for the upward spike in gasoline prices?

As we have seen, the variables in the demand and supply functions in Equations 2.1 and 2.2 determining equilibrium market price may be grouped into three broad sets of factors affecting use value, cost of production, and resource scarcity.[2] Since crude oil inputs account for $2.96 of the $4.10 final product price of gasoline, resource scarcity was a likely candidate to explain the increase in gasoline prices from $3 to $4.10. Higher crude oil input prices shift the supply curve leftward, leading to higher final product prices for gasoline. Figure 2.5 shows that the previous three times crude oil input prices shot up, supply disruptions in the crude oil input market were involved (i.e., during the first Gulf War in Kuwait in 1991, during an especially effective era for the OPEC cartel 1999–2001, and during the Iraq War in 2004).

In contrast, the extraordinary price rise of crude oil from $40 to $80 per barrel in 2006–2007 reflected demand-side increased usage especially by India and China. Together India and China represent only 9 percent of the 85 million barrels per day (mbd) worldwide, but these two countries have been growing very quickly. Just 2 to 3 percent additional demand can significantly raise equilibrium prices for crude oil resources because at any point in time there is a very thin inventory (8–10 days supply) working its way through the distribution network from wells to pumps to terminals to tankers to refineries. By late 2007, as gasoline headed toward $4.10 per gallon in the United States, $9.16 per gallon in Germany, and $8.80 per gallon in Great Britain, Western drivers substantially cut back consumption.

---

[2]Two additional factors are speculation and government intervention in the form of taxes, subsidies, and regulations.

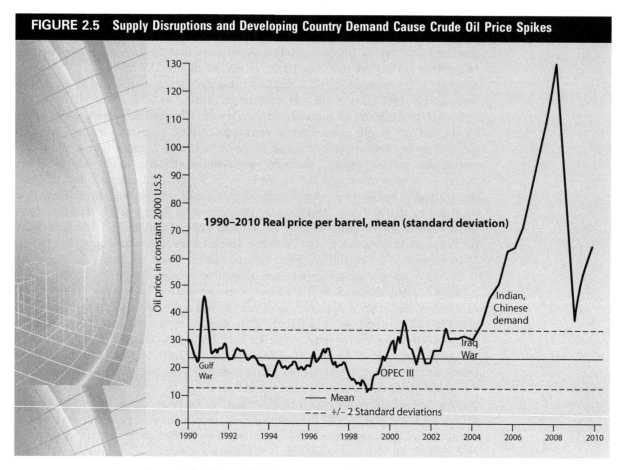

FIGURE 2.5   Supply Disruptions and Developing Country Demand Cause Crude Oil Price Spikes

Source: Federal Reserve Bank, St. Louis, *National Economics Trends*, September 2000; FedDallas, Regional Economic Data, 2006.

Was the $80 crude price in late 2007 the highest price ever in the crude oil input market prior to that time? The answer is "no." In 1981, the equilibrium crude oil price reached $36 per barrel. Using the U.S. consumer price index (CPI), since crude oil transactions worldwide are denominated in U.S. dollars, cumulative price increases between 1981 and 2007 total 228.8 percent, so $36 × a 2.288 inflation-adjustment multiplier equals $82 in 2007, and $80/2.288 equals $35 in 1981. Consequently, the $80 crude oil price in late 2007 was in fact lower than the inflation-adjusted $36 crude price in 1981 at the height of the influence of the OPEC II oil cartel.

However, in early 2008, the equilibrium price of crude continued to spike upward.

When the crude price climbed above $100, large numbers of speculators acquired long positions in the crude oil futures market betting on a further price rise. Speculative demand (supply) is always motivated by the anticipation of equilibrium market prices being higher (lower) tomorrow. Those who "go long" and buy futures contracts to take delivery at prices agreed on today are betting the price will go up, and those who "sell short" and write futures contracts promising to deliver in the future at prices agreed on today are betting the other way. The net long direction of speculative trading in the first half of 2008 added to the growing market demand from India and China and drove the crude oil equilibrium price still higher, eventually reaching $147 per barrel in July 2008.

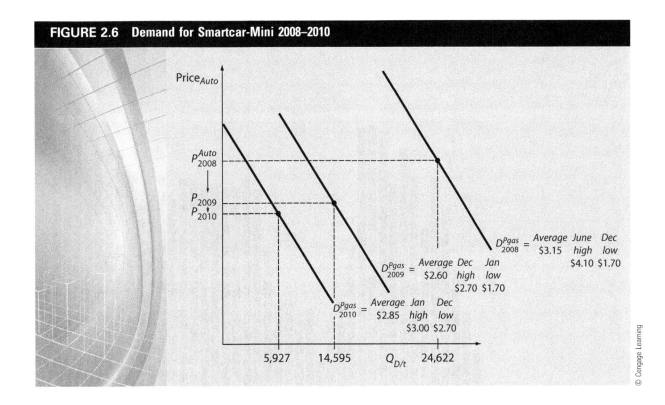

FIGURE 2.6   Demand for Smartcar-Mini 2008–2010

Faced with the need to recover their extraordinary input costs for crude, ExxonMobil, Shell, and other gasoline retailers raised regular prices to $4.10 per gallon. American consumers decided to vacate their SUVs, join carpools, and ride the buses and trains to work. Urban mass transit system ridership shot up 20 percent in a matter of months. Other Americans purchased fuel-efficient hybrids like the Toyota Prius. Figure 2.6 shows 24,622 Smartcar-Mini subcompacts were sold in 2008.

Then, legendary promoter T. Boone Pickens proposed to convert the federal trucking fleet from petroleum-derived fuel oil to natural gas. Fearing an onslaught of feasible substitutes like hybrid electric cars and natural gas-powered trucks, the Saudis decided the equilibrium price of crude had to be driven lower, so they ramped up crude oil production from their average 8.5 mbd 1990–2006. By 2007 and 2008, the Saudi's production capacity rose all the way to 10.5 and 10.9 mbd, respectively (see Figure 2.7).

With U.S. demand for gasoline declining and the capacity to extract and refine expanding, the equilibrium price of crude finally began to reverse course. The late 2008 crude oil price collapse by more than $100 per barrel depicted in Figure 2.8 was caused by a combination of increasing supply fundamentals (shifting the supply curve to the right), slowing demand growth, and a speculative expectation that in the near term crude prices would next be lower (not higher). Saudi capacity eventually grew to 12.5 mbd. Both Saudi Arabia and Kuwait also broke ground on two giant new refining facilities. Over the last two years oil has average about $80/barrel.[3]

---

[3]Appendix 7B explains why a Saudi Arabian oil executive would have preferred the dotted price path in Figure 2.8, with crude oil remaining below $100 a barrel whereas a Texan was delighted to receive all the extra revenue from the price spike to $147.

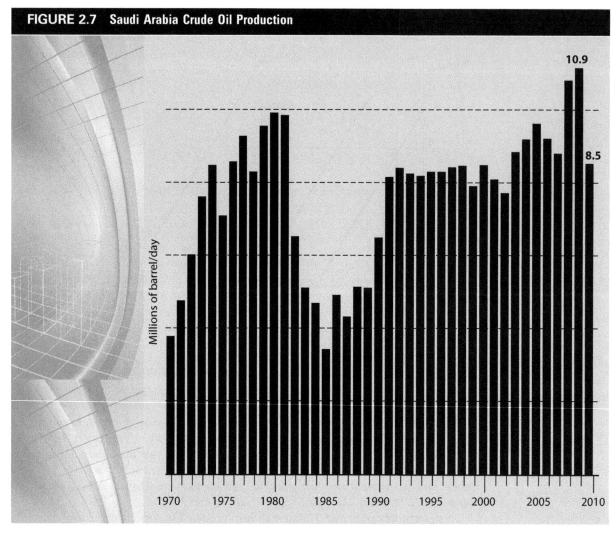

FIGURE 2.7 Saudi Arabia Crude Oil Production

10.9

8.5

Millions of barrel/day

1970   1975   1980   1985   1990   1995   2000   2005   2010

Source: U.S. Energy Information Administration.

Example

Speculation Sends Crude Oil Input Price on a Roller-Coaster Ride at ExxonMobil and Shell

With reversed expectations of lower crude prices in the near term, the speculative bubble in crude oil quickly burst. Despite 5 percent *higher* market demand over the last four months of 2008 (again primarily from China and India), the equilibrium price of crude oil plummeted $107 a barrel from $146 in September 2008 to a low of $39 by January 2009 (see Figure 2.8). By 2009 (Q3), the crude price stood again at $75 per barrel, and regular gasoline was selling for $2.74 per gallon. Figure 2.6 shows Smartcar-Mini demand fell off 10,000 cars to 14,595 in 2009 and another 10,000 to 5,927 in 2010. Over a three-year period, rising Asian demand, massive capacity expansions, a worldwide financial boom, then collapse, and speculative buying followed by speculative selling had taken oil companies and gasoline buyers on quite a roller-coaster ride.

(continued)

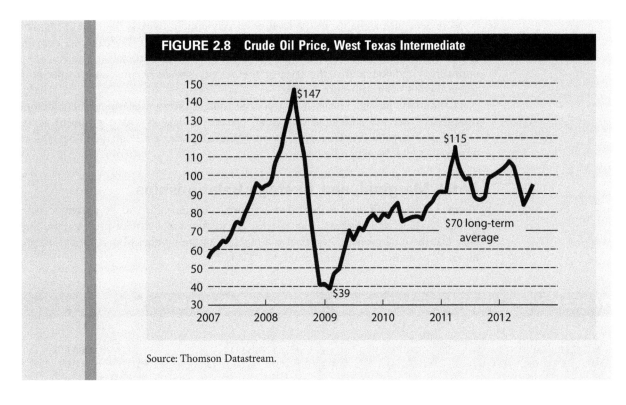

FIGURE 2.8 Crude Oil Price, West Texas Intermediate

Source: Thomson Datastream.

MARGINAL ANALYSIS

marginal analysis
A basis for making various economic decisions that analyzes the additional (marginal) benefits derived from a particular decision and compares them with the additional (marginal) costs incurred.

Marginal analysis is one of the most useful concepts in microeconomics. Resource-allocation decisions typically are expressed in terms of the marginal equilibrium conditions that must be satisfied to attain an optimal solution. The familiar profit-maximization rule for the firm of setting output at the point where "marginal cost equals marginal revenue" is one such example. Long-term investment decisions (capital expenditures) also are made using marginal analysis decision rules. Only if the expected return from an investment project (i.e., the *marginal return* to the firm) exceeds the cost of funds that must be acquired to finance the project (the *marginal cost* of capital), should the project be undertaken. Following this important marginal decision rule leads to the maximization of shareholder wealth.

Example

Tenneco Shipyard Marginal Analysis

Resource-allocation decisions should be made by comparing the marginal (or incremental) benefits of a change in the level of an activity with the incremental costs of the change. For example, the marginal revenue benefit derived from producing and selling one more supertanker is equal to the difference between total revenue, assuming the additional unit is not sold, and total revenue including the additional sale. Similarly, *marginal cost* is defined as the change in total costs that occurs from undertaking some economic activity, such as the production of an additional ship design including the opportunity costs, and therefore may not necessarily always be equal to the cash outlays alone. Perhaps the Tenneco design team has an opportunity for higher net profit as subcontractors on Boeing projects. If so, Tenneco's routine ship-design work should be contracted out to other shipbuilding design firms who can become a trusted subcontractor to Tenneco.

More generally, a change in the level of an economic activity is desirable if the marginal benefits exceed the marginal (i.e., the incremental) costs. If we define *net marginal return* as the *difference* between marginal benefits and marginal costs, then an equivalent optimality condition is that the level of the activity should be increased to the point where the net marginal return is zero.

In summary, marginal analysis instructs decision makers to determine the additional (marginal) costs and additional (marginal) benefits associated with a proposed action. *Only if the marginal benefits exceed the marginal costs* (i.e., if net marginal benefits are positive) should the action be taken.

Total, Marginal, and Average Relationships

Revenue, cost, profit, and many other economic relationships can be presented using tabular, graphic, and algebraic frameworks. Let us first use a tabular presentation. Suppose that the total profit π_T of a firm is a function of the number of units of output produced Q, as shown in columns 1 and 2 of Table 2.4.

TABLE 2.4   TOTAL, MARGINAL, AND AVERAGE PROFIT RELATIONSHIPS

(1)	(2)	(3)	(4)
NUMBER OF UNITS OF OUTPUT PER UNIT OF TIME Q	TOTAL PROFIT $\pi_T(Q)$ (\$)	MARGINAL PROFIT $\Delta\pi(Q) = \pi_T(Q) - \pi_T(Q-1)$ (\$/UNIT)	AVERAGE PROFIT $\pi_A(Q) = \pi_T(Q)/Q$ (\$/UNIT)
0	−200	0	—
1	−150	50	−150.00
2	−25	125	−12.50
3	200	225	66.67
4	475	275	118.75
5	775	300	155.00
6	1,075	300	179.17
7	1,325	250	189.29
8	1,475	150	184.38
9	1,500	25	166.67
10	1,350	−150	135.00

© Cengage Learning

Marginal Analysis and Capital Budgeting Decisions: Sara Lee Corporation

The capital budgeting decision problem facing a typical firm, such as Sara Lee Corporation, can be used to illustrate the application of marginal analysis decision rules. Sara Lee has the following schedule of potential investment projects (all assumed to be of equal risk) available to it:

PROJECT	INVESTMENT REQUIRED (\$ MILLION)	EXPECTED RATE OF RETURN	CUMULATIVE INVESTMENT (\$ MILLION)
A	\$25.0	27.0%	\$ 25.0
B	15.0	24.0	40.0

(continued)

PROJECT	INVESTMENT REQUIRED ($ MILLION)	EXPECTED RATE OF RETURN	CUMULATIVE INVESTMENT ($ MILLION)
C	40.0	21.0	80.0
D	35.0	18.0	115.0
E	12.0	15.0	127.0
F	20.0	14.0	147.0
G	18.0	13.0	165.0
H	13.0	11.0	178.0
I	7.0	8.0	185.0

Sara Lee has estimated the cost of acquiring the funds needed to finance these investment projects as follows:

BLOCK OF FUNDS ($ MILLION)	COST OF CAPITAL (%)	CUMULATIVE FUNDS RAISED ($ MILLION)
First 50.0	10.0	50.0
Next 25.0	10.5	75.0
Next 40.0	11.0	115.0
Next 50.0	12.2	165.0
Next 20.0	14.5	185.0

The expected rate of return on the projects listed above can be thought of as the marginal (or incremental) return available to Sara Lee as it undertakes each additional investment project. Similarly, the cost-of-capital schedule may be thought of as the incremental cost of acquiring the needed funds. Following the marginal analysis rules means that Sara Lee should invest in additional projects as long as the expected rate of return on the project exceeds the marginal cost of capital funds needed to finance the project.

Project A, which offers an expected return of 27 percent and requires an outlay of $25 million, is acceptable because the marginal return exceeds the marginal cost of capital (10.0 percent for the first $50 million of funds raised by Sara Lee). In fact, an examination of the tables indicates that projects A through G all meet the marginal analysis test because the marginal return from each of these projects exceeds the marginal cost of capital funds needed to finance these projects. In contrast, projects H and I should not be undertaken because they offer returns of 11 percent and 8 percent, respectively, compared with a marginal cost of capital of 14.5 percent for the $20 million in funds needed to finance those projects.

Example

Marginal Analysis of Driving a Mini Cooper versus a Chevy Volt

Urban sprawl and flight to the suburbs have now resulted in the mean commuter trip in the United States rising to 33 miles one way. With the housing density in most American cities well below what would be required to support extensive light rail

(continued)

and subway lines, the typical household must find economical ways to get at least one worker from a suburban home to the central business district and back each day. A fuel-efficient, small commuter car like the Mini Cooper is one alternative. Others have recently been introduced—the Chevy Volt and Nissan Leaf, both all-electric vehicles that are recharged at the end of each 40-mile commuting trip. Technically, the Leaf and the Volt are e-REVs, extended-range electric vehicles. Each contains a small gasoline-driven internal combustion engine that runs an electric generator, but unlike hybrids such as the Ford Fusion and Toyota Prius, these e-REVs have no mechanical connection between the gasoline engine and the drivetrain. Instead, the Chevy Volt goes 40 miles on the charge contained in 220 lithium ion (L-ion) batteries which are plugged in for a recharging cycle of 8 hours at 110 volts (or 3 hours at 220 volts) at work and at home. When the battery pack falls to a 30 percent state of charge (SOC), the gasoline engine comes on to turn the generator and maintain battery power.

Automotive engineers calculate that each mile traveled in the Chevy Volt's all-electric mode "burns" 0.26 kilowatt hours of electricity. So, the mean commuter trip of 33 miles requires 8.58 kwh of electricity. The price of electricity in the United States varies from a peak period in the midday and evening to a much cheaper off-peak period late at night, and from a low of $0.07 per kwh in Washington state to $0.12 in Rhode Island. On average, a representative nighttime rate is $0.10, and a representative daytime rate is $0.13. This means that each nighttime charge of a Chevy Volt will cost the household $0.86, and the comparable daytime charge downtown at work will be $1.12 for a total operating cost per day of just under $2 per day. For 300 days of work, that's $600 per year. In contrast, the gasoline-powered Mini Cooper gets 32 mpg, so at $3.00 per gallon, the Mini's operating cost is approximately $6 per day or $1,800 per year. The typical commuter use of e-Rev vehicles will save $4 per day or $1,200 per year relative to popular fuel-efficient gasoline-powered commuter cars.

At an EPA-measured 41 mpg throughout a range of driving conditions, the hybrid-electric Ford Fusion qualifies for a federal tax credit of $3,400. In contrast, at an EPA-measured 238 mpg, the Chevy Volt qualifies for a $7,500 tax credit to offset the $12,000 additional cost of the L-ion battery pack over the cost of a conventional battery. Because the Chevy Volt's battery pack is expected to last 10 years, the $1,200 annual capital cost for the battery pack is equal to the $1,200 energy cost savings even without the federal tax credit. To date, sales volumes have been quite low in part because fleet purchasers (especially rental car companies) are waiting to see if the battery packs are durable, which will determine the Volt's resale value.

Marginal profit, which represents the change in total profit resulting from a one-unit increase in output, is shown in column 3 of the table. (A Δ is used to represent a "change" in some variable.) The marginal profit $\Delta\pi(Q)$ of any level of output Q is calculated by taking the difference between the total profit at this level $\pi_T(Q)$ and at one unit below this level $\pi_T(Q - 1)$.[4] In comparing the marginal and total profit functions, we note that for increasing output levels, the marginal profit values remain positive as long as the total profit function is increasing. Only when the total profit function begins decreasing—that is, at $Q = 10$ units—does the marginal profit become negative. The average profit function values $\pi_A(Q)$, shown in column 4 of Table 2.4, are obtained by

---

[4]Web Appendix A expands upon the idea that the total profit function can be maximized by identifying the level of activity at which the marginal profit function goes to zero.

dividing the total profit figure $\pi_T(Q)$ by the output level Q. In comparing the marginal and the average profit function values, we see that the average profit function $\pi_A(Q)$ is increasing as long as the marginal profit is greater than the average profit—that is, up to $Q = 7$ units. Beyond an output level of $Q = 7$ units, the marginal profit is less than the average profit and the average profit function values are decreasing.

By examining the total profit function $\pi_T(Q)$ in Table 2.4, we see that profit is maximized at an output level of $Q = 9$ units. Given that the objective is to maximize total profit, then the optimal output decision would be to produce and sell 9 units. If the marginal analysis decision rule discussed earlier in this section is used, the same (optimal) decision is obtained. Applying the rule to this problem, the firm would expand production as long as the net marginal return—that is, marginal revenue minus marginal cost (marginal profit)—is positive. From column 3 of Table 2.4, we can see that the marginal profit is positive for output levels up to $Q = 9$. Therefore, the marginal profit decision rule would indicate that 9 units should be produced—the same decision that was obtained from the total profit function.

The relationships among the total, marginal, and average profit functions and the optimal output decision also can be represented graphically. A set of *continuous* profit functions, analogous to those presented in Table 2.4 for discrete integer values of output (Q), is shown in Figure 2.9. At the break-even output level Q_1, both total profits and

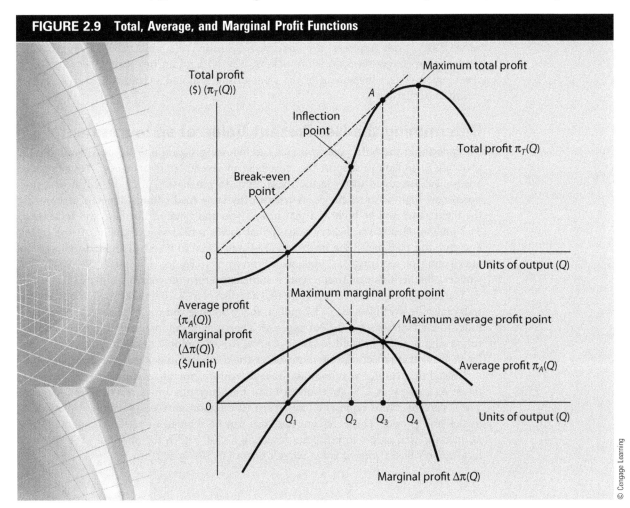

FIGURE 2.9 Total, Average, and Marginal Profit Functions

© Cengage Learning

average profits are zero. The marginal profit function, which equals the slope of the total profit function, takes on its maximum value at an output of Q_2 units. This point corresponds to the *inflection point*. Below the inflection point, total profits are increasing at an increasing rate, and hence marginal profits are increasing. Above the inflection point, up to an output level Q_4, total profits are increasing at a decreasing rate, and consequently marginal profits are decreasing. The average profit function, which represents the slope of a straight line drawn from the origin 0 to each point on the total profit function, takes on its maximum value at an output of Q_3 units. The average profit necessarily equals the marginal profit at this point. This follows because the slope of the $0A$ line, which defines the average profit, is also equal to the slope of the total profit function at point A, which defines the marginal profit. Finally, total profit is maximized at an output of Q_4 units where marginal profit equals 0. Beyond Q_4 the total profit function is decreasing, and consequently the marginal profit function takes on negative values.

THE NET PRESENT VALUE CONCEPT

When costs and benefits occur at approximately the same time, the marginal decision rule (proceed with the action if marginal benefit exceeds marginal cost) applies. But, many economic decisions require that costs be incurred immediately to capture a stream of benefits over several future time periods. In these cases, the *net present value* (NPV) *rule* replaces the marginal decision rule and provides appropriate guidance for longer-term decision makers. The NPV of an investment represents the contribution of that investment to the value of the firm and, accordingly, to shareholder wealth maximization.

Determining the Net Present Value of an Investment

To understand the NPV rule, consider the following situation. You are responsible for investing $1 million to support the retirement of several family members. Your financial advisor has suggested that you use these funds to purchase a piece of land near a proposed new highway interchange. A trustworthy state road commissioner is certain that the interchange will be built and that in one year the value of this land will increase to $1.2 million. Hence, you believe initially that this is a riskless investment. At the end of one year you plan to sell the land. You are being asked to invest $1 million today in the anticipation of receiving $1.2 million a year from today, or a profit of $200,000. You wonder whether this profit represents a sufficient return on your investment.

You feel it is important to recognize that a return of $1.2 million received one year from today must be worth less than $1.2 million today because you could invest your $1 million today to earn interest over the coming year. Therefore, to compare a dollar received in the future with a dollar in hand today, it is necessary to multiply the future dollar by a *discount factor* that reflects the alternative investment opportunities that are available.

Instead of investing $1 million in the land venture, you are aware that you could also invest in a one-year U.S. government bond that currently offers a return of 3 percent. The 3 percent return represents the return (the opportunity cost) forgone by investing in the land project. The 3 percent rate also can be thought of as the compensation to an investor who agrees to postpone receiving a cash return for one year. The discount factor, also called a *present value interest factor* (PVIF), is equal to

$$PVIF = \frac{1}{1+i}$$

present value
The value today of a future amount of money or a series of future payments evaluated at the appropriate discount rate.

where i is the compensation for postponing receipt of a cash return for one year. The **present value** (PV_0) of an amount received one year in the future (FV_1) is equal to that amount times the discount factor, or

$$PV_0 = FV_1 \times (PVIF) \tag{2.3}$$

In the case of the land project, the present value of the promised $1.2 million expected to be received in one year is equal to

$$PV_0 = \$1.2 \text{ million} \left(\frac{1}{1 + 0.03} \right) = \$1,165,049$$

If you invested $1,165,049 today to earn 3 percent for the coming year, you would have $1.2 million at the end of the year. You are clearly better off with the proposed land investment (assuming that it really is riskless like the U.S. government bond investment). How much better off are you?

The answer to this question is at the heart of NPV calculations. The land investment project is worth $1,165,049 today to an investor who demands a 3 percent return on this type of investment. You, however, have been able to acquire this investment for only $1,000,000. Thus, your wealth has increased by undertaking this investment by $165,049 ($1,165,049 present value of the projected investment opportunity payoffs minus the required initial investment of $1,000,000). The NPV of this investment is $165,049. In general, the NPV of an investment is equal to

$$\text{NPV} = \text{Present value of future returns} - \text{Initial outlay} \tag{2.4}$$

This example was simplified by assuming that the returns from the investment were received exactly one year from the date of the initial outlay. If the payoff from the land investment had been not one but two years away, the PVIF would have been $1/(1.03)^2 = 0.942596$, and the NPV would have been $1.2 million (.942596) – $1.0 million = $131,115. The NPV rule can be generalized to cover returns received over any number of future time periods with projected growth or decay and terminal values as salvage or disposal costs. In Appendix A at the end of the book, the present value concept is developed in more detail so that it can be applied in these more complex investment settings.

 Example

Changing a Lightbulb Saves $30 and May Save the Planet[5]

Incandescent lightbulbs replaced oil lamps for interior lighting more than 100 years ago. Thomas Edison himself improved on some basic designs running electric current through a carbonized filament in an oxygen-free vacuum tube, producing less combustion and more light. General Electric had its origins selling long-lasting tungsten filament incandescent bulbs. Still, 12 percent of the typical household's electric bill goes for lighting 30 lightbulbs, and the standard incandescent bulb loses more than 90 percent of its electrical energy in the form of heat created by the white *hot* filament. Today, the new compact fluorescent light (CFL) bulb uses 75 percent less electricity to heat an argon vapor that emits ultraviolet (UV) light. The UV light excites a fluorescent phosphor coating on the inside of the tube, which then emits visible light. The U.S. Department of Energy estimates that if all 105 million U.S. households replaced just 10 heavily used incandescent bulbs with a CFL bulb yielding comparable light, the electricity saved could light 30 million homes. In addition, the energy saved would remove from the environment an amount of greenhouse gases from

(continued)

coal-burning power plants equal to the CO_2 emitted by 8,000,000 cars. The U.K. Department of Business, Enterprise, and Regulatory Reform estimates that replacing the three most frequently used lightbulbs in U.K. households would save the electricity used by all the streetlamps in Britain.

The magnitude of these energy savings is certainly staggering, but at what cost? Bought for $0.50 per bulb, 1,000-hour incandescent 60-watt bulbs cost much less than CFL bulbs that create the same 1,050 lumens of light, last 8,000 hours, burn only 15 watts of electricity (versus 60), but cost $4.99.[6] So, the lifetime cost comparison hinges on whether the extra $4.49 acquisition cost of the CFL bulb is worth the extended lifetime of energy savings. Net present value techniques are designed to answer just such questions of the time value of money (savings) that are delayed.

Table 2.5 shows the initial net investments of $4.49 and $0.50 per bulb in time period zero, the 45 kilowatt hours (kwh) of power saved on average 2¾ hours per day by the CFL bulb, the $0.11 per kwh representative cost of the electricity,[7] and the additional $0.50 incandescent bulb replacement every year (the typical U.S. household's annual usage). Assuming a 6 percent discount rate, the net present value of the $4.96 annual energy savings plus the $0.50 replacement cost for incandescent bulbs avoided each year for seven years yields a net present value cost savings of $33.59, which exceeds the differential $3.99 acquisition cost for the CFL bulb by $29.60. The European Union has found this $30 net present value of the cost savings from switching to CFL bulbs (plus their CO_2 abatement) so compelling that incandescent bulbs are no longer approved for manufacture or import into the EU. The more gradual U.S. phaseout of incandescent bulbs began in 2012. The average American household has 30 lightbulbs, ten of which are used this heavily, a potential savings of $49.60 + $5.00 as a cash flow each year and a net present value savings of $296 over eight years.

---

[5]Based on "Stores Stock New Bulbs for the Light Switch," *Wall Street Journal*, June 1, 2011, p. D3, www.energy.gov and www.energystar.gov.

[6]Philips has discussed charging $50 for the still higher tech LED bulbs that last roughly 25 times as long as incandescent bulbs.

[7]Electric rates for incremental power vary by region from $.07 per kwh in the state of Washington to $.08 in the Carolinas, to $.12 in California, New York, and across New England. Electricity is much more expensive in Europe because of the carbon credits required to burn coal or fuel oil (the principal source of energy for power plants). For example, in Denmark, electricity costs $0.36 per kwh.

Sources of Positive Net Present Value Projects

What causes some projects to have a positive NPV and others to have a negative NPV? When product and factor markets are other than perfectly competitive, it is possible for a firm to earn above-normal profits (economic rents) that result in positive net present value projects. The reasons why these above-normal profits may be available arise from conditions that define each type of product and factor market and distinguish it from a perfectly competitive market. These reasons include the following barriers to entry and other factors:

1. Buyer preferences for established brand names
2. Ownership or control of favored distribution systems (such as exclusive auto dealerships or airline hubs)
3. Patent control of superior product designs or production techniques
4. Exclusive ownership of superior natural resource deposits

TABLE 2.5	LIFETIME COST SAVINGS OF COMPACT FLUORESCENT LIGHT (CFL) BULBS								
	t = 0	t = 1	t = 2	t = 3	t = 4	t = 5	t = 6	t = 7	t = 8
									(END OF PERIOD VALUES)
Incandescent	−$0.50	−$0.50	−$0.50	−$0.50	−$0.50	−$0.50	−$0.50	−$0.50	0
CFL	−$4.49	2 ¾ hrs × 365 × 45 kwh × $0.11 = $4.96	$4.96	$4.96	$4.96	$4.96	$4.96	$4.96	$4.96
Initial Cost difference	−$3.99		NPV (8 years of $4.96 energy savings at d = 6%) = $30.80						
			NPV (7 years of $0.50 incandescent replacement cost at d = 6%) = $2.79						
		NPV (Lifetime cost savings) − Cost difference ($30.80 + $2.79) = $33.59 − $3.99 = $29.60 per bulb								

© Cengage Learning

5. Inability of new firms to acquire necessary factors of production (management, labor, equipment)
6. Superior access to financial resources at lower costs (economies of scale in attracting capital)
7. Economies of large-scale production and distribution arising from
   a. Capital-intensive production processes
   b. High initial start-up costs

These factors can permit a firm to identify positive net present value projects for internal investment. If the barriers to entry are sufficiently high (such as a patent on key technology) so as to prevent any new competition, or if the start-up period for competitive ventures is sufficiently long, then it is possible that a project may have a positive net present value. However, in assessing the viability of such a project, the manager or analyst must consider the likely period of time when above-normal returns can be earned before new competitors emerge and force cash flows back to a more normal level. It is generally unrealistic to expect to be able to earn above-normal returns over the entire life of an investment project.

Risk and the NPV Rule

The previous land investment example assumed that the investment was riskless. Therefore, the rate of return used to compute the discount factor and the net present value was the riskless rate of return available on a U.S. government bond having a one-year maturity. What if you do not believe that the construction of the new interchange is a certainty, or you are not confident about of the value of the land in one year? To compensate for the perceived risk of this investment, you decide that you require a 15 percent rate of return on your investment. Using a 15 percent required rate of return in calculating the discount factor, the present value of the expected $1.2 million sales price of the land is $1,043,478 ($1.2 million times [1/1.15]). Thus, the NPV of this investment declines to $43,478. The increase in the perceived risk of the investment results in a dramatic $121,571 decline from $165,049 in the NPV on a $1 million investment.

A primary problem facing managers is the difficulty of evaluating the risk associated with investments and then translating that risk into a discount rate that reflects an adequate level of risk compensation. In the next section of this chapter, we discuss the risk concept and the factors that affect investment risk and influence the required rate of return on an investment.

MEANING AND MEASUREMENT OF RISK

risk A decision-making situation in which there is variability in the possible outcomes, and the probabilities of these outcomes can be specified by the decision maker.

Risk implies a chance for some unfavorable outcome to occur—for example, the *possibility that actual cash flows will be less than* the expected outcome. When a range of potential outcomes is associated with a decision and the decision maker is able to assign probabilities to each of these possible outcomes, risk is said to exist. A decision is said to be *risk free* if the cash flow outcomes are known with certainty. A good example of a risk-free investment is U.S. Treasury securities. There is virtually no chance that the Treasury will fail to redeem these securities at maturity or that the Treasury will default on any interest payments owed. In contrast, US Airways bonds constitute a *risky* investment because it is possible that US Airways will default on one or more interest payments and will lack sufficient funds at maturity to redeem the bonds at face value. In summary, *risk* refers to the potential variability of outcomes from a decision. The more variable these outcomes are, the greater the risk.

Probability Distributions

probability The percentage chance that a particular outcome will occur.

The **probability** that a particular outcome will occur is defined as the relative frequency or *percentage chance* of its occurrence. Probabilities may be either objectively or subjectively determined. An objective determination is based on past outcomes of similar events, whereas a subjective determination is merely an opinion made by an individual about the likelihood that a given event will occur. In the case of decisions that are frequently repeated, such as the drilling of developmental oil wells in an established oil field, reasonably good objective estimates can be made about the success of a new well. In contrast, for totally new decisions or one-of-a-kind investments, subjective estimates about the likelihood of various outcomes are necessary. The fact that many probability estimates in business are at least partially subjective does not diminish their usefulness.

Using either objective or subjective methods, the decision maker can develop a probability distribution for the possible outcomes. Table 2.6 shows the probability distribution of net cash flows for two sample investments. The lowest estimated annual net cash flow (NCF) for each investment—$200 for Investment I and $100 for Investment II—represents pessimistic forecasts about the investments' performance; the middle values—$300 and $300—could be considered normal performance levels; and the highest values—$400 and $500—are optimistic estimates.

TABLE 2.6 PROBABILITY DISTRIBUTIONS OF THE ANNUAL NET CASH FLOWS (NCF) FROM TWO INVESTMENTS			
INVESTMENT I		INVESTMENT II	
POSSIBLE NCF ($)	PROBABILITY	POSSIBLE NCF ($)	PROBABILITY
200	0.2	100	0.2
300	0.6	300	0.6
400	0.2	500	0.2
	1.0		1.0

Example

Probability Distributions and Risk: US Airways Bonds[8]

Consider an investor who is contemplating the purchase of US Airways bonds. That investor might assign the probabilities associated with the three possible outcomes from this investment, as shown in Table 2.7. These probabilities are interpreted to mean that a 30 percent chance exists that the bonds will not be in default over their life and will be redeemed at maturity, a 65 percent chance of interest default during the life of the bonds, and a 5 percent chance that the bonds will not be redeemed at maturity. In this example, no other outcomes are deemed possible.

TABLE 2.7 POSSIBLE OUTCOMES FROM INVESTING IN US AIRWAYS BONDS	
OUTCOME	PROBABILITY
No default, bonds redeemed at maturity	0.30
Default on interest for one or more periods	0.65
No interest default, but bonds not redeemed at maturity	0.05
	1.00

© Cengage Learning

[8]The annual report for the US Airways Corporation can be found at http://investor.usairways.com

Expected Values

expected value The weighted average of the possible outcomes where the weights are the probabilities of the respective outcomes.

From this information, the expected value of each decision alternative can be calculated. The **expected value** is defined as the weighted average of the possible outcomes. It is the value that is expected to occur on average if the decision (such as an investment) were repeated a large number of times.

Algebraically, the expected value may be defined as

$$\bar{r} = \sum_{j=1}^{n} r_j p_j \qquad [2.5]$$

where $\bar{r}$ is the expected value; r_j is the outcome for the jth case, where there are n possible outcomes; and p_j is the probability that the jth outcome will occur. The expected cash flows for Investments I and II are calculated in Table 2.8 using Equation 2.5. In this example, both investments have expected values of annual net cash flows equaling $300.

TABLE 2.8 COMPUTATION OF THE EXPECTED RETURNS FROM TWO INVESTMENTS					
INVESTMENT I			INVESTMENT II		
r_j	p_j	$r_j \times p_j$	r_j	p_j	$r_j \times p_j$
$200	0.2	$ 40	$100	0.2	$ 20
300	0.6	180	300	0.6	180
400	0.2	80	500	0.2	100
	Expected value: $\bar{r}$ = $300				$\bar{r}$ = $300

© Cengage Learning

Standard Deviation: An Absolute Measure of Risk

The **standard deviation** is a statistical measure of the dispersion of a variable about its mean. It is defined as the square root of the weighted average squared deviations of individual outcomes from the mean:

$$\sigma = \sqrt{\sum_{j=1}^{n} (r_j - \bar{r}_j)^2 p_j} \qquad [2.6]$$

where σ is the standard deviation.

The standard deviation can be used to measure the variability of a decision alternative. As such, it gives an indication of the risk involved in the alternative. The larger the standard deviation, the more variable the possible outcomes and the riskier the decision alternative. A standard deviation of zero indicates no variability and thus no risk.

Table 2.9 shows the calculation of the standard deviations for Investments I and II. These calculations show that Investment II appears to be *riskier* than Investment I because the expected cash flows from Investment II are *more variable*.

Normal Probability Distribution

The possible outcomes from most investment decisions are much more numerous than in Table 2.6 but their effects can be estimated by assuming a continuous probability distribution. Assuming a *normal* probability distribution is often correct or nearly correct, and it greatly simplifies the analysis. The normal probability distribution is characterized by a symmetrical, bell-like curve. A table of the *standard normal probability function* (Table 1 in Appendix B at the end of this book) can be used to compute the probability of occurrence of any particular outcome. From this table, for example, it is apparent that the actual outcome should be between plus and minus 1 standard deviation from the

---

TABLE 2.9   COMPUTATION OF THE STANDARD DEVIATIONS FOR TWO INVESTMENTS

	j	r_j	$\bar{r}$	$r_j - \bar{r}$	$(r_j - \bar{r})^2$	p_j	$(r_j - \bar{r})^2 p_j$
Investment I	1	$200	$300	−$100	$10,000	0.2	$2,000
	2	300	300	0	0	0.6	0
	3	400	300	100	10,000	0.2	2,000
							$\sum_{j=1}^{3} (r_j - \bar{r})^2 p_j = \$4,000$
		$\sigma = \sqrt{\sum_{j=1}^{n} (r_j - \bar{r}_j)^2 p_j} = \sqrt{4,000} = \$63.25$					
Investment II	1	$100	$300	−$200	$40,000	0.2	$8,000
	2	300	300	0	0	0.6	0
	3	500	300	200	40,000	0.2	8,000
							$\sum_{j=1}^{3} (r_j - \bar{r})^2 p_j = \$16,000$
		$\sigma = \sqrt{\sum_{j=1}^{n} (r_j - \bar{r}_j)^2 p_j} = \sqrt{16,000} = \$126.49$					

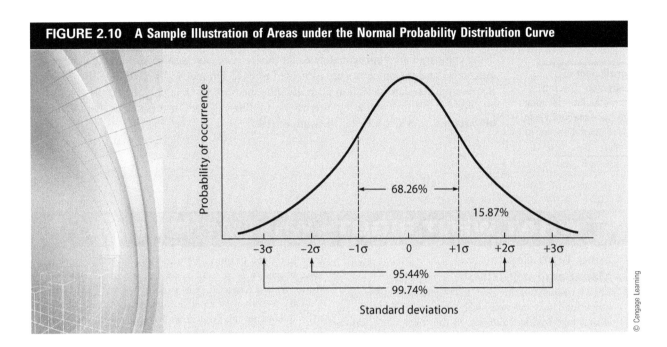

FIGURE 2.10   A Sample Illustration of Areas under the Normal Probability Distribution Curve

expected value 68.26 percent of the time,[9] between plus and minus 2 standard deviations 95.44 percent of the time, and between plus and minus 3 standard deviations 99.74 percent of the time (see Figure 2.10). So a "3 sigma event" occurs less than 1 percent of the time with a relative frequency 0.0026 (i.e., 1.0 − 0.9974), and a "9 sigma event" occurs almost never, with a relative frequency less than 0.0001. Nevertheless, such extraordinary events can and do happen (see following box on LTCM).

The number of standard deviations z that a particular value of r is from the mean $\bar{r}$ can be computed as

$$z = \frac{r - \bar{r}}{\sigma} \qquad [2.7]$$

Table 1 in Appendix B and Equation 2.7 can be used to compute the probability of an annual net cash flow for Investment I being less than some value r—for example, $205. First, the number of standard deviations that $205 is from the mean must be calculated. Substituting the mean and the standard deviation from Tables 2.8 and 2.9 into Equation 2.7 yields

$$z = \frac{\$205 - \$300}{\$63.25}$$

$$= -1.50$$

In other words, the annual cash flow value of $205 is 1.5 standard deviations below the mean. Reading from the 1.5 row in Table 1 gives a value of 0.0668, or 6.68 percent. Thus, a 6.68 percent probability exists that Investment I will have annual net cash flows less than $205. Conversely, there is a 93.32 percent probability (1 − 0.0668) that the investment will have a cash flow greater than $205.

---

[9]For example, Table 1 indicates a probability of 0.1587 of a value occurring that is greater than $+1\sigma$ from the mean and a probability of 0.1587 of a value occurring that is less than -1σ from the mean. Hence the probability of a value between $+1\sigma$ and -1σ is 68.26 percent—that is, $1.00 - (2 \times 0.1587)$.

Coefficient of Variation: A Relative Measure of Risk

The standard deviation is an appropriate measure of risk when the decision alternatives being compared are approximately equal in size (i.e., have similar expected values of the outcomes) and the outcomes are estimated to have symmetrical probability distributions. Because the standard deviation is an *absolute* measure of variability, however, it is generally not suitable for comparing alternatives of differing size. In these cases the **coefficient of variation** provides a better measure of risk.

coefficient of variation The ratio of the standard deviation to the expected value. A relative measure of risk.

WHAT WENT RIGHT • WHAT WENT WRONG

Long-Term Capital Management (LTCM)[10]

LTCM operated from June 1993–September 1998 as a hedge fund that invested highly leveraged private capital in arbitrage trading strategies on the financial derivative markets. LTCM's principal activity was examining interest rate derivative contracts throughout the world for evidence of very minor mispricing and then betting enormous sums on the subsequent convergence of those contracts to predictable equilibrium prices. Since the mispricing might be only several cents per thousand dollars invested, LTCM often needed to risk millions or even billions on each bet to secure a nontrivial absolute dollar return. With sometimes as many as 100 independent bets spread across dozens of different government bond markets, LTCM appeared globally diversified.

In a typical month, 60 such convergence strategies with positions in several thousand counterparty contracts would make money and another 40 strategies with a similar number of counterparties would lose money. Steadily, the profits mounted. From approximately $1 billion net asset value (equity) in February 1994, LTCM reached $7 billion of net asset value in January 1998. LTCM then paid out $2.4 billion in a one-time distribution to non-partners, which equaled a 40 percent annual compound return on their investment (ROI). Shortly thereafter, in August 1998, the remaining $4.6 billion equity shrank by 45 percent, and then one month later shrank by another 82 percent to less than $600 million. In September 1998, the hedge fund was taken over by 14 Wall Street banks who, in exchange for inserting $3.6 billion to cover the firm's debts, acquired 90 percent of the equity ownership. What went wrong?

One potential explanation is that such events are fully expected in an enterprise so risky that it returns a 40 percent ROI. Anticipated risk and expected return are highly positively correlated across different types of investments. However, LTCM's annual return had a standard deviation

from June 1993 to June 1998 of only 11.5 percent per year as compared to 10 percent as the average for all S&P 500 stocks. In this respect, LTCM's return volatility was quite ordinary. Another potential explanation is that LTCM's $129 billion on the June 1998 balance sheet was overwhelmed by excessive off-balance sheet assets and liabilities. Although the absolute size of the numbers is staggering (e.g., $1.2 trillion in interest rate swaps, $28 billion in foreign exchange derivatives, and $36 billion in equity derivatives), LTCM's 9 percent ratio of on-balance sheet to off-balance sheet assets was similar to that of a typical securities firm (about 12 percent). Even LTCM's high financial leverage ($129 billion assets to $4.7 billion equity = 26 to 1) was customary practice for hedge funds.

What appears to have gone wrong for LTCM was that a default of the Russian government on debt obligations in August 1998 set in motion a truly extraordinary "flight to quality." General turmoil in the bond markets caused interest rate volatility to rise to a standard deviation of 36 percent when 3 percent would have been typical. LTCM was caught on the wrong side of many interest rate derivative positions for which no trade was available at any price. Although LTCM had "stress tested" their trading positions against so-called 3 sigma events (a one-day loss of $35 million), this August–September 1998 volatility proved to be a 9 sigma event (i.e., a one day loss of $553 million).

With massive investments highly leveraged and exposed to a 9 sigma event, LTCM hemorrhaged $2 billion in one month. Because liquidity risk exposure of an otherwise fully diversified portfolio was to blame, many investment houses have concluded that leverage should be substantially reduced as a result of the events at LTCM.

---

[10]R. Lowenstein, *When Genius Failed* (New York: Random House, 2000); remarks by Dave Modest, NBER Conference, May 1999; and "Case Study: LTCM," *eRisk*, (2000).

The coefficient of variation (v) considers relative variation and thus is well suited for use when a comparison is being made between two unequally sized decision alternatives. It is defined as the ratio of the standard deviation σ to the expected value $\bar{r}$, or

$$v = \frac{\sigma}{r} \qquad [2.8]$$

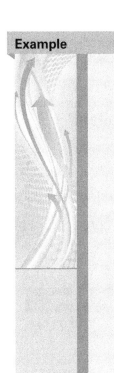

Example

Relative Risk Measurement: Arrow Tool Company

Arrow Tool Company is considering two investments, T and S. Investment T has expected annual net cash flows of $100,000 and a standard deviation of $20,000, whereas Investment S has expected annual net cash flows of $4,000 and a $2,000 standard deviation. Intuition tells us that Investment T is less risky because its *relative* variation is smaller. As the coefficient of variation increases, so does the relative risk of the decision alternative. The coefficients of variation for Investments T and S are computed as

Investment T:

$$v = \frac{\sigma}{\bar{r}}$$
$$= \frac{\$20,000}{\$100,000}$$
$$= 0.20$$

Investment S:

$$v = \frac{\sigma}{\bar{r}}$$
$$= \frac{\$2,000}{\$4,000}$$
$$= 0.50$$

Cash flows of Investment S have a larger coefficient of variation (0.50) than do cash flows of Investment T (0.20); therefore, even though the standard deviation is smaller, Investment S is the *more* risky of the two alternatives.

RISK AND REQUIRED RETURN

The relationship between risk and required return on an investment can be defined as

$$\text{Required return} = \text{Risk-free return} + \text{Risk premium} \qquad [2.9]$$

The risk-free rate of return refers to the return available on an investment with no risk of default. For debt securities, no default risk means that promised interest and principal payments are guaranteed to be made. The best example of risk-free debt securities are short-term government securities, such as U.S. Treasury bills. The buyer of a U.S. government debt security always is assured of receiving the promised *principal* and *interest* payments because the U.S. government always can print more money. The risk-free return on T-bills equals the real rate of interest plus the expected rate of inflation. The second term in Equation 2.9 is a potential "reward" that an investor can expect to receive from providing capital for a risky investment. This *risk premium* may arise for any number of reasons. The borrower firm may default on its contractual repayment obligations (a default risk premium). The investor may have little seniority in presenting claims against a bankrupt borrower (a seniority risk premium). The investor may be unable to sell his security interest (a liquidity risk premium as we saw in the case of LTCM), or debt repayment may occur early (a maturity risk premium). Finally, the return the investor receives may simply be highly volatile, exceeding expectations during one period and plummeting below expectations during the next period. Investors generally are considered to be *risk averse*; that is, they expect, on average, to be compensated for any and all of these risks they assume when making an investment.

Example

Risk-Return Trade-Offs in Stocks, Bonds, Farmland, and Diamonds

Investors require higher rates of return on debt securities based primarily on their default risk. Bond-rating agencies, such as Moody's, Standard and Poor's, and Fitch, provide evaluations of the default risk of many corporate bonds. Moody's, for example, rates bonds on a 9-point scale from Aaa through C, where Aaa-rated bonds have the lowest expected default risk. As can be seen in Table 2.10, the yields on bonds increase as the risk of default increases, again reflecting the positive relationship between risk and required returns.

TABLE 2.10 RELATIONSHIP BETWEEN RISK AND REQUIRED RETURNS	
DEBT SECURITY	**YIELD (%)**
U.S. Treasury bill	3.8
U.S. Treasury bonds (25 year +)	5.06
Aaa-rated corporate bonds	6.49
Aa-rated bonds	6.93
A-rated bonds	7.18
Baa-rated corporate bonds	7.80
Other investments	
Diamonds	3.0
Farmland	6.5
Stocks	
All U.S. stocks	10.1
Biotech stocks	12.6
Emerging market stocks	16.0

Source: Board of Governors of the Federal Reserve System, *Federal Reserve Bulletin.*

Table 2.10 also shows investment in diamonds has returned 3 percent whereas farmland has returned 6.5 percent, U.S. stocks have returned 10 percent, biotech stocks have returned 12.6 percent, and emerging market stocks have returned 16 percent compounded annually from 1970 to 2010. These compound annual returns mirror the return variance of diamonds (lowest), farmland, U.S. stocks, biotech stocks, and emerging market stocks (highest).

SUMMARY

- Demand and supply simultaneously determine equilibrium market price. The determinants of demand (supply) other than price shift the demand (supply) curve. A change in price alone leads to a change in quantity demanded (supplied) without any shift in demand (supply).
- The offer price demanders are willing to pay is determined by the marginal use value of the purchase being considered. The asking price suppliers are willing to accept is determined by the variable cost of the product or service being supplied.
- The equilibrium price of gasoline fluctuates primarily because of spikes and collapses in crude oil input prices caused at various times by supply disruptions and gluts, increasing demand in developing countries, and speculation.
- Changes in price result in *movement* along the demand curve, whereas changes in any of the other variables in the demand function result in *shifts* of the entire demand curve. Thus "changes in quantity demanded along" a particular demand curve result from price changes. In contrast, when one speaks of "changes in demand," one is referring to shifts in the entire demand curve.
- Some of the factors that cause a shift in the entire demand curve are changes in the income level of consumers, the price of substitute and complemen-

tary goods, the level of advertising, competitors' advertising expenditures, population, consumer preferences, time period of adjustment, taxes or subsidies, and price expectations.
- The *marginal analysis* concept requires that a decision maker determine the additional (marginal) costs and additional (marginal) benefits associated with a proposed action. If the marginal benefits exceed the marginal costs (i.e., if the net marginal benefits are positive), the action should be taken.
- The *net present value* of an investment is equal to the present value of expected future returns (cash flows) minus the initial outlay.
- The net present value of an investment equals the contribution of that investment to the value of the firm and, accordingly, to the wealth of shareholders. The net present value of an investment depends on the return required by investors (the firm), which, in turn, is a function of the perceived risk of the investment.
- *Risk* refers to the potential variability of outcomes from a decision alternative. It can be measured either by the *standard deviation* (an absolute measure of risk) or *coefficient of variation* (a relative measure of risk).
- A positive relationship exists between risk and required rates of return. Investments involving greater risks must offer higher expected returns.

Exercises

Answers to the exercises in blue can be found in Appendix D at the back of the book.

1. For each of the determinants of demand in Equation 2.1, identify an example illustrating the effect on the demand for hybrid gasoline-electric vehicles such as the Toyota Prius. Then do the same for each of the determinants of supply in Equation 2.2. In each instance, would equilibrium market price increase or decrease? Consider substitutes such as plug-in hybrids, the Nissan Leaf and Chevy Volt, and complements such as gasoline and lithium ion laptop computer batteries.

2. Gasoline prices above $3 per gallon have affected what Enterprise Rental Car Co. can charge for various models of rental cars. SUVs are $37 with one-day return and subcompacts are $41 with one-day return. Why would the equilibrium price of SUVs be lower than the equilibrium price of subcompacts?

3. The Ajax Corporation has the following set of projects available to it:

PROJECT*	INVESTMENT REQUIRED ($ MILLION)	EXPECTED RATE OF RETURN (%)
A	500	23.0
B	75	18.0
C	50	21.0
D	125	16.0
E	300	14.0
F	150	13.0
G	250	19.0

*Note: All projects have equal risk.

Ajax can raise funds with the following marginal costs:

First $250 million	14.0%
Next 250 million	15.5
Next 100 million	16.0
Next 250 million	16.5
Next 200 million	18.0
Next 200 million	21.0

Use the marginal cost and marginal revenue concepts developed in this chapter to derive an optimal capital budget for Ajax.

4. ESPN currently pays the NFL $1.1 billion per year for eight years for the right to exclusively televise Monday Night Football. What is the net present value of this investment if the parent Disney Company has an opportunity interest rate equal to its cost of capital of 9 percent. Fox and CBS agreed to pay $712 million and $622 million respectively for six years to televise Sunday afternoon NFC games. What was that worth?

5. The demand for MICHTEC's products is related to the state of the economy. If the economy is expanding next year (an above-normal growth in GNP), the company expects sales to be $90 million. If there is a recession next year (a decline in GNP), sales are expected to be $75 million. If next year is normal (a moderate growth in GNP), sales are expected to be $85 million. MICHTEC's economists have estimated the chances that the economy will be either expanding, normal, or in a recession next year at 0.2, 0.5, and 0.3, respectively.
   a. Compute expected annual sales.
   b. Compute the standard deviation of annual sales.
   c. Compute the coefficient of variation of annual sales.

6. Two investments have the following expected returns (net present values) and standard deviation of returns:

PROJECT	EXPECTED RETURNS ($)	STANDARD DEVIATION ($)
A	50,000	40,000
B	250,000	125,000

Which one is riskier? Why?

7. The manager of the aerospace division of General Aeronautics has estimated the price it can charge for providing satellite launch services to commercial firms. Her most optimistic estimate (a price not expected to be exceeded more than 10 percent of the time) is $2 million. Her most pessimistic estimate (a lower price than this one is not expected more than 10 percent of the time) is $1 million. The expected value estimate is $1.5 million. The price distribution is believed to be approximately normal.
   a. What is the expected price?
   b. What is the standard deviation of the launch price?
   c. What is the probability of receiving a price less than $1.2 million?

Case Exercise

Revenue Management at American Airlines[11]

Airlines face highly cyclical demand; American reported profitability in the strong expansion of 2006–2007 but massive losses in the severe recession of 2008–2009. Demand also fluctuates day to day. One of the ways American copes with random demand is through marginal analysis using revenue management techniques. Revenue or "yield" management (RM) is an integrated demand-management, order-booking, and capacity-planning process.

To win orders in a service industry *without slashing prices* requires that companies create perceived value for segmented classes of customers. Business travelers on airlines, for example, will pay substantial premiums for last-minute responsiveness to their flight change requests. Other business travelers demand exceptional delivery reliability and on-time performance. In contrast, most vacation excursion travelers want commodity-like service at rock-bottom prices. Although only 15–20 percent of most airlines' seats are in the business segment, 65–75 percent of the profit contribution on a typical flight comes from this group.

The management problem is that airline capacity must be planned and allocated well in advance of customer arrivals, often before demand is fully known, yet unsold inventory perishes at the moment of departure. This same issue faces hospitals, consulting firms, TV stations, and printing businesses, all of whom must acquire and schedule capacity before the demands for elective surgeries, a crisis management team, TV ads, or the next week's press run are fully known.

One approach to minimizing unsold inventory and yet capturing all last-minute high-profit business is to auction off capacity to the highest bidder. The auction for free-wheeling electricity works just that way: power companies bid at quarter 'til the hour for excess supplies that other utilities agree to deliver on the hour. However, in airlines, prices cannot be adjusted quickly as the moment of departure approaches. Instead, revenue managers employ large historical databases to predict segmented customer demand in light of current arrivals on the reservation system. They then analyze the expected marginal profit from holding in reserve another seat in business class in anticipation of additional "last-minute" demand and compare that seat by seat to the alternative expected marginal profit from accepting one more advance reservation request from a discount traveler.

[11]Based on Robert Cross, *Revenue Management* (New York: Broadway Books, 1995); and Frederick Harris and Peter Peacock, "Hold My Place Please: Yield Management Improves Capacity Allocation Guesswork," *Marketing Management* (Fall 1995), pp. 34–46.

Suppose on the 9:00 A.M. Dallas to Chicago flight next Monday, 63 of American's 170 seats have been "protected" for first class, business class, and full coach fares but only 50 have been sold; the remaining 107 seats have been authorized for sale at a discount. Three days before departure, another advance reservation request arrives in the discount class, which is presently full. Should American reallocate capacity and take on the new discount passenger? The answer depends on the marginal profit from each class and the predicted probability of excess demand (beyond 63 seats) next Monday in the business classes.

If the $721 full coach fare has a $500 marginal profit and the $155 discount fare has a $100 marginal profit, the seat in question should not be reallocated from business to discount customers unless the probability of "stocking out" in business is less than 0.20 (accounting for the likely incidence of cancellations and no-shows). Therefore, if the probability of stocking out is 0.25, the expected marginal profit from holding an empty seat for another potential business customer is $125, whereas the marginal profit from selling that seat to the discount customer is only $100 with certainty. Even a pay-in-advance no-refund seat request from the discount class should be refused. Every company has some viable orders that should be refused because additional capacity held in reserve for the anticipated arrival of higher profit customers is not "idle capacity" but rather a predictable revenue opportunity waiting to happen.

In this chapter, we developed the marginal analysis approach used in solving American's seat allocation decision problem. The Appendix to Chapter 14 discusses further the application of revenue management to baseball, theatre ticketing, and hotels.

Questions

1. Make a list of some of the issues that will need to be resolved if American Airlines decides to routinely charge different prices to customers in the same class of service.

2. Would you expect these revenue management techniques of charging differential prices based on the target customers' willingness to pay for change order responsiveness, delivery reliability, schedule frequency, and so forth to be more effective in the trucking industry, the outpatient health care industry, or the hotel industry? Why or why not?

3. Sometimes when reservation requests by deep discount travelers are refused, demanders take their business elsewhere; they "balk." At other times, such demanders negotiate and can be "sold up" to higher fare service like United's Economy Plus. If United experiences fewer customers balking when reservation requests for the cheapest seats are refused, should they allocate preexisting capacity to protect fewer seats (or more) for late-arriving full-fare passengers?

CHAPTER 10

Prices, Output, and Strategy: Pure and Monopolistic Competition

CHAPTER PREVIEW

Stockholder wealth-maximizing managers seek a pricing and output strategy that will maximize the present value of the future profit stream to the firm. The determination of the wealth-maximizing strategy depends on the production capacity, cost levels, demand characteristics, and the potential for immediate and longer-term competition. In this chapter, we provide an introduction to competitive strategic analysis and discuss Michael Porter's Five Forces strategic framework. Thereafter, we distinguish pure competition with detailed analyses of the home contractor industry from monopolistic competition with detailed analyses of advertising expenditures in ready-to-eat (RTE) cereals. With asymmetrically informed sellers, the rational hesitation of buyers to pay full price and the resulting problem of adverse selection in a "lemons market" are also discussed.

MANAGERIAL CHALLENGE
Resurrecting Apple in the Tablet World[1]

Apple Computer revolutionized personal computing by adapting Xerox's point and click graphical user interface (GUI) into its 1983 Macintosh 3. The GUI was quickly reverse engineered and imitated by Microsoft, whose point and click Windows operating system (OS) captured a 90 percent plus market share by 1997. IBM and then Compaq, Dell, and Hewlett-Packard (HP) personal computers (PCs) equipped with Windows and Intel computer chips then dominated the PC business for more than 15 years (1997–2012).

But recently, PC sales declined by 8.6 percent. Personal computing is now taking place on the fly. Not just telecommunications and web searches, but document preparation and spreadsheet analysis are increasingly occurring in an on-demand mobile environment wherever the user finds herself. In addition, touchscreen tiles are replacing mice and keypads. Microsoft's Windows 8 release in November 2012 confirms this paradigm shift. Tablet-based mobile computing has displaced the desk-

top computer and laptop. Apple recently sold its 100 millionth 8-inch screen, 11-ounce, 16–64 gigabyte memory, dual camera–laden tablet.

Today, the assembly of personal computers and tablets is outsourced to a wide variety of supply chain partners operating at massive scale worldwide. With fewer outsourced components, more product features, and extensive R&D costs, Apple's PCs sell for $1,100 and up, whereas HP, Dell, and Toshiba's PCs are priced as low as $600. In tablets, Amazon's Kindle Fire and Google's Nexus 7 both at $199 to $249, and Microsoft's Surface sell well against Apple's newest $499 basic iPad and new iPad Mini at $329 to $659. Like the PC market before it, the tablet market has quickly become very competitive. Apple initially sold primarily through retail outlets like Computer Tree, but to target the consumer sector, Apple has launched dozens of company-owned Apple stores. Apple's closed (proprietary, unlicensable) OS (operating system) architecture sacrificed network effects. In contrast, Google's Android telecom

MANAGERIAL CHALLENGE *Continued*

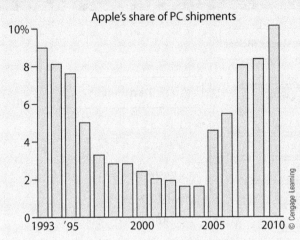

Apple's share of PC shipments

movies. Amazon places a distant third in digital movie sales at 8.5 percent. Microsoft's Surface tablet is projected to garner 20 percent market share by 2016.

system and Microsoft's huge installed base attracted third-party independent software vendors who wrote numerous applications programs. Without compatibility to this Wintel-installed base, Apple's offering stagnated.

Apple PCs retained market leadership only in the education, graphic design, and publishing sectors. Because 55 percent of all PC and OS sales are in corporations, 33 percent are in the home, 7 percent are in government, and only 5 percent are in education, Apple's market share of U.S. PC sales slipped badly from 10 to 3 percent in the late 1990s. In 1999, Steve Jobs oversaw Apple's effort to reinvent itself by introducing the futuristic iMac and the iPod digital music player, merging that technology with the Apple iPad and later the Apple iPhone.

This time, Apple was ready with layer upon layer of enhanced capabilities for each new generation of its resurgent products.[2] The competitive advantages of the iPod and iPad tablet are process-based, rather than product-based. They rely upon cumulative capabilities with its iTunes Music Store, its partnerships with Disney Inc., Paramount, and various record labels. Almost overnight, Apple garnered a 73 percent share of the $9 billion digital music industry and a 56 percent share of digital movie sales. Walmart, the largest seller of DVDs, has achieved a 26 percent market share in head-to-head competition with Apple for digital movies using its Vudu Web site for downloading music and

Discussion Questions

■ In the thrid quarter of 2012 Apple tablet sales of iPads equal to $7.5 billion exceeded Apple personal computer sales of $6.6 billion. Has your use for a PC waned to the point where you would consider owning just a tablet?

■ Have you visited an Apple Store? Did the in-store experience enhance your perceived value for an Apple product?

■ What prices to charge for iMacs, iPods, and iPads remains a central issue for Apple management. On what basis would you justify paying a price premium for an Apple iMac? What about an Apple iPad?

[1]Based on *Apple Inc.*, 2008, Harvard Business School Case Publishing; "Wal-Mart Stores Tries to Play Apple's Game," *Wall Street Journal* (March 19, 2012), p. C8; "iPhone Shines but iPad Dimms," *Wall Street Journal* (October 26, 2012), p. B1; "Tablets on High," *The Economist* (October 27, 2012), p. 63; and "Apple Drops an iPad Mini on Rivals," *Wall Street Journal* (October 24, 2012), p. B1.

[2]In smart phones, Apple has adopted licensable open software architecture to attract apps vendors. It was estimated in 2012 that the iPhone5 incorporated over a quarter million apps, few of which Apple itself had to pay to develop. With 2012 (3Q) sales of $17.1 billion, the iPhone emerged as Apple's most popular product ever.

INTRODUCTION

To remain competitive, many companies today commit themselves to continuous improvement processes and episodes of strategic planning. Competitive strategic analysis provides a framework for thinking proactively about threats to a firm's business model,

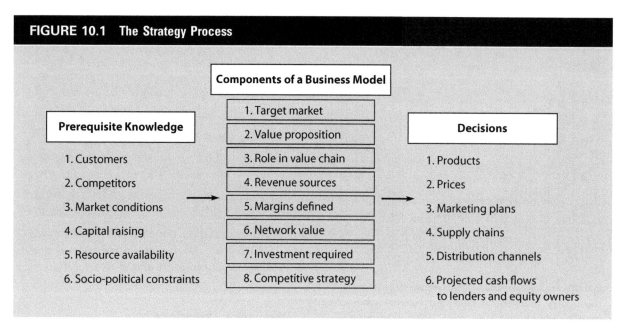

FIGURE 10.1 The Strategy Process

Source: Adapted from H. Chesbrough, *Open Innovation* (Cambridge, MA: Harvard University Press, 2003). Reprinted by permission.

---

core competencies
Technology-based expertise or knowledge on which a company can focus its strategy.

about new business opportunities, and about the future reconfigurations of the firm's resources, capabilities, and **core competencies**.

Figure 10.1 displays the components of a business model in the context of a firm's prerequisite knowledge and strategic decisions. All successful business models begin by identifying *target markets*—that is, what businesses one wants to enter and stay in. Physical assets, human resources, and intellectual property (like patents and licenses) sometimes limit the firm's capabilities, but business models are as unbounded as the ingenuity of entrepreneurial managers in finding ways to identify new opportunities. Next, all successful business models lay out a value proposition grounded in customer expectations of perceived value and then identify what part of the *value chain* leading to end products the firm plans to create. Business models always must clarify *how and when revenue will be realized* and analyze the sensitivity of *gross and net margins* to various possible changes in the firm's cost structure. In specifying the *required investments*, business models also assess the potential for creating *value in network relationships* with complementary businesses and in joint ventures and alliances. Finally, all successful business models develop a *competitive strategy*.

COMPETITIVE STRATEGY

The essence of competitive strategy is threefold: resource-based capabilities, business processes, and adaptive innovation.[3] First, competitive strategy analyzes how the firm can secure differential access to key resources like patents or distribution channels. From humble beginnings as an Internet bookseller that contracted out its warehousing and book delivery service, Amazon managed to become the preferred fulfillment agent

---

[3]This section is based on H. Chesbrough, *Open Innovation* (Boston: Harvard Business School Press, 2003), pp. 73–83.

WHAT WENT RIGHT • WHAT WENT WRONG

Xerox[4]

Xerox invented the chemical paper copier and thereafter realized phenomenal 15 percent compound growth rates for almost two decades. When its initial patents expired, Xerox was ready with a plain paper copier that established a first-mover technology advantage, but ultimately the company failed to receive any broad patent extension. Xerox's target market was large corporations and government installations that valued high-quality, high-volume leased machines with an enormous variety of capabilities and full-service maintenance contracts, even though supplies and usage fees were expensive.

Unable to compete on product capabilities, Japanese competitors Canon and Ricoh realized that tremendous market potential lay in smaller businesses where affordability per copy was a major value proposition. Installation and service were outsourced to highly competitive independent dealer networks, and the smaller-volume Japanese copy machine itself was sold at very low initial cost, with self-service replacement cartridges being the principal source of profitability.

As with later events at Apple, Xerox insisted on closed architecture software and built all of its copier components in-house rather than pursuing partnerships that could reduce cost by realizing scale economies and thereby trigger a larger installed base of Xerox machines. Ricoh and Canon pursued just the opposite open architecture and partnership strategy to achieve network effects and drive down costs.

Both became $2 billion firms in a copier business that Xerox had totally dominated only 15 years earlier.

[4]Based on Chesbrough, op. cit.; and on C. Bartlett and S. Ghoshal, *Transnational Management* (Boston, MA: Irwin-McGraw-Hill, 1995), Case 4–1.

for web-based sales in general. That is, the bookseller Amazon acquired enough regular customers searching for CDs, office products, tools, and toys that companies like Toys "R" Us adopted Amazon as their channel partner. In Japan, 7-Eleven stores won that same role for neighborhood pick-up and delivery of web-based purchases. Second, competitive strategy designs business processes that are difficult to imitate and capable of creating unique value for the target customers. For example, the high-frequency point-to-point streamlined operations processes of Southwest Airlines prove very difficult for hub-and-spoke airlines to imitate, and, as a result, the market capitalization of Southwest often exceeds that of all the other major U.S. carriers combined.

Similarly, both Dell and Compaq at one point in their respective corporate histories, had $12 billion in net sales and approximately $1 billion in net income in 1998. But Compaq's business model required $6 billion in net operating assets (i.e., inventories plus net plant and equipment plus working capital) to earn $1 billion, while Dell's required only $2 billion. How could Dell produce the same net income with one-third as much plant and equipment, inventories, and working capital as Compaq? The answer is that Dell created a direct-to-the-customer sales process; Dell builds to order, with subassembly components bought just in time from outside contractors, and it realizes cash from a sale within 48 hours. These value-creating business processes generated 50 percent ($1B/$2B) return on investment (ROI) at Dell, whereas the comparable ROI at Compaq was just 16 percent ($1B/$6B).[5]

Finally, competitive strategy provides a road map for sustaining a firm's profitability, principally through innovation. Think of Polaroid to digital cameras, calculators to spreadsheets, and mobile radios to handheld smart phones: As such industries emerge, evolve, and morph into other product spaces, firms must anticipate these changes and plan how they will sustain their positioning in the industry, and ultimately migrate their business to new industries. IBM, the dominant mainframe leasing company in the 1970s, has reinvented itself

---

[5]Return on invested capital is defined as net income divided by net operating assets (i.e., net plant and equipment plus inventories plus net accounts receivable).

twice—first in the 1980s as a PC manufacturer, and a second time in the 1990s and 2000s as a systems solution provider for a "smarter planet." In contrast, some firms like Xerox or Kodak became entrenched in outdated competitive strategic positions.

Generic Types of Strategies[6]

industry analysis Assessment of the strengths and weaknesses of a set of competitors or line of businesses.

Strategic thinking initially focuses on **industry analysis**—that is, identifying industries in which it would be attractive to do business. Michael Porter's Five Forces model (discussed later) illustrates this approach. Soon thereafter, however, business strategists want to conduct *competitor analysis* to learn more about how firms can sustain their relative profitability in a *strategic group* of related firms. Efforts to answer these questions are often described as *strategic positioning*. Finally, strategists try to isolate what *core competencies* any particular firm possesses as a result of its *resource-based capabilities* in order to identify **sustainable competitive advantages** vis-à-vis their competitors in a relevant market.

sustainable competitive advantages Difficult-to-imitate features of a company's processes or products.

Product Differentiation Strategy

product differentiation strategy A business-level strategy that relies upon differences in products or processes affecting perceived customer value.

Any one of three generic types of strategies may suffice. A firm may establish a product differentiation strategy, a lowest-delivered-cost strategy, or an information technology (IT) strategy. **Product differentiation strategy** usually involves competing on capabilities, brand names, or product endorsements. Boeing competes on product capabilities. Coca-Cola is by far the world's most widely recognized brand. Gillette, P&G's Pampers, Nestlé, Nescafé, and Kellogg's each has nearly 50 percent market shares. All of these branded products command a price premium worldwide simply because of the product image and lifestyle associated with their successful branding.

Example

Rawlings Sporting Goods Waves Off the Swoosh Sign[7]

Even though $200 million Rawlings competes against heavily branded Nike with annual sales of $14 billion, Rawlings baseball gloves are extremely profitable. The key is that the gloves receive product endorsements by more than 50 percent of major leaguers, such as the California Angles' Pujols and Yankees shortstop Derek Jeter. These superstars receive $20,000 for licensing their autographs to Rawlings for engraving on Little League gloves. But players can talk about a feature of Rawlings' equipment that keeps them coming back year after year. Rawlings is very attentive to this feedback and will lengthen the webbing or stiffen the fingers on a new model in just a few weeks to please its celebrity endorsers. Quick adaptation to the vagaries of the consumer marketplace is a requisite part of any product differentiation strategy.

[7]Based on "I've Got It," *Wall Street Journal* (April 1, 2002), p. A1.

Cost-Based Strategy

cost-based strategy A business-level strategy that relies upon low-cost operations, marketing, or distribution.

Competitive scope decisions are especially pivotal for **cost-based strategy**. For example, a firm like Southwest Airlines with a *focused cost strategy* must limit its business plan to focus narrowly on point-to-point, medium-distance, nonstop routes.

[6]This section is based in part on C. De Kluyver and J. Pearce, *Strategy: A View from the Top* (Upper Saddle River, NJ: Prentice-Hall, 2003).

| Example | ## Think Small to Grow Big: Southwest Airlines |

Think Small to Grow Big: Southwest Airlines

Southwest adopted operations processes for ticket sales, boarding procedures, plane turnarounds, crew scheduling, flight frequency, maintenance, and jet fuel hedging that deliver exceptionally reduced operating costs to target customers in a price-sensitive market niche. Anything that works against this cost-based strategy must be jettisoned from the business plan. Southwest has clearly accomplished its goal. As air travel plummeted in the months following the September 11, 2001, attacks on the World Trade Center, only Southwest had a break-even volume that was low enough to continue to make money. Southwest can cover all of its costs at 64 percent load factors (unit sales/seat capacity), whereas American Airlines, United, Delta, and US Airways often operate well below their break-even points of 75 to 84 percent.

Much has been made of the fact that Southwest has labor costs covered by 36 percent of sales dollars, while United, American, and US Airways have labor costs covered by 48 percent of sales dollars. But the $0.07 gap between United's $0.12 cost per revenue passenger mile (rpm) and Jet Blue's $0.05 and Southwest's $0.07 cost per rpm reflects not just labor costs but hard-to-imitate process differences. Booz, Allen, Hamilton found that only 15 percent of the operating cost difference between full-service and low-cost carriers was labor cost. But the largest source of cost difference between Southwest's $0.07 cost per revenue passenger mile and United's $0.12 is process differences in check-in, boarding, reservations, crew scheduling, and maintenance. These processes make possible the famed 15-minute turnaround time at Southwest.

In contrast, Dell Computers' *cost leadership strategy* allows it to address a wide scope of PC product lines at prices that make its competitors wish to exit the market, as IBM did in 1999. Gateway was also unable to keep pace with Dell's cost-cutting and by 2006 found itself at 5.3 percent market share versus a 10.6 percent peak in 1999. Shortly thereafter Gateway sold off its PC business.

Information Technology Strategy

information technology strategy A business-level strategy that relies on IT capabilities.

Finally, firms can seek their sustainable competitive advantage among relevant market rivals by pursuing an **information technology strategy**. In addition to assisting in the recovery of stolen vehicles, satellite-based GPS has allowed Allstate Insurance to confirm that certain cars on a family policy are not being driven to work, while other less expensive cars are being exposed to the driving hazards of commuting. This allows Allstate to cut some insurance rates and win more business from their competitors. The e-commerce strategy of Southland Corporation's 7-Eleven convenience stores in 6,000 locations across Japan provides another good example.

In conclusion, a company's strategy can result in higher profits if the company configures its resource-based capabilities, business processes, and adaptive innovations in such a way as to obtain a sustainable competitive advantage. Whether cost-based strategy, product differentiation strategy, or IT strategy provides the most effective route to competitive advantage depends in large part on the firm's strategic focus. IT-based strategy is especially conducive to broad target market initiatives. In addition to using IT for merchandizing lunch items, 7-Eleven Japan "drives" customer traffic to its convenience stores by allowing Internet buyers to pick up their web purchases and pay at the 7-Eleven counter. Is 7-Eleven Japan a convenience store, an Internet fulfillment agent like Amazon, or a warehouse and distribution company? In some sense, 7-Eleven Japan is all of these. Unlike Southwest Airlines' cost-focused strategy, 7-Eleven Japan has a much broader IT-based strategy that conveys a competitive advantage across several relevant markets.

Example

The E-Commerce of Lunch at 7-Elevens in Japan[8]

Japanese office workers put in very long hours, often arriving at 8:00 A.M. and staying well into the evening. In the midst of this long day, most take an hour and a quarter break to go out on the street and pick up lunch. Boxed lunches, rice balls, and sandwiches are the routine offerings, but the fashion-conscious Japanese want to be seen eating what's "in." This situation makes an excellent opportunity for Southland Corporation's 7-Eleven stores, which is the biggest retailer in Japan and twice as profitable as the country's second-largest retailer, the clothing outlet Fast Retailing.

7-Eleven Japan collects sales information by proprietary satellite communication networks from its 8,500 locations three times a day. The data are used to improve product packaging and shelf placements with laboratory-like experiments in matched-pair stores throughout the country. But there is more, much more. 7-Eleven Japan has built systems to analyze the entire data inflow in just 20 minutes. Specifically, 7-Eleven forecasts what to prepare for the lunch crowd downtown today based on what sells this morning and what sold yesterday evening in suburban locations. As customers become more fickle, product fashion cycles in sandwiches are shortening from seven weeks to, in some cases, as little time as 10 days. 7-Eleven Japan forecasts the demand daily on an item-by-item, store-by-store basis.

Of course, such short-term demand forecasting would be useless if food preparation were a production-to-stock process with many weeks of lead time required. Instead, supply chain management practices are closely monitored and adapted continuously with electronic commerce tools. Delivery trucks carry bar code readers that upload instantaneously to headquarters databases. Orders for a particular sandwich at a particular store are placed before 10:00 A.M., processed through the supply chain to all component input companies in less than 7 minutes, and delivered by 4:00 P.M. for the next day's sales. Most customers praise the extraordinary freshness, quality ingredients, and minimal incidence of out-of-stock items. All this competitive advantage over rival grocers and noodle shops has led to consistent price premiums for 7-Eleven's in-house brand.

---

[8]Based on "Over the Counter Commerce," *The Economist* (May 26, 2001), pp. 77–78.

Which of the three generic types of strategies (differentiation, cost savings, or IT) will be most effective for a particular company depends in part on a firm's choice of *competitive scope*—that is, on the number and type of product lines and market segments, the number of geographic locations, and the network of horizontally and vertically integrated businesses in which the company decides to invest. For example, the most profitable clothing retailer in the United States, The Gap, once undertook to expand its competitive scope by opening a new chain of retail clothing stores. Unfortunately, Old Navy's bargain-priced khakis, jeans, and sweaters immediately began cannibalizing sales at its mid-priced parent. Even fashion-conscious teens could see little reason to pay $16.50 for a Gap-emblazoned T-shirt when Old Navy's branding offered style and a nearly identical product for $12.50. The configuration of a firm's resource capabilities, its business opportunities relative to its rivals, and a detailed knowledge of its customers intertwine to determine the preferred competitive scope.

The Relevant Market Concept

relevant market A group of firms belonging to the same strategic group of competitors.

A **relevant market** *is a group of firms that interact with each other in a buyer-seller relationship.* Relevant markets often have both spatial and product characteristics. For example, the market for large, prime-rate commercial loans includes large banks and corporations from all areas of the United States, whereas the market for bagged cement is confined to a 250-mile radius around the plant.

The *market structure* within these relevant markets varies tremendously. The four largest producers of breakfast cereals control 86 percent of the total U.S. output—a **concentrated market**. In contrast, the market for brick and concrete block is **fragmented**, with the largest four firms accounting for only 8 percent of the total U.S. output. Recently, the share of the total U.S. output produced by the largest four firms in the women's hosiery industry has **consolidated**, growing from 32 to 58 percent. These differences in market structures and changes in market structure over time have important implications for the determination of price levels, price stability, and the likelihood of sustained profitability in these relevant markets.

concentrated market A relevant market with a majority of total sales occurring in the largest four firms.

fragmented A relevant market whose market shares are uniformly small.

consolidated A relevant market whose number of firms has declined through acquisition, merger, and buyouts.

PORTER'S FIVE FORCES STRATEGIC FRAMEWORK

Michael Porter[9] developed a conceptual framework for industry analysis, identifying the threats to profitability from five forces of competition in a relevant market. Figure 10.2 displays Porter's Five Forces: the threat of substitutes, the threat of entry, the power of buyers, the power of suppliers, and the intensity of rivalry. Today, a sixth force is often added—the threat of a disruptive technology—such as digital file sharing for the recorded music industry, streaming video on demand for the video rental industry, or digital photography for the film industry.

Example

What Went Right What Went Wrong at Fuji and Kodak?

Eastman Kodak of Rochester, New York, once dominated both the camera and the photographic film industries. Founded in 1888, Kodak had a 90 and 85 percent market shares in North American film and disposable camera sales as late as 1976. Similarly, Fuji Film dominated the film and disposable camera markets in Japan. But digital photography and camera-laden smart phones changed all that. Both firms saw their primary products rendered obsolete by the force of disruptive technology. Kodak

(continued)

[9]Michael Porter, *Competitive Strategy* (Cambridge, MA: The Free Press, 1998). See also Cynthia Porter and Michael Porter, eds., *Strategy: Seeking and Securing Competitive Advantage* (Cambridge, MA: Harvard Business School Publishing, 1992).

was persuaded to ignore the inevitable and has shuttered its operations with equity value of only $220 million, whereas Fuji reinvented itself and enjoys a market capitalization of $12.6 billion in 2012. Why such a stark difference?

Rather than pressing a head start in digital cameras, Kodak chose to stay with 70 percent margin traditional chemical film development in light of the comparatively tiny 5 percent margins associated with digital photography services. Fuji, in contrast, shifted its antioxidant chemical compounds to cosmetic use and invested heavily in optical films for liquid crystal display (LCD) flat panel screens. In addition, electronic components for the copier industry proved another profitable Fuji business line. Despite a portfolio of 1,100 highly valuable patents, failing to adapt to a disruptive technology led eventually to Kodak's bankruptcy.

The Threat of Substitutes

First, an incumbent's profitability is determined by the threat of substitutes. Is the product generic, like AAA-grade January wheat, two-bedroom apartments, and office

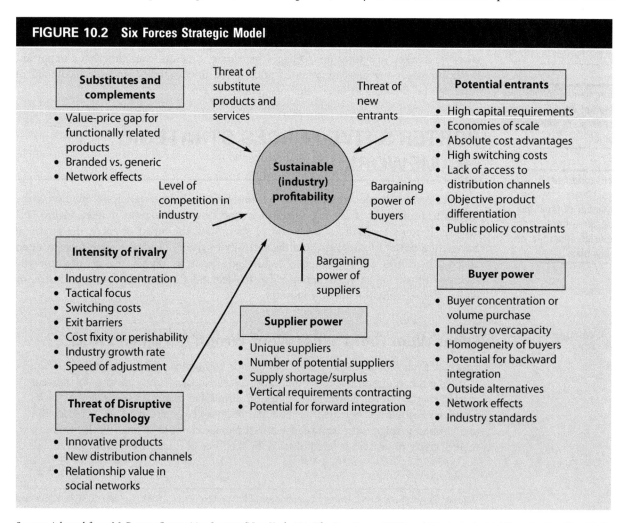

FIGURE 10.2   Six Forces Strategic Model

Source: Adapted from M. Porter, *Competitive Strategy* (New York, NA: The Free Press, 1998); and J. Bain, *Industrial Organization* (New York, NY: John Wiley, 1959).

supplies, or is it branded, like Gillette razors, Pepsi-Cola, and Campbell's soup? The more brand loyalty, the less the threat of substitutes and the higher the incumbent's sustainable profitability will be. Also, the more distant the substitutes outside the relevant market, the less price responsive will be demand, and the larger will be the optimal markups and profit margins. As videoconferencing equipment improves, the margins in business air travel will decline. A videoconferencing projector and sound system now leases for just $279 *per month*. Similarly, flavored and unflavored bottled water and other noncarbonated beverages such as juice, tea, and sports drinks are growing as much as eight times faster than U.S. soda sales. This trend will tend to erode the loyalty of Pepsi and Coke drinkers. If so, profitability will decline.

Network effects are available to enhance profitability if companies can find **complementors**—that is, independent firms that enhance the customer value associated with using the primary firm's product, thereby raising profitability. For example, Microsoft Windows has obtained such a lock-in on PC customers that independent software providers (ISPs) write highly valued applications for Windows for which Microsoft pays nothing. Similarly, Apple's iPad attracts ISPs who enhance the customer value, and thereby support the high price point, and alter the positioning of iPad.

The closeness or distance of substitutes often hinges not only on consumer perceptions created by advertising but also on segmentation of the customers into separate distribution channels. Pantyhose distributed through convenience stores have few substitutes at 9:00 P.M. the night before a business trip, many fewer than pantyhose sold through department store distribution channels. Consequently, the threat of substitutes is reduced, and the sustainable profit margin on convenience store pantyhose is higher. Similarly, one-stop service and nonstop service in airlines are different products with different functionality. United's one-stop service from Chicago provides a distant substitute for Minneapolis-origin air travelers. Consequently, Northwest Airlines (now Delta) enjoys high margins on nonstop service from Minneapolis.

complementors
Independent firms that enhance the focal firm's value proposition.

The Threat of Entry

A second force determining the likely profitability of an industry or product line is the threat of potential entrants. The higher the barriers to entry, the more profitable an incumbent will be. Barriers to entry can arise from several factors. First, consider high capital costs. The bottling and distribution business in the soft drink industry necessitates a $50 million investment. Although a good business plan with secure collateral will always attract loanable funds, unsecured loans become difficult to finance at this size. Fewer potential entrants with the necessary capital imply a lesser threat of entry and higher incumbent profitability.

Second, economies of scale and absolute cost advantages can provide another barrier to entry. An absolute cost advantage arises with proprietary IT that lowers a company's cost (e.g., at 7-Eleven Japan). In the traditional cable TV industry, the huge infrastructure cost of laying wire throughout the community deterred multiple entrants. The first mover had a tremendous scale economy in spreading fixed cost across a large customer base. Of course, wireless technology for satellite-based TV may soon lower this barrier, and then numerous suppliers of TV content will exhibit similar unit cost. These new threats of entry imply lower industry profitability in cable TV.

Third, if customers are brand loyal, the costs of inducing a customer to switch to a new entrant's product may pose a substantial barrier to entry. Year after year, hundreds of millions of dollars of cumulative advertising in the cereal industry maintains the pulling power of the Tony the Tiger Frosted Flakes brand. Unadvertised cereals go unnoticed. To take another example, hotel corporations raise the switching costs for their regular customers when they issue frequent-stayer giveaways. Committing room capacity to promotional giveaways raises barriers to entry. A new entrant therefore has a higher cost associated with becoming an effective entry threat in these markets.

Example

The Relevant Market for Web Browsers: Microsoft's Internet Explorer[10]

One of the recurring antitrust policy questions is the definition of the relevant market for computer software. In 1996, Netscape's user-friendly and pioneering product Navigator had an 82 percent share of the Internet browser market. But during 1996–1999, Microsoft's Internet Explorer made swift inroads. Bundling Explorer with its widely adopted Windows OS, Microsoft marketed an integrated software package preinstalled on PCs. Microsoft quoted higher prices for Windows alone than for Windows with Internet Explorer and threatened PC assemblers like Compaq and Gateway with removal of their Windows license unless they mounted Explorer as a desktop icon. Because most PC customers do want Windows preinstalled on their machines, Explorer penetrated deep into the browser market very quickly. By the start of 2000, some estimates showed Explorer's market share as high as 59 percent.

If the relevant market for these products is an integrated PC OS, then Microsoft has simply incorporated new web browser and media player technology into an already dominant Windows OS product. An analogy might be the interlock between an automobile's ignition and steering system to deter auto theft. If, on the other hand, Internet browsers (or, more recently, media players) are a separate relevant market, like stereo equipment for automobiles, then Microsoft should not be entitled to employ anticompetitive practices like refusals to deal to extend their dominance of PC OS into this new software market.

Microsoft's spectacular growth in sales of Windows 98 was not the issue. Winning a near monopoly of 85 percent market share in the previously fragmented OS software industry indicated a superior product, a great business plan, and good management. But allowing Microsoft to extend that market power into a new line of business using tactics that would be ineffective and self-defeating in the absence of the dominant market share in the original business is just what the antitrust laws were intended to prevent. Twenty state attorneys general in the United States and the European antitrust authorities have pursued a case against Microsoft using this line of reasoning. The European Union insisted on multiple versions of Windows with (and without) Media Player stripped out and fined Microsoft $624 million in March 2004. Appeals were exhausted in 2009, and Microsoft paid the fine plus interest.

---

[10]Based on "U.S. Sues Microsoft over PC Browser" and "Personal Technology," *Wall Street Journal* (October 21 and 30, 1997); "Microsoft's Browser: A Bundle of Trouble," *The Economist* (October 25, 1997); and *U.S. News and World Report,* Business and Technology (December 15, 1997).

Access to distribution channels is another potential barrier that has implications for the profitability of incumbents. The shelf space in grocery stores is very limited; all the slots are filled. A new entrant would therefore have to offer huge trade promotions (i.e., free display racks or slot-in allowances) to induce grocery store chains to displace one of their current suppliers. A related barrier to entry has emerged in the satellite television industry where Direct TV and EchoStar control essentially all the channel slots on satellites capable of reaching the entire U.S. audience. Government regulatory agencies also can approve or deny access to distribution channels. For example, the Food and Drug Administration (FDA) approves prescription drugs for certain therapeutic uses but not for others. The FDA also approves or denies exceptions to the Orphan Drug Act that gives firms patent-like exclusive selling rights when public policy pressure warrants doing so. Biogen's highest sales product, Avonex (a weekly injection for multiple sclerosis patients), received a license under the Orphan Drug Act. Other similarly situated firms have been denied approval; such a barrier to entry may prove insurmountable.

Example

Potential Entry at Office Depot/Staples[11]

Office Depot (a $6 billion company) and Staples (a $4 billion company) proposed to merge. Their combined sales in the $13 billion office supply superstore industry totaled 76 percent. From another perspective, their potential competitors included not only OfficeMax but all small paper goods specialty stores, department stores, discount stores such as Kmart, warehouse clubs like Sam's Club, office supply catalogs, and some computer retailers. This much larger office supply industry is very fragmented, easy to enter, and huge ($185 billion). Using this latter standard, the combined market share of Staples and Office Depot was only 6 percent.

The profit margins of Office Depot, OfficeMax, and Staples are significantly higher when only one office supply superstore locates in a town. This would suggest that the small-scale office suppliers offer little threat of entry into the superstore market. The exceptional ease of entry (and exit) at a small scale moderates the markups and profit margins of incumbent specialty retailers like stationery stores, but not office supply superstores. High capital requirement and scale economies in warehousing and distribution appear responsible for the barriers to entry in the office supply superstore market.

[11]Based on "FTC Rejects Staples' Settlement Offer," *Wall Street Journal* (April 7, 1997), p. A3; and J. Baker, "Econometric Analysis in *FTC* v. *Staples*," *Journal of Public Policy and Marketing* 18, no. 1 (Spring 1999), pp. 11–21.

Preexisting competitors in related product lines provide a substantial threat of entry as well; see the following example.

Example

Eli Lilly Poses a Threat of Potential Entry for AstraZeneca[12]

In 2000, AstraZeneca's cancer treatment Nolvadex became the first drug ever approved for reducing the risk of breast cancer in currently healthy women. Eli Lilly markets a pharmaceutical product, Evista, long approved by the FDA for the treatment of osteoporosis. Preliminary tests have suggested a therapeutic potential for Evista in the prevention of breast cancer. Lilly promptly released an Evista study in which the incidence of developing cancer over a three-year period was reduced 55 percent in 10,575 women with high-risk factors for developing breast cancer. AstraZeneca sued to stop and undoubtedly slowed Lilly's marketing efforts, but the real barrier to entry would come if the FDA denies the use of Evista for breast cancer treatment. Without such a denial, AstraZeneca's Nolvadex faces a formidable direct competitor from a preexisting supplier in an adjacent relevant market.

[12]Zeneca Sues Eli Lilly Over Promotion of Evista for Preventing Breast Cancer, *Wall Street Journal* (February 26, 1999), p. B6.

Finally, a barrier to entry may be posed by product differentiation. Objective product differentiation is subject to reverse engineering, violations of intellectual property, and offshore imitation even of patented technology like the shutter in a Kodak digital camera. In contrast, subjective perceived product differentiation based on customer perceptions of lifestyle images and product positioning (e.g., Pepsi-Cola) can erect effective barriers to entry that allow incumbent firms to better survive competitive attack. In sum, the higher any of these barriers to entry, the lower the threat of potential entrants and the higher the sustainable industry profitability will be.

Objective versus Perceived Product Differentiation: Xerox

Shielded from competition by patents on its landmark dry paper copier, Xerox enjoyed a virtual monopoly and 15 percent compound earnings growth through the 1960s and early 1970s. During this period, its research lab in Palo Alto, California, spun off one breakthrough device after another. One year it was the graphical user interface that Apple later brought to market as a user-friendly PC. Xerox scientists and engineers also developed the Ethernet, the first local area network for connecting computers and printers. Yet, Xerox was able to commercialize almost none of these R & D successes. As a result, Japanese copier companies like Canon and Ikon reverse engineered the Xerox product, imitated its processes, and ultimately developed better and cheaper copiers.

The Power of Buyers and Suppliers

The profitability of incumbents is determined in part by the bargaining power of buyers and suppliers. Buyers may be highly concentrated, like Boeing and Airbus in the purchase of large aircraft engines, or extremely fragmented, like the restaurants that are customers of wholesale grocery companies. If industry capacity approximately equals or exceeds demand, concentrated buyers can force price concessions that reduce an incumbent's profitability. On the other hand, fragmented buyers have little bargaining power unless excess capacity and inventory overhang persist.

Unique suppliers may also reduce industry profitability. The Coca-Cola Co. establishes exclusive franchise arrangements with independent bottlers. No other supplier can provide the secret ingredients in the concentrate syrup. Bottler profitability is therefore rather low. In contrast, Coke's own suppliers are numerous; many potential sugar and flavoring manufacturers would like to win the Coca-Cola account, and the syrup inputs are non-unique commodities. These factors raise the likely profitability of the concentrate manufacturers such as Coca-Cola because of the lack of power among their suppliers.

Supply shortages, stockouts, and a backorder production environment can alter the relative power of buyers and suppliers in the value chain. One of the few levers a supplier has against huge category-killer retailers like Toys "R" Us to prevent their expropriating all the net value is to refuse to guarantee on-time delivery for triple orders of popular products. A deeply discounted wholesale price should never receive 100 percent delivery reliability.

Finally, buyers and suppliers will have more bargaining power and reduce firm profitability when they possess more outside alternatives and can credibly threaten to vertically integrate into the industry. HMOs (health maintenance organizations) can negotiate very low fees from primary care physicians precisely because the HMO has so many outside alternatives. Buyers who control the setting of industry standards can also negotiate substantial reductions in pricing and profitability from manufacturers who may then be in a position to capture network effects. Companies favored by having their product specs adopted as an industry standard often experience increasing returns to their marketing expenditures.

The Intensity of Rivalrous Tactics

In the global economy, few companies can establish and maintain dominance in anything beyond niche markets. Reverse engineering of products, imitation of advertising images, and offshore production at low cost imply that General Motors (GM) cannot hope to rid itself of Ford, and Coca-Cola cannot hope truly to defeat Pepsi. Instead, to sustain profitability in such a setting, companies must avoid intense rivalries and elicit passive, more cooperative responses from close competitors. The intensity of the rivalry in an industry depends on several factors: industry concentration, the tactical focus of competition, switching costs, the presence of exit barriers, the industry growth rate, and the ratio of fixed to total cost (termed the **cost fixity**) in the typical cost structure.

Exactly what firms and what products offer close substitutes for potential customers in the relevant market determine the degree of industry concentration. One measure of industry concentration is the sum of the market shares of the four largest or eight largest firms in an industry. The larger the market shares and the smaller the number of competitors, the more interdependence each firm will perceive, and the less intense the rivalry. The ready-to-eat cereal industry has more intense rivalry than the soft drink industry, in part because Kellogg's (37 percent), General Mills (25 percent), Post (15 percent), and Quaker Oats (8 percent) together comprise 85 percent of the market. When two firms enjoy 60 to 90 percent of industry shipments (e.g., Pepsi and Coke), their transparent interdependence can lead to reduced intensity of rivalry if the firms tacitly collude. Similarly, because Titleist and Spalding dominate the golf ball market, the rivalrous intensity is less than in the fragmented golf club business.

Sustainable profitability is increased by tactics that focus on non-price rather than price competition. Airlines are more profitable when they can avoid price wars and focus their competition for passengers on service quality—for example, delivery reliability, change-order responsiveness, and schedule convenience. But trunk route airlines between major U.S. cities provide generic transportation with nearly identical service quality and departure frequency. Consequently, fare wars are frequent, and the resulting profitability of trunk airline routes is very low. In contrast, long-standing rivals Coca-Cola and Pepsi have never discounted their cola concentrates. This absence of "gain-share discounting" and a diminished focus on price competition tactics in general increases the profitability of the concentrate business. Airlines tried to control gain-share discounting by introducing "frequent flyer" programs to increase the customers' *switching cost* from one competitor to another. This idea to reduce the intensity of rivalry worked well for a time, until business travelers joined essentially all the rival frequent flyer programs.

> **cost fixity** A measure of fixed to total cost that is correlated with gross profit margins.

Example

Price Competition at the Soda Fountain: PepsiCo Inc.[13]

Soft drinks are marketed through several distribution channels at different prices. The channels of distribution include independent beverage resellers, vending machine companies, and company-owned bottlers supplying supermarkets, convenience stores, and vending machines, which account for 31, 12, and 11 percent, respectively, of all

(continued)

soft drink sales. Shelf slots in the store channels are full, and bottlers compete on stocking services and retailer rebates for prime shelf space and vending machine locations in an attempt to grow their brands. With roughly the same percent market shares in the stores, the Coca-Cola- and PepsiCo-owned bottlers attempt to avoid head-to-head price competition, which would simply lower profits for both firms, and instead seek predictable patterns of company-sponsored once-every-other-week discounts. Where independent beverage resellers have established a practice of persistent gain-share discounting, the Coca-Cola Company and PepsiCo have often attempted to purchase the franchises and replace them with company-owned bottlers. Vending operations are very high-margin businesses, and PepsiCo and Coca-Cola increasingly service vending machines directly from their company-owned bottlers. To date, little price competition has emerged in the vending channel, in part because independents must purchase from exclusive franchise bottlers in their areas.

Price competition is heating up, however, in the fountain drink side of the business. As more and more families eat more and more meals outside the household, the fountain drink channel accounted for 37 percent of total sales. Coca-Cola has long dominated the fountain drink business. At restaurants and soda shops in 2000, Coke enjoyed a 59 percent share to Pepsi's 23 percent. Recently, PepsiCo declared an intent to vigorously pursue fountain drink sales through discount pricing tactics if necessary. This development threatens continuing profitability in this important channel of the soft drink industry.

[13]Based on "Cola Wars Continue," Harvard Business School Case Publishing (1994); "Pepsi Hopes to Tap Coke's Fountain Sales," *USA Today* (November 6, 1997), p. 3B; and "Antitrust Suit Focuses on Bottlers' Pricing and Sales Practices," *Wall Street Journal* (January 20, 1999), p. B7.

break-even sales change analysis A calculation of the percentage increase in unit sales required to justify a price discount, given the contribution margin.

Sometimes price versus non-price competition simply reflects the lack of product differentiation available in commodity-like markets (e.g., in selling cement). However, the incidence of price competition is also determined in part by the cost structure prevalent in the industry. Where fixed costs as a percentage of total costs are high, margins will tend to be larger. If so, firms are tempted to fight tooth and nail for incremental customers because every additional unit sale represents a substantial contribution to covering the fixed costs. All other things being the same, gain-share discounting will therefore tend to increase the greater the fixed cost is. For example, gross margins in the airline industry reflect the enormous fixed costs for aircraft leases and terminal facilities, often reaching 80 percent. Consider the following **break-even sales change analysis** for an airline that seeks to increase its total contributions by lowering its prices 10 percent:

$$(P_0 - MC)Q_0 < (0.9\,P_0 - MC)Q_1$$
$$< (0.9\,P_0 - MC)(Q_0 + \Delta Q)$$

[10.1]

where revenue minus variable cost (MC times Q) is the *total contribution*. If discounting is to succeed in raising total contributions, the change in sales ΔQ must be great enough to more than offset the 10 percent decline in revenue per unit sale. Rearranging Equation 10.1 and dividing by P_0 yields

$$\frac{(P_0 - MC)Q_0}{P_0} < \left[\frac{(P_0 - MC)}{P_0} - 0.1\frac{P_0}{P_0}\right](Q_0 + \Delta Q)$$
$$(PCM)Q_0 < (PCM - 0.1)(Q_0 + \Delta Q)$$

where *PCM* is the price-cost margin, often referred to as the contribution margin. That is,

$$\frac{PCM}{(PCM - 0.1)} < \frac{(Q_0 + \Delta Q)}{Q_0}$$

$$\frac{PCM}{(PCM - 0.1)} < 1 + \frac{\Delta Q}{Q_0} \qquad [10.2]$$

Using Equation 10.2, an 80 percent price-cost margin implies that a sales increase of only 15 percent is all that one requires to warrant cutting prices by 10 percent. Here's how one reaches that conclusion:

$$\frac{0.8}{[0.8 - 0.1]} < 1 + \frac{\Delta Q}{Q_0}$$

$$1.14 < 1 + \frac{\Delta Q}{Q_0}$$

$$1.14 < 1 + 0.15$$

barriers to exit
Economic losses resulting from non-redeployable assets or contractual constraints upon business termination.

In contrast, in paperback book publishing, a price-cost margin of 12 percent implies sales must increase by better than 500 percent in order to warrant a 10 percent price cut—that is, $0.12/0.02 < 1 + 5.0^+$. Because a marketing plan that creates a 15 percent sales increase from a 10 percent price cut is much more feasible than one that creates a 500 percent sales increase from a 10 percent price cut, the airline industry is more likely to focus on pricing competition than the paperback book publishing industry.

Example

Contribution Margins at Hanes Discourage Discounting

First-quality white cotton T-shirts and briefs have long been the mainstay of the Hanes Corporation. Selling these "blanks" to other companies that perform value-added finishing, dyeing, embroidering, or custom stitching, Hanes captures only the initial stages in the value chain. At a wholesale price of $1.25 and with $0.85 direct cost of goods sold, the gross margin for Hanes briefs of $0.40 must recover the fixed costs plus the distribution-and-selling expenses to earn a profit. With a $0.15 commission per unit sale as a selling expense, the contribution margin (*CM*) in dollars is $0.25, and the percentage contribution margin (*PCM*) is $0.25/$1.25 = 20%.

Because of very price-elastic demand, price discounted by as little as 15 percent can double unit sales. However, with contribution margins (*PCM*) as low as 20 percent, the additional sales triggered by the discount are much less attractive than one might think. Break-even sales change analysis using Equation 10.2 confirms that a doubling of sales volume is less than the incremental sales change required to restore total contributions to the levels earned before the price cut:

$$PCM/(PCM - \%\Delta P) = 0.20/(0.20 - 0.15) = 4.0 = 1 + 3.0^+$$

The interpretation here is that unit sales must increase by 300 percent $(1 + 300\%\Delta Q)$ in order to restore total contributions to their preexisting level. That is, the price reduction must more than *quadruple* unit sales in order to raise total contributions (operating profit). The data displayed in Table 10.1 demonstrate this conclusion in a spreadsheet format.

Barriers to exit increase the intensity of rivalry in a tight oligopoly. If remote plants specific to a particular line of products (e.g., aluminum smelting plants) are

TABLE 10.1	HANES SALES VOLUME REQUIRED TO MAINTAIN OPERATING PROFIT WITH A 15 PERCENT PRICE CUT				
	GIVEN DATA	WITH 15% PRICE CUT	DOUBLE SALES VOLUME	TRIPLE SALES VOLUME	QUADRUPLE SALES VOLUME
Price	1.25	1.0625	2.125	3.1875	4.25
DCGS (VC only)	−0.85	−0.85	−1.70	−2.55	−3.40
Commission	−0.15	−0.15	−0.30	−0.45	−0.60
CM	0.25	0.0625	0.125	0.1875	0.25

© Cengage Learning

non-redeployable, the tactics will be more aggressive because no competitor can fully recover its sunk cost should margins collapse. In addition to capital equipment, non-redeployable assets can include product-specific display racks (L'eggs); product-specific showrooms (Ethan Allen); and intangible assets that prove difficult to carve up and package for resale (unpatented trade secrets and basic research). Trucking companies, on the other hand, own very redeployable assets—that is, trucks and warehouses. If a trucking company attacks its rivals, encounters aggressive retaliation, and then fails and must liquidate its assets, the owners can hope to receive nearly the full value of the economic working life remaining in their trucks and warehouses. As a result, competitive tactics in the trucking industry are not as effective in threatening rivals, so competitive rivalrous intensity is lower and profitability is higher.

Finally, industry demand growth can influence the intensity of rivalry. When sales to established customers are increasing and new customers are appearing in the market, rival firms are often content to maintain market share and realize high profitability. When demand growth declines, competitive tactics sharpen in many industries, especially if capacity planning has failed to anticipate the decline. Furniture companies discount steeply when housing demand slows. Airline prices and profits declined sharply when demand for air travel leveled off unexpectedly after the Gulf War. Similarly, when soft drink sales in the United States flattened out at a gallon per week, Porter's model predicts that flat soft drink demand would lead to more intense rivalry and lower profitability at PepsiCo Inc. and Coca-Cola Co. Coca-Cola has deflected many competitive initiatives to its fast-growing international division in an attempt to reduce the growing likelihood of intense rivalry with PepsiCo here in the United States.

Example

Intensity of Rivalry at US Airways[14]

The Charlotte hub of US Airways is a very concentrated terminal facility; US Airways has over 92 percent of the flights. Thus, US Airways' market share is comparable to Microsoft's dominance of the OS business with Windows. However, high indirect fixed costs for aircraft leases and facilities imply high margins that make it very tempting for airlines to attract incremental customers through price discounting. In contrast, Windows is seldom, if ever, discounted. Also, exit barriers are high in airlines but rather low in computer software, where massive sunk-cost expenses for research and development create largely patentable trade secrets that can be easily resold. Finally, industry demand growth is low in airlines but extremely high in computer software. Consequently, in one-stop flights from Charlotte, US Airways is subject to intense rivalry but Microsoft Windows is not.

(continued)

> Frequent price competition, high exit barriers, and flat growth all imply tremendous rivalrous intensity in the airline industry and downward competitive pressure on US Airways' profit margins. The opposite is true in Microsoft's OS software business. Windows software is seldom discounted and remains extremely profitable. In short, airlines have industry characteristics that force nearly competitive performance on even dominant firms, whereas a dominant firm in computer OS faces less intense rivalry.

[14]Based on "Flying to Charlotte Is Easy," *Wall Street Journal* (June 14, 1995), p. S1.

Finally, the speed of adjustment of rivalrous actions and reactions matters. Recall that if incumbents are slow to respond to tactical initiatives of hit-and-run entrants, then profitability may be driven down to the break-even levels in so-called contestable markets. In contrast, if incumbents are easily provoked and exhibit fast adjustment speeds, then profitability is often more sustainable.

The Myth of Market Share

In summary, the key to profitability in many businesses is to design a strategy that reduces the threat of substitutes, the power of buyers and suppliers, and the threat of entry. Then, firms must adopt tactics and elicit tactical responses from their rivals so that the profit potential in their effective business strategy is not eroded away. This often means forsaking gain-share discounting and other aggressive tactics that would spiral the industry into price wars. Price premiums reflecting true customer value are very difficult to win back once buyers have grown accustomed to a pattern of deep discount rivalry between the competitors or predictably timed clearance sales. Airlines and department store retailers are painfully aware of these tactical mistakes.

More generally, discounting and excessive promotions designed to grab market share are seldom a source of long-term profitability and often result in lower capitalized value. The soft-drink bottler 7-Up once doubled and tripled its market share largely through discounting. But profits declined, and the company was eventually acquired by Cadbury Schweppes. Hon Industries makes twice the ROI of Steelcase in the office equipment market even though Hon is one-third of Steelcase's size. Boeing was much more profitable allowing a slight majority of wide-bodied orders to go to government-subsidized Airbus rather than tie up their own assembly-line operations with hundreds of additional orders triggered by the low prices.

After the initial penetration of a new product or new technology into a relevant market, market share should never become an end in itself. Increasing market share is the means to achieve scale economies and learning-curve-based cost advantages. But additional share points at any cost almost always mean a reduction in profits, not the reverse.

A CONTINUUM OF MARKET STRUCTURES

The relationship between individual firms and the relevant market as a whole is referred to as the industry's *market structure* and depends upon:

1. The number and relative size of firms in the industry.
2. The similarity of the products sold by the firms of the industry; that is, the degree of product differentiation.

3. The extent to which decision making by individual firms is independent, not inter-dependent or collusive.
4. The conditions of entry and exit.

Four specific market structures are often distinguished: pure competition, monopoly, monopolistic competition, and oligopoly. We discuss each in turn.

| Pure Competition | Monopolistic Competition | Oligopoly | Monopoly |

Pure Competition

pure competition
A market structure characterized by a large number of buyers and sellers of a homo-geneous (nondifferen-tiated) product. Entry and exit from the in-dustry is costless, or nearly so. Information is freely available to all market participants, and there is no collu-sion among firms in the industry.

The **pure competition** industry model has the following characteristics:

1. A large number of buyers and sellers, each of which buys or sells such a small pro-portion of the total industry output that a single buyer's or seller's actions cannot have a perceptible impact on the market price.
2. A homogeneous product produced by each firm; that is, no product differentiation, as with licensed taxi cab services or AAA-grade January wheat.
3. Complete knowledge of all relevant market information by all firms, each of which acts totally independently, such as the 117 home builders of standardized two-bedroom subdivision homes in a large city.
4. Free entry and exit from the market—that is, minimal barriers to entry and exit.

The single firm in a purely competitive industry is, in essence, a price taker. Because the products of each producer are almost perfect substitutes for the products of every other producer, the single firm in pure competition can do nothing but offer its entire output at the going market price. As a result, the individual firm's demand curve approaches perfect elasticity at the market price. It can sell nothing at a higher price because all buyers will rationally shift to other sellers. If the firm sells at a price slightly below the long-run market price, it will lose money.

For example, Figure 10.3 indicates the nature of the industry and firm demand curves under pure competition in tract home building. Line DD' represents the total industry or market demand curve for tract houses and $S'S$ is the market supply curve. At price $175,000, the market price, a total of Q_{DI} houses will be demanded by the sum of all firms in the industry. Line dd' represents the demand curve facing each individual firm. The individual firm sells its entire output, Q_{DF}, at the market price $175,000. By definition, the quantity Q_{DF} represents only a small fraction of the total industry demand of Q_{DI}.

Why get involved in industries where revenues per sale ($175,000 in Figure 10.3) are just sufficient to cover fully allocated unit costs of $175,000? The reason is that these sales at a "razor-thin margin" are the ticket to the occasional windfalls when demand increases and price rises enough to generate excess profits (for a few months in the tract home business, a few weeks in the wildcatter oil business, a few hours in the AAA Kansas City corn business, or a few minutes in the T-bond resale market). Note that the timing and magnitude of these windfalls are not predictable. Otherwise the real estate development land, oil leases, T-bills, and grain silos would rise in value, and the expected excess profit would again reduce to a razor-thin margin above break-even conditions. Also, remember that at competitive equilibrium the business owner-manager is getting a salary or other return as great as could be received in his or her next best activity. In short, this is not the business environment where venture capital

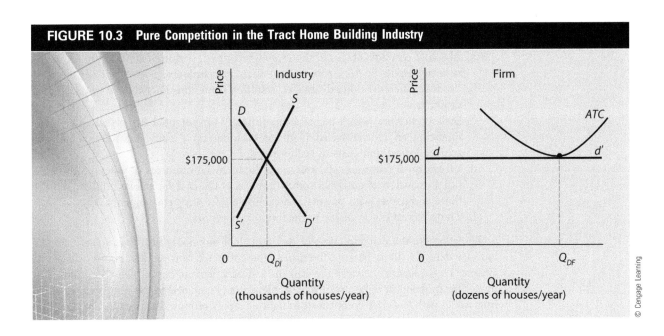

FIGURE 10.3   Pure Competition in the Tract Home Building Industry

and entrepreneurial returns of 40 percent on invested capital occur regularly, but it does provide perhaps a 12 percent return with good managerial skills and cost controls. More importantly, these razor-thin margins are interrupted occasionally when windfall profits of as much as $25,000 on a tract home, $20 per barrel on crude oil, $1.50 per bushel on corn, or $5,000 per $1 million T-bill erupt for a short time.

Contestable Markets   A contestable market is an extreme case of purely competitive markets. In this market structure, break-even performance often occurs with just a handful of firms, perhaps only one. The reason is that entry and exit are free and cost-less. Consequently, the mere threat of "hit-and-run" entry is sufficient to drive prices down to the zero-profit, full cost-covering level. Incumbents in such markets are often slower to react than the hit-and-run firms that impose all this competitive pressure. An example is the bond markets where financial arbitrage by hedge funds triggers enormous bets (perhaps tens of billions of dollars) that any out-of-line government bond or bill prices will converge back to their equilibrium levels. Similarly, airlines might seem to be a contestable market; aircraft would seem to be the ultimate mobile asset, but landing slots are not, and incumbents react quickly and aggressively to hit-and-run entrants in these markets.

Monopoly

monopoly A market structure character-ized by one firm pro-ducing a highly differentiated product in a market with sig-nificant barriers to entry.

The **monopoly** model at the other extreme of the market structure spectrum from pure competition is characterized as follows:

1. Only one firm producing some specific product line (in a specified market area), like an exclusive cable TV franchise.
2. Low cross-price elasticity of demand between the monopolist's product and any other product; that is, no close substitute products.
3. No interdependence with other competitors because the firm is a monopolist in its relevant market.

4. Substantial barriers to entry that prevent competition from entering the industry. These barriers may include any of the following:
   a. Absolute cost advantages of the established firm, resulting from economies in securing inputs or from patented production techniques.
   b. Product differentiation advantages, resulting from consumer loyalty to established products.
   c. Scale economies, which increase the difficulty for potential entrant firms of financing an efficient-sized plant or building up a sufficient sales volume to achieve lowest unit costs in such a plant.
   d. Large capital requirements, exceeding the financial resources of potential entrants.
   e. Legal exclusion of potential competitors, as is the case for public utilities, and for those companies with patents and exclusive licensing arrangements.
   f. Trade secrets not available to potential competitors.

By definition, the demand curve of the individual monopoly firm is identical with the industry demand curve, because the firm is the entire relevant market. As we will see in Chapter 11, the identity between the firm and industry demand curves allows decision making for the monopolist to be a relatively simple matter, compared to the complexity of rivalrous tactics with few close competitors in tight oligopoly groups, discussed in Chapter 12.

Monopolistic Competition

monopolistic competition A market structure very much like pure competition, with the major distinction being the existence of a differentiated product.

E. H. Chamberlin and Joan Robinson coined the term **monopolistic competition** to describe industries with characteristics both of competitive markets (i.e., many firms) and of monopoly (i.e., product differentiation). The market structure of monopolistic competition is characterized as follows:

1. A few dominant firms and a large number of competitive fringe firms.
2. Dominant firms selling products that are differentiated in some manner: real, perceived, or just imagined.
3. Independent decision making by individual firms.
4. Ease of entry and exit from the market as a whole but very substantial barriers to effective entry among the leading brands.

By far the most important distinguishing characteristic of monopolistic competition is that the outputs of each firm are starkly differentiated in some way from those of every other firm. In other words, the cross-price elasticity of demand between the products of individual firms is much lower than in purely competitive markets—that is, among tract home builders, oil wildcatters, AAA January wheat suppliers, or T-bill resellers. Product differentiation may be based on exclusive features (Disney World), trademarks (Nike's swoosh), trade names (BlackBerry), packaging (L'eggs hosiery), quality (Coach handbags), design (Apple iMacs), color and style (Swatch watches), or the conditions of sale (Dooney & Bourke). These conditions may include such factors as credit terms, location of the seller, congeniality of sales personnel, after-sale service, and warranties.

Because each firm produces a differentiated product, it is difficult to define an industry demand curve in monopolistic competition. Thus, rather than well-defined industries, one tends to get something of a continuum of products. Generally, it is rather easy to identify groups of differentiated products that fall in the same industry, like light beers, after-shave colognes, or perfumes.

Oligopoly

oligopoly A market structure in which the number of firms is so small that the actions of any one firm are likely to have noticeable impacts on the performance of other firms in the industry.

The **oligopoly** market structure describes a market having a few closely related firms. The number of firms is so small that actions by an individual firm in the industry with respect to price, output, product style or quality, terms of sale, and so on, have a perceptible impact on the sales of other firms in the industry. In other words, oligopoly is distinguished by a noticeable degree of *interdependence* among firms in the industry. The products or services that are produced by oligopolists may be homogeneous—as in the cases of air travel, 40-foot steel I-beams, aluminum, and cement—or they may be partially differentiated—as in the cases of soft drinks, luxury automobiles, and cruise ships.

Although the lack of product differentiation is an important factor in shaping an oligopolist's demand curve, the degree of interdependence of firms in the industry is of even greater significance. Primarily because of this interdependence, defining a single firm's demand curve is complicated. The relationship between price and output is determined not only by consumer preferences, product substitutability, and level of advertising, *but also by the responses that other competitors may make to a price change by the focal firm.* A full discussion of rival response expectations and their game-theoretic modeling will be deferred until Chapter 12.

PRICE-OUTPUT DETERMINATION UNDER PURE COMPETITION

As discussed in Chapter 2, the individual firm in a purely competitive industry is effectively a price taker because the products of every producer are perfect substitutes for the products of every other producer. This leads to the familiar horizontal or perfectly elastic demand curve of the purely competitive firm. Although we rarely find instances where all the conditions for pure competition are met, tract home real estate, securities exchanges, and the commodity markets approach these conditions. For instance, the individual tract home seller, wheat farmer, or T-bill reseller has little choice but to accept the going market price. In pure competition, the firm must sell at the market price (p_1 or p_2), and its demand curve is represented by a horizontal line (D_1 or D_2) at the market price, as shown in Figure 10.4.

Short Run

A firm in a purely competitive industry may break-even against all economic costs, make transitory profits (in excess of normal returns to capital and entrepreneurial labor), or operate at a temporary loss in the short run. In the purely competitive case, marginal revenue *MR* is equal to price *P*, because the sale of each additional unit increases total revenue by the price of that unit (which remains constant at all levels of output). For instance, if

$$P = \$8/\text{unit}$$

then

$$\text{Total revenue} = TR = P \cdot Q$$
$$= 8Q$$

Marginal revenue is defined as the change in total revenue resulting from the sale of one additional unit of output, or the derivative of total revenue with respect to *Q*:

$$MR = \frac{dTR}{dQ} = \$8/\text{unit}$$

and in competitive markets marginal revenue equals price.

The profit-maximizing firm will produce all those units of output where marginal revenue exceeds or equals marginal cost (the variable cost of the next unit to be produced). Beyond that point, the production and sale of one additional unit would add more to

FIGURE 10.4   The Firm in Pure Competition: The Short Run

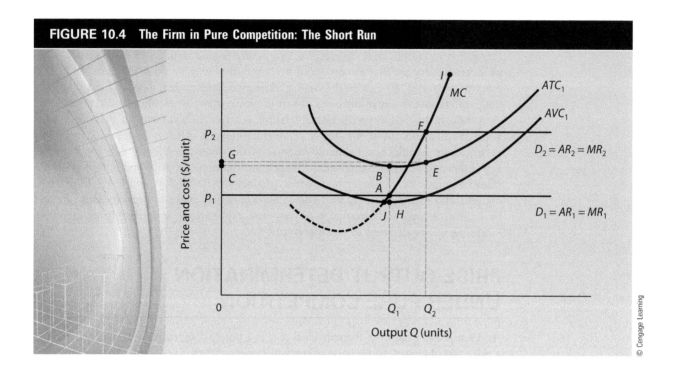

© Cengage Learning

total cost than to total revenue ($MC > MR$), and hence total profit ($TR - TC$) would decline. Up to the point where $MC = MR$, the production and sale of one more unit would increase total revenue more than total cost ($MR > MC$), and total profit would increase as an additional unit is produced and sold. *Producing at the point where marginal revenue* MR *equals marginal cost* MC *maximizes the total profit function.*[15]

The individual firm's supply function in Figure 10.4 is equal to that portion of the MC curve from point J to point I. At any price level below point J, the firm would shut down because it would not even be covering its variable costs (i.e., $P < AVC$). Temporary shutdown would result in limiting the losses to fixed costs alone.

Returning to Figure 10.4, if price $P = p_1$, the firm would produce the level of output Q_1, where $MC = MR$ (profits are maximized or losses minimized). In this case the firm would incur a loss per unit equal to the difference between average total cost ATC and average revenue or price. This is represented by the height BA in Figure 10.4. The total loss incurred by the firm at Q_1 level of output and price p_1 equals the rectangle p_1CBA. This may be conceptually thought of as the loss per unit (BA) times the number of units produced and sold (Q_1).

At price p_1 losses are minimized, because average variable costs AVC have been covered and a contribution remains to cover part of the fixed costs (AH per unit times Q_1 units). If the firm did not produce, it would incur losses equal to the entire amount of fixed costs (BH per unit times Q_1 units). Hence we may conclude that in the short run a

---

[15]This can be proven as follows:

$$\pi = TR - TC$$

$$\frac{d\pi}{dQ} = \frac{dTR}{dQ} - \frac{dTC}{dQ} = MR - MC = 0$$

or $MR = MC$ when profits are maximized.

   Check for profit maximization by taking the second derivative of π with respect to Q, or $\frac{d^2\pi}{dQ^2}$. If it is less than zero, then π is maximized.

firm will produce and sell at that level of output where $MR = MC$, as long as the variable costs and direct fixed costs of production (i.e., the avoidable costs from the point of view of the shutdown/operate decision) are being covered $(P > AVC)$.[16]

Flat Screen Televisions Lose \$126 per Unit Sold: Sony Corporation[17]

Most of the cost of a flat screen TV involves the LCD panel. Globally, 220 million flat screen TVs were sold in 2011 for \$115 billion. Although scale economies in massive factories and volume discounts on electronic input components have driven the cost of LCDs down from \$2,400 to \$500 the last decade, the price has fallen even faster. In 2001, the average selling price of a large LCD panel was over \$4,000. By 2011, this price had fallen below \$600 (see Figure 10.5). Sony Corporation finds its flat screen TVs now fail to cover the full cost of the LCD panels and instead impose an \$126 (\$500 − \$374) loss per TV sold. Nevertheless, the indirect fixed costs of the LCD factories Korean Samsung, Japanese Sharp, Panasonic, and Sony constructed are partially covered by operating. Losses would be greater in the short run if they shut down.

FIGURE 10.5   Price and Long-Run Average Total Cost of LCD Panels

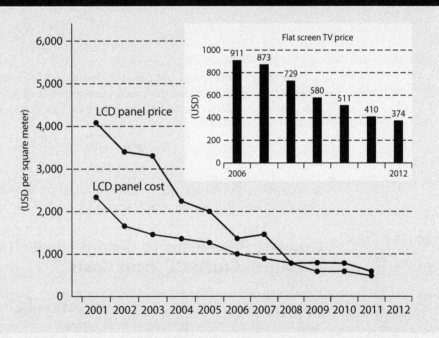

Source: New York Times (December 12, 2008), *CNN Money* (September 9, 2010), *The Economist* (January 21, 2012), p. 47.

---

[17]Based on "Television-Making: Cracking Up," *The Economist* (January 21, 2012), p. 72.

---

[16]Variable costs are defined narrowly by accountants to identify the avoidable costs incurred by the smallest unit sale in the company's business plan. In addition, some other costs that are batch costs (like utilities for the third shift on the factory floor) or direct fixed costs traceable to the decision to operate (like unscheduled maintenance to offset wear and tear on the machinery) are avoidable by the decision in question. Therefore, these costs could be varied (avoided) by the decision to shutdown and should therefore be included in the AVC that must be exceeded in order to decide to operate.

If price were p_2, the firm would produce Q_2 units and make a profit per unit of EF, or a total profit represented by the rectangle $FEGp_2$. The supply curve of the competitive firm is therefore often identified as the marginal cost schedule above minimum AVC. Industry supply is the horizontal summation of these firm supply curves.

Profit Maximization under Pure Competition (Short Run): Adobe Corporation

Assume Adobe Corporation faces the following total revenue and total cost functions:

$$\text{Total revenue}: TR = 8Q$$

$$\text{Total cost}: TC = Q^2 + 4Q + 2$$

Marginal revenue and marginal cost are defined as the first derivative of total revenue and total cost, or

$$\text{Marginal revenue}: MR = \frac{dTR}{dQ} = \$8/\text{unit}$$

$$\text{Marginal cost}: MC = \frac{dTR}{dQ} = 2Q + 4$$

Total profit equals total revenue minus total cost:

$$\text{Total profit}: (\pi) = TR - TC$$

$$= 8Q - (Q^2 + 4Q + 2)$$

$$= -Q^2 + 4Q - 2$$

To maximize total profit, we take the derivative of π with respect to quantity, set it equal to zero, and solve for the profit-maximizing level of Q. (It is also necessary to check the second derivative to be certain we have found a maximum, not a minimum!)[18]

$$\frac{d\pi}{dQ} = -2Q + 4 = 0$$

$$Q^* = 2 \text{ units}$$

Because $MR = \$8/\text{unit}$ and $MC = 2Q + 4 = [2(2) + 4] = \$8/\text{unit}$, when total profit is maximized, note that we are merely setting $MC = MR$.

 Example

Gasoline Price Rises to Record Levels Reflecting a Spike in Crude Oil Input Costs[19]

Throughout 2006, 2007, and early 2008, the price of gasoline in the United States galloped upward to reach $4 per gallon. Why did it happen? Competitive pressure at retail prevents gas station gouging of retail customers. Excise taxes average only $0.40 across the United States and have been largely unchanged for two decades. Refinery and pipeline bottlenecks were partially to blame after Gulf Coast hurricanes Katrina and Rita but not in July 2008. Instead, the principal source of the run-up in gasoline prices was a spectacular increase in crude oil input prices.

(continued)

---

[18]The check for profit maximization goes as follows:

$$\frac{d^2\pi}{dQ^2} = -2$$

Because the second derivative is negative, we know we have found a maximum value for the profit function.

Figure 10.6(a), shows that six times in the past 30 years, crude oil prices have risen steeply. In each prior case, supply disruptions due to armed conflicts in the Middle East or cartel restrictions of output were responsible. In 1973 and 1999–2000, the OPEC I and OPEC III oil cartels successfully enforced reduced output quotas on members, thereby restraining supply and driving the market price of crude oil higher. In 1978, 1980, and 1990, three military conflicts massively restricted the supply of crude oil leaving the Persian Gulf. In 2004–2008, however, not supply but demand factors were involved. Demand growth in India, China, and the United States in 2004–2008 drove scarce input prices right up the rising marginal cost schedule for crude oil supply exhibited in Figure 10.6(b).

Oil in the Persian Gulf region is cheapest to find, develop, and extract at a marginal cost of $3 per barrel. In contrast, Venezuelan and Russian oil recovers its marginal cost at $9 per barrel, West Texas oil at $13 per barrel, and the North Sea fields necessitate offshore rigs and expensive extraction technology that generate $20-per-barrel marginal cost. The delivered costs of incremental oil output from the North Slope of Alaska run $30 per barrel. These oil field production firms and their associated output trace out a traditional upward-sloping long-run supply curve (here a step function) for the crude oil industry—again see Figure 10.6(b).

By mid-year 2006, as crude oil input prices passed through $70 and $80 and headed higher, Missouri and Iowa farmers joined co-ops created to build and operate $65 million corn-fed ethanol plants. The marginal cost at which the booming demand for petroleum products was causing crude oil to be brought to market exceeded the marginal cost of ethanol for the first time ever. For decades, Brazil had been hugely successful with sugarcane-fed ethanol plants—so successful that in 2008 Brazil declared energy independence from foreign oil. But sugarcane has a much higher chemical energy content than corn, so sugarcane-based ethanol is profitable at $40, much lower than the $60 needed to induce suppliers to bring corn-based ethanol to market.

[19]Based on "Special Report: The Oil Industry," *The Economist* (April 22, 2006), pp. 55–73.

Long Run

In the long run, all inputs are free to vary. Hence, no conceptual distinction exists between fixed and variable costs. Under long-run conditions in purely competitive markets, average cost will tend to be just equal to price, and all excessive profits will be eliminated (see Point A where $p_1 = AC_1$ in Figure 10.7). If not, and if, for example, a price above p_1 exceeds average total costs, like p_1' generating temporary quasi-profits, then more firms will enter, the industry supply will increase (as illustrated by the parallel shift outward to the right of the $\Sigma_{SR}S_{FIRM}$ along market demand D^2_{MKT} in Figure 10.7), and market price will again be driven down toward the equilibrium, zero-profit level p_1.

In addition, as more firms bid for the available factors of production (say, skilled carpentry labor or lumber during a housing boom), the cost of these factors will tend to rise. In that event, the entire cost structure of MC_1 and AC_1 will rise to reflect the higher input costs along an upward-sloping input supply schedule like that for crude oil in Figure 10.6(b). This higher input cost results in a shift up of the firm's cost structure to AC_2 (see Figure 10.7) and imposes a two-way squeeze on excess profit. Such a scenario is referred to as an **external diseconomy of scale**. External scale diseconomies

external diseconomy of scale An increase in unit costs reflecting higher input prices.

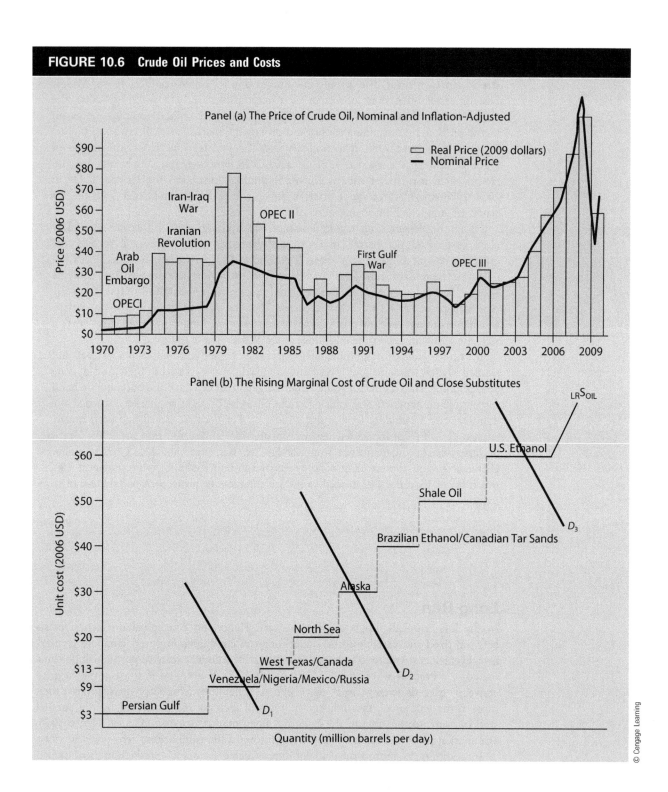

FIGURE 10.6 Crude Oil Prices and Costs

Panel (a) The Price of Crude Oil, Nominal and Inflation-Adjusted

Panel (b) The Rising Marginal Cost of Crude Oil and Close Substitutes

© Cengage Learning

are distinguished from internal scale economies and diseconomies in that the latter reflect unit cost changes as the rate of output increases, *assuming no change in input prices*, whereas the former reflect the bidding up of input prices as the industry expands in response to an increase in market demand.

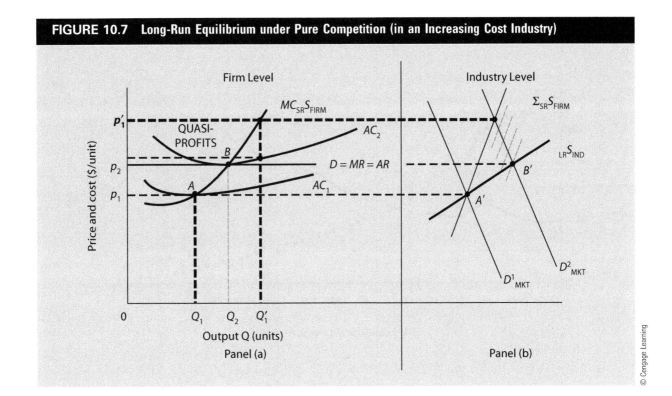

FIGURE 10.7 Long-Run Equilibrium under Pure Competition (in an Increasing Cost Industry)

Copper Price Rise by 400 Percent Contributes to Housing Bubble

Home prices across the United States rose to unsustainable heights in 2006–2008. Part of the reason was demand-pull bid price pressure from lower interest rates on mortgages than ever seen in post-war U.S. markets. But another reason was cost-push asking price pressure from spiking commodity prices. A 2,100-square-foot home incorporates 440 pounds of copper plumbing, sheathing, and wiring. Between 2003 and 2007, copper rose in price 400 percent. Lumber prices have responded the same way in the fall of 2012 in the immediate aftermath of Hurricane Sandy.

Under a constant input price assumption, the long-run industry supply curve $_{LR}S_{IND}$ in Figure 10.7 would be flat, a so-called *constant-cost industry* like coal harvesting. However, with the rising input prices for crude oil depicted in Figure 10.6(b), the long-run supply curve $_{LR}S_{IND}$ for the downstream final product gasoline rises to the right, signifying an *increasing-cost industry*, as depicted in Figure 10.7. (It is also quite possible to have downward-sloping long-run supply curves.) A decreasing-cost industry occurred in the 1980s in calculators and in the 1990s in PCs because computer chip inputs became less expensive as the personal computer market expanded, as shown in Figure 10.8.

The net result is that in the long-run equilibrium, all purely competitive firms will tend to have identical costs, and prices will tend to equal average total costs (i.e., the average total cost curve *AC* will be tangent to the horizontal price line p_2). Thus, we

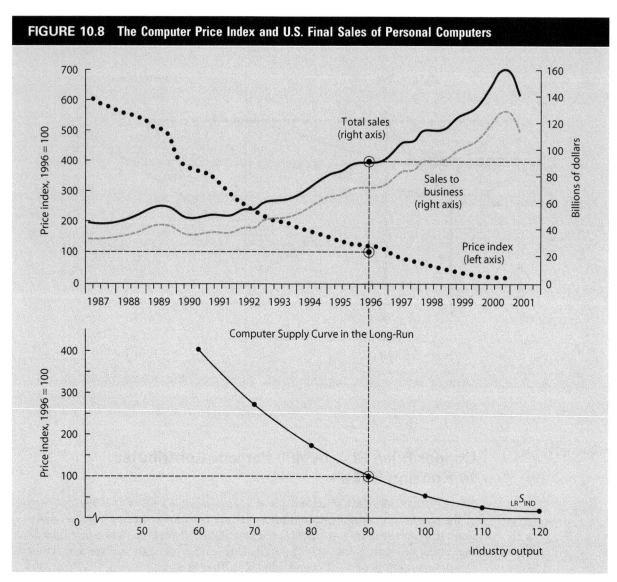

FIGURE 10.8 The Computer Price Index and U.S. Final Sales of Personal Computers

Source: St. Louis Federal Reserve Bank, *National Economic Trends* (May 2001).

may say that at the long-run profit-maximizing level of output under pure competition, equilibrium will be achieved at a point where $P = MR = MC = AC$. In long-run equilibrium, each competitive firm is producing at its most efficient (i.e., its lowest unit cost) level of output and just breaking even.

PRICE-OUTPUT DETERMINATION UNDER MONOPOLISTIC COMPETITION

Monopolistic competition is a market structure with a relatively large number of firms, each selling a product that is differentiated in some manner from the products of its fringe competitors, and with substantial barriers to entry into the group of leading firms.

WHAT WENT RIGHT • WHAT WENT WRONG

The Dynamics of Competition at Amazon.com[20]

Online retailing started very slowly in clothing and other search goods that buyers want to "touch and feel," but it has excelled in one experience good—namely, books. Amazon stocks less than 1,000 bestsellers but displays and provides reviews on 2.5 million popular titles. Using Ingram Book Group, the world's largest book wholesaler, Amazon is able to ship most selections in one to three days. Even though sales have doubled each half year, Amazon.com shares have declined in value.

One difficulty for Amazon.com is that Internet retailing is a classic example of a business with low barriers to entry and exit. As soon as Amazon's business systems for display, order taking, shipping, and payments stabilized, since profits were present, substantial entry activity occurred. For example, Barnes and Noble entered into an exclusive contract with America Online to pitch electronic book sales to AOL's 8.5 million subscribers. And many specialist booksellers of Civil War books, jet plane books, history books, auto books, and so forth have flooded onto the Internet search engines. Even Amazon's wholesale supplier Ingram Book Group has entered the fray; for $2,500, Ingram support services will set up a Web site on behalf of any new book retailer.

Amazon.com responded by offering customized notification and book discussion services to provide value added for readers with special interests. The information revolution has made relationship marketing to established customers a pivotal element in securing repeat purchases. Nevertheless, the numerous open opportunities for fast, easy, and cheap entry likely will erode the profits in electronic book retailing. The imperfect consumer information, limited time for comparison shopping, and brand loyalty that retailers have depended upon are disappearing with Internet search engines. As a result, retailing's traditionally slim profit margins are quickly becoming hairline thin or nonexistent just like tract home building. A competitive rate of return on time, talent, and investment in online retailing might today amount to only 5 percent.

[20]Based on "Web Browsing," *The Economist* (March 29, 1997), p. 71; "In Search of the Perfect Market: A Survey of Electronic Commerce," *The Economist* (May 10, 1997); "The Net: A Market Too Perfect for Profits," *BusinessWeek* (May 11, 1998), p. 20; "Comparison Shopping Is the Web's Virtue—Unless You're a Seller," *Wall Street Journal* (July 23, 1998), p. A1; and *Value Line, Ratings and Reports*, various issues.

Product differentiation may be based on special product characteristics, trademarks, packaging, quality perceptions, distinctive product design, or conditions surrounding the sale, such as location of the seller, warranties, and credit terms. The demand curve for any one firm is expected to have a negative slope and be extremely elastic because of the large number of close substitutes. The firm in monopolistic competition has some limited discretion over price (as distinguished from the firm in pure competition) because of customer loyalties arising from real or perceived product differences. Profit maximization (or loss minimization) again occurs when the firm produces at that level of output and charges that price at which marginal revenue equals marginal cost.

Short Run

Just as in the case of pure competition, a monopolistically competitive firm may or may not generate a profit in the short run. For example, consider a demand curve such as $D'D'$ in Figure 10.9, with marginal revenue equal to MR'. Such a firm will set its prices where $MR' = MC$, resulting in price P_3 and output Q_3. The firm will earn a profit of EC dollars per unit of output. However, the low barriers to entry in a monopolistically competitive industry will not permit these short-run profits to be earned for long. As new firms enter the industry, industry supply will increase, causing the equilibrium price to fall. This is reflected in a downward movement in the demand curve facing any individual firm.

Long Run

With relatively free entry and exit into the competitive fringe, average costs and a firm's demand function will be driven *toward* tangency at a point such as A in Figure 10.9.

FIGURE 10.9   Long-Run Equilibrium in Monopolistic Competition

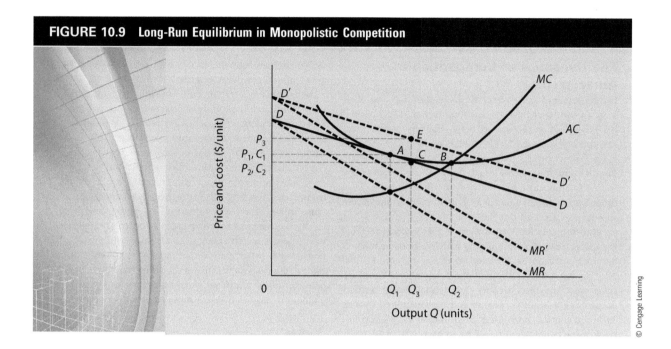

© Cengage Learning

At this price, P_1, and output, Q_1, marginal cost is equal to marginal revenue. Hence a firm selling perfume or beer is producing at its optimal level of output. Any price lower or higher than P_1 will result in a loss to the firm because average costs will exceed price.

Because the monopolistic competitor produces at a level of output where average costs are still declining (between Points A and B in Figure 10.9), monopolistically competitive firms produce with excess capacity. Of course, this argument overlooks the extent to which idle capacity may be a source of product differentiation. Idle capacity means a firm such as Singapore Airlines can operate with high delivery reliability and change-order responsiveness, which can be very important to business travelers and that warrants a price premium relative to competitive fringe airlines.

Example

Long-Run Price and Output Determination: Blockbuster, Inc.

The market for DVD rentals in Charlotte, North Carolina, can best be described as monopolistically competitive. The demand for DVD rentals is estimated to be

$$P = 10 - 0.004Q$$

where Q is the number of weekly DVD rentals. The long-run average cost function for Blockbuster (now owned by Dish Network) is estimated to be

$$LRAC = 8 - 0.006Q + 0.000002Q^2$$

Blockbuster's managers want to know the profit-maximizing price and output levels, and the level of expected total profits at these price and output levels.

First, compute total revenue (TR) as

$$TR = P \cdot Q = 10Q - 0.004Q^2$$

(continued)

Next, compute marginal revenue (*MR*) by taking the first derivative of *TR*:

$$MR = \frac{dTR}{dQ} = 10 - 0.008Q$$

Compute total cost (*TC*) by multiplying *LRAC* by *Q*:

$$TC = LRAC \cdot Q = 8Q - 0.006Q^2 + 0.000002Q^3$$

Compute marginal cost (*MC*) by taking the first derivative of *TC*:

$$MC = \frac{dTC}{dQ} = 8 - 0.012Q + 0.000006Q^2$$

Next, set *MR* = *MC*

$$10 - 0.008Q = 8 - 0.012Q + 0.000006Q^2$$

$$0.000006Q^2 - 0.004Q - 2 = 0$$

Use the quadratic formula to solve for *Q*. *Q** is equal to 1,000.[21] At this quantity, price is equal to

$$P^* = 10 - 0.004(1,000)$$
$$= 10 - 4$$
$$= \$6$$

Total profit is equal to the difference between *TR* and *TC*, or

$$\pi = TR - TC$$
$$= 10Q - 0.004Q^2 - [8Q - 0.006Q^2 + 0.000002Q^3]$$
$$= 10(1,000) - 0.004(1,000)^2 - [8(1,000) - 0.006(1,000)^2 + 0.000002(1,000)^3]$$
$$= \$2,000$$

The *MR* and *MC* at these price and output levels are $2.

The fact that Blockbuster expects to earn a profit of $2,000 suggests that the firm can anticipate additional competition, resulting in price cutting that will ultimately eliminate this profit amount.[22]

---

[21]The solution of the quadratic formula, $aQ^2 + bQ + c = 0$, is

$$Q = \frac{-b \pm \sqrt{b^2 - 4ac}}{2a} = \frac{-(-0.004) \pm \sqrt{(-0.004)^2 - 4(0.000006)(1-2)}}{2(0.000006)}$$

$$= 1,000 \text{ or } -333.33$$

Only the positive solution is feasible.

[22]Recall that the *TC* function includes a "normal" level of profit. Hence, this $2,000 represents an economic *rent* above a normal profit level.

SELLING AND PROMOTIONAL EXPENSES

In addition to varying price and quality characteristics of their products, firms may also vary the amount of their advertising and other promotional expenses in their search for profits. This selling and promotional activity generates two distinct types of benefits. First, demand for the general product group may be shifted upward to the right.

The second, more widespread incentive for advertising is the desire to shift the demand function of a particular firm at the expense of other firms offering similar products. This strategy will be pursued both by oligopolists like Philip Morris and General Mills and by firms in more monopolistically competitive industries such as beer—e.g., Anheuser-Busch, Miller, and Coors.

Determining the Optimal Level of Selling and Promotional Outlays

To illustrate the effects of advertising expenditures and to determine the optimal selling expenses of a firm, consider the case where price and product characteristics already have been determined, and all retailers are selling at the manufacturer's suggested retail price.

The determination of the optimal advertising outlay is a straightforward application of the marginal decision-making rules followed by profit-maximizing firms. Define *MR* to be the change in total revenue received from a one-unit increase in output (and the sale of that output). For fixed-price settings, *MR* just equals the price, *P*. Define *MC* to be the change in total costs of producing and distributing (but not of advertising) an additional unit of output. The marginal profit or contribution margin from an additional unit of output is (from Chapter 9):

$$\text{Contribution Margin } (PCM) = P - MC \qquad [10.3]$$

The marginal cost of advertising (*MCA*) associated with the sale of an additional unit of output is defined as the change in advertising expenditures (ΔAk) where k is the unit cost of an advertising message, *A*, or

$$MCA = \frac{\Delta Ak}{\Delta Q} \qquad [10.4]$$

The optimal level of advertising outlays is the level of advertising where the marginal profit contribution (*PCM*) is equal to the *MCA*, or

$$PCM = MCA \qquad [10.5]$$

As long as a firm receives a greater contribution margin than the *MCA* it incurs to sell an additional unit of output, the advertising outlay should be made. If *PCM* is less than *MCA*, the advertising outlay should not be made and the level of advertising should be reduced until *PCM* = *MCA*. This marginal analysis also applies to other types of non-price competition like after-sale service and product replacement guarantees.

Example

Optimal Advertising at Parkway Ford

The marginal profit contribution from selling Ford automobiles at Parkway Ford averages $1,000 across the various models it sells. Parkway estimates that it will have to incur $550 of additional promotional expenses per vehicle to increase its sales by 1 unit per day. Should the outlay for promotions be made?

Because *PCM* > *MCA* (i.e., $1,000 > $550), Parkway's operating profit will be increased by $450 if it incurs an additional $550 of promotional expenses. Parkway should continue to make additional promotional outlays (which are likely to be less

(continued)

and less effective at triggering additional sales per day) up to the point where the *MCA* equals the expected (marginal profit) contribution margin.

If Parkway were then to find that *MCA* was greater than *PCM*, it should cut back on promotional outlays until the contribution margin rose enough to again equate *PCM* = *MCA*.

Optimal Advertising Intensity

Optimal expenditure on demand-increasing costs like promotions, couponing, direct mail, and media advertising can be compared across firms. For example, the total contributions from incremental sales relative to the advertising cost of beer ads can be compared to the total contributions relative to the advertising cost of cereal ads. Advertising is often placed in five media (network TV, local TV, radio, newspapers, and magazines). The reach of a TV ad is measured as audience thousands per minute of advertising message; reach is directly related to the advertising message's cost (k). Consider the following contribution analysis of the decision to purchase an ad. A manager should fully fund in her marketing budget any ad campaign for which

$$(P - MC)(\Delta Q/\Delta A) > k \qquad [10.6]$$

where ($P - MC$) is the contribution margin and ($\Delta Q/\Delta A$) is the incremental increase in demand (i.e., a shift outward in demand) attributable to the advertising.[23]

Example

Ford and P&G Tie Ad Agency Pay to Sales

Historically, ad agencies have earned more income each time their clients buy another expensive 30-second slot on network TV (or other media), whatever the performance of the ad in generating incremental sales. More recently, Ford and Procter & Gamble, two of the world's biggest advertisers, announced that henceforth all agency billings would need to be performance based. These incentive payment plans include a fixed fee for designing ad campaigns plus incentive pay based on the incremental sales traceable to the ad. The idea is to encourage agencies to search for database marketing, Internet, and event sponsorships that far exceed the marginal media buy-in advertising productivity, $\Delta Q/\Delta A$.

Expanding Equation 10.6, by multiplying both sides by A and dividing both sides by PQ, identifies the two determinants of the optimal advertising expenditure per dollar sales or "advertising intensity." Ak/PQ is determined by the contribution margin percentage ($P - MC$)/P and by the advertising elasticity of demand E_a:

$$\frac{Ak}{PQ} = \frac{(P - MC)}{P}\frac{A}{Q}(\Delta Q/\Delta A) \qquad [10.7]$$

$$\frac{Ak}{PQ} = \frac{(P - MC)}{P}E_a \qquad [10.8]$$

---

[23]Sometimes the price points at which the product can be sold change after a successful ad campaign. If so, the appropriate valuation of the incremental sales in Equation 10.6 is the new contribution margin.

Both factors are important. With high margins (near 70 percent) and very effective ads, Kellogg's spends almost 30 percent of every dollar of sales revenue on cereal advertising (e.g., 0.294 = 0.70 × 0.42, where 0.42 is the estimated E_a). In contrast, the jewelry industry has 92 percent margins, the highest of all four-digit industries, but Zales's advertising inserts in the weekend paper simply do not trigger many jewelry sales. Because the advertising elasticity in jewelry is so low (only 0.11), a company like Zales spends only 10 percent of its sales revenue on advertising (i.e., 0.92 × 0.11 = 0.10). Campbell's Soup has relatively high advertising elasticity of demand (0.32) given its strong brand name, but the margins on canned goods are very low (less than 10 percent); consequently, Campbell's Soup spends just one-tenth of what Kellogg's spends on advertising as a percentage of sales revenue—just 3 percent of sales revenue.

Example

Optimal Advertising Intensity at Kellogg's and General Mills[24]

The ready-to-eat (RTE) cereal industry spends 55 percent of its sales revenue on marketing and promotion—30 percent on advertising alone. In part, this resource allocation decision reflects the fact that cereal demand is very sensitive to successful ad campaigns like Kellogg's Tony the Tiger or General Mills' Wheaties, the Breakfast of Champions. In addition, however, RTE cereal margins are among the highest of any four-digit industry. Kellogg's Raisin Bran sells for $4.49 and has a direct fixed plus variable manufacturing cost of $1.63. That calculates as a (4.49 − 1.63)/4.49 = 70 percent gross margin. Frosted Flakes' margin is 72 percent, and Fruit Loops' margin is 68 percent. These margins reflect brand loyalties built up over many years of advertising investments. In the highly concentrated RTE cereal industry, Quaker Oats (8 percent), Post (15 percent), General Mills (25 percent), and Kellogg's (37 percent) control 85 percent of the market.

Until recently, advertising and retail displays were the predominant forms of competition in cereals. Like Coca-Cola and PepsiCo, the dominant RTE cereal companies had concluded that price discounting would be mutually ruinous and ultimately ineffective. Therefore, each company decided independently to refrain from discounting prices in attempting to gain market share. However, in June 1996, 20 percent price cuts swept through the industry, in part in response to the growth of private-label cereals (e.g., Target Corn Flakes) that had collectively grabbed close to 10 percent of the market. Margins on some leading brand-name products fell from 70 to 50 percent, with licensing (15 percent), packaging (10 percent), wages (10 percent), and distribution (15 percent) accounting for the rest of the selling price.

[24]Based on "Cereals," *Winston-Salem Journal* (March 8, 1995), p. A1; and "Denial in Battle Creek," *Forbes* (October 7, 1996), pp. 44–46.

The Net Value of Advertising

Although advertising can raise entry barriers and maintain market power of dominant firms, the economics of information argues that by giving consumers information, advertising can reduce the prices paid. The discovery of price information may be costly and time consuming in the absence of price advertising. For example, Benham[25] found the

[25]Lee Benham, "The Effect of Advertising on the Price of Eyeglasses," *Journal of Law and Economics* (October 1972), pp. 337–352.

price of eyeglasses to be substantially lower in states that permitted price advertising than in those that prohibited such advertising. Also, because advertising creates brand awareness (both for good and inferior brands), advertisers who misrepresent their product will not be successful in generating repeat business.

COMPETITIVE MARKETS UNDER ASYMMETRIC INFORMATION

In competitive markets for T-shirts, crude oil, auto rentals, and delivered pizza, both buyers and sellers have full knowledge of the capabilities and after-sale performance of the standard products. Equilibrium price just covers the supplier's cost of production for a product of known reliable quality. If suppliers were to charge more, rival offers and entry would quickly erode their sales. If suppliers were to charge less, they could not afford to stay in business. This has been the message so far of this chapter—in competitive markets under ideal information conditions, you get what you pay for. Such markets differ enormously from competitive markets under asymmetric information, which are sometimes called **lemons markets**. One prominent example of asymmetric information in a lemons market is used automobiles, in which the true quality of mechanical repairs, or other features, often is known only to the seller. Other goods sold under asymmetric information include house paint, mail-order computer components, and common cold remedies.

lemons markets
Asymmetric information exchange leads to the low-quality products and services driving out the higher-quality products and services.

In a lemons market, the buyers discount all unverifiable claims by the sellers, who market only lower-quality products at the reduced prices buyers are willing to offer. This disappearance of higher-quality products from the marketplace illustrates the concept of adverse selection—that is, the lower-quality products are selected in and the higher-quality products are adversely selected out. To resolve the marketing problems posed by adverse selection requires credible commitment mechanisms such as warranties, brand-name reputations, collateral, or price premiums for reliable repeat-purchase transactions.

Incomplete versus Asymmetric Information

One distinction that can sharpen our understanding of these complicating factors in competitive exchange is that between asymmetric information and **incomplete information**. Incomplete information is associated with uncertainty, and uncertainty is pervasive. Practically all exchanges, whether for products, financial claims, or labor services, are conducted under conditions of uncertainty. On the one hand, decision makers often face uncertainty as to the effect of random disturbances on the outcome of their actions. This uncertainty typically leads to insurance markets. On the other hand, decision makers are sometimes uncertain as to the payoffs or even types of choices they face. This condition typically leads to intentionally incomplete contracting.

incomplete information Uncertain knowledge of payoffs, choices, and so forth.

asymmetric information Unequal, dissimilar knowledge.

Asymmetric information exchange, in contrast, refers to situations in which either the buyer or the seller possesses information that the other party cannot verify or to which the other party does not have access. For example, mail-order suppliers of computer components or personal sellers of used cars often have an informationally advantaged position relative to the buyers. The sellers know the machine's capabilities, deficiencies, and most probable failure rate, but these are difficult matters for the buyer to assess from reading magazine ads or kicking the tires. And the typical 90-day warranty does nothing to alter this information asymmetry. Both buyer and seller face uncertainty against which they may choose to insure, but one has more information or better information than the other.

Search Goods versus Experience Goods

In services, retailing, and many manufacturing industries, buyers generally search the market to identify low-price suppliers. Sometimes this search is accomplished by asking for recommendations from recent purchasers, by scouring the catalogs and ads, or by visiting showrooms and sales floors. In selecting a supplier, many customers are also intensely interested in multiple dimensions of product and service quality, including product design, durability, image, conformance to specifications, order delay, delivery reliability, change-order responsiveness, and after-sale service. Customers often spend as much time and effort searching the market for the desired quality mix as they do searching for lowest price. Retailers and service providers understand this and often offer many quality combinations at various prices to trigger a purchase of these **search goods**. Consider, for example, the many price-quality alternatives available in clothing, sporting goods, and furniture stores as well as across hotel chains.

On the other hand, some products and services have important quality dimensions that *cannot* be observed at the point of purchase. Consider, again, used cars and other resale machinery, nonprescription remedies for the common cold, house paint, and mail-order computer components. The quality of these items can be detected only through experience in using the products. Hence, products and services of this type are termed **experience goods** and are distinguished from search goods.

Ultimately, the problem with experience goods in competitive market exchange is the unverifiability of asymmetric information. The seller knows how to detect the difference between high-quality and low-quality products (e.g., between lemons and cream puffs in the used-car market), but cannot credibly relay this information to buyers, at least not in chance encounters between strangers. Fraudulent sellers will claim high quality when it is absent, and realizing this, buyers rationally discount all such information. Because of the private, impacted nature of the product quality information, the seller's claims and omissions can never be verified without experiencing for oneself the reliability of the auto, the efficacy of the common cold remedy, the durability of the house paint, or the capability of the computer component.

All of this is not to say that the buyers of experience goods are without recourse or that the sellers are without ingenuity as to how to market their products. Warranties and investments in reputations provide mechanisms whereby the sellers of house paint and computer components can credibly commit to delivering a high-quality product. The essential point is that in the absence of these bonding or hostage mechanisms, the experience-good buyer will rationally disbelieve the seller's claims. Consequently, the honest seller of truly high-quality experience goods will find little market for his or her higher-cost, higher-priced product. The "bad apples drive out the good" in many experience-good markets.

Adverse Selection and the Notorious Firm

Suppose customers recognize that unverifiable private information about experience-good quality is present, yet knowledge of any fraudulent high-price sale of low-quality products spreads almost instantaneously throughout the marketplace. Is this extreme reputational effect sufficient to restore the exchange of high-quality/high-price experience goods? Or, can the notorious firm continue to defraud customers here and elsewhere? The answer depends on the conditions of entry and exit discussed earlier in this chapter, but not in the way you might expect.

Consider the cost structure and profits of such a notorious firm, depicted in Figure 10.10. If offered the low price P_l, the firm operates in competitive equilibrium at Q_1, where the price just covers the marginal cost and average total cost ($SAC_{\text{low quality}}$) for

search goods
Products and services whose quality can be detected through market search.

experience goods Products and services whose quality is undetectable when purchased.

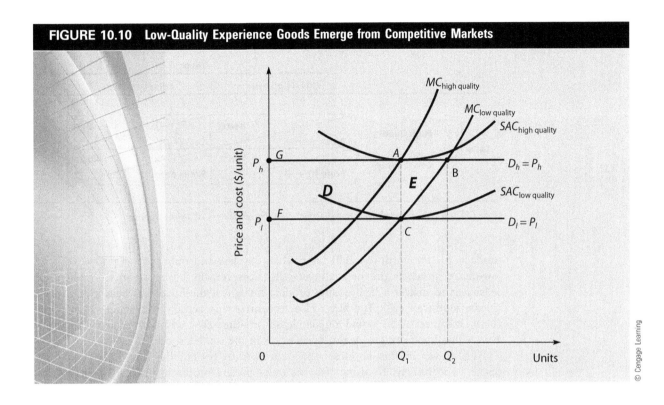

FIGURE 10.10   Low-Quality Experience Goods Emerge from Competitive Markets

Q_1 units of the low-quality product. Alternatively, if offered the high price P_h, either the firm can competitively supply Q_1 of the high-quality experience good and again just break even against the higher costs of $SAC_{\text{high quality}}$,[26] or the firm can deliver a low-quality experience good at Q_2 and continue to incur the lower costs of $SAC_{\text{low quality}}$. The third alternative entails an expansion of output along $MC_{\text{low quality}}$ in response to the price rise and generates profits. That is, the incremental output $(Q_2 - Q_1)$ earns incremental profit equal to the difference between P_h and $MC_{\text{low quality}}$—namely, the shaded area ABC (labeled bold E)—and in addition, the original output Q_1 earns a fraudulent rent of area $GACF$ (labeled bold D). Although the supplier observes his own cost directly and therefore detects the availability of $D + E$, the problem for the experience-good buyer is that in terms of point-of-sale information, high-price transactions at Point B on $MC_{\text{low quality}}$ and at Point A on $MC_{\text{high quality}}$ are indistinguishable. Both types of products have an asking price of P_h, and only the seller observes the output rate Q_1 versus Q_2.

Of course, the supplier is not indifferent between the two alternatives. The high-quality transaction offers a cash flow from operations just sufficient to cover capital costs and break even at Point A, whereas the fraudulent transaction (a low-quality product at a high price at Point B) offers a net profit for at least one period. Table 10.2 depicts this interaction between experience-good buyers and a potentially fraudulent firm as a payoff matrix. The seller can produce either low or high quality, and the buyer can offer either low or high prices. The row player (the seller) gets the below-diagonal payoffs in each cell, and the column player (the buyer) gets the above-diagonal payoffs in each cell. The buyer prefers to cover the high cost of high-quality

---

[26]The minimum cost output for the plant configuration and cost structure associated with high quality could shift right or left, but to simplify, assume that the SAC just increases vertically from Point C to Point A.

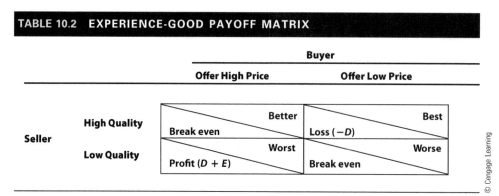

Note: Column-player payoffs are above diagonal. Row-player payoffs are below diagonal.

products (in the northwest cell) rather than pay less and only cover the lower cost of low-quality products (in the southeast cell). However, the buyer is worst off when the seller fails to deliver a high-quality product for which the buyer has paid a high price (in the southwest cell). The buyer also recognizes that getting more than she pays for (in the northeast cell) would impose losses on the seller who would prefer to break even with a low-price/low-quality transaction in the southeast cell.

Each player in this business game attempts to predict the other's behavior and respond accordingly. Knowing that the seller prefers profits to breaking even at high prices and that the seller prefers breaking even to losses at low prices, the buyer predicts that low-quality product will be forthcoming irrespective of the price offered. Therefore, the buyer makes only low-price offers. Only those who wish to be repeatedly defrauded offer to pay high prices for one-shot transactions with strangers offering experience goods.

adverse selection A limited choice of lower-quality alternatives attributable to asymmetric information.

This reasoning motivates **adverse selection** by the rational seller in an experience-good market. Because sellers can anticipate only low-price offers from buyers, the sellers never produce high-quality products—that is, the market for experience goods will be incomplete in that not all product qualities will be available for sale. Anticipating that buyers will radically discount their unverifiable high-quality "cream puffs," individual sellers of used cars choose to place only low-quality "lemons" on the market. The "cream puffs" often are given away to relatives. Similarly, jewelers in vacation locations, anticipating that out-of-town buyers will suspect uncertified spectacular gemstones are fakes, choose to sell only lower-quality gemstones. And unbranded mail-order computer components are inevitably of lower quality. Adverse selection always causes competitive markets with asymmetric information to be incomplete. Again, the bad apples drive out the good.

Insuring and Lending under Asymmetric Information: Another Lemons Market

This same adverse selection reasoning applies beyond experience-good product markets whenever asymmetric information is prominent. Consider the transaction between a bank loan officer and a new commercial borrower, or between an insurance company and a new auto insurance policyholder. Through an application and interview process and with access to various databases and credit references, the lender or insurer attempts to uncover the private, impacted information about the applicant's credit or driving history. Nevertheless, just as in the case of claims made by the itinerant seller of an experience good, verification remains a problem. The applicant has an incentive to omit facts that would tend to result in loan or insurance denial (e.g., prior business failures or unreported accidents), and knowing this, the lender may offer only higher-rate loans and the insurer higher-rate policies.

The problem is that higher-rate loans and expensive insurance policies tend to affect the composition of the applicant pool, resulting in adverse selection. Some honest, well-intentioned borrowers and good-risk insurance applicants will now drop out of the applicant pool because of concern about their inability to pay principal and interest and insurance premiums on time as promised. But other applicants who never intended to repay (or drive carefully), or more problematically, those who will try less hard to avoid default or accidents, are undeterred by the higher rates. The asymmetric information and higher rates have adversely selected out precisely those borrowers and drivers the lender and auto insurance company wanted to attract to their loan portfolio and insurance risk pool. Recognizing this problem, the creditors and insurers offer a restricted and incomplete set of loan and insurance contracts. Credit rationing that excludes large segments of the population of potential borrowers and state-mandated protection against uninsured motorists are reflections of the adverse selection problem resulting from asymmetric information in these commercial lending and auto insurance markets.

SOLUTIONS TO THE ADVERSE SELECTION PROBLEM

In both theory and practice, there are two approaches to eliciting the exchange of high-quality experience goods, commercial loans to new borrowers, or auto insurance policies to new residents. The first involves regulatory agencies such as the Federal Trade Commission, the Food and Drug Administration, and the Consumer Product Safety Commission. These agencies can attempt to set quotas (e.g., on minimum product durability, on minimum lending in "red-lined" underprivileged communities, or on minimum auto liability insurance coverage). They may also impose restrictions (e.g., on the sale of untested pharmaceuticals), enforce product safety standards (e.g., on the flammability of children's sleepwear), and monitor truth-in-advertising laws. We discuss public regulation at greater length in Chapter 16.

Mutual Reliance: Hostage Mechanisms Support Asymmetric Information Exchange

reliance relationships Long-term, mutually beneficial agreements, often informal.

A second, quite different approach involves self-enforcing private solution mechanisms where each party relies on the other. Such **reliance relationships** often involve the exchange of some sort of hostage, such as a reputational asset, an escrow account, or a surety bond. In general, **hostage or bonding mechanisms** are necessary to induce unregulated asymmetric information exchange. For this second approach to the adverse selection problem to succeed, buyers must be convinced that fraud is more costly to the seller than the cost of delivering the promised product quality. Then, and only then, will the customers pay for the seller's additional expected costs attributable to the higher-quality products.

bonding mechanism A procedure for establishing trust by pledging valuable property contingent on your nonperformance of an agreement.

One simple illustration of the use of a hostage mechanism to support asymmetric information exchange is a product warranty, perhaps for an auto tire. Tires are an experience good in that blowout protection and tread wear life are product qualities not detectable at the point of purchase. Only by driving many thousands of miles and randomly encountering many road hazards can the buyer ascertain these tire qualities directly. However, if a tread wear replacement warranty and a tire blowout warranty make the sellers conspicuously worse off should they fail to deliver high-quality tires, then buyers can rely on that manufacturer's product claims. As a consequence, buyers will be willing to offer higher prices for the unverifiably higher-quality product.

Hostage mechanisms can be either self-enforcing or enforced by third parties. Like warranties, a seller's representations about after-sale service and product replacement guarantees are ultimately contractual agreements that will be enforced by the courts. However, other hostage mechanisms require no third-party enforcement. Suppose Du-Pont's industrial chemicals division reveals to potential new customers the names and addresses of several satisfied current customers. This practice of providing references is not only to assist potential buyers in gauging the quality of the product or service for sale but also to deliver an irretrievable hostage. Once new customers have the easy ability to contact regular customers and blow the whistle on product malfunctions or misrepresentations, the seller has an enhanced incentive to deliver high quality to both sets of buyers. Connecting all suppliers and customers in a real-time information system is a natural extension of this familiar practice of providing references. The total quality management's (TQM's) ISO 9000 standards recommend that companies insist on just such information links to their suppliers' other customers.

Example

Credible Product Replacement Claims: Dooney & Bourke

The women's handbag market has a wide selection of brand names, prices, and qualities. Leather products have several search-good characteristics in that one can touch and feel the material in order to assess the fineness or coarseness of the grain, the evenness of the tanning process, the suppleness of the leather, and so forth. In these respects, one can search for just that quality for which one is willing to pay. However, the susceptibility to discoloring with age or exposure to the elements and the quality of the stitching are much harder to detect at the point of purchase. As a result, some aspects of handbag purchase are an experience-good exchange. Therefore, one wonders how the wide variety of prices and qualities can be sustained.

Dooney & Bourke resolved this question by offering an almost preposterous replacement guarantee. Like Revo sunglasses, Dooney & Bourke offered to replace any handbag for the life of the customer. Because each state attorney general will assist any customer in enforcing this promise, the commitment was credible, and the replacement guarantee provides a hostage that supports high-price, high-quality exchanges. In particular, customers can easily discern that Dooney & Bourke is better off producing an exceptionally high-quality handbag to deliver at the first transaction rather than an unlimited series of replacements.

Brand-Name Reputations as Hostages

A marketing mechanism that supports asymmetric information exchange is a brand-name reputation such as Sony Trinitron Wega digital televisions, Apple Macintosh computers, Pepperidge Farm snacks, and Toyota Lexus automobiles. Branding requires a substantial investment over extended periods of time. Moreover, brand names are capital assets that provide future net cash flows from repeat-purchase customers as long as the brand reputation holds up. Defrauding customers by delivering less quality than the brand reputation promised would destroy the capitalized market value of the brand name. Buyers anticipate that value-maximizing managers will not intentionally destroy brand-name capital. Brand names therefore deliver a hostage, providing assurances to buyers that the seller will not misrepresent the quality of an experience good.

Ultimately, brand-name capital provides such a hostage because the disreputation effects on the brand name that result from delivering fraudulent product quality cannot be separated from the salable brand asset. Successful brands can be extended to sell other products; Nestlé's original hot chocolate brand can be extended to sell cereal-based candy bars, and Oreo cookies can be extended to sell ice cream. But the product failure of Texas Instruments (TI) personal computers means that now the TI brand name cannot be easily extended to other consumer electronic products. All the potential buyers have to figure out is whether the seller would be worse off sacrificing the value of the brand name but economizing on production expenses rather than simply incurring the extra expense to produce a high-quality product while retaining the brand value. A brand-name asset such as Pepperidge Farm may suggest one answer, whereas Joe's Garage suggests another.

Example

Customers for Life at Sewell Cadillac[27]

The most profitable luxury automobile dealership in the United States is operated in Dallas, Texas, by Carl Sewell. Several decades ago, Mr. Sewell realized that the critical success factor in his business was establishing repeat-purchase transactions with regular customers. Many potential buyers shop for lowest price in the new automobile market, sometimes with no more inconvenience than fingertip browsing of the Internet. And because the alternatives are many, and the information on posted prices is great, many dealerships spend several hundred dollars per car on personal selling costs with little prospect of repeat business.

Carl Sewell decided instead to expend similarly large amounts attracting "customers for life." He began by making the apparently preposterous claim that he would dispatch Sewell Cadillac emergency roadside service to any Sewell Cadillac customer experiencing car trouble anywhere in the state of Texas. Texas is geographically quite a large state. To economize on the need for such trips, Sewell developed an extensive dealer-based maintenance schedule and instituted in his service department one of the first total quality management (TQM) programs in the auto industry.

Because TQM introduced new process-based competitive advantages, they were difficult for other dealers to imitate. These process innovations cost plenty, but the word-of-mouth reputation effects every time the dealership delivered on its promise spread the name and quality image of Sewell Cadillac across North Texas. Soon customers were driving in from surrounding cities for the privilege of doing high-margin business with Carl Sewell. And even more importantly, these same customers came back time and time again with very little additional selling cost to the dealership.

---

[27]See Carl Sewell and Paul B. Brown, *Customers for Life* (New York: Simon & Schuster, 1992).

If brand-name assets could be sold independently of their reputations (or disreputations), then this hostage mechanism would cease to support experience-good exchange. Assets that can be redeployed at the grantor's wish are not hostages in this reliance contracting sense. The implication is that easy entry and exit, which works to ensure break-even prices just sufficient to cover costs in the normal competitive markets, may have undesirable consequences in markets with asymmetric information experience goods.

Price Premiums with Non-Redeployable Assets[28]

Recall that if sellers are offered prices that just cover high-quality cost, sellers of experience goods prefer the profit from defrauding customers by delivering low-quality products. But suppose buyers offered reliable sellers a continuing price premium above the cost of high-quality products. At P_{hh} in Figure 10.11, the non-notorious firm produces Q'_1 high-quality product and earns a continuous stream of profits ($IJAG + JKA$), labeled $T + U$. This perpetuity may now exceed (in present value) the notorious firm's onetime-only fraudulent rent from production at Q'_2—namely, $D + T$, plus incremental profit $E + U + V$. That is,

$$(T + U)/d > [(D + T) + (E + U + V)]/(1 + d) \qquad [10.9]$$

where d is an appropriate discount rate (e.g., the firm's weighted average cost of capital, perhaps 12 percent). By Equation 10.9, lower discount rates or faster rising marginal cost (i.e., a smaller incremental profit from the expansion of output, shaded area V in Figure 10.11) decreases the likelihood of fraudulent behavior. If reliable delivery of a high-quality product does in fact earn long-term net profit in excess of the onetime-only profit from fraud, sellers will offer both low- and high-quality products at P_l and P_{hh}, respectively, and some buyers will purchase in each market.

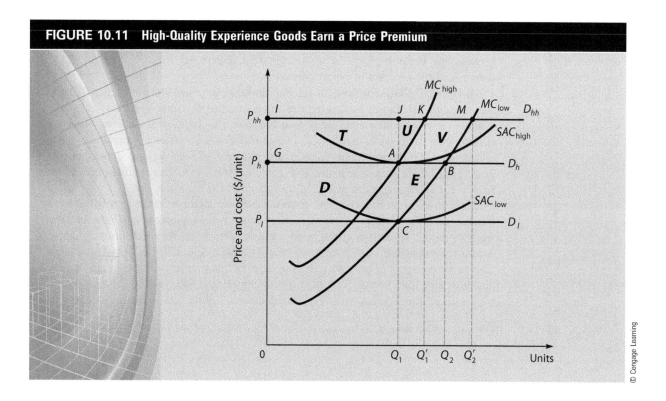

FIGURE 10.11   High-Quality Experience Goods Earn a Price Premium

© Cengage Learning

---

[28]See B. Klein and K. Leffler, "The Role of Market Forces in Assuring Contractual Performance," *Journal of Political Economy* 89, no. 4 (1981), pp. 615–641.

However, transitory profits alone do not allow an escape from adverse selection. Because profits attract entry in competitive markets, the price premiums will erode, and notorious firm behavior will then return. What is missing is a mechanism to dissipate the rent from the price premiums. If the sellers invest the high-quality price premiums in firm-specific assets, such as Sewell Cadillac's TQM program, L'eggs retail displays for convenience stores, or Ethan Allen's interiors for its showrooms, then new entrants will encounter a higher entry barrier than previously. Such barriers cause potential entrants to perceive much lower potential net profit unless one is planning to deliver a very expensive high-quality product. They therefore deter entry. Sewell Cadillac's, L'eggs, or Ethan Allen's operating profits in excess of production cost can then persist, and high-quality, high-price experience goods can then survive in the marketplace.

The rent-dissipating investments must not be in generic retail sites easily redeployable to the next tenant or capital equipment easily redeployable to the next manufacturer (e.g., corporate jet aircraft). If that were the case, hit-and-run entry would recur each time high-quality prices rose above cost. New entrants would just move in on the business for a short time period and then sell off their assets in thick resale markets when profits eroded. In that event, competitive equilibrium would again induce adverse selection in experience-good markets. Instead, the investment that dissipates the operating profit from high-quality products must be sunk-cost investment in non-redeployable assets.

Example

Hostage Exchange with Efficient Uncut Diamond Sorting at De Beers[29]

Another illustration of experience-good exchange is block booking by the De Beers diamond cartel, which controls over 80 percent of the uncut wholesale diamond business. De Beers offers groupings of diamonds of various grades to approved wholesale buyers. Because buyers are not allowed to cull the less-valuable stones, the quality of the diamonds in any given grouping is unverifiable at the point of purchase, hence the term *sights*. If these arrangements were one time only, no buyer would purchase high-price sights or agree to the culling restrictions. But because block booking economizes on the duplicatory assessments of rejected stones that would otherwise result, De Beers can consistently offer its sights at net costs below the value at which the diamonds grade out. Buyers therefore have a reason for purchasing high-quality experience goods from De Beers.

If a competitor offered no culling restrictions and lower prices, the diamond merchants would carefully weigh the additional cost of sorting the diamonds themselves against the price premiums at De Beers and might well decide to continue doing business with De Beers. Knowing this, very few potential competitors ever enter the uncut diamond wholesale business to challenge De Beers despite its high markups and margins. De Beers' reputation for passing on its cost savings in diamond sorting to buyers is the hostage that brings buyers back time and time again.

[29]Based on R. Kenney and B. Klein, "The Economics of Block Booking," *Journal of Law and Economics* 26 (1983), pp. 497–540.

non-redeployable assets Assets whose value in second-best use is near zero.

Non-redeployable assets are assets whose liquidation value in second-best use is low. Usually this occurs when the assets depend on a firm-specific input such as a Sewell Cadillac, L'eggs, or Ethan Allen brand name. Without the brand name, no firm has a use for the egg-shaped retail racks designed for L'eggs original packaging or the lavish

asset specificity The difference in value between first-best and second-best use.

Ethan Allen showrooms. Non-redeployable assets have high value in their first best use. The difference between value in first best use and liquidation value is a measure of the **asset specificity**. Highly specific assets make the best hostages to convince customers that asymmetric information transactions will be nonfraudulent.

In summary, asymmetric information causes competitive markets for experience goods to differ rather markedly from the competitive markets for search goods. Long-run equilibrium for high-quality experience goods requires revenues in excess of total unit cost. These profits are invested by reliable sellers of experience goods in highly specific assets. Potentially notorious firms with redeployable assets attract only customers seeking low-price/low-quality experience goods. In experience-good markets, you get what you pay for when reputations matter or when other hostage mechanisms establish the seller's credibility.

SUMMARY

- Competitive strategy entails an analysis of the firm's resource-based capabilities, the design of business processes that can secure sustainable competitive advantage, and the development of a road map for innovation.

- Types of strategic thinking include industry analysis, competitor analysis, strategic positioning, and identification of core competencies derived from resource-based capabilities.

- Sustainable competitive advantage may arise from product differentiation strategy (product capabilities, branding, and endorsements), from focused cost or cost leadership strategy, or from information technology strategy.

- The choice of competitive strategy should be congruent with the breadth or narrowness of the firm's strategic focus.

- A successful competitive strategy includes an ongoing process of reinvention and reconfiguration of capabilities and business models.

- A relevant market is a group of economic agents that interact with each other in a buyer-seller relationship. Relevant markets often have both spatial and product characteristics.

- The Five Forces model of business strategy identifies threat of substitutes, threat of entry, power of buyers, power of suppliers, and the intensity of rivalry as the determinants of sustainable incumbent profitability in a particular industry. Such industry analyses are often complemented by an assessment of threats from disruptive technology.

- The threat of substitutes depends upon the number and closeness of substitutes as determined by the product development, advertising, brand-naming, and segmentation strategies of preexisting competitors. Complements in consumption can be an enormous source of network effects, raising sustainable profitability.

- The threat of entry depends upon the height of barriers to potential entrants including capital requirements, economies of scale, absolute cost advantages, switching costs, access to distribution channels, and trade secrets and other difficult-to-imitate forms of product differentiation.

- The bargaining power of buyers and suppliers depends upon their number, their size distribution, the relationship between industry capacity and industry demand, the uniqueness of the inputs, the potential for forward and backward integration, the ability of the buyers to influence the setting of an industry standard, and the extent to which each party to the bargain has outside alternatives.

- The intensity of rivalry depends upon the number and size distribution of sellers in the relevant market, the relative frequency of price versus non-price competition, switching costs, the proportion of fixed to total cost, the barriers to exit, the growth rate of industry demand, and the incumbent's speed of adjustment.

- The *demand* for a good or service is defined as the various quantities of that good or service that consumers are willing and able to purchase during a particular period of time at all possible prices. The *supply* of a good or service is defined as the quantities that sellers are willing to make available to purchasers at all possible prices during a particular period of time.

■ In general, a profit-maximizing firm will desire to operate at that level of output where marginal cost equals marginal revenue.

■ In a purely competitive market structure, the firm will operate in the short run as long as price is greater than average variable cost.

■ In a *purely competitive* market structure, the tendency is toward a long-run equilibrium condition in which firms earn just normal profits, price is equal to marginal cost and average total cost, and average total cost is minimized.

■ In a monopolistically competitive industry, a large number of firms sell a differentiated product. In practice, few market structures can be best analyzed in the context of the *monopolistic competition* model. Most actual market structures have greater similarities to the purely competitive market model or the *oligopolistic* market model.

■ Advertising expenditures are optimal from a profit-maximization perspective if they are carried to the point where the marginal profit contribution from an additional unit of output is equal to the marginal cost of advertising. The optimal level of advertising intensity (the advertising expenditure per sales dollar) varies across products and industries; it is determined by the marginal profit contribution from incremental sales and by the advertising elasticity of demand.

■ Exchange under incomplete information and under asymmetric information differs. *Incomplete information* refers to the uncertainty that is pervasive in practically all transactions and motivates insurance markets. *Asymmetric information*, on the other hand, refers to private information one party possesses that the other party cannot independently verify.

■ Asymmetric information in *experience-good* markets leads to *adverse selection* whereby high-price/high-quality products are driven from the market by low-quality products whose low quality is indistinguishable at the point of sale. Buyers in such *lemons markets* refuse to offer prices high enough to cover the cost of high quality because under competitive conditions suppliers will predictably commit fraud, and then perhaps move on to conduct business with unsuspecting customers under other product or company names.

■ To escape adverse selection and elicit high-quality experience goods necessitates either intrusive and expensive regulation or some sort of bonding mechanism to induce *self-enforcing reliance relationships* between buyers and sellers. Warranties, independent appraisals, leases with a high residual, collateral, irrevocable money-back guarantees, contingent payments, and brand names all provide assurance to buyers that the seller will not misrepresent the product quality. Hostage mechanisms support asymmetric information exchange.

■ Another way to escape adverse selection is for buyers to offer price premiums and repeat-purchase transactions to firms that resist fraudulently selling low-quality experience goods for high prices. These profits are invested by reliable sellers in *non-redeployable, highly specific assets*. Potentially *notorious firms* with redeployable assets continue to attract only customers seeking low-price/low-quality products. Under asymmetric information, at best you get what you pay for, never more.

Exercises

Answers to the exercises in blue can be found in Appendix D at the back of the book.

1. The profitability of the leading cola syrup manufacturers PepsiCo and Coca-Cola and of the bottlers in the cola business is very different. PepsiCo and Coca-Cola enjoy an 81 percent operating profit as a percentage of sales; bottlers experience only a 15 percent operating profit as a percentage of sales. Perform a Porter's Five Forces analysis that explains why one type of business is potentially so profitable relative to the other.

2. Television channel operating profits vary from as high as 45 to 55 percent at MTV and Nickelodeon down to 12 to 18 percent at NBC and ABC. Provide a Porter Five Forces analysis of each type of network. Why is MTV so profitable relative to the major networks?

3. The costs of producing steel have declined substantially from building a conventional hot-rolled steel mill down to the new minimill technology that requires only scrap metal, an electric furnace, and 300 workers rather than iron ore raw materials, enormous blast furnaces, rolling mills, reheating furnaces, and thousands of workers. What effect on the potential industry profitability would Porter's Five Forces framework suggest this new technology had? Why?

4. Ethanol is again viewed as one part of a solution to the problem of shortages of petroleum products. Ethanol is made from a blend of gasoline and alcohol derived from corn or sugarcane. What would you expect the impact of this program to be on the price of corn, soybeans, and wheat?

5. Why invest capital in purely competitive industries with equilibrium margins that are razor thin and entrants that erode quasi-profits? Suppose volume is not exceptionally large, why then?

6. Assume that a firm in a perfectly competitive industry has the following total cost schedule:

OUTPUT (UNITS)	TOTAL COST ($)
10	110
15	150
20	180
25	225
30	300
35	385
40	480

a. Calculate a marginal cost and an average cost schedule for the firm.
b. If the prevailing market price is $17 per unit, how many units will be produced and sold? What are profits per unit? What are total profits?
c. Is the industry in long-run equilibrium at this price?

7. Royersford Knitting Mills, Ltd., sells a line of women's knit underwear. The firm now sells about 20,000 pairs a year at an average price of $10 each. Fixed costs amount to $60,000, and total variable costs equal $120,000. The production department has estimated that a 10 percent increase in output would not affect fixed costs but would reduce average variable cost by 40 cents.

The marketing department advocates a price reduction of 5 percent to increase sales, total revenues, and profits. The arc elasticity of demand with respect to prices is estimated at −2.

a. Evaluate the impact of the proposal to cut prices on (i) total revenue, (ii) total cost, and (iii) total profits.
b. If average variable costs are assumed to remain constant over a 10 percent increase in output, evaluate the effects of the proposed price cut on total profits.

8. The Poster Bed Company believes that its industry can best be classified as monopolistically competitive. An analysis of the demand for its canopy bed has resulted in the following estimated demand function for the bed:

$$P = 1760 - 12Q$$

The cost analysis department has estimated the total cost function for the poster bed as

$$TC = \frac{1}{3}Q^3 - 15Q^2 + 5Q + 24{,}000$$

    a. Calculate the level of output that should be produced to maximize short-run profits.

    b. What price should be charged?

    c. Compute total profits at this price-output level.

    d. Compute the point price elasticity of demand at the profit-maximizing level of output.

    e. What level of fixed costs is the firm experiencing on its bed production?

    f. What is the impact of a $5,000 increase in the level of fixed costs on the price charged, output produced, and profit generated?

9. Jordan Enterprises has estimated the contribution margin $(P - MC)/P$ for its Air Express model of basketball shoes to be 40 percent. Based on market research and past experience, Jordan estimates the following relationship between the sales for Air Express and advertising/promotional outlays:

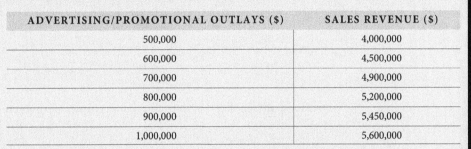

ADVERTISING/PROMOTIONAL OUTLAYS ($)	SALES REVENUE ($)
500,000	4,000,000
600,000	4,500,000
700,000	4,900,000
800,000	5,200,000
900,000	5,450,000
1,000,000	5,600,000

    a. What is the marginal revenue from an additional dollar spent on advertising if the firm is currently spending $1,000,000 on advertising?

    b. What level of advertising would you recommend to Jordan's management?

10. Which of the following products and services are likely to encounter adverse selection problems: golf shirts at traveling pro tournaments, certified gemstones from Tiffany's, graduation gift travel packages, or mail-order auto parts? Why or why not?

11. If notorious firm behavior (i.e., defrauding a buyer of high-priced experience goods by delivering low quality) becomes known throughout the marketplace only with a lag of three periods, profits on high-quality transactions remain the same, and interest rates rise slightly, are customers more likely or less likely to agree to pay high prices for an experience good? Explain.

Case Exercises   ## Netflix and Redbox Compete for Movie Rentals[30]

Charging $17.99 a month for an unlimited number of movie rentals (three at one time), Netflix revolutionized the movie rental business with a one-day mailing service for DVDs and acquired 12 million subscribers and $1.5 billion in revenue. However, Block-buster, the video rental giant from the earlier $5.5 billion bricks-and-mortar movie rental business, decided to enter the mail-in delivery and online-DVD rental businesses. Blockbuster (now a division of Dish Network) drove prices down to $14.99, attracting 2 million subscribers. Netflix responded with a cut-rate service of one movie at a time for $9.99 per month, which drove the net profit right out of the business.

---

[30]"Movies to Go," *The Economist* (July 9, 2005), p. 57; and "Blockbuster Plots a Remake," *Wall Street Journal* (February 24, 2010), p. B1, and "Hollywood: The Price Is Wrong," *Wall Street Journal* (February 9, 2011), p. C14.

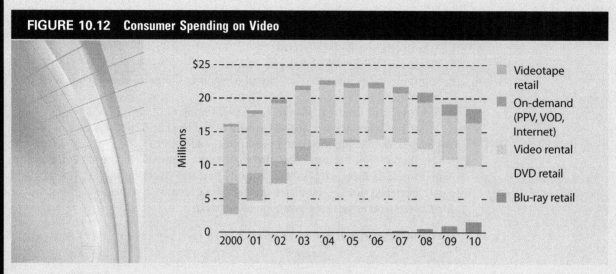

FIGURE 10.12 Consumer Spending on Video

Source: IHS Screen Digest, *Wall Street Journal* (February 9, 2011, p. B14).

Movie studios like Viacom and Time Warner also entered the market with direct-to-the-customer video on demand delivered over the web. Following two months of theatre-only releases, the studios asked $20 to $25 per showing. This fee is five times what it costs to rent a second-run or classic movie from the cable companies and 10 times Netflix's or Redbox's $1.99 or $1 fees for overnight rentals. At such exorbitant prices, the studios earn a 70 percent margin, but studies of price elasticity in home entertainment experiments suggest an eight-fold increase in volume for half-price promotions. On-demand movie rentals and Blu-ray retail sales are the only two growing segments of consumer demand for video (see Figure 10.12).

Use Porter's Five Forces model to answer the following questions:

Questions

1. What disruptive technology has threatened the bricks-and-mortar and mail-in movie rental business?
2. Does easy access to distribution channels at grocery stores for Redbox's 22,000 vending machines indicate a high- or low-entry threat in the movie rental business? Why? Why might McDonald's be an even better distribution channel than grocery stores?
3. Are there any economies of scale in the on-demand video rental business to serve as a barrier to the entry of Amazon?
4. Who are Netflix's and Redbox's suppliers? Are they in a position to appropriate much of the value in the value chain? Why or why not?
5. What factors determine the intensity of rivalry in any industry? Is the intensity of rivalry in the video rental industry high or low? Why?

Saving Sony Music

Explore the crisis that Internet file sharing of copyrighted music recordings has caused for Vivendi Universal, *Sony Music*, *EMI*, and AOL Time Warner Music, which together formerly supplied 70 percent of the global music industry.

Questions

1. How would the Internet firms Napster and Kazaa be reflected in a Porter Five Forces industry analysis?

2. Why was the Internet a disruptive technology for Sony Music? Did the new digital file transfer technology favor album-size transactions which Sony Music understood very well? Or did the new technology favor Steve Jobs's vision of an Apple iTunes Music Store focused on easily accessible 99-cent singles? What aspect of the iTunes Music Store made it more desirable that simply transferring stolen digital music files one by one?

3. What should be Sony Music's competitive strategy in response to this crisis? Include a discussion of resource-based capabilities, business opportunities, and a road map of future innovation.

4. Is your competitive strategy for Sony Music a product-differentiation strategy, a low-cost strategy, or an IT strategy? What is your strategic focus?

The Time Value of Money

APPENDIX

A

INTRODUCTION

Many economic decisions involve benefits and costs that are expected to occur at different future points in time. For example, the construction of a new office complex requires an immediate outlay of cash and results in a stream of expected cash inflows (benefits) over many future years. To determine if the expected future cash inflows are sufficient to justify the initial outlay, we must have a way to compare cash flows occurring at different points in time. Also, recall from Chapter 1 that the value of a firm is equal to the discounted (or present) value of all expected returns. These future returns are discounted at a rate of return that is consistent with the risk of the expected future returns. When future returns are more certain, the discount rate used is lower, resulting in a higher present value of the firm, *all other things being equal.* Conversely, when future returns are riskier or more uncertain, they are discounted at a higher rate, resulting in a lower present value of the firm, *all other things being equal.*

An explicit solution to the problem of comparing the benefits and costs of economic transactions that occur at different points in time requires answers to the following kinds of questions: Is $1 to be received one year from today worth less than $1 in hand today? If so, why is it worth less? How much less is it worth?

The answers to these questions depend on the alternative uses available for the dollar between today and one year from today. Suppose the dollar can be invested in a guaranteed savings account paying a 6 percent annual rate of return (interest rate). The $1 invested today will return $1(1.06) = $1.06 one year from today. To receive exactly $1 one year from today, only $1/(1.06) = $0.943 would have to be invested in the account today. Given the opportunity to invest at a 6 percent rate of return, we see that $1 to be received one year from today is indeed worth less than $1 in hand today, its worth being only $0.943. Thus, the existence of opportunities to invest the dollar at positive rates of return makes $1 to be received at any future point in time worth less than $1 in hand today.[1] This is what is meant by the *time value of money.* The investor's required rate of return is called the *discount rate.*

PRESENT VALUE OF A SINGLE PAYMENT

We can generalize this result for any future series of cash flows and any interest rate. Assume that the opportunity exists to invest at a compound rate of *r* percent per annum. Then the *present value (PV)* (value today) of $1 to be received at the end of year *n*, discounted at *r* percent, is

$$PV_0 = \frac{1}{(1+r)^n} \qquad [A.1]$$

---

[1]In this analysis, we are abstracting from price-level considerations. Changes in the level of prices (the value of the dollar in terms of the quantity of goods and services it will buy) can also affect the worth of the dollar. In theory, future price increases (or decreases) that are anticipated by the market will be reflected in the interest rate.

The term $1/(1 + r)^n$ is often called a present value interest factor, or $PVIF_{r,n}$. Table A.3 at the end of this Appendix contains $PVIF$ values for various interest rates, r, and periods in the future, n.

Example

Present Value

If an opportunity exists to invest at a compound rate of return of 12 percent, then the present value of $1 to be received four years ($n = 4$) from today is

$$PV_0 = \frac{1}{(1 + .12)^4} = (PVIF_{12\%,4})$$

$$= \$1(0.6355)$$

$$= \$0.6355$$

As we see in Table A.1, investing $0.6355 today at an interest rate of 12 percent per annum will give $1 at the end of four years.

Alternatively, the $PVIF$ factors from Table A.3 again could be used to find the present value of $1 expected to be received in four years ($n = 4$), assuming an interest rate of 12 percent ($r = 12\%$), as follows:

$$PV_0 = \$1(PVIF_{12\%,4})$$

$$= \$1(0.63552)$$

$$= \$0.6355$$

TABLE A.1   PRESENT VALUE OF $1 TO BE RECEIVED AT THE END OF FOUR YEARS

YEAR	RETURN RECEIVED AT END OF YEAR ($)	VALUE OF INVESTMENT AT END OF YEAR ($)	
0 (present)	—	0.6355	← Initial amount invested
1	0.6355(0.12) = 0.0762	0.6355 + 0.0762 = 0.7117	
2	0.7117(0.12) = 0.0854	0.7117 + 0.0854 = 0.7971	
3	0.7971(0.12) = 0.0957	0.7971 + 0.0957 = 0.8928	
4	0.8928(0.12) = 0.1072	0.8928 + 0.1072 = 1.000	

© Cengage Learning

Example

Present Value of a Deferred Bequest

What is the present value of an expected bequest of $2 million to your university if the expected remaining life span of the donor is eight years and the university uses an interest rate of 9 percent to evaluate gifts of this type?

$$PV_0 = \$2,000,000(PVIF_{9\%,8})$$

$$= \$2,000,000(0.50187)$$

$$= \$1,003,740$$

Your university would be indifferent between receiving $1,003,740 today or $2 million in eight years.

Solving for the Interest or Growth Rate

PVIF can also be used to solve for interest rates. For example, suppose you wish to borrow $5,000 today from an associate. The associate is willing to loan you the money if you promise to pay back $6,802 four years from today. The compound interest rate your associate is charging can be determined as follows:

$$PV_0 = \$6,802(PVIF_{r,4})$$

$$\$5,000 = \$6,802(PVIF_{r,4})$$

$$PVIF_{r,4} = \frac{\$5,000}{\$6,802}$$

$$= 0.735$$

Reading across the Period 04 row in Table A.3, 0.735 (rounded to three places for simplicity) is found in the 8 percent column. Thus, the effective interest rate on the loan is 8 percent per year, compounded annually.

Example

Calculation of Earnings Growth Rates for Hanamaker Paper

Another common application of the use of *PVIF* factors from Table A.3 is the calculation of the compound rate of growth of an earnings or dividend stream. For example, Hanamaker Paper Company had earnings per share of $2.56 in 2010. Security analysts have forecasted 2015 earnings per share to be $6.37. What is the expected compound annual rate of growth in Hanamaker Paper Company's earnings per share? We can use the *PVIF* factors from Table A.3 to solve this problem as follows:

$$\$2.56 = \$6.37(PVIF_{r,5})$$

$$PVIF_{r,5} = 0.40188$$

Looking across the Period 05 row in Table A.3 we find a *PVIF* equal to 0.40188 under the 20 percent column. Thus, the compound annual growth rate of earnings for Hanamaker Paper Company is 20 percent. (Interpolation can be used for *PVIF* values between the values found in the tables. In practice, financial calculators are normally used for these types of calculations.)

PRESENT VALUE OF A SERIES OF EQUAL PAYMENTS (ANNUITY)

The present value of a series of *equal* $1 payments to be received at the end of each of the next *n* years (an *annuity*), discounted at a rate of *r* percent, is

$$PV_0 = \frac{1}{(1+r)^1} + \frac{1}{(1+r)^2} + \cdots + \frac{1}{(1+r)^n}$$

$$PV_0 = \sum_{t=1}^{n} \frac{1}{(1+r)^t} \qquad [A.2]$$

	RETURN RECEIVED AT	AMOUNT WITHDRAWN AT	VALUE OF INVESTMENT AT	
YEAR	**END OF YEAR ($)**	**END OF YEAR ($)**	**END OF YEAR ($)**	
0 (present)	—	—	3.0374	← Initial amount invested
1	3.0374(0.12) = 0.3645	1.00	3.0374 + 0.3645 − 1.00 = 2.4019	
2	2.4019(0.12) = 0.2882	1.00	2.4019 + 0.2882 − 1.00 = 1.6901	
3	1.6901(0.12) = 0.2028	1.00	1.6901 + 0.2028 − 1.00 = 0.8929	
4	0.8929(0.12) = 0.1071	1.00	0.8929 + 0.1071 − 1.00 = 0.0000	

TABLE A.2 PRESENT VALUE OF $1 TO BE RECEIVED AT THE END OF EACH OF THE NEXT FOUR YEARS

For example, the present value of $1 to be received at the end of each of the next four years, discounted at 12 percent, is

$$PV_0 = \sum_{t=1}^{4} \frac{1}{(1+.12)^t}$$

$$= \frac{1}{(1+.12)^1} + \frac{1}{(1+.12)^2} + \frac{1}{(1+.12)^3} + \frac{1}{(1+.12)^4}$$

$$= 0.89286 + 0.79719 + 0.71178 + 0.63552 = \$3.0374$$

As shown in Table A.2, investing $3.0374 today at 12 percent will return exactly $1 at the end of each of the next four years, with nothing remaining in the account at the end of the fourth year. Again, rather than perform the present-value calculations (Equation A.2), we can use a table to look up the values we need. Table A.4 at the end of this Appendix contains the present values at various interest rates of $1 to be received at the end of each year for various periods of time. The values in Table A.4 are called present value interest factors for annuities, or $PVIFA_{r,n}$, where r is the interest rate per period and n is the number of periods (normally years).

Using the $PVIFA$ factors from Table A.4, the present value of an annuity ($PVAN_0$) can be computed as

$$PVAN_0 = PMT(PVIFA_{r,n}) \qquad [A.3]$$

where PMT = the annuity amount to be received each period.

Example

Present Value of an Annuity

You have recently purchased the winning ticket in the Florida lottery and have won $30 million, to be paid in equal $3 million increments ($PMT$) at the end of each of the next 10 years. What are your winnings worth to you today using an interest rate of 8 percent? The $PVIFA$ factors from Table A.4 can be used to solve this problem as follows:

$$PVAN_0 = \$3,000,000(PVIFA_{8\%,10})$$

$$= \$3,000,000(6.7101)$$

$$= \$20,130,300$$

Thus, your $30 million winnings are worth only $20,130,300 to you today.

Solving for the Interest Rate

PVIFA factors also can be used to solve for the rate of return expected from an investment. This rate of return is often referred to as the *internal rate of return* from an investment. Suppose the Big Spring Tool Company purchases a machine for $100,000. This machine is expected to generate annual cash flows of $23,740 to the firm over the next five years. What is the expected rate of return from this investment?

Using Equation A.3, we can determine the expected rate of return in this example as follows:

$$PVAN_0 = PMT(PVIF_{r,5})$$

$$\$100,000 = \$23,740(PVIFA_{r,5})$$

$$PVIF_{r,5} = 4.2123$$

From the Period 05 row in Table A.4, we see that a *PVIFA* of 4.2123 occurs in the 6 percent column. Hence, this investment offers a 6 percent expected (internal) rate of return.

PRESENT VALUE OF A SERIES OF UNEQUAL PAYMENTS

The present value of a series of *unequal* payments (PMT_t, $t = 1,..., n$) to be received at the end of each of the next n years, discounted at a rate of r percent, is

$$PV_0 = \sum_{t=1}^{n} \frac{PMT_t}{(1+r)^t}$$
$$= \sum_{t=1}^{n} PMT_t(PVIF_{r,t}) \qquad [A.4]$$

The $PVIF_{r,t}$ values are the interest factors from Table A.3. Thus, the present value of a series of unequal payments is equal to the sum of the present value of the individual payments.

Example

Project Evaluation for Intel

Intel Corporation is evaluating an investment in a new chip-manufacturing facility. The facility is expected to have a useful life of five years and yield the following cash flow stream after the initial investment outlay:

END OF YEAR *t*	CASH FLOW *PMT_t*
1	+ $1,000,000
2	+ 1,500,000
3	− 500,000
4	+ 2,000,000
5	+ 1,000,000

The negative cash flow in Year 3 arises because of the expected need to install pollution-control equipment during that year. The present value of this series of

(continued)

unequal payments can be computed using *PVIF* factors from Table A.3 and assuming a 10 percent interest (required) rate on the investment:

$$PV = \$1,000,000(PVIF_{10\%,1}) + \$1,500,000(PVIF_{10\%,2})$$
$$-\$500,000(PVIF_{10\%,3}) + \$2,000,000(PVIF_{10\%,4})$$
$$+\$1,000,000(PVIF_{10\%,5})$$
$$= \$1,000,000(0.90909) + \$1,500,000(0.82645)$$
$$-\$500,000(0.75131) + \$2,000,000(0.68301)$$
$$+\$1,000,000(0.62092)$$
$$= \$3,760,050$$

The present value of these cash flows ($3,760,050) should be compared to the required initial cash outlay to determine whether to invest in the new manufacturing facility.

TABLE A.3   PRESENT VALUE OF $1 (*PVIF*)

PERIOD	1%	2%	3%	4%	5%	6%	7%	8%	9%	10%	PERIOD
01	.99010	.98039	.97007	.96154	.95233	.94340	.93458	.92593	.91743	.90909	01
02	.98030	.96117	.94260	.92456	.90703	.89000	.87344	.85734	.84168	.82645	02
03	.97059	.94232	.91514	.88900	.86384	.83962	.81639	.79383	.77228	.75131	03
04	.96098	.92385	.88849	.85480	.82270	.79209	.76290	.73503	.70883	.68301	04
05	.95147	.90573	.86261	.82193	.78353	.74726	.71299	.68058	.64993	.62092	05
06	.94204	.88797	.83748	.79031	.74622	.70496	.66634	.63017	.59627	.56447	06
07	.93272	.87056	.81309	.75992	.71063	.66506	.62275	.58349	.54705	.51316	07
08	.92348	.85349	.78941	.73069	.67684	.62741	.58201	.54027	.50187	.46651	08
09	.91434	.83675	.76642	.70259	.64461	.59190	.54393	.50025	.46043	.42410	09
10	.90529	.82035	.74409	.67556	.61391	.55839	.50835	.46319	.42241	.38554	10
11	.89632	.80426	.72242	.64958	.58468	.52679	.47509	.42888	.38753	.35049	11
12	.88745	.78849	.70138	.62460	.55684	.49697	.44401	.39711	.35553	.31683	12
13	.87866	.77303	.68095	.60057	.53032	.46884	.41496	.36770	.32618	.28966	13
14	.86996	.75787	.66112	.57747	.50507	.44230	.38782	.34046	.29925	.26333	14
15	.86135	.74301	.64186	.55526	.48102	.41726	.36245	.31524	.27454	.23939	15
16	.85282	.72845	.62317	.53391	.45811	.39365	.33873	.29189	.25187	.21763	16
17	.84436	.71416	.60502	.51337	.43630	.37136	.31657	.27027	.23107	.19784	17
18	.83602	.70016	.58739	.49363	.41552	.35034	.29586	.25025	.21199	.17986	18
19	.82774	.68643	.57029	.47464	.39573	.33051	.27651	.23171	.19449	.16354	19
20	.81954	.67297	.55367	.45639	.37689	.31180	.25842	.21455	.17843	.14864	20
21	.81143	.65978	.53755	.44883	.35894	.29415	.24151	.19866	.16370	.13513	21
22	.80340	.64684	.52189	.42195	.34185	.27750	.22571	.18394	.15018	.12285	22
23	.79544	.63414	.50669	.40573	.32557	.26180	.21095	.17031	.13778	.11168	23
24	.78757	.62172	.49193	.39012	.31007	.24698	.19715	.15770	.12640	.10153	24
25	.77977	.60953	.47760	.37512	.29530	.23300	.18425	.14602	.11597	.09230	25

TABLE A.3   PRESENT VALUE OF $1 (*PVIF*) (CONTINUED)

PERIOD	11%	12%	13%	14%	15%	16%	17%	18%	19%	20%	PERIOD
01	.90090	.89286	.88496	.87719	.86957	.86207	.85470	.84746	.84043	.83333	01
02	.81162	.79719	.78315	.76947	.75614	.74316	.73051	.71818	.70616	.69444	02
03	.73119	.71178	.69305	.67497	.65752	.64066	.62437	.60863	.59342	.57870	03
04	.65873	.63552	.61332	.59208	.57175	.55229	.53365	.51579	.49867	.48225	04
05	.59345	.56743	.54276	.51937	.49718	.47611	.45611	.43711	.41905	.40188	05
06	.53464	.50663	.48032	.45559	.43233	.41044	.38984	.37043	.35214	.33490	06
07	.48166	.45235	.42506	.39964	.37594	.35383	.33320	.31392	.29592	.27908	07
08	.43393	.40388	.37616	.35056	.32690	.30503	.28478	.26604	.24867	.23257	08
09	.39092	.36061	.33288	.30751	.28426	.26295	.24340	.22546	.20897	.19381	09
10	.35218	.32197	.29459	.26974	.24718	.22668	.20804	.19106	.17560	.16151	10
11	.31728	.28748	.26070	.23662	.21494	.19542	.17781	.16192	.14756	.13459	11
12	.28584	.25667	.23071	.20756	.18691	.16846	.15197	.13722	.12400	.11216	12
13	.25751	.22917	.20416	.18207	.16253	.14523	.12989	.11629	.10420	.09346	13
14	.23199	.20462	.18068	.15971	.14133	.12520	.11102	.09855	.08757	.07789	14
15	.20900	.18270	.15989	.14010	.12289	.10793	.09489	.08352	.07359	.06491	15
16	.18829	.16312	.14150	.12289	.10686	.09304	.08110	.07073	.06184	.05409	16
17	.16963	.14564	.12522	.10780	.09293	.08021	.06932	.05998	.05196	.04507	17
18	.15282	.13004	.11081	.09456	.08080	.06914	.05925	.05083	.04367	.03756	18
19	.13768	.11611	.09806	.08295	.07026	.05961	.05064	.04308	.03669	.03130	19
20	.12403	.10367	.08678	.07276	.06110	.05139	.04328	.03651	.03084	.02608	20
21	.11174	.09256	.07680	.06383	.05313	.04430	.03699	.03094	.02591	.02174	21
22	.10067	.08264	.06796	.05599	.04620	.03819	.03162	.02622	.02178	.01811	22
23	.09069	.07379	.06014	.04911	.04017	.03292	.02702	.02222	.01830	.01509	23
24	.08170	.06588	.05322	.04308	.03493	.02838	.02310	.01883	.01538	.01258	24
25	.07361	.05882	.04710	.03779	.03038	.02447	.01974	.01596	.01292	.01048	25

TABLE A.4 PRESENT VALUE OF AN ANNUITY OF $1 (*PVIFA*)

PERIOD	1%	2%	3%	4%	5%	6%	7%	8%	9%	10%	PERIOD
01	.9901	.9804	.9709	.9615	.9524	.9434	.9346	.9259	.9174	.9091	01
02	1.9704	1.9416	1.9135	1.8861	1.8594	1.8334	1.8080	1.7833	1.7591	1.7355	02
03	2.9410	2.8839	2.8286	2.7751	2.7233	2.6730	2.6243	2.5771	2.5313	2.4868	03
04	3.9020	3.8077	3.7171	3.6299	3.5459	3.4651	3.3872	3.3121	3.2397	3.1699	04
05	4.8535	4.7134	4.5797	4.4518	4.3295	4.2123	4.1002	3.9927	3.8896	3.7908	05
06	5.7955	5.6014	5.4172	5.2421	5.0757	4.9173	4.7665	4.6229	4.4859	4.3553	06
07	6.7282	6.4720	6.2302	6.0020	5.7863	5.5824	5.3893	5.2064	5.0329	4.8684	07
08	7.6517	7.3254	7.0196	6.7327	6.4632	6.2093	5.9713	5.7466	5.5348	5.3349	08
09	8.5661	8.1622	7.7861	7.4353	7.1078	6.8017	6.5152	6.2469	5.9852	5.7590	09
10	9.4714	8.9825	8.7302	8.1109	7.7217	7.3601	7.0236	6.7101	6.4176	6.1446	10
11	10.3677	9.7868	9.2526	8.7604	8.3064	7.8868	7.4987	7.1389	6.8052	6.4951	11
12	11.2552	10.5753	9.9589	9.3850	8.8632	8.3838	7.9427	7.5361	7.1601	6.8137	12
13	12.1338	11.3483	10.6349	9.9856	9.3935	8.8527	8.3576	7.9038	7.4869	7.1034	13
14	13.0088	12.1062	11.2960	10.5631	9.8986	9.2950	8.7454	8.2442	7.7860	7.3667	14
15	13.8651	12.8492	11.9379	11.1183	10.3796	9.7122	9.1079	8.5595	8.0607	7.6061	15
16	14.7180	13.5777	12.5610	11.6522	10.8377	10.1059	9.4466	8.8514	8.3126	7.8237	16
17	15.5624	14.2918	13.1660	12.1656	11.2740	10.4772	9.7632	9.1216	8.5435	8.0215	17
18	16.3984	14.9920	13.7534	12.6592	11.6895	10.8276	10.0591	9.3719	8.7556	8.2014	18
19	17.2201	15.2684	14.3237	13.1339	12.0853	11.1581	10.3356	9.6036	8.9501	8.3649	19
20	18.0457	16.3514	14.8774	13.5903	12.4622	11.4699	10.5940	9.8181	9.1285	8.5136	20
21	18.8571	17.0111	15.4149	14.0291	12.8211	11.7640	10.8355	10.0168	9.2922	8.6487	21
22	19.6605	17.6581	15.9368	14.4511	13.1630	12.0416	11.0612	10.2007	9.4424	8.7715	22
23	20.4559	18.2921	16.4435	14.8568	13.4885	12.3033	11.2722	10.3710	9.5802	8.8832	23
24	21.2435	18.9139	16.9355	15.2469	13.7986	12.5503	11.4693	10.5287	9.7066	8.9847	24
25	22.0233	19.5234	17.4181	15.6220	14.9039	12.7833	11.6536	10.6748	9.8226	9.0770	25

TABLE A.4	PRESENT VALUE OF AN ANNUITY OF $1 (*PVIFA*) (CONTINUED)										
PERIOD	**11%**	**12%**	**13%**	**14%**	**15%**	**16%**	**17%**	**18%**	**19%**	**20%**	**PERIOD**
01	.9009	.8929	.8850	.8772	.8696	.8621	.8547	.8475	.8403	.8333	01
02	1.7125	1.6901	1.6681	1.6467	1.6257	1.6052	1.5852	1.5656	1.5465	1.5278	02
03	2.4437	2.4018	2.3612	2.3216	2.2832	2.2459	2.2096	2.1743	2.1399	2.1065	03
04	3.1024	3.0373	2.9745	2.9137	2.8550	2.7982	2.7432	2.6901	2.6386	2.5887	04
05	3.6959	3.6048	3.5172	3.4331	3.3522	3.2743	3.1993	3.1272	3.0576	2.9906	05
06	4.2305	4.1114	3.9976	3.8887	3.7845	3.6847	3.5892	3.4976	3.4098	3.3255	06
07	4.7122	4.5638	4.4226	4.2883	4.1604	4.0386	3.9224	3.8115	3.7057	3.6046	07
08	5.1461	4.9676	4.7988	4.6389	4.4873	4.3436	4.2072	4.0776	3.9544	3.8372	08
09	5.5370	5.3282	5.1317	4.9464	4.7716	4.6065	4.4506	4.3030	4.1633	4.0310	09
10	5.8892	5.6502	5.4262	5.2161	5.0188	4.8332	4.6586	4.4941	4.3389	4.1925	10
11	6.2065	5.9377	5.6869	5.4527	5.2337	5.0286	4.8364	4.6560	4.4865	4.3271	11
12	6.4924	6.1944	5.9176	5.6603	5.4206	5.1971	4.9884	4.7932	4.6105	4.4392	12
13	6.7499	6.4235	6.1218	5.8424	5.5831	5.3423	5.1183	4.9095	4.7147	4.5327	13
14	6.9819	6.6282	6.3025	6.0021	5.7245	5.4675	5.2293	5.0081	4.8023	4.6106	14
15	7.1909	6.8109	6.4624	6.1422	5.8474	5.5755	5.3242	5.0916	4.8759	4.6755	15
16	7.3792	6.9740	6.6039	6.2651	5.9542	5.6685	5.4053	5.1624	4.9377	4.7296	16
17	7.5488	7.1196	6.7291	6.3729	6.0472	5.7487	5.4746	5.2223	4.9897	4.7746	17
18	7.7016	7.2497	6.8389	6.4674	6.1280	5.8178	5.5339	5.2732	5.0333	4.8122	18
19	7.8393	7.3650	6.9380	6.5504	6.1982	5.8775	5.5845	5.3176	5.0700	4.8435	19
20	7.9633	7.4694	7.0248	6.6231	6.2593	5.9288	5.6278	5.3527	5.1009	4.8696	20
21	8.0751	7.5620	7.1016	6.6870	6.3125	5.9731	5.6648	5.3837	5.1268	4.8913	21
22	8.1757	7.6446	7.1695	6.7429	6.3587	6.0113	5.6964	5.4099	5.1486	4.9094	22
23	8.2664	7.7184	7.2297	6.7921	6.3988	6.0442	5.7234	5.4321	5.1668	4.9245	23
24	8.3481	7.7843	7.2829	6.8351	6.4338	6.0726	5.7465	5.4509	5.1822	4.9371	24
25	8.4217	7.8431	7.3300	6.8729	6.4641	6.0971	5.7662	5.4669	5.1951	4.9476	25

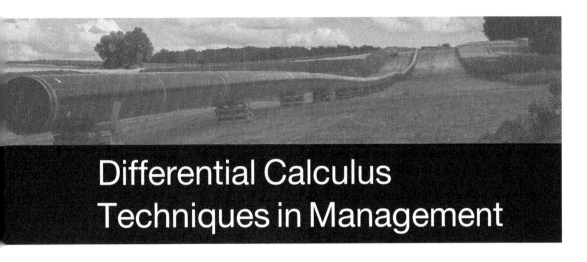

Differential Calculus Techniques in Management

Decision analysis involves determining the action that best achieves a desired goal or objective. It means finding the action that optimizes (i.e., maximizes or minimizes) the value of an objective function. For example, we may be interested in determining the output level that maximizes profits. In a production problem, the goal may be to find the combination of inputs that minimizes the cost of producing a desired level of output. In a capital budgeting problem, the objective may be to select those projects that maximize the net present value of the investments chosen. Many techniques are available for solving optimization problems such as these. This appendix focuses on the use of differential calculus.

RELATIONSHIP BETWEEN MARGINAL ANALYSIS AND DIFFERENTIAL CALCULUS

In Chapter 2, marginal analysis was introduced as one of the fundamental concepts of microeconomic decision making. In the marginal analysis framework, resource allocation decisions are made by comparing the marginal benefits of a proposed change in the level of an activity with the marginal costs of that change. The proposed change should be made as long as the marginal benefits exceed the marginal costs. By following this basic rule, resources can be allocated efficiently, and profits or shareholder wealth can be maximized.

Initially, let us assume that the objective we are seeking to optimize, Y, can be expressed algebraically as a function of *one* decision variable, X.

$$Y = f(X) \qquad [B.1]$$

Recall that marginal profit is defined as the change in profit resulting from a one-unit change in output. In general, the marginal value of any variable Y, which is a function of another variable X, is defined as the change in the value of Y resulting from a one-unit change in X. The marginal value of Y, M_y, can be calculated from the change in Y, ΔY, that occurs as the result of a given change in X, ΔX:

$$M_y = \frac{\Delta Y}{\Delta X} \qquad [B.2]$$

When calculated with this expression, different estimates for the amount ΔY may be obtained, depending on the size of the incremental change in X that we use in the computation. The true marginal value[1] of a function is obtained from Equation B.2 when ΔX is made as small as possible. If ΔX can be thought of as a continuous (rather than a discrete)

---

[1]For example, if X is a continuous variable measured in feet, pounds, and so on, then ΔX can, in theory, take on fractional values such as 0.5, 0.10, 0.05, 0.001, or 0.0001 feet or pounds. When X is a continuous variable, ΔX can be made as small as desired.

MANAGERIAL CHALLENGE
A Skeleton in the Stealth Bomber's Closet[2]

In 1990, the U.S. Air Force publicly unveiled its newest long-range strategic bomber, the B-2 or "Stealth" bomber. This plane is characterized by a unique flying-wing design engineered to evade detection by enemy radar. The plane has been controversial because of its high cost. However, a lesser known controversy relates to its fundamental design.

The flying-wing design originated from a secret study that concluded that a plane's maximum range could be achieved if virtually all the volume were contained in the wing. A complex mathematical appendix was attached to the study.

However, Professor of Engineering Joseph Foa discovered that a fundamental error had been made in the initial report. It turned out that the original researchers had taken the first derivative of a complex equation and found that it had two solutions. The original

researchers mistakenly concluded that the all-wing design was the one that maximized range, when, in fact, it *minimized* range.

In this appendix we introduce some of the same optimization techniques applied to the Stealth bomber project. We develop tools designed to maximize profits or minimize costs. Fortunately, the mathematical functions we deal with in this chapter and throughout the book are much simpler than those that confronted the original "flying-wing" engineers. We introduce techniques that can be used to check whether a function, such as profits or costs, is being minimized or maximized at a particular level of output.

[2]Based on W. Biddle, "Skeleton Alleged in the Stealth Bomber's Closet," *Science* (May 12, 1989), pp. 650–651

derivative A measure of the marginal effect of a change in one variable on the value of a function. Graphically, it represents the slope of the function at a given point.

variable that can take on fractional values, then in calculating M_y by using Equation B.2, we can let ΔX approach zero.

In concept, differential calculus takes this approach. The **derivative**, or, more precisely, *first derivative*,[3] dY/dX, of a function is defined as the *limit* of the ratio $\Delta Y/\Delta X$ as ΔX approaches zero; that is,

$$\frac{dY}{dX} = \lim_{\Delta X \to 0} \frac{\Delta Y}{\Delta X}$$ [B.3]

Graphically, the first derivative of a function represents the *slope* of the curve at a given point on the curve. The definition of a derivative as the limit of the change in Y (i.e., ΔY) as ΔX approaches zero is illustrated in Figure B.1(a).

Suppose we are interested in the derivative of the $Y = f(X)$ function at the point X_0. The derivative dY/dX measures the slope of the tangent line *ECD*. An estimate of this slope, albeit a poor estimate, can be obtained by calculating the marginal value of Y over the interval X_0 to X_2. Using Equation B.2, a value of

$$M_y' = \frac{\Delta Y}{\Delta X} = \frac{Y_2 - Y_0}{X_2 - X_0}$$

is obtained for the slope of the *CA* line. Now let us calculate the marginal value of Y using a smaller interval, for example, X_0 to X_1. The slope of the *CB* line, which is equal to

$$M_y'' = \frac{\Delta Y}{\Delta X} = \frac{Y_1 - Y_0}{X_1 - X_0}$$

gives a much better estimate of the true marginal value as represented by the slope of the *ECD* tangent line. Thus we see that the smaller the ΔX value, the better the estimate of

[3]It is also possible to compute second, third, fourth, and so on, derivatives. Second derivatives are discussed later in this appendix.

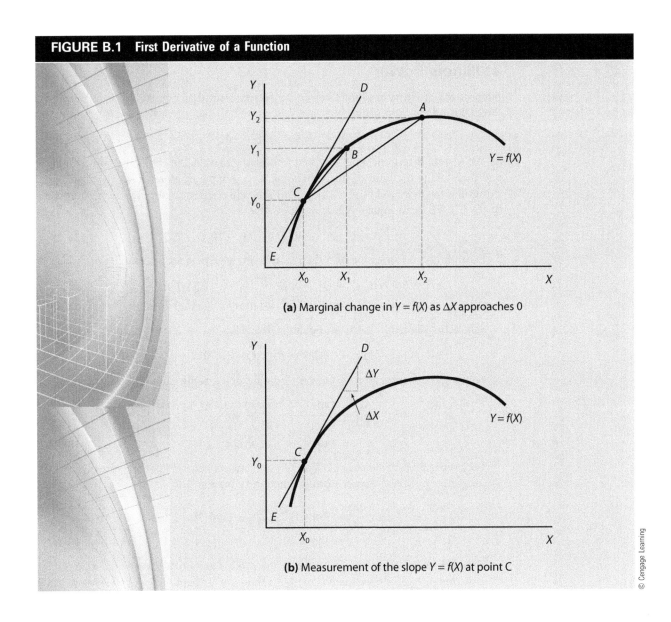

FIGURE B.1   First Derivative of a Function

(a) Marginal change in $Y = f(X)$ as ΔX approaches 0

(b) Measurement of the slope $Y = f(X)$ at point C

© Cengage Learning

the slope of the curve. Letting ΔX approach zero allows us to find the slope of the $Y = f(X)$ curve at point B. As shown in Figure B.1(b), the slope of the ECD tangent line (and the $Y = f(X)$ function at point C) is measured by the change in Y, or rise, ΔY, divided by the change in X, or run, ΔX.

Process of Differentiation

The process of differentiation—that is, finding the derivative of a function—involves determining the limiting value of the ratio $\Delta Y/\Delta X$ as ΔX approaches zero. Before offering some general rules for finding the derivative of a function, we illustrate with an example the algebraic process used to obtain the derivative without the aid of these general rules. The specific rules that simplify this process are presented in the following section.

Example

Process of Differentiation: Profit Maximization at Illinois Power

Suppose the profit, π, of Illinois Power can be represented as a function of the output level Q using the expression

$$\pi = -40 + 140Q - 10Q^2 \qquad [B.4]$$

We wish to determine $d\pi/dQ$ by first finding the marginal profit expression $\Delta\pi/\Delta Q$ and then taking the limit of this expression as ΔQ approaches zero. Let us begin by expressing the new level of profit $(\pi + \Delta\pi)$ that will result from an increase in output to $(Q + \Delta Q)$. From Equation B.4, we know that

$$\pi + \Delta\pi = -40 + 140(Q + \Delta Q) - 10(Q + \Delta Q)^2 \qquad [B.5]$$

Expanding this expression and then simplifying algebraic terms, we obtain

$$\pi + \Delta\pi = -40 + 140Q + 140\Delta Q - 10[Q^2 + 2Q\Delta Q + (\Delta Q)^2]$$
$$= -40 + 140Q - 10Q^2 + 140\Delta Q - 20Q\Delta Q - 10(\Delta Q)^2 \qquad [B.6]$$

Subtracting Equation B.4 from Equation B.6 yields

$$\Delta\pi = 140\Delta Q - 20Q\Delta Q - 10(\Delta Q)^2 \qquad [B.7]$$

Forming the marginal profit ratio $\Delta\pi/\Delta Q$ and doing some canceling, we get

$$\frac{\Delta\pi}{\Delta Q} = \frac{140\Delta Q - 20Q\Delta Q - 10(\Delta Q)^2}{\Delta Q}$$
$$= 140 - 20Q - 10\Delta Q \qquad [B.8]$$

Taking the limit of Equation B.8 as ΔQ approaches zero yields the expression for the derivative of Illinois Power's profit function (Equation B.4).

$$\frac{d\pi}{dQ} = \lim_{\Delta Q \to 0}[140 - 20Q - 10\Delta Q]$$
$$= 140 - 20Q \qquad [B.9]$$

If we are interested in the derivative of the profit function at a particular value of Q, Equation B.9 can be evaluated for this value. For example, suppose we want to know the marginal profit, or slope of the profit function, at $Q = 3$ units. Substituting $Q = 3$ in Equation B.9 yields

$$\text{Marginal profit} = \frac{d\pi}{dQ} = 140 - 20(3) = \$80 \text{ per unit}$$

Rules of Differentiation

Fortunately, we do not need to go through this lengthy process every time we want the derivative of a function. A series of general rules, derived in a manner similar to the process just described, exists for differentiating various types of functions.

Constant Functions   A constant function can be expressed as

$$Y = a \qquad [B.10]$$

where a is a constant (i.e., Y is independent of X). The derivative of a constant function is equal to zero:

$$\frac{dY}{dX} = 0 \qquad [B.11]$$

For example, consider the constant function

$$Y = 4$$

which is graphed in Figure B.2(a). Recall that the first derivative of a function (dY/dX) measures the slope of the function. Because this constant function is a horizontal straight line with zero slope, its derivative (dY/dX) is therefore equal to zero.

Power Functions   A power function takes the form of

$$Y = aX^b \qquad [B.12]$$

where a and b are constants. The derivative of a power function is equal to

$$\frac{dY}{dX} = b \cdot a \cdot X^{b-1} \qquad [B.13]$$

A couple of examples are used to illustrate the application of this rule. First, consider the function

$$Y = 2X$$

which is graphed in Figure B.2(b). Note that the slope of this function is equal to 2 and is constant over the entire range of X values. Applying the power function rule to this example, where $a = 2$ and $b = 1$, yields

$$\frac{dY}{dX} = 1 \cdot 2 \cdot X^{1-1}$$
$$= 2X^0 = 2$$

Note that any variable raised to the zero power, for example, X^0, is equal to 1.

Next, consider the function

$$Y = X^2$$

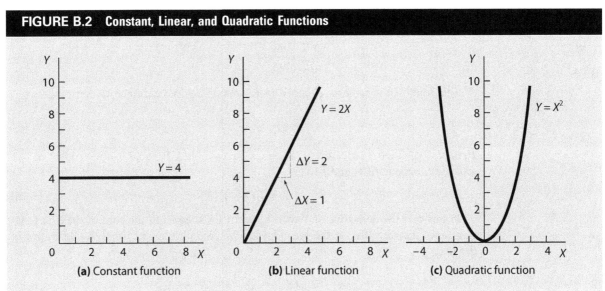

FIGURE B.2   Constant, Linear, and Quadratic Functions

(a) Constant function

(b) Linear function

(c) Quadratic function

© Cengage Learning

which is graphed in Figure B.2(c). Note that the slope of this function varies depending on the value of X. Application of the power function rule to this example yields ($a = 1$, $b = 2$):

$$\frac{dY}{dX} = 2 \cdot 1 \cdot X^{2-1}$$
$$= 2X$$

As we can see, this derivative (or slope) function is negative when $X < 0$, zero when $X = 0$, and positive when $X > 0$.

Sum of Functions Suppose a function $Y = f(X)$ represents the sum of two (or more) separate functions, $f_1(X)$, $f_2(X)$, that is,

$$Y = f_1(X) + f_2(X) \qquad [B.14]$$

The derivative of Y with respect to X is found by differentiating each of the separate functions and then adding the results:

$$\frac{dY}{dX} = \frac{df_1(X)}{dX} + \frac{df_2(X)}{dX} \qquad [B.15]$$

This result can be extended to find the derivative of the sum of any number of functions.

Rules of Differentiation: Profit Maximization at Illinois Power (continued)

As an example of the application of these rules, consider again the profit function for Illinois Power, given earlier in Equation B.4:

$$\pi = -40 + 140Q - 10Q^2$$

In this example Q represents the X variable and π represents the Y variable, that is, $\pi = f(Q)$. The function $f(Q)$ is the sum of *three* separate functions: a constant function, $f_1(Q) = -40$, and two power functions, $f_2(Q) = 140Q$ and $f_3(Q) - 10Q^2$. Therefore, applying the differentiation rules yields

$$\frac{d\pi}{dQ} = \frac{df_1(Q)}{dQ} + \frac{df_2(Q)}{dQ} + \frac{df_3(Q)}{dQ}$$
$$= 0 + 1 \cdot 140 \cdot Q^{1-1} + 2 \cdot (-10) \cdot Q^{2-1}$$
$$= 140 - 20Q$$

This result is the same as obtained in Equation B.9 by the differentiation process.

Product of Two Functions Suppose the variable Y is equal to the product of two separate functions $f_1(X)$ and $f_2(X)$:

$$Y = f_1(X) \cdot f_2(X) \qquad [B.16]$$

In this case the derivative of Y with respect to X is equal to the sum of the first function times the derivative of the second, plus the second function times the derivative of the first.

$$\frac{dY}{dX} = f_1(X) \cdot \frac{df_2(X)}{dX} + f_2(X) \cdot \frac{df_1(X)}{dX} \qquad [B.17]$$

For example, suppose we are interested in the derivative of the expression

$$Y = X^2(2X - 3)$$

Let $f_1(X) = X^2$ and $f_2(X) = (2X - 3)$. By the preceding rule (and the earlier rules for differentiating constant and power functions), we obtain

$$\frac{dY}{dX} = X^2 \cdot \frac{dY}{dX}[(2X - 3)] + (2X - 3) \cdot \frac{dY}{dX}[X^2]$$

$$= X^2 \cdot (2 - 0) + (2X - 3) \cdot (2X)$$

$$= 2X^2 + 4X^2 - 6X$$

$$= 6X^2 - 6X$$

$$= 6X(X - 1)$$

Quotient of Two Functions   Suppose the variable Y is equal to the quotient of two separate functions $f_1(X)$ and $f_2(X)$:

$$Y = \frac{f_1(X)}{f_2(X)} \qquad [B.18]$$

For such a relationship the derivative of Y with respect to X is obtained as follows:

$$\frac{dY}{dX} = \frac{f_2(X) \cdot \dfrac{df_1(X)}{dX} - f_1(X) \cdot \dfrac{df_2(X)}{dX}}{[f_2(X)]^2} \qquad [B.19]$$

As an example, consider the problem of finding the derivative of the expression

$$Y = \frac{10X^2}{5X - 1}$$

Letting $f_1(X) = 10X^2$ and $f_2(X) = 5X - 1$, we have

$$\frac{dY}{dX} = \frac{(5X - 1) \cdot 20X - 10X^2 \cdot 5}{(5X - 1)^2}$$

$$= \frac{100X^2 - 20X - 50X^2}{(5X - 1)^2}$$

$$= \frac{50X^2 - 20X}{(5X - 1)^2}$$

$$= \frac{10X(5X - 2)}{(5X - 1)^2}$$

Function of a Function (Chain Rule)   Suppose Y is a function of the variable Z, $Y = f_1(Z)$; and Z is in turn a function of the variable X, $Z = f_2(X)$. The derivative of Y with respect to X can be determined by first finding dY/dZ and dZ/dX and then multiplying the two expressions together:

$$\frac{dY}{dX} = \frac{dY}{dZ} \cdot \frac{dZ}{dX}$$

$$= \frac{df_1(Z)}{dZ} \cdot \frac{df_2(X)}{dX} \qquad [B.20]$$

TABLE B.1   SUMMARY OF RULES FOR DIFFERENTIATING FUNCTIONS

	FUNCTION	DERIVATIVE
1.	Constant Function $Y = a$	$\dfrac{dY}{dX} = 0$
2.	Power Function $Y = aX^b$	$\dfrac{dY}{dX} = b \cdot a \cdot X^{b-1}$
3.	Sum of Functions $Y = f_1(X) + f_2(X)$	$\dfrac{dY}{dX} = \dfrac{df_1(X)}{dX} + \dfrac{df_2(X)}{dX}$
4.	Product of Two Functions $Y = f_1(X) \cdot f_2(X)$	$\dfrac{dY}{dX} = f_1(X) \cdot \dfrac{df_2(X)}{dX} + f_2(X) \cdot \dfrac{df_1(X)}{dX}$
5.	Quotient of Two Functions $Y = \dfrac{f_1(X)}{f_2 X}$	$\dfrac{dY}{dX} = \dfrac{f_2(X) \cdot \dfrac{df_1(X)}{dX} - f_1(X) \cdot \dfrac{df_2(X)}{dX}}{[f_2(X)]^2}$
6.	Function of a Function $Y = f_1(Z)$, where $Z = f_2(X)$	$\dfrac{dY}{dX} = \dfrac{dY}{dZ} \cdot \dfrac{dZ}{dX}$

To illustrate the application of this rule, suppose we are interested in finding the derivative (with respect to X) of the function

$$Y = 10Z - 2Z^2 - 3$$

where Z is related to X in the following way:[4]

$$Z = 2X^2 - 1$$

First, we find (by the earlier differentiation rules)

$$\frac{dY}{dZ} = 10 - 4Z$$

$$\frac{dZ}{dX} = 4X$$

and then

$$\frac{dY}{dX} = (10 - 4Z) \cdot 4X$$

Substituting the expression for Z in terms of X into this equation yields

$$\begin{aligned}
\frac{dY}{dX} &= [10 - 4(2X^2 - 1)] \cdot 4X \\
&= (10 - 8X^2 + 4) \cdot 4X \\
&= 40X - 32X^3 + 16X \\
&= 56X - 32X^3 \\
&= 8X(7 - 4X^2)
\end{aligned}$$

These rules for differentiating functions are summarized in Table B.1.

---

[4]Alternatively, one can substitute $Z = 2X^2 - 1$ into $Y = 10Z - 2Z^2 - 3$ and differentiate Y with respect to X.

APPLICATIONS OF DIFFERENTIAL CALCULUS TO OPTIMIZATION PROBLEMS

The reason for studying the process of differentiation and the rules for differentiating functions is that these methods can be used to find optimal solutions to many kinds of maximization and minimization problems in managerial economics.

Maximization Problem

first-order condition
A test to locate one or more maximum or minimum points of an algebraic function.

As you recall from the discussion of marginal analysis, a necessary (but not sufficient) condition for finding the maximum point on a curve (e.g., maximum profits) is that the marginal value or slope of the curve at this point must be equal to zero. We can now express this condition within the framework of differential calculus. Because the derivative of a function measures the slope or marginal value at any given point, an equivalent necessary condition for finding the maximum value of a function $Y = f(X)$ is that the derivative dY/dX at this point must be equal to zero. This requirement is known as the **first-order condition** for locating one or more maximum or minimum points of an algebraic function.

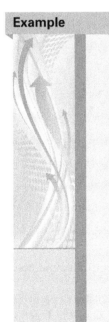

Example

First-Order Condition: Profit Maximization at Illinois Power (continued)

Using the profit function (Equation B.4)

$$\pi = -40 + 140Q - 10Q^2$$

discussed earlier, we can illustrate how to find the profit-maximizing output level Q by means of this condition. Setting the first derivative of this function (which was computed previously) to zero, we obtain

$$\frac{d\pi}{dQ} = 140 - 20Q$$

$$0 = 140 - 20Q$$

Solving this equation for Q yields $Q^* = 7$ units as the profit-maximizing output level. The profit and first derivative functions and optimal solution are shown in Figure B.3. As we can see, profits are maximized at the point where the function is neither increasing nor decreasing, in other words, where the slope (or first derivative) is equal to zero.

Second Derivatives and the Second-Order Condition

second-order condition A test to determine whether a point that has been determined from the first-order condition is either a maximum point or a minimum point of the algebraic function.

Setting the derivative of a function equal to zero and solving the resulting equation for the value of the decision variable does not guarantee that the point will be obtained at which the function takes on its maximum value. (Recall the Stealth bomber example at the start of this appendix.) The slope of a U-shaped function will also be equal to zero at its low point and the function will take on its *minimum* value at the given point. In other words, setting the derivative to zero is only a *necessary* condition for finding the maximum value of a function; it is not a *sufficient* condition. Another condition, known as the **second-order condition**, is required to determine whether a point that has been

FIGURE B.3 Profit and First Derivative Functions

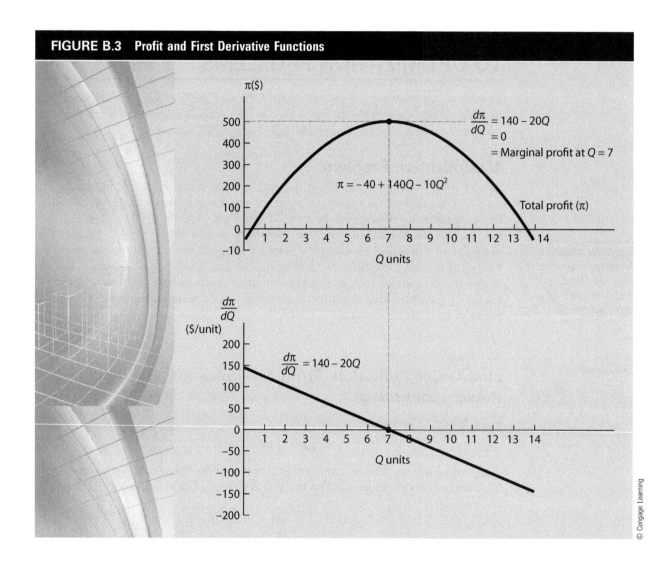

determined from the first-order condition is either a maximum point or minimum point of the algebraic function.

This situation is illustrated in Figure B.4. At both points A and B the slope of the function (first derivative, dY/dX) is zero; however, only at point B does the function take on its maximum value. We note in Figure B.4 that the marginal value (slope) is continually *decreasing* in the neighborhood of the maximum value (point B) of the $Y = f(X)$ function. First the slope is positive up to the point where $dY/dX = 0$, and thereafter the slope becomes negative. Thus we must determine whether the slope's marginal value (slope of the slope) is declining. To test whether the marginal value is decreasing, take the derivative of the marginal value and determine whether it is negative at the given point on the function. In effect, we need to find the derivative of the derivative—that is, the *second derivative* of the function—and then test whether it is less than zero. Formally, the second derivative of the function $Y = f(X)$ is written as d^2Y/dX^2 and is found by applying the previously described differentiation rules to the first derivative. A *maximum point is obtained if the second derivative is negative, that is, $d^2Y/dX^2 < 0$.*

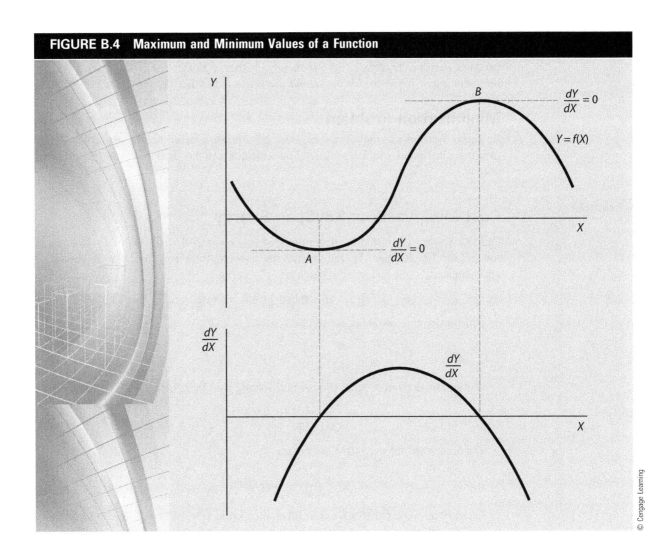

FIGURE B.4   Maximum and Minimum Values of a Function

Example

Second-Order Condition: Profit Maximization at Illinois Power (continued)

In the profit-maximization example, the second derivative is obtained from the first derivative as follows:

$$\frac{d\pi}{dQ} = 140 - 20Q$$

$$\frac{d^2\pi}{dQ^2} = 0 + 1 \cdot (-20) \cdot Q^{1-1}$$

$$= -20$$

Because $d^2\pi/dQ^2 < 0$, we know that a maximum-profit point has been obtained.

An opposite condition holds for obtaining the point at which the function takes on a minimum value. Note again in Figure B.4 that the marginal value (slope) is continually *increasing* in the neighborhood of the minimum value (point *A*) of the $Y = (X)$ function. First the slope is negative up to the point where $dY/dX = 0$, and thereafter the slope becomes positive. Therefore, we test to see whether $d^2Y/dX^2 > 0$ at the given point. *A minimum point is obtained if the second derivative is positive, that is, $d^2Y/dX^2 > 0$.*

Minimization Problem

In some decision-making situations, cost minimization may be the objective. As in profit-maximization problems, differential calculus can be used to locate the optimal points.

Example

Cost Minimization: KeySpan Energy

Suppose we are interested in determining the output level that minimizes average total costs for KeySpan Energy, where the average total cost function might be approximated by the following relationship (*Q* represents output):

$$C = 15 - 0.040Q + 0.000080Q^2$$

Differentiating *C* with respect to *Q* gives

$$\frac{dC}{dQ} = -0.040 + 0.000160Q$$

Setting this derivative equal to zero and solving for *Q* yields

$$0 = 0.040 + 0.000160Q$$
$$Q^* = 250$$

Taking the second derivative, we obtain

$$\frac{d^2C}{dQ^2} = +0.000160$$

Because the second derivative is positive, the output level of $Q = 250$ is indeed the value that minimizes average total costs.

Summarizing, we see that *two* conditions are required for locating a maximum or minimum value of a function using differential calculus. The *first-order* condition determines the point(s) at which the first derivative dY/dX is equal to zero. After we obtain one or more points, a *second-order* condition is used to determine whether the function takes on a maximum or minimum value at the given point(s). The second derivative d^2Y/dX^2 indicates whether a given point is a maximum ($d^2Y/dX^2 < 0$) or a minimum ($d^2Y/dX^2 > 0$) value of the function.

PARTIAL DIFFERENTIATION AND MULTIVARIATE OPTIMIZATION

Thus far in this appendix, the analysis has been limited to a criterion variable *Y* that can be expressed as a function of *one* decision variable *X*. However, many commonly used economic relationships contain two or more decision variables. For example, a *demand function* relates sales of a product or service to such variables as price, advertising, promotion expenses, price of substitutes, and income.

Partial Derivatives

Consider a criterion variable Y that is a function of two decision variables X_1 and X_2:[5]

$$Y = f(X_1, X_2) \qquad [B.21]$$

partial derivative
A measure of the marginal effect of a change in one variable on the value of a multivariate function while holding constant all other variables.

Let us now examine the change in Y that results from a given change in either X_1 or X_2. To isolate the marginal effect on Y from a given change in X_1 (i.e., $\Delta Y/\Delta X_1$), we must hold X_2 constant. Similarly, if we wish to isolate the marginal effect on Y from a given change in X_2 (i.e., $\Delta Y/\Delta X_2$), the variable X_1 must be held constant. A measure of the marginal effect of a change in any one variable on the change in Y, holding all other variables in the relationship constant, is obtained from the **partial derivative** of the function. The partial derivative of Y with respect to X_1 is written as $\partial Y/\partial X_1$ and is found by applying the previously described differentiation rules to the $Y = f(X_1, X_2)$ function, where the variable X_2 is treated as a constant. Similarly, the partial derivative of Y with respect to X_2 is written as $\partial Y/\partial X_2$ and is found by applying the differentiation rules to the function, where the variable X_1 is treated as a constant.

Example

Partial Derivatives: Indiana Petroleum Company

To illustrate the procedure for obtaining partial derivatives, let us consider the following relationship in which the profit variable, π, is a function of the output level of two products (heating oil and gasoline) Q_1 and Q_2:

$$\pi = -60 + 140Q_1 + 100Q_2 - 10Q_1^2 - 8Q_2^2 - 6Q_1Q_2 \qquad [B.22]$$

Treating Q_2 as a constant, the partial derivative of π with respect to Q_1 is obtained:

$$\frac{\partial \pi}{\partial Q_1} = 0 + 140 + 0 + 2 \cdot (-10) \cdot Q_1 - 0 - 6Q_2$$

$$= 140 - 20Q_1 - 6Q_2 \qquad [B.23]$$

Similarly, with Q_1 treated as a constant, the partial derivative of π with respect to Q_2 is equal to

$$\frac{\partial \pi}{\partial Q_1} = 0 + 0 + 100 - 0 + 2 \cdot (-8) \cdot Q_2 - 6Q_1$$

$$= 100 - 16Q_2 - 6Q_1 \qquad [B.24]$$

---

[5]The following analysis is not limited to two decision variables. Relationships containing any number of variables can be analyzed within this framework.

Example

Partial Derivatives: Demand Function for Shield Toothpaste

Partial derivatives can be useful in demand analysis, especially in quantitative studies. Suppose the demand for Shield toothpaste is estimated as tubes per year,

$$Q = 14.6 + 2.2P + 7.4A \qquad [B.25]$$

where Q = quantity sold, P = selling price, and A = advertising campaigns, the partial derivatives of Q with respect to P and A are

$$\frac{\partial Q}{\partial P} = -2.2 \ \text{ and } \frac{\partial Q}{\partial A} = 7.4$$

To take another example, for the multiplicative exponential demand function

$$Q = 3.0P^{-.50}A^{.25}$$

The partial derivative of Q with respect to P is

$$\begin{aligned}
\frac{\partial Q}{\partial P} &= 3.0A^{.25}(-.50P^{-.50-1}) \\
&= -1.5P^{-1.50}A^{.25}
\end{aligned}$$

Similarly, the partial derivative of Q with respect to A is

$$\begin{aligned}
\frac{\partial Q}{\partial A} &= 3.0P^{-.50}(.25A^{.25-1}) \\
&= .75P^{-.50}A^{-.75}
\end{aligned}$$

Maximization Problem

The partial derivatives can be used to obtain the optimal solution to a maximization or minimization problem containing two or more X variables. Analogous to the first-order conditions discussed earlier for the one-variable case, we set *each* of the partial derivatives equal to zero and solve the resulting set of simultaneous equations for the optimal X values.

Example

Profit Maximization: Indiana Petroleum Company (continued)

Suppose we are interested in determining the values of Q_1 and Q_2 that maximize the company's profits given in Equation B.22. In this case, each of the two partial derivative functions (Equations B.23 and B.24) would be set equal to zero:

$$0 = 140 - 20Q_1 - 6Q_2$$
$$0 = 100 - 16Q_2 - 6Q_1$$

This system of equations can be solved for the profit-maximizing values of Q_1 and Q_2.[6] The optimal values are $Q_1^* = 5.77$ units and $Q_2^* = 4.08$ units.[7] The optimal total profit is

$$\pi^* = -60 + 140(5.77) + 100(4.08) + 10(5.77)^2 - 8(4.08)^2 - 6(5.77)(4.08) = 548.45$$

---

[6]The second-order conditions for obtaining a maximum or minimum in the multiple-variable case are somewhat complex. A discussion of these conditions can be found in most basic calculus texts.

[7]Exercise 10 at the end of this appendix requires the determination of these optimal values.

SUMMARY

- *Marginal analysis* is useful in making decisions about the expansion or contraction of an economic activity.
- *Differential calculus*, which bears a close relationship to marginal analysis, can be applied whenever an algebraic relationship can be specified between the decision variables and the objective or criterion variable.
- The *first derivative* measures the slope or rate of change of a function at a given point and is equal to the limiting value of the marginal function as the marginal value is calculated over smaller and smaller intervals, that is, as the interval approaches zero.
- Various rules are available (see Table B.1) for finding the derivative of specific types of functions.

- A necessary, but not sufficient, condition for finding the maximum or minimum points of a function is that the first derivative be equal to zero, which is known as the *first-order condition.*
- A *second-order condition* is required to determine whether a given point is a maximum or minimum. The *second derivative* indicates that a given point is a maximum if the second derivative is less than zero or a minimum if the second derivative is greater than zero.
- The *partial derivative* of a multivariate function measures the marginal effect of a change in one variable on the value of the function, holding constant all other variables.

Exercises

1. Define Q as the level of output produced and sold, and suppose that a firm's total revenue (TR) and total cost (TC) functions can be represented in tabular form as shown here.

OUTPUT (Q)	TOTAL REVENUE (TR)	TOTAL COST (TC)	OUTPUT (Q)	TOTAL REVENUE (TR)	TOTAL COST (TC)
0	0	20	11	264	196
1	34	26	12	276	224
2	66	34	13	286	254
3	96	44	14	294	286
4	124	56	15	300	320
5	150	70	16	304	356
6	174	86	17	306	394
7	196	104	18	306	434
8	216	124	19	304	476
9	234	146	20	300	520
10	250	170			

a. Compute the marginal revenue and average revenue functions.
b. Compute the marginal cost and average cost functions.
c. On a single graph, plot the total revenue, total cost, marginal revenue, and marginal cost functions.
d. Determine the output level in the *graph* that maximizes profits (Profit = Total revenue − Total cost) by finding the point where marginal revenue equals marginal cost.
e. Check your result in part (d) by finding the output level in the *tables* developed in parts (a) and (b) that likewise satisfies the condition that marginal revenue equals marginal cost.

2. Consider again the total revenue and total cost functions shown in tabular form in the previous problem.
   a. Compute the total, marginal, and average profit functions.
   b. On a single graph, plot the total profit and marginal profit functions.
   c. Determine the output level in the graph and table where the total profit function takes on its maximum value.
   d. How does the result in part (c) in this exercise compare with the result in part (d) of the previous exercise?
   e. Determine total profits at the profit-maximizing output level.

3. Differentiate the following functions:
   a. $TC = 50 + 100Q - 6Q^2 + .5Q^3$
   b. $ATC = 50/Q + 100 - 6Q + .5Q^2$
   c. $MC = 100 - 12Q + 1.5Q^2$
   d. $Q = 50 - .75P$
   e. $Q = .40X^{1.50}$

4. Differentiate the following functions:
   a. $Y = 2X^3/(4X^2 - 1)$
   b. $Y = 2X/(4X^2 - 1)$
   c. $Y = 8Z^2 - 4Z + 1$, where $Z = 2X^2 - 1$ (differentiate Y with respect to X)

5. Define Q to be the level of output produced and sold, and assume that the firm's cost function is given by the relationship

$$TC = 20 + 5Q + Q^2$$

Furthermore, assume that the demand for the output of the firm is a function of price P given by the relationship

$$Q = 25 - P$$

   a. Define total profit as the difference between total revenue and total cost, and express in terms of Q the total profit function for the firm. (*Note:* Total revenue equals price per unit times the number of units sold.)
   b. Determine the output level where total profits are maximized.
   c. Calculate total profits and selling price at the profit-maximizing output level.
   d. If fixed costs increase from $20 to $25 in the total cost relationship, determine the effects of such an increase on the profit-maximizing output level and total profits.

6. Use the cost and demand functions in Exercise 5 to calculate the following:
   a. Determine the marginal revenue and marginal cost functions.
   b. Show that, at the profit-maximizing output level determined in part (b) of the previous exercise, marginal revenue equals marginal cost and illustrates the economic principle that profits are maximized at the output level where marginal revenue equals marginal cost.

7. Determine the partial derivatives with respect to all of the variables in the following functions:
   a. $TC = 50 + 5Q_1 + 10Q_2 + .5Q_1Q_2$
   b. $Q = 1.5L^{.60}K^{.50}$
   c. $Q_A = 2.5P_A^{-1.30}Y^{.20}P_B^{.40}$

8. Bounds Inc. determined through regression analysis that its sales (S) are a function of the amount of advertising (measured in units) in two different media. This relationship is given by the following equation (X = newspapers, Y = magazines):

$$S(X, Y) = 200X + 100Y - 10X^2 - 20Y^2 + 20XY$$

   a. Find the level of newspaper and magazine advertising that maximizes the firm's sales.
   b. Calculate the firm's sales at the optimal values of newspaper and magazine advertising determined in part (a).

9. The Santa Fe Cookie Factory is considering an expansion of its retail piñon cookie business to other cities. The firm's owners lack the funds needed to undertake the expansion on their own. They are considering a franchise arrangement for the new outlets. The company incurs variable costs of $6 for each pound of cookies sold. The fixed costs of operating a typical retail outlet are estimated to be $300,000 per year. The demand function facing each retail outlet is estimated to be

$$P = \$50 - .001Q$$

   where P is the price per pound of cookies and Q is the number of pounds of cookies sold. [*Note:* Total revenue equals price (P) times quantity (Q) sold.]

   a. What price, output, total revenue, total cost, and total profit level will each profit-maximizing franchise experience?
   b. Assume that the parent company charges each franchisee a fee equal to 5 percent of total revenues, and recompute the values in part (a).
   c. The Santa Fe Cookie Factory is considering a combined fixed/variable franchise fee structure. Under this arrangement, each franchisee would pay the parent company $25,000 plus 1 percent of total revenues. Recompute the values in part (a).
   d. What franchise fee arrangement do you recommend that the Santa Fe Cookie Factory adopt? What are the advantages and disadvantages of each plan?

10. Show that the optimal solution to the set of simultaneous equations in the Indiana Petroleum example are $Q_1^* = 5.77$ and $Q_2^* = 4.08$.

Tables

TABLE C.1 VALUES OF THE STANDARD NORMAL DISTRIBUTION FUNCTION*

Z	0	1	2	3	4	5	6	7	8	9
−3.0	.0013	.0010	.0007	.0005	.0003	.0002	.0002	.0001	.0001	.0000
−2.9	.0019	.0018	.0017	.0017	.0016	.0016	.0015	.0015	.0014	.0014
−2.8	.0026	.0025	.0024	.0023	.0023	.0022	.0021	.0021	.0020	.0019
−2.7	.0035	.0034	.0033	.0032	.0031	.0030	.0029	.0028	.0027	.0026
−2.6	.0047	.0045	.0044	.0043	.0041	.0040	.0039	.0038	.0037	.0036
−2.5	.0062	.0060	.0059	.0057	.0055	.0054	.0052	.0051	.0049	.0048
−2.4	.0082	.0080	.0078	.0075	.0073	.0071	.0069	.0068	.0066	.0064
−2.3	.0107	.0104	.0102	.0099	.0096	.0094	.0091	.0089	.0087	.0084
−2.2	.0139	.0136	.0132	.0129	.0126	.0122	.0119	.0116	.0113	.0110
−2.1	.0179	.0174	.0170	.0166	.0162	.0158	.0154	.0150	.0146	.0143
−2.0	.0228	.0222	.0217	.0212	.0207	.0202	.0197	.0192	.0188	.0183
−1.9	.0287	.0281	.0274	.0268	.0262	.0256	.0250	.0244	.0238	.0233
−1.8	.0359	.0352	.0344	.0336	.0329	.0322	.0314	.0307	.0300	.0294
−1.7	.0446	.0436	.0427	.0418	.0409	.0401	.0392	.0384	.0375	.0367
−1.6	.0548	.0537	.0526	.0516	.0505	.0495	.0485	.0475	.0465	.0455
−1.5	.0668	.0655	.0643	.0630	.0618	.0606	.0594	.0582	.0570	.0559
−1.4	.0808	.0793	.0778	.0764	.0749	.0735	.0722	.0708	.0694	.0681
−1.3	.0988	.0951	.0934	.0918	.0901	.0885	.0869	.0853	.0838	.0823
−1.2	.1151	.1131	.1112	.1093	.1075	.1056	.1038	.1020	.1003	.0985
−1.1	.1357	.1335	.1314	.1292	.1271	.1251	.1230	.1210	.1190	.1170
−1.0	.1587	.1562	.1539	.1515	.1492	.1469	.1446	.1423	.1401	.1379
−.9	.1841	.1814	.1788	.1762	.1736	.1711	.1685	.1660	.1635	.1611
−.8	.2119	.2090	.2061	.2033	.2005	.1977	.1949	.1922	.1894	.1867
−.7	.2420	.2389	.2358	.2327	.2297	.2266	.2236	.2206	.2177	.2148
−.6	.2743	.2709	.2676	.2643	.2611	.2578	.2546	.2514	.2483	.2451
−.5	.3085	.3050	.3015	.2981	.2946	.2912	.2877	.2843	.2810	.2776
−.4	.3446	.3409	.3372	.3336	.3300	.3264	.3228	.3192	.3156	.3121
−.3	.3821	.3783	.3745	.3707	.3669	.3632	.3594	.3557	.3520	.3483
−.2	.4207	.4168	.4129	.4090	.4052	.4013	.3974	.3936	.3897	.3859
−.1	.4602	.4562	.4522	.4483	.4443	.4404	.4364	.4325	.4286	.4247
−.0	.5000	.4960	.4920	.4880	.4840	.4801	.4761	.4721	.4681	.4641

*Note: Table values give the probability of a value occurring that is *less than z* standard deviations from the mean.

Note 1: If a random variable X is not "standard," its values must be "standardized": $z = \left(\frac{X - \mu}{\sigma}\right)$. That is:

$$P(X \le x) = N\left(\frac{x - \mu}{\sigma}\right)$$

Note 2: For $z \le -4$, $N(z) = 0$ to 4 decimal places; for $z \ge 4$, $N(z) = 1$ to 4 decimal places.

TABLE C.1	VALUES OF THE STANDARD NORMAL DISTRIBUTION FUNCTION (CONTINUED)								
Z	0	1	2	3	4	5	6	7	8	9
.0	.5000	.5040	.5080	.5120	.5160	.5199	.5239	.5279	.5319	.5359
.1	.5398	.5438	.5478	.5517	.5557	.5596	.5636	.5675	.5714	.5753
.2	.5793	.5832	.5871	.5910	.5948	.5987	.6026	.6064	.6103	.6141
.3	.6179	.6217	.6255	.6293	.6331	.6368	.6406	.6443	.6480	.6517
.4	.6554	.6591	.6628	.6664	.6700	.6736	.6772	.6808	.6844	.6879
.5	.6915	.6950	.6985	.7019	.7054	.7088	.7123	.7157	.7190	.7224
.6	.7257	.7291	.7324	.7357	.7389	.7422	.7454	.7486	.7517	.7549
.7	.7580	.7611	.7642	.7673	.7703	.7734	.7764	.7794	.7823	.7852
.8	.7881	.7910	.7939	.7967	.7995	.8023	.8051	.8078	.8106	.8133
.9	.8159	.8186	.8212	.8238	.8264	.8289	.8315	.8340	.8365	.8389
1.0	.8413	.8438	.8461	.8485	.8508	.8531	.8554	.8577	.8599	.8621
1.1	.8643	.8665	.8686	.8708	.8729	.8749	.8770	.8790	.8810	.8830
1.2	.8849	.8869	.8888	.8907	.8925	.8944	.8962	.8980	.8997	.9015
1.3	.9032	.9049	.9066	.9082	.9099	.9115	.9131	.9147	.9162	.9177
1.4	.9192	.9207	.9222	.9236	.9251	.9265	.9278	.9292	.9306	.9319
1.5	.9332	.9345	.9357	.9370	.9382	.9394	.9406	.9418	.9430	.9441
1.6	.9452	.9463	.9474	.9484	.9495	.9505	.9515	.9525	.9535	.9545
1.7	.9554	.9564	.9573	.9582	.9591	.9599	.9608	.9616	.9625	.9633
1.8	.9641	.9648	.9656	.9664	.9671	.9678	.9686	.9693	.9700	.9706
1.9	.9713	.9719	.9726	.9732	.9738	.9744	.9750	.9756	.9762	.9767
2.0	.9772	.9778	.9783	.9788	.9793	.9798	.9803	.9808	.9812	.9817
2.1	.9821	.9826	.9830	.9834	.9838	.9842	.9846	.9850	.9854	.9857
2.2	.9861	.9864	.9868	.9871	.9874	.9878	.9881	.9884	.9887	.9890
2.3	.9893	.9896	.9898	.9901	.9904	.9906	.9909	.9911	.9913	.9916
2.4	.9918	.9920	.9922	.9925	.9927	.9929	.9931	.9932	.9934	.9936
2.5	.9938	.9940	.9941	.9943	.9945	.9946	.9948	.9949	.9951	.9952
2.6	.9953	.9955	.9956	.9957	.9959	.9960	.9961	.9962	.9963	.9964
2.7	.9965	.9966	.9967	.9968	.9969	.9970	.9971	.9972	.9973	.9974
2.8	.9974	.9975	.9976	.9977	.9977	.9978	.9979	.9979	.9980	.9981
2.9	.9981	.9982	.9982	.9983	.9984	.9984	.9985	.9985	.9986	.9986
3.0	.9987	.9990	.9993	.9995	.9997	.9998	.9998	.9999	.9999	1.0000

Source: From CHOU, STATISTICAL ANALYSIS @, 1E. © 1969 Cengage Learning.

TABLE C.3 THE F-DISTRIBUTION—UPPER 5 PERCENT BREAKPOINTS

δ_1 / δ_2	1	2	3	4	5	6	7	8	9	10	12	15	20	24	30	40	60	120	∞
1	161.4	199.5	215.7	224.6	230.2	234.0	236.8	238.9	240.5	241.9	243.9	245.9	248.0	249.1	250.1	251.1	252.2	253.3	254.3
2	18.57	19.00	19.16	19.25	19.30	19.33	19.35	19.37	19.38	19.40	19.41	19.43	19.45	19.45	19.46	19.47	19.48	19.49	19.50
3	10.13	9.55	9.28	9.12	9.01	8.94	8.89	8.85	8.81	8.79	8.74	8.70	8.66	8.64	8.62	8.59	8.57	8.55	8.53
4	7.71	6.94	6.59	6.39	6.26	6.16	6.09	6.04	6.00	5.96	5.91	5.86	5.80	5.77	5.75	5.72	5.69	5.66	5.63
5	6.61	5.79	5.41	5.19	5.05	4.95	4.88	4.82	4.77	4.74	4.68	4.62	4.56	4.53	4.50	4.46	4.43	4.40	4.36
6	5.99	5.14	4.76	4.53	4.39	4.28	4.21	4.15	4.10	4.06	4.00	3.94	3.87	3.84	3.81	3.77	3.74	3.70	3.67
7	5.59	4.74	4.35	4.12	3.97	3.87	3.79	3.73	3.68	3.64	3.57	3.51	3.44	3.41	3.38	3.34	3.30	3.27	3.23
8	5.32	4.46	4.07	3.84	3.69	3.58	3.50	3.44	3.39	3.35	3.28	3.22	3.15	3.12	3.08	3.04	3.01	2.97	2.93
9	5.12	4.26	3.86	3.63	3.48	3.37	3.29	3.23	3.18	3.14	3.07	3.01	2.94	2.90	2.86	2.83	2.79	2.75	2.71
10	4.96	4.10	3.71	3.48	3.33	3.22	3.14	3.07	3.02	2.98	2.91	2.85	2.77	2.74	2.70	2.66	2.62	2.58	2.54
11	4.84	3.98	3.59	3.36	3.20	3.09	3.01	2.95	2.90	2.85	2.79	2.72	2.65	2.61	2.57	2.53	2.49	2.45	2.40
12	4.75	3.89	3.49	3.26	3.11	3.00	2.91	2.85	2.80	2.75	2.69	2.62	2.54	2.51	2.47	2.43	2.38	2.34	2.30
13	4.67	3.81	3.41	3.18	3.03	2.92	2.83	2.77	2.71	2.67	2.60	2.53	2.46	2.42	2.38	2.34	2.30	2.25	2.21
14	4.60	3.74	3.34	3.11	2.96	2.85	2.76	2.70	2.65	2.60	2.53	2.46	2.39	2.35	2.31	2.27	2.22	2.18	2.13
15	4.54	3.68	3.29	3.06	2.90	2.79	2.71	2.64	2.59	2.54	2.48	2.40	2.33	2.29	2.25	2.20	2.16	2.11	2.07
16	4.49	3.63	3.24	3.01	2.85	2.74	2.66	2.59	2.54	2.49	2.42	2.35	2.28	2.24	2.19	2.15	2.11	2.06	2.01
17	4.45	3.59	3.20	2.96	2.81	2.70	2.61	2.55	2.49	2.45	2.38	2.31	2.23	2.19	2.15	2.10	2.06	2.01	1.96
18	4.41	3.55	3.16	2.93	2.77	2.66	2.58	2.51	2.46	2.41	2.34	2.27	2.19	2.15	2.11	2.06	2.02	1.97	1.92
19	4.38	3.52	3.13	2.90	2.74	2.63	2.54	2.48	2.42	2.38	2.31	2.23	2.16	2.11	2.07	2.03	1.98	1.93	1.88
20	4.35	3.49	3.10	2.87	2.71	2.60	2.51	2.45	2.39	2.35	2.28	2.20	2.12	2.08	2.04	1.99	1.95	1.90	1.84
21	4.32	3.47	3.07	2.84	2.68	2.57	2.49	2.42	2.37	2.32	2.25	2.18	2.10	2.05	2.01	1.96	1.92	1.87	1.81
22	4.30	3.44	3.05	2.82	2.66	2.55	2.46	2.40	2.34	2.30	2.23	2.15	2.07	2.03	1.98	1.94	1.89	1.84	1.78
23	4.28	3.42	3.03	2.80	2.64	2.53	2.44	2.37	2.32	2.27	2.20	2.13	2.05	2.01	1.96	1.91	1.86	1.81	1.76
24	4.26	3.40	3.01	2.78	2.62	2.51	2.42	2.36	2.30	2.25	2.18	2.11	2.03	1.98	1.94	1.89	1.84	1.79	1.73
25	4.24	3.39	2.99	2.76	2.60	2.49	2.40	2.34	2.28	2.24	2.16	2.09	2.01	1.96	1.92	1.87	1.82	1.77	1.71
26	4.23	3.37	2.98	2.74	2.59	2.47	2.39	2.32	2.27	2.22	2.15	2.07	1.99	1.95	1.90	1.85	1.80	1.75	1.69
27	4.21	3.35	2.96	2.73	2.57	2.46	2.37	2.31	2.25	2.20	2.13	2.06	1.97	1.93	1.88	1.84	1.79	1.73	1.67
28	4.20	3.34	2.95	2.71	2.56	2.45	2.36	2.29	2.24	2.19	2.12	2.04	1.96	1.91	1.87	1.82	1.77	1.71	1.65
29	4.18	3.33	2.93	2.70	2.55	2.43	2.35	2.28	2.22	2.18	2.10	2.03	1.94	1.90	1.85	1.81	1.75	1.70	1.64
30	4.17	3.32	2.92	2.69	2.53	2.42	2.33	2.27	2.21	2.16	2.09	2.01	1.93	1.89	1.84	1.79	1.74	1.68	1.62
40	4.08	3.23	2.84	2.61	2.45	2.34	2.25	2.18	2.12	2.08	2.00	1.92	1.84	1.79	1.74	1.69	1.64	1.58	1.51
60	4.00	3.15	2.76	2.53	2.37	2.25	2.17	2.10	2.04	1.99	1.92	1.84	1.75	1.70	1.65	1.59	1.53	1.47	1.39
120	3.92	3.07	2.68	2.45	2.29	2.17	2.09	2.02	1.96	1.91	1.83	1.75	1.66	1.61	1.55	1.50	1.43	1.35	1.25
∞	3.84	3.00	2.60	2.37	2.21	2.10	2.01	1.94	1.88	1.83	1.75	1.67	1.57	1.52	1.46	1.39	1.32	1.22	1.00

(continued)

TABLE C.3   THE F-DISTRIBUTION—UPPER 1 PERCENT BREAKPOINTS (CONTINUED)

δ_2 \ δ_1	1	2	3	4	5	6	7	8	9	10	12	15	20	24	30	40	60	120	∞
1	4052	4999.5	5403	5625	5764	5859	5928	5982	6022	6056	6106	6157	6209	6235	6261	6287	6313	6339	6366
2	98.50	99.00	99.17	99.25	99.30	99.33	99.36	99.37	99.39	99.40	99.42	99.43	99.45	99.46	99.47	99.47	99.48	99.49	99.50
3	34.12	30.82	29.46	28.71	28.24	27.91	27.67	27.49	27.35	27.23	27.05	26.87	26.69	26.60	26.50	26.41	26.32	26.22	26.13
4	21.20	18.00	16.69	15.98	15.52	15.21	14.98	14.80	14.66	14.55	14.37	14.20	14.02	13.93	13.84	13.75	13.65	13.56	13.46
5	16.26	13.27	12.06	11.39	10.97	10.67	10.46	10.29	10.16	10.05	9.89	9.72	9.55	9.47	9.38	9.29	9.20	9.11	9.02
6	13.75	10.92	9.78	9.15	8.75	8.47	8.26	8.10	7.98	7.87	7.72	7.56	7.40	7.31	7.23	7.14	7.06	6.97	6.88
7	12.25	9.55	8.45	7.85	7.46	7.19	6.99	6.84	6.72	6.62	6.47	6.31	6.16	6.07	5.99	5.91	5.82	5.74	5.65
8	11.26	8.65	7.59	7.01	6.63	6.37	6.18	6.03	5.91	5.81	5.67	5.52	5.36	5.28	5.20	5.12	5.03	4.95	4.86
9	10.56	8.02	6.99	6.42	6.06	5.80	5.61	5.47	5.35	5.26	5.11	4.96	4.81	4.73	4.65	4.57	4.48	4.40	4.31
10	10.04	7.56	6.55	5.99	5.64	5.39	5.20	5.06	4.94	4.85	4.71	4.56	4.41	4.33	4.25	4.17	4.08	4.00	3.91
11	9.65	7.21	6.22	5.67	5.32	5.07	4.89	4.74	4.63	4.54	4.40	4.25	4.10	4.02	3.94	3.86	3.78	3.69	3.60
12	9.33	6.93	5.95	5.41	5.06	4.82	4.64	4.50	4.39	4.30	4.16	4.01	3.86	3.78	3.70	3.62	3.54	3.45	3.36
13	9.07	6.70	5.74	5.21	4.86	4.62	4.44	4.30	4.19	4.10	3.96	3.82	3.66	3.59	3.51	3.43	3.34	3.25	3.17
14	8.86	6.51	5.56	5.04	4.69	4.46	4.28	4.14	4.03	3.94	3.80	3.66	3.51	3.43	3.35	3.27	3.18	3.09	3.00
15	8.68	6.36	5.42	4.89	4.56	4.32	4.14	4.00	3.89	3.80	3.67	3.52	3.37	3.29	3.21	3.13	3.05	2.96	2.87
16	8.53	6.23	5.29	4.77	4.44	4.20	4.03	3.89	3.78	3.69	3.55	3.41	3.26	3.18	3.10	3.02	2.93	2.84	2.75
17	8.40	6.11	5.18	4.67	4.34	4.10	3.93	3.79	3.68	3.59	3.46	3.31	3.16	3.08	3.00	2.92	2.83	2.75	2.65
18	8.29	6.01	5.09	4.58	4.25	4.01	3.84	3.71	3.60	3.51	3.37	3.23	3.08	3.00	2.92	2.84	2.75	2.66	2.57
19	8.18	5.93	5.01	4.50	4.17	3.94	3.77	3.63	3.52	3.43	3.30	3.15	3.00	2.92	2.84	2.76	2.67	2.58	2.49
20	8.10	5.85	4.94	4.43	4.10	3.87	3.70	3.56	3.46	3.37	3.23	3.09	2.94	2.86	2.78	2.69	2.61	2.52	2.42
21	8.02	5.78	4.87	4.37	4.04	3.81	3.64	3.51	3.40	3.31	3.17	3.03	2.88	2.80	2.72	2.64	2.55	2.46	2.36
22	7.95	5.72	4.82	4.31	3.99	3.76	3.59	3.45	3.35	3.26	3.12	2.98	2.83	2.75	2.67	2.58	2.50	2.40	2.31
23	7.88	5.66	4.76	4.26	3.94	3.71	3.54	3.41	3.30	3.21	3.07	2.93	2.78	2.70	2.62	2.54	2.45	2.35	2.26
24	7.82	5.61	4.72	4.22	3.90	3.67	3.50	3.36	3.26	3.17	3.03	2.89	2.74	2.66	2.58	2.49	2.40	2.31	2.21
25	7.77	5.57	4.68	4.18	3.85	3.63	3.46	3.32	3.22	3.13	2.99	2.85	2.70	2.62	2.54	2.45	2.36	2.27	2.17
26	7.72	5.53	4.64	4.14	3.82	3.59	3.42	3.29	3.18	3.09	2.96	2.81	2.66	2.58	2.50	2.42	2.33	2.23	2.13
27	7.68	5.49	4.60	4.11	3.78	3.56	3.39	3.26	3.15	3.06	2.93	2.78	2.63	2.55	2.47	2.38	2.29	2.20	2.10
28	7.64	5.45	4.57	4.07	3.75	3.53	3.36	3.23	3.12	3.03	2.90	2.75	2.60	2.52	2.44	2.35	2.26	2.17	2.06
29	7.60	5.42	4.54	4.04	3.73	3.50	3.33	3.20	3.09	3.00	2.87	2.73	2.57	2.49	2.41	2.33	2.23	2.14	2.03
30	7.56	5.39	4.51	4.02	3.70	3.47	3.30	3.17	3.07	2.98	2.84	2.70	2.55	2.47	2.39	2.30	2.21	2.11	2.01
40	7.31	5.18	4.31	3.83	3.51	3.29	3.12	2.99	2.89	2.80	2.66	2.52	2.37	2.29	2.20	2.11	2.02	1.92	1.80
60	7.08	4.98	4.13	3.65	3.34	3.12	2.95	2.82	2.72	2.63	2.50	2.35	2.20	2.12	2.03	1.94	1.84	1.73	1.60
120	6.85	4.79	3.95	3.48	3.17	2.96	2.79	2.66	2.56	2.47	2.34	2.19	2.03	1.95	1.86	1.76	1.66	1.53	1.38
∞	6.63	4.61	3.78	3.32	3.02	2.80	2.64	2.51	2.41	2.32	2.18	2.04	1.88	1.79	1.70	1.59	1.47	1.32	1.00

Source: E. S. Pearson and H. O. Hartley, *Biometrika Tables for Statisticians*, Vol. 1, Table 18.

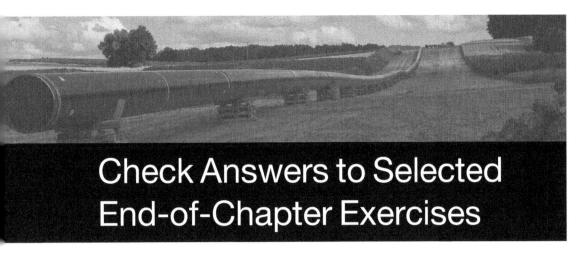

Check Answers to Selected End-of-Chapter Exercises

Chapter 1

Case Exercise—Designing a Managerial Incentives Contract

1. $240 million
7. $167 million
8. $205 million

Chapter 2

3. Budget = $875 million
5. c. $v = 0.067$

Chapter 3

2. 44%
5. $P = \$90$
6. a. $E_D = -0.59$
8. a. $E_X = 1.34$
   Close substitutes.
9. $Q_{2006} = 5,169$
   $Q_{2007} = 3,953$

Chapter 4

3. d. $r^2 = 0.885$
9. a. $Y' = -14.7351 + 3.9214$ Size + 3.5851 Rooms − 0.1181 Age − 2.8317 Garage

Case Exercise—Soft Drink Demand Estimation

2. $E_D = -3.38$

Appendix 4A

2. a. $Y' = 1.210 + 0.838$ Selling Expenses, $r^2 = 0.93$
4. a. (i) $S' = 247.644 + 0.3926$ Advertising − 0.7339 Price
   (ii) $\text{Log}(S') = 2.4482 + 0.7296$ Log Advertising − 0.2406 Log Price

Chapter 5

3. b. Sum(Actual/Forecast)/6 = 636.6%/6 = 106.1%, thus + 6%
4. b. GNP = C + I + G = 635 + 120 + 200 = 955
7. b. $Y'_{2007} = 259.03$
8. a. December 2007 = 468

Chapter 6

1. Both increase
3. Outsource abroad and buy foreign assets
6. 15 percent decline. Relative purchasing power parity

Chapter 7

3. b. 10 or 11 men
5. c. $AP_X = 6X - 0.4X^2$
7. a. 4.88%

Case Exercise—Production Function for Wilson Company

4. $E_K = 0.415$, $E_L = 1.078$

Chapter 8

2. b. ($90,000)

Case Exercise—Cost Analysis

1. $4.55

Chapter 9

2. a. $Q^* = 574.08 (million)

5. a. $30,000,000

Case Exercise—Cost Functions

5. $Q^* = 1,675$

Case Exercise—Charter Airline Operating Decisions

3. Indirect Fixed Cost = $23,900

Chapter 10

8. b. $P^* = $1,220

9. b. $900,000 on advertising

Chapter 11

2. c. $Q^* = 125$

3. e. $\pi^* = $263,625

4. b. $P^* = $60

8. a. $ROI = 14.2\%$

9. a. $ROI = 12.98\%$

Chapter 12

2. a. $P^* = 145
   $Q_A^* = 30$

5. a. $P^* = $9,666.70$, $Q^* = 666.7$

6. c. $P^* = 125, $Q^* = 50$

Chapter 13

3. b. Dominant strategy for AMC is to "Not Abide"

5. {$150, Match}, No

6. Least should pass. More should always attack Most, and knowing that, Most should always attack More. If they pass, Least will get a second opportunity to attack a once stronger but now weakened opponent.

8. {Late, Late} is one of two pure Nash equilibria.

Chapter 14

1. $P_{US} = 80, $P_{OVERSEAS} = 22.50

3. a. $\pi = -20 + 96Q1 + 76Q_2 - 2Q_2^1 - Q_2^2$

Appendix 14A

3. 22 seats

Chapter 15

3. High interest rates, large principal, long term, unsecured

5. Vertical integration if the power plant is dependent on this type of coal. Otherwise, long-term supply contracts.

Case Exercise—Division of Investment Banking Fees in a Syndicate

1. Lead underwriter = $97 million
   Syndicate Co-Manager = 0
   Syndicate Member 3 = $1 million
   Syndicate Member 4 = 0
   Syndicate Member 5 = $2 million

Appendix 15A

4. Electricity, T-bills

5. $1.3 million.
   Use open bidding, multiple rounds, highest-wins-and-pays.

11. Apple's expected profit is $1.5 million less from understatement.

Chapter 16

3. a. HHI before = 1,964. So, in general, no, although off-setting efficiency arguments may come into play as long as 1,984 is below the 2,500 standard.

6. b. $\pi^* = $450 million

11. Coordinate on Nash equilibrium (Lucent Imitate, Motorola Develop) in joint venture with compensation of at least $1 billion to Motorola.

Chapter 17

2. $IRR = 9.1\%$. So, No.

4. b. $NCF_{10} = $5,560

5. a. $IRR = 14.94\%$,
   $NPV = $45,176

6. $k_e = 13.4\%$

7. b. $k_e' = 13\%$

8. $k_a = 12.3\%$

9. b. Power plant:
   $NPV_{@12\%} = -$22.71$ million,
   $NPV_{@5\%} = 62.65 million

Case Exercise—Cost-Benefit Analysis

1. B/C ratio = 1.90

COLLEGE ACCOUNTING

1

Asset, Liability, Owner's Equity, Revenue, and Expense Accounts

Learning Objectives

After you have completed this chapter, you will be able to do the following:

1 Define and identify *asset*, *liability*, and *owner's equity* accounts.

2 Record, in column form, a group of business transactions involving changes in assets, liabilities, and owner's equity.

3 Define and identify *revenue* and *expense* accounts.

4 Record, in column form, a group of business transactions involving all five elements of the fundamental accounting equation.

To: **Amy Roberts, CPA**
Subject: **Starting My New Business**

Hi Amy,

Well, I've given it a lot of thought and have decided to take the "plunge"! I'm going to start my own business. I've been working for many years as a whitewater rafting guide and helping in the business office. I think I'm ready to go out on my own. I know a lot about rafting and operating tours, but I don't know much about accounting. Do you think you could help? Would you recommend I purchase accounting software like QuickBooks®?

Thanks,

Janie

_____

To: **Janie Conner**
Subject: **RE: Starting My New Business**

Hi Janie,

Great! I'm so glad you've finally taken my advice and decided to open your own business. I will definitely help you learn accounting, and I would strongly recommend that you purchase an accounting software package like QuickBooks! There's a lot to learn—so let's take it step by step. I've made a list of some items for you to concentrate on first.

_____ 1. Understand what accounting is—what it does, what its purpose is.

_____ 2. Know the fundamental accounting equation. (This is important!)

_____ 3. Know examples of accounts that are included in each asset, liability, or owner's equity category.

Once you've learned these items, email me, and we'll move on! Good luck.

Amy

Ragnar Th Sigurdsson/Arctic Images/Alamy

As we stated in the Introduction, accounting is the process of analyzing, classifying, recording, summarizing, and interpreting business transactions. In this chapter, we will introduce the analyzing, classifying, and recording steps in the accounting process.

ASSETS, LIABILITIES, AND OWNER'S EQUITY

The Fundamental Accounting Equation

Assets are properties or things of value, such as cash, equipment, copyrights, buildings, and land, owned and controlled by an economic unit or a business entity. By the term business entity, we mean that the business is an economic unit in itself and the assets or properties of the business are completely separate from the owner's personal assets. However, the owner has a claim on the assets of the business and generally has a responsibility for its debts. **The owner's right, claim, or financial interest is expressed by the word equity in the business.** Another term that can be used is capital. Whenever you see the term owner's equity, it means the owner's right to or investment in the business.

Assets	=	Owner's Equity
Properties or things of value owned by the business		Owner's *right* to or investment in the business

Suppose the total value of the assets is $80,000, and the business entity does not owe any amount against the assets. Then,

Assets	=	Owner's Equity
$80,000	=	$80,000

Or suppose the assets consist of a truck that costs $35,000. The owner has invested $12,000 for the truck, and the business entity has borrowed the remainder from the

 Define and identify *asset*, *liability*, and *owner's equity* accounts.

Learning Objective

443

bank, which is a **creditor** (one to whom money is owed). This business transaction or event can be shown as follows:

Assets	=	Liabilities	+	Owner's Equity
Items owned		*Amounts owed to creditors*		*Owner's investment*
$35,000	=	$23,000	+	$12,000

We have now introduced a new classification, **liabilities**, which represent debts. They are the amounts that the business entity owes its creditors. The debts may originate because the business bought goods or services on credit, borrowed money, or otherwise created an obligation to pay. The creditors' claims to the assets have priority over the claims of the owner.

An equation expressing the relationship of assets, liabilities, and owner's equity is called the **fundamental accounting equation**.

> **Assets = Liabilities + Owner's Equity**

We'll deal with this equation constantly from now on. If we know two parts of this equation, we can determine the third. Let's look at some examples.

Determine Assets

Fundamental Accounting Equation Example 1: Millie Adair has $17,000 invested in her travel agency, and the agency owes creditors $5,000; that is, the agency has liabilities of $5,000. Then,

Assets	=	Liabilities	+	Owner's Equity
?	=	$5,000	+	$17,000

We can find the amount of the business's assets by adding the liabilities and the owner's equity.

```
$  5,000 Liabilities
+17,000 Owner's Equity
$22,000 Assets
```

The completed equation now reads as follows:

Assets	=	Liabilities	+	Owner's Equity
$22,000	=	$5,000	+	$17,000

Determine Owner's Equity

Fundamental Accounting Equation Example 2: Larry Roland owns a car repair shop. His business has assets of $40,000, and it owes creditors $16,000; that is, it has liabilities of $16,000. Then,

FYI

Even if the truck is not completely paid for (for example, a loan was taken out to pay for the truck), the truck is still considered an asset. The truck would be recorded at the total costs, and a liability would be recorded for the amount of the loan.

Assets	=	Liabilities	+	Owner's Equity
$40,000	=	$16,000	+	?

We find the owner's equity by subtracting the liabilities from the assets.

$40,000 Assets
−16,000 Liabilities
$24,000 Owner's Equity

The completed equation now reads as follows:

Assets	=	Liabilities	+	Owner's Equity
$40,000	=	$16,000	+	$24,000

Like a balancing scale, the equation stays in balance by making equal or offsetting increases and decreases to one side or both sides.

Determine Liabilities

Fundamental Accounting Equation Example 3: Theo Viero's insurance agency has assets of $86,000; his investment (his equity) amounts to $46,000. Then,

Assets	=	Liabilities	+	Owner's Equity
$86,000	=	?	+	$46,000

To find the firm's total liabilities, we subtract the equity from the assets.

$ 86,000 Assets
−46,000 Owner's Equity
$ 40,000 Liabilities

The completed equation reads as follows:

Assets	=	Liabilities	+	Owner's Equity
$86,000	=	$40,000	+	$46,000

To: **Amy Roberts, CPA**
Subject: **Assets, Liabilities, and Owner's Equity**

Hi Amy,
Thanks for your help! I have purchased QuickBooks, and I am ready to install it on my computer. Do you have any tips for getting started? I am also doing really well with learning the fundamental accounting equation and identifying accounts. I can now identify most accounts as an asset, liability, or owner's equity. How does this knowledge apply to the transactions of my business?
Thanks,
Janie

To: **Janie Conner**

Subject: **RE: Asset, Liabilities, and Owner's Equity**

Hi Janie,

I'm glad to hear you have purchased QuickBooks. I'll provide you with some tips to get started and a demonstration file you can use to practice. Once you have learned a few more of the accounting basics, you will be ready to apply these in QuickBooks. Now that you know the fundamental accounting equation and also examples of accounts included in each asset, liability, or owners' equity category, you are ready to begin analyzing transactions. You will use your knowledge of accounts and apply this to the company's day-to-day transactions by recording these transactions in column form. This can be challenging, but I'll provide you with four easy steps to remember that will help you along the way. Let's get started!

Amy

Recording Business Transactions

Learning Objective

2   Record, in column form, a group of business transactions involving changes in assets, liabilities, and owner's equity.

As explained in the Introduction, business transactions are events that have a direct effect on the operations of an economic unit or enterprise and are expressed in terms of money. Each business transaction must be recorded in the accounting records. As business transactions are recorded, the amounts listed under the headings Assets, Liabilities, and Owner's Equity change. However, **the total of one side of the fundamental accounting equation must equal the total of the other side.** The categories under these three main headings are called **accounts**.

Let's look at a group of business transactions. These transactions are typical of those seen in a service or professional business. In these transactions, let's assume that J. Conner establishes her own business and calls it Conner's Whitewater Adventures. Conner's Whitewater Adventures is a **sole proprietorship**, or a one-owner business.

TRANSACTION (a).   **Owner deposited $90,000 in a bank account in the name of the business.** Conner deposits $90,000 cash in a separate bank account in the name of Conner's Whitewater Adventures. This separate bank account will help Conner keep her business investment separate from her personal funds. This is an example of the **separate entity concept**, which says a business is treated as a separate economic or accounting entity. (See Figure 1.) The business is independent, or stands by itself; it is separate from its owners, creditors, and customers.

The Cash account consists of bank deposits and money on hand. The business now has $90,000 more in cash than before, and Conner's investment has increased by $90,000.

Figure 1
Separate entity concept

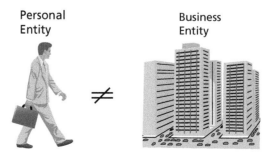

Personal Entity   Business Entity

The account denoted by the owner's name followed by the word *Capital* indicates the amount of the owner's investment, or equity, in the business. The effect of this transaction on the fundamental accounting equation is as follows:

	Assets	=	**Liabilities**	+	**Owner's Equity**
	Items owned		*Amounts owed to creditors*		*Owner's investment*
	Cash	=			J. Conner, Capital
(a)	**+90,000**	=			**+90,000**

Besides cash, an investment may be in the form of goods, such as equipment. Therefore, the word *Capital* used under Owner's Equity does not always mean that cash was invested.

Accounting, as we said before, is the process of analyzing, classifying, recording, summarizing, and interpreting business transactions in terms of money. Look at transaction (a) above and see if you understand that we have gone through certain steps, which are stated below in question form.

STEP 1. What accounts are involved? Cash and J. Conner, Capital are involved.

STEP 2. What are the classifications of the accounts involved? Cash is an asset account, and J. Conner, Capital is an owner's equity account.

STEP 3. Are the accounts increased or decreased? Cash is increased because Conner's Whitewater Adventures has more cash now than it had before. J. Conner, Capital is increased because Conner has a greater investment now than she had before.

STEP 4. Is the equation in balance after the transaction has been recorded? Yes.

We will stress this step-by-step process throughout the text. This example serves as an introduction to **double-entry accounting**. The "double" entry method is demonstrated by the fact that each transaction must be recorded in at least two accounts, keeping the accounting equation in balance.

For example, transaction (a) resulted in a plus $90,000 and a plus $90,000 *on each side of the equation.* **The left side of the equation must always equal the right side of the equation.**

TRANSACTION (b). Company bought equipment, paying cash, $38,000. Conner's first task is to get her company ready for business; to do that, she needs the proper equipment. Accordingly, Conner buys equipment costing $38,000 and pays cash. **Note at this point that Conner does not invest any new money. She simply exchanges part of the business's cash for equipment.** Because equipment is a new type of property for the firm, a new account, Equipment, is created. Equipment is included under Assets because it is something of value owned by the business. As a result of this transaction, the accounting equation changes.

	Assets	=	**Liabilities**	+	**Owner's Equity**
	Items owned		*Amounts owed to creditors*		*Owner's investment*
	Cash + Equipment	=			J. Conner, Capital
Initial Investment	90,000	=			90,000
(b)	**−38,000 + 38,000**				
New balances	52,000 + 38,000	=			90,000
	90,000				90,000

STEP 1. **What accounts are involved?** Cash and Equipment are involved.

STEP 2. **What are the classifications of the accounts involved?** Cash is an asset account, and Equipment is an asset account.

STEP 3. **Are the accounts increased or decreased?** Cash is decreased because Conner used cash to purchase the equipment. Equipment is increased because Conner's Whitewater Adventures has more equipment now than it had before.

STEP 4. **Is the equation in balance after the transaction is recorded?** Yes.

Remember that the recording of each transaction must yield an equation that is in balance. In this example, the transaction was recorded on *the same side*. Is that okay? Yes! For example, transaction (b) resulted in a minus $38,000 and a plus $38,000 on the *same side*, with nothing recorded on the other side. This results in an overall change of $0 ($38,000 – $38,000) for each side. It does not matter whether you change one side or both sides. **The important point is that whenever a transaction is properly recorded, the accounting equation remains in balance.**

TRANSACTION (c). **Company bought equipment on account from a supplier, $4,320.** Conner's Whitewater Adventures buys equipment costing $4,320 on credit from Signal Products.

The Equipment account shows an increase because the business now owns $4,320 more in equipment. The terms *on credit* or *on account* mean that Conner's Whitewater Adventures does not pay cash for the equipment but instead will owe Signal Products money to be paid in the future. This causes an increase in liabilities because the business now owes $4,320. The liability account **Accounts Payable** is used for short-term obligations or charge accounts, usually due within 30 days. Because Conner's Whitewater Adventures owes money to Signal Products, Signal Products is called a creditor of Conner's Whitewater Adventures. A total of $94,320 is now on each side of the equal sign.

	Assets		=	Liabilities	+	Owner's Equity
	Items owned			*Amounts owed to creditors*		*Owner's investment*
	Cash	+ Equipment	=	Accounts Payable	+	J. Conner, Capital
Previous balances	52,000 +	38,000	=			90,000
(c)		+4,320		+4,320		
New balances	52,000 +	42,320	=	4,320	+	90,000
	94,320			94,320		

STEP 1. **What accounts are involved?** Equipment and Accounts Payable are involved.

STEP 2. **What are the classifications of the accounts involved?** Equipment is an asset account, and Accounts Payable is a liability account.

STEP 3. **Are the accounts increased or decreased?** Equipment is increased because Conner's Whitewater Adventures has more equipment now than it had before. Accounts Payable is increased because Conner's owes more to creditors than it owed before.

STEP 4. **Is the equation in balance after the transaction is recorded?** Yes.

TRANSACTION (d). **Company paid a creditor on account, $2,000.** Conner's Whitewater Adventures pays $2,000 to Signal Products to be applied against the firm's liability of $4,320.

	Assets		=	Liabilities	+	Owner's Equity
	Items owned			*Amounts owed to creditors*		*Owner's investment*
	Cash	+ Equipment	=	Accounts Payable	+	J. Conner, Capital
Previous balances	52,000 +	42,320	=	4,320	+	90,000
(d)	−2,000			−2,000		
New balances	50,000 +	42,320	=	2,320	+	90,000
	92,320			92,320		

STEP 1. **What accounts are involved?** Cash and Accounts Payable are involved.

STEP 2. **What are the classifications of the accounts involved?** Cash is an asset account, and Accounts Payable is a liability account.

STEP 3. **Are the accounts increased or decreased?** Cash is decreased because Conner used cash to pay Signal Products. Accounts Payable is decreased because Conner's owes less now than it owed before.

STEP 4. **Is the equation in balance after the transaction is recorded?** Yes.

TRANSACTION (e). **Owner invested equipment in the business.** Conner invested her own computer equipment, having a **fair market value** of $5,200, in Conner's Whitewater Adventures. **Fair market value is the present worth of an asset.** It is the amount that would be received if the asset were sold on the open market. Examples of additional investments by owners may be in the form of equipment, cash, tools, or real estate.

	Assets		=	Liabilities	+	Owner's Equity
	Items owned			*Amounts owed to creditors*		*Owner's investment*
	Cash	+ Equipment	=	Accounts Payable	+	J. Conner, Capital
Previous balances	50,000 +	42,320	=	2,320	+	90,000
(e)		+5,200				+5,200
New balances	50,000 +	47,520	=	2,320	+	95,200
	97,520			97,520		

STEP 1. **What accounts are involved?** Equipment and J. Conner, Capital are involved.

STEP 2. **What are the classifications of the accounts involved?** Equipment is an asset account, and J. Conner, Capital is an owner's equity account.

STEP 3. **Are the accounts increased or decreased?** Equipment is increased because Conner's Whitewater Adventures now has more equipment than it had before. J. Conner, Capital is increased because Conner has a greater investment now than she had before.

STEP 4. **Is the equation in balance after the transaction is recorded?** Yes.

Summary of Transactions

Let's summarize the business transactions of Conner's Whitewater Adventures in column form. To test your understanding of the recording procedure, describe the nature of the transactions that have taken place.

	Assets		=	Liabilities	+	Owner's Equity
	Items owned			*Amounts owed to creditors*		*Owner's investment*
	Cash	+ Equipment	=	Accounts Payable	+	J. Conner, Capital
Transaction (a)	+90,000					+90,000
Transaction (b)	−38,000	+38,000				
Balance	52,000 +	38,000	=			90,000
Transaction (c)		+4,320		+4,320		
Balance	52,000 +	42,320	=	4,320	+	90,000
Transaction (d)	−2,000			−2,000		
Balance	50,000 +	42,320	=	2,320	+	90,000
Transaction (e)		+5,200				+5,200
Balance	50,000 +	47,520	=	2,320	+	95,200
		97,520			97,520	

The following observations apply to all types of business transactions:

1. Every transaction is recorded as an increase and/or decrease in two or more accounts.
2. One side of the equation is always equal to the other side of the equation.

In this chapter, we are using a column arrangement as a practical device to show how transactions are recorded. This arrangement is useful for showing increases and decreases in various accounts as a result of the transactions. We also show new balances after each transaction is recorded.

ACCOUNTING IN YOUR FUTURE

ACCOUNTING SKILLS

You may wonder why taking an accounting class is important. One possible career for students who study accounting is as an entry-level accounting clerk for a company. As an accounting clerk, you would be the financial recordkeeper for the business. Your responsibilities would include maintaining accounting records, such as those you are learning about in this chapter. You might also be responsible for preparing financial statements, making bank deposits, and handling payroll.

Many businesses require that an accounting clerk have a high school diploma and some accounting course work. An associate degree in accounting is highly recommended. Minimum requirements are a knowledge of basic accounting terminology, concepts, and processes, and using a manual accounting system or an automated accounting system such as general ledger accounting software. Skills related to Microsoft® Word®, Excel®, and Outlook® also are helpful.* You need to be able to work with others in the accounting department and be attentive to detail and accuracy. Accounting clerks, sometimes called bookkeepers, can become certified bookkeepers by meeting the requirements of the American Institute of Professional Bookkeepers (www.aipb.org). The U.S. Department of Labor's Bureau of Labor Statistics (www.bls.gov) provides information about this field, including job locations and pay scales.

Microsoft, Encarta, MSN, and Windows are either registered trademarks or trademarks of Microsoft Corporation in the United States and/or other countries.

REVENUE AND EXPENSE ACCOUNTS

Revenues are the amounts earned by a business. Examples of revenues are fees earned for performing services, income from selling merchandise, rent income from tenants for the use of property, and interest income for lending money. Revenues may be in the form of cash or credit card receipts. Revenues may also result from credit sales to charge customers, in which case cash will be received at a later time.

Expenses (or the costs of doing business) are the costs that relate to earning revenue. Examples of expenses are wages expense for labor performed, rent expense for the use of property, interest expense for the use of money, and advertising expense for the use of various media (for example, newspapers, radio, direct mail, and the Internet). Expenses may be paid in cash either when incurred or at a later time. Expenses to be paid at a later time involve Accounts Payable.

Revenues and expenses directly affect owner's equity. **If a business earns revenue, an increase in owner's equity occurs. When a business incurs expenses, owner's equity decreases.** For the present, think of it this way: If the company makes money, the

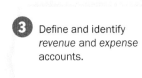
Define and identify *revenue* and *expense* accounts.

Learning Objective

Incurred is another word for *being responsible for* or *having taken place.*

owner's equity is increased. If the company has to pay out money for the costs of doing business, the owner's equity is decreased. Revenues and expenses fall under the umbrella of owner's equity: Revenue increases owner's equity; expenses decrease owner's equity.

Figure 2

The umbrella of owner's equity

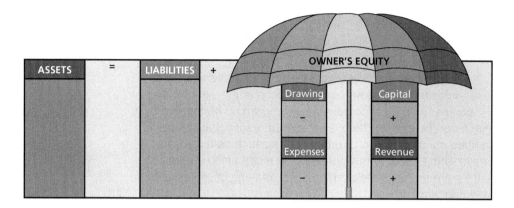

Chart of Accounts

The **chart of accounts** is the official list of accounts *tailor-made* for the business. All of the company's transactions must be recorded using the official account titles. The numbers preceding the account titles are the **account numbers**.

We now present the chart of accounts for Conner's Whitewater Adventures. Some of the accounts are new to you, but they will be explained as we move along. In the numbering of account titles, the 100s are used for assets, the 200s are used for liabilities, the 300s are used for owner's equity accounts, the 400s are used for revenue accounts, and the 500s are used for expense accounts.

CHART OF ACCOUNTS

Assets (100–199)
111 Cash
113 Accounts Receivable
115 Supplies
117 Prepaid Insurance
124 Equipment

Liabilities (200–299)
221 Accounts Payable

Owner's Equity (300–399)
311 J. Conner, Capital
312 J. Conner, Drawing

Revenue (400–499)
411 Income from Tours

Expenses (500–599)
511 Wages Expense
512 Rent Expense
514 Advertising Expense
515 Utilities Expense

While charts of accounts vary from business to business, the beginning numbers for assets, liabilities, owner's equity, revenues, and expenses are standard for a service business. Some account numbers are much longer than three digits. In any case, use the exact account titles listed in the company's chart of accounts.

For merchandising businesses selling goods (versus services), expenses will start with the 600s because accounts starting with the 500s are reserved for accounts related to the cost of the goods being sold.

Most accounting programs, such as QuickBooks, include a standard chart of accounts set up for many different types of businesses.

©Annette Shaff/Shutterstock.com

In the Real World

Every company must have a chart of accounts. For example, the popular Internet search provider Google has a chart of accounts similar to but much bigger than the example we're using. What might be some names of some accounts Google might have in its chart of accounts? Why is a listing of accounts so important?

Recording Business Transactions

Let's examine more transactions of Conner's Whitewater Adventures for the first month of operations. Soon after the opening of Conner's Whitewater Adventures, the first customers arrive, beginning a flow of revenue for the business.

4 Record, in column form, a group of business transactions involving all five elements of the fundamental accounting equation.

Learning Objective

TRANSACTION (f). **Company sold services for cash, $8,000.** Conner's Whitewater Adventures receives cash revenue of $8,000 in return for providing whitewater rafting tours for customers over a two-week period. In other words, the company earns $8,000 for services performed for cash customers. Revenue has the effect of increasing owner's equity, but because the company wants to know how much revenue is earned, we set up a special column for revenue. The revenue account for Conner's Whitewater Adventures is called Income from Tours. The accounting equation is affected as follows (PB stands for previous balance, and NB stands for new balance).

	Assets			=	Liabilities	+	Owner's Equity		
	Cash	+	Equipment	=	Accounts Payable	+	J. Conner, Capital	+	Revenue
PB	50,000	+	47,520	=	2,320	+	95,200		
(f)	+8,000								+8,000 (Income from Tours)
NB	58,000	+	47,520	=	2,320	+	95,200	+	8,000
		105,520					105,520		

Let's review the mental process for formulating the entry.

STEP 1. **What accounts are involved?** In this transaction, they are Cash and Income from Tours.

STEP 2. **What are the classifications of the accounts involved?** Cash is an asset account, and Income from Tours is a revenue account and part of owner's equity.

STEP 3. **Are the accounts increased or decreased?** Cash is increased because Conner's Whitewater Adventures received cash. Income from Tours (revenue) is increased.

STEP 4. **Is the equation in balance after the transaction has been recorded?** Yes.

TRANSACTION (g). **Company paid rent (an expense) for the month, $1,250.** Shortly after opening the business, Conner's Whitewater Adventures pays the month's rent of $1,250. Rent is payment for the privilege of occupying property.

It seems logical that if revenue is added to owner's equity, expenses (the opposite of revenue) must be subtracted from owner's equity. To be consistent, a separate column is set up for expenses.

Because the time period represented by the rent payment is one month or less, we record the $1,250 as an expense. If the payment covered a period longer than one month, we would record the amount under an asset called Prepaid Rent.

	Assets		=	**Liabilities**	+		**Owner's Equity**		
	Cash	+ Equip.	=	Accounts Payable	+	J. Conner, Capital	+ Revenue	− Expenses	
PB	58,000	+ 47,520	=	2,320	+	95,200	+ 8,000		
(g)	−1,250							+1,250 (Rent Expense)	
NB	56,750	+ 47,520	=	2,320	+	95,200	+ 8,000	− 1,250	
		104,270					104,270		

STEP 1. **What accounts are involved?** Cash and Rent Expense are involved.

STEP 2. **What are the classifications of the accounts involved?** Cash is an asset account, and Rent Expense is an owner's equity account.

STEP 3. **Are the accounts increased or decreased?** Cash is decreased because after the payment, Conner's Whitewater Adventures has less cash than before. Rent Expense is increased because now Conner's Whitewater Adventures has more rent expense than before.

STEP 4. **Is the equation in balance after the transaction is recorded?** Yes. Notice that in this equation, it looks as though the account doesn't balance—there is a negative entry on the left and a positive entry on the right. This is deceiving. The entry to Rent Expense is a positive entry in a negative column, thus creating an overall negative entry. It looks like this: $-(+1,250) = -1,250$.

TRANSACTION (h). **Company bought supplies on credit, $675.** Conner's Whitewater Adventures buys office supplies costing $675 on credit from Fineman Company. Computer paper, ink cartridges, invoice pads, pens and pencils, folders, filing cabinets, and calculators are considered supplies to be used by Conner's Whitewater Adventures for the business. Supplies are recorded as an asset until they are used. When supplies are used, they are taken from the asset account and placed in the expense account. We'll talk more about this later. For the time being, because Conner hasn't used the supplies yet, we will record them as an asset.

Assets			=	Liabilities	+	Owner's Equity		
				Accounts		J. Conner,		
Cash	+ Equip.	+ Supplies =		Payable	+	Capital	+ Revenue	− Expenses
PB 56,750	+ 47,520	=		2,320	+	95,200	+ 8,000	− 1,250
(h)		+**675**		+**675**				
NB 56,750	+ 47,520 +	675 =		2,995	+	95,200	+ 8,000	− 1,250
	104,945					104,945		

STEP 1. **What accounts are involved?** Supplies and Accounts Payable are involved.

STEP 2. **What are the classifications of the accounts involved?** Supplies is an asset account, and Accounts Payable is a liability account.

STEP 3. **Are the accounts increased or decreased?** Supplies is increased as Conner's Whitewater Adventures now has more supplies than before. Accounts Payable is increased as Conner's Whitewater Adventures now owes money for the purchase of supplies.

STEP 4. **Is the equation in balance after the transaction has been recorded?** Yes.

TRANSACTION (i). **Company paid cash for insurance, $1,875.** Conner's Whitewater Adventures paid $1,875 for a three-month liability insurance policy. At the time of payment, the company has not used up the insurance; thus, it is not yet an expense. As the insurance expires (is used), it will become an expense. **However, because it is paid in advance for a period longer than one month, it has value over that longer period and is, therefore, recorded as Prepaid Insurance, an asset.**

At the end of the year or accounting period, an adjustment will have to be made to take out the expired portion (that is, coverage for the months that have been used up) and record it as an expense. We discuss this adjustment in a later chapter.

Assets				=	Liabilities	+	Owner's Equity		
			Ppd.		Accounts		J. Conner,		
Cash	+ Equip.	+ Supplies +	Ins. =		Payable	+	Capital	+ Revenue	− Expenses
PB 56,750	+ 47,520	+ 675		=	2,995	+	95,200	+ 8,000	− 1,250
(i) −**1,875**			+**1,875**						
NB 54,875	+ 47,520	+ 675 +	1,875 =		2,995	+	95,200	+ 8,000	− 1,250
	104,945						104,945		

STEP 1. **What accounts are involved?** Cash and Prepaid Insurance are involved.

STEP 2. **What are the classifications of the accounts involved?** Cash and Prepaid Insurance are both asset accounts.

STEP 3. **Are the accounts increased or decreased?** Cash is decreased because Conner's Whitewater Adventures is paying money, and Prepaid Insurance is increased because Conner's Whitewater Adventures has more insurance than before.

STEP 4. **Is the equation in balance after the transaction is recorded?** Yes.

Remember that each time a transaction is recorded, the total amount on one side of the equation **remains equal** to the total amount on the other side. As proof of this equality, look at the following computation:

Cash	$ 54,875	**Accounts Payable**	$ 2,995
Equipment	47,520	**J. Conner, Capital**	95,200
Supplies	675	**Revenue**	8,000
Prepaid Insurance	1,875	**Expenses**	−1,250
	$104,945		$104,945

Steps in Analyzing Transactions

Now that we have recorded transactions in all five classifications of accounts, let's review the steps we followed.

FYI

Think through these steps each time you are presented with a transaction. We'll work through several more examples for Conner's Whitewater Adventures. However, we won't continue to show the steps. If you need extra help, write the steps in the margin.

STEP 1. Read the transaction to understand what is happening and how it affects the business. For example, the business has more revenue or has more expenses or has more cash or owes less to creditors. Identify the accounts involved. Look for Cash first; you will quickly recognize whether cash is coming in or going out.

STEP 2. Decide on the classifications of the accounts involved. For example, Equipment is something the business owns, and it's an asset; Accounts Payable is an amount the business owes, and it's a liability.

STEP 3. Decide whether the accounts are increased or decreased.

STEP 4. After recording the transaction, make sure the accounting equation is in balance.

SMALL BUSINESS **SUCCESS**

Tools to Success—The U.S. Small Business Administration

Throughout the pages of this text, you will occasionally find a feature labeled Small Business Success. This feature is designed to provide insight into accounting issues surrounding small businesses. Some of you may own a small business when you graduate; maybe you are thinking of starting your own small bookkeeping firm. Many of you will work in small businesses such as a local or regional accounting firm. These features contain information that is useful to small and large businesses and will be helpful if you are thinking about owning your own business.

The U.S. Small Business Administration website (www.sba.gov) is a great place to find information about managing, accounting for, and running a small business. Take a moment to go to the website and review the tools that are available to small businesses. Click on the Starting & Managing link, and you will find information that deals with starting a new business, managing a business, and financing a business.

You can also find audio and video podcasts on the website that provide information about business success. If you are interested in hearing about successful small businesses, you can find a series on small business features. The series discusses various small businesses that have used the tools provided by the Small Business Administration and have grown to be successful and profitable entities.

Keep an eye out for the Small Business Success feature! It will give you insight into how businesses use the accounting information you are learning in this course.

TRANSACTION (j). **Company received a bill for an expense, $620.** Conner's Whitewater Adventures receives a bill from *The Times* for newspaper advertising, $620. **Conner's Whitewater Adventures has received the bill for advertising; it has not paid any cash.** Previously, we described an expense as cash paid or to be paid for the cost of doing business. An expense of $620 has now been incurred (or has taken place), and it should be recorded as an increase in expenses (Advertising Expense). Also, because the company owes $620 more than it did before and it intends to pay at a later time, this amount should be recorded as an increase in Accounts Payable. Notice that Cash is not used because the bill has not been paid.

	Assets					=	Liabilities	+	Owner's Equity			
	Cash	+ Equip.	+ Supplies	+	Ppd. Ins.	=	Accounts Payable	+	J. Conner, Capital	+ Revenue	−	Expenses
PB	54,875	+ 47,520	+ 675	+	1,875	=	2,995	+	95,200	+ 8,000	−	1,250
(j)							+620					+620 (Advertising Expense)
NB	54,875	+ 47,520	+ 675	+	1,875	=	3,615	+	95,200	+ 8,000	−	1,870
	104,945								104,945			

TRANSACTION (k). **Company sold services on account, $6,750.** Conner's Whitewater Adventures signs a contract with Crystal River Lodge to provide rafting adventures for guests. Conner's Whitewater Adventures provides 27 one-day rafting tours and bills Crystal River Lodge for $6,750.

A company uses the **Accounts Receivable** account to record the amounts due from (legal claims against) charge customers. Because Conner's Whitewater Adventures' claim against Crystal River Lodge of $6,750 is promised to be paid, it is recorded in Accounts Receivable. Revenue is earned or recognized when the service is performed even though the $6,750 has not been received in cash. We count the $6,750 as an increase in revenue and an increase in Accounts Receivable. Keep in mind that Accounts Receivable is an asset, or something that is owned. Conner's Whitewater Adventures owns a claim of $6,750 against Crystal River Lodge.

	Assets						=	Liabilities	+	Owner's Equity		
	Cash	+ Equip.	+ Supplies	+	Ppd. Ins.	+ Accts. Rec.	=	Accounts Payable	+	J. Conner, Capital	+ Revenue	− Expenses
PB	54,875	+ 47,520	+ 675	+	1,875		=	3,615	+	95,200	+ 8,000	− 1,870
(k)						+6,750					+6,750 (Income from Tours)	
NB	54,875	+ 47,520	+ 675	+	1,875	+ 6,750	=	3,615	+	95,200	+ 14,750	− 1,870
	111,695									111,695		

When Crystal River Lodge pays the $6,750 bill in cash, Conner's Whitewater Adventures records this transaction as an increase in Cash and a decrease in Accounts Receivable. At that time, Conner's Whitewater Adventures will *not* have to make an entry for the revenue because the **revenue was earned and recorded when the service was performed.**

TRANSACTION (l). Company paid creditor on account. Conner's Whitewater Adventures pays $1,500 to Signal Products, its creditor (the party to whom it owes money), as partial payment on account for the liability recorded in transaction (c).

	Cash	+	Equip.	+	Supplies	+	Ppd. Ins.	+	Accts. Rec.	=	Accounts Payable	+	J. Conner, Capital	+	Revenue	−	Expenses
PB	54,875	+	47,520	+	675	+	1,875	+	6,750	=	3,615	+	95,200	+	14,750	−	1,870
(l)	−1,500										−1,500						
NB	53,375	+	47,520	+	675	+	1,875	+	6,750	=	2,115	+	95,200	+	14,750	−	1,870

110,195   110,195

TRANSACTION (m). Company paid an expense in cash, $225. Conner's Whitewater Adventures receives a bill from Solar Power, Inc., for $225. Because the bill was not previously recorded as a liability and is to be paid immediately, we record the amount directly as an expense.

	Cash	+	Equip.	+	Supplies	+	Ppd. Ins.	+	Accts. Rec.	=	Accounts Payable	+	J. Conner, Capital	+	Revenue	−	Expenses
PB	53,375	+	47,520	+	675	+	1,875	+	6,750	=	2,115	+	95,200	+	14,750	−	1,870
(m)	−225																+225 (Utilities Expense)
NB	53,150	+	47,520	+	675	+	1,875	+	6,750	=	2,115	+	95,200	+	14,750	−	2,095

109,970   109,970

TRANSACTION (n). Company paid creditor on account, $620. Conner's Whitewater Adventures pays $620 to *The Times* for advertising. Recall that this bill had previously been recorded as a liability in transaction (j).

	Cash	+	Equip.	+	Supplies	+	Ppd. Ins.	+	Accts. Rec.	=	Accounts Payable	+	J. Conner, Capital	+	Revenue	−	Expenses
PB	53,150	+	47,520	+	675	+	1,875	+	6,750	=	2,115	+	95,200	+	14,750	−	2,095
(n)	−620										−620						
NB	52,530	+	47,520	+	675	+	1,875	+	6,750	=	1,495	+	95,200	+	14,750	−	2,095

109,350   109,350

TRANSACTION (o). Company paid an expense in cash, $2,360. Conner's Whitewater Adventures pays wages of a part-time employee, $2,360.

	Assets					=	Liabilities	+		Owner's Equity		
	Cash	+ Equip.	+ Supplies	+ Ppd. Ins.	+ Accts. Rec.	=	Accounts Payable	+	J. Conner, Capital	+ Revenue	− Expenses
PB	52,530	+ 47,520	+ 675	+ 1,875	+ 6,750	=	1,495	+	95,200	+ 14,750	− 2,095
(o)	−2,360										+2,360 (Wages Expense)
NB	50,170	+ 47,520	+ 675	+ 1,875	+ 6,750	=	1,495	+	95,200	+ 14,750	− 4,455
			106,990							106,990	

TRANSACTION (p). **Company buys equipment on account for $3,780, making a cash down payment of $1,850 and charging $1,930.** Conner's Whitewater Adventures buys additional equipment from Signal Products for $3,780, paying $1,850 down with the remaining $1,930 on account. Because buying an item *on account* is the same as buying it *on credit,* both terms are used to describe such transactions and involve Accounts Payable.

	Assets					=	Liabilities	+		Owner's Equity		
	Cash	+ Equip.	+ Supplies	+ Ppd. Ins.	+ Accts. Rec.	=	Accounts Payable	+	J. Conner, Capital	+ Revenue	− Expenses
PB	50,170	+ 47,520	+ 675	+ 1,875	+ 6,750	=	1,495	+	95,200	+ 14,750	− 4,455
(p)	−1,850	+3,780					+1,930				
NB	48,320	+ 51,300	+ 675	+ 1,875	+ 6,750	=	3,425	+	95,200	+ 14,750	− 4,455
			108,920							108,920	

Again, because the equipment is expected to last for years, Conner's Whitewater Adventures lists this $3,780 as an increase in the assets. Note that three accounts are involved in this transaction: Cash because cash was paid out, Equipment because the company has more equipment than it had before, and Accounts Payable because the company owes more now than it owed before.

TRANSACTION (q). **Company receives cash on account from credit customer, $2,500.** Conner's Whitewater Adventures receives $2,500 from Crystal River Lodge to apply against the amount billed in transaction (k). Because Crystal River Lodge now owes Conner's Whitewater Adventure less than it did before, Conner's Whitewater Adventures deducts the $2,500 from Accounts Receivable. An exchange of assets has no effect on the totals of the equation.

	Assets					=	Liabilities	+		Owner's Equity		
	Cash	+ Equip.	+ Supplies	+ Ppd. Ins.	+ Accts. Rec.	=	Accounts Payable	+	J. Conner, Capital	+ Revenue	− Expenses
PB	48,320	+ 51,300	+ 675	+ 1,875	+ 6,750	=	3,425	+	95,200	+ 14,750	− 4,455
(q)	+2,500				−2,500						
NB	50,820	+ 51,300	+ 675	+ 1,875	+ 4,250	=	3,425	+	95,200	+ 14,750	− 4,455
			108,920							108,920	

Conner's Whitewater Adventures previously listed the amount as revenue [see transaction (k)], so it should *not* be recorded as revenue again.

TRANSACTION (r). **Company sells services for cash, $8,570.** Conner's Whitewater Adventures receives revenue from cash customers during the rest of the month, $8,570.

	Cash	+ Equip.	+ Supplies	+ Ppd. Ins.	+ Accts. Rec.	= Accounts Payable	+ J. Conner, Capital	+ Revenue	− Expenses
Assets						**= Liabilities +**		**Owner's Equity**	
PB	50,820	+ 51,300	+ 675	+ 1,875	+ 4,250	= 3,425	+ 95,200	+ 14,750	− 4,455
(r)	+8,570							+8,570 (Income from Tours)	
NB	59,390	+ 51,300	+ 675	+ 1,875	+ 4,250	= 3,425	+ 95,200	+ 23,320	− 4,455
			117,490					117,490	

TRANSACTION (s). **Owner makes a cash withdrawal, $3,500.** At the end of the month, Conner withdraws $3,500 in cash from the business for her personal living costs. A **withdrawal** (or drawing) may be considered the opposite of an investment in cash by the owner and is treated as a decrease in owner's equity. Withdrawals are different from expenses. Expenses are paid to someone else for the cost of goods or services used in the business. On the other hand, withdrawals are paid directly to the owner and do not involve the cost of goods or services used in the business. A withdrawal may consist of cash or other assets.

Because the owner takes cash out of the business, there is a decrease of $3,500 in Cash. This withdrawal of cash also decreases owner's equity and is denoted in the account labeled with the owner's name followed by the word *Drawing*. We record $3,500 under J. Conner, Drawing.

	Cash	+ Equip.	+ Supplies	+ Ppd. Ins.	+ Accts. Rec.	= Accounts Payable	+ J. Conner, Capital	− J. Conner, Drawing	+ Revenue	− Expenses
Assets						**= Liabilities +**		**Owner's Equity**		
PB	59,390	+ 51,300	+ 675	+ 1,875	+ 4,250	= 3,425	+ 95,200		+ 23,320	− 4,455
(s)	−3,500							+3,500		
NB	55,890	+ 51,300	+ 675	+ 1,875	+ 4,250	= 3,425	+ 95,200	− 3,500	+ 23,320	− 4,455
			113,990					113,990		

Summary of Transactions (f) through (s)

Figure 3 summarizes business transactions (f) through (s) of Conner's Whitewater Adventures with the transactions identified by letter. To test your understanding of the recording procedure, describe the nature of the transactions.

Figure 3
Summary of transactions (f) through (s)

	Assets					=	Liabilities	+	Owner's Equity				
	Cash	+ Equip.	+ Supplies	+ Ppd. Ins.	+ Accts. Rec.	=	Accounts Payable	+ J. Conner, Capital	− J. Conner, Drawing	+ Revenue	− Expenses			
Bal.	50,000	+ 47,520				=	2,320	+ 95,200					
(f)	+8,000									+8,000 (Income from Tours)			
Bal.	58,000	+ 47,520				=	2,320	+ 95,200		+ 8,000			
(g)	−1,250										+1,250 (Rent Exp.)		
Bal.	56,750	+ 47,520				=	2,320	+ 95,200		+ 8,000	− 1,250		
(h)			+675				+675						
Bal.	56,750	+ 47,520	+ 675			=	2,995	+ 95,200		+ 8,000	− 1,250		
(i)	−1,875			+1,875									
Bal.	54,875	+ 47,520	+ 675	+ 1,875		=	2,995	+ 95,200		+ 8,000	− 1,250		
(j)							+620				+620 (Adv. Exp.)		
Bal.	54,875	+ 47,520	+ 675	+ 1,875		=	3,615	+ 95,200		+ 8,000	− 1,870		
(k)					+6,750					+6,750 (Income from Tours)			
Bal.	54,875	+ 47,520	+ 675	+ 1,875	+ 6,750	=	3,615	+ 95,200		+ 14,750	− 1,870		
(l)	−1,500						−1,500						
Bal.	53,375	+ 47,520	+ 675	+ 1,875	+ 6,750	=	2,115	+ 95,200		+ 14,750	− 1,870		
(m)	−225										+225 (Util. Exp.)		
Bal.	53,150	+ 47,520	+ 675	+ 1,875	+ 6,750	=	2,115	+ 95,200		+ 14,750	− 2,095		
(n)	−620						−620						
Bal.	52,530	+ 47,520	+ 675	+ 1,875	+ 6,750	=	1,495	+ 95,200		+ 14,750	− 2,095		
(o)	−2,360										+2,360 (Wages Exp.)		
Bal.	50,170	+ 47,520	+ 675	+ 1,875	+ 6,750	=	1,495	+ 95,200		+ 14,750	− 4,455		
(p)	−1,850	+3,780					+1,930						
Bal.	48,320	+ 51,300	+ 675	+ 1,875	+ 6,750	=	3,425	+ 95,200		+ 14,750	− 4,455		
(q)	+2,500				−2,500								
Bal.	50,820	+ 51,300	+ 675	+ 1,875	+ 4,250	=	3,425	+ 95,200		+ 14,750	− 4,455		
(r)	+8,570									+8,570 (Income from Tours)			
Bal.	59,390	+ 51,300	+ 675	+ 1,875	+ 4,250	=	3,425	+ 95,200		+ 23,320	− 4,455		
(s)	−3,500								+3,500				
Bal.	55,890	+ 51,300	+ 675	+ 1,875	+ 4,250	=	3,425	+ 95,200	− 3,500	+ 23,320	− 4,455		

Left Side of Equals Sign:		**Right Side of Equals Sign:**	
Cash	$ 55,890	Accounts Payable	$ 3,425
Equipment	51,300	J. Conner, Capital	95,200
Supplies	675	J. Conner, Drawing	−3,500
Prepaid Insurance	1,875	Revenue	23,320
Accounts Receivable	4,250	Expenses	−4,455
	$113,990		$113,990

YOU Make the Call

You've just been hired as an accounting clerk. The other accounting clerk, Sam, has asked you to check some transactions he analyzed. Use the transaction-analysis steps presented earlier in the chapter (see page 26) to determine the accuracy of the following transactions and write your own analysis.

SAM'S ANALYSES—FIND THE ERRORS

TRANSACTION 1. Received a bill for the month's rent, $1,000.

STEP 1. Cash and Rent Expense are the accounts involved.

STEP 2. Cash is an asset, and Rent Expense is an expense.

STEP 3. Cash is decreased, and Rent Expense is decreased.

TRANSACTION 2: Bought equipment on account for $1,800.

STEP 1. Equipment and Accounts Receivable are the accounts involved.

STEP 2. Equipment is an asset, and Accounts Receivable is an asset.

STEP 3. Equipment is decreased, and Accounts Receivable is increased.

SOLUTION

Sam's analyses for both transactions are incorrect.

TRANSACTION 1:

STEP 1. Accounts Payable and Rent Expense are the accounts involved.

STEP 2. The bill was received but not paid, therefore creating a liability. Cash is not involved because the business has not paid the monthly rent.

Accounts Payable is a liability, and Rent Expense is an expense.

STEP 3. Accounts Payable is increased, and Rent Expense is increased. Remember, the bill was only received, not paid; therefore, no cash is involved. Rent Expense increases, but its ultimate effect is a subtraction in the fundamental accounting equation.

TRANSACTION 2:

STEP 1. Equipment and Accounts Payable are the accounts involved.

STEP 2. Accounts Payable is involved because the business owes money to the seller. Accounts Payable is the account used to manage short-term liabilities. Accounts Receivable is the account used to keep track of what customers owe the business.

Equipment is an asset, and Accounts Payable is a liability.

STEP 3. Equipment is increased, and Accounts Payable is increased.

Accounting with *QuickBooks*®

In this text, you will learn how to record transactions and prepare financial reports for various companies using a **manual accounting system.** You will also have an opportunity to use QuickBooks, a **computerized accounting system.** In a manual accounting system, accounting transactions are recorded and financial reports are prepared by hand, rather than on a computer. Using the featured *Accounting with QuickBooks* section throughout this text, you will also learn how to record transactions and process financial reports in a computerized accounting system using QuickBooks.

Characteristics of Computerized Accounting Systems

A computerized accounting system records accounting transactions using a computer and accounting software. There are many types of accounting software. QuickBooks is a software program that is often used by small to medium-sized businesses.

 Identify the advantages and disadvantages of a computerized accounting system.

A majority of companies use some form of a computerized accounting system. They do so because the advantages of a computerized accounting system far outweigh the disadvantages. Some of the advantages of a computerized accounting system are as follows:

- **Automatic**—Computerized accounting systems automatically complete many parts of the accounting cycle. Once a user enters a transaction, the software posts the transaction to the ledger and updates the financial statements. In addition, computerized accounting systems perform financial calculations, such as totaling revenue and expenses and determining net income.

- **Timeliness**—Computerized accounting systems allow companies to prepare up-to-date financial reports quickly. Also, accountants can easily locate specific transactions they want to review or investigate.

- **Accuracy**—Errors, such as out-of-balance transactions, are eliminated using a computerized accounting system. The software alerts the user when a transaction is out of balance and will not let the user proceed until the transaction is balanced.

- **Ease of use**—Basic accounting systems, like QuickBooks, are easy to use and often require the user to have little previous accounting knowledge.

- **Security measures**—Computerized accounting systems provide a series of security measures that include passwords to restrict access and built-in error checks.

- **Analysis**—Companies can easily analyze their financial statements to identify performance measurements, including determining which services are and are not

Learning Objectives

After you have completed this section, you will be able to do the following:

1 Identify the advantages and disadvantages of a computerized accounting system.

2 Install and register QuickBooks.

3 Open or restore a company.

Learning Objective

4 Modify a company name.

5 View and use a chart of accounts.

6 Back up QuickBooks.

7 Close a company and exit QuickBooks.

ACCOUNTING WITH *QuickBooks*®

profitable, the percentage of cash spent on expenses, and comparisons between the current and previous fiscal periods.

- **Inexpensive**—Basic accounting systems like QuickBooks are relatively inexpensive to purchase and use.

There are also disadvantages to using computerized accounting systems. These include:

- **Security risks**—Even with the security measures accounting software provides, computer systems can still be hacked, and data can be compromised. In addition, data can be lost through power and/or computer failures. Some risks can be lessened by using a virus protection program and by performing routine **backups**. Backups store company data files in a safe place, such as online, or on an external backup device such as a USB flash drive, CD, or external hard drive.

- **User error**—Although QuickBooks and other computerized accounting systems are designed to help reduce certain input errors, such as out-of-balance transactions, errors can still occur. Transactions can be recorded incorrectly, and valuable information can be lost or deleted.

Getting Started with QuickBooks

In the first few chapters of this text, we use Conner's Whitewater Adventures to demonstrate how to record transactions and process reports in a computerized accounting system. We will be using the accounting program QuickBooks Accountant; however, Intuit the company that provides QuickBooks, also offers various other versions, including QuickBooks online. The online version of QuickBooks is an example of **cloud computing**. This version is used via the Internet, rather than a local computer. With cloud computing, authorized users can access software and data anywhere they have an Internet connection. Data and software do not have to be stored on an actual computer. To compare the various QuickBooks financial software packages, you can visit www.intuit.com.

Learning Objective   Install and register QuickBooks.

QuickBooks Tip

Your instructor may want you to use a different version of QuickBooks. Don't worry. Most of the instructions are similar for all versions of QuickBooks, even if the look is a little different.

If your *College Accounting* textbook came with a trial version of QuickBooks software, you will need to install the software CD on your computer. To install QuickBooks, follow these steps:

STEP 1. Be sure to close all open programs on your computer. You may also have to adjust your computer's security settings and/or close your antivirus software prior to installation.

STEP 2. Insert the QuickBooks CD into your computer's CD drive.

STEP 3. The QuickBooks installation should automatically start once the CD is inserted. Follow the installation instructions as prompted on your computer screen. If you have a previous trial version of QuickBooks on your computer, you may need to uninstall the prior version before installing the current version from the CD.

STEP 4. Now enter the license and product numbers that came with your QuickBooks CD. Be sure to put the CD and the license/product numbers in a safe place until your trial version has expired. You may need these items later if you require technical support.

STEP 5. Be sure to register your QuickBooks trial version during installation. Your trial version of QuickBooks is valid for 140 days; however, the software must be registered within 30 days or a certain number of log-ins, for you to receive the entire trial period. It is recommended that you wait until your instructor tells you to install and register your QuickBooks trial software. This will ensure that you have the software available for the entire time period you need for your course.

QuickBooks Tip

If you forget to register your QuickBooks trial version when you install it, click on the Help menu, then click Register QuickBooks. You can also contact Intuit Support at www.intuit.com or 888-859-4056.

Setting up a Company

The first step in using QuickBooks is to set up a company. This involves entering company information, including the name of the company, address, and industry. In addition, the chart of accounts is created. Notice in Figure Q1 that the chart of accounts is similar to the one we have already discussed.

Figure Q1
Chart of accounts

Name		Type
Conner's Whitewater Adventures - Janie Conner - QuickBooks Accountant 20-- [Chart of Accounts]		
File Edit View Lists Favorites Accountant Company Customers Vendors Employees Banking Reports Window Help		
• 111 Cash		Bank
• 113 Accounts Receivable		Accounts Receivable
• 115 Supplies		Other Current Asset
• 117 Prepaid Insurance		Other Current Asset
• 124 Equipment		Fixed Asset
• 221 Accounts Payable		Accounts Payable
• 311 J. Conner, Capital		Equity
• 312 J. Conner, Drawing		Equity
• 411 Income from Tours		Income
• 511 Wages Expense		Expense
• 512 Rent Expense		Expense
• 514 Advertising Expense		Expense
• 515 Utilities Expense		Expense

This course will not discuss how to set up companies since that is typically covered in a stand-alone computerized accounting course. For all problems in this book, you will be provided with data files that already have the company information set up.

3 Open or restore a company.

Learning Objective

STEP 1. Save the .QBB data file to your computer.
The QuickBooks data files are located on the textbook website at CengageBrain.com. It is recommended that you set up a new folder for your QuickBooks files so they are easy to locate later. The QuickBooks problems for this text will use two types of QuickBooks files: the backup file (.QBB) and the working file (.QBW). Before you can start entering transactions into QuickBooks, you will need to convert the backup file (.QBB) to a working file (.QBW). This will be covered in Step 2.

QuickBooks Tip

You cannot click directly on a QuickBooks backup file (.QBB) to open it. QuickBooks backup files (.QBB) must be restored from the QuickBooks program first.

STEP 2. Restore the file saved in Step 1.

- From the **File** menu or the opening page, click **Open or Restore Company**. (See Figure Q2.)

- Select **Restore a Backup Copy** and click **Next**.

- Now select **Local Backup** and click **Next**.

- Locate the QuickBooks backup file you saved in **Step 1**. Click **Open**.

- When the window **Where do you want to restore the file?** appears, click **Next**.

- Select the location where you want to save your file.

- Name your file per your instructor's instructions. You will now see (.QBW) in the file type. Click **Save**.

- A message will appear that QuickBooks is being restored. Click **OK** when you see the following window: **Your data has been restored successfully**.

Figure Q2
Opening or restoring a company

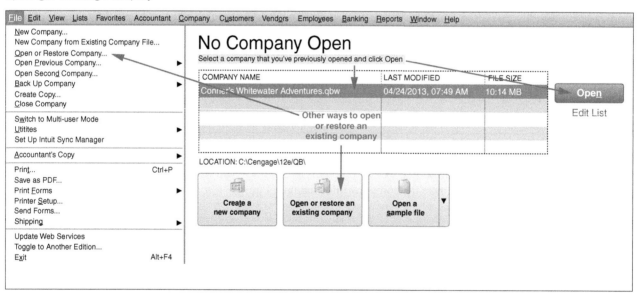

Learning Objective   **4** Modify a company name.

Your instructor may want you to distinguish your company reports from others. To make this distinction, you can insert your name with the company name under **Company Information**.

STEP 1. Select **Company** from the menu bar.

STEP 2. Select **Company Information**. (See Figure Q3.)

Figure Q3
Accessing company information

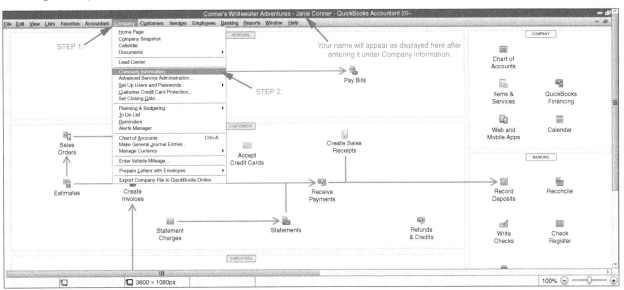

STEP 3. Enter your name as shown in Figure Q4 or according to your instructor's directions. Once you have added your name to the Company Name field, click **OK**.

Figure Q4
Company information screen

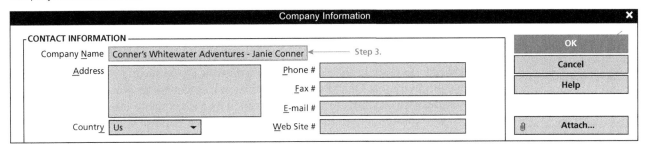

5 View and use a chart of accounts.

Learning Objective

There are three ways to view a chart of accounts in QuickBooks. (See Figure Q5.)

1. Select **Lists** from the menu bar on the home page, and then select **Chart of Accounts** from the dropdown list.
2. Select **Company** from the menu bar on the home page, and then select **Chart of Accounts** from the dropdown list (as shown).
3. Select **Chart of Accounts** directly from the home page.

ACCOUNTING WITH QuickBooks®

Figure Q5
Viewing chart of accounts

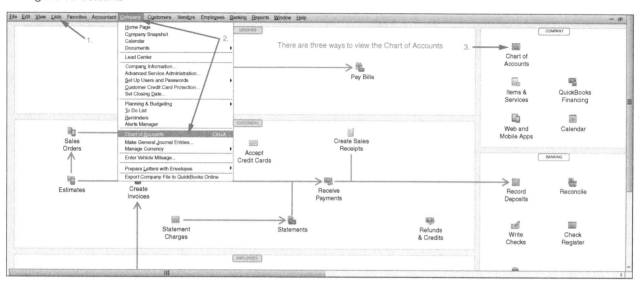

Learning Objective **6** Back up QuickBooks.

It is important to regularly back up your company's QuickBooks data files. You may decide to back up your company's data each time you close your QuickBooks company file, or you may decide to back up your company's data according to a predetermined schedule. Either way, it is important that you back up your company's QuickBooks data files often. As stated previously, be sure to back up and store your QuickBooks company data in a safe place, such as online or on an external backup device. In the real world, you should not back up your QuickBooks company data file to the computer where your original file is located. However, in the classroom, you will typically be storing your data on a flash drive. Be aware that QuickBooks will show a warning message when trying to restore your backup file (.QBB) to the same location as the company file (.QBW). For class purposes, you can ignore this warning message. As a reminder, in the real world you should save a backup copy on a different storage device than the original company file. It is also a good idea to store a backup copy offsite.

To start your backup, insert your external backup device, and then click on **Back Up Company**. A side menu item will appear. Select **Create Local Backup**. (See Figure Q6.)

QuickBooks Tip

Many companies choose to back up to the cloud. This provides the company with a secure offsite copy of its QuickBooks data, which cannot be destroyed by a disaster such as a fire or be intentionally deleted.

Figure Q6
Creating local backup

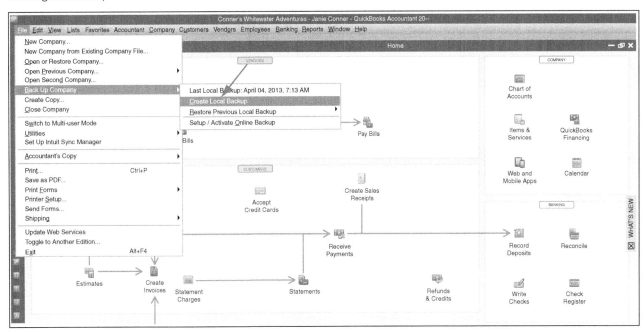

Now select **Local Backup**. Then select **Next** to proceed.

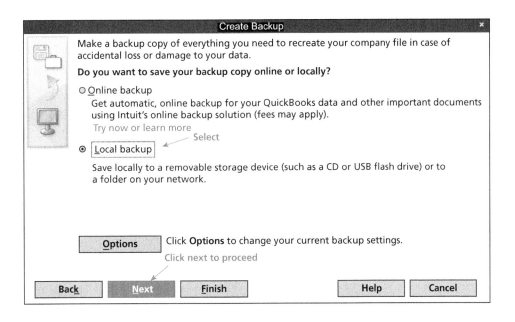

Figure Q7
Local backup

Select **Save It Now**, and then select **Next** to proceed.

Figure Q8
Saving backup copy

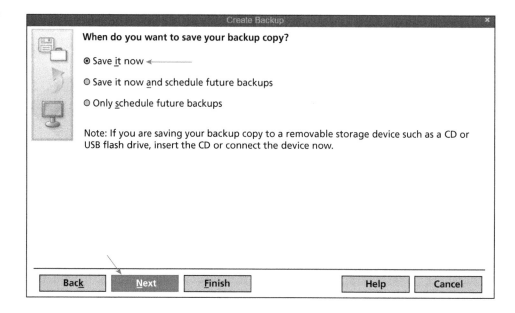

While your QuickBooks company file is backing up, the following message will appear:

Figure Q9
Verifying data integrity

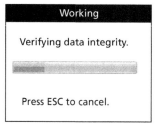

When your QuickBooks backup is complete, the following message will appear. Click **OK**.

Figure Q10
QuickBooks backup completion

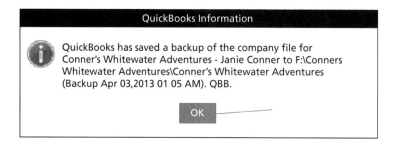

7 Close a company and exit QuickBooks.

Complete the following steps to close a company and exit QuickBooks.

STEP 1. Select **File**.

STEP 2. Select **Close Company**.

STEP 3. Select **Exit**. You can also exit QuickBooks by clicking the [×] in the top right-hand corner of your QuickBooks screen.

Figure Q11
Close and exit company

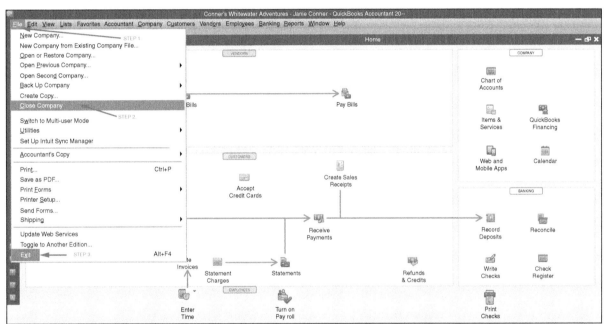

Chapter Review

Study and Practice

1 Define and identify *asset*, *liability*, and *owner's equity* accounts.

Assets are cash, properties, or things of value owned by the business. **Liabilities** are amounts the business owes to creditors. **Owner's equity** is the owner's investment in or rights to the business. The **fundamental accounting equation** expresses the relationship of assets, liabilities, and owner's equity and is represented as:

$$\text{Assets} = \text{Liabilities} + \text{Owner's Equity}$$

PRACTICE EXERCISE 1

Complete the fundamental accounting equation:

Assets	=	Liabilities	+	Owner's Equity
Items owned		*Amounts owed to creditors*		*Owner's investment*
$50,000	=	$12,000	+	?

PRACTICE EXERCISE 1 • SOLUTION

$50,000 Assets
−12,000 Liabilities
$38,000 Owner's Equity

 Learning Objective   Record, in column form, a group of business transactions involving changes in assets, liabilities, and owner's equity.

The accounting equation is stated as assets equals liabilities plus owner's equity. Under the appropriate classification, a separate column is set up for each **account**. Transactions are recorded by listing amounts as additions to or deductions from the various accounts. The equation must remain in balance.

 PRACTICE EXERCISE 2

Write the corresponding amounts for each transaction where you see question marks. Compute the balance to make sure the equation is in balance before proceeding to the next transaction.

	Assets			=	Liabilities	+	Owner's Equity
	Items owned				*Amounts owed to creditors*		*Owner's investment*
	Cash	+	Equipment	=	Accounts Payable	+	J. Lawson, Capital
Transaction (a)	+90,000						?
Transaction (b)	?		+53,000				
Balance	?	+	?	=			?
Transaction (c)			?		+9,000		
Balance	?	+	?	=	?	+	?
Transaction (d)	?				−4,000		
Balance	?	+	?	=	?	+	?
Transaction (e)			?				+5,200
Balance	?	+	?	=	?	+	?
		?				?	

PRACTICE EXERCISE 2 • SOLUTION

	Assets		=	Liabilities	+	Owner's Equity
	Items owned			*Amounts owed to creditors*		*Owner's investment*
	Cash	+ Equipment	=	Accounts Payable	+	J. Lawson, Capital
Transaction (a)	+90,000					+90,000
Transaction (b)	−53,000	+53,000				
Balance	37,000 +	53,000	=			90,000
Transaction (c)		+9,000		+9,000		
Balance	37,000 +	62,000	=	9,000	+	90,000
Transaction (d)	−4,000			−4,000		
Balance	33,000 +	62,000	=	5,000	+	90,000
Transaction (e)		+5,200				+5,200
Balance	33,000 +	67,200	=	5,000	+	95,200
	100,200				100,200	

3 Define and identify *revenue* and *expense* accounts.

Learning Objective

Revenues consist of amounts earned by a business, such as fees earned for performing services, income from selling merchandise, rent income from tenants for the use of property, and interest earned for lending money. **Expenses** are the costs of earning revenue—that is, of doing business—such as wages expense, rent expense, interest expense, and advertising expense.

3 PRACTICE EXERCISE 3

Identify the revenue and expense accounts from the following list of accounts. If the account is a revenue account, write R. If the account is an expense account, write E. If it is neither, leave blank.

___	Accounts Payable	___	Service Income
___	Rent Expense	___	Utilities Expense
___	J. Martin, Drawing	___	Professional Fees Earned
___	Wages Expense	___	Accounts Receivable

PRACTICE EXERCISE 3 • SOLUTION

___	Accounts Payable	R	Service Income
E	Rent Expense	E	Utilities Expense
___	J. Martin, Drawing	R	Professional Fees Earned
E	Wages Expense	___	Accounts Receivable

Learning Objective   **4**   Record, in column form, a group of business transactions involving all five elements of the fundamental accounting equation.

The accounting equation has been expanded and should appear as follows:

$$\text{Assets} = \text{Liabilities} + \text{Capital} - \text{Drawing} + \text{Revenue} - \text{Expenses}$$

Accounts are classified and listed under each heading. Transactions are recorded by listing amounts as additions to or deductions from the various accounts. The equation must remain in balance.

 PRACTICE EXERCISE 4

Record the following transactions in the grid provided below.

Transaction (a).   Company bought equipment for $8,000 on account.
Transaction (b).   Company sold services on account for $6,200.
Transaction (c).   Customer paid $3,000 on account.
Transaction (d).   Company owner invested personal computer system in the business, fair market value, $3,400 (Equipment).

	Assets			=	Liabilities	+	Owner's Equity				
	Cash	+ Equipment +	Accounts Receivable	=	Accounts Payable	+	Capital	– Drawing	+ Revenue	– Expenses
(a)										
(b)										
Bal.										
(c)										
Bal.										
(d)										
Bal.										

PRACTICE EXERCISE 4 • SOLUTION

	Assets			=	Liabilities	+	Owner's Equity				
	Cash	+ Equipment +	Accounts Receivable	=	Accounts Payable	+	Capital	– Drawing	+ Revenue	– Expenses
(a)		+8,000			+8,000					
(b)			+6,200						+6,200	
Bal.		+8,000	+6,200	=	+8,000				+6,200	
(c)	+3,000		–3,000							
Bal.	+3,000	+8,000	+3,200	=	+8,000				+6,200	
(d)		+3,400					+3,400			
Bal.	3,000	+ 11,400	+ 3,200	=	8,000	+	3,400		+ 6,200	

17,600   17,600

Glossary

Account numbers The numbers assigned to accounts according to the chart of accounts. *(p. 22)*

Accounts The categories under the Assets, Liabilities, and Owner's Equity headings. *(p. 16)*

Accounts Payable A liability account used for short-term obligations or charge accounts, usually due within 30 days. *(p. 18)*

Accounts Receivable An account used to record the amounts due from (legal claims against) charge customers. *(p. 27)*

Assets Cash, properties, and other things of value owned by an economic unit or a business entity. *(p. 13)*

Backups Procedures that store company data files in a safe place, such as online or on a flash drive. *(p. 34)*

Business entity A business enterprise, separate and distinct from the persons who supply the assets it uses. *(p. 13)*

Capital The owner's investment, or equity, in an enterprise. *(p. 13)*

Chart of accounts The official list of account titles to be used to record the transactions of a business. *(p. 22)*

Cloud computing Software that is used via the Internet instead of from a local computer. Software and data can be accessed anywhere there is an Internet connection. *(p. 34)*

Computerized accounting An accounting system that records transactions using a computer and accounting software such as QuickBooks. *(p. 33)*

Creditor One to whom money is owed. *(p. 14)*

Double-entry accounting The system by which each business transaction is recorded in at least two accounts and the accounting equation is kept in balance. *(p. 17)*

Equity The value of a right or claim to or financial interest in an asset or group of assets. *(p. 13)*

Expenses The costs that relate to earning revenue (the costs of doing business); examples are wages, rent, interest, and advertising. They may be paid in cash immediately or at a future time (Accounts Payable). *(p. 21)*

Fair market value The present worth of an asset or the amount that would be received if the asset were sold to an outsider on the open market. *(p. 19)*

Fundamental accounting equation (Assets = Liabilities + Owner's Equity) An equation expressing the relationship of assets, liabilities, and owner's equity. *(p. 14)*

Liabilities Debts or amounts owed to creditors. *(p. 14)*

Manual accounting system An accounting system in which transactions are recorded by hand. *(p. 33)*

Owner's equity The owner's right to or investment in the business. *(p. 13)*

Revenues The amounts a business earns; examples are fees earned for performing services, sales of merchandise, rent income, and interest income. They may be in the form of cash, credit card receipts, or accounts receivable (charge accounts). *(p. 21)*

Separate entity concept The concept by which a business is treated as a separate economic or accounting entity. The business stands by itself, separate from its owners, creditors, and customers. *(p. 16)*

Sole proprietorship A one-owner business. *(p. 16)*

Withdrawal The taking of cash or other assets out of a business by the owner for his or her own use. (This is also referred to as drawing.) A withdrawal is treated as a decrease in owner's equity. *(p. 30)*

Quiz Yourself

_____ 1. _____ are properties or things of value owned and controlled by a business entity.
   a. Liabilities
   b. Owner's Equity
   c. Assets
   d. None of the above

_____ 2. Parish Tutoring Services has assets of $25,000 and liabilities of $10,000. What is the amount of owner's equity?
   a. $35,000
   b. $15,000
   c. $12,500
   d. $10,000

_____ 3. Which of the following accounts would increase owner's equity?
   a. Cash
   b. Accounts Payable
   c. Accounts Receivable
   d. Income from Tutoring

_____ 4. Which of the following statements is true?
   a. Every transaction is recorded as an increase and/or decrease in only one account.
   b. One side of the equation does not need to equal the other side of the equation.
   c. Double-entry accounting is demonstrated by the fact that each transaction must be recorded in at least two accounts.
   d. When a business earns revenue, owner's equity decreases.

_____ 5. M. Parish purchased supplies on credit. What is the impact on the accounting equation?
   a. Increase Supplies and decrease Cash.
   b. Increase Supplies Expense and increase Accounts Payable.
   c. Increase Supplies Expense and increase Accounts Receivable.
   d. Increase Supplies and increase Accounts Payable.

Answers:
1. c 2. b 3. d 4. c 5. d

Review It with **QuickBooks**®

_____ 1. Which of the following is *not* an advantage of a computerized accounting system?
   a. Security risks
   b. Timeliness
   c. Security measures
   d. Ease of use

_____ 2. The online version of QuickBooks is an example of cloud computing.
   a. True
   b. False

_____ 3. A QuickBooks file with the extension (.QBB) is
   a. a working file.
   b. a file stored in the cloud.
   c. a backup file.
   d. All of the above

_____ 4. Which file extension would indicate a QuickBooks working file?
   a. .QBB
   b. .QBX
   c. .QBW
   c. None of the above

Answers:
1. a 2. a 3. c 4. c

Chapter Assignments

Discussion Questions

1. Define *assets*, *liabilities*, *owner's equity*, *revenues*, and *expenses*.
2. Explain the separate entity concept.
3. How do Accounts Payable and Accounts Receivable differ?
4. Describe two ways to increase owner's equity and two ways to decrease owner's equity.
5. What is the effect on the fundamental accounting equation if supplies are purchased on account? How will the fundamental accounting equation change if supplies are purchased with cash? Explain how this purchase will or will not change the owner's equity.
6. When an owner withdraws cash or goods from the business, why is this considered an increase to the Drawing account and not an increase to the Wages Expense account?
7. Define *chart of accounts* and identify the categories of accounts.
8. What account titles would you suggest for the chart of accounts for a city touring company owned by W. Sanders? List the accounts by account category and include an appropriate account number for each.

Exercises

LO 1

EXERCISE 1-1 Complete the following equations:

a. Assets of $40,000 = Liabilities of $17,200 + Owner's Equity of $_____
b. Assets of $_____ − Liabilities of $18,000 = Owner's Equity of $22,000
c. Assets of $27,000 − Owner's Equity of $15,000 = Liabilities of $_____

Practice Exercise 1

LO 1

EXERCISE 1-2 Determine the following amounts:

a. The amount of the liabilities of a business that has $60,800 in assets and in which the owner has $34,500 equity.
b. The equity of the owner of a tour bus that cost $57,000 who owes $21,800 on an installment loan payable to the bank.
c. The amount of the assets of a business that has $11,780 in liabilities and in which the owner has $28,500 equity.

Practice Exercise 1

LO 1

EXERCISE 1-3 Dr. L. M. Patton is an ophthalmologist. As of December 31, Dr. Patton owned the following property that related to his professional practice, Patton Eye Clinic:

Practice Exercise 1

Cash, $2,995
Professional Equipment, $63,000
Office Equipment, $8,450

On the same date, he owed the following business creditors:

Munez Supply Company, $3,816
Martin Equipment Sales, $3,728

Compute the following amounts in the accounting equation:

Assets $_____ = Liabilities $_____ + Owner's Equity $_____

LO 1, 3

Practice Exercises 1, 3

EXERCISE 1-4 Describe a business transaction that will do the following:

a. Increase an asset and increase a liability
b. Decrease an asset and decrease a liability
c. Decrease an asset and increase an expense
d. Increase an asset and increase owner's equity
e. Increase an asset and decrease an asset
f. Increase an asset and increase revenue

LO 2

Practice Exercise 2

EXERCISE 1-5 Describe a transaction that resulted in each of the following entries affecting the accounting equation.

	Assets			=	Liabilities	+	Owner's Equity
	Cash	+ Office Equipment +	Professional Equipment =		Accounts Payable	+	B. Lake, Capital
(a)	+18,200						+18,200
(b)	−1,375		+1,375				
Bal.	16,825	+	1,375	=			18,200
(c)		+640			+640		
Bal.	16,825 +	640	+ 1,375	=	640	+	18,200
(d)	−2,200		+7,000		+4,800		
Bal.	14,625 +	640	+ 8,375	=	5,440	+	18,200
(e)	−1,000				−1,000		
Bal.	13,625 +	640	+ 8,375	=	4,440	+	18,200
		22,640				22,640	

LO 1, 3

Practice Exercises 1, 3

EXERCISE 1-6 Label each of the following accounts as asset (A), liability (L), owner's equity (OE), revenue (R), or expense (E).

a. Office Supplies
b. Professional Fees
c. Prepaid Insurance
d. R. Baker, Drawing
e. Accounts Payable
f. Service Income
g. R. Baker, Capital
h. Rent Expense
i. Accounts Receivable
j. Wages Expense

LO 2, 4

Practice Exercises 2, 4

EXERCISE 1-7 Describe a transaction that resulted in the following changes in accounts:

a. Rent Expense is increased by $1,050, and Cash is decreased by $1,050.
b. Advertising Expense is increased by $835, and Accounts Payable is increased by $835.
c. Accounts Receivable is increased by $372, and Service Income is increased by $372.

d. Cash is decreased by $410, and C. Tryon, Drawing, is increased by $410.
e. Equipment is increased by $1,850, Cash is decreased by $850, and Accounts Payable is increased by $1,000.
f. Cash is increased by $1,650, and Accounts Receivable is decreased by $1,650.

LO **2, 4**

EXERCISE 1-8 Describe the transactions that are recorded in the following equation:

Practice Exercise
2, 4

	Assets			=	Liabilities +		Owner's Equity			
Cash	+	Accounts Receivable	+ Equipment =		Accounts Payable	+	J. Onyx, Capital	− J. Onyx, Drawing	+ Revenue	− Expenses
(a) +25,000			+4,500				+29,500			
(b) −1,250										+1,250 (Rent Expense)
Bal. 23,750			+ 4,500 =				29,500			− 1,250
(c)		+2,000							+2,000 (Income from Services)	
Bal. 23,750 +		2,000	+ 4,500 =				29,500		+ 2,000	− 1,250
(d) −3,700			+16,000		+12,300					
Bal. 20,050 +		2,000	+ 20,500 =		12,300	+	29,500		+ 2,000	− 1,250
(e) −2,500								+2,500		
Bal. 17,550 +		2,000	+ 20,500 =		12,300	+	29,500 −	2,500	+ 2,000	− 1,250
		40,050					40,050			

Problem Set A

LO **1, 2, 3, 4**

PROBLEM 1-1A On June 1 of this year, J. Larkin, Optometrist, established the Larkin Eye Clinic. The clinic's account names are presented below. Transactions completed during the month follow.

	Assets			=	Liabilities	+		Owner's Equity		
Cash	+ Supplies	+	Office Equipment	=	Accounts Payable	+	Capital	− Drawing	+ Revenue	− Expenses

a. Larkin deposited $25,000 in a bank account in the name of the business.
b. Paid the office rent for the month, $950, Ck. No. 1001 (Rent Expense).
c. Bought supplies for cash, $357, Ck. No. 1002.

(Continued)

d. Bought office equipment on account from NYC Office Equipment Store, $8,956.
e. Bought a computer from Warden's Office Outfitters, $1,636, paying $750 in cash and placing the balance on account, Ck. No. 1003.
f. Sold professional services for cash, $3,482 (Professional Fees).
g. Paid on account to Warden's Office Outfitters, $886, Ck. No. 1004.
h. Received and paid the bill for utilities, $382, Ck. No. 1005 (Utilities Expense).
i. Paid the salary of the assistant, $1,050, Ck. No. 1006 (Salary Expense).
j. Sold professional services for cash, $3,295 (Professional Fees).
k. Larkin withdrew cash for personal use, $1,250, Ck. No. 1007.

Check Figure
Left side of equals sign total, $37,101

Required
1. In the equation, write the owner's name above the terms *Capital* and *Drawing*.
2. Record the transactions and the balance after each transaction. Identify the account affected when the transaction involves revenues or expenses.
3. Write the account totals from the left side of the equals sign and add them. Write the account totals from the right side of the equals sign and add them. If the two totals are not equal, check the addition and subtraction. If you still cannot find the error, re-analyze each transaction.

 1, 2, 3, 4 ·

PROBLEM 1-2A On July 1 of this year, R. Green established the Green Rehab Clinic. The organization's account headings are presented below. Transactions completed during the month of July follow.

Assets				=	Liabilities	+		Owner's Equity		
		Office	Professional		Accounts		———,	———,		
Cash +	Supplies +	Equipment +	Equipment =		Payable	+	Capital	− Drawing	+ Revenue	− Expenses

a. Green deposited $30,000 in a bank account in the name of the business.
b. Paid the office rent for the month, $1,800, Ck. No. 2001 (Rent Expense).
c. Bought supplies for cash, $362, Ck. No. 2002.
d. Bought professional equipment on account from Rehab Equipment Company, $18,000.
e. Bought office equipment from Hi-Tech Computers, $2,890, paying $890 in cash and placing the balance on account, Ck. No. 2003.
f. Sold professional services for cash, $4,600 (Professional Fees).
g. Paid on account to Rehab Equipment Company, $700, Ck. No. 2004.
h. Received and paid the bill for utilities, $367, Ck. No. 2005 (Utilities Expense).
i. Paid the salary of the assistant, $1,150, Ck. No. 2006 (Salary Expense).
j. Sold professional services for cash, $3,868 (Professional Fees).
k. Green withdrew cash for personal use, $1,800, Ck. No. 2007.

Check Figure
Cash, $31,399

Required
1. In the equation, write the owner's name above the terms *Capital* and *Drawing*.
2. Record the transactions and the balance after each transaction. Identify the account affected when the transaction involves revenues or expenses.
3. Write the account totals from the left side of the equals sign and add them. Write the account totals from the right side of the equals sign and add them. If the two totals are not equal, check the addition and subtraction. If you still cannot find the error, re-analyze each transaction.

LO 1, 2, 3, 4

PROBLEM 1-3A S. Davis, a graphic artist, opened a studio for her professional practice on August 1. The account headings are presented below. Transactions completed during the month follow.

Assets					=	Liabilities	+		Owner's Equity			
	Prepaid	Office	Photo			Accounts		———,	———,			
Cash +	Supplies +	Insurance +	Equipment +	Equipment =		Payable	+	Capital −	Drawing +	Revenue	−	Expenses

a. Davis deposited $20,000 in a bank account in the name of the business.
b. Bought office equipment on account from Starkey Equipment Company, $4,120.
c. Davis invested her personal photographic equipment, $5,370. (Increase the account Photo Equipment and increase the account S. Davis, Capital.)
d. Paid the rent for the month, $1,500, Ck. No. 1000 (Rent Expense).
e. Bought supplies for cash, $215, Ck. No. 1001.
f. Bought insurance for two years, $1,840, Ck. No. 1002.
g. Sold graphic services for cash, $3,616 (Professional Fees).
h. Paid the salary of the part-time assistant, $982, Ck. No. 1003 (Salary Expense).
i. Received and paid the bill for telephone service, $134, Ck. No. 1004 (Telephone Expense).
j. Paid cash for minor repairs to graphics equipment, $185, Ck. No. 1005 (Repair Expense).
k. Sold graphic services for cash, $3,693 (Professional Fees).
l. Paid on account to Starkey Equipment Company, $650, Ck. No. 1006.
m. Davis withdrew cash for personal use, $1,800, Ck. No. 1007.

Required

1. In the equation, write the owner's name above the terms *Capital* and *Drawing*.
2. Record the transactions and the balance after each transaction. Identify the account affected when the transaction involves revenues or expenses.
3. Write the account totals from the left side of the equals sign and add them. Write the account totals from the right side of the equals sign and add them. If the two totals are not equal, check the addition and subtraction. If you still cannot find the error, re-analyze each transaction.

Check Figure
Right side of equals sign total, $31,548

LO 1, 2, 3, 4

PROBLEM 1-4A On March 1 of this year, B. Gervais established Gervais Catering Service. The account headings are presented below. Transactions completed during the month follow.

Assets						=	Liabilities	+		Owner's Equity			
	Accounts		Prepaid		Catering		Accounts		———,	———,			
Cash +	Receivable +	Supplies +	Insurance +	Truck +	Equipment =		Payable	+	Capital −	Drawing +	Revenue	−	Expenses

a. Gervais deposited $25,000 in a bank account in the name of the business.
b. Bought a truck from Kelly Motors for $26,329, paying $8,000 in cash and placing the balance on account, Ck. No. 500.
c. Bought catering equipment on account from Luigi's Equipment, $3,795.
d. Paid the rent for the month, $1,255, Ck. No. 501 (Rent Expense).
e. Bought insurance for the truck for one year, $400, Ck. No. 502.
f. Sold catering services for cash for the first half of the month, $3,012 (Catering Income).

(Continued)

g. Bought supplies for cash, $185, Ck. No. 503.
h. Sold catering services on account, $4,307 (Catering Income).
i. Received and paid the heating bill, $248, Ck. No. 504 (Utilities Expense).
j. Received a bill from GC Gas and Lube for gas and oil for the truck, $128 (Gas and Oil Expense).
k. Sold catering services for cash for the remainder of the month, $2,649 (Catering Income).
l. Gervais withdrew cash for personal use, $1,550, Ck. No. 505.
m. Paid the salary of the assistant, $1,150, Ck. No. 506 (Salary Expense).

Check Figure
Cash, $17,873

Required

1. In the equation, write the owner's name above the terms *Capital* and *Drawing*.
2. Record the transactions and the balance after each transaction. Identify the account affected when the transaction involves revenues or expenses.
3. Write the account totals from the left side of the equals sign and add them. Write the account totals from the right side of the equals sign and add them. If the two totals are not equal, check the addition and subtraction. If you still cannot find the error, re-analyze each transaction.

 1, 2, 3, 4 ···

PROBLEM 1-5A In April, J. Rodriguez established an apartment rental service. The account headings are presented below. Transactions completed during the month of April follow.

Assets						= Liabilities +	Owner's Equity			
Cash +	Accounts Receivable +	Supplies +	Prepaid Insurance +	Truck +	Office Equipment =	Accounts Payable +	Capital −	Drawing +	Revenue −	Expenses

a. Rodriguez deposited $70,000 in a bank account in the name of the business.
b. Paid the rent for the month, $2,000, Ck. No. 101 (Rent Expense).
c. Bought supplies on account, $150.
d. Bought a truck for $23,500, paying $2,500 in cash and placing the remainder on account.
e. Bought insurance for the truck for the year, $2,400, Ck. No. 102.
f. Sold services on account, $4,700 (Service Income).
g. Bought office equipment on account from Stern Office Supply, $1,250.
h. Sold services for cash for the first half of the month, $8,250 (Service Income).
i. Received and paid the bill for utilities, $280, Ck. No. 103 (Utilities Expense).
j. Received a bill for gas and oil for the truck, $130 (Gas and Oil Expense).
k. Paid wages to the employees, $2,680, Ck. Nos. 104–106 (Wages Expense).
l. Sold services for cash for the remainder of the month, $3,500 (Service Income).
m. Rodriguez withdrew cash for personal use, $4,000, Ck. No. 107.

Check Figure
Cash, $67,890

Required

1. In the equation, write the owner's name above the terms *Capital* and *Drawing*.
2. Record the transactions and the balance after each transaction. Identify the account affected when the transaction involves revenues or expenses.
3. Write the account totals from the left side of the equals sign and add them. Write the account totals from the right side of the equals sign and add them. If the two totals are not equal, check the addition and subtraction. If you still cannot find the error, re-analyze each transaction.

Problem Set B

LO **1, 2, 3, 4**

PROBLEM 1-1B In July of this year, M. Wallace established a business called Wallace Realty. The account headings are presented below. Transactions completed during the month follow.

Assets			=	Liabilities	+	Owner's Equity				
Cash +	Supplies +	Office Equipment	=	Accounts Payable	+	Capital	— Drawing	+ Revenue	— Expenses

a. Wallace deposited $24,000 in a bank account in the name of the business.

b. Paid the office rent for the current month, $650, Ck. No. 1000 (Rent Expense).
c. Bought office supplies for cash, $375, Ck. No. 1001.
d. Bought office equipment on account from Dellos Computers, $6,300.
e. Received a bill from the *City Crier* for advertising, $455 (Advertising Expense).
f. Sold services for cash, $3,944 (Service Income).
g. Paid on account to Dellos Computers, $1,500, Ck. No. 1002.
h. Received and paid the bill for utilities, $340, Ck. No. 1003 (Utilities Expense).
i. Paid on account to the *City Crier*, $455, Ck. No. 1004.
j. Paid truck expenses, $435, Ck. No. 1005 (Truck Maintenance Expense).
k. Wallace withdrew cash for personal use, $1,500, Ck. No. 1006.

Required

1. In the equation, write the owner's name above the terms *Capital* and *Drawing*.
2. Record the transactions and the balance after each transaction. Identify the account affected when the transaction involves revenues or expenses.
3. Write the account totals from the left side of the equals sign and add them. Write the account totals from the right side of the equals sign and add them. If the two totals are not equal, check the addition and subtraction. If you still cannot find the error, re-analyze each transaction.

Check Figure
Left side of equals sign total, $29,364

LO **1, 2, 3, 4**

PROBLEM 1-2B In March, K. Haas, M.D., established the Haas Sports Injury Clinic. The clinic's account headings are presented below. Transactions completed during the month of March follow.

Assets				=	Liabilities	+	Owner's Equity				
Cash +	Supplies +	Office Equipment +	Professional Equipment	=	Accounts Payable	+	Capital	— Drawing	+ Revenue	— Expenses

a. Haas deposited $48,000 in a bank account in the name of the business.
b. Paid the rent for the month, $2,200, Ck. No. 1000 (Rent Expense).
c. Bought supplies for cash from Medco Co., $2,138.
d. Bought professional equipment on account from Med-Tech Company, $18,000.
e. Bought office equipment on account from Equipment Depot, $1,955.
f. Sold professional services for cash, $8,960 (Professional Fees).
g. Paid on account to Med-Tech Company, $3,000, Ck. No. 1001.
h. Received and paid the bill for utilities, $472, Ck. No. 1002 (Utilities Expense).
i. Paid the salary of the assistant, $1,738, Ck. No. 1003 (Salary Expense).

(Continued)

j. Sold professional services for cash, $10,196 (Professional Fees).
k. Haas withdrew cash for personal use, $3,500, Ck. No. 1004.

Check Figure
Cash, $54,108

Required

1. In the equation, write the owner's name above the terms *Capital* and *Drawing*.
2. Record the transactions and the balance after each transaction. Identify the account affected when the transaction involves revenue, expenses, or a withdrawal.
3. Write the account totals from the left side of the equals sign and add them. Write the account totals from the right side of the equals sign and add them. If the two totals are not equal, check the addition and subtraction. If you still cannot find the error, re-analyze each transaction.

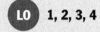

PROBLEM 1-3B P. Schwartz, Attorney at Law, opened his office on October 1. The account headings are presented below. Transactions completed during the month follow.

Assets					= Liabilities +	Owner's Equity				
Cash +	Prepaid Supplies +	Insurance +	Office Equipment +	Library =	Accounts Payable +	Capital −	Drawing +	Revenue −	Expenses

a. Schwartz deposited $25,000 in a bank account in the name of the business.
b. Bought office equipment on account from QuipCo, $9,670.
c. Schwartz invested his personal law library, which cost $2,800.
d. Paid the office rent for the month, $1,700, Ck. No. 2000 (Rent Expense).
e. Bought office supplies for cash, $418, Ck. No. 2001.
f. Bought insurance for two years, $944, Ck. No. 2002.
g. Sold legal services for cash, $8,518 (Professional Fees).
h. Paid the salary of the part-time receptionist, $1,820, Ck. No. 2003 (Salary Expense).
i. Received and paid the telephone bill, $388, Ck. No. 2004 (Telephone Expense).
j. Received and paid the bill for utilities, $368, Ck. No. 2005 (Utilities Expense).
k. Sold legal services for cash, $9,260 (Professional Fees).
l. Paid on account to QuipCo, $2,670, Ck. No. 2006.
m. Schwartz withdrew cash for personal use, $2,500, Ck. No. 2007.

Check Figure
Right side of equals
sign total, $45,802

Required

1. In the equation, write the owner's name above the terms *Capital* and *Drawing*.
2. Record the transactions and the balance after each transaction. Identify the account affected when the transaction involves revenues or expenses.
3. Write the account totals from the left side of the equals sign and add them. Write the account totals from the right side of the equals sign and add them. If the two totals are not equal, check the addition and subtraction. If you still cannot find the error, re-analyze each transaction.

PROBLEM 1-4B In March, T. Carter established Carter Delivery Service. The account headings are presented below. Transactions completed during the month of March follow.

Assets						= Liabilities +	Owner's Equity				
Cash +	Accounts Receivable +	Supplies +	Prepaid Insurance +	Truck +	Equipment =	Accounts Payable +	Capital −	Drawing +	Revenue −	Expenses

a. Carter deposited $25,000 in a bank account in the name of the business.
b. Bought a used truck from Degroot Motors for $15,140, paying $5,140 in cash and placing the remainder on account.

c. Bought equipment on account from Flemming Company, $3,450.
d. Paid the rent for the month, $1,000, Ck. No. 3001 (Rent Expense).
e. Sold services for cash for the first half of the month, $6,927 (Service Income).
f. Bought supplies for cash, $301, Ck. No. 3002.
g. Bought insurance for the truck for the year, $1,200, Ck. No. 3003.
h. Received and paid the bill for utilities, $349, Ck. No. 3004 (Utilities Expense).
i. Received a bill for gas and oil for the truck, $218 (Gas and Oil Expense).
j. Sold services on account, $3,603 (Service Income).
k. Sold services for cash for the remainder of the month, $4,612 (Service Income).
l. Paid wages to the employees, $3,958, Ck. Nos. 3005–3007 (Wages Expense).
m. Carter withdrew cash for personal use, $1,250, Ck. No. 3008.

Required

Check Figure
Cash, $23,341

1. In the equation, write the owner's name above the terms *Capital* and *Drawing*.
2. Record the transactions and the balance after each transaction. Identify the account affected when the transaction involves revenues or expenses.
3. Write the account totals from the left side of the equals sign and add them. Write the account totals from the right side of the equals sign and add them. If the two totals are not equal, check the addition and subtraction. If you still cannot find the error, re-analyze each transaction.

··· **LO 1, 2, 3, 4**

PROBLEM 1-5B In October, A. Nguyen established an apartment rental service. The account headings are presented below. Transactions completed during the month of October follow.

Assets						=	Liabilities +			Owner's Equity		
		Accounts	Prepaid		Office		Accounts	———,	———,			
Cash +	Receivable +	Supplies +	Insurance +	Truck +	Equipment =		Payable	+ Capital −	Drawing +	Revenue −	Expenses	

a. Nguyen deposited $25,000 in a bank account in the name of the business.
b. Paid the rent for the month, $1,200, Ck. No. 2015 (Rent Expense).
c. Bought supplies on account, $225.
d. Bought a truck for $18,000, paying $1,000 in cash and placing the remainder on account.
e. Bought insurance for the truck for the year, $1,400, Ck. No. 2016.
f. Sold services on account, $5,000 (Service Income).
g. Bought office equipment on account from Henry Office Supply, $2,300.
h. Sold services for cash for the first half of the month, $6,050 (Service Income).
i. Received and paid the bill for utilities, $150, Ck. No. 2017 (Utilities Expense).
j. Received a bill for gas and oil for the truck, $80 (Gas and Oil Expense).
k. Paid wages to the employees, $1,400, Ck. Nos. 2018–2020 (Wages Expense).
l. Sold services for cash for the remainder of the month, $4,200 (Service Income).
m. Nguyen withdrew cash for personal use, $2,000, Ck. No. 2021.

Required

Check Figure
Cash, $28,100

1. In the equation, write the owner's name above the terms *Capital* and *Drawing*.
2. Record the transactions and the balance after each transaction. Identify the account affected when the transaction involves revenues or expenses.
3. Write the account totals from the left side of the equals sign and add them. Write the account totals from the right side of the equals sign and add them. If the two totals are not equal, check the addition and subtraction. If you still cannot find the error, re-analyze each transaction.

Try It with **QuickBooks®** (LO 2-7)

QB Exercise 1-1

Install and register the trial version of QuickBooks that came with your text following the steps on pages 34 and 35.
(If you are using a classroom computer with QuickBooks, skip this step.)

1. From the textbook website, CengageBrain.com, locate the QuickBooks data file for Conner's Whitewater Adventures labeled **Student_Data_CH1.QBB**.

2. Save **Student_Data_CH1.QBB** to your computer.

3. Restore the **Student_Data_CH1.QBB** file in QuickBooks.

4. Add your name to the company name (first name, last name) or as directed by your instructor.

5. Locate and open Conner's Whitewater Adventures' chart of accounts.

6. Answer the following questions from the chart of accounts:

    a. The revenue account 411—Income from Tours is identified as what type of account in QuickBooks?

    b. Account 111—Cash is an asset. What type of account is cash identified as in QuickBooks?

    c. What is the account number for J. Conner, Drawing?

    d. Accounts Receivable is an asset. What account type is assigned to this account in QuickBooks?

7. Back up the **Student_Data_CH1.QBW** file to your flash drive or backup device.

8. Close Conner's Whitewater Adventures.

9. Exit QuickBooks.

Activities

Why Does It Matter?

MAC'S CUSTOM CATERING, Eugene, Oregon

Mac's Custom Catering, an award-winning catering business located in Eugene, Oregon, specializes in providing "only the best for you and your guest." Mac's Custom Catering has been in business for over 30 years and is experienced in providing catering services at weddings, corporate events, and large sit-down events. It offers several signature buffet options, including "Northwest Bounty," "Hawaiian Luau," and "Italian Fest."

Imagine that you have been hired to set up the accounting system for a catering business such as Mac's. What accounts would be included in the chart of accounts? As you list the accounts, identify the type of account. Is the account an asset, a liability, or owner's equity?

What Would You Say?

A friend of yours wants to start her own pet-sitting business. She already has a business license that is required in her city. She has had a personal checking account for years. You have told her that she also needs to open a separate account for her business needs, but she does not understand why she needs to have two separate accounts. Explain to her why she should have a business account separate from her personal account. Use some of the language of business you have learned in your text's Introduction and in this chapter.

What Do You Think?

Read the following memorandum and provide the requested information.

MEMORANDUM

TO: Your Name   DATE: July 31, 20--
FROM: J. Perrault, Supervisor   SUBJECT: Calculations for Richter Co.

Please provide the following information ASAP (as soon as possible).

1. The balance of cash in Richter Company's checkbook shows $13,364. I need to know if this ties to or matches the Cash account balance. I do know that total assets amount to $43,560; Office Equipment amounts to $3,896; and other noncash assets are Professional Equipment, $24,375 and Prepaid Insurance, $1,925.
2. D. Richter, the owner, wants to know the amount of his owner's equity. I pulled the outstanding bills, which amount to $7,942.

Please put the information in a memo addressed to me. Thank you for your prompt response.

T Accounts, Debits and Credits, Trial Balance, and Financial Statements

Learning Objectives

After you have completed this chapter, you will be able to do the following:

1. Determine balances of T accounts.

2. Present the fundamental accounting equation using the T account form and label the plus and minus sides.

3. Present the fundamental accounting equation using the T account form and label the debit and credit sides.

4. Record directly in T accounts a group of business transactions involving changes in asset, liability, owner's equity, revenue, and expense accounts for a service business.

5. Prepare a trial balance.

6. Prepare (a) an income statement, (b) a statement of owner's equity, and (c) a balance sheet.

7. Recognize the effect of errors on account balances.

To: **Amy Roberts, CPA**
Subject: **What's Next?**

Hi Amy,
I feel as though I have a good understanding of what accounting is and what the different types of accounts are. I found some flashcards online and have been quizzing myself with the account names and types. I'm getting pretty good! I've also been practicing recording transactions in the column form. I think I'm now ready to learn something new. After I record transactions in the column form, what happens next? Am I ready to start using QuickBooks? Thanks,
Janie

To: **Janie Conner**
Subject: **RE: What's Next?**

Hi Janie,
Using the flashcards was a great idea! It's very important that you recognize the accounts and know whether each is an asset, a liability, or an owner's equity account. We're going to use that knowledge for this next challenge. So here's your list of things to tackle:

_____ 1. Understand what debits and credits are and be able to apply each to the fundamental accounting equation.
_____ 2. Begin recording transactions in T accounts using debits and credits.

This is a lot to learn, but I know that with practice, you'll be successful! You are not quite ready to record entries in QuickBooks yet, but you can review how to prepare financial reports with QuickBooks. You can use the demonstration file I previously sent you to practice.
Amy

In the previous chapter, we introduced the fundamental accounting equation as *Assets = Liabilities + Owner's Equity*. We learned that the fundamental accounting equation includes five account classifications: Assets, Liabilities, Owner's Equity, Revenue, and Expenses. These are the only five classifications in accounting; so whether you are dealing with a small, one-owner business or a large corporation, you will encounter only these five major classifications of accounts. We also discussed the recording of transactions in the column form.

In this chapter, we will record the same transactions from Chapter 1 in T account form and prove the equality of both sides of the fundamental accounting equation using a trial balance. Before we begin, take a moment to review the transactions from Chapter 1 on pages 16–31.

THE T ACCOUNT FORM

In Chapter 1, we recorded business transactions in a column arrangement, which had the following advantages:

1. **In the process of analyzing the transaction, you**
   a. Recognized the need to determine which accounts were involved.
   b. Determined the classification of the accounts involved.
   c. Decided whether the transaction resulted in an increase or a decrease in each of these accounts.
2. **You further realized that after each transaction was recorded, the two sides of the fundamental accounting equation were in balance. In other words, the total of one side of the accounting equation equaled the total of the other side.**

Now instead of recording transactions in a column for each account, we will use a **T account form** for each account. *The T account form has the advantage of providing two sides for each account; one side is used to record increases in the account, and the other side is used to record decreases.* Notice that the Cash account column in the books of Conner's Whitewater Adventures (used in Chapter 1) and the new Cash T account have been presented on the next page. The results are identical. It's just a different way of presenting the same information.

1 Determine balances of T accounts.

Learning Objective

Cash Account Column:		
		Cash
Transaction	**(a)**	90,000
Transaction	**(b)**	−38,000
Balance		52,000
Transaction	**(d)**	−2,000
Balance		50,000
Transaction	**(f)**	+8,000
Balance		58,000
Transaction	**(g)**	−1,250
Balance		56,750
Transaction	**(i)**	−1,875
Balance		54,875
Transaction	**(l)**	−1,500
Balance		53,375
Transaction	**(m)**	−225
Balance		53,150
Transaction	**(n)**	−620
Balance		52,530
Transaction	**(o)**	−2,360
Balance		50,170
Transaction	**(p)**	−1,850
Balance		48,320
Transaction	**(q)**	+2,500
Balance		50,820
Transaction	**(r)**	+8,570
Balance		59,390
Transaction	**(s)**	−3,500
		55,890

Cash T Account:

Cash

	+		−
(a)	90,000	**(b)**	38,000
(f)	8,000	**(d)**	2,000
(q)	2,500	**(g)**	1,250
(r)	8,570	**(i)**	1,875
	109,070	**(l)**	1,500
		(m)	225
		(n)	620
		(o)	2,360
Footings		**(p)**	1,850
		(s)	3,500
			53,180
Bal.	**55,890**		

Steps to calculate balance in T Accounts:

STEP 1. **Add each side separately and record the totals (called footings).**

90,000 + 8,000 + 2,500 + 8,570 = 109,070
38,000 + 2,000 + 1,250 + 1,875 + 1,500 + 225 + 620 + 2,360 + 1,850 + 3,500 = 53,180

STEP 2. **Large footing − Small footing = Balance**

109,070 − 53,180 = 55,890

STEP 3. **Place the balance (from Step 2) on the large footing side and double-underline it.**

55,890 goes on the same side as 109,070.

After we record a group of transactions in a T account, we add both sides and record the totals, called **footings**. Next, we subtract one footing from the other to determine the balance of the account. For the Cash account, shown previously, the balance is $55,890 ($109,070 − $53,180).

We now record the balance on the side of the account having the larger footing, which, with a few minor exceptions, is the plus (+) side. The plus side of a T account is the side that represents the **normal balance** of that account. However, depending on the type of account, the normal balance may fall on either the left or right side of an account.

THE T ACCOUNT FORM WITH PLUS AND MINUS SIDES

To review, we presented the T account for Cash. Cash is classified as an asset account, and all asset accounts look like the following T account:

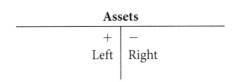

2 Present the fundamental accounting equation using the T account form and label the plus and minus sides.

Learning Objective

However, **not all classifications of accounts have the increase side on the left.** Liability accounts are on the other side of the fundamental accounting equation. So their increase and decrease are opposite those of assets. Liabilities are increased on the right side and decreased on the left side. All liabilities look like the following T account:

Liabilities

−	+
Left	Right

Owner's equity is similar to liabilities. Increases in owner's equity are recorded on the right side of the account. Decreases in owner's equity are recorded on the left side of the account.

Owner's Equity

−	+
Left	Right

Recall that we placed capital, drawing, revenue, and expenses under the umbrella of owner's equity. Capital and revenue increase owner's equity, and drawing and expenses decrease owner's equity. The T accounts for this situation are as follows:

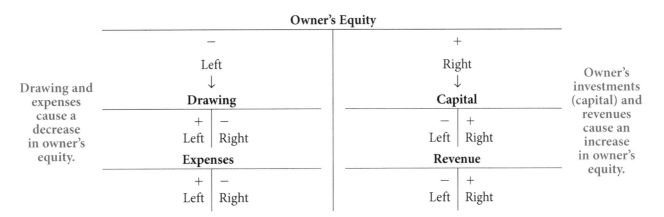

Increases in owner's equity are recorded on the right side of the account. Because capital and revenue increase owner's equity, additions are recorded on the right side.

Decreases in owner's equity are recorded on the left side of the account. Because drawing and expenses decrease owner's equity, additions to drawing and expenses are recorded on the left side.

We can now restate the equation with the T account forms and plus and minus signs for each account classification.

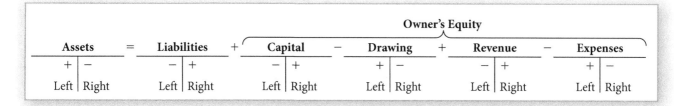

Assets	The *left* side is the *increase* side.
Liabilities	The *right* side is the *increase* side.
Capital	The *right* side is the *increase* side.
Drawing	The *left* side is the *increase* side.
Revenue	The *right* side is the *increase* side.
Expenses	The *left* side is the *increase* side.

Your accounting background up to this point has taught you to analyze business transactions to determine which accounts are involved and to recognize that each amount should be recorded as an increase or a decrease in these accounts. Now the recording process becomes a simple matter of knowing which side of the T accounts should be used to record increases and which should be used to record decreases. **Generally, you will not be using the minus side of the capital, drawing, revenue, and expense accounts because transactions involving these accounts usually result in increases in the accounts.** An exception to this statement is where errors have been made and require correction. Now let's add the last element to the T account before we record the familiar Conner's Whitewater Adventures transactions.

Learning Objective

3 Present the fundamental accounting equation using the T account form and label the debit and credit sides.

THE T ACCOUNT FORM WITH DEBITS AND CREDITS

The left side of a T account is called the **debit** side; the right side is called the **credit** side. The T accounts representing the accounting equation now contain both the signs and the words *Debit* and *Credit*.

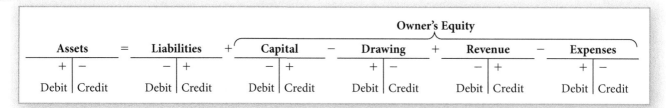

The following table summarizes debits and credits and the way they are affected by increases and decreases. **The critical rule to remember is that the amount placed on the debit side of one or more accounts *must* equal the amount placed on the credit side of another account or other accounts.**

Debits Signify		Credits Signify	
Increases in {	Assets	Decreases in {	Assets
	Drawing		Drawing
	Expenses		Expenses
Decreases in {	Liabilities	Increases in {	Liabilities
	Capital		Capital
	Revenue		Revenue

LEFT   RIGHT

Debit is always the left side of the account, and credit is always the right side of the account. However, the + or − changes with the type of account.

RECORDING BUSINESS TRANSACTIONS IN T ACCOUNTS

Our task now is to learn how to record business transactions in the T account form. First, let's review the steps we've learned so far (Steps 1–3) in analyzing a business transaction. Then we will introduce a new step (Step 4).

STEP 1. What accounts are involved?

STEP 2. What are the classifications of the accounts involved (asset, liability, capital, drawing, revenue, expense)?

STEP 3. Are the accounts increased or decreased?

STEP 4. Write the transaction as a debit to one account (or accounts) and a credit to another account (or accounts).

STEP 5. Is the equation in balance after the transaction has been recorded?

For example, let's analyze the first transaction of the Conner's Whitewater Adventures transactions using this new five-step process. To formulate the entry, you must be able to visualize the fundamental accounting equation in the form of T accounts. With that in mind, the first transaction is as follows:

In transaction (a), Conner deposited $90,000 in a bank account in the name of the business. This transaction results in an increase to Cash with a debit and an increase in the Capital account with a credit.

STEP 1. What accounts are involved? The two accounts involved are Cash and J. Conner, Capital.

STEP 2. What are the classifications of the accounts involved? Cash is an asset account, and J. Conner, Capital, is an owner's equity account.

STEP 3. Are the accounts increased or decreased? Cash is being deposited in the bank account, an increase to Cash. The owner has invested that cash in the business and has increased J. Conner, Capital.

STEP 4. Write the transaction as a debit to one account (or accounts) and a credit to another account (or accounts). Because Cash is an asset account and Cash is increased, Cash is debited. We now need an offsetting credit. J. Conner, Capital, is an owner's equity account and is increased. Thus, J. Conner, Capital, is credited.

4 Record directly in T accounts a group of business transactions involving changes in asset, liability, owner's equity, revenue, and expense accounts for a service business.

Learning Objective

Remember

A business is always treated as a separate economic entity—separate and independent from its owner(s). Notice that we only say "J. Conner" for transactions involving owner investments or drawing. For all other transactions, it is Conner's Whitewater Adventures that is involved in the transaction.

STEP 5. **Is the equation in balance after the transaction has been recorded?** At least one account is debited, and at least one account is credited. And the total amount(s) debited equals the total amount(s) credited. You now have a debit equal to a credit, a $90,000 debit to Cash and a $90,000 credit to J. Conner, Capital.

The resulting transaction in T account form follows.

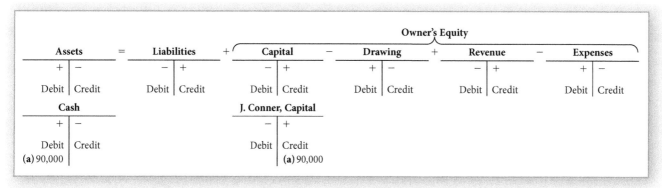

Let's go through the rest of the transactions for Conner's Whitewater Adventures. Because we already worked through Steps 1–3 in Chapter 1, we will discuss only Steps 4 and 5. In transaction (b), Conner's Whitewater Adventures bought equipment, paying cash, $38,000.

STEP 4. **Write the transaction as a debit to one account (or accounts) and a credit to another account (or accounts).**

This transaction results in an increase to Equipment with a debit and a decrease to Cash with a credit.

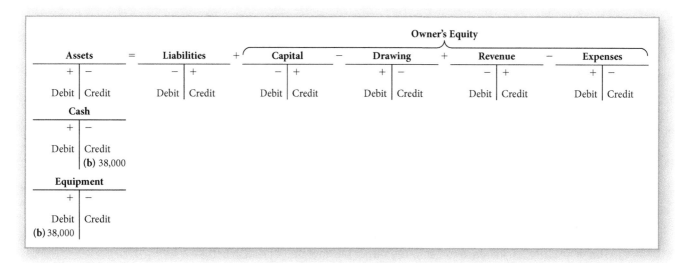

In transaction (c), Conner's Whitewater Adventures bought equipment on account from Signal Products, $4,320.

STEP 4. **Write the transaction as a debit to one account (or accounts) and a credit to another account (or accounts).**

This transaction results in an increase to Equipment with a debit and an increase to Accounts Payable with a credit.

Assets	=	Liabilities	+	Owner's Equity								
				Capital	−	Drawing	+	Revenue	−	Expenses		
+ | −		− | +		− | +		+ | −		− | +		+ | −		
Debit | Credit		Debit | Credit		Debit | Credit		Debit | Credit		Debit | Credit		Debit | Credit		
Equipment		**Accounts Payable**										
+ | −		− | +										
Debit | Credit		Debit | Credit										
(c) 4,320 |		| (c) 4,320										

In transaction (d), Conner's Whitewater Adventures paid Signal Products, a creditor, $2,000.

STEP 4. **Write the transaction as a debit to one account (or accounts) and a credit to another account (or accounts).**

This transaction results in a decrease to Cash with a credit and a decrease to Accounts Payable with a debit.

Assets	=	Liabilities	+	Owner's Equity						
				Capital	−	Drawing	+	Revenue	−	Expenses
+ | −		− | +		− | +		+ | −		− | +		+ | −
Debit | Credit		Debit | Credit		Debit | Credit		Debit | Credit		Debit | Credit		Debit | Credit
Cash		**Accounts Payable**								
+ | −		− | +								
Debit | Credit		Debit | Credit								
| (d) 2,000		(d) 2,000 |								

In transaction (e), J. Conner invests her personal computer, with a fair market value of $5,200, in the business.

STEP 4. **Write the transaction as a debit to one account (or accounts) and a credit to another account (or accounts).**

Equipment, an asset account, increases and is recorded with a debit. J. Conner, Capital, owner's equity, increases and is recorded with a credit.

Assets	=	Liabilities	+	Owner's Equity						
				Capital	−	Drawing	+	Revenue	−	Expenses
+ | −		− | +		− | +		+ | −		− | +		+ | −
Debit | Credit		Debit | Credit		Debit | Credit		Debit | Credit		Debit | Credit		Debit | Credit
Equipment				**J. Conner, Capital**						
+ | −				− | +						
Debit | Credit				Debit | Credit						
(e) 5,200 |				| (e) 5,200						

Here is a restatement of the accounts after recording transactions (a) through (e). To test your understanding of the process, look at each transaction and describe what happened.

Footings or subtotals are required to compute the balances of the accounts. The balances are written in the accounts on the side with the larger total.

							Owner's Equity					
Assets	=	**Liabilities**	+	**Capital**	−	**Drawing**	+	**Revenue**	−	**Expenses**		

Assets + −	Liabilities − +	Capital − +	Drawing + −	Revenue − +	Expenses + −
Debit | Credit	Debit | Credit	Debit | Credit	Debit | Credit	Debit | Credit	Debit | Credit

Cash

Debit +	Credit −
(a) 90,000	(b) 38,000
	(d) 2,000
	40,000
Bal. 50,000	

Equipment

Debit +	Credit −
(b) 38,000	
(c) 4,320	
(e) 5,200	
Bal. 47,520	

Accounts Payable

Debit −	Credit +
(d) 2,000	(c) 4,320
	Bal. 2,320

J. Conner, Capital

Debit −	Credit +
	(a) 90,000
	(e) 5,200
	Bal. 95,200

Let's pause to see if the debits are equal to the credits by listing the balances of the accounts.

STEP 5. Is the equation in balance after the transaction has been recorded?

Yes, the equation is in balance as shown below.

Remember

The normal balance of an account classification is on the plus side of the T account.

Account Name	Accounts with Normal Balances on the Left, or Debit, Side Assets Drawing Expenses	Accounts with Normal Balances on the Right, or Credit, Side Liabilities Capital Revenue
Cash	$50,000	
Equipment	47,520	
Accounts Payable		$ 2,320
J. Conner, Capital		95,200
	$97,520	$97,520

In transaction (f), Conner's Whitewater Adventures sold rafting tours for cash, $8,000.

STEP 4. Write the transaction as a debit to one account (or accounts) and a credit to another account (or accounts).

This transaction results in an increase to Cash with a debit and an increase to Income from Tours with a credit.

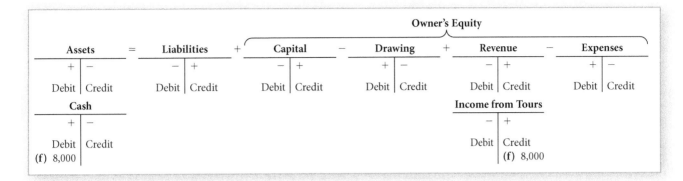

In transaction (g), Conner's Whitewater Adventures paid rent for the month, $1,250.

STEP 4. Write the transaction as a debit to one account (or accounts) and a credit to another account (or accounts).

This transaction results in an increase to Rent Expense with a debit and a decrease to Cash with a credit.

In transaction (h), Conner's Whitewater Adventures bought computer paper, ink cartridges, invoice pads, pens and pencils, folders, filing cabinets, and calculators on account from Fineman Company, $675.

STEP 4. Write the transaction as a debit to one account (or accounts) and a credit to another account (or accounts).

These items are considered supplies to be used by Conner's Whitewater Adventures and are recorded as an asset for $675 on account from Fineman Company. Remember, supplies are considered assets until they are used. When they are used, they are recorded as an expense. This transaction results in an increase to Supplies with a debit and an increase to Accounts Payable with a credit.

In transaction (i), Conner's Whitewater Adventures bought a three-month liability insurance policy, $1,875.

STEP 4. **Write the transaction as a debit to one account (or accounts) and a credit to another account (or accounts).**

This transaction results in an increase to the asset account Prepaid Insurance with a debit and a decrease to Cash with a credit.

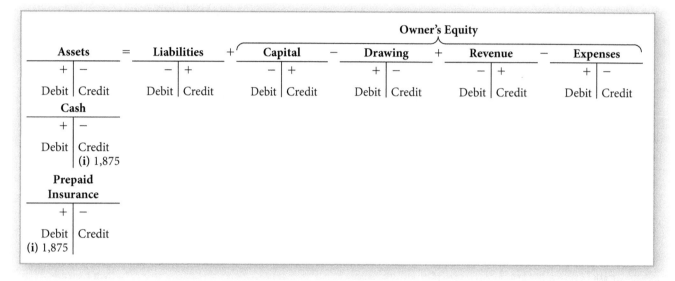

In transaction (j), Conner's Whitewater Adventures received a bill for newspaper advertising from *The Times*, $620.

STEP 4. **Write the transaction as a debit to one account (or accounts) and a credit to another account (or accounts).**

YOU Make the Call

One of your fellow students is having trouble getting his accounting equation to balance after transaction (g). No matter how many times he computes the numbers, he can't get it to balance. When you look at his T accounts, you see that he has been crediting the expenses. He claims that expenses take away from owner's equity, so why should they be under the plus sign? How can you explain that he is partly correct?

SOLUTION
Your fellow student is correct in saying that expenses do take away from owner's equity, but the expense itself is increasing, which requires a debit, or increase, to the expense account. Expenses have the opposite signs of revenues—they are the costs of doing business and act in an opposite way to revenues. So the quick response to your classmate is to make sure the signs on expenses are the opposite of revenues and that expenses are debited when they happen.

This results in an increase to Advertising Expense with a debit and an increase to Accounts Payable with a credit.

	Assets	=	Liabilities	+	Owner's Equity					
					Capital	− Drawing	+ Revenue	− Expenses		
	+ | −		− | +		− | +	+ | −	− | +	+ | −		
	Debit | Credit		Debit | Credit		Debit | Credit	Debit | Credit	Debit | Credit	Debit | Credit		

Accounts Payable
− \| +
Debit \| Credit
(j)   620

Advertising Expense
+ \| −
Debit \| Credit
(j)   620

In transaction (k), Conner's Whitewater Adventures signs a contract with Crystal River Lodge to provide rafting adventures for guests. Conner's Whitewater Adventures provides 27 one-day rafting tours and bills Crystal River Lodge for $6,750.

STEP 4. **Write the transaction as a debit to one account (or accounts) and a credit to another account (or accounts).**

This results in an increase to Accounts Receivable with a debit and an increase to Income from Tours with a credit.

	Assets	=	Liabilities	+	Owner's Equity					
					Capital	− Drawing	+ Revenue	− Expenses		
	+ | −		− | +		− | +	+ | −	− | +	+ | −		
	Debit | Credit		Debit | Credit		Debit | Credit	Debit | Credit	Debit | Credit	Debit | Credit		

Accounts Receivable
+ \| −
Debit \| Credit
(k) 6,750

Income from Tours
− \| +
Debit \| Credit
(k) 6,750

In transaction (l), Conner's Whitewater Adventures pays on account to Signal Products, $1,500.

STEP 4. **Write the transaction as a debit to one account (or accounts) and a credit to another account (or accounts).**

This transaction results in a decrease to Accounts Payable with a debit and a decrease to Cash with a credit.

	Assets	=	Liabilities	+	Owner's Equity					
					Capital	− Drawing	+ Revenue	− Expenses		
	+ | −		− | +		− | +	+ | −	− | +	+ | −		
	Debit | Credit		Debit | Credit		Debit | Credit	Debit | Credit	Debit | Credit	Debit | Credit		

Cash
+ \| −
Debit \| Credit
(l) 1,500

Accounts Payable
− \| +
Debit \| Credit
(l) 1,500

In transaction (m), Conner's Whitewater Adventures received and paid Solar Power, Inc., for the electric bill, $225.

STEP 4. **Write the transaction as a debit to one account (or accounts) and a credit to another account (or accounts).**

The result of this transaction is an increase to Utilities Expense with a debit and a decrease to Cash with a credit.

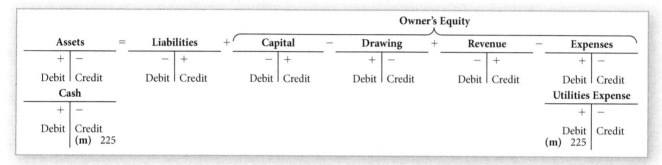

In transaction (n), Conner's Whitewater Adventures paid on account to *The Times*, $620.

STEP 4. **Write the transaction as a debit to one account (or accounts) and a credit to another account (or accounts).**

This transaction results in a decrease to Accounts Payable with a debit and a decrease to Cash with a credit. **Recall that this bill had previously been recorded as a liability in transaction (j).**

In transaction (o), Conner's Whitewater Adventures paid the wages of a part-time employee, $2,360.

STEP 4. **Write the transaction as a debit to one account (or accounts) and a credit to another account (or accounts).**

This transaction results in an increase to Wages Expense with a debit and a decrease to Cash with a credit.

In transaction (p), Conner's Whitewater Adventures bought additional equipment from Signal Products, $3,780, paying $1,850 in cash and placing the balance on account.

STEP 4. **Write the transaction as a debit to one account (or accounts) and a credit to another account (or accounts).**

This transaction results in an increase to Equipment with a debit, an increase to Accounts Payable with a credit, and a decrease to Cash with a credit. This is called a **compound entry**, which always involves more than one debit or more than one credit.

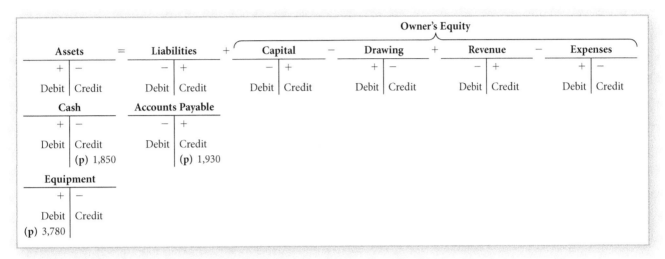

In transaction (q), Conner's Whitewater Adventures received $2,500 cash from Crystal River Lodge to apply against the amount billed in transaction (k).

STEP 4. **Write the transaction as a debit to one account (or accounts) and a credit to another account (or accounts).**

This transaction results in an increase to Cash with a debit and a decrease to Accounts Receivable with a credit.

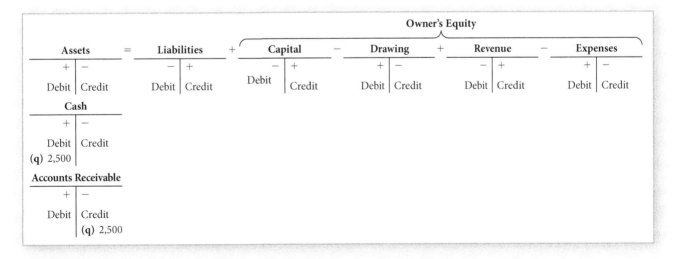

In transaction (r), Conner's Whitewater Adventures sold tours for cash, $8,570.

STEP 4. **Write the transaction as a debit to one account (or accounts) and a credit to another account (or accounts).**

This transaction results in an increase to Cash with a debit and an increase to Income from Tours with a credit.

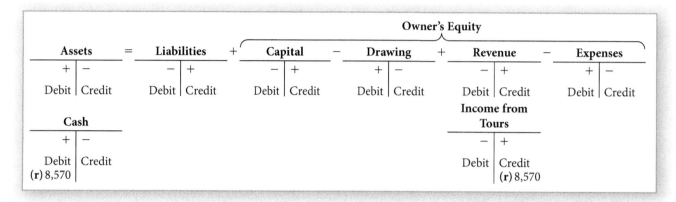

In transaction (s), J. Conner withdrew cash for her personal use, $3,500.

STEP 4. **Write the transaction as a debit to one account (or accounts) and a credit to another account (or accounts).**

This transaction increases J. Conner, Drawing with a debit and decreases Cash with a credit.

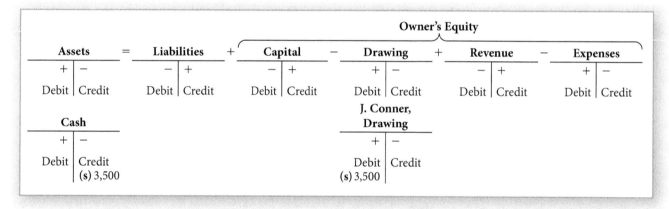

Remember that the Drawing account is used to record any withdrawals by the owner from the business. The Drawing account always decreases owner's equity.

Summary of Transactions

The following T accounts provide a summary of all transactions for Conner's Whitewater Adventures. You will notice that the balance of each account is normally on the plus side. Note that in recording expenses, you normally place the entries only on the plus, or debit, side. Also, in recording revenue, you normally place the entries only on the plus, or credit, side.

Owner's Equity

Assets	=	Liabilities	+	Capital	−	Drawing	+	Revenue	−	Expenses
+ −		− +		− +		+ −		− +		+ −
Debit Credit		Debit Credit		Debit Credit		Debit Credit		Debit Credit		Debit Credit

Cash   **Accounts Payable**   **J. Conner, Capital**   **J. Conner, Drawing**   **Income from Tours**   **Wages Expense**

Cash (+ | −):
- (a) 90,000 | (b) 38,000
- (f) 8,000 | (d) 2,000
- (q) 2,500 | (g) 1,250
- (r) 8,570 | (i) 1,875
- 109,070 | (l) 1,500
- | (m) 225
- | (n) 620
- | (o) 2,360
- | (p) 1,850
- | (s) 3,500
- | 53,180

Bal. 55,890

Accounts Payable (− | +):
- (d) 2,000 | (c) 4,320
- (l) 1,500 | (h) 675
- (n) 620 | (j) 620
- 4,120 | (p) 1,930
- | 7,545
- | Bal. 3,425

J. Conner, Capital (− | +):
- | (a) 90,000
- | (e) 5,200
- | Bal. 95,200

J. Conner, Drawing (+ | −):
- (s) 3,500 |
- Bal. 3,500 |

Income from Tours (− | +):
- | (f) 8,000
- | (k) 6,750
- | (r) 8,570
- | Bal. 23,320

Wages Expense (+ | −):
- (o) 2,360 |
- Bal. 2,360 |

Accounts Receivable (+ | −):
- (k) 6,750 | (q) 2,500
- Bal. 4,250 |

Supplies (+ | −):
- (h) 675 |
- Bal. 675 |

Prepaid Insurance (+ | −):
- (i) 1,875 |
- Bal. 1,875 |

Equipment (+ | −):
- (b) 38,000 |
- (c) 4,320 |
- (e) 5,200 |
- (p) 3,780 |
- Bal. 51,300 |

Rent Expense (+ | −):
- (g) 1,250 |
- Bal. 1,250 |

Advertising Expense (+ | −):
- (j) 620 |
- Bal. 620 |

Utilities Expense (+ | −):
- (m) 225 |
- Bal. 225 |

Figure 1

Accounting memory tool

A memory tool that helps some students memorize debits and credits in T accounts is the equation $A + D + E = L + C + R$. All accounts on the left side of the equation have normal debit balances, and all accounts on the right side have normal credit balances. You can make up a memorable sentence or use this one—All Drippy Eels Love Curly Radishes. Picture an eel dripping with water devouring curly radishes.

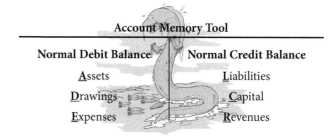

Account Memory Tool

Normal Debit Balance	Normal Credit Balance
Assets	Liabilities
Drawings	Capital
Expenses	Revenues

To: **Amy Roberts, CPA**
Subject: **Debits equal credits?**

Hi Amy,
I've recorded all of my transactions in T accounts using debits and credits. I know that my debits and credits need to equal. Is there an easy way to check this?
Thanks,
Janie

To: **Janie Conner**
Subject: **RE: Debits equal credits?**

Hi Janie,
You're correct! The total debits in the T accounts must always equal the total credits. One way to prove this is by preparing a trial balance. After the trial balance is prepared, you'll be able to prepare financial statements for your business. Financial statements will help you summarize the financial affairs of your business.
Let me know if you have any questions on these next two tasks:
_____ 1. Prepare a trial balance.
_____ 2. Prepare financial statements.
You can also practice preparing these same reports in QuickBooks using the demonstration file I previously sent you.
Thanks.
Amy

THE TRIAL BALANCE

After recording the transactions in the T accounts, you can prepare a trial balance by simply recording the balances of the T accounts in two columns. The **trial balance** is a listing of account balances in two columns—one labeled "Debit" and one labeled "Credit"—and is not considered a financial statement. It is, as the name implies, a trial run by the accountant to prove that the total of the debit balances equals the total of the credit balances. This is evidence of the equality of the two sides of the fundamental accounting equation. The accountant must prove that the accounts are in balance before preparing the company's financial statements.

⑤ Prepare a trial balance.

In preparing a trial balance, shown in Figure 2, record the accounts with balances in the same order they are listed in the chart of accounts.

- Assets
- Liabilities
- Owner's Equity
- Revenue
- Expenses

Conner's Whitewater Adventures
Trial Balance
June 30, 20--

Column headings identify information in each column

Account Name	Debit	Credit
Cash	55,890	
Accounts Receivable	4,250	
Supplies	675	
Prepaid Insurance	1,875	
Equipment	51,300	
Accounts Payable		3,425
J. Conner, Capital		95,200
J. Conner, Drawing	3,500	
Income from Tours		23,320
Wages Expense	2,360	
Rent Expense	1,250	
Advertising Expense	620	
Utilities Expense	225	
	121,945	121,945

Accounts listed in order of the chart of accounts

Dollar signs not used on a trial balance

Single underline beneath figures to be added

Double underline beneath column totals

Figure 2
Trial balance

Remember, the normal balance of each account is on its plus side. The following table indicates where each of the account balances would normally be shown in a trial balance.

	TRIAL BALANCE	
Account Titles	**Left, or Debit, Balances**	**Right, or Credit, Balances**
Assets	Assets	
Liabilities		Liabilities
Capital		Capital
Drawing	Drawing	
Revenue		Revenue
Expenses	Expenses	
Totals		

MAJOR FINANCIAL STATEMENTS

Earlier we listed summarizing as one of the five basic tasks of the accounting process. To accomplish this task, accountants use financial statements. A **financial statement** is a report prepared by accountants to summarize the financial affairs of a business for managers and others (both inside and outside the business).

Note that the headings of all financial statements require three lines:

1. Name of the company (or owner if there is no company name)
2. Title of the financial statement
3. Period of time covered by the financial statement, or its date

Also note that dollar signs are placed at the head of each column and with each total. Single lines are used to show that the figures above are being added or subtracted. Lines should be drawn across the entire column. A double line is drawn under the final total in a column.

The financial statements are all interconnected. The income statement must be prepared first, followed by the statement of owner's equity and then the balance sheet.

The Income Statement

The **income statement** shows total revenue minus total expenses, which yields the net income or net loss. The income statement reports the results of business transactions involving revenue and expense accounts—in other words, how the business has performed—over a period of time, usually a month or a year. When total revenue exceeds total expenses over the period, the result is **net income**, or profit. When the total revenue is less than total expenses, the result is a **net loss**.

The income statement in Figure 3 shows the results of the first month of operations for Conner's Whitewater Adventures.

For convenience, the individual expense amounts are recorded in the first amount column. Thus, the total expenses ($4,455) may be subtracted directly from the total revenue ($23,320).

The income statement covers a period of time, whereas the balance sheet has only one date: the end of the financial period. On the income statement, the revenue for June less the expenses for June shows the results of operations—a net income of $18,865

In the Real World

Where to open a new location is an important business decision. For companies such as Apple, a manufacturer and seller of computers, iPads, iPods, and iPhones, the decision to expand to a new retail store location—as well as other operating decisions—is made from financial statements such as the income statement. You can find a copy of Apple's financial statements on the Internet at http://investor.apple.com. For fiscal year ended September 29, 2012, Apple reported net income of $41,733,000,000 on its income statement. Dell is a competitor of Apple. Would you expect the financial statements of Dell to look similar to Apple's? If so, why might this be beneficial to users of the financial statements?

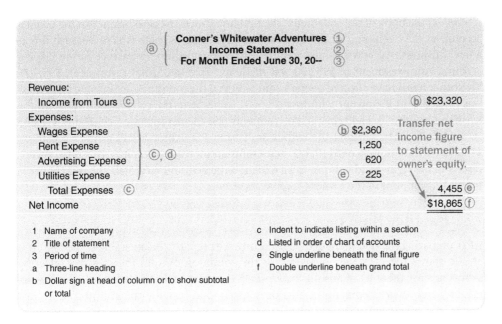

Figure 3
Income statement

FYI

Compare the third line of the income statement heading with the third line of the balance sheet heading shown in Figure 5. Notice that the lines are different—the income statement covers a period of time, and the balance sheet has only one date: the end of the financial period.

To the accountant, the term *net income* means "clear" income, or profit after all expenses have been deducted. Expenses are usually listed in the same order as in the chart of accounts. Revenue and expense amounts are taken directly from the trial balance. If total expenses were greater than the revenue, then a net loss would be recorded.

The Statement of Owner's Equity

In the previous chapter, we said that revenue and expenses are connected with owner's equity through the financial statements. Now let's demonstrate this using a statement of owner's equity, shown in Figure 4, which the accountant prepares after he or she has determined the net income or net loss on the income statement.

The **statement of owner's equity** shows how—and why—the owner's equity, or Capital account, has changed over a stated period of time (in this case, the month of June). Notice the third line in the heading of Figure 4. It shows that the statement of owner's equity covers the same period of time as the income statement.

6b Prepare a statement of owner's equity.

Learning Objective

QuickBooks Tip

The statement of owner's equity is not a standard report in QuickBooks. A customized report can be created if desired.

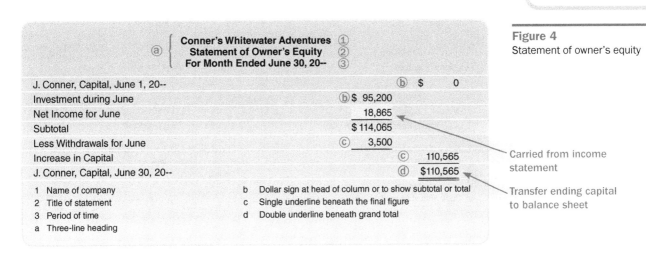

Figure 4
Statement of owner's equity

Carried from income statement

Transfer ending capital to balance sheet

Remember

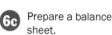

Here's another memory tool for recalling the order of statement preparation: Izzy Swung Off Every Branch (Income, Statement of Owner's Equity, Balance Sheet).

Learning Objective

6c Prepare a balance sheet.

Look at the body of the statement. The first line shows the zero balance in the Capital account at the beginning of the month. The beginning balance is zero because this is a new business. All new businesses start with a zero beginning balance in the Capital account. An investment of $95,200 was made by J. Conner: total investment, $95,200. Two other items have affected owner's equity during the month: A net income of $18,865 was earned, and the owner withdrew $3,500. To perform the calculations, move to the left-hand column and add the total investments and the net income ($95,200 + $18,865 = $114,065). Then subtract the withdrawals from the subtotal ($114,065 − $3,500 = $110,565). The difference ($110,565) represents an increase in capital. This difference is placed in the right-hand column to be added to the beginning capital. The final figure is the ending amount in the owner's Capital account.

The Balance Sheet

After preparing the statement of owner's equity, we prepare a balance sheet. The **balance sheet** shows the **financial position**, or the condition of a business's assets offset by claims against them *as of one particular date*. It summarizes the balances of the asset, liability, and owner's equity accounts on a given date (usually the end of a month or year). Thus, the balance sheet is like a snapshot—a picture of the financial condition of the business at that particular date.

The ending capital balance on the balance sheet is taken from the statement of owner's equity. Note that the accounts appear in the same order as in the chart of accounts.

In the **report form** of the balance sheet, the elements in the accounting equation are presented one on top of the other. A balance sheet prepared on June 30 for Conner's Whitewater Adventures in report form is shown in Figure 5.

Figure 5
Balance sheet

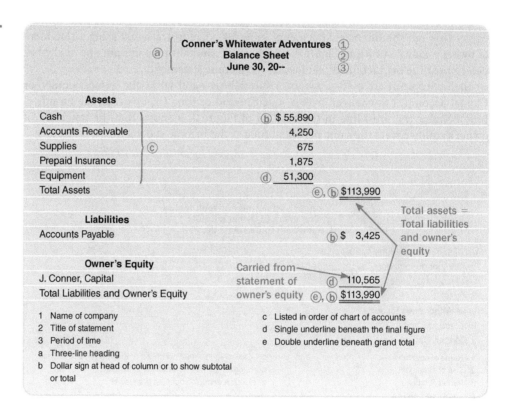

ERRORS EXPOSED BY THE TRIAL BALANCE

If the debit and credit columns in a trial balance are not equal, it is evident that we have made an error. Possible mistakes include the following:

- Making errors in arithmetic, such as errors in adding the trial balance columns or in finding the balances of the accounts.
- Recording only half an entry, such as a debit without a corresponding credit or vice versa.
- Recording both halves of the entry on the same side, such as two debits rather than a debit and a credit.
- Recording one or more amounts incorrectly.

It's important to note that even when debits equal credits, this does not necessarily mean that no errors were made in recording the transactions. For example, a transaction may have been forgotten, it may have been included twice, or it may have been written for an incorrect amount. Although using a computer greatly reduces the occurrence of addition and subtraction errors, it does not prevent the occurrence of other kinds of errors, such as an incorrect amount being recorded.

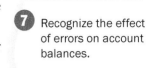

7 Recognize the effect of errors on account balances.

Learning Objective

QuickBooks Tip

Computerized accounting software, like QuickBooks, prevents out-of-balance errors by requiring transactions to balance before updating.

ACCOUNTING IN YOUR FUTURE

ACCOUNTING CLERK

One of many variations in accounting jobs you might find is an accounting clerk. Responsibilities might include invoicing for customers' fees, collecting fees, and maintaining customer accounts. The job might also include some marketing and customer service activities; therefore, people skills would be vital.

As the accounting clerk, you would be required to provide the accountant with weekly reports so that the accountant could correctly report revenue. You would also need to manage financial information regarding collection expenses and marketing expenses, as well as any expenses related to customer service. Consider how knowing the accounting cycle would be beneficial in this position.

The future is yours

iStockPhoto.com/klikk

Procedure for Locating Errors

Suppose you are in a business situation where you have recorded transactions for a month in the account books and the accounts do not balance. To save yourself time, you need to have a definite procedure for tracking down the errors. The best method is to do everything in reverse, as follows:

STEP 1. Look at the pattern of balances to see if a normal balance was placed in the wrong column on the trial balance.

STEP 2. Re-add the trial balance columns.

STEP 3. Check the transferring of the figures from the accounts to the trial balance.

STEP 4. Verify the footings and balances of the accounts.

As an added precaution, form the habit of verifying all addition and subtraction as you go along. You can then correct many mistakes *before* the time comes to prepare a trial balance.

When the trial balance totals do not balance, the difference might indicate that you forgot to record half an entry in the accounts. For example, if the difference in the trial balance totals is $20, you may have recorded $20 on the debit side of one account without recording $20 on the credit side of another account.

Another possibility is to divide the difference by 2; this may provide a clue that you accidentally recorded half an entry twice. For example, if the difference in the trial balance is $600, you may have recorded $300 on the debit side of one account and an additional $300 on the debit side of another account. Look for a transaction that involved $300 and see if you recorded both a debit and a credit. By knowing which transactions to check, you can save a lot of time.

Transpositions and Slides

If the difference is evenly divisible by 9, the discrepancy may be either a transposition or a slide. A **transposition** means that the digits have been transposed, or switched around, when the numbers were copied from one place to another. For example, one transposition of digits in 916 can be written as 619.

Correct Number	Number Copied	Difference	Difference Divided by 9
$916	$619	$297	$297 ÷ 9 = $33

A **slide** is an error in placing the decimal point (in other words, a slide in the decimal point). For example, $27,000 could be inadvertently written as $2,700.

Correct Number	Number Copied	Difference	Difference Divided by 9
$27,000	$2,700	$24,300	$24,300 ÷ 9 = $2,700

Or the error may be a combination of a transposition and a slide, as when $450 is written as $54.

Correct Number	Number Copied	Difference	Difference Divided by 9
$450	$54	$396	$396 ÷ 9 = $44

Again, the difference is evenly divisible by 9 (with no remainder).

Accounting with *QuickBooks*®

Viewing and Printing Financial Reports with QuickBooks

QuickBooks allows users to print several types of financial reports. In this section, you will learn how to print standardized reports such as the trial balance, income statement (profit and loss statement in QuickBooks), and the balance sheet. The statement of owner's equity is not a standardized report in QuickBooks; however, a customized report can be created. In this text, we will use the **Reports** tab to access the reports in QuickBooks. Reports can also be accessed through the **Report Center**.

---

1 View and print a trial balance report.   **Learning Objective**

Similar to manual accounting, the trial balance is prepared after recording transactions. To view and print the trial balance, follow these steps. (See Figure Q1.)

STEP 1. Click the **Reports** tab.

STEP 2. Click **Accountant & Taxes**.

STEP 3. Click **Trial Balance**.

Learning Objectives

After you have completed this section, you will be able to do the following:

1 View and print a trial balance report.

2 View and print a profit and loss (income) statement.

3 View and print a balance sheet.

4 Save report as a PDF.

5 Export QuickBooks reports into Excel.

Figure Q1
Viewing a trial balance report

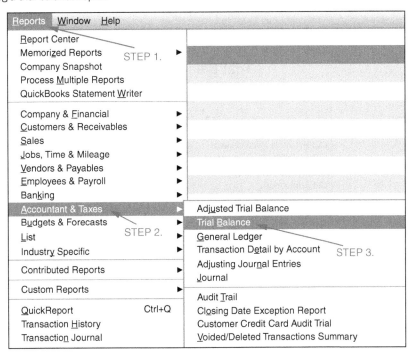

QuickBooks Tip

Remember to refresh reports after making changes to ensure report information has been updated.

STEP 4. Adjust the **From** and **To** dates and click **Refresh**.

Figure Q2
Adjusting report dates

STEP 5. To print the report, click the **Print** button.

Figure Q3
Printing a report

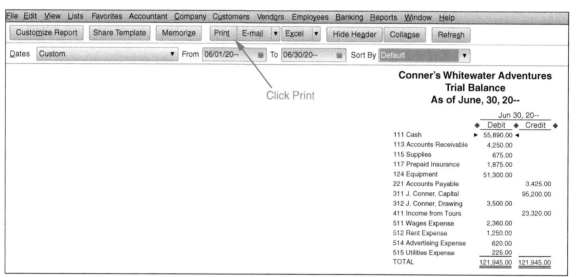

Figure Q4 shows the QuickBooks trial balance report for Conner's Whitewater Adventures.

Figure Q4
Trial balance report

Conner's Whitewater Adventures
Trial Balance
As of June 30, 20--

	Jun 30, 20--	
	Debit	Credit
111 Cash	55,890.00	
113 Accounts Receivable	4,250.00	
115 Supplies	675.00	
117 Prepaid Insurance	1,875.00	
124 Equipment	51,300.00	
221 Accounts Payable		3,425.00
311 J. Conner, Capital		95,200.00
312 J. Conner, Drawing	3,500.00	
411 Income from Tours		23,320.00
511 Wages Expense	2,360.00	
512 Rent Expense	1,250.00	
514 Advertising Expense	620.00	
515 Utilities Expense	225.00	
TOTAL	121,945.00	121,945.00

2 View and print a profit and loss (income) statement.

QuickBooks refers to the income statement as the **profit and loss statement**. To view and print the profit and loss statement, follow these steps. (See Figure Q5.)

STEP 1. Click the **Reports** tab.

STEP 2. Click **Company & Financial**.

STEP 3. Click **Profit & Loss Standard**.

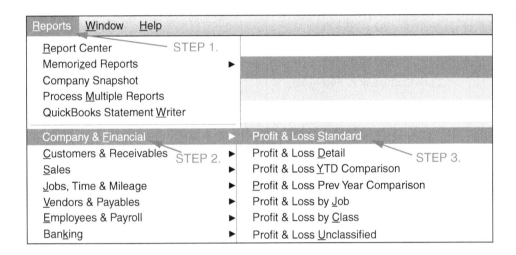

Reports Window Help	
Report Center ⟍ STEP 1.	
Memori**z**ed Reports ▶	
Company Snapshot	
Process **M**ultiple Reports	
QuickBooks Statement **W**riter	
Company & **F**inancial ▶	Profit & Loss **S**tandard
Customers & Receivables STEP 2. ▶	Profit & Loss **D**etail ⟍ STEP 3.
Sales ▶	Profit & Loss **Y**TD Comparison
Jobs, Time & Mileage ▶	**P**rofit & Loss Prev Year Comparison
Vendors & Payables ▶	Profit & Loss by **J**ob
Employees & Payroll ▶	Profit & Loss by **C**lass
Ban**k**ing ▶	Profit & Loss **U**nclassified

Figure Q5
Viewing a profit and loss statement

STEP 4. Adjust the **From** and **To** dates and click **Refresh**.

STEP 5. To print the report, click the **Print** button.

Figure Q6 shows the profit and loss statement for Conner's Whitewater Adventures.

Conner's Whitewater Adventures
Profit & Loss
June 20--

	◆ Jun 20-- ◆
▾ Income	
411 Income from Tours	▸ 23,320.00 ◂
Total Income	23,320.00
▾ Expense	
511 Wages Expense	2,360.00
512 Rent Expense	1,250.00
514 Advertising Expense	620.00
515 Utilities Expense	225.00
Total Expense	4,455.00
Net Income	18,865.00

Figure Q6
Profit and loss statement

PREPARE THE STATEMENT OF OWNER'S EQUITY

The statement of owner's equity is not a standard option in QuickBooks. Your instructor may or may not want you to prepare a report that contains this information. If your instructor wants you to prepare a statement of owner's equity, a customized balance sheet report can be used to display this information. A statement of owner's equity is not a required QuickBooks report for this text.

Learning Objective   View and print a balance sheet.

The next statement to print is the balance sheet. To view and print the balance sheet, follow these steps. (See Figure Q7.)

STEP 1. Click the **Reports** tab.

STEP 2. Click **Company & Financial**.

STEP 3. Click **Balance Sheet Standard**.

Figure Q7
Viewing a balance sheet

QuickBooks Tip

For the balance sheet, you will enter only the ending date of the report.

Reports Window Help	
Report Center — STEP 1.	
Memorized Reports ▶	
Company Snapshot	
Process Multiple Reports	
QuickBooks Statement Writer	
Company & Financial ▶	Profit & Loss Standard
Customers & Receivables STEP 2. ▶	Profit & Loss Detail
Sales ▶	Profit & Loss YTD Comparison
Jobs, Time & Mileage ▶	Profit & Loss Prev Year Comparison
Vendors & Payables ▶	Profit & Loss by Job
Employees & Payroll ▶	Profit & Loss by Class
Banking ▶	Profit & Loss Unclassified
Accountant & Taxes ▶	Income by Customer Summary
Budgets & Forecasts ▶	Income by Customer Detail
List ▶	Expenses by Vendor Summary
Industry Specific ▶	Expenses by Vendor Detail
	Income & Expense Graph
Contributed Reports ▶	
Custom Reports ▶	Balance Sheet Standard
	Balance Sheet Detail — STEP 3.
QuickReport Ctrl+Q	Balance Sheet Summary
Transaction History	Balance Sheet Prev Year Comparison
Transaction Journal	Balance Sheet by Class
	Net Worth Graph

STEP 4. Adjust the **As of** date and click **Refresh**.

STEP 5. To print the report, click the **Print** button.

Figure Q8 shows the balance sheet for Conner's Whitewater Adventures.

Conner's Whitewater Adventures
Balance Sheet
As of June 30, 20--

	Jun 30, 20--
ASSETS	
Current Assets	
Checking/Savings	
111 Cash	55,890.00
Total Checking/Savings	55,890.00
Accounts Receivable	
113 Accounts Receivable	4,250.00
Total Accounts Receivable	4,250.00
Other Current Assets	
115 Supplies	675.00
117 Prepaid Insurance	1,875.00
Total Other Current Assets	2,550.00
Total Current Assets	62,690.00
Fixed Assets	
124 Equipment	51,300.00
Total Fixed Assets	51,300.00
TOTAL ASSETS	113,990.00
LIABILITIES & EQUITY	
Liabilites	
Current Liabilities	
Accounts Payable	
221 Accounts Payable	3,425.00
Total Accounts Payable	3,425.00
Total Current Liabilities	3,425.00
Total Liabilities	3,425.00
Equity	
311 J. Conner, Capital	95,200.00
312 J. Conner, Drawing	-3,500.00
Net Income	18,865.00
Total Equity	110,565.00
TOTAL LIABILITIES & EQUITY	113,990.00

Figure Q8
Balance sheet

4 Save report as a PDF.

Learning Objective

Many times, QuickBooks users will want to save a report electronically rather than printing the report in paper format. Using an electronic file format called **PDF (portable document format)** that converts a printed document into an electronic image is one way to do this. The easiest way to save any report as a PDF in QuickBooks is to click on **File** and then select **Save as PDF**. Next, you will be asked to name and save the PDF file to your computer. As an alternative, you may prefer to install a "virtual" printer using PDF software. Several types of PDF software can be downloaded to your computer, including free versions such as CutePDF™ Writer (www.cutepdf.com). To save a QuickBooks' report in PDF format, follow the previous steps to view and print a report. When you click the **Print** button, select the PDF software installed on your computer as your "virtual" printer. Then click **Print**. (See Figure Q9.)

QuickBooks Tip

Reports can also be saved to a PDF format through the email feature in QuickBooks.

Figure Q9
Printing reports as a PDF

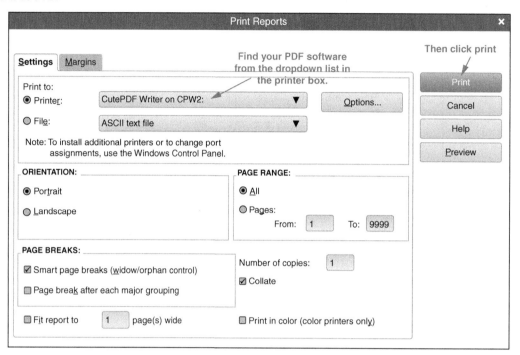

Learning Objective   (5)   Export QuickBooks reports into Excel.

QuickBooks Tip

Reports can also be saved in an Excel format through the email feature in QuickBooks.

QuickBooks users may also want to export financial report information into Excel. To export QuickBooks reports into Excel, follow the previous steps for viewing and printing a report. Then click **Excel** and **Create New Worksheet**. (See Figure Q10.)

Figure Q10
Creating an Excel worksheet

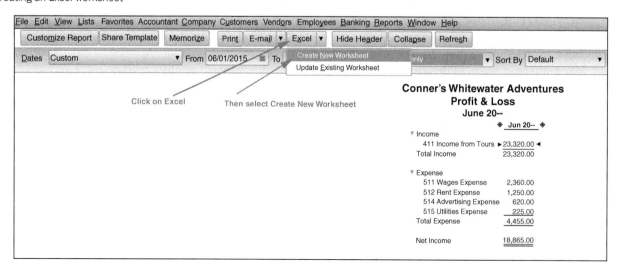

Chapter Review

Study and Practice

 1 Determine balances of T accounts.   **Learning Objective**

To determine balances of T accounts, add the amounts listed on each side of the T account. The totals are called footings. To get the account balance, subtract the total of the smaller side from the total of the larger side. Record the account balance on the larger side.

1 PRACTICE EXERCISE 1

Using the T accounts presented below, determine the balances.

	Cash				Accounts Payable				J. Jay, Capital			J. Jay, Drawing	
(a)	90,000	(b)	38,000	(d)	1,500	(c)	4,500		(a)	90,000	(f)	1,200	
		(f)	1,200						(e)	5,000			

	Equipment		
(b)	38,000	(d)	1,500
(c)	4,500		
(e)	5,000		

PRACTICE EXERCISE 1 · SOLUTION

	Cash				Accounts Payable				J. Jay, Capital			J. Jay, Drawing	
(a)	90,000	(b)	38,000	(d)	1,500	(c)	4,500		(a)	90,000	(f)	1,200	
		(f)	1,200			Bal.	3,000		(e)	5,000	Bal.	1,200	
			39,200						Bal.	95,000			
Bal.	50,800												

	Equipment		
(b)	38,000	(d)	1,500
(c)	4,500		
(e)	5,000		
	47,500		
Bal.	46,000		

 2 Present the fundamental accounting equation using the T account form and label the plus and minus sides.   **Learning Objective**

The fundamental accounting equation can be restated in T account form using plus and minus sides. The following table summarizes the rules:

Assets	The *left* side is the *increase* side.
Liabilities	The *right* side is the *increase* side.

Capital	The *right* side is the *increase* side.
Drawing	The *left* side is the *increase* side.
Revenue	The *right* side is the *increase* side.
Expenses	The *left* side is the *increase* side.

② PRACTICE EXERCISE 2

Using the fundamental accounting equation in T account form, label each side with plus and minus.

PRACTICE EXERCISE 2 • SOLUTION

Owner's Equity

Assets	=	Liabilities	+	Capital	−	Drawing	+	Revenue	−	Expenses
+ −		− +		− +		+ −		− +		+ −

Learning Objective   ③   Present the fundamental accounting equation using the T account form and label the debit and credit sides.

Each account category in the fundamental accounting equation has a debit and credit. The left side of a T account, regardless of the account category, is called the **debit** side. The right side is called the **credit** side. A debit or credit could signify either an increase or a decrease—it depends on the account category. The following table summarizes these rules:

Debits Signify		Credits Signify	
Increases in	Assets Drawing Expenses	Decreases in	Assets Drawing Expenses
Decreases in	Liabilities Capital Revenue	Increases in	Liabilities Capital Revenue

③ PRACTICE EXERCISE 3

Using the fundamental accounting equation in T account form label each side as debit and credit.

PRACTICE EXERCISE 3 • SOLUTION

Owner's Equity

Assets	=	Liabilities	+	Capital	−	Drawing	+	Revenue	−	Expenses
+ −		− +		− +		+ −		− +		+ −
Debit Credit		Debit Credit		Debit Credit		Debit Credit		Debit Credit		Debit Credit

4 Record directly in T accounts a group of business transactions involving changes in asset, liability, owner's equity, revenue, and expense accounts for a service business.

Learning Objective

Transactions can be recorded directly into the T accounts. When analyzing a business transaction, follow these steps:

STEP 1. What accounts are involved?

STEP 2. What are the classifications of the accounts involved (asset, liability, capital, drawing, revenue, expense)?

STEP 3. Are the accounts increased or decreased?

STEP 4. Write the transaction as a debit to one account (or accounts) and a credit to another account (or accounts).

STEP 5. Is the equation in balance after the transaction has been recorded?

4 PRACTICE EXERCISE 4

Record the following transactions directly into the appropriate T accounts and determine the balance in each account.

a. J. Molson deposited $90,000 in the name of the business.

b. Bought equipment for cash, $38,000.

c. Bought advertising on account, $4,320.

d. Paid $2,000 on account.

e. J. Molson invested his personal equipment, valued at $5,200, in the business.

f. The business received cash from customers, $4,000.

g. J. Molson withdrew $1,200 from the business for personal use.

PRACTICE EXERCISE 4 • SOLUTION

	Assets	=	Liabilities	+	Capital	–	Drawing	+	Revenue	–	Expenses
	+ | –		– | +		– | +		+ | –		– | +		+ | –
	Debit | Credit		Debit | Credit		Debit | Credit		Debit | Credit		Debit | Credit		Debit | Credit

	Cash		Accounts Payable		J. Molson, Capital		J. Molson, Drawing		Fees Earned		Advertising Expense
	+ | –		– | +		– | +		+ | –		– | +		+ | –
	Debit | Credit		Debit | Credit		Debit | Credit		Debit | Credit		Debit | Credit		Debit | Credit
(a) 90,000	(b) 38,000	(d) 2,000	(c) 4,320		(a) 90,000	(g) 1,200			(f) 4,000	(c) 4,320	
(f) 4,000	(d) 2,000		Bal. 2,320		(e) 5,200	Bal. 1,200			Bal. 4,000	Bal. 4,320	
94,000	(g) 1,200				Bal. 95,200						
	41,200										

Bal. 52,800

	Equipment
	+ | –
	Debit | Credit
(b) 38,000	
(e) 5,200	
Bal. 43,200	

Learning Objective   **5** Prepare a trial balance.

A **trial balance** is a list of all account balances in two columns—one labeled "Debit" and one labeled "Credit." The trial balance shows that both sides of the accounting equation are equal. The heading consists of the company name, the title of the form (trial balance), and the date.

5 PRACTICE EXERCISE 5

Using the following account balances, prepare a trial balance for Collins's Backpack Adventures as of July 31, 20--.

Accounts Payable	$ 3,325	J. Collins, Drawing	$3,400
Accounts Receivable	4,150	Prepaid Insurance	1,675
Advertising Expense	680	Rent Expense	1,350
Cash	55,830	Supplies	575
Equipment	51,500	Utilities Expense	325
Income from Treks	23,220	Wages Expense	2,460
J. Collins, Capital	95,400		

PRACTICE EXERCISE 5 • SOLUTION

Collins's Backpack Adventures
Trial Balance
July 31, 20—

Account Name	Debit	Credit
Cash	55,830	
Accounts Receivable	4,150	
Supplies	575	
Prepaid Insurance	1,675	
Equipment	51,500	
Accounts Payable		3,325
J. Collins, Capital		95,400
J. Collins, Drawing	3,400	
Income from Treks		23,220
Wages Expense	2,460	
Rent Expense	1,350	
Advertising Expense	680	
Utilities Expense	325	
	121,945	121,945

Learning Objective   **6** Present the fundamental accounting equation using the T account form and label the debit and credit sides.

(a) An **income statement** shows the results of operations of a business for a period of time. It includes revenue and expense accounts and reports either a **net income** or a **net loss**. (b) A **statement of owner's equity** shows the activity in the owner's equity, or Capital account, for a period of time. It includes the balance in the Capital account at the beginning of the period plus any additional investments and any increase or decrease in capital as the result of a net income (or a net loss) minus any withdrawals. (c) A **balance sheet** shows the financial condition of a business at a particular date in time. It summarizes the balances of the asset, liability, and owner's equity accounts on a given date.

PRACTICE EXERCISE 6

Use the trial balance in Practice Exercise 5 to prepare (a) an income statement, (b) a statement of owner's equity, and (c) a balance sheet. Assume that Collins's Backpack Adventures started business on July 1, 20--.

PRACTICE EXERCISE 6 • SOLUTION

(a)

Collins's Backpack Adventures Income Statement For Month Ended July 31, 20--		
Revenue:		
Income from Treks		$23,220
Expenses:		
Wages Expense	$2,460	
Rent Expense	1,350	
Advertising Expense	680	
Utilities Expense	325	
Total Expenses		4,815
Net Income		$18,405

(b)

Collins's Backpack Adventures Statement of Owner's Equity For Month Ended July 31, 20--		
J. Collins, Capital, July 1, 20--		$ 0
Investments during July	$ 95,400	
Net Income for July	18,405	
Subtotal	$113,805	
Less Withdrawals for July	3,400	
Increase in Capital		110,405
J. Collins, Capital, July 31, 20--		$ 110,405

(c)

Collins's Backpack Adventures Balance Sheet July 31, 20--		
Assets		
Cash	$55,830	
Accounts Receivable	4,150	
Supplies	575	
Prepaid Insurance	1,675	
Equipment	51,500	
Total Assets		$ 113,730
Liabilities		
Accounts Payable		$ 3,325
Owner's Equity		
J. Collins, Capital		110,405
Total Liabilities and Owner's Equity		$ 113,730

CHAPTER REVIEW

Learning Objective

7 Recognize the effect of errors on account balances.

Transpositions and slides account for many trial balance errors. The clue is whether the difference in account balances or trial balance totals is evenly divisible by 9.

  a. A **transposition** occurs when digits are switched around, such as 541 written as 415.
  b. A **slide** is an error in placing the decimal point (in other words, a *slide* in the decimal point). For example, $62,000 could be inadvertently written as $6,200.
  c. An error in a trial balance may be a combination of a transposition and a slide, as when $230 is written as $32.

 PRACTICE EXERCISE 7

Identify the following errors as transpositions or slides and indicate the amount of the difference and whether it is divisible by 9.

  a. The amount of supplies bought totaled $341, but it was written as $431.
  b. Equipment was purchased for $3,500, but it was written as $35.
  c. An error was made in the trial balance because $35 was written as $530.

PRACTICE EXERCISE 7 • SOLUTION

a. Transposition: The difference is $90 and can be evenly divided by 9.

Correct Number	Number Copied	Difference	Difference Divided by 9
$341	$431	$90	$90 ÷ 9 = $10

b. Slide: The difference is $3,465 and can be evenly divided by 9.

Correct Number	Number Copied	Difference	Difference Divided by 9
$3,500	$35	$3,465	$3,465 ÷ 9 = $385

c. Transposition and slide: The difference is $495 and can be evenly divided by 9.

Correct Number	Number Copied	Difference	Difference Divided by 9
$35	$530	$495	$495 ÷ 9 = $55

Glossary

Balance sheet A financial statement showing the financial position of an organization on a given date, such as June 30 or December 31. The balance sheet lists the balances in the asset, liability, and owner's equity accounts. *(p. 78)*

Compound entry A transaction that requires more than one debit or more than one credit to be recorded. *(p. 71)*

Credit The right side of a T account; to credit is to record an amount on the right side of a T account. Credits represent increases in liability, capital, or revenue accounts and decreases in asset, drawing, or expense accounts. *(p. 62)*

Debit The left side of a T account; to debit is to record an amount on the left side of a T account. Debits represent increases in asset, drawing, or expense accounts and decreases in liability, capital, or revenue accounts. *(p. 62)*

Financial position The resources or assets owned by an organization at a point in time, offset by the claims against those resources and owner's equity; shown on a balance sheet. *(p. 78)*

Financial statement A report prepared by accountants that summarizes the financial affairs of a business. *(p. 76)*

Footings The totals of each side of a T account. *(p. 60)*

Income statement A financial statement showing the results of business transactions involving revenue and expense accounts over a period of time. *(p. 76)*

Net income The result when total revenue exceeds total expenses over a period of time. *(p. 76)*

Net loss The result when total expenses exceed total revenue over a period of time. *(p. 76)*

Normal balance The plus side of a T account. *(p. 60)*

PDF (portable document format) An electronic file format that converts a printed document into an electronic image. *(p. 85)*

Profit and loss statement Another term for an income statement. *(p. 83)*

Report form The form of the balance sheet in which assets are placed at the top and liabilities and owner's equity are placed below. *(p. 78)*

Slide An error in placing the decimal point in a number. *(p. 80)*

Statement of owner's equity A financial statement showing the activity in the owner's equity, or Capital account, over the financial period. *(p. 77)*

T account form A form of account shaped like the letter T in which increases and decreases in the account may be recorded. One side of the T is for entries on the debit or left side. The other side of the T is for entries on the credit or right side. *(p. 59)*

Transposition An error that involves interchanging, or switching around, digits during the recording of a number. *(p. 80)*

Trial balance A list of all account balances to prove that the total of all debit balances equals the total of all credit balances. *(p. 75)*

Quiz Yourself

_____ 1. Determine the balance of the following T account:

Cash	
90,000	38,000
3,500	1,200
600	

   a. 94,100 debit
   b. 54,900 debit
   c. 133,300 credit
   d. 54,900 credit
   e. 133,300 debit

_____ 2. Which of the following statements is correct?
   a. Increases to cash are shown on the right side of the account.
   b. Decreases to accounts payable are shown on the right side of the account.
   c. Decreases to supplies are shown on the right side of the account.
   d. Increases to rent expense are shown on the right side of the account.

_____ 3. Which of the following statements is false?
   a. R. Flores, Capital is increased with a credit.
   b. Prepaid Insurance is decreased with a credit.
   c. Professional Fees is increased with a debit.
   d. Rent Expense is increased with a debit.

_____ 4. R. Nelson invests his personal computer, with a fair market value of $2,500, in the business. How would this transaction be recorded?
   a. A debit to R. Nelson, Capital, $2,500.
   b. A credit to Cash, $2,500.
   c. A credit to Professional Fees, $2,500
   d. A debit to Computer, $2,500.

_____ 5. When preparing a trial balance, which of the following is correct?
   a. The purpose of the trial balance is to prove that the total of all debit balances equals the total of all credit balances.
   b. Advertising Expense would normally be recorded as a credit.
   c. The trial balance is considered to be a financial statement.
   d. Supplies would normally be recorded as a credit.

(Continued)

Use the following information for questions 6–8:

Flores's Catering
Trial Balance
February 28, 20—

Account Name	Debit	Credit
Cash	20,500	
Accounts Receivable	2,300	
Supplies	500	
Equipment	13,000	
Accounts Payable		3,500
R. Flores, Capital		22,000
R. Flores, Drawing	6,000	
Professional Fees		20,000
Rent Expense	2,400	
Advertising Expense	800	
	45,500	45,500

6. What would be the net income for Flores's Catering?
   a. $45,500
   b. $16,800
   c. $19,800
   d. $10,800

7. On which financial statement(s) would R. Flores, Drawing appear?
   a. Income statement
   b. Balance sheet
   c. Statement of owner's equity
   d. Income statement and statement of owner's equity

8. What is the amount of ending capital shown on the balance sheet for Flores's Catering?
   a. $22,000
   b. $20,000
   c. $45,500
   d. $32,800

9. Flores's Catering purchased equipment that cost $2,500 but it was recorded as $520. Which of the following statement(s) are correct?
   a. This is a transposition error.
   b. This is a slide error.
   c. This is neither a transposition error nor a slide error.
   d. Both a and b are correct.

Answers:
1. b 2. c 3. c 4. d 5. a 6. b 7. c 8. d 9. d

Review It with **QuickBooks**®

1. The trial balance report is located under _____ in QuickBooks.
   a. Company & Financial
   b. Accountant & Taxes
   c. Custom Reports
   d. All of the above

2. The income statement is also known as the _____ in QuickBooks.
   a. Balance sheet
   b. Trial balance
   c. Profit and loss statement
   d. Company & Financial

_____ 3. The balance sheet report is located under _____ in QuickBooks.
a. Company & Financial
b. Accountant & Taxes
c. Custom Reports
d. All of the above

_____ 4. QuickBooks reports can be printed or saved as _____ files.
a. PDF
b. Excel
c. Custom
d. Both a and b are correct.

Answers:
1. b 2. c 3. a 4. d

Chapter Assignments

Discussion Questions

1. Explain how a trial balance and a balance sheet differ.
2. Explain why the term *debit* doesn't always mean "increase" and why the term *credit* doesn't always mean "decrease."
3. What are footings in accounting?
4. How are the three financial statements shown in this chapter connected?
5. What is a compound entry?
6. List two reasons why the debits and credits in the trial balance might not balance.
7. Give an example of a slide and an example of a transposition. Explain how you might decide whether an error is a slide or a transposition.
8. What do we mean when we say that capital, drawing, revenue, and expense accounts are under the umbrella of owner's equity?

Exercises

LO 2, 3

EXERCISE 2-1 On a sheet of paper, draw the fundamental accounting equation with T accounts under each of the account classifications, with plus and minus signs and debit and credit on the appropriate side of each account. Under each of the classifications, draw T accounts, again with the correct plus and minus signs and debit and credit, for each of the following accounts of Barlow Engine Repair.

Practice Exercise 2, 3

Cash
Accounts Receivable
Supplies
Equipment
Accounts Payable
D. Barlow, Capital

D. Barlow, Drawing
Income from Repairs
Wages Expense
Rent Expense
Utilities Expense
Miscellaneous Expense

CHAPTER ASSIGNMENTS

Practice Exercises 2, 3

EXERCISE 2-2 List the classification of each of the following accounts as A (asset), L (liability), OE (owner's equity), R (revenue), or E (expense). Write *Debit* or *Credit* to indicate the increase side, the decrease side, and the normal balance side.

Account	Classification	Increase Side	Normal Balance Side	Decrease Side
0. Cash	A	Debit	Debit	Credit
1. Wages Expense				
2. Equipment				
3. L. Cross, Capital				
4. Service Revenue				
5. L. Cross, Drawing				
6. Accounts Receivable				
7. Rent Expense				
8. Fees Earned				
9. Accounts Payable				

Practice Exercise 4

EXERCISE 2-3 R. Dalberg operates Dalberg's Tours. The company has the following chart of accounts:

Assets	Liabilities	Revenue
Cash	Accounts Payable	Income from Tours
Accounts Receivable		
Supplies	**Owner's Equity**	**Expenses**
Prepaid Insurance	R. Dalberg, Capital	Wages Expense
Display Equipment	R. Dalberg, Drawing	Gas Expense
Van		Advertising Expense
Office Equipment		Utilities Expense

Using the chart of accounts, record the following transactions in pairs of T accounts. Give the T account to be debited first and the account to be credited to the right. Show debit and credit and plus and minus signs. (Example: Received and paid the bill for the month's rent, $480.)

Rent Expense		Cash	
+	−	+	−
Debit	Credit	Debit	Credit
480			480

a. Received and paid the electric bill, $175.
b. Bought supplies on account, $135.
c. Paid for insurance for one year, $580.
d. Made a payment on account to a creditor, $65.
e. Received and paid the telephone bill, $186.
f. Sold services on account, $1,375.
g. Received and paid the gasoline bill for the van, $130.
h. Received cash on account from customers, $1,458.
i. Dalberg withdrew cash for personal use, $700.

CHAPTER ASSIGNMENTS

LO 4

Practice Exercise 4

EXERCISE 2-4 During the first month of operation, Graham Expeditions recorded the following transactions. Describe what has happened in each of the transactions (a) through (k).

Cash	
(a) 4,500	(b) 525
(k) 1,125	(c) 98
	(e) 75
	(g) 500
	(i) 220
	(j) 1,500

Accounts Receivable	
(h) 615	

Supplies	
(d) 680	

Equipment	
(f) 3,510	
(g) 2,000	

Accounts Payable	
	(d) 680
	(g) 1,500

C. M. Graham, Capital	
	(a) 4,500
	(f) 3,510

C. M. Graham, Drawing	
(j) 1,500	

Income from Tours	
	(h) 615
	(k) 1,125

Rent Expense	
(b) 525	

Advertising Expense	
(c) 98	

Utilities Expense	
(i) 220	

Miscellaneous Expense	
(e) 75	

LO 5

Practice Exercise 5

EXERCISE 2-5 Speedy Sewing Services, owned by T. Nguyen, hired a new bookkeeper who is not entirely familiar with the process of preparing a trial balance. All of the accounts have normal balances. Find the errors and prepare a corrected trial balance for December 31 of this year.

Speedy Sewing Services
Trial Balance
December 31, 20—

Account Name	Debit	Credit
Accounts Receivable		10,700
Cash	3,200	
Accounts Payable		9,500
Equipment	24,000	
T. Nguyen, Capital		22,800
T. Nguyen, Drawing		1,900
Prepaid Insurance		1,300
Income from Services		36,000
Wages Expense	17,500	
Rent Expense		4,500
Supplies	1,800	
Utilities Expense	3,400	
	49,900	86,700

LO 5, 6

Practice Exercises
5, 6

EXERCISE 2-6 During the first month of operations, Landish Modeling Agency recorded transactions in T account form. Foot and balance the accounts; then prepare a trial balance, an income statement, a statement of owner's equity, and a balance sheet dated March 31, 20--.

Cash		
(a)	8,200	(b) 350
(c)	8,400	(d) 1,600
(i)	7,580	(f) 175
		(g) 3,400
		(h) 2,200

Accounts Payable	
	(k) 2,800
	(j) 82

Salary Expense	
(g) 3,400	

R. Landish, Capital	
	(a) 8,200

Rent Expense	
(d) 1,600	

Accounts Receivable	
(e) 2,600	

R. Landish, Drawing	
(h) 2,200	

Supplies	
(j) 82	

Modeling Fees	
	(c) 8,400
	(e) 2,600
	(i) 7,580

Utilities Expense	
(f) 175	

Office Furniture	
(b) 350	

Office Equipment	
(k) 2,800	

LO 7

Practice Exercise 7

EXERCISE 2-7 The following errors were made in journalizing transactions. In each case, calculate the amount of the error and indicate whether the debit or the credit column of the trial balance will be understated or overstated.

	Amount of Difference	Debit or Credit Column of Trial Balance Understated or Overstated
0. Example: A $149 debit to Accounts Receivable was not recorded.	$149	Debit column understated
a. A $42 debit to Supplies was recorded as $420.		
b. A $155 debit to Accounts Receivable was recorded twice.		
c. A $179 debit to Prepaid Insurance was not recorded.		
d. A $65 credit to Cash was not recorded.		
e. A $190 debit to Equipment was recorded twice.		
f. A $57 debit to Utilities Expense was recorded as $75.		

LO 7

Practice Exercise 7

EXERCISE 2-8 Would the following errors cause the trial balance to have equal or unequal totals? As a result of the errors, which accounts are overstated (by how much) or understated (by how much)?

a. A purchase of office equipment for $380 was recorded as a debit to Office Equipment for $38 and a credit to Cash for $38.

b. A payment of $280 to a creditor was debited to Accounts Receivable and credited to Cash for $280 each.

c. A purchase of supplies for $245 was recorded as a debit to Equipment for $245 and a credit to Cash for $245.

d. A payment of $76 to a creditor was recorded as a debit to Accounts Payable for $76 and a credit to Cash for $67.

Problem Set A

LO 1, 2, 3, 4

PROBLEM 2-1A During December of this year, G. Elden established Ginny's Gym. The following asset, liability, and owner's equity accounts are included in the chart of accounts:

Cash

Exercise Equipment

Store Equipment	Income from Services
Office Equipment	Advertising Expense
Accounts Payable	During December, the following
G. Elden, Capital	transactions occurred:

a. Elden deposited $35,000 in a bank account in the name of the business.
b. Bought exercise equipment for cash, $8,150, Ck. No. 1001.
c. Bought advertising on account from Hazel Company, $105.
d. Bought a display rack (Store Equipment) on account from Cyber Core, $790.
e. Bought office equipment on account from Office Aids, $185.
f. Elden invested her exercise equipment with a fair market value of $1,200 in the business.
g. Made a payment to Cyber Core, $200, Ck. No. 1002.
h. Sold services for the month of December for cash, $800.

Required
1. Write the account classifications (Assets, Liabilities, Capital, Drawing, Revenue, Expense) in the fundamental accounting equation, as well as the plus and minus signs and *Debit* and *Credit*.
2. Write the account names on the T accounts under the classifications, place the plus and minus signs for each T account, and label the debit and credit sides of the T accounts.
3. Record the amounts in the proper positions in the T accounts. Write the letter next to each entry to identify the transaction.
4. Foot and balance the accounts.

Check Figure
Balance of Cash, $27,450

LO 1, 2, 3, 4, 5

PROBLEM 2-2A B. Kelso established Computer Wizards during November of this year. The accountant prepared the following chart of accounts:

Assets	**Owner's Equity**	**Expenses**
Cash	B. Kelso, Capital	Wages Expense
Supplies	B. Kelso, Drawing	Rent Expense
Computer Software		Advertising Expense
Office Equipment	**Revenue**	Utilities Expense
Neon Sign	Income from Services	Miscellaneous Expense

Liabilities
Accounts Payable

(Continued)

The following transactions occurred during the month:

a. Kelso deposited $45,000 in a bank account in the name of the business.
b. Paid the rent for the current month, $1,800, Ck. No. 2001.
c. Bought office desks and filing cabinets for cash, $790, Ck. No. 2002.
d. Bought a computer and printer (Office Equipment) from Cyber Center for use in the business, $2,700, paying $1,700 in cash and placing the balance on account, Ck. No. 2003.
e. Bought a neon sign on account from Signage Co., $1,350.
f. Kelso invested her personal computer software with a fair market value of $600 in the business.
g. Received a bill from *Country News* for newspaper advertising, $365.
h. Sold services for cash, $1,245.
i. Received and paid the electric bill, $345, Ck. No. 2004.
j. Paid on account to *Country News*, a creditor, $285, Ck. No. 2005.
k. Sold services for cash, $1,450.
l. Paid wages to an employee, $925, Ck. No. 2006.
m. Received and paid the bill for the city business license, $75, Ck. No. 2007 (Miscellaneous Expense).
n. Kelso withdrew cash for personal use, $850, Ck. No. 2008.
o. Bought printer paper and letterhead stationery on account from Office Aids, $115.

Check Figure
Trial balance total,
$50,840

Required

1. Record the owner's name in the Capital and Drawing T accounts.
2. Correctly place the plus and minus signs for each T account and label the debit and credit sides of the accounts.
3. Record the transactions in T accounts. Write the letter of each entry to identify the transaction.
4. Foot the T accounts and show the balances.
5. Prepare a trial balance, with a three-line heading, dated November 30, 20--.

LO 1, 2, 3, 4, 5, 6 ···

PROBLEM 2-3A S. Myers, a speech therapist, opened a clinic in the name of Myers Clinic. Her accountant prepared the following chart of accounts:

Assets	**Owner's Equity**	**Expenses**
Cash	S. Myers, Capital	Salary Expense
Accounts Receivable	S. Myers, Drawing	Rent Expense
Office Equipment		Utilities Expense
Office Furniture	**Revenue**	Miscellaneous Expense
	Professional Fees	
Liabilities		
Accounts Payable		

The following transactions occurred during June of this year:

a. Myers deposited $40,000 in a bank account in the name of the business.
b. Bought waiting room chairs and tables (Office Furniture) on account, $1,330.
c. Bought a fax/copier/scanner combination (Office Equipment) from Max's Equipment for $595, paying $200 in cash and placing the balance on account, Ck. No. 1001.
d. Bought an intercom system (Office Equipment) on account from Regan Office Supply, $375.

e. Received and paid the telephone bill, $155, Ck. No. 1002.
f. Sold professional services on account, $1,484.
g. Received and paid the electric bill, $190, Ck. No. 1003.
h. Received and paid the bill for the state speech therapy convention, $450, Ck. No. 1004 (Miscellaneous Expense).
i. Sold professional services for cash, $2,575.
j. Paid on account to Regan Office Supply, $300, Ck. No. 1005.
k. Paid the rent for the current month, $940, Ck. No. 1006.
l. Paid salary of the receptionist, $880, Ck. No. 1007.
m. Myers withdrew cash for personal use, $800, Ck. No. 1008.
n. Received $885 on account from patients who were previously billed.

Required

Check Figure
Net Income, $1,444

1. Record the owner's name in the Capital and Drawing T accounts.
2. Correctly place the plus and minus signs for each T account and label the debit and credit sides of the accounts.
3. Record the transactions in the T accounts. Write the letter of each entry to identify the transaction.
4. Foot the T accounts and show the balances.
5. Prepare a trial balance as of June 30, 20--.
6. Prepare an income statement for June 30, 20--.
7. Prepare a statement of owner's equity for June 30, 20--.
8. Prepare a balance sheet as of June 30, 20--.

LO 1, 2, 3, 4, 5, 6

PROBLEM 2-4A On May 1, B. Bangle opened Self-Wash Laundry. His accountant listed the following chart of accounts:

Cash	B. Bangle, Drawing
Supplies	Laundry Revenue
Prepaid Insurance	Wages Expense
Equipment	Rent Expense
Furniture and Fixtures	Utilities Expense
Accounts Payable	Miscellaneous Expense
B. Bangle, Capital	

The following transactions were completed during May:

a. Bangle deposited $35,000 in a bank account in the name of the business.
b. Bought chairs and tables (Furniture and Fixtures), paying cash, $1,870, Ck. No. 1000.
c. Bought supplies on account from Barnes Supply Company, $225.
d. Paid the rent for the current month, $875, Ck. No. 1001.
e. Bought washing machines and dryers (Equipment) from Lara Equipment Company, $12,500, paying $3,600 in cash and placing the balance on account, Ck. No. 1002.
f. Sold services for cash for the first half of the month, $1,925.
g. Bought insurance for one year, $1,560, Ck. No. 1003.
h. Paid on account to Lara Equipment Company, $1,800, Ck. No. 1004.
i. Received and paid electric bill, $285, Ck. No. 1005.
j. Sold services for cash for the second half of the month, $1,835.
k. Paid wages to an employee, $940, Ck. No. 1006.
l. Bangle withdrew cash for his personal use, $800, Ck. No. 1007.
m. Paid on account to Barnes Supply Company, $225, Ck. No. 1008.
n. Received and paid bill from the county for sidewalk repair assessment, $280, Ck. No. 1009 (Miscellaneous Expense).

(Continued)

Check Figure
Trial balance total,
$45,860

Required

1. Record the owner's name in the Capital and Drawing T accounts.
2. Correctly place the plus and minus signs for each T account and label the debit and credit sides of the accounts.
3. Record the transactions in the T accounts. Write the letter of each entry to identify the transaction.
4. Foot the T accounts and show the balances.
5. Prepare a trial balance as of May 31, 20--.
6. Prepare an income statement for May 31, 20--.
7. Prepare a statement of owner's equity for May 31, 20--.
8. Prepare a balance sheet as of May 31, 20--.

 LO 6 ··

PROBLEM 2-5A The financial statements for Daniels' Custom Haircuts for the month of October follow.

Daniels' Custom Haircuts Income Statement (a)		
Revenue:		
Professional Fees		$25,000
Expenses:		
Salary Expense	$1,200	
Rent Expense	3,000	
Utilities Expense	600	
Miscellaneous Expense	450	
Total Expenses		(b)
Net Income		$19,750

(c) Statement of Owner's Equity (d)		
Q. Daniels, Capital, October 1, 20--		$ 0
Investments during October	$ (e)	
Net Income for October	(f)	
Subtotal	$29,750	
Less Withdrawals for October	4,000	
Increase in Capital		(g)
Q. Daniels, Capital, October 31, 20--		$25,750

Daniels' Custom Haircuts
Balance Sheet
(h)

Assets		
Cash	$16,000	
Accounts Receivable	2,400	
Office Equipment	10,000	
Office Furniture	8,000	
Total Assets		$ (i)
Liabilities		
Accounts Payable		$ 10,650
Owner's Equity		
Q. Daniels, Capital		(j)
Total Liabilities and Owner's Equity		$ (k)

Required

Solve for the missing information.

Problem Set B

LO 1, 2, 3, 4

PROBLEM 2-1B During February of this year, H. Rose established Rose Shoe Hospital. The following asset, liability, and owner's equity accounts are included in the chart of accounts:

Cash	Accounts Payable
Shop Equipment	H. Rose, Capital
Store Equipment	Income from Services
Office Equipment	Advertising Expense

The following transactions occurred during the month of February:

a. Rose deposited $25,000 cash in a bank account in the name of the business.
b. Bought shop equipment for cash, $1,525, Ck. No. 1000.
c. Bought advertising on account from Milland Company, $325.
d. Bought store shelving on account from Inger Hardware, $750.
e. Bought office equipment from Shara's Office Supply, $625, paying $225 in cash and placing the balance on account, Ck. No. 1001.
f. Paid on account to Inger Hardware, $750, Ck. No. 1002.
g. Rose invested his personal leather working tools with a fair market value of $800 in the business.
h. Sold services for the month of February for cash, $250.

(Continued)

Check Figure
Cash balance,
$22,750

Required

1. Write the account classifications (Assets, Liabilities, Capital, Drawing, Revenue, Expense) in the fundamental accounting equation, as well as the plus and minus signs and *Debit* and *Credit*.
2. Write the account names on the T accounts under the classifications, place the plus and minus signs for each T account, and label the debit and credit sides of the T accounts.
3. Record the amounts in the proper positions in the T accounts. Write the letter next to each entry to identify the transaction.
4. Foot and balance the accounts.

LO 1, 2, 3, 4, 5 ··

PROBLEM 2-2B J. Carrie established Carrie's Photo Tours during June of this year. The accountant prepared the following chart of accounts:

Assets	Owner's Equity	Expenses
Cash	J. Carrie, Capital	Wages Expense
Supplies	J. Carrie, Drawing	Rent Expense
Computer Software		Advertising Expense
Office Equipment	**Revenue**	Utilities Expense
Neon Sign	Income from Services	Miscellaneous Expense

Liabilities
Accounts Payable

The following transactions occurred during the month of June:

a. Carrie deposited $30,000 cash in a bank account in the name of the business.
b. Bought office equipment for cash, $1,850, Ck. No. 1001.
c. Bought computer software from Morey's Computer Center, $640, paying $350 in cash and placing the balance on account, Ck. No. 1002.
d. Paid current month's rent, $950, Ck. No. 1003.
e. Sold services for cash, $1,575.
f. Bought a neon sign from The Sign Company, $1,335, paying $435 in cash and placing the balance on account, Ck. No. 1004.
g. Received bill from *The Gossiper* for advertising, $445.
h. Bought supplies on account from City Supply, $460.
i. Received and paid the electric bill, $380, Ck. No. 1005.
j. Paid on account to *The Gossiper*, $245, Ck. No. 1006.
k. Sold services for cash, $3,474.
l. Paid wages to an employee, $930, Ck. No. 1007.
m. Carrie invested his personal computer (Office Equipment) with a fair market value of $1,000 in the business.
n. Carrie withdrew cash for personal use, $800, Ck. No. 1008.
o. Received and paid the bill for city business license, $75, Ck. No. 1009 (Miscellaneous Expense).

Check Figure
Trial balance total,
$37,899

Required

1. Record the owner's name in the Capital and Drawing T accounts.
2. Correctly place the plus and minus signs for each T account and label the debit and credit sides of the accounts.

3. Record the transactions in the T accounts. Write the letter of each entry to identify the transaction.
4. Foot the T accounts and show the balances.
5. Prepare a trial balance, with a three-line heading, dated June 30, 20--.

LO   **1, 2, 3, 4, 5, 6**

PROBLEM 2-3B D. Johnston, a physical therapist, opened Johnston's Clinic. His accountant provided the following chart of accounts:

Assets	**Owner's Equity**	**Expenses**
Cash	D. Johnston, Capital	Salary Expense
Accounts Receivable	D. Johnston, Drawing	Rent Expense
Office Equipment		Utilities Expense
Office Furniture	**Revenue**	Miscellaneous Expense
	Professional Fees	
Liabilities		
Accounts Payable		

The following transactions occurred during July of this year:

a. Johnston deposited $35,000 in a bank account in the name of the business.
b. Bought filing cabinets (Office Equipment) on account from Muller Office Supply, $560.
c. Paid cash for chairs and carpeting (Office Furniture) for the waiting room, $835, Ck. No. 1000.
d. Bought a photocopier from Rob's Office Equipment, $650, paying $250 in cash and placing the balance on account, Ck. No. 1001.
e. Received and paid the telephone bill, which included installation charges, $185, Ck. No. 1002.
f. Sold professional services on account, $2,255.
g. Received and paid the bill for the state physical therapy convention, $445, Ck. No. 1003 (Miscellaneous Expense).
h. Received and paid the electric bill, $335, Ck. No. 1004.
i. Received cash on account from credit customers, $1,940.
j. Paid on account to Muller Office Supply, $250, Ck. No. 1005.
k. Paid the office rent for the current month, $1,245, Ck. No. 1006.
l. Sold professional services for cash, $1,950.
m. Paid the salary of the receptionist, $960, Ck. No. 1007.
n. Johnston withdrew cash for personal use, $1,200, Ck. No. 1008.

Required
1. Record the owner's name in the Capital and Drawing T accounts.
2. Correctly place the plus and minus signs for each T account and label the debit and credit sides of the accounts.
3. Record the transactions in the T accounts. Write the letter of each entry to identify the transaction.
4. Foot the T accounts and show the balances.
5. Prepare a trial balance as of July 31, 20--.
6. Prepare an income statement for July 31, 20--.
7. Prepare a statement of owner's equity for July 31, 20--.
8. Prepare a balance sheet as of July 31, 20--.

Check Figure
Net Income, $1,035

LO 1, 2, 4, 5, 6 ....

PROBLEM 2-4B On July 1, K. Resser opened Resser's Business Services. Resser's accountant listed the following chart of accounts:

Cash	K. Resser, Drawing
Supplies	Business Services Revenue
Prepaid Insurance	Wages Expense
Equipment	Rent Expense
Furniture and Fixtures	Utilities Expense
Accounts Payable	Miscellaneous Expense
K. Resser, Capital	

The following transactions were completed during July:

a. Resser deposited $25,000 in a bank account in the name of the business.
b. Bought tables and chairs (Furniture and Fixtures) for cash, $725, Ck. No. 1200.
c. Paid the rent for the current month, $1,750, Ck. No. 1201.
d. Bought computers and copy machines (Equipment) from Ferber Equipment, $15,700, paying $4,000 in cash and placing the balance on account, Ck. No. 1202.
e. Bought supplies on account from Wiggins's Distributors, $535.
f. Sold services for cash, $1,742.
g. Bought insurance for one year, $1,375, Ck. No. 1203.
h. Paid on account to Ferber Equipment, $700, Ck. No. 1204.
i. Received and paid the electric bill, $438, Ck. No. 1205.
j. Paid on account to Wiggins's Distributors, $315, Ck. No. 1206.
k. Sold services to customers for cash for the second half of the month, $820.
l. Received and paid the bill for the business license, $75, Ck. No. 1207 (Miscellaneous Expense).
m. Paid wages to an employee, $1,200, Ck. No. 1208.
n. Resser withdrew cash for personal use, $700, Ck. No. 1209.

Check Figure
K. Resser, Capital,
July 31, 20--, $23,399

Required

1. Record the owner's name in the Capital and Drawing T accounts.
2. Correctly place the plus and minus signs for each T account and label the debit and credit sides of the accounts.
3. Record the transactions in the T accounts. Write the letter of each entry to identify the transaction.
4. Foot the T accounts and show the balances.
5. Prepare a trial balance as of July 31, 20--.
6. Prepare an income statement for July 31, 20--.
7. Prepare a statement of owner's equity for July 31, 20--.
8. Prepare a balance sheet as of July 31, 20--.

LO 6

PROBLEM 2-5B The financial statements for Baker Custom Catering for the month of April are presented below.

Baker Custom Catering Income Statement (a)		
Revenue:		
Professional Fees		$12,000
Expenses:		
Salary Expense	$ 800	
Rent Expense	1,200	
Utilities Expense	360	
Miscellaneous Expense	80	
Total Expenses		(b)
Net Income		$ 9,560

(c) Statement of Owner's Equity (d)		
L. Baker, Capital, April 1, 20--		$ 0
Investments during April	$ (e)	
Net Income for April	(f)	
Subtotal	$14,560	
Less Withdrawals for April	1,000	
Increase in Capital		(g)
L. Baker, Capital, April 30, 20--		$13,560

Baker Custom Catering Balance Sheet (h)		
Assets		
Cash	$8,000	
Accounts Receivable	800	
Office Equipment	4,000	
Office Furniture	2,000	
Total Assets		$ (i)
Liabilities		
Accounts Payable		$ 1,240
Owner's Equity		
L. Baker, Capital		(j)
Total Liabilities and Owner's Equity		$ (k)

Required

Solve for the missing information.

Try It with **QuickBooks**® (LO 2–7)

QB Exercise 2-1

Using the Conner's Whitewater Adventures demonstration file from Chapter 1, complete the following activities with QuickBooks. Use the dates June 1, 20--, to June 30, 20--, for all reports.

1. View and print the trial balance report for Conner's Whitewater Adventures.
   a. What is the total of the Debit column on the trial balance?
2. View and print the standard profit and loss statement for Conner's Whitewater Adventures.
   a. What is the net income or net loss for Conner's Whitewater Adventures?
3. View and print the standard balance sheet for Conner's Whitewater Adventures.
   a. What is the amount of Conner's Whitewater Adventures total assets?
4. Save the profit and loss statement as a PDF.
5. Save the profit and loss statement as an Excel file.

Activities

Why Does It Matter?

SOLID ROCK GYM, San Diego, California

Individuals and groups of all ages come to Solid Rock Gym for fun and fitness. Services include several types of indoor rock-climbing experiences such as individual and group instruction, team development, and fitness programs. Solid Rock Gym also offers bouldering (climbing close to the bottom—no rope or hardware), top-roping (climbing while protected by a rope running through anchors above the intended route), and lead climbing (climbing while protected by a rope clipped to anchors as the climber ascends a route).

List five transactions that Solid Rock Gym might record during the month. Determine what accounts are involved and whether the accounts are debited or credited.

Example: Transaction 0. Owner invested cash in the business. Accounts involved: Cash and Capital. Cash is debited, and Capital is credited.

What Would You Say?

A fellow accounting student has difficulty understanding how the fundamental accounting equation stays in balance when a compound entry with one debit and two credits is recorded. Consider, for example, that a business bought equipment for $7,000, paid $3,000 in cash, and placed the remainder on account.

This means that there are two credits and one debit—one debit and one credit on the left side of the equation and the other credit on the right side of the equation. Explain to your fellow student how the equation stays in balance.

What Would You Do?

A new bookkeeper can't find the errors that are causing the company's month-end trial balance to be out of balance. The bookkeeper is too shy to ask for help at the office, so she takes the financial records home and asks her uncle, a retired bookkeeper, to help her locate the errors. Even with the help of her uncle, the trial balance is still out of balance, and now she is too embarrassed to return to the office and ask for help. What is wrong with this practice, if anything?

3

The General Journal and the General Ledger

Learning Objectives

After you have completed this chapter, you will be able to do the following:

1 Record a group of transactions pertaining to a service business in a two-column general journal.

2 Post entries from a two-column general journal to general ledger accounts.

3 Prepare a trial balance from the ledger accounts.

4 Explain the importance of source documents.

5 Correct entries using the ruling or correcting entry method.

To: **Amy Roberts, CPA**
Subject: **Recording Transactions**

Hi Amy,
This accounting stuff can be tough! But I think I am finally getting the hang of recording transactions using T accounts. Is this how accountants actually record transactions? As I have been looking around in QuickBooks, I don't see T accounts anywhere! Help!
Thanks,
Janie

To: **Janie Conner**
Subject: **RE: Recording Transactions**

Hi Janie,
You're right—you won't find T accounts in QuickBooks. That's because recording transactions using T accounts is a beginning step. Are you ready to learn how accountants actually record transactions—in journal entries? Using what you've learned so far about T accounts and debits and credits, you're ready to move on. Here's what you'll need to do:

_____ 1. Begin recording transactions using journal entries.
_____ 2. Learn how to post journal entries into the ledger.

Your knowledge of T accounts and debits and credits is very important for this next challenge and will help you prepare the journal entries correctly. Before you get started, take some time to review the rules of debits and credits. This will really help! You are now ready to start using QuickBooks to record transactions. I will send you some hints to help you get started.
Amy

Jose Luis Pelaez Inc/Blend Images/Getty Images

Accounting Language

Cost principle (p. 115)

Cross-reference (p. 120)

General ledger (p. 118)

Journal (p. 111)

Journalizing (p. 111)

Ledger account (p. 118)

Posting (p. 120)

Source documents (p. 111)

Two-column general journal (p. 113)

In Chapter 2, we learned how to use T accounts as a tool for practicing debits and credits. We also used the trial balance as a means of making sure the debits equal the credits. In this chapter, we will further formalize our accounting procedures by learning about the general journal and the posting procedure.

Recall that *recording* is a step in the definition of accounting. Here we introduce the journal as the official record of business transactions. We have recorded business transactions as debits and credits to T accounts because it's easier to visualize these debits and credits as the plus and minus sides of the T accounts involved. **Determining the appropriate transaction debits and credits is the most important element in the accounting process.** It represents the very basic foundation of accounting, and all of the structure represented by financial statements and other reports is entirely dependent upon it. After determining the debits and credits, the accountant records the transactions in a journal.

The initial steps in the accounting process are as follows:

STEP 1. Record business transactions in a journal.

STEP 2. Post entries to accounts in the ledger.

STEP 3. Prepare a trial balance.

In this chapter, we explain all three steps.

THE GENERAL JOURNAL

We have seen that an accountant must keep a record of each transaction. In Chapter 2, we recorded the transactions directly in T accounts; however, only part of the transaction would be listed in each T account. A **journal** is a book in which business transactions are recorded as they happen. In the journal, both the debits and the credits of the entire transaction are recorded in one place. Actually, the journal is a diary for the business in which you record in day-by-day or chronological order all the events involving financial affairs. A journal is called a *book of original entry*. In other words, a transaction is always recorded first in the journal. The process of recording a business transaction in the journal is called **journalizing**. The information about transactions comes from **source documents** such as checks, invoices, receipts, letters, and memos. These source

1 Record a group of transactions pertaining to a service business in a two-column general journal.

Learning Objective

documents furnish proof (objective evidence) that a transaction has taken place, and they should be identified in the journal entry whenever possible.

Remember the first transaction for Conner's Whitewater Adventures?

TRANSACTION (a). June 1: Conner deposited $90,000 in a bank account in the name of the business.

When the business receives the cash from J. Conner, the accountant creates a source document—in this case, a receipt. See Figure 1 for an example of the source document that would be created.

Figure 1
Source document

Receipt	Date *June 1*	20 ―	No.
Received From *J. Conner*			*90,000.00*
Ninety thousand and 00/100 ★★★★★★★★★★★★★★★★★★★★★★★★★			Dollars
For *Owner investment*			

Next, the accountant needs to analyze this transaction. We already know how to do this by following the steps presented in Chapter 2.

STEP 1. **What accounts are involved?** Cash and J. Conner, Capital are involved.

STEP 2. **What are the classifications of the accounts involved?** Cash is an asset account, and J. Conner, Capital is an owner's equity account.

STEP 3. **Are the accounts increased or decreased?** Cash is increased because Conner's Whitewater Adventures has more cash now than it had before. J. Conner, Capital is increased because Conner has a greater investment now than it had before.

STEP 4. **Write the transaction as a debit to one account (or accounts) and a credit to another account (or accounts).** Cash is increased, and the increase side of Cash is the left, or debit, side. J. Conner, Capital is an owner's equity account and is increased. The increase side of Capital is the right, or credit, side.

STEP 5. **Is the equation in balance after the transaction has been recorded?** Yes.

Let's show these entries by referring to our reliable fundamental accounting equation with the accompanying T accounts.

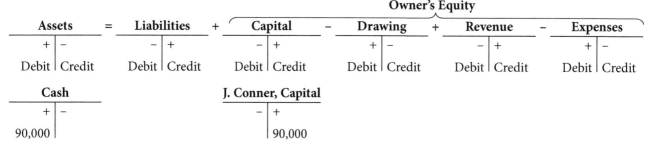

Now the accountant is ready to journalize the transaction. He or she records the business transaction in the journal. The basic form of the journal is the

two-column general journal. The term *two-column* refers to the two columns used for debit and credit amounts. The pages of the journal are numbered in consecutive order.

Let's take a look at completed transaction (a) in the journal.

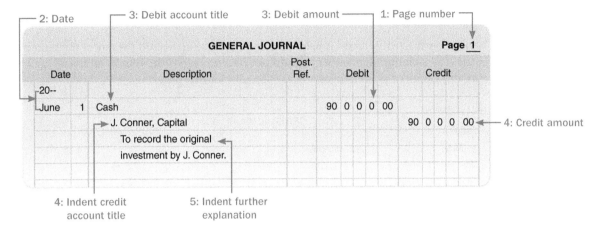

To explain the entry, we will break it down line by line. All journal entries contain the following:

STEP 1. *Page Number:* At the top of the page, record the page number.

STEP 2. *Date:* On the first line, record the year in the left part of the Date column. On the second line, record the month in the left part of the Date column and the day of the month in the right part of the Date column. *You don't have to repeat the year and month until you start a new page or until the year or month changes.*

STEP 3. *Debit:* **The debit part of the entry is always recorded first**. Insert the account title in the Description column and the dollar amount in the Debit column.

STEP 4. *Credit:* **The credit part of the entry is always indented and inserted on the line below the debit entry**. Insert the account title in the Description column and the dollar amount in the Credit column.

STEP 5. *Explanation:* **The explanation, indented further, is inserted on the line below the last line of the entry**. The explanation should refer to source documents, providing information such as check numbers, receipt numbers, or invoice numbers. You may also list names of charge customers or creditors or terms of payment.

For an entry in the general journal to be complete, it must contain (1) the date, (2) a debit entry, (3) a credit entry, and (4) an explanation. To anyone thoroughly familiar with the accounts, the explanation may seem obvious. Nevertheless, record the explanation as a required, integral part of the entry. To make the journal entries easier to read, leave one blank line between each transaction in your homework.

TRANSACTION (b). June 2: Conner's Whitewater Adventures bought equipment, paying cash, $38,000. Decide which accounts are involved. Then determine which of the five possible classifications each part of the transaction applies to. Visualize the plus and minus signs for each classification. Decide whether the accounts are increased or decreased. When you use T accounts to analyze the transaction, the results are as follows:

Equipment		Cash	
+	−	+	−
Debit	Credit	Debit	Credit
38,000			38,000

Now journalize this analysis below the first transaction. Record the day of the month in the Date column. Remember, you do not have to record the month and year again until the month or year changes or you use a new journal page.

			GENERAL JOURNAL								Page 1				
Date		Description		Post. Ref.		Debit					Credit				
20--															
June	1	Cash			90	0	0	0	00						
		J. Conner, Capital									90	0	0	0	00
		To record the original													
		investment by J. Conner.													
	2	Equipment			38	0	0	0	00						
		Cash									38	0	0	0	00
		Bought equipment for cash.													

Skip a line between entries in your homework →

TRANSACTION (c). **June 3: Conner's Whitewater Adventures bought equipment on account from Signal Products, $4,320.** Again, start with the T accounts.

Equipment		Accounts Payable	
+	−	−	+
Debit	Credit	Debit	Credit
4,320			4,320

After skipping a line in the journal, record the day of the month and then the entry. In journalizing a transaction involving Accounts Payable, state the name of the creditor in the explanation. Similarly, in journalizing a transaction involving Accounts Receivable, in the explanation, state the name of the customer who charged the amount.

Remember

In trying to figure out how a transaction should be recorded, first decide on the accounts involved. Then classify the accounts as A, L, OE, R, or E. Finally, ask yourself whether the accounts are increased or decreased and think of the related accounts with their plus and minus sides. This process will make the debits and credits of the transaction fall into place.

			GENERAL JOURNAL								Page 1				
Date		Description		Post. Ref.		Debit					Credit				
	3	Equipment			4	3	2	0	00						
		Accounts Payable									4	3	2	0	00
		Bought equipment on account													
		from Signal Products.													

When a business buys an asset, the asset should be recorded at the actual cost (the agreed amount of a transaction). This is called the **cost principle**. For example, suppose that the $4,320 that Conner's Whitewater Adventures paid for the equipment from Signal Products was a bargain price, as Signal Products had been asking $7,500 for the equipment. Conner's Whitewater Adventures *should record the cost of the equipment as the actual amount paid ($4,320) in the transaction that occurred.* This is true even though the asking price was $7,500.

TRANSACTION (d). **June 4: Conner's Whitewater Adventures paid Signal Products, a creditor, $2,000.** Picture the T accounts like this:

Cash			Accounts Payable		
+	–		–	+	
Debit	Credit		Debit	Credit	
	2,000		2,000		

In this case, we see that cash is decreasing, so we record it on the minus side. We now have a credit to Cash and have completed half of the entry. Next, we recognize that Accounts Payable is involved. We ask ourselves, "Do we owe more or less as a result of this transaction?" The answer is "less," so we record it on the minus, or debit, side of the account.

ACCOUNTING IN YOUR FUTURE

ACCOUNTING SKILLS

I f you decide to work in the field of accounting, there are a number of skills that you need to bring to the position. Of course, you will need to be able to write well and have solid communication and interpersonal skills—those skills are assumed capabilities for nearly every job. However, if you are in the accounting department, you will be expected to be skilled at analyzing transactions, debiting and crediting accounts accurately as you journalize, and posting those transactions too.

You may also be required to prepare a trial balance and financial statements. While your work will be primarily on the computer using general ledger software, you still need to understand what goes on behind the screen. This is especially important when totals don't balance or some other error needs to be uncovered and corrected. That is why the first three chapters in this textbook are particularly critical to building your accounting skills.

Remember

Get in the T account habit. Picture the T accounts in your mind, or draw T accounts on paper with their plus and minus signs. The T account habit is very helpful.

GENERAL JOURNAL — Page 1

Date		Description	Post. Ref.	Debit	Credit
	4	Accounts Payable		2 000 00	
		Cash			2 000 00
		Paid Signal Products on account.			

Because you have already determined the debits and credits in Chapter 2, we will now simply list the transactions for June for Conner's Whitewater Adventures with the date of each transaction. The journal entries are illustrated in Figures 2, 3, and 4.

June 1 Conner deposited $90,000 in a bank account in the name of her business.
2 Conner's Whitewater Adventures buys equipment, paying cash, $38,000.
3 Buys equipment on account from Signal Products, $4,320.
4 Pays $2,000 on account to Signal Products, a creditor.
4 Conner invests her personal computer, with a fair market value of $5,200, in the business.
7 Conner's Whitewater Adventures sells rafting tours for cash, $8,000.

Figure 2
Journal entries for Conner's Whitewater Adventures, June 1–7

GENERAL JOURNAL — Page 1

Date		Description	Post. Ref.	Debit	Credit
20--					
June	1	Cash		90 000 00	
		J. Conner, Capital			90 000 00
		To record the original			
		investment by J. Conner.			
	2	Equipment		38 000 00	
		Cash			38 000 00
		Bought equipment for cash.			
	3	Equipment		4 320 00	
		Accounts Payable			4 320 00
		Bought equipment on account			
		from Signal Products.			
	4	Accounts Payable		2 000 00	
		Cash			2 000 00
		Paid Signal Products on account.			
	4	Equipment		5 200 00	
		J. Conner, Capital			5 200 00
		To record the investment by J. Conner			
		in Conner's Whitewater Adventures.			
	7	Cash		8 000 00	
		Income from Tours			8 000 00
		Received cash for rafting tour sales.			

June   8   Conner's Whitewater Adventures pays rent for the month, $1,250.

10   Buys supplies on account from Fineman Company, $675.

10   Buys a three-month liability insurance policy, $1,875.

14   Receives a bill for newspaper advertising from *The Times*, $620.

15   Signs a contract with Crystal River Lodge to provide rafting adventures for guests. Conner's Whitewater Adventures provides 27 one-day rafting tours and bills Crystal River Lodge for $6,750.

15   Pays on account to Signal Products, $1,500.

18   Receives and pays Solar Power, Inc., for the electric bill, $225.

Remember

In recording business transactions in the journal, you must use the exact account titles as listed in the company's chart of accounts.

GENERAL JOURNAL				Page 2	
Date	Description	Post. Ref.	Debit	Credit	
20--					
June 8	Rent Expense		1 2 5 0 00		
	Cash			1 2 5 0 00	
	Paid rent for June.				
10	Supplies		6 7 5 00		
	Accounts Payable			6 7 5 00	
	Bought supplies on account				
	from Fineman Company.				
10	Prepaid Insurance		1 8 7 5 00		
	Cash			1 8 7 5 00	
	Paid premium for three-month				
	liability insurance policy.				
14	Advertising Expense		6 2 0 00		
	Accounts Payable			6 2 0 00	
	Received bill from				
	advertising with *The Times*.				
15	Accounts Receivable		6 7 5 0 00		
	Income from Tours			6 7 5 0 00	
	Billed Crystal River Lodge for				
	services performed.				
15	Accounts Payable		1 5 0 0 00		
	Cash			1 5 0 0 00	
	Paid Signal Products on account.				
18	Utilities Expense		2 2 5 00		
	Cash			2 2 5 00	
	Paid Solar Power, Inc., bill for utilities.				

Figure 3

Journal entries for Conner's Whitewater Adventures, June 8–18

Figure 4
Journal entries for Conner's Whitewater Adventures, June 20–30

Remember

In each journal entry, debits must equal credits.

Date		Description	Post. Ref.	Debit	Credit
20--					
June	20	Accounts Payable		6 2 0 00	
		Cash			6 2 0 00
		Paid *The Times* in full.			
	24	Wages Expense		2 3 6 0 00	
		Cash			2 3 6 0 00
		Paid wages of part-time employee.			
	26	Equipment		3 7 8 0 00	
		Cash			1 8 5 0 00
		Accounts Payable			1 9 3 0 00
		Bought equipment on account			
		from Signal Products.			
	30	Cash		2 5 0 0 00	
		Accounts Receivable			2 5 0 0 00
		Received from Crystal River Lodge			
		to apply on account.			
	30	Cash		8 5 7 0 00	
		Income from Tours			8 5 7 0 00
		Cash revenue.			
	30	J. Conner, Drawing		3 5 0 0 00	
		Cash			3 5 0 0 00
		Withdrew cash for personal use.			

GENERAL JOURNAL — Page 3

June 20 Conner's Whitewater Adventures pays on account to *The Times*, $620. (This bill was recorded previously.)

24   Pays wages of part-time employee, $2,360.

26   Buys additional equipment from Signal Products for $3,780, paying $1,850 in cash and placing the balance on account.

30   Receives $2,500 cash from Crystal River Lodge to apply against amount billed on June 15.

30   Sells tours for cash, $8,570.

30   J. Conner withdraws cash for her personal use, $3,500.

POSTING TO THE GENERAL LEDGER

You know that the journal is the *book of original entry*. Each transaction must first be recorded in the journal in full. However, it is difficult to determine the balance of any one account, such as Cash, from the general journal entries. So the **ledger account** has been devised to give a complete record of the transactions recorded in each account. The **general ledger** contains all of the ledger accounts and contains detailed information about the increases and decreases in each of those accounts.

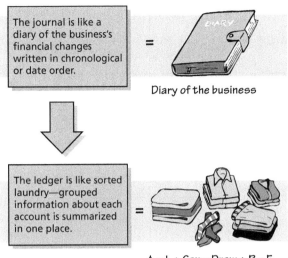

The journal is like a diary of the business's financial changes written in chronological or date order.

=

Diary of the business

The ledger is like sorted laundry—grouped information about each account is summarized in one place.

=

A = L + Cap − Draw + R − E

The Ledger Account Form (Running Balance Format)

We have been looking at accounts in the simple T account form primarily because T accounts illustrate situations so well. The debit and credit sides are specifically labeled, making the T account form a good way to picture account activity. However, determining the balance of an account using the T account form is difficult. You must add both columns and subtract the smaller total from the larger. To overcome this disadvantage, accountants generally use the four-column account form with Balance columns in the general ledger. Let's look at the Cash account of Conner's Whitewater Adventures in four-column form (Figure 5) compared with the T account form. *Leave the Post. Ref. column blank for now.*

GENERAL LEDGER

ACCOUNT **Cash**   ACCOUNT NO. **111**

Date	Item	Post. Ref.	Debit	Credit	Balance Debit	Balance Credit
20--						
June 1			90 0 0 0 00		90 0 0 0 00	
2				38 0 0 0 00	52 0 0 0 00	
4				2 0 0 0 00	50 0 0 0 00	
7			8 0 0 0 00		58 0 0 0 00	
8				1 2 5 0 00	56 7 5 0 00	
10				1 8 7 5 00	54 8 7 5 00	
15				1 5 0 0 00	53 3 7 5 00	
18				2 2 5 00	53 1 5 0 00	
20				6 2 0 00	52 5 3 0 00	
24				2 3 6 0 00	50 1 7 0 00	
26				1 8 5 0 00	48 3 2 0 00	
30			2 5 0 0 00		50 8 2 0 00	
30			8 5 7 0 00		59 3 9 0 00	
30				3 5 0 0 00	55 8 9 0 00	

Transaction amount   Running balance

Figure 5
General ledger for Conner's Whitewater Adventures

Cash

	+		−
(a)	90,000	(b)	38,000
(f)	8,000	(d)	2,000
(q)	2,500	(g)	1,250
(r)	8,570	(i)	1,875
	109,070	(l)	1,500
		(m)	225
		(n)	620
		(o)	2,360
		(p)	1,850
Footings		(s)	3,500
			53,180
Bal.	**55,890**		

Note the calculation of the running balance. In the abbreviated form, it looks like this:

GENERAL LEDGER

ACCOUNT **Cash**   ACCOUNT NO. **111**

Date		Item	Post. Ref.	Debit	Credit	Balance Debit	Balance Credit
20--							
June	1			90 0 0 0 00		90 0 0 0 00	
	2				38 0 0 0 00	52 0 0 0 00	
	4				2 0 0 0 00	50 0 0 0 00	

90,000 – 38,000 = 52,000
52,000 – 2,000 = 50,000

The Posting Process

The process of transferring information from the journal to the ledger accounts is called **posting**. In the posting process, you must transfer the following information from the journal to the ledger accounts: the *date of the transaction,* the *debit and credit amounts,* and the *page number* of the journal. **Post each account separately,** using the following steps. Post the debit part of the entry first.

STEP 1. Write the date of the transaction in the account's Date column.

STEP 2. Write the amount of the transaction in the Debit or Credit column and enter the new balance in the Balance columns under *Debit* or *Credit.*

STEP 3. Write the page number of the journal in the Post. Ref. column of the ledger account. (This is a **cross-reference**; it tells where the amount came from.)

STEP 4. Record the ledger account number in the Post. Ref. column of the journal. (This is also a cross-reference; it tells where the amount was posted.)

Entering the account number in the Post. Ref. column of the journal should be the last step. It acts as a verification of the three preceding steps.

The June 1 transaction for Conner's Whitewater Adventures is illustrated in Figure 6. Let's look at the posting of the debit part of the entry.

② Post entries from a two-column general journal to general ledger accounts.

Learning Objective

QuickBooks Tip

The Post Reference column is not used with computerized accounting software like QuickBooks.

Figure 6
Posting from the general journal to the general ledger—debit entry (June 1 transaction)

① Date of transaction
② Amount of transaction
③ Page number of the journal
④ Ledger account number

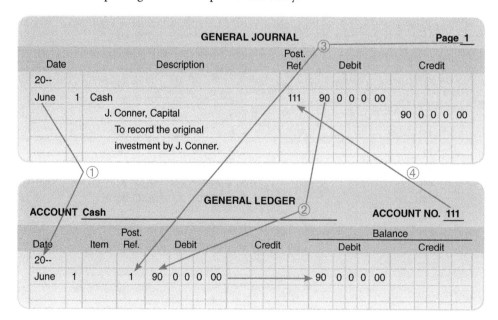

Next, we post the credit part of the entry, as shown in Figure 7.

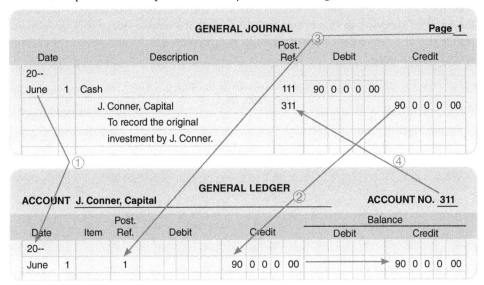

Figure 7
Posting from the general
journal to the general
ledger—credit entry
(June 1 transaction)

① Date of transaction
② Amount of transaction
③ Page number of the journal
④ Ledger account number

The accountant normally uses the Item column only at the end of a financial period. The following words may appear in this column: *balance, closing, adjusting,* and *reversing.* We will explain the use of these terms later.

Incidentally, some accountants use running balance-type ledger account forms that have only one balance column. However, we have used the two-balance-column arrangement to show clearly the appropriate balance of an account. For example, in Figure 6, Cash has a $90,000 balance recorded in the Debit column (normal balance). In Figure 7, J. Conner, Capital, has a $90,000 balance recorded in the Credit column (normal balance).

In the recording of the June 2 transaction, shown in Figure 8, see if you can identify in order the four steps in the posting process.

GENERAL JOURNAL   Page 1

Date	Description	Post. Ref.	Debit	Credit
2	Equipment	124	38 0 0 0 00	
	Cash	111		38 0 0 0 00
	Bought equipment for cash.			

Figure 8
Posting from the general
journal to the general ledger
(June 2 transaction)

GENERAL LEDGER

ACCOUNT **Cash**   ACCOUNT NO. **111**

Date	Item	Post. Ref.	Debit	Credit	Balance Debit	Balance Credit
20--						
June 1		1	90 0 0 0 00		90 0 0 0 00	
2		1		38 0 0 0 00	52 0 0 0 00	

ACCOUNT **Equipment**   ACCOUNT NO. **124**

Date	Item	Post. Ref.	Debit	Credit	Balance Debit	Balance Credit
20--						
June 2		1	38 0 0 0 00		38 0 0 0 00	

Remember

Posting is simply
transferring or copying
the same date and the
debits and credits listed
in the journal entry from
the journal to the ledger.

QuickBooks **Tip**

Posting from the journal
to the ledger is done
automatically in QuickBooks.

If the temporary balance of an account happens to be zero, insert long dashes through both the Debit Balance and the Credit Balance columns. **We'll use another business, the Becker Company, in this example**. Its Accounts Receivable ledger account follows. Notice that the zero balance on October 29 is represented by long dashes in the Debit and Credit columns.

GENERAL LEDGER

ACCOUNT Accounts Receivable ACCOUNT NO. 113

Date		Item	Post. Ref.	Debit	Credit	Balance Debit	Balance Credit
20--							
Oct.	7		96	1 5 0 00		1 5 0 00	
	19		97	2 4 8 00		3 9 8 00	
	21		97		1 5 0 00	2 4 8 00	
	29		98		2 4 8 00	——	——
	31		98	1 8 2 00		1 8 2 00	

Returning to Conner's Whitewater Adventures, let's look at the journal entries for the first month of operation. As you can see in Figure 9, the Post. Ref. column has been filled in because the posting was completed. Immediately after the journal entries, the ledger accounts and entries for Conner's Whitewater Adventures are shown in Figure 10. Take a moment to review all of the journal entries and the related postings.

Figure 9
Journal entries for Conner's Whitewater Adventures (first month of operation)

GENERAL JOURNAL Page 1

Date		Description	Post. Ref.	Debit	Credit
20--					
June	1	Cash	111	90 0 0 0 00	
		J. Conner, Capital	311		90 0 0 0 00
		To record the original			
		investment by J. Conner.			
	2	Equipment	124	38 0 0 0 00	
		Cash	111		38 0 0 0 00
		Bought equipment for cash.			
	3	Equipment	124	4 3 2 0 00	
		Accounts Payable	221		4 3 2 0 00
		Bought equipment on account			
		from Signal Products.			
	4	Accounts Payable	221	2 0 0 0 00	
		Cash	111		2 0 0 0 00
		Paid Signal Products on account.			

	4	Equipment	124	5 2 0 0 00	
		J. Conner, Capital	311		5 2 0 0 00
		To record the investment by J. Conner			
		in Conner's Whitewater Adventures.			
	7	Cash	111	8 0 0 0 00	
		Income from Tours	411		8 0 0 0 00
		Received cash for rafting tour sales.			

Figure 9
(Continued)

GENERAL JOURNAL — Page 2

Date		Description	Post. Ref.	Debit	Credit
20--					
June	8	Rent Expense	512	1 2 5 0 00	
		Cash	111		1 2 5 0 00
		Paid rent for June.			
	10	Supplies	115	6 7 5 00	
		Accounts Payable	221		6 7 5 00
		Bought supplies on account			
		from Fineman Company.			
	10	Prepaid Insurance	117	1 8 7 5 00	
		Cash	111		1 8 7 5 00
		Paid premium for three-month			
		liability insurance policy.			
	14	Advertising Expense	514	6 2 0 00	
		Accounts Payable	221		6 2 0 00
		Received bill from			
		advertising with *The Times*.			
	15	Accounts Receivable	113	6 7 5 0 00	
		Income from Tours	411		6 7 5 0 00
		Billed Crystal River Lodge for			
		services performed.			
	15	Accounts Payable	221	1 5 0 0 00	
		Cash	111		1 5 0 0 00
		Paid Signal Products on account.			
	18	Utilities Expense	515	2 2 5 00	
		Cash	111		2 2 5 00
		Paid Solar Power, Inc., bill for utilities.			

Figure 9
(Concluded)

GENERAL JOURNAL   Page 3

Date	Description	Post. Ref.	Debit	Credit
20--				
June 20	Accounts Payable	221	6 2 0 00	
	Cash	111		6 2 0 00
	Paid *The Times* in full.			
24	Wages Expense	511	2 3 6 0 00	
	Cash	111		2 3 6 0 00
	Paid wages of part-time employee.			
26	Equipment	124	3 7 8 0 00	
	Cash	111		1 8 5 0 00
	Accounts Payable	221		1 9 3 0 00
	Bought equipment on account			
	from Signal Products.			
30	Cash	111	2 5 0 0 00	
	Accounts Receivable	113		2 5 0 0 00
	Received from Crystal River Lodge			
	to apply on account.			
30	Cash	111	8 5 7 0 00	
	Income from Tours	411		8 5 7 0 00
	Received cash for rafting tour sales.			
30	J. Conner, Drawing	312	3 5 0 0 00	
	Cash	111		3 5 0 0 00
	Withdrew cash for personal use.			

Figure 10
General ledger for Conner's Whitewater Adventures (first month of operation)

GENERAL LEDGER

ACCOUNT Cash   **ACCOUNT NO. 111**

Date	Item	Post. Ref.	Debit	Credit	Balance Debit	Balance Credit
20--						
June 1		1	90 0 0 0 00		90 0 0 0 00	
2		1		38 0 0 0 00	52 0 0 0 00	
4		1		2 0 0 0 00	50 0 0 0 00	
7		1	8 0 0 0 00		58 0 0 0 00	
8		2		1 2 5 0 00	56 7 5 0 00	
10		2		1 8 7 5 00	54 8 7 5 00	
15		2		1 5 0 0 00	53 3 7 5 00	
18		2		2 2 5 00	53 1 5 0 00	
20		3		6 2 0 00	52 5 3 0 00	
24		3		2 3 6 0 00	50 1 7 0 00	
26		3		1 8 5 0 00	48 3 2 0 00	
30		3	2 5 0 0 00		50 8 2 0 00	
30		3	8 5 7 0 00		59 3 9 0 00	
30		3		3 5 0 0 00	55 8 9 0 00	

Figure 10
(Continued)

ACCOUNT Accounts Receivable   **ACCOUNT NO. 113**

Date		Item	Post. Ref.	Debit	Credit	Balance Debit	Balance Credit
20--							
June	15		2	6 7 5 0 00		6 7 5 0 00	
	30		3		2 5 0 0 00	4 2 5 0 00	

ACCOUNT Supplies   **ACCOUNT NO. 115**

Date		Item	Post. Ref.	Debit	Credit	Balance Debit	Balance Credit
20--							
June	10		2	6 7 5 00		6 7 5 00	

ACCOUNT Prepaid Insurance   **ACCOUNT NO. 117**

Date		Item	Post. Ref.	Debit	Credit	Balance Debit	Balance Credit
20--							
June	10		2	1 8 7 5 00		1 8 7 5 00	

ACCOUNT Equipment   **ACCOUNT NO. 124**

Date		Item	Post. Ref.	Debit	Credit	Balance Debit	Balance Credit
20--							
June	2		1	38 0 0 0 00		38 0 0 0 00	
	3		1	4 3 2 0 00		42 3 2 0 00	
	4		1	5 2 0 0 00		47 5 2 0 00	
	26		3	3 7 8 0 00		51 3 0 0 00	

ACCOUNT Accounts Payable   **ACCOUNT NO. 221**

Date		Item	Post. Ref.	Debit	Credit	Balance Debit	Balance Credit
20--							
June	3		1		4 3 2 0 00		4 3 2 0 00
	4		1	2 0 0 0 00			2 3 2 0 00
	10		2		6 7 5 00		2 9 9 5 00
	14		2		6 2 0 00		3 6 1 5 00
	15		2	1 5 0 0 00			2 1 1 5 00
	20		3	6 2 0 00			1 4 9 5 00
	26		3		1 9 3 0 00		3 4 2 5 00

Figure 10
(Continued)

ACCOUNT J. Conner, Capital   ACCOUNT NO. 311

Date		Item	Post. Ref.	Debit	Credit	Balance Debit	Balance Credit
20--							
June	1		1		90 0 0 0 00		90 0 0 0 00
	4		1		5 2 0 0 00		95 2 0 0 00

ACCOUNT J. Conner, Drawing   ACCOUNT NO. 312

Date		Item	Post. Ref.	Debit	Credit	Balance Debit	Balance Credit
20--							
June	30		3	3 5 0 0 00		3 5 0 0 00	

ACCOUNT Income from Tours   ACCOUNT NO. 411

Date		Item	Post. Ref.	Debit	Credit	Balance Debit	Balance Credit
20--							
June	7		1		8 0 0 0 00		8 0 0 0 00
	15		2		6 7 5 0 00		14 7 5 0 00
	30		3		8 5 7 0 00		23 3 2 0 00

ACCOUNT Wages Expense   ACCOUNT NO. 511

Date		Item	Post. Ref.	Debit	Credit	Balance Debit	Balance Credit
20--							
June	24		3	2 3 6 0 00		2 3 6 0 00	

ACCOUNT Rent Expense   ACCOUNT NO. 512

Date		Item	Post. Ref.	Debit	Credit	Balance Debit	Balance Credit
20--							
June	8		2	1 2 5 0 00		1 2 5 0 00	

Figure 10
(Continued)

ACCOUNT Advertising Expense   **ACCOUNT NO. 514**

Date		Item	Post. Ref.	Debit	Credit	Balance Debit	Balance Credit
20--							
June	14		2	6 2 0 00		6 2 0 00	

ACCOUNT Utilities Expense   **ACCOUNT NO. 515**

Date		Item	Post. Ref.	Debit	Credit	Balance Debit	Balance Credit
20--							
June	18		2	2 2 5 00		2 2 5 00	

THE TRIAL BALANCE

Preparation of the Trial Balance

After the journal entries have been posted, a trial balance must be prepared. The trial balance is simply a list of the ledger accounts that have balances. A trial balance is presented in Figure 11.

Remember that the trial balance proves only that the total ledger debit balances equal the total ledger credit balances. Even when the debit and credit balances are equal, other types of errors may slip through such as:

1. Posting the correct debit or credit amounts to the incorrect account or
2. Neglecting to journalize or post an entire transaction.

3 Prepare a trial balance from the ledger accounts.

Learning Objective

Figure 11
Trial balance for Conner's Whitewater Adventures

Conner's Whitewater Adventures
Trial Balance
June 30, 20—

Account Name	Debit	Credit
Cash	55,890	
Accounts Receivable	4,250	
Supplies	675	
Prepaid Insurance	1,875	
Equipment	51,300	
Accounts Payable		3,425
J. Conner, Capital		95,200
J. Conner, Drawing	3,500	
Income from Tours		23,320
Wages Expense	2,360	
Rent Expense	1,250	
Advertising Expense	620	
Utilities Expense	225	
	121,945	121,945

Steps in the Accounting Process

So far, you have learned the first three steps in the accounting process.

STEP 1. **Record the transactions of a business in a journal (book of original entry or day-by-day record of the transactions of a firm).** An entry should be based on some source document or evidence that a transaction has occurred, such as an invoice, a receipt, or a check.

STEP 2. **Post entries to the accounts in the ledger.** Transfer the amounts from the journal to the Debit or Credit columns of the specified accounts in the ledger. Use a cross-reference system. Accounts are organized in the ledger according to the account numbers assigned to them in the chart of accounts.

STEP 3. **Prepare a trial balance.** Record the balances of the ledger accounts in the appropriate column, Debit or Credit, of the trial balance form. Prove that the total of the debit balances equals the total of the credit balances.

SOURCE DOCUMENTS

Learning Objective

4 Explain the importance of source documents.

As mentioned earlier, a source document can be an invoice, a receipt, or a check, for example. We now add an important detail in the recording of a journal entry. This detail consists of listing the related source document number, which is used as a reference for the proof of a transaction. For example, Figure 12 is an example of a source document followed by the journal entry (Figure 13) and ledger accounts (Figure 14).

Using the source document, the accountant records the entry in the journal (Figure 13). Note how the explanation includes important information from the source document. The explanation now includes the invoice number.

The journal entry is then posted to the ledger (Figure 14).

Figure 12
Source document

INVOICE

FINEMAN COMPANY   No. 4-962
220 East Ames Street, Denver CO 80012
Sold By: 203 Date: 6/10/20--
Name: Conner's Whitewater Adventures
Address: 1701 East Delaware Street
Colorado Springs, CO 80902
Terms: Net 30 days

Quantity	Description	Unit Price	Amount
10 bx	Invoice forms	12 00	120 00
5 bx	Ink cartridges	32 00	160 00
3 bx	8 x 11 copy paper	20 00	60 00
2	File cabinets, 2-drawer	32 00	64 00
4 bx	3-tab folders	12 00	48 00
3	10-key electric calculators	24 00	72 00
5 bx	12-count black ink pens	12 00	60 00
5 bx	10-count mechanical pencils	10 00	50 00
	SUBTOTAL		634 00
	SALES TAX		41 00
	SHIPPING—free		0 00
	TOTAL		675 00

GENERAL JOURNAL					Page 1	
Date	Description	Post. Ref.	Debit		Credit	
10	Supplies	115	6 7 5 00			
	Accounts Payable	221			6 7 5 00	
	Bought supplies on account					
	from Fineman Company,					
	Invoice No. 4-962.					

Figure 13
Journal entry related to source document

SMALL BUSINESS **SUCCESS**

Paperwork—Why It's Worth Keeping Track of!

As you analyze transactions for a business, you learned that each transaction must be evidenced by a source document. Source documents, or the paperwork for transactions, are very important to all businesses. This is because all accounting transactions are developed from source documents. What are some examples of source documents? Bills from vendors, checks from customers, deposit slips, credit card receipts, bank statements, and customer invoices are all examples of source documents.

Many times businesses use accounting software to create source documents that can be printed for the businesses' or customers' records. Source documents should include the name and address of the business, as well as the date, amount, and description of the transaction. The documents should also include any customer information. The detail provided on the source documents will help the accountant record the transactions.

Source documents are also needed to substantiate the transactions should the business be audited. Internal and external auditors will review the paperwork when determining whether the transactions recorded by the business are accurate. The Internal Revenue Service (IRS) will also require the business to provide proof of transactions for income and deductions shown on the entity's tax return.

Is it necessary for the business to keep source documents forever? Well, that depends on what the source document is and to whom you talk with. Most accountants agree on the following guidelines:

Source Document	Time Period
Support for your tax return	3 years
Related to assets purchased, such as a business vehicle or computer	Keep until you sell or dispose
Documents such as accounts receivable or accounts payable ledgers, bank statements, canceled checks, and invoices	7 years
Items such as loan documents, tax returns, and financial statements	Indefinitely

Source documents are an important part of the accounting cycle. Take a moment to make sure you are comfortable with the information provided on the documents and that you are familiar with the most common documents used in accounting, such as invoices, deposit slips, receipts, and bills from vendors. As you work through the chapters of the textbook, you will be introduced to many types of source documents. Be sure to review them—important information is included on these documents!

Figure 14
Ledger posting

ACCOUNT Supplies   **ACCOUNT NO.** 115

Date	Item	Post. Ref.	Debit	Credit	Balance Debit	Balance Credit
20--						
June 10		2	6 7 5 00		6 7 5 00	

ACCOUNT Accounts Payable   **ACCOUNT NO.** 221

Date	Item	Post. Ref.	Debit	Credit	Balance Debit	Balance Credit
20--						
June 3		1		4 3 2 0 00		4 3 2 0 00
4		1	2 0 0 0 00			2 3 2 0 00
10		2		6 7 5 00		2 9 9 5 00

Previous Postings {

To: **Amy Roberts, CPA**
Subject: **Errors?**

Hi Amy,
I was thinking about recording transactions and wondered what happens if I make an error? Do I simply delete the error and then correct the entry?
Thanks,
Janie

To: **Janie Conner**
Subject: **RE: Errors?**

Hi Janie,
Errors happen even when you are extra careful. Once you find an error, it's important that you don't delete the error, but instead correct it using specific procedures. Using these procedures will ensure that you are properly documenting the error and the corresponding correction.
Amy

CORRECTION OF ERRORS—MANUAL AND COMPUTERIZED

Errors are occasionally made in recording journal entries and posting to the ledger accounts whether recording them manually or on a computer. Never erase or delete the errors because it may look as if you were trying to hide something. The method for correcting errors depends on how and when the errors were made. The two methods for correcting errors are as follows:

5 Correct entries using the ruling or correcting entry method.

Learning Objective

1. The ruling method (can be used only for manual entry).
2. The correcting entry method (can be used for manual and computerized entry).

The Ruling Method

You can use the ruling method to correct an error in the journal before posting or to correct an error in the ledger after an entry has been posted, but only if the entry was recorded manually (with paper and pencil).

CORRECTING ERRORS BEFORE POSTING HAS TAKEN PLACE

When an error has been made in recording an account title in a journal entry, draw a line through the incorrect account title in the journal entry and write the correct account title immediately above it. Include your initials with the correction. For example, an entry to record payment of $1,500 rent was incorrectly debited to Salary Expense.

	GENERAL JOURNAL				Page 1	
Date	Description	Post. Ref.	Debit		Credit	
20--	Rent Expense					
Mar. 1	~~Salary Expense~~ DJM		1 5 0 0 00			
	Cash				1 5 0 0 00	
	Paid rent for the month.					

When an error has been made in recording an amount, draw a line through the incorrect amount in the journal entry and write the correct amount immediately above it. For example, an entry for a $120 payment for office supplies was recorded as $210. Include your initials with the correction.

	GENERAL JOURNAL				Page 1	
Date	Description	Post. Ref.	Debit		Credit	
20--			DJM 1 2 0 00			
Apr. 6	Supplies		~~2 1 0 00~~	DJM 1 2 0 00		
	Cash				~~2 1 0 00~~	
	Bought office supplies.					

CORRECTING ERRORS AFTER POSTING HAS TAKEN PLACE

When an entry was journalized correctly but one of the amounts was posted incorrectly, correct the error by drawing a single line through the amount and recording the correct amount above it. For example, an entry to record cash received for professional fees was correctly journalized as $400. However, it was posted as a debit to Cash for $400 and a credit to Professional Fees for $4,000. In the Professional Fees account, draw a line through $4,000 and insert $400 above or next to the incorrect amount. Change the running balance of the account and initial the corrections.

Order this item today
& it ships within 24 hours.

In the Real World

Even large businesses make accounting errors. When a large corporation makes an error and discovers it after the financial statements have been published, the corporation is required to restate its financial statements. Some of these restatements can be huge. For example, Overstock.com once announced that it would be restating its financial statements for errors made in a previous year. Corrections of these errors affected net income by approximately $1,500,000!

ACCOUNT	Professional Fees						ACCOUNT NO. 411	
		Post.				Balance		
Date	Item	Ref.	Debit	Credit		Debit		Credit
				DJM 4 0 0 00		*DJM* 25 6 0 0 00		
6		94		~~4 0 0 0 00~~		~~29 2 0 0 00~~		

Correcting Entry Method—Manual or Computerized

If the transaction was journalized incorrectly and the amounts were posted, you should use the correcting entry method.

Use this entry when working with computerized accounting software. **Never delete or "fix" the original incorrect entry in a computerized accounting program.**

Following are the two correcting entry methods:

1. *One-step method.* One entry undoes the error and provides the correct account.
2. *Two-step method.* The first step reverses the error made by the original entry. The second step includes the correct entry.

When recording a correcting entry using either the one-step or two-step method, you must include an explanation. For example, on January 9, a $620 payment for advertising was incorrectly journalized and posted as a debit to Miscellaneous Expense for $620 and a credit to Cash for $620. The error was discovered and corrected on January 27 as follows using the one-step method.

		GENERAL JOURNAL				Page 1	
Date		Description	Post. Ref.	Debit		Credit	
20--							
Jan.	27	Advertising Expense		6 2 0 00			
		Miscellaneous Expense				6 2 0 00	
		To correct error of January 9 in which					
		a payment for Advertising Expense					
		was debited to Miscellaneous Expense.					

Following the two-step method, if the original entry was recorded as a debit to Miscellaneous Expense and a credit to Cash, reverse this entry by debiting Cash and crediting Miscellaneous Expense, then record the correct entry.

	GENERAL JOURNAL			Page 1	
Date	Description	Post. Ref.	Debit	Credit	
20--					
Jan. 27	Cash		6 2 0 00		
	Miscellaneous Expense			6 2 0 00	
	To reverse out an incorrect				
	entry recorded January 9.				
27	Advertising Expense		6 2 0 00		
	Cash			6 2 0 00	
	To correct error of January 9				
	in which a payment for				
	Advertising Expense was				
	debited to Miscellaneous Expense.				

YOU Make the Call

Imagine you are an accounting clerk. You find that your trial balance balances, but something doesn't seem quite right. The amount of Miscellaneous Expense is much higher than it was last month, but you don't recall making an entry that would cause this discrepancy. In checking the journal entries, you find that an entry for $724 was accidentally debited to Miscellaneous Expense and credited to Accounts Payable. The $724 should have been debited to Utilities Expense. Explain how you would correct this entry and why you chose that method.

SOLUTION

Because this is a correction after the information was posted, two methods can be used to make the correction.

1. The first method is to simply make a journal entry to correct the original error. In this case, make a journal entry to debit Utilities Expense for $724 and credit Miscellaneous Expense for $724. This is called the one-step method.

2. Another method is to "back out," or reverse, the entry that contains the error and journalize the correct entry. That is, debit Accounts Payable for $724 and credit Miscellaneous Expense for $724. Finally, the correct journal entry is to debit Utilities Expense for $724 and credit Accounts Payable for $724.

These two methods can be used in a manual or computerized system.

Accounting with **QuickBooks**®

Learning Objectives

After you have completed this section, you will be able to do the following:

1 Record a transaction in the general journal.

2 Record a transaction involving Accounts Payable or Accounts Receivable.

3 View and print the general journal.

4 View and print the general ledger.

In Chapter 3, you learned how to prepare journal entries manually using paper and pencil. Today, most journal entries are prepared using computerized accounting software such as QuickBooks. QuickBooks contains a journal that allows you to record transactions the same way you entered them manually for Conner's Whitewater Adventures. There's even room to include a journal explanation in the memo field.

So if the same number of steps is needed to record journal entries in the computer as is needed when using paper and pencil, why do businesses use computerized accounting programs like QuickBooks? There are several reasons. First, when entering the transaction, the user will not be required to remember the exact account name—QuickBooks allows the user to select from a list of accounts. Second, the computerized accounting software checks that the debit and credit balances are equal prior to updating a transaction. If the balances are not equal, the computer will alert the user of the error. QuickBooks does not allow out-of-balance transactions to be updated.

The best part about using a computerized accounting program, such as QuickBooks, may be that the computer automatically takes care of posting to the ledger. This means that the instant the user enters the transaction into QuickBooks and clicks **Save & Close** or **Save & New**, the transaction is posted to the ledger accounts. This saves the accountant a lot of time by eliminating repetitive data entry and helps prevent posting errors. In addition, computerized accounting programs prepare the financial statements based on the journal entries entered.

It's important to remember that even if you will be using a computerized accounting program like QuickBooks, you still need to know how to record and post journal entries as well as how to prepare financial statements. This knowledge will help ensure that you understand the information prepared, using the software, and recognize errors.

Learning Objective

 1 Record a transaction in the general journal.

QuickBooks Tip

Journal explanations for transactions are recorded in the memo field in Quick-Books.

Recording Transactions with Quickbooks

There are two ways of recording transactions in QuickBooks. The journal entry method can be used, or a *Getting Around* screen is available on the home page. This book will demonstrate the journal entry method, but let's take a moment to discuss the *Getting Around* screen on the QuickBooks home page. The *Getting Around* screen (see Figure Q1) provides shortcuts to help users enter transactions.

QuickBooks is organized around centers such as Customers, Vendors, Employees, Banking, and Reports. Each center handles transactions related to the specific area. For example, the Customers center handles transactions related to creating invoices, statements, and sales receipts. Centers allow users to enter transactions in the accounting software without needing to know debits and credits. The software takes the information that has been entered and records the journal entry automatically.

Figure Q1
Getting Around screen

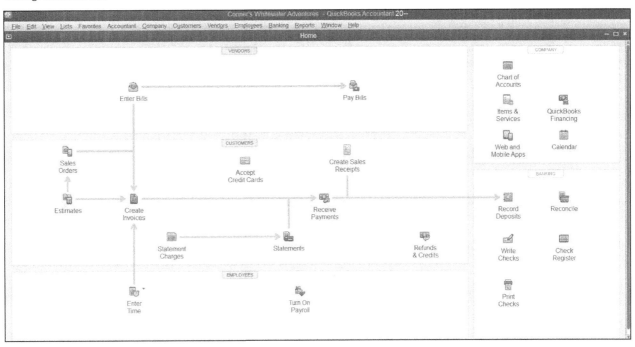

Since you know your debits and credits, you are going to learn how to enter transactions using the journal entry method. Let's analyze the first transaction for Conner's Whitewater Adventures.

June 1 Conner deposited $90,000 in a bank account in the name of the business. To record the transaction in QuickBooks, follow these steps:

STEP 1. Click the **Company** tab. Then click **Make General Journal Entries**.

STEP 2. **Enter the date.** 06/01/20-- (When preparing reports, QuickBooks will automatically default to the current date. To avoid reporting errors, be sure to verify that the report dates in QuickBooks match the actual transactions dates. For this exercise, we will use the year 2015.)

STEP 3. **Select the account to be debited using the drop-down box arrow.** 111 Cash

STEP 4. **Enter the dollar amount in the Debit column.** 90,000

STEP 5. **Enter the transaction description in the Memo box.** (You will only need to enter the description in the first memo line. QuickBooks automatically repeats the description for the next account in the transaction unless changed.)

STEP 6. **Select the account to be credited using the drop-down box arrow.** 311 J. Conner, Capital. (The debit amount is automatically filled into the Credit column. For compound transactions, the credit amount may need to be changed.)

STEP 7. **Review the transaction and click Save & New to proceed to the next entry.**

> **QuickBooks Tip**
>
> In QuickBooks you do not need to enter dollar signs or commas. You can also eliminate entering cents when the entry is a whole number.

ACCOUNTING WITH *QuickBooks*®

The steps have been summarized for you in Figure Q2.

Figure Q2
Recording transactions in the general journal

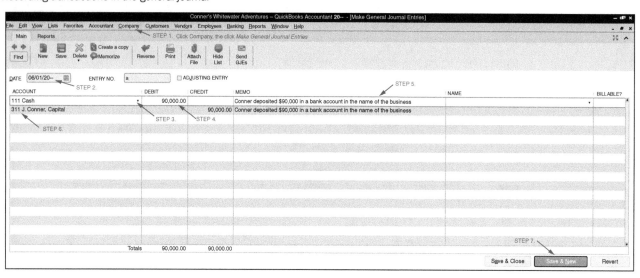

Learning Objective

2   Record a transaction involving Accounts Payable or Accounts Receivable.

When entering a transaction in QuickBooks that involves Accounts Receivable or Accounts Payable, a name must be entered for the Customer (Accounts Receivable) or the Vendor (Accounts Payable). Let's take a look at Figure Q3 for the transaction on June 3 for Conner's Whitewater Adventures.

Figure Q3
Transactions involving accounts receivable or accounts payable

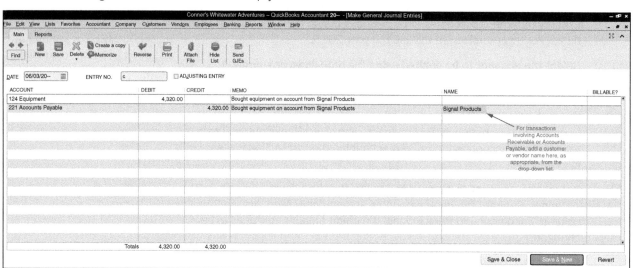

ACCOUNTING WITH *QuickBooks®*

June 3 Conner's Whitewater Adventures bought equipment on account from Signal Products, $4,320. Notice that this transaction involves Accounts Payable and that the vendor is Signal Products. When the user enters the transaction in QuickBooks, he or she must select a vendor in the name box. This is completed by selecting the down arrow and then clicking the vendor name.

 3 View and print the general journal.   **Learning Objective**

View and Print Reports

The general journal in QuickBooks is the same as the journal in a manual accounting system. Both journals contain transactions in chronological order. To view and print the transactions recorded in the general journal, follow these steps:

STEP 1. Click the **Reports** tab.

STEP 2. Click **Accountant & Taxes**.

STEP 3. Click **Journal**.

STEP 4. Adjust the **From:** and **To:** dates and click **Refresh**.

STEP 5. To print the report, click the **Print** button.

QuickBooks Tip

Want to go "green"? Print reports electronically with the Save as PDF option.

Figure Q4 shows the QuickBooks Journal report for Conner's Whitewater Adventures.

Figure Q4
General journal

Conner's Whitewater Adventures
Journal
June 20--

Trans #	Type	Date	Num	Name	Memo	Account	Debit	Credit
1	General Journal	06/01/20--	a		To record the original investment by J. Conner	111 Cash	90,000.00	
					To record the original investment by J. Conner	311 J. Conner, Capital		90,000.00
							90,000.00	90,000.00
2	General Journal	06/02/20--	b		Bought equipment for cash	124 Equipment	38,000.00	
					Bought equipment for cash	111 Cash		38,000.00
							38,000.00	38,000.00
4	General Journal	06/04/20--	d	Signal Products	Paid Signal Products on account	221 Accounts Payable	2,000.00	
				Signal Products	Paid Signal Products on account	111 Cash		2,000.00
							2,000.00	2,000.00
5	General Journal	06/04/20--	e		To record the investment by J. Conner in Conner's Whitewater Adventures	124 Equipment	5,200.00	
					To record the investment by J. Conner in Conner's Whitewater Adventures	311 J. Conner, Capital		5,200.00
							5,200.00	5,200.00
6	General Journal	06/07/20--	f		Received cash for rafting tour sales	111 Cash	8,000.00	
					Received cash for rafting tour sales	411 Income from Tours		8,000.00
							8,000.00	8,000.00

Learning Objective View and print the general ledger.

To view and print the details of the general ledger accounts in QuickBooks, follow these steps:

STEP 1. Click the **Reports** tab.

STEP 2. Click **Accountant & Taxes**.

STEP 3. Click **General Ledger**.

STEP 4. Adjust the **From:** and **To:** dates and click **Refresh**.

STEP 5. To print the report, click the **Print** button.

Figure Q5 shows the QuickBooks General Ledger report for Conner's Whitewater Adventures.

Figure Q5
General ledger

Conner's Whitewater Adventures
General Ledger
As of June 30, 20--

Type	Date	Num	Name	Memo	Split	Debit	Credit	Balance
111 Cash								0.00
General Journal	06/01/20–	a		To record the original investment by J.Coner	311 J. Conner, Capital	90,000.00		90,000.00
General Journal	06/02/20–	b		Bought equipment for cash	124 Equipment		38,000.00	52,000.00
General Journal	06/04/20–	d	Signal Products	Paid Signal Products on account	221 Accounts Payable		2,000.00	50,000.00
General Journal	06/07/20–	f		Received cash for rafting tour sales	411 Income from Tours	8,000.00		58,000.00
General Journal	06/08/20–	g		Paid rent for June	512 Rent Expense		1,250.00	56,750.00
General Journal	06/10/20–	i		Paid premium for three-month liability insurance policy	117 Prepaid Insurance		1,875.00	54,875.00
General Journal	06/15/20–	l	Signal Products	Paid Signal Products on account	221 Accounts Payable		1,500.00	53,375.00
General Journal	06/18/20–	m		Paid Solar Power, Inc. bill for utilities	515 Utilities Expense		225.00	53,150.00
General Journal	06/20/20–	n	The Times	Paid The Times in full	221 Accounts Payable		620.00	52,530.00
General Journal	06/24/20–	o		Paid wages of part-time employee	511 Wages Expense		2,360.00	50,170.00
General Journal	06/26/20–	p		Bought equipment on account from Signal Products	124 Equipment		1,850.00	48,320.00
General Journal	06/30/20–	q		Received from Crystal River Lodge to apply on account	113 Accounts Receivable	2,500.00		50,820.00
General Journal	06/30/20–	r		Received cash for rafting tour sales	411 Income from Tours	8,570.00		59,390.00
General Journal	06/30/20–	s		Withdrew cash for personal use	312 J. Conner, Drawing		3,500.00	55,890.00
Total 111 Cash						109,070.00	53,180.00	55,890.00
113 Accounts Receivable								0.00
General Journal	06/15/20–	k	Crystal River Lodge	Billed Crystal River Lodge for services performed	411 Income from Tours	6,750.00		6,750.00
General Journal	06/30/20–	q	Crystal River Lodge	Received from Crystal River Lodge to apply on account	111 Cash		2,500.00	4,250.00
Total 113 Accounts Receivable						6,750.00	2,500.00	4,250.00

Chapter Review

Study and Practice

 1 Record a group of transactions pertaining to a service business in a two-column general journal.

Learning Objective

Based on **source documents**, the transactions are analyzed to determine what accounts are involved and whether the accounts are debited or credited. For each transaction, total debits must equal total credits. The **journal** is a book of original entry in which a day-by-day record of business transactions is maintained. The parts of a journal entry consist of the transaction date, the title of the account(s) debited, the title of the account(s) credited, the amounts recorded in the Debit and Credit columns, and an explanation.

1 **PRACTICE EXERCISE 1**

Journalize the following transactions for the month of June:

June   1   J. Jonah deposited $35,000 in the bank in the name of the business (Jonah Company).

       2   The business purchased $8,000 in equipment, paying $2,000 in cash and placing the remainder on account.

       4   The business purchased supplies for cash, $250.

     10   The business received cash revenue, $3,250.

     20   The business paid the monthly rent, $1,800.

     24   J. Jonah withdrew $500 for personal use.

PRACTICE EXERCISE 1 • SOLUTION

	GENERAL JOURNAL				Page 1
Date	**Description**	**Post. Ref.**	**Debit**		**Credit**
20--					
June 1	Cash		35 0 0 0 00		
	J. Jonah, Capital				35 0 0 0 00
	Jonah invested cash.				
2	Equipment		8 0 0 0 00		
	Cash				2 0 0 0 00
	Accounts Payable				6 0 0 0 00
	Purchased equipment.				
4	Supplies		2 5 0 00		
	Cash				2 5 0 00
	Purchased supplies.				
10	Cash		3 2 5 0 00		
	Income from Services				3 2 5 0 00
	Cash revenue.				

(Continued)

				Debit	Credit
20	Rent Expense			1 8 0 0 00	
		Cash			1 8 0 0 00
		Paid the monthly rent.			
24	J. Jonah, Drawing			5 0 0 00	
		Cash			5 0 0 00
		Withdrawal for personal use.			

Learning Objective   **2**   Post entries from a two-column general journal to general ledger accounts.

The **general ledger** is a book that contains all of the accounts, arranged according to the chart of accounts. **Posting** is the process of transferring information from the journal to the **ledger accounts**. The posting process consists of four steps:

STEP 1. Write the date of the transaction in the account's Date column.

STEP 2. Write the amount of the transaction in the Debit or Credit column and enter the new balance in the Balance columns under *Debit* or *Credit*.

STEP 3. Write the page number of the journal in the Post. Ref. column of the ledger account.

STEP 4. Record the ledger account number in the Post. Ref. column of the journal.

 PRACTICE EXERCISE 2

Post the journal entries from Practice Exercise 1 to the following general ledger accounts:

Assets	Liabilities	Revenue
111 Cash	221 Accounts Payable	411 Income from Services
115 Supplies		
124 Equipment	**Owner's Equity**	**Expenses**
	311 J. Jonah, Capital	512 Rent Expense
	312 J. Jonah, Drawing	

PRACTICE EXERCISE 2 • SOLUTION

GENERAL LEDGER

ACCOUNT **Cash**   ACCOUNT NO. **111**

Date	Item	Post. Ref.	Debit	Credit	Balance Debit	Balance Credit
20--						
June 1		1	35 0 0 0 00		35 0 0 0 00	
2		1		2 0 0 0 00	33 0 0 0 00	
4		1		2 5 0 00	32 7 5 0 00	
10		1	3 2 5 0 00		36 0 0 0 00	
20		1		1 8 0 0 00	34 2 0 0 00	
24		1		5 0 0 00	33 7 0 0 00	

ACCOUNT Supplies   **ACCOUNT NO.** 115

Date	Item	Post. Ref.	Debit	Credit	Balance Debit	Balance Credit
20--						
June 4		1	2 5 0 00		2 5 0 00	

ACCOUNT Equipment   **ACCOUNT NO.** 124

Date	Item	Post. Ref.	Debit	Credit	Balance Debit	Balance Credit
20--						
June 2		1	8 0 0 0 00		8 0 0 0 00	

ACCOUNT Accounts Payable   **ACCOUNT NO.** 221

Date	Item	Post. Ref.	Debit	Credit	Balance Debit	Balance Credit
20--						
June 2		1		6 0 0 0 00		6 0 0 0 00

ACCOUNT J. Jonah, Capital   **ACCOUNT NO.** 311

Date	Item	Post. Ref.	Debit	Credit	Balance Debit	Balance Credit
20--						
June 1		1		35 0 0 0 00		35 0 0 0 00

ACCOUNT J. Jonah, Drawing   **ACCOUNT NO.** 312

Date	Item	Post. Ref.	Debit	Credit	Balance Debit	Balance Credit
20--						
June 24		1	5 0 0 00		5 0 0 00	

ACCOUNT Income from Services   **ACCOUNT NO.** 411

Date	Item	Post. Ref.	Debit	Credit	Balance Debit	Balance Credit
20--						
June 10		1		3 2 5 0 00		3 2 5 0 00

ACCOUNT Rent Expense   **ACCOUNT NO.** 512

Date	Item	Post. Ref.	Debit	Credit	Balance Debit	Balance Credit
20--						
June 20		1	1 8 0 0 00		1 8 0 0 00	

Learning Objective   **3** Prepare a trial balance from the ledger accounts.

The trial balance consists of a listing of account balances in two columns—one labeled Debit and one labeled Credit. The balances come from the ledger accounts.

3 **PRACTICE EXERCISE 3**

Prepare a trial balance from the ledger accounts in Practice Exercise 2.

PRACTICE EXERCISE 3 • SOLUTION

Jonah Company
Trial Balance
June 30, 20--

Account Name	Debit	Credit
Cash	33,700	
Supplies	250	
Equipment	8,000	
Accounts Payable		6,000
J. Jonah, Capital		35,000
J. Jonah, Drawing	500	
Income from Services		3,250
Rent Expense	1,800	
	44,250	44,250

Learning Objective   **4** Explain the importance of source documents.

Source documents provide proof of a transaction. Examples of source documents include invoices, receipts, checks, and deposit slips.

 PRACTICE EXERCISE 4

What is a possible source document for each of the following transactions?

June   1   J. Jonah deposited $35,000 in the bank in the name of the business (Jonah Company).
       2   The business purchased $8,000 in equipment, paying $2,000 in cash and placing the remainder on account.
       4   The business purchased supplies for cash, $250.
      10   The business received cash revenue, $3,250.
      20   The business paid the monthly rent, $1,800.
      24   J. Jonah withdrew $500 for personal use.

PRACTICE EXERCISE 4 • SOLUTION

June   1   Deposit slip and receipt
       2   Receipt
       4   Vendor invoice (bill) and check
      10   Customer receipt and deposit slip
      20   Vendor invoice (bill) and check
      24   Withdrawal slip or ATM receipt

CHAPTER REVIEW

5 Correct entries using the ruling or correcting entry method.

The ruling method can be used if an error is discovered before or after an entry was posted. A line is drawn through the incorrect account title or amount and the correct account title or amount written immediately above. The person making the correction also includes his or her initials with the correction.

The correcting entry method is used if an error is discovered after an incorrectly journalized entry was posted. If the error consists of the wrong account(s), an entry is made to cancel out or reverse the incorrect account(s) and insert the correct account(s). The correcting entry must include an explanation.

PRACTICE EXERCISE 5

On July 9, a $380 payment for Supplies was incorrectly journalized and posted as a debit to Supplies Expense for $380 and a credit to Cash for $380. Provide the correcting entry following the one-step method.

PRACTICE EXERCISE 5 • SOLUTION

			GENERAL JOURNAL				Page 1	
Date			Description	Post. Ref.	Debit		Credit	
20--								
July	9		Supplies		3 8 0 00			
			Supplies Expense				3 8 0 00	
			To correct error of July 9					
			in which a payment for Supplies					
			was debited to Supplies Expense.					

Glossary

Cost principle The principle that a purchased asset should be recorded at its actual cost. *(p. 115)*

Cross-reference The ledger account number in the Post. Ref. column of the journal and the journal page number in the Post. Ref. column of the ledger account. *(p. 120)*

General ledger A book or file containing the activity (by accounts), either manual or computerized, of a business. *(p. 118)*

Journal The book in which a person makes the original record of a business transaction; commonly referred to as a *book of original entry*. *(p. 111)*

Journalizing The process of recording a business transaction in a journal. *(p. 111)*

Ledger account A complete record of the transactions recorded in an individual account. *(p. 118)*

Posting The process of transferring figures from the journal to the ledger accounts. *(p. 120)*

Source documents Business papers, such as checks, invoices, receipts, letters, and memos, that furnish proof that a transaction has taken place. *(p. 111)*

Two-column general journal A general journal in which there are two amount columns, one used for debit amounts and one used for credit amounts. *(p. 113)*

CHAPTER REVIEW

Quiz Yourself

_____ 1. A _____ is a book in which business transactions are recorded.
   a. journal
   b. ledger
   c. trial balance
   d. balance sheet

_____ 2. Transferring information from the journal to the ledger is called
   a. preparing the financial statements.
   b. journalizing.
   c. posting.
   d. tracking.

_____ 3. For a journal entry to be complete, it must contain
   a. the date.
   b. a debit entry.
   c. a credit entry.
   d. an explanation.
   e. all of the above.

_____ 4. The _____ is used to determine where the amount in the ledger comes from.
   a. debit amount
   b. posting reference (or cross-reference)
   c. journal
   d. none of the above

_____ 5. Which of the following is an example of source documents?
   a. Canceled checks
   b. Vendor invoices
   c. Receipts
   d. All of the above

_____ 6. A $250 payment for salaries expense was incorrectly journalized and posted as a debit to Salaries Expense for $2,500 and a credit to Cash for $2,500. Using the one-step method, how would the entry be corrected?
   a. Cash   2,500
         Salaries Expense   2,500
   b. Salaries Expense   250
         Cash   250
   c. Cash   2,250
         Salaries Expense   2,250
   d. Salaries Expense   2,250
         Cash   2,250

Answers:
1. a 2. c 3. e 4. b 5. d 6. c

Review It with **QuickBooks**®

_____ 1. The general journal report is located under _____ in QuickBooks.
   a. Company & Financial
   b. Accountant & Taxes
   c. Custom Reports
   d. All of the above

_____ 2. Transactions can be recorded in QuickBooks by _____ or _____.
   a. journal entry method; general ledger method
   b. _Getting Around_ screen; general ledger method
   c. journal entry method; _Getting Around_ screen
   d. scanning method; journal entry method

_____ 3. The general ledger report is located under _____ in QuickBooks.
   a. Company & Financial
   b. Accountant & Taxes
   c. Custom Reports
   d. All of the above

_____ 4. Which of the following transactions requires using a name when recording them in QuickBooks?
   a. Providing services for cash
   b. Purchasing equipment for cash
   c. Receiving and paying the utility bill
   d. Purchasing supplies on account

Answers:
1. b 2. c 3. b 4. d

Chapter Assignments

Discussion Questions

1. Why is the journal called a book of original entry?
2. How does the journal differ from the ledger?
3. What is the purpose of providing a ledger account for each account?
4. List by account classification the order of the accounts in the general ledger.
5. Arrange the following steps in the posting process in correct order:
    a. Write the ledger account number in the Post. Ref. column of the journal.
    b. Write the amount of the transaction.
    c. Write the date of the transaction.
    d. Write the page number of the journal in the Post. Ref. column of the ledger account.
6. What does cross-referencing mean in the posting process?
7. Why is a source document important? List some examples of source documents.

Exercises

EXERCISE 3-1 In the following two-column journal, the capital letters represent where parts of a journal entry appear. Write the numbers 1 through 8 on a sheet of paper. After each number, match the capital letter where these items appear with the number of the item. (Not all letters will be used.)

LO 1

Practice Exercise 1

		GENERAL JOURNAL			Page 1
Date		Description	Post. Ref.	Debit	Credit
G					
H	I	J	O	M	
		K	P		N
		L			

1. Year
2. Month
3. Explanation
4. Title of account debited
5. Ledger account number of account credited
6. Amount of debit
7. Day of the month
8. Title of account credited

LO 1
Practice Exercise 1

EXERCISE 3-2 Decor Services completed the following transactions. Journalize the transactions in general journal form, including brief explanations.

Oct. 7   Received cash on account from Randy Hill, a customer, Inv. No. 312, $970.
     15   Paid on account to Miller Ideas, a creditor, $725, Ck. No. 2242.
     20   B. Brown, the owner, withdrew cash for personal use, $1,200, Ck. No. 2243.
     23   Bought store supplies for $150 and office supplies for $70 on account from Williams Office Supply, Inv. No. 1040.
     29   B. Brown, the owner, invested $3,000 cash and $1,500 of his personal equipment.

LO 1
Practice Exercise 1

EXERCISE 3-3 Montoya Tutoring Service completed the following transactions. Journalize the transactions in general journal form, including brief explanations.

Mar. 1   Bought equipment for $5,798 from Teaching Suppliers, paying $3,798 in cash and placing the balance on account, Ck. No. 3230.
     10   Paid the wages for the first week of March, $1,536, Ck. No. 3231.
     15   Sold services for cash to Mason District, $1,481, Sales Inv. 121.
     26   Sold services on account to Tempe School, $1,400, Sales Inv. 122.
     31   Paid on account to Teaching Suppliers, $725, Ck. No. 3232.

LO 2
Practice Exercise 2

EXERCISE 3-4 The following February journal entries all involved cash.

Increases to Cash—Debits		Decreases to Cash—Credits	
2/1	6,400	2/3	640
2/9	1,748	2/6	952
2/16	4,600	2/12	1,200
2/21	980	2/25	3,842
2/28	5,900		

Post the amounts to the ledger account for Cash, Account No. 111. Assume that all transactions appeared on page 1 of the general journal.

LO 2
Practice Exercise 2

EXERCISE 3-5 Arrange the following steps in the posting process in correct order:

a. The amount of the balance of the ledger account is recorded in the Debit Balance or Credit Balance column.
b. The amount of the transaction is recorded in the Debit or Credit column of the ledger account.
c. The ledger account number is recorded in the Post. Ref. column of the journal.
d. The date of the transaction is recorded in the Date column of the ledger account.
e. The page number of the journal is recorded in the Post. Ref. column of the ledger account.

LO **3**

Practice Exercise 3

EXERCISE 3-6 The bookkeeper for Nevado Company has prepared the following trial balance:

Nevado Company Trial Balance June 30, 20—		
Account Name	**Debit**	**Credit**
Cash		2,500
Accounts Receivable	8,300	
Supplies	600	
Prepaid Insurance	650	
Equipment	15,300	
Accounts Payable		2,700
M. Nevado, Capital		12,500
M. Nevado, Drawing	4,890	
Professional Fees		17,540
Rent Expense	500	
Miscellaneous Expense	1,800	
	32,040	35,240

The bookkeeper has asked for your help. In examining the company's journal and ledger, you discover the following errors. Use this information to construct a corrected trial balance.

a. The debits to the Cash account total $8,000, and the credits total $3,300.

b. A $500 payment to a creditor was entered in the journal correctly but was not posted to the Accounts Payable account.

c. The first two numbers in the balance of the Accounts Receivable account were transposed when the balance was copied from the ledger to the trial balance.

d. The $1,500 amount withdrawn by the owner for personal use was debited to Miscellaneous Expense by mistake—it was correctly credited to Cash.

LO **5**

Practice Exercise 5

EXERCISE 3-7 Determine the effect of the following errors on a company's total revenue, total expenses, and net income. Indicate the effect by writing O for Overstated (too much), U for Understated (too little), or NA for Not Affected.

Transactions	Total Revenue	Total Expenses	Net Income
Example: A check for $325 was written to pay on account. The accountant debited Rent Expense for $325 and credited Cash for $325.	NA	O	U
a. $420 was received on account from customers. The accountant debited Cash for $420 and credited Professional Fees for $420.			
b. The owner withdrew $1,200 for personal use. The accountant debited Wages Expense for $1,200 and credited Cash for $1,200.			
c. A check was written for $1,250 to pay the rent. The accountant debited Rent Expense for $1,520 and credited Cash for $1,520.			

(Continued)

Transactions	Total Revenue	Total Expenses	Net Income
d. $1,800 was received on account from customers. The accountant debited Cash for $1,800 and credited the Capital account for $1,800.			
e. A check was written for $225 to pay the phone bill received and recorded earlier in the month. The accountant debited Phone Expense for $225 and credited Cash for $225.			

LO 5

EXERCISE 3-8 Journalize correcting entries for each of the following errors and include a brief explanation.

a. A cash purchase of office equipment for $680 was journalized as a cash purchase of store equipment for $680. (Use the ruling method; assume that the entry has not been posted.)

b. An entry for a $180 payment for office supplies was journalized as $810. (Use the ruling method; assume that the entry has not been posted.)

c. A $620 payment for repairs was journalized and posted as a debit to Equipment instead of a debit to Repair Expense. (Use the correcting entry method to journalize the correction.)

d. A $750 bill for vehicle insurance was received and immediately paid. It was journalized and posted as $660. (Use the correcting entry method to journalize the correction.)

Problem Set A

LO 1

PROBLEM 3-1A The chart of accounts of the Barnes School is shown here, followed by the transactions that took place during October of this year.

Assets
111 Cash
113 Accounts Receivable
115 Prepaid Insurance
124 Equipment
127 Furniture

Liabilities
221 Accounts Payable

Owner's Equity
311 R. Barnes, Capital
312 R. Barnes, Drawing

Revenue
411 Tuition Income

Expenses
511 Salary Expense
512 Rent Expense
513 Gas and Oil Expense
514 Advertising Expense
515 Repair Expense
516 Telephone Expense
517 Utilities Expense
529 Miscellaneous Expense

Oct.   1   Bought liability insurance for one year, $1,850, Ck. No. 1527.
       3   Received a bill for advertising from *Business Summary*, $415.
       4   Paid the rent for the current month, $1,870, Ck. No. 1528.
       7   Received a bill for equipment repair from Fix-It Service, $318, Inv. No. 436.

Oct. 10 Received and deposited tuition from students, $6,375.

11 Received and paid the telephone bill $312, Ck. No. 1529.

15 Bought desks and chairs from The Oak Center, $1,980, paying $980 in cash and placing the balance on account, Ck. No. 1530.

18 Paid on account to *Business Summary*, $415, Ck. No. 1531.

21 R. Barnes withdrew $1,000 for personal use, Ck. No. 1532.

24 Received a bill for gas and oil from Wagner Oil Company, $225, Inv. No. 682.

25 Received and deposited tuition from students, $6,380.

27 Paid the salary of the part-time office assistant, $1,150. Ck. No. 1533.

28 Bought a photocopier on account from Gorst Office Machines, $1,950, Inv. No. 417.

29 Received $950 tuition from a student who had charged the tuition on account in September.

30 Received and paid the bill for utilities, $623, Ck. No. 1534.

31 Paid for flower arrangements for front office, $87, Ck. No. 1535.

31 R. Barnes invested his personal computer and printer, with a fair market value of $1,549, in the business.

Required

Record these transactions in the general journal, including a brief explanation for each entry. Number the journal pages 31 and 32.

Check Figure
Equipment increased by
$3,499 in October

PROBLEM 3-2A The journal entries for August, Carley's Car Care's second month of business, have been journalized in the general journal in your Working Papers and in CengageNow. The balances of the accounts as of July 31 have been recorded in the general ledger in your Working Papers and in CengageNow. Notice the word *Balance* in the Item column, the check mark in the Post. Ref. column, and the fact that the amount is in the Balance column only. This indicates a balance brought forward from a prior page or month.

Required

1. Write the owner's name, M. Carley, in the Capital and Drawing accounts.
2. Post the general journal entries to the general ledger accounts.
3. Prepare a trial balance as of August 31, 20--.
4. Prepare an income statement for the two months ended August 31, 20--.
5. Prepare a statement of owner's equity for the two months ended August 31, 20--.
6. Prepare a balance sheet as of August 31, 20--.

Check Figure
Net Income. $11,649

PROBLEM 3-3A Following is the chart of accounts of the C. Lucern Clinic:

Assets
111 Cash
113 Accounts Receivable
115 Supplies
117 Prepaid Insurance
124 Equipment

Liabilities
221 Accounts Payable

Owner's Equity
311 C. Lucern, Capital
312 C. Lucern, Drawing

Revenue
411 Professional Fees

Expenses
511 Salary Expense
512 Rent Expense
513 Laboratory Expense
514 Utilities Expense

(Continued)

Dr. Lucern completed the following transactions during July:

July   1   Bought laboratory equipment on account from Laser Surgical Supply Company, $3,660, paying $1,660 in cash and placing the remainder on account, Ck. No. 1730.

        3   Paid the office rent for the current month, $1,300, Ck. No. 1731.

        5   Received cash on account from patients, $360.

        6   Bought supplies on account from McRae Supply Company, $315, Inv. No. 3455.

        7   Received and paid the bill for laboratory services, $1,380, Ck. No. 1732.

        8   Bought insurance for one year, $2,650, CK. No. 1733.

     12   Performed medical services for patients on account, $5,886.

     15   Performed medical services for patients for cash, $4,793.

     16   The equipment purchased on July 1 was found to be broken. Dr. Lucern returned the damaged part and received a reduction in his bill, $518, Inv. No. 3162, Credit Memo No. 141. (Credit Equipment.)

     18   Paid the salary of the part-time nurse, $2,100, Ck. No. 1734.

     24   Received and paid the telephone bill for the month, $624, Ck. No. 1735.

     28   Performed medical services for patients on account, $7,381.

     29   Dr. Lucern withdrew cash for his personal use, $2,000, Ck. No. 1736.

Check Figure
Trial balance total, $62,679

Required

1. Journalize the transactions for July in the general journal, beginning on page 21.
2. Write the name of the owner next to the Capital and Drawing accounts in the general ledger. The balances of the accounts as of June 30 have been recorded in the general ledger in your Working Papers and in CengageNow. Notice the word *Balance* in the Item column, the check mark in the Post. Ref. column, and the fact that the amount is in the Balance column only. This indicates a balance brought forward from a prior page or month.
3. Post the entries to the general ledger accounts.
4. Prepare a trial balance.

LO   **1, 2, 3** ··

PROBLEM 3-4A   Lara's Landscaping Service has the following chart of accounts:

Assets
111 Cash
113 Accounts Receivable
115 Supplies
117 Prepaid Insurance
124 Equipment

Liabilities
221 Accounts Payable

Owner's Equity
311 J. Lara, Capital
312 J. Lara, Drawing

Revenue
411 Landscaping Income

Expenses
511 Salary Expense
512 Rent Expense
513 Gas and Oil Expense
514 Utilities Expense

The following transactions were completed by Lara's Landscaping Service:

Mar.   1   Lara deposited $35,000 in a bank account in the name of the business.

        4   Lara invested his personal landscaping equipment, with a fair market value of $1,325, in the business.

        6   Bought a used trailer on account from Tow Sales, $915, Inv. No. 314.

        7   Paid the rent for the current month, $950, Ck. No. 1000.

        9   Bought a used backhoe from Digger's Equipment, $5,300, paying $3,000 in cash and placing the balance on account, Inv. 4166, Ck. No. 1001.

Mar. 10 Bought liability insurance for one year, $1,800, Ck. No. 1002.

13 Sold landscaping services on account to Fredkey's, $3,895, Inv. No. 100.

14 Bought supplies on account from Office Requip, $380, Inv. No. 5172.

15 Sold landscaping services on account to C. Endel, $2,832, Inv. No. 101.

17 Received and paid the bill from Commercial Services for gas and oil for the equipment, $180, Ck. No. 1003.

19 Sold landscaping services for cash to Riston Company, $1,864, Inv. No. 102.

22 Paid on account to Tow Sales, $500, Inv. No. 314, Ck. No. 1004.

24 Received on account from Fredkey's, $800, Inv. No. 100.

28 Sold landscaping services on account to Stevens, Inc., $1,830, Inv. No. 103.

29 Received and paid the telephone bill, $260, Ck. No. 1005.

30 Paid the salary of the employee, $1,850, Ck. No. 1006.

31 Lara withdrew cash for his personal use, $1,500, Ck. No. 1007.

Required

1. Journalize the transactions in the general journal. Provide a brief explanation for each entry.

2. Write the name of the owner on the Capital and Drawing accounts. (Skip this step if you are using QuickBooks or general ledger.)

3. Post the journal entries to the general ledger accounts. (Skip this step if you are using QuickBooks or general ledger.)

4. Prepare a trial balance dated March 31, 20--. (If you are using QuickBooks or general ledger, use the year 2015.)

Check Figure
Trial balance total, $49,841

PROBLEM 3-5A Following is the chart of accounts of Sanchez Realty Company:

LO 1, 2, 3

Assets
111 Cash
113 Accounts Receivable
115 Supplies
117 Prepaid Insurance
124 Office Furniture

Liabilities
221 Accounts Payable

Owner's Equity
311 T. Sanchez, Capital
312 T. Sanchez, Drawing

Revenue
411 Professional Fees

Expenses
511 Salary Expense
512 Rent Expense
513 Advertising Expense
514 Utilities Expense

Sanchez completed the following transactions during April (the first month of business):

Apr. 1 Sanchez deposited $20,000 in a bank account in the name of the business.

5 Sold realty services on account to R. Miller, $7,500, Inv. No. 100.

7 Paid a bill for advertising, $250, Ck. No. 1001.

8 Bought supplies on account from Taylor Supply, $420, Inv. No. 2340.

9 Performed realty services for clients for cash, $2,530.

15 Received and paid the bill for utilities, $280, Ck. No. 1002.

17 Bought a desk and chair from Lewis Furniture, $1,800, paying $300 in cash and placing the balance on account, Ck. No. 1003.

20 Bought liability insurance for one year, $1,800, Ck. No. 1004.

21 Paid the rent for the current month, $1,000, Ck. No. 1005.

(Continued)

Apr. 25 Paid on account to Taylor Supply, $420, for supplies purchased on April 8, Ck. No. 1006.
   27 Received $7,500 from R. Miller for services performed on April 5.
   28 Received and paid the telephone bill for the month, $150, Ck. No. 1007.
   29 Paid the salary of the office assistant, $1,030, Ck. No. 1008.
   30 Sanchez withdrew cash for his personal use, $3,000, Ck. No. 1009.

Check Figure
Trial balance total,
$31,530

Required

1. Journalize the transactions for April in the general journal.
2. Post the entries to the general ledger accounts. (Skip this step if you are using QuickBooks or general ledger.)
3. Prepare a trial balance as of April 30, 20--.
4. Prepare an income statement for the month ended April 30, 20--.
5. Prepare a statement of owner's equity for the month ended April 30, 20--. (Skip this step if you are using QuickBooks.)
6. Prepare a balance sheet as of April 30, 20--.

*If you are using QuickBooks or general ledger , use the year 2015 when preparing all reports.

Problem Set B

LO 1

PROBLEM 3-1B The chart of accounts of Ethan Academy is shown here, followed by the transactions that took place during December of this year.

Assets
111 Cash
113 Accounts Receivable
114 Supplies
115 Prepaid Insurance
124 Equipment
127 Furniture

Liabilities
221 Accounts Payable

Owner's Equity
311 R. Ethan, Capital
312 R. Ethan, Drawing

Revenue
411 Tuition Income

Expenses
511 Salary Expense
512 Rent Expense
513 Gas and Oil Expense
514 Advertising Expense
515 Repair Expense
516 Telephone Expense
517 Utilities Expense
529 Miscellaneous Expense

Dec. 1 Bought liability insurance for one year, $2,260, Ck. No. 1627.
   11 Received a bill for advertising from the *City News*, $415, Statement No. 4267.
   12 Paid the rent for the current month, $1,850, Ck. No. 1628.
   13 Received a bill for equipment repair from Electronic Services, $345, Inv. No. 547.
   16 Received and deposited tuition from students, $5,850.
   17 Received and paid the telephone bill, $305, Ck. No. 1629.
   18 Bought desks and chairs from School Furniture, $1,625, paying $625 in cash and placing the balance on account, Ck. No. 1630.
   20 Paid on account to the *City News,* $415, Statement No. 4267, Ck. No. 1631.

Dec. 21 R. Ethan withdrew $1,000 for personal use, Ck. No. 1632.

26 Received a bill for gas and oil from Discount Oil Company, $210, Inv. No. 591.

27 Received and deposited tuition from students, $6,045.

31 Paid the salary of the office assistant, $1,375, Ck. No. 1633.

31 Bought a fax machine on account from EquipCo, $118, Inv. No. 529.

31 Received $1,150 tuition from a student who had charged the tuition on account last month.

31 Received and paid the bill for utilities, $470, Ck. No. 1634.

31 R. Ethan invested her personal computer and printer, with a fair market value of $1,150, in the business.

31 Bought supplies, $295, Ck. No. 1635.

Required

Record these transactions in the general journal, including a brief explanation for each entry. Number the journal pages 31 and 32.

Check Figure
Equipment increased by
$1,268 in December

PROBLEM 3-2B The journal entries for May, Kiddy Day Care's second month of business, have been journalized in the general journal in your Working Papers and in CengageNow. The balances of the accounts as of April 30 have been recorded in the general ledger in your Working Papers and in CengageNow. Notice the word *Balance* in the Item column, the check mark in the Post. Ref. column, and the fact that the amount is in the Balance column only. This indicates a balance brought forward from a prior page or month.

Required

1. Write the owner's name, R. Ramirez, in the Capital and Drawing accounts.
2. Post the general journal entries to the general ledger accounts.
3. Prepare a trial balance as of May 31, 20--.
4. Prepare an income statement for the two months ended May 31, 20--.
5. Prepare a statement of owner's equity for the two months ended May 31, 20--.
6. Prepare a balance sheet as of May 31, 20--.

Check Figure
Net Income, $12,261

PROBLEM 3-3B Following is the chart of accounts of Vance Rehab Clinic:

Assets
111 Cash
113 Accounts Receivable
115 Supplies
117 Prepaid Insurance
124 Equipment

Revenue
411 Professional Fees

Expenses
511 Salary Expense
512 Rent Expense
513 Laboratory Expense
514 Utilities Expense

Liabilities
221 Accounts Payable

Owner's Equity
311 J. Vance, Capital
312 J. Vance, Drawing

Vance completed the following transactions during July:

July 1 Bought laboratory equipment on account from Sage Surgical Supply Company, $6,520, paying $1,520 in cash and placing the remainder on account, Inv. No. 2071, Ck. No. 1930.

3 Paid the office rent for the current month, $1,550, Ck. No. 1931.

(Continued)

July   5   Received cash on account from patients, $3,045.

       6   Bought supplies on account from Allround Supply, $320, Inv. No. 3455.

       9   Received and paid the bill for laboratory services, $1,484, Ck. No. 1932.

     10   Bought insurance for one year, $2,600, Ck. No. 1933.

     12   Performed rehab services for patients on account, $5,185.

     14   Performed rehab services for patients for cash, $5,050.

     18   Part of the equipment purchased on July 1 was found to be broken. Vance returned the damaged part and received a reduction in her bill, $410, Inv. No. 2071, Credit Memo No. 218. (Credit Equipment.)

     20   Paid the salary of the part-time nurse, $2,200, Ck. No. 1934.

     22   Received and paid the telephone bill for the month, $380, Ck. No. 1935.

     24   Performed rehab services for patients on account, $4,235.

     30   Vance withdrew cash for her personal use, $2,000, Ck. No. 1936.

Check Figure
Trial balance total, $46,028

Required

1. Journalize the transactions for July in the general journal, beginning on page 21.
2. Write the name of the owner next to the Capital and Drawing accounts in the general ledger. The balances of the accounts as of June 30 have been recorded in the general ledger in your Working Papers and in CengageNow. Notice the word *Balance* in the Item column, the check mark in the Post. Ref. column, and the fact that the amount is in the Balance column only. This indicates a balance brought forward from a prior page or month.
3. Post the entries to the general ledger accounts.
4. Prepare a trial balance.

LO 1, 2, 3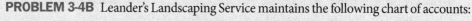

QuickBooks

PROBLEM 3-4B Leander's Landscaping Service maintains the following chart of accounts:

Assets
111 Cash
113 Accounts Receivable
117 Prepaid Insurance
124 Equipment

Liabilities
221 Accounts Payable

Owner's Equity
311 O. Leander, Capital
312 O. Leander, Drawing

Revenue
411 Landscaping Income

Expenses
511 Salary Expense
512 Rent Expense
513 Gas and Oil Expense
514 Utilities Expense
515 Supplies Expense

The following transactions were completed by Leander:

Apr.   1   Leander deposited $30,000 in a bank account in the name of the business.

      4   Leander invested his personal landscaping equipment, with a fair market value of $1,750, in the business.

      6   Bought a used trailer on account from Used Mart, $1,450, Inv. No. 415.

      7   Paid the rent for the current month, $925, Ck. No. 100.

      9   Bought a used bulldozer from Dray's Equipment, $5,100, paying $2,100 in cash and placing the balance on account, Inv. No. 3255, Ck. No. 101.

     10   Bought liability insurance for one year, $2,800, Ck. No. 102.

     13   Sold landscaping services on account to Fulton Homes, $4,595, Inv. No. 100.

     14   Bought supplies on account from Perry's Supply, $427, Inv. No. 4281.

Apr. 15   Sold landscaping services on account to D. D. Mau Inc., $3,997, Inv. No. 101.

     17   Received and paid the bill from Pumpers for gas and oil for the equipment, $227, Ck. No. 103.

     19   Sold landscaping services for cash to Cliff's House, $1,437, Inv. No. 102.

     22   Paid on account to Used Mart, $450, Inv. No. 415, Ck. No. 104.

     24   Received on account from Fulton Homes, $800, Inv. No. 100.

     28   Sold landscaping services on account to H. Ron, $1,785, Inv. No. 103.

     29   Received and paid the telephone bill, $321, Ck. No. 105.

     30   Paid the salary of the employee, $1,836, Ck. No. 106.

     30   Leander withdrew cash for his personal use, $1,500, Ck. No. 107.

Required

1. Journalize the transactions in the general journal. Prepare a brief explanation for each entry.
2. Write the name of the owner on the Capital and Drawing accounts. (Skip this step if you are using QuickBooks or general ledger.)
3. Post the journal entries to the general ledger accounts. (Skip this step if you are using QuickBooks or general ledger.)
4. Prepare a trial balance dated April 30, 20--. (If you are using QuickBooks or general ledger, use the year 2015.)

Check Figure
Trial balance total, $47,991

LO   **1, 2, 3**

PROBLEM 3-5B Following is the chart of accounts of Smith Financial Services:

Assets
111 Cash
113 Accounts Receivable
115 Supplies
117 Prepaid Insurance
124 Office Furniture

Liabilities
221 Accounts Payable

Owner's Equity
311 A. Smith, Capital
312 A. Smith, Drawing

Revenue
411 Professional Fees

Expenses
511 Salary Expense
512 Rent Expense
513 Advertising Expense
514 Utilities Expense

Smith completed the following transactions during June (the first month of business):

June   1   Smith deposited $10,000 in a bank account in the name of the business.

     3   Sold financial services on account to W. Johnson, $3,030, Inv. No. 001.

     8   Paid a bill for advertising, $100, Ck. No. 200.

     9   Bought supplies on account from Jones Supply, $75, Inv. No. 405.

     13   Performed financial services for clients for cash, $3,200.

     17   Received and paid the bill for utilities, $104, Ck. No. 201.

     19   Bought a desk and chair from Davis Furniture, $600, paying $50 in cash and placing the balance on account, Ck. No. 202.

     20   Bought liability insurance for one year, $600, Ck. No. 203.

     23   Paid the rent for the current month, $400, Ck. No. 204.

     27   Paid on account to Jones Supply, $75, for supplies purchased on June 9, Ck. No. 205.

     29   Received $3,030 from W. Johnson for services performed on June 3.

(Continued)

June 29   Received and paid the telephone bill for the month, $80, Ck. No. 206.
     30   Paid the salary of the office assistant, $600, Ck. No. 207.
     30   Smith withdrew cash for her personal use, $800, Ck. No. 208.

Check Figure
Trial balance total,
$16,780

Required

1. Journalize the transactions for June in the general journal.
2. Post the entries to the general ledger accounts. (Skip this step if you are using QuickBooks or general ledger.)
3. Prepare a trial balance as of June 30, 20--.
4. Prepare an income statement for the month ended June 30, 20--.
5. Prepare a statement of owner's equity for the month ended June 30, 20--. (Skip this step if you are using QuickBooks.)
6. Prepare a balance sheet as of June 30, 20--.

*If you are using QuickBooks or general ledger , use the year 2015 when preparing all reports.

Try It with **QuickBooks®** (LO 1–4)

QB Exercise 3-1

Using the Conner's Whitewater Adventures demonstration file from Chapter 1, complete the following activities with QuickBooks. Use the dates June 1, 2015, to June 30, 2015, for all reports.

1. View and print the general journal report for Conner's Whitewater Adventures.

    a. What is the ending balance of the Debit column for the journal?

2. View and print the general ledger report for Conner's Whitewater Adventures.

    a. What is the ending balance in the Cash account? Is this balance a debit or a credit?

    b. What is the total amount of revenues during the month of June for Conner's Whitewater Adventures?

    c. What is the total amount of expenses during the month of June for Conner's Whitewater Adventures?

Activities

Why Does It Matter?

ECOTOUR EXPEDITIONS, INC., Jamestown, Rhode Island
You probably have never imagined the possibility of being an accountant who could have a direct impact on improving global ecosystems. Accountants who work for Ecotour Expeditions, Inc., an ecotourism company, might manage accounting details for guest air travel and accommodations, tour guide compensation, expedition revenue, and a variety of expenses. What type of accounting transactions would Ecotour Expeditions have? List 3 to 4 transactions and then record the journal entry for each transaction. Example: *Purchase safari jeep with cash, $42,500.*

Safari Jeep	42,500	
Cash		42,500

What Would You Say?

You are the new bookkeeper for a small business. The bookkeeper whose job you are taking is training you on the business's manual system. As he journalizes, he writes the account number in the Post. Ref. column because he believes it's easier. His thinking is that, when he posts, he won't be bothered writing the account numbers. How would you explain why he should *not* write the account number in the Post. Ref. column immediately and instead should enter the account number after he has posted the amount to the ledger?

What Do You Think?

You work as an accounting clerk. You have received the following information supplied by a client, S. Winston, from the client's bank statement, the client's tax returns, and a variety of other July documents. The client wants you to prepare an income statement, a statement of owner's equity, and a balance sheet for the month of July for Winston Company.

Income from Services	$ 9,570	Utilities Expense	$ 388
Beginning Capital	50,000	Drawing	2,500
Cash	24,940	Supplies	635
Truck	?	Equipment	16,148
Accounts Payable	?	Total Liabilities and Owner's	
Rent Expense	1,200	Equity	57,473
Wages Expense	4,200		

What Would You Do?

You are responsible for preparing all of the journal entries for Regional Financial Services. You have correctly prepared the following entry for financial services provided on December 15:

Dec. 15	Cash	10,000	
	Fees Earned		10,000

Your boss has asked you to change the date from December 15 to January 15 so that the business's profit, and thus taxes, would be lower. Are you allowed to do this? What is your response to your boss? How should you handle this situation?

BEFORE A TEST CHECK: Chapters 1–3

PART 1 : Multiple-Choice Questions

_____ 1. Which of the following is not considered an account?
   a. Cash
   b. Prepaid Insurance
   c. Equipment
   d. Assets
   e. Accounts Receivable

_____ 2. In which of the following transactions would an expense be recorded?
   a. Received a bill for advertising.
   b. Paid on an account payable for the utility bill.
   c. Received and paid a bill for repairs.
   d. All of these should be recorded as an expense.
   e. Only a and c should be recorded as an expense.

_____ 3. The ending capital balance appears on which of the following statements?
   a. Statement of owner's equity
   b. Balance sheet
   c. Income statement
   d. Statement of owner's equity and balance sheet
   e. Statement of owner's equity and income statement

_____ 4. On a statement of owner's equity, if beginning capital is $42,000 and there is an additional investment of $5,000, a net loss of $9,000, and owner withdrawals of $15,000, the ending capital amount would be
   a. $70,000.
   b. $23,000.
   c. $40,000.
   d. $54,000.
   e. none of these.

_____ 5. If a $260 payment of rent is recorded as a $620 debit to Rent Expense and a $620 credit to Cash, what will the result be?
   a. The trial balance will be in balance.
   b. The Rent Expense account will be overstated.
   c. The Cash account will be understated.
   d. Rent Expense will be overstated and Cash will be understated.
   e. All of the above are true.

_____ 6. A person who wanted to know the balance of an account would look in
   a. the ledger.
   b. the chart of accounts.
   c. the journal.
   d. the source documents.
   e. none of these.

PART II: The Accounting Cycle
Journalizing, Posting, Trial Balance, and Financial Statements

The accounts and their balances as of December 1 of this year for Antec Services are as follows:

111 Cash	$18,900		311 J. Dunn, Capital	$49,590
113 Accounts Receivable	6,300		312 J. Dunn, Drawing	11,200
115 Supplies	870			
116 Prepaid Insurance	1,230		411 Service Income	39,600
124 Equipment	31,200			
			511 Wages Expense	10,450
221 Accounts Payable	6,340		512 Utilities Expense	2,760
			513 Rent Expense	12,620

Check Figure
Net Income, $22,315

Required

1. Journalize the following December transactions in general journal form on journal page 31.

Dec. 1 Sold services for cash, $9,500.
     4 Received and paid the bill for the rent for December, $1,000, Ck. No. 2331.

Dec. 11 Received $1,750 on account from customers, Cash Receipt Nos. 1430–1438.
   19 Sold services on account, $2,075, Sales Inv. No. 2591.
   22 Received and paid the bill for utilities, $255, Ck. No. 2332.
   23 Bought supplies on account from Office Works, $292, Inv. No. 2606.
   31 Paid the wages for the month, $1,775, Ck. No. 2333.
   31 Dunn withdrew $1,500 for personal use, Ck. No. 2334.

2. Label T accounts with the above account names.
3. Correctly place the plus and minus signs under all T accounts and label the debit and credit sides of each T account.
4. Post the entries to the T accounts by date and foot and balance the accounts.
5. Prepare a trial balance as of December 31.
6. Prepare an income statement for the year ended December 31.
7. Prepare a statement of owner's equity for the year ended December 31.
8. Prepare a balance sheet as of December 31.

Answers: Part I

1. d   2. e   3. d   4. b   5. e   6. a

Answers: Part II

1.

GENERAL JOURNAL				Page 3	
Date	Description	Post. Ref.	Debit	Credit	
20--					
Dec. 1	Cash	111	9 5 0 0 00		
	Service Income	411		9 5 0 0	00
	Sold services for cash.				
4	Rent Expense	513	1 0 0 0 00		
	Cash	111		1 0 0 0	00
	Ck. No. 2331.				
11	Cash	111	1 7 5 0 00		
	Accounts Receivable	113		1 7 5 0	00
	Cash on account from customers,				
	Cash Receipt Nos. 1430–1438.				
19	Accounts Receivable	113	2 0 7 5 00		
	Service Income	411		2 0 7 5	00
	Sales Inv. No. 2591.				
22	Utilities Expense	512	2 5 5 00		
	Cash	111		2 5 5	00
	Ck. No. 2332.				
23	Supplies	115	2 9 2 00		
	Accounts Payable	221		2 9 2	00
	Office Works, Inv. No. 2606.				
31	Wages Expense	511	1 7 7 5 00		
	Cash	111		1 7 7 5	00
	Paid month's wages, Ck. No. 2333.				
31	J. Dunn, Drawing	312	1 5 0 0 00		
	Cash	111		1 5 0 0	00
	Ck. No. 2334.				

BEFORE A TEST CHECK

2., 3., and 4.

Owner's Equity

Assets = Liabilities + Capital − Drawing + Revenue − Expenses

Assets

Cash 111

Debit +		Credit −	
Bal.	18,900	12/4	1,000
12/1	9,500	12/22	255
12/11	1,750	12/31	1,775
	30,150	12/31	1,500
			4,530

Bal. 25,620

Accounts Receivable 113

Debit +		Credit −	
Bal.	6,300	12/11	1,750
12/19	2,075		
	8,375		

Bal. 6,625

Supplies 115

Debit +		Credit −	
Bal.	870		
12/23	292		

Bal. 1,162

Prepaid Insurance 116

Debit +		Credit −

Bal. 1,230

Equipment 124

Debit +		Credit −

Bal. 31,200

Liabilities

Accounts Payable 221

Debit −		Credit +	
		Bal.	6,340
		12/23	292
		Bal.	6,632

Capital

J. Dunn, Capital 311

Debit −		Credit +	
		Bal.	49,590

Drawing

J. Dunn, Drawing 312

Debit +		Credit −
Bal.	11,200	
12/31	1,500	
Bal.	**12,700**	

Revenue

Service Income 411

Debit −		Credit +	
		Bal.	39,600
		12/1	9,500
		12/19	2,075
		Bal.	**51,175**

Expenses

Wages Expense 511

Debit +		Credit −
Bal.	10,450	
12/31	1,775	
Bal.	**12,225**	

Utilities Expense 512

Debit +		Credit −
Bal.	2,760	
12/22	255	
Bal.	**3,015**	

Rent Expense 513

Debit +		Credit −
Bal.	12,620	
12/4	1,000	
Bal.	**13,620**	

5.

Antec Services
Trial Balance
December 31, 20—

Account Name	Debit	Credit
Cash	25,620	
Accounts Receivable	6,625	
Supplies	1,162	
Prepaid Insurance	1,230	
Equipment	31,200	
Accounts Payable		6,632
J. Dunn, Capital		49,590
J. Dunn, Drawing	12,700	
Service Income		51,175
Wages Expense	12,225	
Utilities Expense	3,015	
Rent Expense	13,620	
	107,397	107,397

6.

Antec Services
Income Statement
For Year Ended December 31, 20--

Revenue:		
Service Income		$51,175
Expenses:		
Wages Expense	$12,225	
Utilities Expense	3,015	
Rent Expense	13,620	
Total Expenses		28,860
Net Income		$22,315

7.

Antec Services
Statement of Owner's Equity
For Year Ended December 31, 20--

J. Dunn, Capital, January 1, 20--		$49,590
Investments during Year	$ 0	
Net Income for Year	22,315	
Subtotal	$22,315	
Less Withdrawals for Year	12,700	
Increase in Capital		9,615
J. Dunn, Capital, December 31, 20--		$59,205

8.

Antec Services Balance Sheet December 31, 20--		
Assets		
Cash	$25,620	
Accounts Receivable	6,625	
Supplies	1,162	
Prepaid Insurance	1,230	
Equipment	31,200	
Total Assets		$65,837
Liabilities		
Accounts Payable		$ 6,632
Owner's Equity		
J. Dunn, Capital		59,205
Total Liabilities and Owner's Equity		$65,837

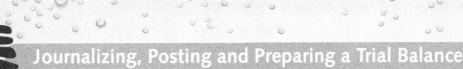

Journalizing, Posting and Preparing a Trial Balance

QuickBooks

A friend of yours, Anika Valli, has decided to open a spa to serve her small resort town of about 7,000 people and 4 million tourists annually. She has named the business All About You Spa to convey the idea that the business intends to pamper those who enter its doors. She will operate the spa five days a week, Tuesday through Saturday, but a phone line will always be available to answer questions and schedule appointments. Hours will be from 8 A.M. to 8 P.M. She has asked you to be the bookkeeper for this new business. At the end of the month of June, the owner, Anika Valli, would like you to provide the following:

1. General journal
2. General ledger
3. Trial balance
4. Income statement (This is the profit and loss statement in QuickBooks.)
5. Statement of owner's equity (Ignore this step if you are using QuickBooks.)
6. Balance sheet

She has kept a checkbook and a file folder with summary evidence of June's spa activity: a check register, a summary report of charges by customers for services provided, all receipts that were issued, and a summary of charges made by All About You Spa. Most of the income from services is received in cash and as charges to credit cards. No checks are accepted, except from approved clients (primarily conference planners and other organizations that book packages as prizes for attendees or gifts for employees, speakers, or other people they want to thank with a spa service or package of services). Anika deposits cash receipts on customer's accounts on the 7th, 14th, 21st, and last day of each month.

The first page in the file folder contains the following chart of accounts. Currently, you will not use or may not be familiar with some of the accounts listed here. Ignore those accounts for now; we will use them later.

CHART OF ACCOUNTS FOR ALL ABOUT YOU SPA

Assets	Liabilities	Revenue	
111 Cash	211 Accounts Payable	411 Income from Services	616 Advertising Expense
113 Accounts Receivable	212 Wages Payable		617 Utilities Expense
114 Office Supplies		**Expenses**	618 Insurance Expense
115 Spa Supplies	**Owner's Equity**	611 Wages Expense	619 Depr. Expense—
117 Prepaid Insurance	311 A. Valli, Capital	612 Rent Expense	Office Equipment
124 Office Equipment	312 A. Valli, Drawing	613 Office Supplies	620 Depr. Expense—Spa
125 Accum. Depr.—	313 Income Summary	Expense	Equipment
Office Equipment		614 Spa Supplies Expense	630 Miscellaneous
128 Spa Equipment		615 Laundry Expense	Expense
129 Accum. Depr.—Spa			
Equipment			

All About You
Spa

The basis of your entries will be the following documents:

Checkbook Entries
(Deposits made and checks written)

Check No.	Date	Explanation	√	Deposits	Check Amount
	6/1	Invested cash in business.		15,000.00	
1011	6/3	Bought 6-month liability insurance policy.			960.00
1012	6/3	Bought spa equipment for $4,235, putting $2,000 cash down.			2,000.00
1013	6/3	Paid June rent.			1,650.00
1014	6/5	Bought office supplies.			248.00
1015	6/5	Purchased flowers and balloons for grand opening (Misc. Exp.).			112.00
1016	6/7	Paid first week's wages.			1,847.50
	6/7	Deposited first week's cash revenue.		2,630.00	
1017	6/11	Paid on account payable for spa equipment (June 3).			873.00
	6/14	Deposited second week's cash revenue.		3,703.00	
1018	6/14	Paid second week's wages.			1,847.50
1019	6/18	Paid on account payable for spa equipment (June 3).			1,200.00
	6/21	Deposited third week's cash revenue.		4,758.00	
1020	6/21	Paid third week's wages.			1,847.50
1021	6/25	Paid on account payable for spa equipment (June 3).			73.00
1022	6/28	Paid fourth week's wages.			1,847.50
1023	6/28	Paid month's laundry bill.			84.00
	6/30	Deposited end of month's cash revenue.		5,992.00	
1024	6/30	A. Valli withdrew $1,850 for personal use.			1,850.00
1025	6/30	Paid June telephone bill.			225.00
1026	6/30	Paid June power and water bill.			248.00

Other information that require journal entries:

Receipt	
6/1 A. Valli, owner of All About You Spa, invested her personal spa equipment	$3,158.00

All About You Spa

June Accounts Payable Charges Summary Report

6/3 Bought spa supplies on account from Spa Supplies, Inc., Inv. No. 804	$492.00
6/5 Bought office equipment on account from Office Equipment Company, Inv. No. 3415	$318.00
6/5 Bought advertising pamphlets on account from Adco, Inc., Inv. No. 512	$397.00
6/5 Bought office equipment on account from Office Equipment, Company, Inv. No. 3445	$832.00
6/5 Bought office supplies on account from Office Staples, Inv. No. 522	$120.00

If you are using QuickBooks you will need to select a vendor when recording Accounts Payable transactions.

June Sales to Customers on Account Summary Report

6/7	Jill Anson	$325.00
6/14	Jack Morgan	$486.00
6/21	Tory Ligman	$344.00
6/30	Judy Wilcox	$109.00

If you are using QuickBooks, you will need to select a customer when recording Accounts Receivable transactions.

Required

1. Journalize the transactions for June (in date order) in the general journal.

    — If you are using QuickBooks or general ledger, review the instructions for the program on the textbook website. If you are preparing the journal entries manually, enter your transactions beginning on page 1.

2. Post the entries to the general ledger accounts.

    — Ignore this step if you are using QuickBooks or general ledger.

3. Prepare a trial balance as of June 30, 20--.

4. Prepare an income statement for the month ended June 30, 20--.

5. Prepare a statement of owner's equity for the month ended June 30, 20--. Skip this step if you are using QuickBooks.

6. Prepare a balance sheet as of June 30, 20--.

* If you are using QuickBooks or general ledger, use the year 2015 when preparing all reports.

Note: The trial balance and financial statements are unadjusted. In the next chapter, you will learn that certain accounts need to be adjusted. These adjustments will change some of the figures in these reports.

595

4 Adjusting Entries and the Work Sheet

Learning Objectives

After you have completed this chapter, you will be able to do the following:

1. *Define* fiscal period *and* fiscal year and explain the accounting cycle.

2. List the classifications of the accounts that occupy each column of a ten-column work sheet.

3. Complete a work sheet for a service enterprise, involving adjustments for supplies, expired insurance, depreciation, and accrued wages.

4. Journalize and post the adjusting entries.

5. Prepare an income statement, a statement of owner's equity, and a balance sheet for a service business directly from the work sheet.

6. Prepare (a) an income statement involving more than one revenue account and a net loss, (b) a statement of owner's equity with an additional investment and either a net income or a net loss, and (c) a balance sheet for a business having more than one accumulated depreciation account.

To: **Amy Roberts, CPA**
Subject: **What's Next?**

Hi Amy,
I've recorded all of my transactions for the month of June. So now I need to prepare the financial statements for the bank—I'm thinking about applying for a loan. Am I ready to prepare the financial statements because I have all of the transactions recorded?
Thanks,
Janie

To: Janie Conner
Subject: RE: What's Next?

Hi Janie,
One more step needs to take place before you can prepare the financial statements: prepare and record adjusting entries. Adjusting entries update the accounts for any internal transactions that haven't yet been recorded, such as usage of supplies, expiration of prepaid insurance, and wages that are owed. Adjusting entries need to be recorded before you can prepare the financial statements to ensure that your accounts are up to date. The easiest way to learn how to prepare adjusting entries is by using a work sheet; this will also help you learn to prepare the financial statements. So here's what you need to know before you're ready to give your financial statements to the bank:

_____ 1. Prepare a work sheet to help in recording adjusting entries
_____ 2. Record adjusting entries in the journal

Let me know if you need help!

Amy

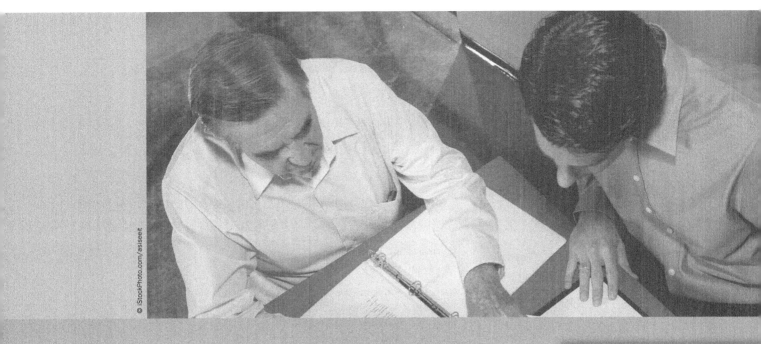

As part of the *summarizing* step in the definition of accounting, we now introduce the work sheet and the financial statements. Now that you are familiar with the classifying and recording phases of accounting for a service business, let's look at the remaining steps in the accounting process.

FISCAL PERIOD

A **fiscal period** is any period of time covering a complete accounting cycle. A **fiscal year** is a fiscal period consisting of 12 consecutive months. It does not have to coincide with the calendar year. If a business has seasonal peaks, it is a good idea to complete the accounting operations at the end of the most active season. At that time, management wants to know what the results of the year are and where the business stands financially. The fiscal year of a resort that operates during the summer may be from October 1 of one year to September 30 of the next year. The government has a fiscal year from October 1 of one year to September 30 of the following year. Department stores often use a fiscal period from February 1 of one year to January 31 of the next year.

THE ACCOUNTING CYCLE

The **accounting cycle** represents the sequence of steps in the accounting process completed during the fiscal period. Figure 1 shows how we introduce these steps on a chapter-by-chapter basis. This outline brings you up to date on what we have accomplished so far, as well as what will be covered in Chapter 5, and how each chapter fits into the steps in the accounting cycle.

THE WORK SHEET

The **work sheet** is an optional working paper used by accountants, in a manual accounting system, to record necessary adjustments and provide up-to-date account balances needed to prepare the financial statements. **The work sheet is a tool that accountants use to help in preparing the financial statements.** As a tool, the work sheet serves as a central place for bringing together the information needed to record the adjustments. With up-to-date account balances, the accountant can then prepare the financial statements.

Accounting Language

Accounting cycle (p. 167)

Accrual (p. 175)

Accrued wages (p. 175)

Adjusting entries (p. 181)

Adjustments (p. 170)

Book value (carrying value) (p. 173)

Contra account (p. 172)

Depreciation (p. 171)

Fiscal period (p. 167)

Fiscal year (p. 167)

Matching principle (p. 181)

Mixed accounts (p. 175)

Straight-line depreciation (p. 171)

Work sheet (p. 167)

1 *Define* fiscal period *and* fiscal year and explain the accounting cycle.

Learning Objective

QuickBooks Tip

When using accounting software such as QuickBooks, the work sheet is not needed.

Figure 1
The accounting cycle
by chapter

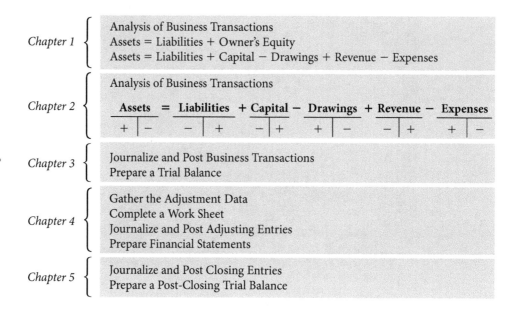

Chapter 1	Analysis of Business Transactions Assets = Liabilities + Owner's Equity Assets = Liabilities + Capital − Drawings + Revenue − Expenses

Chapter 2

Analysis of Business Transactions

Assets		=	**Liabilities**		+	**Capital**		−	**Drawings**		+	**Revenue**		−	**Expenses**	
+	−		−	+		−	+		+	−		−	+		+	−

Chapter 3	Journalize and Post Business Transactions Prepare a Trial Balance
Chapter 4	Gather the Adjustment Data Complete a Work Sheet Journalize and Post Adjusting Entries Prepare Financial Statements
Chapter 5	Journalize and Post Closing Entries Prepare a Post-Closing Trial Balance

Remember

Accounting steps: Analyzing: Which accounts are involved?
Classifying: assets, liabilities, capital, drawing, revenue, and expenses
Recording: journalizing
Summarizing: financial statements
Interpreting: drawing conclusions

First, we present the work sheet form so that you can see the big picture. Then, we describe and show examples of adjustments. Finally, we show how the adjustments are entered on the work sheet and how the work sheet is completed.

We will use a ten-column work sheet—so called because two amount columns are provided for each of the work sheet's five major sections. Work sheets are most often prepared using a spreadsheet program, such as Microsoft Excel®. We will explain the function of each of these sections, again basing our discussion on the accounting activities of Conner's Whitewater Adventures. But first we need to fill in the heading, which consists of three lines: (1) the name of the company, (2) the title of the working paper, and (3) the period of time covered.

	A	B	C	D	E	F	G	H	I	J	K
1						Conner's Whitewater Adventures					
2						Work Sheet					
3						For Month Ended June 30, 20--					
4											
5		TRIAL BALANCE		ADJUSTMENTS		ADJUSTED TRIAL BALANCE		INCOME STATEMENT		BALANCE SHEET	
6	ACCOUNT NAME	DEBIT	CREDIT	DEBIT	CREDIT	DEBIT	CREDIT	DEBIT	CREDIT	DEBIT	CREDIT
7											

Next, we want to point out the account classifications that are placed in each column. We start with the Trial Balance columns and then move across the work sheet, discussing each pair of columns separately.

The Columns of the Work Sheet

TRIAL BALANCE COLUMNS

② List the classifications of the accounts that occupy each column of a ten-column work sheet.

Learning Objective

When you use a work sheet, you do not have to prepare a trial balance on a separate sheet of paper. Instead, you enter the account balances from the general ledger in the first two amount columns of the work sheet. List the accounts that have balances in the Account Name column in the same order in which they appear in the chart of accounts. Assuming **normal balances,** the amount of each account is listed in the Trial Balance Debit and Credit columns of the work sheet according to its classification, as shown on page 169.

	A	B	C	D	E	F	G	H	I	J	K
1				Conner's Whitewater Adventures							
2				Work Sheet							
3				For Month Ended June 30, 20--							
4											
5		TRIAL BALANCE		ADJUSTMENTS		ADJUSTED TRIAL BALANCE		INCOME STATEMENT		BALANCE SHEET	
6	ACCOUNT NAME	DEBIT	CREDIT	DEBIT	CREDIT	DEBIT	CREDIT	DEBIT	CREDIT	DEBIT	CREDIT
7		Assets →				→ Assets					
8			Liabilities →				→ Liabilities				
9			Capital →				→ Capital				
10		Drawing →				→ Drawing					
11			Revenue →				→ Revenue				
12		Expenses →				→ Expenses					
13											

As we move along in this chapter, we will discuss the adjustments. The Adjusted Trial Balance columns contain the same account classifications as the Trial Balance columns. **The Adjusted Trial Balance columns are merely extensions of the Trial Balance columns, plus or minus any adjustment amounts.** If an adjustment is required, the amounts are carried from the Trial Balance columns through the Adjustments columns and into the Adjusted Trial Balance columns.

INCOME STATEMENT COLUMNS

An income statement contains the revenues minus the expenses. Revenue accounts have credit balances, so they are recorded in the Income Statement Credit column. Expense accounts have debit balances, so they are recorded in the Income Statement Debit column.

	A	B	C	D	E	F	G	H	I	J	K
1				Conner's Whitewater Adventures							
2				Work Sheet							
3				For Month Ended June 30, 20--							
4											
5		TRIAL BALANCE		ADJUSTMENTS		ADJUSTED TRIAL BALANCE		INCOME STATEMENT		BALANCE SHEET	
6	ACCOUNT NAME	DEBIT	CREDIT	DEBIT	CREDIT	DEBIT	CREDIT	DEBIT	CREDIT	DEBIT	CREDIT
7		Assets →				→ Assets					
8			Liabilities →				→ Liabilities				
9			Capital →				→ Capital				
10		Drawing →				→ Drawing					
11			Revenue →				→ Revenue →			Revenue	
12		Expenses →				→ Expenses →		Expenses			
13											

BALANCE SHEET COLUMNS

As you may recall, the balance sheet is a statement showing assets, liabilities, and owner's equity. Asset accounts have debit balances, so they are recorded in the Balance Sheet Debit column. Liability accounts have credit balances, so they are recorded in the Balance Sheet Credit column. The Capital account has a credit balance, so it is recorded in the Balance Sheet Credit column. Because the Drawing account is a deduction from Capital, it has a debit balance and is recorded in the Balance Sheet Debit column (the opposite column from that in which Capital is recorded).

	A	B	C	D	E	F	G	H	I	J	K
1				Conner's Whitewater Adventures							
2				Work Sheet							
3				For Month Ended June 30, 20--							
4											
5		TRIAL BALANCE		ADJUSTMENTS		ADJUSTED TRIAL BALANCE		INCOME STATEMENT		BALANCE SHEET	
6	ACCOUNT NAME	DEBIT	CREDIT	DEBIT	CREDIT	DEBIT	CREDIT	DEBIT	CREDIT	DEBIT	CREDIT
7		Assets →				→ Assets →				Assets	
8			Liabilities →				→ Liabilities →				Liabilities
9			Capital →				→ Capital →				Capital
10		Drawing →				→ Drawing →				Drawing	
11			Revenue →				→ Revenue →		Revenue		
12		Expenses →				→ Expenses →		Expenses			
13											

ADJUSTMENTS

Adjustments are a way of updating the ledger accounts. They may be considered *internal transactions*. They have not been recorded in the accounts up to this time because no outside party has been involved. Adjustments are determined after the trial balance has been prepared. Adjustments fine-tune the accounts to present a more accurate report of the accounts.

Only a few accounts are adjusted. To describe the reasons for making adjustments, let's return to Conner's Whitewater Adventures. First, we select the accounts that require adjustments. Then, we show the adjustments recorded in T accounts so that you can see the effect on the accounts. **However, bear in mind that the adjustments are first recorded on the work sheet when using a manual accounting system.** When using general ledger software, adjustments are recorded in the general journal. The adjustments are made at the end of the company's accounting period—in the case of Conner's Whitewater Adventures, June 30.

The Financial Picture
Before Adjustments

The Financial Picture
After Adjustments

Without adjustments, the financial statements would be unclear.

SMALL BUSINESS **SUCCESS**

Choosing Accounting Software

Choosing accounting software is an important decision for small businesses. One popular software package designed for small businesses is QuickBooks. When picking accounting software, it's important to consider the needs of the business, such as:

- How many individuals will use the software?
- What tools are available?
- Can the software handle inventory?
- Is it easy to use?
- What is the cost of the program?
- Can the software be used online?

QuickBooks can handle most basic small business accounting transactions. This software program includes a general ledger, subsidiary ledgers, and financial statements. QuickBooks also has the ability to export data into Excel and Word. Differences in general ledger software packages typically relate to their look and how transactions are entered. For example, QuickBooks uses a more "forms"-based approach, which is identified by different "centers," such as vendors, customers, employees, company, and banking.

It is highly recommended that all small business owners and accounting majors take at least one course in how to use accounting software, such as QuickBooks. Knowledge of accounting software, such as QuickBooks, can easily be applied to other general ledger software packages and is a skill needed for success in the business world.

Supplies

Remember that when a business buys supplies for cash or on credit, the supplies account is debited. An asset is recorded because the supplies have not yet been used. At the end of the accounting period, the amount of supplies that have been used during the period must be deducted from the Supplies account and added to Supplies Expense. During June, Conner's Whitewater Adventures purchased $675 of supplies. At the end of the time period, the company counted its supplies and determined that it had $215 worth of supplies remaining. Thus, $460 ($675 − $215) worth of supplies were used during the period. The amount used, $460, must be deducted from the Supplies account and added to the Supplies Expense account.

	Supplies				Supplies Expense	
	+	−			+	−
(Old) Balance	675	Adjusting 460		Adjusting	460	
(New) Balance	215					

Notice that the new balance of the Supplies account is the amount remaining, $215 ($675 − $460). The $460 amount in Supplies Expense represents the cost of supplies used during the time period.

Prepaid Insurance

The $1,875 balance in Prepaid Insurance represents the premium paid in advance for a three-month liability insurance policy. One month ($625) of the three months of premium has now expired.

$$\$1,875 \text{ premium} \div 3 \text{ months} = \$625 \text{ per month}$$

In the adjustment, Conner's Whitewater Adventures deducts the expired, or used, portion from Prepaid Insurance and adds it to Insurance Expense.

	Prepaid Insurance				Insurance Expense	
	+	−			+	−
(Old) Balance	1,875	Adjusting 625		Adjusting	625	
(New) Balance	1,250					

The new balance of Prepaid Insurance, $1,250 ($1,875 − $625), represents the cost of insurance that remains paid in advance and should therefore appear in the Balance Sheet Debit column. The $625 amount in Insurance Expense represents the cost of insurance that has expired and should appear in the Income Statement Debit column.

Remember

For the adjustment of insurance, you are given the amount used (expired). So in the adjusting entry, take the amount used directly out of Prepaid Insurance and put it into Insurance Expense.

Depreciation of Equipment

We have recorded durable items, such as appliances and fixtures, under Equipment because they will last longer than one year. The benefits of these assets will eventually be used up. (The assets will either wear out or become obsolete.) Therefore, we should systematically spread the cost of these assets over their useful lives. That is, we allocate the cost of the equipment as an expense *over its estimated useful life* and call this **depreciation** because, over time, such equipment loses its usefulness. A part of this depreciation expense is allotted to each fiscal period. In the case of Conner's Whitewater Adventures, the Equipment account has a balance of $51,300. Suppose we estimate that the equipment will have a useful life of seven years, with a trade-in (salvage) value of $8,292 at the end of that time. Using **straight-line depreciation**, we can allocate the cost of an asset, less any trade-in value, evenly over the useful life of the asset. Depreciation for one month is figured like this:

STEP 1. Cost − Trade-in (salvage) value = Full depreciation

$51,300 − $8,292 = $43,008 full depreciation

STEP 2. Full depreciation ÷ Number of years in the asset's useful life = Depreciation for one year

$43,008 full depreciation ÷ 7 years = $6,144 per year

STEP 3. Depreciation for one year ÷ 12 = Depreciation for one month

$6,144 per year ÷ 12 months = $512 per month

When depreciation is recorded, we do not subtract it directly from the asset account. In asset accounts, such as Equipment and Building, we must keep the original cost recorded in the account. Instead, a **contra account** is used. Such accounts are contrary to, or deducted from, other accounts and are used to provide more information to financial statement users. In this case, the amount of depreciation must be recorded in another account; that account is Accumulated Depreciation. If you were to record depreciation incorrectly by crediting the asset account, the balance of your asset account would eventually reach zero or the trade-in value, which is not correct. You would still have the equipment and need to maintain the original cost in the account. The credit should be to the contra-asset account, Accumulated Depreciation. Accumulated Depreciation, Equipment is contrary to, or a deduction from, Equipment.

Always record the adjusting entry for depreciation as a debit to Depreciation Expense (an income statement item) and a credit to Accumulated Depreciation (a balance sheet item), which increases both accounts. The adjustment in T account form would appear as follows:

Depreciation Expense, Equipment		Accumulated Depreciation, Equipment	
+	−	−	+
Adjusting 512			Adjusting 512

To show the accounts under their proper headings, let's look at the fundamental accounting equation. Brackets indicate that Accumulated Depreciation, Equipment is a deduction from the Equipment account. Note that the plus and minus signs are opposite.

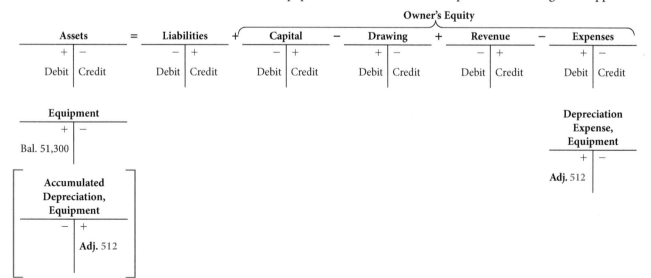

On the work sheet, Equipment (an asset) appears in the Balance Sheet Debit column. Accumulated Depreciation (a deduction from an asset) appears in the opposite column, which is the Balance Sheet Credit column.

Accumulated Depreciation, Equipment, as the title implies, is the total depreciation the company has taken since the original purchase of the asset. Rather than crediting the Equipment account, Conner's Whitewater Adventures uses a separate account to keep track of the total depreciation taken since it first acquired the asset. The maximum depreciation it could take would be the cost of the equipment, $51,300, less the trade-in value of $8,292. So for the first year, Accumulated Depreciation, Equipment will increase at the rate of $512 per month, assuming that no additional equipment has been purchased. For example, at the end of the second month, Accumulated Depreciation, Equipment will amount to $1,024 ($512 + $512).

On the balance sheet, the balance of Accumulated Depreciation is deducted from the balance of the related asset account, as illustrated on the following partial balance sheet for Conner's Whitewater Adventures. The net amount shown, $50,788, is referred to as the book value of the asset. Thus, **book value** (or **carrying value**) is the cost of an asset minus its accumulated depreciation ($51,300 − $512).

Conner's Whitewater Adventures
Partial Balance Sheet
June 30, 20--

Assets

Equipment	$51,300	
Less Accumulated Depreciation	512	$50,788

Wages Expense

The end of the fiscal period and the end of the employees' payroll period rarely fall on the same day. A diagram of the situation looks like this:

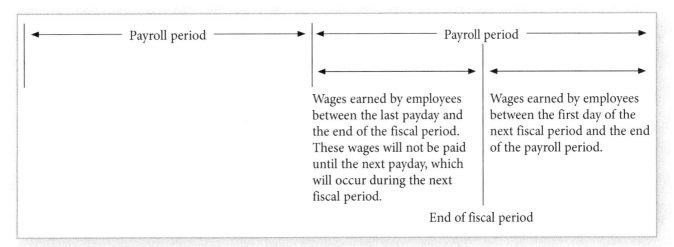

Because the last day of the fiscal period falls in the middle of the payroll period, we must split up the wages earned in that payroll period between the fiscal period just ended and the next fiscal period. We will use another company for this example.

Assume that Brown Company pays its employees $400 per day and that payday falls on Friday. The employees work a five-day week. When employees pick up their paychecks on Friday, the amount of the checks includes their wages for that day and for the preceding four days. Suppose that the last day of the fiscal period falls on Wednesday, December 31. The diagram on the next page illustrates this situation.

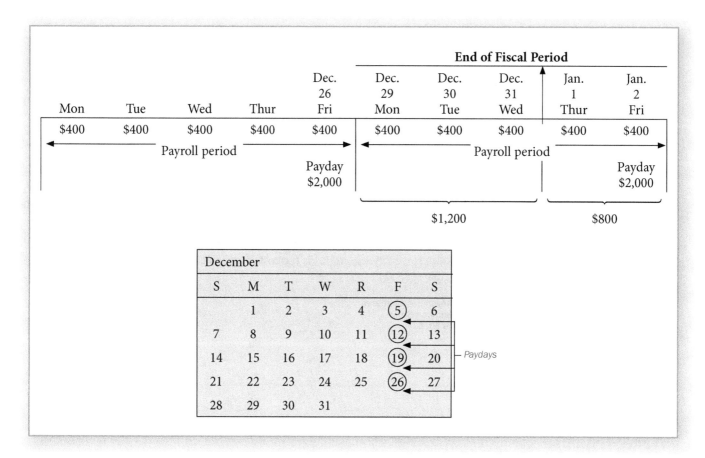

So that the Wages Expense account shows an accurate balance for the fiscal period, you need to add $1,200 for the cost of labor between the last payday, December 26, and the end of the year, December 31 ($400 for December 29; $400 for December 30; $400 for December 31). Because the $1,200 will not be paid at this time but is owed to the employees as of December 31, you also need to add $1,200 to Wages Payable, a liability account, because the company owes this amount to employees.

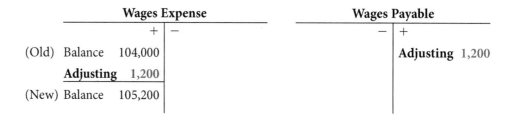

Returning to our illustration of Conner's Whitewater Adventures, the amount of wages that has been paid so far for the month of June is $2,360. However, the last payday was June 24. Between June 24 and the end of the month, Conner's Whitewater Adventures has determined that it owes an additional $472 in wages to its employees. The additional $472 will need to be added to the Wages Expense account and also the Wages Payable. It might be tempting to decrease cash in this adjustment, but cash is not used in this case because the wages have yet not been paid.

Accountants refer to this extra amount that has not been recorded at the end of the month as **accrued wages**. In accounting terms, **accrual** means recognition of an expense or a revenue that has been incurred (expense) or earned (revenue) but has not yet been recorded.

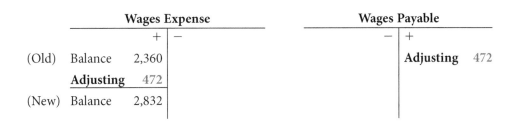

	Wages Expense				Wages Payable	
		+	−		−	+
(Old)	Balance	2,360				Adjusting 472
	Adjusting	472				
(New)	Balance	2,832				

> **Remember**
>
> In the adjusting entry for accrued wages, increase both the Wages Expense and the Wages Payable accounts.

MIXED ACCOUNTS

At this point, take special notice of the fact that each **adjusting entry contains an income statement account (revenue or expense) and a balance sheet account (asset, contra asset, or liability).** Accountants refer to these accounts as **mixed accounts**—accounts with balances that are partly income statement amounts and partly balance sheet amounts. The income statement and balance sheet accounts involved are separate accounts having a part of their name in common, such as Prepaid Insurance and Insurance Expense. Prepaid Insurance is recorded as $1,875 in the Trial Balance columns but is apportioned as $625 in Insurance Expense in the Income Statement columns and $1,250 in Prepaid Insurance in the Balance Sheet columns. In other words, portions of these trial balance amounts are recorded in each section.

Placement of Accounts on the Work Sheet

We now have to enter the adjustments on the work sheet, but before doing so, let's briefly discuss the Drawing and Accumulated Depreciation accounts, as well as net income, and their effect on the work sheet.

CAPITAL AND DRAWING ACCOUNT BALANCES

The Drawing account is a contra account (contrary to Capital). In the statement of owner's equity, Drawing is deducted from Capital. To show one account as a deduction from another, the plus and minus signs are switched. The T accounts look like this:

	J. Conner, Capital			J. Conner, Drawing	
	−	+		+	−
	Debit	Credit		Debit	Credit
		Balance		Balance	

The normal balance for the Capital account is recorded in the Credit columns of the Trial Balance, the Adjusted Trial Balance, and the Balance Sheet sections. The normal balance for the Drawing account is recorded in the Debit columns of the Trial Balance, the Adjusted Trial Balance, and the Balance Sheet sections.

EQUIPMENT AND ACCUMULATED DEPRECIATION, EQUIPMENT ACCOUNT BALANCES

The Accumulated Depreciation, Equipment account is a contra account (contrary to Equipment). On the balance sheet, Accumulated Depreciation, Equipment is deducted from Equipment. The T accounts look like this:

The normal balance for the Equipment account is recorded in the Debit columns of the Trial Balance, the Adjusted Trial Balance, and the Balance Sheet sections. The normal balance for the Accumulated Depreciation, Equipment account is recorded in the Credit columns of the Trial Balance, the Adjusted Trial Balance, and the Balance Sheet sections.

NET INCOME

Net income (or net loss) is the difference between revenue and expenses. It is used to balance the Income Statement columns; because revenue is normally larger than expenses, the balancing amount must be added to the expense side. Net income (or net loss) is also used to balance the Balance Sheet columns. On the statement of owner's equity, you add net income to the owner's beginning Capital balance. Because the Capital balance is located in the Balance Sheet Credit column, net income must also be added to that side. The following diagram shows these relationships:

	A	B	C	D	E	F	G	H	I	J	K
1					Conner's Whitewater Adventures						
2					Work Sheet						
3					For Month Ended June 30, 20--						
4											
5			TRIAL BALANCE		ADJUSTMENTS		ADJUSTED TRIAL BALANCE		INCOME STATEMENT		BALANCE SHEET	
6	ACCOUNT NAME	DEBIT	CREDIT	DEBIT	CREDIT	DEBIT	CREDIT	DEBIT	CREDIT	DEBIT	CREDIT
7		Assets	Accum. Depr.			Assets	Accum. Depr.			Assets	Accum. Depr.
8		+	+			+	+			+	+
9		Drawing	Liabilities			Drawing	Liabilities			Drawing	Liabilities
10		+	+			+	+				+
11		Expenses	Capital			Expenses	Capital	Expenses			Capital
12			+				+				
13			Revenue				Revenue		Revenue		
14		Total	Total			Total	Total	Total	Total	Total	Total
15	Net Income							(NI)			(NI)
16								Total	Total	Total	Total
17											
18								Totals equal each other.		Totals equal each other.	
19											

On the other hand, if expenses are larger than revenue, the result is a net loss. You must add net loss to the revenue side to balance the Income Statement columns. Also, because a net loss is deducted from the owner's beginning Capital balance, you must include net loss on the debit side of the Balance Sheet columns, thereby balancing these columns. To show this, let's look at the Income Statement and Balance Sheet columns diagrammed here.

		INCOME STATEMENT		BALANCE SHEET	
5					
6	ACCOUNT NAME	DEBIT	CREDIT	DEBIT	CREDIT
7				Assets	Accum. Depr.
8				+	+
9				Drawing	Liabilities
10					+
11		Expenses			Capital
12					
13			Revenue		
14		Total	Total	Total	Total
15	Net Loss	(NL) ←		→ (NL)	
16		Total =	Total	Total =	Total
17		Totals equal each other.		Totals equal each other.	
18					
19					
20					
21					

STEPS IN THE COMPLETION OF THE WORK SHEET

The recommended steps to complete the work sheet are as follows:

STEP 1. Complete the Trial Balance columns, total, and rule (single-underline before double-underlining totals).

STEP 2. Complete the Adjustments columns, total, and rule.

STEP 3. Complete the Adjusted Trial Balance columns, total, and rule.

STEP 4. Record balances in the Income Statement and Balance Sheet columns and total each column.

STEP 5. Record net income or net loss in the Income Statement columns by subtracting the smaller side from the larger side and adding the difference to the smaller side, total, and rule.

STEP 6. Record net income or net loss in the Balance Sheet columns by subtracting the smaller side from the larger side and adding the difference to the smaller side (the amount should be the same as the difference between the Income Statement column totals—if not, there is an error), total, and rule.

The work sheet can be prepared using a computer spreadsheet program, such as Microsoft Excel®, or the work sheet can be prepared manually. Whether the work sheet is prepared manually or on a computer, the columns must be completed, totaled, and ruled.

Remember

The Trial Balance columns are the same as in the Trial Balance presented in Chapter 3.

STEP 1: TRIAL BALANCE COLUMNS

Note that the trial balance in Figure 2 is the same trial balance presented earlier for Conner's Whitewater Adventures. You will be able to follow the completion of the entire work sheet for Conner's Whitewater Adventures in Figure 3.

STEP 2: ADJUSTMENTS COLUMNS

When we write the adjustments, we identify them as (a), (b), (c), and (d) to indicate the relationships between the debit and credit sides and the sequence of the individual adjusting entries. (See Figures 2 and 3.)

Note that Supplies Expense; Insurance Expense; Depreciation Expense, Equipment; Accumulated Depreciation, Equipment; and Wages Payable did not appear in the trial balance because there were no balances in the accounts at that time. We wrote them below the Trial Balance totals to complete the work sheet. In this chapter, the business is in its first accounting period. Therefore, these accounts had no balance until the end of the fiscal period adjustments, which means they were not in the trial balance prior to adjustments. After the first fiscal period, these accounts could have a balance and would be listed in the Trial Balance columns in the order of the chart of accounts.

Here is a brief review of the adjustments:

a. To record $460 worth of supplies used during June.
b. To record the $625 cost of insurance expired during June.
c. To record $512 depreciation for the month of June.
d. To record $472 of accrued wages owed at the end of June.

Again, we emphasize that the work sheet is strictly a tool used to gather all of the up-to-date information needed to prepare the financial statements. **The adjustments must still be recorded in the journal.**

Figure 2
Partial work sheet for Conner's Whitewater Adventures

	A	B	C	D	E
1					Conner's
2					
3		Step 1		Step 2	
4					
5		TRIAL BALANCE		ADJUSTMENTS	
6	ACCOUNT NAME	DEBIT	CREDIT	DEBIT	CREDIT
7			*Accum. Depr.*		
8		*A + Draw. + E*	*+ L + Cap. + R*		
9	Cash	55,890.00			
10	Accounts Receivable	4,250.00			
11	Supplies	675.00			(a) 460.00
12	Prepaid Insurance	1,875.00			(b) 625.00
13	Equipment	51,300.00			
14	Accounts Payable		3,425.00		
15	J. Conner, Capital		95,200.00		
16	J. Conner, Drawing	3,500.00			
17	Income from Tours		23,320.00		
18	Wages Expense	2,360.00		(d) 472.00	
19	Rent Expense	1,250.00			
20	Advertising Expense	620.00			
21	Utilities Expense	225.00			
22		121,945.00	121,945.00		
23	Supplies Expense			(a) 460.00	
24	Insurance Expense			(b) 625.00	
25	Depr. Exp., Equip.			(c) 512.00	
26	Accum. Depr., Equip.				(c) 512.00
27	Wages Payable				(d) 472.00
28				2,069.00	2,069.00

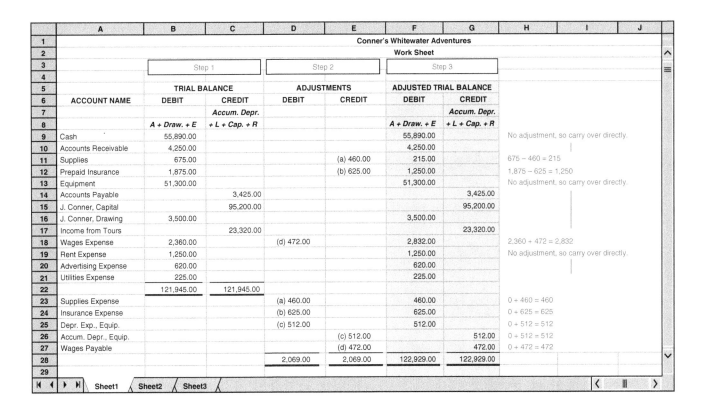

	A	B	C	D	E	F	G	H	I	J
1					Conner's Whitewater Adventures					
2					Work Sheet					
3			Step 1		Step 2		Step 3			
4										
5		TRIAL BALANCE		ADJUSTMENTS		ADJUSTED TRIAL BALANCE				
6	ACCOUNT NAME	DEBIT	CREDIT	DEBIT	CREDIT	DEBIT	CREDIT			
7			Accum. Depr.				Accum. Depr.			
8		A + Draw. + E	+ L + Cap. + R			A + Draw. + E	+ L + Cap. + R			
9	Cash	55,890.00				55,890.00		No adjustment, so carry over directly.		
10	Accounts Receivable	4,250.00				4,250.00				
11	Supplies	675.00			(a) 460.00	215.00		675 − 460 = 215		
12	Prepaid Insurance	1,875.00			(b) 625.00	1,250.00		1,875 − 625 = 1,250		
13	Equipment	51,300.00				51,300.00		No adjustment, so carry over directly.		
14	Accounts Payable		3,425.00				3,425.00			
15	J. Conner, Capital		95,200.00				95,200.00			
16	J. Conner, Drawing	3,500.00				3,500.00				
17	Income from Tours		23,320.00				23,320.00			
18	Wages Expense	2,360.00		(d) 472.00		2,832.00		2,360 + 472 = 2,832		
19	Rent Expense	1,250.00				1,250.00		No adjustment, so carry over directly.		
20	Advertising Expense	620.00				620.00				
21	Utilities Expense	225.00				225.00				
22		121,945.00	121,945.00							
23	Supplies Expense			(a) 460.00		460.00		0 + 460 = 460		
24	Insurance Expense			(b) 625.00		625.00		0 + 625 = 625		
25	Depr. Exp., Equip.			(c) 512.00		512.00		0 + 512 = 512		
26	Accum. Depr., Equip.				(c) 512.00		512.00	0 + 512 = 512		
27	Wages Payable				(d) 472.00		472.00	0 + 472 = 472		
28				2,069.00	2,069.00	122,929.00	122,929.00			
29										

Sheet1   Sheet2   Sheet3

STEP 3: ADJUSTED TRIAL BALANCE COLUMNS

Once the Adjustments columns are totaled and ruled, extend each Trial Balance amount, plus or minus any adjustment from the Adjustments columns, to the Adjusted Trial Balance columns as shown in Figure 3.

STEP 4: INCOME STATEMENT AND BALANCE SHEET COLUMNS

Extend the balances in the Adjusted Trial Balance columns to either the Income Statement or the Balance Sheet columns. (See Figure 4.)

STEP 5: NET INCOME OR NET LOSS—INCOME STATEMENT COLUMNS

Total each of the two Income Statement columns. Subtract the smaller side from the larger side, write the difference under the smaller Income Statement column total, and total and rule as shown in Figure 4.

If there is a net income, the credit side of the Income Statement columns will be larger than the debit side—more revenue than expenses. In this case, write *Net Income* in the Account Name column on the same line as the difference you calculated. If there is a net loss, the debit side of the Income Statement columns will be larger than the credit side—more expenses than revenue. In that case, write *Net Loss* in the Account Name column on the same line as the difference you calculated.

STEP 6: NET INCOME OR NET LOSS—BALANCE SHEET COLUMNS

Total the two Balance Sheet columns. Subtract the smaller side from the larger side, write the difference under the smaller Balance Sheet column total (the amount should equal the difference between the Income Statement column totals—if not, there is an error), and total and rule as shown in Figure 4.

Figure 3
Work sheet with steps of completion explained for Conner's Whitewater Adventures

Figure 4

Work sheet for Conner's Whitewater Adventures—Excel version

Conner's Whitewater Adventures
Work Sheet
For Month Ended June 30, 20–

ACCOUNT NAME	TRIAL BALANCE DEBIT (A + Draw. + E)	TRIAL BALANCE CREDIT (+L + Cap. + R / Accum. Depr.)	ADJUSTMENTS DEBIT	ADJUSTMENTS CREDIT	ADJUSTED TRIAL BALANCE DEBIT (A + Draw. + E)	ADJUSTED TRIAL BALANCE CREDIT (+L + Cap. + R / Accum. Depr.)	INCOME STATEMENT DEBIT (E)	INCOME STATEMENT CREDIT (R)	BALANCE SHEET DEBIT (A + Draw.)	BALANCE SHEET CREDIT (+L + Cap. / Accum. Depr.)
Cash	55,890.00				55,890.00				55,890.00	
Accounts Receivable	4,250.00				4,250.00				4,250.00	
Supplies	675.00			(a) 460.00	215.00				215.00	
Prepaid Insurance	1,875.00			(b) 625.00	1,250.00				1,250.00	
Equipment	51,300.00				51,300.00				51,300.00	
Accounts Payable		3,425.00				3,425.00				3,425.00
J. Conner, Capital		95,200.00				95,200.00				95,200.00
J. Conner, Drawing	3,500.00				3,500.00				3,500.00	
Income from Tours		23,320.00				23,320.00		23,320.00		
Wages Expense	2,360.00		(d) 472.00		2,832.00		2,832.00			
Rent Expense	1,250.00				1,250.00		1,250.00			
Advertising Expense	620.00				620.00		620.00			
Utilities Expense	225.00				225.00		225.00			
	121,945.00	121,945.00								
Supplies Expense			(a) 460.00		460.00		460.00			
Insurance Expense			(b) 625.00		625.00		625.00			
Depr. Exp., Equip.			(c) 512.00		512.00		512.00			
Accum. Depr., Equip.				(c) 512.00		512.00				512.00
Wages Payable				(d) 472.00		472.00				472.00
			2,069.00	2,069.00	122,929.00	122,929.00	6,524.00	23,320.00	116,405.00	99,609.00
Net Income							16,796.00			16,796.00
							23,320.00	23,320.00	116,405.00	116,405.00

Step 1 — In the Account name column, lists the accounts that have balances. Enter the account balances in the Trial Balance columns. Total and rule the columns.

Step 2 — Enter the adjustments, labeling each adjustment as (a), (b), (c), and so on. Total and rule the columns.
(a) Supplies used, $460.
(b) Insurance expired, $625.
(c) Depr. of equip., $512.
(d) Accrued wages, $472.

Step 3 — Carry amounts across from the Trial Balance columns, plus or minus any amounts appearing in the Adjustments columns. Total and rule the columns.

Step 4 — From the top of the Adjusted Trial Balance columns, go down line by line, carrying each amount over to the Income Statement or Balance Sheet columns. Total the columns.

Step 5 — Write Net Income or Net Loss in the Account Name column and the amount in the appropriate Income Statement column. Total and rule the columns.

Step 6 — Enter the net income or loss amount in the appropriate Balance Sheet column. Total, balance, and rule the columns.

Sheet1　Sheet2　Sheet3

Finding Errors in the Income Statement and Balance Sheet Columns

As you have seen, the amount of the net income or net loss must be recorded in both an Income Statement column and a Balance Sheet column. Suppose that after the net income is added to the Balance Sheet Credit column, the Balance Sheet columns are not equal. To find the error, follow this procedure:

STEP 1. Check that the amount of the net income or loss is recorded in the correct columns. For example, net income is placed in the Income Statement Debit column and the Balance Sheet Credit column.

STEP 2. Verify the addition of all columns.

STEP 3. Check that the appropriate amounts have been recorded in the Income Statement and Balance Sheet columns. For example, asset amounts should be listed in the Balance Sheet Debit column, expense amounts should be listed in the Income Statement Debit column, and so on.

STEP 4. Verify by adding or subtracting across each line that the amounts carried over from the Trial Balance columns through the Adjustments columns into the Adjusted Trial Balance columns are correct.

STEP 5. Verify that the correct amounts of the revenue and expense accounts are transferred to the Income Statement columns.

STEP 6. Verify that the correct amounts of assets, liabilities, and owner's equity accounts are transferred to the Balance Sheet columns.

Generally, one of these steps will expose the error.

JOURNALIZING ADJUSTING ENTRIES

To change the balance of a ledger account, you need a journal entry as evidence of the change. So far, we have been listing adjustments only in the Adjustments columns of the work sheet. The work sheet is not a journal, so we must journalize adjusting entries to update the ledger accounts. **Take the information for these entries directly from the Adjustments columns of the work sheet, debiting and crediting the same accounts and amounts in the journal entries.**

In the Description column of the general journal, write *Adjusting Entries* before you begin making these entries. This eliminates the need to write an explanation for each entry. The adjusting entries for Conner's Whitewater Adventures are shown in Figure 5 on page 182.

When you post the adjusting entries to the ledger accounts, write the abbreviation *Adj.* in the Item column of the ledger account. The adjusting entry for Prepaid Insurance is posted below the adjusting entries on page 182.

In the adjusted accounts for Conner's Whitewater Adventures, notice that the intent is to make sure that the expenses recorded match up or are reported with the revenues for the same period of time. In other words, for the month of June, we record all of the revenues for June and all of the expenses for June. Thus, the revenues and expenses for the same time period are matched. This is called the matching principle.

4 Journalize and post the adjusting entries.

Learning Objective

Figure 5
Adjusting entries for Conner's Whitewater Adventures

Remember

Each adjusting entry consists of an income statement account and a balance sheet account.

		GENERAL JOURNAL			Page 4
Date		Description	Post. Ref.	Debit	Credit
20--		Adjusting Entries			
June	30	Supplies Expense	513	4 6 0 00	
		Supplies	115		4 6 0 00
	30	Insurance Expense	516	6 2 5 00	
		Prepaid Insurance	117		6 2 5 00
	30	Depr. Expense, Equipment	517	5 1 2 00	
		Accum. Depr., Equipment	125		5 1 2 00
	30	Wages Expense	511	4 7 2 00	
		Wages Payable	222		4 7 2 00

ACCOUNT Prepaid Insurance　　　　　　　　　　　　　**ACCOUNT NO. 117**

Date	Item	Post. Ref.	Debit	Credit	Balance Debit	Balance Credit
20--						
June	10	2	1 8 7 5 00		1 8 7 5 00	
	30 Adj.	4		6 2 5 00	1 2 5 0 00	

ACCOUNT Insurance Expense　　　　　　　　　　　　**ACCOUNT NO. 516**

Date	Item	Post. Ref.	Debit	Credit	Balance Debit	Balance Credit
20--						
June	30 Adj.	4		6 2 5 00		6 2 5 00

In the Real World

Do large companies such as Rhapsody, a popular online music subscription service, need to make adjusting entries? You bet! All companies regardless of size are required to make adjusting entries so that their financial statements are reported accurately. Rhapsody makes similar adjusting entries to the ones we made in this chapter (for example, Prepaid Insurance, Depreciation, and Wages). So regardless of the size of the company, adjusting entries are an important part of the accounting cycle.

YOU Make the Call

Imagine that you have just been hired as an accounting clerk for a local tour bus company. Part of your job is to prepare adjusting entries prior to producing the financial statements. You have spent the week familiarizing yourself with the accounting system. You find the following preliminary adjusting notes left by the prior accounting clerk:

(a) The tour bus company pays weekly salaries of $606.65 for a five-day workweek. The end of the accounting period is on a Thursday. The amount of wages per day was computed to be $121.33.

(b) The depreciation for the buses using the straight-line method is $33,392.86 per year and $2,782.74 per month. (The buses cost $275,000, with an estimated useful life of seven years and a trade-in value of $41,250 at the end of that time.)

(c) The balance of the Prepaid Insurance account is $2,480, which covers one year. The amount of the adjusting entry for Insurance Expense for this one-month period is $206.67.

As the new accounting clerk, your job is to review these figures for accuracy and then record the appropriate adjusting entries in the general journal.

SOLUTION

(a) $606.65 ÷ 5 = $121.33
$121.33 × 4 days = $485.32 adjustment amount

(b) 1. $275,000 − $41,250 = $233,750 full depreciation
2. $233,750 full depreciation ÷ 7 years = $33,392.86 per year
3. $33,392.86 per year ÷ 12 months = $2,782.74 per month

(c) $2,480 per year ÷ 12 months = $206.67 per month

		GENERAL JOURNAL				Page ___
Date		Description	Post. Ref.	Debit		Credit
		Adjusting Entries				
	(a)	Wages Expense		4 8 5 32		
		Wages Payable				4 8 5 32
	(b)	Depreciation Expense, Equipment		2 7 8 2 74		
		Accumulated Depreciation, Equipment				2 7 8 2 74
	(c)	Insurance Expense		2 0 6 67		
		Prepaid Insurance				2 0 6 67

To: **Amy Roberts, CPA**
Subject: **Financial Statements Review**

Hi Amy,
I have completed the adjusting entries using the work sheet, recorded them in the general journal, and posted them to the ledger. I know we've talked before about financial statements, but I probably need a short review. Can you help?
Thanks,
Janie

To: **Janie Conner**
Subject: **RE: Financial Statements Review**

Hi Janie,
I am glad that you have the adjusting entries recorded in the general journal and also posted to the ledger. Now that the accounts are up to date, you are ready to prepare the financial statements. Remember, from what we talked about earlier, the income statement is prepared first, followed by the statement of owner's equity, and then the balance sheet. Let's review each of these statements so that you are ready to give them to the bank. Let me know if you need help.
Amy

Completion of the Financial Statements

Learning Objective

5 Prepare an income statement, a statement of owner's equity, and a balance sheet for a service business directly from the work sheet.

As we stated, the purpose of the work sheet is to help the accountant prepare the financial statements. Now that we have recorded the adjusting entries, we can use the work sheet to prepare the income statement, the statement of owner's equity, and the balance sheet. The figures for the financial statements are taken directly from the work sheet. These statements are shown in Figure 6.

Note that you record Accumulated Depreciation, Equipment in the asset section of the balance sheet as a direct deduction from Equipment. As we have said, accountants refer to this as a contra account because it is contrary to its companion asset account. The difference, $50,788, is called the book value or carrying value because it represents the cost of the asset after Accumulated Depreciation has been deducted.

When preparing the statement of owner's equity, remember to check the beginning balance of Capital against the balance shown in the Capital account in the general ledger. An additional investment may have been made during the fiscal period, and you need to report any such investment in the statement of owner's equity.

Conner's Whitewater Adventures
Income Statement
For Month Ended June 30, 20--

Revenue:		
Income from Tours		$23,320
Expenses:		
Wages Expense	$2,832	
Rent Expense	1,250	
Supplies Expense	460	
Advertising Expense	620	
Utilities Expense	225	
Insurance Expense	625	
Depreciation Expense, Equipment	512	
Total Expenses		6,524
Net Income		$16,796

Conner's Whitewater Adventures
Statement of Owner's Equity
For Month Ended June 30, 20--

J. Conner, Capital, June 1, 20--		$ 0
Investment during June	$ 95,200	
Net Income for June	16,796	
Subtotal	$111,996	
Less Withdrawals for June	3,500	
Increase in Capital		108,496
J. Conner, Capital, June 30, 20--		$108,496

Conner's Whitewater Adventures
Balance Sheet
June 30, 20--

Assets		
Cash		$ 55,890
Accounts Receivable		4,250
Supplies		215
Prepaid Insurance		1,250
Equipment	$51,300	
Less Accumulated Depreciation	512	50,788
Total Assets		$112,393
Liabilities		
Accounts Payable	$ 3,425	
Wages Payable	472	
Total Liabilities		$ 3,897
Owner's Equity		
J. Conner, Capital		108,496
Total Liabilities and Owner's Equity		$112,393

Figure 6
Financial statements for Conner's Whitewater Adventures

Remember

The columns shown on the financial statements do not represent Debit or Credit. Each column simply shows account balances. Amounts in these columns are either added or subtracted.

Remember

Total assets must always equal total liabilities and owner's equity.

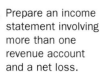

Income Statement Involving More Than One Revenue Account and a Net Loss

When an organization has more than one distinct source of revenue, a separate revenue account is set up for each source. See, for example, the income statement of Harris Miniature Golf presented in Figure 7. Also note that expenses are greater than revenues, resulting in a net loss.

Figure 7
Income statement for Harris Miniature Golf

Harris Miniature Golf Income Statement For Month Ended September 30, 20--		
Revenues:		
Admissions Fees	$2,624	
Concession Fees	1,512	
Total Revenues		$ 4,136
Expenses:		
Wages Expense	$3,123	
Supplies Expense	317	
Advertising Expense	1,000	
Rent Expense	1,900	
Miscellaneous Expense	128	
Total Expenses		6,468
Net Loss		$(2,332)

Statement of Owner's Equity with an Additional Investment and a Net Income

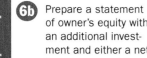

Any additional investment by the owner during the period covered by the financial statements is shown on the statement of owner's equity because such a statement should show everything that has affected the Capital account from the *beginning* until the *end* of the period covered by the financial statements. For example, in Figure 8, assume that the following information is true for L. A. Grand Company, which has a net income:

Balance of L. A. Grand, Capital, on April 1	$86,000
Additional investment by L. A. Grand on April 12	8,000
Net income for the month (from income statement)	6,200
Total withdrawals for the month	4,000

Figure 8
Statement of owner's equity for L. A. Grand Company

L. A. Grand Company Statement of Owner's Equity For Month Ended April 30, 20--		
L. A. Grand, Capital, April 1, 20--		$86,000
Investment during April	$ 8,000	
Net Income for April	6,200	
Subtotal	$14,200	
Less Withdrawals for April	4,000	
Increase in Capital		10,200
L. A. Grand, Capital, April 30, 20--		$96,200

Statement of Owner's Equity with an Additional Investment and a Net Loss

Assume the following for J. D. Ross Company, which has a net loss:

J. D. Ross, Capital, on Oct. 1	$75,000
Additional investment by J. D. Ross on Oct. 25	10,000
Net loss for the month (from income statement)	1,500
Total withdrawals for the month	5,100

The statement of owner's equity in Figure 9 shows this information. Notice that the net loss is subtracted from the additional investment during October.

J. D. Ross Company
Statement of Owner's Equity
For Month Ended October 31, 20--

J. D. Ross, Capital, October 1, 20--		$75,000
Investment during October	$10,000	
Net Loss for October	1,500	
Subtotal	$ 8,500	
Less Withdrawals for October	5,100	
Increase in Capital		3,400
J. D. Ross, Capital, October 31, 20--		$78,400

FYI

The information normally shown on the statement of owner's equity is sometimes included as part of the owner's equity section of the balance sheet in computerized general ledger systems.

Figure 9
Statement of owner's equity for J. D. Ross Company

Businesses with More Than One Depreciation Expense Account and More Than One Accumulated Depreciation Account

Figures 10 and 11 show the income statement and the balance sheet for Molen Veterinary Clinic. In Figure 11, note that the company has two assets subject to depreciation: Building and Equipment. In the financial statements, Depreciation Expense and Accumulated Depreciation must be listed for each asset.

 6c Prepare a balance sheet for a business having more than one accumulated depreciation account.

Learning Objective

Figure 10
Income statement for Molen Veterinary Clinic

Molen Veterinary Clinic
Income Statement
For Month Ended December 31, 20--

Revenue:		
Professional Fees	$332,300	
Boarding Fees	65,270	
Total Revenue		$397,570
Expenses:		
Salary Expense	$250,000	
Depreciation Expense, Building	19,450	
Depreciation Expense, Equipment	11,500	
Supplies Expense	11,380	
Insurance Expense	2,240	
Miscellaneous Expense	4,420	
Total Expenses		298,990
Net Income		$ 98,580

Figure 11
Balance sheet for Molen
Veterinary Clinic

Molen Veterinary Clinic		
Balance Sheet		
December 31, 20--		
Assets		
Cash		$ 21,320
Land		15,200
Building	$349,100	
Less Accumulated Depreciation	112,200	236,900
Equipment	$124,800	
Less Accumulated Depreciation	87,600	37,200
Total Assets		$310,620
Liabilities		
Accounts Payable		$ 7,400
Owner's Equity		
R. N. Molen, Capital		303,220
Total Liabilities and Owner's Equity		$310,620

Accounting with *QuickBooks*®

Adjusting Entries and Reports

Learning Objective	**1** Record adjusting entries in QuickBooks.

Learning Objectives

After you have completed this section, you will be able to do the following:

1 Record adjusting entries in QuickBooks.

2 View and print the adjusting journal entries.

3 View and print the adjusted trial balance.

4 Memorize transactions and reports.

Adjusting entries are recorded in the same manner as general journal entries. The only difference is that the *Adjusting Entry* box is checked in the journal entry screen as shown in Figure Q2.

Adjusting Entry (a) from page 178. As of June 30, supplies remaining totaled $215.

Remember that the Supplies account has a balance of $675, requiring an adjustment of $460 ($675 – $215) to the account.

To record adjusting entries, follow the steps in Figures Q1 and Q2.

STEP 1. Click the **Company** tab. Then select **Make General Journal Entries**.

Company	Customers	Vendors	Employees

Home Page
Company Snapshot
Calendar
Documents

Lead Center

Company Information...
Advanced Service Administration...
Set Up Users and Passwords
Customer Credit Card Protection...
Set Closing Date...

Planning & Budgeting
To Do List
Reminders
Alerts Manager

Chart of Accounts   Ctrl+A
Make General Journal Entries...
Manage Currency

Enter Vehicle Mileage...

Prepare Letters with Envelopes

Export Company File to QuickBooks Online

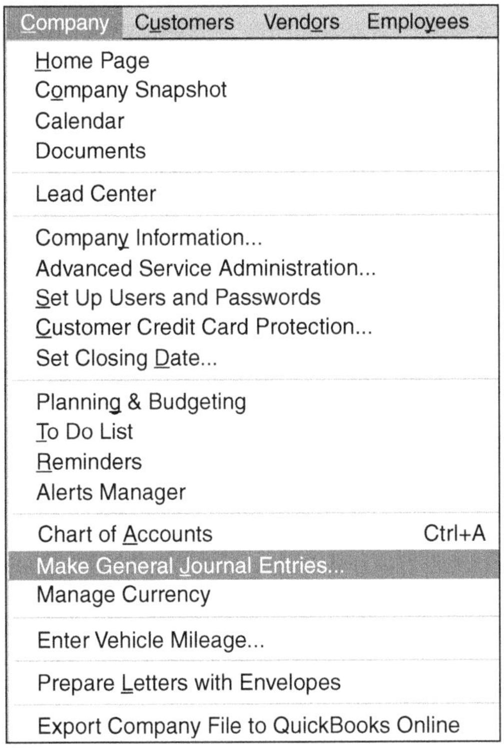

Figure Q1
Make general journal entries

QuickBooks Tip

Make General Journal Entries can also be accessed under Accountant.

STEP 2. Select or enter the **date**.
The date used for Figure Q2 (on the following page) is June 30, 20--.

STEP 3. Enter the **Entry No**.
In Figure Q2, ADJ20--.06a is used for the *Entry No.* The journal entry and adjusting journal entry numbering system can vary by company. QuickBooks has the option to automatically assign the *Entry No.*, or a company may choose to use its own system. For Conner's Whitewater Adventures, the *Entry No.* used for this adjusting entry is ADJ (for adjustment), followed by the year, then the month, and finally the adjustment transaction (a).

STEP 4. Check the **Adjusting Entry** box.

STEP 5. Select the **account to be debited**, enter the **debit amount** and then enter the **description in the memo field**.

STEP 6. Select the **account to be credited**. Then enter the **credit amount**.
The memo field should automatically appear with the information from Step 5. If not, manually enter the description in the credited account memo field.

STEP 7. Select **Save & Close** (to save the transaction and stop recording entries) or **Save & New** (to save the transaction and continue recording entries).

QuickBooks Tip

The memo field provides descriptive information in the journal, as well as other reports.

Figure Q2
Record adjusting entries in the general journal

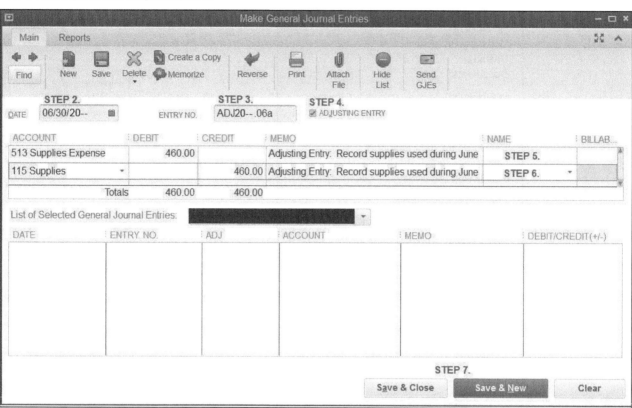

Learning Objective (2)   View and print the adjusting journal entries.

To view and print the adjusting journal entries, follow the steps in Figures Q3 and Figure Q4 (on the next page), after recording the entries.

STEP 1. Select **Reports, Accountant & Taxes**, and then **Adjusting Journal Entries**.

STEP 2. Adjust the **From:** and **To:** dates and click **Refresh**.

STEP 3. To print the report, click the **Print** button.

Figure Q4 shows the adjusting journal entries report for Conner's Whitewater Adventures.

Figure Q4
View adjusting journal entries report

Conner's Whitewater Adventures					
Adjusting Journal Entries					
June 30, 20–					
Date	Num	Memo	Account	Debit	Credit
▸ 06/30/20–	ADJ2013.06a	Adjusting Entry: Record supplies used during June	513 Supplies Expense	460.00	◂
		Adjusting Entry: Record supplies used during June	115 Supplies		460.00
				460.00	460.00
06/30/20–	ADJ2013.06b	Adjusting Entry: Record insurance expired during June	516 Insurance Expense	625.00	
		Adjusting Entry: Record insurance expired during June	117 Prepaid Insurance		625.00
				625.00	625.00
06/30/20–	ADJ2013.06c	Adjusting Entry: Depreciation for the month of June	517 Depreciation Expense, Equip.	512.00	
		Adjusting Entry: Depreciation for the month of June	125 Accum. Depr., Equipment		512.00
				512.00	512.00
06/30/20–	ADJ2013.06d	Adjusting Entry: Accrued wages owned at the end of June	511 Wages Expense	472.00	
		Adjusting Entry: Accrued wages owned at the end of June	222 Wages Payable		472.00
				472.00	472.00
TOTAL				2,069.00	2,069.00

ACCOUNTING WITH QuickBooks®

Learning Objective   View and print the adjusted trial balance.

To view and print the adjusted trial balance, follow the steps in Figures Q5 and Q6.

STEP 1. Select **Reports, Accountant & Taxes**, and then **Adjusted Trial Balance**.

Figure Q5
View the adjusted trial balance

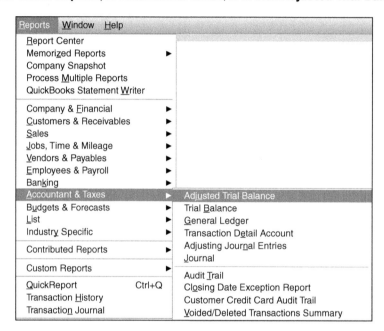

STEP 2. Adjust the **From:** and **To:** dates and click **Refresh**.

STEP 3. To print the report, click the **Print** button.

Figure Q6 shows the adjusted trial balance report for Conner's Whitewater Adventures.

Figure Q6
Adjusted trial balance report

	Unadjusted Balance		Adjustments		Adjusted Balance	
	Debit	Credit	Debit	Credit	Debit	Credit
115 Supplies				460.00		460.00
117 Prepaid Insurance				625.00		625.00
124 Equipment: 125 Accum. Depr., Equipment				512.00		512.00
222 Wages Payable				472.00		472.00
511 Wages Expenses			472.00		472.00	
513 Supplies Expenses			460.00		460.00	
516 Insurance Expenses			625.00		625.00	
517 Depreciation Expenses, Equipment			512.00		512.00	
Total	0.00	0.00	2,069.00	2,069.00	2,069.00	2,069.00

Conner's Whitewater Adventures
Adjusted Trial Balance
June 30, 20--

Learning Objective   Memorize transactions and reports.

MEMORIZE TRANSACTIONS IN THE GENERAL JOURNAL

When a transaction occurs on a regular basis, it is helpful to save or memorize the transaction to retrieve for future use. To memorize a transaction in the general journal, simply click on *Memorize* after entering the information. See Figure Q7.

Figure Q7
Memorize transactions in the general journal

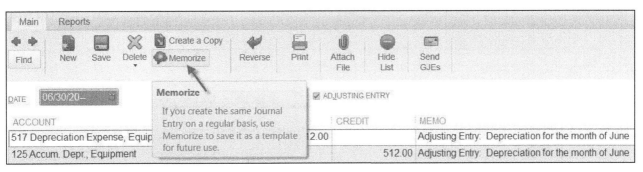

MEMORIZE REPORTS

When reports are used on a regular basis, it is also helpful to save or memorize the reports for future use. To memorize reports, follow the steps in either Figures Q8 or Q9.

STEP 1. After preparing the report, click the **Memorize** tab in the report screen.

STEP 2. Enter the **report name**.

STEP 3. Check the box **Save in Memorized Report Group**.

STEP 4. Select the **classification** where you want to save your report.

STEP 5. Click **OK**.

Figure Q8
Memorize reports

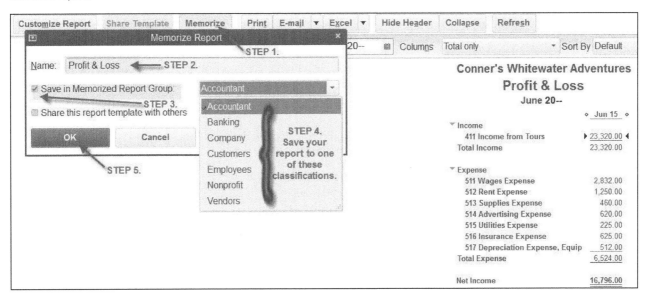

Unless disabled, QuickBooks also has a feature to remind users about memorizing reports when leaving the report area. Upon exiting any report, a message **Would you like to memorize this report?** will appear. To memorize the report, click Y̲es and follow the steps in Figure Q8. To exit the report without memorizing it, click N̲o.

Figure Q9
Memorize report prompt

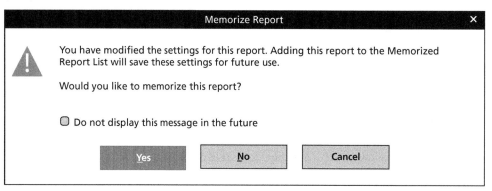

Chapter Review

Study and Practice

Learning Objective   **1**   *Define* fiscal period *and* fiscal year and explain the accounting cycle.

A **fiscal period** is any period of time covering a complete accounting cycle. A **fiscal year** consists of 12 consecutive months. The accounting cycle represents the sequence of steps in the accounting process completed during the fiscal period.

 PRACTICE EXERCISE 1

Which of the following would be considered a fiscal year?

(a) July 1, 20-- to June 30, 20--
(b) October 1, 20-- to August 31, 20--
(c) April 1, 20-- to January 31, 20--
(d) January 1, 20-- to December 31, 20--

PRACTICE EXERCISE 1 • SOLUTION

(a) and (d)

2 List the classifications of the accounts that occupy each column of a ten-column work sheet.

Trial Balance Debit	Assets + Drawing + Expenses
Trial Balance Credit	Accum. Depr. + Liabilities + Capital + Revenue
Adjusted Trial Balance Debit	Assets + Drawing + Expenses
Adjusted Trial Balance Credit	Accum. Depr. + Liabilities + Capital + Revenue
Income Statement Debit	Expenses
Income Statement Credit	Revenue
Balance Sheet Debit	Assets + Drawing
Balance Sheet Credit	Accum. Depr. + Liabilities + Capital

PRACTICE EXERCISE 2

Using a ten-column work sheet, list the classifications of accounts that are found in each column, with the exception of the Adjustments columns (Trial Balance, Adjusted Trial Balance, Income Statement, and Balance Sheet).

PRACTICE EXERCISE 2 • SOLUTION

	A	B	C	D	E	F	G	H	I	J	K
4											
5		TRIAL BALANCE		ADJUSTMENTS		ADJUSTED TRIAL BALANCE		INCOME STATEMENT		BALANCE SHEET	
6	ACCOUNT NAME	DEBIT	CREDIT	DEBIT	CREDIT	DEBIT	CREDIT	DEBIT	CREDIT	DEBIT	CREDIT
7		Assets	Accum. Depr.			Assets	Accum. Depr.			Assets	Accum. Depr.
8		Drawing	Liabilities			Drawing	Liabilities			Drawing	Liabilities
9		Expenses	Capital			Expenses	Capital	Expenses			Capital
10			Revenue				Revenue		Revenue		
11											

Sheet1 Sheet2 Sheet3

3 Complete a work sheet for a service enterprise, involving adjustments for supplies, expired insurance, depreciation, and accrued wages.

Adjustment for supplies used: debit Supplies Expense and credit Supplies.
Adjustment for expired insurance: debit Insurance Expense and credit Prepaid Insurance.
Adjustment for **depreciation**: debit Depreciation Expense and credit Accumulated Depreciation.
Adjustment for accrued wages: debit Wages Expense and credit Wages Payable.

PRACTICE EXERCISE 3

Complete the work sheet on page 196 for Fun and Games for the month of September. Adjustment information:

(a) Supplies used during September, $500.

(b) Insurance expired during September, $175.

(c) Depreciation of equipment for the month of September, $540.

(d) Accrued wages owed at the end of September, $260.

PRACTICE EXERCISE 3 • SOLUTION

See the completed work sheet on page 197.

Fun and Games
Work Sheet
For Month Ended September 30, 20–

ACCOUNT NAME	TRIAL BALANCE		ADJUSTMENTS		ADJUSTED TRIAL BALANCE		INCOME STATEMENT		BALANCE SHEET	
	DEBIT	CREDIT	DEBIT	CREDIT	DEBIT	CREDIT	DEBIT	CREDIT	DEBIT	CREDIT
Cash	24,770.00									
Accounts Receivable	5,750.00									
Supplies	630.00									
Prepaid Insurance	2,100.00									
Equipment	36,000.00									
Accum. Depr., Equip.		540.00								
Accounts Payable		3,985.00								
J. Jay, Capital		54,075.00								
J. Jay, Drawing	5,000.00									
Income from Services		21,000.00								
Wages Expense	2,670.00									
Rent Expense	1,950.00									
Advertising Expense	450.00									
Utilities Expense	280.00									
	79,600.00	79,600.00								
Supplies Expense										
Insurance Expense										
Depr. Exp., Equip.										
Wages Payable										
Net Income										

Sheet1 | Sheet2 | Sheet3

Fun and Games
Work Sheet
For Month Ended September 30, 20–

ACCOUNT NAME	TRIAL BALANCE DEBIT	TRIAL BALANCE CREDIT	ADJUSTMENTS DEBIT	ADJUSTMENTS CREDIT	ADJUSTED TRIAL BALANCE DEBIT	ADJUSTED TRIAL BALANCE CREDIT	INCOME STATEMENT DEBIT	INCOME STATEMENT CREDIT	BALANCE SHEET DEBIT	BALANCE SHEET CREDIT
Cash	24,770.00				24,770.00				24,770.00	
Accounts Receivable	5,750.00				5,750.00				5,750.00	
Supplies	630.00			(a) 500.00	130.00				130.00	
Prepaid Insurance	2,100.00			(b) 175.00	1,925.00				1,925.00	
Equipment	36,000.00				36,000.00				36,000.00	
Accum. Depr., Equip.		540.00		(c) 540.00		1,080.00				1,080.00
Accounts Payable		3,985.00				3,985.00				3,985.00
J. Jay, Capital		54,075.00				54,075.00				54,075.00
J. Jay, Drawing	5,000.00				5,000.00				5,000.00	
Income from Services		21,000.00				21,000.00		21,000.00		
Wages Expense	2,670.00		(d) 260.00		2,930.00		2,930.00			
Rent Expense	1,950.00				1,950.00		1,950.00			
Advertising Expense	450.00				450.00		450.00			
Utilities Expense	280.00				280.00		280.00			
	79,600.00	79,600.00								
Supplies Expense			(a) 500.00		500.00		500.00			
Insurance Expense			(b) 175.00		175.00		175.00			
Depr. Exp., Equip.			(c) 540.00		540.00		540.00			
Wages Payable				(d) 260.00		260.00				260.00
			1,475.00	1,475.00	80,400.00	80,400.00	6,825.00	21,000.00	73,575.00	59,400.00
Net Income							14,175.00			14,175.00
							21,000.00	21,000.00	73,575.00	73,575.00

Sheet1 | Sheet2 | Sheet3

Learning Objective

 4 Journalize and post the adjusting entries.

Adjustments are a way of updating the ledger accounts. They are determined after the trial balance has been prepared. To change the balance of the ledger accounts, **adjusting entries** are needed in the general journal as evidence of the changes. The information for these entries are taken directly from the Adjustments columns of the work sheet, debiting and crediting the same accounts and amounts in the journal entries. Therefore, each adjusting entry consists of an income statement account and a balance sheet account. When the adjusting entries are posted to the ledger accounts, the abbreviation *Adj.* is written in the Item column of the ledger account.

4 PRACTICE EXERCISE 4

Journalize and post the adjusting entries for Fun and Games from Practice Exercise 3.

PRACTICE EXERCISE 4 • SOLUTION

GENERAL JOURNAL											Page 4		
Date		Description	Post. Ref.	Debit					Credit				
20--		Adjusting Entries											
Sept.	30	Supplies Expense	513	5	0	0	00						
		Supplies	115						5	0	0	00	
	30	Insurance Expense	516	1	7	5	00						
		Prepaid Insurance	117						1	7	5	00	
	30	Depr. Expense, Equipment	517	5	4	0	00						
		Accum. Depr., Equipment	125						5	4	0	00	
	30	Wages Expense	511	2	6	0	00						
		Wages Payable	222						2	6	0	00	

ACCOUNT Supplies   **ACCOUNT NO. 115**

Date		Item	Post. Ref.	Debit				Credit				Balance Debit				Balance Credit		
20--																		
Sept.	30	Bal.		6	3	0	00					6	3	0	00			
		Adj.						5	0	0	00	1	3	0	00			

ACCOUNT Prepaid Insurance   **ACCOUNT NO. 117**

Date		Item	Post. Ref.	Debit				Credit				Balance Debit				Balance Credit		
20--																		
Sept.	15		2	2	1	0	0	00				2	1	0	0	00		
	30	Adj.	4					1	7	5	00	1	9	2	5	00		

ACCOUNT Accumulated Depreciation, Equipment **ACCOUNT NO. 125**

Date		Item	Post. Ref.	Debit	Credit	Balance Debit	Balance Credit
20--							
Sept.		Bal.			5 4 0 00		5 4 0 00
	30	Adj.	4		5 4 0 00		1 0 8 0 00

ACCOUNT Wages Payable **ACCOUNT NO. 222**

Date		Item	Post. Ref.	Debit	Credit	Balance Debit	Balance Credit
20--							
Sept.	30	Adj.	4		2 6 0 00		2 6 0 00

ACCOUNT Wages Expense **ACCOUNT NO. 511**

Date		Item	Post. Ref.	Debit	Credit	Balance Debit	Balance Credit
20--							
Sept.	15		2	2 6 7 0 00		2 6 7 0 00	
	30	Adj.	4	2 6 0 00		2 9 3 0 00	

ACCOUNT Supplies Expense **ACCOUNT NO. 513**

Date		Item	Post. Ref.	Debit	Credit	Balance Debit	Balance Credit
20--							
Sept.	30	Adj.	4	5 0 0 00		5 0 0 00	

ACCOUNT Insurance Expense **ACCOUNT NO. 516**

Date		Item	Post. Ref.	Debit	Credit	Balance Debit	Balance Credit
20--							
Sept.	30	Adj.	4	1 7 5 00		1 7 5 00	

ACCOUNT Depreciation Expense, Equipment **ACCOUNT NO. 517**

Date		Item	Post. Ref.	Debit	Credit	Balance Debit	Balance Credit
20--							
Sept.	30	Adj.	4	5 4 0 00		5 4 0 00	

5 Prepare an income statement, a statement of owner's equity, and a balance sheet for a service business directly from the work sheet.

Learning Objective

The income statement is prepared directly from the amounts listed in the Income Statement Debit and Credit columns. The net income should equal the net income previously determined on the **work sheet**. For the statement of owner's equity, use the amount of the beginning capital listed in the Balance Sheet Credit column after checking the general ledger for any additional investment(s), the amount of the net income from the Balance Sheet Credit column, and the amount of Drawing from the Balance Sheet Debit column. Prepare the balance sheet directly from the amounts listed in the Balance Sheet Debit and Credit columns (except Drawing and Capital).

PRACTICE EXERCISE 5

Prepare an income statement, a statement of owner's equity, and a balance sheet for Fun and Games using the information from Practice Exercise 3.

PRACTICE EXERCISE 5 • SOLUTION

Fun and Games Income Statement For Month Ended September 30, 20--		
Revenue:		
Income from Services		$21,000
Expenses:		
Wages Expense	$2,930	
Rent Expense	1,950	
Supplies Expense	500	
Advertising Expense	450	
Utilities Expense	280	
Insurance Expense	175	
Depreciation Expense, Equipment	540	
Total Expenses		6,825
Net Income		$14,175

Fun and Games Statement of Owner's Equity For Month Ended September 30, 20--		
J. Jay, Capital, September 1, 20--		$54,075
Investment during September	$ 0	
Net Income for September	14,175	
Subtotal	$14,175	
Less Withdrawals for September	5,000	
Increase in Capital		9,175
J. Jay, Capital, September 30, 20--		$63,250

Fun and Games
Balance Sheet
September 30, 20--

Assets

Cash		$24,770
Accounts Receivable		5,750
Supplies		130
Prepaid Insurance		1,925
Equipment	$36,000	
Less Accumulated Depreciation	1,080	34,920
Total Assets		$67,495

Liabilities

Accounts Payable	$ 3,985	
Wages Payable	260	
Total Liabilities		$ 4,245

Owner's Equity

J. Jay, Capital		63,250
Total Liabilities and Owner's Equity		$67,495

6 Prepare (a) an income statement involving more than one revenue account and a net loss, (b) a statement of owner's equity with an additional investment and either a net income or a net loss, and (c) a balance sheet for a business having more than one accumulated depreciation account.

Learning Objective

(a) An income statement containing more than one revenue account requires an additional line for each type of revenue, followed by a total amount of revenue.

(b) A statement of owner's equity involving an additional investment requires a line for each additional investment beneath the beginning capital amount, followed by a total amount of investment.

(c) Businesses that have more than one type of asset subject to depreciation must show a separate account for each asset on the balance sheet.

6a **PRACTICE EXERCISE 6a**

Using the following information, prepare an income statement for the month of September for The Swim Shack:

Depreciation Expense, Equipment	$ 525
Income from Concessions	4,000
Income from Service	1,500
Insurance Expense	200
Rent Expense	1,950
Utilities Expense	790
Wages Expense	3,580
Supplies Expense	100

PRACTICE EXERCISE 6a • SOLUTION

The Swim Shack
Income Statement
For Month Ended September 30, 20--

Revenue:		
Income from Concessions	$4,000	
Income from Services	1,500	
Total Revenue		$ 5,500
Expenses:		
Wages Expense	$3,580	
Rent Expense	1,950	
Supplies Expense	100	
Utilities Expense	790	
Insurance Expense	200	
Depreciation Expense, Equipment	525	
Total Expenses		7,145
Net Loss		$(1,645)

6b **PRACTICE EXERCISE 6b**

Using the following information, prepare a statement of owner's equity for the month of July for Stanley's Computers and Electronics.

P. Stanley, Capital, on July 1	$205,077
Additional investment by P. Stanley on July 21	15,500
Net loss for the month (from income statement)	1,850
Total withdrawals for the month	3,500

PRACTICE EXERCISE 6b • SOLUTION

Stanley's Computers and Electronics
Statement of Owner's Equity
For Month Ended July 31, 20--

P. Stanley, Capital, July 1, 20--		$205,077
Investment during July	$15,500	
Net Loss for July	1,850	
Subtotal	$13,650	
Less Withdrawals for July	3,500	
Increase in Capital		10,150
P. Stanley, Capital, July 31, 20--		$215,227

PRACTICE EXERCISE 6c

Using the following information, prepare a year-end balance sheet for Moreland Clinic as of December 31.

Accounts Payable	$ 7,380
Accumulated Depreciation, Building	112,200
Accumulated Depreciation, Equipment	87,600
Building	339,100
Cash	31,345
Equipment	114,800
Land	25,000
Supplies	175
W. Moreland, Capital	303,240

PRACTICE EXERCISE 6c • SOLUTION

Moreland Clinic
Balance Sheet
December 31, 20--

Assets		
Cash		$ 31,345
Supplies		175
Land		25,000
Building	$339,100	
Less Accumulated Depreciation	112,200	226,900
Equipment	$114,800	
Less Accumulated Depreciation	87,600	27,200
Total Assets		$310,620
Liabilities		
Accounts Payable		$ 7,380
Owner's Equity		
W. Moreland, Capital		303,240
Total Liabilities and Owner's Equity		$310,620

Glossary

Accounting cycle The sequence of steps in the accounting process completed during the fiscal period. *(p. 167)*

Accrual Recognition of an expense or a revenue that has been incurred or earned but has not yet been recorded. *(p. 175)*

Accrued wages Unpaid wages owed to employees for the time between the end of the last pay period and the end of the fiscal period. *(p. 175)*

Adjusting entries Entries that bring the books up to date at the end of the fiscal period. *(p. 181)*

Adjustments Internal transactions that bring ledger accounts up to date as a planned part of the accounting procedure. *(p. 170)*

Book value or carrying value The cost of an asset minus the accumulated depreciation. *(p. 173)*

Contra account An account that is contrary to, or a deduction from, another account; for example,

Accumulated Depreciation, Equipment is listed as a deduction from Equipment. *(p. 172)*

Depreciation An expense based on the expectation that an asset will gradually decline in usefulness due to time, wear and tear, or obsolescence; the cost of the asset is therefore spread out over its estimated useful life. A part of depreciation expense is apportioned to each fiscal period. *(p. 171)*

Fiscal period Any period of time covering a complete accounting cycle, generally consisting of 12 consecutive months. *(p. 167)*

Fiscal year A fiscal period consisting of 12 consecutive months. *(p. 167)*

Matching principle The principle that the expenses for one time period are matched up with the related revenues for the same time period. *(p. 181)*

Mixed accounts Certain accounts that appear on the trial balance with balances that are partly income statement amounts and partly balance sheet amounts—for example, Prepaid Insurance and Insurance Expense. *(p. 175)*

Straight-line depreciation A means of calculating depreciation in which the cost of an asset, less any trade-in value, is allocated evenly over the useful life of the asset. *(p. 171)*

Work sheet A working paper used by accountants to record necessary adjustments and provide up-to-date account balances needed to prepare the financial statements. *(p. 167)*

Quiz Yourself

_____ 1. The _____ represents the sequence of steps in the accounting process.
   a. fiscal year
   b. fiscal period
   c. accounting cycle
   d. work sheet

_____ 2. The _____ is a working paper used by accountants to record necessary adjustments and provide up-to-date account balances needed to prepare the financial statements.
   a. journal
   b. balance sheet
   c. accounting cycle
   d. work sheet

_____ 3. On the work sheet, assets are recorded in which of the following columns?
   a. Trial Balance, Credit
   b. Income Statement, Debit
   c. Balance Sheet, Debit
   d. Adjusted Trial Balance, Credit

_____ 4. Rainy Day Services had $430 of supplies reported on its unadjusted trial balance as of March 31. During the month of March, Rainy Day Services used $175 worth of supplies. What is the entry to adjust supplies?

   a. Supplies Expense   175
         Cash   175
   b. Supplies   430
         Supplies Expense   430
   c. Supplies Expense   255
         Supplies   255
   d. Supplies Expense   175
         Supplies   175

_____ 5. On the work sheet, Accumulated Depreciation, Equipment would be recorded in which of the following columns?
   a. Adjusted Trial Balance, Credit
   b. Income Statement, Debit
   c. Balance Sheet, Debit
   d. Income Statement, Credit

_____ 6. The _____ requires that expenses be matched up with revenue for the same period of time.
   a. matching principle
   b. expense principle
   c. revenue recognition principle
   d. separate entity concept

_____ 7. Accumulated Depreciation, Equipment is reported
   a. on the income statement as an expense.
   b. on the balance sheet as an addition to total assets.
   c. on the income statement as a revenue.
   d. on the balance sheet as a subtraction from the related asset account.

Answers:
1. c 2. d 3. c 4. d 5. a 6. a 7. d

Review It with **QuickBooks**

_____ 1. Adjusting entries are recorded in the same manner as general journal entries, except for
   a. the point of entry to the general journal is different.
   b. the account name must include adjusting entry.
   c. the box marked *Adjusting Entry* is checked.
   d. All of the above

_____ 2. How is the Entry No. field in QuickBooks completed?
   a. QuickBooks can automatically assign the number.
   b. The company can have its own numbering system.
   c. Both a and b
   d. Neither a nor b

_____ 3. The Adjusted Trial Balance report is located under _____ in QuickBooks.
   a. Company & Financial
   b. Accountant & Taxes
   c. Custom Reports
   d. All of the above

_____ 4. Which transactions and reports should be memorized in QuickBooks?
   a. Those that occur one time
   b. Those that occur every five years
   c. Those that occur on a regular basis
   d. Due to security concerns, companies should never memorize transactions or reports.

Answers:
1. c   2. c   3. b   4. c

Chapter Assignments

Discussion Questions

1. What is the purpose of a work sheet?
2. What is the purpose of adjusting entries?
3. What is a mixed account? A contra account? Give an example of each.
4. In which column of the work sheet—Income Statement (IS) or Balance Sheet (BS)— would the adjusted balances of the following accounts appear?

Account	IS or BS?	Account	IS or BS?
a. Prepaid Insurance		e. Accumulated Depreciation, Equipment	
b. Wages Expense		f. J. Karl, Drawing	
c. Wages Payable		g. Insurance Expense	
d. Income from Services		h. Depreciation Expense, Equipment	

5. Why is it necessary to make an adjustment if wages for work performed for the pay period Monday through Friday are paid on Friday and the accounting period ends on a Wednesday?
6. Define depreciation as it relates to a van you bought for your business.
7. Define an internal transaction and provide an example.
8. Why is it necessary to journalize and post adjusting entries?

Exercises

Practice Exercise 2

EXERCISE 4-1 List the following classifications of accounts in all of the columns in which they appear on the work sheet, with the exception of the Adjustments columns. (Example: Assets)

Assets   Capital
Accumulated Depreciation   Drawing
   (with previous balance)   Revenue
Liabilities   Expenses

Write *Net Income* in the appropriate columns.

	A	B	C	D	E	F	G	H	I	J	K
4											
5		TRIAL BALANCE		ADJUSTMENTS		ADJUSTED TRIAL BALANCE		INCOME STATEMENT		BALANCE SHEET	
6	ACCOUNT NAME	DEBIT	CREDIT	DEBIT	CREDIT	DEBIT	CREDIT	DEBIT	CREDIT	DEBIT	CREDIT
7		Assets				Assets				Assets	
8											
9											
10											
11											
12											
13											
14											
15	Net Income										

Sheet1 Sheet2 Sheet3

Practice Exercise 2

EXERCISE 4-2 Classify each of the accounts listed below as assets (A), liabilities (L), owner's equity (OE), revenue (R), or expenses (E). Indicate the normal debit or credit balance of each account. Indicate whether each account will appear in the Income Statement columns (IS) or the Balance Sheet columns (BS) of the work sheet. Item 0 is given as an example.

Account	Classification	Normal Balance	IS or BS Columns
0. Example: Wages Expense	E	Debit	IS
a. Prepaid Insurance			
b. Accounts Payable			
c. Wages Payable			
d. T. Bristol, Capital			
e. Accumulated Depreciation, Building			
f. T. Bristol, Drawing			
g. Rental Income			
h. Equipment			
i. Depreciation Expense, Equipment			
j. Supplies Expense			

LO 3

EXERCISE 4-3 Place a check mark next to any account(s) requiring adjustment. Explain why those accounts must be adjusted.

✓	Account Name (in trial balance order)	Reason for Adjusting This Account
	a. Cash	
	b. Prepaid Insurance	
	c. Equipment	
	d. Accumulated Depreciation, Equipment	
	e. Wages Payable	
	f. R. Wesley, Capital	
	g. R. Wesley, Drawing	
	h. Wages Expense	

LO 3

Practice Exercise 3

EXERCISE 4-4 A partial work sheet for Marge's Place is shown below. Prepare the following adjustments on this work sheet for the month ended June 30, 20--.
a. Expired or used-up insurance, $450.
b. Depreciation expense on equipment, $750. (Remember to credit the Accumulated Depreciation account for equipment, not Equipment.)
c. Wages accrued or earned since the last payday, $380 (owed and to be paid on the next payday).
d. Supplies used, $110.

	A	B	C	D	E
1	Marge's Place				
2	Work Sheet				
3	For Month Ended June 30, 20--				
4					
5		TRIAL BALANCE		ADJUSTMENTS	
6	ACCOUNT NAME	DEBIT	CREDIT	DEBIT	CREDIT
7	Cash	4,370.00			
8	Supplies	250.00			
9	Prepaid Insurance	1,800.00			
10	Equipment	4,880.00			
11	Accumulated Depreciation, Equipment		1,350.00		
12	Accounts Payable		2,539.00		
13	M. Benson, Capital		4,544.00		
14	M. Benson, Drawing	2,000.00			
15	Income from Services		6,937.00		
16	Rent Expense	1,086.00			
17	Supplies Expense	256.00			
18	Wages Expense	660.00			
19	Miscellaneous Expense	68.00			
20		15,370.00	15,370.00		
21					

H ◀ ▶ H   Sheet1 / Sheet2 / Sheet3 /

Practice Exercise 3

EXERCISE 4-5 Complete the work sheet for Ramey Company, dated December 31, 20--, through the adjusted trial balance using the following adjustment information:

a. Expired or used-up insurance, $460.
b. Depreciation expense on equipment, $870. (Remember to credit the Accumulated Depreciation account for equipment, not Equipment.)
c. Wages accrued or earned since the last payday, $120 (owed and to be paid on the next payday).
d. Supplies remaining, $80.

	A	B	C	D	E	F	G
1	Ramey Company						
2	Work Sheet						
3	For Month Ended December 31, 20--						
4							
5		TRIAL BALANCE		ADJUSTMENTS		ADJUSTED TRIAL BALANCE	
6	ACCOUNT NAME	DEBIT	CREDIT	DEBIT	CREDIT	DEBIT	CREDIT
7	Cash	5,190.00					
8	Supplies	430.00					
9	Prepaid Insurance	1,200.00					
10	Equipment	4,678.00					
11	Accumulated. Depr., Equip.		1,556.00				
12	Accounts Payable		1,875.00				
13	S. Ramey, Capital		6,026.00				
14	S. Ramey, Drawing	1,700.00					
15	Service Fees		5,836.00				
16	Rent Expense	965.00					
17	Supplies Expense	267.00					
18	Wages Expense	765.00					
19	Miscellaneous Expense	98.00					
20		15,293.00	15,293.00				
21							

Sheet1 / Sheet2 / Sheet3

Practice Exercise 4

EXERCISE 4-6 Journalize the four adjusting entries from the partial work sheet on the next page for Brady Company for the month ended May 31. (*Hint:* Use what you know about opening new accounts for adjusting entries.)

	A	H	I	J	K	
1		Brady Company				^
2		Work Sheet				
3		For Month Ended May 31, 20--				
4						
5		INCOME STATEMENT		BALANCE SHEET		
6	ACCOUNT NAME	DEBIT	CREDIT	DEBIT	CREDIT	
7	Cash			5,501.00		
8	Supplies			230.00		
9	Prepaid Insurance			841.00		
10	Equipment			4,832.00		
11	Accumulated Depreciation, Equipment				1,720.00	
12	Accounts Payable				1,085.00	
13	S. Brady, Capital				6,800.00	
14	S. Brady, Drawing			2,150.00		≡
15	Professional Fees		9,673.00			
16	Salary Expense	3,787.00				
17	Rent Expense	1,484.00				
18	Miscellaneous Expense	134.00				
19						
20	Insurance Expense	200.00				
21	Depreciation Expense, Equipment	364.00				
22	Salaries Payable				330.00	
23	Supplies Expense	85.00				
24		6,054.00	9,673.00	13,554.00	9,935.00	
25	Net Income	3,619.00			3,619.00	
26		9,673.00	9,673.00	13,554.00	13,554.00	
27						v

H ◄ ► H \ Sheet1 / Sheet2 / Sheet3 /   ‹ III ›

LO 4

EXERCISE 4-7 Journalize the adjustments for Newkirk Company as of August 31.

Practice Exercise 4

	A	B	C	D	E	
1		Newkirk Company				^
2		Work Sheet				
3		For Month Ended August 31, 20--				
4						
5		TRIAL BALANCE		ADJUSTMENTS		
6	ACCOUNT NAME	DEBIT	CREDIT	DEBIT	CREDIT	
7	Cash	3,526.00				
8	Supplies	345.00			(d) 65.00	
9	Prepaid Insurance	3,973.00			(a) 300.00	
10	Equipment	3,678.00				
11	Accumulated Depreciation, Equipment		645.00		(b) 206.00	
12	Accounts Payable		1,843.00			
13	J. Newkirk, Capital		10,752.00			
14	J. Newkirk, Drawing	3,000.00				≡
15	Service Fees		5,683.00			
16	Rent Expense	2,458.00				
17	Wages Expense	1,865.00		(c) 268.00		
18	Miscellaneous Expense	78.00				
19		18,923.00	18,923.00			
20	Insurance Expense			(a) 300.00		
21	Depreciation Expense, Equipment			(b) 206.00		
22	Wages Payable				(c) 268.00	
23	Supplies Expense			(d) 65.00		
24				839.00	839.00	
25						v

H ◄ ► H \ Sheet1 / Sheet2 / Sheet3 /   ‹ III ›

LO 4

Practice Exercise 4

EXERCISE 4-8 Journalize the following adjusting entries that were included on the work sheet for the month ended December 31.

Dec. 31   Salaries for three days are unpaid at December 31, $2,700. Salaries are $4,500 for a five-day week.

31   Insurance was bought on September 1 for $3,600 for 12 months' coverage. Four months' coverage has expired, $1,200.

31   Depreciation for the month on equipment, $50, based on an asset costing $3,200 with a trade-in value of $200 and an estimated life of five years.

31   The balance in supplies before adjustment totaled $154. The amount of supplies on hand at the end of the year is $72.

LO 5

EXERCISE 4-9 Determine on which financial statement each account listed below is reported. Use the following abbreviations: Income Statement (IS), Statement of Owner's Equity (OE), and Balance Sheet (BS).

a.   S. Beagle, Capital
b.   Cash
c.   Miscellaneous Expense
d.   Accumulated Depreciation, Equipment
e.   Wages Payable
f.   S. Beagle, Drawing

g.   Equipment
h.   Supplies
i.   Depreciation Expense
j.   Supplies Expense
k.   Service Fees
l.   Accounts Receivable

Problem Set A

LO 3

PROBLEM 4-1A The trial balance of Morgan's Insurance Agency as of September 30, after the firm has completed its first month of operations, is as follows:

Morgan's Insurance Company Trial Balance September 30, 20—		
Account Name	**Debit**	**Credit**
Cash	3,337	
Accounts Receivable	1,428	
Supplies	487	
Prepaid Insurance	775	
Office Equipment	5,146	
Accounts Payable		1,367
S. Morgan, Capital		9,528
S. Morgan, Drawing	1,000	
Commissions Earned		2,843
Rent Expense	885	
Travel Expense	388	
Utilities Expense	227	
Miscellaneous Expense	65	
	13,738	13,738

Required
1. Record the amounts in the Trial Balance columns of the work sheet.
2. Complete the work sheet by making the following adjustments and lettering each adjustment:
   a. Expired or used-up insurance, $300.
   b. Depreciation expense on office equipment, $600.
   c. Supplies used, $150.

Check Figure
Net Income, $228

LO 3, 4
QuickBooks

PROBLEM 4-2A The trial balance of Clayton Cleaners for the month ended September 30 is as follows:

Clayton Cleaners
Trial Balance
September 30, 20—

Account Name	Debit	Credit
Cash	2,589	
Supplies	652	
Prepaid Insurance	1,136	
Equipment	21,752	
Accumulated Depreciation, Equipment		14,357
Accounts Payable		2,647
K. Clayton, Capital		28,169
K. Clayton, Drawing	21,359	
Income from Services		40,850
Wages Expense	23,983	
Rent Expense	11,673	
Utilities Expense	1,254	
Telephone Expense	1,144	
Miscellaneous Expense	481	
	86,023	86,023

Data for the adjustments are as follows:
a. Expired or used-up insurance, $800.
b. Depreciation expense on equipment, $2,700.
c. Wages accrued or earned since the last payday, $585 (owed and to be paid on the next payday).
d. Supplies remaining at the end of month, $230.

Required
1. Complete a work sheet. (Skip this step if using QuickBooks or general ledger.)
2. Journalize the adjusting entries.

Check Figure
Net Loss, $2,192

LO 4, 5

PROBLEM 4-3A The completed work sheet for Chelsey Decorators for the month of March is in your Working Papers or in CengageNow.

Required
1. Journalize the adjusting entries.
2. If using QuickBooks, prepare an adjusting journal entries report and an adjusted trial balance.
3. Prepare an income statement.
4. Prepare a statement of owner's equity. Assume that no additional investments were made in March. (Skip this step if using QuickBooks.)
5. Prepare a balance sheet.

Check Figure
Total Assets, $15,003

CHAPTER ASSIGNMENTS

LO   3, 4, 5, 6 ···

PROBLEM 4-4A The trial balance for Game Time on July 31 is as follows:

Account Name	Debit	Credit
Game Time		
Trial Balance		
July 31, 20—		
Cash	14,721	
Supplies	257	
Prepaid Insurance	1,295	
Equipment	17,642	
Accumulated Depreciation, Equipment		2,287
Repair Equipment	1,265	
Accumulated Depreciation, Repair Equipment		880
Accounts Payable		942
B. Ryan, Capital		23,871
B. Ryan, Drawing	2,000	
Game Fees		7,954
Concession Fees		3,752
Wages Expense	1,068	
Rent Expense	980	
Utilities Expense	246	
Repair Expense	180	
Miscellaneous Expense	32	
	39,686	39,686

Data for month-end adjustments are as follows:

a. Expired or used-up insurance, $480.
b. Depreciation expense on equipment, $850.
c. Depreciation expense on repair equipment, $120.
d. Wages accrued or earned since the last payday, $525 (owed and to be paid on the next payday).
e. Supplies used, $70.

Check Figure
Net Income, $7,155

Required

1. Complete a work sheet for the month. (Skip this step if using QuickBooks or general ledger.)
2. Journalize the adjusting entries.
3. If using QuickBooks, prepare an adjusting journal entries report and an adjusted trial balance.
4. Prepare an income statement, a statement of owner's equity*, and a balance sheet. Assume that no additional investments were made during July.

*If using QuickBooks, skip preparing the statement of owner's equity.

LO   3, 4, 5, 6

PROBLEM 4-5A The trial balance for Benner Hair Salon on March 31 is as follows:

Benner Hair Salon Trial Balance March 31, 20—		
Account Name	**Debit**	**Credit**
Cash	4,440	
Supplies	150	
Prepaid Insurance	2,354	
Equipment	10,507	
Accumulated Depreciation, Equipment		1,000
Accounts Payable		240
A. Benner, Capital		13,449
A. Benner, Drawing	1,500	
Salon Fees		6,230
Wages Expense	1,036	
Rent Expense	650	
Utilities Expense	130	
Repair Expense	65	
Miscellaneous Expense	87	
	20,919	20,919

Data for month-end adjustments are as follows:
a. Expired or used-up insurance, $300.
b. Depreciation expense on equipment, $500.
c. Wages accrued or earned since the last payday, $235 (owed and to be paid on the next payday).
d. Supplies remaining at the end of the month, $65.

Required

Check Figure
Net Income, $3,142

1. Complete a work sheet for the month. (Skip this step if using QuickBooks or general ledger.)
2. Journalize the adjusting entries.
3. Prepare an income statement, a statement of owner's equity*, and a balance sheet. Assume that no additional investments were made during March.

*If using QuickBooks, skip preparing the statement of owner's equity.

Problem Set B

LO   3

PROBLEM 4-1B The trial balance for Mason's Insurance Agency as of August 31, after the firm has completed its first month of operations, is shown on the next page.

(Continued)

Mason's Insurance Company
Trial Balance
August 31, 20—

Account Name	Debit	Credit
Cash	3,527	
Accounts Receivable	1,219	
Supplies	492	
Prepaid Insurance	1,362	
Office Equipment	3,939	
Accounts Payable		2,071
C. Mason, Capital		9,020
C. Mason, Drawing	1,900	
Commissions Earned		3,520
Rent Expense	1,695	
Travel Expense	225	
Utilities Expense	198	
Miscellaneous Expense	54	
	14,611	14,611

Check Figure

Net Loss, $12

Required

1. Record amounts in the Trial Balance columns of the work sheet.
2. Complete the work sheet by making the following adjustments and lettering each adjustment:
   a. Expired or used-up insurance, $260.
   b. Depreciation expense on office equipment, $900.
   c. Supplies used, $200.

LO 3, 4

QuickBooks

PROBLEM 4-2B The trial balance of The New Decors for the month ended September 30 is as follows:

The New Decors
Trial Balance
September 30, 20—

Account Name	Debit	Credit
Cash	4,378	
Supplies	1,864	
Prepaid Insurance	1,345	
Equipment	30,978	
Accumulated Depreciation, Equipment		15,235
Accounts Payable		3,751
R. Becker, Capital		44,208
R. Becker, Drawing	20,445	
Income from Services		44,791
Wages Expense	29,761	
Rent Expense	15,932	
Utilities Expense	1,573	
Telephone Expense	1,271	
Miscellaneous Expense	438	
	107,985	107,985

Data for the adjustments are as follows:
a. Expired or used-up insurance, $425.
b. Depreciation expense on equipment, $2,750.
c. Wages accrued or earned since the last payday, $475 (owed and to be paid on the next payday).
d. Supplies remaining at end of month, $215.

Required
1. Complete a work sheet. (Skip this step if using QuickBooks or general ledger.)
2. Journalize the adjusting entries.

Check Figure
Net Loss, $9,483

LO 4, 5

PROBLEM 4-3B The completed work sheet for Juarez Design for the month of March is in your Working Papers, CengageNow or general ledger.

Required
1. Journalize the adjusting entries.
2. Prepare an income statement.
3. Prepare a statement of owner's equity*. Assume that no additional investments were made in March.
4. Prepare a balance sheet.

*If using QuickBooks, skip preparing the statement of owner's equity.

QuickBooks

Check Figure
Total Assets, $21,997

LO 3, 4, 5, 6

PROBLEM 4-4B The trial balance for Harris Pitch and Putt on June 30 is as follows: Data for month-end adjustments are as follows:

QuickBooks

Harris Pitch and Putt Trial Balance June 30, 20—		
Account Name	**Debit**	**Credit**
Cash	5,532	
Supplies	246	
Prepaid Insurance	1,284	
Equipment	21,687	
Accumulated Depreciation, Equipment		1,478
Repair Equipment	5,289	
Accumulated Depreciation, Repair Equipment		1,285
Accounts Payable		860
W. Harris, Capital		23,110
W. Harris, Drawing	2,565	
Golf Fees		11,487
Concession Fees		3,763
Wages Expense	3,163	
Rent Expense	1,350	
Utilities Expense	457	
Repair Expense	171	
Miscellaneous Expense	239	
	41,983	41,983

a. Expired or used-up insurance, $380.
b. Depreciation expense on equipment, $1,950.
c. Depreciation expense on repair equipment, $1,650.

(*Continued*)

d. Wages accrued or earned since the last payday, $585 (owed and to be paid on the next payday).
e. Supplies remaining at end of month, $120.

Check Figure
Net Income, $5,179

Required
1. Complete a work sheet for the month. (Skip this step if using QuickBooks or general ledger.)
2. Journalize the adjusting entries.
3. If using QuickBooks, prepare an adjusting journal entries report and an adjusted trial balance.
4. Prepare an income statement, a statement of owner's equity*, and a balance sheet. Assume that no additional investments were made during June.

*If using QuickBooks, skip preparing the statement of owner's equity.

LO 3, 4, 5, 6

PROBLEM 4-5B The trial balance for Wilson Financial Services on January 31 is as follows:

Wilson Financial Services
Trial Balance
January 31, 20—

Account Name	Debit	Credit
Cash	17,910	
Supplies	650	
Prepaid Insurance	4,500	
Equipment	15,400	
Accumulated Depreciation, Equipment		3,500
Accounts Payable		2,450
L. Wilson, Capital		25,800
L. Wilson, Drawing	3,000	
Financial Services Fees		15,550
Wages Expense	4,025	
Rent Expense	1,200	
Utilities Expense	430	
Repair Expense	110	
Miscellaneous Expense	75	
	47,300	47,300

Data for month-end adjustments are as follows:
a. Expired or used-up insurance, $750.
b. Depreciation expense on equipment, $300.
c. Wages accrued or earned since the last payday, $1,055 (owed and to be paid on the next payday).
d. Supplies used, $535.

Check Figure
Net Income, $7,070

Required
1. Complete a work sheet for the month. (Skip this step if using QuickBooks or general ledger.)
2. Journalize the adjusting entries.
3. If using QuickBooks, prepare an adjusting journal entries report and an adjusted trial balance.
4. Prepare an income statement, a statement of owner's equity*, and a balance sheet. Assume that no additional investments were made during January.

*If using QuickBooks, skip preparing the statement of owner's equity.

Try It with **QuickBooks**® (LO 1, 2, 3, 4)

QB Exercise 4-1

Using the Conner's Whitewater Adventures demonstration file from Chapter 4, complete the following activities with QuickBooks. Use the dates June 1, 2015, to June 30, 2015, for all reports.

1. Record the following adjusting entries in the QuickBooks general journal:
   a. $460 worth of supplies used during June.
   b. $625 expired insurance during June.
   c. $512 depreciation for the month of June.
   d. $472 accrued wages owed, but not recorded at the end of June.

2. View and print the adjusting entries report for Conner's Whitewater Adventures.
   a. What is the ending balance of the Debit column for this report?

3. View and print the adjusted trial balance report for Conner's Whitewater Adventures.
   a. What is the adjusted balance in the Supplies account? Is this balance a debit or a credit?
   b. What is the adjusted balance in the Wages Payable account? Is this balance a debit or a credit?
   c. What is the total debit amount of the unadjusted trial balance?
   d. What is the total credit amount of the adjusted trial balance?

Activities

Why Does It Matter?

RIDE THE DUCKS OF SEATTLE, Seattle, Washington

Ride the Ducks of Seattle may seem like an unlikely name for a thriving business—but it is the name of a real business! The year-round Seattle tour company uses vehicles that can be providing a road tour one minute and plying the waters of Elliott Bay the next. One of Ride the Ducks' employees is a bookkeeper who also serves as a reservationist, tour vehicle cleaner, and computer specialist. In addition to recording and posting journal entries each month, he makes adjusting entries. What are some of the adjusting entries this bookkeeper might make for Ride the Ducks of Seattle?

What Would You Say?

You are the bookkeeper for a small but thriving business. You have asked the owner for the information you need to make adjusting entries for depreciation, supplies, insurance, and wages. He says that he's really busy and that what you've done so far is "close enough." Explain the need for adjusting entries and their effect on the owner's balance sheet and the "bottom line" on the income statement.

What Do You Think?

Your supervisor just finished a work sheet for the month of June, but all of the columns except the following were left unreadable because of a spilled latte. You have been asked to journalize the adjusting entries using the surviving partial work sheet below.

ACCOUNT NAME	INCOME STATEMENT		BALANCE SHEET	
	DEBIT	CREDIT	DEBIT	CREDIT
Cash			8,476.00	
Accounts Receivable			1,486.00	
Equipment			12,367.00	
Accumulated Depreciation, Equipment				3,610.00
Accounts Payable				2,813.00
G. Kramer, Capital				11,707.00
G. Kramer, Drawing			1,100.00	
Income from Services		11,216.00		
Rent Expense	2,510.00			
Wages Expense	2,467.00			
Insurance Expense	210.00			
Depreciation Expense, Equipment	750.00			
Wages Payable				620.00
	5,937.00	11,216.00	24,029.00	18,750.00
Net Income	5,279.00			5,279.00
	11,216.00	11,216.00	24,029.00	24,029.00

What Would You Do?

Your client is preparing financial statements to show the bank. You know that he has incurred a refrigeration repair expense during the month, but you see no such expense on the books. When you question the client, he tells you that he has not yet paid the $1,255 bill. Your client is on the accrual basis of accounting. He does not want the refrigeration repair expense on the books as of the end of the month because he wants his profits to look good for the bank. Is your client behaving ethically by suggesting that the refrigeration repair expense not be booked until the $1,255 is paid? Are you behaving ethically if you agree to the client's request? What principle is involved here?

Adjustments

Although you printed the trial balance and financial statements to get an idea of how All About You Spa is doing financially, some accounts are not accurate. You need to make adjusting entries to provide a clearer picture of how the spa is doing.

HOW TO COMPUTE THE ADJUSTMENTS

Compute the adjustment amounts for the month of June, using the following information:

Adjustment (a): Liability insurance for six months was purchased during the first days of the month. That protection for one month has been used or expended.

Adjustments (b) and (c): Office equipment and spa equipment have depreciated. That means they have been in use for a month and have, for accounting purposes, lost some usefulness. This is an estimate, of course, which allows us to expense the depreciation and, in effect, lowers the book value (value on the books) of both types of equipment.

(b): The owner, Anika Valli, purchased office equipment totaling $1,150. The office equipment will be depreciated using the straight-line method. The office equipment is estimated to have a salvage (trade-in) value of $550 and is expected to last five years. Remember, you want to compute the depreciation for one month, not one year.

(c): Anika Valli invested spa equipment totaling $7,393 in the business ($3,158 of her own spa equipment plus $4,235 of new spa equipment purchased). The spa equipment will be depreciated using the straight-line method. The spa equipment is estimated to have a trade-in, or salvage, value of $3,500 and is expected to last five years. Remember, you want to compute the depreciation for one month, not one year.

Adjustment (d): All About You Spa owes one day of wages to its employees. The month's total wages paid in June amounted to $7,390. The employees worked 21 days but were paid for only 20 days because the payday for the last day worked is in the next pay period.

Adjustments (e) and (f): After a count of supplies at the end of the month, All About You Spa has $130 remaining in Office Supplies and $205 remaining in Spa Supplies.

Required

1. Complete a work sheet for the month (if required by your instructor).

2. Journalize the adjusting entries in the general journal.

   - If you are preparing the adjusting entries manually, enter your transactions beginning on page 4.

(*Continued*)

All About You
Spa

CONTINUING PROBLEM

Check Figures
4. Adjusted trial balance total, $39,197.38
5. Net income, $7,111.62
6. A. Valli, Capital, ending balance, $23,419.62
7. Total assets, $26,037.12

3. Post the adjusting entries to the general ledger accounts.

   • Ignore this step if you are using QuickBooks or general ledger.

4. Prepare an adjusted trial balance as of June 30, 20--.

5. Prepare an income statement (after adjustment) for the month ended June 30, 20--.

6. Prepare a statement of owner's equity* (after adjustment) for the month ended June 30, 20--.

7. Prepare a balance sheet (after adjustment) as of June 30, 20--.

   *If using QuickBooks, skip preparing the statement of owner's equity.

Closing Entries and the Post-Closing Trial Balance

After you have completed this chapter, you will be able to do the following:

1. List the steps in the accounting cycle.

2. Journalize and post closing entries for a service enterprise.

3. Prepare a post-closing trial balance.

4. Define cash basis and accrual basis accounting.

5. Prepare interim statements.

To: **Amy Roberts, CPA**
Subject: **It's the End of the Year!**

Hi Amy,
Well, I made it! The business has been successful this year, and I am even earning a profit! I can't begin to thank you enough for all the help you've given me. I guess I'll just continue to record transactions using everything we've talked about so far. Is there anything else that still needs to be completed?
Thanks,
Janie

To: **Janie Conner**
Subject: **RE: It's the End of the Year!**

Hi Janie,
I'm glad to hear the business has been successful! At the end of each fiscal period, two more steps need to take place to finish the accounting work: closing entries and post-closing trial balance. Let's start with closing entries. Closing entries are completed to prepare the accounts for next year. Like last time, we'll be looking at the work sheet to help us prepare closing entries. Here are the steps to learn:

_____ 1. Understand the steps of the accounting cycle (which is what you've been learning all along).

_____ 2. Learn how to record and post closing entries.

Let me know if you need help!
Amy

Let's review the steps in the accounting cycle for an entire fiscal period. Remember that a fiscal period is generally 12 consecutive months.

STEP 1. Analyze source documents and record business transactions in a journal.

STEP 2. Post journal entries to the accounts in the ledger.

STEP 3. Prepare a trial balance.

STEP 4. Gather adjustment data and record the adjusting entries on a work sheet.

STEP 5. Complete the work sheet.

STEP 6. Journalize and post the adjusting entries from the data on the work sheet.

STEP 7. Prepare financial statements from the data on the work sheet.

STEP 8. Journalize and post the closing entries.

STEP 9. Prepare a post-closing trial balance.

Accrual basis of accounting (p. 235)

Cash basis of accounting (p. 234)

Closing entries (p. 224)

Income Summary account (p. 225)

Interim statements (p. 235)

Nominal (temporary-equity) accounts (p. 229)

Post-closing trial balance (p. 233)

Real (permanent) accounts (p. 229)

This chapter explains the procedure for completing the final steps: journalizing and posting the closing entries and preparing the post-closing trial balance.

Adjusting entries, closing entries, and a post-closing trial balance are prepared at the end of a fiscal period. To introduce you to these final steps in the accounting cycle, we assume that the fiscal period for Conner's Whitewater Adventures ends after one month. We make this assumption so that we can thoroughly cover the material and give you a chance to practice its application. The entire accounting cycle is outlined in Figure 1 on the next page.

① List the steps in the accounting cycle.

Learning Objective

CLOSING ENTRIES

To help you understand the reason for the closing entries, let's take a look at a version of the fundamental accounting equation.

$$\text{Assets} = \text{Liabilities} + \text{Capital} - \text{Drawing} + \text{Revenue} - \text{Expenses}$$

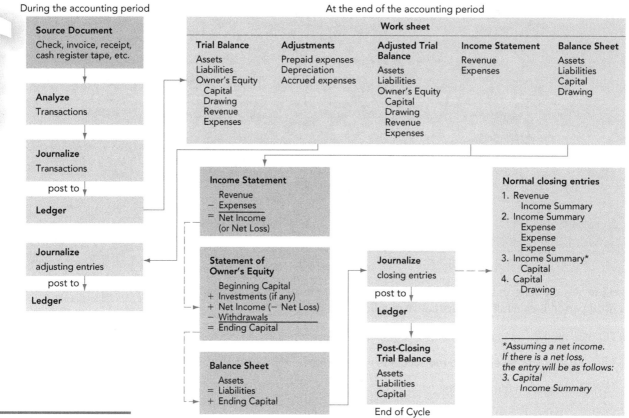

Figure 1
The accounting cycle

We know that the income statement, as stated in the third line of its heading, covers a period of time. The income statement consists of revenue minus expenses for this period of time only. So when the next fiscal period begins, we should start with zero balances. We start over again each period.

Purpose of Closing Entries

This brings us to the *purpose* of the **closing entries**, which is to close (or zero out) revenue, expense, and Drawing accounts. We do this because their balances apply to only one fiscal period. Closing entries are made after the last adjusting entry and after the financial statements have been prepared. With the coming of the next fiscal period, we want to start from zero, recording revenue and expenses for the new fiscal period. The closing entries also update the owner's Capital account.

Closing entries empty, or zero out, temporary owner's equity accounts and prepare the accounts for the new accounting period—much like when you empty the information from your tax folders one year so that you can fill the folders with the new year's revenue and expense receipts.

Accountants also refer to closing the accounts as *clearing the accounts*. For income tax purposes, this is certainly understandable. No one wants to pay income tax more than once on the same income, and the Internal Revenue Service doesn't allow you to count an expense more than once. So now we have this:

$$\text{Assets} = \text{Liabilities} + \text{Capital} - \overset{\text{(closed)}}{\cancel{\text{Drawing}}} + \overset{\text{(closed)}}{\cancel{\text{Revenue}}} - \overset{\text{(closed)}}{\cancel{\text{Expenses}}}$$

The assets, liabilities, and owner's Capital accounts remain open. The balance sheet gives the present balances of these accounts. The accountant carries the asset, liability, and Capital account balances over to the next fiscal period.

Procedure for Closing

The procedure for closing is simply to balance off the account (in other words, to make the balance *equal to zero*). This meets our objective, which is to start from zero in the next fiscal period. Let's illustrate this first with T accounts. Suppose an account to be closed has a debit balance of $870. To make the balance equal to zero, we *credit* the account for $870.

Debit		Credit	
Balance	870	Closing	870
New Balance	0		

Now suppose an account to be closed has a credit balance of $1,400. To make the balance equal to zero, we *debit* the account for $1,400.

Debit		Credit	
Closing	1,400	Balance	1,400
		New Balance	0

Remember, every entry must have at least one debit and one credit. So to record the other half of the closing entry, we bring into existence the **Income Summary account**. The Income Summary account does not have plus and minus signs and does not have a normal balance, just debit and credit.

There are four steps in the closing procedure:

STEP 1. Close the revenue account(s) into Income Summary.

STEP 2. Close the expense account(s) into Income Summary.

STEP 3. Close the Income Summary account into the Capital account, transferring the net income or net loss to the Capital account.

STEP 4. Close the Drawing account into the Capital account.

To illustrate, we return to Conner's Whitewater Adventures. For the purpose of the illustration, assume that Conner's Whitewater Adventures' fiscal period ends after one month. We have the following T account balances in the revenue and expense accounts after the adjustments have been posted.

Income from Tours				Advertising Expense		
−	+			+	−	
	Balance	23,320	Balance	620		

Wages Expense			Utilities Expense		
+	−		+	−	
Balance	2,832	Balance	225		

Rent Expense			Insurance Expense		
+	−		+	−	
Balance	1,250	Balance	625		

Supplies Expense			Depreciation Expense, Equipment		
+	−		+	−	
Balance	460	Balance	512		

STEP 1. Close the revenue account(s) into Income Summary.

To make the balance of Income from Tours equal to zero, we *balance it off*, or debit it, in the amount of $23,320. Because we need an offsetting credit, we credit Income Summary for the same amount. Notice that there are no signs in Income Summary, only debit and credit.

Income from Tours				Income Summary		
	−	+				
Closing	23,320	Balance	23,320		(Revenue)	23,320

The balance of Income from Tours is transferred to Income Summary.

STEP 2. Close the expense account(s) into Income Summary.

To make the balances of the expense accounts equal to zero, we need to *balance them off*, or credit them. Again, the T accounts are useful for formulating this journal entry.

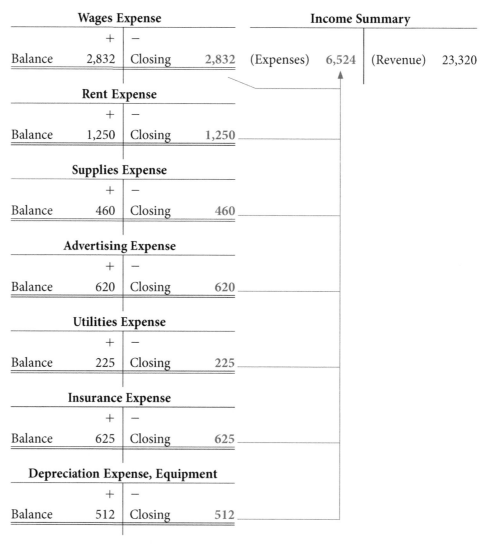

Wages Expense				Income Summary		
	+	−				
Balance	2,832	Closing	2,832	(Expenses) 6,524	(Revenue)	23,320

Rent Expense			
	+	−	
Balance	1,250	Closing	1,250

Supplies Expense			
	+	−	
Balance	460	Closing	460

Advertising Expense			
	+	−	
Balance	620	Closing	620

Utilities Expense			
	+	−	
Balance	225	Closing	225

Insurance Expense			
	+	−	
Balance	625	Closing	625

Depreciation Expense, Equipment			
	+	−	
Balance	512	Closing	512

STEP 3. Close the Income Summary account into the Capital account, transferring the net income or net loss to the Capital account.

Recall that we created Income Summary so that we could have a debit and a credit in each closing entry. Now that it has done its job, we close it out. We use the same procedure as before, making the balance equal to zero, or balancing off the account. We transfer, or close, the balance of the Income Summary account into the Capital account, as shown in the T accounts below. In addition, Figure 2 shows the closing entries recorded in the general journal for steps 1 through 3.

Income Summary		**J. Conner, Capital**	
		− | +	
(Expenses) 6,524 | (Revenue) 23,320		Balance 95,200	
Closing 16,796 | Balance 16,796		Closing 16,796	

GENERAL JOURNAL				Page 4
Date	Description	Post. Ref.	Debit	Credit
	Closing Entries			
Step 1 — 30	Income from Tours		23 3 2 0 00	
	Income Summary			23 3 2 0 00
30	Income Summary		6 5 2 4 00	
	Wages Expense			2 8 3 2 00
	Rent Expense			1 2 5 0 00
Step 2 —	Supplies Expense			4 6 0 00
	Advertising Expense			6 2 0 00
	Utilities Expense			2 2 5 00
	Insurance Expense			6 2 5 00
	Depreciation Expense, Equipment			5 1 2 00
Step 3 — 30	Income Summary		16 7 9 6 00	
	J. Conner, Capital			16 7 9 6 00

Figure 2
Closing entries for Conner's Whitewater Adventures

Income Summary is always closed into the Capital account by the amount of revenue minus expenses (the net income or the net loss). Comparing net income or net loss on the work sheet with the closing entry for Income Summary can serve as a checkpoint or verification for you.

Net income is added (credited) to the Capital account because, as shown in the statement of owner's equity, net income is treated as an addition. Net loss, on the other hand, is subtracted from (debited to) the Capital account, because net loss is treated as a deduction in the statement of owner's equity. Assuming that J. Doe Company had a net loss of $600, here's how to close Income Summary:

Income Summary		**J. Doe, Capital**	
		− | +	
(Expenses) 3,000 | (Revenue) 2,400	(Net Loss) 600	Balance 42,000	
Balance 600 | Closing 600			

The entry to close Income Summary into J. Doe's Capital account for a net loss would look like the following:

GENERAL JOURNAL					Page 3
Date	Description	Post. Ref.	Debit		Credit
	Closing Entries				
31	J. Doe, Capital		6 0 0 00		
	Income Summary				6 0 0 00

STEP 4. Close the Drawing account into the Capital account.

Let's return to the example of Conner's Whitewater Adventures. The Drawing account applies to only one fiscal period, so it too must be closed. Drawing is not an expense because it did not help the business generate revenue. **And because Drawing is not an expense, it cannot affect net income or net loss.** It appears in the statement of owner's equity as a deduction from the Capital account, so it is closed directly into the Capital account. We balance off the Drawing account, or make its balance equal to zero, by transferring the balance of Drawing to the Capital account.

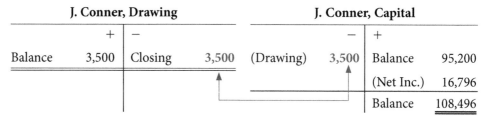

The entire set of journal entries in the closing procedure for Conner's Whitewater Adventures is shown below.

Figure 3
Closing entries for Conner's Whitewater Adventures

GENERAL JOURNAL						Page 4
	Date	Description	Post. Ref.	Debit		Credit
		Closing Entries				
Step 1	30	Income from Tours		23 3 2 0 00		
		Income Summary				23 3 2 0 00
	30	Income Summary		6 5 2 4 00		
		Wages Expense				2 8 3 2 00
		Rent Expense				1 2 5 0 00
		Supplies Expense				4 6 0 00
Step 2		Advertising Expense				6 2 0 00
		Utilities Expense				2 2 5 00
		Insurance Expense				6 2 5 00
		Depreciation Expense, Equipment				5 1 2 00
Step 3	30	Income Summary		16 7 9 6 00		
		J. Conner, Capital				16 7 9 6 00
Step 4	30	J. Conner, Capital		3 5 0 0 00		
		J. Conner, Drawing				3 5 0 0 00

These closing entries show that Conner's Whitewater Adventures has net income of $16,796; the owner has withdrawn $3,500 for personal expenses; and $13,296 ($16,796 − $3,500) has been retained in the business, thereby increasing capital.

Closing Entries Using Accounting Software

Making closing entries using accounting software, such as QuickBooks, is frequently an automatic procedure. The accounting software automatically updates the capital account. If you are using accounting software, at the end of each fiscal period, you should perform the following steps:

1. Make a backup copy of the file.
2. Print all financial statements.
3. Set a closing date and password-protect the books for that fiscal year.

The purpose of setting a closing date and password-protecting the books at the end of the fiscal year is to prevent changes from being made to transactions that have already been closed. This will ensure that no accidental changes are made to the previous fiscal year after it has been closed.

Closing Entries Using the Work Sheet

You can gather the information for the closing entries directly from the ledger accounts or from the work sheet. Because the Income Statement columns of the work sheet consist entirely of revenues and expenses, you can pick up the figures for three of the four closing entries from these columns. Figure 4, on page 230, shows a partial work sheet for Conner's Whitewater Adventures.

You can plan the closing entries by balancing off all of the figures that appear in the Income Statement columns. For example, in the Income Statement Credit column, there is a credit for $23,320 (Income from Tours), so we debit that account for $23,320 and credit Income Summary for $23,320.

There are debits for $2,832, $1,250, $620, $225, $460, $625, and $512 (expense accounts). So now we *credit* these accounts for the same amounts and debit Income Summary for the total ($6,524).

Next, we close Income Summary into Capital, using the net income figure ($16,796) already shown on the work sheet in Figure 4.

We do, of course, have to get the last closing entry from the Balance Sheet columns to close Drawing.

Incidentally, accountants call the accounts that are to be closed (such as revenue, expenses, and Drawing) **nominal (temporary-equity) accounts**. These accounts are temporary in that their balances apply to only one fiscal period. The *equity* aspect pertains because all of these accounts come under the umbrella of owner's equity.

On the other hand, accountants call the accounts that remain open (such as assets, liabilities, and Capital) **real (permanent) accounts**. These accounts have balances that will be carried over to the next fiscal period. They are *permanent* because as long as the company exists, these accounts will retain their balances.

> **Remember**
>
> The temporary-equity accounts (revenue, expenses, and Drawing) are closed out because they apply to only one fiscal period.

Posting the Closing Entries

In the Item column of the ledger account, we write the word *Closing*. To show that the balance of an account is zero, we draw a line through both the Debit Balance and the Credit Balance columns.

Figure 4

Partial work sheet for Conner's Whitewater Adventures

Conner's Whitewater Adventures
Work Sheet
For Month Ended June 30, 20--

ACCOUNT NAME	TRIAL BALANCE DEBIT (A + Draw. + E)	TRIAL BALANCE CREDIT (+ L + Cap. + R / Accum. Depr.)	ADJUSTMENTS DEBIT	ADJUSTMENTS CREDIT	ADJUSTED TRIAL BALANCE DEBIT (A + Draw. + E)	ADJUSTED TRIAL BALANCE CREDIT (+ L + Cap. + R / Accum. Depr.)	INCOME STATEMENT DEBIT (E)	INCOME STATEMENT CREDIT (R)	BALANCE SHEET DEBIT (A + Draw.)	BALANCE SHEET CREDIT (+ L + Cap. / Accum. Depr.)
Cash	55,890.00				55,890.00				55,890.00	
Accounts Receivable	4,250.00				4,250.00				4,250.00	
Supplies	675.00			(a) 460.00	215.00				215.00	
Prepaid Insurance	1,875.00			(b) 625.00	1,250.00				1,250.00	
Equipment	51,300.00				51,300.00				51,300.00	
Accounts Payable		3,425.00				3,425.00				3,425.00
J. Conner, Capital		95,200.00				95,200.00				95,200.00
J. Conner, Drawing	3,500.00				3,500.00				3,500.00	
Income from Tours		23,320.00				23,320.00		23,320.00		
Wages Expense	2,360.00		(d) 472.00		2,832.00		2,832.00			
Rent Expense	1,250.00				1,250.00		1,250.00			
Advertising Expense	620.00				620.00		620.00			
Utilities Expense	225.00				225.00		225.00			
	121,945.00	121,945.00								
Supplies Expense			(a) 460.00		460.00		460.00			
Insurance Expense			(b) 625.00		625.00		625.00			
Depr. Exp., Equip.			(c) 512.00		512.00		512.00			
Accum. Depr., Equip.				(c) 512.00		512.00				512.00
Wages Payable				(d) 472.00		472.00				472.00
			2,069.00	2,069.00	122,929.00	122,929.00	6,524.00	23,320.00	116,405.00	99,609.00
Net Income							16,796.00			16,796.00
							23,320.00	23,320.00	116,405.00	116,405.00

Sheet1 | Sheet2 | Sheet3

After we have posted the closing entries, the Capital, Drawing, Income Summary, revenue, and expense accounts of Conner's Whitewater Adventures appear as follows:

GENERAL LEDGER

ACCOUNT J. Conner, Capital   **ACCOUNT NO. 311**

Date		Item	Post. Ref.	Debit	Credit	Balance Debit	Balance Credit
20--							
June	1		1		90 0 0 0 00		90 0 0 0 00
	4		1		5 2 0 0 00		95 2 0 0 00
	30	Closing	4		16 7 9 6 00		111 9 9 6 00
	30	Closing	4	3 5 0 0 00			108 4 9 6 00

ACCOUNT J. Conner, Drawing   **ACCOUNT NO. 312**

Date		Item	Post. Ref.	Debit	Credit	Balance Debit	Balance Credit
20--							
June	30		3	3 5 0 0 00		3 5 0 0 00	
	30	Closing	4		3 5 0 0 00	———	———

ACCOUNT Income Summary   **ACCOUNT NO. 313**

Date		Item	Post. Ref.	Debit	Credit	Balance Debit	Balance Credit
20--							
June	30	Closing	4		23 3 2 0 00		23 3 2 0 00
	30	Closing	4	6 5 2 4 00			16 7 9 6 00
	30	Closing	4	16 7 9 6 00		———	———

ACCOUNT Income from Tours   **ACCOUNT NO. 411**

Date		Item	Post. Ref.	Debit	Credit	Balance Debit	Balance Credit
20--							
June	7		1		8 0 0 0 00		8 0 0 0 00
	15		2		6 7 5 0 00		14 7 5 0 00
	30		3		8 5 7 0 00		23 3 2 0 00
	30	Closing	4	23 3 2 0 00		———	———

ACCOUNT Wages Expense   **ACCOUNT NO. 511**

Date		Item	Post. Ref.	Debit	Credit	Balance Debit	Balance Credit
20--							
June	24		2	2 3 6 0 00		2 3 6 0 00	
	30	Adj.	4	4 7 2 00		2 8 3 2 00	
	30	Closing	4		2 8 3 2 00	———	———

ACCOUNT Rent Expense   **ACCOUNT NO. 512**

Date		Item	Post. Ref.	Debit	Credit	Balance Debit	Balance Credit
20--							
June	8		1	1 2 5 0 00		1 2 5 0 00	
	30	Closing	4		1 2 5 0 00		

ACCOUNT Supplies Expense   **ACCOUNT NO. 513**

Date		Item	Post. Ref.	Debit	Credit	Balance Debit	Balance Credit
20--							
June	30	Adj.	4	4 6 0 00		4 6 0 00	
	30	Closing	4		4 6 0 00		

ACCOUNT Advertising Expense   **ACCOUNT NO. 514**

Date		Item	Post. Ref.	Debit	Credit	Balance Debit	Balance Credit
20--							
June	14		2	6 2 0 00		6 2 0 00	
	30	Closing	4		6 2 0 00		

ACCOUNT Utilities Expense   **ACCOUNT NO. 515**

Date		Item	Post. Ref.	Debit	Credit	Balance Debit	Balance Credit
20--							
June	18		2	2 2 5 00		2 2 5 00	
	30	Closing	4		2 2 5 00		

ACCOUNT Insurance Expense   **ACCOUNT NO. 516**

Date		Item	Post. Ref.	Debit	Credit	Balance Debit	Balance Credit
20--							
June	30	Adj.	4	6 2 5 00		6 2 5 00	
	30	Closing	4		6 2 5 00		

ACCOUNT Depreciation Expense, Equipment   **ACCOUNT NO. 517**

Date		Item	Post. Ref.	Debit	Credit	Balance Debit	Balance Credit
20--							
June	30	Adj.	4	5 1 2 00		5 1 2 00	
	30	Closing	4		5 1 2 00		

To: **Amy Roberts, CPA**
Subject: **Closing Entries Recorded and Posted**

Hi Amy,

I have recorded and posted the closing entries. Last time we talked, you mentioned that we need to prepare a post-closing trial balance after the closing entries. What's the purpose of that trial balance?
Thanks,
Janie

To: **Janie Conner**
Subject: **RE: Closing Entries Recorded and Posted**

Hi Janie,

That's right. The post-closing trial balance is the next step. It is prepared after the closing entries have been recorded and posted, and it will help ensure the debit balances equal the credit balances. Let's take a look at the post-closing trial balance. As always, email me back if you have questions.
Amy

THE POST-CLOSING TRIAL BALANCE

After posting the closing entries and before going on to the next fiscal period, it is important to verify the balances of the accounts that remain open. To do so, prepare a **post-closing trial balance** using the final balance figures from the ledger accounts. The purpose of the post-closing trial balance is to make sure the debit balances equal the credit balances.

Note that the accounts listed in the post-closing trial balance (assets, liabilities, and Capital) are the *real*, or *permanent*, *accounts*. (See Figure 5.) The accountant carries the balances of the permanent accounts forward from one fiscal period to another.

3 Prepare a post-closing trial balance.

Learning Objective

Figure 5
Post-closing trial balance for Conner's Whitewater Adventures

Conner's Whitewater Adventures Post-Closing Trial Balance June 30, 20—		
Account Name	**Debit**	**Credit**
Cash	55,890	
Accounts Receivable	4,250	
Supplies	215	
Prepaid Insurance	1,250	
Equipment	51,300	
Accumulated Depreciation, Equipment		512
Accounts Payable		3,425
Wages Payable		472
J. Conner, Capital		108,496
	112,905	112,905

Notice that the *nominal*, or *temporary-equity*, *accounts* (revenue, expenses, Income Summary, and Drawing), which are closed at the end of each fiscal period, are not shown on the post-closing trial balance. These accounts are not shown because they have zero balances.

If the total debits and total credits of the post-closing trial balance are not equal, here's a recommended procedure for tracking down the error.

1. Re-add the trial balance columns.

2. Check that the figures were correctly transferred from the ledger accounts to the post-closing trial balance.

3. Verify the posting of the adjusting entries and the recording of the new balances.

4. Check that the closing entries have been posted and that all revenue, expense, Income Summary, and Drawing accounts have zero balances.

THE BASES OF ACCOUNTING: CASH AND ACCRUAL

Learning Objective

4 Define cash basis and accrual basis accounting.

The basis of accounting that a company chooses has a direct effect on the company's net income and the company's income tax. The business must use the same basis of accounting from year to year, and the basis of accounting must clearly reflect the net income of the business.

Under the **cash basis of accounting**, revenue is recorded when it is received in cash and expenses are recorded when they are paid in cash. Many small businesses' and individuals' personal income taxes are recorded on the cash basis.

SMALL BUSINESS **SUCCESS**

Do I Need an Accountant?

If you are not taking this class because you want to be an accountant or a bookkeeper, you might be taking the class because you plan on owning and operating a small business. Many new small business owners take on the responsibilities of being the accountant for their business. However, at some point, your business will begin to grow, and you may need to consider hiring someone to manage your accounting books so that your time is free to run the business.

An accountant can help you in many areas of your small business, such as:

- What should my business structure be—sole proprietorship, partnership, S corporation, or corporation?

- What software should I use for my accounting?
- How do I handle the payroll for employees?
- What are my requirements for filing taxes?
- What expenses are deductible for tax purposes?
- How do I prepare financial statements when applying for a loan?

So how do you find an accountant? The best way is by referrals. Ask other businesses in your industry for references or visit your local Certified Public Accounting Society website for more recommendations (www.aicpa.org/yellow/ypascpa.htm).

Under the **accrual basis of accounting**, revenue is recorded when it is earned and expenses are recorded when they are incurred (when they occur or when the bill is received). For example, in the sale of goods, revenue is counted by the seller when the buyer accepts delivery of the goods. Expenses are recorded by the seller of the goods when the costs are incurred. Recall that this is called the matching principle because revenue in one fiscal period is matched to expenses incurred in the same period. If your business produces, purchases, or sells merchandise, the business must keep an inventory and use the accrual method for sales and purchases of merchandise.

Let's look at this example of the differences between cash and accrual. Roby Hair Salon pays $6,000 cash in July for the current month (July) and the following five months of rent (August–December). If Roby uses the cash basis of accounting, the full $6,000 will be recorded as rent expense in July. If Roby uses the accrual basis of accounting instead, the expense will be spread over the six months. The amount of $1,000 ($6,000/6) will be recorded each month.

	Cash Basis	Accrual Basis
July	$6,000	$1,000
August		1,000
September		1,000
October		1,000
November		1,000
December		1,000
TOTAL	$6,000	$6,000

Notice that the total expense recorded under both methods is the same, $6,000. The difference between the cash and the accrual basis is simply an issue of *when* the expense is recorded.

Most businesses use the same method of accounting for their financial statements and income tax reporting. Some businesses, though, are not allowed to use the cash basis method for reporting income tax. For example, corporations that average annual gross receipts of more than $5 million may not use the cash basis method. However, there are some important exceptions to this general rule. A business may use a combination of cash and accrual bases of accounting, called the *hybrid method*. Selecting a basis of accounting can often be complicated and confusing. IRS Publication 538, Accounting Periods and Methods, provides information that makes this decision less confusing. Publication 538 is available on the IRS website at www.irs.gov.

INTERIM STATEMENTS

The owner of a business understandably does not want to wait until the end of the 12-month fiscal period to determine whether the company is making a profit or a loss. Instead, most owners want financial statements at the end of each month. Financial statements prepared during the fiscal year, for periods of less than 12 months, are called **interim statements**. (They are given this name because they are prepared within the fiscal period.) For example, a business may prepare the income statement, the statement of owner's equity, and the balance sheet *monthly*. These statements provide up-to-date

 Prepare interim statements.

Learning Objective

YOU Make the Call

Using the information you know about the cash basis versus the accrual basis, review the four types of businesses listed below. Consider the type of accounting transactions the following businesses might make. Then suggest whether the cash basis or the accrual basis would be a logical fit for the business.

1. An investment advisory corporation owned by outside investors with $12 million in annual gross receipts

2. A crane sales company with $1 million in annual gross receipts

3. A travel agency owned by one individual with $60,000 in annual gross receipts

4. A tractor sales company with $6 million in annual gross receipts

SOLUTION

The travel agency would probably be on the cash basis because it is a sole proprietorship. However, the investment advisory corporation would likely be on the accrual basis because its annual gross receipts exceed $5 million. The crane sales company and the tractor sales company would also use the accrual basis because both companies have inventory.

information about the results and status of operations. A company might have the following interim statements:

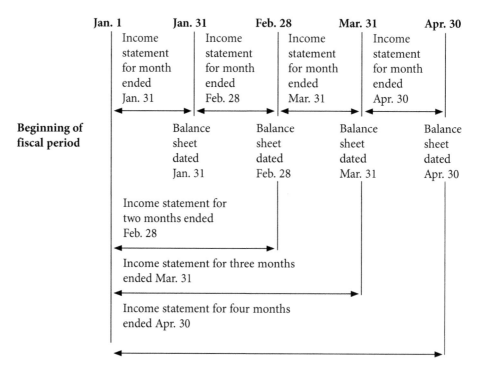

In this case, the accountant would prepare a work sheet at the end of each month. Next, based on these work sheets, he or she would journalize and post the adjusting entries and prepare the financial statements. However, the remaining steps—preparing closing entries and the post-closing trial balance—would be performed only at the end of the year.

© iStockPhoto.com/ranplett

In the Real World

Publicly traded corporations such as Electronic Arts, Inc., a leading video game publisher, are required to file interim financial statements. These interim financial statements are filed using Form 10-Q and present the quarterly (every three months) financial position of the corporation. The interim financial statements are similar to the annual financial statements but are not as detailed and are typically not verified by an auditor.

Accounting with *QuickBooks*®

Closing Entries and the Post-Closing Trial Balance

1 Close the fiscal period.

In QuickBooks, closing entries are completed automatically by the software. This saves users time and helps prevent errors. When using a general ledger software package, such as QuickBooks, it is important to prevent users from unintentionally posting to a prior accounting period. The QuickBooks administrator has two options to help prevent prior-period posting errors: (1) the administrator can enter a closing date in the system, which prompts QuickBooks to alert users who are entering information into a prior accounting period, or (2) the administrator can further restrict user access by requiring a password to gain access to a prior accounting period. The combination of both is recommended.

To close the fiscal period, follow the steps in Figures Q1, Q2, and Q3.

STEP 1. Click on the **Company** tab.

STEP 2. Select **Set Up Users and Passwords**.

STEP 3. Select **Set Up Users**.

Learning Objectives

After you have completed this section, you will be able to do the following:

1 Close the fiscal period.

2 View and print the post-closing trial balance.

ACCOUNTING WITH *QuickBooks*®

Figure Q1
Set up users and passwords

STEP 4. Click on **Closing Date**.

Figure Q2
Set the closing date

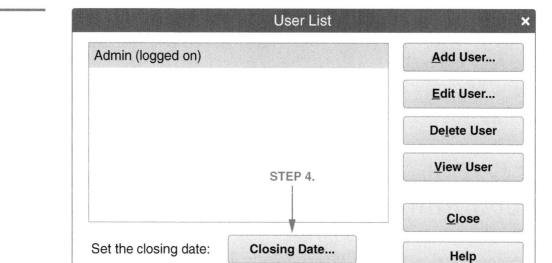

QuickBooks Tip

The closing date and password can also be entered from the **Accountant** tab.

STEP 5. Select **Closing Date**. This is the last day of the fiscal period.

STEP 6. Enter a **Closing Date Password** and **Confirm Password**.

STEP 7. Click **OK**.

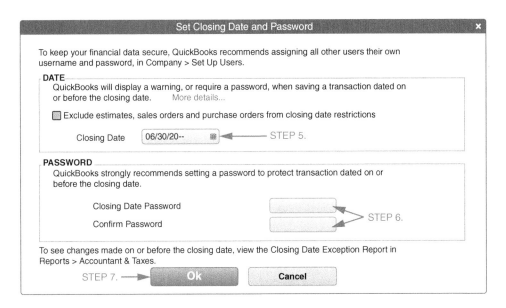

Figure Q3
Set closing date and password

2 View and print the post-closing trial balance.

Learning Objective

To view and print the post-closing trial balance, follow the steps in Figures Q4, Q5, and Q6.

STEP 1. Click **Reports**.

STEP 2. Select **Accountant & Taxes**.

STEP 3. Select **Trial Balance**.

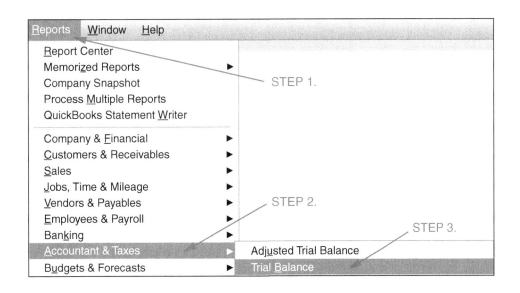

Figure Q4
View post-closing trial balance

STEP 4. Change the **From** and **To** dates and click **Refresh**.

STEP 5. Click **Customize Report**.

STEP 6. Select **Header/Footer** tab.

STEP 7. Change the **Report Title** to **Post-Closing Trial Balance**.

STEP 8. Click **OK**.

STEP 9. Click **Print**.

Figure Q5
Modify trial balance report
to create a post-closing trial
balance report

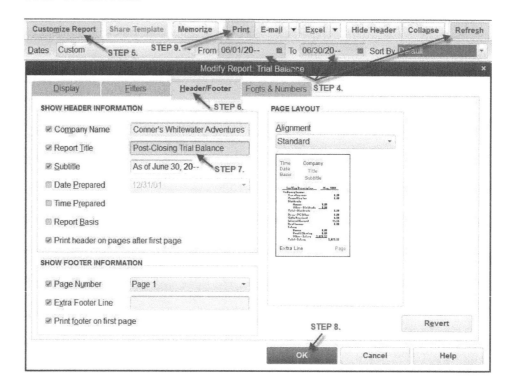

Figure Q6 shows the post-closing trial balance report for Conner's Whitewater Adventures.

Conner's Whitewater Adventures Post-Closing Trial Balance As of June 30, 20--		
	Jun 30, 20--	
	Debit	Credit
111 Cash	55,890.00	
113 Accounts Receivable	4,250.00	
115 Supplies	215.00	
117 Prepaid Insurance	1,250.00	
124 Equipment	51,300.00	
125 Accum. Depr., Equipment		512.00
221 Accounts Payable		3,425.00
222 Wages Payable		472.00
311 J. Conner, Capital		108,496.00
312 J. Conner, Drawing	0.00	
411 Income from Tours	0.00	
511 Wages Expense	0.00	
512 Rent Expense	0.00	
513 Supplies Expense	0.00	
514 Advertising Expense	0.00	
515 Utilities Expense	0.00	
516 Insurance Expense	0.00	
517 Depreciation Expense, Equip	0.00	
TOTAL	112,905.00	112,905.00

Figure Q6
Post-closing trial balance report

ACCOUNTING WITH *QuickBooks*®

Chapter Review

Study and Practice

1 List the steps in the accounting cycle.

Learning Objective

STEP 1. Analyze source documents and record business transactions in a journal.

STEP 2. Post journal entries to the accounts in the ledger.

STEP 3. Prepare a trial balance.

STEP 4. Gather adjustment data and record the adjusting entries on a work sheet.

STEP 5. Complete the work sheet.

STEP 6. Journalize and post the adjusting entries from the data on the work sheet.

STEP 7. Prepare financial statements from the data on the work sheet.

STEP 8. Journalize and post the closing entries.

STEP 9. Prepare a post-closing trial balance.

1 **PRACTICE EXERCISE 1**

Match the steps of the accounting cycle to their corresponding number.

____ 1. Step 1 a. Journalize and post the closing entries.
____ 2. Step 2 b. Prepare a trial balance.

(*Continued*)

CHAPTER REVIEW

	3. Step 3	c. Analyze source documents and record business transactions in a journal.
	4. Step 4	
	5. Step 5	d. Prepare a post-closing trial balance.
	6. Step 6	e. Prepare financial statements from the data on the work sheet.
	7. Step 7	f. Post journal entries to the accounts in the ledger.
	8. Step 8	g. Complete the work sheet.
	9. Step 9	h. Journalize and post the adjusting entries from the data on the work sheet.
		i. Gather adjustment data and record the adjusting entries on a work sheet.

PRACTICE EXERCISE 1 • SOLUTION

1. c   2. f   3. b   4. i   5. g   6. h   7. e   8. a   9. d

Learning Objective   **2** Journalize and post closing entries for a service enterprise.

The four steps in the closing procedure are as follows:

STEP 1. Close the revenue account(s) into Income Summary.

STEP 2. Close the expense account(s) into Income Summary.

STEP 3. Close the Income Summary account into the Capital account, transferring the net income or net loss to the Capital account.

STEP 4. Close the Drawing account into the Capital account.

 PRACTICE EXERCISE 2

The adjusted trial balance for Larson Floral is listed below. Using this information, journalize the four closing entries.

Larson Floral Adjusted Trial Balance June 30, 20—		
Account Name	**Debit**	**Credit**
Cash	14,600	
Accounts Receivable	500	
Supplies	335	
Prepaid Insurance	320	
Delivery Van	28,275	
Accumulated Depreciation, Delivery Van		810
Accounts Payable		750
Wages Payable		300
E. Larson, Capital		37,435
E. Larson, Drawing	1,500	
Income from Services		12,170
Wages Expense	3,600	
Rent Expense	775	
Supplies Expense	710	
Advertising Expense	270	
Utilities Expense	250	
Insurance Expense	30	
Depreciation Expense, Delivery Van	300	
	51,465	51,465

PRACTICE EXERCISE 2 • SOLUTION

GENERAL JOURNAL					Page 4	
Date		Description	Post. Ref.	Debit	Credit	
20--		Closing Entries				
June	30	Income from Services		12 1 7 0 00		
		Income Summary			12 1 7 0 00	
	30	Income Summary		5 9 3 5 00		
		Wages Expense			3 6 0 0 00	
		Rent Expense			7 7 5 00	
		Supplies Expense			7 1 0 00	
		Advertising Expense			2 7 0 00	
		Utilities Expense			2 5 0 00	
		Insurance Expense			3 0 00	
		Depreciation Expense, Delivery Van			3 0 0 00	
	30	Income Summary		6 2 3 5 00		
		E. Larson, Capital			6 2 3 5 00	
	30	E. Larson, Capital		1 5 0 0 00		
		E. Larson, Drawing			1 5 0 0 00	

③ Prepare a post-closing trial balance.

Learning Objective

A **post-closing trial balance** consists of the final balances of the accounts remaining open. It is the final proof that the debit balances equal the credit balances before the posting for the new fiscal period begins.

③ PRACTICE EXERCISE 3

Using the information in Practice Exercise 2, prepare a post-closing trial balance for Larson Floral.

PRACTICE EXERCISE 3 • SOLUTION

Larson Floral
Post-Closing Trial Balance
June 30, 20—

Account Name	Debit	Credit
Cash	14,600	
Accounts Receivable	500	
Supplies	335	
Prepaid Insurance	320	
Delivery Van	28,275	
Accumulated Depreciation, Delivery Van		810
Accounts Payable		750
Wages Payable		300
E. Larson, Capital		42,170
	44,030	44,030

Learning Objective   Define cash basis and accrual basis accounting.

Under the **cash basis of accounting**, revenue is recorded when it is received in cash, and expenses are recorded when they are paid in cash. Under the **accrual basis of accounting**, revenue is recorded when earned, even if cash is received at an earlier or a later date, and expenses are recorded when incurred, even if cash is to be paid at an earlier or a later date.

 PRACTICE EXERCISE 4

Considering the following events, determine which month the revenue or expenses would be recorded using the accounting method specified.

a. Crane Company uses the *accrual basis of accounting*. Crane prepays cash in June for insurance that covers the following month, July, only.
b. Loggins & Rogers Tax Services uses the *cash basis of accounting*. Loggins & Rogers receives cash from customers in January for services to be performed in March.
c. Red Tractor Supplies Company uses the *accrual basis of accounting*. Red Tractor Supplies makes a sale to a customer in September but does not expect payment until November.
d. Norton Company uses the *cash basis of accounting*. Norton prepays cash in February for insurance that covers the following month, March, only.

PRACTICE EXERCISE 4 · SOLUTION

a. July
b. January
c. September
d. February

Learning Objective   Prepare interim statements.

Interim statements consist of year-to-date income statements, statements of owner's equity, and balance sheets as of various dates during the fiscal period.

 PRACTICE EXERCISE 5

Assume that Larson Floral's fiscal period does not end on June 30 but rather December 31. Using the information from Practice Exercise 2, complete an interim balance sheet for June for Larson Floral.

PRACTICE EXERCISE 5 • SOLUTION

Larson Floral
Balance Sheet
June 30, 20--

Assets

Cash		$14,600
Accounts Receivable		500
Supplies		335
Prepaid Insurance		320
Delivery Van	$28,275	
Less Accumulated Depreciation	810	27,465
Total Assets		$43,220

Liabilities

Accounts Payable	$ 750	
Wages Payable	300	
Total Liabilities		$ 1,050

Owner's Equity

E. Larson, Capital		42,170
Total Liabilities and Owner's Equity		$43,220

Glossary

Accrual basis of accounting An accounting method under which revenue is recorded when it is earned, regardless of when it is received, and expenses are recorded when they are incurred, regardless of when they are paid. (*p. 235*)

Cash basis of accounting An accounting method under which revenue is recorded only when it is received in cash, and expenses are recorded only when they are paid in cash. (*p. 234*)

Closing entries Entries made at the end of a fiscal period to close off the revenue, expense, and Drawing accounts—that is, to make the balances of the temporary-equity accounts equal to zero. Closing is also called *clearing the accounts*. (*p. 224*)

Income Summary account An account brought into existence as a debit to balance expense accounts or as a credit to balance revenue accounts in the closing entry process. The revenue and expense account

balances are transferred to this account to allow calculations of net income or net loss. (*p. 225*)

Interim statements Financial statements, covering a period that is less than 12 months, that are prepared during the fiscal year. (*p. 235*)

Nominal (temporary-equity) accounts Accounts that apply to only one fiscal period and that are to be closed at the end of that fiscal period. These are the revenue, expense, and Drawing accounts. This category may also be described as all accounts except assets, liabilities, and the Capital account. (*p. 229*)

Post-closing trial balance The listing of the final balances of the real accounts at the end of the fiscal period. (*p. 233*)

Real (permanent) accounts The accounts that remain open (assets, liabilities, and the Capital account in owner's equity) and have balances that will be carried over to the next fiscal period. (*p. 229*)

Quiz Yourself

_____ 1. What is the third step in the accounting cycle?
   a. Analyze source documents and record business transactions in a journal.
   b. Prepare a post-closing trial balance.
   c. Journalize and post the closing entries.
   d. Prepare a trial balance.

_____ 2. Which of the following accounts would be closed during the closing process?
   a. Service Revenue
   b. Cash
   c. B. Williams, Capital
   d. Accumulated Depreciation, Equipment

_____ 3. If Income from Services had a $20,400 credit balance before closing entries, which of the following would be the appropriate closing entry to close revenues?
   a. Income from Services　20,400
       Cash　　　　　　　　　　　　20,400
   b. Income from Services　20,400
       Income Summary　　　　　　　20,400
   c. Income Summary　　　20,400
       J. Crestview, Capital　　　　　20,400
   d. J. Crestview, Capital　20,400
       Income from Services　　　　　20,400

_____ 4. Which of the following accounts would appear on a post-closing trial balance?
   a. Depreciation Expense, Equipment
   b. Income from Services
   c. R. McDonald, Drawing
   d. R. McDonald, Capital

_____ 5. Under the cash basis method of accounting, which of the following statements is true?
   a. Revenue is recorded when it is earned regardless of when the cash is received.
   b. Expenses are recorded when they are paid.
   c. Expenses are recorded when they are incurred regardless of when the cash is paid.
   d. The cash basis of accounting is allowed for all corporations.

_____ 6. _____ are prepared during the fiscal year for periods of less than 12 months.
   a. Work sheets
   b. Intermediary statements
   c. Interim statements
   d. In-between statements

Answers:
1.d 2.a 3.b 4.d 5.b 6.c

Review It with **QuickBooks**®

_____ 1. In QuickBooks, closing entries are completed
   a. manually, using the General Journal.
   b. automatically, using the General Journal.
   c. automatically, setting the closing date.
   d. All of the above

_____ 2. The QuickBooks administrator can prevent prior-period posting errors by
   a. entering the closing date to alert users they are in a prior period.
   b. requiring a password to gain access to a prior accounting period.
   c. Both a and b
   d. Neither a nor b

_____ 3. In QuickBooks, the post-closing trial balance report is located under
   a. Company & Financial.
   b. Accountant & Taxes.
   c. Custom Reports.
   d. All of the above

_____ 4. _____ allows the modification of a report title.
   a. Lists
   b. Help
   c. Favorites
   d. Customize Report

Answers:
1.c 2.c 3.b 4.d

Chapter Assignments

Discussion Questions

1. Number in order the following steps in the accounting cycle.
    a. Prepare a trial balance.
    b. Post journal entries to the accounts in the ledger.
    c. Journalize and post the adjusting entries from the data on the work sheet.
    d. Analyze source documents and record business transactions in a journal.
    e. Prepare financial statements from the data on the work sheet.
    f. Gather adjustment data and record the adjusting entries on a work sheet.
    g. Journalize and post the closing entries.
    h. Prepare a post-closing trial balance.
    i. Complete the work sheet.
2. List the steps in the closing procedure in the correct order.
3. What is the purpose of closing entries? What is a consequence of forgetting to make closing entries?
4. What are real accounts? What are nominal accounts? Give examples of each.
5. What is the purpose of the Income Summary account? How does it relate to the revenue and expense accounts?
6. What is the purpose of the post-closing trial balance? What is the difference between a trial balance and a post-closing trial balance?
7. Write the third closing entry to transfer the net income or net loss to the P. Hernandez, Capital account, assuming the following:
    a. A net income of $3,842 during the first quarter (Jan.–Mar.)
    b. A net loss of $1,781 during the second quarter (Apr.–Jun.)
8. When would revenue and expenses be recorded if a business used a cash basis of accounting? If a business used an accrual basis of accounting?
9. What are interim financial statements? Why would a business want to prepare them?

Exercises

LO 2

Practice Exercise 2

EXERCISE 5-1 Classify the following accounts as real (permanent) or nominal (temporary) and indicate with an X whether the account is closed. Also indicate the financial statement in which each account will appear. The Building account is given as an example.

(Continued)

Account Title	Real	Nominal	Closed Yes	Closed No	Income Statement	Balance Sheet
0. Example: Building	X			X		X
a. Prepaid Insurance						
b. Accounts Payable						
c. Wages Payable						
d. Services Revenue						
e. Rent Expense						
f. Supplies Expense						
g. Accum. Depr., Equipment						

LO 2

Practice Exercise 2

EXERCISE 5–2 The ledger accounts after adjusting entries for Cortez Services are presented below.
a. Journalize the following closing entries and number as steps 1 through 4.
b. What is the new balance of J. Cortez, Capital after closing? Show your calculations.

Owner's Equity

Assets	=	Liabilities	+	Capital	−	Drawing	+	Revenue	−	Expenses
+ | −		− | +		− | +		+ | −		− | +		+ | −
Debit | Credit		Debit | Credit		Debit | Credit		Debit | Credit		Debit | Credit		Debit | Credit

Cash
Bal. 8,500

Wages Payable
(a) 210

J. Cortez, Capital
Bal. 24,000

J. Cortez, Drawing
Bal. 400

Professional Fees
Bal. 3,850

Wages Expense
Bal. 2,900
(a) 210
Bal. 3,110

Prepaid Insurance
Bal. 990 | (c) 460
Bal. 530

Insurance Expense
(c) 460

Equipment
Bal. 18,125

Depr. Expense, Equipment
(b) 750

Accum. Depr., Equipment
Bal. 3,200
(b) 750
Bal. 3,950

Misc. Expense
Bal. 135

LO 2
Practice Exercise 2

EXERCISE 5-3 As of December 31, the end of the current year, the ledger of Harris Company contained the following account balances after adjustment. All accounts have normal balances. Journalize the closing entries.

Cash	$ 8,440	C. Harris, Drawing	$1,498
Equipment	11,586	Professional Fees	7,075
Accumulated Depreciation,		Wages Expense	1,268
Equipment	2,587	Rent Expense	1,090
Accounts Payable	1,674	Depreciation Expense,	
Wages Payable	658	Equipment	1,143
C. Harris, Capital	13,376	Miscellaneous Expense	345

LO 2
Practice Exercise 2

EXERCISE 5-4 The Income Statement columns of the work sheet of Dunn Company for the fiscal year ended June 30 follow. During the year, K. Dunn withdrew $4,000. Journalize the closing entries.

	A	H	I
		INCOME STATEMENT	
5			
6	ACCOUNT NAME	DEBIT	CREDIT
7	Service Revenue		6,797.00
8	Rental Revenue		3,576.00
9	Rent Expense	2,800.00	
10	Wages Expense	1,854.00	
11	Utilities Expense	465.00	
12	Miscellaneous Expense	59.00	
13		5,178.00	10,373.00
14	Net Income	5,195.00	
15		10,373.00	10,373.00
16			

Sheet1 / Sheet2 / Sheet3

LO 2
Practice Exercise 2

EXERCISE 5-5 The Income Statement columns of the work sheet of Cederblom Company for the fiscal year ended December 31 follow. During the year, S. Cederblom withdrew $17,000. Journalize the closing entries.

	A	H	I
		INCOME STATEMENT	
5			
6	ACCOUNT NAME	DEBIT	CREDIT
7	Service Revenue		29,960.00
8	Rental Revenue		22,000.00
9	Wages Expense	48,520.00	
10	Utilities Expense	7,130.00	
11	Miscellaneous Expense	2,200.00	
12		57,850.00	51,960.00
13	Net Income		5,890.00
14		57,850.00	57,850.00
15			

Sheet1 / Sheet2 / Sheet3

CHAPTER ASSIGNMENTS

Practice Exercise 2

LO 2

EXERCISE 5-6 After all revenue and expenses have been closed at the end of the fiscal period ended December 31, Income Summary has a debit of $45,550 and a credit of $36,520. On the same date, D. Mau, Drawing has a debit balance of $12,000 and D. Mau, Capital had a beginning credit balance of $63,410.

a. Journalize the entries to close the remaining temporary accounts.

b. What is the new balance of D. Mau, Capital after closing the remaining temporary accounts? Show your calculations.

Practice Exercise 3

LO 3

EXERCISE 5-7 Identify whether the following accounts would be included on a post-closing trial balance.

Account Title	Post-Closing Trial Balance	
	Yes	No
0. Example: Cash	X	
a. Income from Services		
b. Prepaid Insurance		
c. Supplies Expense		
d. Accounts Payable		
e. F. Oz, Drawing		
f. Depreciation Expense, Equipment		
g. Wages Payable		
h. Accounts Receivable		
i. Wages Expense		
j. Accumulated Depreciation, Equipment		
k. F. Oz, Capital		

Practice Exercise 4

LO 4

EXERCISE 5-8 Considering the following events, determine which month the revenue or expenses would be recorded using the accounting method specified.

a. Gerber Company uses the *cash basis of accounting*. Gerber prepays cash in April for insurance that covers the following month, May, only.

b. Matthews and Dudley Attorneys uses the *accrual basis of accounting*. Matthews and Dudley Attorneys receives cash from customers in March for services to be performed in April.

c. Eckstein Company uses the *accrual basis of accounting*. Eckstein prepays cash in October for rent that covers the following month, November, only.

d. Gerbino Company uses the *cash basis of accounting*. Gerbino makes a sale to a customer in July but does not expect payment until August.

Practice Exercise 5

LO 5

EXERCISE 5-9 Indicate with an X whether each of the following would appear on the income statement, statement of owner's equity, or balance sheet. An item may appear on more than one statement. The first item is provided as an example.

Item	Income Statement	Statement of Owner's Equity	Balance Sheet
0. Example: The total liabilities of the business at the end of the year.			X
a. The amount of the owner's Capital balance at the end of the year.			
b. The amount of depreciation expense on equipment during the year.			
c. The amount of the company's net income for the year.			
d. The book value of the equipment.			
e. Total insurance expired during the year.			
f. Total accounts receivable at the end of the year.			
g. Total withdrawals by the owner.			
h. The cost of utilities used during the year.			
i. The amount of the owner's Capital balance at the beginning of the year.			

LO 5

Practice Exercise 5

EXERCISE 5-10 Prepare a statement of owner's equity for The Lindal Clinic for the year ended December 31. P. Lindal's capital amount on January 1 was $124,000, and there was an additional investment of $7,000 on May 12 and withdrawals of $31,500 for the year. Net income for the year was $20,418.

Problem Set A

LO 2

PROBLEM 5-1A After the accountant posted the adjusting entries for B. Lyon, Designer, the work sheet contained the following account balances on May 31:

	A	F	G
5		ADJUSTED TRIAL BALANCE	
6	ACCOUNT NAME	DEBIT	CREDIT
7	Cash	2,018.00	
8	Supplies	300.00	
9	Accounts Receivable	1,408.00	
10	Prepaid Insurance	987.00	
11	Office Equipment	5,790.00	
12	Accumulated Depreciation, Office Equipment		1,372.00
13	Accounts Payable		880.00
14	B. Lyon, Capital		7,520.00
15	B. Lyon, Drawing	1,550.00	
16	Commissions Earned		4,679.00
17	Rent Expense	995.00	
18	Supplies Expense	575.00	
19	Depreciation Expense, Office Equipment	462.00	
20	Utilities Expense	269.00	
21	Miscellaneous Expense	97.00	
22		14,451.00	14,451.00
23			

Sheet1 / Sheet2 / Sheet3

(Continued)

Check Figure
Net Income, $2,281

Required
1. Write the owner's name on the Capital and Drawing T accounts.
2. Record the account balances in the T accounts for owner's equity, revenue, and expenses.
3. Journalize the closing entries using the four steps in correct order. Number the closing entries 1 through 4.
4. Post the closing entries to the T accounts immediately after you journalize each one to see the effect of the closing entries. Number the closing entries 1 through 4.

 LO 2

PROBLEM 5-2A The partial work sheet for Ho Consulting for May follows:

	A	H	I	J	K	
5		**INCOME STATEMENT**		**BALANCE SHEET**		
6	**ACCOUNT NAME**	**DEBIT**	**CREDIT**	**DEBIT**	**CREDIT**	
7	Cash			5,710.00		
8	Supplies			209.00		
9	Prepaid Insurance			1,123.00		
10	Equipment			5,731.00		
11	Accumulated Depreciation, Equipment				1,444.00	
12	Accounts Payable				1,841.00	
13	G. Ho, Capital				4,302.00	
14	G. Ho, Drawing			2,400.00		
15	Consulting Revenue		13,060.00			
16	Rent Expense	2,200.00				
17	Wages Expense	1,828.00				
18	Supplies Expense	422.00				
19	Miscellaneous Expense	230.00				
20						
21	Insurance Expense	325.00				
22	Depreciation Expense, Equipment	835.00				
23	Wages Payable				366.00	
24		5,840.00	13,060.00	15,173.00	7,953.00	
25	Net Income	7,220.00			7,220.00	
26		13,060.00	13,060.00	15,173.00	15,173.00	
27						

Sheet1 / Sheet2 / Sheet3

Check Figure
Debit to Income Summary, second entry, $5,840

Required
1. Write the owner's name on the Capital and Drawing T accounts.
2. Record the account balances in the T accounts for owner's equity, revenue, and expenses.
3. Journalize the closing entries using the four steps in correct order. Number the closing entries 1 through 4.
4. Post the closing entries to the T accounts immediately after you journalize each one to see the effect of the closing entries. Number the closing entries 1 through 4.

 LO 1, 2, 3

PROBLEM 5-3A The completed work sheet for Valerie Insurance Agency as of December 31 is presented in your Working Papers or in CengageNow, along with the general ledger as of December 31 before adjustments.

Required

1. Write the name of the owner, M. Valerie, in the Capital and Drawing accounts.
2. Write the balances from the unadjusted trial balance in the general ledger.
3. Journalize and post the adjusting entries.
4. Journalize and post the closing entries in the correct order.
5. Prepare a post-closing trial balance.

Check Figure
Post-closing trial balance
total, $10,170

LO 1, 2, 3

QuickBooks

PROBLEM 5-4A The account balances of Bryan Company as of June 30, the end of the current fiscal year, are as follows:

	A	B	C	
5		TRIAL BALANCE		∧
6	**ACCOUNT NAME**	**DEBIT**	**CREDIT**	
7	Cash	5,491.00		
8	Accounts Receivable	624.00		
9	Supplies	397.00		
10	Prepaid Insurance	1,280.00		
11	Equipment	6,497.00		
12	Accumulated Depreciation, Equipment		2,672.00	≡
13	Van	10,989.00		
14	Accumulated Depreciation, Van		4,368.00	
15	Accounts Payable		1,036.00	
16	B. Bryan, Capital		18,583.00	
17	B. Bryan, Drawing	18,000.00		
18	Fees Earned		38,417.00	
19	Salary Expense	18,600.00		
20	Advertising Expense	1,887.00		
21	Van Operating Expense	462.00		
22	Utilities Expense	685.00		
23	Miscellaneous Expense	164.00		
24		65,076.00	65,076.00	∨
25				
◄ ◄ ► ►◄ Sheet1 Sheet2 Sheet3			‹ ⦀ ›	

Required

1. Data for the adjustments are as follows:
   a. Expired or used up insurance, $495
   b. Depreciation expense on equipment, $670.
   c. Depreciation expense on the van, $1,190.
   d. Salary accrued (earned) since the last payday, $540 (owed and to be paid on the next payday).
   e. Supplies used during the period, $97.
   Your instructor may want you to use a work sheet for these adjustments.
2. Journalize the adjusting entries.
3. Prepare an income statement.
4. Prepare a statement of owner's equity; assume that there was an additional investment of $2,000 on June 10. (Skip this step if using QuickBooks. The additional investment assumption has already been completed in the data file.)
5. Prepare a balance sheet.
6. Journalize the closing entries using the four steps in the correct sequence.

Check Figure
Net Income, $13,627

CHAPTER ASSIGNMENTS

LO 2, 3, 5

PROBLEM 5-5A Williams Mechanic Services prepared the following work sheet for the year ended March 31, 20--.

	A	B	C	D	E	F	G
1	Williams Mechanic Services						
2	Work Sheet						
3	For Year Ended March 31, 20—						
4							
5		TRIAL BALANCE		ADJUSTMENTS		ADJUSTED TRIAL BALANCE	
6	ACCOUNT NAME	DEBIT	CREDIT	DEBIT	CREDIT	DEBIT	CREDIT
7	Cash	6,500.00				6,500.00	
8	Accounts Receivable	1,250.00				1,250.00	
9	Supplies	415.00			(e) 200.00	215.00	
10	Prepaid Insurance	2,175.00			(a) 175.00	2,000.00	
11	Equipment	3,500.00				3,500.00	
12	Accumulated Depreciation, Equipment		1,200.00		(b) 75.00		1,275.00
13	Truck	18,300.00				18,300.00	
14	Accumulated Depreciation, Truck		4,000.00		(c) 300.00		4,300.00
15	Accounts Payable		800.00				800.00
16	J. Williams, Capital		16,940.00				16,940.00
17	J. Williams, Drawing	3,000.00				3,000.00	
18	Fees Earned		15,000.00				15,000.00
19	Salary Expense	1,200.00		(d) 125.00		1,325.00	
20	Advertising Expense	600.00				600.00	
21	Truck Operating Expense	250.00				250.00	
22	Utilities Expense	600.00				600.00	
23	Miscellaneous Expense	150.00				150.00	
24		37,940.00	37,940.00				
25	Insurance Expense			(a) 175.00		175.00	
26	Depreciation Expense, Equipment			(b) 75.00		75.00	
27	Depreciation Expense, Truck			(c) 300.00		300.00	
28	Salaries Payable				(d) 125.00		125.00
29	Supplies Expense			(e) 200.00		200.00	
30				875.00	875.00	38,440.00	38,440.00
31							

Sheet1 / Sheet2 / Sheet3

Check Figure
Post-closing trial balance total, $31,765

Required
1. Complete the work sheet. (Skip this step if using QuickBooks or general ledger.)
2. Prepare an income statement.
3. Prepare a statement of owner's equity; assume that there was an additional investment of $5,000 on March 13. (Skip this step if using QuickBooks. The additional investment assumption has already been completed in the data file.)
4. Prepare a balance sheet.
5. Journalize the closing entries using the four steps in the correct sequence.
6. Prepare a post-closing trial balance. (For QuickBooks, select the trial balance report, then modify the report name to *Post-Closing Trial Balance*.)

Problem Set B

LO 2

PROBLEM 5-1B After the accountant posted the adjusting entries for M. Wally, Designer, the work sheet contained the following account balances on May 31:

	A	F	G
5		ADJUSTED TRIAL BALANCE	
6	**ACCOUNT NAME**	**DEBIT**	**CREDIT**
7	Cash	2,029.00	
8	Accounts Receivable	886.00	
9	Supplies	400.00	
10	Prepaid Insurance	1,460.00	
11	Office Equipment	4,672.00	
12	Accumulated Depreciation, Office Equipment		1,170.00
13	Accounts Payable		943.00
14	M. Wally, Capital		9,221.00
15	M. Wally, Drawing	1,600.00	
16	Commissions Earned		1,997.00
17	Rent Expense	990.00	
18	Supplies Expense	480.00	
19	Depreciation Expense, Office Equipment	420.00	
20	Utilities Expense	286.00	
21	Miscellaneous Expense	108.00	
22		13,331.00	13,331.00
23			

Sheet1 / Sheet2 / Sheet3

Required

1. Write the owner's name on the Capital and Drawing T accounts.
2. Record the account balances in the T accounts for owner's equity, revenue, and expenses.
3. Journalize the closing entries using the four steps in correct order. Number the closing entries 1 through 4.
4. Post the closing entries to the T accounts immediately after you journalize each one to see the effect of the closing entries. Number the closing entries 1 through 4.

PROBLEM 5-2B The partial work sheet for Emil Consulting for June is as follows:

	A	H	I	J	K
5		INCOME STATEMENT		BALANCE SHEET	
6	**ACCOUNT NAME**	**DEBIT**	**CREDIT**	**DEBIT**	**CREDIT**
7	Cash			6,000.00	
8	Supplies			104.00	
9	Prepaid Insurance			1,344.00	
10	Equipment			6,751.00	
11	Accumulated Depreciation, Equipment				4,212.00
12	Accounts Payable				1,356.00
13	W. Emil, Capital				5,367.00
14	W. Emil, Drawing			1,700.00	
15	Consulting Fees		9,546.00		
16	Rent Expense	1,800.00			
17	Wages Expense	1,533.00			
18	Miscellaneous Expense	168.00			
19					
20	Supplies Expense	365.00			
21	Insurance Expense	364.00			
22	Depreciation Expense, Equipment	700.00			
23	Wages Payable				348.00
24		4,930.00	9,546.00	15,899.00	11,283.00
25	Net Income	4,616.00			4,616.00
26		9,546.00	9,546.00	15,899.00	15,899.00
27					

Sheet1 / Sheet2 / Sheet3

(Continued)

Check Figure
Debit to Income
Summary, second entry,
$4,930

Required

1. Write the owner's name on the Capital and Drawing T accounts.
2. Record the account balances in the T accounts for owner's equity, revenue, and expenses.
3. Journalize the closing entries using the four steps in correct order. Number the closing entries 1 through 4.
4. Post the closing entries to the T accounts immediately after you journalize each one to see the effect of the closing entries. Number closing entries 1 through 4.

 LO **1, 2, 3** ···

PROBLEM 5-3B The completed work sheet for Oliver Tour Company as of December 31 is presented in your Working Papers or in CengageNow, along with the general ledger as of December 31 before adjustments.

Check Figure
Post-closing trial balance
total, $9,147

Required

1. Write the name of the owner, S. Oliver, in the Capital and Drawing accounts.
2. Write the balances from the unadjusted trial balance in the general ledger.
3. Journalize and post the adjusting entries.
4. Journalize and post the closing entries in the correct order.
5. Prepare a post-closing trial balance.

 LO **1, 2, 3** ···

PROBLEM 5-4B The account balances of Miss Beverly's Tutoring Service as of June 30, the end of the current fiscal year, are as follows:

	A	B	C	
5		TRIAL BALANCE		
6	ACCOUNT NAME	DEBIT	CREDIT	
7	Cash	6,491.00		
8	Accounts Receivable	624.00		
9	Supplies	527.00		
10	Prepaid Insurance	1,280.00		
11	Equipment	5,497.00		
12	Accumulated Depreciation, Equipment		2,472.00	
13	Van	13,674.00		
14	Accumulated Depreciation, Van		4,168.00	
15	Accounts Payable		1,436.00	
16	B. Morrow, Capital		14,848.00	
17	B. Morrow, Drawing	18,000.00		
18	Fees Earned		43,680.00	
19	Salary Expense	16,000.00		
20	Advertising Expense	2,200.00		
21	Van Operating Expense	705.00		
22	Utilities Expense	1,248.00		
23	Miscellaneous Expense	358.00		
24		66,604.00	66,604.00	
25				

Sheet1 / Sheet2 / Sheet3

Check Figure
Net income, $19,567

Required

1. Data for the adjustments are as follows:
   a. Expired or used up insurance, $470.
   b. Depreciation expense on equipment, $948.
   c. Depreciation expense on the van, $1,490.
   d. Salary accrued (earned) since the last payday, $574 (owed and to be paid on the next payday).
   e. Supplies remaining as of June 30, $407.

Your instructor may want you to use a work sheet for these adjustments.

2. Journalize the adjusting entries.
3. Prepare an income statement.
4. Prepare a statement of owner's equity; assume that there was an additional investment of $3,000 on June 10. (Skip this step if using QuickBooks. The additional investment assumption has already been completed in the data file.)
5. Prepare a balance sheet.
6. Journalize the closing entries using the four steps in the proper sequence.

LO 2, 3, 5

PROBLEM 5-5B Tom's Catering Services prepared the following work sheet for the year ended December 31, 20--.

	A	B	C	E	G	I	K
1			Tom's Catering Services				
2			Work Sheet				
3			For Year Ended December 31, 20--				
4							
5		TRIAL BALANCE		ADJUSTMENTS		ADJUSTED TRIAL BALANCE	
6	ACCOUNT NAME	DEBIT	CREDIT	DEBIT	CREDIT	DEBIT	CREDIT
7	Cash	2,400.00				2,400.00	
8	Accounts Receivable	800.00				800.00	
9	Supplies	225.00			(e) 80.00	145.00	
10	Prepaid Insurance	1,200.00			(a) 100.00	1,100.00	
11	Equipment	2,220.00				2,220.00	
12	Accumulated Depreciation, Equipment		370.00		(b) 185.00		555.00
13	Truck	25,000.00				25,000.00	
14	Accumulated Depreciation, Truck		5,000.00		(c) 1,000.00		6,000.00
15	Accounts Payable		250.00				250.00
16	Y. Tom, Capital		26,500.00				26,500.00
17	Y. Tom, Drawing	1,500.00				1,500.00	
18	Fees Earned		2,400.00				2,400.00
19	Salary Expense	640.00		(d) 80.00		720.00	
20	Advertising Expense	130.00				130.00	
21	Truck Operating Expense	125.00				125.00	
22	Utilities Expense	200.00				200.00	
23	Miscellaneous Expense	80.00				80.00	
24		34,520.00	34,520.00				
25	Insurance Expense			(a) 100.00		100.00	
26	Depreciation Expense, Equipment			(b) 185.00		185.00	
27	Depreciation Expense, Truck			(c) 1,000.00		1,000.00	
28	Salaries Payable				(d) 80.00		80.00
29	Supplies Expense			(e) 80.00		80.00	
30				1,445.00	1,445.00	35,785.00	35,785.00
31							

Sheet1 / Sheet2 / Sheet3

Required
1. Complete the work sheet. (Skip this step if using QuickBooks or general ledger.)
2. Prepare an income statement.
3. Prepare a statement of owner's equity; assume that there was an additional investment of $2,500 on December 1. (Skip this step if using QuickBooks. The additional investment assumption has already been completed in the data file.)
4. Prepare a balance sheet.
5. Journalize the closing entries with the four steps in the correct sequence.
6. Prepare a post-closing trial balance. (For QuickBooks, select the trial balance report, then modify the report name to *Post-Closing Trial Balance*.)

QuickBooks

Check Figure
Post-closing trial balance total, $31,665

Try It with **QuickBooks**® (LO 1, 2)

QB Exercise 5-1

Using the Conner's Whitewater Adventures demonstration file for Chapter 5, complete the following activities with QuickBooks:

1. Set the closing date to June 30, 2015.
2. Record the closing entry for J. Conner, Drawing to J. Conner, Capital.
3. View and print the post-closing trial balance report for Conner's Whitewater Adventures as of July 1, 2015. (Both the From and To dates should be July 1, 2015. Be sure to change the report title to *Post-Closing Trial Balance*.)

   a. What is the ending balance of the Debit column for the post-closing trial balance?
   b. What is the ending balance in the J. Conner, Drawing account?
   c. What is the ending balance of the Wages Payable account on the post-closing trial balance? Is this a debit or a credit? What is the classification of this account?
   d. What is the total owner's equity for Conner's Whitewater Adventures as of July 1, 2015?

For the problem listed above, the QuickBooks data file is not set up to automatically close the temporary accounts. Journalize the closing entries using *Make General Journal Entries*. In the memo field, identify the entry as *Closing Entry*.

Activities

Why Does It Matter?

REAL GAP EXPERIENCE, Tunbridge Wells, Kent (UK)

Rather than going directly to college, some students take time off to travel abroad, learn new skills, or volunteer. This period is known as a "gap year." Real Gap Experience provides hundreds of gap year traveling opportunities in over 45 countries around the world. The company offers everything from volunteering to building houses in Guatemala to teaching in China (for pay) to taking a year-long, around-the-world trip. What does this have to do with accounting, and why is it important? Every company needs to keep a record of its financial activities so that financial statements can be presented and used for decision making. Real Gap Experience's accounting records are most likely computerized, but the company still needs to go through the closing process. Why is the closing process important to a company such as Real Gap Experience? What types of accounts would be used during the closing process for this company?

What Would You Say?

Your uncle owns a small sole proprietorship. He does his own bookkeeping, although he didn't finish the chapter on closing entries before he opened his business. He mentions to you that closing entries look like they take a long time. He wonders why he should bother to do them because all he really looks at is the checkbook. What would you say to convince him that closing entries are necessary?

What Do You Think?

On the next page is the post-closing trial balance submitted to you by the bookkeeper of Tafoya Consulting Company. Assume that the debit total ($41,048) is correct.
a. Analyze the work and prepare a response to what you have reviewed.
b. Journalize the closing entries.
c. What is the net income or net loss?
d. Is there an increase or a decrease in Capital?
e. What would be the ending amount of Capital?
f. What is the new balance of the post-closing trial balance?

Tafoya Consulting Company
Post-Closing Trial Balance
December 31, 20--

Account Name	Debit	Credit
Cash	3,412	
Accounts Receivable	1,693	
Prepaid Insurance	2,147	
Accounts Payable		?
C. Tafoya, Capital		13,818
C. Tafoya, Drawing	6,360	
Consulting Fees		25,603
Wages Expense	11,994	
Rent Expense	9,600	
Advertising Expense	2,582	
Supplies Expense	914	
Insurance Expense	1,610	
Miscellaneous Expense	736	
	41,048	41,048

What Would You Do?

You are preparing a post-closing trial balance for the company where you work, but it doesn't balance. You are tired, and besides, you don't think the company pays you for this much hassle and extra time. You decide to increase the balance of an asset account to make the totals balance. Discuss this action and explain whether it is ethical or illegal.

What's Wrong with This Picture?

The bookkeeper has completed a work sheet and has journalized and posted the closing entries, but he forgot to journalize and post the adjusting entries from the work sheet. What are the effects of these actions and omissions? How would these actions and omissions affect the accounting records and the resulting financial statements?

BEFORE A TEST CHECK: Chapters 4–5

PART 1: Multiple-Choice Questions

_____ 1. The net income appears on all of the following statements except
   a. the statement of owner's equity.
   b. the balance sheet.
   c. the income statement.
   d. all of the above.
   e. none of the above.

_____ 2. Which of the following entries records the withdrawal of cash for personal use by Dolan, the owner of a business firm?
   a. Debit Cash and credit Drawing.
   b. Debit Salary Expense and credit Cash.
   c. Debit Cash and credit Salary Expense.
   d. Debit Drawing and credit Cash.
   e. None of the above.

_____ 3. Which of the following errors, considered individually, would cause the trial balance totals to be unequal?
   a. A payment of $52 for supplies was posted as a debit of $52 to Supplies Expense and a credit of $25 to Cash.
   b. A payment of $625 to a creditor was posted as a debit of $625 to Accounts Payable and a debit of $625 to Cash.
   c. Cash received from customers on account was posted as a debit of $380 to Cash and a credit of $38 to Accounts Receivable.
   d. All of the above.
   e. None of the above.

_____ 4. The balance in the Prepaid Insurance account before adjustment at the end of the year is $600. This represents six months' insurance paid on November 1. No adjusting entry was made on November 30. The adjusting entry required on December 31 is
   a. debit Insurance Expense, $200; credit Prepaid Insurance, $200.
   b. debit Prepaid Insurance, $100; credit Insurance Expense, $100.
   c. debit Prepaid Insurance, $600; credit Insurance Expense, $600.
   d. debit Insurance Expense, $600; credit Prepaid Insurance, $600.
   e. none of the above.

_____ 5. If an accountant fails to make an adjusting entry to record expired insurance at the end of a fiscal period, the omission will cause
   a. total expenses to be understated.
   b. total revenue to be understated.
   c. total assets to be understated.
   d. all of the above.
   e. none of the above.

_____ 6. Farmer Company bought equipment on January 2 of this year for $9,000. At the time of purchase, the equipment was estimated to have a useful life of eight years and a trade-in value of $1,000 at the end of eight years. Using the straight-line method, the amount of depreciation for the first year is
   a. $900.
   b. $1,000.
   c. $800.
   d. $950.
   e. none of the above.

_____ 7. If expenses are greater than revenue, the Income Summary account will be closed by a debit to
   a. Cash and a credit to Income Summary.
   b. Income Summary and a credit to Cash.
   c. Capital and a credit to Income Summary.
   d. Income Summary and a credit to Capital.
   e. none of the above.

_____ 8. In preparing closing entries, it is helpful to refer to which of the following columns of the work sheet first?
   a. The Balance Sheet columns
   b. The Adjusted Trial Balance columns
   c. The Income Statement columns
   d. Both the Adjusted Trial Balance and the Income Statement columns
   e. None of the above

PART II: Practical Application

On December 31, the ledger accounts of Kristopher's Upholstery Shop have the following balances after all adjusting entries have been posted.

Cash	$ 3,600
Supplies	400
Equipment	13,000
Accumulated Depreciation, Equipment	1,100
Accounts Payable	300
K. Payton, Capital	16,500
K. Payton, Drawing	16,400
Income Summary	
Income from Services	35,900
Wages Expense	11,500
Rent Expense	2,400
Supplies Expense	4,100
Utilities Expense	1,000
Depreciation Expense, Equipment	500
Miscellaneous Expense	900

Required
Journalize the four closing entries in the proper order.

PART III: Matching Questions

_____ 1. Creditor
_____ 2. Business entity
_____ 3. Fundamental accounting equation
_____ 4. Income statement
_____ 5. Owner's equity
_____ 6. Accounts Receivable
_____ 7. Net loss
_____ 8. Ledger
_____ 9. Credit
_____ 10. Compound entry
_____ 11. Trial balance
_____ 12. Journalizing
_____ 13. Posting
_____ 14. Cross-reference
_____ 15. Journal
_____ 16. Work sheet
_____ 17. Book value
_____ 18. Depreciation
_____ 19. Accounting cycle
_____ 20. Fiscal year
_____ 21. Contra account
_____ 22. Mixed accounts
_____ 23. Temporary-equity accounts
_____ 24. Real accounts
_____ 25. Debit

a. The book of original entry
b. One to whom money is owed.
c. Accounts that are partly income statement and partly balance sheet accounts
d. Assets – Liabilities
e. A listing of the ending balances of all ledger accounts that proves the equality of total debits and total credits
f. The process of recording transactions in a journal
g. The left side of a T account
h. A business enterprise, separate and distinct from the person who owns its assets.
i. The process of transferring accounts and amounts and amounts from the journal to the ledger
j. An account that is deducted from another account
k. Amounts owed by charge customers
l. Balance sheet accounts
m. Assets = Liabilities + Owner's Equity
n. A bookkeeping device for referring from journal to ledger or ledger to journal
o. The right side of a T account

(_Continued_)

p. Allocation of the cost of a plant asset over its estimated life

q. Financial statement that shows the net results of operations

r. Accounts that belong to only one fiscal period and are closed out at the end of each fiscal period

s. A transaction that has two or more debits and/or credits

t. Spreadsheet used to record adjustments and provide balances to prepare financial statements

u. Excess of total expenses over total revenues

v. A period of 12 consecutive months

w. A book containing all of the accounts of a business

x. The cost of an asset minus its accumulated depreciation

y. Steps in the accounting process, completed during the fiscal period

Answers: Part I

1. b   2. d   3. d   4. a   5. a   6. b   7. c   8. c

Answers: Part II

			GENERAL JOURNAL								Page 4			
Date		Description	Post. Ref.	Debit					Credit						
20--		Closing Entries													
Dec.	31	Income from Services		35	9	0	0	00							
		Income Summary							35	9	0	0	00		
	31	Income Summary		20	4	0	0	00							
		Wages Expense							11	5	0	0	00		
		Rent Expense							2	4	0	0	00		
		Supplies Expense							4	1	0	0	00		
		Utilities Expense							1	0	0	0	00		
		Depreciation Expense, Equipment								5	0	0	00		
		Miscellaneous Expense								9	0	0	00		
	31	Income Summary		15	5	0	0	00							
		K. Payton, Capital							15	5	0	0	00		
	31	K. Payton, Capital		16	4	0	0	00							
		K. Payton, Drawing							16	4	0	0	00		

Answers: Part III

1. b   2. h   3. m   4. q   5. d   6. k   7. u   8. w   9. o   10. s   11. e   12. f   13. i   14. n
15. a   16. t   17. x   18. p   19. y   20. v   21. j   22. c   23. r   24. l   25. g

Accounting Cycle Review Problem A

This problem is designed to enable you to apply the knowledge you have acquired in the preceding chapters. In accounting, the ultimate test is being able to handle data in real-life situations. This problem will give you valuable experience.

QuickBooks

CHART OF ACCOUNTS

Assets
111 Cash
112 Accounts Receivable
114 Prepaid Insurance
121 Land
122 Building
123 Accumulated Depreciation, Building
124 Pool/Slide Facility
125 Accumulated Depreciation, Pool/ Slide Facility
126 Pool Furniture
127 Accumulated Depreciation, Pool Furniture

Liabilities
221 Accounts Payable
222 Wages Payable
223 Mortgage Payable

Owner's Equity
311 L. Judar, Capital
312 L. Judar, Drawing
313 Income Summary

Revenue
411 Income from Services
412 Concessions Income

Expenses
511 Pool Maintenance Expense
512 Wages Expense
513 Advertising Expense
514 Utilities Expense
515 Interest Expense
517 Insurance Expense
518 Depreciation Expense, Building
519 Depreciation Expense, Pool/Slide Facility
520 Depreciation Expense, Pool Furniture
522 Miscellaneous Expense

You are to record transactions in a two-column general journal. Assume that the fiscal period is one month. You will then be able to complete all of the steps in the accounting cycle.

When you are analyzing the transactions, think them through by visualizing the T accounts or by writing them down on scratch paper. For unfamiliar types of transactions, specific instructions for recording them are included. However, reason them out for yourself as well. Check off each transaction as it is recorded.

July 1 Judar deposited $135,000 in a bank account for the purpose of buying Blast Off! The business is a recreation area offering three large waterslides (called "tubes")—one children's slide, an inner tube run, and a looping extreme slide.

2 Bought Blast Off! in its entirety for a total price of $540,800. The assets include pool furniture, $3,800; the pool/slide facility (includes filter system, pools, pump, and slides), $148,800; building, $96,200; and land, $292,000. Paid $120,000 down and signed a mortgage note for the remainder.

2 Received and paid the bill for a one-year premium for insurance, $12,240.

2 Bought 125 inner tubes from Worn Tires for $1,225, paying $500 down, with the remainder due in 20 days.

3 Signed a contract with a video game company to lease space for video games and to provide a food concession. The rental income agreed upon is 10 percent of the revenues generated from the machines and food, with the estimated monthly rental income paid in advance. Received cash payment for July, $250.

(Continued)

July   5   Received bills totaling $1,320 for the grand opening/Fourth of July party. The bill from Party Rentals for the promotional handouts, balloons, decorations, and prizes was $620, and the newspaper advertising bills from the *City Star* were $700. (These expenses should all be considered advertising expense.)

      6   Signed a one-year contract for the pool maintenance with All-Around Maintenance and paid the maintenance fee for July of $1,600.

      6   Paid cash for employee picnic food and beverages, $128. (Debit Miscellaneous Expense.)

      7   Received $12,086 in cash as income for the use of the facilities.

      9   Bought parts for the filter system on account from Arlen's Pool Supply, $646. (Debit Pool Maintenance Expense.)

    14   Received $10,445 in cash as income for the use of the facilities.

    15   Paid wages to employees for the period ended July 14, $9,460.

    16   Paid $1,150 cash as partial payment on account for promotional expenses recorded on July 5. Party Rentals was paid $620 and City Star was paid the remainder of $530.

    16   Judar withdrew cash for personal use, $2,500.

    17   Bought additional pool furniture from Pool Suppliers for $2,100; payment due in 30 days.

    18   Paid cash to seamstress for alterations and repairs to the character costumes, $328. (Debit Miscellaneous Expense.)

    21   Received $10,330 in cash as income for the use of the facilities.

    21   Paid cash to Worn Tires as partial payment on account, $600.

    23   Received a $225 reduction of our account from Pool Suppliers for lawn chairs received in damaged condition.

    25   Received and paid telephone bill, $292.

    29   Paid wages for the period July 15 through 28 of $8,227.

    31   Received $11,870 in cash as income for the use of the facilities.

    31   Paid cash to Arlen's Pool Supply to apply on account, $360.

    31   Received and paid water bill, $684.

    31   Paid cash as an installment payment on the mortgage, $3,890. Of this amount, $1,910 represents a reduction in the principal and the remainder is interest.

    31   Received and paid electric bill, $942.

    31   Bought additional inner tubes from Worn Tires for $480, paying $100 down, with the remainder due in 30 days.

    31   Judar withdrew cash for personal use, $3,200.

    31   Sales for the video and food concessions amounted to $4,840, and 10 percent of $4,840 equals $484. Because you have already recorded $250 as concessions income, record the additional $234 revenue due from the concessionaire. (Cash was not received.)

Check Figure
Trial balance total, $601,941; net income, $16,293; post-closing trial balance total, $569,614

Required

1. Journalize the transactions. (Start on page 1 of the general journal if using Excel or Working Papers.)
2. Post the transactions to the ledger accounts. (Skip this step if using QuickBooks or general ledger.)
3. Prepare a trial balance. (If using a work sheet, use the first two columns.)
4. Data for the adjustments are as follows:
   a. Insurance expired during the month, $1,020.
   b. Depreciation of building for the month, $480.

    c. Depreciation of pool/slide facility for the month, $675.
    d. Depreciation of pool furniture for the month, $220.
    e. Wages accrued at July 31, $920.
    Your instructor may want you to use a work sheet for these adjustments.
  5. Journalize adjusting entries.
  6. Post adjusting entries to the ledger accounts. (Skip this step if using QuickBooks or general ledger.)
  7. Prepare an adjusted trial balance.
  8. Prepare the income statement.
  9. Prepare the statement of owner's equity. (Skip this step if using QuickBooks)
 10. Prepare the balance sheet.
 11. Journalize closing entries.
 12. Post closing entries to the ledger accounts. (Skip this step if using QuickBooks or general ledger.)
 13. Prepare a post-closing trial balance. (If using QuickBooks, select the trial balance report and modify the report name to *Post-Closing Trial Balance*.)

Accounting Cycle Review Problem B

This problem is designed to enable you to apply the knowledge you have acquired in the preceding chapters. In accounting, the ultimate test is being able to handle data in real-life situations. This problem will give you valuable experience.

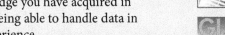

CHART OF ACCOUNTS

Assets
111 Cash
112 Accounts Receivable
114 Prepaid Insurance
121 Land
125 Pool Structure
126 Accumulated Depreciation, Pool Structure
127 Fan System
128 Accumulated Depreciation, Fan System
129 Sailboats
130 Accumulated Depreciation, Sailboats

Liabilities
221 Accounts Payable
222 Wages Payable
223 Mortgage Payable

Owner's Equity
311 R. Cury, Capital
312 R. Cury, Drawing
313 Income Summary

Revenue
411 Income from Services
412 Concessions Income

Expenses
511 Sailboat Rental Expense
512 Wages Expense
513 Advertising Expense
514 Utilities Expense
515 Interest Expense
516 Insurance Expense
517 Depreciation Expense, Pool Structure
518 Depreciation Expense, Fan System
519 Depreciation Expense, Sailboats
522 Miscellaneous Expense

You are to record transactions in a two-column general journal. Assume that the fiscal period is one month. You will then be able to complete all of the steps in the accounting cycle.

When you are analyzing the transactions, think them through by visualizing the T accounts or by writing them down on scratch paper. For unfamiliar types of transactions, specific instructions for recording them are included. However, reason them out for yourself as well. Check off each transaction as it is recorded.

June	1	Cury deposited $95,000 in a bank account for the purpose of buying Wind In Your Sails, a business offering the use of small sailboats to the public at a large indoor pool with a fan system that provides wind.
	2	Bought Wind In Your Sails in its entirety for a total price of $216,100. The assets include sailboats, $25,800; fan system, $13,300; pool structure, $140,000; and land, $37,000. Paid $60,000 down and signed a mortgage note for the remainder.
	3	Received and paid bill for newspaper advertising, $350.
	3	Received and paid bill for a one-year premium for insurance, $12,000.
	3	Bought additional boats from Louis Manufacturing Co. for $7,200, paying $3,200 down, with the remainder due in 30 days.
	3	Signed a contract with a vending machine service to lease space for vending machines. The rental income agreed upon is 10 percent of the sales generated from the machines, with the estimated total rental income payable in advance. Received estimated cash payment for June, $150.
	3	Received bill from Quick Printing for promotional handouts, $540 (Advertising Expense).
	3	Signed a contract for leasing sailboats from K. Einstein Boat Co. and paid rental fee for June, $700.
	5	Paid cash for miscellaneous expenses, $104.
	8	Received $2,855 in cash as income for the use of the boats.
	9	Bought an addition for the fan system on account from Stark Pool Supply, $745.
	15	Paid wages to employees for the period ended June 14, $3,900.
	16	Paid on account for promotional handouts already recorded on June 3, $540.
	16	Cury withdrew cash for personal use, $2,500.
	16	Bought additional sails from Canvas Products, Inc., $850; payment due in 30 days.
	16	Received $6,850 in cash as income for the use of the boats.
	19	Paid cash for miscellaneous expenses, $40.
	20	Paid cash to Louis Manufacturing Co. as part payment on account, $1,300.
	22	Received $8,260 in cash for the use of the boats.
	23	Received a reduction in the outstanding bill from Louis Manufacturing Co. for a boat received in damaged condition, $380.
	24	Received and paid telephone bill, $324.
	29	Paid wages for period June 15 through 28, $4,973.
	30	Paid cash to Stark Pool Supply to apply on account, $475.
	30	Received and paid electric bill, $345.
	30	Paid cash as an installment payment on the mortgage, $1,848. Of this amount, $497 represents a reduction in the principal and the remainder is interest.
	30	Received and paid water bill, $590.
	30	Bought additional boats from Riddle and Son for $5,320, paying $1,550 down, with the remainder due in 30 days.

(Continued)

June 30   Cury withdrew cash for personal use, $1,800.

    30   Received $5,902 in cash as income for the use of the boats.

    30   Sales from vending machines for the month amounted to $1,780. Ten percent of $1,780 equals $178. Because you have already recorded $150 as concessions income, list the additional $28 revenue earned from the vending machine operator. (Cash was not received.)

Required

1. Journalize the transactions. (Start on page 1 of the general journal if using Excel or Working Papers.)
2. Post the transactions to the ledger accounts. (Skip this step if using QuickBooks or general ledger.)
3. Prepare a trial balance. (If using a work sheet, use the first two columns.)
4. Data for the adjustments are as follows:
   a. Insurance expired during the month, $1,000.
   b. Depreciation of pool structure for the month, $715.
   c. Depreciation of fan system for the month, $260.
   d. Depreciation of sailboats for the month, $900.
   e. Wages accrued at June 30, $810.

   Your instructor may want you to use a work sheet for these adjustments.
5. Journalize adjusting entries.
6. Post adjusting entries to the ledger accounts. (Skip this step if using QuickBooks or general ledger.)
7. Prepare an adjusted trial balance.
8. Prepare the income statement.
9. Prepare the statement of owner's equity. (Skip this step if using QuickBooks.)
10. Prepare the balance sheet.
11. Journalize closing entries.
12. Post closing entries to the ledger accounts. (Skip this step if using QuickBooks or general ledger.)
13. Prepare a post-closing trial balance. (If using QuickBooks, select the trial balance report and modify the report name to *Post-Closing Trial Balance.*)

Check Figure
Trial balance total, $281,858; net income, $7,143; post-closing trial balance total, $263,341

CONTINUING PROBLEM

QuickBooks

Closing Entries

After the adjusting entries are recorded and posted and the financial statements have been prepared, you are ready to perform the closing entries. Closing entries zero out the temporary owner's equity accounts (revenue(s), expenses(s), and Drawing). This process transfers the net income to or deducts the net loss and the withdrawals from the Capital account. In addition, the closing process prepares the records for the new fiscal period.

Required

1. Journalize the closing entries in the general journal.
   (If you are preparing the closing entries manually, enter your transactions beginning on page 5.)
2. Post the closing entries to the general ledger accounts.
   (Skip this step if you are using QuickBooks or general ledger.)
3. Prepare a post-closing trial balance as of June 30, 20--. (If using QuickBooks, select the trial balance report and modify the report name to *Post-Closing Trial Balance*.)

Check Figures
1. Debit to Income Summary second entry, $11,235.38
3. Post-closing trial balance total, $26,112

Methods of Depreciation

A

1 Prepare a schedule of depreciation using the straight-line method.

2 Prepare a schedule of depreciation using the double-declining-balance method.

3 Prepare a schedule of depreciation for five-year property under the Modified Accelerated Cost Recovery System.

Accounting Language

Double-declining-balance method (p. A-2)

Modified Accelerated Cost Recovery System (MACRS) (p. A-2)

Straight-line method (p. A-1)

As you have learned, depreciation is the the process of allocating the cost of an asset to an expense over its useful life. In this appendix, we will illustrate three methods of depreciation (straight-line, double-declining-balance, and Modified Accelerated Cost Recovery System) using the example of a delivery truck. Assume that the truck was bought at the beginning of Year 1 at a cost of $24,000. The truck is estimated to have a useful life of five years and a trade-in value of $6,000 at the end of the five-year period.

STRAIGHT-LINE METHOD

The **straight-line method** was demonstrated in Chapter 4. This method is popular because it is easy to use and allows a business to calculate an equal amount of depreciation expense for each year of service anticipated. The accountant computes the annual depreciation by dividing the depreciation base (cost minus salvage value, if any) by the number of years of useful life predicted for the asset. See the illustration of the straight-line method below.

1 Prepare a schedule of depreciation using the straight-line method.

$$\text{Yearly Depreciation} = \frac{\text{Cost of Asset} - \text{Trade-in Value}}{\text{Years of Life}} = \frac{\$24,000 - \$6,000}{5 \text{ years}}$$

$$= \frac{\$18,000}{5 \text{ years}} = \$3,600 \text{ per year}$$

Year	Depreciation for the Year	Accumulated Depreciation	Book Value (Cost Less Accumulated Depreciation)
1	$18,000 ÷ 5 years = $ 3,600	$ 3,600	$24,000 − $ 3,600 = $20,400
2	18,000 ÷ 5 years = 3,600	$ 3,600 + $3,600 = 7,200	24,000 − 7,200 = 16,800
3	18,000 ÷ 5 years = 3,600	7,200 + 3,600 = 10,800	24,000 − 10,800 = 13,200
4	18,000 ÷ 5 years = 3,600	10,800 + 3,600 = 14,400	24,000 − 14,400 = 9,600
5	18,000 ÷ 5 years = 3,600	14,400 + 3,600 = 18,000	24,000 − 18,000 = 6,000
	$18,000		

DOUBLE-DECLINING-BALANCE METHOD

The **double-declining-balance method** is an accelerated method of depreciation that allows larger amounts of depreciation to be taken in the early years of an asset's life. In accelerated depreciation, larger amounts of depreciation are taken during the early life of an asset, and smaller amounts are taken during the later years of an asset's life. Some accountants reason that the amount charged to depreciation should be higher during an asset's early years, when it is more productive and efficient, to offset the higher repair and maintenance expenses of the asset's later years. This way the total annual expense tends to be equalized over the entire life of the asset.

The double-declining-balance method calculates depreciation at double the straight-line rate. In the illustration below, with an estimated useful life of five years, the straight-line rate is 1/5, or 0.20. Twice, or double, the straight-line rate is 2/5 (1/5 × 2), or 0.40. Note that the trade-in value is not taken into account until the end of the schedule. To calculate depreciation using the double-declining-balance method, multiply the *book value* at the beginning of each year by twice the straight-line rate.

Year	Depreciation for the Year	Accumulated Depreciation	Book Value (Cost Less Accumulated Depreciation)
1	$24,000 × 0.40 = $ 9,600	$ 9,600	$24,000 − $ 9,600 = $14,400
2	$14,400 × 0.40 = 5,760	$ 9,600 + $5,760 = 15,360	24,000 − 15,360 = 8,640
3	$8,640 − $6,000 = 2,640	15,360 + 2,640 = 18,000	24,000 − 18,000 = 6,000
4	0	18,000	24,000 − 18,000 = 6,000
5	0	18,000	24,000 − 18,000 = 6,000
	$18,000		

If the 40% depreciation rate is applied to Year 3, depreciation expense would be $3,456 ($8,640 × 0.40), accumulated depreciation would be $18,816 ($15,360 + $3,456), and book value would be $5,184 ($24,000 − $18,816). However, the book value cannot drop below the established salvage, or trade-in, value of $6,000. So for Year 3, an adjustment must be made limiting the depreciation for the year to $2,640, which will bring the accumulated depreciation up to $18,000. Consequently, the book value at the end of the year will be $6,000 ($24,000 cost − $18,000 accumulated depreciation) and no further depreciation will be taken.

TAX REQUIREMENT—MACRS

Business firms are entitled to deduct depreciation on their income tax returns. However, the amount recorded on a company's income statement (based on the depreciation method, straight-line method, double-declining-balance, or another method) may differ from the amount recorded on the company's income tax return.

For property acquired after 1986, a schedule of depreciation called the **Modified Accelerated Cost Recovery System (MACRS)** has been established. The term *recovery* is used because MACRS is a means of recovering or deducting the cost of an asset. Most small businesses use MACRS for financial statement reporting and tax reporting. MACRS is a combination of the declining-balance and straight-line depreciation methods. For more information, see IRS Publication 946, available at www.irs.gov.

According to MACRS, property is divided into eight classes, as follows:

Property Class	Description
3-year property	Certain horses and tractor units for use over the road
5-year property	Autos, light- and heavy-duty general-purpose trucks, computers, and office equipment (copiers, etc.); also, furniture, appliances, window treatments, and carpeting used in residential rental buildings
7-year property	Office furniture and fixtures and any property that does not have a class life and that is not, by law, in any other class
10-year property	Vessels, barges, tugs, and similar water transportation equipment
15-year property	Wharves, roads, fences, and any municipal wastewater treatment plant
20-year property	Certain farm buildings and municipal sewers
27.5-year residential rental property	Rental houses and apartments
39-year real property	Office buildings, store buildings, and warehouses

Under MACRS, trade-in value is ignored. The following table lists the depreciation rates that a business may use for tax purposes.

Depreciation for Recovery Period				
Year	3-Year	5-Year	7-Year	10-Year
1	33.33%	20.00%	14.29%	10.00%
2	44.45	32.00	24.49	18.00
3	14.81	19.20	17.49	14.40
4	7.41	11.52	12.49	11.52
5		11.52	8.93	9.22
6		5.76	8.92	7.37
7			8.93	6.55
8			4.46	6.55
9				6.56
10				6.55
11				3.28

Our delivery truck qualifies as five-year property.

Year	Depreciation for the Year	Accumulated Depreciation	Book Value (Cost Less Accumulated Depreciation)
1	$24,000 × 0.20 = $ 4,800.00	$ 4,800.00	$24,000.00 − $ 4,800.00 = $19,200.00
2	24,000 × 0.32 = 7,680.00	$ 4,800.00 + $7,680.00 = 12,480.00	24,000.00 − 12,480.00 = 11,520.00
3	24,000 × 0.192 = 4,608.00	12,480.00 + 4,608.00 = 17,088.00	24,000.00 − 17,088.00 = 6,912.00
4	24,000 × 0.1152 = 2,764.80	17,088.00 + 2,764.80 = 19,852.80	24,000.00 − 19,852.80 = 4,147.20
5	24,000 × 0.1152 = 2,764.80	19,852.80 + 2,764.80 = 22,617.60	24,000.00 − 22,617.60 = 1,382.40
6	24,000 × 0.0576 = 1,382.40	22,617.60 + 1,382.40 = 24,000.00	24,000.00 − 24,000.00 = 0
	$24,000.00		

Glossary

Double-declining balance method An accelerated depreciation method that calculates depreciation at double the straight-line rate. *(p. A-2)*

Modified Accelerated Cost Recovery System (MACRS) A variety of tax rate schedules established by the Internal Revenue Service. MACRS is a combination of declining-balance and straight-line methods. *(p. A-2)*

Straight-line method A popular method of depreciation because it is easy to use and allows a business to calculate an equal amount of depreciation expense for each year of service anticipated. Annual depreciation is calculated by dividing the depreciation base (cost minus salvage value, if any) by the number of years of useful life predicted for the asset. *(p. A-1)*

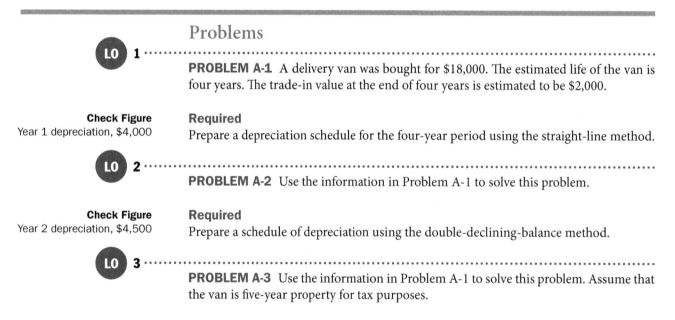

Problems

LO 1

PROBLEM A-1 A delivery van was bought for $18,000. The estimated life of the van is four years. The trade-in value at the end of four years is estimated to be $2,000.

Check Figure
Year 1 depreciation, $4,000

Required
Prepare a depreciation schedule for the four-year period using the straight-line method.

LO 2

PROBLEM A-2 Use the information in Problem A-1 to solve this problem.

Check Figure
Year 2 depreciation, $4,500

Required
Prepare a schedule of depreciation using the double-declining-balance method.

LO 3

PROBLEM A-3 Use the information in Problem A-1 to solve this problem. Assume that the van is five-year property for tax purposes.

Check Figure
Year 3 depreciation, $3,456

Required
Prepare a schedule of depreciation under MACRS. Round figures to the nearest whole dollar.

Bad Debts

After you have completed this appendix, you will be able to do the following:

1 Prepare the adjusting entry for bad debts using the allowance method, based on a percentage of credit sales.

2 Prepare the entry to write off an account as uncollectible when the allowance method is used.

3 Prepare the entry to write off an account as uncollectible when the specific charge-off method is used.

Accounting Language

Allowance method of accounting for bad debts expense (p. B-1)

Specific charge-off method of accounting for bad debts expense (p. B-3)

As you know, not all credit customers pay their bills. In this appendix, we turn our attention to the accounts receivable that will not be collected. There are two basic methods of providing for writing or charging off credit customers' accounts that are considered uncollectible. They are the allowance method and the specific charge-off method.

ALLOWANCE METHOD

The **allowance method of accounting for bad debts expense** provides for bad debts expense in advance by estimating them. Although there are a number of ways to estimate the amount of future expenses from open accounts, we will base our estimate on a percentage of credit sales.

For example, based on its experience with bad debts expense, Miami Printing estimates that 1 percent of its revenue from services on account for the year will be uncollectible. Obviously, Miami Printing does not know which credit customers will not pay their bills. If the company were certain that a particular customer would not pay his or her bill, it wouldn't perform services without requiring cash in advance.

Adjusting Entry and Writing Off an Account

Miami Printing's total income from services on account for last year was $500,000. One percent of $500,000 is $5,000 ($500,000 × 0.01 = $5,000). On its work sheet, Miami Printing makes an adjusting entry. We also show this in T account form assuming a credit balance of $170 in the Allowance for Doubtful Accounts account.

1 Prepare the adjusting entry for bad debts using the allowance method, based on a percentage of credit sales.

Bad Debts Expense			Allowance for Doubtful Accounts	
+	−		−	+
Dec. 31 Adj. 5,000				Bal. 170
				Dec. 31 Adj. 5,000

The general journal entry is shown below.

	GENERAL JOURNAL				Page ___
Date	Description	Post. Ref.	Debit	Credit	
20—	Adjusting Entry				
Dec. 31	Bad Debts Expense		5 0 0 0 00		
	Allowance for Doubtful Accounts			5 0 0 0 00	

Allowance for Doubtful Accounts is treated as a deduction from Accounts Receivable. Consequently, Allowance for Doubtful Accounts is a contra account. The adjusting entry is similar to the entry for depreciation in that there is a debit to an expense account and a credit to a contra-asset account.

Assume that Miami Printing's Accounts Receivable balance is $90,000. Let's show the accounts and the adjusting entries in T account form.

Owner's Equity

Assets	=	Liabilities	+	Capital	−	Drawing	+	Revenue	−	Expenses
+ | −		− | +		− | +		+ | −		− | +		+ | −
Debit | Credit		Debit | Credit		Debit | Credit		Debit | Credit		Debit | Credit		Debit | Credit

Accounts Receivable

+	−
Bal. 90,000	

Income from Services

−	+
	Bal. 500,000

Bad Debts Expense

+	−
Adj. 5,000	

Allowance for Doubtful Accounts

−	+
	Bal. 170
	Adj. 5,000
	Bal. 5,170

Learning Objective

2 Prepare the entry to write off an account as uncollectible when the allowance method is used.

The Bad Debts Expense account comes into existence as an adjusting entry, and it is immediately closed during the closing process.

As certain credit customers' accounts are determined to be uncollectible and are written off, the losses are taken out of Allowance for Doubtful Accounts. Think of the Allowance for Doubtful Accounts as a reservoir. By means of the adjusting entry, the account is filled up at the end of the year and is gradually drained off (reduced) during the next year by write-offs of credit customer accounts. The $170 balance in Allowance for Doubtful Accounts at the end of the year (prior to the adjusting entry of $5,000) indicates that less accounts receivable were actually written off as uncollectible during the year than previously estimated. As a result, Bad Debts Expense in the period was overstated and net income thus understated.

Let's go on to the next year. On January 2, Miami Printing finally gives up on its attempts to collect $720 from its credit customer Ace Computer, which is included in Accounts Receivable. Miami Printing now writes off the account in the amount of $720, shown in T account form.

	Accounts Receivable				Allowance for Doubtful Accounts		
	+	−		−	+		
Bal.	90,000	Jan. 2 (write-off)	720	Jan. 2 (write-off) 720	Bal.	5,170	
Bal.	89,280				Bal.	4,450	

As you can see, the write-off has reduced both the balance of Accounts Receivable and the balance of Allowance for Doubtful Accounts but has not changed the net realizable value of accounts receivable. The general journal entry is shown below.

GENERAL JOURNAL — Page ___

Date		Description	Post. Ref.	Debit	Credit
20—					
Jan.	2	Allowance for Doubtful Accounts		7 2 0 00	
		Accounts Receivable			7 2 0 00
		Wrote off the account of Ace			
		Computer as uncollectible.			

An Advantage and a Disadvantage of the Allowance Method

The allowance method is consistent with the accrual basis of accounting in that it matches revenues of one year with expenses of the same year. The bad debts expense potential is provided in the same year in which the revenue is earned. The conformity with the matching principle places the allowance method in compliance with generally accepted accounting principles as recognized by the FASB.

SPECIFIC CHARGE-OFF METHOD

Under the **specific charge-off method of accounting for bad debts expense**, when a credit customer's account is determined to be uncollectible, the account is simply written off. The terms *write-off* and *charge-off* mean the same thing. No allowance account is used with the specific charge-off method because no estimate of uncollectible accounts receivable is calculated. As an illustration, Walter Company uses the specific charge-off method. On May 5, Walter Company writes off the account of Garber Construction, $1,220. For the purpose of this example, we will use a separate Accounts Receivable account for Garber Construction. T accounts pertaining to Garber's account look like this:

3 Prepare the entry to write off an account as uncollectible when the specific charge-off method is used.

Learning Objective

	Accounts Receivable, Garber Construction			Bad Debts Expense		
	+	−		+	−	
Bal.	1,220	May 5 (write-off)	1,220	May 5 (write-off) 1,220		

The general journal entry is shown below.

GENERAL JOURNAL					Page ___
Date	Description	Post. Ref.	Debit	Credit
20—					
May 5	Bad Debts Expense		1 2 2 0 00	
	Accounts Receivable			1 2 2 0 00
	Wrote off the account of			
	Garber Construction as			
	uncollectible.			

Under this method, entries will be made directly into the Bad Debts Expense account during the year. No adjusting entry is needed, and Allowance for Doubtful Accounts is not used.

Advantages of the Specific Charge-off Method

The main advantage is that the method may be used for federal income tax purposes. It is not necessary to make an adjusting entry. Also, one less account (Allowance for Doubtful Accounts) is required.

A Disadvantage of the Specific Charge-off Method

This method is not consistent with the accrual basis of accounting (recognizing revenue when it is earned and expenses when they are incurred). The method does not match up the revenues of one year with the expenses of the same year. This lack of conformity with the matching principle places the specific charge-off method in violation of generally accepted accounting principles. For example, the sale of services on account to Garber Construction could have been made two years ago. Because the account receivable will never be collected, the revenue for that year was too high (overstated). Consequently, net income is also overstated during that year. Now, two years later, $1,220 is written off as an expense. So net income for this year is too low (understated) because of the added expense.

Glossary

Allowance method of accounting for bad debts expense A method that requires an adjusting entry to debit Bad Debts Expense and to credit Allowance for Doubtful Accounts to match expenses from uncollectible accounts with sales of the same period. Write-offs of uncollectible accounts are debited to Allowance for Doubtful Accounts and credited to Accounts Receivable. *(p. B-1)*

Specific charge-off method of accounting for bad debts expense A method of recognizing bad debts that requires no adjusting entry. The accountant debits Bad Debts Expense and credits Accounts Receivable, when an uncollectable account is written off. This method is required for federal income tax reporting but is not allowed under GAAP. *(p. B-3)*

Problems

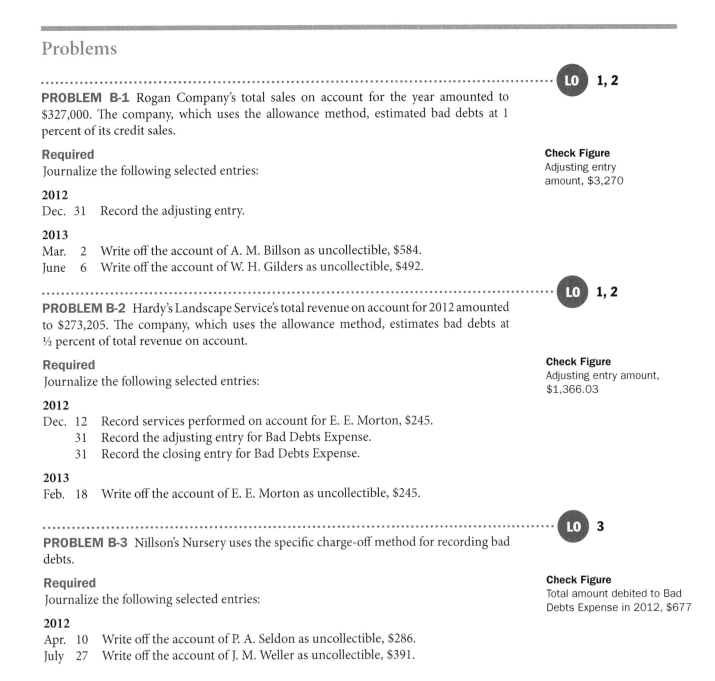

LO 1, 2

PROBLEM B-1 Rogan Company's total sales on account for the year amounted to $327,000. The company, which uses the allowance method, estimated bad debts at 1 percent of its credit sales.

Required
Journalize the following selected entries:

Check Figure
Adjusting entry
amount, $3,270

2012
Dec. 31   Record the adjusting entry.

2013
Mar. 2   Write off the account of A. M. Billson as uncollectible, $584.
June 6   Write off the account of W. H. Gilders as uncollectible, $492.

LO 1, 2

PROBLEM B-2 Hardy's Landscape Service's total revenue on account for 2012 amounted to $273,205. The company, which uses the allowance method, estimates bad debts at ½ percent of total revenue on account.

Required
Journalize the following selected entries:

Check Figure
Adjusting entry amount,
$1,366.03

2012
Dec. 12   Record services performed on account for E. E. Morton, $245.
     31   Record the adjusting entry for Bad Debts Expense.
     31   Record the closing entry for Bad Debts Expense.

2013
Feb. 18   Write off the account of E. E. Morton as uncollectible, $245.

LO 3

PROBLEM B-3 Nillson's Nursery uses the specific charge-off method for recording bad debts.

Required
Journalize the following selected entries:

Check Figure
Total amount debited to Bad
Debts Expense in 2012, $677

2012
Apr. 10   Write off the account of P. A. Seldon as uncollectible, $286.
July 27   Write off the account of J. M. Weller as uncollectible, $391.

Inventory Methods

1 Determine the amount of the ending merchandise inventory by the weighted-average-cost method.

3 Determine the amount of the ending merchandise inventory by the last-in, first-out (LIFO) method.

2 Determine the amount of the ending merchandise inventory by the first-in, first-out (FIFO) method.

Accounting Language

First-in, first-out (FIFO) method (p. C-2)

Last-in, first-out (LIFO) method (p. C-2)

Weighted-average-cost method (p. C-2)

To determine the dollar amount of the ending merchandise inventory under the periodic inventory system, it is necessary to take a physical count of the various items in stock and match them up with their costs. In other words, the ending inventory consists of the number of units of each type of item on hand multiplied by the cost of each unit.

If each unit were purchased at the same price, the job of determining the total cost of the inventory would be simple. For example, if there are 100 units of Product A on hand and all 100 units were bought at $15, the total cost of the ending inventory is $1,500 (100 × $15). However, over a period of time, costs of individual purchases of units may differ. Changes in costs of individual units make the different methods of inventory valuation necessary.

We will use Bruce Medical Supply, a distributor of medical supplies, to illustrate the three methods of inventory valuation. Bruce records inventory on a periodic inventory system. Bruce's ending inventory consists of 176 Standard 2.5v diagnostic sets acquired through various purchases, as follows:

Specific Purchase	Number of Units	Cost per Unit	Total Cost
Beginning inventory	34	$145	$ 4,930
First purchase	60	152	9,120
Second purchase	256	156	39,936
Third purchase	164	162	26,568
Total units available	514		$80,554

Of the 514 units available for sale, 176 units are still on hand and 338 have been sold (514 – 176 = 338 units sold).

Bruce Medical Supply may choose any one of the following three methods of recording the total cost of the 176 units in the ending inventory of medical supplies.

WEIGHTED-AVERAGE-COST METHOD

An alternative to keeping track of the cost of each item purchased is to use the **weighted-average-cost method**. This method averages the cost per unit of all like articles available for sale during the period. The first step is to find the total cost of the merchandise on hand during the year by multiplying the number of units by their respective purchase costs. (See page C-1.) From this information, you can find the average cost per unit, which will be used to determine the ending inventory value, as shown below:

$$\text{Average Cost per Unit} = \frac{\text{Total Cost}}{\text{Total Units Available}} = \frac{\$80,554}{514} = \$156.72 \text{ (rounded)}$$

Cost of Ending Inventory (176 units) = 156.72×176 units = $27,582.72

FIRST-IN, FIRST-OUT METHOD

The **first-in, first-out (FIFO) method** is based on the assumption that the first units of diagnostic sets purchased will be sold first. The costs of the units left will be those of the most recently purchased units. You may think of this as the way a grocery store sells milk. Because milk will sour, the oldest milk is moved to the front of the display shelf and is sold first. Consequently, the cartons of milk remaining on the shelf are the freshest milk.

Relating to our illustration of diagnostic sets:

Specific Purchase	Number of Units	Cost per Unit	Total Cost
Beginning inventory	34	$145	$ 4,930
First purchase	60	152	9,120
Second purchase	256	156	39,936
Third purchase	164	162	26,568
Total units available	514		$80,554

The cost of ending merchandise inventory, or the 176 diagnostic sets on hand (most recently purchased), is as follows:

164	units (third purchase)	@ $162 each =	$26,568
12	units (second purchase)	@ $156 each =	1,872
176	units		$28,440

LAST-IN, FIRST-OUT METHOD

The **last-in, first-out (LIFO) method** is based on the assumption that the last units of diagnostic sets purchased will be sold first. The costs of the units left over will be those of the earliest purchased units. You may think of this as the way a coal yard sells coal. When the coal yard sells coal to its customers, it takes coal off the top of the pile. Consequently, the tons of coal in the ending inventory consist of those first few tons at the bottom of the pile.

Relating to our illustration of diagnostic sets shown above, the cost of the ending merchandise inventory, or the 176 diagnostic sets on hand (earliest purchased), is as follows:

34	units (beginning inventory)	@ $145 each =	$ 4,930
60	units (first purchase)	@ $152 each =	9,120
82	units (second purchase)	@ $156 each =	12,792
176	units		$26,842

COMPARISON OF METHODS

If prices don't change very much, all inventory methods give about the same results. However, in a dynamic market where prices are constantly rising and falling, each method may yield different amounts. Here is a comparison of the results of the sale of diagnostic sets using the three methods we described.

Comparison of Three Methods		
Method	Ending Inventory (176 units)	Cost of Goods Sold (Goods Available for Sale − Ending Inventory) (338 units = 514 − 176)
Weighted-average-cost	$27,582.72	$52,971.28 ($80,554.00 − $27,582.72)
First-in, first-out	28,440.00	52,114.00 ($80,554.00 − $28,440.00)
Last-in, first-out	26,842.00	53,712.00 ($80,554.00 − $26,842.00)

A summary of the effects of the methods is as follows:

1. Weighted-average-cost is a compromise between LIFO and FIFO for both the amount of the ending inventory and the Cost of Goods Sold.
2. FIFO provides the most realistic amount for ending merchandise inventory in the Current Assets section of the balance sheet. The ending inventory is valued at the most recent costs, referred to as replacement cost.
3. LIFO provides the most realistic amount for the Cost of Goods Sold section of the income statement because the items that have been sold must be replaced at the most recent costs.

Now assume that the diagnostic sets were sold for $245 each.

	Weighted-Average-Cost	First-in, First-out	Last-in, First-out
Sales (338 units × $245 each)	$82,810.00	$82,810.00	$82,810.00
Less: Cost of Goods Sold	52,971.28	52,114.00	53,712.00
Gross Profit	$29,838.72	$30,696.00	$29,098.00

As you can see, the inventory method used can have an effect on the gross profit of a business. Once an inventory method is adopted by a business, the method must be used consistently. If a company wants to change its inventory method for tax purposes, the company must request permission from the Internal Revenue Service.

Glossary

First-in, first-out (FIFO) method An inventory costing method that assumes the first units purchased will be sold first and the costs of the units left in inventory will be from the most recently purchased items. *(p. C-2)*

Last-in, first-out (LIFO) method An inventory costing method that assumes the last units purchased will be sold first and the costs of the units left in inventory will be from the earliest purchased items. *(p. C-2)*

Weighted-average-cost method An inventory costing method that averages the costs of items purchased. The average unit price is then used to determine the total cost of goods sold and total cost of remaining inventory. *(p. C-2)*

Problems

LO 1

PROBLEM C-1 Bean Nursery sells bark to its customers at retail. Bean buys bark from a plywood mill in bulk and transports the bark in its own trucks. Information relating to the beginning inventory and purchases of bark is as follows:

Beginning inventory	1,500 cubic yards @ $0.40 per cubic yard
First purchase	2,100 cubic yards @ $0.42 per cubic yard
Second purchase	1,400 cubic yards @ $0.46 per cubic yard
Third purchase	1,000 cubic yards @ $0.47 per cubic yard

Check Figure
Cost of ending inventory,
$519.24

Required
Find the cost of 1,200 cubic yards in the ending inventory by the weighted-average-cost method. Carry average cost per cubic yard to four decimals.

LO 2

PROBLEM C-2 Use the information presented in Problem C-1 to solve this problem.

Check Figure
Cost of ending inventory,
$562

Required
Find the cost of the ending inventory by the first-in, first-out method.

LO 3

PROBLEM C-3 Use the information presented in Problem C-1 to solve this problem.

Check Figure
Cost of ending inventory,
$480

Required
Find the cost of the ending inventory by the last-in, first-out method.

Notes Payable and Notes Receivable

D

Learning Objectives

After you have completed this appendix, you will be able to do the following:

1 Calculate the interest on promissory notes.

2 Determine the due dates of promissory notes.

3a Record journal entries for notes given to secure an extension of time on an open account.

3b Record journal entries for payment of an interest-bearing note at maturity.

3c Record journal entries for notes given to secure a cash loan when the bank discounts the note.

3d Record journal entries for payment of a discounted note at maturity.

4a Record the journal entry for receipt of a note from a charge customer.

4b Record the journal entry for receipt of payment of an interest-bearing note at maturity.

4c Record the journal entry for discounting an interest-bearing note receivable.

4d Record the journal entry for a dishonored note receivable.

Accounting Language

Discount (p. D-4)

Discount period (p. D-7)

Discounting a notes payable (p. D-4)

Discounting notes receivable (p. D-6)

Dishonored note receivable (p. D-8)

Duration (p. D-2)

Interest (p. D-2)

Maker (p. D-1)

Maturity date (p. D-2)

Maturity value (p. D-4)

Payee (p. D-1)

Principal (p. D-2)

Proceeds (p. D-4)

Promissory note (p. D-1)

Credit plays an extremely important role in the operation of most business enterprises. Credit may be extended on a charge-account basis, with payment generally due in 25 to 30 days. This type of credit involves the Accounts Payable and Accounts Receivable accounts. Credit may also be granted by giving or receiving notes for specific transactions. This sort of credit involves the Notes Payable and Notes Receivable accounts. The notes which represent formal instruments of credit are known as a **promissory note**. A promissory note – usually referred to simply as a *note* – is a written promise to pay a certain sum at a fixed or determinable future time. They are customarily used as evidence of credit transactions for periods longer than 30 days. For example, promissory notes may be used in sales of equipment on the installment plan and for transactions involving large amounts of money. Promissory notes are also used to grant extensions of credit beyond the original credit terms. Like a check, notes must be payable to the order of a particular person or firm, known as the **payee**. It must also be signed by the person or firm making the promise, known as the **maker**.

Most companies become involved with notes at one time or another by issuing notes to creditors, by receiving notes from customers, or by issuing notes to banks in order to borrow money. Consequently, an accountant must be acquainted with the procedures for handling promissory notes.

CALCULATING INTEREST

1 Calculate the interest on promissory notes.

Interest is a charge made for the use of money. To the maker of the note, interest is an expense. The amount of interest a maker pays is expressed as a certain percentage of the principal of the note for a period of one year (or less). The following formula is used to calculate interest:

$$\underset{\substack{\text{(in dollars)}}}{\textbf{Interest}} = \underset{\substack{\text{(in dollars)}}}{\textbf{Principal} \text{ of Note}} \times \underset{\substack{\text{(as a percentage} \\ \text{of the principal)}}}{\textbf{Rate} \text{ of Interest}} \times \underset{\substack{\text{(expressed as a} \\ \text{year or fraction} \\ \text{of a year)}}}{\textbf{Time} \text{ of Note}}$$

FYI

Agencies of the federal government use the actual number of days in the year.

The **principal** is the face amount of the note. The *rate of interest* is a percentage of the principal. *Time,* or the length of life of the note, is usually expressed in days or months. It is the period between the note's date of issue (starting date) and its **maturity date** (the due date or interest payment date). It is stated in terms of a year or fraction of a year. The usual commercial practice is to use a 360-day year, making the denominator of the fraction 360.

Example: $80,000, 6 percent, 60 days

Interest = Principal × Rate × Time

$$\text{Interest} = \$80,000 \times 0.06 \times \frac{60}{360} = \underline{\$800}$$

DETERMINING DUE DATES

2 Determine the due dates of promissory notes.

The period of time between a promissory note's issue date and its maturity date is called the **duration** of the note. The duration of a note may be expressed in days or moths. If the time of the note is expressed in months, the maturity date is the corresponding day in the month after the specified number of months has elapsed. When counting the number of days, begin with the day *after* the date the note was issued and end with the last day of the note.

Example

Let's say that the due date of a promissory note is specified as 60 days after April 8. The due date is June 7.

The due date is determined by the following steps:

STEP 1. Determine the number of days remaining in the month of issue by subtracting the date of the note from the number of days in the month in which it is dated.

STEP 2. Add as many full months as possible without exceeding the number of days in the note, counting the full number of days in these months.

STEP 3. Determine the number of days remaining in the month in which the note matures by subtracting the total days counted so far from the number of days in the note, as shown on the following page.

April								May								June						
S	M	T	W	T	F	S		S	M	T	W	T	F	S		S	M	T	W	T	F	S
		1	2	3	4	5						1	2	3		1	2	3	4	5	6	7
6	7	8	9	10	11	12		4	5	6	7	8	9	10		8	9	10	11	12	13	14
13	14	15	16	17	18	19		11	12	13	14	15	16	17		15	16	17	18	19	20	21
20	21	22	23	24	25	26		18	19	20	21	22	23	24		22	23	24	25	26	27	28
27	28	29	30					25	26	27	28	29	30	31		29	30					

22 days
8th through the 30th
30 − 8 = 22 days left

+ 31 days

= 53 days have passed
60 − 53 = 7 days remaining after May 31
June 7 due date

STEP 1. April (30 − 8)   = 22 days left in April

STEP 2. May   = 31 days
            _____
            Total days so far   = 53 days

STEP 3. June (60 − 53)   = 7th day of June (due date)

In addition to determining the due date using the method above, you can find a loan calculator on the Internet that will automatically find the due dat. These calculators require you to input the starting date and time period of the loan; the software then determines the due date.

TRANSACTIONS FOR NOTES PAYABLE

We assume that all notes are due within one year; thus, they are classified on the balance sheet as Current Liabilities. However, if notes are not due within one year, the portion of the note that is due within one year is a Current Liability and the remainder is classified as a Long-Term Liability. Interest expense is classified on the income statement as Interest Expense (if significant) or Other Expense.

Note Given to Secure an Extension of Time on an Open Account

When a company wants to obtain an extension of time for the payment of an account, the company may ask a supplier to accept a note for all or part of the amount due. For example, assume that Whitewater Raft Supply prefers not to pay its open account with Dana Manufacturing Company when the account becomes due. Dana Manufacturing Company agrees to accept a 60-day, 6 percent, $900 note from Whitewater Raft Supply in settlement of the account. The entry that caused the account to be put on Dana Manufacturing Company's books came about when Whitewater Raft Supply bought merchandise on account on April 12, with terms 2/10, n/30.

3a Record journal entries for notes given to secure an extension of time on an open account.

Learning Objective

ORIGINAL PURCHASE
In general journal form, the entry looks like this:

		GENERAL JOURNAL			Page ___	
Date		Description	Post. Ref.	Debit	Credit	
20—						
Apr.	12	Purchase		9 0 0 00		
		Accounts Payable, Dana				
		Manufacturing Company			9 0 0 00	
		Terms 2/10, n/30.				

PAYMENT BY NOTE

On May 12, Whitewater Raft Supply records the issuance of the note in its general journal.

			GENERAL JOURNAL			Page ___
	Date		Description	Post. Ref.	Debit	Credit
20—						
May	12		Accounts Payable, Dana			
			Manufacturing Company		9 0 0 00	
			Notes Payable			9 0 0 00
			Gave a 60-day, 6 percent			
			note in settlement of our			
			open account.			

Observe that the previous entry cancels the Accounts Payable, Dana Manufacturing Company account and substitutes Notes Payable. The note does not *pay* the debt; it merely changes the liability status from an account payable to a note payable.

Payment of an Interest-Bearing Note at Maturity

3b Record journal entries for payment of an interest-bearing note at maturity.

When a note payable falls due, payment must be made to the holder. The maker must make payment for the principal of the note plus the interest, or **maturity value**.

Whitewater Raft Supply pays the note on July 11. In general journal form, the entry is as follows:

			GENERAL JOURNAL			Page ___
	Date		Description	Post. Ref.	Debit	Credit
20—						
July	11		Notes Payable		9 0 0 00	
			Interest Expense		9 00	
			Cash			9 0 9 00
			Paid note to Dana			
			Manufacturing Company.			

Because Interest = Principal × Rate × Time, we perform this calculation:

$$\text{Interest} = \$900 \times 0.06 \times \frac{60}{360} = \underline{\underline{\$9}}$$

Borrowing from a Bank When Bank Discounts Note (Deducts Interest in Advance)

3c Record journal entries for notes given to secure a cash loan when the bank discounts the note.

In another type of bank loan, called **discounting a note payable**, the bank deducts the interest in advance. For example, also on June 7, Whitewater Raft Supply borrows $10,000 for 120 days from Westmore National Bank and the bank requires Whitewater Raft Supply to sign a note. From the face value of the note, the bank deducts 6 percent interest for 120 days, so Whitewater Raft Supply actually gets only $9,800 (($10,000 − $200). This interest deducted in advance by a bank is called the **discount**. The principal of the loan left after the discount has been subtracted is called the **proceeds**, which is the amount the borrower has available to use. Because all of the interest is deducted at the time the loan is made, the note must state that only the face amount is to be paid at maturity. The calculation for the discount is as follows:

$$\text{Interest} = \text{Principal} \times \text{Rate} \times \text{Time}$$

$$\text{Interest} = \$10,000 \times 0.06 \times \frac{120}{360} = \underline{\$200}$$

The bank deducts the discount from the face amount of the note before making the money available to the borrower.

Principal	$10,000
– Discount	200
Proceeds	$ 9,800

		GENERAL JOURNAL				Page __	
Date		Description	Post. Ref.	Debit		Credit	
20—							
June	7	Cash		9 8 0 0 00			
		Interest Expense		2 0 0 00			
		Notes Payable				10 0 0 0 00	
		Discounted our 120-day, non-					
		interest-bearing note at Westmore					
		National Bank, discount rate					
		6 percent.					

Note Paid to the Bank at Maturity

When the note becomes due, Whitewater Raft Supply pays the bank only the *face value of the note* and records the transaction as follows:

		GENERAL JOURNAL				Page __	
Date		Description	Post. Ref.	Debit		Credit	
20—							
Oct.	5	Notes Payable		10 0 0 0 00			
		Cash				10 0 0 0 00	
		Paid Westmore National					
		Bank on our note payable					
		discounted June 7.					

 Record journal entries for payment of a discounted note at maturity.

TRANSACTIONS FOR NOTES RECEIVABLE

 Record the journal entry for receipt of a note from a charge customer.

Now let's see how to journalize tranctions involving notes receivable for Whitewater Raft Supply. The accounts involved are Notes Receivable (classified as a current asset on the balance sheet in our examples, although it could be classified as a long-term asset if the repayment period is longer than a year) and Interest Income (classified as other income on the income statement).

Note from a Charge Customer to Extend Time on Account

On March 7, Whitewater Raft Supply sold $930 worth of merchandise to Green River Rafts, with the customary terms of 2/10, n/30, and made the original entry in its sales journal. On April 6, Green River Rafts sent Whitewater Raft Supply a note for $930, payable within 30 days, at 6 percent interest. The note, dated April 6, was in settlement of the transaction of March 7. Whitewater Raft Supply recorded this new development in its general journal as follows:

	GENERAL JOURNAL				Page___	
Date	Description	Post. Ref.	Debit		Credit	
20—						
Apr. 6	Notes Receivable		9 3 0 00			
	Accounts Receivable, Green					
	River Rafts				9 3 0 00	
	Received a 30-day, 6 percent					
	note, dated April 6, in					
	settlement of open account.					

4b Record the journal entry for receipt of payment of an interest-bearing note at maturity.

RECEIPT OF PAYMENT OF AN INTEREST-BEARING NOTE AT MATURITY

On May 6, Green River Rafts paid Whitewater Raft Supply in full: principal plus interest. Whitewater Raft Supply recorded the transaction in the general journal as follows:

	GENERAL JOURNAL				Page___	
Date	Description	Post. Ref.	Debit		Credit	
20—						
May 6	Cash		9 3 4 65			
	Notes Receivable				9 3 0 00	
	Interest Income				4 65	
	Received full payment of					
	Green River Rafts' note.					
	($930 × 0.06 × 30/360)					

As a reminder, if special journals were used, this transaction would be recorded directly in the cash receipts journal rather than in the general journal. But for the sake of simplicity and clarity, we will use the general journal format to illustrate entries throughout this chapter.

DISCOUNTING NOTE RECEIVABLE

4c Record the journal entry for discounting an interest-bearing note receivable.

Instead of keeping notes receivable until they come due, a firm can raise cash by selling its notes receivable to a bank or finance company. This type of financing is called **discounting notes receivable** because the bank deducts the interest or discount from the maturity value of the note to determine the proceeds (that is, the amount of money received by the payee). In the process of discounting a note receivable, the payee endorses the note (as it would a check) and delivers it to the financial institution.

The financial institution gives out cash now in exchange for the right to collect the principal and interest when the note comes due. The discount rate is the annual rate (percentage of maturity value) charged by the financial institution for buying the note. The financial institution generally discounts at a higher interest rate than stated in the note because the financial institution assumes increased risk of the maker's possible default.

Whitewater Raft Supply granted an extension on an open account by accepting a 60-day, 5 percent note for $1,800, dated April 20, from Bowers River Co. To raise cash to buy additional merchandise, Whitewater Raft Supply sold the note to New National Bank on May 5. The bank charged a discount rate of 6 percent. In handling discounted notes receivable, you should follow a definite step-by-step procedure.

STEP 1. Diagram the Situation. A diagram of the Situation looks like this:

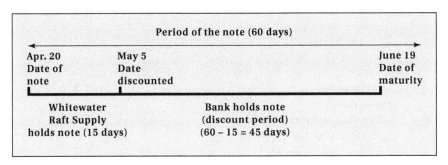

STEP 2. Determine the discount period. The discount period of the note consists of the interval between the date the note is given to the bank and the maturity date of the note. (In other words, the discount period is the time the note has left to run.)

Days held by endorser:			**Discount period (bank holds note):**
April 30 − 20	=	10 days left in April	(Total days − Days held by endorser)
May	=	5 days in May	60 days − 15 days = 45 days
Days held by endorser	=	15 days	

STEP 3. Record the formula. Next, we determine the value of the note at maturity and deduct the amount of the bank's discount from it, using the following formula:

    Principal ($1,800)

\+   Interest to maturity date (5%, 60 days)

    Value at maturity

−   Discount (6%, 45 days)

    Proceeds

STEP 4. Complete the formula. After we set up the problem, we can complete the calculation.

Principal	$1,800.00	Interest = Principal × Rate × Time
\+ Interest (5%, 60 days)	15.00	
Value at maturity	$1,815.00	Interest = $1,800.00 × 0.05 × $\frac{60}{360}$ = $15.00
− Discount (6%, 45 days)	13.61	
Proceeds	$1,801.39	Discount = $1,815.00 × 0.06 × $\frac{45}{360}$ = $13.61

Note that in our calculations, we figure the discount on the value of the note at maturity ($1,815). The proceeds are the amount that Whitewater Raft Supply receives from the bank; this amount is therefore debited to Cash. *If the amount of the proceeds is greater than the amount of the principal, the difference represents Interest Income* because Whitewater Raft Supply made money on the deal. *If the amount of the proceeds is less than the principal, on the other hand, the deficiency represents Interest Expense* because Whitewater Raft Supply lost money in the deal.

STEP 5. Record the entry. Look at the entry in Whitewater Raft Supply's general journal.

GENERAL JOURNAL						Page ___
Date		Description	Post. Ref.	Debit	Credit	
20—						
May	5	Cash		1 8 0 1 39		
		Notes Receivable			1 8 0 0 00	
		Interest Income			1 39	
		Discounted at the bank Bowers River				
		Co.'s note, dated April 20. The bank				
		discount rate is 6 percent.				

DISHONORED NOTES RECEIVABLE

4d Record the journal entry for a dishonored note receivable.

When the maker of a note fails to pay the principal amount or to renew the note at maturity, the note is said to be a **dishonored note receivable**. The maker of the note is still obligated to pay the principal plus interest, and the creditor should take legal steps to collect the debt. However, the balance of the Notes Receivable account shows only the principal of notes that have not yet matured. A note that is past due, or dishonored, should be removed from the Notes Receivable account and added to the Accounts Receivable account; the amount listed should be the principal plus interest. In other words, once a note receivable comes due and is not collected, it is "in default." Bu the maker still owes the payee, so the amount owed (principal plus interest) is put back into Accounts Receivable.

For example, Whitewater Raft Supply holds a 60-day, 5 percent note for $950, dated April 20, from Hartman Guides, which fails to pay by the due date. Thus, the note is dishonored at maturity. Whitewater Raft Supply then makes the following entry in its general journal to remove the dishonored note from the Notes Receivable account.

GENERAL JOURNAL						Page ___
Date		Description	Post. Ref.	Debit	Credit	
20—						
June	19	Accounts Receivable, Hartman				
		Guides		9 5 7 92		
		Notes Receivable			9 5 0 00	
		Interest Income			7 92	
		Hartman Guides dishonored				
		its 60-day, 5 percent note for				
		$950, dated April 20.				
		($950 × 0.05 × 60/360)				

Glossary

Discount Interest deducted in advance by a bank that makes a loan (p. D-4)

Discount period The time between the date a note receivable is discounted and the date it matures. (p. D-7)

Discounting a notes payable The procedure by which a bank deducts interest in advance when it loans money with a note. (p. D-4)

Discounting notes receivable The process by which a firm may raise cash by selling a note receivable to a bank or finance company. The bank deducts the discount from the maturity value of the note to determine the proceeds (*amount of money*) the firm receives. (p. D-6)

Dishonored note receivable A note whose maker fails to pay the principal amount or to renew the note at maturity. (p. D-8)

Duration The period of time a note is outstanding; the length of time in days or months from a note's issue date to its maturity date. (p. D-2)

Interest A charge made for the use of money. (p. D-2)

Maker An individual or a firm that signs a promissory note. (p. D-1)

Maturity date The due date of a promissory note. (p. D-2)

Maturity value The principal (*face value*) of note plus interest from the date of the note until the due date. (p. D-4)

Payee The party receiving payment, such as on a note receivable or an account receivable. (p. D-1)

Principal The face amount of a note. (p. D-2)

Proceeds The principal of a loan less the discount. (p. D-4)

Promissory note A written promise to pay a certain sum at a fixed or determinable future time. (p. D-1)

Problems

LO 1, 2

PROBLEM D-1 Part A: Calculate the interest on the following notes:

Principal	Interest Rate (percent)	Number of Days
1. $14,600	5.5%	30 days
2. 11,200	6.5	60 days
3. 6,400	5	90 days
4. 9,500	6	120 days
5. 3,500	7	3 months

Part B: Determine the maturity dates on the following notes:

Date of Issue	Life of Note
1. January 18	90 days
2. February 12	6 months
3. June 21	60 days
4. September 10	4 months
5. November 17	30 days

LO 1, 2, 3a, 3b

PROBLEM D-2 Andy Cooke gave a 60-day, 5.5 percent note, dated February 14, to Key Company, a creditor, in the amount of $10,500.

a. What is the due date of the note?
b. How much interest is to be paid on the note at maturity?
c. Write the entries in general journal form to record issuance of the note by the maker and payment of the note at maturity as they would appear on Cooke's books.

LO 3c, 3d

PROBLEM D-3 As a result of a loan from Plateau State Bank, Trent Company signed a 90-day note, dated March 12, for $12,700 that the bank discounted at 7 percent. Journalize the entries for the maker in general journal form to record the following, assuming that the note is paid in the same fiscal period.

a. Issuance of the note on March 12.
b. Payment of the note at maturity.

LO 3c, 3d

PROBLEM D-4 On August 5, M. Valenty borrowed $8,500 from Costner State Bank for 45 days, with a discount rate of 7 percent. Accordingly, M. Valenty signed a note for $8,500, dated August 5. Write entries in general journal form to record the following transactions:

a. Issuance of the note on August 5.
b. Payment of the note at maturity on September 19.

LO 4a, 4b

PROBLEM D-5 On March 11, Rainz Company received a 90-day, 6 percent note for $1,500, dated March 11, from J. Rose, a charge customer, to satisfy his open account receivable.

a. What is the due date of the note?
b. How much interest is due at maturity?
Given the preceding data, write entries in general journal form on the books of Rainz Company to record the following:
c. Receipt of the note from J. Rose in settlement of his account.
d. Receipt of the principal and interest at maturity.
Given the same data, write entries in general journal form on Rose's books to record the following:
e. Issuance of the note by Rose in settlement of his account.
f. Payment of the note at maturity.

LO 4a, 4c

Problem D-6 Prepare entries in general journal form to record the following:

June 12 Sold merchandise on account to K. Perrot; terms 3/10, n/30; $1,740.
July 12 Received $740 in cash from K. Perrot and a 60-day, 7 percent note for $1,000, dated July 12.
Aug. 17 Discounted the note at the bank at 7.5 percent.

LO 4a, 4b

PROBLEM D-7 The following T accounts show a series of four transactions concerning a sale of merchandise on account and subsequent payment of the amount owed. Describe what happened in each transaction.

Cash			Accounts Receivable			Sales		
+	−		+	−		−	+	
(d) 1,090			(a) 1,200	(b) 120			(a) 1,200	
				(c) 1,080				

Interest Income			Notes Receivable			Sales Returns and Allowances		
−	+		+	−		+	−	
	(d) 10		(c) 1,080	(d) 1,080		(b) 120		

LO 4d

PROBLEM D-8 Prepare entries in general journal form to record the following:

Aug. 6 Woodard Company failed to pay its 30-day, 5 percent note for $480, dated July 7. The note is thus dishonored at maturity.

FINANCIAL
& MANAGERIAL
ACCOUNTING

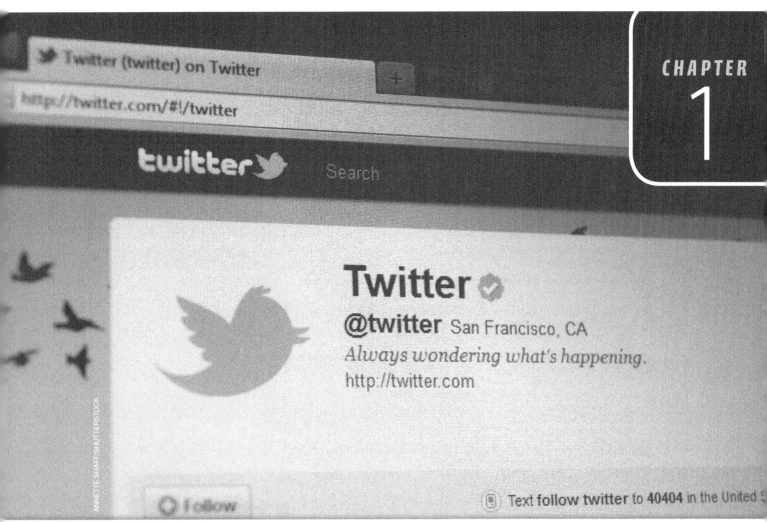

Introduction to Accounting and Business

Twitter

When two teams pair up for a game of football, there is often a lot of noise. The band plays, the fans cheer, and fireworks light up the scoreboard. Obviously, the fans are committed and care about the outcome of the game. Just like fans at a football game, the owners of a business want their business to "win" against their competitors in the marketplace. While having your football team win can be a source of pride, winning in the marketplace goes beyond pride and has many tangible benefits. Companies that are winners are better able to serve customers, provide good jobs for employees, and make money for their owners.

Twitter is one of the most visible companies on the Internet. It provides a real-time information network where members can post messages, called Tweets, of up to 140 characters for free. Millions post Tweets every day throughout the world.

Do you think Twitter is a successful company? Does it make money? How would you know? Accounting helps to answer these questions.

This textbook introduces you to accounting, the language of business. Chapter 1 begins by discussing what a business is, how it operates, and the role that accounting plays.

OBJ 1 Describe the nature of business and the role of accounting and ethics in business.

Nature of Business and Accounting

A **business**[1] is an organization in which basic resources (inputs), such as materials and labor, are assembled and processed to provide goods or services (outputs) to customers. Businesses come in all sizes, from a local coffee house to **Starbucks**, which sells over $10 billion of coffee and related products each year.

The objective of most businesses is to earn a **profit**. Profit is the difference between the amounts received from customers for goods or services and the amounts paid for the inputs used to provide the goods or services. This text focuses on businesses operating to earn a profit. However, many of the same concepts and principles also apply to not-for-profit organizations such as hospitals, churches, and government agencies.

Types of Businesses

Three types of businesses operating for profit include service, merchandising, and manufacturing businesses. Some examples of each type of business are given below.

Service businesses provide services rather than products to customers.
    Delta Air Lines (transportation services)
    The Walt Disney Company (entertainment services)

---

1 A complete glossary of terms appears at the end of the text.

Merchandising businesses sell products they purchase from other businesses to customers.

> Walmart (general merchandise)
> Amazon.com (Internet books, music, videos)

Manufacturing businesses change basic inputs into products that are sold to customers.

> Ford Motor Co. (cars, trucks, vans)
> Dell, Inc. (personal computers)

Role of Accounting in Business

The role of accounting in business is to provide information for managers to use in operating the business. In addition, accounting provides information to other users in assessing the economic performance and condition of the business.

Thus, **accounting** can be defined as an information system that provides reports to users about the economic activities and condition of a business. You could think of accounting as the "language of business." This is because accounting is the means by which businesses' financial information is communicated to users.

Note:
Accounting is an information system that provides reports to users about the economic activities and condition of a business.

The process by which accounting provides information to users is as follows:

1. Identify users.
2. Assess users' information needs.
3. Design the accounting information system to meet users' needs.
4. Record economic data about business activities and events.
5. Prepare accounting reports for users.

As illustrated in Exhibit 1, users of accounting information can be divided into two groups: internal users and external users.

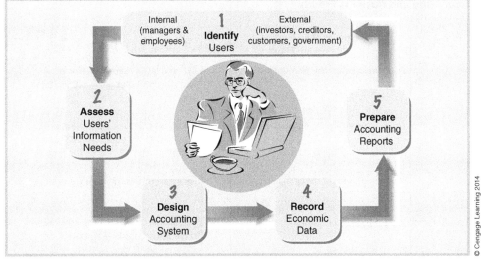

EXHIBIT 1

Accounting as an Information System

© Cengage Learning 2014

Internal users of accounting information include managers and employees. These users are directly involved in managing and operating the business. The area of accounting that provides internal users with information is called **managerial accounting**, or **management accounting**.

The objective of managerial accounting is to provide relevant and timely information for managers' and employees' decision-making needs. Oftentimes, such information is sensitive and is not distributed outside the business. Examples of sensitive information might include information about customers, prices, and plans to expand the business. Managerial accountants employed by a business are employed in **private accounting**.

External users of accounting information include investors, creditors, customers, and the government. These users are not directly involved in managing and operating the business. The area of accounting that provides external users with information is called **financial accounting**.

The objective of financial accounting is to provide relevant and timely information for the decision-making needs of users outside of the business. For example, financial reports on the operations and condition of the business are useful for banks and other creditors in deciding whether to lend money to the business. **General-purpose financial statements** are one type of financial accounting report that is distributed to external users. The term *general-purpose* refers to the wide range of decision-making needs that these reports are designed to serve. Later in this chapter, general-purpose financial statements are described and illustrated.

Role of Ethics in Accounting and Business

The objective of accounting is to provide relevant, timely information for user decision making. Accountants must behave in an ethical manner so that the information they provide users will be trustworthy and, thus, useful for decision making. Managers and employees must also behave in an ethical manner in managing and operating a business. Otherwise, no one will be willing to invest in or loan money to the business.

Ethics are moral principles that guide the conduct of individuals. Unfortunately, business managers and accountants sometimes behave in an unethical manner. Many of the managers of the companies listed in Exhibit 2 engaged in accounting or business fraud. These ethical violations led to fines, firings, and lawsuits. In some cases, managers were criminally prosecuted, convicted, and sent to prison.

EXHIBIT 2	Accounting and Business Frauds

Company	Nature of Accounting or Business Fraud	Result
Computer Associates International, Inc.	Fraudulently inflated its financial results.	CEO and senior executives indicted. Five executives pled guilty. $225 million fine.
Enron	Fraudulently inflated its financial results.	Bankrupcty. Senior executives criminally convicted. Over $60 billion in stock market losses.
HealthSouth	Overstated performance by $4 billion in false entries.	Senior executives criminally convicted.
Qwest Communications International, Inc.	Improperly recognized $3 billion in false receipts.	CEO and six other executives criminally convicted of "massive financial fraud." $250 million SEC fine.
Xerox Corporation	Recognized $3 billion in revenue prior to when it should have been recorded.	$10 million fine to SEC. Six executives forced to pay $22 million.

© Cengage Learning 2014

What went wrong for the managers and companies listed in Exhibit 2? The answer normally involved one or both of the following two factors:

> *Failure of Individual Character.* An ethical manager and accountant is honest and fair. However, managers and accountants often face pressures from

supervisors to meet company and investor expectations. In many of the cases in Exhibit 2, managers and accountants justified small ethical violations to avoid such pressures. However, these small violations became big violations as the company's financial problems became worse.

Culture of Greed and Ethical Indifference. By their behavior and attitude, senior managers set the company culture. In most of the companies listed in Exhibit 2, the senior managers created a culture of greed and indifference to the truth.

As a result of the accounting and business frauds shown in Exhibit 2, Congress passed new laws to monitor the behavior of accounting and business. For example, the **Sarbanes-Oxley Act of 2002 (SOX)** was enacted. SOX established a new oversight body for the accounting profession called the **Public Company Accounting Oversight Board (PCAOB)**. In addition, SOX established standards for independence, corporate responsibility, and disclosure.

How does one behave ethically when faced with financial or other types of pressure? Guidelines for behaving ethically are shown in Exhibit 3.[2]

---

1. Identify an ethical decision by using your personal ethical standards of honesty and fairness.
2. Identify the consequences of the decision and its effect on others.
3. Consider your obligations and responsibilities to those who will be affected by your decision.
4. Make a decision that is ethical and fair to those affected by it.

EXHIBIT 3

Guidelines for Ethical Conduct

© Cengage Learning 2014

Integrity, Objectivity, and Ethics in Business

BERNIE MADOFF

In June 2009, Bernard L. "Bernie" Madoff was sentenced to 150 years in prison for defrauding thousands of investors in one of the biggest frauds in American history. Madoff's fraud started several decades earlier when he began a "Ponzi scheme" in his investment management firm, Bernard L. Madoff Investment Securities LLC.

In a Ponzi scheme, the investment manager uses funds received from new investors to pay a return to existing investors, rather than basing investment returns on the fund's actual performance. As long as the investment manager is able to attract new investors, he or she will have new funds to pay existing investors and continue the fraud. While most Ponzi schemes collapse quickly when the investment manager runs out of new investors, Madoff's reputation, popularity, and personal contacts provided a steady stream of investors, which allowed the fraud to survive for decades.

© Cengage Learning 2014

Opportunities for Accountants

Numerous career opportunities are available for students majoring in accounting. Currently, the demand for accountants exceeds the number of new graduates entering the job market. This is partly due to the increased regulation of business caused by the accounting and business frauds shown in Exhibit 2. Also, more and more businesses have come to recognize the importance and value of accounting information.

As indicated earlier, accountants employed by a business are employed in private accounting. Private accountants have a variety of possible career options within a company. Some of these career options are shown in Exhibit 4 along with their

---

2 Many companies have ethical standards of conduct for managers and employees. In addition, the Institute of Management Accountants and the American Institute of Certified Public Accountants have professional codes of conduct.

EXHIBIT 4	Accounting Career Paths and Salaries			
Accounting Career Track	**Description**	**Career Options**	**Annual Starting Salaries***	**Certification**
Private Accounting	Accountants employed by companies, government, and not-for-profit entities.	Bookkeeper	$38,500	
		Payroll clerk	$37,000	Certified Payroll Professional (CPP)
		General accountant	$44,625	
		Budget analyst	$47,250	
		Cost accountant	$46,625	Certified Management Accountant (CMA)
		Internal auditor	$51,875	Certified Internal Auditor (CIA)
		Information technology auditor	$60,750	Certified Information Systems Auditor (CISA)
Public Accounting	Accountants employed individually or within a public accounting firm in tax or audit services.	Local firms	$47,313	Certified Public Accountant (CPA)
		National firms	$57,250	Certified Public Accountant (CPA)

Source: Robert Half 2012 U.S. Salary Guide (Finance and Accounting), Robert Half International, Inc. (http://www.rhi.com/salaryguides)
*Mean salaries of a reported range. Private accounting salaries are reported for large companies. Salaries may vary by region.

starting salaries. Accountants who provide audit services, called auditors, verify the accuracy of financial records, accounts, and systems. As shown in Exhibit 4, several private accounting careers have certification options.

Accountants and their staff who provide services on a fee basis are said to be employed in **public accounting**. In public accounting, an accountant may practice as an individual or as a member of a public accounting firm. Public accountants who have met a state's education, experience, and examination requirements may become **Certified Public Accountants (CPAs)**. CPAs typically perform general accounting, audit, or tax services. As can be seen in Exhibit 4, CPAs have slightly better starting salaries than private accountants. Career statistics indicate, however, that these salary differences tend to disappear over time.

Because all functions within a business use accounting information, experience in private or public accounting provides a solid foundation for a career. Many positions in industry and in government agencies are held by individuals with accounting backgrounds.

 Summarize the development of accounting principles and relate them to practice.

Generally Accepted Accounting Principles

If a company's management could record and report financial data as it saw fit, comparisons among companies would be difficult, if not impossible. Thus, financial accountants follow **generally accepted accounting principles (GAAP)** in preparing reports. These reports allow investors and other users to compare one company to another.

Accounting principles and concepts develop from research, accepted accounting practices, and pronouncements of regulators. Within the United States, the **Financial Accounting Standards Board (FASB)** has the primary responsibility for developing accounting principles. The FASB publishes *Statements of Financial Accounting Standards* as well as *Interpretations* of these Standards. In addition, the **Securities and Exchange Commission (SEC),** an agency of the U.S. government, has authority over the accounting and financial disclosures for companies whose shares of ownership (stock) are traded and sold to the public. The SEC normally accepts the accounting principles set forth by the FASB. However, the SEC may issue *Staff Accounting Bulletins* on accounting matters that may not have been addressed by the FASB.

Many countries outside the United States use generally accepted accounting principles adopted by the **International Accounting Standards Board (IASB)**. The IASB issues *International Financial Reporting Standards (IFRSs)*. Differences currently exist between FASB and IASB accounting principles. However, the FASB and IASB are working together to reduce and eliminate these differences into a single set of accounting principles. Such a set of worldwide accounting principles would help facilitate investment and business in an increasingly global economy.

See Appendix C for more information.

In this chapter and text, accounting principles and concepts are emphasized. It is through this emphasis on the "why" as well as the "how" that you will gain an understanding of accounting.

International Connection

INTERNATIONAL FINANCIAL REPORTING STANDARDS (IFRS)

IFRS are considered to be more "principles-based" than U.S. GAAP, which is considered to be more "rules-based." For example, U.S. GAAP consists of approximately 17,000 pages, which include numerous industry-specific accounting rules. In contrast, IFRS allow more judgment in deciding how business transactions are recorded. Many believe that the strong regulatory and litigation environment in the United States is the cause for the more rules-based GAAP approach. Regardless, IFRS and GAAP share many common principles.*

*Differences between U.S. GAAP and IFRS are further discussed and illustrated in Appendix C.

© Cengage Learning 2014

Business Entity Concept

The **business entity concept** limits the economic data in an accounting system to data related directly to the activities of the business. In other words, the business is viewed as an entity separate from its owners, creditors, or other businesses. For example, the accountant for a business with one owner would record the activities of the business only and would not record the personal activities, property, or debts of the owner.

A business entity may take the form of a proprietorship, partnership, corporation, or limited liability company (LLC). Each of these forms and their major characteristics are listed below.

Note:
Under the business entity concept, the activities of a business are recorded separately from the activities of its owners, creditors, or other businesses.

Form of Business Entity	Characteristics
Proprietorship is owned by one individual.	• 70% of business entities in the United States. • Easy and cheap to organize. • Resources are limited to those of the owner. • Used by small businesses.
Partnership is owned by two or more individuals.	• 10% of business organizations in the United States (combined with limited liability companies). • Combines the skills and resources of more than one person.
Corporation is organized under state or federal statutes as a separate legal taxable entity.	• Generates 90% of business revenues. • 20% of the business organizations in the United States. • Ownership is divided into shares called *stock*. • Can obtain large amounts of resources by issuing stock. • Used by large businesses.
Limited liability company (LLC) combines the attributes of a partnership and a corporation.	• 10% of business organizations in the United States (combined with partnerships). • Often used as an alternative to a partnership. • Has tax and legal liability advantages for owners.

The three types of businesses discussed earlier—service, merchandising, and manufacturing—may be organized as proprietorships, partnerships, corporations, or limited liability companies. Because of the large amount of resources required to operate a manufacturing business, most manufacturers such as **Ford Motor Company** are corporations. Most large retailers such as **Walmart** and **Home Depot** are also corporations. Companies organized as corporations often include *Inc.* as part of their name to indicate that they are incorporated. For example, Apple's legal name is Apple Inc.

Cost Concept

Under the **cost concept**, amounts are initially recorded in the accounting records at their cost or purchase price. To illustrate, assume that Aaron Publishers purchased the following building on February 20, 2012, for $150,000:

Price listed by seller on January 1, 2012	$160,000
Aaron Publishers' initial offer to buy on January 31, 2012	140,000
Purchase price on February 20, 2012	150,000
Estimated selling price on December 31, 2014	220,000
Assessed value for property taxes, December 31, 2014	190,000

Under the cost concept, Aaron Publishers records the purchase of the building on February 20, 2012, at the purchase price of $150,000. The other amounts listed above have no effect on the accounting records.

The fact that the building has an estimated selling price of $220,000 on December 31, 2014, indicates that the building has increased in value. However, to use the $220,000 in the accounting records would be to record an illusory or unrealized profit. If Aaron Publishers sells the building on January 9, 2016, for $240,000, a profit of $90,000 ($240,000 − $150,000) is then realized and recorded. The new owner would record $240,000 as its cost of the building.

The cost concept also involves the objectivity and unit of measure concepts. The **objectivity concept** requires that the amounts recorded in the accounting records be based on objective evidence. In exchanges between a buyer and a seller, both try to get the best price. Only the final agreed-upon amount is objective enough to be recorded in the accounting records. If amounts in the accounting records were constantly being revised upward or downward based on offers, appraisals, and opinions, accounting reports could become unstable and unreliable.

The **unit of measure concept** requires that economic data be recorded in dollars. Money is a common unit of measurement for reporting financial data and reports.

Example Exercise 1-1 **Cost Concept**

On August 25, Gallatin Repair Service extended an offer of $125,000 for land that had been priced for sale at $150,000. On September 3, Gallatin Repair Service accepted the seller's counteroffer of $137,000. On October 20, the land was assessed at a value of $98,000 for property tax purposes. On December 4, Gallatin Repair Service was offered $160,000 for the land by a national retail chain. At what value should the land be recorded in Gallatin Repair Service's records?

Follow My Example 1-1

$137,000. Under the cost concept, the land should be recorded at the cost to Gallatin Repair Service.

Practice Exercises: **PE 1-1A, PE 1-1B**

 State the accounting equation and define each element of the equation.

The Accounting Equation

The resources owned by a business are its **assets**. Examples of assets include cash, land, buildings, and equipment. The rights or claims to the assets are divided into two types: (1) the rights of creditors and (2) the rights of owners. The rights of creditors are the debts of the business and are called **liabilities**. The rights of the owners are called **stockholders' equity** for a corporation and **owner's equity** for a proprietorship, partnership, or limited liability company. Throughout this text, we use the corporate form of business. However, most of the concepts and principles described and illustrated also apply to proprietorships, partnerships, and limited liability companies.

The following equation shows the relationship among assets, liabilities, and stockholders' equity:

$$\text{Assets} = \text{Liabilities} + \text{Stockholders' Equity}$$

This equation is called the **accounting equation**. Liabilities usually are shown before stockholders' equity in the accounting equation because creditors have first rights to the assets.

Given any two amounts, the accounting equation may be solved for the third unknown amount. To illustrate, if the assets owned by a business amount to $100,000 and the liabilities amount to $30,000, the stockholders' equity is equal to $70,000, as shown below.

$$\text{Assets} - \text{Liabilities} = \text{Stockholders' Equity}$$
$$\$100,000 - \$30,000 = \$70,000$$

Example Exercise 1-2 Accounting Equation

You're A Star is a motivational consulting business. At the end of its accounting period, December 31, 2013, You're A Star has assets of $800,000 and liabilities of $350,000. Using the accounting equation, determine the following amounts:

a. Stockholders' equity as of December 31, 2013.
b. Stockholders' equity as of December 31, 2014, assuming that assets increased by $130,000 and liabilities decreased by $25,000 during 2014.

Follow My Example 1-2

a.　　　Assets = Liabilities + Stockholders' Equity
　　　$800,000 = $350,000 + Stockholders' Equity
　　Stockholders' Equity = $450,000

b. First, determine the change in stockholders' equity during 2014 as follows:

　　　Assets = Liabilities + Stockholders' Equity
　　　$130,000 = -$25,000 + Stockholders' Equity
　　Stockholders' Equity = $155,000

Next, add the change in stockholders' equity during 2014 to the stockholders' equity on December 31, 2013 to arrive at stockholders' equity on December 31, 2014, as shown below.

Stockholders' Equity on December 31, 2014 = $450,000 + $155,000 = $605,000

Practice Exercises: **PE 1-2A, PE 1-2B**

Business Transactions and the Accounting Equation

OBJ 4 Describe and illustrate how business transactions can be recorded in terms of the resulting change in the elements of the accounting equation.

Paying a monthly bill, such as a telephone bill of $168, affects a business's financial condition because it now has less cash on hand. Such an economic event or condition that directly changes an entity's financial condition or its results of operations is a **business transaction**. For example, purchasing land for $50,000 is a business transaction. In contrast, a change in a business's credit rating does not directly affect cash or any other asset, liability, or stockholders' equity amount.

All business transactions can be stated in terms of changes in the elements of the accounting equation. How business transactions affect the accounting equation can be illustrated by using some typical transactions. As a basis for illustration, a business organized by Chris Clark is used.

Note:
All business transactions can be stated in terms of changes in the elements of the accounting equation.

Assume that on November 1, 2013, Chris Clark organizes a corporation that will be known as NetSolutions. The first phase of Chris's business plan is to operate Net-Solutions as a service business assisting individuals and small businesses in developing Web pages and installing computer software. Chris expects this initial phase of the business to last one to two years. During this period, Chris plans on gathering information on the software and hardware needs of customers. During the second phase of the business plan, Chris plans to expand NetSolutions into a personalized retailer of software and hardware for individuals and small businesses.

Each transaction during NetSolutions' first month of operations is described in the following paragraphs. The effect of each transaction on the accounting equation is then shown.

Transaction A

Nov. 1, 2013   Chris Clark deposited $25,000 in a bank account in the name of NetSolutions in exchange for shares of stock in the corporation.

Stock issued to stockholders' (owners), such as Chris Clark, is referred to as **capital stock**. This transaction increases assets by increasing Cash (on the left side of the equation) by $25,000. To balance the equation, Capital Stock under stockholders' equity (on the right side of the equation) increases by the same amount.

The effect of this transaction on NetSolutions' accounting equation is shown below.

$$\left.\begin{array}{c} \textbf{Assets} \\ \text{Cash} \\ \text{a. } 25{,}000 \end{array}\right\} = \left\{\begin{array}{c} \textbf{Stockholders' Equity} \\ \text{Capital Stock} \\ 25{,}000 \end{array}\right.$$

The accounting equation shown above is only for the corporation, NetSolutions. Under the business entity concept, Chris Clark's personal assets, such as a home or personal bank account, and personal liabilities are excluded from the equation.

Transaction B

Nov. 5, 2013   NetSolutions paid $20,000 for the purchase of land as a future building site.

The land is located in a business park with access to transportation facilities. Chris Clark plans to rent office space and equipment during the first phase of the business plan. During the second phase, Chris plans to build an office and a warehouse for NetSolutions on the land.

Business Connection

THE ACCOUNTING EQUATION

The accounting equation serves as the basic foundation for the accounting systems of all companies. From the smallest business, such as the local convenience store, to the largest business, such as **Ford Motor Company**, companies use the accounting equation. Some examples taken from recent financial reports of well-known companies are shown below.

Company	Assets*	=	Liabilities	+	Stockholders' Equity
The Coca-Cola Company	$72,921	=	$41,918	+	$31,003
Dell, Inc.	$38,599	=	$30,833	+	$7,766
eBay, Inc.	$22,004	=	$6,702	+	$15,302
Google	$57,851	=	$11,610	+	$46,241
McDonald's	$31,975	=	$17,341	+	$14,634
Microsoft Corporation	$86,113	=	$39,938	+	$46,175
Southwest Airlines Co.	$15,463	=	$9,226	+	$6,237
Walmart	$180,663	=	$109,416	+	$71,247

*Amounts are shown in millions of dollars.

The purchase of the land changes the makeup of the assets, but it does not change the total assets. The items in the equation prior to this transaction and the effect of the transaction are shown below. The new amounts are called *balances*.

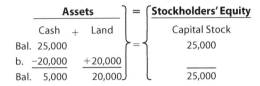

	Assets		=	Stockholders' Equity
	Cash	+	Land		Capital Stock
Bal.	25,000				25,000
b.	−20,000		+20,000		
Bal.	5,000		20,000		25,000

Nov. 10, 2013 NetSolutions purchased supplies for $1,350 and agreed to pay the supplier in the near future. Transaction C

You have probably used a credit card to buy clothing or other merchandise. In this type of transaction, you received clothing for a promise to pay your credit card bill in the future. That is, you received an asset and incurred a liability to pay a future bill. NetSolutions entered into a similar transaction by purchasing supplies for $1,350 and agreeing to pay the supplier in the near future. This type of transaction is called a purchase *on account* and is often described as follows: *Purchased supplies on account, $1,350.*

The liability created by a purchase on account is called an **account payable**. Items such as supplies that will be used in the business in the future are called **prepaid expenses**, which are assets. Thus, the effect of this transaction is to increase assets (Supplies) and liabilities (Accounts Payable) by $1,350, as follows:

	Assets				=	Liabilities +	Stockholders' Equity
	Cash	+ Supplies +	Land			Accounts Payable +	Capital Stock
Bal.	5,000		20,000				25,000
c.		+1,350				+1,350	
Bal.	5,000	1,350	20,000			1,350	25,000

Nov. 18, 2013 NetSolutions received cash of $7,500 for providing services to customers. Transaction D

You may have earned money by painting houses or mowing lawns. If so, you received money for rendering services to a customer. Likewise, a business earns money by selling goods or services to its customers. This amount is called **revenue**.

During its first month of operations, NetSolutions received cash of $7,500 for providing services to customers. The receipt of cash increases NetSolutions' assets and also increases stockholders' equity in the business. The revenues of $7,500 are recorded in a Fees Earned column to the right of Capital Stock. The effect of this transaction is to increase Cash and Fees Earned by $7,500, as follows.

	Assets				=	Liabilities +	Stockholders' Equity	
	Cash	+ Supplies +	Land			Accounts Payable +	Capital Stock +	Fees Earned
Bal.	5,000	1,350	20,000			1,350	25,000	
d.	+7,500							+7,500
Bal.	12,500	1,350	20,000			1,350	25,000	7,500

Different terms are used for the various types of revenues. As illustrated above, revenue from providing services is recorded as **fees earned**. Revenue from the sale of merchandise is recorded as **sales**. Other examples of revenue include rent, which is recorded as **rent revenue**, and interest, which is recorded as **interest revenue**.

Instead of receiving cash at the time services are provided or goods are sold, a business may accept payment at a later date. Such revenues are described as *fees earned on account* or *sales on account*. For example, if NetSolutions had provided services on account instead of for cash, transaction (d) would have been described as follows: *Fees earned on account, $7,500.*

In such cases, the firm has an **account receivable**, which is a claim against the customer. An account receivable is an asset, and the revenue is earned and recorded as if cash had been received. When customers pay their accounts, Cash increases and Accounts Receivable decreases.

Transaction E   *Nov. 30, 2013   NetSolutions paid the following expenses during the month: wages, $2,125; rent, $800; utilities, $450; and miscellaneous, $275.*

During the month, NetSolutions spent cash or used up other assets in earning revenue. Assets used in this process of earning revenue are called **expenses**. Expenses include supplies used and payments for employee wages, utilities, and other services.

NetSolutions paid the following expenses during the month: wages, $2,125; rent, $800; utilities, $450; and miscellaneous, $275. Miscellaneous expenses include small amounts paid for such items as postage, coffee, and newspapers. The effect of expenses is the opposite of revenues in that expenses reduce assets and stockholders' equity. Like fees earned, the expenses are recorded in columns to the right of Capital Stock. However, since expenses reduce stockholders' equity, the expenses are entered as negative amounts. The effect of this transaction is shown below.

	Assets			=	Liabilities +		Stockholders' Equity				
	Cash	+ Supplies	+ Land	=	Accounts Payable +	Capital Stock	+ Fees Earned −	Wages Exp. −	Rent Exp. −	Utilities Exp. −	Misc. Exp.
Bal.	12,500	1,350	20,000		1,350	25,000	7,500				
e.	−3,650							−2,125	−800	−450	−275
Bal.	8,850	1,350	20,000		1,350	25,000	7,500	−2,125	−800	−450	−275

Businesses usually record each revenue and expense transaction as it occurs. However, to simplify, NetSolutions' revenues and expenses are summarized for the month in transactions (d) and (e).

Transaction F   *Nov. 30, 2013   NetSolutions paid creditors on account, $950.*

When you pay your monthly credit card bill, you decrease the cash and decrease the amount you owe to the credit card company. Likewise, when NetSolutions pays $950 to creditors during the month, it reduces assets and liabilities, as shown below.

	Assets			=	Liabilities +		Stockholders' Equity				
	Cash	+ Supplies	+ Land	=	Accounts Payable +	Capital Stock	+ Fees Earned −	Wages Exp. −	Rent Exp. −	Utilities Exp. −	Misc. Exp.
Bal.	8,850	1,350	20,000		1,350	25,000	7,500	−2,125	−800	−450	−275
f.	−950				−950						
Bal.	7,900	1,350	20,000		400	25,000	7,500	−2,125	−800	−450	−275

Paying an amount on account is different from paying an expense. The paying of an expense reduces stockholders' equity, as illustrated in transaction (e). Paying an amount on account reduces the amount owed on a liability.

Transaction G   *Nov. 30, 2013   Chris Clark determined that the cost of supplies on hand at the end of the month was $550.*

The cost of the supplies on hand (not yet used) at the end of the month is $550. Thus, $800 ($1,350 − $550) of supplies must have been used during the month. This decrease in supplies is recorded as an expense, as shown below.

	Assets			=	Liabilities +		Stockholders' Equity					
	Cash	+ Supplies	+ Land	=	Accounts Payable +	Capital Stock	+ Fees Earned −	Wages Exp. −	Rent Exp. −	Supplies Exp. −	Utilities Exp. −	Misc. Exp.
Bal.	7,900	1,350	20,000		400	25,000	7,500	−2,125	−800		−450	−275
g.		−800								−800		
Bal.	7,900	550	20,000		400	25,000	7,500	−2,125	−800	−800	−450	−275

Nov. 30, 2013 NetSolutions paid $2,000 to stockholders (Chris Clark) as dividends. Transaction H

Dividends are distributions of earnings to stockholders. The payment of dividends decreases cash and stockholders' equity. Like expenses, dividends are recorded in a separate column to the right of Capital Stock as a negative amount. The effect of the payment of dividends of $2,000 is shown below.

	Assets			=	Liabilities +				Stockholders' Equity					
					Accounts	Capital			Fees	Wages	Rent	Supplies	Utilities	Misc.
	Cash +	Supp. +	Land	=	Payable +	Stock	− Dividends +	Earned −	Exp. −	Exp. −	Exp. −	Exp. −	Exp. −	Exp.
Bal.	7,900	550	20,000		400	25,000		7,500	-2,125	-800	-800	-450	-275	
h.	-2,000						-2,000							
Bal.	5,900	550	20,000		400	25,000	-2,000	7,500	-2,125	-800	-800	-450	-275	

Dividends should not be confused with expenses. Dividends do not represent assets or services used in the process of earning revenues. Instead, dividends are considered a distribution of earnings to stockholders.

The transactions of NetSolutions are summarized below. Each transaction is identi- Summary
fied by letter, and the balance of each accounting equation element is shown after every transaction.

	Assets			= Liabilities +				Stockholders' Equity					
				Accounts	Capital		Fees	Wages	Rent	Supplies	Utilities	Misc.	
	Cash	+ Supp. +	Land	= Payable +	Stock	− Dividends +	Earned −	Exp. −	Exp. −	Exp. −	Exp. −	Exp.	
a.	+25,000				+25,000								
b.	-20,000		+20,000										
Bal.	5,000		20,000		25,000								
c.		+1,350		+1,350									
Bal.	5,000	+1,350	20,000	+1,350	25,000								
d.	+7,500						+7,500						
Bal.	12,500	1,350	20,000	1,350	25,000		7,500						
e.	-3,650							-2,125	-800		-450	-275	
Bal.	8,850	1,350	20,000	1,350	25,000		7,500	-2,125	-800		-450	-275	
f.	-950			-950									
Bal.	7,900	1,350	20,000	400	25,000		7,500	-2,125	-800		-450	-275	
g.		-800								-800			
Bal.	7,900	550	20,000	400	25,000		7,500	-2,125	-800	-800	-450	-275	
h.	-2,000					-2,000							
Bal.	5,900	550	20,000	400	25,000	-2,000	7,500	-2,125	-800	-800	-450	-275	

You should note the following:

1. The effect of every transaction *is an increase or a decrease in one or more of the accounting equation elements.*
2. The two sides of the accounting equation are *always equal.*
3. The stockholders' equity (owner's equity) is *increased by amounts invested by stockholders (capital stock).*
4. The stockholders' equity (owner's equity) is *increased by revenues and decreased by expenses.*
5. The stockholders' equity (owner's equity) is *decreased by dividends paid to stockholders.*
   Stockholders' equity is classified as:

1. Capital Stock
2. Retained Earnings.

Capital stock is shares of ownership distributed to investors of a corporation. It represents the portion of stockholders' equity contributed by investors. For NetSolutions, shares of capital stock of $25,000 were distributed to Chris Clark in exchange for investing in the business.

Retained earnings is the stockholders' equity created from business operations through revenue and expense transactions. For NetSolutions, retained earnings of $3,050 were created by its November operations (revenue and expense transactions), as shown below.

NetSolutions
Retained Earnings
November Operations
(Revenue and Expense Transactions)

	Fees Earned	−	Wages Exp.	−	Rent Exp.	−	Supplies Exp.	−	Utilities Exp.	−	Misc. Exp.
Trans, d.	+7,500										
Trans, e.			−2,125		−800				−450		−275
Trans, g.							−800				
Balance, Nov. 30	7,500		−2,125		−800		−800		−450		−275

$3,050

Stockholders' equity created by investments by stockholders (capital stock) and by business operations (retained earnings) is reported separately. Since dividends are distributions of earnings to stockholders, dividends reduce retained earnings. NetSolutions paid $2,000 in dividends during November, thus reducing retained earnings to $1,050 ($3,050 − $2,000).

The effects of investments by stockholders, dividends, revenues, and expenses on stockholders' equity are illustrated in Exhibit 5.

EXHIBIT 5

Effects of Transactions on Stockholders' Equity

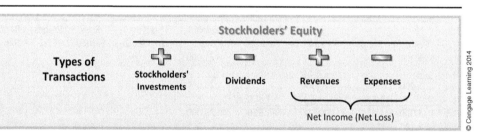

© Cengage Learning 2014

Example Exercise 1-3   Transactions   OBJ 4

Salvo Delivery Service is owned and operated by Joel Salvo. The following selected transactions were completed by Salvo Delivery Service during February:

1. Received cash from owner as additional investment in exchange for capital stock, $35,000.
2. Paid creditors on account, $1,800.
3. Billed customers for delivery services on account, $11,250.
4. Received cash from customers on account, $6,740.
5. Paid dividends, $1,000.

Indicate the effect of each transaction on the accounting equation elements (Assets, Liabilities, Stockholders' Equity Capital Stock, Dividends, Revenue, and Expense). Also indicate the specific item within the accounting equation element that is affected. To illustrate, the answer to (1) is shown below.

(1) Asset (Cash) increases by $35,000; Stockholders' Equity (Capital Stock) increases by $35,000.

Follow My Example 1-3

(2) Asset (Cash) decreases by $1,800; Liability (Accounts Payable) decreases by $1,800.
(3) Asset (Accounts Receivable) increases by $11,250; Revenue (Delivery Service Fees) increases by $11,250.
(4) Asset (Cash) increases by $6,740; Asset (Accounts Receivable) decreases by $6,740.
(5) Asset (Cash) decreases by $1,000; Dividends increases by $1,000.

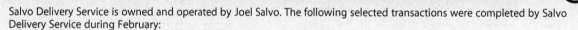

Practice Exercises: **PE 1-3A, PE 1-3B**

OBJ 5 Describe the financial statements of a corporation and explain how they interrelate.

Financial Statements

After transactions have been recorded and summarized, reports are prepared for users. The accounting reports providing this information are called **financial statements**. The primary financial statements of a corporation are the income statement, the retained earnings statement, the balance sheet, and the statement of cash flows. The order in which the financial statements are prepared and the nature of each statement are described as follows.

Order Prepared	Financial Statement	Description of Statement
1.	**Income statement**	A summary of the revenue and expenses *for a specific period of time*, such as a month or a year.
2.	**Retained earnings statement**	A summary of the changes in retained earnings that have occurred *during a specific period of time*, such as a month or a year.
3.	**Balance sheet**	A list of the assets, liabilities, and stockholders' equity *as of a specific date*, usually at the close of the last day of a month or a year.
4.	**Statement of cash flows**	A summary of the cash receipts and cash payments for a *specific period of time*, such as a month or a year.

The four financial statements and their interrelationships are illustrated in Exhibit 6, on page 17. The data for the statements are taken from the summary of transactions of NetSolutions on page 13.

All financial statements are identified by the name of the business, the title of the statement, and the *date* or *period of time*. The data presented in the income statement, the retained earnings statement, and the statement of cash flows are for a period of time. The data presented in the balance sheet are for a specific date.

Income Statement

The income statement reports the revenues and expenses for a period of time, based on the **matching concept**. This concept is applied by *matching* the expenses incurred during a period with the revenue that those expenses generated. The excess of the revenue over the expenses is called **net income**, net profit, or **earnings**. If the expenses exceed the revenue, the excess is a **net loss**.

Note: When revenues exceed expenses, it is referred to as *net income, net profit,* or *earnings.* When expenses exceed revenues, it is referred to as *net loss.*

The revenue and expenses for NetSolutions were shown in the equation as separate increases and decreases. Net income for a period increases the stockholders' equity (retained earnings) for the period. A net loss decreases the stockholders' equity (retained earnings) for the period.

The revenue, expenses, and the net income of $3,050 for NetSolutions are reported in the income statement in Exhibit 6. The order in which the expenses are listed in the income statement varies among businesses. Most businesses list expenses in order of size, beginning with the larger items. Miscellaneous expense is usually shown as the last item, regardless of the amount.

Example Exercise 1-4 Income Statement

OBJ 5

The revenues and expenses of Chickadee Travel Service for the year ended April 30, 2014, are listed below.

Fees earned	$263,200
Miscellaneous expense	12,950
Office expense	63,000
Wages expense	131,700

Prepare an income statement for the current year ended April 30, 2014.

Follow My Example 1-4

Chickadee Travel Service
Income Statement
For the Year Ended April 30, 2014

Fees earned.............................		$263,200
Expenses:		
Wages expense......................	$131,700	
Office expense.......................	63,000	
Miscellaneous expense................	12,950	
Total expenses		207,650
Net income		$ 55,550

Practice Exercises: **PE 1-4A, PE 1-4B**

Retained Earnings Statement

The retained earnings statement reports the changes in the retained earnings for a period of time. It is prepared *after* the income statement because the net income or net loss for the period must be reported in this statement. Similarly, it is prepared *before* the balance sheet, since the amount of retained earnings at the end of the period must be reported on the balance sheet. Because of this, the retained earnings statement is often viewed as the connecting link between the income statement and balance sheet.

The following two types of transactions affected NetSolutions' retained earnings during November:

1. Revenues and expenses, which resulted in net income of $3,050.
2. Dividends of $2,000 paid to stockholders (Chris Clark).

These transactions are summarized in the retained earnings statement for NetSolutions shown in Exhibit 6.

Since NetSolutions has been in operation for only one month, it has no retained earnings at the beginning of November. For December, however, there is a beginning balance—the balance at the end of November. This balance of $1,050 is reported on the retained earnings statement.

To illustrate, assume that NetSolutions earned net income of $4,155 and paid dividends of $2,000 during December. The retained earnings statement for NetSolutions for December is shown below.

NetSolutions Retained Earnings Statement For the Month Ended December 31, 2013		
Retained earnings, December 1, 2013		$1,050
Net income for November	$4,155	
Less dividends	2,000	
Increase in retained earnings		2,155
Retained earnings, December 31, 2013		$3,205

Example Exercise 1-5 Retained Earnings Statement OBJ 5

Using the income statement for Chickadee Travel Service shown in Example Exercise 1-4, prepare a retained earnings statement for the year ended April 30, 2014. Adam Cellini, the owner, invested an additional $50,000 in the business in exchange for capital stock, and dividends of $30,000 were paid during the year. Retained earnings were $30,000 on May 1, 2013, the beginning of the current year.

Follow My Example 1-5

Chickadee Travel Service Retained Earnings Statement For the Year Ended April 30, 2014		
Retained earnings, May 1, 2013		$30,000
Net income for the year	$55,550	
Less dividends	30,000	
Increase in retained earnings		25,550
Retained earnings, April 30, 2014		$55,550

Practice Exercises: **PE 1-5A, PE 1-5B**

Balance Sheet

The balance sheet in Exhibit 6 reports the amounts of NetSolutions' assets, liabilities, and stockholders' equity as of November 30, 2013. The asset and liability amounts are taken from the last line of the summary of transactions on page 13.

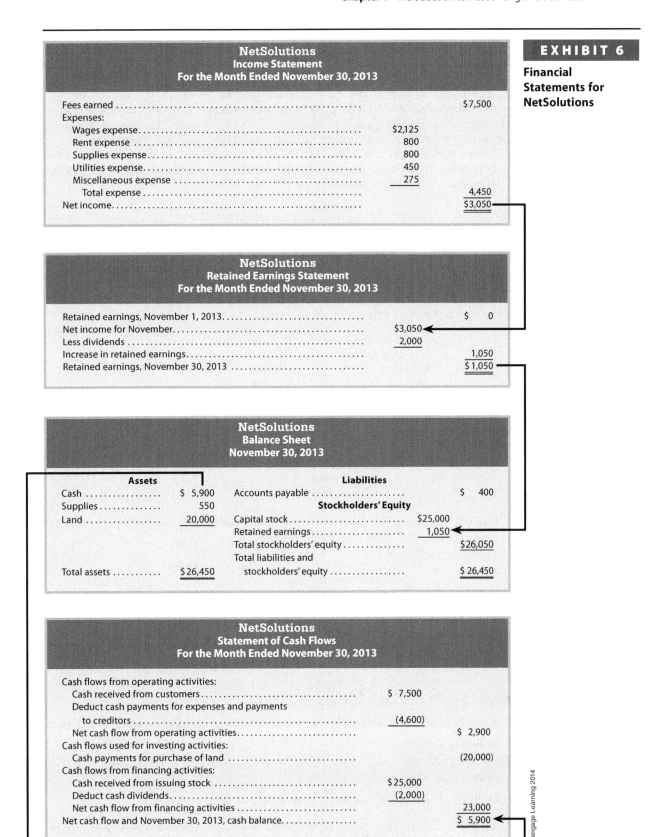

NetSolutions
Income Statement
For the Month Ended November 30, 2013

Fees earned		$7,500
Expenses:		
Wages expense	$2,125	
Rent expense	800	
Supplies expense	800	
Utilities expense	450	
Miscellaneous expense	275	
Total expense		4,450
Net income		$3,050

NetSolutions
Retained Earnings Statement
For the Month Ended November 30, 2013

Retained earnings, November 1, 2013		$ 0
Net income for November	$3,050	
Less dividends	2,000	
Increase in retained earnings		1,050
Retained earnings, November 30, 2013		$1,050

NetSolutions
Balance Sheet
November 30, 2013

Assets		**Liabilities**	
Cash	$ 5,900	Accounts payable	$ 400
Supplies	550	**Stockholders' Equity**	
Land	20,000	Capital stock	$25,000
		Retained earnings	1,050
		Total stockholders' equity	$26,050
		Total liabilities and	
Total assets	$26,450	stockholders' equity	$ 26,450

NetSolutions
Statement of Cash Flows
For the Month Ended November 30, 2013

Cash flows from operating activities:		
Cash received from customers	$ 7,500	
Deduct cash payments for expenses and payments		
to creditors	(4,600)	
Net cash flow from operating activities		$ 2,900
Cash flows used for investing activities:		
Cash payments for purchase of land		(20,000)
Cash flows from financing activities:		
Cash received from issuing stock	$ 25,000	
Deduct cash dividends	(2,000)	
Net cash flow from financing activities		23,000
Net cash flow and November 30, 2013, cash balance		$ 5,900

© Cengage Learning 2014

EXHIBIT 6

Financial Statements for NetSolutions

Retained earnings as of November 30, 2013, is taken from the retained earnings statement. The form of balance sheet shown in Exhibit 6 is called the **account form**. This is because it resembles the basic format of the accounting equation, with assets on the left side and the liabilities and stockholders' equity sections on the right side.[3]

The assets section of the balance sheet presents assets in the order that they will be converted into cash or used in operations. Cash is presented first, followed by receivables, supplies, prepaid insurance, and other assets. The assets of a more permanent nature are shown next, such as land, buildings, and equipment.

In the liabilities section of the balance sheet in Exhibit 6, accounts payable is the only liability. When there are two or more liabilities, each should be listed and the total amount of liabilities presented as follows:

	Liabilities	
Accounts payable	$12,900	
Wages payable	2,570	
Total liabilities		$15,470

Example Exercise 1-6 Balance Sheet

Using the following data for Chickadee Travel Service as well as the retained earnings statement shown in Example Exercise 1-5, prepare a balance sheet as of April 30, 2014.

Accounts payable	$ 12,200
Accounts receivable	31,350
Capital stock	100,000
Cash	53,050
Land	80,000
Supplies	3,350

Follow My Example 1-6

Chickadee Travel Service
Balance Sheet
April 30, 2014

Assets		**Liabilities**	
Cash..................................	$ 53,050	Accounts payable...........................	$ 12,200
Accounts receivable	31,350		
Supplies	3,350	**Stockholders' Equity**	
Land.................................	80,000	Capital stock...............................	$100,000
		Retained earnings	55,550
		Total stockholders' equity..................	155,550
Total assets..........................	$167,750	Total liabilities and stockholders' equity.....	$167,750

Practice Exercises: **PE 1-6A, PE 1-6B**

Statement of Cash Flows

The statement of cash flows consists of the following three sections, as shown in Exhibit 6:

1. operating activities
2. investing activities
3. financing activities

Each of these sections is briefly described below.

Cash Flows from Operating Activities This section reports a summary of cash receipts and cash payments from operations. The net cash flow from operating activities normally differs from the amount of net income for the period. In Exhibit 6, NetSolutions

---

3 An alternative form of balance sheet, called the *report form,* is illustrated in Chapter 5. It presents the liabilities and stockholders' equity sections below the assets section.

reported net cash flows from operating activities of $2,900 and net income of $3,050. This difference occurs because revenues and expenses may not be recorded at the same time that cash is received from customers or paid to creditors.

Cash Flows from Investing Activities This section reports the cash transactions for the acquisition and sale of relatively permanent assets. Exhibit 6 reports that NetSolutions paid $20,000 for the purchase of land during November.

Cash Flows from Financing Activities This section reports the cash transactions related to cash investments by stockholders, borrowings, and cash dividends. Exhibit 6 shows that Chris Clark invested $25,000 in exchange for capital stock and dividends of $2,000 were paid during November.

Preparing the statement of cash flows requires that each of the November cash transactions for NetSolutions be classified as an operating, investing, or financing activity. Using the summary of transactions shown on page 13, the November cash transactions for NetSolutions are classified as follows:

Transaction	Amount	Cash Flow Activity
a.	$25,000	Financing (Issuance of capital stock)
b.	−20,000	Investing (Purchase of land)
d.	7,500	Operating (Fees earned)
e.	−3,650	Operating (Payment of expenses)
f.	−950	Operating (Payment of account payable)
h.	−2,000	Financing (Paid dividends)

Transactions (c) and (g) are not listed above since they did not involve a cash receipt or payment. In addition, the payment of accounts payable in transaction (f) is classified as an operating activity since the account payable arose from the purchase of supplies, which are used in operations. Using the preceding classifications of November cash transactions, the statement of cash flows is prepared as shown in Exhibit 6.[4]

The ending cash balance shown on the statement of cash flows is also reported on the balance sheet as of the end of the period. To illustrate, the ending cash of $5,900 reported on the November statement of cash flows in Exhibit 6 is also reported as the amount of cash on hand in the November 30, 2013, balance sheet.

Since November is NetSolutions' first period of operations, the net cash flow for November and the November 30, 2013, cash balance are the same amount, $5,900, as shown in Exhibit 6. In later periods, NetSolutions will report in its statement of cash flows a beginning cash balance, an increase or a decrease in cash for the period, and an ending cash balance. For example, assume that for December NetSolutions has a decrease in cash of $3,835. The last three lines of NetSolutions' statement of cash flows for December would be as follows:

Decrease in cash	$(3,835)
Cash as of December 1, 2013	5,900
Cash as of December 31, 2013	$ 2,065

Example Exercise 1-7 Statement of Cash Flows

A summary of cash flows for Chickadee Travel Service for the year ended April 30, 2014, is shown below.

Cash receipts:	
Cash received from customers	$251,000
Cash received from issuing capital stock	50,000
Cash payments:	
Cash paid for expenses	210,000
Cash paid for land	80,000
Cash paid for dividends	30,000

The cash balance as of May 1, 2013, was $72,050. Prepare a statement of cash flows for Chickadee Travel Service for the year ended April 30, 2014.

(Continued)

4 This method of preparing the statement of cash flows is called the "direct method." This method and the indirect method are discussed further in Chapter 14.

Follow My Example 1-7

Chickadee Travel Service
Statement of Cash Flows
For the Year Ended April 30, 2014

Cash flows from operating activities:		
Cash received from customers	$251,000	
Deduct cash payments for expenses	(210,000)	
Net cash flows from operating activities....................		$ 41,000
Cash flows used for investing activities:		
Cash payments for purchase of land		(80,000)
Cash flows from financing activities:		
Cash received issuing capital stock.........................	$ 50,000	
Deduct cash dividends....................................	(30,000)	
Net cash flows from financing activities		20,000
Net decrease in cash during year		$(19,000)
Cash as of May 1, 2013		72,050
Cash as of April 30, 2014		$ 53,050

Practice Exercises: **PE 1-7A, PE 1-7B**

Interrelationships Among Financial Statements

Financial statements are prepared in the order of the income statement, retained earnings statement, balance sheet, and statement of cash flows. This order is important because the financial statements are interrelated. These interrelationships for NetSolutions are shown in Exhibit 6 and are described below.[5]

Financial Statements	Interrelationship	NetSolutions Example (Exhibit 6)
Income Statement *and* Retained Earnings Statement	Net income or net loss reported on the income statement is also reported on the retained earnings statement as either an addition (net income) to or deduction (net loss) from the beginning retained earnings.	NetSolutions' net income of $3,050 for November is added to the beginning retained earnings on November 1, 2013, in the retained earnings statement.
Retained Earnings Statement *and* Balance Sheet	Retained earnings at the end of the period reported on the retained earnings statement is also reported on the balance sheet as retained earnings.	NetSolutions' retained earnings of $1,050 as of November 30, 2013, on the retained earnings statement also appears on the November 30, 2013, balance sheet as retained earnings.
Balance Sheet *and* Statement of Cash Flows	The cash reported on the balance sheet is also reported as the end-of-period cash on the statement of cash flows.	Cash of $5,900 reported on the balance sheet as of November 30, 2013, is also reported on the November statement of cash flows as the end-of-period cash.

The preceding interrelationships are important in analyzing financial statements and the impact of transactions on a business. In addition, these interrelationships serve as a check on whether the financial statements are prepared correctly. For example, if the ending cash on the statement of cash flows does not agree with the balance sheet cash, then an error has occurred.

---

5 Depending on the method of preparing the cash flows from operating activities section of the statement of cash flows, net income (or net loss) may also appear on the statement of cash flows. This interrelationship or method of preparing the statement of cash flows, called the "indirect method," is described and illustrated in Chapter 14.

Financial Analysis and Interpretation: Ratio of Liabilities to Stockholders' Equity

OBJ 6 Describe and illustrate the use of the ratio of liabilities to stockholders' equity in evaluating a company's financial condition.

The basic financial statements illustrated in this chapter are useful to bankers, creditors, stockholders, and others in analyzing and interpreting the financial performance and condition of a company. Throughout this text, various tools and techniques that are often used to analyze and interpret a company's financial performance and condition are described and illustrated. The first such tool that is discussed is useful in analyzing the ability of a company to pay its creditors.

The relationship between liabilities and stockholders' equity, expressed as a **ratio of liabilities to stockholders' equity**, is computed as follows:

$$\text{Ratio of Liabilities to Stockholders' Equity} = \frac{\text{Total Liabilities}}{\text{Total Stockholders' Equity}}$$

NetSolutions' ratio of liabilities to stockholders' equity at the end of November is 0.015, as computed below.

$$\text{Ratio of Liabilities to Stockholders' Equity} = \frac{\$400}{\$26,050} = 0.015$$

To illustrate, recent balance sheet data (in millions) for **Google Inc.** and **McDonald's Corporation** are shown below.

	Recent Year	Prior Year
Google Inc.		
Total liabilities	$11,610	$ 4,493
Total stockholders' equity	46,241	36,004
McDonald's Corporation		
Total liabilities	$17,341	$16,191
Total stockholders' equity	14,634	14,034

The ratio of liabilities to stockholders' equity for Google and McDonald's for a recent year and the prior year is computed below.

	Recent Year	Prior Year
Google Inc.		
Total liabilities	$11,610	$ 4,493
Total stockholders' equity	46,241	36,004
Ratio of liabilities to stockholders' equity	0.25	0.12
	($11,610/$46,241)	($4,493/$36,004)
McDonald's Corporation		
Total liabilities	$ 17,341	$16,191
Total stockholders' equity	14,634	14,034
Ratio of liabilities to stockholders' equity	1.18	1.15
	($17,341/$14,634)	($16,191/$14,034)

The rights of creditors to a business's assets come before the rights of the owners or stockholders. Thus, the lower the ratio of liabilities to stockholders' equity, the better able the company is to withstand poor business conditions and to pay its obligations to creditors.

Google is unusual in that it has a very low amount of liabilities; thus, its ratio of liabilities to stockholders' equity of 0.25 in the recent year and 0.12 in the prior year is low. In contrast, McDonald's has more liabilities; its ratio of liabilities to stockholders' equity is 1.18 in the recent year and 1.15 in the prior year. Since McDonald's ratio of liabilities to stockholders' equity increased slightly, its creditors are slightly more at risk at the end of the recent year. Also, McDonald's creditors are more at risk than are Google's creditors. The creditors of both companies are, however, well protected against the risk of nonpayment.

Example Exercise 1-8   Ratio of Liabilities to Stockholders' Equity

The following data were taken from Hawthorne Company's balance sheet:

	Dec. 31, 2014	Dec. 31, 2013
Total liabilities	$120,000	$105,000
Total stockholders' equity	80,000	75,000

a. Compute the ratio of liabilities to stockholders' equity.

b. Has the creditors' risk increased or decreased from December 31, 2013, to December 31, 2014?

Follow My Example 1-8

a.

	Dec. 31, 2014	Dec. 31, 2013
Total liabilities	$120,000	$105,000
Total stockholders' equity	80,000	75,000
Ratio of liabilities to stockholders' equity	1.50	1.40
	($120,000/$80,000)	($105,000/$75,000)

b. Increased

Practice Exercises: **PE 1-8A, PE 1-8B**

At a Glance 1

Describe the nature of a business and the role of accounting and ethics in business.

Key Points   A business provides goods or services (outputs) to customers with the objective of earning a profit. Three types of businesses include service, merchandising, and manufacturing businesses.

Accounting is an information system that provides reports to users about the economic activities and condition of a business.

Ethics are moral principles that guide the conduct of individuals. Good ethical conduct depends on individual character and firm culture.

Accountants are engaged in private accounting or public accounting.

Learning Outcomes	Example Exercises	Practice Exercises
• Distinguish among service, merchandising, and manufacturing businesses.		
• Describe the role of accounting in business, and explain why accounting is called the "language of business."		
• Define ethics, and list two factors affecting ethical conduct.		
• Differentiate between private and public accounting.		

Summarize the development of accounting principles and relate them to practice.

Key Points Generally accepted accounting principles (GAAP) are used in preparing financial statements. Accounting principles and concepts develop from research, practice, and pronouncements of authoritative bodies.

The business entity concept views the business as an entity separate from its owners, creditors, or other businesses. Businesses may be organized as proprietorships, partnerships, corporations, and limited liability companies. The cost concept requires that purchases of a business be recorded in terms of actual cost. The objectivity concept requires that the accounting records and reports be based on objective evidence. The unit of measure concept requires that economic data be recorded in dollars.

Learning Outcomes	Example Exercises	Practice Exercises
• Explain what is meant by generally accepted accounting principles.		
• Describe how generally accepted accounting principles are developed.		
• Describe and give an example of what is meant by the business entity concept.		
• Describe the characteristics of a proprietorship, partnership, corporation, and limited liability company.		
• Describe and give an example of what is meant by the cost concept.	**EE1-1**	**PE1-1A, 1-1B**
• Describe and give an example of what is meant by the objectivity concept.		
• Describe and give an example of what is meant by the unit of measure concept.		

State the accounting equation and define each element of the equation.

Key Points The resources owned by a business and the rights or claims to these resources may be stated in the form of an equation, as follows:

Assets = Liabilities + Stockholders' Equity

Learning Outcomes	Example Exercises	Practice Exercises
• State the accounting equation.		
• Define assets, liabilities, and stockholders' equity.		
• Given two elements of the accounting equation, solve for the third element.	**EE1-2**	**PE1-2A, 1-2B**

Describe and illustrate how business transactions can be recorded in terms of the resulting change in the elements of the accounting equation.

Key Points All business transactions can be stated in terms of the change in one or more of the three elements of the accounting equation.

Learning Outcomes	Example Exercises	Practice Exercises
• Define a business transaction.		
• Using the accounting equation as a framework, record transactions.	**EE1-3**	**PE1-3A, 1-3B**

OBJ 5 Describe the financial statements of a proprietorship and explain how they interrelate.

Key Points The primary financial statements of a corporation are the income statement, the retained earnings statement, the balance sheet, and the statement of cash flows. The income statement reports a period's net income or net loss, which is also reported on the retained earnings statement. The ending retained earnings reported on the retained earnings statement is also reported on the balance sheet. The ending cash balance is reported on the balance sheet and the statement of cash flows.

Learning Outcomes	Example Exercises	Practice Exercises
• List and describe the financial statements of a corporation.		
• Prepare an income statement.	**EE1-4**	**PE1-4A, 1-4B**
• Prepare a retained earnings statement.	**EE1-5**	**PE1-5A, 1-5B**
• Prepare a balance sheet.	**EE1-6**	**PE1-6A, 1-6B**
• Prepare a statement of cash flows.	**EE1-7**	**PE1-7A, 1-7B**
• Explain how the financial statements of a corporation are interrelated.		

OBJ 6 Describe and illustrate the use of the ratio of liabilities to stockholders' equity in evaluating a company's financial condition.

Key Points A ratio useful in analyzing the ability of a business to pay its creditors is the ratio of liabilities to stockholders' equity. The lower the ratio of liabilities to stockholders' equity, the better able the company is to withstand poor business conditions and to pay its obligations to creditors.

Learning Outcomes	Example Exercises	Practice Exercises
• Describe the usefulness of the ratio of liabilities to stockholders' equity.		
• Compute the ratio of liabilities to stockholders' equity.	**EE1-8**	**PE1-8A, 1-8B**

Key Terms

account form (18)
account payable (11)
account receivable (12)
accounting (3)
accounting equation (9)
assets (8)
balance sheet (15)
business (2)
business entity concept (7)
business transaction (9)
capital stock (10)
Certified Public Accountant (CPA) (6)
corporation (7)

cost concept (8)
dividends (13)
earnings (15)
ethics (4)
expenses (12)
fees earned (11)
financial accounting (4)
Financial Accounting Standards Board (FASB) (6)
financial statements (14)
generally accepted accounting principles (GAAP) (6)
general-purpose financial statements (4)

income statement (15)
interest revenue (11)
International Accounting Standards Board (IASB) (7)
liabilities (8)
limited liability company (LLC) (7)
management (or managerial) accounting (3)
manufacturing business (3)
matching concept (15)
merchandising business (3)
net income (or net profit) (15)
net loss (15)

objectivity concept (8)
owner's equity (9)
partnership (7)
prepaid expenses (11)
private accounting (4)
profit (2)
proprietorship (7)

public accounting (6)
ratio of liabilities to
    stockholders' equity (21)
rent revenue (11)
retained earnings (13)
retained earnings statement (15)
revenue (11)

sales (11)
Securities and Exchange
    Commission (SEC) (6)
service business (2)
statement of cash flows (15)
stockholders' equity (9)
unit of measure concept (8)

Illustrative Problem

Cecil Jameson, Attorney-at-Law, is organized as a corporation and operated by Cecil Jameson. On July 1, 2013, the company has the following assets, liabilities, and capital stock: cash, $1,000; accounts receivable, $3,200; supplies, $850; land, $10,000; accounts payable, $1,530; capital stock, $10,000. Office space and office equipment are currently being rented, pending the construction of an office complex on land purchased last year. Business transactions during July are summarized as follows:

a. Received cash from clients for services, $3,928.

b. Paid creditors on account, $1,055.

c. Received cash from Cecil Jameson as an additional investment in exchange for capital stock, $3,700.

d. Paid office rent for the month, $1,200.

e. Charged clients for legal services on account, $2,025.

f. Purchased supplies on account, $245.

g. Received cash from clients on account, $3,000.

h. Received invoice for paralegal services from Legal Aid Inc. for July (to be paid on August 10), $1,635.

i. Paid the following: wages expense, $850; utilities expense, $325; answering service expense, $250; and miscellaneous expense, $75.

j. Determined that the cost of supplies on hand was $980; therefore, the cost of supplies used during the month was $115.

k. Paid dividends, $1,000.

Instructions

1. Determine the amount of retained earnings as of July 1, 2013.

2. State the assets, liabilities, and stockholders' equity as of July 1 in equation form similar to that shown in this chapter. In tabular form below the equation, indicate the increases and decreases resulting from each transaction and the new balances after each transaction.

3. Prepare an income statement for July, a retained earnings statement for July, and a balance sheet as of July 31, 2013.

4. (Optional). Prepare a statement of cash flows for July.

Solution

1.

$$\text{Assets} - \text{Liabilities} = \text{Stockholders' Equity}$$
$$(\$1,000 + \$3,200 + \$850 + \$10,000) - \$1,530 = \text{Capital Stock} + \text{Retained Earnings}$$
$$\$15,050 - \$1,530 = \$10,000 + \text{Retained Earnings}$$
$$\$3,520 = \text{Retained Earnings}$$

2.

		Assets			=	**Liabilities +**						**Stockholders' Equity**						
	Cash +	Accts. Rec. +	Supp. +	Land =		Accts. Pay. +	Capital Stock +	Retained Earnings -	Dividends +	Fees Earned -	Paralegal Exp. -	Rent Exp. -	Wages Exp. -	Utilities Exp. -	Answering Service Exp. -	Supp. Exp. -	Misc. Exp.
Bal.	1,000	3,200	850	10,000		1,530	10,000	3,520									
a.	+3,928									3,928							
Bal.	4,928	3,200	850	10,000		1,530				3,928							
b.	−1,055					−1,055											
Bal.	3,873	3,200	850	10,000		475				3,928							
c.	+3,700						+3,700										
Bal.	7,573	3,200	850	10,000		475	13,700			3,928							
d.	−1,200											−1,200					
Bal.	6,373	3,200	850	10,000		475				3,928		−1,200					
e.		+ 2,025								+ 2,025							
Bal.	6,373	5,225	850	10,000		475				5,953		−1,200					
f.			+245			+245											
Bal.	6,373	5,225	1,095	10,000		720				5,953		−1,200					
g.	+3,000	−3,000															
Bal.	9,373	2,225	1,095	10,000		720				5,953		−1,200					
h.						+1,635					−1,635						
Bal.	9,373	2,225	1,095	10,000		2,355				5,953	−1,635	−1,200					
i.	−1,500												−850	−325	−250		−75
Bal.	7,873	2,225	1,095	10,000		2,355				5,953	−1,635	−1,200	−850	−325	−250		−75
j.			−115													−115	
Bal.	7,873	2,225	980	10,000		2,355				5,953	−1,635	−1,200	−850	−325	−250	−115	−75
k.	−1,000								−1,000								
Bal.	6,873	2,225	980	10,000		2,355	13,700	3,520	−1,000	5,953	−1,635	−1,200	−850	−325	−250	−115	−75

3.

Cecil Jameson, Attorney-at-Law
Income Statement
For the Month Ended July 31, 2013

Fees earned..		$5,953
Expenses:		
Paralegal expense..	$1,635	
Rent expense...	1,200	
Wages expense	850	
Utilities expense	325	
Answering service expense	250	
Supplies expense	115	
Miscellaneous expense	75	
Total expenses..		4,450
Net income		$1,503

Cecil Jameson, Attorney-at-Law
Retained Earnings Statement
For the Month Ended July 31, 2013

Retained earnings, July 1, 2013......................................		$3,520
Net income for the month	$1,503	
Less dividends	1,000	
Increase in retained earnings		503
Retained earnings, July 31, 2013....................................		$4,023

(Continued)

Cecil Jameson, Attorney-at-Law
Balance Sheet
July 31, 2013

Assets		Liabilities	
Cash	$ 6,873	Accounts payable	$ 2,355
Accounts receivable	2,225	**Stockholders' Equity**	
Supplies	980	Capital stock	$13,700
Land	10,000	Retained earnings	4,023
Total assets	$20,078	Total stockholders' equity	17,723
		Total liabilities and stockholders' equity	$20,078

4. Optional.

Cecil Jameson, Attorney-at-Law
Statement of Cash Flows
For the Month Ended July 31, 2013

Cash flows from operating activities:		
Cash received from customers	$6,928*	
Deduct cash payments for operating expenses	(3,755)**	
Net cash flows from operating activities		$3,173
Cash flows from investing activities		—
Cash flows from financing activities:		
Cash received from issuing capital stock	$3,700	
Deduct cash dividends	(1,000)	
Net cash flows from financing activities		2,700
Net increase in cash during year		$5,873
Cash as of July 1, 2013		1,000
Cash as of July 31, 2013		$6,873

*$6,928 = $3,928 + $3,000

**$3,755 = $1,055 + $1,200 + $1,500

© Cengage Learning 2014

Discussion Questions

1. Name some users of accounting information.

2. What is the role of accounting in business?

3. Why are most large companies like **Microsoft**, **PepsiCo**, **Caterpillar**, and **AutoZone** organized as corporations?

4. Josh Reilly is the owner of Dispatch Delivery Service. Recently Josh paid interest of $4,500 on a personal loan of $75,000 that he used to begin the business. Should Dispatch Delivery Service record the interest payment? Explain.

5. On July 12, Reliable Repair Service extended an offer of $150,000 for land that had been priced for sale at $185,000. On September 3, Reliable Repair Service accepted the seller's counteroffer of $167,500. Describe how Reliable Repair Service should record the land.

6. a. Land with an assessed value of $750,000 for property tax purposes is acquired by a business for $900,000. Ten years later, the plot of land has an assessed value of $1,200,000 and the business receives an offer of $2,000,000 for it. Should the monetary amount assigned to the land in the business records now be increased?

   b. Assuming that the land acquired in (a) was sold for $2,125,000, how would the various elements of the accounting equation be affected?

7. Describe the difference between an account receivable and an account payable.

8. A business had revenues of $679,000 and operating expenses of $588,000. Did the business (a) incur a net loss or (b) realize net income?

9. A business had revenues of $640,000 and operating expenses of $715,000. Did the business (a) incur a net loss or (b) realize net income?

10. The financial statements are interrelated. (a) What item of financial or operating data appears on both the income statement and the retained earnings statement? (b) What item appears on both the balance sheet and the retained earnings statement? (c) What item appears on both the balance sheet and the statement of cash flows?

Practice Exercises

*Example
Exercises*

EE 1-1 *p.8*
EE 1-1 *p.8*
EE 1-2 *p.9*
EE 1-2 *p.9*
EE 1-3 *p.14*

PE 1-1A   Cost concept OBJ. 2

On May 19, Integrity Repair Service extended an offer of $335,000 for land that had been priced for sale at $363,000. On June 4, Integrity Repair Service accepted the seller's counteroffer of $345,000. On October 10, the land was assessed at a value of $290,000 for property tax purposes. On February 5 of the next year, Integrity Repair Service was offered $380,000 for the land by a national retail chain. At what value should the land be recorded in Integrity Repair Service's records?

PE 1-1B   Cost concept OBJ. 2

On March 31, Higgins Repair Service extended an offer of $415,000 for land that had been priced for sale at $460,000. On April 15, Higgins Repair Service accepted the seller's counteroffer of $437,500. On September 9, the land was assessed at a value of $375,000 for property tax purposes. On December 8, Higgins Repair Service was offered $475,000 for the land by a national retail chain. At what value should the land be recorded in Higgins Repair Service's records?

PE 1-2A   Accounting equation OBJ. 3

Ultima is a motivational consulting business. At the end of its accounting period, December 31, 2013, Ultima has assets of $942,000 and liabilities of $584,000. Using the accounting equation, determine the following amounts:

a. Stockholders' equity as of December 31, 2013.

b. Stocholders' equity as of December 31, 2014, assuming that assets increased by $113,000 and liabilities increased by $44,000 during 2014.

PE 1-2B   Accounting equation OBJ. 3

Be-The-One is a motivational consulting business. At the end of its accounting period, December 31, 2013, Be-The-One has assets of $395,000 and liabilities of $97,000. Using the accounting equation, determine the following amounts:

a. Stockholders' equity as of December 31, 2013.

b. Stockholders' equity as of December 31, 2014, assuming that assets decreased by $65,000 and liabilities increased by $36,000 during 2014.

PE 1-3A   Transactions OBJ. 4

Arrowhead Delivery Service is owned and operated by Gates Deeter. The following selected transactions were completed by Arrowhead Delivery Service during August:

1. Received cash in exchange for capital stock, $25,000.

2. Paid creditors on account, $3,750.

*Example
Exercises*

3. Billed customers for delivery services on account, $22,400.

4. Received cash from customers on account, $11,300.

5. Paid dividends, $6,000.

Indicate the effect of each transaction on the accounting equation elements (Assets, Liabilities, Stockholders' Equity Capital Stock, Dividends, Revenue, and Expense). Also indicate the specific item within the accounting equation element that is affected. To illustrate, the answer to (1) is shown below.

(1) Asset (Cash) increases by $25,000; Stockholders' Equity (Capital Stock) increases by $25,000.

EE 1-3 *p. 14* **PE 1-3B Transactions**   OBJ. 4

Interstate Delivery Service is owned and operated by Katie Wyer. The following selected transactions were completed by Interstate Delivery Service during May:

1. Received cash in exchange for capital stock, $18,000.

2. Paid advertising expense, $4,850.

3. Purchased supplies on account, $2,100.

4. Billed customers for delivery services on account, $14,700.

5. Received cash from customers on account, $8,200.

Indicate the effect of each transaction on the accounting equation elements (Assets, Liabilities, Stockholders' Equity Capital Stock, Dividends, Revenue, and Expense). Also indicate the specific item within the accounting equation element that is affected. To illustrate, the answer to (1) is shown below.

(1) Asset (Cash) increases by $18,000; Stockholders' Equity (Capital Stock) increases by $18,000.

EE 1-4 *p. 15* **PE 1-4A Income statement**   OBJ. 5

The revenues and expenses of Sunset Travel Service for the year ended April 30, 2014, are listed below.

Fees earned	$1,673,000
Office expense	488,000
Miscellaneous expense	34,000
Wages expense	660,000

Prepare an income statement for the current year ended April 30, 2014.

EE 1-4 *p. 15* **PE 1-4B Income statement**   OBJ. 5

The revenues and expenses of Sentinel Travel Service for the year ended August 31, 2014, are listed below.

Fees earned	$750,000
Office expense	295,000
Miscellaneous expense	12,000
Wages expense	450,000

Prepare an income statement for the current year ended August 31, 2014.

EE 1-5 *p. 16* **PE 1-5A Retained earnings statement**   OBJ. 5

Using the income statement for Sunset Travel Service shown in Practice Exercise 1-4A, prepare a retained earnings statement for the current year ended April 30, 2014. Craig Daws, the owner, invested an additional $75,000 in the business in exchange for capital stock and cash dividends of $55,000 were paid during the year. Retained earnings as of May 1, 2013, was $250,000.

Example Exercises

EE 1-5 *p. 16*   **PE 1-5B**   **Retained earnings statement**   OBJ. 5

Using the income statement for Sentinel Travel Service shown in Practice Exercise 1-4B, prepare a retained earnings statement for the current year ended August 31, 2014. Barb Schroeder, the owner, invested an additional $36,000 in the business in exchange for capital stock and cash dividends of $18,000 were paid during the year. Retained earnings as of September 1, 2013, was $300,000.

EE 1-6 *p. 18*   **PE 1-6A**   **Balance sheet**   OBJ. 5

Using the following data for Sunset Travel Service as well as the retained earnings statement shown in Practice Exercise 1-5A, prepare a balance sheet as of April 30, 2014.

Accounts payable	$ 61,000
Accounts receivable	124,000
Capital stock	125,000
Cash	274,000
Land	450,000
Supplies	13,000

EE 1-6 *p. 18*   **PE 1-6B**   **Balance sheet**   OBJ. 5

Using the following data for Sentinel Travel Service as well as the retained earnings statement shown in Practice Exercise 1-5B, prepare a balance sheet as of August 31, 2014.

Accounts payable	$ 44,600
Accounts receivable	75,500
Capital stock	116,000
Cash	45,400
Land	310,000
Supplies	4,700

EE 1-7 *p. 19*   **PE 1-7A**   **Statement of cash flows**   OBJ. 5

A summary of cash flows for Sunset Travel Service for the year ended April 30, 2014, is shown below.

Cash receipts:	
Cash received from customers	$1,500,000
Cash received from issuing capital stock	75,000
Cash payments:	
Cash paid for operating expenses	1,215,000
Cash paid for land	240,000
Cash paid for dividends	66,000

The cash balance as of May 1, 2013, was $220,000.

Prepare a statement of cash flows for Sunset Travel Service for the year ended April 30, 2014.

EE 1-7 *p. 19*   **PE 1-7B**   **Statement of cash flows**   OBJ. 5

A summary of cash flows for Sentinel Travel Service for the year ended August 31, 2014, is shown below.

Cash receipts:	
Cash received from customers	$734,000
Cash received from issuing capital stock	36,000
Cash payments:	
Cash paid for operating expenses	745,600
Cash paid for land	50,000
Cash paid for dividends	18,000

The cash balance as of September 1, 2013, was $89,000.

Prepare a statement of cash flows for Sentinel Travel Service for the year ended August 31, 2014.

EE 1-8 *p. 22*

PE 1-8A   Ratio of liabilities to stockholders' equity   OBJ. 6
The following data were taken from Mesa Company's balance sheet:

	Dec. 31, 2014	Dec. 31, 2013
Total liabilities	$547,800	$518,000
Total stockholders' equity	415,000	370,000

a. Compute the ratio of liabilities to stockholders' equity.

b. Has the creditor's risk increased or decreased from December 31, 2013, to December 31, 2014?

EE 1-8 *p. 22*

PE 1-8B   Ratio of liabilities to stockholders' equity   OBJ. 6
The following data were taken from Alvarado Company's balance sheet:

	Dec. 31, 2014	Dec. 31, 2013
Total liabilities	$4,085,000	$2,880,000
Total stockholders' equity	4,300,000	3,600,000

a. Compute the ratio of liabilities to stockholders' equity.

b. Has the creditor's risk increased or decreased from December 31, 2013, to December 31, 2014?

Exercises

EX 1-1   Types of businesses   OBJ. 1
The following is a list of well-known companies.

1. Alcoa Inc.
2. Boeing
3. Caterpillar
4. Citigroup Inc.
5. CVS
6. Dow Chemical Company
7. eBay Inc.
8. FedEx
9. Ford Motor Company
10. Gap Inc.
11. H&R Block
12. Hilton Hospitality, Inc.
13. Procter & Gamble
14. SunTrust
15. Walmart Stores, Inc.

a. Indicate whether each of these companies is primarily a service, merchandise, or manufacturing business. If you are unfamiliar with the company, use the Internet to locate the company's home page or use the finance Web site of Yahoo (http://finance.yahoo.com).

b. For which of the preceding companies is the accounting equation relevant?

EX 1-2   Professional ethics   OBJ. 1
A fertilizer manufacturing company wants to relocate to Yellowstone County. A report from a fired researcher at the company indicates the company's product is releasing toxic by-products. The company suppressed that report. A later report commissioned by the company shows there is no problem with the fertilizer.

Should the company's chief executive officer reveal the content of the unfavorable report in discussions with Yellowstone County representatives? Discuss.

EX 1-3   Business entity concept

OBJ. 2

Ozark Sports sells hunting and fishing equipment and provides guided hunting and fishing trips. Ozark Sports is owned and operated by Eric Griffith, a well-known sports enthusiast and hunter. Eric's wife, Linda, owns and operates Lake Boutique, a women's clothing store. Eric and Linda have established a trust fund to finance their children's college education. The trust fund is maintained by Missouri State Bank in the name of the children, Mark and Steffy.

a. For each of the following transactions, identify which of the entities listed should record the transaction in its records.

Entities	
L	Lake Boutique
M	Missouri State Bank
O	Ozark Sports
X	None of the above

1. Linda authorized the trust fund to purchase mutual fund shares.
2. Linda purchased two dozen spring dresses from a St. Louis designer for a special spring sale.
3. Eric paid a breeder's fee for an English springer spaniel to be used as a hunting guide dog.
4. Linda deposited a $2,000 personal check in the trust fund at Missouri State Bank.
5. Eric paid a local doctor for his annual physical, which was required by the workmen's compensation insurance policy carried by Ozark Sports.
6. Eric received a cash advance from customers for a guided hunting trip.
7. Linda paid her dues to the YWCA.
8. Linda donated several dresses from inventory for a local charity auction for the benefit of a women's abuse shelter.
9. Eric paid for dinner and a movie to celebrate their twelfth wedding anniversary.
10. Eric paid for an advertisement in a hunters' magazine.

b. What is a business transaction?

✔ Starbucks, $3,675

EX 1-4   Accounting equation

OBJ. 3

The total assets and total liabilities of Peet's Coffee & Tea Inc. and Starbucks Corporation are shown below.

	Peet's Coffee & Tea (in millions)	Starbucks (in millions)
Assets	$209	$6,386
Liabilities	36	2,711

Determine the stockholders' equity of each company.

✔ Dollar Tree, $1,459

EX 1-5   Accounting equation

OBJ. 3

The total assets and total liabilities of Dollar Tree Inc. and Target Corporation are shown below.

	Dollar Tree (in millions)	Target Corporation (in millions)
Assets	$2,381	$43,705
Liabilities	922	28,218

Determine the stockholders' equity of each company.

✔ a. $456,100

EX 1-6   Accounting equation

OBJ. 3

Determine the missing amount for each of the following:

	Assets	=	Liabilities	+	Stockholders' Equity
a.	X	=	$118,000	+	$338,100
b.	$766,750	=	X	+	$411,740
c.	$3,250,300	=	$1,178,100	+	X

EX 1-7 Accounting equation   OBJ. 3, 4

✔ b. $890,000

Mega Concepts is a motivational consulting business. At the end of its accounting period, December 31, 2013, Mega Concepts has assets of $1,250,000 and liabilities of $475,000. Using the accounting equation and considering each case independently, determine the following amounts:

a. Stockholders' equity as of December 31, 2013.

b. Stockholders' equity as of December 31, 2014, assuming that assets increased by $225,000 and liabilities increased by $110,000 during 2014.

c. Stockholders' equity as of December 31, 2014, assuming that assets decreased by $300,000 and liabilities increased by $90,000 during 2014.

d. Stockholders' equity as of December 31, 2014, assuming that assets increased by $550,000 and liabilities decreased by $135,000 during 2014.

e. Net income (or net loss) during 2014, assuming that as of December 31, 2014, assets were $1,500,000, liabilities were $375,000, and no additional capital stock was issued or dividends paid.

EX 1-8 Asset, liability, and stockholders' equity items   OBJ. 3

Indicate whether each of the following is identified with (1) an asset, (2) a liability, or (3) stockholders' equity:

a. accounts payable

b. cash

c. fees earned

d. land

e. supplies

f. wages expense

EX 1-9 Effect of transactions on accounting equation   OBJ. 4

Describe how the following business transactions affect the three elements of the accounting equation.

a. Invested cash in business.

b. Paid for utilities used in the business.

c. Purchased supplies for cash.

d. Purchased supplies on account.

e. Received cash for services performed.

EX 1-10 Effect of transactions on accounting equation   OBJ. 4

✔ a. (1) increase
$260,000

a. A vacant lot acquired for $180,000 is sold for $440,000 in cash. What is the effect of the sale on the total amount of the seller's (1) assets, (2) liabilities, and (3) stockholders' equity?

b. Assume that the seller owes $69,000 on a loan for the land. After receiving the $440,000 cash in (a), the seller pays the $69,000 owed. What is the effect of the payment on the total amount of the seller's (1) assets, (2) liabilities, and (3) stockholders' equity?

c. Is it true that a transaction always affects at least two elements (Assets, Liabilities, or Stockholders' Equity) of the accounting equation? Explain.

EX 1-11 Effect of transactions on stockholders' equity   OBJ. 4

Indicate whether each of the following types of transactions will either (a) increase stockholders' equity or (b) decrease stockholders' equity:

1. expenses

2. issuing capital stock in exchange for cash

3. dividends

4. revenues

EX 1-12   Transactions   OBJ. 4

The following selected transactions were completed by Reuben's Delivery Service during October:

1. Received cash from owner in exchange for capital stock, $20,000.
2. Purchased supplies for cash, $900.
3. Paid rent for October, $3,000.
4. Paid advertising expense, $2,500.
5. Received cash for providing delivery services, $23,100.
6. Billed customers for delivery services on account, $41,750.
7. Paid creditors on account, $4,500.
8. Received cash from customers on account, $36,200.
9. Determined that the cost of supplies on hand was $175 and $725 of supplies had been used during the month.
10. Paid dividends, $1,000.

Indicate the effect of each transaction on the accounting equation by listing the numbers identifying the transactions, (1) through (10), in a column, and inserting at the right of each number the appropriate letter from the following list:

a. Increase in an asset, decrease in another asset.

b. Increase in an asset, increase in a liability.

c. Increase in an asset, increase in stockholders' equity.

d. Decrease in an asset, decrease in a liability.

e. Decrease in an asset, decrease in stockholders' equity.

EX 1-13   Nature of transactions   OBJ. 4

✔ d. $7,200

Angela Howard operates her own catering service. Summary financial data for July are presented in equation form as follows. Each line designated by a number indicates the effect of a transaction on the equation. Each increase and decrease in stockholders' equity, except transaction (5), affects net income.

	Assets			= Liabilities +		Stockholders' Equity			
	Cash	+ Supplies +	Land	= Accounts Payable +	Capital Stock +	Retained Earning −	Dividends +	Fees Earned −	Expenses
Bal.	30,000	2,000	80,000	12,000	30,000	70,000			
1.	+33,000							+33,000	
2.	−20,000		+20,000						
3.	−24,000								−24,000
4.		+1,000		+1,000					
5.	−3,000						−3,000		
6.	−6,000			−6,000					
7.		−1,800							−1,800
Bal.	10,000	1,200	100,000	7,000	30,000	70,000	−3,000	33,000	−25,800

a. Describe each transaction.

b. What is the amount of the net decrease in cash during the month?

c. What is the amount of the net increase in stockholders' equity during the month?

d. What is the amount of the net income for the month?

e. How much of the net income for the month was retained in the business?

EX 1-14   Net income and dividends   OBJ. 5

The income statement for the month of February indicates a net income of $17,500. During the same period, $25,500 in cash dividends was paid.

➤ Would it be correct to say that the business incurred a net loss of $8,000 during the month? Discuss.

EX 1-15 Net income and stockholders' equity for four businesses

OBJ. 5

✔ Kilo: Net income, $230,000

Four different corporations, Juliet, Kilo, Lima, and Mike, show the same balance sheet data at the beginning and end of a year. These data, exclusive of the amount of stockholders' equity, are summarized as follows:

	Total Assets	Total Liabilities
Beginning of the year	$ 600,000	$150,000
End of the year	1,125,000	500,000

On the basis of the above data and the following additional information for the year, determine the net income (or loss) of each company for the year. (*Hint:* First determine the amount of increase or decrease in stockholders' equity during the year.)

Juliet: No additional capital stock was issued, and no dividends were paid.

Kilo: No additional capital stock was issued, but dividends of $55,000 were paid.

Lima: Additional capital stock of $100,000 was issued, but no dividends were paid.

Mike: Additional capital stock of $100,000 was issued, and dividends of $55,000 were paid.

EX 1-16 Balance sheet items

OBJ. 5

From the following list of selected items taken from the records of Hoosier Appliance Service as of a specific date, identify those that would appear on the balance sheet:

1. Accounts Receivable
2. Cash
3. Fees Earned
4. Land
5. Capital Stock
6. Supplies
7. Supplies Expense
8. Utilities Expense
9. Wages Expense
10. Wages Payable

EX 1-17 Income statement items

OBJ. 5

Based on the data presented in Exercise 1-16, identify those items that would appear on the income statement.

EX 1-18 Retained earnings statement

OBJ. 5

✔ Retained earnings, November 30, 2014: $635,000

Financial information related to Infra-Systems Company for the month ended November 30, 2014, is as follows:

Net income for November	$275,000
Dividends paid during November	40,000
Retained earnings, November 1, 2014	400,000

a. Prepare a retained earnngs statement for the month ended November 30, 2014.

b. Why is the retained earnings statement prepared before the November 30, 2014, balance sheet?

EX 1-19 Income statement

OBJ. 5

✔ Net income: $284,000

Exploration Services was organized on March 1, 2014. A summary of the revenue and expense transactions for March follows:

Fees earned	$1,100,000
Wages expense	715,000
Rent expense	80,000
Supplies expense	9,000
Miscellaneous expense	12,000

Prepare an income statement for the month ended March 31.

EX 1-20 Missing amounts from balance sheet and income statement data OBJ. 5

One item is omitted in each of the following summaries of balance sheet and income statement data for the following four different corporations:

	Freeman	Heyward	Jones	Ramirez
Beginning of the year:				
Assets	$ 900,000	$490,000	$115,000	(d)
Liabilities	360,000	260,000	81,000	$120,000
End of the year:				
Assets	1,260,000	675,000	100,000	270,000
Liabilities	330,000	220,000	80,000	136,000
During the year:				
Additional issuance of capital stock	(a)	150,000	10,000	55,000
Dividends	75,000	32,000	(c)	39,000
Revenue	570,000	(b)	115,000	115,000
Expenses	240,000	128,000	122,500	128,000

Determine the missing amounts, identifying them by letter. (*Hint:* First determine the amount of increase or decrease in stockholders' equity during the year.)

EX 1-21 Balance sheets, net income OBJ. 5

Financial information related to Ebony Interiors for February and March 2014 is as follows:

	February 28, 2014	March 31, 2014
Accounts payable	$310,000	$400,000
Accounts receivable	800,000	960,000
Capital stock	200,000	200,000
Cash	320,000	380,000
Retained earnings	?	?
Supplies	30,000	35,000

a. Prepare balance sheets for Ebony Interiors as of February 28 and March 31, 2014.

b. Determine the amount of net income for March, assuming that no additional capital stock was issued and no dividends were paid during the month.

c. Determine the amount of net income for March, assuming that no additional capital stock was issued but dividends of $50,000 were paid during the month.

EX 1-22 Financial statements OBJ. 5

Each of the following items is shown in the financial statements of Exxon Mobil Corporation.

1. Accounts payable
2. Cash equivalents
3. Crude oil inventory
4. Equipment
5. Exploration expenses
6. Income taxes payable
7. Investments
8. Long-term debt

9. Marketable securities
10. Notes and loans payable
11. Notes receivable
12. Operating expenses
13. Prepaid taxes
14. Sales
15. Selling expenses

a. Identify the financial statement (balance sheet or income statement) in which each item would appear.

b. Can an item appear on more than one financial statement?

c. Is the accounting equation relevant for Exxon Mobil Corporation?

EX 1-23 Statement of cash flows OBJ. 5

Indicate whether each of the following activities would be reported on the statement of cash flows as (a) an operating activity, (b) an investing activity, or (c) a financing activity:

1. Cash received from fees earned.
2. Cash paid for expenses.

3. Cash paid for land.

4. Cash paid for dividends.

EX 1-24 Statement of cash flows   OBJ. 5

A summary of cash flows for Ethos Consulting Group for the year ended May 31, 2014, is shown below.

Cash receipts:	
Cash received from customers	$637,500
Cash received from issuing capital stock	62,500
Cash payments:	
Cash paid for operating expenses	475,000
Cash paid for land	90,000
Cash paid for dividends	17,500

The cash balance as of June 1, 2013, was $58,000.

Prepare a statement of cash flows for Ethos Consulting Group for the year ended May 31, 2014.

EX 1-25 Financial statements   OBJ. 5

✔ Correct amount of total assets is $51,500.

We-Sell Realty, organized August 1, 2014, is owned and operated by Omar Farah. How many errors can you find in the following statements for We-Sell Realty, prepared after its first month of operations?

We-Sell Realty
Income Statement
August 31, 2014

Sales commissions		$140,000
Expenses:		
Office salaries expense	$87,000	
Rent expense	18,000	
Automobile expense	7,500	
Miscellaneous expense	2,200	
Supplies expense	1,150	
Total expenses		115,850
Net income		$ 25,000

Omar Farah
Retained Earnings Statement
August 31, 2013

Retained earnings, August 1, 2014	$ 0
Less dividends during August	10,000
	$(10,000)
Additional issuance of capital stock on August 1, 2014	15,000
	$ 5,000
Net income for August	25,000
Retained earnings, August 31, 2014	$ 30,000

Balance Sheet
For the Month Ended August 31, 2014

Assets		Liabilities	
Cash	$ 8,900	Accounts receivable	$38,600
Accounts payable	22,350	Supplies	4,000
		Stockholders' Equity	
		Retained earnings	30,000
Total assets	$31,250	Total liabilities and stockholders' equity...	$72,600

EX 1-26 Ratio of liabilities to stockholders' equity   OBJ. 6

The Home Depot, Inc., is the world's largest home improvement retailer and one of the largest retailers in the United States based on net sales volume. The Home Depot operates over 2,200 Home Depot® stores that sell a wide assortment of building materials and home improvement and lawn and garden products.

The Home Depot recently reported the following balance sheet data (in millions):

	Year 2	Year 1
Total assets	$40,125	$40,877
Total stockholders' equity	18,889	19,393

a. Determine the total liabilities at the end of Years 2 and 1.

b. Determine the ratio of liabilities to stockholders' equity for Year 2 and Year 1. Round to two decimal places.

c. What conclusions regarding the margin of protection to the creditors can you draw from (b)?

EX 1-27 Ratio of liabilities to stockholders' equity   OBJ. 6

Lowe's Companies Inc., a major competitor of The Home Depot in the home improvement business, operates over 1,700 stores. Lowe's recently reported the following balance sheet data (in millions):

	Year 2	Year 1
Total assets	$33,699	$33,005
Total liabilities	15,587	13,936

a. Determine the total stockholders' equity as of at the end of Years 2 and 1.

b. Determine the ratio of liabilities to stockholders' equity for Year 2 and Year 1. Round to two decimal places.

c. What conclusions regarding the risk to the creditors can you draw from (b)?

d. Using the balance sheet data for The Home Depot in Exercise 1-26, how does the ratio of liabilities to stockholders' equity of Lowe's compare to that of The Home Depot?

Problems Series A

✔ Cash bal. at end of June: $29,250

PR 1-1A Transactions   OBJ. 4

On June 1 of the current year, Bret Eisen established a business to manage rental property. He completed the following transactions during June:

a. Opened a business bank account with a deposit of $30,000 in exchange for capital stock.

b. Purchased office supplies on account, $1,200.

c. Received cash from fees earned for managing rental property, $7,200.

d. Paid rent on office and equipment for the month, $3,000.

e. Paid creditors on account, $750.

f. Billed customers for fees earned for managing rental property, $5,000.

g. Paid automobile expenses (including rental charges) for month, $600, and miscellaneous expenses, $300.

h. Paid office salaries, $1,800.

i. Determined that the cost of supplies on hand was $700; therefore, the cost of supplies used was $500.

j. Paid dividends $1,500.

Instructions

1. Indicate the effect of each transaction and the balances after each transaction, using the following tabular headings:

Assets			= Liabilities +		Stockholders' Equity							
	Accounts		Accounts	Capital		Fees	Rent	Salaries	Supplies	Auto	Misc.	
Cash +	Receivable +	Supplies =	Payable +	Stock	− Dividends	+ Earned	− Expense	− Expense	− Expense	− Expense	− Expense	

2. Briefly explain why issuance of capital stock and revenues increased stock-holders' equity, while dividends and expenses decreased stockholders' equity.

3. Determine the net income for June.

4. How much did June's transactions increase or decrease retained earnings?

PR 1-2A Financial statements

OBJ. 5

✔ 1. Net income: $360,000

SPREADSHEET

Following are the amounts of the assets and liabilities of Oriental Travel Agency at December 31, 2014, the end of the current year, and its revenue and expenses for the year. The retained earnings was $400,000 on January 1, 2014, the beginning of the current year. During the current year, dividends of $25,000 were paid.

Accounts payable	$ 115,000	Miscellaneous expense	$ 7,000
Accounts receivable	370,000	Rent expense	150,000
Capital stock	50,000	Supplies	20,000
Cash	210,000	Supplies expense	14,000
Fees earned	1,100,000	Utilities expense	79,000
Land	300,000	Wages expense	490,000

Instructions

1. Prepare an income statement for the current year ended December 31, 2014.

2. Prepare a retained earnings statement for the current year ended December 31, 2014.

3. Prepare a balance sheet as of December 31, 2014.

4. What item appears on both the retained earnings statement and the balance sheet?

PR 1-3A Financial statements

OBJ. 5

✔ 1. Net income: $31,200

SPREADSHEET

Seth Feye established Reliance Financial Services on July 1, 2014. Reliance Financial Services offers financial planning advice to its clients. The effect of each transaction and the balances after each transaction for July are shown below.

	Assets			= Liabilities +			Stockholders' Equity					
	Cash +	Accounts Receivable +	Supplies =	Accounts Payable +	Capital Stock	− Dividends +	Fees Earned	− Salaries Expense	− Rent Expense	− Auto Expense	− Supplies Expense	− Misc. Expense
a.	+50,000				+50,000							
b.			+7,000	+7,000								
Bal.	50,000		7,000	7,000	50,000							
c.	−3,600			−3,600								
Bal.	46,400		7,000	3,400	50,000							
d.	+110,000						+110,000					
Bal.	156,400		7,000	3,400	50,000		110,000					
e.	−33,000								−33,000			
Bal.	123,400		7,000	3,400	50,000		110,000		−33,000			
f.	−20,800									−16,000		−4,800
Bal.	102,600		7,000	3,400	50,000		110,000		−33,000	−16,000		−4,800
g.	−55,000							−55,000				
Bal.	47,600		7,000	3,400	50,000		110,000	−55,000	−33,000	−16,000		−4,800
h.			−4,500								−4,500	
Bal.	47,600		2,500	3,400	50,000		110,000	−55,000	−33,000	−16,000	−4,500	−4,800
i.		+34,500					+ 34,500					
Bal.	47,600	34,500	2,500	3,400	50,000		144,500	−55,000	−33,000	−16,000	−4,500	−4,800
j.	−15,000					−15,000						
Bal.	32,600	34,500	2,500	3,400	50,000	−15,000	144,500	−55,000	−33,000	−16,000	−4,500	−4,800

Instructions

1. Prepare an income statement for the month ended July 31, 2014.

2. Prepare a retained earnings statement for the month ended July 31, 2014.

3. Prepare a balance sheet as of July 31, 2014.

4. (Optional). Prepare a statement of cash flows for the month ending July 31, 2014.

PR 1-4A   Transactions; financial statements   OBJ. 4, 5

✔ 2. Net income: $23,650

On October 1, 2014, Kevin Bosley established Sunrise Realty. Kevin completed the following transactions during the month of October:

a. Opened a business bank account with a deposit of $18,000 in exchange for capital stock.

b. Purchased office supplies on account, $3,200.

c. Paid creditor on account, $1,800.

d. Earned sales commissions, receiving cash, $36,750.

e. Paid rent on office and equipment for the month, $4,000.

f. Paid dividends, $3,000.

g. Paid automobile expenses (including rental charge) for month, $2,500, and miscellaneous expenses, $1,200.

h. Paid office salaries, $3,750.

i. Determined that the cost of supplies on hand was $1,550; therefore, the cost of supplies used was $1,650.

Instructions

1. Indicate the effect of each transaction and the balances after each transaction, using the following tabular headings:

Assets		= Liabilities +				Stockholders' Equity					
		Accounts	Capital			Sales	Rent	Salaries	Auto	Supplies	Misc.
Cash +	Supplies =	Payable +	Stock	– Dividends +	Commissions	– Expense	– Expense	– Expense	– Expense	– Expense

2. Prepare an income statement for October, a retained earnings statement for October, and a balance sheet as of October 31.

PR 1-5A   Transactions; financial statements   OBJ. 4, 5

✔ 3. Net income: $63,775

SPREADSHEET

D'Lite Dry Cleaners is owned and operated by Joel Palk. A building and equipment are currently being rented, pending expansion to new facilities. The actual work of dry cleaning is done by another company at wholesale rates. The assets, liabilities, and capital stock of the business on July 1, 2014, are as follows: Cash, $45,000; Accounts Receivable, $93,000; Supplies, $7,000; Land, $75,000; Accounts Payable, $40,000; Capital Stock, $60,000. Business transactions during July are summarized as follows:

a. Joel Palk invested additional cash in exchange for capital stock with a deposit of $35,000 in the business bank account.

b. Paid $50,000 for the purchase of land adjacent to land currently owned by D'Lite Dry Cleaners as a future building site.

c. Received cash from cash customers for dry cleaning revenue, $32,125.

d. Paid rent for the month, $6,000.

e. Purchased supplies on account, $2,500.

f. Paid creditors on account, $22,800.

g. Charged customers for dry cleaning revenue on account, $84,750.

h. Received monthly invoice for dry cleaning expense for July (to be paid on August 10), $29,500.

i. Paid the following: wages expense, $7,500; truck expense, $2,500; utilities expense, $1,300; miscellaneous expense, $2,700.

j. Received cash from customers on account, $88,000.

k. Determined that the cost of supplies on hand was $5,900; therefore, the cost of supplies used during the month was $3,600.

l. Paid dividends, $12,000.

Instructions

1. Determine the amount of retained earnings as of July 1 of the current year.

2. State the assets, liabilities, and stockholders' equity as of July 1 in equation form similar to that shown in this chapter. In tabular form below the equation, indicate increases and decreases resulting from each transaction and the new balances after each transaction.

3. Prepare an income statement for July, a retained earnings statement for July, and a balance sheet as of July 31.

4. (Optional). Prepare a statement of cash flows for July.

PR 1-6A   Missing amounts from financial statements   OBJ. 5

✔ k. $750,000

The financial statements at the end of Wolverine Realty's first month of operations are as follows:

Wolverine Realty
Income Statement
For the Month Ended April 30, 2014

Fees earned...		$ (a)
Expenses:		
Wages expense...	$300,000	
Rent expense..	100,000	
Supplies expense..	(b)	
Utilities expense..	20,000	
Miscellaneous expense......................................	25,000	
Total expenses...		475,000
Net income..		$275,000

Wolverine Realty
Retained Earnings Statement
For the Month Ended April 30, 2014

Retained earnings, April 1, 2014...................................		$ (c)
Net income for April...	$ (d)	
Less dividends...	125,000	
Increase in retained earnings.....................................		(e)
Retained earnings, April 30, 2014.................................		$ (f)

Wolverine Realty
Balance Sheet
April 30, 2014

Assets		Liabilities	
Cash	$462,500	Accounts payable	$100,000
Supplies......................	12,500	**Stockholders' Equity**	
Land	150,000	Capital stock....................	$375,000
Total assets	$ (g)	Retained earnings...............	(h)
		Total stockholders' equity........	(i)
		Total liabilities and stockholders' equity .... $ (j)	

Wolverine Realty
Statement of Cash Flows
For the Month Ended April 30, 2014

Cash flows from operating activities:		
Cash received from customers...................................	$ (k)	
Deduct cash payments for expenses and payments to creditors.....	(387,500)	
Net cash flows from operating activities...........................		$ (l)
Cash flows used for investing activities:		
Cash payments for acquisition of land		(m)
Cash flows from financing activities:		
Cash received from issuing capital stock	$ (n)	
Deduct cash dividends	(o)	
Net cash flows from financing activities...........................		(p)
Net increase (decrease) in cash and April 30, 2014, cash balance		$ (q)

Instructions

By analyzing the interrelationships among the four financial statements, determine the proper amounts for (a) through (q).

Problems Series B

PR 1-1B Transactions

OBJ. 4

✔ Cash bal. at end of March: $48,650

Amy Austin established an insurance agency on March 1 of the current year and completed the following transactions during March:

a. Opened a business bank account with a deposit of $50,000 in exchange for capital stock.

b. Purchased supplies on account, $4,000.

c. Paid creditors on account, $2,300.

d. Received cash from fees earned on insurance commissions, $13,800.

e. Paid rent on office and equipment for the month, $5,000.

f. Paid automobile expenses for month, $1,150, and miscellaneous expenses, $300.

g. Paid office salaries, $2,500.

h. Determined that the cost of supplies on hand was $2,700; therefore, the cost of supplies used was $1,300.

i. Billed insurance companies for sales commissions earned, $12,500.

j. Paid dividends, $3,900.

Instructions

1. Indicate the effect of each transaction and the balances after each transaction, using the following tabular headings:

Assets			=	Liabilities	+			Stockholders' Equity					
	Accounts			Accounts		Capital		Fees	Rent	Salaries	Supplies	Auto	Misc.
Cash +	Receivable +	Supplies	=	Payable	+	Stock	– Dividends +	Earned	– Expense	– Expense	– Expense	– Expense	– Expense

2. ━━━▶ Briefly explain why the issuance of capital stock and revenues increased stockholders' equity, while dividends and expenses decreased stockholders' equity.

3. Determine the net income for March.

4. How much did March's transactions increase or decrease retained earnings?

PR 1-2B   Financial statements   OBJ. 5

✔ 1. Net income:
$200,000

The amounts of the assets and liabilities of Wilderness Travel Service at April 30, 2014, the end of the current year, and its revenue and expenses for the year are listed below. The retained earnings was $145,000 at May 1, 2013, the beginning of the current year, and dividends of $40,000 were paid during the current year.

Accounts payable	$ 25,000	Rent expense	$ 75,000
Accounts receivable	210,000	Supplies	9,000
Capital stock	35,000	Supplies expense	12,000
Cash	146,000	Taxes expense	10,000
Fees earned	875,000	Utilities expense	38,000
Miscellaneous expense	15,000	Wages expense	525,000

Instructions

1. Prepare an income statement for the current year ended April 30, 2014.

2. Prepare a retained earnings statement for the current year ended April 30, 2014.

3. Prepare a balance sheet as of April 30, 2014.

4. What item appears on both the income statement and retained earnings statement?

PR 1-3B   Financial statements   OBJ. 5

✔ 1. Net income:
$10,900

SPREADSHEET

Jose Loder established Bronco Consulting on August 1, 2014. The effect of each transaction and the balances after each transaction for August are shown below.

	Assets				= Liabilities +			Stockholders' Equity						
	Cash +	Accounts Receivable +	Supplies	=	Accounts Payable +	Capital Stock	– Dividends +	Fees Earned	– Salaries Expense	– Rent Expense	– Auto Expense	– Supplies Expense	– Misc. Expense
a.	+75,000					+75,000							
b.			+9,000		+9,000								
Bal.	75,000		9,000		9,000	75,000							
c.	+92,000							+92,000					
Bal.	167,000		9,000		9,000	75,000		92,000					
d.	–27,000									–27,000			
Bal.	140,000		9,000		9,000	75,000		92,000		–27,000			
e.	–6,000				–6,000								
Bal.	134,000		9,000		3,000	75,000		92,000		–27,000			
f.		+33,000						+33,000					
Bal.	134,000	33,000	9,000		3,000	75,000		125,000		–27,000			
g.	–23,000										–15,500		–7,500
Bal.	111,000	33,000	9,000		3,000	75,000		125,000		–27,000	–15,500		–7,500
h.	–58,000								–58,000				
Bal.	53,000	33,000	9,000		3,000	75,000		125,000	–58,000	–27,000	–15,500		–7,500
i.			–6,100									–6,100	
Bal.	53,000	33,000	2,900		3,000	75,000		125,000	–58,000	–27,000	–15,500	–6,100	–7,500
j.	–5,000						–5,000						
Bal.	48,000	33,000	2,900		3,000	75,000	–5,000	125,000	–58,000	–27,000	–15,500	–6,100	–7,500

Instructions

1. Prepare an income statement for the month ended August 31, 2014.

2. Prepare a retained earnings statement for the month ended August 31, 2014.

3. Prepare a balance sheet as of August 31, 2014.

4. (Optional). Prepare a statement of cash flows for the month ending August 31, 2014.

PR 1-4B   Transactions; financial statements   OBJ. 4, 5

✔ 2. Net income:
$10,850

On April 1, 2014, Maria Adams established Custom Realty. Maria completed the following transactions during the month of April:

a. Opened a business bank account with a deposit of $24,000 in exchange for capital stock.

b. Paid rent on office and equipment for the month, $3,600.

c. Paid automobile expenses (including rental charge) for month, $1,350, and miscellaneous expenses, $600.

d. Purchased office supplies on account, $1,200.

e. Earned sales commissions, receiving cash, $19,800.

f. Paid creditor on account, $750.

g. Paid office salaries, $2,500.

h. Paid dividends, $3,500.

i. Determined that the cost of supplies on hand was $300; therefore, the cost of supplies used was $900.

Instructions

1. Indicate the effect of each transaction and the balances after each transaction, using the following tabular headings:

Assets		= Liabilities +		Stockholders' Equity						
Cash + Supplies	=	Accounts Payable +	Capital Stock – Dividends +	Sales Commissions –	Rent Expense –	Salaries Expense –	Auto Expense –	Supplies Expense –	Misc. Expense

2. Prepare an income statement for April, a retained earnings statement for April, and a balance sheet as of April 30.

PR 1-5B Transactions; financial statements

OBJ. 4, 5

Bev's Dry Cleaners is owned and operated by Beverly Zahn. A building and equipment are currently being rented, pending expansion to new facilities. The actual work of dry cleaning is done by another company at wholesale rates. The assets, liabilities, and capital stock of the business on November 1, 2014, are as follows: Cash, $39,000; Accounts Receivable, $80,000; Supplies, $11,000; Land, $50,000; Accounts Payable, $31,500; Capital Stock, $50,000. Business transactions during November are summarized as follows:

a. Beverly Zahn invested additional cash in exchange for capital stock with a deposit of $21,000 in the business bank account.

b. Purchased land adjacent to land currently owned by Bev's Dry Cleaners to use in the future as a parking lot, paying cash of $35,000.

c. Paid rent for the month, $4,000.

d. Charged customers for dry cleaning revenue on account, $72,000.

e. Paid creditors on account, $20,000.

f. Purchased supplies on account, $8,000.

g. Received cash from cash customers for dry cleaning revenue, $38,000.

h. Received cash from customers on account, $77,000.

i. Received monthly invoice for dry cleaning expense for November (to be paid on December 10), $29,450.

j. Paid the following: wages expense, $24,000; truck expense, $2,100; utilities expense, $1,800; miscellaneous expense, $1,300.

k. Determined that the cost of supplies on hand was $11,800; therefore, the cost of supplies used during the month was $7,200.

l. Paid dividends, $5,000.

Instructions

1. Determine the amount of retained earnings as of November 1.

2. State the assets, liabilities, and stockholders' equity as of November 1 in equation form similar to that shown in this chapter. In tabular form below the equation, indicate increases and decreases resulting from each transaction and the new balances after each transaction.

3. Prepare an income statement for November, a retained earnings statement for November, and a balance sheet as of November 30.

4. (Optional). Prepare a statement of cash flows for November.

PR 1-6B Missing amounts from financial statements OBJ. 5

✔ i. $208,000

The financial statements at the end of Atlas Realty's first month of operations are shown below.

Atlas Realty
Income Statement
For the Month Ended May 31, 2014

Fees earned..		$400,000
Expenses:		
Wages expense..	$ (a)	
Rent expense...	48,000	
Supplies expense	17,600	
Utilities expense..	14,400	
Miscellaneous expense......................................	4,800	
Total expenses		288,000
Net income		$ (b)

Atlas Realty
Retained Earnings Statement
For the Month Ended May 31, 2014

Retained earnings, May 1, 2014.....................................		$ (c)
Net income	$ (d)	
Less dividends	(e)	
Increase in retained earnings.......................................		(f)
Retained earnings, May 31, 2014		$ (g)

Atlas Realty
Balance Sheet
May 31, 2014

Assets		Liabilities	
Cash	$123,200	Accounts payable	$48,000
Supplies......................	12,800	**Stockholders' Equity**	
Land	(h)	Capital stock...........................	$ (j)
Total assets	$ (i)	Retained earnings......................	(k)
		Total stockholders' equity..............	(l)
		Total liabilities and stockholders' equity	$ (m)

Atlas Realty
Statement of Cash Flows
For the Month Ended May 31, 2014

Cash flows from operating activities:		
Cash received from customers	$ (n)	
Deduct cash payments for expenses and payments to creditors	(252,800)	
Net cash flows from operating activities		$ (o)
Cash flows from investing activities:		
Cash payments for acquisition of land............................		(120,000)
Cash flows from financing activities:		
Cash received from issuing capital stock..........................	$ 160,000	
Deduct cash dividends..	(64,000)	
Net cash flows from financing activities		(p)
Net increase (decrease) in cash and May 31, 2014, cash balance.......		$ (q)

Instructions

By analyzing the interrelationships among the four financial statements, determine the proper amounts for (a) through (q).

Continuing Problem

✔ 2. Net income: $1,340

Peyton Smith enjoys listening to all types of music and owns countless CDs. Over the years, Peyton has gained a local reputation for knowledge of music from classical to rap and the ability to put together sets of recordings that appeal to all ages.

During the last several months, Peyton served as a guest disc jockey on a local radio station. In addition, Peyton has entertained at several friends' parties as the host deejay.

On June 1, 2014, Peyton established a corporation known as PS Music. Using an extensive collection of music MP3 files, Peyton will serve as a disc jockey on a fee basis for weddings, college parties, and other events. During June, Peyton entered into the following transactions:

June 1. Deposited $4,000 in a checking account in the name of PS Music in exchange for capital stock.

2. Received $3,500 from a local radio station for serving as the guest disc jockey for June.

2. Agreed to share office space with a local real estate agency, Pinnacle Realty. PS Music will pay one-fourth of the rent. In addition, PS Music agreed to pay a portion of the salary of the receptionist and to pay one-fourth of the utilities. Paid $800 for the rent of the office.

4. Purchased supplies from City Office Supply Co. for $350. Agreed to pay $100 within 10 days and the remainder by July 5, 2014.

6. Paid $500 to a local radio station to advertise the services of PS Music twice daily for two weeks.

8. Paid $675 to a local electronics store for renting digital recording equipment.

12. Paid $350 (music expense) to Cool Music for the use of its current music demos to make various music sets.

13. Paid City Office Supply Co. $100 on account.

16. Received $300 from a dentist for providing two music sets for the dentist to play for her patients.

22. Served as disc jockey for a wedding party. The father of the bride agreed to pay $1,000 in July.

25. Received $500 for serving as the disc jockey for a cancer charity ball hosted by the local hospital.

29. Paid $240 (music expense) to Galaxy Music for the use of its library of music demos.

30. Received $900 for serving as PS disc jockey for a local club's monthly dance.

30. Paid Pinnacle Realty $400 for PS Music's share of the receptionist's salary for June.

30. Paid Pinnacle Realty $300 for PS Music's share of the utilities for June.

30. Determined that the cost of supplies on hand is $170. Therefore, the cost of supplies used during the month was $180.

30. Paid for miscellaneous expenses, $415.

30. Paid $1,000 royalties (music expense) to National Music Clearing for use of various artists' music during the month.

30. Paid dividends of $500.

Instructions

1. Indicate the effect of each transaction and the balances after each transaction, using the following tabular headings:

Assets			=	Liabilities +				Stockholders' Equity								
											Office	Equipment					
Cash +	Accts. Rec. +	Supplies	=	Accounts Payable +	Capital Stock	– Dividends	+ Fees Earned	– Music Exp.	– Rent Exp.	– Rent Exp.	– Advertising Exp.	– Wages Exp.	– Utilities Exp.	– Supplies Exp.	– Misc. Exp.

2. Prepare an income statement for PS Music for the month ended June 30, 2014.

3. Prepare a retained earnings statement for PS Music for the month ended June 30, 2014.

4. Prepare a balance sheet for PS Music as of June 30, 2014.

Cases & Projects

CP 1-1 Ethics and professional conduct in business

Group Project

Colleen Fernandez, president of Rhino Enterprises, applied for a $175,000 loan from First Federal Bank. The bank requested financial statements from Rhino Enterprises as a basis for granting the loan. Colleen has told her accountant to provide the bank with a balance sheet. Colleen has decided to omit the other financial statements because there was a net loss during the past year.

In groups of three or four, discuss the following questions:

1. Is Colleen behaving in a professional manner by omitting some of the financial statements?

2. a. What types of information about their businesses would owners be willing to provide bankers? What types of information would owners not be willing to provide?

   b. What types of information about a business would bankers want before extending a loan?

   c. What common interests are shared by bankers and business owners?

CP 1-2 Net income

On January 1, 2013, Dr. Marcie Cousins established Health-Wise Medical, a medical practice organized as a corporation. The following conversation occurred the following August between Dr. Cousins and a former medical school classmate, Dr. Avi Abu, at an American Medical Association convention in Seattle.

Dr. Abu: Marcie, good to see you again. Why didn't you call when you were in Miami? We could have had dinner together.

Dr. Cousins: Actually, I never made it to Miami this year. My husband and kids went up to our Vail condo twice, but I got stuck in Jacksonville. I opened a new consulting practice this January and haven't had any time for myself since.

Dr. Abu: I heard about it . . . Health . . . something . . . right?

Dr. Cousins: Yes, Health-Wise Medical. My husband chose the name.

Dr. Abu: I've thought about doing something like that. Are you making any money? I mean, is it worth your time?

Dr. Cousins: You wouldn't believe it. I started by opening a bank account with $25,000, and my July bank statement has a balance of $80,000. Not bad for six months—all pure profit.

Dr. Abu: Maybe I'll try it in Miami! Let's have breakfast together tomorrow and you can fill me in on the details.

Comment on Dr. Cousins' statement that the difference between the opening bank balance ($25,000) and the July statement balance ($80,000) is pure profit.

CP 1-3 Transactions and financial statements

Lisa Duncan, a junior in college, has been seeking ways to earn extra spending money. As an active sports enthusiast, Lisa plays tennis regularly at the Phoenix Tennis Club, where her family has a membership. The president of the club recently approached Lisa with the proposal that she manage the club's tennis courts. Lisa's primary duty would be to supervise the operation of the club's four indoor and 10 outdoor courts, including court reservations.

In return for her services, the club would pay Lisa $325 per week, plus Lisa could keep whatever she earned from lessons. The club and Lisa agreed to a one-month trial, after which both would consider an arrangement for the remaining two years of Lisa's college career. On this basis, Lisa organized Serve-N-Volley. During September 2014, Lisa managed the tennis courts and entered into the following transactions:

a. Opened a business account by depositing $950.

b. Paid $300 for tennis supplies (practice tennis balls, etc.).

c. Paid $275 for the rental of video equipment to be used in offering lessons during September.

d. Arranged for the rental of two ball machines during September for $250. Paid $100 in advance, with the remaining $150 due October 1.

e. Received $1,750 for lessons given during September.

f. Received $600 in fees from the use of the ball machines during September.

g. Paid $800 for salaries of part-time employees who answered the telephone and took reservations while Lisa was giving lessons.

h. Paid $290 for miscellaneous expenses.

i. Received $1,300 from the club for managing the tennis courts during September.

j. Determined that the cost of supplies on hand at the end of the month totaled $180; therefore, the cost of supplies used was $120.

k. Withdrew $400 for personal use on September 30.

As a friend and accounting student, you have been asked by Lisa to aid her in assessing the venture.

1. Indicate the effect of each transaction and the balances after each transaction, using the following tabular headings:

Assets		=	Liabilities	+				Owner's Equity				
Cash +	Supplies	=	Accounts Payable	+	Lisa Duncan, Capital	−	Lisa Duncan, Drawing	+	Fees Earned	− Salaries Expense	− Rent Expense	− Supplies Expense	− Misc. Expense

2. Prepare an income statement for September.

3. Prepare a statement of owner's equity for September. The statement of owner's equity for a proprietorship is similar to the retained earnings statement for a corporation. The balance of the owner's capital as of the beginning of the period is listed first. Any investments made by the owner during the period are then listed and the net income (net loss) is added (subtracted) to determine a subtotal. From this subtotal, the owner's withdrawals are subtracted to determine the increase (decrease) in owner's equity for the period. This increase (decrease) is then added to (subtracted from) the beginning owner's equity to determine the owner's equity as of the end of the period.

4. Prepare a balance sheet as of September 30.

5. a. Assume that Lisa Duncan could earn $10 per hour working 30 hours a week as a waitress. Evaluate which of the two alternatives, working as a waitress or operating Serve-N-Volley, would provide Lisa with the most income per month.

   b. ◖▬▬▶ Discuss any other factors that you believe Lisa should consider before discussing a long-term arrangement with the Phoenix Tennis Club.

CP 1-4 Certification requirements for accountants

Internet Project

By satisfying certain specific requirements, accountants may become certified as public accountants (CPAs), management accountants (CMAs), or internal auditors (CIAs). Find the certification requirements for one of these accounting groups by accessing the appropriate Internet site listed below.

Site	Description
http://www.ais-cpa.com	This site lists the address and/or Internet link for each state's board of accountancy. Find your state's requirements.
http://www.imanet.org	This site lists the requirements for becoming a CMA.
http://www.theiia.org	This site lists the requirements for becoming a CIA.

CP 1-5 Cash flows

Amazon.com, an Internet retailer, was incorporated and began operation in the mid-90s. On the statement of cash flows, would you expect Amazon.com's net cash flows from operating, investing, and financing activities to be positive or negative for its first three years of operations? Use the following format for your answers, and briefly explain your logic.

	First Year	Second Year	Third Year
Net cash flows from operating activities	negative		
Net cash flows from investing activities			
Net cash flows from financing activities			

CP 1-6 Financial analysis

The now defunct Enron Corporation, once headquartered in Houston, Texas, provided products and services for natural gas, electricity, and communications to wholesale and retail customers. Enron's operations were conducted through a variety of subsidiaries and affiliates that involved transporting gas through pipelines, transmitting electricity, and managing energy commodities. The following data were taken from Enron's financial statements:

	In millions
Total revenues	$100,789
Total costs and expenses	98,836
Operating income	1,953
Net income	979
Total assets	65,503
Total liabilities	54,033
Total stockholders' equity	11,470
Net cash flows from operating activities	4,779
Net cash flows from investing activities	(4,264)
Net cash flows from financing activities	571
Net increase in cash	1,086

The market price of Enron's stock was approximately $83 per share when the prior financial statement data were taken. Before it went bankrupt, Enron's stock sold for $0.22 per share.

Review the preceding financial statement data and search the Internet for articles on Enron Corporation. Briefly explain why Enron's stock dropped so dramatically.

Corporations: Organization, Stock Transactions, and Dividends

Google

If you purchase a share of stock from Google, you own a small interest in the company. You may request a Google stock certificate as an indication of your ownership.

Google is one of the most visible companies on the Internet. Many of us cannot visit the Web without using Google to power a search or to retrieve our e-mail using Google's gmail. Yet Google's Internet tools are free to online browsers. Google generates most of its revenue through online advertising.

Purchasing a share of stock from Google may be a great gift idea for the "hard-to-shop-for person." However, a stock certificate represents more than just a picture that you can frame. In fact, the stock certificate is a document that reflects legal ownership of the future financial prospects of Google. In addition, as a shareholder, it represents your claim against the assets and earnings of the corporation.

If you are purchasing Google stock as an investment, you should analyze Google financial statements and management's plans for the future. For example, Google first offered its stock to the public on August 19, 2004, for $100 per share. Google's stock recently sold for over $600 per share, even though it pays no dividends. In addition, Google recently expanded into developing and offering free software platforms for mobile devices such as cell phones. For example, your cell phone may use Google's Android™ operating system. So, should you purchase Google stock?

This chapter describes and illustrates the nature of corporations, including the accounting for stock and dividends. This discussion will aid you in making decisions such as whether or not to buy Google stock.

OBJ 1 Describe the nature of the corporate form of organization.
Nature of a Corporation
   Characteristics of a Corporation
   Forming a Corporation

OBJ 2 Describe and illustrate the characteristics of stock, classes of stock, and entries for issuing stock.
Paid-In Capital from Issuing Stock
   Characteristics of Stock
   Classes of Stock   **EE 11-1**
   Issuing Stock   **EE 11-2**
   Premium on Stock   **EE 11-2**
   No-Par Stock   **EE 11-2**

OBJ 3 Describe and illustrate the accounting for cash dividends and stock dividends.
Accounting for Dividends
   Cash Dividends   **EE 11-3**
   Stock Dividends   **EE 11-4**

OBJ 4 Describe and illustrate the accounting for treasury stock transactions.
Treasury Stock Transactions   **EE 11-5**

OBJ 5 Describe and illustrate the reporting of stockholders' equity.
Reporting Stockholders' Equity
   Stockholders' Equity on the Balance Sheet   **EE 11-6**
   Reporting Retained Earnings   **EE 11-7**
   Statement of Stockholders' Equity
   Reporting Stockholders' Equity for Mornin' Joe

OBJ 6 Describe the effect of stock splits on corporate financial statements.
Stock Splits

OBJ 7 Describe and illustrate the use of earnings per share in evaluating a company's profitability.
Financial Analysis and Interpretation: Earnings per Share   **EE 11-8**

At a Glance 11   Page 517

 **OBJ 1** Describe the nature of the corporate form of organization.

Nature of a Corporation

Most large businesses are organized as corporations. As a result, corporations generate more than 90% of the total business dollars in the United States. In contrast, most small businesses are organized as proprietorships, partnerships, or limited liability companies.

Characteristics of a Corporation

A corporation was defined in the Dartmouth College case of 1819, in which Chief Justice Marshall of the U.S. Supreme Court stated: "A corporation is an artificial being, invisible, intangible, and existing only in contemplation of the law."

A *corporation* is a legal entity, distinct and separate from the individuals who create and operate it. As a legal entity, a corporation may acquire, own, and dispose of property in its own name. It may also incur liabilities and enter into contracts. Most importantly, it can sell shares of ownership, called **stock**. This characteristic gives corporations the ability to raise large amounts of capital.

The **stockholders** or *shareholders* who own the stock own the corporation. They can buy and sell stock without affecting the corporation's operations or continued existence. Corporations whose shares of stock are traded in public markets are called *public corporations*. Corporations whose shares are not traded publicly are usually owned by a small group of investors and are called *nonpublic* or *private corporations*.

The stockholders of a corporation have *limited liability*. This means that creditors usually may not go beyond the assets of the corporation to satisfy their claims. Thus, the financial loss that a stockholder may suffer is limited to the amount invested.

The stockholders control a corporation by electing a *board of directors*. This board meets periodically to establish corporate policies. It also selects the chief executive officer (CEO) and other major officers to manage the corporation's day-to-day affairs. Exhibit 1 shows the organizational structure of a corporation.

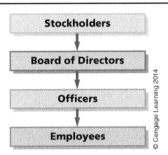

Stockholders
↓
Board of Directors
↓
Officers
↓
Employees

© Cengage Learning 2014

As a separate entity, a corporation is subject to taxes. For example, corporations must pay federal income taxes on their income.[1] Thus, corporate income that is distributed to stockholders in the form of *dividends* has already been taxed. In turn, stockholders must pay income taxes on the dividends they receive. This *double taxation* of corporate earnings is a major disadvantage of the corporate form. The advantages and disadvantages of the corporate form are listed in Exhibit 2.

Note:
Corporations have a separate legal existence, transferable units of ownership, and limited stockholder liability.

EXHIBIT 2   **Advantages and Disadvantages of the Corporate Form**

Advantages	Explanation
Separate legal existence	A corporation exists separately from its owners.
Continuous life	A corporation's life is separate from its owners; therefore, it exists indefinitely.
Raising large amounts of capital	The corporate form is suited for raising large amounts of money from shareholders.
Ownership rights are easily transferable	A corporation sells shares of ownership, called *stock*. The stockholders of a public company can transfer their shares of stock to other stockholders through stock markets, such as the New York Stock Exchange.
Limited liability	A corporation's creditors usually may not go beyond the assets of the corporation to satisfy their claims. Thus, the financial loss that a stockholder may suffer is limited to the amount invested.

Disadvantages	Explanation
Owner is separate from management	Stockholders control management through a board of directors. The board of directors should represent shareholder interests; however, the board is often more closely tied to management than to shareholders. As a result, the board of directors and management may not always behave in the best interests of stockholders.
Double taxation of dividends	As a separate legal entity, a corporation is subject to taxation. Thus, net income distributed as dividends will be taxed once at the corporation level, and then again at the individual level.
Regulatory costs	Corporations must satisfy many requirements, such as those required by the Sarbanes-Oxley Act of 2002.

© Cengage Learning 2014

Forming a Corporation

The first step in forming a corporation is to file an *application of incorporation* with the state. State incorporation laws differ, and corporations often organize in those states with the more favorable laws. For this reason, more than half of the largest companies are incorporated in Delaware. Exhibit 3 lists some corporations, their states of incorporation, and the location of their headquarters.

After the application of incorporation has been approved, the state grants a *charter* or *articles of incorporation*. The articles of incorporation formally create the corporation.[2]

1 A majority of states also require corporations to pay income taxes.

2 The articles of incorporation may also restrict a corporation's activities in certain areas, such as owning certain types of real estate, conducting certain types of business activities, or purchasing its own stock.

Corporation	State of Incorporation	Headquarters
Caterpillar	Delaware	Peoria, Ill.
Delta Air Lines	Delaware	Atlanta, Ga.
The Dow Chemical Company	Delaware	Midland, Mich.
Google	Delaware	Mountain View, Calif.
General Electric Company	New York	Fairfield, Conn.
The Home Depot	Delaware	Atlanta, Ga.
Kellogg Company	Delaware	Battle Creek, Mich.
R.J. Reynolds Tobacco Company	Delaware	Winston-Salem, N.C.
Starbucks Corporation	Washington	Seattle, Wash.
Sun Microsystems, Inc.	Delaware	Palo Alto, Calif.
3M	Delaware	St. Paul, Minn.
The Washington Post Company	Delaware	Washington, D.C.
Whirlpool Corporation	Delaware	Benton Harbor, Mich.

© Cengage Learning 2014

The corporate management and board of directors then prepare a set of *bylaws*, which are the rules and procedures for conducting the corporation's affairs.

Costs may be incurred in organizing a corporation. These costs include legal fees, taxes, state incorporation fees, license fees, and promotional costs. Such costs are debited to an expense account entitled *Organizational Expenses.*

To illustrate, a corporation's organizing costs of $8,500 on January 5 are recorded as shown below.

Jan.	5	Organizational Expenses	8,500	
		Cash		8,500
		Paid costs of organizing the corporation.		

Paid-In Capital from Issuing Stock

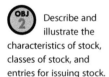

OBJ 2 Describe and illustrate the characteristics of stock, classes of stock, and entries for issuing stock.

The two main sources of stockholders' equity are paid-in capital (or contributed capital) and retained earnings. The main source of paid-in capital is from issuing stock.

Characteristics of Stock

The number of shares of stock that a corporation is *authorized* to issue is stated in its charter. The term *issued* refers to the shares issued to the stockholders. A corporation may reacquire some of the stock that it has issued. The stock remaining in the hands of stockholders is then called **outstanding stock**. The relationship between authorized, issued, and outstanding stock is shown in the graphic at the right.

Number of shares authorized, issued, and outstanding

© Cengage Learning 2014

Upon request, corporations may issue stock certificates to stockholders to document their ownership. Printed on a stock certificate is the name of the company, the name of the stockholder, and the number of shares owned. The stock certificate may also indicate a dollar amount assigned to each share of stock, called **par** value. Stock may be issued without par, in which case it is called *no-par stock*. In some states, the board of directors of a corporation is required to assign a *stated value* to no-par stock.

Corporations have limited liability and, thus, creditors have no claim against stockholders' personal assets. To protect creditors, however, some states require corporations to maintain a minimum amount of paid-in capital. This minimum amount, called *legal capital*, usually includes the par or stated value of the shares issued.

The major rights that accompany ownership of a share of stock are as follows:

1. The right to vote in matters concerning the corporation.
2. The right to share in distributions of earnings.
3. The right to share in assets upon liquidation.

These stock rights normally vary with the class of stock.

Classes of Stock

When only one class of stock is issued, it is called **common stock**. Each share of common stock has equal rights.

A corporation may also issue one or more classes of stock with various preference rights such as a preference to dividends. Such a stock is called a **preferred stock**. The dividend rights of preferred stock are stated either as dollars per share or as a percent of par. For example, a $50 par value preferred stock with a $4 per share dividend may be described as either:[3]

> preferred $4 stock, $50 par
> or
> preferred 8% stock, $50 par

Because they have first rights (preference) to any dividends, preferred stockholders have a greater chance of receiving dividends than common stockholders. However, since dividends are normally based on earnings, a corporation cannot guarantee dividends even to preferred stockholders.

The payment of dividends is authorized by the corporation's board of directors. When authorized, the directors are said to have *declared* a dividend.

Cumulative preferred stock has a right to receive regular dividends that were not declared (paid) in prior years. Noncumulative preferred stock does not have this right.

Cumulative preferred stock dividends that have not been paid in prior years are said to be **in arrears**. Any preferred dividends in arrears must be paid before any common stock dividends are paid. In addition, any dividends in arrears are normally disclosed in notes to the financial statements.

To illustrate, assume that a corporation has issued the following preferred and common stock:

> 1,000 shares of cumulative preferred $4 stock, $50 par
> 4,000 shares of common stock, $15 par

The corporation was organized on January 1, 2012, and paid no dividends in 2012 and 2013. In 2014, the corporation paid $22,000 in dividends, of which $12,000 was paid to preferred stockholders and $10,000 was paid to common stockholders as shown below.

Total dividends paid		$22,000
Preferred stockholders:		
2012 dividends in arrears (1,000 shares × $4)	$4,000	
2013 dividends in arrears (1,000 shares × $4)	4,000	
2014 dividend (1,000 shares × $4)	4,000	
Total preferred dividends paid		(12,000)
Dividends available to common stockholders		$10,000

As a result, preferred stockholders received $12.00 per share ($12,000 ÷ 1,000 shares) in dividends, while common stockholders received $2.50 per share ($10,000 ÷ 4,000 shares).

In addition to dividend preference, preferred stock may be given preferences to assets if the corporation goes out of business and is liquidated. However, claims of creditors must be satisfied first. Preferred stockholders are next in line to receive any remaining assets, followed by the common stockholders.

---

3 In some cases, preferred stock may receive additional dividends if certain conditions are met. Such stock, called *participating preferred stock*, is not often issued.

Example Exercise 11-1 Dividends per Share

Sandpiper Company has 20,000 shares of cumulative preferred 1% stock of $100 par and 100,000 shares of $50 par common stock. The following amounts were distributed as dividends:

Year 1 $10,000
Year 2   45,000
Year 3   80,000

Determine the dividends per share for preferred and common stock for each year.

Follow My Example 11-1

	Year 1	Year 2	Year 3
Amount distributed	$10,000	$45,000	$80,000
Preferred dividend (20,000 shares)	10,000	30,000*	20,000
Common dividend (100,000 shares)	$ 0	$15,000	$60,000
*($10,000 + $20,000)			
Dividends per share:			
Preferred stock	$0.50	$1.50	$1.00
Common stock	None	$0.15	$0.60

Practice Exercises: **PE 11-1A, PE 11-1B**

Issuing Stock

A separate account is used for recording the amount of each class of stock issued to investors in a corporation. For example, assume that a corporation is authorized to issue 10,000 shares of $100 par preferred stock and 100,000 shares of $20 par common stock. The corporation issued 5,000 shares of preferred stock and 50,000 shares of common stock at par for cash. The corporation's entry to record the stock issue is as follows:[4]

Cash		1,500,000	
Preferred Stock			500,000
Common Stock			1,000,000
Issued preferred stock and common stock at par for cash.			

Stock is often issued by a corporation at a price other than its par. The price at which stock is sold depends on a variety of factors, such as the following:

1. The financial condition, earnings record, and dividend record of the corporation.
2. Investor expectations of the corporation's potential earning power.
3. General business and economic conditions and expectations.

If stock is issued (sold) for a price that is more than its par, the stock has been sold at a **premium**. For example, if common stock with a par of $50 is sold for $60 per share, the stock has sold at a premium of $10.

If stock is issued (sold) for a price that is less than its par, the stock has been sold at a **discount**. For example, if common stock with a par of $50 is sold for $45 per share, the stock has sold at a discount of $5. Many states do not permit stock to be sold at a discount. In other states, stock may be sold at a discount in only unusual cases. Since stock is rarely sold at a discount, it is not illustrated.

In order to distribute dividends, financial statements, and other reports, a corporation must keep track of its stockholders. Large public corporations normally use

4 The accounting for investments in stocks from the point of view of the investor is discussed in Chapter 13.

a financial institution, such as a bank, for this purpose.⁵ In such cases, the financial institution is referred to as a *transfer agent* or *registrar*.

Premium on Stock

When stock is issued at a premium, Cash is debited for the amount received. Common Stock or Preferred Stock is credited for the par amount. The excess of the amount paid over par is part of the paid-in capital. An account entitled *Paid-In Capital in Excess of Par* is credited for this amount.

To illustrate, assume that Caldwell Company issues 2,000 shares of $50 par preferred stock for cash at $55. The entry to record this transaction is as follows:

Cash	110,000	
Preferred Stock		100,000
Paid-In Capital in Excess of Par—Preferred Stock		10,000
Issued $50 par preferred stock at $55.		

When stock is issued in exchange for assets other than cash, such as land, buildings, and equipment, the assets acquired are recorded at their fair market value. If this value cannot be determined, the fair market price of the stock issued is used.

To illustrate, assume that a corporation acquired land with a fair market value that cannot be determined. In exchange, the corporation issued 10,000 shares of its $10 par common stock. If the stock has a market price of $12 per share, the transaction is recorded as follows:

Land	120,000	
Common Stock		100,000
Paid-In Capital in Excess of Par		20,000
Issued $10 par common stock, valued		
at $12 per share, for land.		

No-Par Stock

In most states, no-par preferred and common stock may be issued. When no-par stock is issued, Cash is debited and Common Stock is credited for the proceeds. As no-par stock is issued over time, this entry is the same even if the issuing price varies.

To illustrate, assume that on January 9 a corporation issues 10,000 shares of no-par common stock at $40 a share. On June 27, the corporation issues an additional 1,000 shares at $36. The entries to record these issuances of the no-par stock are as follows:

Jan.	9	Cash	400,000	
		Common Stock		400,000
		Issued 10,000 shares of no-par		
		common stock at $40.		
June	27	Cash	36,000	
		Common Stock		36,000
		Issued 1,000 shares of no-par		
		common stock at $36.		

5 Small corporations may use a subsidiary ledger, called a *stockholders ledger*. in this case, the stock accounts (Preferred Stock and Common Stock) are controlling accounts for the subsidiary ledger.

In some states, no-par stock may be assigned a *stated value per share.* The stated value is recorded like a par value. Any excess of the proceeds over the stated value is credited to *Paid-In Capital in Excess of Stated Value.*

To illustrate, assume that in the preceding example the no-par common stock is assigned a stated value of $25. The issuance of the stock on January 9 and June 27 is recorded as follows:

Jan.	9	Cash	400,000	
		Common Stock		250,000
		Paid-In Capital in Excess of Stated Value		150,000
		Issued 10,000 shares of no-par common stock at $40; stated value, $25.		
June	27	Cash	36,000	
		Common Stock		25,000
		Paid-In Capital in Excess of Stated Value		11,000
		Issued 1,000 shares of no-par common stock at $36; stated value, $25.		

Business Connection

GOOGLE INC.

Some excepts from Google's bylaws are shown below.

ARTICLE I—CORPORATE OFFICES

1.1 REGISTERED OFFICE.
The registered office of Google Inc. shall be fixed in the corporation's certificate of incorporation. ...

1.2 OTHER OFFICES.
The corporation's Board of Directors (the "Board") may at any time establish other offices at any place or places where the corporation is qualified to do business.

ARTICLE II—MEETINGS OF STOCKHOLDERS

2.2 ANNUAL MEETING.
The annual meeting of stockholders shall be held each year on a date and at a time designated by the Board. At the annual meeting, directors shall be elected and any other proper business may be transacted.

2.4 NOTICE OF STOCKHOLDERS' MEETINGS.
All notices of meetings of stockholders shall be sent ... not less than ten (10) nor more than sixty (60) days before the date of the meeting to each stockholder entitled to vote at such meeting. ... The notice shall specify the place, if any, date and hour of the meeting, the means of remote communication, if any, by which stockholders and proxy holders may be deemed to be present in person and vote at such meeting. ...

2.8 ADMINISTRATION OF THE MEETING.
Meetings of stockholders shall be presided over by the chairman of the Board. ...

ARTICLE V—OFFICERS

5.1 OFFICERS.
The officers of the corporation shall be a chief executive officer, one or more presidents (at the discretion of the Board), a chairman of the Board and a secretary. The corporation may also have, at the discretion of the Board, a vice chairman of the Board, a chief financial officer, a treasurer, one or more vice presidents, one or more assistant vice presidents, one or more assistant treasurers, one or more assistant secretaries, and any such other officers as may be appointed in accordance with the provisions of these bylaws.

5.6 CHAIRMAN OF THE BOARD.
The chairman of the Board shall be a member of the Board and, if present, preside at meetings of the Board. ...

5.7 CHIEF EXECUTIVE OFFICER.
Subject to the control of the Board, ... the chief executive officer shall, together with the president or presidents of the corporation, have general supervision, direction, and control of the business and affairs of the corporation. ... The chief executive officer shall ... preside at all meetings of the stockholders.

5.11 CHIEF FINANCIAL OFFICER.
The chief financial officer shall keep and maintain ... adequate and correct books and records of accounts of the properties and business transactions of the corporation, including accounts of its assets, liabilities, receipts, disbursements, gains, losses, capital, retained earnings and shares. ...

5.12 TREASURER.
The treasurer shall deposit all moneys and other valuables in the name and to the credit of the corporation. ...

Source: Amended and Restated Bylaws of Google Inc., July 18, 2012. (Accessed at http://investor.google.com/corporate/bylaws.html.)

Example Exercise 11-2 Entries for Issuing Stock

On March 6, Limerick Corporation issued for cash 15,000 shares of no-par common stock at $30. On April 13, Limerick issued at par 1,000 shares of preferred 4% stock, $40 par for cash. On May 19, Limerick issued for cash 15,000 shares of 4%, $40 par preferred stock at $42.
    Journalize the entries to record the March 6, April 13, and May 19 transactions.

Follow My Example 11-2

Mar. 6	Cash	450,000	
	Common Stock		450,000
	(15,000 shares × $30).		
Apr. 13	Cash	40,000	
	Preferred Stock		40,000
	(1,000 shares × $40).		
May 19	Cash	630,000	
	Preferred Stock		600,000
	Paid-In Capital in Excess of Par		30,000
	(15,000 shares × $42).		

Practice Exercises: **PE 11-2A, PE 11-2B**

Accounting for Dividends

OBJ 3 Describe and illustrate the accounting for cash dividends and stock dividends.

When a board of directors declares a cash dividend, it authorizes the distribution of cash to stockholders. When a board of directors declares a stock dividend, it authorizes the distribution of its stock. In both cases, declaring a dividend reduces the retained earnings of the corporation.[6]

Cash Dividends

A cash distribution of earnings by a corporation to its shareholders is a **cash dividend**. Although dividends may be paid in other assets, cash dividends are the most common.
    Three conditions for a cash dividend are as follows:

1. Sufficient retained earnings
2. Sufficient cash
3. Formal action by the board of directors

International Connection

IFRS FOR SMEs

In 2010, the International Accounting Standards Board (IASB) issued a set of accounting standards specifically designed for small- and medium-sized enterprises (SMEs) called International Financial Reporting Standards (IFRS) for SMEs. SMEs in the United States are private companies and such small corporations that they do not report to the Securities and Exchange Commission (SEC). IFRS for SMEs consist of only 230 pages, compared to 2,700 pages for full IFRS. These standards are designed to be cost effective for SMEs. Thus, IFRS for SMEs require fewer disclosures and contain no industry-specific standards or exceptions.

    The American Institute of CPAs (AICPA) has accepted IFRS for SMEs as part of U.S. generally accepted accounting principles (GAAP) for private companies not reporting to the SEC. If users, such as bankers and investors, accept these financial statements, IFRS for SMEs may become popular in the United States.*

*Differences between U.S. GAAP and IFRS are further discussed and illustrated in Appendix C.

6 In rare cases, when a corporation is reducing its operations or going out of business, a dividend may be a distribution of paid-in capital. Such a dividend is called a *liquidating dividend*.

There must be a sufficient (large enough) balance in Retained Earnings to declare a cash dividend. That is, the balance of Retained Earnings must be large enough so that the dividend does not create a debit balance in the retained earnings account. However, a large Retained Earnings balance does not mean that there is cash available to pay dividends. This is because the balances of Cash and Retained Earnings are often unrelated.

Even if there are sufficient retained earnings and cash, a corporation's board of directors is not required to pay dividends. Nevertheless, many corporations pay quarterly cash dividends to make their stock more attractive to investors. *Special* or *extra* dividends may also be paid when a corporation experiences higher than normal profits.

Three dates included in a dividend announcement are as follows:

1. Date of declaration
2. Date of record
3. Date of payment

The *date of declaration* is the date the board of directors formally authorizes the payment of the dividend. On this date, the corporation incurs the liability to pay the amount of the dividend.

Microsoft Corporation declared a dividend of $0.20 per share on March 13, 2012, to common stockholders of record as of May 17, 2012, payable on June 14, 2012.

The *date of record* is the date the corporation uses to determine which stockholders will receive the dividend. During the period of time between the date of declaration and the date of record, the stock price is quoted as selling *with-dividends*. This means that any investors purchasing the stock before the date of record will receive the dividend.

The *date of payment* is the date the corporation will pay the dividend to the stockholders who owned the stock on the date of record. During the period of time between the record date and the payment date, the stock price is quoted as selling *ex-dividends*. This means that since the date of record has passed, any new investors will not receive the dividend.

To illustrate, assume that on October 1 Hiber Corporation declares the cash dividends shown below with a date of record of November 10 and a date of payment of December 2.

	Dividend per Share	Total Dividends
Preferred stock, $100 par, 5,000 shares outstanding....................	$2.50	$12,500
Common stock, $10 par, 100,000 shares outstanding	$0.30	30,000
Total		$42,500

On October 1, the declaration date, Hiber Corporation records the following entry:

Declaration Date

Oct.	1	Cash Dividends	42,500	
		Cash Dividends Payable		42,500
		Declared cash dividends.		

Date of Record   On November 10, the date of record, no entry is necessary. This date merely determines which stockholders will receive the dividends.

On December 2, the date of payment, Hiber Corporation records the payment of the dividends as follows:

Date of Payment

Dec.	2	Cash Dividends Payable	42,500	
		Cash		42,500
		Paid cash dividends.		

At the end of the accounting period, the balance in Cash Dividends will be transferred to Retained Earnings as part of the closing process. This closing entry debits Retained Earnings and credits Cash Dividends for the balance of the cash dividends account. If the cash dividends have not been paid by the end of the period, Cash Dividends Payable will be reported on the balance sheet as a current liability.

Example Exercise 11-3 Entries for Cash Dividends

The important dates in connection with a cash dividend of $75,000 on a corporation's common stock are February 26, March 30, and April 2. Journalize the entries required on each date.

Follow My Example 11-3

Feb. 26	Cash Dividends...	75,000	
	Cash Dividends Payable................................		75,000
Mar. 30	No entry required.		
Apr. 2	Cash Dividends Payable...................................	75,000	
	Cash...		75,000

Practice Exercises: **PE 11-3A, PE 11-3B**

Integrity, Objectivity, and Ethics in Business

THE PROFESSOR WHO KNEW TOO MUCH

A major Midwestern university released a quarterly "American Customer Satisfaction Index" based on its research of customers of popular U.S. products and services. Before the release of the index to the public, the professor in charge of the research bought and sold stocks of some of the companies in the report. The professor was quoted as saying that he thought it was important to test his theories of customer satisfaction with "real" [his own] money.

Is this proper or ethical? Apparently, the dean of the Business School didn't think so. In a statement to the press, the dean stated: "I have instructed anyone affiliated with the (index) not to make personal use of information gathered in the course of producing the quarterly index, prior to the index's release to the general public, and they [the researchers] have agreed."

Sources: Jon E. Hilsenrath and Dan Morse, "Researcher Uses Index to Buy, Short Stocks," *The Wall Street Journal*, February 18, 2003; and Jon E. Hilsenrath, "Satisfaction Theory: Mixed Results," *The Wall Street Journal*, February 19, 2003.

Stock Dividends

A **stock dividend** is a distribution of shares of stock to stockholders. Stock dividends are normally declared only on common stock and issued to common stockholders.

A stock dividend affects only stockholders' equity. Specifically, the amount of the stock dividend is transferred from Retained Earnings to Paid-In Capital. The amount transferred is normally the fair value (market price) of the shares issued in the stock dividend.[7]

To illustrate, assume that the stockholders' equity accounts of Hendrix Corporation as of December 15 are as follows:

Common Stock, $20 par (2,000,000 shares issued)	$40,000,000
Paid-In Capital in Excess of Par—Common Stock	9,000,000
Retained Earnings	26,600,000

On December 15, Hendrix Corporation declares a stock dividend of 5% or 100,000 shares (2,000,000 shares × 5%) to be issued on January 10 to stockholders of record on December 31. The market price of the stock on December 15 (the date of declaration) is $31 per share.

---

7 The use of fair market value is justified as long as the number of shares issued for the stock dividend is small (less than 25% of the shares outstanding).

The entry to record the stock dividend is as follows:

Dec.	15	Stock Dividends	3,100,000	
		Stock Dividends Distributable		2,000,000
		Paid-In Capital in Excess of Par—Common Stock		1,100,000
		Declared 5% (100,000 shares) stock		
		dividend on $20 par common stock		
		with a market price of $31 per share.		

After the preceding entry is recorded, Stock Dividends will have a debit balance of $3,100,000. Like cash dividends, the stock dividends account is closed to Retained Earnings at the end of the accounting period. This closing entry debits Retained Earnings and credits Stock Dividends.

At the end of the period, the *stock dividends distributable* and *paid-in capital in excess of par—common stock* accounts are reported in the Paid-In Capital section of the balance sheet. Thus, the effect of the preceding stock dividend is to transfer $3,100,000 of retained earnings to paid-in capital.

On January 10, the stock dividend is distributed to stockholders by issuing 100,000 shares of common stock. The issuance of the stock is recorded by the following entry:

Jan.	10	Stock Dividends Distributable	2,000,000	
		Common Stock		2,000,000
		Issued stock as stock dividend.		

A stock dividend does not change the assets, liabilities, or total stockholders' equity of a corporation. Likewise, a stock dividend does not change an individual stockholder's proportionate interest (equity) in the corporation.

To illustrate, assume a stockholder owns 1,000 of a corporation's 10,000 shares outstanding. If the corporation declares a 6% stock dividend, the stockholder's proportionate interest will not change, as shown below.

	Before **Stock Dividend**	*After* **Stock Dividend**
Total shares issued	10,000	10,600 [10,000 + (10,000 × 6%)]
Number of shares owned	1,000	1,060 [1,000 + (1,000 × 6%)]
Proportionate ownership	10% (1,000/10,000)	10% (1,060/10,600)

Example Exercise 11-4 Entries for Stock Dividends

Vienna Highlights Corporation has 150,000 shares of $100 par common stock outstanding. On June 14, Vienna Highlights declared a 4% stock dividend to be issued August 15 to stockholders of record on July 1. The market price of the stock was $110 per share on June 14.

Journalize the entries required on June 14, July 1, and August 15.

Follow My Example 11-4

June 14	Stock Dividends (150,000 × 4% × $110).........................	660,000	
	Stock Dividends Distributable (6,000 × $100)		600,000
	Paid-In Capital in Excess of Par—Common Stock		
	($660,000 – $600,000).....................................		60,000
July 1	No entry required.		
Aug. 15	Stock Dividends Distributable	600,000	
	Common Stock		600,000

Practice Exercises: **PE 11-4A, PE 11-4B**

Treasury Stock Transactions

OBJ 4
Describe and illustrate the accounting for treasury stock transactions.

Treasury stock is stock that a corporation has issued and then reacquired. A corporation may reacquire (purchase) its own stock for a variety of reasons, including the following:

1. To provide shares for resale to employees
2. To reissue as bonuses to employees, or
3. To support the market price of the stock

The *cost method* is normally used for recording the purchase and resale of treasury stock.[8] Using the cost method, *Treasury Stock* is debited for the cost (purchase price) of the stock. When the stock is resold, Treasury Stock is credited for its cost. Any difference between the cost and the selling price is debited or credited to *Paid-In Capital from Sale of Treasury Stock*.

The 2011 edition of *Accounting Trends & Techniques* indicated that 64.6% of the companies surveyed reported treasury stock.

To illustrate, assume that a corporation has the following paid-in capital on January 1:

Common stock, $25 par (20,000 shares authorized and issued)	$500,000
Excess of issue price over par	150,000
	$650,000

On February 13, the corporation purchases 1,000 shares of its common stock at $45 per share. The entry to record the purchase of the treasury stock is as follows:

Feb.	13	Treasury Stock	45,000	
		Cash		45,000
		Purchased 1,000 shares of treasury stock at $45.		

On April 29, the corporation sells 600 shares of the treasury stock for $60. The entry to record the sale is as follows:

Apr.	29	Cash	36,000	
		Treasury Stock		27,000
		Paid-In Capital from Sale of Treasury Stock		9,000
		Sold 600 shares of treasury stock at $60.		

A sale of treasury stock may result in a decrease in paid-in capital. To the extent that Paid-In Capital from Sale of Treasury Stock has a credit balance, it is debited for any such decrease. Any remaining decrease is then debited to the retained earnings account.

To illustrate, assume that on October 4, the corporation sells the remaining 400 shares of treasury stock for $40 per share. The entry to record the sale is as follows:

Oct.	4	Cash	16,000	
		Paid-In Capital from Sale of Treasury Stock	2,000	
		Treasury Stock		18,000
		Sold 400 shares of treasury stock at $40.		

The October 4 entry shown above decreases paid-in capital by $2,000. Since Paid-In Capital from Sale of Treasury Stock has a credit balance of $9,000, the entire $2,000 was debited to Paid-In Capital from Sale of Treasury Stock.

No dividends (cash or stock) are paid on the shares of treasury stock. To do so would result in the corporation earning dividend revenue from itself.

---

8 Another method that is infrequently used, called the *par value method*, is discussed in advanced accounting texts.

Example Exercise 11-5 **Entries for Treasury Stock**

On May 3, Buzz Off Corporation reacquired 3,200 shares of its common stock at $42 per share. On July 22, Buzz Off sold 2,000 of the reacquired shares at $47 per share. On August 30, Buzz Off sold the remaining shares at $40 per share. Journalize the transactions of May 3, July 22, and August 30.

Follow My Example 11-5 ▶▶

May 3	Treasury Stock (3,200 × $42)...	134,400	
	Cash		134,400
July 22	Cash (2,000 × $47)	94,000	
	Treasury Stock (2,000 × $42)..		84,000
	Paid-In Capital from Sale of Treasury Stock [2,000 × ($47 – $42)]		10,000
Aug. 30	Cash (1,200 × $40)	48,000	
	Paid-In Capital from Sale of Treasury Stock [1,200 × ($42 – $40)]	2,400	
	Treasury Stock (1,200 × $42)..		50,400

Practice Exercises: **PE 11-5A, PE 11-5B**

 Describe and illustrate the reporting of stockholders' equity.

Reporting Stockholders' Equity

As with other sections of the balance sheet, alternative terms and formats may be used in reporting stockholders' equity. Also, changes in retained earnings and paid-in capital may be reported in separate statements or notes to the financial statements.

Stockholders' Equity on the Balance Sheet

Exhibit 4 shows two methods for reporting stockholders' equity for the December 31, 2014, balance sheet for Telex Inc.

Method 1. Each class of stock is reported, followed by its related paid-in capital accounts. Retained earnings is then reported followed by a deduction for treasury stock.

Method 2. The stock accounts are reported, followed by the paid-in capital reported as a single item, Additional paid-in capital. Retained earnings is then reported followed by a deduction for treasury stock.

EXHIBIT 4

Stockholders' Equity Section of a Balance Sheet

Telex Inc.
Balance Sheet
December 31, 2014

Stockholders' Equity

Paid-in capital:			
Preferred 10% stock, $50 par (2,000 shares authorized and issued)...............................	$100,000		
Excess of issue price over par	10,000	$ 110,000	
Common stock, $20 par (50,000 shares authorized, 45,000 shares issued)	$900,000		
Excess of issue price over par	190,000	1,090,000	
From sale of treasury stock................................		2,000	
Total paid-in capital..................................			$1,202,000
Retained earnings...			350,000
Total			$1,552,000
Deduct treasury stock (600 shares at cost)....................			27,000
Total stockholders' equity			$1,525,000

— **Method 1**

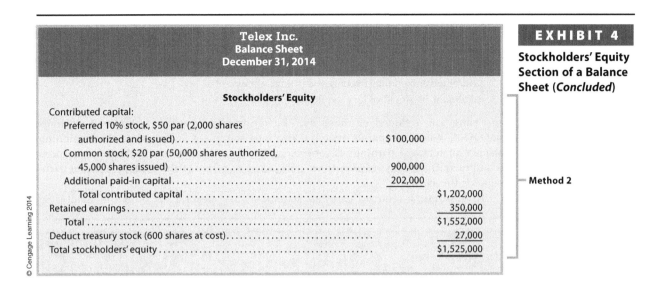

EXHIBIT 4

Stockholders' Equity Section of a Balance Sheet (*Concluded*)

Telex Inc.
Balance Sheet
December 31, 2014

Stockholders' Equity

Contributed capital:		
Preferred 10% stock, $50 par (2,000 shares authorized and issued)	$100,000	
Common stock, $20 par (50,000 shares authorized, 45,000 shares issued)	900,000	
Additional paid-in capital	202,000	
Total contributed capital		$1,202,000
Retained earnings		350,000
Total		$1,552,000
Deduct treasury stock (600 shares at cost)		27,000
Total stockholders' equity		$1,525,000

Method 2

© Cengage Learning 2014

Significant changes in stockholders' equity during a period may also be presented in a statement of stockholders' equity or in the notes to the financial statements. The statement of stockholders' equity is illustrated later in this section.

Relevant rights and privileges of the various classes of stock outstanding should also be reported.[9] Examples include dividend and liquidation preferences, conversion rights, and redemption rights. Such information may be disclosed on the face of the balance sheet or in the notes to the financial statements.

Example Exercise 11-6 Reporting Stockholders' Equity

Using the following accounts and balances, prepare the Stockholders' Equity section of the balance sheet. Forty thousand shares of common stock are authorized, and 5,000 shares have been reacquired.

Common Stock, $50 par	$1,500,000
Paid-In Capital from Sale of Treasury Stock	44,000
Paid-In Capital in Excess of Par	160,000
Retained Earnings	4,395,000
Treasury Stock	120,000

Follow My Example 11-6

Stockholders' Equity

Paid-in capital:		
Common stock, $50 par (40,000 shares authorized, 30,000 shares issued)	$1,500,000	
Excess of issue price over par	160,000	$1,660,000
From sale of treasury stock		44,000
Total paid-in capital		$1,704,000
Retained earnings		4,395,000
Total		$6,099,000
Deduct treasury stock (5,000 shares at cost)		120,000
Total stockholders' equity		$5,979,000

Practice Exercises: **PE 11-6A, PE 11-6B**

9 *FASB Accounting Standards Codification,* Section 505-10-50.

Reporting Retained Earnings

Changes in retained earnings may be reported using one of the following:

1. Separate retained earnings statement
2. Combined income and retained earnings statement
3. Statement of stockholders' equity

Changes in retained earnings may be reported in a separate retained earnings statement. When a separate retained earnings statement is prepared, the beginning balance of retained earnings is reported. The net income is then added (or net loss is subtracted) and any dividends are subtracted to arrive at the ending retained earnings for the period.

To illustrate, a retained earnings statement for Telex Inc. is shown in Exhibit 5.

EXHIBIT 5 **Retained Earnings Statement**	**Telex Inc.** **Retained Earnings Statement** **For the Year Ended December 31, 2014**		
	Retained earnings, January 1, 2014			$245,000
	Net income		$180,000	
	Less dividends:			
	Preferred stock.	$10,000		
	Common stock.	65,000	75,000	
	Increase in retained earnings.			105,000
	Retained earnings, December 31, 2014.			$350,000

© Cengage Learning 2014

Changes in retained earnings may also be reported in combination with the income statement. This format emphasizes net income as the connecting link between the income statement and ending retained earnings. Since this format is not often used, we do not illustrate it.

Changes in retained earnings may also be reported in a statement of stockholders' equity. An example of reporting changes in retained earnings in a statement of stockholders' equity for Telex Inc. is shown in Exhibit 6.

Example Exercise 11-7   **Retained Earnings Statement**   OBJ 5

Dry Creek Cameras Inc. reported the following results for the year ending March 31, 2014:

Retained earnings, April 1, 2013	$3,338,500
Net income	461,500
Cash dividends declared	80,000
Stock dividends declared	120,000

Prepare a retained earnings statement for the fiscal year ended March 31, 2014.

Follow My Example 11-7

Dry Creek Cameras Inc.
Retained Earnings Statement
For the Year Ended March 31, 2014

Retained earnings, April 1, 2013		$3,338,500
Net income	$461,500	
Less dividends declared	200,000	
Increase in retained earnings		261,500
Retained earnings, March 31, 2014		$3,600,000

Practice Exercises: **PE 11-7A, PE 11-7B**

Restrictions The use of retained earnings for payment of dividends may be restricted by action of a corporation's board of directors. Such **restrictions**, sometimes called *appropriations,* remain part of the retained earnings.

Restrictions of retained earnings are classified as:

1. *Legal.* State laws may require a restriction of retained earnings.

    Example: States may restrict retained earnings by the amount of treasury stock purchased. In this way, legal capital cannot be used for dividends.

2. *Contractual.* A corporation may enter into contracts that require restrictions of retained earnings.

    Example: A bank loan may restrict retained earnings so that money for repaying the loan cannot be used for dividends.

3. *Discretionary.* A corporation's board of directors may restrict retained earnings voluntarily.

    Example: The board may restrict retained earnings and, thus, limit dividend distributions so that more money is available for expanding the business.

Restrictions of retained earnings must be disclosed in the financial statements. Such disclosures are usually included in the notes to the financial statements.

Prior Period Adjustments An error may arise from a mathematical mistake or from a mistake in applying accounting principles. Such errors may not be discovered within the same period in which they occur. In such cases, the effect of the error should not affect the current period's net income. Instead, the correction of the error, called a **prior period adjustment**, is reported in the retained earnings statement. Such corrections are reported as an adjustment to the beginning balance of retained earnings.[10]

Statement of Stockholders' Equity

When the only change in stockholders' equity is due to net income or net loss and dividends, a retained earnings statement is sufficient. However, when a corporation also has changes in stock and paid-in capital accounts, a **statement of stockholders' equity** is normally prepared.

A statement of stockholders' equity is normally prepared in a columnar format. Each column is a major stockholders' equity classification. Changes in each classification are then described in the left-hand column. Exhibit 6 illustrates a statement of stockholders' equity for Telex Inc.

EXHIBIT 6	**Statement of Stockholders' Equity**

Telex Inc. Statement of Stockholders' Equity For the Year Ended December 31, 2014						
	Preferred Stock	Common Stock	Additional Paid-In Capital	Retained Earnings	Treasury Stock	Total
Balance, January 1, 2014	$100,000	$850,000	$177,000	$245,000	$(17,000)	$1,355,000
Net income				180,000		180,000
Dividends on preferred stock				(10,000)		(10,000)
Dividends on common stock				(65,000)		(65,000)
Issuance of additional common stock		50,000	25,000			75,000
Purchase of treasury stock					(10,000)	(10,000)
Balance, December 31, 2014	$100,000	$900,000	$202,000	$350,000	$(27,000)	$1,525,000

© Cengage Learning 2014

10 Prior period adjustments are illustrated in advanced texts.

Reporting Stockholders' Equity for Mornin' Joe

Mornin' Joe reports stockholders' equity in its balance sheet. Mornin' Joe also includes a retained earnings statement and statement of stockholders' equity in its financial statements.

The Stockholders' Equity section of Mornin' Joe's balance sheet as of December 31, 2014, is shown below.

Mornin' Joe Balance Sheet December 31, 2014			
Stockholders' Equity			
Paid-in capital:			
Preferred 10% stock, $50 par (6,000 shares authorized and issued)		$ 300,000	
Excess of issue price over par		50,000	$ 350,000
Common stock, $20 par (50,000 shares authorized, 45,000 shares issued)		$ 900,000	
Excess of issue price over par		1,450,000	2,350,000
Total paid-in capital			$2,700,000
Retained earnings			1,200,300
Total			$3,900,300
Deduct treasury stock (1,000 shares at cost)			46,000
Total stockholders' equity			$3,854,300
Total liabilities and stockholders' equity			$6,169,700

© Cengage Learning 2014

Mornin' Joe's retained earnings statement for the year ended December 31, 2014, is as follows:

Mornin' Joe Retained Earnings Statment For the Year Ended December 31, 2014			
Retained earnings, January 1, 2014			$ 852,700
Net income		$421,600	
Less dividends:			
Preferred stock	$30,000		
Common stock	44,000	74,000	
Increase in retained earnings			347,600
Retained earnings, December 31, 2014			$1,200,300

© Cengage Learning 2014

The statement of stockholders' equity for Mornin' Joe is shown below.

Mornin' Joe Statement of Stockholders' Equity For the Year Ended December 31, 2014						
	Preferred Stock	Common Stock	Additional Paid-In Capital	Retained Earnings	Treasury Stock	Total
Balance, January 1, 2014	$300,000	$800,000	$1,325,000	$ 852,700	$(36,000)	$3,241,700
Net income				421,600		421,600
Dividends on preferred stock				(30,000)		(30,000)
Dividends on common stock				(44,000)		(44,000)
Issuance of additional common stock		100,000	175,000			275,000
Purchase of treasury stock					(10,000)	(10,000)
Balance, December 31, 2014	$300,000	$900,000	$1,500,000	$1,200,300	$(46,000)	$3,854,300

© Cengage Learning 2014

Stock Splits

OBJ 6 Describe the effect of stock splits on corporate financial statements.

A **stock split** is a process by which a corporation reduces the par or stated value of its common stock and issues a proportionate number of additional shares. A stock split applies to all common shares including the unissued, issued, and treasury shares.

A major objective of a stock split is to reduce the market price per share of the stock. This attracts more investors and broadens the types and numbers of stockholders.

To illustrate, assume that Rojek Corporation has 10,000 shares of $100 par common stock outstanding with a current market price of $150 per share. The board of directors declares the following stock split:

1. Each common shareholder will receive 5 shares for each share held. This is called a 5-for-1 stock split. As a result, 50,000 shares (10,000 shares × 5) will be outstanding.
2. The par of each share of common stock will be reduced to $20 ($100/5).

The par value of the common stock outstanding is $1,000,000 both before and after the stock split as shown below.

	Before Split	After Split
Number of shares	10,000	50,000
Par value per share	× $100	× $20
Total	$1,000,000	$1,000,000

In addition, each Rojek Corporation shareholder owns the same total par amount of stock before and after the stock split. For example, a stockholder who owned 4 shares of $100 par stock before the split (total par of $400) would own 20 shares of $20 par stock after the split (total par of $400). Only the number of shares and the par value per share have changed.

Since there are more shares outstanding after the stock split, the market price of the stock should decrease. For example, in the preceding example, there would be 5 times as many shares outstanding after the split. Thus, the market price of the stock would be expected to fall from $150 to about $30 ($150 ÷ 5).

Stock splits do not require a journal entry, since only the par (or stated) value and number of shares outstanding have changed. However, the details of stock splits are normally disclosed in the notes to the financial statements.

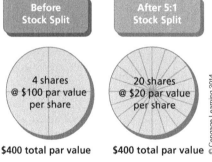

Note:
A stock split does not require a journal entry.

Business Connection

BUFFETT ON STOCK SPLITS

Warren E. Buffett, chairman and chief executive officer of Berkshire Hathaway Inc., opposes stock splits on the basis that they add no value to the company. Since its inception, Berkshire Hathaway has never declared a stock split on its primary (Class A) common stock. As a result, Berkshire Hathaway's Class A common stock sells well above $100,000 per share, which is the most expensive stock on the New York Stock Exchange. Such a high price doesn't bother Buffet, since he believes that high stock prices attract more sophisticated and long-term investors and discourage stock speculators and short-term investors.

In contrast, Microsoft Corporation has split its stock nine times since it went public in 1986. As a result, one share of Microsoft purchased in 1986 is equivalent to 288 shares today, which would be worth over $8,500.

Financial Analysis and Interpretation: Earnings per Share

Describe and illustrate the use of earnings per share in evaluating a company's profitability.

Net income is often used by investors and creditors in evaluating a company's profitability. However, net income by itself is difficult to use in comparing companies of different sizes. Also, trends in net income may be difficult to evaluate if there have been significant changes in a company's stockholders' equity. Thus, the profitability of companies is often expressed as earnings per share.

Earnings per common share (EPS), sometimes called *basic earnings per share,* is the net income per share of common stock outstanding during a period.[11] Corporations whose stock is traded in a public market must report earnings per common share on their income statements.

Earnings per share is computed as follows:

$$\text{Earnings per Share} = \frac{\text{Net Income} - \text{Preferred Dividends}}{\text{Average Number of Common Shares Outstanding}}$$

If a company has preferred stock outstanding, any preferred dividends are subtracted from net income. This is because the numerator represents only those earnings available to the common shareholders.

To illustrate, the following data (in thousands) were taken from recent financial statements of Google:

	Year 2	Year 1
Net income.............................	$8,505,000	$6,520,000
Average number of common shares outstanding	318,702 shares	316,221 shares
Earnings per share.......................	$26.69	$20.62
	($8,505,000 ÷ 318,702 shares)	($6,520,000 ÷ 316,221 shares)

Google had no preferred stock outstanding; thus, no preferred dividends were subtracted in computing earnings per share. As shown above, Google's earnings per share increased from $20.62 in Year 1 to $26.69 in Year 2. An increase in earnings per share is generally considered a favorable trend.

Earnings per share can be used to compare two companies with different net incomes. For example, the following data (in millions) were taken from a recent year's financial statements for Goldman Sachs Group, Inc., and Wells Fargo & Company.

	Goldman Sachs	Wells Fargo
Net income..................................	$8,354	$12,362
Preferred dividends..........................	$641	$730
Average number of common shares outstanding........................	545.0 shares	5,226.8 shares

Goldman Sachs:

$$\text{Earnings per Share} = \frac{\text{Net Income} - \text{Preferred Dividends}}{\text{Average Number of Common Shares Outstanding}} = \frac{\$8,354 - \$641}{545.0 \text{ shares}} = \frac{\$7,713}{545.0 \text{ shares}} = \$14.15$$

Wells Fargo:

$$\text{Earnings per Share} = \frac{\text{Net Income} - \text{Preferred Dividends}}{\text{Average Number of Common Shares Outstanding}} = \frac{\$12,362 - \$730}{5,226.8 \text{ shares}} = \frac{\$11,632}{5,226.8 \text{ shares}} = \$2.23$$

Based on earnings per share, Goldman Sachs is more profitable than Wells Fargo.

---

11 For complex capital structures, earnings per share assuming dilution may also be reported as described in Chapter 15.

Example Exercise 11-8 Earnings per Share

Financial statement data for years ending December 31 for Finnegan Company are shown below.

	2014	2013
Net income	$350,000	$195,000
Preferred dividends	$20,000	$15,000
Average number of common shares outstanding	75,000 shares	50,000 shares

a. Determine earnings per share for 2014 and 2013.

b. Does the change in the earnings per share from 2013 to 2014 indicate a favorable or an unfavorable trend?

Follow My Example 11-8

a.

2014:

$$\text{Earnings per Share} = \frac{\text{Net Income} - \text{Preferred Dividends}}{\text{Average Number of Common Shares Outstanding}} = \frac{\$350,000 - \$20,000}{75,000 \text{ shares}} = \frac{\$330,000}{75,000 \text{ shares}} = \$4.40$$

2013:

$$\text{Earnings per Share} = \frac{\text{Net Income} - \text{Preferred Dividends}}{\text{Average Number of Common Shares Outstanding}} = \frac{\$195,000 - \$15,000}{50,000 \text{ shares}} = \frac{\$180,000}{50,000 \text{ shares}} = \$3.60$$

b. The increase in the earnings per share from $3.60 to $4.40 indicates a favorable trend in the company's profitability.

Practice Exercises: **PE 11-8A, PE 11-8B**

At a Glance 11

Describe the nature of the corporate form of organization.

Key Points   Corporations have a separate legal existence, transferable units of stock, unlimited life, and limited stockholders' liability. The advantages and disadvantages of the corporate form are summarized in Exhibit 2. Costs incurred in organizing a corporation are debited to Organizational Expenses.

Learning Outcomes	Example Exercises	Practice Exercises
• Describe the characteristics of corporations.		
• List the advantages and disadvantages of the corporate form.		
• Prepare a journal entry for the costs of organizing a corporation.		

Describe and illustrate the characteristics of stock, classes of stock, and entries for issuing stock.

Key Points The main source of paid-in capital is from issuing common and preferred stock. Stock issued at par is recorded by debiting Cash and crediting the class of stock issued for its par amount. Stock issued for more than par is recorded by debiting Cash, crediting the class of stock for its par, and crediting Paid-In Capital in Excess of Par for the difference. When no-par stock is issued, the entire proceeds are credited to the stock account. No-par stock may be assigned a stated value per share, and the excess of the proceeds over the stated value may be credited to Paid-In Capital in Excess of Stated Value.

Learning Outcomes	Example Exercises	Practice Exercises
• Describe the characteristics of common and preferred stock including rights to dividends.	**EE11-1**	**PE11-1A, 11-1B**
• Journalize the entry for common and preferred stock issued at par.	**EE11-2**	**PE11-2A, 11-2B**
• Journalize the entry for common and preferred stock issued at more than par.	**EE11-2**	**PE11-2A, 11-2B**
• Journalize the entry for issuing no-par stock.	**EE11-2**	**PE11-2A, 11-2B**

Describe and illustrate the accounting for cash dividends and stock dividends.

Key Points The entry to record a declaration of cash dividends debits Dividends and credits Dividends Payable. When a stock dividend is declared, Stock Dividends is debited for the fair value of the stock to be issued. Stock Dividends Distributable is credited for the par or stated value of the common stock to be issued. The difference between the fair value of the stock and its par or stated value is credited to Paid-In Capital in Excess of Par—Common Stock. When the stock is issued on the date of payment, Stock Dividends Distributable is debited and Common Stock is credited for the par or stated value of the stock issued.

Learning Outcomes	Example Exercises	Practice Exercises
• Journalize the entries for the declaration and payment of cash dividends.	**EE11-3**	**PE11-3A, 11-3B**
• Journalize the entries for the declaration and payment of stock dividends.	**EE11-4**	**PE11-4A, 11-4B**

Describe and illustrate the accounting for treasury stock transactions.

Key Points When a corporation buys its own stock, the cost method of accounting is normally used. Treasury Stock is debited for its cost, and Cash is credited. If the stock is resold, Treasury Stock is credited for its cost and any difference between the cost and the selling price is normally debited or credited to Paid-In Capital from Sale of Treasury Stock.

Learning Outcomes	Example Exercises	Practice Exercises
• Define treasury stock.		
• Describe the accounting for treasury stock.		
• Journalize entries for the purchase and sale of treasury stock.	**EE11-5**	**PE11-5A, 11-5B**

Describe and illustrate the reporting of stockholders' equity.

Key Points   Two alternatives for reporting stockholders' equity are shown in Exhibit 4. Changes in retained earnings are reported in a retained earnings statement, as shown in Exhibit 5. Restrictions to retained earnings should be disclosed. Any prior period adjustments are reported in the retained earnings statement. Changes in stockholders' equity may be reported on a statement of stockholders' equity, as shown in Exhibit 6.

Learning Outcomes	Example Exercises	Practice Exercises
• Prepare the Stockholders' Equity section of the balance sheet.	**EE11-6**	**PE11-6A, 11-6B**
• Prepare a retained earnings statement.	**EE11-7**	**PE11-7A, 11-7B**
• Describe retained earnings restrictions and prior period adjustments.		
• Prepare a statement of stockholders' equity.		

Describe the effect of stock splits on corporate financial statements.

Key Points   When a corporation reduces the par or stated value of its common stock and issues a proportionate number of additional shares, a stock split has occurred. There are no changes in the balances of any accounts, and no entry is required for a stock split.

Learning Outcomes	Example Exercises	Practice Exercises
• Define and give an example of a stock split.		
• Describe the accounting for and effects of a stock split on the financial statements.		

Describe and illustrate the use of earnings per share in evaluating a company's profitability.

Key Points   The profitability of companies is often expressed as earnings per share. Earnings per share is computed by subtracting preferred dividends from net income and dividing by the average number of common shares outstanding.

Learning Outcomes	Example Exercises	Practice Exercises
• Describe the use of earnings per share in evaluating a company's profitability.		
• Compute and interpret earnings per share.	**EE11-8**	**PE11-8A, 11-8B**

Key Terms

cash dividend (505)
common stock (501)
cumulative preferred
  stock (501)
discount (502)
earnings per common
  share (EPS) (516)

in arrears (501)
outstanding stock (500)
par (500)
preferred stock (501)
premium (502)
prior period adjustments (513)
restrictions (513)

statement of stockholders'
  equity (513)
stock (498)
stock dividend (507)
stock split (515)
stockholders (498)
treasury stock (509)

Illustrative Problem

Altenburg Inc. is a lighting fixture wholesaler located in Arizona. During its current fiscal year, ended December 31, 2014, Altenburg Inc. completed the following selected transactions:

Feb. 3. Purchased 2,500 shares of its own common stock at $26, recording the stock at cost. (Prior to the purchase, there were 40,000 shares of $20 par common stock outstanding.)

May 1. Declared a semiannual dividend of $1 on the 10,000 shares of preferred stock and a $0.30 dividend on the common stock to stockholders of record on May 31, payable on June 15.

June 15. Paid the cash dividends.

Sept. 23. Sold 1,000 shares of treasury stock at $28, receiving cash.

Nov. 1. Declared semiannual dividends of $1 on the preferred stock and $0.30 on the common stock. In addition, a 5% common stock dividend was declared on the common stock outstanding, to be capitalized at the fair market value of the common stock, which is estimated at $30.

Dec. 1. Paid the cash dividends and issued the certificates for the common stock dividend.

Instructions

Journalize the entries to record the transactions for Altenburg Inc.

Solution

2014					
Feb.	3	Treasury Stock		65,000	
		Cash			65,000
May	1	Cash Dividends		21,250	
		Cash Dividends Payable			21,250
		(10,000 × $1) + [(40,000 − 2,500) × $0.30].			
June	15	Cash Dividends Payable		21,250	
		Cash			21,250
Sept.	23	Cash		28,000	
		Treasury Stock			26,000
		Paid-In Capital from Sale of Treasury Stock			2,000
Nov.	1	Cash Dividends		21,550	
		Cash Dividends Payable			21,550
		(10,000 × $1) + [(40,000 − 1,500) × $0.30].			
	1	Stock Dividends		57,750*	
		Stock Dividends Distributable			38,500
		Paid-In Capital in Excess of			
		Par—Common Stock			19,250
		*(40,000 − 1,500) × 5% × $30.			
Dec.	1	Cash Dividends Payable		21,550	
		Stock Dividends Distributable		38,500	
		Cash			21,550
		Common Stock			38,500

Discussion Questions

1. Of two corporations organized at approximately the same time and engaged in competing businesses, one issued $80 par common stock, and the other issued $1 par common stock. Do the par designations provide any indication as to which stock is preferable as an investment? Explain.

2. A stockbroker advises a client to "buy preferred stock. . . . With that type of stock, . . . [you] will never have to worry about losing the dividends." Is the broker right?

3. A corporation with both preferred stock and common stock outstanding has a substantial credit balance in its retained earnings account at the be-ginning of the current fiscal year. Although net income for the current year is sufficient to pay the preferred dividend of $150,000 each quarter and a common dividend of $90,000 each quarter, the board of directors declares dividends only on the preferred stock. Suggest possible reasons for passing the dividends on the common stock.

4. An owner of 2,500 shares of Simmons Company common stock receives a stock dividend of 50 shares.

   a. What is the effect of the stock dividend on the stockholder's proportionate interest (equity) in the corporation?

b. How does the total equity of 2,550 shares compare with the total equity of 2,500 shares before the stock dividend?

5. a. Where should a declared but unpaid cash dividend be reported on the balance sheet?

   b. Where should a declared but unissued stock dividend be reported on the balance sheet?

6. A corporation reacquires 60,000 shares of its own $10 par common stock for $3,000,000, recording it at cost.

   a. What effect does this transaction have on revenue or expense of the period?

   b. What effect does it have on stockholders' equity?

7. The treasury stock in Discussion Question 6 is resold for $3,750,000.

   a. What is the effect on the corporation's revenue of the period?

   b. What is the effect on stockholders' equity?

8. What are the three classifications of restrictions of retained earnings, and how are such restrictions normally reported on the financial statements?

9. Indicate how prior period adjustments would be reported on the financial statements presented only for the current period.

10. What is the primary purpose of a stock split?

Practice Exercises

Example Exercises
EE 11-1 *p. 502*

PE 11-1A   Dividends per share
OBJ. 2

Swan Creek Company has 40,000 shares of cumulative preferred 2% stock, $60 par and 50,000 shares of $50 par common stock. The following amounts were distributed as dividends:

Year 1	$ 30,000
Year 2	90,000
Year 3	125,000

Determine the dividends per share for preferred and common stock for each year.

EE 11-1 *p. 502*

PE 11-1B   Dividends per share
OBJ. 2

Zero Calories Company has 16,000 shares of cumulative preferred 1% stock, $40 par and 80,000 shares of $150 par common stock. The following amounts were distributed as dividends:

Year 1	$ 21,600
Year 2	4,000
Year 3	100,800

Determine the dividends per share for preferred and common stock for each year.

EE 11-2 *p. 505*

PE 11-2A   Entries for issuing stock
OBJ. 2

On May 10, Century Realty Inc. issued for cash 90,000 shares of no-par common stock (with a stated value of $30) at $42. On September 3, Century Realty Inc. issued at par value 36,000 shares of preferred 1% stock, $25 par for cash. On December 1, Century Realty Inc. issued for cash 14,000 shares of preferred 1% stock, $25 par at $33.

Journalize the entries to record the May 10, September 3, and December 1 transactions.

EE 11-2 *p. 505*

PE 11-2B   Entries for issuing stock
OBJ. 2

On January 22, Zentric Corporation issued for cash 180,000 shares of no-par common stock at $4. On February 14, Zentric Corporation issued at par value 44,000 shares of preferred 2% stock, $55 par for cash. On August 30, Zentric Corporation issued for cash 9,000 shares of preferred 2% stock, $55 par at $60.

Journalize the entries to record the January 22, February 14, and August 30 transactions.

EE 11-3 *p. 507* | **PE 11-3A   Entries for cash dividends** | OBJ. 3

The declaration, record, and payment dates in connection with a cash dividend of $1,250,000 on a corporation's common stock are August 1, October 15, and November 14. Journalize the entries required on each date.

EE 11-3 *p. 507* | **PE 11-3B   Entries for cash dividends** | OBJ. 3

The declaration, record, and payment dates in connection with a cash dividend of $480,000 on a corporation's common stock are February 1, March 18, and May 1. Journalize the entries required on each date.

EE 11-4 *p. 508* | **PE 11-4A   Entries for stock dividends** | OBJ. 3

Olde Wine Corporation has 250,000 shares of $40 par common stock outstanding. On February 15, Olde Wine Corporation declared a 2% stock dividend to be issued May 2 to stockholders of record on March 27. The market price of the stock was $52 per share on February 15.

Journalize the entries required on February 15, March 27, and May 2.

EE 11-4 *p. 508* | **PE 11-4B   Entries for stock dividends** | OBJ. 3

Antique Buggy Corporation has 820,000 shares of $35 par common stock outstanding. On June 8, Antique Buggy Corporation declared a 5% stock dividend to be issued August 12 to stockholders of record on July 13. The market price of the stock was $63 per share on June 8.

Journalize the entries required on June 8, July 13, and August 12.

EE 11-5 *p. 510* | **PE 11-5A   Entries for treasury stock** | OBJ. 4

On January 31, Wilderness Resorts Inc. reacquired 22,500 shares of its common stock at $31 per share. On April 20, Wilderness Resorts sold 12,800 of the reacquired shares at $40 per share. On October 4, Wilderness Resorts sold the remaining shares at $28 per share.

Journalize the transactions of January 31, April 20, and October 4.

EE 11-5 *p. 510* | **PE 11-5B   Entries for treasury stock** | OBJ. 4

On May 27, Hydro Clothing Inc. reacquired 75,000 shares of its common stock at $8 per share. On August 3, Hydro Clothing sold 54,000 of the reacquired shares at $11 per share. On November 14, Hydro Clothing sold the remaining shares at $7 per share.

Journalize the transactions of May 27, August 3, and November 14.

EE 11-6 *p. 511* | **PE 11-6A   Reporting stockholders' equity** | OBJ. 5

Using the following accounts and balances, prepare the Stockholders' Equity section of the balance sheet. Two hundred fifty thousand shares of common stock are authorized, and 17,500 shares have been reacquired.

Common Stock, $60 par	$12,000,0000
Paid-In Capital from Sale of Treasury Stock	320,000
Paid-In Capital in Excess of Par—Common Stock	3,200,000
Retained Earnings	18,500,000
Treasury Stock	1,137,500

Example
Exercises

EE 11-6 *p. 511*   **PE 11-6B**   **Reporting stockholders' equity**   OBJ. 5

Using the following accounts and balances, prepare the Stockholders' Equity section of the balance sheet. Five-hundred thousand shares of common stock are authorized, and 40,000 shares have been reacquired.

Common Stock, $120 par	$48,000,000
Paid-In Capital from Sale of Treasury Stock	4,500,000
Paid-In Capital in Excess of Par—Common Stock	6,400,000
Retained Earnings	63,680,000
Treasury Stock	5,200,000

EE 11-7 *p. 512*   **PE 11-7A**   **Retained earnings statement**   OBJ. 5

Rockwell Inc. reported the following results for the year ended June 30, 2014:

Retained earnings, July 1, 2013	$3,900,000
Net income	714,000
Cash dividends declared	100,000
Stock dividends declared	50,000

Prepare a retained earnings statement for the fiscal year ended June 30, 2014.

EE 11-7 *p. 512*   **PE 11-7B**   **Retained earnings statement**   OBJ. 5

Noric Cruises Inc. reported the following results for the year ended October 31, 2014:

Retained earnings, November 1, 2013	$12,400,000
Net income	2,350,000
Cash dividends declared	175,000
Stock dividends declared	300,000

Prepare a retained earnings statement for the fiscal year ended October 31, 2014.

EE 11-8 *p. 518*   **PE 11-8A**   **Earnings per share**   OBJ. 7

Financial statement data for the years ended December 31 for Dovetail Corporation are shown below.

	2014	2013
Net income	$448,750	$376,000
Preferred dividends	$40,000	$40,000
Average number of common shares outstanding	75,000 shares	60,000 shares

a. Determine the earnings per share for 2014 and 2013.

b. Does the change in the earnings per share from 2013 to 2014 indicate a favorable or an unfavorable trend?

EE 11-8 *p. 518*   **PE 11-8B**   **Earnings per share**   OBJ. 7

Financial statement data for the years ended December 31 for Black Bull Inc. are shown below.

	2014	2013
Net income	$2,485,700	$1,538,000
Preferred dividends	$50,000	$50,000
Average number of common shares outstanding	115,000 shares	80,000 shares

a. Determine the earnings per share for 2014 and 2013.

b. Does the change in the earnings per share from 2013 to 2014 indicate a favorable or an unfavorable trend?

Exercises

EX 11-1   **Dividends per share**   OBJ. 2

✔ Preferred stock,
1st year: $0.80

Wallace Inc., a developer of radiology equipment, has stock outstanding as follows: 30,000 shares of cumulative preferred 2% stock, $90 par and 125,000 shares of $10 par common. During its first four years of operations, the following amounts were distributed as dividends:

first year, $24,000; second year, $81,000; third year, $92,000; fourth year, $139,000. Calculate the dividends per share on each class of stock for each of the four years.

✔ Preferred stock,
1st year: $0.90

EX 11-2 Dividends per share OBJ. 2

Lightfoot Inc., a software development firm, has stock outstanding as follows: 40,000 shares of cumulative preferred 1% stock, $125 par, and 100,000 shares of $150 par common. During its first four years of operations, the following amounts were distributed as dividends: first year, $36,000; second year, $58,000; third year, $75,000; fourth year, $124,000. Calculate the dividends per share on each class of stock for each of the four years.

EX 11-3 Entries for issuing par stock OBJ. 2

On February 25, Madison County Rocks Inc., a marble contractor, issued for cash 120,000 shares of $36 par common stock at $40, and on June 3, it issued for cash 50,000 shares of preferred stock, $8 par at $9.

a. Journalize the entries for February 25 and June 3.

b. What is the total amount invested (total paid-in capital) by all stockholders as of June 3?

EX 11-4 Entries for issuing no-par stock OBJ. 2

On August 5, Synthetic Carpet Inc., a carpet wholesaler, issued for cash 500,000 shares of no-par common stock (with a stated value of $1) at $3, and on December 17, it issued for cash 5,000 shares of preferred stock, $180 par at $200.

a. Journalize the entries for August 5 and December 17, assuming that the common stock is to be credited with the stated value.

b. What is the total amount invested (total paid-in capital) by all stockholders as of December 17?

EX 11-5 Issuing stock for assets other than cash OBJ. 2

On May 10, First Lift Corporation, a wholesaler of hydraulic lifts, acquired land in exchange for 3,600 shares of $4 par common stock with a current market price of $28. Journalize the entry to record the transaction.

EX 11-6 Selected stock transactions OBJ. 2

Heavenly Sounds Corp., an electric guitar retailer, was organized by Mickey Blessing, John Frey, and Nancy Stein. The charter authorized 750,000 shares of common stock with a par of $20. The following transactions affecting stockholders' equity were completed during the first year of operations:

a. Issued 45,000 shares of stock at par to John Frey for cash.

b. Issued 400 shares of stock at par to Mickey Blessing for promotional services provided in connection with the organization of the corporation, and issued 60,000 shares of stock at par to Mickey Blessing for cash.

c. Purchased land and a building from Nancy Stein in exchange for stock issued at par. The building is mortgaged for $450,000 for 20 years at 4%, and there is accrued interest of $1,500 on the mortgage note at the time of the purchase. It is agreed that the land is to be priced at $150,000 and the building at $600,000, and that Nancy Stein's equity will be exchanged for stock at par. The corporation agreed to assume responsibility for paying the mortgage note and the accrued interest.

Journalize the entries to record the transactions.

EX 11-7 Issuing stock OBJ. 2

Willow Creek Nursery, with an authorization of 75,000 shares of preferred stock and 200,000 shares of common stock, completed several transactions involving its stock on October 1, the first day of operations. The trial balance at the close of the day follows:

(Continued)

Cash	3,780,000	
Land	840,000	
Buildings	2,380,000	
Preferred 1% Stock, $80 par		2,800,000
Paid-In Capital in Excess of Par—Preferred Stock		420,000
Common Stock, $30 par		3,600,000
Paid-In Capital in Excess of Par—Common Stock		180,000
	7,000,000	7,000,000

All shares within each class of stock were sold at the same price. The preferred stock was issued in exchange for the land and buildings.

Journalize the two entries to record the transactions summarized in the trial balance.

EX 11-8 Issuing stock   OBJ. 2

Workplace Products Inc., a wholesaler of office products, was organized on February 1 of the current year, with an authorization of 10,000 shares of preferred 2% stock, $120 par and 250,000 shares of $25 par common stock. The following selected transactions were completed during the first year of operations:

Feb. 1. Issued 180,000 shares of common stock at par for cash.

  1. Issued 400 shares of common stock at par to an attorney in payment of legal fees for organizing the corporation.

Mar. 9. Issued 30,000 shares of common stock in exchange for land, buildings, and equipment with fair market prices of $200,000, $550,000, and $135,000, respectively.

Apr. 13. Issued 8,500 shares of preferred stock at $131 for cash.

Journalize the transactions.

EX 11-9 Entries for cash dividends   OBJ. 3

The declaration, record, and payment dates in connection with a cash dividend of $187,500 on a corporation's common stock are July 10, August 9, and September 18. Journalize the entries required on each date.

EX 11-10 Entries for stock dividends   OBJ. 3

✔ b. (1) $6,900,000
  (3) $84,900,000

Healthy Living Co. is an HMO for businesses in the Seattle area. The following account balances appear on the balance sheet of Healthy Living Co.: Common stock (400,000 shares authorized; 300,000 shares issued), $18 par, $5,400,000; Paid-in capital in excess of par—common stock, $1,500,000; and Retained earnings, $78,000,000. The board of directors declared a 5% stock dividend when the market price of the stock was $40 a share. Healthy Living Co. reported no income or loss for the current year.

a. Journalize the entries to record (1) the declaration of the dividend, capitalizing an amount equal to market value, and (2) the issuance of the stock certificates.

b. Determine the following amounts before the stock dividend was declared: (1) total paid-in capital, (2) total retained earnings, and (3) total stockholders' equity.

c. Determine the following amounts after the stock dividend was declared and closing entries were recorded at the end of the year: (1) total paid-in capital, (2) total retained earnings, and (3) total stockholders' equity.

EX 11-11 Treasury stock transactions   OBJ. 4

✔ b. $118,000 credit

Crystal Lake Inc. bottles and distributes spring water. On March 4 of the current year, Crystal Lake reacquired 33,000 shares of its common stock at $84 per share. On August 27, Crystal Lake Inc. sold 25,000 of the reacquired shares at $90 per share. The remaining 8,000 shares were sold at $80 per share on November 11.

a. Journalize the transactions of March 4, August 27, and November 11.

b. What is the balance in Paid-In Capital from Sale of Treasury Stock on December 31 of the current year?

c. ▱▱▱▱▱▶ For what reasons might Crystal Lake have purchased the treasury stock?

EX 11-12 Treasury stock transactions OBJ. 4, 5

✔ b. $153,000 credit

Irrigate Smart Inc. develops and produces spraying equipment for lawn maintenance and industrial uses. On February 17 of the current year, Irrigate Smart Inc. reacquired 50,000 shares of its common stock at $12 per share. On April 29, 31,000 of the reacquired shares were sold at $15 per share, and on July 31, 12,000 of the reacquired shares were sold at $17.

a. Journalize the transactions of February 17, April 29, and July 31.

b. What is the balance in Paid-In Capital from Sale of Treasury Stock on December 31 of the current year?

c. What is the balance in Treasury Stock on December 31 of the current year?

d. How will the balance in Treasury Stock be reported on the balance sheet?

EX 11-13 Treasury stock transactions OBJ. 4, 5

✔ b. $55,500 credit

Biscayne Bay Water Inc. bottles and distributes spring water. On May 14 of the current year, Biscayne Bay Water Inc. reacquired 23,500 shares of its common stock at $75 per share. On September 6, Biscayne Bay Water Inc. sold 14,000 of the reacquired shares at $81 per share. The remaining 9,500 shares were sold at $72 per share on November 30.

a. Journalize the transactions of May 14, September 6, and November 30.

b. What is the balance in Paid-In Capital from Sale of Treasury Stock on December 31 of the current year?

c. Where will the balance in Paid-In Capital from Sale of Treasury Stock be reported on the balance sheet?

d. ➤ For what reasons might Biscayne Bay Water Inc. have purchased the treasury stock?

EX 11-14 Reporting paid-in capital OBJ. 5

✔ Total paid-in capital, $13,615,000

The following accounts and their balances were selected from the unadjusted trial balance of Point Loma Group Inc., a freight forwarder, at October 31, the end of the current fiscal year:

Common Stock, no par, $14 stated value	$ 4,480,000
Paid-In Capital from Sale of Treasury Stock	45,000
Paid-In Capital in Excess of Par—Preferred Stock	210,000
Paid-In Capital in Excess of Stated Value—Common Stock	480,000
Preferred 2% Stock, $120 par	8,400,000
Retained Earnings	39,500,000

Prepare the Paid-In Capital portion of the Stockholders' Equity section of the balance sheet using Method 1 of Exhibit 4. There are 375,000 shares of common stock authorized and 85,000 shares of preferred stock authorized.

EX 11-15 Stockholders' Equity section of balance sheet OBJ. 5

✔ Total stockholders' equity, $23,676,000

The following accounts and their balances appear in the ledger of Goodale Properties Inc. on June 30 of the current year:

Common Stock, $45 par	$ 3,060,000
Paid-In Capital from Sale of Treasury Stock	115,000
Paid-In Capital in Excess of Par—Common Stock	272,000
Retained Earnings	20,553,000
Treasury Stock	324,000

Prepare the Stockholders' Equity section of the balance sheet as of June 30. Eighty thousand shares of common stock are authorized, and 9,000 shares have been reacquired.

EX 11-16 Stockholders' Equity section of balance sheet

OBJ. 5

✔ Total stockholders' equity, $89,100,000

Specialty Auto Racing Inc. retails racing products for BMWs, Porsches, and Ferraris. The following accounts and their balances appear in the ledger of Specialty Auto Racing Inc. on July 31, the end of the current year:

Common Stock, $36 par	$10,080,000
Paid-In Capital from Sale of Treasury Stock—Common	340,000
Paid-In Capital in Excess of Par—Common Stock	420,000
Paid-In Capital in Excess of Par—Preferred Stock	384,000
Preferred 1% Stock, $150 par	7,200,000
Retained Earnings	71,684,000
Treasury Stock—Common	1,008,000

Fifty thousand shares of preferred and 300,000 shares of common stock are authorized. There are 24,000 shares of common stock held as treasury stock.

Prepare the Stockholders' Equity section of the balance sheet as of July 31, the end of the current year using Method 1 of Exhibit 4.

EX 11-17 Retained earnings statement

OBJ. 5

✔ Retained earnings, January 31, $55,040,000

Atlas Pumps Corporation, a manufacturer of industrial pumps, reports the following results for the year ended January 31, 2014:

Retained earnings, February 1, 2013	$48,110,000
Net income	9,330,000
Cash dividends declared	2,000,000
Stock dividends declared	400,000

Prepare a retained earnings statement for the fiscal year ended January 31, 2014.

EX 11-18 Stockholders' Equity section of balance sheet

OBJ. 5

✔ Corrected total stockholders' equity, $122,800,000

List the errors in the following Stockholders' Equity section of the balance sheet prepared as of the end of the current year:

Stockholders' Equity

Paid-in capital:		
Preferred 2% stock, $80 par		
(125,000 shares authorized and issued)	$10,000,000	
Excess of issue price over par	500,000	$ 10,500,000
Retained earnings		96,700,000
Treasury stock (75,000 shares at cost)		1,755,000
Dividends payable		430,000
Total paid-in capital		$ 109,385,000
Common stock, $20 par (1,000,000 shares		
authorized, 825,000 shares issued)		17,655,000
Organizing costs		300,000
Total stockholders' equity		$127,340,000

EX 11-19 Statement of stockholders' equity

OBJ. 5

✔ Total stockholders' equity, Dec. 31, $21,587,000

SPREADSHEET

The stockholders' equity T accounts of I-Cards Inc. for the current fiscal year ended December 31, 2014, are as follows. Prepare a statement of stockholders' equity for the fiscal year ended December 31, 2014.

COMMON STOCK

Jan.	1	Balance	4,800,000
Apr.	14	Issued	
		30,000 shares	1,200,000
Dec.	31	Balance	6,000,000

PAID-IN CAPITAL IN EXCESS OF PAR

	Jan. 1	Balance	960,000
	Apr. 14	Issued	
		30,000 shares	300,000
	Dec. 31	Balance	1,260,000

TREASURY STOCK

Aug. 7	Purchased		
	12,000 shares	552,000	

RETAINED EARNINGS

Mar. 31	Dividend	69,000	Jan. 1	Balance	11,375,000
June 30	Dividend	69,000	Dec. 31	Closing	
Sept. 30	Dividend	69,000		(net income)	3,780,000
Dec. 31	Dividend	69,000	Dec. 31	Balance	14,879,000

EX 11-20 Effect of stock split
OBJ. 6

Ironhaus Restaurant Corporation wholesales ovens and ranges to restaurants throughout the Southwest. Ironhaus Restaurant Corporation, which had 40,000 shares of common stock outstanding, declared a 4-for-1 stock split.

a. What will be the number of shares outstanding after the split?

b. If the common stock had a market price of $300 per share before the stock split, what would be an approximate market price per share after the split?

EX 11-21 Effect of cash dividend and stock split
OBJ. 3, 6

Indicate whether the following actions would (+) increase, (–) decrease, or (0) not affect Indigo Inc.'s total assets, liabilities, and stockholders' equity:

	Assets	Liabilities	Stockholders' Equity
(1) Authorizing and issuing stock certificates in a stock split	_____	_____	_____
(2) Declaring a stock dividend	_____	_____	_____
(3) Issuing stock certificates for the stock dividend declared in (2)	_____	_____	_____
(4) Declaring a cash dividend	_____	_____	_____
(5) Paying the cash dividend declared in (4)	_____	_____	_____

EX 11-22 Selected dividend transactions, stock split
OBJ. 3, 6

Selected transactions completed by Canyon Ferry Boating Corporation during the current fiscal year are as follows:

Jan. 8. Split the common stock 2 for 1 and reduced the par from $80 to $40 per share. After the split, there were 150,000 common shares outstanding.

Apr. 30. Declared semiannual dividends of $0.75 on 18,000 shares of preferred stock and $0.28 on the common stock payable on July 1.

July 1. Paid the cash dividends.

Oct. 31. Declared semiannual dividends of $0.75 on the preferred stock and $0.14 on the common stock (before the stock dividend). In addition, a 5% common stock dividend was declared on the common stock outstanding. The fair market value of the common stock is estimated at $52.

Dec. 31. Paid the cash dividends and issued the certificates for the common stock dividend.

Journalize the transactions.

EX 11-23 EPS
OBJ. 7

Junkyard Arts, Inc., had earnings of $316,000 for 2014. The company had 40,000 shares of common stock outstanding during the year. In addition, the company issued 15,000 shares of $50 par value preferred stock on January 9, 2014. The preferred stock has a

(Continued)

dividend of $1.60 per share. There were no transactions in either common or preferred stock during 2014.

Determine the basic earnings per share for Junkyard Arts.

EX 11-24 EPS OBJ. 7

Pacific Gas and Electric Company is a large gas and electric utility operating in northern and central California. Three recent years of financial data for Pacific Gas and Electric Company are as follows:

	Fiscal Years Ended (in millions)		
	Year 3	Year 2	Year 1
Net income	$1,105	$1,208	$1,312
Preferred dividends	$14	$14	$14
Average number of common shares outstanding	382	368	357

a. Determine the earnings per share for fiscal Year 3, Year 2, and Year 1. Round to the nearest cent.

b. Evaluate the growth in earnings per share for the three years in comparison to the growth in net income for the three years.

EX 11-25 EPS OBJ. 7

For a recent year, OfficeMax and Staples are two companies competing in the retail office supply business. OfficeMax had a net income of $71,155,000, while Staples had a net income of $881,948,000. OfficeMax had preferred stock of $30,901,000 with preferred dividends of $2,527,000. Staples had no preferred stock. The average outstanding common shares for each company were as follows:

	Average Number of Common Shares Outstanding
OfficeMax	84,908,000
Staples	715,596,000

a. Determine the earnings per share for each company. Round to the nearest cent.

b. Evaluate the relative profitability of the two companies.

Problems Series A

PR 11-1A Dividends on preferred and common stock OBJ. 2

✔ 1. Common dividends in 2011: $48,000

Partridge Theatre Inc. owns and operates movie theaters throughout Texas and Oklahoma. Partridge Theatre Inc. has declared the following annual dividends over a six-year period: 2009, $18,000; 2010, $40,000; 2011, $80,000; 2012, $120,000; 2013, $150,000; and 2014, $228,000. During the entire period ended December 31 of each year, the outstanding stock of the company was composed of 40,000 shares of cumulative, preferred 1% stock, $75 par, and 200,000 shares of common stock, $5 par.

Instructions

1. Calculate the total dividends and the per-share dividends declared on each class of stock for each of the six years. There were no dividends in arrears on January 1, 2009. Summarize the data in tabular form, using the following column headings:

Year	Total Dividends	Preferred Dividends		Common Dividends	
		Total	Per Share	Total	Per Share
2009	$ 18,000				
2010	40,000				
2011	80,000				
2012	120,000				
2013	150,000				
2014	228,000				

2. Calculate the average annual dividend per share for each class of stock for the six-year period.

3. Assuming a market price per share of $125 for the preferred stock and $7.60 for the common stock, calculate the average annual percentage return on initial shareholders' investment, based on the average annual dividend per share (a) for preferred stock and (b) for common stock.

PR 11-2A Stock transactions for corporate expansion   OBJ. 2

On December 1 of the current year, the following accounts and their balances appear in the ledger of Latte Corp., a coffee processor:

Preferred 2% Stock, $50 par (250,000 shares authorized, 80,000 shares issued)...	$ 4,000,000
Paid-In Capital in Excess of Par—Preferred Stock	560,000
Common Stock, $35 par (1,000,000 shares authorized, 400,000 shares issued)...	14,000,000
Paid-In Capital in Excess of Par—Common Stock	1,200,000
Retained Earnings...	180,000,000

At the annual stockholders' meeting on March 31, the board of directors presented a plan for modernizing and expanding plant operations at a cost of approximately $11,000,000. The plan provided (a) that a building, valued at $3,375,000, and the land on which it is located, valued at $1,500,000, be acquired in accordance with preliminary negotiations by the issuance of 125,000 shares of common stock, (b) that 40,000 shares of the unissued preferred stock be issued through an underwriter, and (c) that the corporation borrow $4,000,000. The plan was approved by the stockholders and accomplished by the following transactions:

May 11. Issued 125,000 shares of common stock in exchange for land and a building, according to the plan.

20. Issued 40,000 shares of preferred stock, receiving $52 per share in cash.

31. Borrowed $4,000,000 from Laurel National, giving a 5% mortgage note.

Instructions
Journalize the entries to record the May transactions.

PR 11-3A Selected stock transactions   OBJ. 2, 3, 4

✔ f. Cash dividends, $71,750

The following selected accounts appear in the ledger of Orion Inc. on February 1, 2014, the beginning of the current fiscal year:

Preferred 1% Stock, $40 par (75,000 shares authorized, 45,000 shares issued)	$ 1,800,000
Paid-In Capital in Excess of Par—Preferred Stock............................	72,000
Common Stock, $12 par (2,000,000 shares authorized, 1,250,000 shares issued)	15,000,000
Paid-In Capital in Excess of Par—Common Stock............................	3,750,000
Retained Earnings	45,450,000

During the year, the corporation completed a number of transactions affecting the stockholders' equity. They are summarized as follows:

a. Issued 360,000 shares of common stock at $22, receiving cash.

b. Issued 14,000 shares of preferred 1% stock at $43.

c. Purchased 66,000 shares of treasury common for $18 per share.

d. Sold 51,000 shares of treasury common for $21 per share.

e. Sold 10,000 shares of treasury common for $16 per share.

f. Declared cash dividends of $0.40 per share on preferred stock and $0.03 per share on common stock.

g. Paid the cash dividends.

(Continued)

Instructions

Journalize the entries to record the transactions. Identify each entry by letter.

PR 11-4A   Entries for selected corporate transactions   OBJ. 2, 3, 4, 5

Morrow Enterprises Inc. manufactures bathroom fixtures. The stockholders' equity accounts of Morrow Enterprises Inc., with balances on January 1, 2014, are as follows:

✔ 4. Total stockholders' equity, $44,436,200

Common Stock, $20 stated value (500,000 shares authorized, 375,000 shares issued)	$ 7,500,000
Paid-In Capital in Excess of Stated Value—Common Stock	825,000
Retained Earnings	33,600,000
Treasury Stock (25,000 shares, at cost)	450,000

The following selected transactions occurred during the year:

Jan. 22.   Paid cash dividends of $0.08 per share on the common stock. The dividend had been properly recorded when declared on December 1 of the preceding fiscal year for $28,000.

Apr. 10.   Issued 75,000 shares of common stock for $24 per share.

June 6.   Sold all of the treasury stock for $26 per share.

July   5.   Declared a 4% stock dividend on common stock, to be capitalized at the market price of the stock, which is $25 per share.

Aug. 15.   Issued the certificates for the dividend declared on July 5.

Nov. 23.   Purchased 30,000 shares of treasury stock for $19 per share.

Dec. 28.   Declared a $0.10-per-share dividend on common stock.

       31.   Closed the credit balance of the income summary account, $1,125,000.

       31.   Closed the two dividends accounts to Retained Earnings.

Instructions

1. Enter the January 1 balances in T accounts for the stockholders' equity accounts listed. Also prepare T accounts for the following: Paid-In Capital from Sale of Treasury Stock; Stock Dividends Distributable; Stock Dividends; Cash Dividends.

2. Journalize the entries to record the transactions, and post to the eight selected accounts.

3. Prepare a retained earnings statement for the year ended December 31, 2014.

4. Prepare the Stockholders' Equity section of the December 31, 2014, balance sheet.

PR 11-5A   Entries for selected corporate transactions   OBJ. 2, 3, 4, 6

Selected transactions completed by Primo Discount Corporation during the current fiscal year are as follows:

✔ Oct. 1, cash dividends, $202,800

Jan.   9.   Split the common stock 3 for 1 and reduced the par from $75 to $25 per share. After the split, there were 1,200,000 common shares outstanding.

Feb. 28.   Purchased 40,000 shares of the corporation's own common stock at $28, recording the stock at cost.

May   1.   Declared semiannual dividends of $0.80 on 75,000 shares of preferred stock and $0.12 on the common stock to stockholders of record on June 1, payable on July 10.

July 10.   Paid the cash dividends.

Sept. 7.   Sold 30,000 shares of treasury stock at $34, receiving cash.

Oct.   1.   Declared semiannual dividends of $0.80 on the preferred stock and $0.12 on the common stock (before the stock dividend). In addition, a 2% common stock dividend was declared on the common stock outstanding. The fair market value of the common stock is estimated at $36.

Dec.   1.   Paid the cash dividends and issued the certificates for the common stock dividend.

Instructions

Journalize the transactions.

Problems Series B

✔ 1. Common
dividends in 2011:
$25,000

PR 11-1B Dividends on preferred and common stock OBJ. 2

Yosemite Bike Corp. manufactures mountain bikes and distributes them through retail outlets in California, Oregon, and Washington. Yosemite Bike Corp. has declared the following annual dividends over a six-year period ended December 31 of each year: 2009, $24,000; 2010, $10,000; 2011, $126,000; 2012, $100,000; 2013, $125,000; and 2014, $125,000. During the entire period, the outstanding stock of the company was composed of 25,000 shares of cumulative preferred 2% stock, $90 par, and 100,000 shares of common stock, $4 par.

Instructions

1. Determine the total dividends and the per-share dividends declared on each class of stock for each of the six years. There were no dividends in arrears on January 1, 2009. Summarize the data in tabular form, using the following column headings:

Year	Total Dividends	Preferred Dividends		Common Dividends	
		Total	Per Share	Total	Per Share
2009	$ 24,000				
2010	10,000				
2011	126,000				
2012	100,000				
2013	125,000				
2014	125,000				

2. Determine the average annual dividend per share for each class of stock for the six-year period.

3. Assuming a market price of $100 for the preferred stock and $5 for the common stock, calculate the average annual percentage return on initial shareholders' investment, based on the average annual dividend per share (a) for preferred stock and (b) for common stock.

PR 11-2B Stock transaction for corporate expansion OBJ. 2

Pulsar Optics produces medical lasers for use in hospitals. The accounts and their balances appear in the ledger of Pulsar Optics on April 30 of the current year as follows:

Preferred 1% Stock, $120 par (300,000 shares authorized, 36,000 shares issued)	$ 4,320,000
Paid-In Capital in Excess of Par—Preferred Stock	180,000
Common Stock, $15 par (2,000,000 shares authorized, 1,400,000 shares issued)	21,000,000
Paid-In Capital in Excess of Par—Common Stock	3,500,000
Retained Earnings	78,000,000

At the annual stockholders' meeting on August 5, the board of directors presented a plan for modernizing and expanding plant operations at a cost of approximately $9,000,000. The plan provided (a) that the corporation borrow $1,500,000, (b) that 20,000 shares of the unissued preferred stock be issued through an underwriter, and (c) that a building, valued at $4,150,000, and the land on which it is located, valued at $800,000, be acquired in accordance with preliminary negotiations by the issuance of 300,000 shares of common stock. The plan was approved by the stockholders and accomplished by the following transactions:

Oct. 9. Borrowed $1,500,000 from St. Peter City Bank, giving a 4% mortgage note.

17. Issued 20,000 shares of preferred stock, receiving $126 per share in cash.

28. Issued 300,000 shares of common stock in exchange for land and a building, according to the plan.

Instructions

Journalize the entries to record the October transactions.

PR 11-3B Selected stock transactions

OBJ. 2, 3, 4

Diamondback Welding & Fabrication Corporation sells and services pipe welding equipment in Illinois. The following selected accounts appear in the ledger of Diamondback Welding & Fabrication Corporation on July 1, 2014, the beginning of the current fiscal year:

Preferred 2% Stock, $80 par (100,000 shares authorized, 60,000 shares issued)	$ 4,800,000
Paid-In Capital in Excess of Par—Preferred Stock	210,000
Common Stock, $9 par (3,000,000 shares authorized, 1,750,000 shares issued)	15,750,000
Paid-In Capital in Excess of Par—Common Stock	1,400,000
Retained Earnings	52,840,000

During the year, the corporation completed a number of transactions affecting the stockholders' equity. They are summarized as follows:

a. Purchased 87,500 shares of treasury common for $8 per share.

b. Sold 55,000 shares of treasury common for $11 per share.

c. Issued 20,000 shares of preferred 2% stock at $84.

d. Issued 400,000 shares of common stock at $13, receiving cash.

e. Sold 18,000 shares of treasury common for $7.50 per share.

f. Declared cash dividends of $1.60 per share on preferred stock and $0.05 per share on common stock.

g. Paid the cash dividends.

Instructions

Journalize the entries to record the transactions. Identify each entry by letter.

PR 11-4B Entries for selected corporate transactions

OBJ. 2, 3, 4, 5

Nav-Go Enterprises Inc. produces aeronautical navigation equipment. The stockholders' equity accounts of Nav-Go Enterprises Inc., with balances on January 1, 2014, are as follows:

Common Stock, $5 stated value (900,000 shares authorized, 620,000 shares issued)	$3,100,000
Paid-In Capital in Excess of Stated Value—Common Stock	1,240,000
Retained Earnings	4,875,000
Treasury Stock (48,000 shares, at cost)	288,000

The following selected transactions occurred during the year:

Jan. 15. Paid cash dividends of $0.06 per share on the common stock. The dividend had been properly recorded when declared on December 1 of the preceding fiscal year for $34,320.

Mar. 15. Sold all of the treasury stock for $6.75 per share.

Apr. 13. Issued 200,000 shares of common stock for $8 per share.

June 14. Declared a 3% stock dividend on common stock, to be capitalized at the market price of the stock, which is $7.50 per share.

July 16. Issued the certificates for the dividend declared on June 14.

Oct. 30. Purchased 50,000 shares of treasury stock for $6 per share.

Dec. 30. Declared a $0.08-per-share dividend on common stock.

31. Closed the credit balance of the income summary account, $775,000.

31. Closed the two dividends accounts to Retained Earnings.

Instructions

1. Enter the January 1 balances in T accounts for the stockholders' equity accounts listed. Also prepare T accounts for the following: Paid-In Capital from Sale of Treasury Stock; Stock Dividends Distributable; Stock Dividends; Cash Dividends.

2. Journalize the entries to record the transactions, and post to the eight selected accounts.

3. Prepare a retained earnings statement for the year ended December 31, 2014.

4. Prepare the Stockholders' Equity section of the December 31, 2014, balance sheet.

✔ Sept. 1, Cash
dividends, $95,200

GENERAL LEDGER

PR 11-5B Entries for selected corporate transactions

OBJ. 2, 3, 4, 6

West Yellowstone Outfitters Corporation manufactures and distributes leisure clothing. Selected transactions completed by West Yellowstone Outfitters during the current fiscal year are as follows:

Jan. 15. Split the common stock 4 for 1 and reduced the par from $120 to $30 per share. After the split, there were 800,000 common shares outstanding.

Mar. 1. Declared semiannual dividends of $0.25 on 100,000 shares of preferred stock and $0.07 on the 800,000 shares of $30 par common stock to stockholders of record on March 31, payable on April 30.

Apr. 30. Paid the cash dividends.

May 31. Purchased 60,000 shares of the corporation's own common stock at $32, recording the stock at cost.

Aug. 17. Sold 40,000 shares of treasury stock at $38, receiving cash.

Sept. 1. Declared semiannual dividends of $0.25 on the preferred stock and $0.09 on the common stock (before the stock dividend). In addition, a 1% common stock dividend was declared on the common stock outstanding, to be capitalized at the fair market value of the common stock, which is estimated at $40.

Oct. 31. Paid the cash dividends and issued the certificates for the common stock dividend.

Instructions
Journalize the transactions.

Cases & Projects

CP 11-1 Board of directors' actions

Bernie Ebbers, the CEO of WorldCom, a major telecommunications company, was having personal financial troubles. Ebbers pledged a large stake of his WorldCom stock as security for some personal loans. As the price of WorldCom stock sank, Ebbers' bankers threatened to sell his stock in order to protect their loans. To avoid having his stock sold, Ebbers asked the board of directors of WorldCom to loan him nearly $400 million of corporate assets at 2.5% interest to pay off his bankers. The board agreed to lend him the money.

➤ Comment on the decision of the board of directors in this situation.

CP 11-2 Ethics and professional conduct in business

Lou Hoskins and Shirley Crothers are organizing Red Lodge Metals Unlimited Inc. to undertake a high-risk gold-mining venture in Canada. Lou and Shirley tentatively plan to request authorization for 400,000,000 shares of common stock to be sold to the general public. Lou and Shirley have decided to establish par of $0.03 per share in order to appeal to a wide variety of potential investors. Lou and Shirley feel that investors would be more willing to invest in the company if they received a large quantity of shares for what might appear to be a "bargain" price.

➤ Discuss whether Lou and Shirley are behaving in a professional manner.

CP 11-3 Issuing stock

Epstein Engineering Inc. began operations on January 5, 2014, with the issuance of 500,000 shares of $80 par common stock. The sole stockholders of Epstein Engineering Inc. are Barb Abrams and Dr. Amber Epstein, who organized Epstein Engineering Inc. with the objective of developing a new flu vaccine. Dr. Epstein claims that the flu vaccine, which is nearing the final development stage, will protect individuals against

(Continued)

90% of the flu types that have been medically identified. To complete the project, Epstein Engineering Inc. needs $25,000,000 of additional funds. The local banks have been unwilling to loan the funds because of the lack of sufficient collateral and the riskiness of the business.

The following is a conversation between Barb Abrams, the chief executive officer of Epstein Engineering Inc., and Amber Epstein, the leading researcher.

Barb: What are we going to do? The banks won't loan us any more money, and we've got to have $25 million to complete the project. We are so close! It would be a disaster to quit now. The only thing I can think of is to issue additional stock. Do you have any suggestions?

Amber: I guess you're right. But if the banks won't loan us any more money, how do you think we can find any investors to buy stock?

Barb: I've been thinking about that. What if we promise the investors that we will pay them 5% of net sales until they have received an amount equal to what they paid for the stock?

Amber: What happens when we pay back the $25 million? Do the investors get to keep the stock? If they do, it'll dilute our ownership.

Barb: How about, if after we pay back the $25 million, we make them turn in their stock for $120 per share? That's one and one-half times what they paid for it, plus they would have already gotten all their money back. That's a $120 profit per share for the investors.

Amber: It could work. We get our money, but don't have to pay any interest, dividends, or the $80 per share until we start generating net sales. At the same time, the investors could get their money back plus $120 per share profit.

Barb: We'll need current financial statements for the new investors. I'll get our accountant working on them and contact our attorney to draw up a legally binding contract for the new investors. Yes, this could work.

In late 2014, the attorney and the various regulatory authorities approved the new stock offering, and 312,500 shares of common stock were privately sold to new investors at the stock's par of $80.

In preparing financial statements for 2014, Barb Abrams and Dan Fisher, the controller for Epstein Engineering Inc., have the following conversation:

Dan: Barb, I've got a problem.

Barb: What's that, Dan?

Dan: Issuing common stock to raise that additional $25 million was a great idea. But . . .

Barb: But what?

Dan: I've got to prepare the 2014 annual financial statements, and I am not sure how to classify the common stock.

Barb: What do you mean? It's common stock.

Dan: I'm not so sure. I called the auditor and explained how we are contractually obligated to pay the new stock-holders 5% of net sales until $80 per share is paid. Then, we may be obligated to pay them $120 per share.

Barb: So . . .

Dan: So the auditor thinks that we should classify the additional issuance of $25 million as debt, not stock! And, if we put the $25 million on the balance sheet as debt, we will violate our other loan agreements with the banks. And, if these agreements are violated, the banks may call in all our debt immediately. If they do that, we are in deep trouble. We'll probably have to file for bankruptcy. We just don't have the cash to pay off the banks.

1. ▰▰▰▰▶ Discuss the arguments for and against classifying the issuance of the $25 million of stock as debt.

2. ▰▰▰▰▶ What do you think might be a practical solution to this classification problem?

CP 11-4 Interpret stock exchange listing

The following stock exchange data for Microsoft Corporation were taken from the Yahoo! Finance Web site on February 29, 2012:

Microsoft Corporation (MSFT)			
Last Trade:	31.74	Prev. Clos:	31.87
Trade Time:	4:00 PM EST	1y Target Est:	31.96
		Day's Range:	31.61–32.00
		52wk Range:	23.65–31.93
		Volume:	58,178,568
		Div & Yield:	0.80 (2.60%)

a. If you owned 500 shares of Mircosoft, what amount would you receive as a quarterly dividend?

b. Compute the percentage decrease in price from the Previous Close to the Last Trade. Round to two decimal places.

c. What is Microsoft's percentage change in market price from the 52-week low to the Previous Close on February 28, 2012? Round to one decimal place.

d. If you bought 500 shares of GE at the Last Trade price on February 29, 2012, how much would it cost, and who gets the money?

CP 11-5 Dividends

Motion Designs Inc. has paid quarterly cash dividends since 2003. These dividends have steadily increased from $0.05 per share to the latest dividend declaration of $0.50 per share. The board of directors would like to continue this trend and is hesitant to suspend or decrease the amount of quarterly dividends. Unfortunately, sales dropped sharply in the fourth quarter of 2014 because of worsening economic conditions and increased competition. As a result, the board is uncertain as to whether it should declare a dividend for the last quarter of 2014.

On October 1, 2014, Motion Designs Inc. borrowed $4,000,000 from Valley National Bank to use in modernizing its retail stores and to expand its product line in reaction to its competition. The terms of the 10-year, 6% loan require Motion Designs Inc. to:

a. Pay monthly interest on the last day of the month.

b. Pay $400,000 of the principal each October 1, beginning in 2015.

c. Maintain a current ratio (current assets/current liabilities) of 2.

d. Maintain a minimum balance (a compensating balance) of $100,000 in its Valley National Bank account.

On December 31, 2014, $1,000,000 of the $4,000,000 loan had been disbursed in modernization of the retail stores and in expansion of the product line. Motion Designs Inc.'s balance sheet as of December 31, 2014, is shown below.

Motion Designs Inc.
Balance Sheet
December 31, 2014

Assets			
Current assets:			
Cash		$ 250,000	
Marketable securities		3,000,000	
Accounts receivable	$ 800,000		
Less allowance for doubtful accounts	50,000	750,000	
Merchandise inventory		2,980,000	
Prepaid expenses		20,000	
Total current assets			$ 7,000,000
Property, plant, and equipment:			
Land		$1,500,000	
Buildings	$5,050,000		
Less accumulated depreciation...........	1,140,000	3,910,000	
Equipment	$3,320,000		
Less accumulated depreciation	730,000	2,590,000	
Total property, plant, and equipment			8,000,000
Total assets.....................................			$15,000,000

(Continued)

Liabilities

Current liabilities:

Accounts payable	$1,590,000	
Notes payable (Valley National Bank).	400,000	
Salaries payable.	10,000	
Total current liabilities.		$2,000,000

Long-term liabilities:

Notes payable (Valley National Bank).	3,600,000	
Total liabilities		$ 5,600,000

Stockholders' Equity

Paid-in capital:

Common stock, $25 par (200,000 shares authorized, 180,000 shares issued)	$4,500,000		
Excess of issue price over par	270,000		
Total paid-in capital		$4,770,000	
Retained earnings.		4,630,000	
Total stockholders' equity			9,400,000
Total liabilities and stockholders' equity.			$15,000,000

The board of directors is scheduled to meet January 10, 2015, to discuss the results of operations for 2014 and to consider the declaration of dividends for the fourth quarter of 2014. The chairman of the board has asked for your advice on the declaration of dividends.

1. ━━━▶ What factors should the board consider in deciding whether to declare a cash dividend?

2. ━━━▶ The board is considering the declaration of a stock dividend instead of a cash dividend. Discuss the issuance of a stock dividend from the point of view of (a) a stockholder and (b) the board of directors.

CP 11-6 Profiling a corporation

Group Project

Internet Project

Select a public corporation you are familiar with or which interests you. Using the Internet, develop a short (1 to 2 pages) profile of the corporation. Include in your profile the following information:

1. Name of the corporation.
2. State of incorporation.
3. Nature of its operations.
4. Total assets for the most recent balance sheet.
5. Total revenues for the most recent income statement.
6. Net income for the most recent income statement.
7. Classes of stock outstanding.
8. Market price of the stock outstanding.
9. High and low price of the stock for the past year.
10. Dividends paid for each share of stock during the past year.

In groups of three or four, discuss each corporate profile. Select one of the corporations, assuming that your group has $100,000 to invest in its stock. Summarize why your group selected the corporation it did and how financial accounting information may have affected your decision. Keep track of the performance of your corporation's stock for the remainder of the term.

Note: Most major corporations maintain "home pages" on the Internet. This home page provides a variety of information on the corporation and often includes the corporation's financial statements. In addition, the New York Stock Exchange Web site **(http://www.nyse .com)** includes links to the home pages of many listed companies that can be assessed by clicking on "Listings Directory." Financial statements can also be accessed using EDGAR, the electronic archives of financial statements filed with the Securities and Exchange Commission (SEC).

SEC documents can also be retrieved using the EdgarScan™ service at **http://www.sec .gov/edgar/searchedgar/companysearch.html.** To obtain annual report information, key in a company name in the appropriate space. Edgar will list the reports available to you for the company you've selected. Select the most recent annual report filing, identified as a 10-K or 10-K405.

Statement of Cash Flows

Jones Soda Co.

Suppose you were to receive $100 from an event. Would it make a difference what the event was? Yes, it would! If you received $100 for your birthday, then it's a gift. If you received $100 as a result of working part time for a week, then it's the result of your effort. If you received $100 as a loan, then it's money that you will have to pay back in the future. If you received $100 as a result of selling your iPod, then it's the result of selling an asset. Thus, $100 received can be associated with different types of events, and these events have different meanings to you, and different implications for your future. You would much rather receive a $100 gift than take out a $100 loan. Likewise, company stakeholders view inflows and outflows of cash differently, depending on their source.

Companies are required to report information about the events causing a change in cash over a period of time. This information is reported in the statement of cash flows. One such company is Jones Soda Co. Jones began in the late 1980s as an

alternative beverage company, known for its customer-provided labels, unique flavors, and support for extreme sports. You have probably seen Jones Soda at Barnes & Noble, Panera Bread, or Starbucks, or maybe sampled some of its unique flavors, such as Fufu Berry®, Blue Bubblegum®, or Lemon Drop®. As with any company, cash is important to Jones Soda. Without cash, Jones would be unable to expand its brands, distribute its product, support extreme sports, or provide a return for its owners. Thus, its managers are concerned about the sources and uses of cash.

In previous chapters, we have used the income statement, balance sheet, statement of retained earnings, and other information to analyze the effects of management decisions on a business's financial position and operating performance. In this chapter, we focus on the events causing a change in cash by presenting the preparation and use of the statement of cash flows.

OBJ 1 Describe the cash flow activities reported in the statement of cash flows.

Reporting Cash Flows

The **statement of cash flows** reports a company's cash inflows and outflows for a period.[1] The statement of cash flows provides useful information about a company's ability to do the following:

1. Generate cash from operations
2. Maintain and expand its operating capacity
3. Meet its financial obligations
4. Pay dividends

The statement of cash flows is used by managers in evaluating past operations and in planning future investing and financing activities. It is also used by external users such as investors and creditors to assess a company's profit potential and ability to pay its debt and pay dividends.

The statement of cash flows reports three types of cash flow activities, as follows:

Cash flows from operating activities are the cash flows from transactions that affect the net income of the company.

    Example: Purchase and sale of merchandise by a retailer.

Cash flows from investing activities are the cash flows from transactions that affect investments in the noncurrent assets of the company.

    Example: Purchase and sale of fixed assets, such as equipment and buildings.

---

1 As used in this chapter, *cash* refers to cash and cash equivalents. Examples of cash equivalents include short-term, highly liquid investments, such as money market accounts, bank certificates of deposit, and U.S. Treasury bills.

Cash flows from financing activities are the cash flows from transactions that affect the debt and equity of the company.

Example: Issuing or retiring equity and debt securities.

The cash flows are reported in the statement of cash flows as follows:

Cash flows from operating activities	$XXX
Cash flows from investing activities	XXX
Cash flows from financing activities	XXX
Net increase or decrease in cash for the period	$XXX
Cash at the beginning of the period	XXX
Cash at the end of the period	$XXX

The ending cash on the statement of cash flows equals the cash reported on the company's balance sheet at the end of the year.

Exhibit 1 illustrates the sources (increases) and uses (decreases) of cash by each of the three cash flow activities. A *source* of cash causes the cash flow to increase and is called a *cash inflow*. A *use* of cash causes cash flow to decrease and is called *cash outflow*.

Note:
The statement of cash flows reports cash flows from operating, investing, and financing activities.

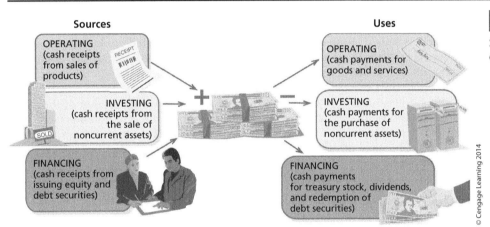

Sources

Uses

OPERATING (cash receipts from sales of products)

OPERATING (cash payments for goods and services)

INVESTING (cash receipts from the sale of noncurrent assets)

INVESTING (cash payments for the purchase of noncurrent assets)

FINANCING (cash receipts from issuing equity and debt securities)

FINANCING (cash payments for treasury stock, dividends, and redemption of debt securities)

© Cengage Learning 2014

EXHIBIT 1

Sources and Uses of Cash

Cash Flows from Operating Activities

Cash flows from operating activities reports the cash inflows and outflows from a company's day-to-day operations. Companies may select one of two alternative methods for reporting cash flows from operating activities in the statement of cash flows:

1. The direct method
2. The indirect method

Both methods result in the same amount of cash flows from operating activities. They differ in the way they report cash flows from operating activities.

The **direct method** reports operating cash inflows (receipts) and cash outflows (payments) as follows:

Cash flows from operating activities:		
Cash received from customers		$XXX
Less: Cash payments for merchandise	$XXX	
Cash payments for operating expenses	XXX	
Cash payments for interest	XXX	
Cash payments for income taxes	XXX	XXX
Net cash flow from operating activities		$XXX

The primary operating cash inflow is cash received from customers. The primary operating cash outflows are cash payments for merchandise, operating expenses, interest, and income tax payments. The cash received from operating activities less the cash payments for operating activities is the net cash flow from operating activities.

The primary advantage of the direct method is that it *directly* reports cash receipts and cash payments in the statement of cash flows. Its primary disadvantage is that these data may not be readily available in the accounting records. Thus, the direct method is normally more costly to prepare and, as a result, is used infrequently in practice.

The **indirect method** reports cash flows from operating activities by beginning with net income and adjusting it for revenues and expenses that do not involve the receipt or payment of cash, as follows:

Cash flows from operating activities:		
Net income	$XXX	
Adjustments to reconcile net income to net cash flow from operating activities	XXX	
Net cash flow from operating activities		$XXX

The adjustments to reconcile net income to net cash flow from operating activities include such items as depreciation and gains or losses on fixed assets. Changes in current operating assets and liabilities such as accounts receivable or accounts payable are also added or deducted, depending on their effect on cash flows. In effect, these additions and deductions adjust net income, which is reported on an accrual accounting basis, to cash flows from operating activities, which is a cash basis.

A primary advantage of the indirect method is that it reconciles the differences between net income and net cash flows from operations. In doing so, it shows how net income is related to the ending cash balance that is reported on the balance sheet.

Because the data are readily available, the indirect method is less costly to prepare than the direct method. As a result, the indirect method of reporting cash flows from operations is most commonly used in practice.

Exhibit 2 illustrates the Cash Flows from Operating Activities section of the statement of cash flows for NetSolutions. Exhibit 2 shows the direct and indirect methods using the NetSolutions data from Chapter 1. As Exhibit 2 illustrates, both methods report the same amount of net cash flow from operating activities, $2,900.

EXHIBIT 2   **Cash Flow from Operations: Direct and Indirect Methods—NetSolutions**

Direct Method

Cash flows from operating activities:	
Cash received from customers	$7,500
Deduct cash payments for expenses and payments to creditors	4,600
Net cash flow from operating activities	$2,900

Indirect Method

Cash flows from operating activities:	
Net income	$3,050
Add increase in accounts payable	400
	$3,450
Deduct increase in supplies	550
Net cash flow from operating activities	$2,900

the same

© Cengage Learning 2014

In October 2008, the U.S. government invested $250 billion of cash into U.S. banks to help stabilize the financial system.

Cash Flows from Investing Activities

Cash flows from investing activities show the cash inflows and outflows related to changes in a company's long-term assets. Cash flows from investing activities are reported on the statement of cash flows as follows:

Cash flows from investing activities:		
Cash inflows from investing activities	$XXX	
Less cash used for investing activities	XXX	
Net cash flows from investing activities		$XXX

Cash inflows from investing activities normally arise from selling fixed assets, investments, and intangible assets. Cash outflows normally include payments to purchase fixed assets, investments, and intangible assets.

In fiscal 2011, Apple Inc. generated $37.5 billion in net cash flow from operating activities.

Cash Flows from Financing Activities

Cash flows from financing activities show the cash inflows and outflows related to changes in a company's long-term liabilities and stockholders' equity. Cash flows from financing activities are reported on the statement of cash flows as follows:

Cash flows from financing activities:
Cash inflows from financing activities	$XXX	
Less cash used for financing activities	XXX	
Net cash flow from financing activities		$XXX

Cash inflows from financing activities normally arise from issuing long-term debt or equity securities. For example, issuing bonds, notes payable, preferred stock, and common stock creates cash inflows from financing activities. Cash outflows from financing activities include paying cash dividends, repaying long-term debt, and acquiring treasury stock.

Noncash Investing and Financing Activities

A company may enter into transactions involving investing and financing activities that do not *directly* affect cash. For example, a company may issue common stock to retire long-term debt. Although this transaction does not directly affect cash, it does eliminate future cash payments for interest and for paying the bonds when they mature. Because such transactions *indirectly* affect cash flows, they are reported in a separate section of the statement of cash flows. This section usually appears at the bottom of the statement of cash flows.

Example Exercise 13-1 Classifying Cash Flows OBJ 1

Identify whether each of the following would be reported as an operating, investing, or financing activity in the statement of cash flows.

a. Purchase of patent
b. Payment of cash dividend
c. Disposal of equipment
d. Cash sales
e. Purchase of treasury stock
f. Payment of wages expense

Follow My Example 13-1

a. Investing
b. Financing
c. Investing
d. Operating
e. Financing
f. Operating

Practice Exercises: **PE 13-1A, PE 13-1B**

No Cash Flow per Share

Cash flow per share is sometimes reported in the financial press. As reported, cash flow per share is normally computed as *cash flow from operations per share*. However, such reporting may be misleading because of the following:

1. Users may misinterpret cash flow per share as the per-share amount available for dividends. This would not be the case if the cash generated by operations is required for repaying loans or for reinvesting in the business.
2. Users may misinterpret cash flow per share as equivalent to (or better than) earnings per share.

For these reasons, the financial statements, including the statement of cash flows, should not report cash flow per share.

Statement of Cash Flows— The Indirect Method

The indirect method of reporting cash flows from operating activities uses the logic that a change in any balance sheet account (including cash) can be analyzed in terms of changes in the other balance sheet accounts. Thus, by analyzing changes in noncash balance sheet accounts, any change in the cash account can be *indirectly* determined.

To illustrate, the accounting equation can be solved for cash as shown below.

$$\text{Assets} = \text{Liabilities} + \text{Stockholders' Equity}$$
$$\text{Cash} + \text{Noncash Assets} = \text{Liabilities} + \text{Stockholders' Equity}$$
$$\text{Cash} = \text{Liabilities} + \text{Stockholders' Equity} - \text{Noncash Assets}$$

Therefore, any change in the cash account can be determined by analyzing changes in the liability, stockholders' equity, and noncash asset accounts as shown below.

$$\textit{Change} \text{ in Cash} = \textit{Change} \text{ in Liabilities} + \textit{Change} \text{ in Stockholders' Equity}$$
$$- \textit{Change} \text{ in Noncash Assets}$$

Under the indirect method, there is no order in which the balance sheet accounts must be analyzed. However, net income (or net loss) is the first amount reported on the statement of cash flows. Since net income (or net loss) is a component of any change in Retained Earnings, the first account normally analyzed is Retained Earnings.

To illustrate the indirect method, the income statement and comparative balance sheets for Rundell Inc., shown in Exhibit 3, are used. Ledger accounts and other data supporting the income statement and balance sheet are presented as needed.[2]

EXHIBIT 3   **Income Statement and Comparative Balance Sheet**

Rundell Inc. Income Statement For the Year Ended December 31, 2014		
Sales		$1,180,000
Cost of merchandise sold		790,000
Gross profit		$ 390,000
Operating expenses:		
Depreciation expense	$ 7,000	
Other operating expenses	196,000	
Total operating expenses		203,000
Income from operations		$ 187,000
Other income:		
Gain on sale of land	$ 12,000	
Other expense:		
Interest expense	8,000	4,000
Income before income tax		$ 191,000
Income tax expense		83,000
Net income		$ 108,000

(Continued)

---

2 An appendix that discusses using a spreadsheet (work sheet) as an aid in assembling data for the statement of cash flows is presented at the end of this chapter. This appendix illustrates the use of this spreadsheet in reporting cash flows from operating activities using the indirect method.

EXHIBIT 3	**Income Statement and Comparative Balance Sheet** *(concluded)*

Rundell Inc.
Comparative Balance Sheet
December 31, 2014 and 2013

	2014	2013	Increase (Decrease)
Assets			
Cash	$ 97,500	$ 26,000	$ 71,500
Accounts receivable (net)	74,000	65,000	9,000
Inventories	172,000	180,000	(8,000)
Land	80,000	125,000	(45,000)
Building	260,000	200,000	60,000
Accumulated depreciation—building.	(65,300)	(58,300)	7,000**
Total assets	$618,200	$537,700	$ 80,500
Liabilities			
Accounts payable (merchandise creditors)	$ 43,500	$ 46,700	$ (3,200)
Accrued expenses payable (operating expenses)	26,500	24,300	2,200
Income taxes payable	7,900	8,400	(500)
Dividends payable	14,000	10,000	4,000
Bonds payable	100,000	150,000	(50,000)
Total liabilities	$191,900	$239,400	$ 47,500*
Stockholders' Equity			
Common stock ($2 par)	$ 24,000	$ 16,000	$ 8,000
Paid-in capital in excess of par.	120,000	80,000	40,000
Retained earnings.	282,300	202,300	80,000
Total stockholders' equity	$426,300	$298,300	$128,000
Total liabilities and stockholders' equity.	$618,200	$537,700	$ 80,500

**There is a $7,000 increase to Accumulated Depreciation—Building, which is a contra asset account. As a result, the $7,000 increase in this account must be subtracted in summing to the increase in Total assets of $80,500.

© Cengage Learning 2014

Retained Earnings

The comparative balance sheet for Rundell Inc. shows that retained earnings increased $80,000 during the year. The retained earnings account shown below indicates how this change occurred.

Account *Retained Earnings*					**Account No.**	
					Balance	
Date		**Item**	**Debit**	**Credit**	**Debit**	**Credit**
2014 Jan.	1	Balance				202,300
Dec.	31	Net income		108,000		310,300
	31	Cash dividends	28,000			282,300

The retained earnings account indicates that the $80,000 ($108,000 − $28,000) change resulted from net income of $108,000 and cash dividends of $28,000. The net income of $108,000 is the first amount reported in the Cash Flows from Operating Activities section.

Adjustments to Net Income

The net income of $108,000 reported by Rundell Inc. does not equal the cash flows from operating activities for the period. This is because net income is determined using the accrual method of accounting.

Under the accrual method of accounting, revenues and expenses are recorded at different times from when cash is received or paid. For example, merchandise may be sold on account and the cash received at a later date. Likewise, insurance premiums may be paid in the current period, but expensed in a following period.

Thus, under the indirect method, adjustments to net income must be made to determine cash flows from operating activities. The typical adjustments to net income are shown in Exhibit 4.[3]

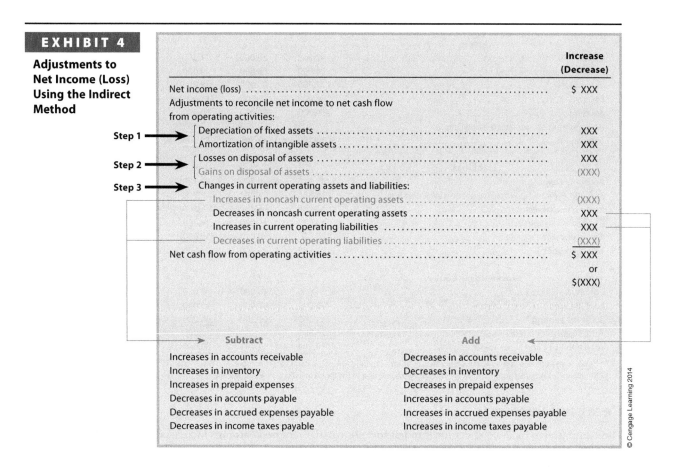

EXHIBIT 4

Adjustments to Net Income (Loss) Using the Indirect Method

	Increase (Decrease)
Net income (loss)	$ XXX
Adjustments to reconcile net income to net cash flow from operating activities:	
Step 1 → Depreciation of fixed assets	XXX
Amortization of intangible assets	XXX
Step 2 → Losses on disposal of assets	XXX
Gains on disposal of assets	(XXX)
Step 3 → Changes in current operating assets and liabilities:	
Increases in noncash current operating assets	(XXX)
Decreases in noncash current operating assets	XXX
Increases in current operating liabilities	XXX
Decreases in current operating liabilities	(XXX)
Net cash flow from operating activities	$ XXX
	or
	$(XXX)

Subtract	Add
Increases in accounts receivable	Decreases in accounts receivable
Increases in inventory	Decreases in inventory
Increases in prepaid expenses	Decreases in prepaid expenses
Decreases in accounts payable	Increases in accounts payable
Decreases in accrued expenses payable	Increases in accrued expenses payable
Decreases in income taxes payable	Increases in income taxes payable

© Cengage Learning 2014

Net income is normally adjusted to cash flows from operating activities, using the following steps:

Step 1. Expenses that do not affect cash are added. Such expenses decrease net income but do not involve cash payments and, thus, are added to net income.

Examples: *Depreciation* of fixed assets and *amortization* of intangible assets are added to net income.

Step 2. Losses on the disposal of assets are added and gains on the disposal of assets are deducted. The disposal (sale) of assets is an investing activity rather than an operating activity. However, such losses and gains are reported as part of net income. As a result, any *losses* on disposal of assets are *added* back to net income. Likewise, any *gains* on disposal of assets are *deducted* from net income.

Example: Land costing $100,000 is sold for $90,000. The loss of $10,000 is added back to net income.

---

3 Other items that also require adjustments to net income to obtain cash flows from operating activities include amortization of bonds payable discounts (add), losses on debt retirement (add), amortization of bonds payable premiums (deduct), and gains on retirement of debt (deduct).

Step 3. Changes in current operating assets and liabilities are added or deducted as follows:

Increases in noncash current operating assets are deducted.
Decreases in noncash current operating assets are added.
Increases in current operating liabilities are added.
Decreases in current operating liabilities are deducted.

Example: A sale of $10,000 on account increases sales, accounts receivable, and net income by $10,000. However, cash is not affected. Thus, the $10,000 increase in accounts receivable is deducted. Similar adjustments are required for the changes in the other current asset and liability accounts, such as inventory, prepaid expenses, accounts payable, accrued expenses payable, and income taxes payable, as shown in Exhibit 4.

Example Exercise 13-2   Adjustments to Net Income—Indirect Method   OBJ 2

Omni Corporation's accumulated depreciation increased by $12,000, while $3,400 of patent amortization was recognized between balance sheet dates. There were no purchases or sales of depreciable or intangible assets during the year. In addition, the income statement showed a gain of $4,100 from the sale of land. Reconcile Omni's net income of $50,000 to net cash flow from operating activities.

Follow My Example 13-2

Net income	$50,000
Adjustments to reconcile net income to net cash flow from operating activities:	
Depreciation	12,000
Amortization of patents	3,400
Gain from sale of land	(4,100)
Net cash flow from operating activities	$61,300

Practice Exercises: **PE 13-2A, PE 13-2B**

The Cash Flows from Operating Activities section of Rundell's statement of cash flows is shown in Exhibit 5. Rundell's net income of $108,000 is converted to cash flows from operating activities of $100,500 as follows:

EXHIBIT 5

Cash Flows from Operating Activities—Indirect Method

Cash flows from operating activities:	
Net income	$108,000
Adjustments to reconcile net income to net cash flow from operating activities:	
Step 1 → Depreciation	7,000
Step 2 → Gain on sale of land	(12,000)
Changes in current operating assets and liabilities:	
Increase in accounts receivable	(9,000)
Decrease in inventories..	8,000
Step 3 → Decrease in accounts payable	(3,200)
Increase in accrued expenses payable	2,200
Decrease in income taxes payable	(500)
Net cash flow from operating activities	$100,500

© Cengage Learning 2014

Step 1. Add depreciation of $7,000.

Analysis: The comparative balance sheet in Exhibit 3 indicates that Accumulated Depreciation—Building increased by $7,000. The account, shown on the following page, indicates that depreciation for the year was $7,000 for the building.

Account *Accumulated Depreciation—Building*					Account No.	
					Balance	
Date		**Item**	**Debit**	**Credit**	**Debit**	**Credit**
2014 Jan.	1	Balance				58,300
Dec.	31	Depreciation for year		7,000		65,300

Step 2. Deduct the gain on the sale of land of $12,000.

Analysis: The income statement in Exhibit 3 reports a gain of $12,000 from the sale of land. The proceeds, which include the gain, are reported in the Investing section of the statement of cash flows.[4] Thus, the gain of $12,000 is deducted from net income in determining cash flows from operating activities.

Step 3. Add and deduct changes in current operating assets and liabilities.

Analysis: The increases and decreases in the current operating asset and current liability accounts are shown below.

	December 31		**Increase**
Accounts	**2014**	**2013**	**Decrease***
Accounts Receivable (net)	$ 74,000	$ 65,000	$9,000
Inventories	172,000	180,000	8,000*
Accounts Payable (merchandise creditors)	43,500	46,700	3,200*
Accrued Expenses Payable (operating expenses)	26,500	24,300	2,200
Income Taxes Payable	7,900	8,400	500*

Accounts receivable (net): The $9,000 increase is deducted from net income. This is because the $9,000 increase in accounts receivable indicates that sales on account were $9,000 more than the cash received from customers. Thus, sales (and net income) includes $9,000 that was not received in cash during the year.

Business Connection

CASH CRUNCH!

Automobile manufacturers such as Chrysler Group LLC sell their cars and trucks through a network of independently owned and operated dealerships. The vehicles are sold to the dealerships on credit by issuing a trade receivable, which is repaid to Chrysler Group LLC after the vehicles are sold by the dealership. The economic crisis of 2008 created a slump in car sales that lasted well into 2009. By spring 2009, Chrysler dealers around the world found themselves with large inventories of unsold cars and trucks,

resulting in their inability to repay their trade receivables from Chrysler Group LLC. This led to a significant decline in Chrysler's cash flow from operating activities that forced the company into a financial restructuring. Ultimately, the company was rescued by a significant investment (cash inflow from financing activities) from Fiat and loans and investments (cash inflow from financing activities) from the U.S. and Canadian governments. Chrysler's cash position improved in the years that followed. In May 2011, the company repaid the majority of the loans outstanding from the U.S. and Canadian governments (cash used for financing activities).

Source: "Chrysler Restructuring Plan for Long-Term Viability," Chrysler Group LLC, February 17, 2009.

Inventories: The $8,000 decrease is added to net income. This is because the $8,000 decrease in inventories indicates that the cost of merchandise *sold* exceeds the cost of the merchandise *purchased* during the year by $8,000. In other words, the cost of merchandise sold includes $8,000 of goods from inventory that were not purchased (used cash) during the year.

Accounts payable (merchandise creditors): The $3,200 decrease is deducted from net income. This is because a decrease in accounts payable indicates that the cash *payments* to merchandise creditors exceed the merchandise *purchased on account* by $3,200. Therefore, the cost of merchandise sold is $3,200 less than the cash paid to merchandise creditors during the year.

4 The reporting of the proceeds (cash flows) from the sale of land as part of investing activities is discussed later in this chapter.

Accrued expenses payable (operating expenses): The $2,200 increase is added to net income. This is because an increase in accrued expenses payable indicates that operating expenses exceed the cash payments for operating expenses by $2,200. In other words, operating expenses reported on the income statement include $2,200 that did not require a cash outflow during the year.

Income taxes payable: The $500 decrease is deducted from net income. This is because a decrease in income taxes payable indicates that taxes paid exceed the amount of taxes incurred during the year by $500. In other words, the amount reported on the income statement for income tax expense is less than the amount paid by $500.

Example Exercise 13-3 **Changes in Current Operating Assets and Liabilities—Indirect Method**

OBJ 2

Victor Corporation's current operating assets and liabilities from the company's comparative balance sheet were as follows:

	Dec. 31, 2015	Dec. 31, 2014
Accounts receivable	$ 6,500	$ 4,900
Inventory	12,300	15,000
Accounts payable	4,800	5,200
Dividends payable	5,000	4,000

Adjust Victor's net income of $70,000 for changes in operating assets and liabilities to arrive at cash flows from operating activities.

Follow My Example 13-3

Net income	$70,000
Adjustments to reconcile net income to net cash flow from operating activities:	
Changes in current operating assets and liabilities:	
Increase in accounts receivable	(1,600)
Decrease in inventory	2,700
Decrease in accounts payable	(400)
Net cash flow from operating activities	$70,700

Note: The change in dividends payable impacts the cash paid for dividends, which is disclosed under financing activities.

Practice Exercises: **PE 13-3A, PE 13-3B**

Using the preceding analyses, Rundell's net income of $108,000 is converted to cash flows from operating activities of $100,500 as shown in Exhibit 5, on page 537.

Integrity, Objectivity, and Ethics in Business

CREDIT POLICY AND CASH FLOW

One would expect customers to pay for products and services sold on account. Unfortunately, that is not always the case. Collecting accounts receivable efficiently is the key to turning a current asset into positive cash flow. Most entrepreneurs would rather think about the exciting aspects of their business—such as product development, marketing, sales, and advertising—than credit collection. This can be a mistake. Hugh McHugh of Overhill Flowers, Inc., decided that he would have no more trade accounts after dealing with Christmas orders that weren't paid for until late February, or sometimes not paid at all. As stated by one collection service, "One thing business owners always tell me is that they never thought about [collections] when they started their own business." To the small business owner, the collection of accounts receivable may mean the difference between succeeding and failing.

Source: Paulette Thomas, "Making Them Pay: The Last Thing Most Entrepreneurs Want to Think About Is Bill Collection; It Should Be One of the First Things," *The Wall Street Journal*, September 19, 2005, p. R6.

Example Exercise 13-4 **Cash Flows from Operating Activities—Indirect Method**

OBJ 2

Omicron Inc. reported the following data:

Net income	$120,000
Depreciation expense	12,000
Loss on disposal of equipment	15,000
Increase in accounts receivable	5,000
Decrease in accounts payable	2,000

Prepare the Cash Flows from Operating Activities section of the statement of cash flows, using the indirect method.

Follow My Example 13-4

Cash flows from operating activities:
Net income $120,000
Adjustments to reconcile net income to net cash flow
from operating activities:
 Depreciation expense................................... 12,000
 Loss on disposal of equipment........................... 15,000
Changes in current operating assets and liabilities:
 Increase in accounts receivable .... (5,000)
 Decrease in accounts payable........................ (2,000)
Net cash flow from operating activities......................... $140,000

Practice Exercises: **PE 13-4A, PE 13-4B**

Dividends

The retained earnings account of Rundell Inc., shown on page 535, indicates cash dividends of $28,000 were declared during the year. However, the dividends payable account, shown below, indicates that only $24,000 of dividends were paid during the year.

Account Dividends Payable					Account No.	
					Balance	
Date		**Item**	**Debit**	**Credit**	**Debit**	**Credit**
2014 Jan.	1	Balance				10,000
	10	Cash paid	10,000		—	—
June	20	Dividends declared		14,000		14,000
July	10	Cash paid	14,000		—	—
Dec.	20	Dividends declared		14,000		14,000

Since dividend payments are a financing activity, the dividend payment of $24,000 is reported in the Financing Activities section of the statement of cash flows, as shown below.

Cash flows from financing activities:
Cash paid for dividends..................................... $24,000

Common Stock

The common stock account increased by $8,000, and the paid-in capital in excess of par—common stock account increased by $40,000, as shown below. These increases were from issuing 4,000 shares of common stock for $12 per share.

Account Common Stock					**Account No.**	
					Balance	
Date		**Item**	**Debit**	**Credit**	**Debit**	**Credit**
2014 Jan.	1	Balance				16,000
Nov.	1	4,000 shares issued for cash		8,000		24,000

Account Paid-In Capital in Excess of Par—Common Stock					**Account No.**	
					Balance	
Date		**Item**	**Debit**	**Credit**	**Debit**	**Credit**
2014 Jan.	1	Balance				80,000
Nov.	1	4,000 shares issued for cash		40,000		120,000

This cash inflow is reported in the Financing Activities section as follows:

```
Cash flows from financing activities:
     Cash received from sale of common stock . . . . . . . . . . . . . . . . . .     $48,000
```

Bonds Payable

The bonds payable account decreased by $50,000, as shown below. This decrease is from retiring the bonds by a cash payment for their face amount.

Account Bonds Payable					**Account No.**	
					Balance	
Date		**Item**	**Debit**	**Credit**	**Debit**	**Credit**
2014 Jan.	1	Balance				150,000
June	1	Retired by payment of cash at face amount	50,000			100,000

This cash outflow is reported in the Financing Activities section as follows:

```
Cash flows from financing activities:
     Cash paid to retire bonds payable . . . . . . . . . . . . . . . . . . . . . . . . . .     $50,000
```

Building

The building account increased by $60,000, and the accumulated depreciation—building account increased by $7,000, as shown below.

Account Building						Account No.	
						Balance	
Date		**Item**	**Debit**	**Credit**	**Debit**	**Credit**	
2014 Jan.	1	Balance			200,000		
Dec.	27	Purchased for cash	60,000		260,000		

Account Accumulated Depreciation—Building						Account No.	
						Balance	
Date		**Item**	**Debit**	**Credit**	**Debit**	**Credit**	
2014 Jan.	1	Balance				58,300	
Dec.	31	Depreciation for the year		7,000		65,300	

The purchase of a building for cash of $60,000 is reported as an outflow of cash in the Investing Activities section as follows:

Cash flows from investing activities:
Cash paid for purchase of building $60,000

The credit in the accumulated depreciation—building account represents depreciation expense for the year. This depreciation expense of $7,000 on the building was added to net income in determining cash flows from operating activities, as reported in Exhibit 5, on page 537.

Land

The $45,000 decline in the land account was from two transactions, as shown below.

Account Land						Account No.	
						Balance	
Date		**Item**	**Debit**	**Credit**	**Debit**	**Credit**	
2014 Jan.	1	Balance			125,000		
June	8	Sold for $72,000 cash		60,000	65,000		
Oct.	12	Purchased for $15,000 cash	15,000		80,000		

The June 8 transaction is the sale of land with a cost of $60,000 for $72,000 in cash. The $72,000 proceeds from the sale are reported in the Investing Activities section, as follows:

Cash flows from investing activities:
Cash received from sale of land $72,000

The proceeds of $72,000 include the $12,000 gain on the sale of land and the $60,000 cost (book value) of the land. As shown in Exhibit 5, on page 537, the $12,000 gain is deducted from net income in the Cash Flows from Operating Activities section. This is so that the $12,000 cash inflow related to the gain is not included twice as a cash inflow.

The October 12 transaction is the purchase of land for cash of $15,000. This transaction is reported as an outflow of cash in the Investing Activities section, as follows:

Cash flows from investing activities:
Cash paid for purchase of land $15,000

Example Exercise 13-5   Land Transactions on the Statement of Cash Flows   ⟩⟩ (OBJ 2)

Alpha Corporation purchased land for $125,000. Later in the year, the company sold a different piece of land with a book value of $165,000 for $200,000. How are the effects of these transactions reported on the statement of cash flows?

Follow My Example 13-5 ⟩⟩

The gain on the sale of the land is deducted from net income, as shown below.

Gain on sale of land .... $(35,000)

The purchase and sale of land is reported as part of cash flows from investing activities, as shown below.

Cash received from sale of land   200,000
Cash paid for purchase of land ....   (125,000)

Practice Exercises: **PE 13-5A, PE 13-5B**

Preparing the Statement of Cash Flows

The statement of cash flows for Rundell Inc., using the indirect method, is shown in Exhibit 6. The statement of cash flows indicates that cash increased by $71,500 during the year. The most significant increase in net cash flows ($100,500) was from operating activities. The most significant use of cash ($26,000) was for financing activities. The ending balance of cash on December 31, 2014, is $97,500. This ending cash balance is also reported on the December 31, 2014, balance sheet shown in Exhibit 3 on pages 534–535.

EXHIBIT 6

Statement of Cash Flows—Indirect Method

Rundell Inc.
Statement of Cash Flows
For the Year Ended December 31, 2014

Cash flows from operating activities:			
Net income...		$108,000	
Adjustments to reconcile net income to net cash flow from operating activities:			
Depreciation		7,000	
Gain on sale of land..............................		(12,000)	
Changes in current operating assets and liabilities:			
Increase in accounts receivable.................		(9,000)	
Decrease in inventories.........................		8,000	
Decrease in accounts payable		(3,200)	
Increase in accrued expenses payable...........		2,200	
Decrease in income taxes payable		(500)	
Net cash flow from operating activities			$100,500
Cash flows from investing activities:			
Cash received from sale of land		$ 72,000	
Less: Cash paid for purchase of land	$15,000		
Cash paid for purchase of building	60,000	75,000	
Net cash flow used for investing activities..............			(3,000)
Cash flows from financing activities:			
Cash received from sale of common stock...............		$ 48,000	
Less: Cash paid to retire bonds payable	$50,000		
Cash paid for dividends.........................	24,000	74,000	
Net cash flow used for financing activities			(26,000)
Increase in cash			$ 71,500
Cash at the beginning of the year......................			26,000
Cash at the end of the year............................			$ 97,500

Prepare a
statement of
cash flows, using the direct
method.

Statement of Cash Flows—The Direct Method

The direct method reports cash flows from operating activities as follows:

Cash flows from operating activities:		
Cash received from customers		$ XXX
Less: Cash payments for merchandise	$ XXX	
Cash payments for operating expenses.......................	XXX	
Cash payments for interest	XXX	
Cash payments for income taxes	XXX	XXX
Net cash flow from operating activities		$ XXX

The Cash Flows from Investing and Financing Activities sections of the statement of cash flows are exactly the same under both the direct and indirect methods. The amount of net cash flow from operating activities is also the same, but the manner in which it is reported is different.

Under the direct method, the income statement is adjusted to cash flows from operating activities as follows:

Income Statement	Adjusted to	Cash Flows from Operating Activities
Sales	→	Cash received from customers
Cost of merchandise sold	→	Cash payments for merchandise
Operating expenses:		
Depreciation expense	N/A	N/A
Other operating expenses	→	Cash payments for operating expenses
Gain on sale of land	N/A	N/A
Interest expense	→	Cash payments for interest
Income tax expense	→	Cash payments for income taxes
Net income	→	Net cash flow from operating activities

N/A—Not applicable

As shown above, depreciation expense is not adjusted or reported as part of cash flows from operating activities. This is because deprecation expense does not involve a cash outflow. The gain on the sale of the land is also not adjusted and is not reported as part of cash flows from operating activities. This is because the cash flow from operating activities is determined directly, rather than by reconciling net income. The cash proceeds from the sale of the land are reported as an investing activity.

To illustrate the direct method, the income statement and comparative balance sheet for Rundell Inc., shown in Exhibit 3 on pages 534–535, are used.

Cash Received from Customers

The income statement (shown in Exhibit 3) of Rundell Inc. reports sales of $1,180,000. To determine the *cash received from customers*, the $1,180,000 is adjusted for any increase or decrease in accounts receivable. The adjustment is summarized below.

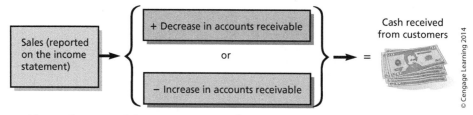

The cash received from customers is $1,171,000, computed as follows:

Sales	$1,180,000
Less increase in accounts receivable	9,000
Cash received from customers	$1,171,000

The increase of $9,000 in accounts receivable (shown in Exhibit 3) during 2014 indicates that sales on account exceeded cash received from customers by $9,000. In other words, sales include $9,000 that did not result in a cash inflow during the year. Thus, $9,000 is deducted from sales to determine the *cash received from customers*.

Example Exercise 13-6 Cash Received from Customers—Direct Method

OBJ 3

Sales reported on the income statement were $350,000. The accounts receivable balance declined $8,000 over the year. Determine the amount of cash received from customers.

Follow My Example 13-6

Sales..	$350,000
Add decrease in accounts receivable	8,000
Cash received from customers.....................................	$358,000

Practice Exercises: **PE 13-6A, PE 13-6B**

Cash Payments for Merchandise

The income statement (shown in Exhibit 3) for Rundell Inc. reports cost of merchandise sold of $790,000. To determine the *cash payments for merchandise*, the $790,000 is adjusted for any increases or decreases in inventories and accounts payable. Assuming the accounts payable are owed to merchandise suppliers, the adjustment is summarized below.

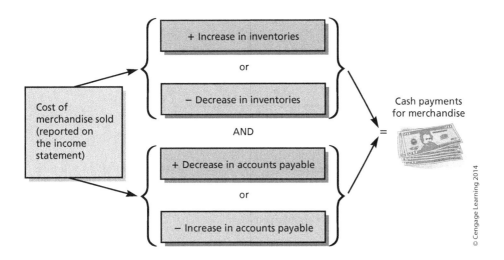

The cash payments for merchandise are $785,200, computed as follows:

Cost of merchandise sold	$790,000
Deduct decrease in inventories	(8,000)
Add decrease in accounts payable	3,200
Cash payments for merchandise	$785,200

The $8,000 decrease in inventories (from Exhibit 3) indicates that the merchandise sold exceeded the cost of the merchandise purchased by $8,000. In other words, the cost of merchandise sold includes $8,000 of goods sold from inventory that did not require a cash outflow during the year. Thus, $8,000 is deducted from the cost of merchandise sold in determining the *cash payments for merchandise*.

The $3,200 decrease in accounts payable (from Exhibit 3) indicates that cash payments for merchandise were $3,200 more than the purchases on account during 2014. Therefore, $3,200 is added to the cost of merchandise sold in determining the *cash payments for merchandise*.

Example Exercise 13-7 **Cash Payments for Merchandise—Direct Method**

The cost of merchandise sold reported on the income statement was $145,000. The accounts payable balance increased by $4,000, and the inventory balance increased by $9,000 over the year. Determine the amount of cash paid for merchandise.

Follow My Example 13-7

Cost of merchandise sold...	$145,000
Add increase in inventories...	9,000
Deduct increase in accounts payable	(4,000)
Cash paid for merchandise	$150,000

Practice Exercises: **PE 13-7A, PE 13-7B**

Cash Payments for Operating Expenses

The income statement (from Exhibit 3) for Rundell Inc. reports total operating expenses of $203,000, which includes depreciation expense of $7,000. Since depreciation expense does not require a cash outflow, it is omitted from *cash payments for operating expenses*.

To determine the *cash payments for operating expenses*, the other operating expenses (excluding depreciation) of $196,000 ($203,000 − $7,000) are adjusted for any increase or decrease in accrued expenses payable. Assuming that the accrued expenses payable are all operating expenses, this adjustment is summarized below.

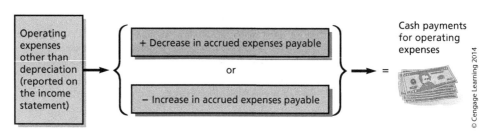

The cash payments for operating expenses are $193,800, computed as follows:

Operating expenses other than depreciation	$196,000
Deduct increase in accrued expenses payable	(2,200)
Cash payments for operating expenses	$193,800

The increase in accrued expenses payable (from Exhibit 3) indicates that the cash payments for operating expenses were $2,200 less than the amount reported for operating expenses during the year. Thus, $2,200 is deducted from the operating expenses in determining the *cash payments for operating expenses*.

Gain on Sale of Land

The income statement for Rundell Inc. (from Exhibit 3) reports a gain of $12,000 on the sale of land. The sale of land is an investing activity. Thus, the proceeds from the sale, which include the gain, are reported as part of the cash flows from investing activities.

Interest Expense

The income statement (from Exhibit 3) for Rundell Inc. reports interest expense of $8,000. To determine the *cash payments for interest*, the $8,000 is adjusted for any increases or decreases in interest payable. The adjustment is summarized as follows:

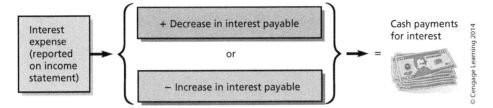

The comparative balance sheet of Rundell Inc. in Exhibit 3 indicates no interest payable. This is because the interest expense on the bonds payable is paid on June 1 and December 31. Since there is no interest payable, no adjustment of the interest expense of $8,000 is necessary.

Cash Payments for Income Taxes

The income statement (from Exhibit 3) for Rundell Inc. reports income tax expense of $83,000. To determine the *cash payments for income taxes*, the $83,000 is adjusted for any increases or decreases in income taxes payable. The adjustment is summarized below.

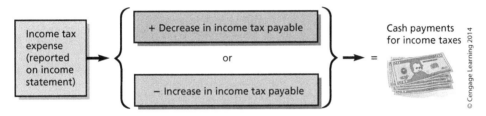

The cash payments for income taxes are $83,500, computed as follows:

Income tax expense	$83,000
Add decrease in income taxes payable	500
Cash payments for income taxes	$83,500

The $500 decrease in income taxes payable (from Exhibit 3) indicates that the cash payments for income taxes were $500 more than the amount reported for income tax expense during 2014. Thus, $500 is added to the income tax expense in determining the *cash payments for income taxes*.

Reporting Cash Flows from Operating Activities—Direct Method

The statement of cash flows for Rundell Inc., using the direct method for reporting cash flows from operating activities, is shown in Exhibit 7. The portions of the statement that differ from those prepared under the indirect method are highlighted in color.

Rundell Inc.
Statement of Cash Flows
For the Year Ended December 31, 2014

Cash flows from operating activities:			
Cash received from customers		$1,171,000	
Deduct: Cash payments for merchandise	$785,200		
Cash payments for operating expenses	193,800		
Cash payments for interest	8,000		
Cash payments for income taxes	83,500	1,070,500	
Net cash flow from operating activities		$100,500	

(Continued)

EXHIBIT 7				
Statement of Cash Flows—Direct Method *(concluded)*				

EXHIBIT 7

Statement of Cash Flows—Direct Method *(concluded)*

Rundell Inc.
Statement of Cash Flows
For the Year Ended December 31, 2014

Cash flows from investing activities:			
Cash received from sale of land		$ 72,000	
Less: Cash paid for purchase of land	$ 15,000		
Cash paid for purchase of building	60,000	75,000	
Net cash flow used for investing activities..............			(3,000)
Cash flows from financing activities:			
Cash received from sale of common stock...............		$ 48,000	
Less: Cash paid to retire bonds payable	$ 50,000		
Cash paid for dividends	24,000	74,000	
Net cash flow used for financing activities			(26,000)
Increase in cash			$ 71,500
Cash at the beginning of the year........................			26,000
Cash at the end of the year...............................			$ 97,500
Schedule Reconciling Net Income with Cash			
Flows from Operating Activities:			
Cash flows from operating activities:			
Net income...			$108,000
Adjustments to reconcile net income to net cash			
flow from operating activities:			
Depreciation.....................................			7,000
Gain on sale of land..............................			(12,000)
Changes in current operating assets and			
liabilities:			
Increase in accounts receivable			(9,000)
Decrease in inventory			8,000
Decrease in accounts payable.................			(3,200)
Increase in accrued expenses payable			2,200
Decrease in income taxes payable.............			(500)
Net cash flow from operating activities			$100,500

© Cengage Learning 2014

Exhibit 7 also includes the separate schedule reconciling net income and net cash flow from operating activities. This schedule is included in the statement of cash flows when the direct method is used. This schedule is similar to the Cash Flows from Operating Activities section prepared under the indirect method.

IFRS

International 🌐 Connection

IFRS FOR STATEMENT OF CASH FLOWS

The statement of cash flows is required under International Financial Reporting Standards (IFRS). The statement of cash flows under IFRS is similar to that reported under U.S. GAAP in that the statement has separate sections for operating, investing, and financing activities. Like U.S. GAAP, IFRS also allow the use of either the indirect or direct method of reporting cash flows from operating activities. IFRS differ from U.S. GAAP in some minor areas, including:

- Interest paid can be reported as either an operating or a financing activity, while interest received can be reported as either an operating or an investing activity. In contrast, U.S. GAAP reports interest paid or received as an operating activity.
- Dividends paid can be reported as either an operating or a financing activity, while dividends received can be reported as either an operating or an investing activity. In contrast, U.S. GAAP reports dividends paid as a financing activity and dividends received as an operating activity.
- Cash flows to pay taxes are reported as a separate line in the operating activities, in contrast to U.S. GAAP, which does not require a separate line disclosure.

*IFRS are further discussed and illustrated in Appendix C.

© Cengage Learning 2014

Financial Analysis and Interpretation: Free Cash Flow

A valuable tool for evaluating the cash flows of a business is free cash flow. **Free cash flow** measures the operating cash flow available to a company to use after purchasing the property, plant, and equipment (PP&E) necessary to maintain current productive capacity.[5] It is computed as follows:

OBJ 4 Describe and illustrate the use of free cash flow in evaluating a company's cash flow.

Cash flow from operating activities	$XXX
Less: Investments in PP&E needed to maintain current production	XXX
Free cash flow	$XXX

Analysts often use free cash flow, rather than cash flows from operating activities, to measure the financial strength of a business. Industries such as airlines, railroads, and telecommunications companies must invest heavily in new equipment to remain competitive. Such investments can significantly reduce free cash flow. For example, Verizon Communications Inc.'s free cash flow is approximately 51% of the cash flow from operating activities. In contrast, Apple Inc.'s free cash flow is approximately 89% of the cash flow from operating activities.

To illustrate, the cash flow from operating activities for Research in Motion, Inc., maker of BlackBerry® smartphones, was $4,009 million in a recent fiscal year. The statement of cash flows indicated that the cash invested in property, plant, and equipment was $1,039 million. Assuming that the amount invested in property, plant, and equipment is necessary to maintain productive capacity, free cash flow would be computed as follows (in millions):

Cash flow from operating activities	$4,009
Less: Investments in PP&E needed to maintain current production	1,039
Free cash flow	$2,970

Research in Motion's free cash flow was 74% of cash flow from operations and over 15% of sales. Compare this to the calculation of free cash flows for Apple Inc. (a computer company), The Coca-Cola Company (a beverage company), and Verizon Communications, Inc. (a telecommunications company), shown below (in millions):

	Apple Inc.	The Coca-Cola Company	Verizon Communications, Inc.
Sales	$65,225	$35,119	$106,565
Cash flow from operating activities	$18,595	$ 9,352	$ 33,363
Less: Investments in PP&E needed to maintain current production	2,005	2,215	16,458
Free cash flow	$16,590	$ 7,137	$ 16,905
Free cash flow as a percentage of cash flow from operations	89%	76%	51%
Free cash flow as a percentage of sales	25%	20%	16%

Positive free cash flow is considered favorable. A company that has free cash flow is able to fund internal growth, retire debt, pay dividends, and benefit from financial flexibility. A company with no free cash flow is unable to maintain current productive capacity. Lack of free cash flow can be an early indicator of liquidity problems. As one analyst notes, "Free cash flow gives the company firepower to reduce debt and ultimately generate consistent, actual income."[6]

5 Productive capacity is the number of goods the company is currently producing and selling.

6 Jill Krutick, *Fortune*, March 30, 1998, p. 106.

Example Exercise 13-8   Free Cash Flow

Omnicron Inc. reported the following on the company's cash flow statement in 2014 and 2013:

	2014	2013
Net cash flow from operating activities	$140,000	$120,000
Net cash flow used for investing activities	(120,000)	(80,000)
Net cash flow used for financing activities	(20,000)	(32,000)

Seventy-five percent of the net cash flow used for investing activities was used to replace existing capacity.

a. Determine Omnicron's free cash flow.

b. Has Omnicron's free cash flow improved or declined from 2013 to 2014?

Follow My Example 13-8

a.

	2014	2013
Net cash flow from operating activities	$140,000	$120,000
Less: Investments in fixed assets to maintain current production	90,000[1]	60,000[2]
Free cash flow	$ 50,000	$ 60,000

[1] $120,000 × 75%
[2] $80,000 × 75%

b. The change from $60,000 to $50,000 indicates an unfavorable trend.

Practice Exercises: **PE 13-8A, PE 13-8B**

A P P E N D I X

Spreadsheet (Work Sheet) for Statement of Cash Flows—The Indirect Method

A spreadsheet (work sheet) may be used in preparing the statement of cash flows. However, whether or not a spreadsheet (work sheet) is used, the concepts presented in this chapter are not affected.

The data for Rundell Inc., presented in Exhibit 3 on pages 534–535, are used as a basis for illustrating the spreadsheet (work sheet) for the indirect method. The steps in preparing this spreadsheet (work sheet), shown in Exhibit 8, are as follows:

Step 1. List the title of each balance sheet account in the Accounts column.

Step 2. For each balance sheet account, enter its balance as of December 31, 2013, in the first column and its balance as of December 31, 2014, in the last column. Place the credit balances in parentheses.

Step 3. Add the December 31, 2013 and 2014 column totals, which should total to zero.

Step 4. Analyze the change during the year in each noncash account to determine its net increase (decrease) and classify the change as affecting cash flows from operating activities, investing activities, financing activities, or noncash investing and financing activities.

Step 5. Indicate the effect of the change on cash flows by making entries in the Transactions columns.

EXHIBIT 8   End-of-Period Spreadsheet (Work Sheet) for Statement of Cash Flows—Indirect Method

Step 2

A	B	C	D	E	F	G
1	Rundell Inc.					
2	End-of-Period Spreadsheet (Work Sheet) for Statement of Cash Flows					
3	For the Year Ended December 31, 2014					
4 Accounts	Balance,		Transactions			Balance,
5	Dec. 31, 2013		Debit		Credit	Dec. 31, 2014
6 Cash	26,000	(o)	71,500			97,500
7 Accounts receivable (net)	65,000	(n)	9,000			74,000
8 Inventories	180,000			(m)	8,000	172,000
9 Land	125,000	(k)	15,000	(l)	60,000	80,000
10 Building	200,000	(j)	60,000			260,000
11 Accumulated depreciation—building	(58,300)			(i)	7,000	(65,300)
12 Accounts payable (merchandise creditors)	(46,700)	(h)	3,200			(43,500)
13 Accrued expenses payable (operating expenses)	(24,300)			(g)	2,200	(26,500)
14 Income taxes payable	(8,400)	(f)	500			(7,900)
15 Dividends payable	(10,000)			(e)	4,000	(14,000)
16 Bonds payable	(150,000)	(d)	50,000			(100,000)
17 Common stock	(16,000)			(c)	8,000	(24,000)
18 Paid-in capital in excess of par	(80,000)			(c)	40,000	(120,000)
19 Retained earnings	(202,300)	(b)	28,000	(a) 108,000		(282,300)
20 Totals	0		237,200		237,200	0
21 Operating activities:						
22 Net income		(a)	108,000			
23 Depreciation of building		(i)	7,000			
24 Gain on sale of land				(l)	12,000	
25 Increase in accounts receivable				(n)	9,000	
26 Decrease in inventories		(m)	8,000			
27 Decrease in accounts payable				(h)	3,200	
28 Increase in accrued expenses payable		(g)	2,200			
29 Decrease in income taxes payable				(f)	500	
30 Investing activities:						
31 Sale of land		(l)	72,000			
32 Purchase of land				(k)	15,000	
33 Purchase of building				(j)	60,000	
34 Financing activities:						
35 Issued common stock		(c)	48,000			
36 Retired bonds payable				(d)	50,000	
37 Declared cash dividends				(b)	28,000	
38 Increase in dividends payable		(e)	4,000			
39 Net increase in cash				(o)	71,500	
40 Totals			249,200		249,200	

Step 1 (rows 6–19); Step 3 (row 20 Totals); Steps 4–7

Step 6. After all noncash accounts have been analyzed, enter the net increase (decrease) in cash during the period.

Step 7. Add the Debit and Credit Transactions columns. The totals should be equal.

Analyzing Accounts

In analyzing the noncash accounts (Step 4), try to determine the type of cash flow activity (operating, investing, or financing) that led to the change in the account. As each noncash account is analyzed, an entry (Step 5) is made on the spreadsheet (work sheet) for the type of cash flow activity that caused the change. After all noncash accounts have been analyzed, an entry (Step 6) is made for the increase (decrease) in cash during the period.

The entries made on the spreadsheet are not posted to the ledger. They are only used in preparing and summarizing the data on the spreadsheet.

The order in which the accounts are analyzed is not important. However, it is more efficient to begin with Retained Earnings and proceed upward in the account listing.

Retained Earnings

The spreadsheet (work sheet) shows a Retained Earnings balance of $202,300 at December 31, 2013, and $282,300 at December 31, 2014. Thus, Retained Earnings increased $80,000 during the year. This increase is from the following:

1. Net income of $108,000
2. Declaring cash dividends of $28,000

To identify the cash flows from these activities, two entries are made on the spreadsheet.

The $108,000 is reported on the statement of cash flows as part of "cash flows from operating activities." Thus, an entry is made in the Transactions columns on the spreadsheet, as follows:

(a)	Operating Activities—Net Income.................................	108,000	
	Retained Earnings...		108,000

The preceding entry accounts for the net income portion of the change to Retained Earnings. It also identifies the cash flow in the bottom portion of the spreadsheet as related to operating activities.

The $28,000 of dividends is reported as a financing activity on the statement of cash flows. Thus, an entry is made in the Transactions columns on the spreadsheet, as follows:

(b)	Retained Earnings..	28,000	
	Financing Activities—Declared Cash Dividends		28,000

The preceding entry accounts for the dividends portion of the change to Retained Earnings. It also identifies the cash flow in the bottom portion of the spreadsheet as related to financing activities. The $28,000 of declared dividends will be adjusted later for the actual amount of cash dividends paid during the year.

Other Accounts

The entries for the other noncash accounts are made in the spreadsheet in a manner similar to entries (a) and (b). A summary of these entries is as follows:

(c)	Financing Activities—Issued Common Stock......................	48,000		
	Common Stock		8,000	
	Paid-In Capital in Excess of Par—Common Stock		40,000	
(d)	Bonds Payable	50,000		
	Financing Activities—Retired Bonds Payable...................		50,000	
(e)	Financing Activities—Increase in Dividends Payable...............	4,000		
	Dividends Payable		4,000	
(f)	Income Taxes Payable	500		
	Operating Activities—Decrease in Income Taxes Payable........		500	
(g)	Operating Activities—Increase in Accrued Expenses Payable	2,200		
	Accrued Expenses Payable		2,200	

(h)	Accounts Payable	3,200	
	Operating Activities—Decrease in Accounts Payable		3,200
(i)	Operating Activities—Depreciation of Building	7,000	
	Accumulated Depreciation—Building		7,000
(j)	Building	60,000	
	Investing Activities—Purchase of Building		60,000
(k)	Land	15,000	
	Investing Activities—Purchase of Land		15,000
(l)	Investing Activities—Sale of Land	72,000	
	Operating Activities—Gain on Sale of Land		12,000
	Land		60,000
(m)	Operating Activities—Decrease in Inventories	8,000	
	Inventories		8,000
(n)	Accounts Receivable	9,000	
	Operating Activities—Increase in Accounts Receivable		9,000
(o)	Cash	71,500	
	Net Increase in Cash		71,500

After all the balance sheet accounts are analyzed and the entries made on the spreadsheet (work sheet), all the operating, investing, and financing activities are identified in the bottom portion of the spreadsheet. The accuracy of the entries is verified by totaling the Debit and Credit Transactions columns. The totals of the columns should be equal.

Preparing the Statement of Cash Flows

The statement of cash flows prepared from the spreadsheet is identical to the statement in Exhibit 6 on page 543. The data for the three sections of the statement are obtained from the bottom portion of the spreadsheet.

At a Glance 13

Describe the cash flow activities reported in the statement of cash flows.

Key Points   The statement of cash flows reports cash receipts and cash payments by three types of activities: operating activities, investing activities, and financing activities. Cash flows from operating activities reports the cash inflows and outflows from a company's day-to-day operations. Cash flows from investing activities reports the cash inflows and outflows related to changes in a company's long-term assets. Cash flows from financing activities reports the cash inflows and outflows related to changes in a company's long-term liabilities and stockholders' equity. Investing and financing for a business may be affected by transactions that do not involve cash. The effect of such transactions should be reported in a separate schedule accompanying the statement of cash flows.

Learning Outcome	Example Exercises	Practice Exercises
• Classify transactions that either provide or use cash into either operating, investing, or financing activities.	**EE13-1**	**PE13-1A, 13-1B**

Prepare a statement of cash flows, using the indirect method.

Key Points   The indirect method reports cash flows from operating activities by adjusting net income for revenues and expenses that do not involve the receipt or payment of cash. Noncash expenses such as depreciation are added back to net income. Gains and losses on the disposal of assets are added to or deducted from net income. Changes in current operating assets and liabilities are added to or subtracted from net income, depending on their effect on cash. Cash flows from investing activities and cash flows from financing activities are reported below cash flows from operating activities in the statement of cash flows.

Learning Outcomes	Example Exercises	Practice Exercises
• Determine cash flows from operating activities under the indirect method by adjusting net income for noncash expenses and gains and losses from asset disposals.	EE13-2	PE13-2A, 13-2B
• Determine cash flows from operating activities under the indirect method by adjusting net income for changes in current operating assets and liabilities.	EE13-3	PE13-3A, 13-3B
• Prepare the Cash Flows from Operating Activities section of the statement of cash flows, using the indirect method.	EE13-4	PE13-4A, 13-4B
• Prepare the Cash Flows from Investing Activities and Cash Flows from Financing Activities sections of the statement of cash flows.	EE13-5	PE13-5A, 13-5B

Prepare a statement of cash flows, using the direct method.

Key Points   The amount of cash flows from operating activities is the same under both the direct and indirect methods, but the manner in which cash flows operating activities is reported is different. The direct method reports cash flows from operating activities by major classes of operating cash receipts and cash payments. The difference between the major classes of total operating cash receipts and total operating cash payments is the net cash flow from operating activities. The Cash Flows from Investing and Financing Activities sections of the statement are the same under both the direct and indirect methods.

Learning Outcome	Example Exercises	Practice Exercises
• Prepare the cash flows from operating activities section of the statement of cash flows under the direct method.	EE13-6 EE13-7	PE13-6A, 13-6B PE13-7A, 13-7B

Describe and illustrate the use of free cash flow in evaluating a company's cash flow.

Key Points   Free cash flow measures the operating cash flow available for company use after purchasing the fixed assets that are necessary to maintain current productive capacity. It is calculated by subtracting these fixed asset purchases from net cash flow from operating activities. A company with strong free cash flow is able to fund internal growth, retire debt, pay dividends, and enjoy financial flexibility. A company with weak free cash flow has much less financial flexibility.

Learning Outcomes	Example Exercises	Practice Exercises
• Describe free cash flow.		
• Calculate and evaluate free cash flow.	EE13-8	PE13-8A, 13-8B

Key Terms

cash flow per share (533)
cash flows from financing
   activities (531)
cash flows from investing
   activities (530)

cash flows from operating
   activities (530)
direct method (531)
free cash flow (549)

indirect method (532)
statement of cash flows (530)

Illustrative Problem

The comparative balance sheet of Dowling Company for December 31, 2014 and 2013, is as follows:

Dowling Company
Comparative Balance Sheet
December 31, 2014 and 2013

	2014	2013
Assets		
Cash	$ 140,350	$ 95,900
Accounts receivable (net)	95,300	102,300
Inventories	165,200	157,900
Prepaid expenses	6,240	5,860
Investments (long-term)	35,700	84,700
Land	75,000	90,000
Buildings	375,000	260,000
Accumulated depreciation—buildings	(71,300)	(58,300)
Machinery and equipment	428,300	428,300
Accumulated depreciation—machinery and equipment	(148,500)	(138,000)
Patents	58,000	65,000
Total assets	$1,159,290	$1,093,660
Liabilities and Stockholders' Equity		
Accounts payable (merchandise creditors)	$ 43,500	$ 46,700
Accrued expenses payable (operating expenses)	14,000	12,500
Income taxes payable	7,900	8,400
Dividends payable	14,000	10,000
Mortgage note payable, due 2023	40,000	0
Bonds payable	150,000	250,000
Common stock, $30 par	450,000	375,000
Excess of issue price over par—common stock	66,250	41,250
Retained earnings	373,640	349,810
Total liabilities and stockholders' equity	$1,159,290	$1,093,660

The income statement for Dowling Company is shown here.

Dowling Company
Income Statement
For the Year Ended December 31, 2014

Sales		$1,100,000
Cost of merchandise sold		710,000
Gross profit		$ 390,000
Operating expenses:		
Depreciation expense	$ 23,500	
Patent amortization	7,000	
Other operating expenses	196,000	
Total operating expenses		226,500
Income from operations		$ 163,500
Other income:		
Gain on sale of investments	$ 11,000	
Other expense:		
Interest expense	26,000	(15,000)
Income before income tax		$ 148,500
Income tax expense		50,000
Net income		$ 98,500

An examination of the accounting records revealed the following additional information applicable to 2014:

a. Land costing $15,000 was sold for $15,000.

b. A mortgage note was issued for $40,000.

c. A building costing $115,000 was constructed.

d. 2,500 shares of common stock were issued at $40 in exchange for the bonds payable.

e. Cash dividends declared were $74,670.

Instructions

1. Prepare a statement of cash flows, using the indirect method of reporting cash flows from operating activities.

2. Prepare a statement of cash flows, using the direct method of reporting cash flows from operating activities.

Solution

1.

Dowling Company **Statement of Cash Flows—Indirect Method** **For the Year Ended December 31, 2014**		

Cash flows from operating activities:			
Net income......................................		$ 98,500	
Adjustments to reconcile net income to net cash flow from operating activities:			
Depreciation.................................		23,500	
Amortization of patents.......................		7,000	
Gain on sale of investments		(11,000)	
Changes in current operating assets and liabilities:			
Decrease in accounts receivable		7,000	
Increase in inventories		(7,300)	
Increase in prepaid expenses		(380)	
Decrease in accounts payable............		(3,200)	
Increase in accrued expenses payable		1,500	
Decrease in income taxes payable........		(500)	
Net cash flow from operating activities			$115,120
Cash flows from investing activities:			
Cash received from sale of:			
Investments.....................................	$60,000[1]		
Land...	15,000	$ 75,000	
Less: Cash paid for construction of building............		115,000	
Net cash flow used for investing activities..............			(40,000)
Cash flows from financing activities:			
Cash received from issuing mortgage note payable.....		$ 40,000	
Less: Cash paid for dividends..........................		70,670[2]	
Net cash flow used for financing activities			(30,670)
Increase in cash			$ 44,450
Cash at the beginning of the year........................			95,900
Cash at the end of the year..............................			$140,350
Schedule of Noncash Investing and Financing Activities:			
Issued common stock to retire bonds payable..........			$100,000

[1] $60,000 = $11,000 gain + $49,000 (decrease in investments)
[2] $70,670 = $74,670 – $4,000 (increase in dividends)

2.

Dowling Company **Statement of Cash Flows—Direct Method** **For the Year Ended December 31, 2014**			
Cash flows from operating activities:			
Cash received from customers[1]		$1,107,000	
Deduct: Cash paid for merchandise[2]	$720,500		
Cash paid for operating expenses[3]	194,880		
Cash paid for interest expense	26,000		
Cash paid for income tax[4]	50,500	991,880	
Net cash flow from operating activities			$115,120
Cash flows from investing activities:			
Cash received from sale of:			
Investments	$ 60,000[5]		
Land	15,000	$ 75,000	
Less: Cash paid for construction of building		115,000	
Net cash flow used for investing activities			(40,000)
Cash flows from financing activities:			
Cash received from issuing mortgage note payable		$ 40,000	
Less: Cash paid for dividends[6]		70,670	
Net cash flow used for financing activities			(30,670)
Increase in cash			$ 44,450
Cash at the beginning of the year			95,900
Cash at the end of the year			$140,350
Schedule of Noncash Investing and			
Financing Activities:			
Issued common stock to retire bonds payable			$100,000
Schedule Reconciling Net Income with Cash Flows			
from Operating Activities[7]			

Computations:

[1]$1,100,000 + $7,000 = $1,107,000

[2]$710,000 + $3,200 + $7,300 = $720,500

[3]$196,000 + $380 – $1,500 = $194,880

[4]$50,000 + $500 = $50,500

[5]$60,000 = $11,000 gain + $49,000 (decrease in investments)

[6]$74,670 + $10,000 – $14,000 = $70,670

[7]The content of this schedule is the same as the Operating Activities section of part (1) of this solution and is not reproduced here for the sake of brevity.

Discussion Questions

1. What is the principal disadvantage of the direct method of reporting cash flows from operating activities?

2. What are the major advantages of the indirect method of reporting cash flows from operating activities?

3. A corporation issued $2,000,000 of common stock in exchange for $2,000,000 of fixed assets. Where would this transaction be reported on the statement of cash flows?

4. A retail business, using the accrual method of accounting, owed merchandise creditors (accounts payable) $320,000 at the beginning of the year and $350,000 at the end of the year. How would the $30,000 increase be used to adjust net income in determining the amount of cash flows from operating activities by the indirect method? Explain.

5. If salaries payable was $100,000 at the beginning of the year and $75,000 at the end of the year, should $25,000 be added to or deducted from income to determine the amount of cash flows from operating activities by the indirect method? Explain.

6. A long-term investment in bonds with a cost of $500,000 was sold for $600,000 cash. (a) What was the gain or loss on the sale? (b) What was the effect of the transaction on cash flows? (c) How should the transaction be reported on the statement of cash flows if cash flows from operating activities are reported by the indirect method?

7. A corporation issued $2,000,000 of 20-year bonds for cash at 98. How would the transaction be reported on the statement of cash flows?

8. Fully depreciated equipment costing $50,000 was discarded. What was the effect of the transaction on cash flows if (a) $15,000 cash is received, (b) no cash is received?

9. For the current year, Packers Company decided to switch from the indirect method to the direct method for reporting cash flows from operating activities on the statement of cash flows. Will the change cause the amount of net cash flow from operating activities to be larger, smaller, or the same as if the indirect method had been used? Explain.

10. Name five common major classes of operating cash receipts or operating cash payments presented on the statement of cash flows when the cash flows from operating activities are reported by the direct method.

Practice Exercises

Example Exercises

EE 13-1 *p. 533* | **PE 13-1A   Classifying cash flows** | OBJ. 1

Identify whether each of the following would be reported as an operating, investing, or financing activity on the statement of cash flows.

a. Payment of accounts payable

b. Payment for administrative expenses

c. Purchase of land

d. Issuance of common stock

e. Retirement of bonds payable

f. Cash received from customers

EE 13-1 *p. 533* | **PE 13-1B   Classifying cash flows** | OBJ. 1

Identify whether each of the following would be reported as an operating, investing, or financing activity on the statement of cash flows.

a. Purchase of investments

b. Disposal of equipment

c. Payment for selling expenses

d. Collection of accounts receivable

e. Cash sales

f. Issuance of bonds payable

EE 13-2 *p. 537* | **PE 13-2A   Adjustments to net income—indirect method** | OBJ. 2

Carlyn Corporation's accumulated depreciation—furniture account increased by $7,500, while $2,750 of patent amortization was recognized between balance sheet dates. There were no purchases or sales of depreciable or intangible assets during the year. In addition, the income statement showed a loss of $4,000 from the sale of land. Reconcile a net income of $107,500 to net cash flow from operating activities.

EE 13-2 *p. 537* | **PE 13-2B   Adjustments to net income—indirect method** | OBJ. 2

Ya Wen Corporation's accumulated depreciation—equipment account increased by $8,750, while $3,250 of patent amortization was recognized between balance sheet dates. There were no purchases or sales of depreciable or intangible assets during the year. In addition, the income statement showed a gain of $18,750 from the sale of investments. Reconcile a net income of $175,000 to net cash flow from operating activities.

Example
Exercises

EE 13-3 *p. 539* **PE 13-3A   Changes in current operating assets and liabilities—indirect method**   OBJ. 2

Macavoy Corporation's comparative balance sheet for current assets and liabilities was as follows:

	Dec. 31, 2014	Dec. 31, 2013
Accounts receivable	$33,000	$39,600
Inventory	22,000	18,920
Accounts payable	19,800	17,380
Dividends payable	60,500	64,900

Adjust net income of $253,000 for changes in operating assets and liabilities to arrive at net cash flow from operating activities.

EE 13-3 *p. 539* **PE 13-3B   Changes in current operating assets and liabilities—indirect method**   OBJ. 2

Huluduey Corporation's comparative balance sheet for current assets and liabilities was as follows:

	Dec. 31, 2014	Dec. 31, 2013
Accounts receivable	$18,000	$14,400
Inventory	34,800	29,700
Accounts payable	27,600	20,700
Dividends payable	8,400	10,800

Adjust net income of $160,000 for changes in operating assets and liabilities to arrive at net cash flow from operating activities.

EE 13-4 *p. 540* **PE 13-4A   Cash flows from operating activities—indirect method**   OBJ. 2

Avenger Inc. reported the following data:

Net income	$270,000
Depreciation expense	30,000
Gain on disposal of equipment	24,600
Decrease in accounts receivable	16,800
Decrease in accounts payable	4,320

Prepare the Cash Flows from Operating Activities section of the statement of cash flows, using the indirect method.

EE 13-4 *p. 540* **PE 13-4B   Cash flows from operating activities—indirect method**   OBJ. 2

Staley Inc. reported the following data:

Net income	$280,000
Depreciation expense	48,000
Loss on disposal of equipment	19,520
Increase in accounts receivable	17,280
Increase in accounts payable	8,960

Prepare the Cash Flows from Operating Activities section of the statement of cash flows, using the indirect method.

EE 13-5 *p. 543* **PE 13-5A   Land transactions on the statement of cash flows**   OBJ. 2

Rainbow Corporation purchased land for $360,000. Later in the year, the company sold a different piece of land with a book value of $180,000 for $120,000. How are the effects of these transactions reported on the statement of cash flows?

Example Exercises

EE 13-5 *p. 543* **PE 13-5B** **Land transactions on the statement of cash flows** OBJ. 2

IZ Corporation purchased land for $400,000. Later in the year, the company sold a different piece of land with a book value of $200,000 for $240,000. How are the effects of these transactions reported on the statement of cash flows?

EE 13-6 *p. 545* **PE 13-6A** **Cash received from customers—direct method** OBJ. 3

Sales reported on the income statement were $480,000. The accounts receivable balance increased $54,000 over the year. Determine the amount of cash received from customers.

EE 13-6 *p. 545* **PE 13-6B** **Cash received from customers—direct method** OBJ. 3

Sales reported on the income statement were $112,000. The accounts receivable balance decreased $10,500 over the year. Determine the amount of cash received from customers.

EE 13-7 *p. 546* **PE 13-7A** **Cash payments for merchandise—direct method** OBJ. 3

The cost of merchandise sold reported on the income statement was $770,000. The accounts payable balance decreased $44,000, and the inventory balance decreased by $66,000 over the year. Determine the amount of cash paid for merchandise.

EE 13-7 *p. 546* **PE 13-7B** **Cash payments for merchandise—direct method** OBJ. 3

The cost of merchandise sold reported on the income statement was $240,000. The accounts payable balance increased $12,000, and the inventory balance increased by $19,200 over the year. Determine the amount of cash paid for merchandise.

EE 13-8 *p. 550* **PE 13-8A** **Free cash flow** OBJ. 4

McMahon Inc. reported the following on the company's statement of cash flows in 2014 and 2013:

	2014	2013
Net cash flow from operating activities	$ 294,000	$ 280,000
Net cash flow used for investing activities	(224,000)	(252,000)
Net cash flow used for financing activities	(63,000)	(42,000)

Seventy percent of the net cash flow used for investing activities was used to replace existing capacity.

a. Determine McMahon's free cash flow for both years.

b. Has McMahon's free cash flow improved or declined from 2013 to 2014?

EE 13-8 *p. 550* **PE 13-8B** **Free cash flow** OBJ. 4

Dillin Inc. reported the following on the company's statement of cash flows in 2014 and 2013:

	2014	2013
Net cash flow from operating activities	$ 476,000	$ 455,000
Net cash flow used for investing activities	(427,000)	(378,000)
Net cash flow used for financing activities	(42,000)	(58,800)

Eighty percent of the net cash flow used for investing activities was used to replace existing capacity.

a. Determine Dillin's free cash flow for both years.

b. Has Dillin's free cash flow improved or declined from 2013 to 2014?

Exercises

EX 13-1 Cash flows from operating activities—net loss   OBJ. 1

On its income statement for a recent year, Continental Airlines, Inc., reported a net *loss* of $471 million from operations. On its statement of cash flows, it reported $1,241 million of cash flows from operating activities.

➤ Explain this apparent contradiction between the loss and the positive cash flows.

EX 13-2 Effect of transactions on cash flows   OBJ. 1

✔ c. Cash payment, $475,000

State the effect (cash receipt or payment and amount) of each of the following transactions, considered individually, on cash flows:

a. Sold equipment with a book value of $78,000 for $94,000.

b. Sold a new issue of $250,000 of bonds at 102.

c. Retired $400,000 of bonds, on which there was $4,000 of unamortized discount, for $475,000.

d. Purchased 3,000 shares of $30 par common stock as treasury stock at $40 per share.

e. Sold 4,000 shares of $25 par common stock for $50 per share.

f. Paid dividends of $1.50 per share. There were 40,000 shares issued and 5,000 shares of treasury stock.

g. Purchased land for $287,000 cash.

h. Purchased a building by paying $60,000 cash and issuing a $50,000 mortgage note payable.

EX 13-3 Classifying cash flows   OBJ. 1

Identify the type of cash flow activity for each of the following events (operating, investing, or financing):

a. Redeemed bonds

b. Purchased patents

c. Purchased buildings

d. Purchased treasury stock

e. Sold long-term investments

f. Paid cash dividends

g. Issued common stock

h. Issued preferred stock

i. Net income

j. Issued bonds

k. Sold equipment

EX 13-4 Cash flows from operating activities—indirect method   OBJ. 2

Indicate whether each of the following would be added to or deducted from net income in determining net cash flow from operating activities by the indirect method:

a. Increase in notes payable due in 90 days to vendors

b. Decrease in prepaid expenses

c. Increase in merchandise inventory

d. Loss on disposal of fixed assets

e. Decrease in accounts receivable

f. Decrease in salaries payable

g. Gain on retirement of long-term debt

h. Increase in notes receivable due in 90 days from customers

i. Depreciation of fixed assets

j. Amortization of patent

k. Decrease in accounts payable

EX 13-5 Cash flows from operating activities—indirect method OBJ. 2

The net income reported on the income statement for the current year was $600,000. Depreciation recorded on store equipment for the year amounted to $24,000. Balances of the current asset and current liability accounts at the beginning and end of the year are as follows:

	End of Year	Beginning of Year
Cash	$62,400	$57,600
Accounts receivable (net)	45,600	42,000
Merchandise inventory	60,000	66,000
Prepaid expenses	7,200	5,400
Accounts payable (merchandise creditors)	60,000	54,000
Wages payable	31,800	36,000

a. Prepare the Cash Flows from Operating Activities section of the statement of cash flows, using the indirect method.

b. ▬▬▬➤ Briefly explain why net cash flow from operating activities is different than net income.

EX 13-6 Cash flows from operating activities—indirect method OBJ. 1, 2

The net income reported on the income statement for the current year was $240,000. Depreciation recorded on equipment and a building amounted to $72,000 for the year. Balances of the current asset and current liability accounts at the beginning and end of the year are as follows:

	End of Year	Beginning of Year
Cash	$ 67,200	$ 72,000
Accounts receivable (net)	84,000	88,800
Inventories	168,000	150,000
Prepaid expenses	9,600	10,800
Accounts payable (merchandise creditors)	72,000	78,000
Salaries payable	12,000	10,200

a. Prepare the Cash Flows from Operating Activities section of the statement of cash flows, using the indirect method.

b. ▬▬▬➤ If the direct method had been used, would the net cash flow from operating activities have been the same? Explain.

EX 13-7 Cash flows from operating activities—indirect method OBJ. 1, 2

The income statement disclosed the following items for 2014:

Depreciation expense	$ 72,000
Gain on disposal of equipment	42,000
Net income	635,000

Balances of the current assets and current liability accounts changed between December 31, 2013, and December 31, 2014, as follows:

Accounts receivable	$11,200
Inventory	6,400*
Prepaid insurance	2,400*
Accounts payable	7,600*
Income taxes payable	2,400
Dividends payable	1,700

*Decrease

a. Prepare the Cash Flows from Operating Activities section of the statement of cash flows, using the indirect method.

b. ▬▬▬➤ Briefly explain why net cash flows from operating activities is different than net income.

EX 13-8 **Determining cash payments to stockholders**   OBJ. 2

The board of directors declared cash dividends totaling $364,000 during the current year. The comparative balance sheet indicates dividends payable of $104,300 at the beginning of the year and $91,000 at the end of the year. What was the amount of cash payments to stockholders during the year?

EX 13-9 **Reporting changes in equipment on statement of cash flows**   OBJ. 2

An analysis of the general ledger accounts indicates that office equipment, which cost $144,000 and on which accumulated depreciation totaled $60,000 on the date of sale, was sold for $72,000 during the year. Using this information, indicate the items to be reported on the statement of cash flows.

EX 13-10 **Reporting changes in equipment on statement of cash flows**   OBJ. 2

An analysis of the general ledger accounts indicates that delivery equipment, which cost $80,000 and on which accumulated depreciation totaled $36,000 on the date of sale, was sold for $37,200 during the year. Using this information, indicate the items to be reported on the statement of cash flows.

EX 13-11 **Reporting land transactions on statement of cash flows**   OBJ. 2

On the basis of the details of the following fixed asset account, indicate the items to be reported on the statement of cash flows:

ACCOUNT *Land*   ACCOUNT NO.

Date		Item	Debit	Credit	Balance	
					Debit	Credit
2014						
Jan.	1	Balance			496,000	
Apr.	6	Purchased for cash	60,200		556,200	
Nov.	23	Sold for $54,600		36,480	519,720	

EX 13-12 **Reporting stockholders' equity items on statement of cash flows**   OBJ. 2

On the basis of the following stockholders' equity accounts, indicate the items, exclusive of net income, to be reported on the statement of cash flows. There were no unpaid dividends at either the beginning or the end of the year.

ACCOUNT *Common Stock, $50 par*   ACCOUNT NO.

Date		Item	Debit	Credit	Balance	
					Debit	Credit
2014						
Jan.	1	Balance, 150,000 shares				7,500,000
Mar.	7	37,500 shares issued for cash		1,875,000		9,375,000
June	30	5,500-share stock dividend		275,000		9,650,000

ACCOUNT *Paid-In Capital in Excess of Par—Common Stock*   ACCOUNT NO.

Date		Item	Debit	Credit	Balance	
					Debit	Credit
2014						
Jan.	1	Balance				500,000
Mar.	7	37,500 shares issued for cash		3,000,000		3,500,000
June	30	Stock dividend		495,000		3,995,000

ACCOUNT *Retained Earnings*   ACCOUNT NO.

Date		Item	Debit	Credit	Balance Debit	Balance Credit
2014						
Jan.	1	Balance				2,500,000
June	30	Stock dividend	770,000			1,730,000
Dec.	30	Cash dividend	723,750			1,006,250
	31	Net income		1,800,000		2,806,250

**EX 13-13   Reporting land acquisition for cash and mortgage note on statement of   OBJ. 2
cash flows**

On the basis of the details of the following fixed asset account, indicate the items to be reported on the statement of cash flows:

ACCOUNT *Land*   ACCOUNT NO.

Date		Item	Debit	Credit	Balance Debit	Balance Credit
2014						
Jan.	1	Balance			156,000	
Feb.	10	Purchased for cash	246,000		402,000	
Nov.	20	Purchased with long-term mortgage note	324,000		726,000	

EX 13-14   Reporting issuance and retirement of long-term debt   OBJ. 2

On the basis of the details of the following bonds payable and related discount accounts, indicate the items to be reported in the Financing Activities section of the statement of cash flows, assuming no gain or loss on retiring the bonds:

ACCOUNT *Bonds Payable*   ACCOUNT NO.

Date		Item	Debit	Credit	Balance Debit	Balance Credit
2014						
Jan.	1	Balance				400,000
	2	Retire bonds	80,000			320,000
June	30	Issue bonds		240,000		560,000

ACCOUNT *Discount on Bond Payable*   ACCOUNT NO.

Date		Item	Debit	Credit	Balance Debit	Balance Credit
2014						
Jan.	1	Balance			18,000	
	2	Retire bonds		6,400	11,600	
June	30	Issue bonds	16,000		27,600	
Dec.	31	Amortize discount		1,400	26,200	

✔ Net income,
$341,770

EX 13-15 **Determining net income from net cash flow from operating activities** OBJ. 2

Curwen Inc. reported net cash flow from operating activities of $357,500 on its statement of cash flows for the year ended December 31, 2014. The following information was reported in the Cash Flows from Operating Activities section of the statement of cash flows, using the indirect method:

Decrease in income taxes payable	$ 7,700
Decrease in inventories	19,140
Depreciation	29,480
Gain on sale of investments	13,200
Increase in accounts payable	5,280
Increase in prepaid expenses	2,970
Increase in accounts receivable	14,300

a. Determine the net income reported by Curwen Inc. for the year ended December 31, 2014.

b.   Briefly explain why Curwen's net income is different than net cash flow from operating activities.

✔ Net cash flow
from operating
activities, $(3,465)

EX 13-16 **Cash flows from operating activities—indirect method** OBJ. 2

Selected data derived from the income statement and balance sheet of Jones Soda Co. for a recent year are as follows:

Income statement data (in thousands):	
Net earnings (loss)	$(6,106)
Losses on inventory write-down and fixed assets	379
Depreciation expense	799
Stock-based compensation expense (noncash)	830
Balance sheet data (in thousands):	
Increase in accounts receivable	278
Decrease in inventory	1,252
Decrease in prepaid expenses	131
Decrease in accounts payable	472

a. Prepare the Cash Flows from Operating Activities section of the statement of cash flows, using the indirect method for Jones Soda Co.

b.   Interpret your results in part (a).

✔ Net cash flow from
operating activities,
$120

EX 13-17 **Statement of cash flows—indirect method** OBJ. 2

The comparative balance sheet of Wedge Industries Inc. for December 31, 2014 and 2013, is as follows:

	Dec. 31, 2014	Dec. 31, 2013
Assets		
Cash	$ 392	$128
Accounts receivable (net)	224	160
Inventories	140	88
Land	320	360
Equipment	180	140
Accumulated depreciation—equipment	(48)	(24)
Total	$1,208	$852
Liabilities and Stockholders' Equity		
Accounts payable (merchandise creditors)	$ 140	$128
Dividends payable	24	—
Common stock, $10 par	80	40
Paid-in capital: Excess of issue price over par—common stock	200	100
Retained earnings	764	584
Total	$1,208	$852

The following additional information is taken from the records:

1. Land was sold for $100.

2. Equipment was acquired for cash.

3. There were no disposals of equipment during the year.

4. The common stock was issued for cash.

5. There was a $260 credit to Retained Earnings for net income.

6. There was an $80 debit to Retained Earnings for cash dividends declared.

a. Prepare a statement of cash flows, using the indirect method of presenting cash flows from operating activities.

b. ━━━▶ Was Wedge Industries Inc. net cash flow from operations more or less than net income? What is the source of this difference?

EX 13-18   Statement of cash flows—indirect method   OBJ. 2

List the errors you find in the following statement of cash flows. The cash balance at the beginning of the year was $240,000. All other amounts are correct, except the cash balance at the end of the year.

Shasta Inc.
Statement of Cash Flows
For the Year Ended December 31, 2014

Cash flows from operating activities:			
Net income		$360,000	
Adjustments to reconcile net income to net			
cash flow from operating activities:			
Depreciation.		100,800	
Gain on sale of investments		17,280	
Changes in current operating assets and liabilities:			
Increase in accounts receivable		27,360	
Increase in inventories		(36,000)	
Increase in accounts payable		(3,600)	
Decrease in accrued expenses payable		(2,400)	
Net cash flow from operating activities			$463,440
Cash flows from investing activities:			
Cash received from sale of investments		$240,000	
Less: Cash paid for purchase of land	$259,200		
Cash paid for purchase of equipment	432,000	691,200	
Net cash flow used for investing activities			(415,200)
Cash flows from financing activities:			
Cash received from sale of common stock		$312,000	
Cash paid for dividends		132,000	
Net cash flow from financing activities			180,000
Increase in cash			$ 47,760
Cash at the end of the year			192,240
Cash at the beginning of the year			$240,000

✔ a. $801,900

EX 13-19   Cash flows from operating activities—direct method   OBJ. 3

The cash flows from operating activities are reported by the direct method on the statement of cash flows. Determine the following:

a. If sales for the current year were $753,500 and accounts receivable decreased by $48,400 during the year, what was the amount of cash received from customers?

b. If income tax expense for the current year was $50,600 and income tax payable decreased by $5,500 during the year, what was the amount of cash payments for income taxes?

c. ━━━▶ Briefly explain why the cash received from customers in (a) is different than sales.

EX 13-20 Cash paid for merchandise purchases OBJ. 3

The cost of merchandise sold for Kohl's Corporation for a recent year was $15,480 million. The balance sheet showed the following current account balances (in millions):

	Balance, End of Year	Balance, Beginning of Year
Merchandise inventories	$4,050	$3,420
Accounts payable	1,494	1,260

Determine the amount of cash payments for merchandise.

EX 13-21 Determining selected amounts for cash flows from operating activities—direct method OBJ. 3

✔ a. $1,025,800

Selected data taken from the accounting records of Ginis Inc. for the current year ended December 31 are as follows:

	Balance, December 31	Balance, January 1
Accrued expenses payable (operating expenses)	$ 12,650	$ 14,030
Accounts payable (merchandise creditors)	96,140	105,800
Inventories	178,020	193,430
Prepaid expenses	7,360	8,970

During the current year, the cost of merchandise sold was $1,031,550, and the operating expenses other than depreciation were $179,400. The direct method is used for presenting the cash flows from operating activities on the statement of cash flows.

Determine the amount reported on the statement of cash flows for (a) cash payments for merchandise and (b) cash payments for operating expenses.

EX 13-22 Cash flows from operating activities—direct method OBJ. 3

✔ Net cash flow from operating activities, $96,040

The income statement of Booker T Industries Inc. for the current year ended June 30 is as follows:

Sales		$511,000
Cost of merchandise sold		290,500
Gross profit		$220,500
Operating expenses:		
Depreciation expense	$ 39,200	
Other operating expenses	105,000	
Total operating expenses		144,200
Income before income tax		$ 76,300
Income tax expense		21,700
Net income		$ 54,600

Changes in the balances of selected accounts from the beginning to the end of the current year are as follows:

	Increase (Decrease)
Accounts receivable (net)	$(11,760)
Inventories	3,920
Prepaid expenses	(3,780)
Accounts payable (merchandise creditors)	(7,980)
Accrued expenses payable (operating expenses)	1,260
Income tax payable	(2,660)

a. Prepare the Cash Flows from Operating Activities section of the statement of cash flows, using the direct method.

b. ▬▬▶ What does the direct method show about a company's cash flows from operating activities that is not shown using the indirect method?

EX 13-23 Cash flows from operating activities—direct method

OBJ. 3

The income statement for Rhino Company for the current year ended June 30 and balances of selected accounts at the beginning and the end of the year are as follows:

Sales	$445,500
Cost of merchandise sold	154,000
Gross profit	$291,500
Operating expenses:	
Depreciation expense .... $ 38,500	
Other operating expenses 115,280	
Total operating expenses	153,780
Income before income tax	$137,720
Income tax expense	39,600
Net income	$ 98,120

	End of Year	Beginning of Year
Accounts receivable (net)	$36,300	$31,240
Inventories	92,400	80,300
Prepaid expenses	14,520	15,840
Accounts payable (merchandise creditors)	67,540	62,700
Accrued expenses payable (operating expenses)	19,140	20,900
Income tax payable..	4,400	4,400

✔ Net cash flow from operating activities, $123,860

Prepare the Cash Flows from Operating Activities section of the statement of cash flows, using the direct method.

EX 13-24 Free cash flow

OBJ. 4

Sweeter Enterprises Inc. has cash flows from operating activities of $539,000. Cash flows used for investments in property, plant, and equipment totaled $210,000, of which 75% of this investment was used to replace existing capacity.

a. Determine the free cash flow for Sweeter Enterprises Inc.

b. ━━━▶ How might a lender use free cash flow to determine whether or not to give Sweeter Enterprises Inc. a loan?

EX 13-25 Free cash flow

OBJ. 4

The financial statements for Nike, Inc., are provided in Appendix B at the end of the text.

a. Determine the free cash flow for the most recent fiscal year. Assume that 90% of the additions to property, plant, and equipment were used to maintain productive capacity.

b. ━━━▶ How might a lender use free cash flow to determine whether or not to give Nike, Inc., a loan?

c. ━━━▶ Would you feel comfortable giving Nike a loan, based on the free cash flow calculated in (a)?

EX 13-26 Free cash flow

OBJ. 4

Lovato Motors Inc. has cash flows from operating activities of $720,000. Cash flows used for investments in property, plant, and equipment totaled $440,000, of which 85% of this investment was used to replace existing capacity.

Determine the free cash flow for Lovato Motors Inc.

Problems Series A

✔ Net cash flow from operating activities, $148,280

SPREADSHEET

PR 13-1A   Statement of cash flows—indirect method   OBJ. 2

The comparative balance sheet of Charles Inc. for December 31, 2014 and 2013, is shown as follows:

	Dec. 31, 2014	Dec. 31, 2013
Assets		
Cash	$ 469,320	$ 439,440
Accounts receivable (net)	170,880	156,720
Inventories	481,320	462,840
Investments	0	180,000
Land	246,000	0
Equipment	528,840	414,840
Accumulated depreciation—equipment	(124,800)	(111,000)
	$1,771,560	$1,542,840
Liabilities and Stockholders' Equity		
Accounts payable (merchandise creditors)	$ 318,360	$ 303,720
Accrued expenses payable (operating expenses)	31,680	39,480
Dividends payable	18,000	14,400
Common stock, $2 par	95,000	75,000
Paid-in capital: Excess of issue price over par—common stock	290,000	210,000
Retained earnings	1,018,520	900,240
	$1,771,560	$1,542,840

Additional data obtained from an examination of the accounts in the ledger for 2014 are as follows:

a. The investments were sold for $210,000 cash.

b. Equipment and land were acquired for cash.

c. There were no disposals of equipment during the year.

d. The common stock was issued for cash.

e. There was a $190,280 credit to Retained Earnings for net income.

f. There was a $72,000 debit to Retained Earnings for cash dividends declared.

Instructions

Prepare a statement of cash flows, using the indirect method of presenting cash flows from operating activities.

✔ Net cash flow from operating activities, $328,800

SPREADSHEET

PR 13-2A   Statement of cash flows—indirect method   OBJ. 2

The comparative balance sheet of Lankau Enterprises Inc. at December 31, 2014 and 2013, is as follows:

	Dec. 31, 2014	Dec. 31, 2013
Assets		
Cash	$ 219,900	$ 269,700
Accounts receivable (net)	336,900	363,000
Merchandise inventory	482,400	448,800
Prepaid expenses	20,100	14,400
Equipment	982,500	805,500
Accumulated depreciation—equipment	(256,200)	(198,300)
	$1,785,600	$1,703,100
Liabilities and Stockholders' Equity		
Accounts payable (merchandise creditors)	$ 375,300	$ 356,400
Mortgage note payable	0	504,000
Common stock, $25 par	411,000	36,000
Paid-in capital: Excess of issue price over par—common stock	705,000	480,000
Retained earnings	294,300	326,700
	$1,785,600	$1,703,100

Additional data obtained from the income statement and from an examination of the accounts in the ledger for 2014 are as follows:

a. Net income, $198,000.

b. Depreciation reported on the income statement, $125,100.

c. Equipment was purchased at a cost of $244,200, and fully depreciated equipment costing $67,200 was discarded, with no salvage realized.

d. The mortgage note payable was not due until 2016, but the terms permitted earlier payment without penalty.

e. 15,000 shares of common stock were issued at $40 for cash.

f. Cash dividends declared and paid, $230,400.

Instructions

Prepare a statement of cash flows, using the indirect method of presenting cash flows from operating activities.

PR 13-3A   Statement of cash flows—indirect method OBJ. 2

✔ Net cash flow from operating activities, $(169,600)

The comparative balance sheet of Whitman Co. at December 31, 2014 and 2013, is as follows:

	Dec. 31, 2014	Dec. 31, 2013
Assets		
Cash	$ 918,000	$ 964,800
Accounts receivable (net)	828,900	761,940
Inventories	1,268,460	1,162,980
Prepaid expenses	29,340	35,100
Land	315,900	479,700
Buildings	1,462,500	900,900
Accumulated depreciation—buildings	(408,600)	(382,320)
Equipment	512,280	454,680
Accumulated depreciation—equipment	(141,300)	(158,760)
	$4,785,480	$4,219,020
Liabilities and Stockholders' Equity		
Accounts payable (merchandise creditors)	$ 922,500	$ 958,320
Bonds payable	270,000	0
Common stock, $25 par	317,000	117,000
Paid-in capital: Excess of issue price over par—common stock	758,000	558,000
Retained earnings	2,517,980	2,585,700
	$4,785,480	$4,219,020

The noncurrent asset, noncurrent liability, and stockholders' equity accounts for 2014 are as follows:

ACCOUNT *Land* **ACCOUNT NO.**

Date		Item	Debit	Credit	Balance Debit	Balance Credit
2014						
Jan.	1	Balance			479,700	
Apr.	20	Realized $151,200 cash from sale		163,800	315,900	

ACCOUNT *Buildings* **ACCOUNT NO.**

Date		Item	Debit	Credit	Balance Debit	Balance Credit
2014						
Jan.	1	Balance			900,900	
Apr.	20	Acquired for cash	561,600		1,462,500	

(Continued)

ACCOUNT *Accumulated Depreciation—Buildings*   **ACCOUNT NO.**

Date		Item	Debit	Credit	Balance Debit	Balance Credit
2014						
Jan.	1	Balance				382,320
Dec.	31	Depreciation for year		26,280		408,600

ACCOUNT *Equipment*   **ACCOUNT NO.**

Date		Item	Debit	Credit	Balance Debit	Balance Credit
2014						
Jan.	1	Balance			454,680	
	26	Discarded, no salvage		46,800	407,880	
Aug.	11	Purchased for cash	104,400		512,280	

ACCOUNT *Accumulated Depreciation—Equipment*   **ACCOUNT NO.**

Date		Item	Debit	Credit	Balance Debit	Balance Credit
2014						
Jan.	1	Balance				158,760
	26	Equipment discarded	46,800			111,960
Dec.	31	Depreciation for year		29,340		141,300

ACCOUNT *Bonds Payable*   **ACCOUNT NO.**

Date		Item	Debit	Credit	Balance Debit	Balance Credit
2014						
May	1	Issued 20-year bonds		270,000		270,000

ACCOUNT *Common Stock, $25 par*   **ACCOUNT NO.**

Date		Item	Debit	Credit	Balance Debit	Balance Credit
2014						
Jan.	1	Balance				117,000
Dec.	7	Issued 8,000 shares of common stock for $50 per share		200,000		317,000

ACCOUNT *Paid-In Capital in Excess of Par—Common Stock*   **ACCOUNT NO.**

Date		Item	Debit	Credit	Balance Debit	Balance Credit
2014						
Jan.	1	Balance				558,000
Dec.	7	Issued 8,000 shares of common stock for $50 per share		200,000		758,000

ACCOUNT *Retained Earnings*   **ACCOUNT NO.**

Date		Item	Debit	Credit	Balance Debit	Balance Credit
2014						
Jan.	1	Balance				2,585,700
Dec.	31	Net loss	35,320			2,550,380
	31	Cash dividends	32,400			2,517,980

Instructions

Prepare a statement of cash flows, using the indirect method of presenting cash flows from operating activities.

PR 13-4A Statement of cash flows—direct method   OBJ. 3

✔ Net cash flow from operating activities, $293,600

SPREADSHEET

GENERAL LEDGER

The comparative balance sheet of Canace Products Inc. for December 31, 2014 and 2013, is as follows:

	Dec. 31, 2014	Dec. 31, 2013
Assets		
Cash	$ 643,400	$ 679,400
Accounts receivable (net)	566,800	547,400
Inventories	1,011,000	982,800
Investments	0	240,000
Land	520,000	0
Equipment...	880,000	680,000
Accumulated depreciation	(244,400)	(200,400)
	$3,376,800	$2,929,200
Liabilities and Stockholders' Equity		
Accounts payable (merchandise creditors)	$ 771,800	$ 748,400
Accrued expenses payable (operating expenses)	63,400	70,800
Dividends payable..	8,800	6,400
Common stock, $2 par..	56,000	32,000
Paid-in capital: Excess of issue price over par—common stock	408,000	192,000
Retained earnings..	2,068,800	1,879,600
	$3,376,800	$2,929,200

The income statement for the year ended December 31, 2014, is as follows:

Sales		$5,980,000
Cost of merchandise sold		2,452,000
Gross profit...		$3,528,000
Operating expenses:		
Depreciation expense	$ 44,000	
Other operating expenses	3,100,000	
Total operating expenses		3,144,000
Operating income..		$ 384,000
Other expense:		
Loss on sale of investments		(64,000)
Income before income tax		$ 320,000
Income tax expense		102,800
Net income		$ 217,200

Additional data obtained from an examination of the accounts in the ledger for 2014 are as follows:

a. Equipment and land were acquired for cash.

b. There were no disposals of equipment during the year.

(Continued)

c. The investments were sold for $176,000 cash.

d. The common stock was issued for cash.

e. There was a $28,000 debit to Retained Earnings for cash dividends declared.

Instructions

Prepare a statement of cash flows, using the direct method of presenting cash flows from operating activities.

PR 13-5A   Statement of cash flows—direct method applied to PR 13-1A   OBJ. 3

✔ Net cash flow from operating activities, $148,280

The comparative balance sheet of Charles Inc. for December 31, 2014 and 2013, is as follows:

	Dec. 31, 2014	Dec. 31, 2013
Assets		
Cash	$ 469,320	$ 439,440
Accounts receivable (net)	170,880	156,720
Inventories	481,320	462,840
Investments	0	180,000
Land	246,000	0
Equipment.	528,840	414,840
Accumulated depreciation—equipment	(124,800)	(111,000)
	$1,771,560	$1,542,840
Liabilities and Stockholders' Equity		
Accounts payable (merchandise creditors)	$ 318,360	$ 303,720
Accrued expenses payable (operating expenses)	31,680	39,480
Dividends payable.	18,000	14,400
Common stock, $2 par.	95,000	75,000
Paid-in capital: Excess of issue price over par—common stock	290,000	210,000
Retained earnings.	1,018,520	900,240
	$1,771,560	$1,542,840

The income statement for the year ended December 31, 2014, is as follows:

Sales		$ 5,261,701
Cost of merchandise sold		3,237,970
Gross profit		$2,023,731
Operating expenses:		
Depreciation expense	$ 13,800	
Other operating expenses	1,722,798	
Total operating expenses		1,736,598
Operating income.		$ 287,133
Other income:		
Gain on sale of investments.		30,000
Income before income tax		$ 317,133
Income tax expense		126,853
Net income		$ 190,280

Additional data obtained from an examination of the accounts in the ledger for 2014 are as follows:

a. The investments were sold for $210,000 cash.

b. Equipment and land were acquired for cash.

c. There were no disposals of equipment during the year.

d. The common stock was issued for cash.

e. There was a $72,000 debit to Retained Earnings for cash dividends declared.

Instructions

Prepare a statement of cash flows, using the direct method of presenting cash flows from operating activities.

Problems Series B

PR 13-1B **Statement of cash flows—indirect method** OBJ. 2

✔ Net cash flow from operating activities, $154,260

The comparative balance sheet of Merrick Equipment Co. for December 31, 2014 and 2013, is as follows:

	Dec. 31, 2014	Dec. 31, 2013
Assets		
Cash	$ 70,720	$ 47,940
Accounts receivable (net)	207,230	188,190
Inventories	298,520	289,850
Investments	0	102,000
Land	295,800	0
Equipment..	438,600	358,020
Accumulated depreciation—equipment	(99,110)	(84,320)
	$1,211,760	$901,680
Liabilities and Stockholders' Equity		
Accounts payable (merchandise creditors)	$ 205,700	$194,140
Accrued expenses payable (operating expenses)	30,600	26,860
Dividends payable.......................................	25,500	20,400
Common stock, $1 par...................................	202,000	102,000
Paid-in capital: Excess of issue price over par—common stock	354,000	204,000
Retained earnings.......................................	393,960	354,280
	$1,211,760	$901,680

Additional data obtained from an examination of the accounts in the ledger for 2014 are as follows:

a. Equipment and land were acquired for cash.

b. There were no disposals of equipment during the year.

c. The investments were sold for $91,800 cash.

d. The common stock was issued for cash.

e. There was a $141,680 credit to Retained Earnings for net income.

f. There was a $102,000 debit to Retained Earnings for cash dividends declared.

Instructions

Prepare a statement of cash flows, using the indirect method of presenting cash flows from operating activities.

PR 13-2B **Statement of cash flows—indirect method** OBJ. 2

✔ Net cash flow from operating activities, $561,400

The comparative balance sheet of Harris Industries Inc. at December 31, 2014 and 2013, is as follows:

	Dec. 31, 2014	Dec. 31, 2013
Assets		
Cash	$ 443,240	$ 360,920
Accounts receivable (net)	665,280	592,200
Inventories	887,880	1,022,560
Prepaid expenses	31,640	25,200
Land	302,400	302,400
Buildings	1,713,600	1,134,000
Accumulated depreciation—buildings....................	(466,200)	(414,540)
Machinery and equipment...............................	781,200	781,200
Accumulated depreciation—machinery and equipment.....	(214,200)	(191,520)
Patents...	106,960	112,000
	$4,251,800	$3,724,420

(Continued)

Liabilities and Stockholders' Equity

Accounts payable (merchandise creditors)	$ 837,480	$ 927,080
Dividends payable..	32,760	25,200
Salaries payable...	78,960	87,080
Mortgage note payable, due 2017	224,000	0
Bonds payable	0	390,000
Common stock, $5 par....................................	200,400	50,400
Paid-in capital: Excess of issue price over par—common stock	366,000	126,000
Retained earnings.......................................	2,512,200	2,118,660
	$4,251,800	$3,724,420

An examination of the income statement and the accounting records revealed the following additional information applicable to 2014:

a. Net income, $524,580.

b. Depreciation expense reported on the income statement: buildings, $51,660; machinery and equipment, $22,680.

c. Patent amortization reported on the income statement, $5,040.

d. A building was constructed for $579,600.

e. A mortgage note for $224,000 was issued for cash.

f. 30,000 shares of common stock were issued at $13 in exchange for the bonds payable.

g. Cash dividends declared, $131,040.

Instructions

Prepare a statement of cash flows, using the indirect method of presenting cash flows from operating activities.

PR 13-3B   Statement of cash flows—indirect method   OBJ. 2

✔ Net cash flow from operating activities, $162,800

The comparative balance sheet of Coulson, Inc. at December 31, 2014 and 2013, is as follows:

	Dec. 31, 2014	Dec. 31, 2013
Assets		
Cash	$ 300,600	$ 337,800
Accounts receivable (net)	704,400	609,600
Inventories	918,600	865,800
Prepaid expenses	18,600	26,400
Land	990,000	1,386,000
Buildings	1,980,000	990,000
Accumulated depreciation—buildings.....................	(397,200)	(366,000)
Equipment	660,600	529,800
Accumulated depreciation—equipment	(133,200)	(162,000)
	$5,042,400	$4,217,400
Liabilities and Stockholders' Equity		
Accounts payable (merchandise creditors)	$ 594,000	$ 631,200
Income taxes payable	26,400	21,600
Bonds payable	330,000	0
Common stock, $20 par..................................	320,000	180,000
Paid-in capital: Excess of issue price over par—common stock	950,000	810,000
Retained earnings.......................................	2,822,000	2,574,600
	$5,042,400	$4,217,400

The noncurrent asset, noncurrent liability, and stockholders' equity accounts for 2014 are as follows:

ACCOUNT *Land*   **ACCOUNT NO.**

Date		Item	Debit	Credit	Balance Debit	Balance Credit
2014						
Jan.	1	Balance			1,386,000	
Apr.	20	Realized $456,000 cash from sale		396,000	990,000	

ACCOUNT *Buildings*   **ACCOUNT NO.**

Date		Item	Debit	Credit	Balance Debit	Balance Credit
2014						
Jan.	1	Balance			990,000	
Apr.	20	Acquired for cash	990,000		1,980,000	

ACCOUNT *Accumulated Depreciation—Buildings*   **ACCOUNT NO.**

Date		Item	Debit	Credit	Balance Debit	Balance Credit
2014						
Jan.	1	Balance				366,000
Dec.	31	Depreciation for year		31,200		397,200

ACCOUNT *Equipment*   **ACCOUNT NO.**

Date		Item	Debit	Credit	Balance Debit	Balance Credit
2014						
Jan.	1	Balance			529,800	
	26	Discarded, no salvage		66,000	463,800	
Aug.	11	Purchased for cash	196,800		660,600	

ACCOUNT *Accumulated Depreciation—Equipment*   **ACCOUNT NO.**

Date		Item	Debit	Credit	Balance Debit	Balance Credit
2014						
Jan.	1	Balance				162,000
	26	Equipment discarded	66,000			96,000
Dec.	31	Depreciation for year		37,200		133,200

ACCOUNT *Bonds Payable*   **ACCOUNT NO.**

Date		Item	Debit	Credit	Balance Debit	Balance Credit
2014						
May	1	Issued 20-year bonds		330,000		330,000

(Continued)

ACCOUNT *Common Stock, $10 par*   ACCOUNT NO.

Date		Item	Debit	Credit	Balance Debit	Balance Credit
2014						
Jan.	1	Balance				180,000
Dec.	7	Issued 7,000 shares of common stock for $40 per share		140,000		320,000

ACCOUNT *Paid-In Capital in Excess of Par—Common Stock*   ACCOUNT NO.

Date		Item	Debit	Credit	Balance Debit	Balance Credit
2014						
Jan.	1	Balance				810,000
Dec.	7	Issued 7,000 shares of common stock for $40 per share		140,000		950,000

ACCOUNT *Retained Earnings*   ACCOUNT NO.

Date		Item	Debit	Credit	Balance Debit	Balance Credit
2014						
Jan.	1	Balance				2,574,600
Dec.	31	Net income		326,600		2,901,200
	31	Cash dividends	79,200			2,822,000

Instructions

Prepare a statement of cash flows, using the indirect method of presenting cash flows from operating activities.

PR 13-4B Statement of cash flows—direct method   OBJ. 3

✔ Net cash flow from operating activities, $509,220

The comparative balance sheet of Martinez Inc. for December 31, 2014 and 2013, is as follows:

	Dec. 31, 2014	Dec. 31, 2013
Assets		
Cash	$ 661,920	$ 683,100
Accounts receivable (net)	992,640	914,400
Inventories	1,394,400	1,363,800
Investments	0	432,000
Land	960,000	0
Equipment..	1,224,000	984,000
Accumulated depreciation—equipment	(481,500)	(368,400)
	$4,751,460	$4,008,900
Liabilities and Stockholders' Equity		
Accounts payable (merchandise creditors)	$1,080,000	$ 966,600
Accrued expenses payable (operating expenses)	67,800	79,200
Dividends payable.......................................	100,800	91,200
Common stock, $5 par	130,000	30,000
Paid-in capital: Excess of issue price over par—common stock	950,000	450,000
Retained earnings.......................................	2,422,860	2,391,900
	$4,751,460	$4,008,900

The income statement for the year ended December 31, 2014, is as follows:

Sales		$4,512,000
Cost of merchandise sold		2,352,000
Gross profit		$2,160,000
Operating expenses:		
Depreciation expense	$ 113,100	
Other operating expenses	1,344,840	
Total operating expenses		1,457,940
Operating income.......................................		$ 702,060
Other income:		
Gain on sale of investments...........................		156,000
Income before income tax		$ 858,060
Income tax expense		299,100
Net income		$ 558,960

Additional data obtained from an examination of the accounts in the ledger for 2014 are as follows:

a. Equipment and land were acquired for cash.

b. There were no disposals of equipment during the year.

c. The investments were sold for $588,000 cash.

d. The common stock was issued for cash.

e. There was a $528,000 debit to Retained Earnings for cash dividends declared.

Instructions
Prepare a statement of cash flows, using the direct method of presenting cash flows from operating activities.

✔ Net cash flow from operating activities, $154,260

PR 13-5B   Statement of cash flows—direct method applied to PR 13-1B   OBJ. 3

The comparative balance sheet of Merrick Equipment Co. for Dec. 31, 2014 and 2013, is:

	Dec. 31, 2014	Dec. 31, 2013
Assets		
Cash	$ 70,720	$ 47,940
Accounts receivable (net)	207,230	188,190
Inventories	298,520	289,850
Investments	0	102,000
Land	295,800	0
Equipment..	438,600	358,020
Accumulated depreciation—equipment	(99,110)	(84,320)
	$1,211,760	$ 901,680
Liabilities and Stockholders' Equity		
Accounts payable (merchandise creditors)	$ 205,700	$ 194,140
Accrued expenses payable (operating expenses)	30,600	26,860
Dividends payable...	25,500	20,400
Common stock, $1 par.....................................	202,000	102,000
Paid-in capital: Excess of issue price over par—common stock	354,000	204,000
Retained earnings...	393,960	354,280
	$1,211,760	$ 901,680

(Continued)

The income statement for the year ended December 31, 2014, is as follows:

Sales		$2,023,898
Cost of merchandise sold		1,245,476
Gross profit		$ 778,422
Operating expenses:		
Depreciation expense	$ 14,790	
Other operating expenses	517,299	
Total operating expenses		532,089
Operating income		$ 246,333
Other expenses:		
Loss on sale of investments		(10,200)
Income before income tax		$ 236,133
Income tax expense		94,453
Net income		$ 141,680

Additional data obtained from an examination of the accounts in the ledger for 2014 are as follows:

a. Equipment and land were acquired for cash.

b. There were no disposals of equipment during the year.

c. The investments were sold for $91,800 cash.

d. The common stock was issued for cash.

e. There was a $102,000 debit to Retained Earnings for cash dividends declared.

Instructions

Prepare a statement of cash flows, using the direct method of presenting cash flows from operating activities.

Cases & Projects

CP 13-1 Ethics and professional conduct in business

Lucas Hunter, president of Simmons Industries Inc., believes that reporting operating cash flow per share on the income statement would be a useful addition to the company's just completed financial statements. The following discussion took place between Lucas Hunter and Simmons' controller, John Jameson, in January after the close of the fiscal year.

Lucas: I've been reviewing our financial statements for the last year. I am disappointed that our net income per share has dropped by 10% from last year. This won't look good to our shareholders. Is there anything we can do about this?

John: What do you mean? The past is the past, and the numbers are in. There isn't much that can be done about it. Our financial statements were prepared according to generally accepted accounting principles, and I don't see much leeway for significant change at this point.

Lucas: No, no. I'm not suggesting that we "cook the books." But look at the cash flow from operating activities on the statement of cash flows. The cash flow from operating activities has increased by 20%. This is very good news—and, I might add, useful information. The higher cash flow from operating activities will give our creditors comfort.

John: Well, the cash flow from operating activities is on the statement of cash flows, so I guess users will be able to see the improved cash flow figures there.

Lucas: This is true, but somehow I feel that this information should be given a much higher profile. I don't like this information being "buried" in the statement of cash flows. You know as well as I do that many users will focus on the income statement. Therefore, I think we ought to include an operating cash flow per share number on the face of the income statement—someplace under the earnings per share number. In this way, users will get the complete picture of our operating performance. Yes, our earnings per share dropped this year, but our cash flow from operating activities improved! And all the information is in one place where users can see and compare the figures. What do you think?

John: I've never really thought about it like that before. I guess we could put the operating cash flow per share on the income statement, under the earnings per share. Users would really benefit from this disclosure. Thanks for the idea—I'll start working on it.

Lucas: Glad to be of service.

How would you interpret this situation? Is John behaving in an ethical and professional manner?

CP 13-2 Using the statement of cash flows

You are considering an investment in a new start-up company, Giraffe Inc., an Internet service provider. A review of the company's financial statements reveals a negative retained earnings. In addition, it appears as though the company has been running a negative cash flow from operating activities since the company's inception.

How is the company staying in business under these circumstances? Could this be a good investment?

CP 13-3 Analysis of statement of cash flows

Dillip Lachgar is the president and majority shareholder of Argon Inc., a small retail store chain. Recently, Dillip submitted a loan application for Argon Inc. to Compound Bank. It called for a $600,000, 9%, 10-year loan to help finance the construction of a building and the purchase of store equipment, costing a total of $750,000. This will enable Argon Inc. to open a store in the town of Compound. Land for this purpose was acquired last year. The bank's loan officer requested a statement of cash flows in addition to the most recent income statement, balance sheet, and retained earnings statement that Dillip had submitted with the loan application.

As a close family friend, Dillip asked you to prepare a statement of cash flows. From the records provided, you prepared the following statement:

Argon Inc.
Statement of Cash Flows
For the Year Ended December 31, 2014

Cash flows from operating activities:		
Net income	$ 300,000	
Adjustments to reconcile net income to net cash flow from operating activities:		
Depreciation.	84,000	
Gain on sale of investments	(30,000)	
Changes in current operating assets and liabilities:		
Decrease in accounts receivable	21,000	
Increase in inventories	(42,000)	
Increase in accounts payable	30,000	
Decrease in accrued expenses payable	(6,000)	
Net cash flow from operating activities		$ 357,000
Cash flows from investing activities:		
Cash received from investments sold	$ 180,000	
Less: Cash paid for purchase of store equipment.	(120,000)	
Net cash flow from investing activities		60,000
Cash flows from financing activities:		
Cash paid for dividends.	$ (126,000)	
Net cash flow used for financing activities.		(126,000)
Increase in cash		$ 291,000
Cash at the beginning of the year.		108,000
Cash at the end of the year.		$ 399,000

Schedule of Noncash Financing and Investing Activities:

Issued common stock for land	$ 240,000

(Continued)

After reviewing the statement, Dillip telephoned you and commented, "Are you sure this statement is right?" Dillip then raised the following questions:

1. "How can depreciation be a cash flow?"

2. "Issuing common stock for the land is listed in a separate schedule. This transaction has nothing to do with cash! Shouldn't this transaction be eliminated from the statement?"

3. "How can the gain on the sale of investments be a deduction from net income in determining the cash flow from operating activities?"

4. "Why does the bank need this statement anyway? They can compute the increase in cash from the balance sheets for the last two years."

After jotting down Dillip's questions, you assured him that this statement was "right." But to alleviate Dillip's concern, you arranged a meeting for the following day.

a. ➤ How would you respond to each of Dillip's questions?

b. ➤ Do you think that the statement of cash flows enhances the chances of Argon Inc. receiving the loan? Discuss.

CP 13-4 Analysis of cash flow from operations

The Commercial Division of Tidewater Inc. provided the following information on its cash flow from operations:

Net income	$ 945,000
Increase in accounts receivable	(1,134,000)
Increase in inventory	(1,260,000)
Decrease in accounts payable	(189,000)
Depreciation	210,000
Cash flow from operating activities	$(1,428,000)

The manager of the Commercial Division provided the accompanying memo with this report:

From: Senior Vice President, Commercial Division

I am pleased to report that we had earnings of $945,000 over the last period. This resulted in a return on invested capital of 8%, which is near our targets for this division. I have been aggressive in building the revenue volume in the division. As a result, I am happy to report that we have increased the number of new credit card customers as a result of an aggressive marketing campaign. In addition, we have found some excellent merchandise opportunities. Some of our suppliers have made some of their apparel merchandise available at a deep discount. We have purchased as much of these goods as possible in order to improve profitability. I'm also happy to report that our vendor payment problems have improved. We are nearly caught up on our overdue payables balances.

➤ Comment on the senior vice president's memo in light of the cash flow information.

CP 13-4 Statement of cash flows

Group Project

This activity will require two teams to retrieve cash flow statement information from the Internet. One team is to obtain the most recent year's statement of cash flows for Johnson & Johnson, and the other team the most recent year's statement of cash flows for JetBlue Airways Corp.

The statement of cash flows is included as part of the annual report information that is a required disclosure to the Securities and Exchange Commission (SEC). SEC documents can be retrieved using the EdgarScan™ service at **http://www.sec.gov/edgar/searchedgar/companysearch.html.**

To obtain annual report information, key in a company name in the appropriate space. EdgarScan will list the reports available to you for the company you've selected. Select the most recent annual report filing, identified as a 10-K or 10-K405. EdgarScan provides an outline of the report, including the separate financial statements. You can double-click the income statement and balance sheet for the selected company into an Excel™ spreadsheet for further analysis.

As a group, compare the two statements of cash flows.

a. ⬤➤ How are Johnson & Johnson and JetBlue Airways Corp. similar or different regarding cash flows?

b. Compute and compare the free cash flow for each company, assuming additions to property, plant, and equipment replace current capacity.

Financial Statement Analysis

Nike, Inc.

"**J**ust do it." These three words identify one of the most recognizable brands in the world, **Nike**. While this phrase inspires athletes to "compete and achieve their potential," it also defines the company.

Nike began in 1964 as a partnership between University of Oregon track coach Bill Bowerman and one of his former student-athletes, Phil Knight. The two began by selling shoes imported from Japan out of the back of Knight's car to athletes at track and field events. As sales grew, the company opened retail outlets, calling itself **Blue Ribbon Sports**. The company also began to develop its own shoes. In 1971, the company commissioned a graphic design student at Portland State University to develop the swoosh logo for a fee of $35. In 1978, the company changed its name to Nike, and in 1980, it sold its first shares of stock to the public.

Nike would have been a great company to invest in at the time. If you had invested in Nike's

common stock back in 1990, you would have paid $5.00 per share. As of April 2011, Nike's stock was worth $109.23 per share. Unfortunately, you can't invest using hindsight.

How can you select companies in which to invest? Like any significant purchase, you should do some research to guide your investment decision. If you were buying a car, for example, you might go to **Edmunds.com** to obtain reviews, ratings, prices, specifications, options, and fuel economies to evaluate different vehicles. In selecting companies to invest in, you can use financial analysis to gain insight into a company's past performance and future prospects. This chapter describes and illustrates common financial data that can be analyzed to assist you in making investment decisions such as whether or not to invest in Nike's stock.

Source: http://www.nikebiz.com/.

(OBJ 1) Describe basic financial statement analytical methods.

Basic Analytical Methods

Users analyze a company's financial statements using a variety of analytical methods. Three such methods are as follows:

1. Horizontal analysis
2. Vertical analysis
3. Common-sized statements

Horizontal Analysis

The percentage analysis of increases and decreases in related items in comparative financial statements is called **horizontal analysis**. Each item on the most recent statement is compared with the same item on one or more earlier statements in terms of the following:

1. *Amount* of increase or decrease
2. *Percent* of increase or decrease

When comparing statements, the earlier statement is normally used as the base year for computing increases and decreases.

Exhibit 1 illustrates horizontal analysis for the December 31, 2014 and 2013, balance sheets of Lincoln Company. In Exhibit 1, the December 31, 2013, balance sheet (the earliest year presented) is used as the base year.

Exhibit 1 indicates that total assets decreased by $91,000 (7.4%), liabilities decreased by $133,000 (30.0%), and stockholders' equity increased by $42,000 (5.3%).

Lincoln Company
Comparative Balance Sheet
December 31, 2014 and 2013

	Dec. 31, 2014	Dec. 31, 2013	Increase (Decrease) Amount	Percent
Assets				
Current assets....................................	$ 550,000	$ 533,000	$ 17,000	3.2%
Long-term investments...........................	95,000	177,500	(82,500)	(46.5%)
Property, plant, and equipment (net)	444,500	470,000	(25,500)	(5.4%)
Intangible assets................................	50,000	50,000	—	—
Total assets	$1,139,500	$1,230,500	$ (91,000)	(7.4%)
Liabilities				
Current liabilities...............................	$ 210,000	$ 243,000	$ (33,000)	(13.6%)
Long-term liabilities............................	100,000	200,000	(100,000)	(50.0%)
Total liabilities	$ 310,000	$ 443,000	$(133,000)	(30.0%)
Stockholders' Equity				
Preferred 6% stock, $100 par	$ 150,000	$ 150,000	—	—
Common stock, $10 par.........................	500,000	500,000	—	—
Retained earnings..............................	179,500	137,500	$ 42,000	30.5%
Total stockholders' equity......................	$ 829,500	$ 787,500	$ 42,000	5.3%
Total liabilities and stockholders' equity...........	$1,139,500	$1,230,500	$ (91,000)	(7.4%)

EXHIBIT 1

Comparative Balance Sheet—Horizontal Analysis

Since the long-term investments account decreased by $82,500, it appears that most of the decrease in long-term liabilities of $100,000 was achieved through the sale of long-term investments.

The balance sheets in Exhibit 1 may be expanded or supported by a separate schedule that includes the individual asset and liability accounts. For example, Exhibit 2 is a supporting schedule of Lincoln's current asset accounts.

Exhibit 2 indicates that while cash and temporary investments increased, accounts receivable and inventories decreased. The decrease in accounts receivable could be caused by improved collection policies, which would increase cash. The decrease in inventories could be caused by increased sales.

Lincoln Company
Comparative Schedule of Current Assets
December 31, 2014 and 2013

	Dec. 31, 2014	Dec. 31, 2013	Increase (Decrease) Amount	Percent
Cash	$ 90,500	$ 64,700	$ 25,800	39.9%
Temporary investments.........................	75,000	60,000	15,000	25.0%
Accounts receivable (net).......................	115,000	120,000	(5,000)	(4.2%)
Inventories	264,000	283,000	(19,000)	(6.7%)
Prepaid expenses	5,500	5,300	200	3.8%
Total current assets............................	$550,000	$533,000	$ 17,000	3.2%

EXHIBIT 2

Comparative Schedule of Current Assets—Horizontal Analysis

Exhibit 3 illustrates horizontal analysis for the 2014 and 2013 income statements of Lincoln Company. Exhibit 3 indicates an increase in sales of $296,500, or 24.0%. However, the percentage increase in sales of 24.0% was accompanied by an even greater percentage increase in the cost of goods (merchandise) sold of 27.2%.[1] Thus, gross profit increased by only 19.7% rather than by the 24.0% increase in sales.

1 The term *cost of goods sold* is often used in practice in place of *cost of merchandise sold*. Such usage is followed in this chapter.

© Cengage Learning 2014

EXHIBIT 3

Comparative
Income
Statement—
Horizontal Analysis

Lincoln Company
Comparative Income Statement
For the Years Ended December 31, 2014 and 2013

			Increase (Decrease)	
	2014	**2013**	**Amount**	**Percent**
Sales	$1,530,500	$1,234,000	$296,500	24.0%
Sales returns and allowances	32,500	34,000	(1,500)	(4.4%)
Net sales	$1,498,000	$1,200,000	$298,000	24.8%
Cost of goods sold	1,043,000	820,000	223,000	27.2%
Gross profit	$ 455,000	$ 380,000	$ 75,000	19.7%
Selling expenses	$ 191,000	$ 147,000	$ 44,000	29.9%
Administrative expenses	104,000	97,400	6,600	6.8%
Total operating expenses	$ 295,000	$ 244,400	$ 50,600	20.7%
Income from operations	$ 160,000	$ 135,600	$ 24,400	18.0%
Other income	8,500	11,000	(2,500)	(22.7%)
	$ 168,500	$ 146,600	$ 21,900	14.9%
Other expense (interest)	6,000	12,000	(6,000)	(50.0%)
Income before income tax	$ 162,500	$ 134,600	$ 27,900	20.7%
Income tax expense	71,500	58,100	13,400	23.1%
Net income	$ 91,000	$ 76,500	$ 14,500	19.0%

Exhibit 3 also indicates that selling expenses increased by 29.9%. Thus, the 24.0% increases in sales could have been caused by an advertising campaign, which increased selling expenses. Administrative expenses increased by only 6.8%, total operating expenses increased by 20.7%, and income from operations increased by 18.0%. Interest expense decreased by 50.0%. This decrease was probably caused by the 50.0% decrease in long-term liabilities (Exhibit 1). Overall, net income increased by 19.0%, a favorable result.

Exhibit 4 illustrates horizontal analysis for the 2014 and 2013 retained earnings statements of Lincoln Company. Exhibit 4 indicates that retained earnings increased by 30.5% for the year. The increase is due to net income of $91,000 for the year, less dividends of $49,000.

EXHIBIT 4

Comparative
Retained Earnings
Statement—
Horizontal Analysis

Lincoln Company
Comparative Retained Earnings Statement
For the Years Ended December 31, 2014 and 2013

			Increase (Decrease)	
	2014	**2013**	**Amount**	**Percent**
Retained earnings, January 1	$137,500	$100,000	$37,500	37.5%
Net income for the year	91,000	76,500	14,500	19.0%
Total	$228,500	$176,500	$52,000	29.5%
Dividends:				
On preferred stock	$ 9,000	$ 9,000	—	—
On common stock	40,000	30,000	$10,000	33.3%
Total	$ 49,000	$ 39,000	$10,000	25.6%
Retained earnings, December 31	$179,500	$137,500	$42,000	30.5%

© Cengage Learning 2014

Example Exercise 14-1 Horizontal Analysis

The comparative cash and accounts receivable balances for a company are provided below.

	Dec. 31, 2014	Dec. 31, 2013
Cash	$62,500	$50,000
Accounts receivable (net)	74,400	80,000

Based on this information, what is the amount and percentage of increase or decrease that would be shown on a balance sheet with horizontal analysis?

Follow My Example 14-1

Cash $12,500 increase ($62,500 – $50,000), or 25%
Accounts receivable $5,600 decrease ($74,400 – $80,000), or (7%)

Practice Exercises: **PE 14-1A, PE 14-1B**

Vertical Analysis

The percentage analysis of the relationship of each component in a financial statement to a total within the statement is called **vertical analysis**. Although vertical analysis is applied to a single statement, it may be applied on the same statement over time. This enhances the analysis by showing how the percentages of each item have changed over time.

In vertical analysis of the balance sheet, the percentages are computed as follows:

1. Each asset item is stated as a percent of the total assets.
2. Each liability and stockholders' equity item is stated as a percent of the total liabilities and stockholders' equity.

Exhibit 5 illustrates the vertical analysis of the December 31, 2014 and 2013, balance sheets of Lincoln Company. Exhibit 5 indicates that current assets have increased from 43.3% to 48.3% of total assets. Long-term investments decreased from 14.4% to 8.3% of total assets. Stockholders' equity increased from 64.0% to 72.8%, with a comparable decrease in liabilities.

EXHIBIT 5

Comparative
Balance Sheet—
Vertical Analysis

Lincoln Company
Comparative Balance Sheet
December 31, 2014 and 2013

	Dec. 31, 2014		Dec. 31, 2013	
	Amount	Percent	Amount	Percent
Assets				
Current assets	$ 550,000	48.3%	$ 533,000	43.3%
Long-term investments	95,000	8.3	177,500	14.4
Property, plant, and equipment (net)	444,500	39.0	470,000	38.2
Intangible assets	50,000	4.4	50,000	4.1
Total assets	$1,139,500	100.0%	$1,230,500	100.0%
Liabilities				
Current liabilities	$ 210,000	18.4%	$ 243,000	19.7%
Long-term liabilities	100,000	8.8	200,000	16.3
Total liabilities	$ 310,000	27.2%	$ 443,000	36.0%
Stockholders' Equity				
Preferred 6% stock, $100 par	$ 150,000	13.2%	$ 150,000	12.2%
Common stock, $10 par	500,000	43.9	500,000	40.6
Retained earnings	179,500	15.7	137,500	11.2
Total stockholders' equity	$ 829,500	72.8%	$ 787,500	64.0%
Total liabilities and stockholders' equity	$1,139,500	100.0%	$1,230,500	100.0%

© Cengage Learning 2014

In a vertical analysis of the income statement, each item is stated as a percent of net sales. Exhibit 6 illustrates the vertical analysis of the 2014 and 2013 income statements of Lincoln Company.

Exhibit 6 indicates a decrease in the gross profit rate from 31.7% in 2013 to 30.4% in 2014. Although this is only a 1.3 percentage point (31.7% – 30.4%) decrease, in dollars of potential gross profit, it represents a decrease of $19,500 (1.3% × $1,498,000) based on 2014 net sales. Thus, a small percentage decrease can have a large dollar effect.

EXHIBIT 6		
Comparative Income Statement— Vertical Analysis		

Lincoln Company
Comparative Income Statement
For the Years Ended December 31, 2014 and 2013

	2014 Amount	2014 Percent	2013 Amount	2013 Percent
Sales	$1,530,500	102.2%	$1,234,000	102.8%
Sales returns and allowances	32,500	2.2	34,000	2.8
Net sales	$1,498,000	100.0%	$1,200,000	100.0%
Cost of goods sold	1,043,000	69.6	820,000	68.3
Gross profit	$ 455,000	30.4%	$ 380,000	31.7%
Selling expenses	$ 191,000	12.8%	$ 147,000	12.3%
Administrative expenses	104,000	6.9	97,400	8.1
Total operating expenses	$ 295,000	19.7%	$ 244,400	20.4%
Income from operations	$ 160,000	10.7%	$ 135,600	11.3%
Other income	8,500	0.6	11,000	0.9
	$ 168,500	11.3%	$ 146,600	12.2%
Other expense (interest)	6,000	0.4	12,000	1.0
Income before income tax	$ 162,500	10.9%	$ 134,600	11.2%
Income tax expense	71,500	4.8	58,100	4.8
Net income	$ 91,000	6.1%	$ 76,500	6.4%

© Cengage Learning 2014

Example Exercise **14-2** **Vertical Analysis** OBJ 1

Income statement information for Lee Corporation is provided below.

Sales	$100,000
Cost of goods sold	65,000
Gross profit	$ 35,000

Prepare a vertical analysis of the income statement for Lee Corporation.

Follow My Example 14-2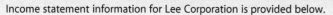

	Amount	Percentage	
Sales	$100,000	100%	($100,000 ÷ $100,000)
Cost of goods sold	65,000	65	($65,000 ÷ $100,000)
Gross profit	$ 35,000	35%	($35,000 ÷ $100,000)

Practice Exercises: **PE 14-2A, PE 14-2B**

Common-Sized Statements

In a **common-sized statement**, all items are expressed as percentages, with no dollar amounts shown. Common-sized statements are often useful for comparing one company with another or for comparing a company with industry averages.

Exhibit 7 illustrates common-sized income statements for Lincoln Company and Madison Corporation. Exhibit 7 indicates that Lincoln Company has a slightly higher

EXHIBIT 7

Common-Sized Income Statements

	Lincoln Company	Madison Corporation
Sales	102.2%	102.3%
Sales returns and allowances	2.2	2.3
Net sales	100.0%	100.0%
Cost of goods sold	69.6	70.0
Gross profit	30.4%	30.0%
Selling expenses	12.8%	11.5%
Administrative expenses	6.9	4.1
Total operating expenses	19.7%	15.6%
Income from operations	10.7%	14.4%
Other income	0.6	0.6
	11.3%	15.0%
Other expense (interest)	0.4	0.5
Income before income tax	10.9%	14.5%
Income tax expense	4.8	5.5
Net income	6.1%	9.0%

© Cengage Learning 2014

rate of gross profit (30.4%) than Madison Corporation (30.0%). However, Lincoln has a higher percentage of selling expenses (12.8%) and administrative expenses (6.9%) than does Madison (11.5% and 4.1%). As a result, the income from operations of Lincoln (10.7%) is less than that of Madison (14.4%).

The unfavorable difference of 3.7 (14.4% – 10.7%) percentage points in income from operations would concern the managers and other stakeholders of Lincoln. The underlying causes of the difference should be investigated and possibly corrected. For example, Lincoln Company may decide to outsource some of its administrative duties so that its administrative expenses are more comparative to that of Madison Corporation.

Other Analytical Measures

Other relationships may be expressed in ratios and percentages. Often, these relationships are compared within the same statement and, thus, are a type of vertical analysis. Comparing these items with items from earlier periods is a type of horizontal analysis.

Analytical measures are not a definitive conclusion. They are only guides in evaluating financial and operating data. Many other factors, such as trends in the industry and general economic conditions, should also be considered when analyzing a company.

Liquidity and Solvency Analysis

OBJ 2 Use financial statement analysis to assess the solvency of a business.

All users of financial statements are interested in the ability of a company to do the following:

1. Maintain **liquidity** and **solvency**
2. Earn income, called **profitability**

The ability of a company to convert assets into cash is called liquidity, while the ability of a company to pay its debts is called solvency. Liquidity, solvency, and profitability are interrelated. For example, a company that cannot convert assets into cash may have difficulty taking advantage of profitable courses of action requiring immediate cash outlays. Likewise, a company that cannot pay its debts will have difficulty obtaining credit. A lack of credit will, in turn, limit the company's ability to purchase merchandise or expand operations, which decreases its profitability.

Liquidity and solvency are normally assessed using the following:

1. Current position analysis
    Working capital
    Current ratio
    Quick ratio

One popular printed source for industry ratios is *Annual Statement Studies* from Risk Management Association. Online analysis is available from Zacks Investment Research site, which is linked to the text's Web site at **www.cengagebrain.com.**

2. Accounts receivable analysis
    Accounts receivable turnover
    Number of days' sales in receivables

3. Inventory analysis
    Inventory turnover
    Number of days' sales in inventory

4. The ratio of fixed assets to long-term liabilities
5. The ratio of liabilities to stockholders' equity
6. The number of times interest charges are earned

The Lincoln Company financial statements presented earlier are used to illustrate the preceding analyses.

Current Position Analysis

A company's ability to pay its current liabilities is called **current position analysis**. It is a solvency measure of special interest to short-term creditors and includes the computation and analysis of the following:

1. Working capital
2. Current ratio
3. Quick ratio

Working Capital A company's **working capital** is computed as follows:

$$\text{Working Capital} = \text{Current Assets} - \text{Current Liabilities}$$

To illustrate, the working capital for Lincoln Company for 2014 and 2013 is computed below.

	2014	2013
Current assets	$550,000	$533,000
Less current liabilities	210,000	243,000
Working capital	$340,000	$290,000

The working capital is used to evaluate a company's ability to pay current liabilities. A company's working capital is often monitored monthly, quarterly, or yearly by creditors and other debtors. However, it is difficult to use working capital to compare companies of different sizes. For example, working capital of $250,000 may be adequate for a local hardware store, but it would be inadequate for The Home Depot.

Current Ratio The **current ratio**, sometimes called the *working capital ratio*, is computed as follows:

$$\text{Current Ratio} = \frac{\text{Current Assets}}{\text{Current Liabilities}}$$

To illustrate, the current ratio for Lincoln Company is computed below.

	2014	2013
Current assets	$550,000	$533,000
Current liabilities	$210,000	$243,000
Current ratio	2.6 ($550,000/$210,000)	2.2 ($533,000/$243,000)

The current ratio is a more reliable indicator of a company's ability to pay its current liabilities than is working capital, and it is much easier to compare across companies. To illustrate, assume that as of December 31, 2014, the working capital of a competitor is much greater than $340,000, but its current ratio is only 1.3. Considering these facts alone, Lincoln Company, with its current ratio of 2.6, is in a more favorable position to obtain short-term credit than the competitor, which has the greater amount of working capital.

Quick Ratio One limitation of working capital and the current ratio is that they do not consider the types of current assets a company has and how easily they can be turned in to cash. Because of this, two companies may have the same working capital and current ratios, but differ significantly in their ability to pay their current liabilities.

To illustrate, the current assets and liabilities for Lincoln Company and Jefferson Corporation as of December 31, 2014, are as follows:

	Lincoln Company	Jefferson Corporation
Current assets:		
Cash	$ 90,500	$ 45,500
Temporary investments	75,000	25,000
Accounts receivable (net)	115,000	90,000
Inventories	264,000	380,000
Prepaid expenses	5,500	9,500
Total current assets	$550,000	$550,000
Total current assets	$550,000	$550,000
Less current liabilities	210,000	210,000
Working capital	$340,000	$340,000
Current ratio ($550,000/$210,000)	2.6	2.6

Lincoln and Jefferson both have a working capital of $340,000 and current ratios of 2.6. Jefferson, however, has more of its current assets in inventories. These inventories must be sold and the receivables collected before all the current liabilities can be paid. This takes time. In addition, if the market for its product declines, Jefferson may have difficulty selling its inventory. This, in turn, could impair its ability to pay its current liabilities.

In contrast, Lincoln's current assets contain more cash, temporary investments, and accounts receivable, which can easily be converted to cash. Thus, Lincoln is in a stronger current position than Jefferson to pay its current liabilities.

A ratio that measures the "instant" debt-paying ability of a company is the **quick ratio**, sometimes called the *acid-test ratio*. The quick ratio is computed as follows:

$$\text{Quick Ratio} = \frac{\text{Quick Assets}}{\text{Current Liabilities}}$$

Quick assets are cash and other current assets that can be easily converted to cash. Quick assets normally include cash, temporary investments, and receivables, but exclude inventories and prepaid assets.

To illustrate, the quick ratio for Lincoln Company is computed below.

	2014	2013
Quick assets:		
Cash	$ 90,500	$ 64,700
Temporary investments	75,000	60,000
Accounts receivable (net)	115,000	120,000
Total quick assets	$280,500	$244,700
Current liabilities	$210,000	$243,000
Quick ratio	1.3 ($280,500 ÷ $210,000)	1.0 ($244,700 ÷ $243,000)

Example Exercise 14-3   Current Position Analysis

The following items are reported on a company's balance sheet:

Cash	$300,000
Temporary investments	100,000
Accounts receivable (net)	200,000
Inventory	200,000
Accounts payable	400,000

Determine (a) the current ratio and (b) the quick ratio.

Follow My Example 14-3 ⟩⟩

a. Current Ratio = Current Assets ÷ Current Liabilities

Current Ratio = ($300,000 + $100,000 + $200,000 + $200,000) ÷ $400,000

Current Ratio = 2.0

b. Quick Ratio = Quick Assets ÷ Current Liabilities

Quick Ratio = ($300,000 + $100,000 + $200,000) ÷ $400,000

Quick Ratio = 1.5

Practice Exercises: **PE 14-3A, PE 14-3B**

Accounts Receivable Analysis

A company's ability to collect its accounts receivable is called **accounts receivable analysis**. It includes the computation and analysis of the following:

1. Accounts receivable turnover
2. Number of days' sales in receivables

Collecting accounts receivable as quickly as possible improves a company's liquidity. In addition, the cash collected from receivables may be used to improve or expand operations. Quick collection of receivables also reduces the risk of uncollectible accounts.

Accounts Receivable Turnover   The **accounts receivable turnover** is computed as follows:

$$\text{Accounts Receivable Turnover} = \frac{\text{Net Sales}^2}{\text{Average Accounts Receivable}}$$

To illustrate, the accounts receivable turnover for Lincoln Company for 2014 and 2013 is computed below. Lincoln's accounts receivable balance at the beginning of 2013 is $140,000.

	2014	2013
Net sales	$1,498,000	$1,200,000
Accounts receivable (net):		
Beginning of year	$ 120,000	$ 140,000
End of year	115,000	120,000
Total	$ 235,000	$ 260,000
Average accounts receivable	$117,500 ($235,000 ÷ 2)	$130,000 ($260,000 ÷ 2)
Accounts receivable turnover	12.7 ($1,498,000 ÷ $117,500)	9.2 ($1,200,000 ÷ $130,000)

The increase in Lincoln's accounts receivable turnover from 9.2 to 12.7 indicates that the collection of receivables has improved during 2014. This may be due to a change in how credit is granted, collection practices, or both.

For Lincoln Company, the average accounts receivable was computed using the accounts receivable balance at the beginning and the end of the year. When sales

2 If known, *credit* sales should be used in the numerator. Because credit sales are not normally known by external users, we use net sales in the numerator.

are seasonal and, thus, vary throughout the year, monthly balances of receivables are often used. Also, if sales on account include notes receivable as well as accounts receivable, notes and accounts receivable are normally combined for analysis.

Number of Days' Sales in Receivables The **number of days' sales in receivables** is computed as follows:

$$\text{Number of Days' Sales in Receivables} = \frac{\text{Average Accounts Receivable}}{\text{Average Daily Sales}}$$

where

$$\text{Average Daily Sales} = \frac{\text{Net Sales}}{365 \text{ days}}$$

To illustrate, the number of days' sales in receivables for Lincoln Company is computed below.

	2014	2013
Average accounts receivable	$117,500 ($235,000 ÷ 2)	$130,000 ($260,000 ÷ 2)
Average daily sales	$4,104 ($1,498,000 ÷ 365)	$3,288 ($1,200,000 ÷ 365)
Number of days' sales in receivables	28.6 ($117,500 ÷ $4,104)	39.5 ($130,000 ÷ $3,288)

The number of days' sales in receivables is an estimate of the time (in days) that the accounts receivable have been outstanding. The number of days' sales in receivables is often compared with a company's credit terms to evaluate the efficiency of the collection of receivables.

To illustrate, if Lincoln's credit terms are 2/10, n/30, then Lincoln was very *inefficient* in collecting receivables in 2013. In other words, receivables should have been collected in 30 days or less, but were being collected in 39.5 days. Although collections improved during 2014 to 28.6 days, there is probably still room for improvement. On the other hand, if Lincoln's credit terms are n/45, then there is probably little room for improving collections.

Example Exercise 14-4 **Accounts Receivable Analysis**

A company reports the following:

Net sales	$960,000
Average accounts receivable (net)	48,000

Determine (a) the accounts receivable turnover and (b) the number of days' sales in receivables. Round to one decimal place.

Follow My Example 14-4

a. Accounts Receivable Turnover = Net Sales ÷ Average Accounts Receivable
    Accounts Receivable Turnover = $960,000 ÷ $48,000
    Accounts Receivable Turnover = 20.0
b. Number of Days' Sales in Receivables = Average Accounts Receivable ÷ Average Daily Sales
    Number of Days' Sales in Receivables = $48,000 ÷ ($960,000 ÷ 365) = $48,000 ÷ $2,630
    Number of Days' Sales in Receivables = 18.3 days

Practice Exercises: **PE 14-4A, PE 14-4B**

Inventory Analysis

A company's ability to manage its inventory effectively is evaluated using **inventory analysis**. It includes the computation and analysis of the following:

1. Inventory turnover
2. Number of days' sales in inventory

Excess inventory decreases liquidity by tying up funds (cash) in inventory. In addition, excess inventory increases insurance expense, property taxes, storage costs, and other related expenses. These expenses further reduce funds that could be used elsewhere to improve or expand operations.

Excess inventory also increases the risk of losses because of price declines or obsolescence of the inventory. On the other hand, a company should keep enough inventory in stock so that it doesn't lose sales because of lack of inventory.

Inventory Turnover The **inventory turnover** is computed as follows:

$$\text{Inventory Turnover} = \frac{\text{Cost of Goods Sold}}{\text{Average Inventory}}$$

To illustrate, the inventory turnover for Lincoln Company for 2014 and 2013 is computed below. Lincoln's inventory balance at the beginning of 2013 is $311,000.

	2014	**2013**
Cost of goods sold	$1,043,000	$820,000
Inventories:		
Beginning of year	$ 283,000	$311,000
End of year	264,000	283,000
Total	$ 547,000	$594,000
Average inventory	$273,500 ($547,000 ÷ 2)	$297,000 ($594,000 ÷ 2)
Inventory turnover	3.8 ($1,043,000 ÷ $273,500)	2.8 ($820,000 ÷ $297,000)

The increase in Lincoln's inventory turnover from 2.8 to 3.8 indicates that the management of inventory has improved in 2014. The inventory turnover improved because of an increase in the cost of goods sold, which indicates more sales, and a decrease in the average inventories.

What is considered a good inventory turnover varies by type of inventory, companies, and industries. For example, grocery stores have a higher inventory turnover than jewelers or furniture stores. Likewise, within a grocery store, perishable foods have a higher turnover than the soaps and cleansers.

Number of Days' Sales in Inventory The **number of days' sales in inventory** is computed as follows:

$$\text{Number of Days' Sales in Inventory} = \frac{\text{Average Inventory}}{\text{Average Daily Cost of Goods Sold}}$$

where

$$\text{Average Daily Cost of Goods Sold} = \frac{\text{Cost of Goods Sold}}{365 \text{ days}}$$

To illustrate, the number of days' sales in inventory for Lincoln Company is computed below.

	2014	**2013**
Average inventory	$273,500 ($547,000 ÷ 2)	$297,000 ($594,000 ÷ 2)
Average daily cost of goods sold	$2,858 ($1,043,000 ÷ 365)	$2,247 ($820,000 ÷ 365)
Number of days' sales in inventory	95.7 ($273,500 ÷ $2,858)	132.2 ($297,000 ÷ $2,247)

The number of days' sales in inventory is a rough measure of the length of time it takes to purchase, sell, and replace the inventory. Lincoln's number of days' sales in inventory improved from 132.2 days to 95.7 days during 2014. This is a major improvement in managing inventory.

Example Exercise 14-5   Inventory Analysis

A company reports the following:

Cost of goods sold	$560,000
Average inventory	112,000

Determine (a) the inventory turnover and (b) the number of days' sales in inventory. Round to one decimal place.

Follow My Example 14-5

a. Inventory Turnover = Cost of Goods Sold ÷ Average Inventory

    Inventory Turnover = $560,000 ÷ $112,000

    Inventory Turnover = 5.0

b. Number of Days' Sales in Inventory = Average Inventory ÷ Average Daily Cost of Goods Sold

    Number of Days' Sales in Inventory = $112,000 ÷ ($560,000 ÷ 365) = $112,000 ÷ $1,534

    Number of Days' Sales in Inventory = 73.0 days

Practice Exercises: **PE 14-5A, PE 14-5B**

Ratio of Fixed Assets to Long-Term Liabilities

The **ratio of fixed assets to long-term liabilities** provides a measure of whether noteholders or bondholders will be paid. Since fixed assets are often pledged as security for long-term notes and bonds, it is computed as follows:

$$\text{Ratio of Fixed Assets to Long-Term Liabilities} = \frac{\text{Fixed Assets (net)}}{\text{Long-Term Liabilities}}$$

To illustrate, the ratio of fixed assets to long-term liabilities for Lincoln Company is computed below.

	2014	**2013**
Fixed assets (net)	$444,500	$470,000
Long-term liabilities	$100,000	$200,000
Ratio of fixed assets to long-term liabilities	4.4 ($444,500 ÷ $100,000)	2.4 ($470,000 ÷ $200,000)

During 2014, Lincoln's ratio of fixed assets to long-term liabilities increased from 2.4 to 4.4. This increase was due primarily to Lincoln paying off one-half of its long-term liabilities in 2014.

Ratio of Liabilities to Stockholders' Equity

The **ratio of liabilities to stockholders' equity** measures how much of the company is financed by debt and equity. It is computed as follows:

$$\text{Ratio of Liabilities to Stockholders' Equity} = \frac{\text{Total Liabilities}}{\text{Total Stockholders' Equity}}$$

To illustrate, the ratio of liabilities to stockholders' equity for Lincoln Company is computed below.

	2014	**2013**
Total liabilities	$310,000	$443,000
Total stockholders' equity	$829,500	$787,500
Ratio of liabilities to stockholders' equity	0.4 ($310,000 ÷ $829,500)	0.6 ($443,000 ÷ $787,500)

Lincoln's ratio of liabilities to stockholders' equity decreased from 0.6 to 0.4 during 2014. This is an improvement and indicates that Lincoln's creditors have an adequate margin of safety.

Example Exercise 14-6 **Long-Term Solvency Analysis**

The following information was taken from Acme Company's balance sheet:

Fixed assets (net)	$1,400,000
Long-term liabilities	400,000
Total liabilities	560,000
Total stockholders' equity	1,400,000

Determine the company's (a) ratio of fixed assets to long-term liabilities and (b) ratio of liabilities to total stockholders' equity.

Follow My Example 14-6

a. Ratio of Fixed Assets to Long-Term Liabilities = Fixed Assets ÷ Long-Term Liabilities

Ratio of Fixed Assets to Long-Term Liabilities = $1,400,000 ÷ $400,000

Ratio of Fixed Assets to Long-Term Liabilities = 3.5

b. Ratio of Liabilities to Total Stockholders' Equity = Total Liabilities ÷ Total Stockholders' Equity

Ratio of Liabilities to Total Stockholders' Equity = $560,000 ÷ $1,400,000

Ratio of Liabilities to Total Stockholders' Equity = 0.4

Practice Exercises: **PE 14-6A, PE 14-6B**

Number of Times Interest Charges Are Earned

The **number of times interest charges are earned**, sometimes called the *fixed charge coverage ratio*, measures the risk that interest payments will not be made if earnings decrease. It is computed as follows:

$$\text{Number of Times Interest Charges Are Earned} = \frac{\text{Income Before Income Tax} + \text{Interest Expense}}{\text{Interest Expense}}$$

Interest expense is paid before income taxes. In other words, interest expense is deducted in determining taxable income and, thus, income tax. For this reason, income *before taxes* is used in computing the number of times interest charges are earned.

The *higher* the ratio the more likely interest payments will be paid if earnings decrease. To illustrate, the number of times interest charges are earned for Lincoln Company is computed below.

	2014	2013
Income before income tax	$162,500	$134,600
Add interest expense	6,000	12,000
Amount available to pay interest	$168,500	$146,600
Number of times interest charges are earned	28.1 ($168,500 ÷ $6,000)	12.2 ($146,600 ÷ $12,000)

The number of times interest charges are earned improved from 12.2 to 28.1 during 2014. This indicates that Lincoln Company has sufficient earnings to pay interest expense.

The number of times interest charges are earned can be adapted for use with dividends on preferred stock. In this case, the *number of times preferred dividends are earned* is computed as follows:

$$\text{Number of Times Preferred Dividends Are Earned} = \frac{\text{Net Income}}{\text{Preferred Dividends}}$$

Since dividends are paid after taxes, net income is used in computing the number of times preferred dividends are earned. The *higher* the ratio, the more likely preferred dividend payments will be paid if earnings decrease.

Example Exercise 14-7 **Times Interest Charges Are Earned**

A company reports the following:

Income before income tax	$250,000
Interest expense	100,000

Determine the number of times interest charges are earned.

Follow My Example 14-7 ▶▶

Number of Times Interest Charges Are Earned = (Income Before Income Tax + Interest Expense) ÷ Interest Expense
Number of Times Interest Charges Are Earned = ($250,000 + $100,000) ÷ $100,000
Number of Times Interest Charges Are Earned = 3.5

Practice Exercises: **PE 14-7A, PE 14-7B**

Profitability Analysis

 Use financial statement analysis to assess the profitability of a business.

Profitability analysis focuses on the ability of a company to earn profits. This ability is reflected in the company's operating results, as reported in its income statement. The ability to earn profits also depends on the assets the company has available for use in its operations, as reported in its balance sheet. Thus, income statement and balance sheet relationships are often used in evaluating profitability.

Common profitability analyses include the following:

1. Ratio of net sales to assets
2. Rate earned on total assets
3. Rate earned on stockholders' equity
4. Rate earned on common stockholders' equity
5. Earnings per share on common stock
6. Price-earnings ratio
7. Dividends per share
8. Dividend yield

Note:
Profitability analysis focuses on the relationship between operating results and the resources available to a business.

Ratio of Net Sales to Assets

The **ratio of net sales to assets** measures how effectively a company uses its assets. It is computed as follows:

$$\text{Ratio of Net Sales to Assets} = \frac{\text{Net Sales}}{\substack{\text{Average Total Assets} \\ \text{(excluding long-term investments)}}}$$

As shown above, any long-term investments are excluded in computing the ratio of net sales to assets. This is because long-term investments are unrelated to normal operations and net sales.

To illustrate, the ratio of net sales to assets for Lincoln Company is computed below. Total assets (excluding long-term investments) are $1,010,000 at the beginning of 2013.

	2014	2013
Net sales	$1,498,000	$1,200,000
Total assets (excluding long-term investments):		
Beginning of year	$1,053,000*	$1,010,000
End of year	1,044,500**	1,053,000***
Total	$2,097,500	$2,063,000
Average total assets	$1,048,750 ($2,097,500 ÷ 2)	$1,031,500 ($2,063,000 ÷ 2)
Ratio of net sales to assets	1.4 ($1,498,000 ÷ $1,048,750)	1.2 ($1,200,000 ÷ $1,031,500)

  *($1,230,500 – $177,500)
  **($1,139,500 – $95,000)
  ***($1,230,500 – $177,500)

For Lincoln Company, the average total assets was computed using total assets (excluding long-term investments) at the beginning and end of the year. The average total assets could also be based on monthly or quarterly averages.

The ratio of net sales to assets indicates that Lincoln's use of its operating assets has improved in 2014. This was primarily due to the increase in net sales in 2014.

Example Exercise 14-8 **Net Sales to Assets** **OBJ 3**

A company reports the following:

Net sales	$2,250,000
Average total assets	1,500,000

Determine the ratio of net sales to assets.

Follow My Example 14-8

Ratio of Net Sales to Assets = Net Sales ÷ Average Total Assets
Ratio of Net Sales to Assets = $2,250,000 ÷ $1,500,000
Ratio of Net Sales to Assets = 1.5

Practice Exercises: **PE 14-8A, PE 14-8B**

Rate Earned on Total Assets

The **rate earned on total assets** measures the profitability of total assets, without considering how the assets are financed. In other words, this rate is not affected by the portion of assets financed by creditors or stockholders. It is computed as follows:

$$\text{Rate Earned on Total Assets} = \frac{\text{Net Income} + \text{Interest Expense}}{\text{Average Total Assets}}$$

The rate earned on total assets is computed by adding interest expense to net income. By adding interest expense to net income, the effect of whether the assets are financed by creditors (debt) or stockholders (equity) is eliminated. Because net income includes any income earned from long-term investments, the average total assets includes long-term investments as well as the net operating assets.

To illustrate, the rate earned on total assets by Lincoln Company is computed below. Total assets are $1,187,500 at the beginning of 2013.

	2014	2013
Net income	$ 91,000	$ 76,500
Plus interest expense	6,000	12,000
Total	$ 97,000	$ 88,500
Total assets:		
Beginning of year	$1,230,500	$1,187,500
End of year	1,139,500	1,230,500
Total	$2,370,000	$2,418,000
Average total assets	$1,185,000 ($2,370,000 ÷ 2)	$1,209,000 ($2,418,000 ÷ 2)
Rate earned on total assets	8.2% ($97,000 ÷ $1,185,000)	7.3% ($88,500 ÷ $1,209,000)

The rate earned on total assets improved from 7.3% to 8.2% during 2014.

The *rate earned on operating assets* is sometimes computed when there are large amounts of nonoperating income and expense. It is computed as follows:

$$\text{Rate Earned on Operating Assets} = \frac{\text{Income from Operations}}{\text{Average Operating Assets}}$$

Since Lincoln Company does not have a significant amount of nonoperating income and expense, the rate earned on operating assets is not illustrated.

Example Exercise 14-9 Rate Earned on Total Assets

A company reports the following income statement and balance sheet information for the current year:

Net income	$ 125,000
Interest expense	25,000
Average total assets	2,000,000

Determine the rate earned on total assets.

Follow My Example 14-9

Rate Earned on Total Assets = (Net Income + Interest Expense) ÷ Average Total Assets
Rate Earned on Total Assets = ($125,000 + $25,000) ÷ $2,000,000
Rate Earned on Total Assets = $150,000 ÷ $2,000,000
Rate Earned on Total Assets = 7.5%

Practice Exercises: **PE 14-9A, PE 14-9B**

Rate Earned on Stockholders' Equity

The **rate earned on stockholders' equity** measures the rate of income earned on the amount invested by the stockholders. It is computed as follows:

$$\text{Rate Earned on Stockholders' Equity} = \frac{\text{Net Income}}{\text{Average Total Stockholders' Equity}}$$

To illustrate, the rate earned on stockholders' equity for Lincoln Company is computed below. Total stockholders' equity is $750,000 at the beginning of 2013.

	2014	2013
Net income	$ 91,000	$ 76,500
Stockholders' equity:		
Beginning of year	$ 787,500	$ 750,000
End of year	829,500	787,500
Total	$1,617,000	$1,537,500
Average stockholders' equity	$808,500 ($1,617,000 ÷ 2)	$768,750 ($1,537,500 ÷ 2)
Rate earned on stockholders' equity	11.3% ($91,000 ÷ $808,500)	10.0% ($76,500 ÷ $768,750)

The rate earned on stockholders' equity improved from 10.0% to 11.3% during 2014.

Leverage involves using debt to increase the return on an investment. The rate earned on stockholders' equity is normally higher than the rate earned on total assets. This is because of the effect of leverage.

For Lincoln Company, the effect of leverage for 2014 is 3.1% and for 2013 is 2.7% computed as follows:

	2014	2013
Rate earned on stockholders' equity	11.3%	10.0%
Less rate earned on total assets	8.2	7.3
Effect of leverage	3.1%	2.7%

Exhibit 8 shows the 2014 and 2013 effects of leverage for Lincoln Company.

Rate Earned on Common Stockholders' Equity

The **rate earned on common stockholders' equity** measures the rate of profits earned on the amount invested by the common stockholders. It is computed as follows:

$$\text{Rate Earned on Common Stockholders' Equity} = \frac{\text{Net Income} - \text{Preferred Dividends}}{\text{Average Common Stockholders' Equity}}$$

EXHIBIT 8

Effect of Leverage

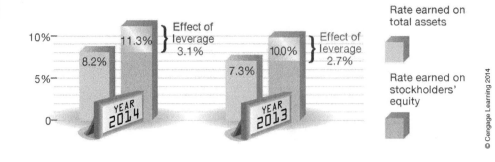

Because preferred stockholders rank ahead of the common stockholders in their claim on earnings, any preferred dividends are subtracted from net income in computing the rate earned on common stockholders' equity.

Lincoln Company had $150,000 of 6% preferred stock outstanding on December 31, 2014 and 2013. Thus, preferred dividends of $9,000 ($150,000 × 6%) are deducted from net income. Lincoln's common stockholders' equity is determined as follows:

	December 31		
	2014	**2013**	**2012**
Common stock, $10 par	$500,000	$500,000	$500,000
Retained earnings	179,500	137,500	100,000
Common stockholders' equity	$679,500	$637,500	$600,000

The retained earnings on December 31, 2012, of $100,000 is the same as the retained earnings on January 1, 2013, as shown in Lincoln's retained earnings statement in Exhibit 4.

Using this information, the rate earned on common stockholders' equity for Lincoln Company is computed below.

	2014	**2013**
Net income	$ 91,000	$ 76,500
Less preferred dividends	9,000	9,000
Total	$ 82,000	$ 67,500
Common stockholders' equity:		
Beginning of year	$ 637,500	$ 600,000
End of year	679,500*	637,500**
Total	$1,317,000	$1,237,500
Average common stockholders' equity	$658,500 ($1,317,000 ÷ 2)	$618,750 ($1,237,500 ÷ 2)
Rate earned on common stockholders' equity	12.5% ($82,000 ÷ $658,500)	10.9% ($67,500 ÷ $618,750)

*($829,500 – $150,000)
**($787,500 – $150,000)

Lincoln Company's rate earned on common stockholders' equity improved from 10.9% to 12.5% in 2014. This rate differs from the rates earned by Lincoln Company on total assets and stockholders' equity as shown below.

	2014	2013
Rate earned on total assets	8.2%	7.3%
Rate earned on stockholders' equity	11.3%	10.0%
Rate earned on common stockholders' equity	12.5%	10.9%

These rates differ because of leverage, as discussed in the preceding section.

Example Exercise 14-10 **Common Stockholders' Profitability Analysis**

A company reports the following:

Net income	$ 125,000
Preferred dividends	5,000
Average stockholders' equity	1,000,000
Average common stockholders' equity	800,000

Determine (a) the rate earned on stockholders' equity and (b) the rate earned on common stockholders' equity.

Follow My Example 14-10 〉〉

a. Rate Earned on Stockholders' Equity = Net Income ÷ Average Stockholders' Equity

  Rate Earned on Stockholders' Equity = $125,000 ÷ $1,000,000

  Rate Earned on Stockholders' Equity = 12.5%

b. Rate Earned on Common Stockholders' Equity = (Net Income – Preferred Dividends) ÷ Average
  Common Stockholders' Equity

  Rate Earned on Common Stockholders' Equity = ($125,000 – $5,000) ÷ $800,000

  Rate Earned on Common Stockholders' Equity = 15%

Practice Exercises: **PE 14-10A, PE 14-10B**

Earnings per Share on Common Stock

Earnings per share (EPS) on common stock measures the share of profits that are earned by a share of common stock. Earnings per share must be reported in the income statement. As a result, earnings per share (EPS) is often reported in the financial press. It is computed as follows:

$$\text{Earnings per Share (EPS) on Common Stock} = \frac{\text{Net Income} - \text{Preferred Dividends}}{\text{Shares of Common Stock Outstanding}}$$

When preferred and common stock are outstanding, preferred dividends are subtracted from net income to determine the income related to the common shares.

To illustrate, the earnings per share (EPS) of common stock for Lincoln Company is computed below.

	2014	**2013**
Net income	$91,000	$76,500
Preferred dividends	9,000	9,000
Total	$82,000	$67,500
Shares of common stock outstanding	50,000	50,000
Earnings per share on common stock	$1.64 ($82,000 ÷ 50,000)	$1.35 ($67,500 ÷ 50,000)

Lincoln Company had $150,000 of 6% preferred stock outstanding on December 31, 2014 and 2013. Thus, preferred dividends of $9,000 ($150,000 × 6%) are deducted from net income in computing earnings per share on common stock.

Lincoln did not issue any additional shares of common stock in 2014. If Lincoln had issued additional shares in 2014, a weighted average of common shares outstanding during the year would have been used.

Lincoln's earnings per share (EPS) on common stock improved from $1.35 to $1.64 during 2014.

Lincoln Company has a simple capital structure with only common stock and preferred stock outstanding. Many corporations, however, have complex capital structures with various types of equity securities outstanding, such as convertible preferred stock,

stock options, and stock warrants. In such cases, the possible effects of such securities on the shares of common stock outstanding are considered in reporting earnings per share. These possible effects are reported separately as *earnings per common share assuming dilution* or *diluted earnings per share*. This topic is described and illustrated in advanced accounting courses and textbooks.

Price-Earnings Ratio

The **price-earnings (P/E) ratio** on common stock measures a company's future earnings prospects. It is often quoted in the financial press and is computed as follows:

$$\text{Price-Earnings (P/E) Ratio} = \frac{\text{Market Price per Share of Common Stock}}{\text{Earnings per Share on Common Stock}}$$

To illustrate, the price-earnings (P/E) ratio for Lincoln Company is computed below.

	2014	2013
Market price per share of common stock	$41.00	$27.00
Earnings per share on common stock	$1.64	$1.35
Price-earnings ratio on common stock	25 ($41 ÷ $1.64)	20 ($27 ÷ $1.35)

The price-earnings ratio improved from 20 to 25 during 2014. In other words, a share of common stock of Lincoln Company was selling for 20 times earnings per share at the end of 2013. At the end of 2014, the common stock was selling for 25 times earnings per share. This indicates that the market expects Lincoln to experience favorable earnings in the future.

Example Exercise 14-11 **Earnings per Share and Price-Earnings Ratio**

A company reports the following:

Net income	$250,000
Preferred dividends	$15,000
Shares of common stock outstanding	20,000
Market price per share of common stock	$35.25

a. Determine the company's earnings per share on common stock.

b. Determine the company's price-earnings ratio. Round to one decimal place.

Follow My Example 14-11

a. Earnings per Share on Common Stock = (Net Income – Preferred Dividends) ÷ Shares of Common Stock Outstanding

Earnings per Share = ($250,000 – $15,000) ÷ 20,000

Earnings per Share = $11.75

b. Price-Earnings Ratio = Market Price per Share of Common Stock ÷ Earnings per Share on Common Stock

Price-Earnings Ratio = $35.25 ÷ $11.75

Price-Earnings Ratio = 3.0

Practice Exercises: **PE 14-11A, PE 14-11B**

Dividends per Share

Dividends per share measures the extent to which earnings are being distributed to common shareholders. It is computed as follows:

$$\text{Dividends per Share} = \frac{\text{Dividends on Common Stock}}{\text{Shares of Common Stock Outstanding}}$$

To illustrate, the dividends per share for Lincoln Company are computed below.

	2014	2013
Dividends on common stock	$40,000	$30,000
Shares of common stock outstanding	50,000	50,000
Dividends per share of common stock	$0.80 ($40,000 ÷ 50,000)	$0.60 ($30,000 ÷ 50,000)

The dividends per share of common stock increased from $0.60 to $0.80 during 2014.

Dividends per share are often reported with earnings per share. Comparing the two per-share amounts indicates the extent to which earnings are being retained for use in operations. To illustrate, the dividends and earnings per share for Lincoln Company are shown in Exhibit 9.

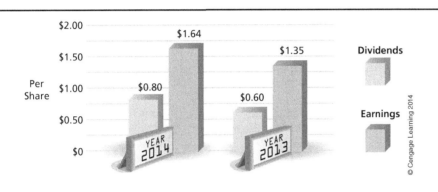

© Cengage Learning 2014

EXHIBIT 9

Dividends and Earnings per Share of Common Stock

Dividend Yield

The **dividend yield** on common stock measures the rate of return to common stockholders from cash dividends. It is of special interest to investors whose objective is to earn revenue (dividends) from their investment. It is computed as follows:

$$\text{Dividend Yield} = \frac{\text{Dividends per Share of Common Stock}}{\text{Market Price per Share of Common Stock}}$$

To illustrate, the dividend yield for Lincoln Company is computed below.

	2014	2013
Dividends per share of common stock	$0.80	$0.60
Market price per share of common stock	$41.00	$27.00
Dividend yield on common stock	2.0% ($0.80 ÷ $41)	2.2% ($0.60 ÷ $27)

The dividend yield declined slightly from 2.2% to 2.0% in 2014. This decline was primarily due to the increase in the market price of Lincoln's common stock.

The dividends per share, dividend yield, and P/E ratio of a common stock are normally quoted on the daily listing of stock prices in *The Wall Street Journal* and on Yahoo!'s finance Web site.

Summary of Analytical Measures

Exhibit 10 shows a summary of the solvency and profitability measures discussed in this chapter. The type of industry and the company's operations usually affect which measures are used. In many cases, additional measures are used for a specific industry. For example, airlines use *revenue per passenger mile* and *cost per available seat* as profitability measures. Likewise, hotels use *occupancy rates* as a profitability measure.

The analytical measures shown in Exhibit 10 are a useful starting point for analyzing a company's solvency and profitability. However, they are not a substitute for sound judgment. For example, the general economic and business environment should always be considered in analyzing a company's future prospects. In addition, any trends and interrelationships among the measures should be carefully studied.

EXHIBIT 10 **Summary of Analytical Measures**

Liquidity and solvency measures:	**Method of Computation**	**Use**
Working Capital	Current Assets – Current Liabilities	To indicate the ability to meet currently maturing obligations (measures solvency)
Current Ratio	$\dfrac{\text{Current Assets}}{\text{Current Liabilities}}$	
Quick Ratio	$\dfrac{\text{Quick Assets}}{\text{Current Liabilities}}$	To indicate instant debt-paying ability (measures solvency)
Accounts Receivable Turnover	$\dfrac{\text{Net Sales}}{\text{Average Accounts Receivable}}$	To assess the efficiency in collecting receivables and in the management of credit (measures liquidity)
Numbers of Days' Sales in Receivables	$\dfrac{\text{Average Accounts Receivable}}{\text{Average Daily Sales}}$	
Inventory Turnover	$\dfrac{\text{Cost of Goods Sold}}{\text{Average Inventory}}$	To assess the efficiency in the management of inventory (measures liquidity)
Number of Days' Sales in Inventory	$\dfrac{\text{Average Inventory}}{\text{Average Daily Cost of Goods Sold}}$	
Ratio of Fixed Assets to Long-Term Liabilities	$\dfrac{\text{Fixed Assets (net)}}{\text{Long-Term Liabilities}}$	To indicate the margin of safety to long-term creditors (measures solvency)
Ratio of Liabilities to Stockholders' Equity	$\dfrac{\text{Total Liabilities}}{\text{Total Stockholders' Equity}}$	To indicate the margin of safety to creditors (measures solvency)
Number of Times Interest Charges Are Earned	$\dfrac{\text{Income Before Income Tax + Interest Expense}}{\text{Interest Expense}}$	To assess the risk to debtholders in terms of number of times interest charges were earned (measures solvency)
Number of Times Preferred Dividends Are Earned	$\dfrac{\text{Net Income}}{\text{Preferred Dividends}}$	To assess the risk to preferred stockholders in terms of the number of times preferred dividends were earned (measures solvency)
Profitability measures: Ratio of Net Sales to Assets	$\dfrac{\text{Net Sales}}{\text{Average Total Assets (excluding long-term investments)}}$	To assess the effectiveness in the use of assets
Rate Earned on Total Assets	$\dfrac{\text{Net Income + Interest Expense}}{\text{Average Total Assets}}$	To assess the profitability of the assets
Rate Earned on Stockholders' Equity	$\dfrac{\text{Net Income}}{\text{Average Total Stockholders' Equity}}$	To assess the profitability of the investment by stockholders
Rate Earned on Common Stockholders' Equity	$\dfrac{\text{Net Income – Preferred Dividends}}{\text{Average Common Stockholders' Equity}}$	To assess the profitability of the investment by common stockholders
Earnings per Share (EPS) on Common Stock	$\dfrac{\text{Net Income – Preferred Dividends}}{\text{Shares of Common Stock Outstanding}}$	
Price-Earnings (P/E) Ratio	$\dfrac{\text{Market Price per Share of Common Stock}}{\text{Earnings per Share on Common Stock}}$	To indicate future earnings prospects, based on the relationship between market value of common stock and earnings
Dividends per Share	$\dfrac{\text{Dividends on Common Stock}}{\text{Shares of Common Stock Outstanding}}$	To indicate the extent to which earnings are being distributed to common stockholders
Dividend Yield	$\dfrac{\text{Dividends per Share of Common Stock}}{\text{Market Price per Share of Common Stock}}$	To indicate the rate of return to common stockholders in terms of dividends

Integrity, Objectivity, and Ethics in Business

CHIEF FINANCIAL OFFICER BONUSES

A recent study by compensation experts at Temple University found that chief financial officer salaries are correlated with the complexity of a company's operations, but chief financial officer bonuses are correlated with the company's ability to meet analysts' earnings forecasts. These results suggest that financial bonuses may provide chief financial officers with an incentive to use

questionable accounting practices to improve earnings. While the study doesn't conclude that bonuses lead to accounting fraud, it does suggest that bonuses give chief financial officers a reason to find ways to use accounting to increase apparent earnings.

Source: E. Jelesiewicz, "Today's CFO: More Challenge but Higher Compensation," *News Communications* (Temple University, August 2009).

Corporate Annual Reports

Describe the contents of corporate annual reports.

Public corporations issue annual reports summarizing their operating activities for the past year and plans for the future. Such annual reports include the financial statements and the accompanying notes. In addition, annual reports normally include the following sections:

See Appendix C for more information

- Management discussion and analysis
- Report on internal control
- Report on fairness of the financial statements

Management Discussion and Analysis

Management's Discussion and Analysis (MD&A) is required in annual reports filed with the Securities and Exchange Commission. It includes management's analysis of current operations and its plans for the future. Typical items included in the MD&A are as follows:

- Management's analysis and explanations of any significant changes between the current and prior years' financial statements.
- Important accounting principles or policies that could affect interpretation of the financial statements, including the effect of changes in accounting principles or the adoption of new accounting principles.
- Management's assessment of the company's liquidity and the availability of capital to the company.
- Significant risk exposures that might affect the company.
- Any "off-balance-sheet" arrangements such as leases not included directly in the financial statements. Such arrangements are discussed in advanced accounting courses and textbooks.

Report on Internal Control

The Sarbanes-Oxley Act of 2002 requires a report on internal control by management. The report states management's responsibility for establishing and maintaining internal control. In addition, management's assessment of the effectiveness of internal controls over financial reporting is included in the report.

Sarbanes-Oxley also requires a public accounting firm to verify management's conclusions on internal control. Thus, two reports on internal control, one by management and one by a public accounting firm, are included in the annual report. In some situations, these may be combined into a single report on internal control.

Report on Fairness of the Financial Statements

All publicly held corporations are required to have an independent audit (examination) of their financial statements. The Certified Public Accounting (CPA) firm that conducts the audit renders an opinion, called the *Report of Independent Registered Public Accounting Firm*, on the fairness of the statements.

An opinion stating that the financial statements present fairly the financial position, results of operations, and cash flows of the company is said to be an *unqualified opinion*, sometimes called a *clean opinion*. Any report other than an unqualified opinion raises a "red flag" for financial statement users and requires further investigation as to its cause.

The annual report of Nike, Inc. is shown in Appendix B. The Nike report includes the financial statements as well as the MD&A Report on Internal Control, and the Report on Fairness of the Financial Statements.

Integrity, Objectivity, and Ethics in Business

BUY LOW, SELL HIGH

Research analysts work for banks, brokerages, or other financial institutions. Their job is to estimate the value of a company's common stock by reviewing and evaluating the company's business model, strategic plan, and financial performance. Based on this analysis, the analyst develops an estimate of a stock's value, which is called its *fundamental value*. Analysts then advise their clients to "buy" or "sell" a company's stock based on the following guidelines:

Current market price is greater than fundamental value	Sell
Current market price is lower than fundamental value	Buy

If analysts are doing their job well, their clients will enjoy large returns by buying stocks at low prices and selling them at high prices.

© Cengage Learning 2014

A P P E N D I X

Unusual Items on the Income Statement

Generally accepted accounting principles require that unusual items be reported separately on the income statement. This is because such items do not occur frequently and are typically unrelated to current operations. Without separate reporting of these items, users of the financial statements might be misled about current and future operations.

Unusual items on the income statement are classified as one of the following:

1. Affecting the *current period* income statement
2. Affecting a *prior period* income statement

Unusual Items Affecting the Current Period's Income Statement

Unusual items affecting the current period's income statement include the following:

1. Discontinued operations
2. Extraordinary items

These items are reported separately on the income statement for any period in which they occur.

Discontinued Operations A company may discontinue a segment of its operations by selling or abandoning the segment's operations. For example, a retailer might decide to sell its product only online and, thus, discontinue selling its merchandise at its retail outlets (stores).

Any gain or loss on discontinued operations is reported on the income statement as a *Gain (or loss) from discontinued operations*. It is reported immediately following *Income from continuing operations*.

To illustrate, assume that Jones Corporation produces and sells electrical products, hardware supplies, and lawn equipment. Because of a lack of profits, Jones discontinues its electrical products operation and sells the remaining inventory and other assets at a loss of $100,000. Exhibit 11 illustrates the reporting of the loss on discontinued operations.[3]

Jones Corporation Income Statement For the Year Ended December 31, 2014		**EXHIBIT 11** **Unusual Items in the Income Statement**
Net sales.	$12,350,000	
Cost of merchandise sold	5,800,000	
Gross profit	$ 6,550,000	
Selling and administrative expenses	5,240,000	
Income from continuing operations before income tax.	$ 1,310,000	
Income tax expense	620,000	
Income from continuing operations	$ 690,000	
Loss on discontinued operations	100,000	
Income before extraordinary items	$ 590,000	
Extraordinary items:		
Gain on condemnation of land	150,000	
Net income	$ 740,000	

© Cengage Learning 2014

In addition, a note accompanying the income statement should describe the operations sold, including such details as the date operations were discontinued, the assets sold, and the effect (if any) on current and future operations.

Extraordinary Items An **extraordinary item** is defined as an event or a transaction that has both of the following characteristics:

1. Unusual in nature
2. Infrequent in occurrence

Gains and losses from natural disasters such as floods, earthquakes, and fires are normally reported as extraordinary items, provided that they occur infrequently. Gains or losses from land or buildings taken (condemned) for public use are also reported as extraordinary items.

Any gain or loss from extraordinary items is reported on the income statement as *Gain (or loss) from extraordinary item*. It is reported immediately following *Income from continuing operations* and any *Gain (or loss) on discontinued operations*.

To illustrate, assume that land owned by Jones Corporation was taken for public use (condemned) by the local government. The condemnation of the land resulted in a gain of $150,000. Exhibit 11 illustrates the reporting of the extraordinary gain.[4]

Reporting Earnings per Share Earnings per common share should be reported separately for discontinued operations and extraordinary items. To illustrate, a partial income statement for Jones Corporation is shown in Exhibit 12. The company has 200,000 shares of common stock outstanding.

Exhibit 12 reports earnings per common share for income from continuing operations, discontinued operations, and extraordinary items. However, only earnings per share for income from continuing operations and net income are required by generally accepted accounting principles. The other per-share amounts may be presented in the notes to the financial statements.

---

3 The gain or loss on discontinued operations is reported net of any tax effects. To simplify, the tax effects are not specifically identified in Exhibit 11.

4 The gain or loss on extraordinary operations is reported net of any tax effects.

EXHIBIT 12

Income Statement with Earnings per Share

Jones Corporation Income Statement For the Year Ended December 31, 2014	
Earnings per common share:	
Income from continuing operations.	$3.45
Loss on discontinued operations	0.50
Income before extraordinary items	$2.95
Extraordinary items:	
Gain on condemnation of land	0.75
Net income	$3.70

Unusual Items Affecting the Prior Period's Income Statement

An unusual item may occur that affects a prior period's income statement. Two such items are as follows:

1. Errors in applying generally accepted accounting principles
2. Changes from one generally accepted accounting principle to another

If an error is discovered in a prior period's financial statement, the prior-period statement and all following statements are restated and thus corrected.

A company may change from one generally accepted accounting principle to another. In this case, the prior-period financial statements are restated as if the new accounting principle had always been used.[5]

For both of the preceding items, the current-period earnings are not affected. That is, only the earnings reported in prior periods are restated. However, because the prior earnings are restated, the beginning balance of Retained Earnings may also have to be restated. This, in turn, may cause the restatement of other balance sheet accounts. Illustrations of these types of adjustments and restatements are provided in advanced accounting courses.

5 Changes from one acceptable depreciation method to another acceptable depreciation method are an exception to this general rule and are to be treated prospectively as a change in estimate.

At a Glance 14

OBJ 1

Describe basic financial statement analytical methods.

Key Points The basic financial statements provide much of the information users need to make economic decisions. Analytical procedures are used to compare items on a current financial statement with related items on earlier statements, or to examine relationships within a financial statement.

Learning Outcomes	Example Exercises	Practice Exercises
• Prepare a vertical analysis from a company's financial statements.	EE14-1	PE14-1A, 14-1B
• Prepare a horizontal analysis from a company's financial statements.	EE14-2	PE14-2A, 14-2B
• Prepare common-sized financial statements.		

Use financial statement analysis to assess the solvency of a business.

Key Points   All users of financial statements are interested in the ability of a business to convert assets into cash (liquidity), pay its debts (solvency), and earn income (profitability). Liquidity, solvency, and profitability are interrelated. Liquidity and solvency are normally assessed by examining the following: current position analysis, accounts receivable analysis, inventory analysis, the ratio of fixed assets to long-term liabilities, the ratio of liabilities to stockholders' equity, and the number of times interest charges are earned.

Learning Outcomes	Example Exercises	Practice Exercises
• Determine working capital.		
• Compute and interpret the current ratio.	EE14-3	PE14-3A, 14-3B
• Compute and interpret the quick ratio.	EE14-3	PE14-3A, 14-3B
• Compute and interpret accounts receivable turnover.	EE14-4	PE14-4A, 14-4B
• Compute and interpret the number of days' sales in receivables.	EE14-4	PE14-4A, 14-4B
• Compute and interpret inventory turnover.	EE14-5	PE14-5A, 14-5B
• Compute and interpret the number of days' sales in inventory.	EE14-5	PE14-5A, 14-5B
• Compute and interpret the ratio of fixed assets to long-term liabilities.	EE14-6	PE14-6A, 14-6B
• Compute and interpret the ratio of liabilities to stockholders' equity.	EE14-6	PE14-6A, 14-6B
• Compute and interpret the number of times interest charges are earned.	EE14-7	PE14-7A, 14-7B

Use financial statement analysis to assess the profitability of a business.

Key Points   Profitability analysis focuses on the ability of a company to earn profits. This ability is reflected in the company's operating results as reported on the income statement and resources available as reported on the balance sheet. Major analyses include the ratio of net sales to assets, the rate earned on total assets, the rate earned on stockholders' equity, the rate earned on common stockholders' equity, earnings per share on common stock, the price-earnings ratio, dividends per share, and dividend yield.

Learning Outcomes	Example Exercises	Practice Exercises
• Compute and interpret the ratio of net sales to assets.	EE14-8	PE14-8A, 14-8B
• Compute and interpret the rate earned on total assets.	EE14-9	PE14-9A, 14-9B
• Compute and interpret the rate earned on stockholders' equity.	EE14-10	PE14-10A, 14-10B
• Compute and interpret the rate earned on common stockholders' equity.	EE14-10	PE14-10A, 14-10B
• Compute and interpret the earnings per share on common stock.	EE14-11	PE14-11A, 14-11B
• Compute and interpret the price-earnings ratio.	EE14-11	PE14-11A, 14-11B
• Compute and interpret the dividends per share and dividend yield.		
• Describe the uses and limitations of analytical measures.		

Describe the contents of corporate annual reports.

Key Points   Corporations normally issue annual reports to their stockholders and other interested parties. Such reports summarize the corporation's operating activities for the past year and plans for the future.

Learning Outcome	Example Exercises	Practice Exercises
• Describe the elements of a corporate annual report.		

Key Terms

accounts receivable analysis (594)

accounts receivable turnover (594)

common-sized statement (590)

current position analysis (592)

current ratio (592)

dividend yield (605)

dividends per share (604)

earnings per share (EPS) on common stock (603)

extraordinary item (609)

horizontal analysis (586)

inventory analysis (595)

inventory turnover (596)

leverage (601)

liquidity (591)

Management's Discussion and Analysis (MD&A) (607)

number of days' sales in inventory (596)

number of days' sales in receivables (595)

number of times interest charges are earned (598)

price-earnings (P/E) ratio (604)

profitability (591)

quick assets (593)

quick ratio (593)

rate earned on common stockholders' equity (601)

rate earned on stockholders' equity (601)

rate earned on total assets (600)

ratio of fixed assets to long-term liabilities (597)

ratio of liabilities to stockholders' equity (597)

ratio of net sales to assets (599)

solvency (591)

vertical analysis (589)

working capital (592)

Illustrative Problem

Rainbow Paint Co.'s comparative financial statements for the years ending December 31, 2014 and 2013, are as follows. The market price of Rainbow Paint Co.'s common stock was $25 on December 31, 2014, and $30 on December 31, 2013.

Rainbow Paint Co. Comparative Income Statement For the Years Ended December 31, 2014 and 2013		
	2014	**2013**
Sales	$5,125,000	$3,257,600
Sales returns and allowances	125,000	57,600
Net sales	$5,000,000	$3,200,000
Cost of goods sold	3,400,000	2,080,000
Gross profit	$1,600,000	$1,120,000
Selling expenses	$ 650,000	$ 464,000
Administrative expenses	325,000	224,000
Total operating expenses	$ 975,000	$ 688,000
Income from operations	$ 625,000	$ 432,000
Other income	25,000	19,200
	$ 650,000	$ 451,200
Other expense (interest)	105,000	64,000
Income before income tax	$ 545,000	$ 387,200
Income tax expense	300,000	176,000
Net income	$ 245,000	$ 211,200

Rainbow Paint Co.
Comparative Retained Earnings Statement
For the Years Ended December 31, 2014 and 2013

	2014	2013
Retained earnings, January 1	$723,000	$581,800
Add net income for year	245,000	211,200
Total	$968,000	$793,000
Deduct dividends:		
On preferred stock	$ 40,000	$ 40,000
On common stock	45,000	30,000
Total	$ 85,000	$ 70,000
Retained earnings, December 31	$883,000	$723,000

Rainbow Paint Co.
Comparative Balance Sheet
December 31, 2014 and 2013

	Dec. 31, 2014	Dec. 31, 2013
Assets		
Current assets:		
Cash	$ 175,000	$ 125,000
Temporary investments	150,000	50,000
Accounts receivable (net)	425,000	325,000
Inventories	720,000	480,000
Prepaid expenses	30,000	20,000
Total current assets	$1,500,000	$1,000,000
Long-term investments	250,000	225,000
Property, plant, and equipment (net)	2,093,000	1,948,000
Total assets	$3,843,000	$3,173,000
Liabilities		
Current liabilities	$ 750,000	$ 650,000
Long-term liabilities:		
Mortgage note payable, 10%, due 2017	$ 410,000	—
Bonds payable, 8%, due 2020	800,000	$ 800,000
Total long-term liabilities	$1,210,000	$ 800,000
Total liabilities	$1,960,000	$1,450,000
Stockholders' Equity		
Preferred 8% stock, $100 par	$ 500,000	$ 500,000
Common stock, $10 par	500,000	500,000
Retained earnings	883,000	723,000
Total stockholders' equity	$1,883,000	$1,723,000
Total liabilities and stockholders' equity	$3,843,000	$3,173,000

Instructions

Determine the following measures for 2014:

1. Working capital

2. Current ratio

3. Quick ratio

4. Accounts receivable turnover

5. Number of days' sales in receivables

6. Inventory turnover

7. Number of days' sales in inventory

8. Ratio of fixed assets to long-term liabilities

9. Ratio of liabilities to stockholders' equity

10. Number of times interest charges are earned

11. Number of times preferred dividends are earned

12. Ratio of net sales to assets

13. Rate earned on total assets

14. Rate earned on stockholders' equity

15. Rate earned on common stockholders' equity

16. Earnings per share on common stock

17. Price-earnings ratio

18. Dividends per share

19. Dividend yield

Solution

(Ratios are rounded to the nearest single digit after the decimal point.)

1. Working capital: $750,000
   $1,500,000 − $750,000

2. Current ratio: 2.0
   $1,500,000 ÷ $750,000

3. Quick ratio: 1.0
   $750,000 ÷ $750,000

4. Accounts receivable turnover: 13.3
   $5,000,000 ÷ [($425,000 + $325,000) ÷ 2]

5. Number of days' sales in receivables: 27.4 days
   $5,000,000 ÷ 365 days = $13,699
   $375,000 ÷ $13,699

6. Inventory turnover: 5.7
   $3,400,000 ÷ [($720,000 + $480,000) ÷ 2]

7. Number of days' sales in inventory: 64.4 days
   $3,400,000 ÷ 365 days = $9,315
   $600,000 ÷ $9,315

8. Ratio of fixed assets to long-term liabilities: 1.7
   $2,093,000 ÷ $1,210,000

9. Ratio of liabilities to stockholders' equity: 1.0
   $1,960,000 ÷ $1,883,000

10. Number of times interest charges are earned: 6.2
    ($545,000 + $105,000) ÷ $105,000

11. Number of times preferred dividends are earned: 6.1
    $245,000 ÷ $40,000

12. Ratio of net sales to assets: 1.5
    $5,000,000 ÷ [($3,593,000 + $2,948,000) ÷ 2]

13. Rate earned on total assets: 10.0%
    ($245,000 + $105,000) ÷ [($3,843,000 + $3,173,000) ÷ 2]

14. Rate earned on stockholders' equity: 13.6%
    $245,000 ÷ [($1,883,000 + $1,723,000) ÷ 2]

15. Rate earned on common stockholders' equity: 15.7%
    ($245,000 − $40,000) ÷ [($1,383,000 + $1,223,000) ÷ 2]

16. Earnings per share on common stock: $4.10
    ($245,000 − $40,000) ÷ 50,000 shares

17. Price-earnings ratio: 6.1
    $25 ÷ $4.10

18. Dividends per share: $0.90
    $45,000 ÷ 50,000 shares

19. Dividend yield: 3.6%
    $0.90 ÷ $25

Discussion Questions

1. What is the difference between horizontal and vertical analysis of financial statements?

2. What is the advantage of using comparative statements for financial analysis rather than statements for a single date or period?

3. The current year's amount of net income (after income tax) is 25% larger than that of the preceding year. Does this indicate an improved operating performance? Discuss.

4. How would the current and quick ratios of a service business compare?

5. a. Why is it advantageous to have a high inventory turnover?
   b. Is it possible to have a high inventory turnover and a high number of days' sales in inventory? Discuss.

6. What do the following data taken from a comparative balance sheet indicate about the company's ability to borrow additional funds on a long-term basis in the current year as compared to the preceding year?

	Current Year	Preceding Year
Fixed assets (net)	$1,260,000	$1,360,000
Total long-term liabilities	300,000	400,000

7. a. How does the rate earned on total assets differ from the rate earned on stockholders' equity?
   b. Which ratio is normally higher? Explain.

8. a. Why is the rate earned on stockholders' equity by a thriving business ordinarily higher than the rate earned on total assets?
   b. Should the rate earned on common stockholders' equity normally be higher or lower than the rate earned on total stockholders' equity? Explain.

9. The net income (after income tax) of McCants Inc. was $2 per common share in the latest year and $6 per common share for the preceding year. At the beginning of the latest year, the number of shares outstanding was doubled by a stock split. There were no other changes in the amount of stock outstanding. What were the earnings per share in the preceding year, adjusted for comparison with the latest year?

10. Describe two reports provided by independent auditors in the annual report to shareholders.

Practice Exercises

Example Exercises

EE 14-1 *p. 589*

PE 14-1A **Horizontal analysis**   OBJ. 1

The comparative temporary investments and inventory balances of a company are provided below.

	2014	2013
Temporary investments	$46,400	$40,000
Inventory	73,600	80,000

Based on this information, what is the amount and percentage of increase or decrease that would be shown in a balance sheet with horizontal analysis?

EE 14-1 *p. 589*

PE 14-1B **Horizontal analysis**   OBJ. 1

The comparative accounts payable and long-term debt balances for a company are provided below.

	2014	2013
Accounts payable	$111,000	$100,000
Long-term debt	132,680	124,000

Based on this information, what is the amount and percentage of increase or decrease that would be shown in a balance sheet with horizontal analysis?

EE 14-2 *p. 590*

PE 14-2A **Vertical analysis**   OBJ. 1

Income statement information for Thain Corporation is provided below.

Sales	$850,000
Cost of goods sold	493,000
Gross profit	357,000

Prepare a vertical analysis of the income statement for Thain Corporation.

EE 14-2 *p. 590*

PE 14-2B **Vertical analysis**   OBJ. 1

Income statement information for Einsworth Corporation is provided below.

Sales	$1,200,000
Cost of goods sold	780,000
Gross profit	420,000

Prepare a vertical analysis of the income statement for Einsworth Corporation.

EE 14-3 *p. 590*

PE 14-3A **Current position analysis**   OBJ. 2

The following items are reported on a company's balance sheet:

Cash	$130,000
Marketable securities	50,000
Accounts receivable (net)	60,000
Inventory	120,000
Accounts payable	150,000

Determine (a) the current ratio and (b) the quick ratio. Round to one decimal place.

Example
Exercises

EE 14-3 *p. 594*

PE 14-3B   Current position analysis   OBJ. 2

The following items are reported on a company's balance sheet:

Cash	$210,000
Marketable securities	120,000
Accounts receivable (net)	110,000
Inventory	160,000
Accounts payable	200,000

Determine (a) the current ratio and (b) the quick ratio. Round to one decimal place.

EE 14-4 *p. 595*

PE 14-4A   Accounts receivable analysis   OBJ. 2

A company reports the following:

Net sales	$1,200,000
Average accounts receivable (net)	100,000

Determine (a) the accounts receivable turnover and (b) the number of days' sales in receivables. Round to one decimal place.

EE 14-4 *p. 595*

PE 14-4B   Accounts receivable analysis   OBJ. 2

A company reports the following:

Net sales	$3,150,000
Average accounts receivable (net)	210,000

Determine (a) the accounts receivable turnover and (b) the number of days' sales in receivables. Round to one decimal place.

EE 14-5 *p. 597*

PE 14-5A   Inventory analysis   OBJ. 2

A company reports the following:

Cost of goods sold	$630,000
Average inventory	90,000

Determine (a) the inventory turnover and (b) the number of days' sales in inventory. Round to one decimal place.

EE 14-5 *p. 597*

PE 14-5B   Inventory analysis   OBJ. 2

A company reports the following:

Cost of goods sold	$435,000
Average inventory	72,500

Determine (a) the inventory turnover and (b) the number of days' sales in inventory. Round to one decimal place.

EE 14-6 *p. 598*

PE 14-6A   Long-term solvency analysis   OBJ. 2

The following information was taken from Einar Company's balance sheet:

Fixed assets (net)	$1,800,000
Long-term liabilities	600,000
Total liabilities	900,000
Total stockholders' equity	750,000

Determine the company's (a) ratio of fixed assets to long-term liabilities and (b) ratio of liabilities to stockholders' equity.

EE 14-6 *p. 598*   **PE 14-6B   Long-term solvency analysis**   OBJ. 2

The following information was taken from Charu Company's balance sheet:

Fixed assets (net)	$2,000,000
Long-term liabilities	800,000
Total liabilities	1,000,000
Total stockholders' equity	625,000

Determine the company's (a) ratio of fixed assets to long-term liabilities and (b) ratio of liabilities to stockholders' equity.

EE 14-7 *p. 599*   **PE 14-7A   Times interest charges are earned**   OBJ. 2

A company reports the following:

Income before income tax	$4,000,000
Interest expense	400,000

Determine the number of times interest charges are earned.

EE 14-7 *p. 599*   **PE 14-7B   Times interest charges are earned**   OBJ. 2

A company reports the following:

Income before income tax	$8,000,000
Interest expense	500,000

Determine the number of times interest charges are earned.

EE 14-8 *p. 600*   **PE 14-8A   Net sales to assets**   OBJ. 3

A company reports the following:

Net sales	$1,800,000
Average total assets	1,125,000

Determine the ratio of net sales to assets.

EE 14-8 *p. 600*   **PE 14-8B   Net sales to assets**   OBJ. 3

A company reports the following:

Net sales	$4,400,000
Average total assets	2,000,000

Determine the ratio of net sales to assets.

EE 14-9 *p. 601*   **PE 14-9A   Rate earned on total assets**   OBJ. 3

A company reports the following income statement and balance sheet information for the current year:

Net income	$ 250,000
Interest expense	100,000
Average total assets	2,500,000

Determine the rate earned on total assets.

EE 14-9 *p. 601*   **PE 14-9B   Rate earned on total assets**   OBJ. 3

A company reports the following income statement and balance sheet information for the current year:

Net income	$ 410,000
Interest expense	90,000
Average total assets	5,000,000

Determine the rate earned on total assets.

*Example
Exercises*
EE 14-10 *p. 603*

PE 14-10A Common stockholders' profitability analysis   OBJ. 3

A company reports the following:

Net income	$ 375,000
Preferred dividends	75,000
Average stockholders' equity	2,500,000
Average common stockholders' equity	1,875,000

Determine (a) the rate earned on stockholders' equity and (b) the rate earned on common stockholders' equity. Round to one decimal place.

EE 14-10 *p. 603*

PE 14-10B Common stockholders' profitability analysis   OBJ. 3

A company reports the following:

Net income	$1,000,000
Preferred dividends	50,000
Average stockholders' equity	6,250,000
Average common stockholders' equity	3,800,000

Determine (a) the rate earned on stockholders' equity and (b) the rate earned on common stockholders' equity. Round to one decimal place.

EE 14-11 *p. 604*

PE 14-11A Earnings per share and price-earnings ratio   OBJ. 3

A company reports the following:

Net income	$185,000
Preferred dividends	$25,000
Shares of common stock outstanding	100,000
Market price per share of common stock	$20

a. Determine the company's earnings per share on common stock.

b. Determine the company's price-earnings ratio.

EE 14-11 *p. 604*

PE 14-11B Earnings per share and price-earnings ratio   OBJ. 3

A company reports the following:

Net income	$410,000
Preferred dividends	$60,000
Shares of common stock outstanding	50,000
Market price per share of common stock	$84

a. Determine the company's earnings per share on common stock.

b. Determine the company's price-earnings ratio.

Exercises

EX 14-1 Vertical analysis of income statement   OBJ. 1

✔ a. 2014 net income: $30,000; 2.0% of sales

Revenue and expense data for Soldner Inc. are as follows:

	2014	2013
Sales	$1,500,000	$1,450,000
Cost of goods sold	930,000	812,000
Selling expenses	210,000	261,000
Administrative expenses	255,000	232,000
Income tax expense	52,500	72,500

(Continued)

a. Prepare an income statement in comparative form, stating each item for both 2014 and 2013 as a percent of sales. Round to one decimal place.

b. ▰▰▰▸Comment on the significant changes disclosed by the comparative income statement.

EX 14-2   Vertical analysis of income statement OBJ. 1

✔ a. Current fiscal year income from continuing operations, 14.2% of revenues

The following comparative income statement (in thousands of dollars) for the two recent fiscal years was adapted from the annual report of Speedway Motorsports, Inc., owner and operator of several major motor speedways, such as the Atlanta, Texas, and Las Vegas Motor Speedways.

	Current Year	Previous Year
Revenues:		
Admissions	$139,125	$163,087
Event-related revenue	156,691	178,805
NASCAR broadcasting revenue	178,722	173,803
Other operating revenue	27,705	34,827
Total revenue	$502,243	$550,522
Expenses and other:		
Direct expense of events	$100,843	$100,922
NASCAR purse and sanction fees	120,273	123,078
Other direct expenses	21,846	26,208
General and administrative	188,196	266,252
Total expenses and other	$431,158	$516,460
Income from continuing operations	$ 71,085	$ 34,062

a. Prepare a comparative income statement for these two years in vertical form, stating each item as a percent of revenues. Round to one decimal place.

b. ▰▰▰▸Comment on the significant changes.

EX 14-3   Common-sized income statement OBJ. 1

✔ a. Bull Run net income: $60,000; 3.0% of sales

Revenue and expense data for the current calendar year for Bull Run Company and for the electronics industry are as follows. The Bull Run Company data are expressed in dollars. The electronics industry averages are expressed in percentages.

	Bull Run Company	Electronics Industry Average
Sales	$2,100,000	105.0%
Sales returns and allowances	100,000	5.0
Net sales	$2,000,000	100.0%
Cost of goods sold	1,040,000	60.0
Gross profit	$ 960,000	40.0%
Selling expenses	$ 560,000	22.0%
Administrative expenses	300,000	12.0
Total operating expenses	$ 860,000	34.0%
Operating income	$ 100,000	6.0%
Other income	60,000	3.0
	$ 160,000	9.0%
Other expense	40,000	2.0
Income before income tax	$ 120,000	7.0%
Income tax expense	60,000	6.0
Net income	$ 60,000	1.0%

a. Prepare a common-sized income statement comparing the results of operations for Bull Run Company with the industry average. Round to one decimal place.

b. ▰▰▰▸As far as the data permit, comment on significant relationships revealed by the comparisons.

EX 14-4 Vertical analysis of balance sheet OBJ. 1

✔ Retained earnings,
Dec. 31, 2014, 36.0%

Balance sheet data for Peacock Company on December 31, the end of the fiscal year, are shown below.

	2014	2013
Current assets	$1,050,000	$ 750,000
Property, plant, and equipment	1,960,000	2,100,000
Intangible assets	490,000	150,000
Current liabilities	630,000	420,000
Long-term liabilities	1,260,000	1,200,000
Common stock	350,000	300,000
Retained earnings	1,260,000	1,080,000

Prepare a comparative balance sheet for 2014 and 2013, stating each asset as a percent of total assets and each liability and stockholders' equity item as a percent of the total liabilities and stockholders' equity. Round to one decimal place.

EX 14-5 Horizontal analysis of the income statement OBJ. 1

✔ a. Net income
increase, 125.0%

Income statement data for Bezos Company for the years ended December 31, 2014 and 2013, are as follows:

	2014	2013
Sales	$ 840,000	$600,000
Cost of goods sold	724,500	525,000
Gross profit	$ 115,500	$ 75,000
Selling expenses	$ 52,500	$ 37,500
Administrative expenses	41,400	30,000
Total operating expenses	$ 93,900	$ 67,500
Income before income tax	$ 21,600	$ 7,500
Income tax expense	10,800	2,700
Net income	$ 10,800	$ 4,800

a. Prepare a comparative income statement with horizontal analysis, indicating the increase (decrease) for 2014 when compared with 2013. Round to one decimal place.

b. ▬▬▬▬▶What conclusions can be drawn from the horizontal analysis?

EX 14-6 Current position analysis OBJ. 2

✔ a. 2014 working
capital, $2,420,000

The following data were taken from the balance sheet of Mossberg Company:

	Dec. 31, 2014	Dec. 31, 2013
Cash	$ 700,000	$ 600,000
Marketable securities	800,000	620,000
Accounts and notes receivable (net)	920,000	780,000
Inventories	600,000	500,000
Prepaid expenses	500,000	500,000
Total current assets	$ 3,520,000	$ 3,000,000
Accounts and notes payable (short-term)	$ 800,000	$ 750,000
Accrued liabilities	300,000	250,000
Total current liabilities	$1,100,000	$1,000,000

a. Determine for each year (1) the working capital, (2) the current ratio, and (3) the quick ratio. Round ratios to one decimal place.

b. ▬▬▬▬▶What conclusions can be drawn from these data as to the company's ability to meet its currently maturing debts?

EX 14-7 Current position analysis

✔ a. (1) Current year's current ratio, 0.8

OBJ. 2

PepsiCo, Inc., the parent company of Frito-Lay snack foods and Pepsi beverages, had the following current assets and current liabilities at the end of two recent years:

	Current Year (in millions)	Prior Year (in millions)
Cash and cash equivalents	$ 5,943	$3,943
Short-term investments, at cost	426	192
Accounts and notes receivable, net	6,323	4,624
Inventories	3,372	2,618
Prepaid expenses and other current assets	1,505	1,194
Short-term obligations	4,898	8,292
Accounts payable	10,994	464

a. Determine the (1) current ratio and (2) quick ratio for both years. Round to one decimal place.

b. ➤ What conclusions can you draw from these data?

EX 14-8 Current position analysis

OBJ. 2

The bond indenture for the 10-year, 9% debenture bonds issued January 2, 2013, required working capital of $100,000, a current ratio of 1.5, and a quick ratio of 1.0 at the end of each calendar year until the bonds mature. At December 31, 2014, the three measures were computed as follows:

1. Current assets:

Cash......................................	$102,000
Temporary investments	48,000
Accounts and notes receivable (net)...........	120,000
Inventories................................	36,000
Prepaid expenses...........................	24,000
Intangible assets	124,800
Property, plant, and equipment..............	55,200

Total current assets (net)		$510,000
Current liabilities:		
Accounts and short-term notes payable	$ 96,000	
Accrued liabilities...........................	204,000	
Total current liabilities		300,000
Working capital		$210,000
2. Current ratio	1.7	$510,000 ÷ $300,000
3. Quick ratio.....................................	1.2	$115,200 ÷ $ 96,000

a. List the errors in the determination of the three measures of current position analysis.

b. ➤ Is the company satisfying the terms of the bond indenture?

EX 14-9 Accounts receivable analysis

OBJ. 2

✔ a. Accounts receivable turnover, 2014, 7.0

The following data are taken from the financial statements of Krawcheck Inc. Terms of all sales are 2/10, n/55.

	2014	2013	2012
Accounts receivable, end of year	$ 500,000	$ 475,000	$440,000
Net sales on account	3,412,500	2,836,500	

a. For 2013 and 2014, determine (1) the accounts receivable turnover and (2) the number of days' sales in receivables. Round to the nearest dollar and one decimal place.

b. ➤ What conclusions can be drawn from these data concerning accounts receivable and credit policies?

EX 14-10 Accounts receivable analysis

OBJ. 2

Xavier Stores Company and Lestrade Stores Inc. are large retail department stores. Both companies offer credit to their customers through their own credit card operations. Information from the financial statements for both companies for two recent years is as follows (all numbers are in millions):

	Xavier	Lestrade
Merchandise sales	$8,500,000	$4,585,000
Credit card receivables—beginning	820,000	600,000
Credit card receivables—ending	880,000	710,000

a. Determine the (1) accounts receivable turnover and (2) the number of days' sales in receivables for both companies. Round to one decimal place.

b. ━━━━━▶ Compare the two companies with regard to their credit card policies.

EX 14-11 Inventory analysis

OBJ. 2

✔ a. Inventory turnover, current year, 7.5

The following data were extracted from the income statement of Saleh Inc.:

	Current Year	Preceding Year
Sales	$12,750,000	$13,284,000
Beginning inventories	840,000	800,000
Cost of goods sold	6,375,000	7,380,000
Ending inventories	860,000	840,000

a. Determine for each year (1) the inventory turnover and (2) the number of days' sales in inventory. Round to the nearest dollar and one decimal place.

b. ━━━━━▶ What conclusions can be drawn from these data concerning the inventories?

EX 14-12 Inventory analysis

OBJ. 2

✔ a. Dell inventory turnover, 42.6

Dell Inc. and Hewlett-Packard Company (HP) compete with each other in the personal computer market. Dell's primary strategy is to assemble computers to customer orders, rather than for inventory. Thus, for example, Dell will build and deliver a computer within four days of a customer entering an order on a Web page. Hewlett-Packard, on the other hand, builds some computers prior to receiving an order, then sells from this inventory once an order is received. Below is selected financial information for both companies from a recent year's financial statements (in millions):

	Dell Inc.	Hewlett-Packard Company
Sales	$61,494	$126,033
Cost of goods sold	50,098	96,089
Inventory, beginning of period	1,051	6,128
Inventory, end of period	1,301	6,466

a. Determine for both companies (1) the inventory turnover and (2) the number of days' sales in inventory. Round to one decimal place.

b. ━━━━━▶ Interpret the inventory ratios by considering Dell's and Hewlett-Packard's operating strategies.

EX 14-13 Ratio of liabilities to stockholders' equity and number of times interest charges are earned

OBJ. 2

✔ a. Ratio of liabilities to stockholders' equity, Dec. 31, 2014, 0.9

The following data were taken from the financial statements of Hunter Inc. for December 31, 2014 and 2013:

	Dec. 31, 2014	Dec. 31, 2013
Accounts payable	$ 924,000	$ 800,000
Current maturities of serial bonds payable	200,000	200,000
Serial bonds payable, 10%, issued 2009, due 2019	1,000,000	1,200,000
Common stock, $10 par value	250,000	250,000
Paid-in capital in excess of par	1,250,000	1,250,000
Retained earnings	860,000	500,000

(*Continued*)

The income before income tax was $480,000 and $420,000 for the years 2014 and 2013, respectively.

a. Determine the ratio of liabilities to stockholders' equity at the end of each year. Round to one decimal place.

b. Determine the number of times the bond interest charges are earned during the year for both years. Round to one decimal place.

c. ━━━━▶What conclusions can be drawn from these data as to the company's ability to meet its currently maturing debts?

EX 14-14 **Ratio of liabilities to stockholders' equity and number of times interest charges are earned** OBJ. 2

✔ a. Hasbro, 1.5

Hasbro and Mattel, Inc., are the two largest toy companies in North America. Condensed liabilities and stockholders' equity from a recent balance sheet are shown for each company as follows (in thousands):

	Hasbro	Mattel
Current liabilities	$ 718,801	$ 1,350,282
Long-term debt	1,397,681	950,000
Deferred liabilities	361,324	488,867
Total liabilities	$ 2,477,806	$ 2,789,149
Shareholders' equity:		
Common stock	$ 104,847	$ 441,369
Additional paid in capital	625,961	1,706,461
Retained earnings	2,978,317	2,720,645
Accumulated other comprehensive loss and other equity items	8,149	(359,199)
Treasury stock, at cost	(2,101,854)	(1,880,692)
Total stockholders' equity	$ 1,615,420	$ 2,628,584
Total liabilities and stockholders' equity	$ 4,093,226	$ 5,417,733

The income from operations and interest expense from the income statement for each company were as follows (in thousands):

	Hasbro	Mattel
Income from operations	$397,752	$684,863
Interest expense	82,112	64,839

a. Determine the ratio of liabilities to stockholders' equity for both companies. Round to one decimal place.

b. Determine the number of times interest charges are earned for both companies. Round to one decimal place.

c. ━━━━▶Interpret the ratio differences between the two companies.

EX 14-15 **Ratio of liabilities to stockholders' equity and ratio of fixed assets to long-term liabilities** OBJ. 2

✔ a. H.J. Heinz, 2.9

Recent balance sheet information for two companies in the food industry, H.J. Heinz Company and The Hershey Company, is as follows (in thousands of dollars):

	H.J. Heinz	Hershey
Net property, plant, and equipment	$2,505,083	$1,437,702
Current liabilities	4,161,460	1,298,845
Long-term debt	3,078,128	1,541,825
Other long-term liabilities	1,757,426	529,746
Stockholders' equity	3,108,962	902,316

a. Determine the ratio of liabilities to stockholders' equity for both companies. Round to one decimal place.

b. Determine the ratio of fixed assets to long-term liabilities for both companies. Round to one decimal place.

c. ━━━━▶Interpret the ratio differences between the two companies.

EX 14-16 Ratio of net sales to assets OBJ. 3

✔ a. YRC Worldwide, 1.5

Three major segments of the transportation industry are motor carriers, such as YRC Worldwide; railroads, such as Union Pacific; and transportation arrangement services, such as C.H. Robinson Worldwide Inc. Recent financial statement information for these three companies is shown as follows (in thousands of dollars):

	YRC Worldwide	Union Pacific	C.H. Robinson Worldwide Inc.
Net sales	$4,334,640	$16,965,000	$9,274,305
Average total assets	2,812,504	42,636,000	1,914,974

a. Determine the ratio of net sales to assets for all three companies. Round to one decimal place.

b. ➤ Assume that the ratio of net sales to assets for each company represents their respective industry segment. Interpret the differences in the ratio of net sales to assets in terms of the operating characteristics of each of the respective segments.

EX 14-17 Profitability ratios OBJ. 3

✔ a. Rate earned on total assets, 2014, 12.0%

The following selected data were taken from the financial statements of Robinson Inc. for December 31, 2014, 2013 and 2012:

	December 31		
	2014	2013	2012
Total assets	$4,800,000	$4,400,000	$4,000,000
Notes payable (8% interest)	2,250,000	2,250,000	2,250,000
Common stock.......................................	250,000	250,000	250,000
Preferred 4% stock, $100 par			
(no change during year)	500,000	500,000	500,000
Retained earnings....................................	1,574,000	1,222,000	750,000

The 2014 net income was $372,000, and the 2013 net income was $492,000. No dividends on common stock were declared between 2012 and 2014.

a. Determine the rate earned on total assets, the rate earned on stockholders' equity, and the rate earned on common stockholders' equity for the years 2013 and 2014. Round to one decimal place.

b. ➤ What conclusions can be drawn from these data as to the company's profitability?

EX 14-18 Profitability ratios OBJ. 3

✔ a. Year 3 rate earned on total assets, 12.2%

Ralph Lauren Corp. sells men's apparel through company-owned retail stores. Recent financial information for Ralph Lauren is provided below (all numbers in thousands).

	Fiscal Year 3	Fiscal Year 2	
Net income	$567,600	$479,500	
Interest expense	18,300	22,200	
	Fiscal Year 3	Fiscal Year 2	Fiscal Year 1
Total assets (at end of fiscal year)	$4,981,100	$4,648,900	$4,356,500
Total stockholders' equity (at end of fiscal year)	3,304,700	3,116,600	2,735,100

Assume the apparel industry average rate earned on total assets is 8.0%, and the average rate earned on stockholders' equity is 10.0% for the year ended April 2, Year 3.

a. Determine the rate earned on total assets for Ralph Lauren for fiscal Years 2 and 3. Round to one digit after the decimal place.

b. Determine the rate earned on stockholders' equity for Ralph Lauren for fiscal Years 2 and 3. Round to one decimal place.

c. ➤ Evaluate the two-year trend for the profitability ratios determined in (a) and (b).

d. ➤ Evaluate Ralph Lauren's profit performance relative to the industry.

EX 14-19 Six measures of solvency or profitability

✔ c. Ratio of net sales to assets, 4.2

OBJ. 2, 3

The following data were taken from the financial statements of Gates Inc. for the current fiscal year. Assuming that long-term investments totaled $3,000,000 throughout the year and that total assets were $7,000,000 at the beginning of the current fiscal year, determine the following: (a) ratio of fixed assets to long-term liabilities, (b) ratio of liabilities to stockholders' equity, (c) ratio of net sales to assets, (d) rate earned on total assets, (e) rate earned on stockholders' equity, and (f) rate earned on common stockholders' equity. Round to one decimal place.

Property, plant, and equipment (net)			$ 3,200,000
Liabilities:			
Current liabilities		$ 1,000,000	
Mortgage note payable, 6%, issued 2003, due 2019		2,000,000	
Total liabilities			$ 3,000,000
Stockholders' equity:			
Preferred $10 stock, $100 par (no change during year)			$ 1,000,000
Common stock, $10 par (no change during year)			2,000,000
Retained earnings:			
Balance, beginning of year	$1,570,000		
Net income	930,000	$2,500,000	
Preferred dividends	$ 100,000		
Common dividends	400,000	500,000	
Balance, end of year			2,000,000
Total stockholders' equity			$ 5,000,000
Net sales			$18,900,000
Interest expense			$ 120,000

EX 14-20 Six measures of solvency or profitability

✔ d. Price-earnings ratio, 10.0

OBJ. 2, 3

The balance sheet for Garcon Inc. at the end of the current fiscal year indicated the following:

Bonds payable, 8% (issued in 2004, due in 2024)	$5,000,000
Preferred $4 stock, $50 par	2,500,000
Common stock, $10 par	5,000,000

Income before income tax was $3,000,000, and income taxes were $1,200,000 for the current year. Cash dividends paid on common stock during the current year totaled $1,200,000. The common stock was selling for $32 per share at the end of the year. Determine each of the following: (a) number of times bond interest charges are earned, (b) number of times preferred dividends are earned, (c) earnings per share on common stock, (d) price-earnings ratio, (e) dividends per share of common stock, and (f) dividend yield. Round to one decimal place, except earnings per share, which should be rounded to two decimal places.

EX 14-21 Earnings per share, price-earnings ratio, dividend yield

✔ b. Price-earnings ratio, 15.0

OBJ. 3

The following information was taken from the financial statements of Tolbert Inc. for December 31 of the current fiscal year:

Common stock, $20 par (no change during the year)	$10,000,000
Preferred $4 stock, $40 par (no change during the year)	2,500,000

The net income was $1,750,000 and the declared dividends on the common stock were $1,125,000 for the current year. The market price of the common stock is $45 per share.

For the common stock, determine (a) the earnings per share, (b) the price-earnings ratio, (c) the dividends per share, and (d) the dividend yield. Round to one decimal place, except earnings per share, which should be rounded to two decimal places.

EX 14-22   Price-earnings ratio; dividend yield   OBJ. 3

The table below shows the stock price, earnings per share, and dividends per share for three companies for a recent year:

	Price	Earnings per Share	Dividends per Share
Deere & Co.	$ 65.70	$ 4.40	$1.16
Google	528.33	27.72	0.00
The Coca-Cola Company	69.05	5.37	1.88

a. Determine the price-earnings ratio and dividend yield for the three companies. Round to one decimal place.

b. ━━━▶ Explain the differences in these ratios across the three companies.

Appendix

EX 14-23   Earnings per share, extraordinary item

✔ b. Earnings per share on common stock, $7.60

The net income reported on the income statement of Cutler Co. was $4,000,000. There were 500,000 shares of $10 par common stock and 100,000 shares of $2 preferred stock outstanding throughout the current year. The income statement included two extraordinary items: an $800,000 gain from condemnation of land and a $400,000 loss arising from flood damage, both after applicable income tax. Determine the per-share figures for common stock for (a) income before extraordinary items and (b) net income.

Appendix

EX 14-24   Extraordinary item

Assume that the amount of each of the following items is material to the financial statements. Classify each item as either normally recurring (NR) or extraordinary (E).

a. Loss on the disposal of equipment considered to be obsolete because of the development of new technology.

b. Uninsured loss on building due to hurricane damage. The building was purchased by the company in 1910 and had not previously incurred hurricane damage.

c. Gain on sale of land condemned by the local government for a public works project.

d. Uninsured flood loss. (Flood insurance is unavailable because of periodic flooding in the area.)

e. Interest revenue on notes receivable.

f. Uncollectible accounts expense.

g. Loss on sale of investments in stocks and bonds.

Appendix

EX 14-25   Income statement and earnings per share for extraordinary items and discontinued operations

Cruz Inc. reports the following for 2014:

Income from continuing operations before income tax	$1,000,000
Extraordinary property loss from hurricane	$140,000*
Loss from discontinued operations	$240,000*
Weighted average number of shares outstanding	20,000
Applicable tax rate	40%
*Net of any tax effect.	

a. Prepare a partial income statement for Cruz Inc., beginning with income from continuing operations before income tax.

b. Calculate the earnings per common share for Cruz Inc., including per-share amounts for unusual items.

Appendix

EX 14-26   Unusual items

Discuss whether Colston Company correctly reported the following items in the financial statements:

a. In 2014, the company discovered a clerical error in the prior year's accounting records. As a result, the reported net income for 2013 was overstated by $45,000. The company corrected this error by restating the prior-year financial statements.

b. In 2014, the company voluntarily changed its method of accounting for long-term construction contracts from the percentage of completion method to the completed contract method. Both methods are acceptable under generally acceptable accounting principles. The cumulative effect of this change was reported as a separate component of income in the 2014 income statement.

Problems Series A

PR 14-1A   Horizontal analysis of income statement   OBJ. 1

✔ 1. Net sales, 15.0% increase

For 2014, Lindell Company reported its most significant decline in net income in years. At the end of the year, H. Finn, the president, is presented with the following condensed comparative income statement:

Lindell Company
Comparative Income Statement
For the Years Ended December 31, 2014 and 2013

	2014	2013
Sales	$1,092,500	$950,000
Sales returns and allowances	57,500	50,000
Net sales	$1,035,000	$900,000
Cost of goods sold	625,000	500,000
Gross profit	$ 410,000	$400,000
Selling expenses	$ 153,600	$120,000
Administrative expenses	97,600	80,000
Total operating expenses	$ 251,200	$200,000
Income from operations	$ 158,800	$200,000
Other income	15,000	10,000
Income before income tax	$ 173,800	$210,000
Income tax expense	23,000	20,000
Net income	$ 150,800	$190,000

Instructions

1. Prepare a comparative income statement with horizontal analysis for the two-year period, using 2013 as the base year. Round to one decimal place.

2. ▬▬▶To the extent the data permit, comment on the significant relationships revealed by the horizontal analysis prepared in (1).

PR 14-2A   Vertical analysis of income statement   OBJ. 1

✔ 1. Net income, 2014, 12.0%

For 2014, Kasay Company initiated a sales promotion campaign that included the expenditure of an additional $30,000 for advertising. At the end of the year, Scott Brown, the president, is presented with the following condensed comparative income statement:

Kasay Company
Comparative Income Statement
For the Years Ended December 31, 2014 and 2013

	2014	2013
Sales	$922,500	$820,000
Sales returns and allowances	22,500	20,000
Net sales	$900,000	$800,000
Cost of goods sold	360,000	340,000
Gross profit	$540,000	$460,000
Selling expenses	$216,000	$176,000
Administrative expenses	81,000	72,000
Total operating expenses	$297,000	$248,000
Income from operations	$243,000	$212,000
Other income	135,000	92,000
Income before income tax	$378,000	$304,000
Income tax expense	270,000	240,000
Net income	$108,000	$ 64,000

Instructions

1. Prepare a comparative income statement for the two-year period, presenting an analysis of each item in relationship to net sales for each of the years. Round to one decimal place.

2. ➤ To the extent the data permit, comment on the significant relationships revealed by the vertical analysis prepared in (1).

✔ 2. c. Current
ratio, 2.0

PR 14-3A   Effect of transactions on current position analysis   OBJ. 2

Data pertaining to the current position of Forte Company are as follows:

Cash	$412,500
Marketable securities	187,500
Accounts and notes receivable (net)	300,000
Inventories	700,000
Prepaid expenses	50,000
Accounts payable	200,000
Notes payable (short-term)	250,000
Accrued expenses	300,000

Instructions

1. Compute (a) the working capital, (b) the current ratio, and (c) the quick ratio. Round to one decimal place.

2. List the following captions on a sheet of paper:

Transaction	Working Capital	Current Ratio	Quick Ratio

Compute the working capital, the current ratio, and the quick ratio after each of the following transactions, and record the results in the appropriate columns. *Consider each transaction separately* and assume that only that transaction affects the data given above. Round to one decimal place.

a. Sold marketable securities at no gain or loss, $70,000.

b. Paid accounts payable, $125,000.

c. Purchased goods on account, $110,000.

d. Paid notes payable, $100,000.

e. Declared a cash dividend, $150,000.

f. Declared a common stock dividend on common stock, $50,000.

g. Borrowed cash from bank on a long-term note, $225,000.

h. Received cash on account, $125,000.

i. Issued additional shares of stock for cash, $600,000.

j. Paid cash for prepaid expenses, $10,000.

✔ 5. Number of days'
sales in receivables,
36.5

PR 14-4A **Nineteen measures of solvency and profitability** OBJ. 2, 3

The comparative financial statements of Bettancort Inc. are as follows. The market price
of Bettancort Inc. common stock was $71.25 on December 31, 2014.

Bettancort Inc.
Comparative Retained Earnings Statement
For the Years Ended December 31, 2014 and 2013

	2014	2013
Retained earnings, January 1	$2,655,000	$2,400,000
Add net income for year	300,000	280,000
Total	$2,955,000	$2,680,000
Deduct dividends:		
On preferred stock	$ 15,000	$ 15,000
On common stock	10,000	10,000
Total	$ 25,000	$ 25,000
Retained earnings, December 31	$2,930,000	$2,655,000

Bettancort Inc.
Comparative Income Statement
For the Years Ended December 31, 2014 and 2013

	2014	2013
Sales (all on account)	$1,212,000	$1,010,000
Sales returns and allowances	12,000	10,000
Net sales	$1,200,000	$1,000,000
Cost of goods sold	500,000	475,000
Gross profit	$ 700,000	$ 525,000
Selling expenses	$ 240,000	$ 200,000
Administrative expenses	180,000	150,000
Total operating expenses	$ 420,000	$ 350,000
Income from operations	$ 280,000	$ 175,000
Other income	166,000	225,000
	$ 446,000	$ 400,000
Other expense (interest)	66,000	60,000
Income before income tax	$ 380,000	$ 340,000
Income tax expense	80,000	60,000
Net income	$ 300,000	$ 280,000

Bettancort Inc.
Comparative Balance Sheet
December 31, 2014 and 2013

	Dec. 31, 2014	Dec. 31, 2013
Assets		
Current assets:		
Cash	$ 450,000	$ 400,000
Marketable securities	300,000	260,000
Accounts receivable (net)	130,000	110,000
Inventories	67,000	58,000
Prepaid expenses	153,000	139,000
Total current assets	$1,100,000	$ 967,000
Long-term investments	2,350,000	2,200,000
Property, plant, and equipment (net)	1,320,000	1,188,000
Total assets	$4,770,000	$4,355,000
Liabilities		
Current liabilities	$ 440,000	$ 400,000
Long-term liabilities:		
Mortgage note payable, 8%, due 2019	$ 100,000	$ 0
Bonds payable, 10%, due 2015	1,000,000	1,000,000
Total long-term liabilities	$1,100,000	$1,000,000
Total liabilities	$1,540,000	$1,400,000
Stockholders' Equity		
Preferred $0.75 stock, $10 par	$ 200,000	$ 200,000
Common stock, $10 par	100,000	100,000
Retained earnings	2,930,000	2,655,000
Total stockholders' equity	$3,230,000	$2,955,000
Total liabilities and stockholders' equity	$4,770,000	$4,355,000

Instructions

Determine the following measures for 2014, rounding to one decimal place:

1. Working capital
2. Current ratio
3. Quick ratio
4. Accounts receivable turnover
5. Number of days' sales in receivables
6. Inventory turnover
7. Number of days' sales in inventory
8. Ratio of fixed assets to long-term liabilities
9. Ratio of liabilities to stockholders' equity
10. Number of times interest charges are earned
11. Number of times preferred dividends are earned
12. Ratio of net sales to assets
13. Rate earned on total assets
14. Rate earned on stockholders' equity
15. Rate earned on common stockholders' equity
16. Earnings per share on common stock
17. Price-earnings ratio
18. Dividends per share of common stock
19. Dividend yield

PR 14-5A Solvency and profitability trend analysis   OBJ. 2, 3

Addai Company has provided the following comparative information:

	2014	2013	2012	2011	2010
Net income	$ 273,406	$ 367,976	$ 631,176	$ 884,000	$ 800,000
Interest expense	616,047	572,003	528,165	495,000	440,000
Income tax expense	31,749	53,560	106,720	160,000	200,000
Total assets (ending balance)	4,417,178	4,124,350	3,732,443	3,338,500	2,750,000
Total stockholders' equity (ending balance)	3,706,557	3,433,152	3,065,176	2,434,000	1,550,000
Average total assets	4,270,764	3,928,396	3,535,472	3,044,250	2,475,000
Average total stockholders' equity	3,569,855	3,249,164	2,749,588	1,992,000	1,150,000

You have been asked to evaluate the historical performance of the company over the last five years.

Selected industry ratios have remained relatively steady at the following levels for the last five years:

	2010–2014
Rate earned on total assets	28%
Rate earned on stockholders' equity	18%
Number of times interest charges are earned	2.7
Ratio of liabilities to stockholders' equity	0.4

Instructions

1. Prepare four line graphs with the ratio on the vertical axis and the years on the horizontal axis for the following four ratios (rounded to one decimal place):

   a. Rate earned on total assets
   b. Rate earned on stockholders' equity
   c. Number of times interest charges are earned
   d. Ratio of liabilities to stockholders' equity

   Display both the company ratio and the industry benchmark on each graph. That is, each graph should have two lines.

2. ▬▬▬▶ Prepare an analysis of the graphs in (1).

Problems Series B

PR 14-1B Horizontal analysis of income statement OBJ. 1

✔ 1. Net sales,
30.0% increase

For 2014, Macklin Inc. reported its most significant increase in net income in years. At the end of the year, John Mayer, the president, is presented with the following condensed comparative income statement:

Macklin Inc.
Comparative Income Statement
For the Years Ended December 31, 2014 and 2013

	2014	2013
Sales	$936,000	$720,000
Sales returns and allowances	26,000	20,000
Net sales	$910,000	$700,000
Cost of goods sold	441,000	350,000
Gross profit	$469,000	$350,000
Selling expenses	$ 139,150	$115,000
Administrative expenses	99,450	85,000
Total operating expenses	$238,600	$200,000
Income from operations	$230,400	$150,000
Other income	65,000	50,000
Income before income tax	$295,400	$200,000
Income tax expense	65,000	50,000
Net income	$230,400	$150,000

Instructions

1. Prepare a comparative income statement with horizontal analysis for the two-year period, using 2013 as the base year. Round to one decimal place.

2. ▬▬▶ To the extent the data permit, comment on the significant relationships revealed by the horizontal analysis prepared in (1).

PR 14-2B Vertical analysis of income statement OBJ. 1

✔ 1. Net income,
2013, 14.0%

For 2014, Fielder Industries Inc. initiated a sales promotion campaign that included the expenditure of an additional $40,000 for advertising. At the end of the year, Leif Grando, the president, is presented with the following condensed comparative income statement:

Fielder Industries Inc.
Comparative Income Statement
For the Years Ended December 31, 2014 and 2013

	2014	2013
Sales	$1,325,000	$1,200,000
Sales returns and allowances	25,000	20,000
Net sales	$1,300,000	$1,180,000
Cost of goods sold	682,500	613,600
Gross profit	$ 617,500	$ 566,400
Selling expenses	$ 260,000	$ 188,800
Adminstrative expenses	169,000	177,000
Total operating expenses	$ 429,000	$ 365,800
Income from operations	$ 188,500	$ 200,600
Other income	78,000	70,800
Income before income tax	$ 266,500	$ 271,400
Income tax expense	117,000	106,200
Net income	$ 149,500	$ 165,200

Instructions

1. Prepare a comparative income statement for the two-year period, presenting an analysis of each item in relationship to net sales for each of the years. Round to one decimal place.

2. ▬▬▶ To the extent the data permit, comment on the significant relationships revealed by the vertical analysis prepared in (1).

PR 14-3B   Effect of transactions on current position analysis

OBJ. 2

Data pertaining to the current position of Lucroy Industries Inc. are as follows:

✔ 2. g. Quick
ratio, 1.6

Cash	$ 800,000
Marketable securities	550,000
Accounts and notes receivable (net)	850,000
Inventories	700,000
Prepaid expenses	300,000
Accounts payable	1,200,000
Notes payable (short-term)	700,000
Accrued expenses	100,000

Instructions

1. Compute (a) the working capital, (b) the current ratio, and (c) the quick ratio. Round to one decimal place.

2. List the following captions on a sheet of paper:

Transaction	Working Capital	Current Ratio	Quick Ratio

Compute the working capital, the current ratio, and the quick ratio after each of the following transactions, and record the results in the appropriate columns. *Consider each transaction separately* and assume that only that transaction affects the data given above. Round to one decimal place.

a. Sold marketable securities at no gain or loss, $500,000.

b. Paid accounts payable, $287,500.

c. Purchased goods on account, $400,000.

d. Paid notes payable, $125,000.

e. Declared a cash dividend, $325,000.

f. Declared a common stock dividend on common stock, $150,000.

g. Borrowed cash from bank on a long-term note, $1,000,000.

h. Received cash on account, $75,000.

i. Issued additional shares of stock for cash, $2,000,000.

j. Paid cash for prepaid expenses, $200,000.

PR 14-4B   Nineteen measures of solvency and profitability

OBJ. 2, 3

The comparative financial statements of Stargel Inc. are as follows. The market price of Stargel Inc. common stock was $119.70 on December 31, 2014.

✔ 9. Ratio of
liabilities to
stockholders'
equity, 0.4

Stargel Inc.
Comparative Retained Earnings Statement
For the Years Ended December 31, 2014 and 2013

	2014	2013
Retained earnings, January 1	$5,375,000	$4,545,000
Add net income for year	900,000	925,000
Total	$6,275,000	$5,470,000
Deduct dividends:		
On preferred stock	$ 45,000	$ 45,000
On common stock	50,000	50,000
Total	$ 95,000	$ 95,000
Retained earnings, December 31	$6,180,000	$5,375,000

(Continued)

Stargel Inc.
Comparative Income Statement
For the Years Ended December 31, 2014 and 2013

	2014	2013
Sales (all on account)	$10,050,000	$9,450,000
Sales returns and allowances.......................................	50,000	50,000
Net sales...	$10,000,000	$9,400,000
Cost of goods sold..	5,350,000	4,950,000
Gross profit	$ 4,650,000	$4,450,000
Selling expenses	$ 2,000,000	$1,880,000
Administrative expenses...	1,500,000	1,410,000
Total operating expenses	$ 3,500,000	$3,290,000
Income from operations	$ 1,150,000	$1,160,000
Other income...	150,000	140,000
	$ 1,300,000	$1,300,000
Other expense (interest)	170,000	150,000
Income before income tax	$ 1,130,000	$1,150,000
Income tax expense	230,000	225,000
Net income	$ 900,000	$ 925,000

Stargel Inc.
Comparative Balance Sheet
December 31, 2014 and 2013

	Dec. 31, 2014	Dec. 31, 2013
Assets		
Current assets:		
Cash	$ 500,000	$ 400,000
Marketable securities	1,010,000	1,000,000
Accounts receivable (net)......................................	740,000	510,000
Inventories..	1,190,000	950,000
Prepaid expenses..	250,000	229,000
Total current assets..	$3,690,000	$3,089,000
Long-term investments..	2,350,000	2,300,000
Property, plant, and equipment (net)	3,740,000	3,366,000
Total assets	$9,780,000	$8,755,000
Liabilities		
Current liabilities...	$ 900,000	$ 880,000
Long-term liabilities:		
Mortgage note payable, 8%, due 2019..........................	$ 200,000	$ 0
Bonds payable, 10%, due 2015.................................	1,500,000	1,500,000
Total long-term liabilities	$1,700,000	$1,500,000
Total liabilities	$2,600,000	$2,380,000
Stockholders' Equity		
Preferred $0.90 stock, $10 par..................................	$ 500,000	$ 500,000
Common stock, $5 par...	500,000	500,000
Retained earnings...	6,180,000	5,375,000
Total stockholders' equity......................................	$7,180,000	$6,375,000
Total liabilities and stockholders' equity........................	$9,780,000	$8,755,000

Instructions

Determine the following measures for 2014, rounding to one decimal place, except per share amounts which should be rounded to the nearest penny:

1. Working capital
2. Current ratio
3. Quick ratio
4. Accounts receivable turnover
5. Number of days' sales in receivables
6. Inventory turnover
7. Number of days' sales in inventory
8. Ratio of fixed assets to long-term liabilities

9. Ratio of liabilities to stockholders' equity

10. Number of times interest charges are earned

11. Number of times preferred dividends are earned

12. Ratio of net sales to assets

13. Rate earned on total assets

14. Rate earned on stockholders' equity

15. Rate earned on common stockholders' equity

16. Earnings per share on common stock

17. Price-earnings ratio

18. Dividends per share of common stock

19. Dividend yield

PR 14-5B   Solvency and profitability trend analysis   OBJ. 2, 3

Crosby Company has provided the following comparative information:

	2014	2013	2012	2011	2010
Net income	$ 5,571,720	$ 3,714,480	$ 2,772,000	$ 1,848,000	$ 1,400,000
Interest expense	1,052,060	891,576	768,600	610,000	500,000
Income tax expense	1,225,572	845,222	640,320	441,600	320,000
Total assets (ending balance)	29,378,491	22,598,839	17,120,333	12,588,480	10,152,000
Total stockholders' equity (ending balance)	18,706,200	13,134,480	9,420,000	6,648,000	4,800,000
Average total assets	25,988,665	19,859,586	14,854,406	11,370,240	8,676,000
Average total stockholders' equity	15,920,340	11,277,240	8,034,000	5,724,000	4,100,000

You have been asked to evaluate the historical performance of the company over the last five years.

Selected industry ratios have remained relatively steady at the following levels for the last five years:

	2010–2014
Rate earned on total assets	19%
Rate earned on stockholders' equity	26%
Number of times interest charges are earned	3.4
Ratio of liabilities to stockholders' equity	1.4

Instructions

1. Prepare four line graphs with the ratio on the vertical axis and the years on the horizontal axis for the following four ratios (rounded to one decimal place):

   a. Rate earned on total assets

   b. Rate earned on stockholders' equity

   c. Number of times interest charges are earned

   d. Ratio of liabilities to stockholders' equity

   Display both the company ratio and the industry benchmark on each graph. That is, each graph should have two lines.

2. ➤ Prepare an analysis of the graphs in (1).

Nike, Inc., Problem

Financial Statement Analysis

The financial statements for Nike, Inc., are presented in Appendix B at the end of the text. The following additional information (in thousands) is available:

Accounts receivable at May 31, 2008	$ 2,884
Inventories at May 31, 2008	2,357
Total assets at May 31, 2008	13,249
Stockholders' equity at May 31, 2008	8,693

Instructions

1. Determine the following measures for the fiscal years ended May 31, 2011 (fiscal 2010), and May 31, 2010 (fiscal 2009), rounding to one decimal place.

   a. Working capital

   b. Current ratio

   c. Quick ratio

   d. Accounts receivable turnover

   e. Number of days' sales in receivables

   f. Inventory turnover

   g. Number of days' sales in inventory

   h. Ratio of liabilities to stockholders' equity

   i. Ratio of net sales to assets

   j. Rate earned on total assets, assuming interest expense is $4 million for the year ending May 31, 2011, and $6 million for the year ending May 31, 2010

   k. Rate earned on common stockholders' equity

   l. Price-earnings ratio, assuming that the market price was $75.70 per share on May 31, 2011, and $73.50 per share on May 31, 2010

   m. Percentage relationship of net income to net sales

2. ➤ What conclusions can be drawn from these analyses?

Cases & Projects

CP 14-1   Analysis of financing corporate growth

Assume that the president of Freeman Industries Inc. made the following statement in the Annual Report to Shareholders:

"The founding family and majority shareholders of the company do not believe in using debt to finance future growth. The founding family learned from hard experience during Prohibition and the Great Depression that debt can cause loss of flexibility and eventual loss of corporate control. The company will not place itself at such risk. As such, all future growth will be financed either by stock sales to the public or by internally generated resources."

➤ As a public shareholder of this company, how would you respond to this policy?

CP 14-2   Receivables and inventory turnover

Rodgers Industries Inc. has completed its fiscal year on December 31, 2014. The auditor, Josh McCoy, has approached the CFO, Aaron Mathews, regarding the year-end receivables and inventory levels of Rodgers Industries. The following conversation takes place:

Josh: We are beginning our audit of Rodgers Industries and have prepared ratio analyses to determine if there have been significant changes in operations or financial position. This helps us guide the audit process. This analysis indicates that the inventory turnover has decreased from 5.1 to 2.7, while the accounts receivable turnover has decreased from 11 to 7. I was wondering if you could explain this change in operations.

Aaron: There is little need for concern. The inventory represents computers that we were unable to sell during the holiday buying season. We are confident, however, that we will be able to sell these computers as we move into the next fiscal year.

Josh: What gives you this confidence?

Aaron: We will increase our advertising and provide some very attractive price concessions to move these machines. We have no choice. Newer technology is already out there, and we have to unload this inventory.

Josh: … and the receivables?

Aaron: As you may be aware, the company is under tremendous pressure to expand sales and profits. As a result, we lowered our credit standards to our commercial customers so that we would be able to sell products to a broader customer base. As a result of this policy change, we have been able to expand sales by 35%.

Josh: Your responses have not been reassuring to me.

Aaron: I'm a little confused. Assets are good, right? Why don't you look at our current ratio? It has improved, hasn't it? I would think that you would view that very favorably.

➤ Why is Josh concerned about the inventory and accounts receivable turnover ratios and Aaron's responses to them? What action may Josh need to take? How would you respond to Aaron's last comment?

CP 14-3   Vertical analysis

The condensed income statements through income from operations for Dell Inc. and Apple Inc. are reproduced below for recent fiscal years (numbers in millions of dollars).

	Dell Inc.	Apple Inc.
Sales (net)	$61,494	$65,225
Cost of sales	50,098	39,541
Gross profit	$11,396	$25,684
Selling, general, and administrative expenses	$ 7,302	$ 5,517
Research and development	661	1,782
Operating expenses	$ 7,963	$ 7,299
Income from operations	$ 3,433	$18,385

➤ Prepare comparative common-sized statements, rounding percents to one decimal place. Interpret the analyses.

CP 14-4 Profitability and stockholder ratios

Deere & Co. manufactures and distributes farm and construction machinery that it sells around the world. In addition to its manufacturing operations, Deere & Co.'s credit division loans money to customers to finance the purchase of their farm and construction equipment.

The following information is available for three recent years (in millions except per-share amounts):

	Year 3	Year 2	Year 1
Net income (loss)	$1,865	$874	$2,053
Preferred dividends	$0.00	$0.00	$0.00
Interest expense	$811	$1,042	$1,137
Shares outstanding for computing earnings per share	424	423	431
Cash dividend per share	$1.16	$1.12	$1.06
Average total assets	$42,200	$39,934	$38,655
Average stockholders' equity	$5,555	$5,676	$6,844
Average stock price per share	$60.95	$47.06	$58.01

1. Calculate the following ratios for each year:

   a. Rate earned on total assets

   b. Rate earned on stockholders' equity

   c. Earnings per share

   d. Dividend yield

   e. Price-earnings ratio

2. What is the ratio of average liabilities to average stockholders' equity for Year 3?

3. Based on these data, evaluate Deere & Co.'s performance.

CP 14-5 Comprehensive profitability and solvency analysis

Marriott International, Inc., and Hyatt Hotels Corporation are two major owners and managers of lodging and resort properties in the United States. Abstracted income statement information for the two companies is as follows for a recent year:

	Marriott (in millions)	Hyatt (in millions)
Operating profit before other expenses and interest	$ 677	$ 39
Other income (expenses)	54	118
Interest expense	(180)	(54)
Income before income taxes	$ 551	$103
Income tax expense	93	37
Net income	$ 458	$ 66

Balance sheet information is as follows:

	Marriott (in millions)	Hyatt (in millions)
Total liabilities	$7,398	$2,125
Total stockholders' equity	1,585	5,118
Total liabilities and stockholders' equity	$8,983	$7,243

The average liabilities, average stockholders' equity, and average total assets were as follows:

	Marriott (in millions)	Hyatt (in millions)
Average total liabilities	$7,095	$2,132
Average total stockholders' equity	1,364	5,067
Average total assets	8,458	7,199

1. Determine the following ratios for both companies (round to one decimal place after the whole percent):

   a. Rate earned on total assets

   b. Rate earned on stockholders' equity

   c. Number of times interest charges are earned

   d. Ratio of liabilities to stockholders' equity

2. ➤ Analyze and compare the two companies, using the information in (1).

Appendix A

Interest Tables

Present Value of $1 at Compound Interest Due in *n* Periods

Periods	4.0%	4.5%	5%	5.5%	6%	6.5%	7%
1	0.96154	0.95694	0.95238	0.94787	0.94340	0.93897	0.93458
2	0.92456	0.91573	0.90703	0.89845	0.89000	0.88166	0.87344
3	0.88900	0.87630	0.86384	0.85161	0.83962	0.82785	0.81630
4	0.85480	0.83856	0.82270	0.80722	0.79209	0.77732	0.76290
5	0.82193	0.80245	0.78353	0.76513	0.74726	0.72988	0.71299
6	0.79031	0.76790	0.74622	0.72525	0.70496	0.68533	0.66634
7	0.75992	0.73483	0.71068	0.68744	0.66506	0.64351	0.62275
8	0.73069	0.70319	0.67684	0.65160	0.62741	0.60423	0.58201
9	0.70259	0.67290	0.64461	0.61763	0.59190	0.56735	0.54393
10	0.67556	0.64393	0.61391	0.58543	0.55839	0.53273	0.50835
11	0.64958	0.61620	0.58468	0.55491	0.52679	0.50021	0.47509
12	0.62460	0.58966	0.55684	0.52598	0.49697	0.46968	0.44401
13	0.60057	0.56427	0.53032	0.49856	0.46884	0.44102	0.41496
14	0.57748	0.53997	0.50507	0.47257	0.44230	0.41410	0.38782
15	0.55526	0.51672	0.48102	0.44793	0.41727	0.38883	0.36245
16	0.53391	0.49447	0.45811	0.42458	0.39365	0.36510	0.33873
17	0.51337	0.47318	0.43630	0.40245	0.37136	0.34281	0.31657
18	0.49363	0.45280	0.41552	0.38147	0.35034	0.32189	0.29586
19	0.47464	0.43330	0.39573	0.36158	0.33051	0.30224	0.27651
20	0.45639	0.41464	0.37689	0.34273	0.31180	0.28380	0.25842
21	0.43883	0.39679	0.35894	0.32486	0.29416	0.26648	0.24151
22	0.42196	0.37970	0.34185	0.30793	0.27751	0.25021	0.22571
23	0.40573	0.36335	0.32557	0.29187	0.26180	0.23494	0.21095
24	0.39012	0.34770	0.31007	0.27666	0.24698	0.22060	0.19715
25	0.37512	0.33273	0.29530	0.26223	0.23300	0.20714	0.18425
26	0.36069	0.31840	0.28124	0.24856	0.21981	0.19450	0.17220
27	0.34682	0.30469	0.26785	0.23560	0.20737	0.18263	0.16093
28	0.33348	0.29157	0.25509	0.22332	0.19563	0.17148	0.15040
29	0.32065	0.27902	0.24295	0.21168	0.18456	0.16101	0.14056
30	0.30832	0.26700	0.23138	0.20064	0.17411	0.15119	0.13137
31	0.29646	0.25550	0.22036	0.19018	0.16425	0.14196	0.12277
32	0.28506	0.24450	0.20987	0.18027	0.15496	0.13329	0.11474
33	0.27409	0.23397	0.19987	0.17087	0.14619	0.12516	0.10723
34	0.26355	0.22390	0.19035	0.16196	0.13791	0.11752	0.10022
35	0.25342	0.21425	0.18129	0.15352	0.13011	0.11035	0.09366
40	0.20829	0.17193	0.14205	0.11746	0.09722	0.08054	0.06678
45	0.17120	0.13796	0.11130	0.08988	0.07265	0.05879	0.04761
50	0.14071	0.11071	0.08720	0.06877	0.05429	0.04291	0.03395

Present Value of $1 at Compound Interest Due in *n* Periods

Periods	8%	9%	10%	11%	12%	13%	14%
1	0.92593	0.91743	0.90909	0.90090	0.89286	0.88496	0.87719
2	0.85734	0.84168	0.82645	0.81162	0.79719	0.78315	0.76947
3	0.79383	0.77218	0.75131	0.73119	0.71178	0.69305	0.67497
4	0.73503	0.70843	0.68301	0.65873	0.63552	0.61332	0.59208
5	0.68058	0.64993	0.62092	0.59345	0.56743	0.54276	0.51937
6	0.63017	0.59627	0.56447	0.53464	0.50663	0.48032	0.45559
7	0.58349	0.54703	0.51316	0.48166	0.45235	0.42506	0.39964
8	0.54027	0.50187	0.46651	0.43393	0.40388	0.37616	0.35056
9	0.50025	0.46043	0.42410	0.39092	0.36061	0.33288	0.30751
10	0.46319	0.42241	0.38554	0.35218	0.32197	0.29459	0.26974
11	0.42888	0.38753	0.35049	0.31728	0.28748	0.26070	0.23662
12	0.39711	0.35553	0.31863	0.28584	0.25668	0.23071	0.20756
13	0.36770	0.32618	0.28966	0.25751	0.22917	0.20416	0.18207
14	0.34046	0.29925	0.26333	0.23199	0.20462	0.18068	0.15971
15	0.31524	0.27454	0.23939	0.20900	0.18270	0.15989	0.14010
16	0.29189	0.25187	0.21763	0.18829	0.16312	0.14150	0.12289
17	0.27027	0.23107	0.19784	0.16963	0.14564	0.12522	0.10780
18	0.25025	0.21199	0.17986	0.15282	0.13004	0.11081	0.09456
19	0.23171	0.19449	0.16351	0.13768	0.11611	0.09806	0.08295
20	0.21455	0.17843	0.14864	0.12403	0.10367	0.08678	0.07276
21	0.19866	0.16370	0.13513	0.11174	0.09256	0.07680	0.06383
22	0.18394	0.15018	0.12285	0.10067	0.08264	0.06796	0.05599
23	0.17032	0.13778	0.11168	0.09069	0.07379	0.06014	0.04911
24	0.15770	0.12640	0.10153	0.08170	0.06588	0.05323	0.04308
25	0.14602	0.11597	0.09230	0.07361	0.05882	0.04710	0.03779
26	0.13520	0.10639	0.08391	0.06631	0.05252	0.04168	0.03315
27	0.12519	0.09761	0.07628	0.05974	0.04689	0.03689	0.02908
28	0.11591	0.08955	0.06934	0.05382	0.04187	0.03264	0.02551
29	0.10733	0.08215	0.06304	0.04849	0.03738	0.02889	0.02237
30	0.09938	0.07537	0.05731	0.04368	0.03338	0.02557	0.01963
31	0.09202	0.06915	0.05210	0.03935	0.02980	0.02262	0.01722
32	0.08520	0.06344	0.04736	0.03545	0.02661	0.02002	0.01510
33	0.07889	0.05820	0.04306	0.03194	0.02376	0.01772	0.01325
34	0.07305	0.05339	0.03914	0.02878	0.02121	0.01568	0.01162
35	0.06763	0.04899	0.03558	0.02592	0.01894	0.01388	0.01019
40	0.04603	0.03184	0.02209	0.01538	0.01075	0.00753	0.00529
45	0.03133	0.02069	0.01372	0.00913	0.00610	0.00409	0.00275
50	0.02132	0.01345	0.00852	0.00542	0.00346	0.00222	0.00143

Present Value of Ordinary Annuity of $1 per Period

Periods	4.0%	4.5%	5%	5.5%	6%	6.5%	7%
1	0.96154	0.95694	0.95238	0.94787	0.94340	0.93897	0.93458
2	1.88609	1.87267	1.85941	1.84632	1.83339	1.82063	1.80802
3	2.77509	2.74896	2.72325	2.69793	2.67301	2.64848	2.62432
4	3.62990	3.58753	3.54595	3.50515	3.46511	3.42580	3.38721
5	4.45182	4.38998	4.32948	4.27028	4.21236	4.15568	4.10020
6	5.24214	5.15787	5.07569	4.99553	4.91732	4.84101	4.76654
7	6.00205	5.89270	5.78637	5.68297	5.58238	5.48452	5.38929
8	6.73274	6.59589	6.46321	6.33457	6.20979	6.08875	5.97130
9	7.43533	7.26879	7.10782	6.95220	6.80169	6.65610	6.51523
10	8.11090	7.91272	7.72173	7.53763	7.36009	7.18883	7.02358
11	8.76048	8.52892	8.30641	8.09254	7.88687	7.68904	7.49867
12	9.38507	9.11858	8.86325	8.61852	8.38384	8.15873	7.94269
13	9.98565	9.68285	9.39357	9.11708	8.85268	8.59974	8.35765
14	10.56312	10.22283	9.89864	9.58965	9.29498	9.01384	8.74547
15	11.11839	10.73955	10.37966	10.03758	9.71225	9.40267	9.10791
16	11.65230	11.23402	10.83777	10.46216	10.10590	9.76776	9.44665
17	12.16567	11.70719	11.27407	10.86461	10.47726	10.11058	9.76322
18	12.65930	12.15999	11.68959	11.24607	10.82760	10.43247	10.05909
19	13.13394	12.59329	12.08532	11.60765	11.15812	10.73471	10.33560
20	13.59033	13.00794	12.46221	11.95038	11.46992	11.01851	10.59401
21	14.02916	13.40472	12.82115	12.27524	11.76408	11.28498	10.83553
22	14.45112	13.78442	13.16300	12.58317	12.04158	11.53520	11.06124
23	14.85684	14.14777	13.48857	12.87504	12.30338	11.77014	11.27219
24	15.24696	14.49548	13.79864	13.15170	12.55036	11.99074	11.46933
25	15.62208	14.82821	14.09394	13.41393	12.78336	12.19788	11.65358
26	15.98277	15.14661	14.37519	13.66250	13.00317	12.39237	11.82578
27	16.32959	15.45130	14.64303	13.89810	13.21053	12.57500	11.98671
28	16.66306	15.74287	14.89813	14.12142	13.40616	12.74648	12.13711
29	16.98371	16.02189	15.14107	14.33310	13.59072	12.90749	12.27767
30	17.29203	16.28889	15.37245	14.53375	13.76483	13.05868	12.40904
31	17.58849	16.54439	15.59281	14.72393	13.92909	13.20063	12.53181
32	17.87355	16.78889	15.80268	14.90420	14.08404	13.33393	12.64656
33	18.14765	17.02286	16.00255	15.07507	14.23023	13.45909	12.75379
34	18.41120	17.24676	16.19290	15.23703	14.36814	13.57661	12.85401
35	18.66461	17.46101	16.37419	15.39055	14.49825	13.68696	12.94767
40	19.79277	18.40158	17.15909	16.04612	15.04630	14.14553	13.33171
45	20.72004	19.15635	17.77407	16.54773	15.45583	14.48023	13.60552
50	21.48218	19.76201	18.25593	16.93152	15.76186	14.72452	13.80075

Present Value of Ordinary Annuity of $1 per Period

Periods	8%	9%	10%	11%	12%	13%	14%
1	0.92593	0.91743	0.90909	0.90090	0.89286	0.88496	0.87719
2	1.78326	1.75911	1.73554	1.71252	1.69005	1.66810	1.64666
3	2.57710	2.53129	2.48685	2.44371	2.40183	2.36115	2.32163
4	3.31213	3.23972	3.16987	3.10245	3.03735	2.97447	2.91371
5	3.99271	3.88965	3.79079	3.69590	3.60478	3.51723	3.43308
6	4.62288	4.48592	4.35526	4.23054	4.11141	3.99755	3.88867
7	5.20637	5.03295	4.86842	4.71220	4.56376	4.42261	4.28830
8	5.74664	5.53482	5.33493	5.14612	4.96764	4.79677	4.63886
9	6.24689	5.99525	5.75902	5.53705	5.32825	5.13166	4.94637
10	6.71008	6.41766	6.14457	5.88923	5.65022	5.42624	5.21612
11	7.13896	6.80519	6.49506	6.20652	5.93770	5.68694	5.45273
12	7.53608	7.16073	6.81369	6.49236	6.19437	5.91765	5.66029
13	7.90378	7.48690	7.10336	6.74987	6.42355	6.12181	5.84236
14	8.22424	7.78615	7.36669	6.96187	6.62817	6.30249	6.00207
15	8.55948	8.06069	7.60608	7.19087	6.81086	6.46238	6.14217
16	8.85137	8.31256	7.82371	7.37916	6.97399	6.60388	6.26506
17	9.12164	8.54363	8.02155	7.54879	7.11963	6.72909	6.37286
18	9.37189	8.75563	8.20141	7.70162	7.24967	6.83991	6.46742
19	9.60360	8.95011	8.36492	7.83929	7.36578	6.93797	6.55037
20	9.81815	9.12855	8.51356	7.96333	7.46944	7.02475	6.62313
21	10.01680	9.29224	8.64869	8.07507	7.56200	7.10155	6.68696
22	10.20074	9.44243	8.77154	8.17574	7.64465	7.16951	6.74294
23	10.37106	9.58021	8.88322	8.26643	7.71843	7.22966	6.79206
24	10.52876	9.70661	8.98474	8.34814	7.78432	7.28288	6.83514
25	10.67478	9.82258	9.07704	8.42174	7.84314	7.32998	6.87293
26	10.80998	9.92897	9.16095	8.48806	7.89566	7.37167	6.90608
27	10.93516	10.02658	9.23722	8.54780	7.94255	7.40856	6.93515
28	11.05108	10.11613	9.30657	8.60162	7.98442	7.44120	6.96066
29	11.15841	10.19828	9.36961	8.65011	8.02181	7.47009	6.98304
30	11.25778	10.27365	9.42691	8.69379	8.05518	7.49565	7.00266
31	11.34980	10.34280	9.47901	8.73315	8.08499	7.51828	7.01988
32	11.43500	10.40624	9.52638	8.76860	8.11159	7.53830	7.03498
33	11.51389	10.46444	9.56943	8.80054	8.13535	7.55602	7.04823
34	11.58693	10.51784	9.60857	8.82932	8.15656	7.57170	7.05985
35	11.65457	10.56682	9.64416	8.85524	8.17550	7.58557	7.07005
40	11.92461	10.75736	9.77905	8.95105	8.24378	7.63438	7.10504
45	12.10840	10.88120	9.86281	9.00791	8.28252	7.66086	7.12322
50	12.23348	10.96168	9.91481	9.04165	8.30450	7.67524	7.13266

NIKE INC

FORM 10-K
(Annual Report)

Filed 07/22/11 for the Period Ending 05/31/11

Address	ONE BOWERMAN DR
	BEAVERTON, OR 97005-6453
Telephone	5036713173
CIK	0000320187
Symbol	NKE
SIC Code	3021 - Rubber and Plastics Footwear
Industry	Footwear
Sector	Consumer Cyclical
Fiscal Year	05/31

Source: Nike, Inc. Annual Report pursuant to Section 13 or 15(b) of the Securities Exchange Act of 1934. For the fiscal year ended May 31, 2011. United States Securities and Exchange Commission, Washington D.C. 20549.

Table of Contents

Management's Annual Report on Internal Control Over Financial Reporting

Management is responsible for establishing and maintaining adequate internal control over financial reporting, as such term is defined in Rule 13a-15(f) and Rule 15d-15(f) of the Securities Exchange Act of 1934, as amended. Internal control over financial reporting is a process designed to provide reasonable assurance regarding the reliability of financial reporting and the preparation of the financial statements for external purposes in accordance with generally accepted accounting principles in the United States of America. Internal control over financial reporting includes those policies and procedures that: (i) pertain to the maintenance of records that, in reasonable detail, accurately and fairly reflect the transactions and dispositions of assets of the company; (ii) provide reasonable assurance that transactions are recorded as necessary to permit preparation of financial statements in accordance with generally accepted accounting principles, and that receipts and expenditures of the company are being made only in accordance with authorizations of our management and directors; and (iii) provide reasonable assurance regarding prevention or timely detection of unauthorized acquisition, use or disposition of assets of the company that could have a material effect on the financial statements.

While "reasonable assurance" is a high level of assurance, it does not mean absolute assurance. Because of its inherent limitations, internal control over financial reporting may not prevent or detect every misstatement and instance of fraud. Controls are susceptible to manipulation, especially in instances of fraud caused by the collusion of two or more people, including our senior management. Also, projections of any evaluation of effectiveness to future periods are subject to the risk that controls may become inadequate because of changes in conditions, or that the degree of compliance with the policies or procedures may deteriorate.

Under the supervision and with the participation of our Chief Executive Officer and Chief Financial Officer, our management conducted an evaluation of the effectiveness of our internal control over financial reporting based upon the framework in *Internal Control — Integrated Framework* issued by the Committee of Sponsoring Organizations of the Treadway Commission (COSO). Based on the results of our evaluation, our management concluded that our internal control over financial reporting was effective as of May 31, 2011.

PricewaterhouseCoopers LLP, an independent registered public accounting firm, has audited (1) the consolidated financial statements and (2) the effectiveness of our internal control over financial reporting as of May 31, 2011, as stated in their report herein.

Mark G. Parker
Chief Executive Officer and President

Donald W. Blair
Chief Financial Officer

54

REPORT OF INDEPENDENT REGISTERED PUBLIC ACCOUNTING FIRM

To the Board of Directors and
Shareholders of NIKE, Inc.:

In our opinion, the consolidated financial statements listed in the index appearing under Item 15(a)(1) present fairly, in all material respects, the financial position of NIKE, Inc. and its subsidiaries at May 31, 2011 and 2010, and the results of their operations and their cash flows for each of the three years in the period ended May 31, 2011 in conformity with accounting principles generally accepted in the United States of America. In addition, in our opinion, the financial statement schedule listed in the appendix appearing under Item 15(a)(2) presents fairly, in all material respects, the information set forth therein when read in conjunction with the related consolidated financial statements. Also in our opinion, the Company maintained, in all material respects, effective internal control over financial reporting as of May 31, 2011, based on criteria established in *Internal Control — Integrated Framework* issued by the Committee of Sponsoring Organizations of the Treadway Commission (COSO). The Company's management is responsible for these financial statements and financial statement schedule, for maintaining effective internal control over financial reporting and for its assessment of the effectiveness of internal control over financial reporting, included in Management's Annual Report on Internal Control Over Financial Reporting appearing under Item 8. Our responsibility is to express opinions on these financial statements, on the financial statement schedule, and on the Company's internal control over financial reporting based on our integrated audits. We conducted our audits in accordance with the standards of the Public Company Accounting Oversight Board (United States). Those standards require that we plan and perform the audits to obtain reasonable assurance about whether the financial statements are free of material misstatement and whether effective internal control over financial reporting was maintained in all material respects. Our audits of the financial statements included examining, on a test basis, evidence supporting the amounts and disclosures in the financial statements, assessing the accounting principles used and significant estimates made by management, and evaluating the overall financial statement presentation. Our audit of internal control over financial reporting included obtaining an understanding of internal control over financial reporting, assessing the risk that a material weakness exists, and testing and evaluating the design and operating effectiveness of internal control based on the assessed risk. Our audits also included performing such other procedures as we considered necessary in the circumstances. We believe that our audits provide a reasonable basis for our opinions.

A company's internal control over financial reporting is a process designed to provide reasonable assurance regarding the reliability of financial reporting and the preparation of financial statements for external purposes in accordance with generally accepted accounting principles. A company's internal control over financial reporting includes those policies and procedures that (i) pertain to the maintenance of records that, in reasonable detail, accurately and fairly reflect the transactions and dispositions of the assets of the company; (ii) provide reasonable assurance that transactions are recorded as necessary to permit preparation of financial statements in accordance with generally accepted accounting principles, and that receipts and expenditures of the company are being made only in accordance with authorizations of management and directors of the company; and (iii) provide reasonable assurance regarding prevention or timely detection of unauthorized acquisition, use, or disposition of the company's assets that could have a material effect on the financial statements.

Because of its inherent limitations, internal control over financial reporting may not prevent or detect misstatements. Also, projections of any evaluation of effectiveness to future periods are subject to the risk that controls may become inadequate because of changes in conditions, or that the degree of compliance with the policies or procedures may deteriorate.

/s/   P RICEWATERHOUSE C OOPERS LLP

Portland, Oregon
July 22, 2011

NIKE, INC.
CONSOLIDATED STATEMENTS OF INCOME

	Year Ended May 31,		
	2011	2010	2009
	(In millions, except per share data)		
Revenues	$20,862	$19,014	$19,176
Cost of sales	11,354	10,214	10,572
Gross margin	9,508	8,800	8,604
Demand creation expense	2,448	2,356	2,352
Operating overhead expense	4,245	3,970	3,798
Total selling and administrative expense	6,693	6,326	6,150
Restructuring charges (Note 16)	—	—	195
Goodwill impairment (Note 4)	—	—	199
Intangible and other asset impairment (Note 4)	—	—	202
Interest expense (income), net (Notes 6, 7 and 8)	4	6	(10)
Other (income), net (Note 17)	(33)	(49)	(89)
Income before income taxes	2,844	2,517	1,957
Income taxes (Note 9)	711	610	470
Net income	$ 2,133	$ 1,907	$ 1,487
Basic earnings per common share (Notes 1 and 12)	$ 4.48	$ 3.93	$ 3.07
Diluted earnings per common share (Notes 1 and 12)	$ 4.39	$ 3.86	$ 3.03
Dividends declared per common share	$ 1.20	$ 1.06	$ 0.98

The accompanying notes to consolidated financial statements are an integral part of this statement.

56

NIKE, INC.
CONSOLIDATED BALANCE SHEETS

	May 31,	
	2011	**2010**
	(In millions)	
ASSETS		
Current assets:		
Cash and equivalents	$ 1,955	$ 3,079
Short-term investments (Note 6)	2,583	2,067
Accounts receivable, net (Note 1)	3,138	2,650
Inventories (Notes 1 and 2)	2,715	2,041
Deferred income taxes (Note 9)	312	249
Prepaid expenses and other current assets	594	873
Total current assets	11,297	10,959
Property, plant and equipment, net (Note 3)	2,115	1,932
Identifiable intangible assets, net (Note 4)	487	467
Goodwill (Note 4)	205	188
Deferred income taxes and other assets (Notes 9 and 17)	894	873
Total assets	$14,998	$14,419
LIABILITIES AND SHAREHOLDERS' EQUITY		
Current liabilities:		
Current portion of long-term debt (Note 8)	$ 200	$ 7
Notes payable (Note 7)	187	139
Accounts payable (Note 7)	1,469	1,255
Accrued liabilities (Notes 5 and 17)	1,985	1,904
Income taxes payable (Note 9)	117	59
Total current liabilities	3,958	3,364
Long-term debt (Note 8)	276	446
Deferred income taxes and other liabilities (Notes 9 and 17)	921	855
Commitments and contingencies (Note 15)	—	—
Redeemable Preferred Stock (Note 10)	—	—
Shareholders' equity:		
Common stock at stated value (Note 11):		
Class A convertible — 90 and 90 shares outstanding	—	—
Class B — 378 and 394 shares outstanding	3	3
Capital in excess of stated value	3,944	3,441
Accumulated other comprehensive income (Note 14)	95	215
Retained earnings	5,801	6,095
Total shareholders' equity	9,843	9,754
Total liabilities and shareholders' equity	$14,998	$14,419

The accompanying notes to consolidated financial statements are an integral part of this statement.

57

NIKE, INC.
CONSOLIDATED STATEMENTS OF CASH FLOWS

| | Year Ended May 31, | | |
	2011	2010	2009
		(In millions)	
Cash provided by operations:			
Net income	$ 2,133	$ 1,907	$ 1,487
Income charges (credits) not affecting cash:			
Depreciation	335	324	335
Deferred income taxes	(76)	8	(294)
Stock-based compensation (Note 11)	105	159	171
Impairment of goodwill, intangibles and other assets (Note 4)	—	—	401
Amortization and other	23	72	48
Changes in certain working capital components and other assets and liabilities excluding the impact of acquisition and divestitures:			
(Increase) decrease in accounts receivable	(273)	182	(238)
(Increase) decrease in inventories	(551)	285	32
(Increase) decrease in prepaid expenses and other current assets	(35)	(70)	14
Increase (decrease) in accounts payable, accrued liabilities and income taxes payable	151	297	(220)
Cash provided by operations	1,812	3,164	1,736
Cash used by investing activities:			
Purchases of short-term investments	(7,616)	(3,724)	(2,909)
Maturities of short-term investments	4,313	2,334	1,280
Sales of short-term investments	2,766	453	1,110
Additions to property, plant and equipment	(432)	(335)	(456)
Disposals of property, plant and equipment	1	10	33
Increase in other assets, net of other liabilities	(30)	(11)	(47)
Settlement of net investment hedges	(23)	5	191
Cash used by investing activities	(1,021)	(1,268)	(798)
Cash used by financing activities:			
Reductions in long-term debt, including current portion	(8)	(32)	(7)
Increase (decrease) in notes payable	41	(205)	177
Proceeds from exercise of stock options and other stock issuances	345	364	187
Excess tax benefits from share-based payment arrangements	64	58	25
Repurchase of common stock	(1,859)	(741)	(649)
Dividends — common and preferred	(555)	(505)	(467)
Cash used by financing activities	(1,972)	(1,061)	(734)
Effect of exchange rate changes	57	(47)	(47)
Net (decrease) increase in cash and equivalents	(1,124)	788	157
Cash and equivalents, beginning of year	3,079	2,291	2,134
Cash and equivalents, end of year	$ 1,955	$ 3,079	$ 2,291
Supplemental disclosure of cash flow information:			
Cash paid during the year for:			
Interest, net of capitalized interest	$ 32	$ 48	$ 47
Income taxes	736	537	765
Dividends declared and not paid	145	131	121

The accompanying notes to consolidated financial statements are an integral part of this statement.

58

Table of Contents

NIKE, INC.
CONSOLIDATED STATEMENTS OF SHAREHOLDERS' EQUITY

	Class A Shares	Class A Amount	Class B Shares	Class B Amount	Capital in Excess of Stated Value	Accumulated Other Comprehensive Income	Retained Earnings	Total
					(In millions, except per share data)			
Balance at May 31, 2008	97	$ —	394	$ 3	$ 2,498	$ 251	$ 5,073	$ 7,825
Stock options exercised			4		167			167
Conversion to Class B Common Stock	(2)		2					—
Repurchase of Class B Common Stock			(11)		(6)		(633)	(639)
Dividends on Common stock ($0.98 per share)							(475)	(475)
Issuance of shares to employees			1		45			45
Stock-based compensation (Note 11):					171			171
Forfeiture of shares from employees			—		(4)		(1)	(5)
Comprehensive income:								
Net income							1,487	1,487
Other comprehensive income:								
Foreign currency translation and other (net of tax benefit of $178)						(335)		(335)
Net gain on cash flow hedges (net of tax expense of $168)						454		454
Net gain on net investment hedges (net of tax expense of $55)						106		106
Reclassification to net income of previously deferred net gains related to hedge derivatives (net of tax expense of $40)						(108)		(108)
Total comprehensive income						117	1,487	1,604
Balance at May 31, 2009	95	$ —	390	$ 3	$ 2,871	$ 368	$ 5,451	$ 8,693
Stock options exercised			9		380			380
Conversion to Class B Common Stock	(5)		5					—
Repurchase of Class B Common Stock			(11)		(7)		(747)	(754)
Dividends on Common stock ($1.06 per share)							(515)	(515)
Issuance of shares to employees			1		40			40
Stock-based compensation (Note 11):					159			159
Forfeiture of shares from employees			—		(2)		(1)	(3)
Comprehensive income:								
Net income							1,907	1,907
Other comprehensive income (Notes 14 and 17):								
Foreign currency translation and other (net of tax benefit of $72)						(159)		(159)
Net gain on cash flow hedges (net of tax expense of $28)						87		87
Net gain on net investment hedges (net of tax expense of $21)						45		45
Reclassification to net income of previously deferred net gains related to hedge derivatives (net of tax expense of $42)						(122)		(122)
Reclassification of ineffective hedge gains to net income (net of tax expense of $1)						(4)		(4)
Total comprehensive income						(153)	1,907	1,754
Balance at May 31, 2010	90	$ —	394	$ 3	$ 3,441	$ 215	$ 6,095	$ 9,754
Stock options exercised			7		368			368
Repurchase of Class B Common Stock			(24)		(14)		(1,857)	(1,871)
Dividends on Common stock ($1.20 per share)							(569)	(569)
Issuance of shares to employees			1		49			49
Stock-based compensation (Note 11):					105			105
Forfeiture of shares from employees			—		(5)		(1)	(6)
Comprehensive income:								
Net income							2,133	2,133
Other comprehensive income (Notes 14 and 17):								
Foreign currency translation and other (net of tax expense of $121)						263		263
Net loss on cash flow hedges (net of tax benefit of $66)						(242)		(242)
Net loss on net investment hedges (net of tax benefit of $28)						(57)		(57)
Reclassification to net income of previously deferred net gains related to hedge derivatives (net of tax expense of $24)						(84)		(84)
Total comprehensive income						(120)	2,133	2,013
Balance at May 31, 2011	90	$ —	378	$ 3	$ 3,944	$ 95	$ 5,801	$ 9,843

The accompanying notes to consolidated financial statements are an integral part of this statement.

59

Table of Contents

NIKE, INC.
NOTES TO CONSOLIDATED FINANCIAL STATEMENTS

Note 1 — Summary of Significant Accounting Policies

Description of Business

NIKE, Inc. is a worldwide leader in the design, marketing and distribution of athletic and sports-inspired footwear, apparel, equipment and accessories. Wholly-owned NIKE subsidiaries include Cole Haan, which designs, markets and distributes dress and casual shoes, handbags, accessories and coats; Converse Inc., which designs, markets and distributes athletic and casual footwear, apparel and accessories; Hurley International LLC, which designs, markets and distributes action sports and youth lifestyle footwear, apparel and accessories; and Umbro International Limited, which designs, distributes and licenses athletic and casual footwear, apparel and equipment, primarily for the sport of soccer.

Basis of Consolidation

The consolidated financial statements include the accounts of NIKE, Inc. and its subsidiaries (the "Company"). All significant intercompany transactions and balances have been eliminated.

Recognition of Revenues

Wholesale revenues are recognized when title passes and the risks and rewards of ownership have passed to the customer, based on the terms of sale. This occurs upon shipment or upon receipt by the customer depending on the country of the sale and the agreement with the customer. Retail store revenues are recorded at the time of sale. Provisions for sales discounts, returns and miscellaneous claims from customers are made at the time of sale. As of May 31, 2011 and 2010, the Company's reserve balances for sales discounts, returns and miscellaneous claims were $423 million and $371 million, respectively.

Shipping and Handling Costs

Shipping and handling costs are expensed as incurred and included in cost of sales.

Demand Creation Expense

Demand creation expense consists of advertising and promotion costs, including costs of endorsement contracts, television, digital and print advertising, brand events, and retail brand presentation. Advertising production costs are expensed the first time an advertisement is run. Advertising placement costs are expensed in the month the advertising appears, while costs related to brand events are expensed when the event occurs. Costs related to retail brand presentation are expensed when the presentation is completed and delivered. A significant amount of the Company's promotional expenses result from payments under endorsement contracts. Accounting for endorsement payments is based upon specific contract provisions. Generally, endorsement payments are expensed on a straight-line basis over the term of the contract after giving recognition to periodic performance compliance provisions of the contracts. Prepayments made under contracts are included in prepaid expenses or other assets depending on the period to which the prepayment applies.

Through cooperative advertising programs, the Company reimburses retail customers for certain costs of advertising the Company's products. The Company records these costs in selling and administrative expense at the point in time when it is obligated to its customers for the costs, which is when the related revenues are recognized. This obligation may arise prior to the related advertisement being run.

Total advertising and promotion expenses were $2,448 million, $2,356 million, and $2,352 million for the years ended May 31, 2011, 2010 and 2009, respectively. Prepaid advertising and promotion expenses recorded in prepaid expenses and other assets totaled $291 million and $261 million at May 31, 2011 and 2010, respectively.

Table of Contents

NIKE, INC.
NOTES TO CONSOLIDATED FINANCIAL STATEMENTS — (Continued)

Cash and Equivalents

Cash and equivalents represent cash and short-term, highly liquid investments with maturities of three months or less at date of purchase. The carrying amounts reflected in the consolidated balance sheet for cash and equivalents approximate fair value.

Short-Term Investments

Short-term investments consist of highly liquid investments, including commercial paper, U.S. treasury, U.S. agency, and corporate debt securities, with maturities over three months from the date of purchase. Debt securities that the Company has the ability and positive intent to hold to maturity are carried at amortized cost. At May 31, 2011 and 2010, the Company did not hold any short-term investments that were classified as trading or held-to-maturity.

At May 31, 2011 and 2010, short-term investments consisted of available-for-sale securities. Available-for-sale securities are recorded at fair value with unrealized gains and losses reported, net of tax, in other comprehensive income, unless unrealized losses are determined to be other than temporary. The Company considers all available-for-sale securities, including those with maturity dates beyond 12 months, as available to support current operational liquidity needs and therefore classifies all securities with maturity dates beyond three months at the date of purchase as current assets within short-term investments on the consolidated balance sheet.

See Note 6 — Fair Value Measurements for more information on the Company's short term investments.

Allowance for Uncollectible Accounts Receivable

Accounts receivable consists primarily of amounts receivable from customers. We make ongoing estimates relating to the collectability of our accounts receivable and maintain an allowance for estimated losses resulting from the inability of our customers to make required payments. In determining the amount of the allowance, we consider our historical level of credit losses and make judgments about the creditworthiness of significant customers based on ongoing credit evaluations. Accounts receivable with anticipated collection dates greater than 12 months from the balance sheet date and related allowances are considered non-current and recorded in other assets. The allowance for uncollectible accounts receivable was $124 million and $117 million at May 31, 2011 and 2010, respectively, of which $50 million and $43 million was classified as long-term and recorded in other assets.

Inventory Valuation

Inventories are stated at lower of cost or market and valued on a first-in, first-out ("FIFO") or moving average cost basis.

Property, Plant and Equipment and Depreciation

Property, plant and equipment are recorded at cost. Depreciation for financial reporting purposes is determined on a straight-line basis for buildings and leasehold improvements over 2 to 40 years and for machinery and equipment over 2 to 15 years. Computer software (including, in some cases, the cost of internal labor) is depreciated on a straight-line basis over 3 to 10 years.

Impairment of Long-Lived Assets

The Company reviews the carrying value of long-lived assets or asset groups to be used in operations whenever events or changes in circumstances indicate that the carrying amount of the assets might not be recoverable. Factors that would necessitate an impairment assessment include a significant adverse change in the

NIKE, INC.

NOTES TO CONSOLIDATED FINANCIAL STATEMENTS — (Continued)

extent or manner in which an asset is used, a significant adverse change in legal factors or the business climate that could affect the value of the asset, or a significant decline in the observable market value of an asset, among others. If such facts indicate a potential impairment, the Company would assess the recoverability of an asset group by determining if the carrying value of the asset group exceeds the sum of the projected undiscounted cash flows expected to result from the use and eventual disposition of the assets over the remaining economic life of the primary asset in the asset group. If the recoverability test indicates that the carrying value of the asset group is not recoverable, the Company will estimate the fair value of the asset group using appropriate valuation methodologies which would typically include an estimate of discounted cash flows. Any impairment would be measured as the difference between the asset groups carrying amount and its estimated fair value.

Identifiable Intangible Assets and Goodwill

The Company performs annual impairment tests on goodwill and intangible assets with indefinite lives in the fourth quarter of each fiscal year, or when events occur or circumstances change that would, more likely than not, reduce the fair value of a reporting unit or an intangible asset with an indefinite life below its carrying value. Events or changes in circumstances that may trigger interim impairment reviews include significant changes in business climate, operating results, planned investments in the reporting unit, or an expectation that the carrying amount may not be recoverable, among other factors. The impairment test requires the Company to estimate the fair value of its reporting units. If the carrying value of a reporting unit exceeds its fair value, the goodwill of that reporting unit is potentially impaired and the Company proceeds to step two of the impairment analysis. In step two of the analysis, the Company measures and records an impairment loss equal to the excess of the carrying value of the reporting unit's goodwill over its implied fair value should such a circumstance arise.

The Company generally bases its measurement of fair value of a reporting unit on a blended analysis of the present value of future discounted cash flows and the market valuation approach. The discounted cash flows model indicates the fair value of the reporting unit based on the present value of the cash flows that the Company expects the reporting unit to generate in the future. The Company's significant estimates in the discounted cash flows model include: its weighted average cost of capital; long-term rate of growth and profitability of the reporting unit's business; and working capital effects. The market valuation approach indicates the fair value of the business based on a comparison of the reporting unit to comparable publicly traded companies in similar lines of business. Significant estimates in the market valuation approach model include identifying similar companies with comparable business factors such as size, growth, profitability, risk and return on investment, and assessing comparable revenue and operating income multiples in estimating the fair value of the reporting unit.

The Company believes the weighted use of discounted cash flows and the market valuation approach is the best method for determining the fair value of its reporting units because these are the most common valuation methodologies used within its industry; and the blended use of both models compensates for the inherent risks associated with either model if used on a stand-alone basis.

Indefinite-lived intangible assets primarily consist of acquired trade names and trademarks. In measuring the fair value for these intangible assets, the Company utilizes the relief-from-royalty method. This method assumes that trade names and trademarks have value to the extent that their owner is relieved of the obligation to pay royalties for the benefits received from them. This method requires the Company to estimate the future revenue for the related brands, the appropriate royalty rate and the weighted average cost of capital.

Foreign Currency Translation and Foreign Currency Transactions

Adjustments resulting from translating foreign functional currency financial statements into U.S. dollars are included in the foreign currency translation adjustment, a component of accumulated other comprehensive income in shareholders' equity.

Table of Contents

NIKE, INC.
NOTES TO CONSOLIDATED FINANCIAL STATEMENTS — (Continued)

The Company's global subsidiaries have various assets and liabilities, primarily receivables and payables, that are denominated in currencies other than their functional currency. These balance sheet items are subject to remeasurement, the impact of which is recorded in other (income), net, within our consolidated statement of income.

Accounting for Derivatives and Hedging Activities

The Company uses derivative financial instruments to limit exposure to changes in foreign currency exchange rates and interest rates. All derivatives are recorded at fair value on the balance sheet and changes in the fair value of derivative financial instruments are either recognized in other comprehensive income (a component of shareholders' equity), debt or net income depending on the nature of the underlying exposure, whether the derivative is formally designated as a hedge, and, if designated, the extent to which the hedge is effective. The Company classifies the cash flows at settlement from derivatives in the same category as the cash flows from the related hedged items. For undesignated hedges and designated cash flow hedges, this is within the cash provided by operations component of the consolidated statements of cash flows. For designated net investment hedges, this is generally within the cash used by investing activities component of the cash flow statement. As our fair value hedges are receive-fixed, pay-variable interest rate swaps, the cash flows associated with these derivative instruments are periodic interest payments while the swaps are outstanding, which are reflected in net income within the cash provided by operations component of the cash flow statement.

See Note 17 — Risk Management and Derivatives for more information on the Company's risk management program and derivatives.

Stock-Based Compensation

The Company estimates the fair value of options and stock appreciation rights granted under the NIKE, Inc. 1990 Stock Incentive Plan (the "1990 Plan") and employees' purchase rights under the Employee Stock Purchase Plans ("ESPPs") using the Black-Scholes option pricing model. The Company recognizes this fair value, net of estimated forfeitures, as selling and administrative expense in the consolidated statements of income over the vesting period using the straight-line method.

See Note 11 — Common Stock and Stock-Based Compensation for more information on the Company's stock programs.

Income Taxes

The Company accounts for income taxes using the asset and liability method. This approach requires the recognition of deferred tax assets and liabilities for the expected future tax consequences of temporary differences between the carrying amounts and the tax basis of assets and liabilities. United States income taxes are provided currently on financial statement earnings of non-U.S. subsidiaries that are expected to be repatriated. The Company determines annually the amount of undistributed non-U.S. earnings to invest indefinitely in its non-U.S. operations. The Company recognizes interest and penalties related to income tax matters in income tax expense.

See Note 9 — Income Taxes for further discussion.

Earnings Per Share

Basic earnings per common share is calculated by dividing net income by the weighted average number of common shares outstanding during the year. Diluted earnings per common share is calculated by adjusting weighted average outstanding shares, assuming conversion of all potentially dilutive stock options and awards.

NIKE, INC.

NOTES TO CONSOLIDATED FINANCIAL STATEMENTS — (Continued)

See Note 12 — Earnings Per Share for further discussion.

Management Estimates

The preparation of financial statements in conformity with generally accepted accounting principles requires management to make estimates, including estimates relating to assumptions that affect the reported amounts of assets and liabilities and disclosure of contingent assets and liabilities at the date of financial statements and the reported amounts of revenues and expenses during the reporting period. Actual results could differ from these estimates.

Recently Adopted Accounting Standards

In January 2010, the Financial Accounting Standards Board ("FASB") issued guidance to amend the disclosure requirements related to recurring and nonrecurring fair value measurements. The guidance requires additional disclosures about the different classes of assets and liabilities measured at fair value, the valuation techniques and inputs used, the activity in Level 3 fair value measurements, and the transfers between Levels 1, 2, and 3 of the fair value measurement hierarchy. This guidance became effective for the Company beginning March 1, 2010, except for disclosures relating to purchases, sales, issuances and settlements of Level 3 assets and liabilities, which will be effective for the Company beginning June 1, 2011. As this guidance only requires expanded disclosures, the adoption did not and will not impact the Company's consolidated financial position or results of operations.

In June 2009, the FASB issued a new accounting standard that revised the guidance for the consolidation of variable interest entities ("VIE"). This new guidance requires a qualitative approach to identifying a controlling financial interest in a VIE, and requires an ongoing assessment of whether an entity is a VIE and whether an interest in a VIE makes the holder the primary beneficiary of the VIE. This guidance became effective for the Company beginning June 1, 2010. The adoption of this guidance did not have an impact on the Company's consolidated financial position or results of operations.

Recently Issued Accounting Standards

In June 2011, the FASB issued new guidance on the presentation of comprehensive income. This new guidance requires the components of net income and other comprehensive income to be either presented in one continuous statement, referred to as the statement of comprehensive income, or in two separate, but consecutive statements. This new guidance eliminates the current option to report other comprehensive income and its components in the statement of shareholders' equity. While the new guidance changes the presentation of comprehensive income, there are no changes to the components that are recognized in net income or other comprehensive income under current accounting guidance. This new guidance is effective for the Company beginning June 1, 2012. As this guidance only amends the presentation of the components of comprehensive income, the adoption will not have an impact on the Company's consolidated financial position or results of operations.

In April 2011, the FASB issued new guidance to achieve common fair value measurement and disclosure requirements between U.S. GAAP and International Financial Reporting Standards. This new guidance, which is effective for the Company beginning June 1, 2012, amends current U.S. GAAP fair value measurement and disclosure guidance to include increased transparency around valuation inputs and investment categorization. The Company does not expect the adoption will have a material impact on its consolidated financial position or results of operations.

64

NIKE, INC.

NOTES TO CONSOLIDATED FINANCIAL STATEMENTS — (Continued)

In October 2009, the FASB issued new standards that revised the guidance for revenue recognition with multiple deliverables. These new standards impact the determination of when the individual deliverables included in a multiple-element arrangement may be treated as separate units of accounting. Additionally, these new standards modify the manner in which the transaction consideration is allocated across the separately identified deliverables by no longer permitting the residual method of allocating arrangement consideration. These new standards are effective for the Company beginning June 1, 2011. The Company does not expect the adoption will have a material impact on its consolidated financial position or results of operations.

Note 2 — Inventories

Inventory balances of $2,715 million and $2,041 million at May 31, 2011 and 2010, respectively, were substantially all finished goods.

Note 3 — Property, Plant and Equipment

Property, plant and equipment included the following:

	As of May 31,	
	2011	2010
	(In millions)	
Land	$ 237	$ 223
Buildings	1,124	952
Machinery and equipment	2,487	2,217
Leasehold improvements	931	821
Construction in process	127	177
	4,906	4,390
Less accumulated depreciation	2,791	2,458
	$2,115	$1,932

Capitalized interest was not material for the years ended May 31, 2011, 2010, and 2009.

Note 4 — Identifiable Intangible Assets, Goodwill and Umbro Impairment

Identified Intangible Assets and Goodwill

The following table summarizes the Company's identifiable intangible asset balances as of May 31, 2011 and 2010:

	May 31, 2011			May 31, 2010		
	Gross Carrying Amount	Accumulated Amortization	Net Carrying Amount	Gross Carrying Amount	Accumulated Amortization	Net Carrying Amount
	(In millions)					
Amortized intangible assets:						
Patents	$ 80	$ (24)	$ 56	$ 69	$ (21)	$ 48
Trademarks	44	(25)	19	40	(18)	22
Other	47	(22)	25	32	(18)	14
Total	$ 171	$ (71)	$ 100	$ 141	$ (57)	$ 84
Unamortized intangible assets —						
Trademarks			387			383
Identifiable intangible assets, net			$ 487			$ 467

65

NIKE, INC.

NOTES TO CONSOLIDATED FINANCIAL STATEMENTS — (Continued)

The effect of foreign exchange fluctuations for the year ended May 31, 2011 increased unamortized intangible assets by approximately $4 million.

Amortization expense, which is included in selling and administrative expense, was $16 million, $14 million, and $12 million for the years ended May 31, 2011, 2010, and 2009, respectively. The estimated amortization expense for intangible assets subject to amortization for each of the years ending May 31, 2012 through May 31, 2016 are as follows: 2012: $16 million; 2013: $14 million; 2014: $12 million; 2015: $8 million; 2016: $7 million.

All goodwill balances are included in the Company's "Other" category for segment reporting purposes. The following table summarizes the Company's goodwill balance as of May 31, 2011 and 2010:

	Goodwill	Accumulated Impairment (In millions)	Goodwill, net
May 31, 2009	$ 393	$ (199)	$ 194
Other [(1)]	(6)	—	(6)
May 31, 2010	387	(199)	188
Umbro France [(2)]	10	—	10
Other [(1)]	7	—	7
May 31, 2011	$ 404	$ (199)	$ 205

[(1)]   Other consists of foreign currency translation adjustments on Umbro goodwill.

[(2)]   In March 2011, Umbro acquired the remaining 51% of the exclusive licensee and distributor of the Umbro brand in France for approximately $15 million.

Umbro Impairment in Fiscal 2009

The Company performs annual impairment tests on goodwill and intangible assets with indefinite lives in the fourth quarter of each fiscal year, or when events occur or circumstances change that would, more likely than not, reduce the fair value of a reporting unit or intangible assets with an indefinite life below its carrying value. As a result of a significant decline in global consumer demand and continued weakness in the macroeconomic environment, as well as decisions by Company management to adjust planned investment in the Umbro brand, the Company concluded sufficient indicators of impairment existed to require the performance of an interim assessment of Umbro's goodwill and indefinite lived intangible assets as of February 1, 2009. Accordingly, the Company performed the first step of the goodwill impairment assessment for Umbro by comparing the estimated fair value of Umbro to its carrying amount, and determined there was a potential impairment of goodwill as the carrying amount exceeded the estimated fair value. Therefore, the Company performed the second step of the assessment which compared the implied fair value of Umbro's goodwill to the book value of goodwill. The implied fair value of goodwill is determined by allocating the estimated fair value of Umbro to all of its assets and liabilities, including both recognized and unrecognized intangibles, in the same manner as goodwill was determined in the original business combination.

The Company measured the fair value of Umbro by using an equal weighting of the fair value implied by a discounted cash flow analysis and by comparisons with the market values of similar publicly traded companies. The Company believes the blended use of both models compensates for the inherent risk associated with either model if used on a stand-alone basis, and this combination is indicative of the factors a market participant would consider when performing a similar valuation. The fair value of Umbro's indefinite-lived trademark was

66

NIKE, INC.

NOTES TO CONSOLIDATED FINANCIAL STATEMENTS — (Continued)

estimated using the relief from royalty method, which assumes that the trademark has value to the extent that Umbro is relieved of the obligation to pay royalties for the benefits received from the trademark. The assessments of the Company resulted in the recognition of impairment charges of $199 million and $181 million related to Umbro's goodwill and trademark, respectively, for the year ended May 31, 2009. A tax benefit of $55 million was recognized as a result of the trademark impairment charge. In addition to the above impairment analysis, the Company determined an equity investment held by Umbro was impaired, and recognized a charge of $21 million related to the impairment of this investment. These charges are included in the Company's "Other" category for segment reporting purposes.

The discounted cash flow analysis calculated the fair value of Umbro using management's business plans and projections as the basis for expected cash flows for the next 12 years and a 3% residual growth rate thereafter. The Company used a weighted average discount rate of 14% in its analysis, which was derived primarily from published sources as well as our adjustment for increased market risk given current market conditions. Other significant estimates used in the discounted cash flow analysis include the rates of projected growth and profitability of Umbro's business and working capital effects. The market valuation approach indicates the fair value of Umbro based on a comparison of Umbro to publicly traded companies in similar lines of business. Significant estimates in the market valuation approach include identifying similar companies with comparable business factors such as size, growth, profitability, mix of revenue generated from licensed and direct distribution, and risk of return on investment.

Holding all other assumptions constant at the test date, a 100 basis point increase in the discount rate would reduce the adjusted carrying value of Umbro's net assets by an additional 12%.

Note 5 — Accrued Liabilities

Accrued liabilities included the following:

	May 31,	
	2011	2010
	(In millions)	
Compensation and benefits, excluding taxes	$ 628	$ 599
Endorser compensation	284	267
Taxes other than income taxes	214	158
Fair value of derivatives	186	164
Dividends payable	145	131
Advertising and marketing	139	125
Import and logistics costs	98	80
Other [1]	291	380
	$1,985	$1,904

---

[1] Other consists of various accrued expenses and no individual item accounted for more than 5% of the balance at May 31, 2011 and 2010.

Note 6 — Fair Value Measurements

The Company measures certain financial assets and liabilities at fair value on a recurring basis, including derivatives and available-for-sale securities. Fair value is a market-based measurement that should be determined based on the assumptions that market participants would use in pricing an asset or liability. As a basis for

67

NIKE, INC.

NOTES TO CONSOLIDATED FINANCIAL STATEMENTS — (Continued)

considering such assumptions, the Company uses a three-level hierarchy established by the FASB that prioritizes fair value measurements based on the types of inputs used for the various valuation techniques (market approach, income approach, and cost approach).

The levels of hierarchy are described below:

- Level 1: Observable inputs such as quoted prices in active markets for identical assets or liabilities.

- Level 2: Inputs other than quoted prices that are observable for the asset or liability, either directly or indirectly; these include quoted prices for similar assets or liabilities in active markets and quoted prices for identical or similar assets or liabilities in markets that are not active.

- Level 3: Unobservable inputs in which there is little or no market data available, which require the reporting entity to develop its own assumptions.

The Company's assessment of the significance of a particular input to the fair value measurement in its entirety requires judgment and considers factors specific to the asset or liability. Financial assets and liabilities are classified in their entirety based on the most stringent level of input that is significant to the fair value measurement.

The following table presents information about the Company's financial assets and liabilities measured at fair value on a recurring basis as of May 31, 2011 and 2010 and indicates the fair value hierarchy of the valuation techniques utilized by the Company to determine such fair value.

	May 31, 2011				
	Fair Value Measurements Using			Assets /Liabilities	
	Level 1	Level 2	Level 3	at Fair Value	Balance Sheet Classification
			(In millions)		
Assets					
Derivatives:					
Foreign exchange forwards and options	$ —	$ 38	$ —	$ 38	Other current assets and other long-term assets
Interest rate swap contracts	—	15	—	15	Other current assets and other long-term assets
Total derivatives	—	53	—	53	
Available-for-sale securities:					
U.S. Treasury securities	125	—	—	125	Cash equivalents
Commercial paper and bonds	—	157	—	157	Cash equivalents
Money market funds	—	780	—	780	Cash equivalents
U.S. Treasury securities	1,473	—	—	1,473	Short-term investments
U.S. Agency securities	—	308	—	308	Short-term investments
Commercial paper and bonds	—	802	—	802	Short-term investments
Total available-for-sale securities	1,598	2,047	—	3,645	
Total Assets	$ 1,598	$ 2,100	$ —	$ 3,698	
Liabilities					
Derivatives:					
Foreign exchange forwards and options	$ —	$ 197	$ —	$ 197	Accrued liabilities and other long-term liabilities
Total Liabilities	$ —	$ 197	$ —	$ 197	

68

NIKE, INC.

NOTES TO CONSOLIDATED FINANCIAL STATEMENTS — (Continued)

			May 31, 2010		
	Fair Value Measurements Using			Assets /Liabilities	
	Level 1	Level 2	Level 3	at Fair Value	Balance Sheet Classification
		(In millions)			
Assets					
Derivatives:					
Foreign exchange forwards and options	$ —	$ 420	$ —	$ 420	Other current assets and other long -term assets
Interest rate swap contracts	—	15	—	15	Other current assets and other long-term assets
Total derivatives	—	435	—	435	
Available-for-sale securities:					
U.S. Treasury securities	1,232	—	—	1,232	Cash equivalents
Commercial paper and bonds	—	462	—	462	Cash equivalents
Money market funds	—	685	—	685	Cash equivalents
U.S. Treasury securities	1,085	—	—	1,085	Short-term investments
U.S. Agency securities	—	298	—	298	Short-term investments
Commercial paper and bonds	—	684	—	684	Short-term investments
Total available-for-sale securities	2,317	2,129	—	4,446	
Total Assets	$ 2,317	$ 2,564	$ —	$ 4,881	
Liabilities					
Derivatives:					
Foreign exchange forwards and options	$ —	$ 165	$ —	$ 165	Accrued liabilities and other long-term liabilities
Total Liabilities	$ —	$ 165	$ —	$ 165	

Derivative financial instruments include foreign currency forwards, option contracts and interest rate swaps. The fair value of these derivatives contracts is determined using observable market inputs such as the forward pricing curve, currency volatilities, currency correlations and interest rates, and considers nonperformance risk of the Company and that of its counterparties. Adjustments relating to these risks were not material for the years ended May 31, 2011 and 2010.

Available-for-sale securities are primarily comprised of investments in U.S. Treasury and agency securities, commercial paper, bonds and money market funds. These securities are valued using market prices on both active markets (level 1) and less active markets (level 2). Level 1 instrument valuations are obtained from real-time quotes for transactions in active exchange markets involving identical assets. Level 2 instrument valuations are obtained from readily-available pricing sources for comparable instruments.

As of May 31, 2011 and 2010, the Company had no material Level 3 measurements and no assets or liabilities measured at fair value on a non-recurring basis.

Short-Term Investments

As of May 31, 2011 and 2010, short-term investments consisted of available-for-sale securities. As of May 31, 2011, the Company held $2,253 million of available-for-sale securities with maturity dates within one year and $330 million with maturity dates over one year and less than five years within short-term investments. As of May 31, 2010, the Company held $1,900 million of available-for-sale securities with maturity dates within one year and $167 million with maturity dates over one year and less than five years within short-term investments.

NIKE, INC.

NOTES TO CONSOLIDATED FINANCIAL STATEMENTS — (Continued)

Short-term investments classified as available-for-sale consist of the following at fair value:

	As of May 31,	
	2011	**2010**
	(In millions)	
Available-for-sale investments:		
U.S. treasury and agencies	$1,781	$1,383
Commercial paper and bonds	802	684
Total available-for-sale investments	$2,583	$2,067

Included in interest expense (income), net for the years ended May 31, 2011, 2010, and 2009 was interest income of $30 million, $30 million, and $50 million, respectively, related to cash and equivalents and short-term investments.

For fair value information regarding notes payable and long-term debt, refer to Note 7 — Short-Term Borrowings and Credit Lines and Note 8 — Long-Term Debt.

Note 7 — Short-Term Borrowings and Credit Lines

Notes payable to banks and interest-bearing accounts payable to Sojitz Corporation of America ("Sojitz America") as of May 31, 2011 and 2010, are summarized below:

	May 31,			
	2011		**2010**	
		Interest		Interest
	Borrowings	**Rate**	**Borrowings**	**Rate**
		(In millions)		
Notes payable:				
U.S. operations	35	—[1]	18	—[1]
Non-U.S. operations	152	7.05%[1]	121	6.35%[1]
	$ 187		$ 139	
Sojitz America	$ 111	0.99%	$ 88	1.07%

[1]   Weighted average interest rate includes non-interest bearing overdrafts.

The carrying amounts reflected in the consolidated balance sheet for notes payable approximate fair value.

The Company purchases through Sojitz America certain athletic footwear, apparel and equipment it acquires from non-U.S. suppliers. These purchases are for the Company's operations outside of the United States, Europe and Japan. Accounts payable to Sojitz America are generally due up to 60 days after shipment of goods from the foreign port. The interest rate on such accounts payable is the 60-day London Interbank Offered Rate ("LIBOR") as of the beginning of the month of the invoice date, plus 0.75%.

As of May 31, 2011 and 2010, the Company had no amounts outstanding under its commercial paper program.

In December 2006, the Company entered into a $1 billion revolving credit facility with a group of banks. The facility matures in December 2012. Based on the Company's current long-term senior unsecured debt ratings of A+ and A1 from Standard and Poor's Corporation and Moody's Investor Services, respectively, the interest

70

NIKE, INC.

NOTES TO CONSOLIDATED FINANCIAL STATEMENTS — (Continued)

rate charged on any outstanding borrowings would be the prevailing LIBOR plus 0.15%. The facility fee is 0.05% of the total commitment. Under this agreement, the Company must maintain, among other things, certain minimum specified financial ratios with which the Company was in compliance at May 31, 2011. No amounts were outstanding under this facility as of May 31, 2011 and 2010.

Note 8 — Long-Term Debt

Long-term debt, net of unamortized premiums and discounts and swap fair value adjustments, is comprised of the following:

	May 31, 2011	May 31, 2010
	(In millions)	
5.66% Corporate bond, payable July 23, 2012	$ 26	$ 27
5.40% Corporate bond, payable August 7, 2012	16	16
4.70% Corporate bond, payable October 1, 2013	50	50
5.15% Corporate bond, payable October 15, 2015	114	112
4.30% Japanese Yen note, payable June 26, 2011	130	116
1.52% Japanese Yen note, payable February 14, 2012	62	55
2.60% Japanese Yen note, maturing August 20, 2001 through November 20, 2020	54	53
2.00% Japanese Yen note, maturing August 20, 2001 through November 20, 2020	24	24
Total	476	453
Less current maturities	200	7
	$276	$446

The scheduled maturity of long-term debt in each of the years ending May 31, 2012 through 2016 are $200 million, $48 million, $58 million, $8 million and $109 million, at face value, respectively.

The Company's long-term debt is recorded at adjusted cost, net of amortized premiums and discounts and interest rate swap fair value adjustments. The fair value of long-term debt is estimated based upon quoted prices for similar instruments. The fair value of the Company's long-term debt, including the current portion, was approximately $482 million at May 31, 2011 and $453 million at May 31, 2010.

In fiscal years 2003 and 2004, the Company issued a total of $240 million in medium-term notes of which $190 million, at face value, were outstanding at May 31, 2011. The outstanding notes have coupon rates that range from 4.70% to 5.66% and maturity dates ranging from July 2012 to October 2015. For each of these notes, except the $50 million note maturing in October 2013, the Company has entered into interest rate swap agreements whereby the Company receives fixed interest payments at the same rate as the notes and pays variable interest payments based on the six-month LIBOR plus a spread. Each swap has the same notional amount and maturity date as the corresponding note. At May 31, 2011, the interest rates payable on these swap agreements ranged from approximately 0.3% to 1.0%.

In June 1996, one of the Company's wholly owned Japanese subsidiaries, NIKE Logistics YK, borrowed ¥10.5 billion (approximately $130 million as of May 31, 2011) in a private placement with a maturity of June 26, 2011. Interest is paid semi-annually. The agreement provides for early retirement of the borrowing.

In July 1999, NIKE Logistics YK assumed a total of ¥13.0 billion in loans as part of its agreement to purchase a distribution center in Japan, which serves as collateral for the loans. These loans mature in equal quarterly installments during the period August 20, 2001 through November 20, 2020. Interest is also paid quarterly. As of May 31, 2011, ¥6.3 billion (approximately $78 million) in loans remain outstanding.

71

NIKE, INC.

NOTES TO CONSOLIDATED FINANCIAL STATEMENTS — (Continued)

In February 2007, NIKE Logistics YK entered into a ¥5.0 billion (approximately $62 million as of May 31, 2011) term loan that replaced certain intercompany borrowings and matures on February 14, 2012. The interest rate on the loan is approximately 1.5% and interest is paid semi-annually.

Note 9 — Income Taxes

Income before income taxes is as follows:

	Year Ended May 31,		
	2011	**2010**	**2009**
		(In millions)	
Income before income taxes:			
United States	$1,084	$ 699	$ 846
Foreign	1,760	1,818	1,111
	$2,844	$2,517	$1,957

The provision for income taxes is as follows:

	Year Ended May 31,		
	2011	**2010**	**2009**
		(In millions)	
Current:			
United States			
Federal	$289	$200	$ 410
State	57	50	46
Foreign	441	349	308
	787	599	764
Deferred:			
United States			
Federal	(61)	18	(251)
State	—	(1)	(8)
Foreign	(15)	(6)	(35)
	(76)	11	(294)
	$711	$610	$ 470

A reconciliation from the U.S. statutory federal income tax rate to the effective income tax rate follows:

	Year Ended May 31,		
	2011	**2010**	**2009**
Federal income tax rate	35.0%	35.0%	35.0%
State taxes, net of federal benefit	1.3%	1.3%	1.2%
Foreign earnings	-10.2%	-13.6%	-14.9%
Other, net	-1.1%	1.5%	2.7%
Effective income tax rate	25.0%	24.2%	24.0%

The effective tax rate for the year ended May 31, 2011 of 25.0% increased from the fiscal 2010 effective tax rate of 24.2% due primarily to the change in geographic mix of earnings. A larger percentage of our earnings before income taxes in the current year are attributable to operations in the United States where the statutory tax rate is generally higher than the tax rate on operations outside of the U.S. This impact was partially offset by

72

NIKE, INC.

NOTES TO CONSOLIDATED FINANCIAL STATEMENTS — (Continued)

changes to uncertain tax positions. Our effective tax rate for the year ended May 31, 2010 of 24.2% increased from the fiscal 2009 effective rate of 24.0%. The effective tax rate for fiscal 2009 includes a tax benefit related to charges recorded for the impairment of Umbro's goodwill, intangible and other assets.

Deferred tax assets and (liabilities) are comprised of the following:

	May 31,	
	2011	2010
	(In millions)	
Deferred tax assets:		
Allowance for doubtful accounts	$ 19	$ 17
Inventories	63	47
Sales return reserves	72	52
Deferred compensation	152	144
Stock-based compensation	148	145
Reserves and accrued liabilities	66	86
Foreign loss carry-forwards	60	26
Foreign tax credit carry-forwards	236	148
Hedges	21	1
Undistributed earnings of foreign subsidiaries	—	128
Other	86	37
Total deferred tax assets	923	831
Valuation allowance	(51)	(36)
Total deferred tax assets after valuation allowance	872	795
Deferred tax liabilities:		
Undistributed earnings of foreign subsidiaries	(40)	—
Property, plant and equipment	(151)	(99)
Intangibles	(97)	(99)
Hedges	(1)	(72)
Other	(20)	(8)
Total deferred tax liability	(309)	(278)
Net deferred tax asset	$ 563	$ 517

The following is a reconciliation of the changes in the gross balance of unrecognized tax benefits:

	May 31,		
	2011	2010	2009
	(In millions)		
Unrecognized tax benefits, as of the beginning of the period	$282	$ 274	$251
Gross increases related to prior period tax positions	13	87	53
Gross decreases related to prior period tax positions	(98)	(122)	(62)
Gross increases related to current period tax positions	59	52	72
Gross decreases related to current period tax positions	(6)	—	—
Settlements	(43)	(3)	(29)
Lapse of statute of limitations	(8)	(9)	(4)
Changes due to currency translation	13	3	(7)
Unrecognized tax benefits, as of the end of the period	$212	$ 282	$274

Table of Contents

NIKE, INC.

NOTES TO CONSOLIDATED FINANCIAL STATEMENTS — (Continued)

As of May 31, 2011, the total gross unrecognized tax benefits, excluding related interest and penalties, were $212 million, $93 million of which would affect the Company's effective tax rate if recognized in future periods. Total gross unrecognized tax benefits, excluding interest and penalties, as of May 31, 2010 and 2009 was $282 million and $274 million, respectively.

The Company recognizes interest and penalties related to income tax matters in income tax expense. The liability for payment of interest and penalties increased $10 million, $6 million, and $2 million during the years ended May 31, 2011, 2010, and 2009, respectively. As of May 31, 2011 and 2010, accrued interest and penalties related to uncertain tax positions was $91 million and $81 million, respectively (excluding federal benefit).

The Company is subject to taxation primarily in the U.S., China and the Netherlands as well as various state and other foreign jurisdictions. The Company has concluded substantially all U.S. federal income tax matters through fiscal year 2009. The Company is currently under audit by the Internal Revenue Service for the 2010 tax year. The Company's major foreign jurisdictions, China and the Netherlands, have concluded substantially all income tax matters through calendar 2000 and fiscal 2005, respectively. The Company estimates that it is reasonably possible that the total gross unrecognized tax benefits could decrease by up to $69 million within the next 12 months as a result of resolutions of global tax examinations and the expiration of applicable statutes of limitations.

The Company has indefinitely reinvested approximately $4.4 billion of the cumulative undistributed earnings of certain foreign subsidiaries. Such earnings would be subject to U.S. taxation if repatriated to the U.S. Determination of the amount of unrecognized deferred tax liability associated with the indefinitely reinvested cumulative undistributed earnings is not practicable.

A portion of the Company's foreign operations are benefitting from a tax holiday that will phase out in 2019. The decrease in income tax expense for the year ended May 31, 2011 as a result of this arrangement was approximately $36 million ($0.07 per diluted share) and $30 million ($0.06 per diluted share) for the year ended May 31, 2010.

Deferred tax assets at May 31, 2011 and 2010 were reduced by a valuation allowance relating to tax benefits of certain subsidiaries with operating losses where it is more likely than not that the deferred tax assets will not be realized. The net change in the valuation allowance was an increase of $15 million and $10 million for the years ended May 31, 2011 and 2010, respectively and a decrease of $15 million for the year ended May 31, 2009.

The Company does not anticipate that any foreign tax credit carry-forwards will expire. The Company has available domestic and foreign loss carry-forwards of $183 million at May 31, 2011. Such losses will expire as follows:

	Year Ending May 31,						
					2017-		
	2013	2014	2015	2016	2028	Indefinite	Total
				(In millions)			
Net Operating Losses	$ 7	$10	$ 4	$10	$ 91	$ 61	$183

During the years ended May 31, 2011, 2010, and 2009, income tax benefits attributable to employee stock-based compensation transactions of $68 million, $57 million, and $25 million, respectively, were allocated to shareholders' equity.

NIKE, INC.
NOTES TO CONSOLIDATED FINANCIAL STATEMENTS — (Continued)

Note 10 — Redeemable Preferred Stock

Sojitz America is the sole owner of the Company's authorized Redeemable Preferred Stock, $1 par value, which is redeemable at the option of Sojitz America or the Company at par value aggregating $0.3 million. A cumulative dividend of $0.10 per share is payable annually on May 31 and no dividends may be declared or paid on the common stock of the Company unless dividends on the Redeemable Preferred Stock have been declared and paid in full. There have been no changes in the Redeemable Preferred Stock in the three years ended May 31, 2011, 2010, and 2009. As the holder of the Redeemable Preferred Stock, Sojitz America does not have general voting rights but does have the right to vote as a separate class on the sale of all or substantially all of the assets of the Company and its subsidiaries, on merger, consolidation, liquidation or dissolution of the Company or on the sale or assignment of the NIKE trademark for athletic footwear sold in the United States.

Note 11 — Common Stock and Stock-Based Compensation

The authorized number of shares of Class A Common Stock, no par value, and Class B Common Stock, no par value, are 175 million and 750 million, respectively. Each share of Class A Common Stock is convertible into one share of Class B Common Stock. Voting rights of Class B Common Stock are limited in certain circumstances with respect to the election of directors.

In 1990, the Board of Directors adopted, and the shareholders approved, the NIKE, Inc. 1990 Stock Incentive Plan (the "1990 Plan"). The 1990 Plan provides for the issuance of up to 163 million previously unissued shares of Class B Common Stock in connection with stock options and other awards granted under the plan. The 1990 Plan authorizes the grant of non-statutory stock options, incentive stock options, stock appreciation rights, restricted stock, restricted stock units, and performance-based awards. The exercise price for stock options and stock appreciation rights may not be less than the fair market value of the underlying shares on the date of grant. A committee of the Board of Directors administers the 1990 Plan. The committee has the authority to determine the employees to whom awards will be made, the amount of the awards, and the other terms and conditions of the awards. Substantially all stock option grants outstanding under the 1990 Plan were granted in the first quarter of each fiscal year, vest ratably over four years, and expire 10 years from the date of grant.

The following table summarizes the Company's total stock-based compensation expense recognized in selling and administrative expense:

| | Year Ended May 31, | | |
	2011	2010	2009
		(in millions)	
Stock options [1]	$ 77	$135	$129
ESPPs	14	14	14
Restricted stock	14	10	8
Subtotal	105	159	151
Stock options and restricted stock expense — restructuring [2]	—	—	20
Total stock-based compensation expense	$105	$159	$171

---

[1]   Expense for stock options includes the expense associated with stock appreciation rights. Accelerated stock option expense is recorded for employees eligible for accelerated stock option vesting upon retirement. In the first quarter of fiscal 2011, the Company changed the accelerated vesting provisions of its stock option plan. Under the new provisions, accelerated stock option expense for year ended May 31, 2011 was $12 million. The accelerated stock option expense for the years ended May 31, 2010 and 2009 was $74 million and $59 million, respectively.

NIKE, INC.

NOTES TO CONSOLIDATED FINANCIAL STATEMENTS — (Continued)

(2)   In connection with the restructuring activities that took place during fiscal 2009, the Company recognized stock-based compensation expense relating to the modification of stock option agreements, allowing for an extended post-termination exercise period, and accelerated vesting of restricted stock as part of severance packages. See Note 16 — Restructuring Charges for further details.

As of May 31, 2011, the Company had $111 million of unrecognized compensation costs from stock options, net of estimated forfeitures, to be recognized as selling and administrative expense over a weighted average period of 2.2 years.

The weighted average fair value per share of the options granted during the years ended May 31, 2011, 2010, and 2009, as computed using the Black-Scholes pricing model, was $17.68, $23.43, and $17.13, respectively. The weighted average assumptions used to estimate these fair values are as follows:

	Year Ended May 31,		
	2011	**2010**	**2009**
Dividend yield	1.6%	1.9%	1.5%
Expected volatility	31.5%	57.6%	32.5%
Weighted average expected life (in years)	5.0	5.0	5.0
Risk-free interest rate	1.7%	2.5%	3.4%

The Company estimates the expected volatility based on the implied volatility in market traded options on the Company's common stock with a term greater than one year, along with other factors. The weighted average expected life of options is based on an analysis of historical and expected future exercise patterns. The interest rate is based on the U.S. Treasury (constant maturity) risk-free rate in effect at the date of grant for periods corresponding with the expected term of the options.

The following summarizes the stock option transactions under the plan discussed above:

	Shares [1] (In millions)	Weighted Average Option Price
Options outstanding May 31, 2008	36.6	$ 40.14
Exercised	(4.0)	35.70
Forfeited	(1.3)	51.19
Granted	7.5	58.17
Options outstanding May 31, 2009	38.8	$ 43.69
Exercised	(8.6)	37.64
Forfeited	(0.6)	51.92
Granted	6.4	52.79
Options outstanding May 31, 2010	36.0	$ 46.60
Exercised	(7.0)	42.70
Forfeited	(0.5)	58.08
Granted	6.3	69.20
Options outstanding May 31, 2011	34.8	$ 51.29
Options exercisable at May 31,		
2009	21.4	$ 36.91
2010	20.4	41.16
2011	20.1	$ 44.05

[1]   Includes stock appreciation rights transactions.

NIKE, INC.

NOTES TO CONSOLIDATED FINANCIAL STATEMENTS — (Continued)

The weighted average contractual life remaining for options outstanding and options exercisable at May 31, 2011 was 6.0 years and 4.5 years, respectively. The aggregate intrinsic value for options outstanding and exercisable at May 31, 2011 was $1,154 million and $811 million, respectively. The aggregate intrinsic value was the amount by which the market value of the underlying stock exceeded the exercise price of the options. The total intrinsic value of the options exercised during the years ended May 31, 2011, 2010, and 2009 was $267 million, $239 million, and $108 million, respectively.

In addition to the 1990 Plan, the Company gives employees the right to purchase shares at a discount to the market price under employee stock purchase plans ("ESPPs"). Employees are eligible to participate through payroll deductions up to 10% of their compensation. At the end of each six-month offering period, shares are purchased by the participants at 85% of the lower of the fair market value at the beginning or the end of the offering period. Employees purchased 0.8 million shares during the years ended May 31, 2011 and 2010, and 1.0 million shares during the year ended May 31, 2009.

From time to time, the Company grants restricted stock and unrestricted stock to key employees under the 1990 Plan. The number of shares granted to employees during the years ended May 31, 2011, 2010, and 2009 were 0.2 million, 0.5 million, and 0.1 million with weighted average values per share of $70.23, $53.16, and $56.97, respectively. Recipients of restricted shares are entitled to cash dividends and to vote their respective shares throughout the period of restriction. The value of all of the granted shares was established by the market price on the date of grant. During the years ended May 31, 2011, 2010, and 2009, the fair value of restricted shares vested was $15 million, $8 million, and $10 million, respectively, determined as of the date of vesting.

Note 12 — Earnings Per Share

The following is a reconciliation from basic earnings per share to diluted earnings per share. Options to purchase an additional 0.2 million, 0.2 million, and 13.2 million shares of common stock were outstanding at May 31, 2011, 2010, and 2009, respectively, but were not included in the computation of diluted earnings per share because the options were anti-dilutive.

	Year Ended May 31,		
	2011	2010	2009
	(In millions, except per share data)		
Determination of shares:			
Weighted average common shares outstanding	475.5	485.5	484.9
Assumed conversion of dilutive stock options and awards	10.2	8.4	5.8
Diluted weighted average common shares outstanding	485.7	493.9	490.7
Basic earnings per common share	$ 4.48	$ 3.93	$ 3.07
Diluted earnings per common share	$ 4.39	$ 3.86	$ 3.03

Note 13 — Benefit Plans

The Company has a profit sharing plan available to most U.S.-based employees. The terms of the plan call for annual contributions by the Company as determined by the Board of Directors. A subsidiary of the Company also has a profit sharing plan available to its U.S.-based employees. The terms of the plan call for annual contributions as determined by the subsidiary's executive management. Contributions of $39 million, $35 million, and $28 million were made to the plans and are included in selling and administrative expense for the years ended May 31, 2011, 2010, and 2009, respectively. The Company has various 401(k) employee savings

77

Table of Contents

NIKE, INC.

NOTES TO CONSOLIDATED FINANCIAL STATEMENTS — (Continued)

plans available to U.S.-based employees. The Company matches a portion of employee contributions. Company contributions to the savings plans were $39 million, $34 million, and $38 million for the years ended May 31, 2011, 2010, and 2009, respectively, and are included in selling and administrative expense.

The Company also has a Long-Term Incentive Plan ("LTIP") that was adopted by the Board of Directors and approved by shareholders in September 1997 and later amended in fiscal 2007. The Company recognized $31 million, $24 million, and $18 million of selling and administrative expense related to cash awards under the LTIP during the years ended May 31, 2011, 2010, and 2009, respectively.

The Company has pension plans in various countries worldwide. The pension plans are only available to local employees and are generally government mandated. The liability related to the unfunded pension liabilities of the plans was $93 million and $113 million at May 31, 2011 and 2010, respectively, which was primarily classified as long-term in other liabilities.

Note 14 — Accumulated Other Comprehensive Income

The components of accumulated other comprehensive income, net of tax, are as follows:

	May 31,	
	2011	2010
	(In millions)	
Cumulative translation adjustment and other	$ 168	$ (95)
Net deferred gain on net investment hedge derivatives	50	107
Net deferred (loss) gain on cash flow hedge derivatives	(123)	203
	$ 95	$215

Note 15 — Commitments and Contingencies

The Company leases space for certain of its offices, warehouses and retail stores under leases expiring from 1 to 24 years after May 31, 2011. Rent expense was $446 million, $416 million, and $397 million for the years ended May 31, 2011, 2010 and 2009, respectively. Amounts of minimum future annual rental commitments under non-cancelable operating leases in each of the five years ending May 31, 2012 through 2016 are $374 million, $310 million, $253 million, $198 million, $174 million, respectively, and $535 million in later years.

As of May 31, 2011 and 2010, the Company had letters of credit outstanding totaling $99 million and $101 million, respectively. These letters of credit were generally issued for the purchase of inventory.

In connection with various contracts and agreements, the Company provides routine indemnifications relating to the enforceability of intellectual property rights, coverage for legal issues that arise and other items where the Company is acting as the guarantor. Currently, the Company has several such agreements in place. However, based on the Company's historical experience and the estimated probability of future loss, the Company has determined that the fair value of such indemnifications is not material to the Company's financial position or results of operations.

In the ordinary course of its business, the Company is involved in various legal proceedings involving contractual and employment relationships, product liability claims, trademark rights, and a variety of other matters. The Company does not believe there are any pending legal proceedings that will have a material impact on the Company's financial position or results of operations.

78

Table of Contents

NIKE, INC.

NOTES TO CONSOLIDATED FINANCIAL STATEMENTS — (Continued)

Note 16 — Restructuring Charges

During fiscal 2009, the Company took necessary steps to streamline its management structure, enhance consumer focus, drive innovation more quickly to market and establish a more scalable, long-term cost structure. As a result, the Company reduced its global workforce by approximately 5% and incurred pre-tax restructuring charges of $195 million, primarily consisting of severance costs related to the workforce reduction. As nearly all of the restructuring activities were completed in fiscal 2009, the Company did not recognize additional costs relating to these actions. The restructuring charge is reflected in the corporate expense line in the segment presentation of earnings before interest and taxes in Note 18 — Operating Segments and Related Information. The restructuring accrual included in accrued liabilities in the consolidated balance sheet was $3 million and $8 million as of May 31, 2011 and 2010, respectively.

Note 17 — Risk Management and Derivatives

The Company is exposed to global market risks, including the effect of changes in foreign currency exchange rates and interest rates, and uses derivatives to manage financial exposures that occur in the normal course of business. The Company does not hold or issue derivatives for trading purposes.

The Company formally documents all relationships between formally designated hedging instruments and hedged items, as well as its risk management objective and strategy for undertaking hedge transactions. This process includes linking all derivatives to either specific firm commitments or forecasted transactions. The Company also enters into foreign exchange forwards to mitigate the change in fair value of specific assets and liabilities on the balance sheet, which are not designated as hedging instruments under the accounting standards for derivatives and hedging. Accordingly, changes in the fair value of these non-designated instruments of recorded balance sheet positions are recognized immediately in other (income), net, on the income statement together with the transaction gain or loss from the hedged balance sheet position. The Company classifies the cash flows at settlement from these undesignated instruments in the same category as the cash flows from the related hedged items, generally within the cash provided by operations component of the cash flow statement.

The majority of derivatives outstanding as of May 31, 2011 are designated as cash flow, fair value or net investment hedges. All derivatives are recognized on the balance sheet at their fair value and classified based on the instrument's maturity date. The total notional amount of outstanding derivatives as of May 31, 2011 was $7 billion, which is primarily comprised of cash flow hedges for Euro/U.S. Dollar, British Pound/Euro, and Japanese Yen/U.S. Dollar currency pairs.

79

Table of Contents

NIKE, INC.

NOTES TO CONSOLIDATED FINANCIAL STATEMENTS — (Continued)

The following table presents the fair values of derivative instruments included within the consolidated balance sheet as of May 31, 2011 and 2010:

		Asset Derivatives				Liability Derivatives		
			May 31,	May 31,			May 31,	May 31,
	Balance Sheet Location		2011	2010	Balance Sheet Location		2011	2010
				(in millions)				
Derivatives formally designated as hedging instruments:								
Foreign exchange forwards and options	Prepaid expenses and other current assets	$	22	$ 316	Accrued liabilities	$	170	$ 25
Foreign exchange forwards and options	Deferred income taxes and other long-term assets		7	—	Deferred income taxes and other long-term liabilities		10	—
Interest rate swap contracts	Deferred income taxes and other long-term assets		15	15	Deferred income taxes and other long-term liabilities		—	—
Total derivatives formally designated as hedging instruments			44	331			180	25
Derivatives not designated as hedging instruments:								
Foreign exchange forwards and options	Prepaid expenses and other current assets	$	9	$ 104	Accrued liabilities	$	16	$ 139
Foreign exchange forwards and options	Deferred income taxes and other long-term assets		—	—	Deferred income taxes and other long-term liabilities		1	1
Total derivatives not designated as hedging instruments			9	104			17	140
Total derivatives		$	53	$ 435		$	197	$ 165

The following tables present the amounts affecting the consolidated statements of income for years ended May 31, 2011, 2010 and 2009:

	Amount of Gain (Loss) Recognized in Other Comprehensive Income on Derivatives [1]				Amount of Gain (Loss) Reclassified From Accumulated Other Comprehensive Income into Income [1]			
	Year Ended May 31,			Location of Gain (Loss) Reclassified From Accumulated Other Comprehensive Income Into Income [1]	Year Ended May 31,		
Derivatives formally designated	2011	2010	2009		2011	2010	2009
				(in millions)			
Derivatives designated as cash flow hedges:							
Foreign exchange forwards and options	$ (87)	$ (30)	$ 106	Revenue	$ (30)	$ 51	$ 93
Foreign exchange forwards and options	(152)	89	350	Cost of sales	103	60	(14)
Foreign exchange forwards and options	(4)	5	—	Selling and administrative expense	1	1	1
Foreign exchange forwards and options	(65)	51	165	Other (income), net	34	56	68
Total designated cash flow hedges	$ (308)	$ 115	$ 621		$ 108	$ 168	$ 148
Derivatives designated as net investment hedges:							
Foreign exchange forwards and options	$ (85)	$ 66	$ 161	Other (income), net	$ —	$ —	$ —

[1] For the year ended May 31, 2011 and 2009, the Company recorded an immaterial amount of ineffectiveness from cash flow hedges in other (income), net. For the year ended May 31, 2010, $5 million of ineffectiveness from cash flow hedges was recorded in other (income), net.

NIKE, INC.

NOTES TO CONSOLIDATED FINANCIAL STATEMENTS — (Continued)

	Amount of Gain (Loss) recognized in Income on Derivatives Year Ended May 31,			Location of Gain (Loss) Recognized in Income on Derivatives
	2011	2010	2009	
	(in millions)			
Derivatives designated as fair value hedges:				
Interest rate swaps [1]	$ 6	$ 7	$ 2	Interest expense (income), net
Derivatives not designated as hedging instruments:				
Foreign exchange forwards and options	$(30)	$(91)	$(83)	Other (income), net

[1] All interest rate swap agreements meet the shortcut method requirements under the accounting standards for derivatives and hedging. Accordingly, changes in the fair values of the interest rate swap agreements are exactly offset by changes in the fair value of the underlying long-term debt. Refer to section "Fair Value Hedges" for additional detail.

Refer to Note 5 — Accrued Liabilities for derivative instruments recorded in accrued liabilities, Note 6 —Fair Value Measurements for a description of how the above financial instruments are valued, Note 14 — Accumulated Other Comprehensive Income and the consolidated statements of shareholders' equity for additional information on changes in other comprehensive income for the years ended May 31, 2011, 2010 and 2009.

Cash Flow Hedges

The purpose of the Company's foreign currency hedging activities is to protect the Company from the risk that the eventual cash flows resulting from transactions in foreign currencies, including revenues, product costs, selling and administrative expense, investments in U.S. dollar-denominated available-for-sale debt securities and intercompany transactions, including intercompany borrowings, will be adversely affected by changes in exchange rates. It is the Company's policy to utilize derivatives to reduce foreign exchange risks where internal netting strategies cannot be effectively employed. Hedged transactions are denominated primarily in Euros, British Pounds and Japanese Yen. The Company hedges up to 100% of anticipated exposures typically 12 months in advance, but has hedged as much as 34 months in advance.

All changes in fair values of outstanding cash flow hedge derivatives, except the ineffective portion, are recorded in other comprehensive income until net income is affected by the variability of cash flows of the hedged transaction. In most cases, amounts recorded in other comprehensive income will be released to net income some time after the maturity of the related derivative. The consolidated statement of income classification of effective hedge results is the same as that of the underlying exposure. Results of hedges of revenue and product costs are recorded in revenue and cost of sales, respectively, when the underlying hedged transaction affects net income. Results of hedges of selling and administrative expense are recorded together with those costs when the related expense is recorded. Results of hedges of forecasted purchases of U.S. dollar-denominated available-for-sale securities are recorded in other (income), net when the securities are sold. Results of hedges of forecasted intercompany transactions are recorded in other (income), net when the transaction occurs. The Company classifies the cash flows at settlement from these designated cash flow hedge derivatives in the same category as the cash flows from the related hedged items, generally within the cash provided by operations component of the cash flow statement.

Premiums paid on options are initially recorded as deferred charges. The Company assesses the effectiveness of options based on the total cash flows method and records total changes in the options' fair value to other comprehensive income to the degree they are effective.

NIKE, INC.

NOTES TO CONSOLIDATED FINANCIAL STATEMENTS — (Continued)

As of May 31, 2011, $120 million of deferred net losses (net of tax) on both outstanding and matured derivatives accumulated in other comprehensive income are expected to be reclassified to net income during the next 12 months as a result of underlying hedged transactions also being recorded in net income. Actual amounts ultimately reclassified to net income are dependent on the exchange rates in effect when derivative contracts that are currently outstanding mature. As of May 31, 2011, the maximum term over which the Company is hedging exposures to the variability of cash flows for its forecasted and recorded transactions is 15 months.

The Company formally assesses both at a hedge's inception and on an ongoing basis, whether the derivatives that are used in the hedging transaction have been highly effective in offsetting changes in the cash flows of hedged items and whether those derivatives may be expected to remain highly effective in future periods. Effectiveness for cash flow hedges is assessed based on forward rates. When it is determined that a derivative is not, or has ceased to be, highly effective as a hedge, the Company discontinues hedge accounting.

The Company discontinues hedge accounting prospectively when (1) it determines that the derivative is no longer highly effective in offsetting changes in the cash flows of a hedged item (including hedged items such as firm commitments or forecasted transactions); (2) the derivative expires or is sold, terminated, or exercised; (3) it is no longer probable that the forecasted transaction will occur; or (4) management determines that designating the derivative as a hedging instrument is no longer appropriate.

When the Company discontinues hedge accounting because it is no longer probable that the forecasted transaction will occur in the originally expected period, but is expected to occur within an additional two-month period of time thereafter, the gain or loss on the derivative remains in accumulated other comprehensive income and is reclassified to net income when the forecasted transaction affects net income. However, if it is probable that a forecasted transaction will not occur by the end of the originally specified time period or within an additional two-month period of time thereafter, the gains and losses that were accumulated in other comprehensive income will be recognized immediately in net income. In all situations in which hedge accounting is discontinued and the derivative remains outstanding, the Company will carry the derivative at its fair value on the balance sheet, recognizing future changes in the fair value in other (income), net. For the year ended May 31, 2011 an immaterial amount of ineffectiveness was recorded to other (income), net. For the years ended May 31, 2010 and 2009, the Company recorded in other (income), net $5 million gain and an immaterial amount of ineffectiveness from cash flow hedges, respectively.

Fair Value Hedges

The Company is also exposed to the risk of changes in the fair value of certain fixed-rate debt attributable to changes in interest rates. Derivatives currently used by the Company to hedge this risk are receive-fixed, pay-variable interest rate swaps. As of May 31, 2011, all interest rate swap agreements are designated as fair value hedges of the related long-term debt and meet the shortcut method requirements under the accounting standards for derivatives and hedging. Accordingly, changes in the fair values of the interest rate swap agreements are exactly offset by changes in the fair value of the underlying long-term debt. The cash flows associated with the Company's fair value hedges are periodic interest payments while the swaps are outstanding, which are reflected in net income within the cash provided by operations component of the cash flow statement. No ineffectiveness has been recorded to net income related to interest rate swaps designated as fair value hedges for the years ended May 31, 2011, 2010, and 2009.

In fiscal 2003, the Company entered into a receive-floating, pay-fixed interest rate swap agreement related to a Japanese Yen denominated intercompany loan with one of the Company's Japanese subsidiaries. This interest rate swap was not designated as a hedge under the accounting standards for derivatives and hedging.

82

NIKE, INC.

NOTES TO CONSOLIDATED FINANCIAL STATEMENTS — (Continued)

Accordingly, changes in the fair value of the swap were recorded to net income each period through maturity as a component of interest expense (income), net. Both the intercompany loan and the related interest rate swap matured during the year ended May 31, 2009.

Net Investment Hedges

The Company also hedges the risk of variability in foreign-currency-denominated net investments in wholly-owned international operations. All changes in fair value of the derivatives designated as net investment hedges, except ineffective portions, are reported in the cumulative translation adjustment component of other comprehensive income along with the foreign currency translation adjustments on those investments. The Company classifies the cash flows at settlement of its net investment hedges within the cash used by investing component of the cash flow statement. The Company assesses hedge effectiveness based on changes in forward rates. The Company recorded no ineffectiveness from its net investment hedges for the years ended May 31, 2011, 2010, and 2009.

Credit Risk

The Company is exposed to credit-related losses in the event of non-performance by counterparties to hedging instruments. The counterparties to all derivative transactions are major financial institutions with investment grade credit ratings. However, this does not eliminate the Company's exposure to credit risk with these institutions. This credit risk is limited to the unrealized gains in such contracts should any of these counterparties fail to perform as contracted. To manage this risk, the Company has established strict counterparty credit guidelines that are continually monitored and reported to senior management according to prescribed guidelines. The Company also utilizes a portfolio of financial institutions either headquartered or operating in the same countries the Company conducts its business.

The Company's derivative contracts contain credit risk related contingent features aiming to protect against significant deterioration in counterparties' creditworthiness and their ultimate ability to settle outstanding derivative contracts in the normal course of business. The Company's bilateral credit related contingent features require the owing entity, either the Company or the derivative counterparty, to post collateral should the fair value of outstanding derivatives per counterparty be greater than $50 million. Additionally, a certain level of decline in credit rating of either the Company or the counterparty could trigger collateral requirements. As of May 31, 2011, the Company was in compliance with all such credit risk related contingent features. The aggregate fair value of derivative instruments with credit risk related contingent features that are in a net liability position at May 31, 2011 was $160 million. The Company, or any counterparty, were not required to post any collateral as a result of these contingent features. As a result of the above considerations, the Company considers the impact of the risk of counterparty default to be immaterial.

Note 18 — Operating Segments and Related Information

Operating Segments.   The Company's operating segments are evidence of the structure of the Company's internal organization. The major segments are defined by geographic regions for operations participating in NIKE Brand sales activity excluding NIKE Golf. Each NIKE Brand geographic segment operates predominantly in one industry: the design, development, marketing and selling of athletic footwear, apparel, and equipment. In fiscal 2009, the Company initiated a reorganization of the NIKE Brand into a new model consisting of six geographies. Effective June 1, 2009, the Company's new reportable operating segments for the NIKE Brand are: North America, Western Europe, Central and Eastern Europe, Greater China, Japan, and Emerging Markets. Previously, NIKE Brand operations were organized into the following four geographic regions: U.S., Europe, Middle East and Africa (collectively, "EMEA"), Asia Pacific, and Americas. The Company's NIKE Brand Direct to Consumer operations are managed within each geographic segment.

Table of Contents

NIKE, INC.

NOTES TO CONSOLIDATED FINANCIAL STATEMENTS — (Continued)

The Company's "Other" category is broken into two components for presentation purposes to align with the way management views the Company. The "Global Brand Divisions" category primarily represents NIKE Brand licensing businesses that are not part of a geographic operating segment, selling, general and administrative expenses that are centrally managed for the NIKE Brand and costs associated with product development and supply chain operations. The "Other Businesses" category primarily consists of the activities of our affiliate brands; Cole Haan, Converse Inc., Hurley International LLC and Umbro International Limited; and NIKE Golf. Activities represented in the "Other" category are immaterial for individual disclosure.

Revenues as shown below represent sales to external customers for each segment. Intercompany revenues have been eliminated and are immaterial for separate disclosure.

Corporate consists of unallocated general and administrative expenses, which includes expenses associated with centrally managed departments, depreciation and amortization related to the Company's headquarters, unallocated insurance and benefit programs, including stock-based compensation, certain foreign currency gains and losses, including hedge gains and losses, certain corporate eliminations and other items.

Effective June 1, 2009, the primary financial measure used by the Company to evaluate performance of individual operating segments is Earnings Before Interest and Taxes (commonly referred to as "EBIT") which represents net income before interest expense (income), net and income taxes in the consolidated statements of income. Reconciling items for EBIT represent corporate expense items that are not allocated to the operating segments for management reporting. Previously, the Company evaluated performance of individual operating segments based on pre-tax income or income before income taxes.

As part of the Company's centrally managed foreign exchange risk management program, standard foreign currency rates are assigned to each NIKE Brand entity in our geographic operating segments and are used to record any non-functional currency revenues or product purchases into the entity's functional currency. Geographic operating segment revenues and cost of sales reflect use of these standard rates. For all NIKE Brand operating segments, differences between assigned standard foreign currency rates and actual market rates are included in Corporate together with foreign currency hedge gains and losses generated from the centrally managed foreign exchange risk management program and other conversion gains and losses. Prior to June 1, 2010, foreign currency results, including hedge results and other conversion gains and losses generated by the Western Europe and Central & Eastern Europe geographies were recorded in their respective geographic results.

Additions to long-lived assets as presented in the following table represent capital expenditures.

Accounts receivable, inventories and property, plant and equipment for operating segments are regularly reviewed by management and are therefore provided below.

Certain prior year amounts have been reclassified to conform to fiscal 2011 presentation, as South Africa became part of the Emerging Markets operating segment beginning June 1, 2010. Previously, South Africa was part of the Central & Eastern Europe operating segment.

84

NIKE, INC.

NOTES TO CONSOLIDATED FINANCIAL STATEMENTS — (Continued)

	Year Ended May 31,		
	2011	**2010**	**2009**
		(In millions)	
Revenue			
North America	$ 7,578	$ 6,696	$ 6,778
Western Europe	3,810	3,892	4,139
Central & Eastern Europe	1,031	993	1,247
Greater China	2,060	1,742	1,743
Japan	766	882	926
Emerging Markets	2,736	2,199	1,828
Global Brand Divisions	123	105	96
Total NIKE Brand	18,104	16,509	16,757
Other Businesses	2,747	2,530	2,419
Corporate	11	(25)	—
Total NIKE Consolidated Revenues	$20,862	$19,014	$19,176
Earnings Before Interest and Taxes			
North America	$ 1,750	$ 1,538	$ 1,429
Western Europe	721	856	939
Central & Eastern Europe	233	253	394
Greater China	777	637	575
Japan	114	180	205
Emerging Markets	688	521	364
Global Brand Divisions	(998)	(867)	(811)
Total NIKE Brand	3,285	3,118	3,095
Other Businesses [1]	334	299	(193)
Corporate [2]	(771)	(894)	(955)
Total NIKE Consolidated Earnings Before Interest and Taxes	2,848	2,523	1,947
Interest expense (income), net	4	6	(10)
Total NIKE Consolidated Earnings Before Taxes	$ 2,844	$ 2,517	$ 1,957
Additions to Long-lived Assets			
North America	$ 79	$ 45	$ 99
Western Europe	75	59	70
Central & Eastern Europe	5	4	7
Greater China	43	80	59
Japan	9	12	10
Emerging Markets	21	11	12
Global Brand Divisions	44	30	37
Total NIKE Brand	276	241	294
Other Businesses	38	52	90
Corporate	118	42	72
Total Additions to Long-lived Assets	$ 432	$ 335	$ 456
Depreciation			
North America	$ 70	$ 65	$ 64
Western Europe	52	57	51
Central & Eastern Europe	4	4	4
Greater China	19	11	7
Japan	22	26	30
Emerging Markets	14	12	10
Global Brand Divisions	39	33	43
Total NIKE Brand	220	208	209
Other Businesses	44	46	38
Corporate	71	70	88
Total Depreciation	$ 335	$ 324	$ 335

NIKE, INC.

NOTES TO CONSOLIDATED FINANCIAL STATEMENTS — (Continued)

---

(1)   During the year ended May 31, 2009, the Other category included a pre-tax charge of $401 million for the impairment of goodwill, intangible and other assets of Umbro, which was recorded in the third quarter of fiscal 2009. See Note 4 — Identifiable Intangible Assets, Goodwill and Umbro Impairment for more information.

(2)   During the year ended May 31, 2009, Corporate expense included pre-tax charges of $195 million for the Company's restructuring activities, which were completed in the fourth quarter of fiscal 2009. See Note 16 — Restructuring Charges for more information.

	Year Ended May 31,	
	2011	2010
	(In millions)	
Accounts Receivable, net		
North America	$ 1,069	$ 848
Western Europe	500	402
Central & Eastern Europe	290	271
Greater China	140	129
Japan	153	167
Emerging Markets	466	350
Global Brand Divisions	23	22
Total NIKE Brand	2,641	2,189
Other Businesses	471	442
Corporate	26	19
Total Accounts Receivable, net	$ 3,138	$ 2,650
Inventories		
North America	$ 1,034	$ 768
Western Europe	434	347
Central & Eastern Europe	145	102
Greater China	152	104
Japan	82	68
Emerging Markets	429	285
Global Brand Divisions	25	20
Total NIKE Brand	2,301	1,694
Other Businesses	414	347
Corporate	—	—
Total Inventories	$ 2,715	$ 2,041
Property, Plant and Equipment, net		
North America	$ 330	$ 325
Western Europe	338	282
Central & Eastern Europe	13	11
Greater China	179	146
Japan	360	333
Emerging Markets	58	48
Global Brand Divisions	116	99
Total NIKE Brand	1,394	1,244
Other Businesses	164	167
Corporate	557	521
Total Property, Plant and Equipment, net	$ 2,115	$ 1,932

86

Table of Contents

NIKE, INC.

NOTES TO CONSOLIDATED FINANCIAL STATEMENTS — (Continued)

Revenues by Major Product Lines.   Revenues to external customers for NIKE Brand products are attributable to sales of footwear, apparel and equipment. Other revenues to external customers primarily include external sales by Cole Haan, Converse, Hurley, NIKE Golf, and Umbro.

	Year Ended May 31,		
	2011	**2010**	**2009**
		(In millions)	
Footwear	$11,493	$10,332	$10,307
Apparel	5,475	5,037	5,245
Equipment	1,013	1,035	1,110
Other	2,881	2,610	2,514
	$20,862	$19,014	$19,176

Revenues and Long-Lived Assets by Geographic Area.   Geographical area information is similar to what was shown previously under operating segments with the exception of the Other activity, which has been allocated to the geographical areas based on the location where the sales originated. Revenues derived in the United States were $8,956 million, $7,914 million, and $8,020 million for the years ended May 31, 2011, 2010, and 2009, respectively. The Company's largest concentrations of long-lived assets primarily consist of the Company's world headquarters and distribution facilities in the United States and distribution facilities in Japan, Belgium and China. Long-lived assets attributable to operations in the United States, which are comprised of net property, plant & equipment, were $1,115 million, $1,070 million, and $1,143 million at May 31, 2011, 2010, and 2009, respectively. Long-lived assets attributable to operations in Japan were $363 million, $336 million, and $322 million at May 31, 2011, 2010 and 2009, respectively. Long-lived assets attributable to operations in Belgium were $182 million, $164 million, and $191 million at May 31, 2011, 2010, and 2009, respectively. Long-lived assets attributable to operations in China were $175 million, $144 million, and $76 million at May 31, 2011, 2010, and 2009, respectively.

Major Customers.   No customer accounted for 10% or more of the Company's net sales during the years ended May 31, 2011, 2010, and 2009.

87

Appendix C

International Financial Reporting Standards (IFRS)

The Need for Global Accounting Standards

As discussed in Chapter 1, the Financial Accounting Standards Board (FASB) establishes generally accepted accounting principles (GAAP) for public companies in the United States. Of course, there is a world beyond the borders of the United States. In recent years, the removal of trade barriers and the growth in cross-border equity and debt issuances have led to a dramatic increase in international commerce. As a result, companies are often reporting financial results to users outside of the United States.

Historically, accounting standards have varied considerably across countries. These variances have been driven by cultural, legal, and political differences, and resulted in financial statements that were not easily comparable and difficult to interpret. These differences caused problems for companies in Europe and Asia, where local economies have become increasingly tied to international commerce.

During the last decade, however, a common set of International Financial Reporting Standards (IFRS) has emerged to reduce cross-country differences in accounting standards, primarily in countries outside of North America. While much of the world has migrated to IFRS, the United States has not. Because of the size of the United States and its significant role in world commerce, however, U.S. GAAP still has a global impact. As a result, there are currently two major accounting standard-setting efforts in the world, U.S. GAAP and IFRS. These two sets of accounting standards add cost and complexity for companies doing business and obtaining financing internationally.

Overview of IFRS

International Financial Reporting Standards have emerged during the last 10 years to meet the financial reporting needs of an increasingly global business environment.

What Is IFRS? International Financial Reporting Standards are a set of global accounting standards developed by an international standard-setting body called the International Accounting Standards Board (IASB). Like the Financial Accounting Standards Board, the IASB is an independent entity that establishes accounting rules. Unlike the FASB, the IASB does not establish accounting rules for any specific country. Rather, it develops accounting rules that can be used by a variety of countries, with the goal of developing a single set of global accounting standards.

Who Uses IFRS? IFRS applies to companies that issue publicly traded debt or equity securities, called **public companies**, in countries that have adopted IFRS as their accounting standards. Since 2005, all 27 countries in the European Union (EU) have been required to prepare financial statements using IFRS. In addition, over 100 other countries have adopted IFRS for public companies (see Exhibit 1). In other major economies, Japan is considering mandatory adoption by 2016, India allows limited use of IFRS, and China is converging its standards with IFRS over time. In addition, the G20 (Group of 20) leadership has called for uniform global accounting standards.

EXHIBIT 1

IFRS Adopters

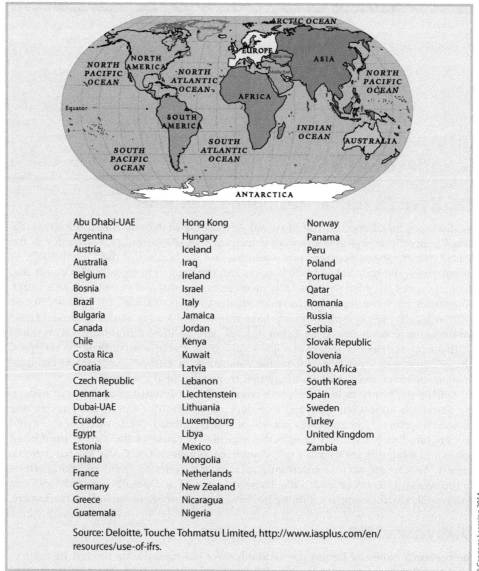

Abu Dhabi-UAE	Hong Kong	Norway
Argentina	Hungary	Panama
Austria	Iceland	Peru
Australia	Iraq	Poland
Belgium	Ireland	Portugal
Bosnia	Israel	Qatar
Brazil	Italy	Romania
Bulgaria	Jamaica	Russia
Canada	Jordan	Serbia
Chile	Kenya	Slovak Republic
Costa Rica	Kuwait	Slovenia
Croatia	Latvia	South Africa
Czech Republic	Lebanon	South Korea
Denmark	Liechtenstein	Spain
Dubai-UAE	Lithuania	Sweden
Ecuador	Luxembourg	Turkey
Egypt	Libya	United Kingdom
Estonia	Mexico	Zambia
Finland	Mongolia	
France	Netherlands	
Germany	New Zealand	
Greece	Nicaragua	
Guatemala	Nigeria	

Source: Deloitte, Touche Tohmatsu Limited, http://www.iasplus.com/en/resources/use-of-ifrs.

U.S. GAAP and IFRS: The Road Forward

The United States has not formally adopted IFRS for U.S. companies. The wide acceptance being gained by IFRS around the world, however, has placed considerable pressure on the United States to align U.S. GAAP with IFRS. There are two possible paths that the United States could take to achieve this: (1) adoption of IFRS by the U.S. Securities and Exchange Commission or (2) convergence of U.S. GAAP and IFRS. These two options are briefly discussed below.

Adoption of IFRS by the SEC The U.S. Securities and Exchange Commission (SEC) is the U.S. governmental agency that has authority over the accounting and financial disclosures for U.S. public companies. Only the SEC has the authority to adopt IFRS for U.S. public companies. In 2008, the SEC presented a "roadmap" to adopting IFRS, which outlined a timetable along with a set of "milestones" that needed to be met before the SEC would be willing to adopt IFRS. In 2010, the SEC reiterated the milestones outlined in the roadmap. According to the work plan, the SEC plans on deciding whether to incorporate IFRS into U.S. GAAP for public companies. The SEC published a Final Report on the issues surrounding IFRS adoption in 2012[1]. A final decision on IFRS adoption by the SEC is anticipated by 2013.

If the SEC adopts IFRS for U.S. GAAP, it has determined that the FASB would retain a "critical and substantive role in achieving the goal of global accounting standards." This suggests that the FASB will not necessarily be eliminated. More likely, the FASB would provide input to the IASB so that U.S. accounting perspectives are considered.

Convergence of U.S. GAAP and IFRS If the SEC does not adopt IFRS, an alternative approach would be for the FASB and IASB to converge U.S. GAAP and IFRS. This would involve aligning IFRS and U.S. GAAP one topic at a time, slowly merging IFRS and U.S. GAAP into two broadly uniform sets of accounting standards. To this end, the FASB and IASB have agreed to work together on a number of difficult and high-profile accounting issues. These issues frame a large portion of the disagreement between the two sets of standards and, if accomplished, will significantly reduce the differences between U.S. GAAP and IFRS. The projects selected for the convergence effort represent some of the more technical topics in accounting and are covered in intermediate and advanced accounting courses. The FASB and IASB have set 2013 as the target for establishing final standards.

One of the major limitations of convergence is that both the FASB and IASB continue to operate as the accounting standard-setting bodies for their respective jurisdictions. As such, convergence would not result in a single set of global accounting standards. Only those standards that go through the joint FASB–IASB standard-setting process would be released as uniform. Standards that do not go through a joint standard-setting process may create inconsistencies between U.S. GAAP and IFRS. Thus, convergence does not guarantee complete uniformity between U.S. GAAP and IFRS. A brief summary of the major U.S. decisions related to IFRS are outlined in the table below.

The Road to IFRS

2002	IASB and FASB jointly agree to work toward making IFRS and U.S. GAAP compatible.
2005	EU adopts IFRS for all companies engaged in international markets.
	SEC and European Commission jointly agree to work toward a "Roadmap for Convergence."
2007	SEC allows foreign (non-U.S.) companies to use IFRS financial statements to meet U.S. filing requirements.
2008	SEC issues proposed "Roadmap" with timeline and key milestones for adopting IFRS.
2010	SEC reiterates milestones in the proposed "Roadmap."
2013	Target date for FASB and IASB convergence on major standard-setting projects.
	Target date for SEC's tentative decision regarding IFRS adoption.
2015	Earliest date the SEC would require IFRS for U.S. public companies.

Differences Between U.S. GAAP and IFRS

U.S. GAAP and IFRS differ both in their approach to standard setting, as well as their financial statement presentation and recording of transactions.

Rules-Based vs. Principles Approach to Standard Setting U.S. GAAP is considered to be a "rules-based" approach to accounting standard setting. The accounting standards provide detailed and specific rules on the accounting for business transactions. There are few exceptions or varying interpretations of the accounting for a business event. This structure is consistent with the U.S. legal and regulatory system, reflecting the social and economic values of the United States.

[1]Work Plan for the Consideration of Incorporating International Financial Accounting Standards into the Financial Reporting System for U.S. Issuers: Final Staff Report, U.S. Securities Exchange Commission, July 13, 2012.

In contrast, IFRS is designed to meet the needs of many countries. Differences in legal, political, and economic systems create different needs for and uses of financial information in different countries. For example, Germany needs a financial reporting system that reflects the central role of banks in its financial system, while the Netherlands needs a financial reporting system that reflects the significant role of outside equity in its financial system.

To accommodate economic, legal, and social diversity, IFRS must be broad enough to capture these differences, while still presenting comparable financial statements. Under IFRS, there is greater opportunity for different interpretations of the accounting treatment of a business event across different business entities. To support this, IFRS often has more extensive disclosures that support alternative assumptions. Thus, IFRS provides more latitude for professional judgment than typically found in comparable U.S. GAAP. Many countries find this feature attractive in reducing regulatory costs associated with using and auditing financial reports. This "principles-based" approach presents one of the most significant challenges to adopting IFRS in the United States.

Technical Differences Between IFRS and U.S. GAAP Although U.S. GAAP is similar to IFRS, differences arise in the presentation format, balance sheet valuations, and technical accounting procedures. The Mornin' Joe International financial statements presented on pages 632–639 highlight the financial statement format, presentation, and recording differences between U.S. GAAP and IFRS. In addition, the International Connection boxes in Chapters 1, 4, 6, 9, 11, and 14 discuss some of the significant differences between U.S. GAAP and IFRS. A more comprehensive summary of the key differences between U.S. GAAP and IFRS that are relevant to an introductory accounting course is provided in the table on the following pages. As standards continue to evolve, this table will be updated periodically online. Visit this book's student Web site at www.cengagebrain.com.

Discussion Questions

1. Briefly discuss why global accounting standards are needed in today's business environment.

2. What are International Financial Reporting Standards? Who uses these accounting standards?

3. What body is responsible for setting International Financial Reporting Standards?

4. Briefly discuss the differences between (a) convergence of U.S. GAAP with IFRS and (b) adoption of IFRS by the U.S. Securities and Exchange Commission.

5. Briefly discuss the difference between (a) a "rules-based" approach to accounting standard setting and (b) a "principles-based" approach to accounting standard setting.

6. How is property, plant, and equipment measured on the balance sheet under IFRS? How does this differ from the way property, plant, and equipment is measured on the balance sheet under U.S. GAAP?

7. What inventory costing methods are allowed under IFRS? How does this differ from the treatment under U.S. GAAP?

Comparison of Accounting for Selected Items Under U.S. GAAP and IFRS

	U.S. GAAP	IFRS	Text Reference
General:			
Financial statement titles	Balance Sheet Statement of Stockholders' Equity Statement of Cash Flows	Statement of Financial Position Statement of Changes in Equity Statement of Cash Flows	 General
Financial periods presented	Public companies must present two years of comparative information for income statement, statement of stockholders' equity, and statement of cash flows	One year of comparative information must be presented	General
Conceptual basis for standard setting	"Rules-based" approach	"Principles-based" approach	General
Internal control requirements	Sarbanes-Oxley Act (SOX) Section 404		Ch 7; LO 1
Balance Sheet:	**Balance Sheet**	**Statement of Financial Position**	
Terminology differences	"Payable" "Stockholders' Equity" "Net Income (Loss)"	"Provision" "Capital and Reserves" "Profit or (Loss)"	Ch 10 Ch 10 General
Inventory—LIFO	LIFO allowed	LIFO prohibited	Ch 6; LO 3, 4, 5
Inventory—valuation	Market is defined as "replacement value" Reversal of lower-of-cost-or-market write-downs not allowed	Market is defined as "fair value" Reversal of write-downs allowed	Ch 6; LO 6 Ch 6; LO 6
Long-lived assets	May NOT be revalued to fair value	May be revalued to fair value on a regular basis	Ch 9; LO 1
			(Continued)

Comparison of Accounting for Selected Items Under U.S. GAAP and IFRS (Continued)

	U.S. GAAP	IFRS	Text Reference
Land held for investment	Treated as held for use or sale, and recorded at historical cost	May be accounted for on a historical cost basis or on a fair value basis with changes in fair value recognized through profit and loss	Ch 9; LO 1
Property, plant, & equipment—valuation	Historical cost	May select between historical cost or revalued amount (a form of fair value)	Ch 9; LO 1
	If impaired, impairment loss may NOT be reversed in future periods	If impaired, impairment loss may be reversed in future periods	
Cost of major overhaul (Capital and revenue expenditures)	Different treatment for ordinary repairs and maintenance, asset improvement, extraordinary repairs	Typically included as part of the cost of the asset if future economic benefit is probable and can be reliably measured	Ch 9; LO 1
Intangible assets—valuation	Acquisition cost, unless impaired	Fair value permitted if the intangible asset trades in an active market	Ch 9; LO 5
Intangible assets—impairment loss reversal	Prohibited	Prohibited for goodwill, but allowed for other intangible assets	Ch 9; LO 5
Deferred tax liability	The amount due within one year classified as current	Always noncurrent	Appendix C
Income Statement:	**Income Statement**	**Statement of Comprehensive Income**	
Revenue recognition	Detailed guidance depending on the transaction	Broad guidance	Ch 3; LO 1
Classification of expenses on income statement	Public companies must present expenses on the income statement by function (e.g., cost of goods sold, selling, administrative)	Expenses may be presented based either by function (e.g., cost of goods sold, selling) or by the nature of expense (e.g., wages expense, interest expense)	Ch 5; LO 1
Research and development costs	Expensed as incurred	Research costs expensed	Ch 9; LO 5
		Development costs capitalized once technical and economic feasibility attained	
Extraordinary items	Allowed for items that are both unusual in nature and infrequent in occurrence	Prohibited	Ch 15; Appendix

(Continued)

Comparison of Accounting for Selected Items Under U.S. GAAP and IFRS *(Concluded)*

	U.S. GAAP	IFRS	Text Reference
Statement of Cash Flows:	*Statement of Cash Flows*	*Statement of Cash Flows*	
Classification of interest paid or received	Treated as an operating activity	Interest paid may be treated as either an operating or a financing activity, interest received may be treated as an operating or investing activity	Ch 14; LO 3
Classification of dividend paid or received	Dividend paid treated as a financing activity, dividend received treated as an operating activity	Dividend paid may be treated as either an operating or a financing activity, dividend received may be treated as an operating or investing activity	Ch 14; LO 3

INDEX

Note: (n) after a page number indicates information in a footnote on that page.